The Mainstream of Civilization
Third Edition

The Mainstream
Third Edition

JOSEPH R. STRAYER
Princeton University

HANS W. GATZKE
Yale University

# of Civilization

Harcourt Brace Jovanovich, Inc.

New York / San Diego / Chicago / San Francisco / Atlanta

The Mainstream of Civilization
Third Edition

Cover photograph: Pier Luigi Nervi, Artist Exhibition Hall, Turin, Italy (1949).
Jerry Cooke, Photo Researchers, Inc.

Maps by Jean Paul Tremblay

Copyright © 1979, 1974, 1969 by Harcourt Brace Jovanovich, Inc.

ISBN: 0-15-551562-4

Library of Congress Catalog Card Number: 78-70777

Printed in the United States of America

Source of Illustrations on pages 836–40 constitutes a continuation of the copyright page.

Preface

It requires a certain amount of courage to attempt to write a history of civilization in one volume. Once the task has been accomplished, however, it is easier to do it a second and then a third time. As before, we have deliberately omitted certain details so that we could discuss as fully as possible the basic characteristics of each civilization and of different periods in the history of each civilization. We have tried to emphasize connections and interrelations—the ways in which politics, economics, art, scholarship, and religion all influence one another. We have tried to capture the flavor of each age—the unique combination of beliefs, activities, and institutions that distinguishes one society from another. In choosing the illustrations and the inserts in the text we have tried to give some idea of the diverse and ever-changing ways in which people have looked at and lived in their world. Finally, we have tried to consider the most difficult of all historical questions—the nature of and the reasons for change in human communities. Why and how do new institutions, new activities, new ideas rise and flourish? Why do they fade away? There are no easy answers to these problems; all we can do is suggest lines of inquiry that the reader may wish to pursue.

Obviously, it is easier to assess the characteristics and achievements of earlier periods than those of the age in which we live. The English Revolution of the seventeenth century ended long ago; the communist revolutions of the twentieth century continue to develop in unpredictable ways. Obviously also, it is more important to know details about the nature and background of problems that are still with us than details about problems that have been solved (at least partially). For these reasons the book broadens as it reaches the nineteenth century. More information is provided and more events are described in the hope that the reader will better understand the present state of the world.

We trust that no one will passively accept our interpretations or believe that our book is an adequate summary of human history. Our work is only an introduction, an attempt to persuade the reader to think deeply about history and to study it in detail. We are convinced that historical-mindedness is a necessity of human life. Consciously or unconsciously, we all base our estimates of the future on our knowledge of the past. It is important, then, that our knowledge of the past be as accurate and as deep as possible.

We remember with gratitude the contribution of the late Professor E. Harris Harbison to the first edition. He left us a framework that has been useful in subsequent revisions. We have also found the contribution of our former collaborator, Professor Edwin L. Dunbaugh, to be helpful in our work.

The authors are greatly indebted to the following historians, who critically read *The Mainstream of Civilization* and made many valuable comments and suggestions: Jeremy du Q. Adams, Southern Methodist University; William Allen, University of Bridgeport; John Eadie, University of Michigan; Erich S. Gruen, University of California at Berkeley; William W. Hallo, Yale University; Karl G. Larew, Towson State College; Ramsay Mac-Mullen, Yale University; Richard Marius, University of Tennessee; Raphael Sealey, University of California at Berkeley; Abraham L. Udovitch, Princeton University; and Christopher R. Friedrichs, University of British Columbia.

J. R. S.
H. W. G.

Foreword *The Study of History*

Consciously or unconsciously, all of us are historians. We can plan for the future only because we remember the past. We can add to our knowledge only because we do not lose memory of former experiences. Everyone, from the peasant to the scholar, tries to meet new situations by discovering familiar elements that make it possible to evoke analogies with the past. An individual who has lost his memory, who has forgotten his own history, is helpless until he has recovered his past or has slowly built up a new past to which he can refer.

What is true of individuals is also true of societies. No community can survive and no institution can function without constant reference to past experience. We are ruled by precedents fully as much as by formal laws, which is to say that we are ruled by memories of the past. It is the memory of common experiences that unites individuals into communities, and it is the memory of his own experiences that makes a child into an adult. Some of the memories may not be happy ones, but in reacting against them we are still linked to the past that produced them.

If everyone is his own historian, if individuals and societies necessarily draw on their memories of the past in order to deal with the present, then what is the need for formal, scholarly history? Isn't it enough to remember only the history that serves our immediate needs?

It is not enough, for two reasons. Human memory is fallible; individuals and societies forget many things that might be useful in solving their problems. This is why we have written records (which are a kind of formal history); this is why illiterate peoples try to preserve their customs and traditions through repeated oral recitations by the elders of the tribe. Second, the more complicated a society becomes, the narrower the range of individual experience in proportion to the total of possible experiences. A peasant living in a medieval village shared most of the experiences of his neighbors, and village custom gave solutions of a sort even to rare and unusual problems. No one living in an urbanized society shares many of the experiences of his neighbors, let alone the experiences of the millions of people throughout the world with whom he is connected by political and economic ties. No one can sum up the past experiences of his society, and of the societies with which his own interacts, with a few customary formulas; and yet these past experiences place a heavy burden on the present. In facing any problem, we look for familiar elements; if these are lacking, we feel fearful and helpless. Knowledge of history increases the chance of finding something familiar in a new and difficult situation.

Certain card games show how this process works at an elementary level. There is almost no chance that one distribution of cards will be repeated in a subsequent deal in bridge. Yet a person who has played several thousand hands of bridge should be able to make intelligent decisions and predictions even though every deal presents a new situation. He should be able to use his high cards and long suits effectively; he should be able to make some shrewd guesses about the location of cards in other hands. Not every experienced player will develop these skills. Some people are unable to generalize from their past experiences, and others cannot see analogies between the present and the past. But, generally speaking, an experienced player will make better use of his cards than a person who has played only ten hands. There is such a thing as a sense of the realities and possibilities of social activity, which can be developed from a knowledge of history.

At the very least, the past has left us the problems that we are trying to solve and the patterns of living that we are seeking to modify. At the most, we may find in the past suggestions for understanding and coping with the present. It is the historian's task to study the behavior of man in the past, to uncover facts, sort them, mass and link them, and so provide connections between past and present.

At the same time the historian must avoid certain pitfalls along the way. Connections with the past cannot be broken, but they can be misrepresented or misunderstood. Primitive peoples have little sense of chronology; they are apt to stir all their memories into a timeless brew of legend. At a more sophisticated level, the past has been used as a means of justifying present values and power structures. Many writers, from ancient times down to the present, have found historical examples to prove that their people were specially favored by the gods, that their state was founded and strengthened by heroes of superhuman ability, that virtue and wisdom (as defined by the author) have always brought success, while folly and vice have led to disaster. "History is philosophy teaching by example," said an ancient Greek (Dionysius of Halicarnassus), and it was more important for the examples to be edifying than for them to be true.

But it is not difficult to avoid deliberate distortions of the past. What *is* difficult is to avoid distortions caused by the incompleteness of our knowledge of the past. Many human activities have left few traces, especially in written records. For example, for thousands of years agriculture has been the chief occupation of the human race, but there are still serious gaps in our knowledge of the history of agriculture. "The short and simple annals of the poor" are short because information is scanty. If we had better information we would probably find that the life of a poor man in any period was anything but simple; it must have been filled with an unending series of nagging problems. In general, we know more about political history than social history, more about the privileged few than the unprivileged masses, more about the history of art than the history of technology, more about the ideas of philosophers and religious leaders than the beliefs of the common people.

Historians have become more skillful in recent years in finding material that gives a better-balanced picture of the past. Archeology reveals not only the palaces of kings, but the homes of ordinary people with their tools, their toys, their cooking utensils, and even fragments of their food. Gods and heroes may dominate the great works of art, but the common folk going about their ordinary business are there too—on Greek vases, Roman tombs, and portals of Gothic cathedrals. Discoveries of hoards of coins reveal unexpected trade relations. Aerial photography can bring out traces of ancient methods of plowing land and dividing fields. Even the written records, which have been studied for centuries, contain hitherto unused facts about such things as family life, migrations, and changes in economic patterns. There are still many holes in the record, but there is no reason to complain about lack of material.

The historian's greatest difficulty is not in discovering facts, but in deciding what facts can be ignored, or merely sampled, or clumped together in a single generalization. No one could master all the facts in yesterday's issue of the *New York Times,* and there are files of newspapers that run back to the eighteenth century. No one could master all the facts brought out in a single session of the Supreme Court, and the records of American courts and of the English courts from which they were derived go back to the twelfth century. To deal with the overwhelming mass of facts, historians have to arrange them, link them together, establish meaningful sequences of causes and effects.

The massing and linking of facts is not only essential, if history is to rise above the level of a catalogue; it is also inevitable, since it is the way the human mind deals with past experience. We do not recall every word we have exchanged when we decide that a certain person is a good friend. We do not remember every paragraph we have read when we decide that we like a certain book. But, while the process of massing and linking is essential and inevitable, this operation is the point of greatest danger in any kind of historical thinking. Consciously or unconsciously, one can mass facts to produce a misleading impression, even though each individual fact is true. Any governmental system can be made to appear obnoxious by discussing only the cases in which there is clear evidence of corruption or oppresion. Any society can be wreathed in a golden haze by dwelling only on its accomplishments in art, literature, and scholarship. Individuals and communities can become convinced that the whole world is conspiring against them if they remember only the occasions when they were treated unjustly. The nature of the sources themselves may cause distortion. For example, it is very easy to find material on political life in the city of Rome during the first century of the Roman Empire. It is difficult to collect evidence on provincial government or on social and economic development. The natural tendency is to overemphasize court intrigues and to pay little attention to such topics as economic growth or the spread of Latin culture throughout the West.

There is no easy way to overcome these problems, but an understanding of the principle of interconnectedness will help. No one is a purely political or economic or ideological being, and societies are composed of such varied human beings. Historians must look for the ways in which these (and other) forces interact. For example, the kind of food men eat can affect their whole social structure: a society dependent on olive oil for its fats will differ in many ways from one that depends on animal products such as lard, butter, and cheese. Religion can have an influence on trade: medieval churchmen aided the growth of Mediterranean commerce by importing silk for the vestments, incense for their ceremonies, and precious stones for their altar vessels and relic boxes. Trade in turn can influence the development of a religion: often it has been the merchant who prepared the way for the missionary. Ideas, technologies, institutions, social patterns, shifts in consumer preferences interact in complicated and bewildering ways. For example, increased use of easily washable cotton clothing in modern Europe improved personal hygiene and thus may have reduced death rates and contributed to growth of population. At the same time, increased demand for cotton encouraged the extension of slavery in the United States and thus was one of the causes of the Civil War.

Full realization of the connections among all human activities should lead to three conclusions. First, there are multiple causes for every event; single explanations for change are almost always wrong. Second, change in any one part of the social pattern may affect any other part of the pattern. Finally, the connections lead back into the past, and therefore the past influences the present.

The relationship between continuity and change is an interaction that the historian must watch with special care. All societies change, and yet all societies retain some connection with the past. The most "traditional" society is less traditional than it realizes; the most "modern" society is more influenced by tradition than it would like to believe. The Anglo-Saxons, theoretically bound by immemorial custom, invented the office of sheriff about the year 1000 A.D. The Americans, theoretically free to create an entirely new political structure, have preserved the office of sheriff with many of its original powers. Conquests and revolutions do not break all the connections with the past. Even where there has apparently been a complete break, the roots of a society may again grow down into its past. Roman law practically vanished from the West after the fifth century A.D.; it reappeared as a powerful force in the thirteenth century.

If there were no continuity, there would be no use in studying history, since nothing in the past would have any bearing on what is done today. If there were no change, there would be no history; a few years of practical experience would teach anyone all he needed to know about human behavior in society at any time and in any place. But, in the world as it is, the forces that would make for change are modified and even distorted by habit and custom, the forces that make for continuity are weakened and limited by new desires and new ideas. It is of some importance to understand where, why, and to what degree the desire for change prevails.

It is easy to see multiple, interlocking activities and rapid rates of change in the modern world. It is less easy to get a sense of the complexity and capacity for change of premodern and non-European societies, which is why the history of such societies often seems flat and uninteresting. The European Middle Ages are summed up as an "Age of Faith"; the history of much of Asia is dismissed with talk of the "unchanging Orient." Yet the Middle Ages were also a period of state building, economic growth, and technological invention—activities that have influenced the modern world fully as much as the Christian Church. The "unchanging Orient" produced all the great world religions, and each of these religions was a powerful force for change. Moreover, there are advantages in studying societies that are less complex and in which rates of change are less rapid than in our own. It is easier to observe and to draw conclusions about human behavior when the number of variables is small and changes do not come so fast that their effects are blurred.

A good historian, then, will try to give adequate attention to a wide variety of human activities, to discuss the interactions among these activities, and to trace the connections between past and present. But these principles cannot be applied mechanically. A writer who is careful to give an exactly equal amount of space to politics, economics, religion, the arts, and scholarship will probably not produce an adequate description of a society. The importance and even the identity of each of these activities varies with time and place. Religion had more influence on Indian than on Chinese society. Economics and politics merge in primitive societies, such as that of the early Germans. It is probably true that the vast majority of the world's scientists were born in the twentieth century; this could not be said of theologians. Thus the impact of scholarship on early societies is different from its impact on modern societies. To understand such variations and transformations, the historian must be more than a meticulous scholar. He must develop a feel for the period he is writing about, a sense of how people lived and worked and thought. It takes time and experience to acquire this feeling for the past, but once it has been acquired historians can give reasonably accurate, and occasionally penetrating, descriptions of earlier societies.

It is this understanding of the development of human society that gives history its chief value. History, even at its worst, gives us the comforting and necessary feeling that there are some familiar elements in a changing world and that there is some hope of understanding the changes that do occur. History at its best gives us a chance of reacting sensibly to problems as they arise. It does not guarantee the correctness of our responses, but it should improve the quality of our judgment. Good judgment about human behavior in society is badly needed today.

Contents

122 Ancient India and China

142 The Germanic Kingdoms in the West

158 Byzantium and Islam

178 The Emergence of a Western European Civilization

14

15

16

23

**522 The French Revolution
and Napoleon**

24

**544 The Search for Stability
1815–1850**

**646 The Period of Promise
1870–1914**

**674 The Struggle
for a European
Equilibrium, 1871–1914**

30

31

33

32

34

**796   From Cold War
to Coexistence**

**824   Epilogue:
The Problems
We Face**

List of Maps

Introduction

This is a history of civilization, with emphasis on the civilization developed by the peoples of Europe. Like all histories, it must be selective. Incomplete as our record of the past is, it is still too full to permit discussion in a single book of all civilizations or even of all events in the history of one civilization. The principles that have guided our selection of topics may be indicated by a definition of our subject. We must answer two questions: What is civilization, and what has been the role of western civilization in creating the conditions that we find in the world today?

Civilization is derived from the Latin word for city, *civitas.* There is reason to emphasize this derivation, for every great civilization has had great cities, and the basic characteristics of civilization are easiest to observe in cities. Civilization is first of all *cooperation*—men working together to satisfy their material and spiritual needs. It requires *organization*—as soon as several people start working together there must be some sort of social, political, or economic pattern to regulate their activity. It encourages *specialization*—as soon as several people begin to cooperate in an organized way there are obvious advantages in dividing the work so that no one man has to do everything for himself. The character of a particular civilization is determined by the type and degree of the organization and specialization of that civilization. Ten thousand Greeks living in a small city-state could accomplish much more than ten thousand Indians scattered through the forests of North America. A few hundred men specializing in science have done more to change our civilization in the last few centuries than millions of artisans working through past ages. Intensive organization and specialization can produce spectacular results, and they can also create spectacular problems.

Civilization requires faith in certain ideals and values as well as skill in organization and techniques. The immediate and direct advantages of organization and specialization are not very apparent to most people. Organization sets limits on personal freedom, and specialization makes a man dependent on other men who may not be wholly trustworthy.

In the long run the advantages are greater than the disadvantages, but farseeing, enlightened self-interest is a very rare human quality, probably rarer than altruism. And if men hesitate to give up present benefits for advantages in their own future, they will be even more hesitant if the advantages are to be gained only by their descendants. There is always resistance to increasing the scale and scope of organization; there is usually resistance to new types of specialization. This resistance can be overcome only by belief that there is something more important than the individual—a religion that emphasizes cooperation, a divinely appointed ruler or ruling class, a nation that has become almost a divinity, a theory of society that has taken on the aspects of a religion. There is a close connection between the dominant beliefs of a people and the kind of civilization it creates.

This history of civilization examines, more than anything else, how and why people have worked together. It is concerned with political history because the political record helps us to understand why people have been more successful at some times than at others in organizing on a large scale, and why some types of organization have proved more effective than others. It is concerned with economic and social history because economic and social organization has a direct effect on both political organization and the type and degree of specialization. It is concerned with the history of ideas and their manifestations in art and literature because organization and specialization are possible only within a framework of accepted beliefs. The interactions among political organizations, economic institutions, and dominant beliefs determine the character and development of a civilization.

Western civilization is only one, and by no means the oldest, of the civilizations that has left a historical record. The earliest civilizations touched Europe and the West only slightly; they centered in the river valleys of Egypt, the Near East, and China. Only with the appearance of the Greek city-states after 1000 B.C. can we see the beginnings of a civilization that belongs to the same family as our own. The Greeks drew heavily on the older civilizations of their neighbors, but they reorganized their borrowed materials and added significant elements to them. Ideas and forms of organization that have remained important in western civilization for over twenty-five hundred years first appear in ancient Greece. The Romans followed the Greeks as the dominant people in the Mediterranean basin. Like the Greeks, they borrowed from their predecessors, rearranged the old materials in new ways, and added ideas of their own, especially in government and law. Roman civilization is the direct ancestor of the civilization of modern European countries. There has never been a time, from the first conquests of the Roman Republic down to the present, when Roman law and Roman political ideas were not being discussed in some parts of the Continent.

Yet, while there is unbroken continuity between the civilization of the Greeks and the Romans and that of the modern West, it is well to remember that continuity is not identity. Much has been added—for example, the ideas brought in by Christianity—and much has been changed. Greco-Roman civilization was neither western nor European; it was Mediterranean. It was most highly developed on the eastern shores of the Mediterranean, and it was greatly influenced by the Orient. France and Spain were colonial outposts that contributed little to Greco-Roman civilization; Germany, Scandinavia, and the Slavic countries were outside the limits of the civilized Mediterranean world.

This Mediterranean civilization ran into trouble in the fourth and fifth centuries A.D. The economic organization proved unsatisfactory, and loyalty to the political organization weakened. As the Roman Empire slowly crumbled, the unity of the Mediterranean basin was destroyed, never to be restored. The southern and eastern shores became part of an Arab empire, part of the non-European Moslem civilization. A remnant of the old Roman Empire, centering around Constantinople, became the Byzantine Empire. This empire developed its own civilization—Christian in belief, Greek in language, but strongly influenced by the East in organization. Byzantine civilization made a great impression on the Slavic peoples of eastern Europe and had some influence on the Latin and Germanic peoples of the West. But it was never fully integrated with the civilization that grew up in western Europe. The western Europeans thought of the Byzantines as remote and somewhat untrustworthy relatives, who might hand out valuable gifts from time to time but who were too eccentric to live with. This attitude, in turn, has made it difficult to integrate eastern and western Europe, since the eastern countries borrowed much more from Byzantium than did those of the West.

With the Arab and Byzantine empires developing separate civilizations, the western European remnant of the old Mediterranean world was thrown back on its own resources. These were at first not very great. Western Europe saved only a fragment of its Roman inheritance, and this Roman inheritance was itself only a fragment of the old Mediterranean civilization. Moreover, the Germanic peoples of northern and central Europe, who had never been included in the Mediterranean world, were for a time dominant in western Europe. They brought in some new ideas and institutions, but they were backward in both political and economic organization. They were slow in assimilating the fragments of Roman civilization that remained, and even slower in developing effective types of organization. In the same way, the Christian religion, which eventually had great influence on European civilization, was only slowly absorbed by the half-barbarized Latins and the half-civilized Germans. For six centuries Europeans struggled with the problems of assimilating the Roman inheritance, integrating Latin and Germanic peoples, and implementing the basic ideas of Christianity. Only when this triple task was done did western Europe at last achieve an independent and consistent civilization. Only then could it profit from its contacts with the more highly developed civilizations of the Arab and Byzantine worlds.

Once it was established as a separate and viable entity, western Europe civilization developed rapidly. Many of our basic institutions and ideas, such as universities and representative assemblies, were worked out in the twelfth and thirteenth centuries. But this western European civilization was confined to a very small area. Its center was in the north, in a triangle bounded by Paris, Cologne, and London. The peripheral countries—Spain, Ireland, Norway, Sweden, Poland, Bohemia, and Italy—did not share in all the manifestations of this civilization, though they accepted its basic ideas. And beyond these countries the influence of western European civilization dropped off sharply. It had little effect on the Moslem world and none whatever on the peoples of Africa and Asia who lived beyond the limits of Moslem influence. It had some impact on Byzantium, but not enough to erase the differences that separated Byzantium from the West. There were some contacts with Russia, but the Russians were probably more influenced by the Byzantines. And the Mongol conquest of the thirteenth century weakened the ties that the Russians had with the West and forced them to face east for two centuries.

Meanwhile, another group of civilizations had developed in the Far East, in India, China, and Japan. Each had its own characteristic values—religious in India, secular and political in China, military in Japan. All three tended to become somewhat self-satisfied and isolated; neither India nor China, for example, was as interested in foreign voyages in the sixteenth century as it had been earlier. In all three the economic system was still based largely on village agriculture. Finally, in spite of promising beginnings, none of the Far Eastern civilizations had developed a strong scientific tradition. These characteristics put the Far Eastern countries at a disadvantage in dealing with Europeans, who were deeply interested in strange lands and peoples, were beginning to develop an economy based on machine production, and were just about to make their first important scientific discoveries.

The great voyages of exploration and the great mechanical inventions, both of which began in the fifteenth century, enabled western European civilization to emerge from its narrow corner and to spread throughout the world. Eastern Europe gradually accepted much of the civilization of the West, though the process was never complete. Three new continents—North America, South America, and Australia—were occupied by Europeans, and a fourth, Africa, was dominated by them. Asia, with its old civilizations and its dense population, was not so easily overrun, but even Asia was profoundly influenced by the European impact. Thus, for the first time, all the peoples of the world were brought into contact with a single civilization. The results of this great experiment are only beginning to be apparent.

There is some justification, then, for the conventional division of history into Ancient, Medieval, and Modern. Ancient history deals with the period in which some of the basic elements of western civilization were developed and passed on to later peoples. But ancient history must be focused on the Near East and the Mediterranean, not on Europe. It must give greater weight to Greece, Asia Minor, Syria, Mesopotamia, and Egypt than to Gaul, Britain, or Germany. Medieval history deals with the period in which a distinct western European civilization appeared. But this civilization was confined to a small part of the European peninsula, and it had little influence outside that area. During the Middle Ages each great region of the world had its own civilization, and no one civilization was able greatly to modify another. Modern history deals not only with the rapid development of western European civilization in its old homeland but also with relations between that civilization and the rest of the world.

This growth and diffusion of western civilization has gone so far that we have perhaps entered a fourth period in its history. This period is marked by the appearance of distinct types of western civilization in the different areas occupied by Europeans, and, even more, by the revitalization of other civilizations following their contact with the West. Both the appearance of different types of western civilization and the revival of old civilizations are stimulating factors; they should help to prevent ossification and decay. Unfortunately, a stimulus can also be an irritant, and the reactions among competing civilizations may lead to efforts for mutual destruction rather than for mutual instruction.

The history of civilization begins in obscurity and ends with a question mark. Yet past experience is our only guide in solving present and future problems, and knowledge of our history may help us answer the great question with which we are faced today, that of the survival of civilization in any form.

EXPLORATION IN SPACE

Uranus
1,782,000,000
miles from sun

VOYAGER 1 & 2 (1977) USA
Launched to investigate outer
planets: Jupiter (1979),
Saturn (1981), Uranus (1986)

Mars
142,000,000
miles from
sun

Pluto
3,664,000,000
miles from sun

VIKING 1 (1975) USA
First soft landing
on Mars (1976)

Mercury
36,000,000
miles from
sun

Neptune
2,792,000,000
miles from sun

MARINER 10 (1973) USA
Flew within 3300 miles
of Venus and 625 miles
of Mercury (1974)

SUN

Venus
67,000,000
miles from
sun

Saturn
886,000,000
miles from sun

PIONEER 5 (1960) USA
First solar orbit

Jupiter
483,000,000
miles from
sun

APOLLO 11 (1969) USA
First men on moon

VENERA 5 (1969) USSR
First probe to impact
on a planet

GALILEO (projected 1981) USA
First satellite to orbit
Jupiter

VENERA 9 (1975) USSR
First definite soft
landing on Venus (1976)

PIONEER 10 (1972-73) USA
Passed within 87,000 miles
of Jupiter. First object
to leave our solar system

Moon
238,900
miles from
Earth

SPUTNIK 1 (1957) USSR
First satellite to
orbit Earth

Earth
93,000,000
miles from
sun

PIONEER 11 (1973) USA
Flew within 25,000 miles
of Jupiter (1974) and is
scheduled to fly by
Saturn (1979)

LUNA 10 (1966) USSR
First lunar orbit

VOSTOK 1 (1961) USSR
First man in orbit

SALYUT (1971) USSR
First space station

ENTERPRISE (1979) USA
First reusable space
shuttle

APOLLO/SOYUZ (1975) USA/USSR
First international space
docking

GEMINI 7 & 6A (1965) USA
First successful space
rendezvous

VOSKHOD 2 (1965) USSR
First "space walk"

george v. kelvin

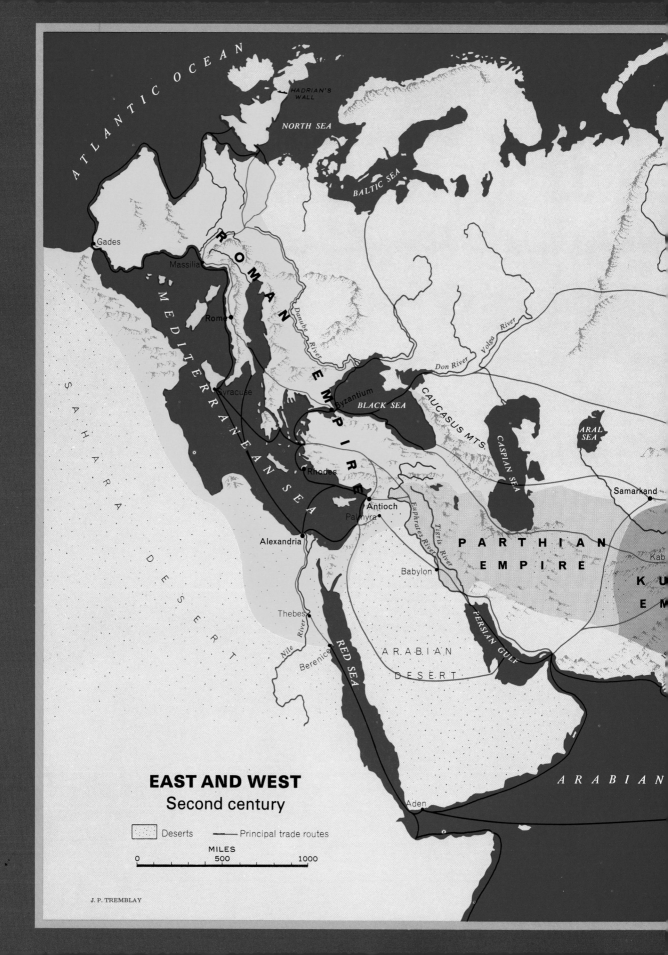

ATLANTIC OCEAN

NORTH SEA

HADRIAN'S WALL

BALTIC SEA

Gades

Massilia

ROMAN EMPIRE

Rome

MEDITERRANEAN SEA

SAHARA DESERT

Danube River

Volga River

Don River

Byzantium

BLACK SEA

CAUCASUS MTS

CASPIAN SEA

ARAL SEA

Samarkand

Syracuse

Rhodes

Antioch

Palmyra

Alexandria

Euphrates River

Tigris River

Babylon

PARTHIAN EMPIRE

Kab

KU
E
M

Thebes

Nile River

Berenice

RED SEA

PERSIAN GULF

ARABIAN DESERT

ARABIAN

Aden

EAST AND WEST

Second century

Deserts ———— Principal trade routes

MILES

0   500   1000

J. P. TREMBLAY

P A C · I F I C   O C E A N

SEA
OF
JAPAN

Amur River

HUNS

ALTAI MTS.

GOBI DESERT

GREAT WALL

LATE   HAN

EMPIRE

Yellow River

Loyang

EAST
CHINA
SEA

TIEN SHAN MTS.

Hankow

Kashgar
Yarkand

Khotan

Yangtze River

HAN
IRE

Brahmaputra River

HIMALAYA MTS.

SOUTH
CHINA
SEA

Ganges River

Pataliputra

EMPIRE
OF THE
ANDHRAS

BAY
OF
BENGAL

EA

Mangalore

INDIAN OCEAN

THE SPREAD OF CHRISTIANITY IN EUROPE To 1417

Christianity to 600
to 900
to 1200
to 1417
Temporarily lost to Islam

☩ Principal cathedral cities
✝ Principal monasteries

MILES
0   100   200   300

osala

Novgorod

Moscow

BALTIC SEA

Gnesen

Vistula River

ROMAN CHURCH
GREEK CHURCH

Kiev

Volga River

Oder River

Cracow

Vienna

Gran

Dnieper River

Don River

Danube River

BLACK SEA

Tigris River

Constantinople

Thessalonica

AEGEAN
SEA

Euphrates River

CYPRUS

CRETE

RANEAN SEA

Nile R.

J. P. TREMBLAY

EUROPEAN CIVILIZATION Fifteenth century

AREAS OF WARFARE

Fall of Granada, 1492

Wars of the Roses, 1454-85

Hussite Wars, 1420-36

Hundred Years' War, 1338-1453

▲ Members of the Hanseatic League

Principal trade routes

MILES
0   100   200   300

NORWAY

ATLANTIC OCEAN

NORTH SEA

DENMARK

IRELAND

Dublin

SCOTLAND

Edinburgh

ENGLAND

Oxford   Cambridge

London

ENGLISH CHANNEL

Leiden
Rotterdam

Bruges   Antwerp
Ghent
Brussels
Louvain

Hamburg   Lübeck

Bremen

Brunswick

Magdeburg

Elbe River

HOLY RO

Noyon

Paris

Cologne

Leipzig

Erfurt

Prague

FRANCE

Fontainebleau

Loire River

Tours

Trier   Mainz

Nuremberg
Regensburg

EMPIRE

BAY OF
BISCAY

Angoulême

Bordeaux

Garonne River

Dijon

Lyons

Basel

Zurich

Geneva

Augsburg

Constance

Trent

BURGUNDY

Rhine R.

Rhône R.

Avignon

Milan

Po River

Venice

Ferrara
Bologna

Genoa

PORTUGAL

Duero River

Ebro R.

NAVARRE

Tagus River

Escorial

Lisbon

Madrid

CASTILE

ARAGON

Barcelona

Marseilles

Pisa
Florence

Siena

Perugia

PAPAL
STATES

ADRIA

CORSICA

SARDINIA
(ARAGON)

Rome

Seville

GRANADA

Palermo

SICILY
(ARAGON)

Nap

MEDIT

EN

Novgorod

Moscow

BALTIC SEA

Danzig

Königsberg

Volga River

Thorn

Vistula River

Oder River

P O L A N D - L I T H U A N I A

Kiev

Cracow

Dnieper River

Don River

Vienna

Buda

H U N G A R Y

Danube River

O T T O M A N

BLACK SEA

Tigris River

Constantinople

Salonika

AEGEAN

SEA

E M P I R E

Euphrates River

RHODES

CYPRUS

CRETE

RRANEAN SEA

Nile R.

J. P. TREMBLAY

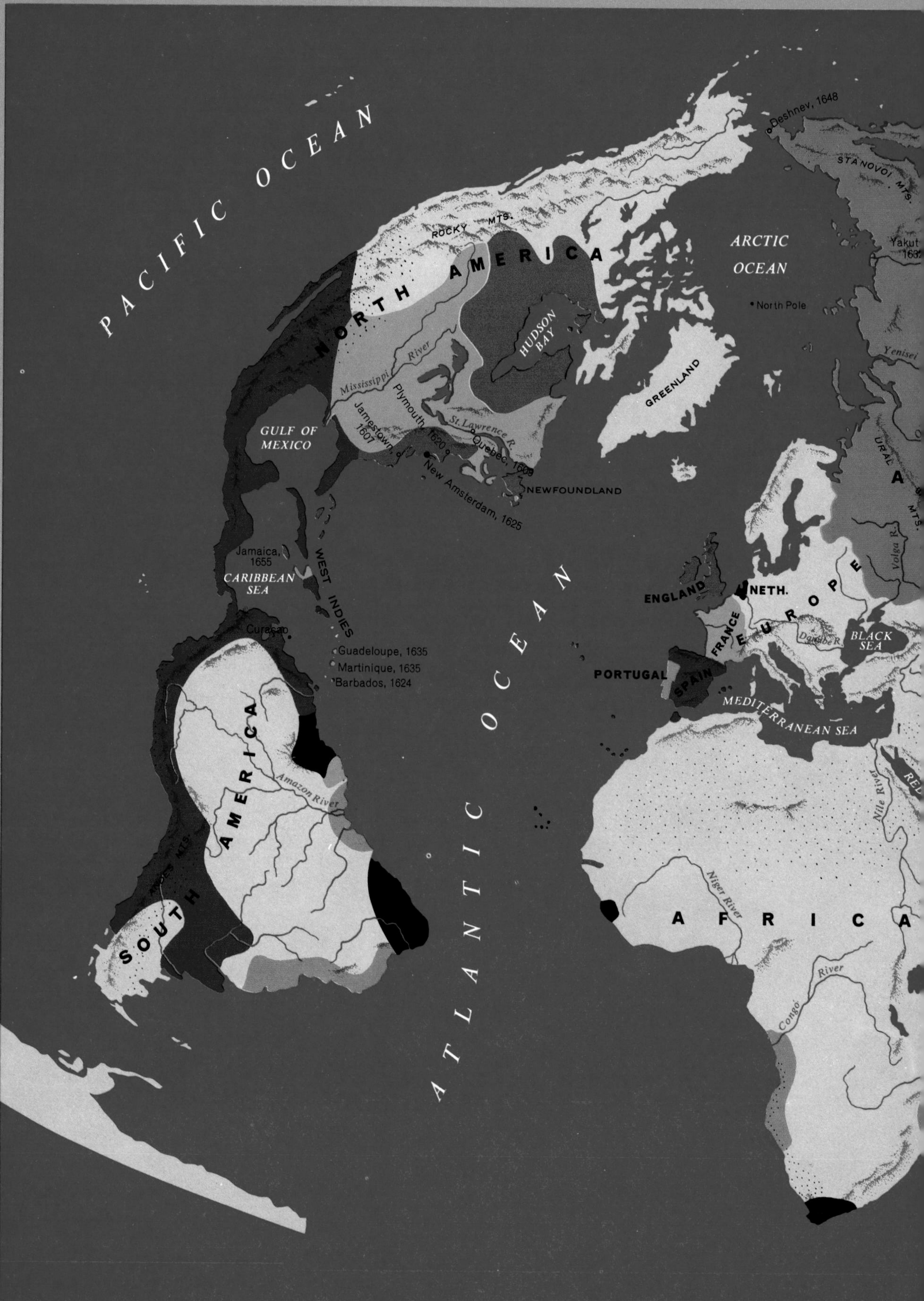

PACIFIC OCEAN

NORTH AMERICA

ROCKY MTS.

ARCTIC
OCEAN

Deshnev, 1648

STANOVOI MTS.

Yakut
163

· North Pole

HUDSON
BAY

GREENLAND

Yenisei

Mississippi River

Plymouth, 1620

St. Lawrence R.

Quebec, 1608

GULF OF
MEXICO

Jamestown,
1607

New Amsterdam, 1625

NEWFOUNDLAND

URAL MTS.

A

Jamaica,
1655

CARIBBEAN
SEA

WEST INDIES

ENGLAND

NETH.

EUROPE

FRANCE

Volga R.

BLACK
SEA

Curaçao

Danube R.

Guadeloupe, 1635
Martinique, 1635
Barbados, 1624

PORTUGAL

SPAIN

MEDITERRANEAN SEA

ATLANTIC OCEAN

SOUTH
AMERICA

Amazon River

ANDES MTS.

Nile River

RED

Niger River

AFRICA

Congo River

River

COLONIZATION   Seventeenth century

English   French   Dutch   Desert

Spanish   Russian   Portuguese

JAPAN

PACIFIC OCEAN

EAST
CHINA
SEA

PHILIPPINE
IS.

SOUTH
CHINA
SEA

SPICE IS.
(MOLUCCAS)

AMBOINA

EAST INDIES

Amur River

Lake
Baykal

Yeniseisk, 1618

C H I N A

Yellow River

Yangtze River

S
I
A

ARAL
SEA

PIAN
SEA

Indus River

HIMALAYA MTS.

Brahmaputra

Ganges R.

Calcutta
1690, 1756

I N D I A

BAY OF
BENGAL

JAVA

AUSTRALIA

Madras, 1639

Bombay,
1661, 1665

Pondicherry, 1674

ARABIAN SEA

INDIAN OCEAN

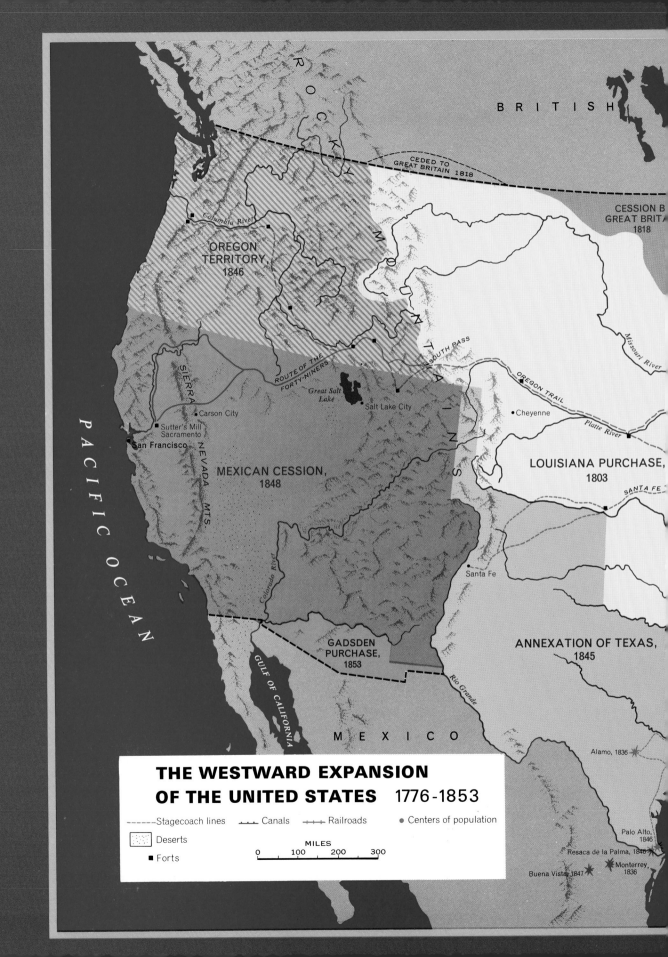

THE WESTWARD EXPANSION OF THE UNITED STATES 1776-1853

----- Stagecoach lines   +-+-+ Canals   +++++ Railroads   ● Centers of population

Deserts

■ Forts

MILES
0   100   200   300

BRITISH

CEDED TO GREAT BRITAIN 1818

CESSION B
GREAT BRIT
1818

OREGON TERRITORY, 1846

R O C K Y

M O U N T A I N S

Columbia River

ROUTE OF THE FORTY-NINERS

SOUTH PASS

Great Salt Lake

Salt Lake City

Missouri River

OREGON TRAIL

● Cheyenne

Platte River

SIERRA

NEVADA MTS.

● Carson City

■ Sutter's Mill
Sacramento
San Francisco

MEXICAN CESSION, 1848

LOUISIANA PURCHASE, 1803

SANTA FE

● Santa Fe

P A C I F I C   O C E A N

Colorado River

GADSDEN PURCHASE, 1853

ANNEXATION OF TEXAS, 1845

Rio Grande

GULF OF CALIFORNIA

M E X I C O

Alamo, 1836

Palo Alto, 1846

Resaca de la Palma, 1846

Buena Vista, 1847

Monterrey, 1836

NORTH AMERICA

LAKE SUPERIOR

LAKE MICHIGAN

LAKE HURON

Northwest Territory

Battle of Lake Erie 181

Detroit

L. ONTARIO

Lundy's Lane 1814

Chippewa, 1814

LAKE ERIE

Buffalo

Toledo

Cleveland

Chicago

St. Lawrence River

Plattsburg, 1814

VT. N.H.

NEW YORK

Albany

MASSACHUSETTS

Boston

CONN. RHODE ISLAND

New Haven

MTS.

New York

PENNSYLVANIA

Harrisburg

Trenton

NEW JERSEY

Philadelphia

New York

Springfield

ROAD

CUMBERLAND

Indianapolis

Columbus 1840

1820

1850

1830

1800

1810

DEL.

Baltimore

Washington

MD.

Washington, 1814

Richmond

VIRGINIA

Kansas City

St. Louis

Ohio River

Mississippi River

WESTWARD EXPANSION TO 1783

APPALACHIAN

NORTH CAROLINA

Memphis

SOUTH CAROLINA

Atlanta

Charleston

GEORGIA

Savannah

Mississippi Territory

ATLANTIC OCEAN

New Orleans, 1815

New Orleans

Galveston

FLORIDA PURCHASE, 1819

GULF OF MEXICO

J. P. TREMBLAY

NAPOLEONIC EUROPE   1812

ATLANTIC OCEAN

NORTH SEA

UNITED KINGDOM
OF
GREAT BRITAIN AND IRELAND

London

ENGLISH CHANNEL

KINGDOM OF DENMARK AND NORWAY

KINGDOM
OF
SWEDEN

Hanover   Berlin

WESTPHALIA

CONFEDERATION

OF THE

RHINE

Leipzig

Jena   SAXONY

Waterloo

Paris

Valmy

Elbe River

Rhine R.

Seine River

Loire River

BAY OF
BISCAY

NAPOLEONIC
EMPIRE

SWITZERLAND

Rhone River

1814-15

1809
1805

1797

Garonne River

1808

Ebro
R.

KINGDOM OF PORTUGAL

Lisbon

Duero River

Salamanca

Tagus River

Madrid

KINGDOM OF SPAIN

Toulon

KINGDOM

OF

ITALY

Po River

Marengo
1800

ADRIAT

ELBA

CORSICA

Rome

KINGD
OF
NAP

Trafalgar

KINGDOM
OF
SARDINIA

KINGDOM
OF
SICILY

MEDIT

Legend

▨	Napoleonic Empire
▨	States under French control
▨	States allied to France
←	Routes of Napoleon

MILES
0   100   200   300

BALTIC SEA

Moscow

Borodino

1812

Tilsit

Friedland

KINGDOM
OF PRUSSIA

DUCHY

Vistula River

1806-07

OF

WARSAW

Oder River

RUSSIAN EMPIRE

Volga River

Dnieper River

Don River

Austerlitz

Wagram

Vienna

AUSTRIAN EMPIRE

BESSARABIA

Danube River

BLACK SEA

Tigris River

PROVINCES

O   T   T   O   M   A   N   E   M   P   I   R   E

AEGEAN
SEA

Euphrates River

1798

RANEAN SEA

1799

Abukir Bay

Nile R.

J. P. TREMBLAY

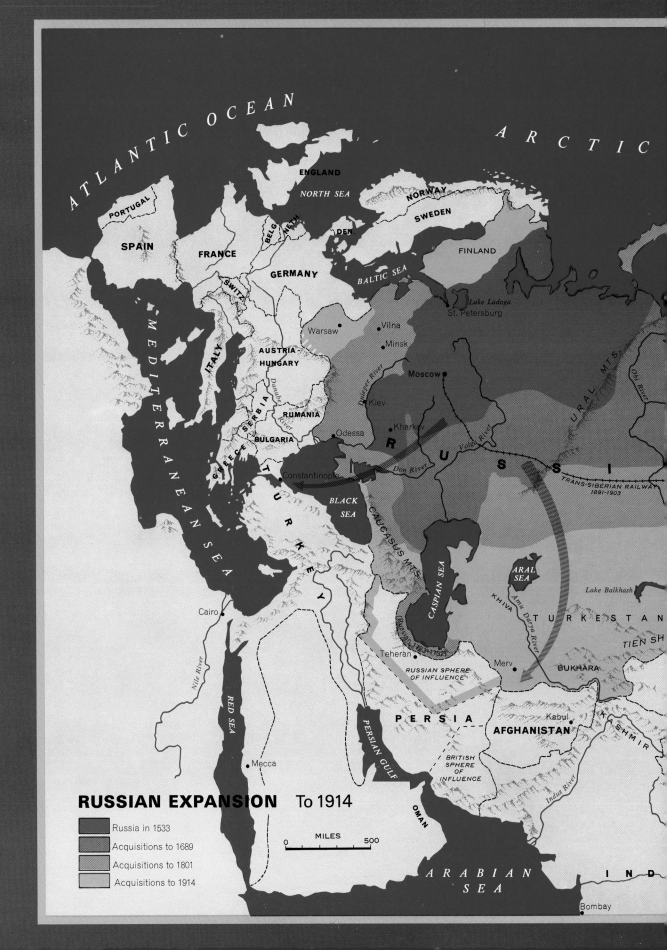

ATLANTIC OCEAN

ARCTIC

ENGLAND

NORTH SEA

NORWAY

SWEDEN

PORTUGAL

SPAIN

FRANCE

BELG.
NETH.

DEN.

FINLAND

GERMANY

Lake Ladoga
St. Petersburg

SWITZ.

BALTIC SEA

Warsaw

Vilna

Minsk

ITALY

AUSTRIA-
HUNGARY

Dnieper River

Moscow

Danube River

SERBIA

RUMANIA

Kiev

Kharkov

Volga River

URAL MTS.

Ob River

GREECE

BULGARIA

Odessa

R

U

S

S

I

A

Don River

TRANS-SIBERIAN RAILWAY
1891-1903

TURKEY

Constantinople

*BLACK
SEA*

CAUCASUS MTS.

MEDITERRANEAN SEA

CASPIAN SEA

ARAL
SEA

Lake Balkhash

KHIVA

Amu Darya River

TURKESTAN

Cairo

Russia 1723-1732

TIEN SH

Teheran

RUSSIAN SPHERE
OF INFLUENCE

Merv

BUKHARA

Nile River

RED SEA

PERSIA

Kabul

K
A
S
H
M
I
R

PERSIAN GULF

AFGHANISTAN

Mecca

BRITISH
SPHERE
OF
INFLUENCE

Indus River

RUSSIAN EXPANSION To 1914

OMAN

Russia in 1533

Acquisitions to 1689

Acquisitions to 1801

Acquisitions to 1914

MILES
0   500

ARABIAN
SEA

I N D

Bombay

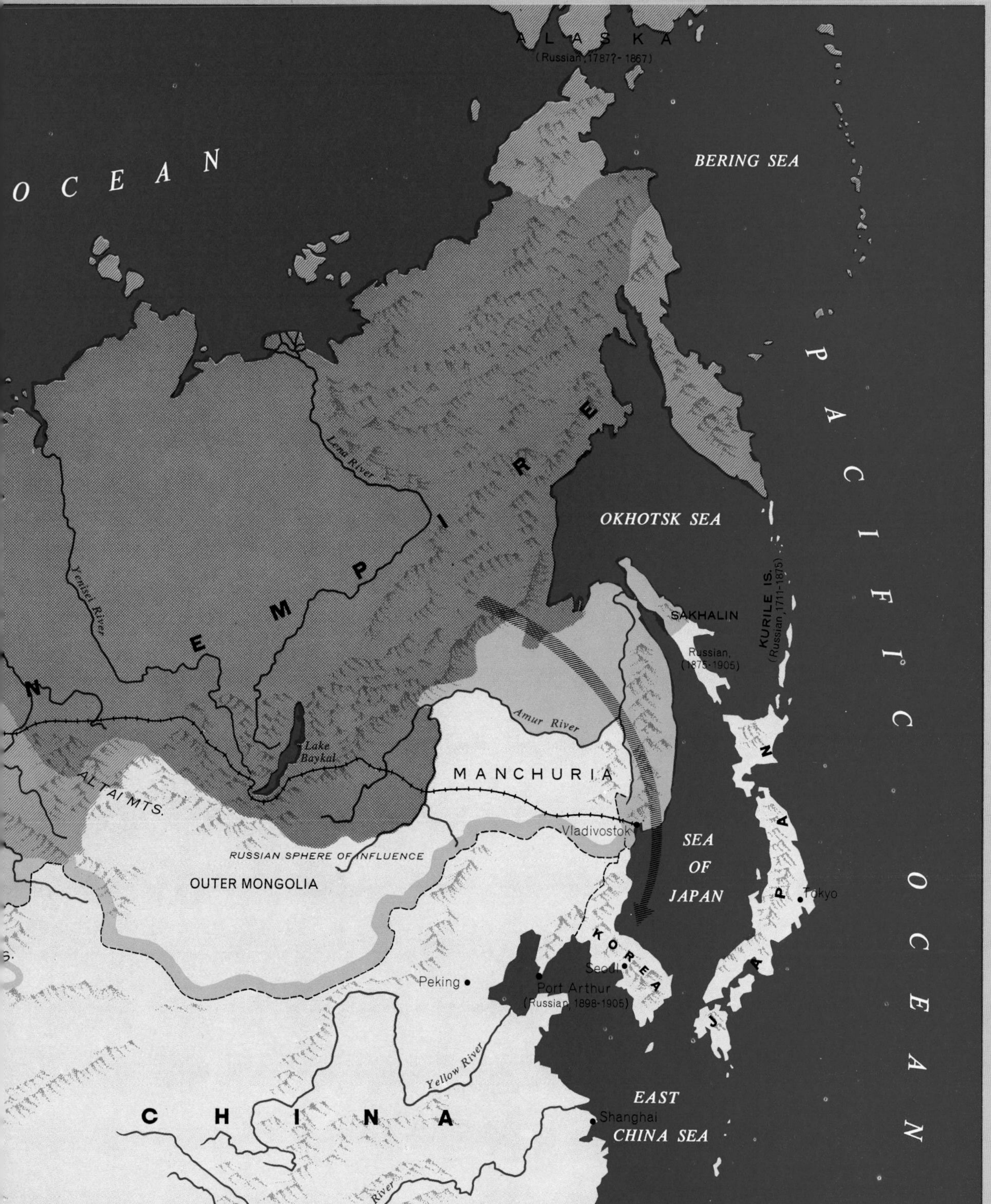

OCEAN

ALASKA
(Russian, 1787?-1867)

BERING SEA

PACIFIC

OKHOTSK SEA

SAKHALIN
Russian,
(1875-1905)

KURILE IS.
(Russian 1711-1875)

Amur River

Lena River

Yenisei River

Lake
Baykal

MANCHURIA

EMPIRE

ALTAI MTS.

RUSSIAN SPHERE OF INFLUENCE

OUTER MONGOLIA

Vladivostok

SEA
OF
JAPAN

JAPAN

Tokyo

KOREA

Seoul

Peking

Port Arthur
(Russian 1898-1905)

Yellow River

EAST
CHINA SEA

Shanghai

OCEAN

CHINA

Brahmaputra   River

LAYA   MOUNTAINS

BHUTAN

ges River

Yangtze River

Mekong River

Hong Kong

Calcutta

BURMA

SIAM

FRENCH
INDO-CHINA

SOUTH
CHINA SEA

BAY OF
BENGAL

J. P. TREMBLAY

WORLD POPULATION

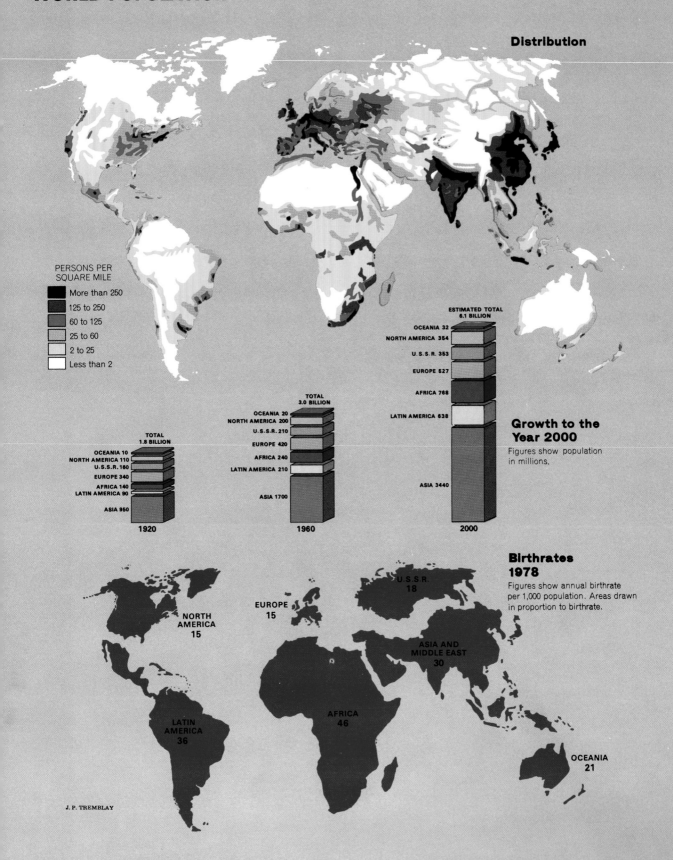

Distribution

PERSONS PER SQUARE MILE

- More than 250
- 125 to 250
- 60 to 125
- 25 to 60
- 2 to 25
- Less than 2

Growth to the Year 2000

Figures show population in millions.

TOTAL 1.8 BILLION

- OCEANIA 10
- NORTH AMERICA 110
- U.S.S.R. 160
- EUROPE 340
- AFRICA 140
- LATIN AMERICA 90
- ASIA 950

1920

TOTAL 3.0 BILLION

- OCEANIA 20
- NORTH AMERICA 200
- U.S.S.R. 210
- EUROPE 420
- AFRICA 240
- LATIN AMERICA 210
- ASIA 1700

1960

ESTIMATED TOTAL 6.1 BILLION

- OCEANIA 32
- NORTH AMERICA 354
- U.S.S.R. 353
- EUROPE 527
- AFRICA 768
- LATIN AMERICA 638
- ASIA 3440

2000

Birthrates 1978

Figures show annual birthrate per 1,000 population. Areas drawn in proportion to birthrate.

NORTH AMERICA 15

EUROPE 15

U.S.S.R. 18

ASIA AND MIDDLE EAST 30

LATIN AMERICA 36

AFRICA 46

OCEANIA 21

J. P. TREMBLAY

The Mainstream of Civilization
Third Edition

The gold-plated inner coffin
of the pharaoh Tutankhamon
(*ca.* 1340 B.C.).

1 The Ancient Middle East to *ca.* 500 B.C.

Human beings have long been interested in their past. But for most peoples the remote past has been very difficult to recover. A few undated monuments, confused mixtures of ancient utensils and ornaments, groups of often contradictory legends were all that was available. As recently as two hundred years ago—or about the time of the American Revolution—western scholars knew almost no history before that of the classical age of Greece (*ca.* 500 B.C.). True, there was some understanding of the historical passages of the Hebrew scriptures, and some awareness that the colossal monuments along the Nile were the remnants of a very early Egyptian civilization. But little attention was given to these evidences of the existence of preclassical societies.

Just at this time, however, the excavations at Pompeii began, and the discoveries made there gave a tremendous impetus to the development of the science of archeology. During the past two centuries it has become clear that thousands of years before the Greeks there were highly developed civilizations in many parts of the Old World. About the year 1800, archeologists and historians began to reconstruct the long and fascinating history of ancient Egypt. More recently, in the nineteenth and twentieth centuries, they uncovered many other civilizations—notably in Mesopotamia, in India, and on the island of Crete—whose existence had not been known before.

Although great cities long unknown have been unearthed and whole libraries and archives discovered, the pace of new excavations continues unabated. Historians of the preclassical civilizations must be constantly prepared to revise their interpretations in the light of new evidence.

PREHISTORY TO *ca.* 3500 B.C.

Human beings, or something akin to human beings, have inhabited the earth for at least 2 million years and perhaps more. All but the last 5500 years of this span is regarded as prehistory, since it antedates the invention of writing. The vast sweep of human prehistory from about 2.5 million to 15,000 B.C. is known as the Old Stone Age because of the primitive pebble and stone tools used by humanlike animals and by humans throughout this era. During the Old Stone Age several species of humanlike

Art of the Old Stone Age:

Harpoon

Dart thrower
of reindeer antler

Baton de commandement
of reindeer antler, showing
wild horses

creatures appeared and disappeared. It was not until about 40,000 B.C. (a relatively recent date in prehistory) that Cro-Magnon man, the species from which all modern people are descended, first wandered into Europe, though we cannot know where or for how long this species may have existed before that time.

The New Stone Age
ca. 10,000–3500 B.C.

It took more than 2 million years to advance from the first crude pebble tools of the Old Stone Age to the precisely made, ground and polished tools characteristic of the New Stone Age. But in the relatively short span of about seven thousand years, there were two basic changes in humans' way of life: the introduction of agriculture shortly before 10,000 B.C. and the emergence of early city-states sometime around 3500 B.C. Both steps seem to have been connected with the drastic changes in climate between about 17,000 and 12,000 B.C. that followed the last of the four great Ice Ages and the subsequent melting of the glaciers that had covered much of the Northern Hemisphere. And both steps were also connected with a rapid growth in population. More people needed more food; with more food, more people could survive, and some of them could leave the land and live in cities.

By about 17,000 B.C. human life seems to have been concentrated in a wide belt embracing southern Europe and northern Africa and extending eastward through

Palestine, Syria, Mesopotamia, and Persia to the Indus River and Yellow River valleys. These regions were fertile then and abounded in the animal life on which people fed. But as the glaciers gradually retreated northward, the rainfall decreased, and the land became dry. The animals either migrated northward or died out. Man's response was the invention of agriculture—the domestication of plants and animals. Recent historians of agriculture have suggested that the first attempt to plant and harvest grain took place somewhere between Palestine and the upper Tigris-Euphrates Valley about 10,000 B.C. Over the next eight thousand years, the knowledge of farming, and later of animal breeding, spread throughout the areas of human habitation, though many primitive peoples in the hills and hinterlands continued to live only by hunting and food gathering.

As hunters, men had moved about as freely as the animals on which they preyed and as widely as the plants that they foraged, traveling in small bands that needed relatively little organization. As farmers, men had to settle down, at least temporarily. The oldest more or less permanent constructed habitations (as opposed to caves and hunting camps) that have been uncovered by archeologists date from about 10,000 B.C., approximately the same time as the introduction of agriculture.

Little is known about life in these early villages, but we can make certain assumptions. With larger numbers of people living and working together, life became quite complex. Crafts developed—the making of cloth from flax and from wool, the working of leather, the manufacture of pottery, and, much later, the smelting and shaping of metals. No one family could produce all these goods, and not every man or

Human skull from the ruins of Jericho (*ca.* 7000 B.C.). The inhabitants of this city developed the art of ''portraiture'' by modeling the features in plaster and inlaying the eyes with shell in an attempt to reconstruct the face of the dead man.

of nature. In short, even in a small village, some organization was needed, and regular patterns of behavior had to be worked out to guide people in their relations with one another. These patterns gradually hardened into fixed customs, which replaced whim and violence in settling disagreements. A chieftain and a council of advisers were needed to enforce these customs and to maintain order; this was the basis of village government. Living in villages, men gave up some of their freedom in return for better protection against human and natural enemies, a more regular supply of food, and a more ordered life. This was, in short, the first step toward civilization.

EARLY CIVILIZATIONS
ca. 3500–1500 B.C.

woman could work at a craft and still raise enough food for a family. Some means of exchanging goods and services had to be devised. Permanent settlements had to be protected against animals, roving plunderers, and the ravages

With improved food supply and better protection, the number of humans continued to increase rapidly. But at the same time the lands they inhabited continued to dry up. Once again, men found that they would have to develop new techniques if they were to survive. In

THE ANCIENT MIDDLE EAST

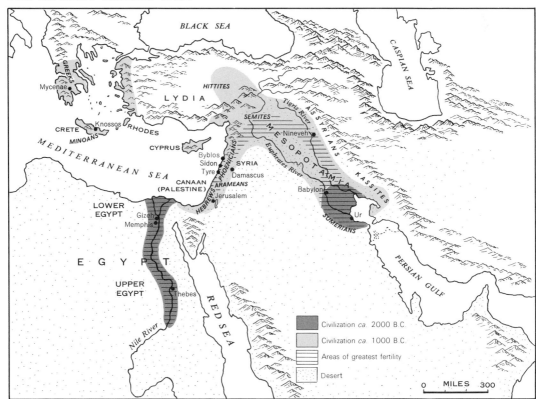

BLACK SEA
CASPIAN SEA
GREEKS
Mycenae
HITTITES
LYDIA
SEMITES
ASSYRIANS
Tigris River
CRETE
Knossos
RHODES
MINOANS
Nineveh
MESOPOTAMIA
CYPRUS
MEDITERRANEAN SEA
Byblos
PHOENICIANS
Sidon
SYRIA
Euphrates River
Tyre
Damascus
KASSITES
CANAAN
(PALESTINE)
ARAMEANS
HEBREWS
Jerusalem
Babylon
LOWER
EGYPT
SUMERIANS
Gizeh
Ur
Memphis
PERSIAN GULF
E G Y P T
UPPER
EGYPT
Thebes
RED SEA
Nile River

Civilization *ca.* 2000 B.C.
Civilization *ca.* 1000 B.C.
Areas of greatest fertility
Desert

0   MILES   300

time some human communities found that they could assure themselves a larger and more regular food supply by cultivating the fertile soil in the valleys of large rivers. But the low-lying lands near the larger rivers provided a far from satisfactory environment. The river banks were too marshy to build on. The steaming swamps along the rivers bred disease. And the floods that came every spring were often strong enough to sweep away whole villages. If men were to make their homes along the rivers, they would have to learn to drain the swamps, control the floodwaters, and irrigate the higher land away from the river beds. To carry out such projects, men would first have to organize into larger communities, accept more complex and more authoritarian forms of government, and acquire greater technical skills than they then had. It was in valleys of the Tigris-Euphrates, Nile, Indus, and Yellow rivers that the first cities and the first civilizations appeared.

A Babylonian boundary stone (*ca.* thirteenth to tenth century B.C.), showing an example of cuneiform writing.

Mesopotamia

The earliest evidences of civilization were found in Mesopotamia (Greek for "between the rivers"), the valley of the Tigris and Euphrates rivers, in what is now Iraq. This Babylonian civilization—as it is often called after the city of Babylon that later dominated the valley—began about 3000 B.C. when a people known as the Sumerians established several city-states in the delta bounded by the two rivers. It is still not known where the Sumerians came from. Some historians believe that they migrated into the delta region from much older agricultural villages in the hilly country further up the valley. More likely, they came to Mesopotamia from somewhere else—perhaps by sea, as their own myths suggest.

The Sumerian cities were united in a loose league. They shared a culture, they spoke a common language, and they worshiped the same gods. A typical Sumerian city-state consisted of the city proper and as much of the surrounding population as the city walls could accommodate in times of crisis. The focal point of each city was a great platform raised above the surrounding residential areas. On it were erected the places of worship, including ultimately the many-storied temples (ziggurats) that became the typical form of Babylonian monumental architecture.

Writing, in the strict sense of the term, was first invented and employed in Mesopotamia about 3100 B.C. New finds suggest that writing may have been preceded by counting. If many objects had to be enumerated, small clay counters could be used to represent them. For a more permanent and more quickly recognizable record, the counters could be impressed in lumps of clay, using different patterns of impressions to represent different numbers. Tallies of this kind have been found from Syria to Iran. If pieces of clay could mean twelve or sixty or six hundred, then they could be marked in other patterns to convey other ideas. The first decipherable attempts to write words appear in southern Mesopotamia.

If the Sumerians did not actually originate this writing, they very soon took it over to represent their language. Most of the earliest examples of Sumerian writing are business records. But school texts appeared almost at once as a means of educating specialists in the new technique. Literary texts and historical records followed in due course. The Sumerians wrote by pressing split reeds on wet clay that was then baked until it was hard. Originally quasi-pictographic, Sumerian writing soon lost all resemblance to pictograms and developed the characteristic symbols called cuneiform (from the Latin word for "wedge-shaped").

The advantages of civilization could not be contained within the confines of the Sumerian city-states. By about 2500 B.C., cities on the Sumerian model had appeared throughout the area from the Tigris-Euphrates Valley to Syria and Palestine on the eastern coast of the Mediterranean—the so-called Fertile Crescent. A recent and startling example of the spread of cities is the discovery of the ruins of Ebla, a thriving city-state in northern Syria at this time.

The people of these newer cities were not Sumerian but Semitic. The Semites, a number of different peoples speaking similar languages, seem to have originated in the Arabian Peninsula, where they had been nomads who lived by breeding animals. As they recognized the superior attractions of the urbanized area of the Fertile Crescent, Semites moved in several waves into Palestine, Syria, and the parts of Mesopotamia north of the Sumerians. By about 2300 B.C. the old Sumerian cities were merely the core of a much larger civilization that embraced the entire Fertile Crescent and whose population was primarily Semitic.

A Semitic warrior named Sargon (ca. 2300 B.C.) was the first to unite the city-states of Mesopotamia into a single empire, though the union survived him by little more than a century. There followed an era of about 150 years when the Sumerians again controlled Mesopotamia. But about 2000 B.C. the valley was conquered by a newly arrived Semitic people called the Amorites ("westerners"). Under the Amorites the Sumerian Empire at first dissolved into a number of small kingdoms. But in time the city-state of Babylon, under its greatest ruler, Hammurabi (ca. 1792–50 B.C.), briefly reunified the entire valley under a single empire.

After Hammurabi's death, Babylon lost its supremacy, and Mesopotamia was again divided into a number of small states. The situation was complicated by the appearance of the Kassites, a people of unknown origin. Babylon itself fell to the Kassites soon after 1600 B.C., and southern Mesopotamia was ruled by the Kassites for more than four hundred years. Little is known about this period; what evidence we have suggests a rather stagnant, if peaceful, civilization. Upper Mesopotamia had a more eventful existence, but Babylonia did not resume its primary role in the development of Mesopotamian civilization until the seventh century B.C.

Hammurabi (*ca.* 1765 B.C.).

Ziggurat at Ur (*ca.* 2250 B.C.).

The economy of the pre-Kassite Babylonian civilization was based on commerce as well as agriculture. There was so much buying and leasing and trading that the Babylonians, earlier than most other peoples, developed a system of commercial law. Over the centuries, many Babylonian rulers attempted to collect the laws of the various cities and collate them into a single legal code. The most extensive and comprehensive of them was the Code of Hammurabi.

Babylonian laws seem harsh today. Some offenses called for the loss of the tongue or a hand. Many were punishable, at least in theory, by death. But we must remember that the Babylonian codes represented an early stage in the evolution of law and that they reflected an even more primitive era when violence was the only recourse for a man who had been offended or cheated. The very creation of written laws, impossible before there were governments strong enough to enforce them, was a major advance toward justice and order.

The Babylonians produced the first known mathematics. They handled rather complicated problems in arithmetic and geometry; they also had some understanding of algebra. Babylonian numbers were ordered on multiples of sixty (unlike our own, which are ordered on multiples of ten), and such Mesopotamian units of measure as the sixty-minute hour and the 360-degree circle are still in use.

The Babylonians also, as did the Egyptians, became interested in astronomy. There were the obvious regularities in the apparent movements of the sun and the moon, from which the concepts of a year, a month, and a week developed. There were the far less obvious regularities in the movements of the planets, which Babylonian astronomers also observed. We may wonder if the concept of laws of nature, from which all science derives, would ever have developed if early astronomers had not studied and tabulated the motions of the heavenly bodies. There are more regularities in heaven than on earth.

Although urban life brought many advantages and a higher level of living for part of the population, no region in Mesopotamia enjoyed long periods of peace and prosperity. The rival states were frequently at war, and often whole cities were razed to the ground. Devastating floods and plagues swept through the lands. These uncertainties were especially shocking to business-oriented communities in which men were seeking individual profit rather than group survival. The Babylonians took a gloomy view of life, seeing their gods as selfish beings who paid little heed to men except to deliver an occasional blow, apparently out of sheer caprice. Babylonian religion was roughly like a business arrangement: the Babylonians believed that if they performed certain ceremonies the gods would leave them in peace. There was a great deal of magic and very little morality in their religious observances. To appease the gods, it was more important to know the right prayers and the appropriate sacrifices than it was to lead an upright life. And yet these same people set very high standards in their business dealings with one another.

The Emergence of Egyptian Civilization

During the same era in which the Mesopotamian city-states were battling the elements, one another, and a succession of foreign invaders, another civilization appeared, matured, and flourished in relative serenity only nine hundred miles away, in Egypt. The Nile Valley, seat of the ancient Egyptian civilization, extends about six hundred miles into Africa, although in Upper (southern) Egypt the fertile belt along the river is rarely more than ten miles wide. The Delta in Lower (northern) Egypt forms a large triangle that widens steadily until it reaches the sea, but much of the land in the Delta is swampy because the Nile splits into many branches. Primitive agricultural communities appeared along the Nile as early as 5000 B.C. when a variety of peoples, including both Negroes and Semites, sought refuge there from the encroaching deserts. About 4000 B.C. these communities began to consolidate into a series of small kingdoms, and by 3000 B.C. the entire Nile Valley had been united under a single monarch.

The civilization that began to appear in Egypt shortly before 3000 B.C. may have received an initial stimulus from Mesopotamia. But Egypt, unlike Mesopotamia, was rapidly united under a single political and economic system, and Egyptian civilization matured more rapidly than that of Mesopotamia. Once established, Egyptian civilization endured as a separate and clearly indentifiable entity until Egypt was absorbed by the Persian Empire in 525 B.C.—a span of 2500 years, as long a period as that from 525 B.C. to the present.

Egypt had many advantages over Mesopotamia, most of them derived from the peculiar nature and position of the Nile Valley. The flooding of the Tigris and Euphrates rivers was irregular and unpredictable. Sometimes there was not enough water to irrigate the crops; at other times heavy floods might wipe out a whole year's harvest. But the Nile flooded every year at the same time and rose to very nearly the same level, and Egyptian life could be geared to the rhythmic regularity of the river. Also, the Mesopotamian plain was open to invasion from all sides, and the frequent incursion of new peoples helped to keep the region divided into warring states. The Nile Valley was exposed to invasion only at its northern and southern extremities. Invasions were less frequent than in Mesopotamia, and when they did occur they could be dealt with easily by a unified military effort.

Thus it was relatively easy and obviously useful for the small kingdoms along the Nile to consolidate into the large states of Upper (southern) and Lower (northern) Egypt. Some sort of struggle obviously preceded the unification of the "Two Lands" (as ancient Egypt was named by its contemporaries), but it occurred so early that only traces of it remain in religious legends. During almost all its history, ancient Egypt was ruled by kings who wore the double crown of the North and the South.

The long expanse of ancient Egyptian history can be divided into four eras, each preceded by a period of transition that began with internal weakness and ended with national consolidation and expansion. Thus the first four centuries of proto-dynastic unification (*ca.* 3100–2700 B.C.) were followed by the Old Kingdom (or the Pyramid Age) from about 2700 to 2150 B.C. Collapse of central power (*ca.* 2150–2050 B.C.) was rapidly reversed by the rise of the Middle Kingdom (*ca.* 2050–1650 B.C.). This era ended with another weakening of central authority and the conquest of Egypt by the Hyksos (*ca.* 1650–1550 B.C.). The expulsion of the Hyksos led to the period of Egypt's greatest expansion under the New Kingdom (*ca.* 1550–1100 B.C.). The next decline was longer (*ca.* 1100–650 B.C.), and the brief revival under the Saïte dynasty (*ca.* 650–525 B.C.) was only a pale reflection of former glories. The Persian conquest of 525 B.C. ended the independence of ancient Egypt.

The Old Kingdom and Middle Kingdom in Egypt ca. 2700–1550 B.C.

The era of the Old Kingdom in Egypt was one of the most dynamic periods in human history. Within three or four centuries after civilization first appeared in the Nile Valley, some of the most notable achievements of the Egyptian civilization had already been realized: the erection of a strong monarchy and a complex bureaucracy capable of maintaining peace and order throughout the country; the introduction of hieroglyphics, a system of writing that, like cuneiform, used both word signs and syllable signs, but that, unlike cuneiform, retained its original pictographic form; the development of sufficient engineering

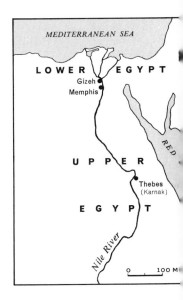

skill to erect large stone structures (including the pyramids) for the first time in history; and the invention of a calendar so accurate that, with minor modifications, it is still in use.

The most important factor in the rapid progress of Egyptian civilization was that all the abundant agricultural resources and ample manpower of the Nile Valley were controlled by a single divine and absolute ruler, known to us, from the Hebrew scriptures, as the pharaoh. The Egyptians believed that the land belonged to the gods. They were grateful to the gods for the gifts of water and grain, and they were beholden to them for the use of the land. They worshiped their pharaoh as one of their gods and as the earthly representative of all the gods, a status accorded to very few Mesopotamian kings. With this unquestioning loyalty of their subjects, the powerful pharaohs of the Old Kingdom were able to administer Egypt almost as a private estate. Agents of the pharaoh—using

their calendars to predict the regular rise and fall of the Nile—told the Egyptian peasants when and where to plant their seed and when to harvest their crops. Such a planned economy ensured a maximum yield, and much of the profit was used to enrich and strengthen the government.

Egyptian peasants seem not to have objected to their servile status. Rather, they accepted the authority of the pharaoh as necessary to their well-being. Unlike the Mesopotamians, who feared the caprice and ill will of many of their deities, the Egyptians thought of their gods—including the pharaoh—as well disposed toward men.

Because the Egyptians buried their dead on the fringes of the desert, in places that were never cultivated, thousands of their tombs have survived. From the contents of these tombs we can get a clearer view of Egyptian religious beliefs than of those of other ancient peoples. It is evident that the Egyptians were tremendously interested in the afterlife and that they devoted much of their energy and wealth to assure survival in the next world. Other peoples believed that the soul might linger in some shady nether world, but the Egyptians were convinced that man participated in the same life-death-rebirth cycle they observed in nature. In Egypt's clear, dry air, dead bodies did not decompose; they turned brown and brittle like the grain stalks. Thus it seemed natural to the Egyptians that if the soul of a man—like the seed of a plant—could be preserved through the human equivalent of a "dry" season, he would be restored to life in another world when the time came for his rebirth.

The Egyptians gave considerable attention to the problem of providing the soul with a suitable place to reside when the body died. In the era of the Old Kingdom, the Egyptians apparently believed that only the pharaoh's soul had to be preserved and that he would take care of the rest of his subjects in the afterworld. It was to provide an elaborate palace for their afterlives that some of the earlier pharaohs built the pyramids between about 2700 and 2200 B.C. In later eras more individualistic views prevailed

Egyptian Religion   Fourteenth century B.C.

Morality and the Last Judgment in the Book of the Dead.

Hail to you, ye gods. . . . Behold, I came to you without sin, without evil, without wrong. . . . I gave bread to the hungry, water to the thirsty, clothing to the naked, and a ferry to him without a boat. I made divine offerings for the gods and food offerings for the dead. Save me! Protect me!

◊   ◊   ◊

Monotheism in the hymn to the sun god (Aton). This was written during the brief period when King Akhnaton (1375–1358 B.C.) was trying to establish the cult of a single sun god.

How manifold are thy works!
They are hidden before men.
O sole God, beside whom is no other,
Thou didst create the earth according to thy heart. . .
Thou didst make the distant sky in order to rise therein,
In order to behold all that thou hast made
While thou wast yet alone.
Shining in thy form as living Aton,
Dawning, glittering, going afar and returning.
Thou makest millions of forms
Through thyself alone.

From James H. Breasted, *The Dawn of Conscience* (New York: Scribner's, 1934), pp. 259, 284–85.

Ramses II, ruler of the Egyptian Empire at its height, built this temple to Amon at Karnak. Below is a colossal statue of Ramses at Karnak. At his knees is his queen, Nefertari.

and even people of moderate means built tombs for themselves, furnished with texts to guide them to the next world and with provisions for the journey.

The pyramids are only the most impressive examples of the remarkable engineering skill of the ancient Egyptians. The concentration of wealth and manpower under a single strong government made it possible for the Egyptians to build many magnificent temples, tombs, and statues on a scale that could be rivaled only in the greatest states of Mesopotamia. Although even the Egyptians did not attempt to build anything as large as the pyramids after the era of the Old Kingdom, structures like the temple at Karnak, built in the era of the New Kingdom, are still awe-inspiring in their size and artistic perfection. The pharaohs, who were gods, built like gods; their temples dominated space just as their statues dominated representations of ordinary men.

Egypt's first long period of peaceful development, under the Old Kingdom, ended about 2150 B.C. when a series of weak pharaohs permitted the government to fall into the hands of powerful local administrators. Without centralized supervision, Egypt experienced an era of local famines and civil wars. After a century of turmoil, the country was reunited under the Middle Kingdom (*ca.* 2050–1650 B.C.). But toward the end of this era, Egypt again experienced a time of troubles, caused largely by foreign invaders. The invaders were known as the Hyksos, and their origin is still not exactly clear. They were probably a Semitic people (perhaps Amorites) whose kinsmen had already conquered the eastern arm of the Fertile Crescent. Aided by their horse-drawn chariots, they gained control of Egypt and then established themselves strongly in the Delta. Elsewhere they were weaker, and they were unable to govern all Egypt for more than a century. Native armies began to push them back, and by about 1550 B.C. the Hyksos had been expelled from Egypt.

It was perhaps no accident that Mesopotamia was overrun by the Kassites at just about the same time that the Hyksos

Ceremonial axe of victory over the Hyksos showing the pharaoh Ahmose smiting an enemy.

attacked Egypt. Growth of population created pressures for expansion, and new military techniques, such as the horse-drawn chariot, facilitated conquest. But Egypt recovered much more rapidly from the Hyksos domination than Mesopotamia did from the Kassite conquests.

Crete

The island of Crete stretches for more than 150 miles across the entrance to the Aegean Sea. The Greeks preserved legends about a great King Minos of Crete who was so powerful that even the city of Athens had to send him an annual tribute. But since the sandy soil of Crete has barely been able to sustain its small population throughout historical times, no one was inclined to take the legend of a powerful kingdom on the island very seriously. Then in 1900 Arthur Evans, an English archeologist, dug into a mound on the northern coast of Crete and uncovered a magnificent palace, the size of a small city, which he assumed to be Knossos, the ancient capital of King Minos.

In addition to the palace at Knossos, Evans and his successors discovered many other sites. They were able to show that a civilization, separate from those of Egypt and Mesopotamia, had flourished on the island from about 2000 to 1400 B.C. This civilization had a style of its own, not monumental like the Egyptian nor stolid like the Mesopotamian, but delicate and cheerful, made for men and not for gods. Evans called it the Minoan civilization after the legendary King Minos. During this era the Minoans seem to have prospered not by farming, but by dominating the trade of the Aegean and the eastern Mediterranean.

The archeologists found that the Minoan civilization must have succumbed to some great catastrophe, for virtually every settlement they discovered showed evidence of violent destruction dating from about 1480 B.C. The palace at Knossos was rebuilt after the catastrophe, but Evans concluded that it was occupied by a people other than its original inhabitants. His main proof was that in the palace he discovered examples of tablets inscribed with two distinct scripts. One of them, which he called Linear Script A, was used throughout the island during the whole era of the Minoan civilization. The second, Linear Script B, was used only at Knossos and only after the rebuilding of the palace.

Many questions still remain unanswered: Who were the Minoan people? Where did they come from, and how did their civilization originate? What was their society like? What form of government did they have? What great disaster overtook Crete about 1480 B.C.? And who were the people who occupied the palace at Knossos after that time?

Two recent discoveries provide some clues to these questions. In 1954 an Englishman named Michael Ventris showed that Linear Script B was actually an old way of writing Greek, which means that the people who occupied the palace after its original destruction were probably Greeks. Then in 1966 a group of American oceanographers discovered a thick layer of volcanic ash at the bottom of the eastern Mediterranean. They were able to demonstrate that around 1480 B.C., on an island about one hundred miles north of Crete, there had been a volcanic eruption four times more violent than any ever recorded. Such a disaster could well account for the destruction of Knossos and other sites on Crete at about that time.

Linear Script A has not yet been conclusively deciphered; until it is, most of the story of the Minoan civilization must

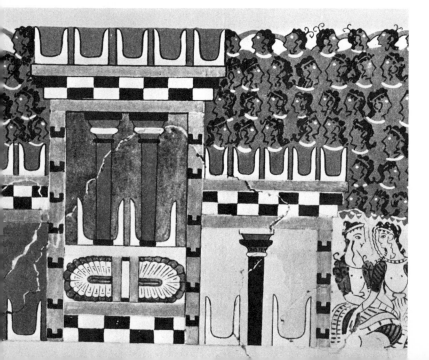

Cretan fresco of court ladies seated around a pillar shrine at a public festival, from the palace at Knossos.

remain a mystery. But with the few clues now available we can attempt a reconstruction, however hypothetical, of Minoan history.

Archeological evidence indicates that the first civilized settlers on Crete arrived from Asia Minor some time after 3000 B.C., that they were at least partly Semitic, and that they had already learned some of the elements of civilization from Mesopotamia. Crete was ideally situated for controlling the commerce between Mesopotamia or Egypt and the more primitive peoples on the shores of Europe. Thus it has been assumed that the Minoan civilization that emerged was based on trade.

The greater part of Minoan trade was apparently with the villages located around the Aegean Sea. The populations of these settlements began to increase rapidly after about 2000 B.C. when the Greeks, migrating south from central Europe, began to settle in the lands around the Aegean (see p. 28). Minoan trade increased proportionately, so that the height of Minoan prosperity, and of Minoan civilization, came after 2000 B.C.

In time the Greeks created a civilization of their own, known as the Mycenaean civilization, which owed a good deal to the Minoan example (see p. 29). By 1500 B.C. Greek traders were competing with the Minoans in the markets of the Aegean and also in Syria and Egypt.

Greeks apparently occupied the palace at Knossos after the Minoan civilization had been weakened by disaster about 1480 B.C. They probably attempted to dominate the island and to take over its commerce. About 1400 B.C. the palace was again destroyed, possibly as a result of a revolt of the Minoans against their Greek rulers. At any rate the Minoan civilization declined rapidly after this time. By about 1200 B.C. it had virtually disappeared, and Crete was nothing more than a part of the Greek civilization.

The Indo-Europeans

The Greeks were but one of several peoples known collectively as Indo-Europeans. The term *Indo-European*, like the term *Semitic*, does not refer to a race of related peoples. Rather it describes a mixture of peoples speaking similar languages. Their ancestors may have come from various parts of the earth, but at some stage in their histories—the stage in which their languages took form—they apparently lived close to one another. For this reason, their cultures as well as their languages developed certain common characteristics.

Shortly before they first appear in history—about 2000 B.C.—the Indo-European peoples seem to have been concentrated somewhere north of the Black Sea between the Danube and the Volga rivers. From this center, as their numbers grew, they spread out in all directions. In the era between about 2000 and 1000 B.C. several waves of Indo-European peoples migrated southward toward the Mediterranean. The westernmost branch—consisting of several separate tribes (including the Latins)—crossed the Alps and settled in Italy.

We have already seen that the Greeks, whose language was similar to Latin, settled in the Aegean area at about the same time that the western tribes settled in Italy. Still further east were the Hittites, who ruled an empire in Asia Minor from about 1800 to 1200 B.C. The Hittites were among the first people to use horses and iron weapons in combat and were one of the most feared military powers of their time. The easternmost branch of the Indo-Europeans settled in Persia, and then in northern India, also in the same era.

By 1000 B.C. Indo-European peoples had occupied all of the continent of Europe. It is from their languages that most tongues spoken in the western world

Above is a seal stone impression of the earliest form of Minoan writing, from which Linear A developed. Below is a Linear A tablet. At bottom is a Linear B tablet.

Race

Race and language are not the same. This should be obvious, for not all who speak Arabic are Arabians and not all who speak English are of the White race. . . . A man's hereditary features and the language he speaks depend on two different sets of circumstances. His hereditary anatomy depends upon his remote ancestors, and his language depends upon the speech he heard as a child.

A race does not move forward as a whole. . . . Race is not a touchstone by which civilized people can be separated from uncivilized. . . . The lesson of history is that pre-eminence in cultural achievement has passed from one race to another, from one continent to another; it has embraced not whole "races" but certain fragments of an ethnic group which were for certain historical reasons favorably situated at the moment.

From Ruth Benedict, *Race: Science and Politics* (New York: Viking, 1945), pp. 9, 18.

today are derived, including the Romance languages (such as Italian, Spanish, and French), the Germanic languages (such as English, German, and Dutch), the Celtic languages (such as Gaelic and Welsh), and the Slavic languages (such as Russian, Polish, and Czech). The Persian and Indic languages spoken in Asia are also of Indo-European origin.

The Spread of Civilization

Before 2000 B.C. civilization was still not very widespread even in the Middle East, where Egypt, Mesopotamia, and Crete were fairly close and had some contacts with one another. There was a civilization in the Indus Valley that traded with Mesopotamia and an even more isolated civilization in the Yellow River Valley of China (see p. 134). The rest of the Eastern Hemisphere was still inhabited by peoples who had not gone much beyond the village level of organization. But the wealth and skills of Egypt, Mesopotamia, and Crete impressed their neighbors and encouraged them to build more complex societies. By 2000 B.C. Mesopotamian civilization, the most dynamic because of its active trade beyond its own frontiers, had spread westward

throughout the Fertile Crescent to include Syria and Palestine as well as the Mesopotamian valley. It became almost contiguous with Egypt. On the east, the Iranians (the inhabitants of what became Persia and is now Iran) had acquired a great deal of technical knowledge from their neighbors and were beginning to develop a civilization of their own. The Iranians also had contacts with India.

By about 1500 B.C. the Greeks and the Hittites were also building cities, organizing states, and engaging in wide-ranging trading ventures. Thus a civilized world extended without a break from the Aegean Sea to the Persian Gulf. With the influx of new peoples and the steady increase in the populations of the older centers, the number of people in this civilized area was probably four or five times greater in 1500 B.C. than it had been in 2000 B.C. Trade increased proportionately, and with it the general standard of living. In the prosperous period between about 1500 and 1200 B.C., the leading power of the ancient world was Egypt. The Minoan civilization disappeared shortly after 1500 B.C., and much of the Mesopotamian world was still under the control of less advanced northern peoples.

THE NEW KINGDOM IN EGYPT
ca. 1550–1100 B.C.

Egypt was freed from foreign domination about 1560 B.C. when an Egyptian nobleman named Ahmose led a successful revolt against the Hyksos rulers and established himself as pharaoh of all Egypt. The reign of Ahmose marked the beginning of the New Kingdom, the most glorious phase of Egypt's long history.

The Egyptian Empire

Ahmose not only expelled the hated Hyksos; he pursued them across the desert to Palestine and Syria. To prevent further invasions, he placed both of these lands under Egyptian protection. Thus for the first time the Egyptians abandoned their centuries-old tradition of isolation and extended their rule to areas beyond their borders. The Egyptian Empire inaugurated by Ahmose later included not only Palestine but also Libya to the west and Nubia to the south.

Under the New Kingdom, Egypt also began to take an active part in the Mediterranean trade that had already enriched the Minoan and Mesopotamian civilizations. After the fall of Crete, Egypt dominated the commerce of the eastern Mediterranean for several centuries.

With tribute from their empire and with commerce to convert their bounteous grain supply into cash, the wealthy and powerful pharaohs of the New Kingdom created the most elaborate architectural monuments in Egyptian history. These pharaohs were no longer content with stark pyramids for their graves; instead, they carved lavishly decorated tombs out of the sandstone cliffs of the Upper Nile. The discovery in 1922 of the tomb of Tutankhamon (*ca.* 1340 B.C.)—the only tomb that had not been completely sacked by thieves over the centuries—provided historians with an invaluable source of information on the life and tastes of the upper classes of the New Kingdom.

Akhnaton
ca. *1375–1358 B.C.*

Throughout most of the history of the New Kingdom, Egypt was at war with the Hittites over the control of Syria and Palestine. Thus most of the pharaohs of the era were warriors. One exception was Akhnaton, who was a religious reformer. Akhnaton tried to superimpose on the ancient and complex religious traditions of Egypt the worship of the Aton, or sun-disk, which he believed to be the supreme and perhaps even the only god. This is the first instance in history of something close to the concept of pure monotheism: the belief in one god. But Akhnaton's religion was never popular in Egypt. The old religious beliefs were deeply ingrained in the thinking of the Egyptian people, and the priests of the old gods, who guarded the formulas for entrance into the afterlife, were far too powerful to be bypassed, even by the pharaoh. As a result, soon after Akhnaton's death the old religion was restored.

THE HITTITE AND EGYPTIAN EMPIRES   *ca.* 1450 B.C.

The Tomb of Tutankhamon

The English archeologist Howard Carter writes of the excitement of uncovering the tomb of the pharaoh Tutankhamon in 1922.

Slowly . . . the remains of passage debris that encumbered the lower part of the doorway were removed, until at last we had the whole door clear before us. The decisive moment had arrived. With trembling hands I made a tiny breach in the upper left hand corner. Darkness and blank space, as far as an iron testing-rod could reach, showed that whatever lay beyond was empty, and not filled like the passage we had just cleared. Candle tests were applied as a precaution against possible foul gases, and then, widening the hole a little, I inserted the candle and peered in. . . . At first I could see nothing, . . . but presently, as my eyes grew accustomed to the light, details of the room within emerged slowly from the mist, strange animals, statues, and gold—everywhere the glint of gold.

From Howard Carter and A. C. Mace, *The Tomb of Tut-ankh-Amen* (London: Cassell, 1923), Vol. I, pp. 95–96.

Head of a colossus of Akhnaton at Karnak (*ca.* 1370 B.C.).

Between about 1250 and 900 B.C. new Indo-European incursions upset the stability of the ancient world. In the Aegean area the invaders were another wave of Greeks, called Dorians (see p. 30), who nearly destroyed the struggling Mycenaean culture that had survived the fall of Crete three centuries earlier. Other Indo-Europeans moved into Asia Minor. They overthrew the Hittite Empire, already weak after its wars with Egypt, and established several smaller kingdoms in its place. Many people of the Aegean area, mostly Greeks, fled from the invaders in fleets of small boats. Ostensibly, these "sea-peoples" were looking for new homes, but they were quite ready to engage in piracy and plundering along the way. Their attacks on Egyptian shipping and their raids in the Nile Delta contributed to the decline of the New Kingdom and ended Egypt's role as a commercial power.

After the decline of the Hittite and Egyptian empires, no strong power appeared in the Middle East until the rise of the Assyrian Empire about four centuries later. During those centuries several small kingdoms and city-states emerged in the lands at the eastern end of the Mediterranean now occupied by Syria, Lebanon, and Israel. Before about 1200 B.C. these lands had been occupied by a Semitic people known as Canaanites, whose culture was derived from that of Mesopotamia. But Ahmose, as we have seen, had placed this area under Egyptian protection. When Egypt declined as a world power and Egyptian garrisons were withdrawn, the Canaanite cities were left defenseless. In the period between about 1200 and 1000 B.C., the "sea-peoples" attacked them from the Mediterranean, while two new waves of Semitic peoples, first the Hebrews and later the Aramaeans, attacked them from the east and south.

Eventually most of the Canaanite cities succumbed to the invaders. One group of the "sea-peoples," known as the Philistines, established a string of independent city-states along the coast of

Akhnaton was a sensitive man given to writing poetry but little interested in affairs of state. Largely as a result of his negligence, Egypt declined as a military power. Syria was lost to the Hittites, and much of Palestine was overrun by bands of invaders called the Habiru. Akhnaton's immediate successors proved as weak as he, and the dynasty founded by Ahmose ended ignominiously as a consequence of a military coup. Subsequent pharaohs regained some of the territory and prestige that Egypt had lost. A series of protracted wars between Egypt and the Hittites over control of Syria was terminated only about 1275 B.C. by a treaty between Ramses II and the Hittite king. This treaty is famous as one of the first recorded international agreements, but it came too late. Both powers, weakened by their struggle, now had to face new dangers of invasion from the north.

the Mediterranean. Inland, the Aramaeans settled in what became the kingdom of Syria, with its capital at Damascus. South of Syria were the two smaller Hebrew kingdoms of Israel and Judah, of which more will be said later.

The Phoenicians

The only Canaanite cities to survive the invasions were those along the rocky coast of Syria that were relatively easy to defend. The inhabitants of these cities were a mixture of Canaanites and "sea-peoples" and were known as Phoenicians. When the raids of the "sea-peoples" subsided, Phoenician ships were the first to venture into the Mediterranean. By about 1100 B.C. the Phoenicians had begun to revive the trade routes abandoned by the Minoans and the Egyptians, and for the next three centuries they controlled Mediterranean commerce.

The ancient trade routes from India and the East were still funneling goods into Mesopotamia. From there, the eastern wares, along with local Mesopotamian produce, moved along the Aramaean caravan routes to one of the Phoenician cities. There they were loaded onto small ships bound for Egypt, Asia Minor, North Africa, or even western Europe. Returning ships carried raw materials from the western Mediterranean to the Phoenician cities, where they were fashioned into finished products and sent to the markets of Mesopotamia.

The Phoenicians were better sailors than any other ancient people, even the Greeks. They were the first people from the Middle East to trade and colonize in western Europe. They were also the first on record to venture beyond Gibraltar into the Atlantic, for their ships sailed regularly to Brittany and Cornwall to obtain the tin needed in the manufacture of bronze. Egyptian sources suggest that the Phoenicians may have sailed around Africa, a feat that would not be repeated until the fifteenth century A.D. Some scholars believe that the Phoenicians may even have reached America.

The largest Phoenician city was Tyre. But by far the oldest—dating from before 2000 B.C.—was Byblos, which specialized in the manufacture of writing materials. It was from Byblos that the Greeks took their word for "book"—*biblion*—and it is from *biblion* that we get such English words as *Bible* and *bibliography*. The Phoenicians also helped to refine and to spread the use of the West Semitic system of writing. Ultimately reduced to only twenty-two letters that could be drawn and recognized without difficulty, the Phoenician alphabet was much easier to use and to understand than either cuneiform or hieroglyphic writing. For the first time in history it was possible for almost anyone to learn to read and write without long years of training. Learning could be more widely diffused, and more men could enter administrative careers. The Phoenician alphabet provided the basis for all three of the major alphabets now in use in the western world: the Hebrew, the Latin (which we use), and the Greek. The Greek alphabet, in turn, is the basis for the Cyrillic alphabet used in Russia and much of eastern Europe. And an Aramaic version of the West Semitic script formed the basis for the writing systems of India. It is curious that so useful a discovery was never duplicated, even by such ingenious people as the Chinese.

Just as the merchants of Europe later brought their civilization to America in their search for new markets and raw materials, the Phoenician traders carried

Typical letters of the alphabet in Phoenician, Greek, and Roman forms. The final Greek letter, omega, is pronounced like the Roman long *o*.

Phoenician	Greek	Roman
⟨	A	A
⟨	B	B
∧	Γ	G
⟨	Δ	D
⟨	E	E
⟨	[Y]	F
⟨	Z	Z
⊕		H
⟨	I	I
Y	K	[K]
L	Λ	L
⟨	M	M
⟨	N	N
o	O	O
⟨	Π	P
⟨		Q
⟨	P	R
W	Σ	S
✕	T	T
	Υ	U,V
	X	X
	Ω	

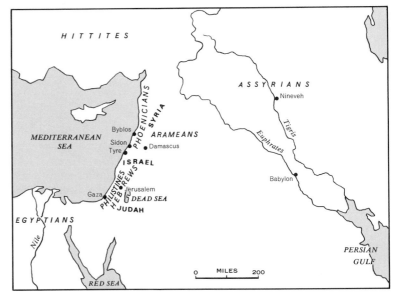

THE MIDDLE EAST *ca.* 800 B.C.

A God of Social Justice

The writings of the prophet Amos contain one of the earliest references (*ca.* 750 B.C.) to Jahweh as a god of social justice.

Hear this, O ye that swallow up the needy,
  even to make the poor of the land to fail,
Saying, When will the new moon be gone, that we may sell corn?
  and the sabbath, that we may set forth wheat,
making the ephah small, and the shekel great,
  and falsifying the balances by deceit?
That we may buy the poor for silver,
  and the needy for a pair of shoes;
  yea, and sell the refuse of the wheat?

Shall not the land tremble for this,
  and every one mourn that dwelleth therein?

From *The Dartmouth Bible*, ed. by Roy B. Chamberlin and Herman Feldman (Boston: Houghton Mifflin, 1961), p. 541.

the civilization of the Middle East to the western Mediterranean. They established colonies and trading posts in many places, particularly on the island of Sicily and in North Africa. The largest Phoenician colony was at Carthage, located near the site of modern Tunis. Here the Phoenician settlers were able to make serfs of the natives and to put them to work on large plantations growing agricultural products for the home markets.

The Phoenician cities came under the domination of the Assyrian Empire after about 750 B.C., and declined rapidly thereafter. At that time the leading merchant families emigrated to Carthage, which became the center of the Phoenician world until it was destroyed by the Romans in 146 B.C.

The Hebrews

Among the peoples of the ancient world, the Hebrews played a relatively unimportant political role. If we were to consider only their significance to their contemporaries, we might dismiss them with a few sentences or perhaps not mention them all. But during the years from about 1200 to 400 B.C. the Hebrews developed a religion that was unique among ancient peoples and that has given their history enormous significance to the modern world. Their religion has helped the Hebrews to maintain their identity, even to the present day, whereas most ancient peoples mixed with one another or with successive waves of conquerors. Moreover, because the ancient Hebrews maintained a detailed record of the evolving relationship between themselves and their God, Jahweh, their scriptures constitute one of the richest original sources for ancient history. The religion developed by the ancient Hebrews provided the basis for three of the major religions of the modern world: Judaism, Christianity, and Islam.

Most of the Hebrew scripture (that part known to Christians as the Old Testament) was written down by many different authors between about 1000 and 150 B.C. It includes rules of law and of religious behavior, legend, history, poetry, prophecy, and apocalyptic visions. But is is given unity by the firm belief in an enduring relationship between God and his people. The first several books recount the stories preserved by the Hebrews about their early history. Although recent archeological discoveries show that many of these stories may well be based on actual historical events (just as archeologists have shown that the poems of Homer, written at about the same time, are probably based on actual events in Greek history), there is not enough evidence to reconstruct the history of the Hebrews before about 1000 B.C. with any certainty.

According to their scriptures, all Hebrews were descended from Abraham, who migrated westward from Ur in Mesopotamia when Jahweh promised him and his descendants the land of Canaan (Palestine). Abraham's grandson Jacob (also called Israel) had twelve sons who were believed to be the progenitors of the twelve tribes into which the Hebrews were later divided. Joseph, one of Jacob's sons, was taken to Egypt as a slave but later rose to a high position in the pharaoh's government. His father and his brothers then joined him in Egypt. The second book of the Old Testament, Exodus, explains that a new pharaoh arose who "knew not Joseph," and who reduced the children of Israel (by then a sizable tribe) to slavery. It is in Exodus that we are introduced to Moses, one of the most impressive figures in literature.

Moses was an Israelite who, according to the account in Exodus, was raised by a daughter of the pharaoh. One day when Moses was alone in the wilderness, Jahweh, the God of Abraham, called to him. While Moses listened in awe and terror, Jahweh renewed his Covenant with the children of Israel: to guide and protect them as long as they worshiped him and him only and obeyed his laws. Jahweh then ordered Moses to lead the Israelites back to the land of Palestine. Moses led the Israelites out of Egypt into the Sinai Desert, where they remained for forty years before trying to enter Palestine. During this sojourn in the desert, Jahweh gave Moses the Law, which included the Ten Commandments and a long catalogue of religious, ethical, and juridical regulations.

Two books, Joshua and Judges, give differing accounts of the Hebrew attack on Palestine after the death of Moses. Here we are on somewhat more solid historical ground, since Egyptian records show that the Canaanite cities were attacked by tribes from the desert during the thirteenth century B.C. Archeological evidence also shows that Jericho and several neighboring cities were besieged and destroyed at about that time. The Hebrew conquest was complicated by the more or less simultaneous arrival of the Philistines, who attacked from the sea. For about a century a three-way battle took place among the Hebrews, the Canaanites, and the Philistines.

In the final stages of the conquest of the Canaanites, the Hebrew tribes decided to unite under a king. Samuel, a religious leader, chose Saul (*ca.* 1000 B.C.) as the first king and later designated David (*ca.* 1000–960 B.C.) as Saul's successor. It was King David who completed the conquest of the Canaanites and the Philistines and united the Hebrew people in a kingdom with its capital at Jerusalem. The Philistines were permitted to maintain their independent cities along the Mediterranean coast, but the Ca-

naanites were eventually absorbed by the Hebrews. Since the Canaanites had been exposed to Mesopotamian influence, they may have been the source of the many Mesopotamian elements in the Hebrew culture, such as the story of the Flood.

Solomon (*ca.* 960–930 B.C.), David's son and successor, built an impressive royal palace and a temple to Jahweh in Jerusalem and established commercial and diplomatic relations with neighboring states. The Hebrew people, however, whose memory of tribal independence was still fresh, resented Solomon's royal pretensions and high taxes. At Solomon's death the ten northern tribes seceded and established the Kingdom of Israel under another dynasty. From about 930 B.C. on, there were two Hebrew kingdoms: Israel in the north, the larger and more prosperous of the two; and Judah in the south, a smaller agricultural kingdom that remained loyal to the house of David.

According to the Bible, the Hebrew concept of monotheism goes back at least to the time of Moses. But monothe-

Semite prisoner inscribed on a relief at the temple of Luxor (perhaps dating from the period of Hebrew residence in Egypt).

ism—the worship of one god—does not necessarily imply that this god is sovereign over the entire earth and is to be worshiped by all peoples. When they first entered Palestine, the Israelites believed that, according to their Covenant, they were to worship only Jahweh and to obey his laws, but that other people might worship other gods. They seem to have conceived of Jahweh as being rather like the gods of other nomadic desert peoples: he protected them from their enemies, he took their side in battles, and he provided them with food and water.

Once the Hebrews had ceased to be desert nomads and had settled down as farmers in Palestine, the worship of a desert god had less meaning for them. Although Jahweh remained the official national god of the Hebrews, many of them turned also to the Baalim, the Canaanite version of the Mesopotamian fertility gods. The conflict between the Baal-worshipers and the defenders of Jahweh produced the first Hebrew prophets, such as Elijah and Elisha. These peripatetic preachers warned that Baal-worship was a breach of the Covenant and would bring the wrath of Jahweh down on all the Hebrew people. The recorded versions of their preaching include some of the most stirring passages in any literature.

The teaching of the prophet Amos (*ca.* 750 B.C.) marks a turning point in the evolution of the Hebrew religion. In powerful measured verse, Amos named the various neighboring peoples known to the Hebrews, listed their sins, and promised that Jahweh would punish them. Although Amos himself may not have realized it, in so preaching he became the first Hebrew teacher—as far as written records show—to speak of Jahweh not merely as the God of the Hebrews but as a god whose law extended to all people.

Amos did not stop, however, after he had listed the sins of Israel's neighbors. He reached a crescendo of fury when he spoke of the sins of the Hebrews them-

THE ASSYRIAN EMPIRE *ca.* 700 B.C.

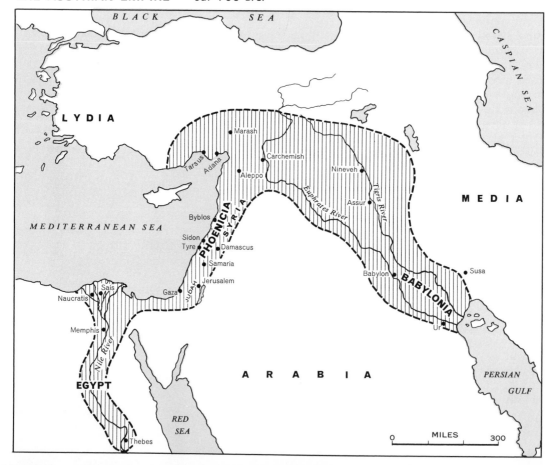

selves. In the time of Amos, many Hebrews were beginning to live in cities and to engage in trade. They were beginning to learn, as the Greeks were learning at the same time, that when a society first turns to a money economy, some men become very rich while others are reduced to poverty or even servitude. The Greeks considered the problem a political matter to be solved through constitutional reforms. For Amos, as for most Hebrews, it was a religious matter. The Hebrews were sinning against Jahweh, he warned, when they "sold the righteous for silver, and the needy for a pair of shoes." Amos gave a new dimension to the worship of Jahweh by stating explicitly something that was already implicit throughout the Law of Moses—namely, that Jahweh was a god of social justice. Thus in Amos we find the first clear expression of the concept of ethical monotheism that made the Hebrew religion unique in the ancient world.

The teachings of such later prophets as Hosea, Isaiah, and Jeremiah reflect a continuing evolution in the Hebrew concept of Jahweh. They presented a universal abstract God, who could be reached by his worshipers wherever they were; a God possessed of infinite power and infinite sanctity and infinite love; a God far above the need for the petty sacrifices of the Baal-worshipers; a God whose relationship to his people was that of a loving father.

The repeated warnings of the prophets that Jahweh would punish the Hebrews for their sins were reinforced by the growing danger from the Assyrians to the east. By the eighth century this militaristic people had gained control of most of Mesopotamia and had already begun to threaten the small states along the Mediterranean coast. There could be no doubt in the minds of the Hebrews just what form Jahweh's punishment would take should it ever come.

A NEW AGE OF EMPIRES
ca. 750–333 B.C.

Such small states as the Phoenician cities and the Hebrew kingdoms had been able to survive only because there were no major powers to threaten them in the period from about 1150 to 750 B.C. Between about 750 and 333 B.C., however, three successive empires dominated the entire Fertile Crescent. These empires brought all the small states of Mesopotamia, Syria, and Palestine under their control and at times even extended their power over Egypt.

The Assyrian Empire
ca. 750–612 B.C.

The first of the new empires was created by the Assyrians, a Semitic people living in the hilly country of the upper Tigris Valley. Located at the northern extreme of the Mesopotamian world, the Assyrians were generally the first to feel the blows of the repeated invasions from the north. They had to become militarily

An alabaster relief showing an Assyrian king on a hunt.

Babylonians and Syrians paying tribute to the Persian emperor Xerxes.

strong in order to survive. In time they built up the most efficient army the ancient world had seen, with long-service professional soldiers and what were probably the first effective cavalry units. About 900 B.C., when barbarian threats from the north temporarily subsided, the Assyrians began to use their army to terrorize and conquer their Mesopotamian neighbors. By about 750 B.C. their empire included the whole Mesopotamian valley. Then in a series of swift and devastating thrusts to the west, they conquered Syria, the Phoenician cities, the Kingdom of Israel, and finally even Egypt.

The Assyrians enforced their rule with cruelty, enslaving and deporting whole peoples and torturing and killing thousands of captives. A large part of the population of Israel, for instance, was either killed or deported, and the land was resettled with people from other parts of the empire. The ten northern Hebrew tribes lost their identity forever. The only Hebrews left were the two tribes of the southern Kingdoms of Judah, which survived as an Assyrian dependency.

Assyrian art (expressed mostly in sculptured reliefs) reflects many of the characteristics of these fierce people. Strong, harsh, and realistic, it abounds in scenes of war, torture, and death. The human figures are somewhat stiff, but no artists have ever surpassed the Assyrians in depicting animals fighting, charging, and writhing in their death agonies.

There were simply not enough Assyrians to garrison a territory stretching from the Nile to the borders of Persia,

and the systematic cruelty of the Assyrians made it impossible for them to control conquered peoples except by force of arms. The Babylonians, eager to regain their old supremacy, launched an uprising and were enthusiastically supported by other subject peoples. Nineveh, the Assyrian capital, fell in 612 B.C., and the great Assyrian Empire crumbled overnight.

The Chaldean Empire
ca. 626–539 B.C.

After the fall of Assyria, most of Mesopotamia came under the short-lived Chaldean Empire, which had its capital in the ancient city of Babylon. Trying to avoid domination by the Chaldeans, the small Kingdom of Judah joined a coalition led by Egypt. But in 587 B.C. Nebuchadnezzar, the Chaldean king, overran Judah, devastated the land, destroyed Solomon's Temple in Jerusalem, and led the king and several thousand leading citizens back to Babylon as captives. During this "Babylonian Captivity," the Hebrews came to believe that Jahweh had a divine plan for his people that was being worked out through history. At first their fate perplexed them. If Jahweh was the only true God, and if the Hebrews were the only ones to worship him and follow his laws, why had they been subjected to conquest and cruelty at the hands of nonbelievers? The answer was provided by the new prophets of the period of exile, such as Joel. The day would soon come, they believed, when Jahweh would reveal himself to all peoples and institute his rule of righteousness. When that time came, the Hebrews would lead the nonbelievers into the paths of Jahweh. Meanwhile, the Hebrews would have to be educated and purified through suffering. Their numbers would be reduced by conquest and slaughter until only a "saving remnant" of dedicated souls was left to carry out the will of Jahweh.

The Book of Daniel gives a dramatic account of the fall of Babylon in 539 B.C. According to this version, a spectral hand began to write on the wall during a banquet given by the crown prince Belshazzar. Only Daniel, a Jew, was able to interpret the message for Belshazzar and his terrified guests. The Chaldean Empire would fall that night. According to other sources, the handwriting on the wall was unnecessary, for the Persian troops were already at the gates, and the citizens of Babylon, frustrated by the weakness of their rulers, were offering no resistance.

The Persian Empire 549–333 B.C.

The Persians, an Indo-European people, lived in a loose federation with the Medes and other neighbors in the hilly region east of Mesopotamia. In 549 B.C. Cyrus, a very able military leader, established himself as king. This was the beginning of the great period of Persian expansion. In 543 B.C. Cyrus conquered and annexed all of Asia Minor. With his victory over the Chaldean Empire in 539 B.C., he added Mesopotamia, Syria, Palestine, and the Phoenician cities to his empire. When his son conquered Egypt in 525 B.C., the Persian Empire embraced almost all of the Middle East.

The organization of the Persian Empire was so successful that it was later used by both the Greeks and the Romans. The Persian system combined a large measure of local autonomy with careful supervision by the central government. Each of the subject peoples was allowed to keep its own customs, its own religion, and often even its own local government. The Hebrews, for instance, were allowed to return to Judah, to reestablish their kingdom, and to rebuild the Temple in Jerusalem. A Persian governor and a Persian garrison were assigned to each of the provinces to maintain order and to supervise the collection of taxes.

THE PERSIAN EMPIRE ca. 500 B.C.

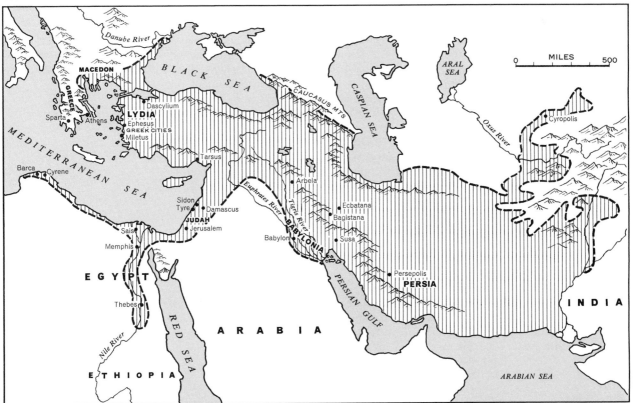

When faced with rebellion, however, the Persians did not hesitate to take extreme military measures.

One result of the Persian conquests was that Persian religious beliefs left a strong mark on the later religions of the western world. The Persian religion, in its earliest known form, was essentially the deification of natural forces. It gave special prominence to Mithra, the sun god. By the time of the Persian conquests, however, the king and most of the leading families had embraced a newer creed based on the teachings of the prophet Zoroaster. According to Zoroaster there were two gods. Ahura-Mazda, the god of good and light, was engaged in a perpetual struggle with Ahriman, the god of evil and darkness. Humans had free will and could ally themselves with either side. After thousands of years, there would be a final struggle in which good would triumph. Those who had chosen to fight on the side of good would go to paradise (a Persian word); the rest would be consumed in eternal fire. Although Zoroastrianism never spread far beyond Persia, it must be counted as one of the most influential religions of history. Its dualism explained one of religion's most difficult problems: How can a good god permit the existence of evil? Although the belief in two separate gods has never been accepted by Jews or Christians, popular Christian concepts of the Devil in the Middle Ages were not much different from Zoroaster's description of Ahriman. Even more influential on both Christianity and Islam were Zoroaster's teachings about paradise, hell, and the Last Judgment.

The Persians first tasted defeat at the battle of Marathon in 490 B.C. when they failed in their attempt to subdue the Greek city-state of Athens (see pp. 38–40). The reason for Persia's defeat was probably not the superior fighting ability of the Athenians, as Greek historians would have us believe, so much as a combination of weaknesses in the Persian system. It placed too much power in the hands of the king. Such a system can succeed only under a man who is both a good administrator and a good general. During the fifth century B.C. the Persian

Persian gold cup (fifth century B.C.).

Empire was ruled by a series of men who were neither. Other factors contributed to a general decline of the eastern civilizations under Persian rule. The Persians were not originators or intellectual leaders; they accepted with little change most of the cultures of their subjects. The Persians created favorable conditions for trade, but they were not themselves great traders. High taxes and subjection to a foreign power apparently dampened the initiative of such trading people as the Phoenicians, whose economic activity declined. The Persians never learned to use their manpower efficiently. In fact, under Persian rule opportunities for the ordinary man decreased. He became a peasant, bound to the soil, rather than a free farmer or a free warrior. This change had a bad effect on the army, which became more and more dependent on mercenaries, many of whom were barbarians from areas outside the Persian Empire.

During the fifth century B.C., the most important advances in commerce, philosophy, art, letters, and social organization were not made in the older civilizations that had come under Persian rule. They came from that small part of the eastern world that had escaped Persian domination: the city-states of the Greek peninsula, whose histories will be examined in the next chapter. Greek strength grew as the Persian Empire decayed, until finally, in 333 B.C., the Greek king Alexander defeated the Persian armies and added all of the Persian Empire to his own domains.

Suggestions for Further Reading

Note: Asterisk denotes a book available in paperback edition.

General Several good texts are devoted specifically to ancient history. Among those are W. E. Caldwell and M. F. Gyles, *The Ancient World,* 3rd ed. (1966), and C. G. Starr, *A History of the Ancient World* (1965). W. H. McNeill, *The Rise of the West** (1963), is more successful than most in placing ancient western history in a framework that includes the ancient world as a whole. For a detailed study, see J. B. Bury et al., eds., *The Cambridge Ancient History* (1923–29). The first two volumes have been issued in a paperback edition. Some works on the ancient world before the Greeks are V. G. Childe, *What Happened in History** (1964); H. Frankfort, *The Birth of Civilization in the Near East** (1956); S. Mascoti, *The Face of the Ancient Orient** (1962); and J. Hawkes, *Life in Mesopotamia, the Indus Valley and Egypt* (1973). L. Cottrell, *The Anvil of Civilization** (1957), is shorter but scholarly and informative.

Archeology and Prehistory There are two works that recount recent archeological discoveries: C. W. Ceram, *Gods, Graves, and Scholars,** rev. ed. (1967), and L. Woolley, *Digging Up the Past** (1940). Ceram is especially helpful in giving references to the work of the great archeologists. R. J. Braidwood, *Prehistoric Men** (1963), and J. Hawkes and L. Woolley, *Prehistory and the Beginnings of Civilization** (1963), are interesting summaries of what is known of human history before the invention of writing.

Mesopotamia A good summary is W. W. Hallo and W. K. Simpson, *The Ancient Near East: A History** (1971). A. L. Oppenheim, *Ancient Mesopotamia* (1964), and H. W. F. Saggs, *The Greatness That Was Babylon* (1962), are detailed surveys of Mesopotamian history. S. Mascoti, *Ancient Semitic Civilizations** (1960), is shorter and includes Syria and Palestine. The two books by S. N. Kramer, *History Begins at Sumer** (1959) and *The Sumerians* (1963), contain excellent source material for the political, social, and religious thinking of the Sumerians, the first people to keep written records. L. Woolley, *Ur of the Chaldees** (1950), is one of many books by a leading authority on Mesopotamian archeology. An interesting description of the Mesopotamian world may be found in G. Contenau, *Everyday Life in Babylon and Assyria* (1954).

Egypt There are two good surveys of ancient Egypt. Of them, A. H. Gardiner, *Egypt of the Pharaohs** (1961), is more factual; J. A. Wilson, *The Culture of Ancient Egypt** (1963), more interpretive. For a study of Egyptian monuments, see either I. E. S. Edwards, *The Pyramids of Egypt,** rev. ed. (1961), or W. S. Smith, *Art and Architecture of Ancient Egypt** (1958). H. Frankfort, *Ancient Egyptian Religion** (1948), largely replaces some of the older standard works on this subject. P. Montet, *Everyday Life in Egypt in the Days of Ramses II* (1958), is a counterpart to Contenau's book on Babylon.

Crete There is no complete and generally accepted history of the Minoan culture, though most of the texts on Greek history mentioned at the end of the next chapter have short surveys. A recent study of the archeological discoveries on Crete is R. W. Hutchinson, *Prehistoric Crete** (1963). L. Cottrell, *The Bull of Minos** (1953), is shorter and more readable.

The Indo-Europeans The best general account is V. G. Childe, *The Aryans: A Study of Indo-European Origins* (1926). O. R. Gurney, *The Hittites** (1952), is a good introduction to the study of the Hittites, and C. W. Ceram, *The Secret of the Hittites* (1956), gives a fascinating account of the archeological expeditions that uncovered the Hittite civilization.

Syria and Palestine Informative studies of the non-Hebrew peoples who inhabited Syria-Palestine can be found in J. Gray, *The Canaanites* (1964); D. Harden, *The Phoenicians* (1962); and R. A. H. Macalister, *The Philistines* (1913). There is such a wealth of material on the ancient Hebrews and their religious evolution that any short list must omit even many standard works. Among the better general histories are W. F. Albright, *The Biblical Period from Abraham to Ezra** (1963); J. Bright, *A History of Israel* (1959); C. H. Gordon, *The Ancient Near East** (1965); A. Lods, *Israel* (1932); and the early chapters of A. L. Sachar, *A History of the Jews** (1966). For a briefer treatment, see E. J. Ehrlich, *A Concise History of Israel** (1965), or H. Orlinsky, *Ancient Israel** (1964).

Assyrians, Chaldeans, and Persians The Assyrians and the Chaldeans are both treated in the general histories of Mesopotamia mentioned above. For studies of the Persians as well as of the diverse peoples they ruled, see either R. N. Frye, *The Heritage of Persia* (1963), or A. T. Olmstead, *A History of the Persian Empire** (1959).

2 Greek Civilization

Even though Persia was weakening when it met its first defeats at the hands of the Greeks, it is still surprising that a few small, loosely allied Greek cities could resist the professional army of a great empire. The Greek success is even more astonishing when we consider that many Greek cities were so afraid of Persia that they took no part in the war. The Greek victories were won by a minority of the Greek people.

The same paradox appears in other Greek achievements. The Greeks were very conscious of their identity, very proud of being Greek, very scornful of the barbarians who did not share their culture. They worshiped the same gods, revered the same oracles, spoke what was basically the same language, met and competed with one another at great festivals such as the Olympic Games. Yet Greece was divided into many quarreling states, and most Greeks were peasant farmers who contributed little to and were little influenced by the high culture of the Greek world. That culture was created by a few men living in a few cities scattered around the rim of the Aegean Sea. It was a long time before Greek culture penetrated very far inland; Boeotia, only thirty miles from Athens, was notorious among the Greeks as the home of dull, ignorant, blundering yokels. Greek culture eventually spread throughout the Mediterranean world, but the Golden Age of Greece was a golden age for only a few hundred thousand men.

Geography helps explain the divisions and uneven development of the Greek people. Rocky mountains enclose fertile plains, emerge from the Aegean Sea to form countless islands, and rise again to form the craggy promontories of Asia Minor. The best harbors were usually not near the best farming land. It was in the seaports that new ideas and new patterns of social organization were most likely to emerge, either through contact with other cities or because of the pressure of growing population. The more fertile areas of Greece, such as Thessaly, had fewer outside contacts and were under less pressure to make innovations.

Geography made it easy for many small states to emerge and to survive. But geography alone cannot account for the particularism of ancient Greeks. Equally important were the intensity of political life in the local communities and the fierce competitiveness of the Greek spirit. It was not impossible to unite Greece, but it was far more difficult than it had been to unite Egypt, and the task took many centuries. Meanwhile the Greeks lived in small, independent communities, each of which developed its own pattern of life. Obviously some patterns would

The Parthenon at Athens.

be more likely to encourage writers, artists, and philosophers than others. Cities that had an active intellectual and artistic life attracted capable men from other parts of the Greek world. Thus small differences became magnified with the passage of time. Early Athens and early Sparta had a good deal in common, but by the middle of the fifth century B.C. Sparta was a garrison state and Athens was the cultural center of the Greek people.

EARLY GREEK HISTORY TO *ca.* 800 B.C.

The Greeks knew little about their own past and were apt to exaggerate the originality and the rapidity of development of their civilization. Their oldest historical records were the two epic poems of Homer—the *Iliad* and the *Odyssey*. These poems celebrate the siege of Troy by a league of Greek warriors. The siege probably took place about 1250 B.C., and its memory was probably preserved in legend, but Homer (or the two or more poets whose work was ascribed to Homer) did not compose the epics before 750 B.C. and perhaps not until a half century or so later. The Greeks were not very conscious of or concerned by these dates. For them the Homeric poems were their earliest historical record, a guide to right conduct, a foundation for their religion, and the fountainhead of a common culture. The epics were works of timeless value, and Homer's heroes were taken as typical of the early Greek character.

Nineteenth-century European scholars saw little historical value in the Homeric legends, except as evidence about the state of Greek society and religion at some date before the classical period. But a German businessman named Heinrich Schliemann was convinced that there had been a siege of Troy. In 1870 he began to excavate a mound near the Dardanelles in Asia Minor that was the traditional site of Troy. To the astonishment of the scholarly world, he found layer after layer of ancient settlements, one of them a large fortified city that had been destroyed shortly before 1200 B.C., and another older and very rich town that had fallen earlier (1800 B.C.). He assumed that the older city was Homer's Troy; actually, layer 7a (the city that fell about 1250 B.C.) was the one he should have selected. Schliemann then went to Mycenae in southern Greece, the legendary home of the Greek leader Agamemnon, and began a search for the king's palace. Here he found evidence of a surprisingly advanced civilization whose roots went back at least as far as 1800 B.C.

Schliemann's successors found similar sites, and it became evident that this Mycenaean civilization was fairly widespread throughout the Greek peninsula. It seemed probable that the Mycenaeans were early Greeks; the decipherment of Linear Script B in 1952 (see p. 12) strengthened this hypothesis. We know that the Greeks reached the Aegean area about 2000 B.C., that they had contacts with the Minoan civilization, that they traded and raided in the Aegean Sea, and that they finally settled in the Greek peninsula, the Aegean islands, and along

The Discovery of Troy

Heinrich Schliemann's discovery of Troy in 1873 helped trigger further archeological expeditions.

He struck into the mound, boldly ripping down walls that to him seemed unimportant. He found weapons and household furnishings, ornaments and vases, overwhelming evidence that a rich city had once occupied the spot. And he found something else as well. . . . Under the ruins of New Ilium he disclosed other ruins, under these still others. The hill was like a tremendous onion, which he proceeded to dismember layer by layer. Each layer seemed to have been inhabited at a different period. Populations had lived and died, cities had been built up only to fall into decay. Sword and fire had raged, one civilization cutting off another, and again and again a city of the living had been raised on a city of the dead.

. . . The question now arose which of these nine cities was the Troy of Homer, of the heroes and the epic war. . . .

Schliemann dug and searched. In the second and third levels from the bottom he found traces of fire, the remains of massive walls, and the ruins of a gigantic gate. He was sure that these walls had once enclosed the palace of Priam. . . .

From C. W. Ceram, *Gods, Graves, and Scholars*, rev. ed. (New York: Knopf, 1967), pp. 36–37.

The earliest representation of Homer, on a fourth-century B.C. coin.

the coast of Asia Minor. These early Greeks spoke an Indo-European language, knew the use of bronze, and were strong enough and numerous enough to conquer and assimilate the earlier inhabitants of the region.

The Mycenaean Civilization
ca. *1650–1150 B.C.*

By about 1600 B.C., or soon thereafter, this early Greek, or Mycenaean, civilization had reached a fairly advanced state. As was to be the case for centuries, there were many small independent political units, each one based on a strongly fortified citadel and ruled by a king and his band of warriors. The Greek city of later centuries did not exist then, but a fairly large merchant class traded throughout the Aegean and with Crete. There was certainly some competition (perhaps violent) with the Minoans for trade, but there must have been periods of peaceful cooperation as well. The great palaces of Mycenae, Tiryns, and Pylos show Minoan influence, and the enormous wealth of the rulers of Mycenae must have come largely from trade.

The Mycenaean Greeks may have contributed to the downfall of Minoan Crete about 1480 B.C.; certainly the Greeks attempted to profit from the disaster. As we have seen in Chapter 1, they probably took over and rebuilt the palace at Knossos; they also must have hoped to take over Minoan trade routes. If so, they were disappointed. It was Egypt under the militant pharaohs of the New Kingdom that became the dominant commercial power of the eastern Mediterranean. The Mycenaeans continued to trade in the Aegean and eastern Mediterranean, and began to penetrate the Black Sea. This may have stirred up rivalry with Troy, which was well placed to block the entrance to the Straits, though the legendary wealth of Troy could also have been a cause of conflict. If there ever was a Trojan War, which some scholars doubt, it would have taken place after the fall of Crete and before the collapse of the Mycenaean civilization—that is, very near the traditional date of 1250 B.C.

THE AEGEAN WORLD   *ca.* 1500–146 B.C.

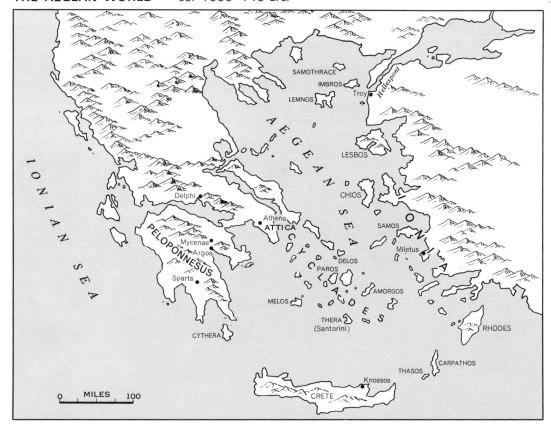

The Mycenaean world was wracked by a series of violent attacks from unknown invaders soon after 1200 B.C. Royal palaces were burned, towns destroyed, and kingdoms overthrown. A few places escaped with little damage, notably Athens, and many Mycenaean Greeks were able to flee to islands in the Aegean or to Greek settlements in Asia Minor. Nevertheless, the Mycenaean ruling class was wiped out and with it Mycenaean art and the Mycenaean system of writing.

The downfall of the Mycenaean civilization was followed by a new invasion of Greek-speaking people, the Dorians. The Dorians may have completed the destruction of the fragments of Mycenaean civilization that had survived the attacks of the earlier invaders; certainly they did nothing to rebuild the old way of life. They were a rustic people who had had little contact with the civilizations of the eastern Mediterranean; their communities were composed of small farmers dominated by groups of warriors. The Dorians were especially numerous in the Peloponnesus, the old center of Mycenaean civilization. As a result, memories of the past faded, especially since there were no written records to preserve old traditions and to report the activities of the new ruling class. Very little is known about Greece during the "Dark Ages" that followed the Dorian invasions.

THE GREEK WORLD
ca. 800–500 B.C.

A little more information is available about the Greek world after 800 B.C., and especially about the Greeks of Ionia, the western coast of Asia Minor. It is evident that an economic revival had occurred and that a number of trading cities had emerged. Some commerce must have existed even during the "Dark Ages," and with both Egypt and the Phoenician cities under Assyrian control, the Greeks had a new opportunity to expand their trade routes throughout the eastern Mediterranean. For example, Miletus and eleven other cities had a seaport in the Nile Delta. Miletus also had a string of trading posts along the shores of the Black Sea where goods from Egypt and western Asia could be sold to the peoples of eastern Europe.

Trade was greatly stimulated by the invention of coined money, which occurred in Asia Minor (probably in the kingdom of Lydia) in the late seventh century B.C. Gold and silver had long been prized, and the value of other goods had often been expressed in terms of specific weights of these precious metals. But testing, weighing, and cutting a bar

GREEK AND PHOENICIAN COLONIZATION AND TRADE   *ca.* 750–550 B.C.

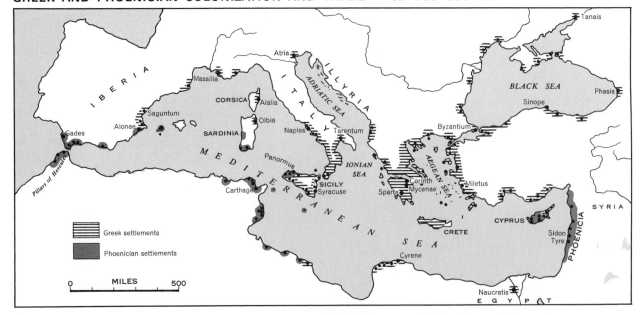

ca. 2000 B.C.	ca. 1700	ca. 1480	ca. 1100	ca. 800	ca. 600	404	323	Conquest by Rome 146 B.C.
Minoan Civilization on Crete			"Dark Ages"	Dominance of City-states of Asia Minor	Dominance of Athens and Sparta		Hellenistic Era	
Arrival of Greeks	Mycenaean Civilization in Aegean Area							

Decline of
City-state System and
Conquest by Macedon

of gold or silver was too tedious for ordinary small transactions. It was eventually discovered that the metal could be cut up into many small bits, stamped to show that a ruler guaranteed their weight and fineness, and then used repeatedly for any sort of business. By making it easier to buy and sell goods of all kinds, this discovery increased the volume of trade.

As Greek trade expanded, towns on the western shore of the Aegean (such as Corinth) began to prosper. Population increased, both in Ionia and in the Greek peninsula. The commercial cities became crowded, and few of them controlled enough agricultural land to guarantee an adequate food supply for all their people. Fortunately, the Mediterranean region was still thinly settled, and there were many districts where small native populations could be subdued or displaced by colonists from the Greek shores of the Aegean. Just as the Phoenicians had taken over North Africa, so, from 750 B.C. on, the Greeks took over southern Italy and eastern Sicily; Naples and Syracuse were both founded by Greeks, and other Greek cities in the region were so numerous that the Romans later called southern Italy Magna Graecia, or Great Greece. Other Greek colonies were even more remote, such as Massilia (Marseilles) in southern France, trading posts in Spain, and Tanais on the north shore of the Black Sea. Greek colonies usually maintained cultural and religious ties with their mother-cities, but they were fully independent and owed no political or military support to their founders.

Cultural Development

Prosperity, as it often does, encouraged cultural development. It was in Ionia that the Greeks rediscovered the art of writing by adapting the Phoenician alphabet to the Greek language in the eighth century B.C. This discovery encouraged poets to put orally transmitted legends into permanent written form, as was done with the story of the Trojan War. In the same way, the works of lyric poets could now be preserved. Writing spread rapidly throughout the Greek-speaking communities, and, as will be seen, Ionia was not the only region that produced famous poets in the seventh and sixth centuries B.C. Nevertheless, until they lost their independence about 540 B.C., the Ionians remained the intellectual leaders of the Greeks.

Throughout the Greek world there was a rapid development of literature and the arts. Not long after the Homeric epics were composed, Hesiod, a small landowner in Boeotia, wrote his long didactic poems describing the origins of the gods and the hard life of the farmer. The first famous woman poet was Sappho of Lesbos; the Spartan commander Tyrtaeus composed martial songs to inspire his soldiers. Even the remote and newly colonized cities of Sicily produced their poets. And in Ionia the foundations were

Scene from a Greek vase (*ca.* 550 B.C.) showing merchants weighing produce. As trade routes multiplied, Greek merchants and wine and oil producers prospered.

being laid for work in philosophy and natural science.

Some remarkable works of art were produced during the seventh and sixth centuries B.C. The Greek temple began to take on its characteristic form—an oblong building framed by pillars with sculptured figures on the doorposts and along the upper walls. Early Greek sculpture owed much to the Egyptians; the figures are stiff and tense, ritualistic rather than realistic. But the Greeks had already learned to depict figures in full profile (which the Egyptians could not or would not do), and they were already showing interest in the beauty of the human figure. Most typical because most common were the vase paintings, which portray lively and realistic pictures of all sorts of human activities.

Greek vase of the late sixth century B.C. depicting a foot race. The vase was awarded to the winner of the foot race contest at the Panathenaic festival in Athens.

Social and Political Change

The rapid growth of trade and population put serious strains on the old political and social system. The *Iliad* and other early Greek writings suggest that a typical Greek community of the "Dark Ages" was ruled by a king or chieftain, who was advised and often contradicted by a council of very independent warriors. The warriors in turn held most of the land and dominated the peasant farmers and herders. The petty kings of the Homeric Age had very little power compared with an Egyptian pharaoh or a Persian emperor, and as time went on they tended to lose what power they had. The community was controlled by the land-holding aristocracy; if the king survived at all it was only because he was needed to perform certain religious rites, or because it was convenient to have a predesignated war-leader ready for sudden emergencies.

In communities with an adequate amount of good land, slow-growing populations, and relatively little commercial activity, this pattern of aristocratic government persisted throughout the period of independent Greek states. But in the trading cities there was more reason for the aristocracy to break up into factions and more friction between rich and poor. Some of the aristocrats became traders and joined forces with merchants of humbler origin; some continued to draw most of their income from their estates. There could be serious policy differences between those who sought to protect and extend trade routes and those who sought to protect and extend their lands. But even those in the latter group were involved in commerce, since they discovered that there was a market for wine and olive oil throughout the Mediterranean. Only a rich landowner could afford the initial investment needed to start a vineyard or an olive grove; the peasants continued to grow grain. But the profits on wine and oil exports could be used to buy cheap grain in Egypt or Sicily, where the soil was more productive. Thus while small farmers and day laborers suffered, landlords, merchants, shipbuilders, and skilled artisans like those who made the great pottery jugs for wine and oil prospered. With grain prices low, peasants fell into debt, and with interest rates running at 16 percent or more, they seldom were able to repay their loans. At best they lost their land and had to join the casual labor force in the city; at worst they and their children were sold into slavery.

The logical outcome of this crisis would have been either a bloody rebellion or the establishment of a society in which a few masters dominated thousands of slaves. But the Greeks had always lived in small tightly knit communities in which every family had its place and every man was known to most of his fellows. Such communities could not fully accept the depersonalizing effects of a commercial economy based on formal business contracts. If anything, economic growth forced people closer together as villages became cities and as the rural population became more dependent on the urban nucleus. The old sense of mutual responsibility and individual dignity persisted and was reinforced by a growing realization that these emerging city-states must make the best use they could of the limited manpower at their disposal. Enslaving half the population was not a good use of manpower; neither was a rebellion that might have killed off most of those who had military, political, and commercial skills. Most Greek cities avoided both these extremes and gradually satisfied the protests of debt-ridden farmers and laborers by a long drawn-out series of political reforms.

One of the first reactions to social strains was the establishment of tyrannies. A tyrant was usually a colorful politician who gained enough support by vague promises of better government to make himself a dictator. Most tyrants were aristocrats with considerable political experience; many of them were quite capable rulers. They usually tried to weaken the landed aristocracy, and in doing so they favored commercial interests and allowed a somewhat larger group of citizens to take part in the political process. For a time they seem to have succeeded in reducing social tensions, but they did not solve the problems of slavery and land reform. Although some tyrants managed to pass their power on

to their sons, no tyranny persisted for any significant length of time. The Greeks disliked the idea of tyranny, not because the tyrants were evil men (though a few of them were), but because they had seized power illegally and behaved arrogantly. The Greeks could accept class differences, but to the very end they remained suspicious of a single man who tried to dominate his fellow citizens. Thus tyranny did not become accepted as a new and desirable form of monarchy; instead it gained a reputation for oppressiveness that has persisted to the present day.

The seventh and sixth centuries B.C. were an age of tyrants, but they were also an age of lawgivers. The latter were rather more successful than the former. Old customs had to be adapted to new conditions, and the ruling classes gave full support to (and usually chose) men who tried to bring the laws up to date. Early laws were rigid and severe (the word *draconian* is still a memorial to the harsh code of the Athenian Draco), but, even so, fixed rules had advantages over decisions based on obsolete customs or whims of kings or aristocratic councils. And later lawgivers were less severe and were more concerned with the welfare of the poorer part of the population. About 590 B.C., for example, Solon of Athens reduced the burden of debt on small farmers and forbade enslavement for debt. Though he was followed by a tyrant, Solon's laws remained in force and formed the basis for a new constitution at the end of the sixth century. Other cities had similar experiences. In time it became a matter of pride to the Greeks that while other peoples were ruled by the will of kings, the Greeks were ruled by laws, not by men. Every Greek knew the laws of his city; they determined and protected his rights; they bound aristocrats and public officials as well as the poor and private citizens. And because the law was known, it was always possible to consider ways in which it could be changed and reformed.

The City-State

By 500 B.C. most of the tyrannies had ended, and many significant codes of law

This stele informed the Athenians of the Law Against Tyranny in 336 B.C.: "Should anyone, in an attempt at absolute power, rise up against the people or try to overthrow the democracy of Athens—whoever kills him shall be blameless."

might be controlled by a handful of aristocrats, but it might also allow most or all of the citizens to participate in the work of government. Whatever the distribution of power, the peak of Greek civilization was reached during the period in which the city-state, like an early Greek kingdom, controlled only a limited area, usually no more than that of a small American county. Much of the land was devoted to farming, but the center of the *polis* was the city itself with its marketplace, its citadel, and its temples. No city-state had a very large population: with more than one hundred thousand inhabitants, Athens was probably the biggest, but many cities had only ten thousand or so.

The smallness of the population was compensated for by the intensity of communal life. The citizens knew one another better and shared one another's experiences more fully than in any modern city of comparable size. Most activities took place in the open, since Greek houses were small and simple—places to eat and sleep, but not to live. Public and private business was transacted on the streets or on the porches of temples and law courts. Artisans and merchants worked in small shops open to the street. Actors gave their performances in unroofed theaters; teachers met their pupils in public gardens; politicians argued in the public squares. Everyone had a chance to know everything that was going on in the city; there was little privacy and apparently little desire for it.

In such close-knit communities it was easy to judge the character and ability of every citizen. And with such small populations it was essential to make the most of these human resources, especially in time of war. The days when a few aristocratic warriors with horses and chariots could carry the main burden of combat were long since gone. Greek armies were now composed of heavy-armed infantry (*hoplites*) fighting in close formation (the *phalanx*); all but the very poorest citizens were supposed to provide their own weapons and serve in the ranks. And when, as in the case of Athens, it was necessary to man a fleet of warships as well as provide an army, even the poorest citizens were needed for service. They

had been drafted. The worst of the social crises caused by rapid changes in the economy was over, although many reforms were still needed. The Greeks were ready to try their great political experiment, the establishment of basically secular governments in which power and responsibility were shared by a considerable part of the citizenry. The kings were gone, and religion was becoming a form of civic patriotism. Basic loyalty went to the *polis*—the city-state—and the *polis* was a republic. It

could pull an oar even if they could not afford shields and weapons.

Men who served in the armed forces at their own expense could scarcely be barred from the political activities of the community. The tendency was to increase the power of the general assembly, to admit more and more citizens (in some cases all citizens) to the assembly, and to increase the number of men eligible for political office. In many cities the officials, or a governing council, were elected by the assembly. Even at their greatest extent, however, these concessions did not produce pure democracy. The franchise was limited to adult males; women were excluded from political life. Slaves, who were numerous in every Greek city, had no rights, and immigrants from other Greek states, who formed a large part of the population in various trading cities such as Athens, could not vote even after many years of residence. Moreover, the aristocratic type of government persisted, with slight modifications, in many states. Overall, however, by the end of the sixth century B.C., a larger percentage of the male citizen population (varying from 100 percent in Athens to 10 percent in Sparta) participated in the political process than in any earlier period.

This increasing participation in politics strengthened the bonds between the citizen and his city. The *polis* was not just an area of land or a group of buildings; it was a way of life that shaped every human activity. As Socrates once put it, the laws and customs of Athens were his parents; they had raised and nurtured him. He was the kind of person he was because he had been born a citizen of Athens. But if the *polis* shaped the lives of its citizens, the citizens also shaped the life of the *polis*. Even in aristocratic states the rulers had to pay some attention to public opinion; elsewhere very little could be done without the approval and active assistance of a considerable part of the body of citizens.

Approval and assistance went far beyond the making and enforcing of laws. The adornment of the city with public buildings, the encouragement of poetry and drama, the support of teachers and scholars all were influenced by public

opinion; and all were, to some degree, dependent on the support of the wealthier classes. Peasants and day laborers were probably not greatly interested in art and literature, but men who had a little money and some leisure could argue endlessly about esthetic and intellectual problems. In fact, one of the excuses for slavery was that it made it possible for the citizen to participate fully in the cultural and political life of his city by freeing him from the routine of daily work. Not all citizens took advantage of their opportunities, even in the most enlightened cities, but enough of them did to enable a sophisticated civilization to develop on a very small population base.

This discussion of life in the Greek city-state has focused exclusively on men. But society then was thoroughly male dominated (which may be why there was a considerable amount of homosexuality). Women stayed home, unless they were courtesans or lesbians, as Sappho reputedly was.

Greek Religion

The religion of the Greeks both bound them together and encouraged strong local patriotisms. Some of the Greek gods probably went back to the religion of pre-Greek inhabitants of the Aegean area; some certainly came in with successive waves of invaders; but by Homeric times they had been combined into a family of twelve major gods who lived on Mount Olympus. Zeus was ruler of the gods and wielder of the thunderbolt; his wife, Hera, was goddess of women and marriage. Strangely enough, Ares, the god of war, was not especially honored by the Greeks, in spite of their belligerent spirit.

Each city gave special honor to one divinity, who was its protector and patron. Thus Athena, goddess of wisdom, was greatly revered in Athens, even though this meant giving second place to Poseidon, god of the sea and the chief god of many communities in Attica. Artemis, the twin sister of Apollo, was worshiped at Sparta as the spirit of bravery and courage. Apollo, god of prophecy, was not so closely tied to any one city; people came from all parts of the Greek

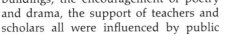

Athena, goddess of wisdom, protector of the home and the citadel, is shown in this bronze statue in military dress (*ca.* seventh century B.C.).

ca. 2000 B.C.	ca. 1700	ca. 1480	ca. 1100	ca. 800	ca. 600	404	323	146 B	Conquest by Rome
Minoan Civilization on Crete			"Dark Ages"	Dominance of City-states of Asia Minor	Dominance of Athens and Sparta			Hellenistic Era	
Arrival of Greeks	Mycenaean Civilization in Aegean Area								

Decline of
City-state System and
Conquest by Macedon

world to seek guidance from his oracle at Delphi, and his shrine on the island of Delos was a center of religious life for many of the Greek islands. Zeus was also widely worshiped. In their great festivals, such as the Olympic and Isthmian games, the Greeks honored all the gods in competitions to determine who was the best poet, the fastest runner, the ablest playwright, the strongest wrestler. But in their frequent wars, the Greeks expected each god to defend his own city, even to the extent of fighting with the god of the opposing city. Religion gave the Greeks cultural but not political unity.

The early Greek religion was not very edifying or inspiring. The gods were simply human beings on a large scale. They had great power and were immortal, but they were also quarrelsome, lustful, and prejudiced. They lied to and

Gorgon from the Temple of Artemis,
goddess of the hunt, at Corfu (600 B.C.).

cheated one another; they interfered in human affairs in unpredictable and whimsical ways; they were completely undisciplined. Zeus had no real control over them (especially when he was off on one of his amorous adventures), and their worshipers could never be sure what would please them. One could only sacrifice and hope for the best.

Educated Greeks tried hard to draw some moral lessons from the confused stories of the gods, but with little success. Something could be done with Apollo as the god of reason and light, and Zeus could be reverenced as the Father of all by ignoring the scandalous stories about him. But while the Greeks were reasonably sure that there were supernatural beings, they were not very sure that they knew much about them. The official religious cult was an excuse for festivals and parades, for building temples and carving statues, for writing poems and plays. It furnished an outlet for civic patriotism. The basic problems of the meaning of life and of the right conduct of life had to be solved in other ways.

It is doubtful that the common people had ever been wholly devoted to the Homeric gods, who were the gods of the old aristocracy. The pre-Greek fertility cults, centered on the worship of Demeter, goddess of grain and fertility, and Dionysus, god of wine and ecstasy, remained popular with them. Both involved secret rituals; both gave some promise of immortality. Through ritual and moral purity the initiate could be united to Demeter and be assured of lasting bliss. Through drinking wine mixed with sacrificial blood, the followers of Dionysus could rise from the dead, as their god had done. Often the two fertility cults were combined, and they spread throughout the Greek world. The most famous Greek dramas were written for the annual festivals of Dionysus, one of the great religious events at Athens.

THE PERSIAN WARS
499–479 B.C.

In the last decades of the sixth century B.C. the Greeks were clearly ready for "take-off"; they had the economic, political, and intellectual base on which to build a great civilization. Precisely at this point came the crisis of the Persian Wars. War can ruin a civilization that is fully developed and set in its ways, but it can stimulate a civilization that is still in its early stage of development. Victory over the Persians confirmed the belief of the Greeks in their uniqueness and in their destiny; the wars were followed immediately by the Golden Age of Greece.

Persian power had been a serious threat ever since Cyrus the Great conquered the Ionian cities about 540 B.C. The Greek world was shocked by this calamity, but an effective response to Persian aggression could come only from the mainland of the Greek peninsula. And leadership there had gradually concentrated in two cities, Athens and Sparta. If they could cooperate, Persia might be resisted; if not, the prospects were dim. But cooperation was not easy, for Athens and Sparta stood at the two extremes of the Greek political system.

Sparta

Sparta in the early period of its history was not very different from other Greek states; like them, it took a prominent part in the early development of Greek art and literature. But Sparta was situated in a fertile agricultural region, one that was not greatly concerned with commerce. It sought to make the most of its favorable agricultural position by dominating other grain-producing communities in its neighborhood. About 650 B.C. one of these neighboring communities, Messenia, revolted and almost destroyed the Spartan state. By 600 B.C. the Spartans were victorious, but they had been badly frightened. They decided to turn the entire male population of their *polis* into a standing army and to suppress any activity that might interfere with military efficiency.

When the reorganization had been completed the population of the Spartan state (called Lacedaemon) was divided into three groups. First were the Spartan male citizens (less than ten thousand men), who had all political rights and enjoyed full equality among themselves. Then came the free citizens of the neighboring communities, who could manage their own affairs but who had nothing to say about decisions of the ruling city. Third were the *helots,* serfs who worked the lands of Lacedaemon for the benefit of Spartan citizens.

The citizens paid a high price for their political and economic privileges. At the age of seven they were taken from their homes to be trained for military service. They entered the army at twenty and were allowed to marry then, but they could not live with their wives until they were thirty. They remained liable for military service until they were sixty.

It is easy to see how this system created the best-disciplined army in the Greek world and how it enabled Sparta to control most of the Peloponnesus, either directly or through an alliance with other cities known as the Peloponnesian League. It is less easy to understand why other Greeks, even in the liberal-minded and unregimented city of Athens, ad-

A procession recorded in marble at the Parthenon (fifth century B.C.). The paraders on their way to the Acropolis carry jars containing sacrificial gifts.

Head of a Spartan warrior believed to be King Leonidas, who commanded the Greek force at Thermopylae (early fifth century B.C.).

mired the Spartans so greatly. Bravery, discipline, frugality, scorn of luxury were characteristic of the Spartans, and it may be that the many Greeks who lacked these qualities found some satisfaction in seeing them embodied in at least one *polis*. Even so, self-discipline is more attractive than discipline imposed by the state; it seems likely that for most people Spartan success was more impressive than Spartan virtue.

Athens

Athens was more like an Ionian city than most of the other Greek states. Dependent on commerce rather early (seventh century B.C.), the Athenians aimed to suppress or control trade rivals rather than add agricultural regions to their holdings. Athens had one asset that most other cities lacked—the silver mines of Laureium, which for many generations yielded enough to pay for great expenses, such as the building of a fleet.

As we have seen, Athens had its early lawgivers (Draco and Solon) and its sixth-century tyrants. The net result of these experiences had been to increase somewhat the number of citizens eligible to take an active role in government, although the wealthy still retained control. A sharp change came after the last tyrant was overthrown in 510 B.C., when the reformer Cleisthenes put through some basic constitutional reforms. Cleisthenes divided the citizens into ten tribes, so arranged that each tribe was a cross section of the whole population, rich and poor, rural and urban. Fifty citizens chosen by lot from each tribe made up the Council of Five Hundred, which prepared business for the assembly. A general assembly of all citizens passed the laws, as had long been customary. The top civil and military offices were open only to the wealthier citizens, and the old Council of the Areopagus, or council of ex-archons (the highest civil officials), had considerable power for a generation or more after Cleisthenes' reforms. But even these officials were elected by popular vote, and since they were not paid, the poorer citizens had no great desire anyway to become archons or generals or treasurers.

The Athenian constitution thus gave every citizen the right to influence the government and to participate in its activities. Almost every citizen took a passionate interest in politics, education, art, and literature. There were, of course, private interests and political factions; the Athenians could be as shortsighted, selfish, and unreasonable as many modern voters. But for almost a century the Athenian system succeeded in releasing the energy of all citizens and in concentrating a good part of it on the common welfare.

The Defeat of Persia

When the Greek cities of Asia Minor revolted against Persia in 499 B.C., Athens sent a fleet to assist them. After the revolt had been put down, the Persian King Darius dispatched a punitive force by sea to Attica. But this force was repulsed by a small Athenian army at Marathon in 490 B.C. The Persian king, unwilling to let such a humiliation go unpunished, planned a full-scale campaign against the cities of the Greek peninsula. Fortunately for the Greeks, Darius died before he could begin his attack. It was only in 480 B.C. that his successor, Xerxes, and a Persian army of over one hundred thousand men crossed the Dardanelles and marched down the Greek peninsula. Faced with such an overwhelming force, most of the small cities north of Athens declared their neutrality. Athens and the Peloponnesian League were left to defend what remained of Greek civilization from envelopment by the Persian Empire.

The Peloponnesian league formed the basis of the Greek defense against the Persians. The Athenians had hoped for Spartan help at Marathon and were quite ready to form a new league in alliance with the Peloponnesians, although in so doing they were forced to accept the leadership of Sparta. As the Persian forces moved southward, a small Spartan detachment at the head of some six thousand Greeks attempted to hold the pass at Thermopylae, north of Athens, until a decisive naval battle could be fought. This battle, which took place off the coast, was a draw. The Greek forces withdrew to take up new positions at the Isthmus of Corinth and the Bay of Salamis. Meanwhile, the Persians broke through the pass at Thermopylae after the entire Spartan detachment had been killed trying to defend it. With Thermopylae unguarded, the Persians had an open road into Athens. The Athenian citizens were quickly evacuated to nearby islands, where they watched in horror as the Persians looted and burned their city.

Though the city was destroyed, Athens was not defeated. Before the Persian attack, Themistocles, an ambitious but farsighted politician, had persuaded the Athenian assembly to put all the income of the silver mines into building a fleet far larger than a city the size of Athens would normally require. He realized that,

while the Greeks could not expect to defeat the massive Persian armies in battle, the Greek peninsula with its islands and inlets could never be conquered except by sea. Shortly after the Persians occupied Athens, a Greek fleet, at least two-thirds of which was Athenian, met the Persian navy in the Bay of Salamis and destroyed it in a single engagement. Cut off from supplies coming by sea from Asia Minor, the Persians were badly crippled. After a final defeat at Plataea by a Spartan-led force (479 B.C.), they retired permanently from the Greek peninsula. In the same year the Greek fleet virtually wiped out the Persian navy in a battle off the coast of Asia Minor.

The defeat of Persia in 479 B.C. meant that the Greek world remained outside Persian control. Since Persia no longer

THE PERSIAN WARS   499–479 B.C.

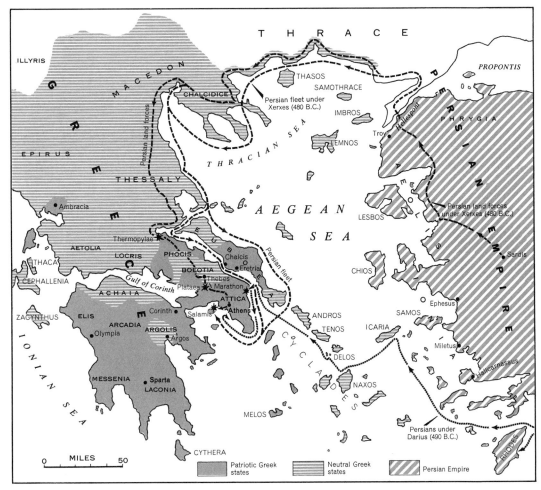

A four drachma coin from Athens showing Athena and her owl (*ca.* sixth century B.C.).

had a strong navy, the Greek cities of Asia Minor were also able to reassert their independence, though they never regained their former strength. The Persian Empire was not completely defeated, however. For the next century and a half, Persia retained its control over the rest of the eastern Mediterranean—Egypt, Palestine, Syria, most of Asia Minor, and Mesopotamia. And the Persian king was able, at times, to influence Greek politics by siding with one or another group of quarreling states.

The victory over the Persians was to the Greeks what the American Revolution was to the colonists, an inexhaustible source of pride and confidence. A few small states had defeated a great empire. Now the Greeks were more sure than ever that they were destined for greatness, that their way of life was superior to that of all other peoples, that they could succeed in any enterprise they undertook. The century following the Persian Wars was the Golden Age, in which the Greeks made their indelible mark on the history of civilization.

THE AGE OF ATHENIAN DOMINATION, 478–431 B.C.

As soon as the Persians retreated, the Athenians rebuilt their city on an even grander scale. Proud of their city, proud of their democracy, proud of their victory over Persia, and prosperous beyond all expectations, the Athenians of the fifth century B.C. not only dominated the Aegean but created one of the most striking cultural patterns in the history of western civilization.

The Athenian Empire

A basic factor in Athens' rise to power and cultural supremacy was wealth. A century earlier, most of the commerce in and out of the Aegean had gone to Miletus or to one of the other Greek cities of Asia Minor. But as these cities declined during the late sixth century, enterprising Athenian merchants began diverting trade to Athens. After the Persian Wars, the Athenians used their large navy to bring former Milesian

trading stations—on the Black Sea and in Syria—under their own control.

In the vast expansion of their trading empire, the Athenians took advantage of their position as leaders of the Delian League. This league was an alliance of the Greek maritime cities around the Aegean. Its original purpose was to continue the naval war against Persia until all Persian forces had been driven from the Aegean Sea and all Greek cities had been freed of Persian control. Delegates met first in 478 B.C. on the island of Delos, from which the league took its name. Each member state was to contribute an annual quota of ships or money. Since Sparta was of no use in naval affairs, the Athenians had no rival power to face in the league. And because they contributed by far the largest fleet, the Athenians were given the right to name the admiral and the administrators of the common treasury.

In time, the navy of the Delian League became almost exclusively Athenian. Other members, with only a few exceptions, contributed cash rather than ships. Naturally, the navy of the league was soon being used primarily to protect and even extend the Athenian economic empire. When one of the member cities resigned in protest, the league's navy appeared in its harbor, besieged the city, and dismantled its fortifications. From that time on, the city was governed by Athens, and the other league members were made to understand that a similar fate awaited other defectors. Finally, in 454 B.C., when the league's treasury was moved from Delos to Athens, it was clear that the league had become an Athenian Empire and that the members were little more than Athenian dependencies.

Although the cities comprising the league had no choice but to remain in it, the other cities of the Greek peninsula became increasingly alarmed at the growth of Athenian power and began to seek closer ties with Sparta and the Peloponnesian League. Between 454 and 431 B.C. most of the cities of the Greek peninsula and around the Aegean became associated with one of the two alliance systems: the Delian League dominated by Athens or the Peloponnesian League dominated by Sparta.

During this time the productive power of Athens was enriched by the influx of thousands of artists, artisans, and merchants from the more sophisticated Greek cities of Asia Minor, who saw greater opportunities in Athens than in their home cities. These immigrants, known as *metics* (that is, Greeks who were not Athenians), provided a labor supply for the expanding Athenian economy. And the many artists, poets, and philosophers among them deserve much of the credit for making the fifth century Athens' Golden Age.

Another source of Athenian postwar prosperity was the large number of prisoners of war brought to Athens as slaves. With *metics* to help produce and sell their wares and with slaves to labor in their shops and mines, all but the poorest Athenian citizens could participate fully in the cultural and political life of the city. And with the wealth derived from tribute paid by the Delian League, plus the income from commerce and mining, the life of the Athenian *polis* was remarkably rich and complex.

Politics

The Athenian constitution, by the middle of the fifth century B.C., gave almost equal rights to all citizens; only a few vestiges of aristocratic privilege remained. In fact, in some areas even the privileges of merit were avoided; for example, the members of the Council of Five Hundred were chosen by lot. The general was the only important elected official—a peculiar and, as it turned out, an unfortunate exception. The Greeks called this system "democracy," and many modern writers have echoed the phrase. But in a population of around one hundred thousand, there were about twenty thousand *metics* and about forty thousand slaves. Neither *metics* nor slaves could vote, nor could the wives and daughters of citizens. Thus only about twenty thousand male citizens (one-fifth of the population) had political rights. This was a high proportion, by standards of the ancient world, but it was not what we would call democracy.

The really significant change in the fifth century was not an increase in the number of voters, but an increase in the political power of the lower classes. These men manned the fleet, which was the source of Athenian wealth and power. Leaders of political factions had to seek the favor of the common citizens, and their favor could shift with alarming rapidity. To prevent a revival of tyranny, the Athenians had invented a device known as ostracism: a majority of citizens could vote the exile for ten years of any politician who seemed to be gaining too much power. Many of the ablest leaders of the city were ostracized, including Themistocles, who had built the fleet that preserved the liberty of Athens. The system of government was unwieldy; the general assembly was too large, and the Council of Five Hundred changed its leadership each month. Policy had to be decided in private conferences among politicians and then be sold to the citizens. It took an extremely able leader to give consistency to Athenian policy without falling into demagogy on the one hand or self-righteous disdain of public opinion on the other. It is remarkable that several men in the fifth century succeeded in this difficult task and that one man, Pericles, was a powerful politician from 463 to 429 B.C. and (because he was annually reelected to the general-

Pericles, from a Roman copy of a Greek bust of the fifth century B.C.

Marble grave relief of a girl with pigeons (*ca.* 450 B.C.).

ship) the unchallenged leader of Athens for the last fifteen years of this period.

The issues discussed by the people ranged all the way from charges of corruption and excessive ambition to basic questions of foreign policy. There were conservatives who feared that the growth of Athenian power was alienating friends of Athens and forcing them to ally with Sparta; there were expansionists who wanted to grab everything in sight. But there were not two organized political parties. The Athenians were too individualistic to fall into rigid political allegiances, and as long as the expansionist policy was successful, the majority did not really want to drop it. Thus Pericles' chief opponent during the early years of his power was Cimon, who can hardly be labeled a conservative or an opponent of expansion. Only when they were faced with the disaster of a losing war did the Athenians think seriously about modifying their basic policies.

Art and Architecture

The destruction of Athens by the Persians meant that the city had to be rebuilt, and the new wealth of Athens allowed it to be rebuilt splendidly. Construction was rather haphazard until Pericles became "boss" of the city and put his friend Phidias, a sculptor, in charge of what might be called city planning. With plenty of money at their disposal from the revenues of the Delian League, Pericles and Phidias were able to attract architects, sculptors, and painters from all over the Greek world. There was nothing at Athens that could not be found in other Greek cities, but there was more of it, and, on the whole, it was better arranged.

Greek art of the fifth century B.C. was an art that had solved its technical problems. Greek architects could construct imposing and well-proportioned buildings; Greek sculptors could represent all the details of the human body with absolute accuracy. It was also an art with definite and limited goals. Greek artists were interested in the finite, not the infinite; they never undertook the hard task of giving concrete form to visions. They idealized life here on earth, not life in a heaven about which they thought little. The ideal man was a demigod, and the god was simply an idealized man. There is little sense of conflict in the Greek art of this period, no antagonism between the real and the ideal. Life in this world at its best could be beautiful and satisfying, and this is what the artists sought to represent.

These characteristics of Greek art are evident in the crowning achievement of the rebuilding of Athens—the temple of the Parthenon,* dedicated to Athena, the patron goddess of the city. The Parthenon did not attempt to impress the beholder through mere size as Egyptian structures had done. Though the Parthenon is almost as large as a football field, its basic qualities are harmony and proportion; it is constructed on a scale that can be measured and understood by the

---

*The Parthenon served as a place of worship for over two thousand years; it was a temple to Athena, then a Christian church, and finally a mosque. It was almost intact until it was blown up in a minor war three hundred years ago. Today only the outer row of columns is standing, though many of the sculptures were saved.

Pericles on Athens and Sparta

This oration, inserted by the Greek historian Thucydides in his *History of the Peloponnesian War*, does not give Pericles' exact words, but it does express admirably the pride of the Athenians in their city and its form of government.

We are called a democracy, for the administration is in the hands of the many and not of the few. But . . . the claim of excellence is also recognized, and when a citizen is in any way distinguished, he is preferred to the public service, not as a matter of privilege, but as the reward of merit. . . . Our city is thrown open to the world, and we never expel a foreigner or prevent him from seeing or learning anything of which the secret, if revealed to an enemy, might profit him. . . . In the matter of education, whereas the Spartans from early youth are always undergoing laborious exercises which are to make them brave, we live at ease, and yet are equally ready to face the perils which they face. . . . For we are lovers of the beautiful, yet simple in our tastes, and we cultivate the mind without loss of manliness. . . . Such is the city for whose sake these men fought and died; . . . and every one of us who survive should gladly toil on her behalf.

From Pericles' Funeral Oration, in Thucydides, *The History of the Peloponnesian War*, trans. by B. Jowett in Francis R. B. Godolphin, ed., *The Greek Historians* (New York: Random House, 1942), Vol. I, pp. 648–50.

human eye. The Parthenon stands on the crest of the Acropolis, the hill that dominates Athens, but it does not reach toward heaven like a Gothic cathedral. It is the crown of an earthly city, not the gateway to a heavenly one.

The sculpture of the Parthenon, carved by Phidias and his followers, represents the gods as well as the people of the city in their processions, their athletic contests, and their military exercises. Here again, the Greeks did not distinguish between the religious and the secular; or, to put it another way, the noblest and best secular activity was also a religious act.

Drama

Built into the side of the Acropolis sloping away from the city was an outdoor amphitheater dedicated to the god Dionysus. Here, during the two annual festivals of Dionysus, the Athenians attended a series of plays. These plays were not staged for amusement. An important part of the religious festival, they were presented by the city to instruct and purge the citizens before they attended the sacred Dionysian rites.

The Greeks had long celebrated religious festivals with semidramatic performances in which a single speaker told a story to which a chorus offered responses. But during the Golden Age the Athenian dramatists transformed these rituals into full-fledged drama by adding a second and then a third speaker. The stories were not new to the audience. Playwrights used themes drawn from ancient Greek legends to illustrate the religious and ethical problems of the present world. What is right conduct? Can a man avoid the fate decreed him by the gods? What course can an individual take when civic and religious laws conflict? These are some of the questions posed by the great Athenian dramatists of the Golden Age: Aeschylus (525–456 B.C.), Sophocles (496?–406 B.C.), and Euripides (480?–406? B.C.).

Running through all the Greek tragedies is the theme that man must remain in harmony with the universe. The Greeks admired a man who was strong and self-sufficient. But the Greek ideal was "moderation in all things," and—as might be expected in a society where most people knew one another—the Greeks could not tolerate a man who believed that he was superior to other men. Thus the greatest fault was *hybris*, or pride. Specifically, *hybris* meant assuming a role reserved for the gods, par-

The Acropolis at Athens.

ticularly in taking the life of another human being, even by accident. Thus most Athenian tragedies deal with guilt and expiation—the misfortunes that must come to a man who defies the gods by not accepting the limitations placed on him as a human.

Best known of the plays of Aeschylus are the blood-chilling tales of the *Oresteia* trilogy, which examine the religious aspects of justice through the story of the downfall of the house of Agamemnon. Agamemnon, betrayed by his wife, is avenged by his son, but the son must suffer for assuming the prerogative of the gods in dealing out retribution. In *Oedipus the King*, Sophocles, the most popular playwright of the period, deals with the problem of the man who has unwittingly done wrong. Not knowing who his parents were, Oedipus killed his own father and married his own mother. In his *Antigone*, Sophocles portrays a conflict that is still acute today—the conflict between the demands of the state and the desire of the individual to follow a higher moral law. Creon, King of Thebes, forbids the burial of his nephew, who had been killed in an unsuccessful rebellion. The body must be left to rot in the fields; anyone who touches it will be put to death. Antigone, sister of the victim, defies the king, for no human order can justify breaking the laws of the gods. Creon decrees that Antigone be confined in a rocky vault, and she kills herself. Creon's subsequent remorse is not enough to save him. His son, who had loved Antigone, commits suicide; his wife kills herself in despair. Human pride, which had defied religion and conscience, has been punished.

Euripides was the youngest of the three great tragedians of the Golden Age. Unlike his predecessors, he was more interested in human emotions than in the problems of sin. His plays were not always well received, for they frequently dealt with unpopular themes. In *Medea*, for instance, Euripides elicits the sympathy of his audience for a half-crazed foreign woman who murders her own children to spite the Greek husband who had abandoned her. And in *The Trojan Women*, presented when Athens was at war and bursting with pride, Euripides

made the Athenians watch a play about the inhuman atrocities perpetrated by a people at war and passed off as patriotic acts.

The writers of comedies were at least as popular as the writers of tragedies, and they probably came closer to reflecting the ideas of ordinary citizens. The only fifth-century comedian whose works have survived was Aristophanes (448?–380? B.C.). Many of his plays have been lost, but those that we possess are witty commentaries on the events of his own day. At times he seems to have been seeking the applause of the lowbrows; for example, the philosopher Socrates appears in one of his plays, *The Clouds*, as a ridiculous figure who talks learned nonsense. But Aristophanes had an honest dislike of humbug and pomposity and a sincere aversion to war. One of his most effective plays is *Lysistrata*, an antiwar comedy in which the women of Athens persuade their husbands to make peace by refusing to sleep with them.

History and Philosophy

Sculpture and architecture, tragedy and comedy, reached their peak in the Athens of the fifth century B.C. History and philosophy, which started later, naturally attained their highest level at a later date. The foundations for both disciplines were laid during the period when Athens was rising to greatness, but the most influential books on these subjects were written after the collapse of the Athenian Empire.

Little is known of the first Greek historians; they seem to have been interested chiefly in genealogies. But with Herodotus of Halicarnassus (*ca.* 480?–420 B.C.), one of the many scholars who visited Athens, we find the historian who is a storyteller and who is interested in the curious differences among the customs of peoples. Herodotus' theme was the war between the Persians and the Greeks, which he saw as the culmination of a long struggle between the culture of the Orient and the culture of Greece. He therefore felt that he should describe the development of all the peoples of the Persian Empire, including the Egyptians and the Babylonians. Herodotus had

Sophocles, popular fifth-century B.C. playwright.

traveled through these countries and had talked to many well-informed men. He preserved many useful facts, but he himself knew that there were as yet no techniques for separating facts from legends. Even his account of the Persian War is so influenced by national pride that it is not entirely reliable, but it is still exciting reading.

Philosophy and science had their roots in the learning of Egypt and Babylonia. In both countries there had been accurate astronomical observations, development of basic principles of mathematics, and some speculation about the nature of the physical world. The Greeks of Ionia, who were a gifted people, probably had ideas of their own about such matters, but they were enormously stimulated by the knowledge they received from the older civilizations of the East. By the sixth century B.C. the Ionians were attempting to organize scattered facts and ideas into coherent systems, to discover first principles and general laws, to express the difference between things as they are and things as they seem. They were somewhat too ready to generalize from insufficient data, somewhat inclined to oversimplify complex problems, somewhat too willing to ascribe human values to mere abstractions (for example, "lucky" or mystical numbers, such as seven). But in beginning to develop the idea of laws of nature, in looking behind appearances to reality, in seeing mathematics as a powerful tool for solving problems, the early Greek philosophers laid the foundations for all later scientific thought in the West.

The search for a single first principle was not very successful as long as it was confined to purely physical entities, such as "water" or "fire." But several Greek philosophers, notably Heraclitus and Anaxagoras, reached the idea of a *logos* or a Mind that governed and permeated the world. Pythagoras, an Ionian who migrated to southern Italy, saw the organizing principle in numbers, naturally enough, since he was a distinguished mathematician. The appearance of change also perplexed early philosophers: How can a flowing river remain the same river? Anaxagoras resolved the paradox by arguing that the world was made up of

countless tiny particles, unchanging themselves, but constantly rearranging to give the appearance of change. This was a forerunner of the "atomic" theory of Democritus, rejected by most of the Greeks but revived by modern scientists.

Athens attracted scholars just as it did artists. The intellectual climate was stimulating, and the Athenians could afford to hire teachers for their youth and to support distinguished writers. By the fifth century B.C. Athens had become the center for the teaching of philosophy, which it remained for many centuries. With so many men arguing about basic truths, opinions were bound to be voiced that shocked conservative citizens. For example, Anaxagoras was accused of atheism because he taught that the sun was simply a ball of fire and that the earth rotated around it. Since Pericles was a patron of Anaxagoras, charges against the philosopher could be used to discredit the statesman.

Even more annoying to many Athenians were the Sophists (the "Wisdomers"), a group of wandering teachers primarily interested in problems of human reason and behavior. They tried to make students think for themselves by asking questions without giving answers. The naive responses of the students were then demolished by logical arguments, so that eventually (at least in theory) the students would begin to think logically themselves and discard prejudices and outworn dogmas.

Teaching students to think for themselves and opposing time-honored beliefs with logic are always dangerous occupations. The Sophists made things worse by being relativists. "Beauty," said one Sophist, "is in the eye of the beholder." If beauty is relative, so is truth, so is justice. And if justice is relative, why should not a bright young man trained in logic and rhetoric go to the law courts and win bad cases with clever arguments?

This is precisely what the enemies of the Sophists feared. Their concern was not unjustified. The Sophists did develop an excellent technique of logical analysis, used by all succeeding Greek philosophers, but they also developed a number of tricks of argument that could thwart

An actor wearing a mask, in a declamatory pose, is depicted in this bronze statue from the Greco-Roman period.

the simple, honest, uneducated man. The Athenians did believe in justice, even if they could not define it logically, and the Sophists offended their civic and religious beliefs. Men of the lower and middle classes, who could not afford to hire tutors for their sons, were also offended by the fact that the Sophists sold "wisdom" for money.

Socrates (469–399 B.C.), one of the few native Athenian philosophers, shared the dislike of many of his fellow citizens for the Sophists. He would not take money for his teaching, and he spent his life trying to prove that the Sophists were wrong. He believed that truth, beauty, and justice were eternal and existed independently of man. If an object was beautiful, it would be beautiful whether or not a human being was there to see it. Similarly, if an action was a crime, it was wrong for all people and for all time. Socrates taught that each man was born with an innate knowledge of eternal truth, but that this knowledge became clouded by his experiences in a selfish and materialistic world. To know the truth, a man must clear away the misconceptions acquired in this world and discover the spark of eternal truth that was in his own soul. To make his point, Socrates borrowed the techniques of the Sophists, asking questions to make people see for themselves where their thinking was unclear or illogical. Although Socrates was beloved by his immediate followers, his methods did not endear him to the populace, most of whom classed him with the Sophists. And in one of the great ironies of history, this opponent of the Sophists was finally executed on charges that, like the Sophists, he was corrupting the youth of the city (see p. 45).

THE PELOPONNESIAN WAR 431–404 B.C.

The Peloponnesian War has been viewed as a Greek tragedy that was acted out in history. It was caused by *hybris*—the ambition of Athens and of Sparta, the desire of politicians for renown, the deliberate renouncement of justice and reason. It was a curse that passed from one generation to the next, an evil that endured when it could soon have been stopped. It ended with the humiliation of one "actor" and the realization by the other that victory led only to new suffering. One might easily see in this tragedy the downfall of classical Greece.

Such a view is, of course, a gross exaggeration. Life is less logical and less coherent than a classical tragedy. Actually, some of the greatest achievements of Greek culture came during and after the war—the plays of Euripides and Aristophanes, the philosophy of Plato and Aristotle. And while the war weakened many Greek city-states, especially Athens and Sparta, the Greek world of competing city-states had always been insecure. It could endure only so long as no great power existed in the eastern Mediterranean. Once the decaying Persian Empire was replaced by new and powerful kingdoms, the Greek cities, strong or

The Trial of Socrates

Plato, in his dialogue *The Apology,* reported the trial of Socrates. In this passage Socrates explains why he cannot change his ways.

Suppose . . . you said to me "Socrates, we shall disregard Anytus and acquit you, but only on one condition, that you give up . . . philosophizing. If we catch you going on in the same way, you shall be put to death." . . . I should reply, "Gentlemen, . . . I owe a greater obedience to God than to you; and so long as I draw breath and have my faculties, I shall never stop practising philosophy and exhorting you and elucidating the truth for everyone that I meet." I shall go on saying . . . , "My very good friend, you are an Athenian and belong to a city which is the greatest and most famous in the world for its wisdom and strength. Are you not ashamed that you give your attention to acquiring as much money as possible, . . . and give no attention or thought to truth and understanding and the perfection of your soul? . . . Wealth does not bring goodness, but goodness brings wealth and every other blessing, both to the individual and to the State." Now if I corrupt the young by this message, the message would seem to be harmful. . . . And so, gentlemen, I would say, "You can please yourselves . . . whether you acquit me or not; you know that I am not going to alter my conduct, not even if I have to die a hundred deaths."

From Plato, *The Last Days of Socrates,* trans. by Hugh Tredennick (Baltimore: Penguin Books, 1959), pp. 61–62.

Socrates, statuette from the Hellenistic period.

weak, could exist only on sufferance. The Peloponnesian War simply underlined a fact that had long been apparent: the Greeks could not unite into a single state. If they could not unite, they were doomed to lose their independence.

The immediate causes of the war were quarrels between Athens and Corinth over the colonies of Corcyra and Poteidaea and the decision of Athens to exclude the merchants of Megara from Athenian markets. These acts did no real damage to Corinth or to Sparta and its allies—none of the disputed cities had great military strength or important trade connections—but they seemed one more proof of the dangers of Athenian imperialism. Sparta and the Peloponnesian League declared war in 431 B.C.

Pericles' war plan was to abandon the Athenian rural areas, concentrate the population inside the city walls, and rely on his navy to harass the enemy and keep open the sea lanes. Since Sparta had no navy, Athens could be sure of an adequate supply of imported food and thus could hold out indefinitely. But in the second year of the war a plague broke out in Athens, killing a considerable part of the population, including Pericles himself. No one could really take his place. There were still able leaders in Athens, but none of them could gain the support of the people long enough to follow a consistent policy. The Athenians did well enough in the early fighting, and Sparta made peace in 421 B.C. But ambitious politicians seeking to gain power by a victorious war reopened the conflict, and from that point it was all downhill. The Athenians took greater and greater risks, such as their disastrous attempt to conquer Syracuse from 415 to 413 B.C., and in the end their naval power was completely destroyed. In 404 B.C. they surrendered to Sparta.

For a brief period Sparta dominated the Greek world. The Spartans put Athens under the control of a brutal oligarchy and tried to set up similar governments in other enemy states. But Sparta also was suffering from the effects of the war, and political dissension at home weakened its power abroad. Athens soon threw off the harsh government imposed by Sparta and reverted to its old political system. Other cities followed the Athenian example. Although Sparta struggled for several decades to maintain its hegemony, its army, never very large, steadily dwindled in a series of losing battles. By 370 B.C. Sparta had become so weak that it could not even defend the Peloponnesus.

The great war between Athens and Sparta produced a great historian, Thucydides (ca. 460–400 B.C.). An Athenian general who had been deprived of his command, Thucydides very early began to collect material for a history of the conflict. He wanted to be absolutely accurate, to write only from his own experience or from the testimony of eyewitnesses. But even more, he wanted to describe the behavior of politicians and states in terms that would have meaning for all future generations. In his own words, his history was to be "an everlasting possession." He succeeded in this high endeavor as few other historians have. The Funeral Speech that he ascribed to Pericles describes what a democratic community can be at its best. The Melian dialogue shows Athens descending to naked imperialism in dealing with a small city. This dialogue portrays so accurately the behavior of a conscienceless conqueror that it was reprinted without changing a word to describe Hitler's takeover of Czechoslovakia in 1938.

GREECE IN THE FOURTH CENTURY B.C.

The Peloponnesian War and the subsequent struggles against Spartan hegemony created a confused political situation in which there was no real center of power in the Greek world. The king of Persia interfered again in Greek affairs and established a loose and intermittent control over the Greek cities of Asia Minor. Athens rebuilt its naval empire, but it was a much weaker one than that of the fifth century. Syracuse dominated the Greeks of Sicily and Italy, but it could not intervene in the Aegean area. None of these states had a political future; in the end the great power of the Near and Middle East was to be the

Plato (426–347 B.C.), Socrates' favorite pupil.

Aristotle (384–322 B.C.), pupil of Plato and organizer of Greek thought.

half-Greek, almost unknown, Kingdom of Macedon.

Plato and Aristotle

Political confusion did not destroy Greek culture; it simply gave the Greeks something more to talk about. The greatest Greek orators were men of the fourth century. They urged the Greeks, eloquently but vainly, to forget their petty quarrels and to unite against common enemies. More lasting than oratory, however, was the work of the philosophers who taught at Athens, the city that had been, and was long to remain, the center of Greek culture.

The beginning was not auspicious. The citizens of Athens, humiliated by their defeat, looked for a scapegoat and picked on the philosopher Socrates. Some of his pupils had been leaders in the unfortunate expeditions that crippled Athenian naval power; moreover, in his persistent questioning, Socrates had challenged many accepted dogmas. He was accused of sacrilege (he believed in "eternal truth" rather than in the gods of the city) and of corrupting the youth. He was arrested in 399 B.C. and condemned to death by a narrow vote of a citizen's court. He could easily have escaped from his prison (which is probably what the authorities wanted him to do), but he refused to renounce his city or to disobey its laws. He died bravely, even cheerfully, and set an example for all his successors.

His memory lived on in his devoted students, and especially in Plato (426–347 B.C.). Most of what we know of Socrates comes from Plato's Dialogues, and Plato's own work was founded on that of his teacher. He took Socrates' concept of the eternal good and expanded it into a more complex philosophy of his own. According to Plato, the only reality was the world of "ideas," where all things had existence in an abstract and perfect form. In the world of ideas the perfect "house" or "table" existed forever as a concept, not as a material object. Here on earth we have but poor and temporary copies of these things. Earthly houses are not true houses. They are but wood or stone that men have tried to shape into a

copy of the true and eternal house; they can burn, blow apart, or deteriorate. The real house—in the world of ideas—can never change or deteriorate. The same, according to Plato, is true of "beauty" and "justice." True justice can exist only in the world of ideas; man may come closer to true justice by contemplating this ideal, but his efforts will always be subject to error. Plato thus provided a solution to the paradox posed by the teaching of Heraclitus, who said that all things were constantly changing, and the teaching of Parmenides, who held that change was impossible and therefore illusory. According to Plato, change was a characteristic only of the physical world. In the world of ideas, all things remain eternally the same.

Like almost all Greeks, Plato believed that the city-state was the best form of political organization and that the character of the citizen was determined by the laws of the city. Plato was an intellectual aristocrat; he disliked Athenian democracy and doubted that the poor and half-educated lower classes could ever be virtuous unless they were controlled by an intellectual elite. His plan for an ideal city-state in the *Republic* showed a clear preference for the Spartan rather than the Athenian example. Each individual's life was to be carefully regulated from birth for the benefit of the whole community. Justice, of course, must be the basis of society, but justice belongs to the eternal world of ideas. It can be understood only by the most intelligent and most carefully educated citizens. Thus the heart of the *Republic* is the description of the training of the "philosopher-kings," who would rule and lead all other citizens to the good life.

Aristotle (384–322 B.C.), Plato's most famous pupil, was the great organizer of Greek thought. By his time the Greeks had accumulated a large amount of information and were trying to arrange it in meaningful order. Aristotle provided a powerful tool for classifying and deriving general propositions from scattered facts. This tool was logic, which he distilled from the somewhat erratic arguments of the Sophists. Aristotle developed rigorous, consistent, and intellectually honest rules of logic and thus gave western thinkers an instrument that could be used for intellectual exploration of any field. Aristotle wrote treatises on everything from biology through political theory to poetics, and he supplied the vocabulary and the basic ideas that were used for centuries in almost every field of learning.

Aristotle was less of an idealist than Plato and was more concerned with observing actual facts. For example, he studied the constitutions of hundreds of Greek cities and came to the conclusion that pure monarchy, pure aristocracy, and pure democracy were good in themselves but were apt to degenerate; democracy, for example, easily falls into dictatorship. Thus the most stable government is a mixed government, in which a strong executive, an aristocratic council, and a democratic assembly balance one another. This idea still influences western society. But Aristotle applied it only to the city-state, in spite of the fact that in his later years the Kingdom of Macedon had gained control of almost all the Greek cities.

Aristotle, unlike Plato, did not believe that ideas were independent entities. He believed in the value of general propositions, but he felt that they grew out of concrete experiences. And in his distinction between Form and Matter he stimulated thought about developmental processes in the universe. Thus the sculptor imposes Form on the Matter of a piece of clay; the Matter of the acorn contains within it the Form of an oak.

Aristotle's logic was not entirely free from flaws; it depended a little too much on words with overtones that went beyond pure description. Yet western theology, law, mathematics, and science were all marked in their formative periods by strict applications of Aristotelian logic. Aristotle tended to generalize too rapidly, and difficulties in taking exact measurements vitiated some of his facts. These weaknesses were especially apparent in his works on the physical sciences; some of his guesses were helpful, but some, such as his theory of motion, were stumbling blocks for centuries. Even at his worst, however, Aristotle posed fundamental problems. For centuries western scholars began their work with a study of his books.

The Rise of Macedon

During the fourth century most of the cities of the Greek peninsula came under the domination of the Kingdom of Macedon. Macedon was a country of peasants ruled by crude, hard-living warriors who formed a loose federation under a king. Its culture was not much above the level of that described in the *Iliad*. These primitive people posed no threat to the Greeks in earlier periods. The Persian and Peloponnesian wars, however, brought the Macedonians into closer contact with the Greeks of the South. These contacts resulted in the Macedonians' rapid progress. During the fourth century, when the Greek city-states were weak, the remarkable King Philip (359–336 B.C.) managed to organize the Macedonian warriors into a powerful and unified fighting force. Once his control of Macedon was secure, Philip began to extend his control over the city-states of the Greek peninsula. Once again, as during the Persian threat more than a century earlier, there was a great debate among the Greek city-states on how best to meet the danger. Demosthenes of Athens, the most famous orator of the golden age of Greek oratory, vainly warned his countrymen of the danger from Macedon, and urged them to unite. But, as so often before, the Greek cities were unable to support any single policy. Many, in fact, looked on Philip as a liberator from the domination of the more powerful Greek cities. Enough cities resisted to provoke a war with Macedon, but they could not cooperate to the extent of presenting a unified defense. As a result, Philip defeated the coalition of Greek city-states in 338 B.C. and turned the Greek peninsula into a Macedonian protectorate. Individual cities clung to their theoretical sovereignty, but they could not oppose Philip's will.

Alexander the Great
336–323 B.C.

Two years later, before Philip could complete his project by reconquering the Greek cities of Asia Minor from Persia, he was assassinated. He was succeeded by his twenty-year-old son, Alexander

Greek coin bearing the likeness of King Philip, conqueror of Athens.

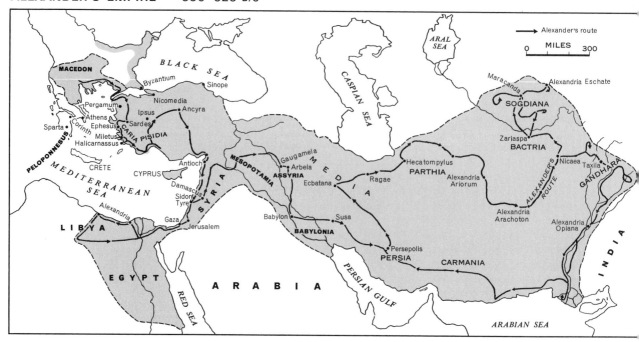

(336–323 B.C.). Conceited, overbearing, undisciplined, and wildly temperamental, Alexander was also brilliant and could display a mesmerizing charm. He was idolized by his soldiers—no small factor in his military success—and even among his enemies he became a legend in his own short lifetime.

Before his death, Philip had planned to unify the Greeks and rally them to his banner by leading a combined Greek army in a war of revenge against the Persians. Determined to carry out his father's plan, Alexander crossed the Hellespont with a Greek army in 334 B.C. and soon proved himself one of the most successful military strategists in history. At the very beginning of his campaign, he won a decisive battle against a Persian force in Asia Minor. The following year he moved eastward into Syria, where he met and routed an army under the Persian king himself. In 332 B.C. Alexander invaded Egypt. After conquering the country, he took two momentous steps. He founded the city of Alexandria, which soon became the leading seaport of the eastern Mediterranean and a center of Greek scholarship. And he visited the ancient oracle of Amon in the Libyan desert, where the priests greeted him as the son of the god. Egypt, at least, had long been ruled by a god-king, and Alexander may have intended to adopt this model as a basis for his position both in Egypt and elsewhere. In Greece an official proclamation of Alexander's divinity was eventually issued; how much of an impression this made is uncertain. Some of the Greeks, at least, may have persuaded themselves that Alexander was the son of Zeus (whom they identified with Amon) and therefore their rightful ruler. In any case, the precedent set by Alexander was followed by his successors. Even the hard-headed Romans eventually accepted the idea that their emperor was divine.

From a military point of view the rest was easy. Alexander proclaimed himself king of Persia, defeated the last Persian army without difficulty, and took his troops on a wild march north to Turkestan, south into the Indus Valley, and back to Babylon. The real problem was political, not military. How could this vast empire, inhabited by such different peoples, be made into a unit? Alexander apparently hoped to use Greek culture to control Asian manpower. Greek colonies were founded everywhere, even in western India; Greeks were encouraged to marry Asian women; and Greek was to be the common language of all the upper classes. Alexander died of fever in 323 B.C., at the age of thirty-three, before he could see how his plan worked. The amazing thing is that even without his guiding hand, even during the bitter quarrels among his successors, his plan did work. For eight hundred years Greek culture was the dominant and unifying culture of the Middle East.

THE HELLENISTIC ERA
323–*ca.* 30 B.C.

Alexander's sudden death meant that he had had no time to consolidate his empire or to arrange for an orderly succession. His Macedonian generals fought among themselves for his conquests. Ptolemy took Egypt immediately, and Seleucus eventually gained control of most of the old Persian Empire, which became known as the Seleucid Empire. Matters could not be arranged so neatly in the old Greek heartland. Antigonus became king of Macedon and protector of the city-states of the Greek peninsula. But he could not hold Asia Minor, where many of the cities were united in the

Kingdom of Pergamum and where the island of Rhodes became an independent naval power. And as time went on, Macedon's control over the southern Balkans and the Greek peninsula steadily diminished.

Political disunity, however, did not interfere with Alexander's vision of a commonwealth of peoples united by Greek culture. All the successor states were dominated by Greeks and by natives who imitated the Greek way of life. Of course the peasants and much of the urban population of the Middle East held fast to their native cultures and native languages. But scholars, administrators, and businessmen all used Greek and were guided, to some degree, by Greek ideas and customs. This era, in which the Middle East was permeated by Greek influence is known as the Hellenistic period.* It ended politically in 30 B.C., when Rome annexed Egypt, the last nominally independent Hellenistic state. But the cultural unity of the Middle East lasted far longer; it was broken only when the Moslems conquered Syria and Egypt in the seventh century A.D.

*The Greeks called themselves Hellenes; *Hellenistic* means "Greek-like."

Idealized statue of Alexander, probably the work of an artist of Pergamum in Asia Minor.

THE PARTITIONING OF ALEXANDER'S EMPIRE   *ca.* 300 B.C.

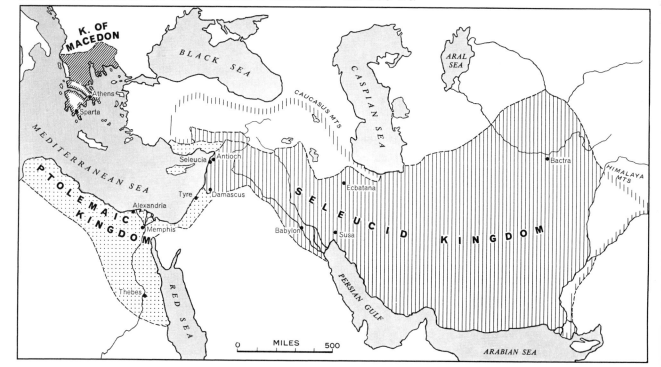

| Persian Empire | Hellenistic Era |
| Independent Greek City-states | |

Rise and Dominance
of Macedon

Egypt was probably the region in which Hellenistic culture flourished most. Alexandria, the capital of the Ptolemies, had a population of about a million; Athens in its prime had had about one hundred thousand. Alexandria profited from the boom in international trade that was one of the great unifying forces of the Hellenistic period. Into its harbor came ships from all parts of the Mediterranean; its caravans crowded the routes that led to Syria, Mesopotamia, and the Red Sea ports that traded with India. Alexandria imported ideas as well as merchandise. Next to the palace of the Ptolemies was a magnificent temple to the Muses (called the Museum) for the study of the arts and sciences, and next to the Museum was a remarkable library. These facilities attracted scholars from all parts of the Hellenistic world and helped make Alexandria the only Greek city that could rival Athens as a cultural center. But Alexandria was more than a Greek city. Native Egyptians made up most of the laboring class, and in its streets one might hear almost any language of the ancient world. There were more Jews in Alexandria than in Jerusalem; it was in Alexandria that the Old Testament was translated into Greek.

Alexandria was by far the largest Hellenistic city, but Antioch, the capital of the Seleucid Empire, was also a great trade center. Rhodes and Pergamum prospered as transshipment points for goods headed for the Aegean and Black Seas. Pergamum also attracted a group of very able artists. Dozens of other Hellenistic cities took part in commercial, intellectual, and artistic activity of the period.

Art and Literature

Hellenistic art naturally differed from that of the fifth century; it had lost the serenity and security of the work of Phidias. It was more emotional and at times almost too emotional in depicting pain and suffering. Occasionally it sought to impress by mere size, as in the statue that stood astride the harbor of Rhodes or the Mausoleum at Halicarnassus. But at its best it created works that are still impressive. The Winged Victory of Samothrace, the Venus of Milo, the Dying Gaul of Pergamum are probably better known than the statues of the Parthenon.

Hellenistic art turned more and more toward realism as time went on. Paintings, mosaics, and statues in this style are not great art, but they are remarkably helpful to the historian. They show men and women as they were, and life as it was lived.

The literature of the period is not as well known. Theocritus was a lyric poet of merit; unfortunately, so many followers imitated his pastoral settings that his originality has been forgotten. Apollonius wrote an epic in the Homeric style, and he too might be better remembered if so many later poets had not done the same thing. Certainly the writer whose influence has lasted longest was Menander. Although his comedies lack the bite of Aristophanes, his plots have amused audiences for two thousand years. Picked up by the Romans and passed down to Shakespeare, they still inspire modern musical comedies.

Science

Many scholars would say that the most striking achievements of the Hellenistic age were in science. Hellenistic scientists performed some remarkable experiments and developed theories that foreshadowed the discoveries of the sixteenth and seventeenth centuries. But science did not have the same significance in the Hellenistic world that it has in ours. It was only an aspect of philoso-

Old Peasant Woman. Sculpture from the Hellenistic era is more emotional and realistic than art of the fifth century B.C.

phy, a speculative pastime with little effect on ordinary life. Herophilus came very close to a theory of the circulation of the blood, but his work did little to change the practice of medicine. Aristarchus of Samos developed a theory of a solar system with planets revolving about the sun, but most people, even scholars, clung to the belief that the earth was the center of the universe. Eratosthenes made an estimate of the circumference of the earth that was very nearly correct, but it was centuries before anyone acted on this proof that the world was not impossibly large and that a voyage from Europe to the Far East would not take an impossible length of time. On the whole, Hellenistic science was not incorporated into the intellectual tradition of the Mediterranean world. Men reverted to the older doctrines of Aristotle, which remained the standard explanations of natural phenomena throughout the Roman and much of the medieval period. The first to take up the work of the Hellenistic scientists were Moslem scholars, and their writings did not reach western Europe until the thirteenth century A.D.

The most important exception to this rule was mathematics. Even practical-minded people could see the value of geometry, and Euclid (*ca.* 300 B.C.), who built scattered propositions about geometry into a coherent system, has been studied from his day to our own. Archimedes of Syracuse (278?–212 B.C.) worked out basic problems concerning mass and motion; he also perfected the theory of machines, such as the compound pulley. Again, there was a practical side to this work: missile-throwing machines built on his principles nearly defeated a Roman attack on Syracuse. This was remembered, but his more theoretical work was long neglected. One of the best tests of a scientific revival in thirteenth-century Europe was the degree to which the works of Archimedes were used.

Philosophy and Religion

Hellenistic philosophy and religion reflected the great problem of the age: What part could an individual play in a society in which individual effort seemed useless? In a small city-state of the fifth century the individual had an important role in his community; he could find meaning and purpose in his life and work. But in the great kingdoms of the Hellenistic world and in the huge cities that were the centers of Hellenistic culture, what could one man do? Would his greatest efforts have any impact on his society? Because of this problem, the three most popular schools of philosophy of the period emphasized private virtues and self-discipline, not participation in public life. The Stoics, whose influence lasted longest, believed in a universal law, which bound all men. Since all men were subject to this law, all men were brothers. Everyone from slave to king must do his duty in the position in which he found himself. Power and wealth, human desires and affections, were dangerous distractions. Public office was not to be sought, though it might be one's duty to accept it. The ideal existence was that of the private citizen, unaffected by external events. The Epicureans went even further. The wise man sought pleasure, but real pleasure came from right conduct, serenity of mind, and moderation in all things. Political ambition and pursuit of wealth caused more pain than they were worth, and the wise man avoided strong attachments to family, friends, or country. The Cynics doubted the possibility of any true knowledge and saw no sense in trying to save a world sunk in hopeless ignorance. Thus the wise man should not worry about wealth and power; he should find peace of mind by withdrawing from worldly concerns.

The philosophers spoke mainly to the middle and upper classes. The mass of the population sought spiritual satisfaction in the mystery cults, with their exotic ceremonies and mystic symbolism. With the active cross-fertilization of culture made possible by trade, new religions traveled from one part of the Hellenistic world to another, and all borrowed concepts and ceremonies from one another. Especially popular were the Dionysian rituals from the Greek cities, Isis worship from Egypt, and the cult of the Great Mother from Asia Minor. Most of these cults offered their initiates a ceremonial purification from earthly sins, the comforts of a personal and loving god or goddess, a mystic community that gave each member a sense of security and personal worth, and a promise of eternity for the soul. The cults did not try to reform the world any more than the philosophies did; they helped the initiates to forget their miseries by giving hope that they would be compensated for present sufferings in a future life.

The Fall of the Hellenistic States

The Hellenistic states were never very strong militarily; and they were further weakened by wars and rebellions. For example, the Seleucid Empire soon lost Bactria and Persia, and in 167 B.C. the Jews, led by the Maccabees, regained their independence. It was easy for Rome, which became the dominant state in the Mediterranean by 200 B.C., to take advantage of quarrels among the fragmented states of the Hellenistic world and to annex them one by one. Rome had effective control of the region by 146 B.C.; with the seizure of Egypt in 30 B.C., it had acquired all of Alexander's empire, except Persia. But the Romans admired Hellenistic culture and, as far as they could, spread it to the West in Latin forms. Greek remained the language of the upper classes in the East, and Athens and Alexandria were the cultural centers of the Roman Empire. In a sense, the Hellenistic culture never ended, though its sphere of influence began to shrink after 500 A.D. It gradually and imperceptibly changed into Byzantine culture, and Byzantine culture ended only after the fall of Constantinople in 1453 A.D.

Suggestions for Further Reading

Note: Asterisk denotes a book available in paperback edition.

General J. B. Bury, *A History of Greece,* remains the most thorough history of the ancient Greeks. Originally published in 1901, it is now available in a Modern Library edition (1972). G. W. Botsford and C. A. Robinson, *Hellenic History,* 5th ed., rev. by D. Kagan (1969), the standard text, is also excellent. R. Sealey, *A History of the Greek City States, 700–338 B.C.** (1976), combines a good introductory narrative with detailed discussion of controversial problems. Among the shorter treatments, M. I. Finley, *The Ancient Greeks** (1963), makes an interesting introduction to Greek history. A. Andrewes, *The Greeks* (1967), and F. J. Frost, *Greek Society* (1972), are interpretive rather than chronological. A representative selection of historical sources can be found in M. I. Finley, ed., *The Greek Historians** (1959). Complete texts of all the Greek writers are available in Greek and English in the *Loeb Classical Library.*

The Mycenaean Era and the Dark Ages The most thorough study of the Greek world before the Golden Age is C. G. Starr, *Origins of Greek Civilization, 1100–650 B.C.* (1961). For the early period, see A. E. Samuel, *The Mycenaeans in History* (1966). M. I. Finley, *Early Greece** (1970), is an excellent short introduction. There have been several recent studies of the Greek world at the time of the Trojan Wars: C. W. Blegen, *Troy and the Trojans* (1963); M. I. Finley, *World of Odysseus** (1954); and D. L. Page, *History and the Homeric Iliad* (1959). G. S. Kirk, *Homer and the Epic** (1965), is also first-rate.

The Greek World from 800 to 500 B.C. A. R. Burn, *The Lyric Age of Greece* (1960), presents a detailed and factual history of the politics and literature of this era. The Greek cities of Ionia and of Sicily and Italy respectively are studied in J. M. Cook, *Greeks in Ionia and the East* (1962), and A. G. Woodhead, *Greeks in the West* (1962). On Greek colonization in general, see J. Boardman, *The Greeks Overseas** (1964). F. de Coulanges, *Ancient City** (1956), is the classic study of the development of the city-state. H. Michell, *Sparta** (1952), helps explain the evolution of Sparta's unique institutions. On political change, see W. G. Forrest, *Emergence of Greek Democracy* (1966), and A. Andrewes, *The Greek Tyrants* (1965).

The Fifth Century Recent studies of the Persian Wars include A. R. Burn, *Persia and the Greeks* (1962), and C. Hignett, *Xerxes' Invasion of Greece* (1963). For the political history of Athens in the Golden Age, see A. E. Zimmern, *The Greek Commonwealth** (1956), considered the classic work on the subject, or one of the excellent shorter treatments, such as A. R. Burn, *Pericles and Athens** (1962); C. A. Robinson, *Athens in the Age of Pericles** (1959); V. Ehrenberg, *From Solon to Socrates** (1968); and W. R. Connor, *The New Politicians of Athens* (1971). H. Michell, *Sparta** (1952), deals with Sparta in the same period. A discussion of Athenian economics may be found in H. Michell, *The Economics of Ancient Greece*, 2nd ed. (1963), or W. S. Ferguson, *Greek Imperialism* (1913). A comprehensive study of the Peloponnesian War is B. W. Henderson, *The Great War Between Athens and Sparta* (1927). See also D. Kagan, *The Origins of the Peloponnesian War* (1969). Difficult, but thorough, is R. Meiggs, *The Athenian Empire* (1972).

Art, Literature, and Drama Excellent introductions to Greek art are J. Boardman, *Greek Art** (1964); G. M. A. Richter, *A Handbook of Greek Art* (1959); and T. B. L. Webster, *Greek Art and Literature** (1939). G. Murray, *The Literature of Ancient Greece* (1956), is standard. Most thorough is A. Lesky, *A History of Greek Literature* (1966). Among the many studies of Greek drama, H. D. F. Kitto, *Greek Tragedy** (1954), and D. L. Page, *History of Greek Tragedy** (1951), are particularly well-written introductions.

Greek Religion A good account is M. Nilsson, *A History of Greek Religion*, 2nd ed. (1949). R. Graves, *The Greek Myth** (1961), presents a new and exciting version of Greek mythology. Two excellent studies of Greek religious beliefs and practices are W. K. C. Guthrie, *The Greeks and Their Gods** (1950), and M. Hadas and M. Smith, *Heroes and Gods* (1965). E. R. Dodds, *The Greeks and the Irrational** (1951), examines Greek religion in the era before and during the Golden Age, and F. C. Grant, *Hellenistic Religions* (1953), covers the era after the Golden Age.

Science and Philosophy The best introductions to Greek philosophy are to be found in general works on the history of philosophy. One of the best is F. Copleston, *A History of Philosophy*, Vol. I (1946). W. Jaeger, *Paidaea* (1944–45), is a remarkable book. The most useful recent summaries of Greek philosophy are W. K. C. Guthrie, *The Greek Philosophers from Thales to Aristotle** (1950), and B. Snell, *Discovery of the Mind: The Greek Origins of European Thought** (1953). G. S. Kirk and J. E. Raven, *Presocratic Philosophers** (1957), and F. M. Cornford, *Before and After Socrates* (1932), both have well-written accounts of the philosophers of the Milesian school. There are many excellent scholarly studies of Socrates, Plato, and Aristotle; for the interested student, A. E. Taylor, *Socrates** (1933); G. M. A. Grube, *Plato's Thought** (1935); and W. Jaeger, *Aristotle** (1962), are recommended.

L. Robin, *Greek Thought and the Origins of the Scientific Spirit* (1948), and B. Farrington, in both *Greek Science* (1949) and *The Origins of Scientific Thought** (1961), trace the development of Greek scientific inquiry. More general is O. Neugebauer, *Exact Sciences in Antiquity* (1957), already a classic.

Alexander the Great and the Hellenistic Era The chief source for the career of Alexander the Great is the Anabasis of Alexander* by Flavius Arrian, a Greek historian. The famous Greek biographer Plutarch wrote a Life of Alexander,* of which there are many editions. Two scholarly but readable modern studies of Alexander are A. R. Burn, *Alexander the Great and the Hellenistic World** (1947), and U. Wilcken, *Alexander the Great* (1967). Beautifully written and well illustrated is P. Green, *Alexander the Great* (1970).

No writer on the Hellenistic era has successfully disentangled himself from the complexities of the politics of the period. For the reader who has learned the art of selectivity in studying political and diplomatic history, however, there are several useful and interesting works. The two standard works on the period are M. Cary, *A History of the Greek World from 323 to 146 B.C.* (1932), and M. I. Rostovtzeff, *Social and Economic History of the Hellenistic World* (1941). W. W. Tarn and G. T. Griffith, *Hellenistic Civilization** (1952), is shorter but thorough. M. Hadas, *Hellenistic Culture: Fusion and Diffusion* (1959), emphasizes the effect of Hellenistic culture on the Jews.

3 Rome and the Unification of the Mediterranean World

Rome succeeded in unifying the ancient world, a feat that neither Darius the Persian, nor Alexander of Macedon, nor the Hellenistic kings had accomplished. In the days of Darius and Alexander, Rome would have seemed a very unlikely candidate for this role. It was a small city without a good harbor and not much given to commerce; it controlled only a part of the Italian peninsula; its inhabitants were, from a Greek point of view, uneducated, unsophisticated barbarians. Even in the western Mediterranean there were cities that were richer, that possessed a higher culture, and that seemed as strong as Rome. The eastern cities and kingdoms were even more advanced. The rise of Rome has puzzled historians in all ages. The Greek Polybius, who witnessed the crucial period of Roman expansion and was the first to ask what made the expansion possible, gave an answer framed largely in terms of politics. Rome conquered because it had a good constitution, knew how to keep the loyalty of its allies, and played the game of international politics with tenacity and ruthless determination. This is not a complete explanation, but it contains enough of the truth to warrant giving more attention to Roman politics than to the politics of earlier empires.

Linguistically the Romans and their Italic allies were closely related to the Greeks. Both were branches of the Indo-European-speaking peoples who had moved toward the Mediterranean from the interior of Europe in the period after 2000 B.C. But the Romans, unlike the Greeks, were far removed from eastern civilizations, and the geography of the Italian peninsula did not encourage long-distance commerce. There were few good natural harbors on either coast; those that did exist, such as Naples, were soon occupied by Greek colonists. However, there was more good farmland in the Italian than in the Greek peninsula; for a long time expansion could be inland rather than overseas. Rome and its Italic neighbors thus tended to resemble the Greek communities that were based on control of agricultural land rather than those based on control of trade routes. Early Rome was more like Sparta than it was like Athens.

The Italian peninsula, though a clearly delimited geographic entity, has never been difficult to invade. It was occupied by a mixture of peoples when the ancestors of the Romans arrived about 2000 B.C., and while these peoples were gradually assimilated by the invaders, other groups continued to try to conquer or to settle in Italy. The Romans were not entirely hypocritical when they claimed that some of their wars were forced on them by the continual influx of aggressive newcomers.

THE ITALIAN PENINSULA TO *ca.* 500 B.C.

By 1000 B.C. most of Italy was held by tribes that spoke Latin or one of the related Indo-European dialects. Soon after 800 B.C., however, two new peoples appeared in Italy: the Greeks, who settled to the south of Rome, and the Etruscans, who settled to the north. Both built walled cities and subdued neighboring Italic tribes; both were active in Mediterranean commerce and brought Italy into closer contact with eastern civilization.

The Etruscans

The Etruscans had a more immediate impact on the Romans and their Latin neighbors than did the Greeks. Unfortunately their origins have not yet been discovered, and most of their surviving inscriptions and writings have not yet been deciphered. Their civilization at its birth seems to have combined a language and certain religious practices from Asia Minor with forms of burial and art native to their center of development in Italy. Out of the mixture the Etruscans evolved an independent and highly sophisticated culture of their own. Their art was as remarkable as that of the Greeks, and sometimes more powerful. Their religion, especially their devices for forecasting the future, long influenced the Romans and other peoples of Italy. As middlemen in trade between the Greek world and the peoples of central Europe, as producers of iron, and as workers in bronze and gold and terra cotta, the Etruscans became very wealthy. Wealth supported

The lid of a bronze container from Praeneste, in Latium (fourth century B.C.). The handle represents two warriors carrying a slain comrade.

Detail from an Etruscan sarcophagus (mid-sixth century B.C.). The deceased couple is shown reclining on a couch, pouring libations as if at their own funeral banquet.

their high civilization and enabled them to dominate Italy from the Po Valley down into Campania, the fertile plain around the Bay of Naples. The peak of Etruscan power and culture (roughly 600–500 B.C.) overlapped the Golden Age of Athens (600–400 B.C.). And like the Athenians, the Etruscans were to be subjugated by a semibarbarous neighboring state.

The Origins of Rome

In 600 B.C. Rome was only the largest of several fortified villages in the surrounding plain of Latium. According to Roman legend, the city was founded by the twins Romulus and Remus in 753 B.C. The site had been occupied long before that date, but archeology suggests that some sort of consolidation or rebuilding did take place in the eighth century B.C.

The early government of Rome resembled that of the Greek states of the eighth and early seventh centuries B.C. A king ruled with the help and advice of a council of leading citizens (the Senate). Major decisions, such as a declaration of war, had to be ratified by an assembly composed of all male citizens old enough for military service.

Within this society, wealth was very unevenly distributed, and the wealthy controlled religion, law, and politics. By the end of the period of the kings and perhaps earlier, a formal split had developed between an upper stratum, called patrician, and the rest of the population, called plebeian. Almost all members of the Senate were patricians, and only patricians could hold public office. A few plebeians were well-to-do, but most of them were small landholders, tenant farmers on patrician estates, and artisans and shopkeepers. There must have been some inhabitants who were not citizens, such as slaves and foreign merchants, but little is known about them in the early period.

Rome came under Etruscan control around 600 B.C., when an Etruscan aristocrat managed to get himself accepted as king. He and his Etruscan successors raised Rome from a citadel and small market town to a city. Greek and Etruscan merchants frequented the town, and the Romans acquired some understanding of the culture and institutions of the civilized world. Cultural benefits, however, seldom make a people grateful for foreign domination, and the Romans were no exception to this rule. About 509 B.C. (this traditional date is as good as any) a group of Roman patricians drove out the Etruscan king and proclaimed Rome an independent republic.

Rome then went through a stage very like that of the Greek cities a few centuries earlier: aristocracy replaced monarchy. All power passed into the hands of the patricians, and these Roman aristocrats were much more careful than their Greek counterparts to make sure that power could never again be concentrated in the hands of a single man. All administrative functions were performed by committees of at least two men, whose term of office, with few exceptions, was limited to one year. Thus the supreme executive authority was given to two consuls, who served both as chief magistrates and as commanders of the army. In times of crisis a single man could be named dictator with absolute authority, but his power lasted only for the duration of the emergency, and in no case for more than six months.

This was a republic, not a democracy. If one man could not rule, neither could the multitude. It is true that officials were elected by the assembly, but only patricians were eligible for office. Moreover, officials serving for only one year were always influenced by the wishes of the Senate, a body that included all former officials. It was hard for anyone to disregard the advice of such an experienced and prestigious group of men.

TERRITORIAL EXPANSION AND POLITICAL REFORM
ca. 500–265 B.C.

The early Roman constitution might have produced complete chaos, with its division of power among short-term officials, an assembly, and a Senate, and with flagrant discrimination against a majority of its citizens. Rome was saved by the good sense of its leaders, who always made concessions in time to avert collapse, and by the patriotism of its citizens, who were willing to accept gradual reform rather than risk armed rebellion. One may wonder whether there would have been so much good sense and so much patriotism if the very life of the community had not been constantly threatened by outside enemies during the first two centuries of the Republic. Nevertheless, the Romans behaved better under pressure than most of their contemporaries; neither internal grievances nor external defeats destroyed the coherence and stability of the community. They were cautious in exploiting their victories and, at least in their early years, skillful in gaining the friendship of defeated enemies. These qualities gave them security at home and, by 265 B.C., control of all the Italian peninsula except for the Po Valley.

Threats from outside enemies began almost as soon as the Etruscans had been expelled. Under the Etruscans, Rome had dominated the other cities of Latium, but with Rome independent these Latin cities wanted independence too. United in the Latin League, they challenged Roman domination (*ca.* 496 B.C.) with sufficient success to gain virtual equality. Rome realized that it had other neighbors who were more dangerous than the Latins and that it needed Latin support. The treaties Rome made with the League formed a pattern for Roman relations with other Italian states. Rome and the League recognized that Roman and Latin citizens had equal rights in one another's courts and that all cities were bound to help one another in war. Thus a relatively large Roman-Latin army was created that acquired a large amount of new territory. "Latin" colonies were established on the conquered lands, new and independent cities inhabited both by Romans and by former citizens of the League. These new cities further increased the military strength of the alliance. This relationship was immensely successful until the fourth century B.C., when it began to break down (see p. 61).

Plebeian Activity and Political Reform

The Roman leaders had shown that they could conciliate outside enemies; they soon had the task of conciliating their own citizens. The plebeians, who formed the bulk of the army, suffered many political and social disabilities. Probably toward the beginning of and certainly later in the fifth century B.C., the plebeians staged a series of sit-down strikes; if they were denied political rights they would not serve in the army. The Romans, like the Athenians in the same period, realized that they needed the full cooperation of all citizens in order to survive. Little by little the plebeians gained most of their demands.

The first concession, and one of the most important, was the election of five (later ten) tribunes to protect the interests of the plebeians. The persons of the tribunes were inviolate; to attack a tribune meant death without trial. A tribune could veto the acts of a consul or any other official, and his veto could not be overridden. Equally important was the fact that the tribunes were elected by an assembly of tribes, not by the old assembly in which citizens were divided into groups based on their wealth. Because the tribes were based on geographical districts, the patricians could not dominate this assembly. Resolutions passed by the assembly of tribes and approved by the Senate had the force of law. It was

Cities of the Latin League, ca. 400 B.C.

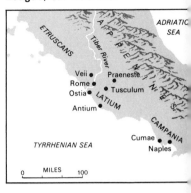

Etruscan kitchen utensils: a water bottle and a spoon.

always difficult for the Senate to withhold such approval, and eventually the requirement was removed (287 B.C.), but long before that date resolutions of the assembly of tribes had become a normal form of Roman legislation. Consuls and other high officials, however, continued to be elected by the older form of assembly, which was led by the wealthier classes.

Plebeian Reforms

Enslavement for debt was a constant threat to the poorer peasants of the ancient world. In this passage, the Roman historian Livy (59 B.C.–17 A.D.) shows how the plebeians gained constitutional safeguards against enslavement for debt by refusing to fight in a time of emergency.

An old man suddenly presented himself in the Forum. . . . Though cruelly changed from what he had once been, he was recognized, and people began to tell each other, compassionately, that he was an old soldier who had once commanded a company and served with distinction. . . . "While I was on service," he said, "during the Sabine War, my crops were ruined by enemy raids, and my cottage was burnt. Everything I had was taken, including my cattle. Then, when I was least able to do so, I was expected to pay taxes, and fell, consequently, into debt. Interest on the borrowed money increased my burden; I lost the land which my father and my grandfather had owned before me, and . . . I was finally seized by my creditor and reduced to slavery. . . ."

The man's story . . . caused a tremendous uproar, which spread swiftly from the Forum through every part of the city. . . .

On top of this highly critical situation came the alarming news . . . that a Volscian army was marching on Rome. . . . For [the plebeians] it seemed like an intervention of providence to crush the pride of the Senate; they went about urging their friends to refuse military service. . . . [One of the consuls then issued] an edict, to the effect that it should be illegal . . . [to] imprison a Roman citizen. . . . As a result of the edict, all "bound" debtors who were present gave their names on the spot, . . . and in the ensuing fight with the Volscians no troops did more distinguished service.

From Livy, *The Early History of Rome*, trans. by Aubrey de Sélincourt (Baltimore: Penguin Books, 1960), pp. 113–16.

Like the Greeks, the Roman plebeians wanted written laws to protect them against arbitrary decisions of patrician officials. About 450 B.C. a committee of ten men was appointed to revise and complete the Roman code of law. All power was turned over to this committee, which drew up the basic laws of Rome, the Twelve Tables. It proved somewhat more difficult to get rid of the commission than to establish it, but its work endured even when its members were driven from power. The Twelve Tables were a rather rudimentary set of laws, but through skillful judicial interpretation they satisfied the needs of the Roman people for many generations. They set the tone and marked the beginning of the greatest Roman intellectual achievement, the Roman law.

Finally, the plebeians gradually gained access to all public offices. This took a little longer than the other reforms; it was only in the fourth century B.C. that restrictions on secular offices were removed and only around 300 B.C. that plebeians were admitted to the priesthood. This last concession was more important than it seems, since a priest could block many political acts by declaring that the auspices were unfavorable.

Rich plebeians gained the most from these reforms: only they could afford the time and money to play the political game. Officials were unpaid, and a seat in the Senate, which regularly followed the holding of high office, was a time-consuming honor. But the plebeians as a whole seem to have been satisfied by their gains. Their tribunes and tribal assemblies gave them considerable power when crucial political decisions had to be made; invidious legal distinctions had been removed; and theoretically all careers were open to all citizens. In actual fact, the Roman ruling class did what many ruling classes have done—it drew the ablest plebeians into its own ranks, accepted them as part of a new senatorial aristocracy, and so deprived poorer citizens of their natural leaders. But during the crucial years of Roman expansion the different Roman classes cooperated enough to avoid serious difficulties.

Rome's Conquest of Italy

The first real test of the Roman system came about 400 B.C. when the Romans decided to end the Etruscan threat to central Italy. After a long and difficult siege (*ca.* 405–396 B.C.) the Romans captured Veii and pushed the Etruscans back from the region of the Tiber, permanently shifting the balance of power between the two peoples. One reason, however, for Etruscan weakness was that they were also being attacked in the north by a new group of invaders, the Gauls. The Gauls were a branch of the Celts, another one of those Indo-European-speaking peoples who had been striking at the civilizations of the Mediterranean, the Middle East, and India ever since 2000 B.C. By the fifth century B.C. the Celts had occupied what is now Germany, the British Isles, and France, which was then called Gaul from the name of the Celtic group that had settled there. The Gauls then crossed into Italy and drove the Etruscans out of the Po Valley. They moved south rapidly, and only a few years after the fall of Veii they destroyed a Roman army on the Tiber (*ca.* 390 B.C.). Rome was abandoned; only the citadel held out. Fortunately for Rome, this was only a raid, and the Gauls withdrew after sacking the city. Rome barely survived this catastrophe; some of its allies fell away, and expansion almost ended for a generation. But the Romans were tough enough to rebuild their city and their power. By the 360s B.C. they were attacking both the Gauls and the Etruscans, and by about 350 they had annexed southern Etruria. The danger from the north had been greatly lessened.

After 350 B.C. the chief threat to Rome came from other Italic peoples, who, like Rome, were expanding. Interests and boundary claims began to conflict especially in the south and east. Even the

Latin allies resented Roman hegemony, and the more distant cities saw no reason to allow Rome to expand indefinitely. Rome, on the other hand, wanted to stop the growth of potential rivals. The situation was complicated by the weakening of the Greek cities of southern Italy. Their trade had declined as a result of wars in Greece and the occupation of western Europe by the Celts, but they were still rich prizes. No Italic people would willingly let one or more of the Greek cities go to a rival. Finally, the more or less Hellenized inhabitants of the Balkans were beginning to cross the Adriatic and mix in Italian affairs, a course that reached its peak with the invasions of King Pyrrhus of Epirus in the years after 280 B.C.

The strongest Italic people were the Samnites, who held much of south-central Italy, including most of the fertile plain of Campania. They were in a much better position to take over Greek cities than the Romans, and they could count on the help of many of the other peoples of Italy. But before Rome could fully concentrate on the Samnites, it had to suppress a rebellion of its own allies. The Latin cities had for some time been treated as inferiors and had been exploited as Rome expanded. They now wanted full independence and joined others peoples around Latium in the Great Latin War (*ca.* 340–338). The Romans crushed the coalition, dissolved the Latin League, and instituted a new and harsher system for controlling subject cities. Most of the Latins had the duties of Roman citizens without the vote or the right to hold office. Some municipalities were governed directly from Rome; others retained limited rights of self-government. Still others became Roman colonies; that is, portions of their land were granted to Roman citizens, who became the ruling class of the city. Rome also retained the system of free, allied cities with full rights of self-government and limited military obligations, but there had to be strong political reasons and a good prospect of faithful cooperation to put a city in this category.

With the Latins under control, the Romans could turn on the Samnites. In a long series of wars (*ca.* 325–290 B.C.) the

This head of a statue of Hermes (*ca.* 500 B.C.) was part of a group of terra cotta figures that adorned the roof of a temple of Apollo in Veii. It became a spoil of war when Veii fell to beseiging Romans in 396 B.C.

Romans finally defeated the Samnites and their allies. It was not an easy task; the Samnites won most of the early battles and, through an alliance with the Etruscans, forced Rome to fight on two fronts. But Rome's superior military organization and tight system of control of subject and allied cities prevailed over the loose Samnite and Etruscan confed-

eracies. After the last Samnite War (298–290 B.C.), there was still a little mopping up to do, but the Romans basically controlled all Italy except for the Gauls in the Po Valley and the Greeks in the south. Some of the Greeks prudently allied themselves with Rome; others, led by Tarentum, called in King Pyrrhus of Epirus to protect their liberties. Like most of Rome's enemies, Pyrrhus won many battles but lost the war.* By 265 B.C. the Greek cities of the peninsula had accepted Roman domination.

Rome's success in war was due to the remarkable staying power of its army. Roman generals were not infallible, but the Roman military system was unbeatable in the long run. The consuls enforced stern discipline: there was no straggling on the march or wavering on the battlefield; disobedience was punished with death. The basic military unit, the legion of about 4300 men, had great striking power and at the same time great flexibility, for it was divided into smaller units that could maneuver independently. Most important of all was Rome's control over its subject and allied cities. The Romans never accepted defeat, not only because they were courageous, but also because they could always raise new armies. Sheer manpower favored Rome; at the time that Alexander was conquering the East with about thirty thousand men, the Romans could deploy an army of about sixty thousand. With this advantage, stubborn perseverance could win more for Rome than brilliant strategy. Even the strongest states of the Mediterranean world could not hold out against the steady pressure that Rome could exert.

ROMAN EXPANSION OVERSEAS, 264–146 B.C.

In acquiring the Greek cities of southern Italy, Rome inherited their struggle with Carthage for the control of Sicily. The resulting "Punic" Wars (Latin *Poenicus* = Phoenician = Carthaginian) tested Rome's staying power even more se-

---

*In 279 B.C. Pyrrhus gained a victory over the Romans that cost a ruinous loss of his forces. Hence the term *Pyrrhic victory*.

verely than had the Samnite Wars; several times Rome came close to total defeat. Since Carthage had been the strongest naval power in the Mediterranean, Roman victories over Carthage meant that Rome became dominant on sea as well as on land. This made it easy for Rome to intervene in the eastern Mediterranean, and long before the destruction of Carthage in 146 B.C., Rome had begun to dominate the Hellenistic world.

The Punic Wars, 264–146 B.C.

The first war with Carthage started in 264 B.C., only a year after Rome's final conquest of southern Italy, and lasted until 241 B.C. Without a fleet, Rome could not contest Carthaginian control of western Sicily, much less attack the center of Carthaginian power in North Africa. With characteristic confidence in their ability to master any military problem, the Romans built a fleet, and made up for lack of naval experience by constructing ships that would let them profit from their skill in hand-to-hand combat. Grappling irons and movable boarding bridges locked hostile ships together and so enabled the Romans to convert a sea battle into something like a land engagement. Even with these advantages, Rome came close to losing the war. After initial victories, the Romans lost three fleets in succession, not to the enemy but to shipwreck and storm. It was all they could do to build a fourth fleet, but this one was victorious in a battle off western Sicily. Carthaginian naval superiority was permanently broken, and Carthage surrendered Sicily to the Romans in 241 B.C.

To make up for the loss of Sicily the Carthaginians decided to take over the rich mines and farmlands of Spain. Under the leadership of one of its best generals, Hamilcar Barca, Carthage gained control of southern and eastern

Symbol of Sicily, found in Ostia, chief port of Rome. The symbol's three legs correspond to the three points of Sicily.

This third-century B.C. coin bears one of the few known contemporary portraits of Hannibal. The elephant appears on the reverse.

Spain. This region was soon producing more revenue for Carthage than Sicily ever had. When Hamilcar died he was succeeded as governor of Spain first by his son-in-law and then by his twenty-five-year-old son Hannibal (221 B.C.).

Roman legend has it that Hannibal as a child swore to his father that he would avenge the Sicilian defeat by destroying Rome. For their part, the Romans were clearly annoyed by Carthaginian success in Spain and were furious when Hannibal attacked a city in northeastern Spain allied to Rome. They determined to crush Carthage in Spain as they had in Sicily. But the fighting had scarcely begun in Spain when Hannibal made one of the most daring strategic moves in all history. In 218 B.C. he left Spain, marched through southern Gaul, and crossed the Alps with a large army including fifty war-elephants. Cut off from his supplies, usually outnumbered, Hannibal repeatedly defeated the massive Roman armies sent against him. For fifteen years he ravaged the Italian countryside and on one occasion came close to Rome. In this desperate war, Rome was saved by the loyalty of its allies in Latium, Samnium, and Etruria, who made it impossible for Hannibal to establish himself in central Italy. In the south, through fear or favor, more of the allied and subject municipalities went over to Hannibal, and it looked as if he could maintain himself there indefinitely.

The deadlock was not broken until the Romans were able to send a first-rate general, Scipio Africanus, into the field. Scipio first went to Spain, where an indecisive war had been dragging on for years, and conquered the province for Rome. He then led a Roman army to North Africa and laid siege to Carthage itself. As he had anticipated, the Carthaginians recalled Hannibal, thus ending his Italian adventures. Losses in Italy and Spain had weakened the Carthaginian army; when Scipio met Hannibal at Zama, a few miles from Carthage, he won a decisive victory (202 B.C.). Carthage had to accept a harsh treaty: Spain was ceded to Rome; a heavy war indemnity was levied; and the Carthaginian fleet was limited to ten ships. Carthage had ceased to be a first-rate power.

Rome and the Hellenistic East

Unlike the Roman conquest of Sicily and Spain, it is hard to find a consistent pattern in Roman expansion in the East. Roman generals certainly wanted triumphs, and Roman pride was flattered by appeals for aid from eastern states that were threatened by their neighbors. One intervention led to another, and withdrawal became almost impossible. There was also great wealth in the East, as Roman generals soon discovered. But Rome did not have a definite plan for conquest and expansion, and again and again it refused to annex defeated states.

As we have seen, the Hellenistic kingdom of Epirus had tried to block Roman expansion in southern Italy, and Macedon gave some assistance to Hannibal when he was operating in the same region. Rome had defeated both kingdoms and in the process had learned a good deal about the richness and the weakness of the Hellenistic world. Because there was no strong state in the area, there was constant bickering among Egypt, the remnant of the Seleucid Empire, the little kingdoms of Asia Minor, Macedon, and leagues of Greek cities. Everyone sought the aid of Rome in their quarrels, but every peace settlement imposed by Rome collapsed. Rome soon found itself hopelessly entangled in a political mess. Roman leaders naturally became exasperated; they could neither keep order in the Hellenistic world nor get out of it.

When the Romans were exasperated they became brutal. Macedon and Epirus were plundered in 167 B.C.; thousands of their inhabitants were sold as slaves. Growing admiration for Greek culture did not keep the Romans from turning savagely on Greek cities that disobeyed Roman orders. Corinth was destroyed; Athens was plundered; and thousands more young men were sent to Italy as slaves. The net result was that Macedon became a Roman province; Rome controlled the Greek cities, allowing them a good deal of autonomy in internal affairs; Asia Minor became a sort of protectorate. Rome was less interested in ruling Syria and Egypt (the Romans had favored Egypt more consistently than any other

Hellenistic state), but Rome made it clear that neither country was to take any initiative without its approval. Most of the Hellenistic world was now in Roman hands.

In the same year that Corinth was destroyed (146 B.C.) the Romans for no apparent reason turned again on Carthage. Carthage had regained some of its wealth but not its military power. Although no threat to Rome, its very existence offended men who remembered stories of the desperate battles against Hannibal. Carthage fell after a six-month siege; every inhabitant was slaughtered or enslaved. The city was destroyed stone by stone, and the lands behind it were made a Roman province. Most of North Africa, however, remained independent under native rulers.

CONSEQUENCES OF EXPANSION

By 146 B.C. Rome controlled Italy, Sicily, Sardinia, Corsica, and parts of Spain and North Africa in the West, and Illyria, Macedon, and Greece in the East. During the next century the gaps in this ring around the Mediterranean were filled in, but the problems of empire existed long before the empire was complete. How could the institutions of a city-state be used to govern the vast territories now ruled by Rome? How could leaders be found who could keep the confidence of the Roman people and gain the obedience of Roman subjects? How could Rome and Italy adjust to the drastic social and economic changes caused by the growth of large agricultural units, rural indebtedness, commerce, the influx of wealth from plundered enemies and tribute-paying provinces, the importation of hundreds of thousands of slaves? How could one find a focus of loyalty in an empire that was also a republic, that had no dominant religion, no god-king, not even a chief of state? These were the questions that the Romans struggled with in the last two centuries before Christ. They found only partial answers at best. The resulting dissatisfaction destroyed the Roman Republic with its multiple leadership and led to the creation of an empire with a single head.

Governing the Provinces

One problem could not be postponed—the government of the provinces. It soon received a workable if not entirely satisfactory answer. The Romans had long found it necessary to use former officials as military commanders. For example, Rome had only two consuls, but it might well have four or five theaters of military operations; in that case former consuls (proconsuls) would command some of the armies. Since most provinces had Roman garrisons, it seemed natural to make the military commander (the proconsul) the governor. This was not an ideal solution. Backed up by an army, an unscrupulous governor could easily enrich himself. In fact, in 149 B.C. the Romans had to establish a special court to try corrupt governors. But not all governors were corrupt, and the mere existence of the court shows that there was some feeling against exploiting the provinces. Moreover, since there were repeated rebellions in some provinces, notably in Spain, military governors were needed to hold the Empire together.

The governors usually had very small staffs and left local affairs to the leaders of local communities. A few allied cities had complete autonomy; elsewhere Roman officials could intervene when they felt it necessary or profitable. The inhabitants of the provinces paid regular taxes to Rome, which, added to the money extorted by corrupt officials, imposed a heavy burden on the provincial economies. Earlier rulers, however, had been no less greedy, and Rome did put an end to the wars that had devastated many parts of the Mediterranean world. After the initial shock of conquest and after the penalties for unsuccessful rebellions had been dealt, the provinces seem to have adjusted fairly well to their new situation.

Changes in Religion, Literature, and Art

Closer contacts with the Hellenistic world brought about changes in Roman art, literature, and religion. Even before the eastern wars, educated Romans had known and been influenced by Greek

Roman Plundering 167–146 B.C.

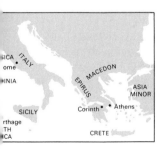

This fresco found in a villa on the outskirts of Pompeii depicts initiation rites of a Dionysian mystery cult, but they are rendered in such a way as to make precise interpretation difficult for the outsider.

In religion, the Romans identified Greek gods with their own; for example, Zeus was Jupiter and Hera was Juno. Historically, these identifications had a foundation in fact: both sets of gods went back to early Indo-European divinities. But in their Greek form the gods were more human and more wayward than the generally faceless and impersonal gods of Rome. In Rome as in Greece, the official religion had been controlled by the aristocracy, and it was already losing its hold on the masses, but it is probable that the introduction of Greek myths made it seem even less applicable to the needs of the people. In any case, some Romans turned, like the Greeks before them, to the mystery religions of the East. During the dark days of the Second Punic War, the Senate itself introduced the Asian cult of Cybele, the Great Mother, in order to bring good fortune to Rome. The cult of Dionysus came in about the same time, even though the Senate disliked its uninhibited ceremonies. But the Oriental religions began to exercise their full influence only after the end of the Republic.

In art, and especially in literature, Greek influence was so great that it is difficult to discover material that does not show signs of Roman imitation of Greek models. The Romans had certainly written poetry and worked up their tribal myths into a sort of history in the early period of the Republic, but one of the first long poems written in Latin was a translation of the *Odyssey*, and around 200 B.C. Romans writing history used Greek. As was pointed out (p. 57), an excellent account of Rome's rise to dominance in the Mediterranean was written in Greek by Polybius, one of the Greek hostages held in Rome. Polybius was deeply impressed by Roman power and by the Roman constitution, but he imitated Thucydides rather than Roman historians. Only with Cato's book on early Roman history (*ca.* 168 B.C.) was a solid historical work attempted in Latin. Cato, who was one of the anti-Greek senators, made a deliberate effort to bring Latin prose up to the Greek level.

The Romans thoroughly enjoyed Greek drama, and the first plays given at Rome were written in Greek. Later the

models, but the sudden arrival of tens of thousands of Greek slaves and hostages in Rome came very close to producing culture shock. Some Romans were horrified at the idea of imitating despised foreigners; they wanted to be more Roman than ever: severe, warlike, unbending lovers of the simple life. Others felt that there was little that was good in the old Roman cultural tradition, and that only the Greek style was worthy of respect. Most Romans, of course, accepted neither of these extreme points of view, but the disagreement ran deep enough to have repercussions in politics. Conservative senators were sure that Greek influence caused political unrest, and this was one of the reasons why they opposed reform movements.

playwrights Plautus and Terence satisfied the Roman desire for amusement by writing comedies in excellent Latin based on earlier works by Hellenistic authors. Little is known about early Roman architecture and not much more about early Roman sculpture, but before 200 B.C. a rough, vigorous native style of architecture and sculpture was being replaced by imitation of Greek originals. Only in works on law was Greek influence minimal. This was the area in which Roman thinkers excelled. Soon after 200 B.C. they were writing solid treatises on basic legal texts and their interpretation. But even in fields related to law, it was only in the first century B.C. that the Romans began to produce important books on political theory and philosophy.

Social, Economic, and Political Change

In addition to providing a constant stream of wealth flowing toward Italy, the provinces supplied Rome with cheap labor. Each conquest and each rebellion was followed by the enslavement of a large part of the defeated people. The result of this influx of money and men was to change the nature of the Roman social and economic system. The upper classes could profit from the new opportunities offered by the acquisition of an empire; the lower classes could not. The gap between rich and poor grew steadily wider. And gaps appeared among the rich as well. War was no longer a fight for existence but a hunt for plunder; public office was no longer a burden but a chance to acquire wealth. As a result, competition for magistracies, army commands, and contracts for public works became intense, and factional struggles among the governing class eventually made it incapable of governing.

The upper classes included the senators and the *equites*, or equestrians. The senators belonged to families, both patrician and plebeian, that had held high public office and hence were entitled to seats in the Senate. Most officials, and consequently most senators, came from old senatorial families; only occasionally could a new man break into this privileged group. It cost a good deal of money to campaign for public office, and the profits began coming in only when a man had reached the higher ranks. On the way up, ambitious men often competed for lower offices by providing expensive amusements for the public. By the first century B.C. bribery of voters had become common, and made campaigning even more costly. Moreover, the great noble families felt that they alone were worthy of office; they used all their influence to exclude lesser men.

The equestrians were those who, in the early years of the Republic, had had enough money to provide their own horses for service in the army. As a class, they were less wealthy than the senators, although the richer equestrians were better off than the poorer senators. Most equestrians were substantial landowners, but some of them were merchants, bankers, and bidders for public contracts. Custom and law forbade senators to engage in these activities, though they often did so by making secret arrangements with businessmen. On the whole, the interests of the senatorial and equestrian classes coincided fairly closely, and each political faction that struggled for office had both senators and equestrians in its ranks.

A major impetus to social and political change was agricultural change. At the beginning of Roman expansion there was a considerable amount of uncultivated land in Italy. Most of this land, as well as cultivated land confiscated from defeated enemies, fell into the hands of the Roman government. Ordinary citizens, especially those who went out to found colonies in the peninsula, received some of the new lands, but the largest part went to the upper classes. They discovered, as rich men in other societies have discovered, that a large estate can be run more efficiently than a small farm, especially when cheap labor is available. The Roman conquests provided them with an almost inexhaustible supply of slaves. Slaves cost little, were given a minimum of food and clothing, and were at times literally worked to death.

Free peasant farmers found it difficult to compete with plantations using slave labor. Their lives were disrupted by continual calls for military service. They

Scenes from everyday life in first-century Rome. Top left: grain from African colonies is being unloaded. Top right: a Greek slave appears to be tutoring his master and mistress. Above: a goldsmith practices his trade. Below: a stooped farmer takes his produce to market.

were under pressure to sell out to rich men seeking a safe, respected, and profitable investment for their money in land. Around the cities, family farms were bought up for specialized agriculture. In the hills and backlands, ranching, which required an investment that a peasant could not make, displaced subsistence farming. The returning veterans or the displaced peasants seldom found work in the countryside, but drifted to Rome, where work was equally scarce. The city was growing rapidly; it had no major export industry, and most of the poor had no permanent jobs. They became "clients" of the rich and especially of the senators. Their duties were to run errands, act as bodyguards, applaud speeches, and start riots when it seemed helpful to their boss or to his faction.

Thus there were two depressed classes in Roman society: the slaves and the poor freemen. Of the two, the slaves caused the less trouble. The agricultural slaves, who were treated most harshly, were carefully watched, even to the point of being locked in underground dungeons at night. Household slaves, such as

the educated Greeks who acted as tutors for rich young Romans, had an easier life. They were often allowed to go into business for themselves and could then buy their freedom, or they might be freed simply because in their long service they had practically become members of the family. Thus the slaves, already divided by race and language, were still further divided by occupation and level of living; it was difficult for them to form an organized resistance. There were remarkably few slave rebellions in the history of the Roman Republic. There were only three really large-scale movements. The slaves rose twice in Sicily, but were crushed by Roman armies. The rebellion of Spartacus in Italy (75–71 B.C.) was more dangerous, but it also failed. Thereafter the brutality of masters and the hopes of slaves lost their edge, and the "peculiar institution" was absorbed into Rome's social structure.

The poor freemen, however, were a constant problem. If they lived in Rome they could vote, and their votes were not always predictable. If they remained on the land as farmers, they were expected to be the backbone of the army, but military requirements were growing, while the number of peasant farmers was probably decreasing. This particular difficulty was resolved in 104 B.C. by permitting landless men to enlist. Such an action, however, merely intensified the problem: the most discontented part of the citizen body now had military as well as political power. Obviously some form of government intervention was needed to save the small farmers and improve the lot of the proletariat, but in spite of long discussions, the ruling class could never agree on a policy. In the end the poorer classes put their faith in soldiers rather than in politicians. The rival generals whose quarrels destroyed the Republic kept the loyalty of their troops by promises of bonuses and grants of land, not by appeals to political programs.

THE COLLAPSE OF THE REPUBLIC 146–59 B.C.

The Gracchi

Tiberius and Gaius Gracchus were the first members of the senatorial class to realize that the problem of the poorer citizens was becoming serious. Even these enlightened men did not fully understand the crisis. They thought more in terms of an idealized early republic than in terms of an empire facing a social crisis. They believed in the old Roman virtues of honesty, self-sacrifice, and devotion to the public welfare, which they thought were incarnate in the class of small farmers. They also believed, more realistically, that the army would be weakened by a decline in the peasant population. Finally, they may have felt that their political group could profit from popular support. The Gracchi were members of the highest aristocracy, grandsons of the great Scipio who had conquered Carthage, but while their birth ensured them high office, it did not confer control of policy. As events were to prove, the Gracchi could never bring many senators to their side; their tragedy was that they could not develop a solid base of political power in any other section of the population.

Tiberius Gracchus was elected tribune in 133 B.C. His first step was to demand that state land virtually owned by rich men with long-term leases should be broken up into small farms. He succeeded in getting the popular assembly to pass a law limiting the amount of public land held by one family, but this action outraged the senators. It not only hurt their interests; it went against an unwritten rule that measures unacceptable to the Senate would not be pushed. The Senate persuaded another tribune to

veto the act; Gracchus, in an unprecedented move, had the tribune voted out of office. To make sure that his reform would endure he ran for a second term as tribune, a violation of custom if not of law. This was more than some senators could swallow; they led their clients in a riot in which Gracchus was lynched.

Some ten years later (123 B.C.) Gaius Gracchus, the younger brother of Tiberius, managed to get himself elected tribune in spite of the hostility of many of the senators. Gaius tried to find a wider political base than his brother had, and for a time he had more success. He gained the support of the impoverished proletariat by providing for state distribution of grain at half-price. This law was so necessary and so popular that no succeeding politician dared to repeal it. He tried to win over the equestrians by giving them control of the juries that judged official corruption. This was a sensible move, since the senators (who had furnished the juries before) held all important offices, and the equestrians were less highhanded in their treatment of the provinces. He continued his brother's policy of land reform and tried to increase the number of small farmers by establishing new colonies.

Gaius also saw a danger that Tiberius had ignored, the discontent of the Italian allies, such as the Samnites, who did not have Roman citizenship. These allies had given Rome faithful service during the Punic and the eastern wars, but they were still treated as inferiors. Their inhabitants could not vote in Roman elections, and they received few material benefits from Roman victories. Although they faced many of the same social and economic problems that Rome did, no one was worrying about them.

Gaius proposed to give Roman citizenship to the Italian allies. This would have relieved them of some of their financial burdens and gained Gracchus a great deal of good will, but it would have been difficult to transform that good will into votes: a citizen could vote only by going to Rome. It is curious that Rome, with its genius for law, never thought of the principle of representation, by which each community could have participated in political decisions by sending one or

A coin minted in 137 B.C. celebrates the private ballot. A Roman is shown dropping a stone tablet into a voting urn.

two men to a central assembly. In any case, Gracchus' proposal was not accepted. Senators, equestrians, and lower classes agreed in rejecting the law, revealing the weakness of his support. Gaius defended his legislation during two terms as tribune, but in the end was lynched like his brother. His death sharply increased tension in Italy and laid the foundation for the bitter civil wars of the next generation.

During the second century B.C., Roman leaders seem to have lost the gift for compromise and accommodation that had held the state together during its early history. Attempts to solve social and economic problems by legal and peaceful means had broken down. A new series of wars, beginning in 107 B.C., was to put still further strains on the Roman system of government and give increasing power to military commanders. Ultimately, decisions would be made and enforced by the generals.

Marius and Sulla

The military difficulties that led to the downfall of the Republic began with a long and bitter war in western North Africa against a recalcitrant ally. As usual, the Romans made a bad start. They began to win only after they discovered a very capable general in an ambitious equestrian from rural Italy named Marius. Elected consul in 107 B.C., Marius ended the African war with a complete victory. It was high time that he did, because a new Indo-European invasion, this time by the Germans, was throwing all of Europe north of the Alps into confusion. Two German tribes appeared in Gaul, raided Spain, and then threatened Italy. After they won several victories over Roman armies, Marius was again called to the rescue. He was reelected consul in 104 B.C., as well as in each of the next four years (103–100 B.C.). Such a series of reelections was unprecedented, but the need to preserve continuity in command was obvious, and there was no real opposition to the break with tradition. Marius justified the confidence placed in him: he annihilated the German armies in two hard-fought battles (102 and 101 B.C.). Thus ended the first,

but by no means the last, of the Roman-German wars.

It was during this crisis that the old connection between ownership of land and military service was broken. Marius had to recruit landless men in order to have sufficient forces. Since the state could not pay these men, Marius rewarded them with bounty from the defeated enemies and grants of land in occupied territories. Most of his successors followed this pattern, but while it provided necessary manpower, it introduced two dangers that endured to the end of Roman history. Troops who received their reward from their general were loyal to that general, not to the state. If land or a substantial bonus was the chief reward for service, then enlistment would be most attractive to the poor and disadvantaged. Over the centuries, fewer and fewer Romans or Italians joined the armed forces. Their places were taken first by provincials, and then by barbarians, men who had little understanding of or loyalty to the Roman state.

Marius was in a strong position after his defeat of the Germans, but he had no political program of his own. Some of his associates wanted to revive the Gracchan policy of land reform; Marius turned against them and helped suppress their movement. This equivocal behavior thoroughly discredited Marius, although other leaders proved no wiser. Nothing was done to allay the grievances of the Italian allies, or the discontent of provincial subjects. As a result, two dangerous uprisings occurred almost simultaneously in Italy and in the East.

The so-called Social War (that is, the war with the Italian allies—*socii* in Latin) began in 90 B.C. The Italian cities formed a confederacy, created their own Senate, raised an army, and held out against Rome for over two years. Marius defended the north, on the whole successfully, but one of his former officers, Sulla, made an even better record in the south. The Romans realized that they had little to gain by devastating Italy, especially since they needed to free their armies for war in the East. They ended the Social War by offering full citizenship to all Italians who would lay down their

Sulla, dictator of Rome from 82 to 79 B.C.

arms, an act that could have prevented the civil war had it been adopted earlier.

The eastern uprising was led by Mithridates, king of a small Hellenistic state on the Black Sea, who hoped to create a new Greek empire. Most of the Greek cities, including Athens, gave him enthusiastic support. They were so embittered by Roman bankers, soldiers, and tax collectors that in 88 B.C., when Mithridates gave the signal, they murdered eighty thousand Romans and Italians in the Greek cities of Asia Minor.

No Roman army was immediately available to avenge this massacre, and a bitter struggle broke out over who was to command an expeditionary force. Sulla, consul in 88 B.C., had the best claim, but while he was away from Rome collecting his forces, Marius obtained the command by a popular vote. Sulla marched on Rome, overturned the vote, and then set out with his army for the East. After three years of hard fighting, he defeated Mithridates and his Greek allies and restored Roman control in Greece and Asia Minor. Sulla demanded an enormous indemnity from his conquered enemies but otherwise was fairly lenient. Mithridates was even allowed to retain his kingdom.

One reason for his leniency was Sulla's eagerness to return to Rome. During his absence opponents had taken over the government and had once more attempted to deprive him of his military command. But when Sulla landed in Italy in 83 B.C. his army of veterans defeated the scattered forces of his opponents one by one. When Sulla took Rome in 82 B.C. he was named dictator for an unlimited period. He proscribed his enemies; that is, he put a price on their heads and confiscated their property. Thousands of "bad citizens," as he called them, were put to death. The property seized from his enemies and from Italian towns that had supported the opposition was distributed among his soldiers. Sulla established colonies throughout Italy and filled them with his adherents.

Although Sulla had full power to revise the Roman constitution, he found no way of overcoming its basic weaknesses. His plan seems to have been to weaken the popular assembly and concentrate power in the Senate, stacked with his own supporters. Once this was done, he retired to his country estate (79 B.C.), where he died the following year. But the new senators were not very different from the old ones; the restrictions on the assembly and the tribunes were gradually removed; and the Roman political system remained inherently unstable.

The New Leaders: Pompey, Crassus, and Cicero

As before, the chief goal of ambitious politicians was to gain the overseas commands that would give them money and control of a loyal army. Danger spots throughout the Roman world offered opportunities for establishing such commands. The East was restless; a bitter opponent of Sulla controlled much of Spain; piracy was rampant in the Mediterranean. The ablest and most popular Roman general was Pompey, who had helped Sulla regain control of Italy in 83 and 82 B.C., but Pompey had some respect for constitutional procedures and some willingness to compromise with his rivals. Thus for almost three decades no one man dominated Rome. Power was held by shifting coalitions of leading politicians, and in a good many cases unaligned majorities in the Senate still had a decisive voice.

Pompey's chief rival was Crassus, a man who had made a fortune in questionable real estate operations. He was never a very good general, but he acquired some military reputation when the one really dangerous slave rebellion in Roman history broke out. Led by the gladiator Spartacus, the slaves at first won several victories, but were finally defeated by Crassus in 71 B.C. Pompey meanwhile had been ending a rebellion in Spain, and there was some danger of a collision between the two victorious generals. They settled their differences, however, and both men were elected consul for the year 70 B.C.

The third political leader to emerge at this time was Cicero, the only civilian in the group. Cicero gained public favor when he secured the conviction of a spectacularly corrupt Roman provincial governor; his whole career depended on

Bust of Pompey showing him late in life.

his skill as a lawyer, orator, and writer. Although he came from an equestrian family, it is not remarkable that he was able to enter the Senate—a good many men of similar background did. But the old senatorial families looked down on these "new men," and most of them went no farther. It was only his extraordinary ability that carried Cicero to the highest office, the consulship.

Cicero was far more honest than most men in that age of corruption. He tried to avoid violence at a time when most problems were settled by civil war. The Romans had already developed a powerful style of oratory; Cicero perfected this style to the point where one of his speeches could sway the entire Senate. As one who thought deeply about Rome's constitutional problems, he tried to halt the drift toward the concentration of powers in the hands of rival politician-generals. Like many successful politicians, Cicero practiced the art of compromise to a degree that often made him seem indecisive, and he knew enough about Roman politics to find it difficult to commit himself to a single faction. In a pinch, he was apt to favor Pompey, who had some of his own qualities (or defects), but as the crisis in Roman government deepened, both men became unable to control events. Cicero was respected to the end, but at the end he had lost most of his political influence.

In 74 B.C. Mithridates again tried to rally the Hellenistic world against Rome, and this time he kept the war going for a decade. Some Roman commanders were incompetent; some conducted brilliant operations; but none of them was able to end the war. This gave Pompey a chance to shine once more. In 66 B.C. the Senate passed a law giving Pompey extraordinary powers (Cicero made a great speech supporting the proposal), which allowed Pompey to end the eastern problem that had plagued Rome since the third century B.C. Mithridates was defeated; parts of Asia Minor and Syria were annexed and the rest put under the control of subject kings. The Jewish kingdom of Palestine was one of these vassal kingdoms. When Pompey returned to Rome in 62 B.C. he had acquired more territory for his country than any previous general.

The Senate gave Pompey a splendid triumphal procession and a cool reception. He had committed Rome to a series of treaties with the eastern kingdoms, and he had promised his soldiers grants of land. The Senate hesitated to ratify these acts, even though Pompey had been given extraconstitutional power to end the war. Pompey was determined to have his promises honored; when the senators refused to satisfy him he had to find ways of putting political pressure on them. The means to do so lay in the person of Gaius Julius Caesar.

THE RISE OF CAESAR 59–44 B.C.

Caesar was a young aristocrat with political ambitions, popularity with the masses—and huge debts. Crassus, who still hoped for power, was aware of his own lack of popularity both in the Senate and with the people, so he decided to back Caesar. By paying off the debts

---

Electioneering in Rome in the Last Days of the Republic

Quintus Cicero to his brother when the latter was running for consul in 64 B.C.

I have said enough about gaining friends, now I should speak of acquiring popular support. The people like to be called by name, flattered, be courted, receive favors, hear about you, feel that you are working for the public good. . . . You must flatter endlessly; this is wrong and shameful in ordinary life, but necessary in running for office. . . . Be in Rome and in the Forum and ask for support. . . . See that you and your friends give parties, widely and to many voting groups. . . . Make it possible for men to see you at any time, day or night. . . .

Let the voters say and think that you know them well, that you greet them by name, that you are generous and open-handed. . . . If possible accuse your competitors of having a bad reputation for crime, vice or bribery. . . . Remember that this is Rome, a city made up of many peoples, in which plots, lies and all kinds of vices abound. You must suffer much arrogance, many insults, much ill-will and the pride and hatred of many people.

Translated from Dante Nardo, *Il Commentariolum Petitionis* (Padua: Liviana, 1970), pp. 213, 215.

Crassus gained a hold on Caesar; by using Crassus' money Caesar gained an enthusiastic personal following and rapid political advancement. He had a reputation as a reformer, although his plans for reform were far from clear; those who knew him best realized that he also had a tremendous desire for power. By 60 B.C. he was ready to run for consul.

The First Triumvirate 59–53 B.C.

Caesar found it an easy matter to bring together Crassus and Pompey, who was still furious with the Senate. Pompey's prestige, Crassus' wealth, and Caesar's popular following made an almost unbeatable combination. The three bosses, or First Triumvirate (to give them their more dignified modern appellation), had about the same degree of power that a similar coalition would have today. They could get most of what they wanted for themselves, and some of what they wanted for their followers, but they were far from having absolute power. And they had to threaten the Senate with force in order to get as much as they did.

The first thing the three wanted was Caesar's election to the consulship for the year 59 B.C. As consul, Caesar saw to it that Pompey's promises were honored, and he distributed land not only to Pompey's veterans, but also to other citizens. Caesar also tried to curb corruption in provincial government by expanding measures taken by Sulla and earlier leaders. He was not entirely successful, but he may have gained some popularity in the provinces.

What Caesar wanted most of all was a military command that would give him a reputation equal to that of Pompey. The one weak link in Rome's control of the Mediterranean was in southern Gaul, where the Romans held only a thin strip of territory linking Italy to Spain. The rest of Gaul was held by Celtic tribes, who were relatively civilized, but who were constantly at war with one another or with Germans pushing in from the East. These wars had a nasty way of spilling over into Roman territory or the territory of Rome's allies. Clearly, it would help Rome if the political situation

Bust of Caesar showing him at the time of his assassination.

in Gaul could be stabilized, but it seemed an unrewarding task. Gaul had neither the wealth nor the splendor of the East. Would a victory over a few Celtic tribes be equivalent to Pompey's triumph over the kings of Asia? Nevertheless, in 58 B.C., a proconsular command over Gaul fell to Caesar's lot, for a period of five years, a term later extended to ten. The

CAESAR IN GAUL   58–49 B.C.

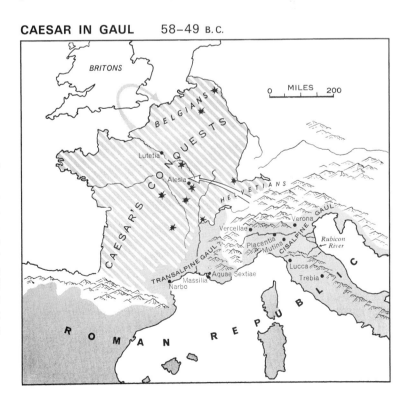

Independent Roman Kingdom	Etruscan Dominance	Rome Conquers Italian Peninsula	Punic Wars	Rome Conquers Entire Mediterranean Area

command included the old Gallic settlements in the Po Valley—a region that was largely Romanized—and Transalpine Gaul, roughly the French Riviera.

It is difficult to say what Caesar's plans were when he first went to Gaul. Certainly he wanted to pacify the tribes living near the Roman frontier and protect the Gauls who seemed friendly to Rome. Probably he wanted to enlarge the Roman province of Transalpine Gaul. But, as often happens in such a situation, one war of pacification led to another, and every time the zone of Roman-protected territory moved northward new enemies appeared. In the end, Caesar conquered all of Gaul and made it a Roman province. As a warning to neighboring peoples, he invaded Britain twice and crossed the Rhine to fight the Germans. All these accomplishments Caesar described in clear terse style in his *Commentaries on the Gallic War.* Any Roman who heard of this book would be convinced that Caesar was a great general and a first-rate administrator.

While Caesar was conquering Gaul, Crassus, still seeking a military reputation, led an army against the Parthians, a people who had taken over Persia. His army was cut to pieces, and Crassus himself was killed (53 B.C.). Meanwhile, Caesar and Pompey had begun to drift apart. The First Triumvirate had come to an end.

Caesar and Pompey

Of the two surviving Triumvirs, Pompey in Rome seemed to have the better position. Mob violence in the city had made orderly government impossible; it created such a dangerous situation that in 52 B.C. Pompey was elected sole consul with practically dictatorial powers. He dominated the Roman government; he was hailed as *Princeps,* or First Citizen. Yet he was not secure as long as Caesar

commanded an intensely loyal army in Gaul and northern Italy.

Pompey's obvious move was to try to deprive Caesar of his military command, an act that would have ended Caesar's political career and perhaps his life. But Caesar had friends in Rome, and the Senate was afraid of starting a civil war. It tried to arrange a compromise by which both Caesar and Pompey would give up their armies, but Pompey would have been perfectly safe in Rome without an army and Caesar would not. Caesar therefore refused to give up his command. In 49 B.C. the Senate ordered Pompey to march against him.

Caesar's outstanding quality as a general was his ability to make quick decisions and to carry them out rapidly. There was no real army in Italy; Pompey's military supporters were mainly in Spain and Greece. Caesar had to strike at once to avoid being caught in a pincers. He marched his army across the Rubicon, a little river marking the boundary between his province of Cisalpine Gaul and Italy, and thundered down on Rome. Pompey, unable to defend the city, fled to Greece with most of the Senate. Caesar had to spend a year securing his position in the West, which gave Pompey time to build a large and well-trained army. When Caesar followed him to Greece, the fighting at first went in Pompey's favor, but Caesar finally won a decisive victory at Pharsalus in 48 B.C. Although Pompey managed to escape to Egypt, he was murdered there by order of the king. Caesar and his lieutenants spent the next three years overcoming supporters of Pompey in Spain, North Africa, and the East. By 45 B.C. Caesar was master of the Roman state.

Caesar's Rule, 48–44 B.C.

Caesar's rule was too short for us to know what his plans were, and it is likely

Richly embossed helmet of an aristocratic warrior of Gaul, at the time of Julius Caesar's conquest.

that he himself was not very sure what was to be done. It was clear that the old constitution had collapsed and that the Roman state must be led by one man. But the Romans still hated the idea of a king, and Caesar had to combine several offices to get the power he needed. He was *imperator* (whence our word *emperor*); that is, he had the *imperium*, the full right of military and civil command. He was dictator for life by vote of the Senate. He enjoyed the privileges and immunity of a tribune. These, and other titles and privileges that he accumulated one by one, made Caesar a king in all but name.

With personal command of the army it was not too difficult to restore order in Rome and in the provinces. Beyond this, Caesar's program was not unlike the programs of Sulla and Pompey, though it was carried out on a larger scale. More land was distributed to veterans, and Roman colonies were established in the provinces. The Senate was enlarged again; this time a few provincial leaders were given seats. Caesar, like his predecessors, tried to lessen corruption in provincial administration, but since he did not change the basic system of giving short-term appointments to proconsuls and other ex-officials, he did little to suppress the temptation to loot and run. Although Caesar managed to speed up the Latinization of the western provinces and gained the support of some of the upper classes in Gaul and Spain, the full incorporation of the provincials into Roman society was still a long way in the future. His most lasting reform was to change the Roman calendar, which was based on an unworkable compromise between a lunar and a solar year. By adopting the 365-day Egyptian year, with an extra day every four years, he introduced the system that, with minor changes, is still used.

Many senators saw their careers blocked because they had opposed Caesar; others, who believed in the old Roman tradition of government, were shocked by the unconstitutional accumulation of power in the hands of one man. The result was a widespread conspiracy. When Caesar entered the Senate on the Ides of March (March 15), 44 B.C., the conspirators, led by Brutus and Cassius, stabbed him to death.

The Murder of Caesar

44 B.C.

The *Lives*, written by the Greek historian Plutarch around 100 A.D., supplies valuable information on Greek and Roman history, particularly on the confusing years of the late Republic. As may be seen from this passage, Plutarch's *Lives* served as a source of Shakespeare's play *Julius Caesar*.

When Caesar entered, the senate stood up to show their respect to him, and of Brutus's confederates, some came about his chair and stood behind it. . . . Tillius, laying hold of his robe with both his hands, pulled it down from his neck, which was the signal for the assault. Casca gave him the first cut in the neck. . . . Those who were not privy to the design were astonished, and their horror and amazement at what they saw were so great that they durst not fly nor assist Caesar, nor so much as speak a word. But those who came prepared for the business enclosed him on every side. For it had been agreed that they should each of them make a thrust at him, and flesh themselves with his blood; for which reason Brutus also gave him one stab in the groin. Some say that he fought and resisted all the rest, shifting his body to avoid the blows, and calling out for help, but that when he saw Brutus's sword drawn, he covered his face with his robe and submitted, letting himself fall . . . at the foot of the pedestal on which Pompey's statue stood. . . .

From Plutarch, *The Lives of Noble Grecians and Romans*, trans. by John Dryden, rev. by Arthur Hugh Clough (New York: Modern Library, n.d.), pp. 892–93.

THE SECOND TRIUMVIRATE 44–36 B.C.

Men like Brutus, who represented the best of the old senatorial class, were convinced that by killing Caesar they could restore the old Republic. But the old system had broken down completely, and the Senate had little popular support. The trouble was that no one else had much support either. Brutus and Cassius left Rome to take up military commands in the East. Mark Antony, who was consul at the time, was loyal to Caesar's memory; he gained the support of the veterans and some of the lower classes by his famous oration at Caesar's funeral. His position was challenged by Octavian, Caesar's grandnephew and adopted son. Octavian, a frail and sickly lad of eighteen, had very little popular support. Cicero and other senators, thinking that it

Coin commemorating the death of Caesar. One side bears the portrait of Brutus; the other side shows the assassins' daggers.

was safe to use him against Mark Antony, accepted him as Caesar's true successor. But Octavian, even at eighteen, was an astute politician and knew where the real power lay. When he had gained all he could from the Senate, he switched sides suddenly and joined Antony and Lepidus (another of Caesar's lieutenants). With Caesar's armies behind them, the three men formed the Second Triumvirate, and marched on Rome in 44 B.C. There the assembly granted them full power for five years.

The first act of the Second Triumvirate was a bloody proscription in which thousands of political opponents were put to death. Cicero, a personal as well as a political enemy of Antony, headed the list. While terrifying the opposition, the Triumvirs divided confiscated lands among veterans and won the support of a new class of landholders. Next, the Triumvirate took its armies across the sea to Macedonia, where they won a quick victory over Brutus and Cassius in 42 B.C.

The three men now divided the Roman world among themselves. Antony had the largest army and controlled both Gaul and the East. Italy was common ground to all three Triumvirs. As neither Octavian nor Lepidus had much military power, Antony paid little attention to his colleagues. In a series of struggles Octavian crushed Lepidus and gradually united Italy behind himself. Lepidus was driven into retirement, but Antony still seemed secure in the East, with its wealth and its tradition of one-man rule.

Antony began to lose support when he became the lover and then the consort of Cleopatra, Queen of Egypt. Although Caesar had also had an affair with Cleopatra, he did not let it interfere with serious business. Antony did: he lived with Cleopatra at the court in Alexandria and rather neglected his other territories. Like many other ill-advised Roman generals, he started a war with the Parthians; nothing of any value was gained, and thousands of Roman soldiers were killed. By 32 B.C. Octavian felt strong enough to move against Antony. He exaggerated and exploited reports that Antony wanted to give Rome's eastern provinces to Cleopatra's children. Then he secured a decree depriving Antony of his com-

THE EXPANSION OF THE ROMAN REPUBLIC BEYOND ITALY   First century B.C.

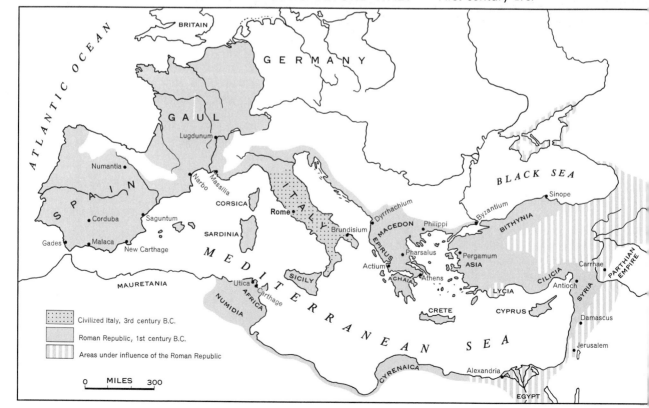

mand. It took some time for each side to marshal its strength, but the two rival forces finally met in the naval battle of Actium in 31 B.C. Octavian's fleet, commanded by his very capable lieutenant, Agrippa, won a decisive victory. Antony fled and later committed suicide; Cleopatra followed his example when she found that she could strike no bargain with Octavian. Egypt was annexed by the victor.

The battle of Actium ended the long period of civil war. Octavian was the master of the Roman world. He proclaimed the restoration of the Republic, but, like Caesar, he occupied all the positions of power. Unlike Caesar, he was able to make his monopoly of power acceptable to the vast majority of citizens and subjects. No military commander opposed him; no politician roused the discontented; no political theorists complained about the break with old traditions. Octavian was to be chief of state for over forty years, and during those years the Roman Empire was born.

Suggestions for Further Reading

Note: Asterisk denotes a book available in paperback edition.

General The surveys of ancient history mentioned at the end of Chapter 1 have sections on the Roman era. There are also many reliable texts devoted specifically to Rome, of which one of the best is H. H. Scullard, *History of the Roman World from 753 to 146* B.C., 3rd ed. (1961). A. E. R. Boak's *A History of Rome to* A.D. *565* has been revised by W. G. Sinnigen (1965), and is useful and clear. Shorter but more vivid are M. I. Rostovtzeff, *Rome** (1964), and D. R. Dudley, *The Civilization of Rome** (1962). M. Grant, *The World of Rome** (1964), emphasizes Roman institutions, customs, and attitudes. A very rich sampling of source readings is collected in the first volume of N. Lewis and M. Reinhold, eds., *Roman Civilization** (1951).

Early Italy, Roman Political Evolution, and Roman Expansion H. H. Scullard, *The Etruscan Cities and Rome* (1967), and R. Bloch, *The Etruscans* (1958), provide up-to-date accounts of a period still quite obscure and complicated. Bloch carries the story further in his *The Origins of Rome* (1966). On the evolution of Rome's constitution, L. Homo, *Roman Political Institutions** (1929, 1962), needs updating but is still the best. Expansion throughout Italy is described in great detail by E. T. Salmon, *Samnium and the Samnites* (1967) and *Roman Colonization under the Republic* (1969). Two recent works unfold Rome's developing power overseas against Carthage and the Hellenistic states: R. M. Errington, *The Dawn of Empire* (1972), and E. Badian, *Roman Imperialism in the Late Republic* (1968).

The Last Century of the Republic, 146–30 B.C. There is such a wealth of material on this complex and chaotic century that only a sampling can be mentioned here. Students interested in a detailed account of the period may consult either F. B. Marsh, *History of the Roman World from 146 to 30* B.C., 2nd ed. (1953), or H. H. Scullard, *From the Gracchi to Nero: A History of Rome from 133* B.C. *to* A.D. *68* (1959). L. R. Taylor, *Party Politics in the Age of Caesar** (1949), gives a clear, concise picture of Roman politics in the later years of this era. R. Syme, *The Roman Revolution** (1939), a classic, offers a detailed but exciting account of the social as well as the political changes that accompanied the failure of the Republic and the creation of the Empire. See also R. E. Smith, *The Failure of the Roman Republic* (1955).

For a description of Roman society in the late Republic, see T. Frank, *Life and Literature in the Roman Republic** (1930). The best studies of Cicero are R. E. Smith, *Cicero the Statesman* (1966), and D. Stockton, *Cicero* (1971). F. R. Crowell, *Cicero and the Roman Republic** (1956), combines a short, lively biography of Cicero with a discussion of the politics of the era. There are many excellent biographies of Caesar as well as many that are not. The most valuable is M. Gelzer, *Caesar, Politician and Statesman* (1968). D. Earl, *The Moral and Political Tradition of Rome* (1967), offers striking insights into the culture and psychology of the times.

4 The Early Roman Empire
27 B.C.–284 A.D.

Returning in triumph to Rome after his victory at Actium, Octavian worked carefully and cautiously to solidify his position. He was quite willing to conciliate the upper classes by preserving old institutions. Consuls were elected every year; the Senate, purged of its recalcitrant members, continued to meet; even the popular assembly was summoned from time to time to give formal approval to Octavian's proposals.

But no one can have been deceived by this facade of republican respectability. Octavian had been given full powers to restore order and stability, and he made all the important decisions. Like Caesar, he was *imperator*, commander of all the armies. Like Caesar, he had the power and immunities of a tribune, including the right to propose laws. He spoke first in the Senate, thus controlling the flow of business through that body; he had his own staff of officials and advisers. He was not quite a sovereign, since theoretically the Senate or the assembly could have voted him out of power if he had ever lost his ability to control them. But he was more than a political boss, because he was surrounded by an aura of sanctity and infallibility that no boss has ever enjoyed.

Octavian himself preferred to be called "Princeps," or First Citizen, and his government and those of his immediate successors are often called the period of the "Principate." But in 27 B.C. the Senate gave him the title of Augustus, and from that time on he was usually referred to by that name. *Augustus* is a word with several layers of meaning. Anyone who was *augustus* was to be looked on with awe and reverence. It was a title that could be used of gods as well as men; it carried overtones of holiness, dignity, wisdom, and authority. Thus, to oppose Augustus was not only politically inexpedient; it was also immoral.

THE PRINCIPATE OF AUGUSTUS
27 B.C.–14 A.D.

Augustus could not have had a very clear concept of the form and extent of imperial authority, since he had only begun the process of developing that authority. But he did have a clear idea of what he wanted to do with his power: there was to be security, a revival of the old Roman virtues, and stability throughout the Roman world.

Theoretically, the Senate was to help Augustus in this task. Rome and Italy would be governed by the Senate and the elected magistrates, and provincial districts that were completely pacified and

The dome of the Pantheon in Rome (*ca.* 125 A.D.), with its oculus at the crown.

needed no armies would be governed by senatorial representatives (proconsuls and the like). Augustus, with permanent proconsular power, had authority over all the provinces in which armies were stationed. These provinces, though backward and poor, were far more numerous than those that were entrusted to senators.

In practice, the division of power, while it secured political tranquility, had some weaknesses. To be secure Augustus had to control Rome and Italy. Many senators, unhappy about their reduced role in government, secretly intrigued against the emperor. At the same time, the Senate could not take any initiatives. Augustus formulated the program of the government. Some of his projects, such as a reform of morals and a revival of the old Roman religion, though they were supported by the upper classes, had little effect. Rome was a cosmopolitan city; even Augustus could not make it revert to the idealized social patterns of the early Republic.

In the provinces the old problem of an inadequate and untrained bureaucracy continued to exist. There were few Roman officials in any province, and most of them served only for short periods. No doubt the lieutenants of Augustus who administered his provinces were somewhat more honest than senatorial governors had been in the past. However, imperial provinces had to support a Roman army, while senatorial provinces did not. In general, Augustus would not permit the flagrant maladministration that had recurred in the last century of the Republic, and under his rule provincial grievances were lessened, though not ended.

Even with these strains, there was no danger that the Roman Empire would fall to pieces. In the first place, there were no longer independent armies, each loyal to its own general. Augustus was com-

mander-in-chief, and his close friend Agrippa was his chief of staff. The army was more or less insulated from the rest of the population, since enlistments were for a period of twenty years. About half of the army was made up of Roman citizens, enrolled in some twenty-five legions of (theoretically) six thousand men each. At the end of their service these men were given large cash bonuses, and occasionally plots of land. The rest of the army was made up of provincials who served as auxiliary troops. The legions were usually under full strength, so Augustus had about 250,000 soldiers. This army was completely loyal to him and numerous enough to put down any uprising.

The second factor that made the inadequate Roman administrative system viable was that it actually had very little administrative work to do. In one way or another, most of the details of government were turned over to local authorities. On the fringes of the Empire were semi-independent kingdoms, like that of Herod in Judea, which controlled their own internal affairs. Even more numerous were the city-states, which administered rural districts from an urban center. As long as local aristocracies kept order in these city-states there was relatively little interference from Roman authorities. In fact, the system worked so well that it was transferred to the less developed parts of the Empire. The Gauls, for example, were encouraged to develop cities that could act as administrative centers for each tribe.

The Frontiers

Augustus wanted to round out the holdings of the Empire in order to make his frontiers more defensible. In most places this was done fairly easily. The border with the Parthians was fixed at the Euphrates, thus ending for a time the

Augustus issued these coins to proclaim the submission of Egypt and Armenia to Roman power.

Parthian wars. It took only a little fighting to establish firm boundaries between Judea and Arabia, Egypt and Ethiopia, and North Africa and the Berber desert tribes.

The one frontier that was never certain and never secure was the frontier with the Germans. The Rhine was not a good boundary. As Caesar had discovered, the Germans frequently pushed across the river into Gaul. The Rhine also made an awkward angle with the Danube, which was a possible frontier against the eastern Germans. It was clearly desirable to push the Germans back from the Rhine, but when an attack was made in 9 A.D. the German chieftain Arminius (Herman) annihilated three Roman legions. Though Arminius became a national hero for modern Germany, his fellow chieftains killed him soon after his great victory. Augustus did not try to take advantage of this act; Germany was not worth risking another three legions. His stepsons, Tiberius and Drusus, did advance toward the Danube line in what are now Switzerland and Austria, and later in the first century, the middle Rhine and the upper Danube were linked by a fortified wall. But on the whole, little German territory was permanently annexed by Rome.

Augustus acquired a considerable amount of territory in creating defensible boundaries for Rome. The lands he acquired, however, had more strategic than economic value. The conquest of Alpine territory, for example, did not produce the flood of gold and highly skilled slaves that had come from the conquest of Asia Minor. There were no magnificent triumphs, such as those celebrated by Pompey. Except for the island of Britain, which was to be conquered in 43 A.D., and some short-lived conquests in the East, Rome had reached the limits of its expansion.

Augustus' Rule

Augustus had not been very popular as a young man, and the Senate was never entirely happy about his dominant position. But, as in many other cases, the mere length of his reign enhanced his popularity; one could scarcely imagine

THE GERMAN PROBLEM
First and second centuries B.C.

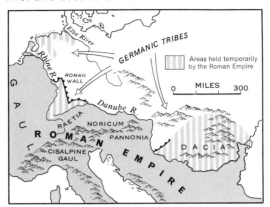

Rome without Augustus. Moreover, Augustus deliberately tried to build up support for his government. New official positions were created for the equestrians, and the class as a whole profited from an increase in commerce and in financial transactions. The lower classes of Rome were kept quiet by increasing

The Deeds of Augustus

This excerpt is from a long epitaph that Augustus composed for himself in his old age, and that was inscribed on brazen columns at Rome and copied in stone in many provincial cities. The only relatively complete copy that has survived is at Ankara (Ancyra). Note how Augustus poses as the preserver of the old Roman Republic.

In my twentieth year, acting upon my own judgment . . . I raised an army by means of which I restored to liberty the Republic which had been oppressed by the tyranny of a faction. . . . Those who killed my father [Julius Caesar], I drove into exile . . . and when they waged war against the Republic I twice defeated them in battle. . . . I have extended the boundaries of all the provinces of the Roman people. . . . I have reduced to a state of peace . . . the lands enclosed by the ocean from Gades [Cadiz] to the mouth of the Elbe. . . . I have added Egypt to the empire of the Roman people. . . . I accepted no office which was contrary to the customs of the country. . . . When I had put an end to the civil wars . . . I transferred the commonwealth from my own power to the authority of the Senate and the Roman people. In return for this favor I was given by decree of the Senate the title Augustus. . . . After that time I excelled all others in dignity, but of power I held no more than those who were my colleagues in any magistracy.

From Augustus, as quoted in *Monumentum Ancyranum: The Deeds of Augustus,* ed. and trans. by William Fairly, *Translations and Reprints* (Philadelphia: University of Pennsylvania Press, 1898), Vol. V, No. 1, pp. 12ff.

the dole of grain and by lavish public entertainments. The inhabitants of Italy had an opportunity to take part in the establishment of new colonies in the thinly settled western provinces. Non-Roman subjects still bore heavy burdens, but at least their lands were no longer ravaged by civil wars, and Augustus had made some effort to improve provincial administration.

Augustus also tried to build up an all-inclusive patriotism that would override local loyalties. Worship of the "spirit" of Rome became an official cult. To this was added worship of the "genius" of the emperor. This was not quite the same thing as saying that the emperor was a god, but it certainly implied that he was guided and imbued by a divine spirit. Such nice distinctions were not important in the East, where rulers had long been worshiped as gods, but they were essential in Italy, which was definitely hostile to the idea of a god-king.

The Golden Age of Latin Literature

In the last years of the Republic and during the first years of the Empire Latin literature reached its peak. Prose writers dealt mainly with history, political the-

Contemporary bust of Cicero, the great orator of the first century B.C.

ory, and philosophy. Cicero covered the widest range—he published his orations and letters as examples of an elegant and polished style, and wrote extensively on ethics, rhetoric, philosophy, and political theory. Caesar's accounts of his wars showed that military communiqués could have both style and political purpose. Sallust (86-34 B.C.) was an enemy of Cicero, and his account of Cicero's consulship is just about as biased as Cicero's defense of his actions. But Sallust was an excellent prose writer and could be a good historian, as he showed in his account of the *Jugurthine War* (a campaign in North Africa). The most influential historian of this period was Livy (59 B.C.–17 A.D.), who summed up the books of earlier writers in a monumental history of Rome. Most of this work has been lost, but enough survives to show that he was chiefly interested in celebrating the piety, civic spirit, and heroism of the early Romans. He accepted legends uncritically, but he retold them splendidly. More than anyone else, Livy created the tradition that Roman character was the source of Roman strength, a tradition that has impressed historians for almost two thousand years.

The poets of the late Republic avoided politics. Catullus (87–54 B.C.) wrote graceful lyrics about his love affairs. The greatest poet of the Republic, and perhaps the most original of all Latin authors, was Lucretius (99–55 B.C.). In his *De rerum natura* he expressed his personal philosophy and his view of the universe in verses of remarkable beauty and power. Although he drew many of his ideas from Hellenistic philosophers, the synthesis was his own. But Lucretius was too speculative to appeal to the practical Roman mind; he had little influence and no successors.

The poets of the early Empire, unlike their predecessors, were deeply involved in politics. Vergil and Horace were not wealthy men; they could devote themselves to writing only because they were patronized by the emperor, or rather by one of his chief advisers, Maecenas. As a result, some of their work has an official flavor. Thus when Vergil (70-19 B.C.) wrote his epic, the *Aeneid*, he was careful to include compliments to the imperial family. The poem itself argues that Rome was founded under divine auspices, that its glorious destiny had long been predicted, and that its brilliant success was due to the virtue of its founders. Vergil imitated the Homeric model, but imitation did not keep him from being a great poet; he wrote some of the most effective lines that appear in the literature of any country. His famous phrase—"Rome is to rule through law, to spare the conquered and put down the mighty from their seats,"—sums up Augustus' vision of the Empire.

Horace (65–8 B.C.) wrote official poems for Augustus' religious festivals and celebrated the virtue of the early Romans. But he was much more than an official poet. He was a shrewd and experienced man, a keen observer of human behavior, and a master of summing up his observations in brief and striking verses.

The fate of Ovid (43 B.C.–17 A.D.) shows why it was well to pay some attention to pleasing the emperor. Drawing on Greek mythology for much of his material, Ovid could tell a good story in graceful verse. But there was little morality in his sources, and Ovid did not bother to add any, which may explain why Ovid was banished from his comfortable life in Rome to a very uncomfortable life on the shores of the Black Sea. His work remained popular, however, and was the chief source of knowledge of Greek mythology during the Middle Ages and the Renaissance.

With the exception of Lucretius, these Latin authors contributed few new ideas to the intellectual tradition of the ancient world. But they did perfect the Latin language by fixing its grammatical rules and by increasing its vocabulary. In their hands Latin became a precise and efficient language. Since much of the world's thinking was to be done in Latin for the next fifteen hundred years, this was no mean achievement. They also introduced eastern ideas to the West in a form in which they could be easily assimilated. Something was lost in the process: Latin was never able to reproduce all the subtle distinctions that could be made in Greek, and the Romans had little interest in Greek scientific work. But by borrowing

Lucretius on Atoms

If you think that basic particles can stand still, and by standing still can beget new motions among things, you are astray and wander far from true reasoning. For since basic particles wander through the void, they must needs all be carried on either by their own weight or by a chance blow from one or other. For when in quick motion they have often met and collided, it follows that they leap apart suddenly in different directions. . . . And to show you more clearly that all the bodies of matter are constantly being tossed about, remember that there is no bottom in the sum of things, and the first bodies have nowhere to rest, since space is without end or limit. . . . Beyond doubt no rest is granted to the first bodies, . . . some after being pressed together then leap back with wide intervals, some again . . . are tossed about within a narrow compass. And those which being held in combination more closely condensed collide and leap back through tiny intervals, . . . these constitute the strong roots of stone and . . . iron and others of this kind. . . . The rest leap far apart and pass far back with long intervals between; these supply thin air for us and the gleaming light of the sun.

From Lucretius, *De rerum natura*, trans. by W. H. D. Rouse (Cambridge, Mass.: Harvard University Press, 1937), Book II, ll. 80–108.

from the Greeks, and by putting what they borrowed into enduring form, Latin authors laid the foundations for much of the later literature of the West.

SUCCESSORS TO AUGUSTUS 14–68 A.D.

It was clear long before Augustus died that his system of government would endure. But who was to succeed him? He was not a hereditary monarch, and he had no son. On the other hand, his own career had shown the value of family connections; he owed his position to the fact that he was the grandnephew and adopted son of Caesar. Therefore, Augustus looked around the circle of his relatives and, after a long series of intrigues and premature deaths of possible successors, settled on his stepson Tiberius. He made Tiberius his associate in the tribunician power and in the *imperium*, so that Tiberius had no trouble in taking over the government when the old emperor died in 14 A.D. But the episode

Relief of a figure thought to be Horace (fragment of a marble frieze, Greco-Roman period).

revealed a weakness in the imperial system that was never cured: the absence of a fixed rule of succession and the danger that the title could be seized through intrigue and violence. The Julio-Claudian emperors* (the first four successors of Augustus) all shared these problems.

Tiberius (14–37 A.D.) and Caligula (37–41 A.D.)

Tiberius was an able administrator and a good general, but he had been embittered by the fact that Augustus had passed him over repeatedly in his search for a successor. Though he came from one of the most distinguished families in Rome (his father was a Claudian), many senators resented his supremacy and intrigued against him. He made more enemies by weeding out subordinates who seemed dishonest or incompetent. Quarrels in his own family over the succession led to several suspicious deaths. Disgusted with Rome and fearful for his life, Tiberius took refuge on the island of Capri near Naples. This move made it easier for intrigue to flourish in Rome. Suspicious of everyone around him, Tiberius ordered the execution of many officials and senators on charges of treason. There was general relief when he died in 37 A.D.

He was succeeded by his grandnephew, Caligula, who seemed as attractive as Tiberius had been morose. Unfortunately, Caligula was also insane. His whimsical cruelty and his lack of military sense disgusted the army and led to a conspiracy in which Caligula was put to death.

Claudius (41–54 A.D.) and Nero (54–68 A.D.)

With the death of Caligula, the Senate hoped to abolish the position of emperor and restore the Republic. They had forgotten that for more than a century real power had rested in the army, and that the army had no great respect for the Senate. While the senators were debating, the palace guard found Caligula's

sickly uncle Claudius and proclaimed him emperor.

Claudius turned out to be a more capable ruler than anyone had expected. He initiated the conquest of Britain and gained good will in the provinces by generous grants of Roman citizenship. He started the reorganization of the imperial government by creating four administrative bureaus, each headed by a freedman (usually a liberated Greek slave). Senators still commanded armies and governed provinces and equestrians handled most of the financial affairs of the Empire, but a new imperial bureaucracy was to grow out of Claudius' group of freedmen.

Claudius married his niece Agrippina, an evil and ruthless woman who persuaded him to disinherit his son by an earlier marriage and to give the succession to her own son, Nero. Nero was self-indulgent and unstable, but at first he left the government of the Empire to his mother and his tutor,

A family portrait. Above: Claudius (*ca.* 50 A.D.). Right: Agrippina, Claudius' wife, with her child Nero.

*These men were all related, by blood or by marriage, to the great Roman families of the Julians and the Claudians

84

Nero as emperor.

own general, and the result was the famous "year of the four emperors" (68–69). Nero, easily overthrown, committed suicide; then three army commanders in succession marched on Rome, claimed the imperial title, and promptly lost it to the next aggressor. The commander in the East, Vespasian, was wiser: he consolidated his hold on his own region and waited for his rivals to kill one another off. When Vespasian's troops gained control of Rome in 69 A.D., little opposition remained, and he was to hold the imperial title until his death ten years later.

THE EMPIRE AT ITS HEIGHT 69–180 A.D.

Vespasian's rule marked a change in the character of the Empire. His predecessors had all come from the old aristocratic families that had held the highest offices in Rome for the last three centuries. Vespasian was not an aristocrat; he came from a middle-class family (the Flavians) in a small Italian town. He had become emperor through his own efforts, not through family connections and palace intrigues. He knew the provinces better than he knew Rome, and he relied on the Roman or Romanized inhabitants of the provinces more than any of his predecessors had done. He maintained correct relations with the Senate, but the Senate with which he had to deal was more and more a new Senate. Proscriptions, executions, and lack of heirs were gradually extinguishing the old Roman aristocratic families. The new senators were drawn from all parts of Italy and eventually of the Empire. Senators as individuals occupied high administrative posts, and served the emperor on various advisory committees. But the Senate as a corporate body had long lost its independent authority.

These tendencies continued under Vespasian's successors. Most of them had had some administrative or military experience. Most of them came from new families. Most of them knew and were concerned with the provinces—two of them were born of Roman families that had settled in Spain.

the philosopher Seneca. When he decided to take power into his own hands he offended most of the leading men of the Empire by his lack of dignity and his cruelty. Believing that he was a great poet and musician, he traveled about the Empire performing his works. When a disastrous fire almost destroyed Rome in 64, there were rumors, almost certainly not true, that Nero had set the blaze to provide a brilliant background for a recitation of his poetry. Seeking a scapegoat, Nero blamed the fire on Rome's small community of Christians and put many of them to death.

Naturally there were plots against such a man, and naturally Nero imagined plots where none existed. He condemned to death his mother, his old friend Seneca, the poet Lucan, and the brilliant general Corbulo, who had defended the eastern frontier against the Parthians. He executed many senators and confiscated their property. And while he was building up a mountain of resentment against himself, he was paying no attention to the administration or to the army.

This time the legions led the rebellion, not the palace guard. This was a new and ominous development. The guard had been able to agree on one man; the scattered legions could not. Each group advanced the claims of its

Vespasian, founder of the Flavian dynasty.

Trajan (*ca.* 100 A.D.).

The Flavian Emperors
69–96 A.D.

Vespasian was an excellent administrator. The Empire was deeply in debt after Nero's extravagances; he made it solvent by reforming the tax structure. The practice of farming taxes to corporations of bankers, which had already been cut back by earlier emperors, was eliminated by Vespasian and his sons. Procurators appointed by the emperor took over financial administration in the provinces. The vast amounts of land owned by the state or confiscated from alleged traitors were organized to produce maximum revenues. The frontiers of the Empire were strengthened in places where defense was difficult.

Vespasian was succeeded by his two sons, Titus (79–81) and Domitian (81–96). Titus was as capable as his father and, with the financial crisis over, could avoid the unpopularity caused by some of Vespasians' financial practices. Domitian seems to have ruled the provinces well, but he was disliked in Rome. The cult of the Republic was about dead, but philosophers were now arguing that the "best man" should rule. Domitian did not seem the best man to many of his subordinates, and he grew more autocratic as he grew older. Writers accused him of wishing to be addressed as "lord and god"; whatever the truth of this accusation, he certainly executed a number of men of high rank on flimsy charges. A palace conspiracy was formed, and Domitian was assassinated in 96 A.D. The armies were taken by surprise and made no move, so that for once the Senate was able to act. With the approval of the palace guard, it chose one of its own members, Nerva, as emperor.

The "Five Good Emperors"
96–180 A.D.

Nerva was an upright and distinguished senator, but he knew that he needed military support. He designated Trajan, commander of the armies on the Rhine, as his successor. With Nerva and Trajan began the era of the "five good emperors," which lasted from 96 to 180 A.D. Gibbon once wrote that this was the happiest period in the history of the human race; certainly it was the most prosperous and least troubled period in the history of the Roman Empire. Partly because of a lack of direct heirs, partly because they shared belief in the rule of "the best man," four emperors in succession passed their power on to adopted sons, and each of the men they chose proved worthy of ruling. The old problem of the succession seemed to be solved; the old jealousy between emperor and Senate almost disappeared; the old distinction between privileged Italy and oppressed provinces was practically eliminated; and the imperial administrative system was greatly improved.

This is not to say that there were no problems or no mistakes on the part of the emperors. The Germans along the lower Danube and the Parthians on the eastern frontier were a constant menace. Trajan (98–117) tried to end this danger by annexing enemy bases. He took Mesopotamia from the Parthians and Dacia (roughly, modern Romania) from the Germans at great cost in both money and lives. Under Trajan the Empire reached its greatest extent, but even Trajan could not hold all of Mesopotamia, and Dacia had to be abandoned in the next century.

Hadrian (117–138) was less a soldier and more an administrator. He abandoned what was left of Mesopotamia and strengthened fortifications along the frontiers. One example of these efforts is Hadrian's Wall, much of which is still visible; it was built to protect northern Britain from raids by the inhabitants of Scotland. But Hadrian's real interest was in perfecting the imperial civil service. He continued earlier trends by appointing equestrians as bureau chiefs instead of freedmen, by organizing a regular hierarchy of positions, and by developing a group of career officers who could be advanced from post to post until they reached the highest positions in the government. He kept careful watch over these men and made long trips through the Empire to inspect provincial government. His success may be measured by the fact that the reign of his successor, Antoninus Pius (138–160), was so uneventful that contemporary writers have little to say about it. The reign of Marcus

Aurelius (161–180), the last of the "good emperors," was not uneventful, but his problems are discussed in a later section.

The Empire in the Second Century

From the time of Vespasian to the death of Marcus Aurelius, most inhabitants of the Empire could go about their business without fearing invasion and without suffering from misgovernment. The letters exchanged by Trajan and the younger Pliny, who was a provincial governor in Asia Minor, show the high standards set for administrators and a real concern for the welfare of the governed. Certainly there were some corrupt officials and some cases of undue severity, but on the whole the provincials could at last feel that they were members of the Roman commonwealth, not subjects of a foreign conqueror.

The distinction between senatorial and imperial provinces had become meaningless; all provincial administration was controlled by the imperial bureaucracy. And while that bureaucracy occasionally interfered in local affairs, the city governments still had most of the responsibility for administering their towns and the surrounding countryside. The city-state was the natural unit of local government in the East, and Rome had tried to build similar units in the western provinces. By the middle of the second century almost all the Empire was divided into these city-states, which proved to be powerful instruments for spreading a common Greek or Latin culture and common loyalties. The Roman city-state was a state in the American, not European, sense; that is, a subordinate, but autonomous, political entity that took care of almost all the needs of the local population. All offices in the cities were reserved for men from the upper classes, who were expected to set an example of good citizenship to the rest of the community. They collected the taxes and made up any deficits in the assigned quota from their own pockets;

Inscription from Trajan's column in the Roman forum (*ca.* 114 A.D.) celebrating his victories over the Germans and Dacians: "The Senate and the Roman people to the *imperator* Caesar, son of the deified Nerva, Nerva Trajan Augustus conqueror of the Germans and the Dacians. . . ."

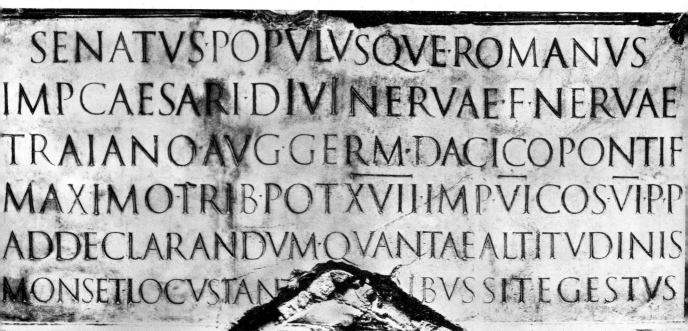

SENATVSPOPVLVSQVEROMANVS
IMPCAESARIDIVINERVAEFNERVAE
TRAIANOAVGGERMDACICOPONTIF
MAXIMOTRIBPOTXVIIIMPVICOSVIPP
ADDECLARANDVMQVANTAEALTITVDINIS
MONSETLOCVSTAN   IBVSSITEGESTVS

Roman soldier fighting on the Danube frontier (108–109 A.D.).

to contend. Even though Hellenization had been going on since the third century B.C., Egyptian and Syrian traditions persisted. Most business, public and private, was conducted in Greek, but the old Oriental languages did not vanish, as Celtic gradually vanished in Gaul.

The Roman authorities, like the Hellenistic rulers of the earlier centuries, had encouraged assimilation and were reasonably satisfied with the results. Roman citizenship was given to the ruling classes of provincial cities and to provincials who served in the Roman army. By the end of the second century, most men of any standing in provincial society were citizens. When, in 212, the emperor Caracalla extended Roman citizenship to all free men in the Empire, he was only giving legal sanction to an already existing psychological reality.

The Jews

Two groups seemed deliberately to avoid assimilation, the Jews and the Christians. The Jews' concept of Jahweh as the one universal God made it impossible for them to accept the idea that in their devotion to Jahweh they were simply worshiping another manifestation of Zeus-Jupiter. The Jewish scriptures gave them an acute sense of their own identity as a people. To be integrated into Greco-Roman culture was to deny the whole meaning of their history and their special relationship with Jahweh.

Most Jews lived together in Judea. Many, however, lived in Hellenistic cities outside Judea, especially in Alexandria. These Jews of the Diaspora (scattering) admired some elements of Greco-Roman culture, but even they remained a people apart. They could not take part in the sacrifices and rituals that demonstrated allegiance to the government. They had to be exempted from the state cults and military service and allowed to live by their own law.

When Rome took over the Hellenistic kingdoms, the special privileges of the Jews were confirmed and Judea was made a client kingdom. But the client kings were not very satisfactory. After wavering back and forth for several generations, Judea became a Roman prov-

they erected public buildings and monuments in the Roman style; they supported the official religion of Rome and the emperor. But to become one of these local notables a man had to accept Latin culture in the West and Greek culture in the East. The imperial government did not trust people who clung to old customs and spoke odd languages.

This gradual assimilation of Greco-Roman culture worked better in the West than in the East. The memory of earlier cultures was disappearing in the West, at least among the urban population. In the cities one either learned Latin and adopted Roman customs or one remained isolated from the mainstream of life. In the rural areas the process took longer. It was only in the fourth century A.D. that Gaul and Spain became thoroughly Latinized. In Britain, which was conquered late and lost early, Latin culture never struck deep roots. The East had plenty of time to assimiliate Greek culture, but stronger survivals with which

ince. This aroused resistance, especially in Galilee, where a group called the Zealots used terrorist techniques. Resistance stirred up a counter-terror by the Romans, which in turn precipitated an open rebellion in 66 A.D. The Jews fought heroically, but in the end the Romans sacked Jerusalem (70 A.D.), destroyed the Temple, and slew thousands of Jews.

The final blow came under Hadrian. With the best of intentions, but with less than his usual sensitivity, he tried to rebuild Jerusalem as a Greco-Roman city, with a temple dedicated to Roman gods. Again Judea rebelled, and again the Jews were slaughtered by the thousands. With Judea largely depopulated, the Jewish communities around the Mediterranean became the centers of Jewish culture. Although there were no more rebellions, there did remain an overwhelming desire to preserve the Law of Moses (the *Torah*) with the teachings concerning the Law (the *Mishna*) and interpretations of the Law (the *Talmud*).

The Beginnings of Christianity

The religion that was eventually accepted by most inhabitants of the Empire was founded in the reigns of Augustus and Tiberius. Jesus of Nazareth was born about 4 B.C.;* his brief period of active teaching and the conversion of the first disciples came during the years from 26 to 30 A.D. Shortly after the birth of Jesus, Augustus had taken direct control of Judea from a client king. Many Jews dreamed of a Messiah who would free them from this foreign rule and prove that theirs was the only true religion. When Jesus began teaching, some Jews accepted him as the Messiah, especially since he quoted passages from the prophets that seemed to refer to such a mission. But most of these followers became discouraged when Jesus made it clear that his kingdom was "not of this world," that he was interested in a new view of the relation between God and man, and not in earthly politics. On the other hand, those who really understood his message were convinced that he was the Christ, the Son of God, and that his teaching of the love of God and the

*Jesus' birth should, of course, have begun the year 1 A.D. But most Church historians now agree that there are errors in the New Testament dating. In any case, the reckoning of years from the birth of Jesus did not begin until the sixth century, and by that time an error of a few years made no great difference.

Spoils taken by the Romans from the Temple in Jerusalem (detail from the Arch of Titus, Rome, 81 A.D.).

This marble relief pictures a small Italian city as it looked in the days of the early Caesars. Blocks of two- and three-story tenements are enclosed by the ancient town wall. At the right, the country villas of the wealthy, with their gardens and colonnades, sprawl across the nearby hillsides.

brotherhood of man was the most important revelation that the human race had ever received.

The dominant group among the Jews at this time was the sect of the Pharisees, strict upholders of the Jewish Law. They were shocked by Jesus' claim that he bore a new revelation that superseded the Law and even more by his assertion that he was the Son of God. They accused Jesus of blasphemy and denounced him to the Roman governor, Pontius Pilate. Pilate was not very sure what he should do, but Judea was a troubled area, and anyone who stirred up strong popular feelings might be dangerous to Roman authority. So about 30 A.D. Jesus was crucified—a Roman form of execution reserved for criminals of the lowest classes.

Pilate and the Pharisees thought that this was the end of the matter. But the disciples remained faithful, for they were convinced that Jesus had risen from the dead and had repeatedly appeared to his followers. The Resurrection gave them courage and confidence. They began to understand the divine purpose: God had become man and had suffered on earth to redeem the sins of mankind. All who believed in Jesus would be saved by his sacrifice. Strong in their faith, they began

to make converts among the Jews of Palestine and Syria. At this time they began to be called Christians.

The new religion was at first only a Jewish sect, ignored by the rest of the world and bitterly opposed by many Jews. At this critical point the conversion of Saul of Tarsus enabled Christianity to broaden its appeal. Saul, though Greek in education and Roman in citizenship, was a fiercely orthodox Jew who felt it was his duty to attack the Christians. In the midst of his campaign he suffered a physical collapse (in the Acts of the Apostles it is said he was blinded); on his recovery he announced his conversion to the faith he had opposed. He took the name of Paul and began preaching Christianity in the cities of Asia Minor and Greece, and eventually in Rome itself.

It was Paul who made Christianity attractive to the non-Jewish inhabitants of the Roman world. He persuaded early Christian leaders that many Jewish ritual practices could be abandoned; one could be a Christian without first having to become a Jew. He also explained Christian doctrine in terms that were understandable to men thinking in terms of Greek philosophy. In his Epistles, he began the work of building a Christian philosophy and theology that could appeal to men of all races.

Meanwhile, other disciples were spreading the faith outside Palestine. Peter, the leader of the group, probably went to Rome; very early tradition holds that he was head of the Roman Church and was martyred there. Other churches were established in Egypt, Asia Minor, Greece, and later in Gaul and in Spain. Stories of the sayings and doings of Jesus were collected and by the end of the first century began to take shape as the Gospels. To these were added the letters and acts of the apostles, and so the body of writings that eventually became the New Testament was formed.

Christianity was a vigorous, active faith at a time when the old state religions were losing their credibility and the mystery cults were not very precise about their doctrines. Its appeal was greatest among the poor and, in the West, among eastern slaves and laborers. There were enough Christians in Rome by 64 A.D. so that they could be blamed

for burning down the city, and during the second century they began to cause problems for imperial governors. Like the Jews, they were a people apart who refused to take part in the public rituals honoring the state and the emperor. Unlike the Jews, the Christians were not protected by ancient privileges. Their religion was an unknown quantity, and their exclusiveness made them objects of suspicion. They were persecuted sporadically, although the most serious attacks against them did not come until the third century.

Society and Economy

By the time the Empire had reached its height, Rome and its environs had a population somewhere around a million. In the East, only Alexandria was as large, but in both East and West there were a few great cities of a hundred thousand or more. The rich could live luxuriously in their town houses, or suburban villas, but without public transportation the

THE ROMAN EMPIRE AT ITS HEIGHT   117 A.D.

A gladiator contends with a wild animal (detail from a fourth-century mosaic).

Greek and Roman merchants traveled freely in the stable world of the first two centuries A.D. Their ships could average more than one hundred miles a day (detail from a sarcophagus from Ostia, *ca.* second or third century A.D.).

cles. The Colosseum, started by Vespasian and dedicated by Titus, held 50,000 spectators. It was used chiefly for combats between gladiators or between slaves, criminals, and wild beasts. The Circus Maximus, which could seat about 150,000 persons, was the center for chariot racing. There were also elegant public baths, though the largest ones were not built until the third century.

Most of the western cities were like Rome—they had forums, temples, arenas, and baths. The eastern cities, with older traditions, had more individuality. But, as archeological excavation shows, there was enough resemblance among the cities so that people traveling through the Empire found themselves at home wherever they went.

The class structure was as rigid as it had been under the Republic. Although few of the old Roman senatorial families had survived the civil wars and the purges of the early emperors, a new senatorial class had replaced them. This class had little political power, but it enjoyed great wealth and held vast estates in Italy and in the provinces. The equestrians, as before, were not far behind the senators. Next came the municipal aristocracies. Far below these privileged groups were the country folk (small farmers, tenants, and laborers), and in the cities, shopkeepers, workers, and unemployed freedmen. And at the very bottom, as in the days of the Republic, were the slaves, who worked in chain gangs in mines and on the great Roman estates.

The imperial government in various ways increased the rigidity of the class structure. By the second century the law

poor had to be crowded into tenements that rose to five or six stories in Rome. The ground floor was used for small shops; the upper stories were divided into small, dark apartments. There was no window glass, so all openings had to be narrow in order to keep out cold and rain. Roman engineers knew how to bring water into a city by aqueducts, but they did not know how to raise it to the upper stories of a tall building. It is not surprising that most people spent as much time in the street as possible. The emperors had to forbid vehicular traffic in Rome during the day; all deliveries were to be made at night when the streets were less crowded.

For the Romans, as for the Greeks before them, the existence of public buildings, market squares, and gardens was an absolute necessity. The old Roman Forum was lined with temples and shops; the emperors built several new forums nearby. They also provided the people with arenas for public specta-

made a strict distinction between upper and lower classes, not only in office-holding but also in judicial procedure. Only the *humiliores* (the more humble) could be tortured or executed in cruel ways, such as by crucifixion. However, some attempts were made to improve the lot of the slaves: they could not be treated as cruelly as they had been under the Republic, and the freeing of slaves was favored. The very poor could improve their position by enlisting in the army.

Internal peace stimulated commerce, especially in the eastern cities. Greeks, Syrians, and Egyptians brought their wares to western markets in Gaul and in Britain. They also went far beyond the borders of the Empire. There was an active trade with India and indirect trade with China, since Chinese merchants brought their silk to Indian markets. There were expeditions into central Africa in search of wild animals to stock the arenas. Germany furnished amber, furs, hides, and slaves.

This prosperity, however, rested on very narrow foundations. The chief occupation of most inhabitants of the Empire remained agriculture, which was not increasing in efficiency. Some areas were declining in population and wealth. Generally speaking, economic growth in the outlying provinces was matched by decline toward the center. For example, when olive trees were planted in Spain and vineyards in Gaul, there was no reason to export oil or wine from Italy or Greece. Agriculture supported the upper classes in luxury and the lower classes at a subsistence level, but it did not produce very much of a surplus for investment.

Industrial production was even less profitable. Famous pottery, for example, was made in Etruria and was widely exported, but this center declined as Roman techniques spread to the provinces. When southern Gaul could produce pottery indistinguishable from the best Italian ware, there was no reason to pay the cost of transport from Italy. Roman manufactures were not very complicated—textiles, metalwares, and pottery. It was easy for each region to become relatively self-sufficient in goods for ordinary consumption. Luxury goods

were another matter, but producers and traders who dealt in these goods formed a very small part of the population.

The Romans were backward in finding new sources of energy. They never learned how to harness horses so that they could pull heavy loads. As a result, land transport was limited to small, two-wheeled carts, usually drawn by oxen. Although water mills were used to grind grain in places like Rome, elsewhere grain was ground by hand. True, the flow of Mediterranean rivers is irregular, but not all Romans lived on the shores of the Mediterranean. The rainy regions of Gaul had few water mills in Roman times, whereas there were thousands of them in the Middle Ages. In a subsistence economy, with a surplus of manpower (at least until the third century), there was no need for labor-saving devices, and Roman conservatism made innovation even more difficult.

The abundance of labor discouraged Roman invention of labor-saving devices. The crane pictured here required the work of many slaves to operate the treadmill (detail from a tomb relief, first century A.D.).

A Roman girl with a writing tablet is depicted in this fresco from Pompeii (*ca.* 70 A.D.).

Art and Literature of the Silver Age

Roman architecture, like Roman law, expressed the Roman desire for order and stability. It reached its peak at the end of the first and the beginning of the second century, a little earlier than the time of the great jurists of the Empire. It was based on two techniques that had long interested the Romans: the use of concrete as a building material and the use of the round arch as the essential unit of construction. As the quality of concrete improved, architects were no longer confined to rectilinear structures of stone columns and beamed ceilings; they could curve their walls and roof their buildings with vaults and domes. The arch had long been used for bridging rivers and carrying aqueducts across deep valleys; when it came to be used in building, it made possible a whole new variety of forms. A series of arches formed a barrel vault over rooms or passageways; an arch at the end of a large enclosed space could be pierced to admit light; a rotated arch formed a dome. The Romans could construct large and magnificent buildings with these techniques—imperial palaces, baths, temples like the Pantheon, which was dedicated to all the gods (and is still in use as a Christian church). Unlike the Greeks, who were interested largely in exteriors (the sanctuary of a Greek temple was often a small, dark room), the Romans achieved their most impressive effects in the interiors of their buildings. The heart of the Pantheon is the great circular sanctuary covered by an enormous dome and lit by windows high in the walls and in the center of the dome itself. It gives a feeling of power, order, and authority; it expresses the majesty of the Roman state and the insignificance of the individual.

This new "imperial style" spread throughout the provinces, from Britain to Syria. Every city had its baths, its temples, its arenas (such as the Colosseum in Rome), which were based on a series of arches. This common style was a unifying force and was so perceived at the time. Both the central and local governments spent large sums of money on public buildings, and thought that it was money well spent. And the "imperial style" left an indelible impression on the European mind. Again and again in the centuries that followed the fall of Rome, architects tried to recreate the vast enclosed spaces of the Roman buildings.

Roman wall frescoes tended to be realistic, and at times merely decorative, as in many of the houses in Pompeii. Roman sculpture was also realistic—busts of emperors and famous men, scenes of battles and processions on triumphal arches. (Here the arch was a sign of power and glory; it had no other function.) But the sculptors at times went beyond realism and expressed the inner character of the people they were portraying.

The literature of the late first century and second century A.D.—sometimes called the Silver Age—gave the Latin style its highest polish. Pungent epigrams and pithy sayings mark the work of the leading writers. In poetry Juvenal satirized and Martial (*ca.* 40–102) exemplified the corruption of Roman society. Tacitus (55–118), the greatest of the Roman historians, was also a master of the epigrammatic style. He was strongly prejudiced in favor of the old aristocracy and against the emperors, and he attached too much importance to gossip about intrigues at court. But few historians have written so well or have been so skilled in characterizing their subjects. His description of one of the ephemeral emperors of 68–69 A.D. as a man who in everyone's opinion was qualified to rule if only he hadn't tried it would fit a good many subsequent politicians. We still see the emperors of the first century through Tacitus' eyes.

Other writers of the period have had somewhat less influence. Seneca (*ca.* 4 B.C.–65 A.D.), Nero's tutor and victim, was a Stoic philosopher; he wrote the only Roman tragedies that have survived—very noble and rather cold. Seneca's nephew and fellow victim Lucan (39–65 A.D.) composed the *Pharsalia*, an epic on republican resistance to Caesar, which has some memorable lines. Suetonius (*ca.* 75–110) in his *Lives of the Twelve Caesars* regaled his readers with amusing anecdotes about Julius Caesar and the emperors through Domitian. Josephus (*ca.* 37–100), a Jewish army officer during the rebellion of 66 A.D. who went over to the Roman side, tried to explain the peculiar history and nature of his people in his *Jewish Antiquities.*

Two promising starts were made at creating the literary form we know as the novel. One was the *Satyricon* by Petronius (d. 65 A.D.), an elegant courtier at the time of Nero. The other was the *Golden Ass* by Apuleius (*ca.* 125–180), who lived in North Africa. Both works bear an extraordinary resemblance to the first novels in modern European languages. Each describes the adventures of a hero whom misfortune dooms to wander among strange, often disreputable, people. But while Petronius and Apuleius had a few successors, the novel never became an established branch of ancient literature.

Pliny (61–113?) was a cultivated gentleman and an honest and conscientious public servant. His *Letters* (modeled somewhat on those of Cicero) show that he knew how to tell a story, as in his description of the eruption of Vesuvius that buried (and so preserved) the towns of Pompeii and Herculaneum. His correspondence as governor of Bithynia with the emperor Trajan shows the extent of imperial control and some lack of initiative on Pliny's part. Pliny asked Trajan's advice on every difficult question—for example, on how to deal with the Chris-

tians—and the emperor seems to have been wearied by all these questions.

The scholarly traditions of the Hellenistic era continued under Roman rule. Athens was still the center for the study of philosophy and Alexandria of science. During the second century the Greek physician Galen wrote his treatises on medicine and Ptolemy his studies in astronomy. Both were regarded as basic texts well into the sixteenth century. Unfortunately, both contained serious errors mixed with useful information. Thus Ptolemy's system made it possible to predict the position of the planets with accuracy, but it was based on a belief

Imperial Administration

The letters between the emperor Trajan and Pliny the Younger, his representative in one of the provinces of Asia Minor, suggest that imperial administrators, however severe, were generally more concerned with achieving justice than with following the letter of the law.

PLINY TO TRAJAN

. . . Having never been present at any of the trials of the Christians, I am unacquainted with the method and limits to be observed either in examining or punishing them. Whether any difference is to be made on account of age, or no distinction allowed between the youngest and the adult; whether repentance admits to a pardon, or if a man has been once a Christian it avails him nothing to recant. . . .

In the meanwhile, the method I have observed . . . is this: I interrogated them whether they were Christians; if they confessed it I repeated the question twice again, adding the threat of capital punishment; if they still persevered, I ordered them to be executed.

TRAJAN TO PLINY

The method you have pursued, my dear Pliny, in sifting the cases of those denounced to you as Christians is extremely proper. It is not possible to lay down any general rule which can be applied as the fixed standard in all cases of this nature. No search should be made for these people; when they are denounced and found guilty they must be punished; with the restriction, however, that if the party denies himself to be a Christian, and shall give proof that he is not (that is, by adoring our Gods) he shall be pardoned on the ground of repentance. . . .

From Pliny, *Letters*, trans. by William Melmoth, rev. by W. M. L. Hutchinson, The Loeb Classical Library (Cambridge, Mass.: Harvard University Press, 1953), pp. 401, 407.

The emperor Marcus Aurelius (160–180) entering Rome in triumph (detail from the column of Marcus Aurelius in Rome).

Philosophy and Theology

Hadrian's reign (117–138) marked a turning point in the history of literature, as in many other activities. For writers in Latin, especially, there was a tendency to imitate past masterpieces and to write in a deliberately archaic style. Poetry, history, and oratory never fully recovered from this blight. At the same time, a tremendous amount of intellectual energy was poured into philosophy and theology. The second century was a century of religious searching, and some of the searchers were able to put their beliefs into words that made a lasting impression on Mediterranean and European societies.

It was in the second century that the first Church Fathers, writing in Greek, increased the appeal of Christianity to the educated classes by deriving a theology and a philosophy from Biblical texts. And by the end of the century Neoplatonism was revived more as a religion than a philosophy. Starting with Plato's belief in eternal, incorporeal Ideas (see p. 48), the Neoplatonists developed a system in which God, who was pure Spirit, generated lesser spirits through whom the physical world was created and through whom the human spirit could reach out toward God. In its lower forms, Neoplatonism came close to magic (which was very popular at this time); in its higher forms, it had some influence on Christian philosophy.

During the second century Stoic philosophy was given its highest expression in the writings of the slave Epictetus (60–140) and the emperor Marcus Aurelius (121–180). The careers of these two men illustrate the basic Stoic doctrine: whether slave or emperor, a man must follow the eternal law. But Stoicism appealed mainly to the upper classes. The masses clung to their traditional and regional religions of infinite variety, in which the worship of Zeus or Jupiter jostled Celtic or Semitic cults.

Roman Law

The long period of political stability and the interest of the emperors in good administration made the second century

that the earth was the center of the solar system.

Plutarch (46?–120) wrote a series of short biographies in Greek—*Parallel Lives of Famous Greeks and Romans.* Plutarch had little primary source material on men such as Pericles or Pompey, but he used, and thus preserved, stories from earlier histories that have since been lost. His biographies are lively reading and are often our only source of information about a good number of episodes in ancient history.

the decisive period in the formulation of Roman law. The Romans, like many other peoples, had started with a few simple rules of law that had been expanded and amended until they covered most of the ordinary problems of Roman citizens. But the Romans also had allied and subject cities, each with its own law. Since inhabitants of different cities often had legal dealings with one another, Roman judges had to discover equitable principles that would be accepted by all reasonable men. Stoic philosophy, which influenced most Roman jurists, helped in this quest. It was easier to discover principles that were valid at all times and in all places if one was first convinced, as the Stoics were, that such principles existed. And as Roman jurists began to formulate these principles in the late Republic and early Empire it seemed reasonable to apply them to all kinds of cases. Rules derived from the common experience of all peoples must be closer to the eternal law of nature than the peculiar and imperfect laws of a single city. Thus the Romans themselves began to prefer the general principles of the law of nations to their own municipal law, which in many respects was out of date.

This process was speeded up in the second century as the emperors began to take increasing responsibility for the administration of justice. The concentration of judicial authority in the hands of the emperor and his appointees naturally led to a greater uniformity in interpreting the law. Able jurists began to produce textbooks that the courts accepted as authoritative. Some emperors, such as Hadrian, asked for official formulations of some parts of the law. This process of putting the law into enduring form continued for many generations; some of the most eminent Roman lawyers wrote in the first half of the third century.

The formulation of Roman law was one of the great achievements of western civilization. It was not perfect—no law is—but it was a great improvement over all earlier legal systems. It was consistent, logical, and complete, and it was based on principles of justice and equity. The Romans themselves described it as "the art of goodness and justice," or "a constant and perpetual will to give every man his due." Roman law did not quite reach this standard; for example, the courts treated the poor much more harshly than the rich, and there were practically no restrictions on the power of the state. These weaknesses were due in part to the fact that the Roman law expounded by the jurists was almost entirely civil law. Criminal law remained crude and harsh. But the majesty of the law impressed even the emperors. They admitted that they should follow the law rather than their own whims, even if they did not always live up to this principle. Roman law, comprehensive and flexible enough to be adapted to any situation, survived all the misfortunes of the Late Empire; Justinian's great compilation in the sixth century (see p. 164) was based largely on the work of Roman jurists of the second and third centuries. Through Justinian's compilation, Roman law has influenced the jurisprudence of every European country, and from Europe this influence spread throughout the world.

Cicero and Ulpian on Justice

Cicero was an able lawyer as well as one of the leading Roman politicians of the first century B.C.

Since reason is given to all men by nature, so right reason is given to them, therefore they are also given law, which is right reason in commanding and forbidding; if law, therefore justice . . . thus a sense of what is right is common to all men.

From Cicero, *De legibus*, I, 33.

Ulpian was one of the great Roman jurists of the early third century A.D. These passages from Ulpian were quoted by Justinian's lawyers at the beginning of the *Digest*, an authoritative treatise on Roman law (see p. 164).

Justice is a constant and perpetual will to give every man his due. The principles of law are these: to live virtuously, not to harm others, to give his due to everyone. Jurisprudence is the knowledge of divine and human things, the science of the just and the unjust.

Law is the art of goodness and justice. By virtue of this we [lawyers] may be called priests, for we cherish justice and we profess knowledge of goodness and equity, separating right from wrong and legal from the illegal. . . .

THE CRISIS OF THE THIRD CENTURY

During the second century the Roman Empire seemed to have found a permanent solution to many of the problems that had long plagued the ancient world. By uniting the peoples living around the Mediterranean into one state the Empire had given peace and security to a vast area. Improvements in imperial administration and the granting of Roman citizenship had almost ended the resentment that subject peoples had felt toward their conquerors. Millions of people shared a culture and had the same tastes; they offered a huge market to enterprising businessmen. The third century should have seen an ever more prosperous and powerful Empire. Instead, it witnessed a series of catastrophes from which the Empire never fully recovered.

Political Weakness

The obvious cause of the troubles of the third century was the old problem of the succession. When Marcus Aurelius died in 180 he was succeeded by his son, Commodus, thus breaking the long chain of adoptions that had produced the "good emperors." Commodus was rather like Nero, vain and capricious, although he fancied himself as a gladiator rather than as a poet. When Commodus was assassinated (192 A.D.) the Senate once more tried to name an emperor, but its nominee was swept away, and the army again divided, with each group of legions supporting a rival emperor. The shrewdest of the generals, Septimius Severus, came out on top; he and members of his family ruled from 193 to 235. Their reign resembles the history of Vespasian and his sons, and Septimius Severus, like Vespasian, undertook many major reforms in government; for example, in the system of collecting taxes. But when the last of the Severi was assassinated, the Senate and the army could not agree on a successor; there was no Nerva, no Trajan. Instead, the army made and unmade emperors with appalling rapidity. Between 235 and 285 there were twenty-six emperors and at least as many unsuccessful pretenders. Many of these em-perors were men of real ability, but few of them remained in power for as long as five years. Rulers whose reigns began with a civil war and ended with assassination could do little to solve the problems of the Empire.

Military Weakness

Joined to the problem of the succession were very serious military problems. Trouble had begun early in the reign of Marcus Aurelius, when the Parthians attacked in the East, while the Germans pushed across the Danube. It took years of fighting to drive back these enemies, and the peace won by Marcus Aurelius lasted less than a generation. The Germans, especially the Goths, renewed their attacks on the Rhine-Danube frontier. In the East the Sassanid ruler of Persia overthrew his overlord, the Parthian emperor, and established a revived and militant Persian Empire. The Parthians had been a rather stable force during their last century of power; the Sassanids were far more dangerous. They plundered the eastern provinces, while the Goths pushed into the Balkans and even built a pirate fleet that disrupted Mediterranean commerce.

The long wars put a severe strain on the finances of the Empire and on the morale of the army. The fighting was desperate, often hopeless. The soldiers, long-term professionals who were out of touch with the civilian population, tended to magnify the virtues of their own general if he were successful, and to despise and rebel against generals or emperors whom they did not know, especially if they seemed incompetent or cowardly. These soldiers led a hard life; they expected bonuses when they completed a campaign or helped their general to become emperor. If money was not available—and often it was not—there would be a mutiny. But not all third-century emperors were assassinated or executed by their soldiers: a good many fell in battle or died on campaigns. Even if the army had been completely united and loyal, there would have been many short reigns.

A considerable part of the army was permanently stationed in frontier prov-

Roman Military Weakness
Late second century

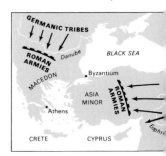

Third-century tomb relief showing an affluent banker and two struggling Roman laborers. The Roman economy was weakened by this gap between the wealthy few and the poor masses.

inces and was recruited from the poorest groups in the population. These characteristics were accentuated when Marcus Aurelius began the practice of inviting Germans into the Empire, giving them land, and enlisting them in the army to defend the frontier against their fellow tribesmen. Such soldiers probably understood little about the institutions or the values of the Empire. But they do not seem to have been any more irresponsible than the crack troops of the imperial bodyguard, who murdered more emperors than did the provincial soldiers.

More and more the quality of the army determined the character of the Empire. Beginning with Septimius Severus, the Roman state became increasingly militarized. Army officers took over civilian tasks, such as tax collection and some kinds of legal jurisdiction. Italy, which was more closely supervised by the emperor in the third century than it had been before the crisis, had a garrison of regular troops. This militarization was necessary in a period in which the Empire was on the defensive, and military men were not necessarily bad administrators. It was, perhaps, more unfortunate that civilians found it necessary to take on military posts. Two of the greatest Roman jurists, Papinian and Ulpian, became commanders of the palace guard, and—like most men who rose to that dangerous eminence—died in rebellions led by their own troops.

Economic Weakness

Economic as well as military problems forced the emperors to militarize the state. As we have seen, even in the second century there were weaknesses in the Roman economy. In a sense, the Empire had simply lived off the profits made by the conquests of the Republic. Areas annexed after the beginning of the Christian era probably never yielded a profit because of the cost of defense. In the third century this cost rose sharply. Army pay had to be increased, and the size of the armed forces increased. Frontier and civil wars devastated many areas and impoverished others. Mediterranean commerce had reached its peak before the appearance of Gothic pirates on the sea; most economic historians agree that it suffered greatly during the third century and never regained its earlier level. Great landowners, high public officials, and a few dealers in luxury goods still had comfortable incomes, but small farmers and middle-class businessmen found it hard to meet extraordinary expenses, and even harder to accumulate capital for new enterprises. Their situation was aggravated by spectacular waves of inflation. Emperors or candidates for the title paid their troops in debased currency. The great increase in the amount of money in circulation raised prices, and fears of further debasement encouraged wild spending that raised prices even more. No government seriously attacked this problem until the end of the third century, and inflation continued to be a problem well into the fourth century.

Weakness in Municipal Government

All these forces tended to weaken local governments. In some respects, the early Empire could have been described as a federation of cities, each responsible for the political and economic welfare of the surrounding territory. During the third century these cities lost population and income. General insecurity affected both local and long-distance trade. Cities far from the frontier had to be fortified; even Rome was protected by encircling walls in the reign of Aurelian (270–275). Municipal government began to break down, since the local aristocracies could no longer afford to hold office. They were responsible for the collection of taxes; when the central government increased its demands, more and more pressure was put on fewer and poorer city leaders. Coercion, harsh laws, and dictatorial bureaucrats left little initiative or independence to city officials. Exploitation had replaced the benevolent care of the "good emperors."

Weakness in Society

The Empire shrank in on itself during the third century. Physically, it lost some of its outposts, such as Dacia; spiritually, it lost some of its vigor and confidence. The ordinary man had long ceased to have political significance, but even well-to-do citizens now had little influence on policy, either in Rome or in provincial cities. Neither the upper nor the lower classes felt much responsibility for the general welfare: that was the business of the emperor and his officials. In a declining economy there was little that anyone could do to improve his lot or to increase productivity; great increases in wealth came largely from service to or favors from the emperor. Repeated outbreaks of plague, beginning in the reign of Marcus Aurelius and continuing into the second half of the third century, may not have greatly reduced the population, but they certainly weakened morale.

Unable to understand or to influence events in this world, a considerable part of the population looked to the next world for hope and consolation. The mystery religions continued to grow. The number of Christians increased enough to worry the emperors; the first large-scale persecutions took place in the third century. None of the eastern religions advocated open opposition to the state, although many of them considered that service to the state was unimportant at best, and an obstacle to salvation at worst. The Empire continued to exist, but it had only the passive loyalty of many of its citizens. And those who were galvanized into resistance were often interested in their own districts, not in the Empire as a whole. Thus Gaul had its own emperors for some fourteen years: they defended only Gaul, not the Danube line or the East.

The Establishment of Military Absolutism

Even its most disillusioned inhabitants could not conceive of a world in which the Empire did not exist. They proved wise in their own generation. After 270 the emperors were still short-lived, but they did their job better. Outside invaders were gradually beaten back, and internal rivals for power were eliminated. Aurelian restored the unity and security of the Roman world; he might have been the founder of the Late Empire if he had not been assassinated in 275. But less than ten years later, in 284, another victorious general, Diocletian, began the reforms that held the Roman world together for another century. Thus, in the end, the generals saved the Empire—by making themselves absolute sovereigns and by imposing a strict, almost military, discipline on their subjects.

The Empire in Decline

This passage, the musings of a trader as he revisits a provincial city in Switzerland in the third century, is from a modern historical novel.

It was a pleasant town. Demetrius paused to look at the Treasury inside its stone wall, and the villas scattered within shady gardens. Yet each year they were a little more neglected; the temple yard had not been properly swept, a latch was hanging loose from a shutter, the gutter was choked by a dirty mass of what had once been somebody's garland. He wondered why the place had changed so much during the six years since his first visit. Then there had been chariots on the streets, and many wagons, an indefinable sense of the city being alive. Was the Empire too big? Yet it had been larger, and nobody had counted the provinces. Were the young so ungrateful? It seemed to him that there was just the same proportion of honest men and rogues as in his childhood. There was constant talk about invasion; nobody now was certain as to who was emperor of what, but the Treasury still functioned reasonably well, most roads got mended, trade went on, yet he could not deny the change. Something had happened; it was as if a sentry had been asked to keep one watch too many, and his fibre had snapped.

From Bryher, *Roman Wall* (New York: Pantheon, 1954), p. 124.

Suggestions for Further Reading

Note: Asterisk denotes a book available in paperback edition.

General

The texts mentioned at the end of the preceding chapter will also serve as introductions to the era of the Roman Empire. A reader seeking a more detailed discussion of the imperial period should consult M. Cary, *History of Rome,* 2nd ed. (1954). Somewhat shorter is J. Wells and R. H. Barrow, *A Short History of the Roman Empire* (1931). Since this book ends with the death of Marcus Aurelius, one might read H. M. D. Parker, *History of the Roman World from A.D. 138 to 337* (1935), or M. Grant, *The Climax of Rome* (1968), for the later period. The classic nonpolitical history of the era is M. I. Rostovtzeff, *The Social and Economic History of the Roman Empire,** rev. ed. (1957). Two short studies of the Roman Empire, both extremely well written, are M. P. Charlesworth, *The Roman Empire** (1951), and H. Mattingly, *Roman Imperial Civilization** (1959). An excellent collection of original source material may be found in N. Lewis and M. Reinhold, eds., *Roman Civilization,* Vol. II (1955).

Government

There are two exhaustive studies of the creation of the Roman Empire: F. B. Marsh, *Founding of the Roman Empire* (1927), and M. Hammond, *The Augustan Principate in Theory and Practice* (1933). See also R. Syme, *The Roman Revolution** (1939), and H. T. Powell, *Rome in the Augustan Age* (1962). The best biography of Augustus is T. R. Holmes, *The Architect of the Roman Empire,* 2 vols. (1928–31), which contains a thorough description of the Empire in the Augustan era. There are many good studies of the individual reigns of the later emperors. V. Scramuzza, *Claudius* (1940), and R. Seager, *Tiberius* (1972), are the best biographies of these two emperors. B. W. Henderson's two lengthy studies, *Life and Principate of the Emperor Nero* (1903) and *Life and Principate of the Emperor Hadrian* (1932), are old but still unsurpassed on these two controversial emperors. For the second century, see M. Hammond, *The Antonine Monarchy* (1959); B. W. Henderson, *Five Roman Emperors* (1927); and A. Birley, *Marcus Aurelius* (1966) and *Septimius Severus* (1970).

The Provinces, Provincial Administration, and Roman Law

For the frontier provinces, see F. Millar, *The Roman Empire and Its Neighbors* (1968). On provincial administration, the most thorough treatment is found in W. T. Arnold, *The Roman System of Administration* (1914). A later, and excellent, survey is G. H. Stevenson, *Roman Provincial Administration* (1939). F. F. Abbott and A. C. Johnson, *Municipal Administration in the Roman Empire* (1926), and A. H. M. Jones, *The Cities of the Eastern Roman Provinces* (1937), both have valuable information on the municipal administrations that were the basis of the Roman provincial administration.

The standard introduction to Roman law is R. W. Buckland, *A Manual of Roman Law* (1925). See also J. A. Crook, *Law and Life of Rome* (1967). A good study of the army is G. Webster, *The Roman Imperial Army* (1969). See also R. MacMullen, *Soldier and Civilian in the Later Roman Empire* (1963).

Society, Literature, and Religion

A comprehensive and interesting description of the society of the early Roman Empire may be found in S. Dill, *Roman Society from Nero to Marcus Aurelius** (1925). Another useful study is J. P. V. Balsdon, *Life and Leisure in Ancient Rome* (1968). A recent and very good book is R. MacMullen, *Roman Social Relations* (1974). Two good introductions to the literature of the era are M. Grant, *Roman Literature** (1954), and M. Hadas, *A History of Latin Literature* (1952). See also the two books by J. W. Duff, *A Literary History of Rome to the Close of the Golden Age,* 3rd ed. (1963) and *A Literary History of Rome in the Silver Age,* 3rd ed. (1964). For the arts, M. Wheeler, *Roman Art and Architecture* (1964), is excellent. So is W. L. MacDonald, *The Architecture of the Roman Empire* (1965).

The most thorough treatment of Roman religion is F. Altheim, *A History of Roman Religion* (1938). The effect of the spread of Hellenistic religions is treated in T. R. Glover, *The Conflict of Religions in the Early Roman Empire** (1960), while the best study of eastern mystery religions in the era of the Roman Empire is F. Cumont, *Oriental Religions in Roman Paganism** (1956). A good recent book is J. Ferguson, *The Religions of the Roman Empire* (1968).

5 The Late Roman Empire
284–476

E ven after the crisis of the third century, the Roman Empire still had two great assets: a formidable army and a well-organized bureaucracy. These two institutions proved strong enough to restore order and unity to the Roman world for another century. The revival of the Roman state had a profound effect on the history of civilization, for it was during the fourth century that Christianity became the official religion of the reunited Roman Empire. Christianity thereby won for itself a firm foothold in the western world.

THE RESTORATION OF ORDER: THE REIGN OF DIOCLETIAN, 284–305

The work of restoration was begun by Aurelian (270–275), who checked the civil wars within the Empire and started the drive to push the Germans and the Persians back to their old frontiers. Aurelian's work was carried on by his successors, even though the army was still making and unmaking emperors at its usual rate. It was not until Diocletian became emperor in 284 that internal stability was fully restored.

Political and Military Reorganization

Diocletian's success was due first of all to his character. Shrewd, tough, and determined, he dominated rival generals as no emperor had been able to do for a century. He was able to keep most of the army on his side and to put down the few commanders who tried to rebel.

In an effort to improve the defense of the borders, Diocletian increased the size of the army and rebuilt the frontier fortifications. To prevent rebellions, he split large armies into smaller units and separated command from supply and payment of troops. To make his personal command over the troops effective, Diocletian abandoned Rome as his official residence and ruled from capitals set up in cities nearer the frontiers. From this time on the city of Rome declined steadily in size and importance.

Just as ingenious, but less successful, were Diocletian's attempts to solve the problem of succession. He realized that the troubled Empire needed more than one high-ranking commander, and he realized that some potential revolts could be warded off by sharing power with able generals. Almost as soon as he was established as emperor, Diocletian named a fellow officer, Maximian, as coemperor. Later, each of the two emperors selected an assistant with the title of Caesar. It was understood that when the emperors retired or died, the Caesars would succeed as emperors and designate new Caesars in turn.

The system of divided authority was also helpful in Diocletian's reorganization of the imperial government. For purposes of administration, each emperor became responsible for half of the Empire: the western half, under Maximian, encompassed Italy, North Africa, Spain, Gaul, Britain, and northern Illyria. The eastern half, under Diocletian himself, consisted essentially of the provinces that had formerly made up the Hellenistic world. Each half was divided into two prefectures, one of which was administered by the Caesar. Consequently, the administrative workload was shared among the emperors and their assistants, and decisions could be made rapidly and intelligently. Diocletian, however, did not give his corulers an entirely free hand; there was never any doubt that he was the senior emperor and that it was he who made the decisions that applied to the Empire as a whole.

In a further effort to increase stability and forestall rebellion, Diocletian emphasized the divine and autocratic nature of the emperor, completing a process that had been going on for generations. By the third century all pretense that the emperor was merely the First Citizen had long been abandoned. But Diocletian became *dominus et deus*, lord and god. Everything that pertained to his household or administration was sacred, and he adopted many of the symbols and ceremonies of the eastern monarchies. Anyone granted an audience with Diocletian was required first to prostrate

The declining creativity and technical skill of the artists of the late Roman Empire can be seen in the Arch of Constantine in Rome (312–315).

himself and then to kiss the hem of the emperor's garment.

Economic Reform

Diocletian tried to stabilize the economy as well as the politics of the Empire. He was almost the only Roman emperor who realized the need for economic planning. Some of his reforms were successful, such as the issue of a new and much improved currency. Some were less successful, such as his attempt to stem inflation by freezing prices and wages. Because he lacked the bureaucracy to enforce the new regulations, his edict soon became a dead letter.

The realization that something should be done about the Roman economy shows Diocletian's perceptiveness, but the means he used to carry out his ideas were harsh and often ineffective. Diocletian was a soldier who believed that a state could be run like an army. He was convinced that an unhealthy economy could be cured by edict; that men could

Diocletian and his coemperor Maximian, each embracing his appointed Caesar (St. Mark's Cathedral, Venice).

be commanded to produce goods at fixed prices just as troops could be commanded to charge an enemy. Since most of Diocletian's successors were also military men with similar approaches to political and economic problems, almost all private activities came under the control of the state during the fourth century.

RELIGION IN THE LATE ROMAN EMPIRE

One of the most baffling problems faced by Diocletian, and one he could not solve, was the growing popularity of the many eastern mystery religions that had first appeared in the Hellenistic era (see p. 53) and of Christianity. All these religions emphasized the afterlife and discouraged the vigorous participation in the affairs of this world on which Diocletian's program of restoration depended. The Christians were particularly offensive to Diocletian, for they continued to refuse to recognize the divine aspect of imperial authority.

The Eastern Mystery Religions

During the first three centuries of the Roman Empire many people in the Mediterranean world had been seeking a faith by which to live. The appeal of the older Greco-Roman gods had been declining since the Hellenistic era; the rituals were still performed, but few people really believed in Jupiter and his fellow gods. The attempt to institute a state religion based on the worship of "the spirit of Rome and the genius of the emperor" had failed when the population lost the intense patriotism that might have given the cult meaning. In the first and second centuries the upper classes had turned to Stoicism. But to the ordinary man Stoicism offered cold comfort. It was too intellectual and too impersonal; it valued eternal law, human brotherhood, and devotion to duty, but it elicited no strong emotional response. There was no individual salvation, no promise of a better life for the poor and the oppressed. Although the Stoics would have denied it, their main motivation was probably pride—pride in doing one's duty for duty's sake, pride in remaining unbroken by worldly problems. During the troubled third century even the upper classes began to abandon Stoicism, and by the end of the century a large part of the population had accepted one of the mystery cults.

Most of the mystery religions were based on very ancient beliefs, though they took on their characteristic forms during the Hellenistic era and the early years of the Roman Empire. Their gods were not the carefree deities of the Greek and Roman pantheons. Instead, they were semidivine heroes who had suffered as men suffer in the age-long struggle against darkness and evil. Most of them

had been killed in the conflict but had returned to life, thus prefiguring victory over death and eternal life for the souls of their followers.

The worship of the Egyptian Isis was widespread throughout the Empire, but even more widespread was Mithraism, a popular form of the Zoroastrian religion of Persia. Mithra was a warrior-god who had been killed by the god of darkness but who rose again and was thus able to bestow immortality on converts who would join him in the eternal war against evil. Mithraism was popular among soldiers and became almost the official religion of the Roman armies. It remained a competitor of Christianity all through the fourth century, and its dualistic theology (a god of good fighting a god of evil) was picked up again by the Manichean heresy that was to trouble medieval Christendom.

A person could join one of these mystic brotherhoods by participating in rituals that cleansed him of the sins of

THE ADMINISTRATIVE DIVISIONS OF DIOCLETIAN   Third and fourth centuries

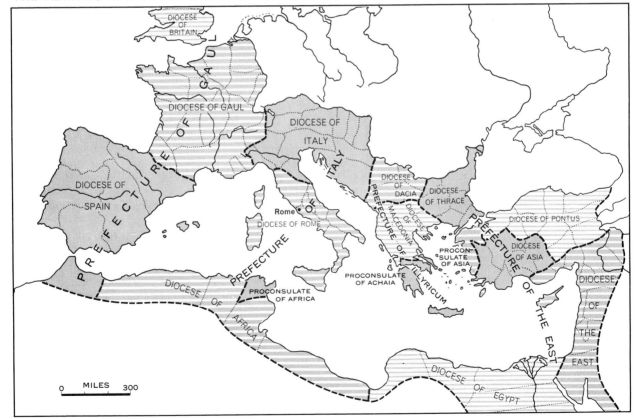

The young boy in this painting (*ca.* 300–350) is an acolyte of the Isis cult. The cup and garland are emblems of his religious belief; the side hairlock was long associated with the child-god Horus.

the physical world and ensured that his unstained soul would become a part of the eternal world of the spirit. An Isis-worshiper was purged of his sins and prepared for his reception by the pure and loving mother-goddess by being immersed in water that symbolized the sacred Nile. An initiate into the religion of Mithra took part in the ritual sacrifice of a bull, and worked upward to deeper knowledge and greater purity by passing through seven grades of instruction.

For many people these religions satisfied a genuine need. The individual felt helpless and insecure in a society over which he had no control, in which his economic and political welfare was determined by remote and unapproachable authorities. He often felt a deep sense of sin, not so much because of personal misconduct as because he was convinced that the misery of the human condition could be explained only by a fundamental blemish on the soul of each man. The eastern religions assured men of their importance as individuals and promised them forgiveness of sin and a happy future life. It is not surprising that these religions won adherents in every part of the Roman world.

The Triumph of Christianity

Another religion that gained large numbers of adherents in the third century was Christianity. Although the Christian refusal to worship "the spirit of Rome and the genius of the emperor" was technically the equivalent of treason, the imperial government paid only intermittent attention to the sect in the first and second centuries. Most Christians belonged to the lower classes during this period, and the government took note of them only when there was political or social unrest (as in Rome under Nero or in Bithynia under Trajan). Even then, it persecuted Christians largely for political reasons; it made no attempt to wipe out the religion.

As a result the early Church had been able to develop its theology and to create a remarkable administrative system, modeled more or less on the administrative system of the Empire. It was important for the scattered members of the new faith to keep in touch with one another and to preserve uniformity of doctrine. The most respected members of each congregation became priests ("elders"), and in each city one priest was designated as bishop ("overseer"). The bishop was responsible for supervising all the Christian congregations in his city and in the surrounding villages. By the end of the second century some bishops (precursors of the later archbishops) were recognized as leaders in their provinces. The systematic organization of the early Church was an innovation in the ancient world and helped establish the supremacy of Christianity over the many other religions of the Empire. No similar system existed for the pagan or mystery cults; the priests of Jupiter in one city, for example, were entirely independent of those in other cities.

During the third century Christianity began to attract members from all classes. Earlier, the educated classes of the Empire, broadminded by tradition, had been offended by the exclusiveness of the Christians, by their unwillingness to admit that there might be truth in other religions. Many people preferred to hedge their bets, so that devotees of the Great Mother (the goddess Cybele) might also join the Isis cult just to play safe. But in the troubled third century—when economic decline, civil war, barbarian raids, and plague affected nearly every family and signaled confusion and decay in almost every aspect of civilized life—the very firmness of Christian beliefs began to make them attractive. Similarly, the unswerving morality of the Christians and their belief in the fatherly love of God offered security in a time of confusion. Finally, the extreme otherworldliness of the Christians, which had seemed mere foolishness to all but the slaves and the poor in the affluent second century, fitted well with the intense desire in the chaotic third century for future happiness.

Christianity grew rapidly enough during the third century to alarm some of the emperors. They were annoyed by Christian lack of patriotism; these zealots would neither sacrifice to the emperor nor serve the state. This disregard of religion (it was even called "atheism") was sure to rouse the anger of the gods. There were some severe and prolonged periods of persecution during the century. The worst and longest began under Diocletian, who hated any kind of disobedience, and reached a peak with Galerius. But this persecution does not seem to have reduced the number of Christians greatly, even in the East, where it was most intense.

THE REIGN OF CONSTANTINE, 307–337

Diocletian, an innovator to the end, abdicated in 305 and became one of the few Roman emperors to die peacefully. But his elaborate provisions for an orderly succession were soon disregarded, and a series of civil wars put five different generals in control of various parts of the Empire. One of these generals was Constantine, who completely reversed Diocletian's policy of persecuting Christians.

The Conversion of Constantine

Scholars have long argued about the reasons for and the sincerity of Constantine's conversion to Christianity. His mother is said to have been a Christian, and certainly he had some idea of the doctrines and the power of the religion before he became emperor. On the other hand, he had held command in Gaul, where Christians were neither numerous nor influential. Constantine cannot have believed that there were enough politically active Christians in his part of the Empire to make any difference in the struggle for power with rival generals. When he invoked the help of the Christian God, he must have been motivated by religious conviction, not by political expediency. Perhaps he thought that he was only tapping a new source of semimagical power, but he surely did not think that he was gaining thousands of Christian recruits for his army. The decisive moment in Constantine's religious life came when he was about to meet his strongest opponent for the imperial title at the battle of the Milvian Bridge (near Rome) in 312. Just before the battle Constantine is said to have had a vision of a

cross in the sky surrounded by the words *in hoc signo vinces* ("in this sign shalt thou conquer"). Convinced that the Christian God had helped him to victory, he ordered his troops to carry Christian insignia from that time on. Soon, in 313, Constantine (and the remaining coemperor who still ruled with him) issued the Edict of Toleration ending the persecution of Christians.

Constantine himself received baptism only on his deathbed, a not uncommon precaution at that time. But, though not a full member, he supported the Church throughout his reign, thus enabling it to become the dominant religion of the Empire during the fourth century. And he apparently hoped that the Empire would be strengthened by strengthening the position of Christianity. Certainly the

Colossal head of Constantine, from his basilica in Rome (*ca.* 320).

Constantine's Religious Beliefs

The official policy of the Empire after 312 was toleration, as shown in a letter sent in the name of both Constantine and his coemperor to the governor of Bithynia in 313.

. . . we resolved to make such decrees as should secure respect and reverence for the Deity; namely, to grant both to the Christians and to all the free choice of following whatever form of worship they pleased, to the intent that all the divine and heavenly powers that be might be favorable to us and all those living under our authority.

◊   ◊   ◊

But Constantine showed stronger personal convictions in a letter written only a year later to the governor of Africa, dealing with the problem of schism in that province.

Since I am assured that you are also a worshipper of the supreme God, I confess to your Excellency that I consider it absolutely wrong that we should pass over in insincerity quarrels and altercations of this kind, whereby perhaps the supreme divinity may be moved not only against the human race, but even against me myself, to whose care He has entrusted rule over all earthly affairs. . . . For then, and only then, shall I be able truly and most fully to feel secure . . . when I shall see all men, in the proper cult of the Catholic religion, venerate the most holy God with hearts joined together like brothers in their worship.

From *Great Problems in European Civilization,* ed. by K. M. Setton and H. R. Winkler (Englewood Cliffs, N.J.: Prentice-Hall, 1954), pp. 75, 79.

Empire was stronger in the fourth century than it had been during much of the third century, but quarrels among theologians proved almost as dangerous as quarrels among generals.

In the face of persecution, the Christians had managed to suppress their differences. After the Edict of Toleration, however, Christian leaders fell into such bitter doctrinal disputes that the unity of the Church was threatened. But Constantine wanted Christianity to promote unity, not destroy it. And since, like any good Roman, he was sure that there must be some single legal formula that would be acceptable to all reasonable men, he often used the force of his imperial office to bring the Church to agreement.

One of the earliest controversies concerned the doctrine of the Trinity. A priest named Arius taught that the Son

and the Holy Spirit had been created by, and were therefore subordinate to, God the Father. Other theologians attacked his teachings, insisting that the three aspects of God must be equal. The quarrels that sprang up were so bitter that Constantine called a council of bishops at Nicaea (in Asia Minor) in 325 to settle the matter. After some argument, the Council of Nicaea produced a confession of faith that completely rejected the teachings of Arius. The Arians were not cowed by this action and remained a powerful force in the Empire (and even more among the Germans) for many generations. And new doctrinal disputes continued to emerge so that councils of bishops had to meet at frequent intervals. The decisions of a majority of a general council were held to be binding on the whole Church. Those who would not accept them were excommunicated—that is, cast out from the Church and the communion of the faithful.

The Extension of Military Absolutism

After his victory at the Milvian Bridge in 312, Constantine established his rule over the western half of the Roman Empire. In 324 he defeated his coemperor and thus gained full control over the entire Empire. Constantine, like Diocletian, was a tough-minded soldier who maintained the order and stability of the Empire with military discipline. Experience, however, had taught him the dangers of sharing the imperial power with other generals. So, although Constantine retained most of Diocletian's reforms, he did not revive the practice of dividing his authority with coemperors.

Realizing, as had many earlier emperors, that the economic and military strength of the ancient world lay in the East—the former Hellenistic world—Constantine sought a new capital that would be easy to defend, that would have access by sea to the commercial routes of the Aegean and the Mediterranean, and that would be near enough to the frontiers for the emperor never to be too far from either his administration or his armies. He chose the site of the ancient Greek city of Byzantium on the

Bosporus. He named his capital New Rome, but after his death it became known as Constantinople (and after its occupation by the Turks in 1453, as Istanbul).

Constantine's efforts to make his new city prosper were successful. He had picked an excellent location, he coerced wealthy men to build there, and he plundered much of the Empire to embellish his new capital. Constantinople soon became one of the leading commercial and cultural centers of the Greco-Roman world. But this move to the East was one more step in downgrading the importance of the western provinces (including Italy) and in leading to a separation between the two sections of the Empire.

THE EMPIRE IN THE FOURTH CENTURY

So towering was Constantine's prestige that for several decades after his death members of his family retained the imperial throne. Except for the brief reign of Julian (361–363), all of Constantine's descendants were Christians. Therefore Christianity came to be more and more the official religion of the Empire. But imperial protection meant imperial intervention in the affairs of the Church. Thus, caesaropapism—the control of the Church by the emperor rather than by the bishops—developed. It was to cause many conflicts between Church and state in later periods. Though Constantine's successors quarreled bitterly among themselves over both politics and religion, most of them were men of military ability, a quality that was badly needed in the fourth century. They succeeded in holding the Empire together and protecting its frontiers.

The Barbarian Threat

Trouble was brewing almost everywhere along the eastern and northern frontiers. The Persians, the oldest and most dangerous of the enemies of the Empire, once more moved to attack the eastern provinces, and the best Roman troops had to be used to repel them. At the same time the Germanic tribes were in turmoil along the Rhine and the Danube. Large groups were migrating in search of better lands or more secure homes, and each migration touched off a series of tribal wars. The victors often raided Roman territory; the vanquished begged permission to settle in Roman frontier zones (as they had done since the time of Marcus Aurelius). Moreover, individual tribes banded together in more or less permanent confederations with such huge reserves of manpower that they could eventually challenge the Roman defenses.

Meanwhile, the Roman army was running short of manpower just when it needed to expand. There was never a time when the inhabitants of the Empire did not outnumber all their barbarian enemies put together. But more and more Roman citizens were being excluded from military service. Senators were barred from army posts because they were needed for civilian jobs; members of the urban aristocracies, because they were needed for local administration. Landlords (and tax collectors) felt that peasants could not be spared from the land, and the city proletariat was useless for military purposes. The frontier provinces still supplied troops, but, since those troops were used almost entirely as border guards, they could not be used as mobile armies to ward off sudden attacks.

To overcome this lack of officers and men, the Empire drew recruits from among the barbarians themselves. The barbarian soldiers acted as the shock

Roman soldier and barbarian warrior (detail from a third-century Roman sarcophagus).

Head of a barbarian found in Gaul, probably representing one of the Helvetian (Swiss) peoples.

Silver-gilt spear mount made for a barbarian warrior, found in a tomb in northern France (*ca.* fourth century).

troops of the Empire, and for the first time in the long history of Rome armies composed of foreigners were valued more highly than armies composed of Roman citizens. But except for a better-organized top command, these barbarian troops were very like the armies of the enemies they were opposing. Consequently, in a battle between armies of equal size it was by no means certain that the barbarized Roman army would prevail. The process that had created this dangerous situation was irreversible, for by the fourth century it was too late to rebuild the army with Roman citizens. There were no mass levies of inhabitants of the Empire and no spontaneous organizations for defense. If barbarian armies could not defend the Empire, then there was no one left to defend it.

Economic and Social Problems

The growing apathy of the people of the Empire was even more dangerous than the barbarizing of the army. Even the upper classes seem to have assumed that the Empire would survive without any great effort on their part. Citizens obeyed orders and paid taxes when they could not evade them, but they showed no readiness to sacrifice life or property to save the state.

As if to reinforce this political apathy, the Roman economy continued to slump. Some parts of the Empire were reasonably prosperous in the fourth century, but in many provinces the depression that had begun in the third century persisted without relief. Population declined in many regions. The towns became less and less able to discharge their economic functions. Large amounts of arable land were permitted to slip out of cultivation, and many peasants tried to avoid the crushing burden of taxation by yielding their farms to great landowners, who could simply defy the tax collector. The peasants saved their money but lost their freedom; most of them became serfs.

Least affected by the depression were the great landlords, especially those of the western provinces. These men were able to ignore the world around them by operating their estates as independent social and economic units. By using the simple home manufactures of their peasants to supply the needs of the estate, they reduced contacts between town and countryside. This was especially disruptive in the West, where the cities were not very strong to begin with. As the cities declined, the landlords took over much of the responsibility for local government, a practice that weakened the authority of imperial officials and eventually led to the autonomous lordships of the early Middle Ages.

Most citizens had long ago given up hope of controlling their political future. During the fourth century they began to give up hope for their economic future as well. They saw no prospect of rising in the world, nor even any assurance that they would be able to hold on to what little they had. This feeling of discouragement was especially strong in the West, and it is not surprising that in that region devotion to the Roman state and to the principles of the Greco-Roman civilization tended to decline.

A State-Controlled Economy

From the time of Diocletian the emperors had been aware of these problems, but they could not trace back through five centuries of history to find the roots of the people's indifference. They could deal only with the current symptoms. And since many of them were military men and all of them were occupied with military affairs, they tried to solve their problems by running the Empire like an army. If the people failed to do their duty voluntarily, they would have to do it under compulsion. If self-interested economic motivations were no longer enough to get essential work done, then it must be done under state control.

The emperors' treatment of municipal governments offers a good example of their attitude. The chief function of municipal government was to collect taxes for the imperial government. These taxes were a heavy burden on the poor and the middle class, especially in a period of declining economy. The city officials who were responsible for collecting the taxes in their communities were in a precarious position; if some inhabitants failed to pay, then the officials had to dig into their own pockets to make up the deficit. Predictably, well-to-do town dwellers tried to avoid municipal office. But the central government, instead of easing their burden, simply ruled that all municipal officials had to stay in office and that their sons had to succeed them when they died. Thus the government attempted to keep the municipalities operating through sheer compulsion. This policy alienated the landholding class of officials, who had formerly been generous contributors to civic projects. It did nothing to halt the decline of commerce. Many western cities were dwindling away by the end of the fourth century.

At the same time the government passed laws to bind the peasants to the soil. Rural slaves had not been a major part of the labor force for centuries, and transplanted barbarians filled the gap only partially and only in the northern frontier zones. Elsewhere the supply of agricultural labor was declining, and land was passing out of cultivation. To avoid the consequent loss of tax revenues, the central government forbade tenant farmers to leave the estates they were working on. In the end, the tenant farmer became something more than a slave but something less than a freeman; to use the later medieval expression, he became a serf. Though not bound to personal service, he was tied to a particular piece of land, and he and his heirs were bound to cultivate that land forever.

Some groups of artisans suffered a similar fate. Bakers in Rome and Constantinople, for instance, were bound to remain in their trade and to furnish a son to succeed them. In fact, by the middle of the fourth century a large part of the population of the Empire was probably

THE LATE ROMAN EMPIRE   *ca.* 395 A.D.

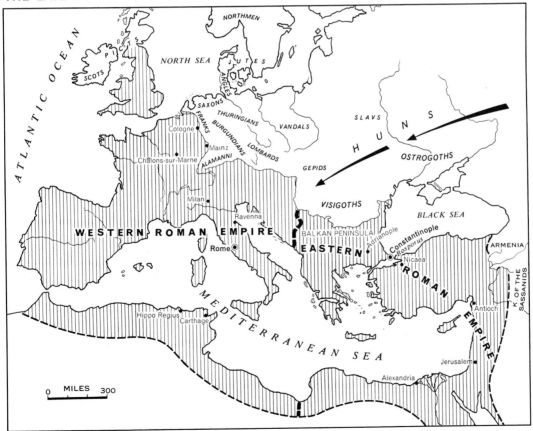

frozen in permanent hereditary occupations. The laws could be evaded, but economic decline reduced opportunities and so reinforced the effects of legislation.

The Church

We are apt to exaggerate the number of Christians in the Empire during the fourth century. There were wide areas, especially in the West, where Christianity had scarcely penetrated. Christianity was at first a city religion; it had yet to develop the parish organization that was later to make it successful in rural areas. The cities of the predominantly rural West were smaller, fewer, and weaker than those of the East. Thus hundreds of thousands of country dwellers had little contact with the new religion. As late as the early sixth century, missionaries could still make numerous converts in Italy and southern Gaul.

At the same time, to the detriment of both literature and politics, theological controversies absorbed the energies of the best thinkers and the ablest writers of the more urban and urbane East. Good Christians might, and did, say that this was only right, that it was better to study the things of God than the problems of the world, but concentration on theological disputes stirred up passions that injured both the Church and the Empire. This was especially true in the East, where there was strong rivalry among the religious leaders of Constantinople, Antioch, and Alexandria. The people of these cities supported their own clergy and argued vehemently over disputed doctrines. The Syrians and the Egyptians voiced their resentment against centuries of Greek domination by adopting theologies that infuriated the Greeks. Religious separatism and local patriotism went hand in hand, and during the next two centuries the loyalty of the eastern provinces to Constantinople diminished steadily.

The West, with the exception of North Africa, was less shaken by religious controversy. Beginning with Tertullian in the second century, Latin theologians had shown a tendency to make clear and simple definitions rather than

Symbol of Christianity, incorporating the Greek letters chi and rho (the monogram for Christ that forms the shape of the cross) and alpha and omega (meaning beginning and end).

to speculate on fine points of doctrine. Fortunately, the definitions they made proved acceptable to the Church councils. The bishop of Rome, now regularly called the pope, was the heir to this Latin tradition and was therefore always on the side of orthodoxy. Since no other bishop in the West had anything like the pope's authority, his interpretation of doctrine was usually accepted in the Latin-speaking provinces. The eastern provinces, attached to their own definitions of orthodox belief, were much less ready to accept papal pronouncements. Thus in religious matters, as in many others, East and West were drifting apart.

THE END OF THE EMPIRE IN THE WEST

In the last quarter of the fourth century the threat to the Rhine and Danube frontiers of the Empire reached a new intensity. To the familiar German raids was added a fresh menace: the advance of the Huns from Central Asia.

The Huns

The Huns were typical of the Asian nomads who for centuries threatened the civilized peoples of the Eurasian continent. These nomads lived in a harsh land of scant rainfall and great extremes of temperature. Often the distance between their summer and winter pastures was over a thousand miles, so they had to become expert horsemen. Living in the saddle, they invented most of the equipment that made cavalry an effective fighting force. For example, they used horseshoes and stirrups long before these devices were known in the West. If one imagines riding a horse into battle without stirrups, one can see why the Asian nomads long had supremacy in cavalry fighting. But even after their equipment was adopted by other peoples, the nomads were still almost unbeatable as horse soldiers; they were unafraid of death and as pitiless as the land in which they lived.

Fortunately for their neighbors, the nomads usually lived in small bands of no great striking force. But every now and then bands threatened by a common danger would join together, or a leader of genius would manage to unite several groups. Once this process started, it was almost irreversible. The ruler of some thousands of nomads could force all the smaller groups in an area of thousands of square miles either to join him or perish. Thus were built up the great human avalanches that thundered down from the high plateaus of Central Asia onto the coasts of China, Europe, and India.

The Huns who attacked Europe were a part of one of these avalanches. As they moved west across the steppes their army snowballed until at last they broke out onto the Russian plain in the second half of the fourth century. No Germanic people could withstand them. Some of the resident population joined the Huns as satellite troops; others fled in terror to the shelter of the Empire.

The Goths

The first Germanic people to be struck by the Huns were the Goths, who had come from the north and had settled around the Black Sea. Since they were on reasonably good terms with the Romans, they turned to Rome for aid. The East Goths (Ostrogoths) were overrun by the Huns, but the West Goths (Visigoths) managed to cross the Danube and take refuge in the Empire. Unfortunately, some imperial officials regarded the West Goths as a new source of forced labor, and mistreatment soon led to revolt. After routing a hastily gathered Roman army in the battle of Adrianople (378), the Goths occupied a large part of the Balkan Peninsula.

This was not the first time that Germans had defeated a Roman army and occupied Roman territory. The time-

THE GERMANIC MIGRATIONS   Fourth to sixth centuries

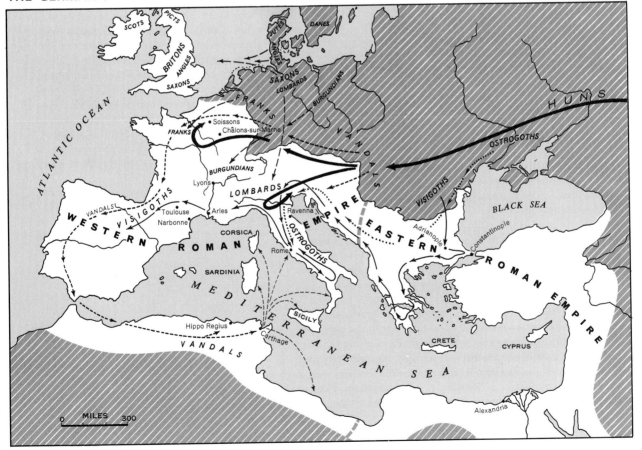

Silver commemorative plate depicting Theodosius and his two sons (*ca.* 390).

A Christian Priest on Social Conditions in the Late Empire

Salvian was a priest who lived in southern Gaul in the fifth century A.D. The passage is not entirely sincere—Salvian really disliked the barbarians—but the fact that he thought that praise of the barbarians would impress his readers shows that there was little loyalty to the Empire in his region.

But as for the way of life among the Goths and the Vandals, how can we consider ourselves superior to them, or even worthy of comparison? To speak first of affection and charity . . . almost all barbarians, at least those who belong to one tribe . . . love one another, while almost all the Romans are at strife with one another. What citizen does not envy his fellows? Who shows complete charity to his neighbors? . . . Worse, the many are persecuted by the few, who use public taxes for their own individual gain. . . . Where can one find cities or even villages in which there are not as many tyrants as officials? . . .

The poor are robbed, widows groan, orphans are oppressed until many, even persons of good birth and education, flee to the enemy to escape . . . persecution. They seek Roman humanity among the barbarians since they cannot endure the barbarian inhumanity they find among the Romans. . . . They do not regret their exile, for they would rather live as free men, though seeming to be in captivity, than as captives in seeming liberty. Hence the name of Roman citizen, once highly valued and dearly bought, is now voluntarily repudiated and shunned.

From Salvian, *On the Government of God,* trans. by Eva M. Sanford (New York: Columbia University Press, 1930), pp. 138–42.

honored tactic in such a case was to settle the invaders in a frontier province, and to integrate them gradually into Roman society. This was the policy adopted by the emperor Theodosius (378–395), and it very nearly succeeded. He concentrated the Goths in a small strip of land south of the Danube in the Balkans, where they lived as Roman allies under their own kings. Their most promising young men were sent to Constantinople for education; some of them received posts in the army. For the remainder of Theodosius' reign the Goths remained quiet.

Theodosius tried to preserve the religious as well as the political unity of the Roman state, but here again he ran into the problem of the barbarians. After a half-century of conflict, Arius and his followers had been crushed by the authorities of the Empire, but before their final defeat Arian bishops had converted some of the Goths. One of these Goths, Ulfila, translated the Scriptures into Gothic and so gave the Arians an advantage in missionary work among the Germans. By the time of Theodosius most of the Goths, and an increasingly large number of other Germans, had accepted the Arian form of Christianity. Theodosius tried to suppress Arianism among his own subjects, but he could not interfere with the religious beliefs of his allies. Most German settlers and most German soldiers were Arians. Their heretical belief offended the Romans and was one of the factors that delayed the merging of the two peoples.

Although Theodosius was a defender of the orthodox faith, he was the first European ruler to do public penance for offending the Church. He had ordered a massacre of the people of Thessalonica because they had killed one of his officers. St. Ambrose, bishop of Milan, refused to give Theodosius communion until he had done penance, and, in spite of threats, forced the emperor to admit his fault. Theodosius' submission demonstrated the growing power of the Church. Medieval popes were to use the event as a precedent in their struggles with lay rulers.

Theodosius was the last emperor to control the whole Roman world and the last to keep the frontiers reasonably intact. He achieved this success, however, only by strengthening the barbarian element in the army and in the border regions. Theodosius himself was strong enough to control his generals, but his weak successors were puppets of the army commanders, most of whom were of Germanic origin.

The Division of the Empire

When Theodosius died in 395, he was succeeded by his two sons, Arcadius in the East and Honorius in the West. This division of the Empire was not meant to be permanent; during the last century there had usually been more than one emperor. While each ruler had been primarily responsible for one part of the Empire, the coemperors had always cooperated to some extent and in emergencies had acted in each other's territories. But the division between Arcadius and Honorius proved to be rather different. The army commanders who held real power under the two young emperors were suspicious of each other and would not cooperate. The Germans (both those in the army and those pushing across the frontiers) grew so strong in the West that the eastern ruler could not step in and reunite the two halves of the Empire when his western colleague died.

Theoretically, the Empire remained one state, but in fact it was permanently divided after 395, and each half had a different fate. The West fell completely under the power of the Germans and for centuries remained backward in political organization and economic activity. In the East the Empire continued, and, though it gradually became quite un-Roman, it was far more stable and prosperous than the barbarian kingdoms of the West.

The Sack of Rome

When Theodosius died, the Visigoths left their Balkan reservation and began raiding again. They might have been crushed if the western and eastern army commanders had cooperated, but each was afraid the other might gain an advantage. In fact, it seems likely that the eastern government persuaded the Goths to move west in order to spare the Balkans from further looting. When the Visigoths stormed down into the Italian peninsula, the emperor Honorius shut himself up in the fortified city of Ravenna and made no move to stop them. The Goths occupied Rome in 410—a catastrophe that sent a last feeble impulse of patriotism through the Empire.

True, Rome had not been the real capital for many years, but it was still the symbol of the Empire. No enemy had touched it for almost eight centuries, and its fall shocked men who otherwise cared little about imperial affairs. Adherents of pagan religions said bitterly that this disaster occurred only after the Empire had forsaken its old, protecting deities for the powerless Christian God. St. Augustine, the ablest Christian writer of the period, was spurred into writing his most famous book, *The City of God* (see p. 119), in order to refute this argument. He insisted that the eternal City of God inhabited by the saints was far more important than any earthly city of sinners. Yet even St. Augustine admitted that the Romans had created the best secular government that had ever existed, and less devout Christians must surely have been worried by signs that this government was failing.

The Visigoths, perhaps seeking more fertile land, abandoned Italy and moved to southwestern Gaul. Here they settled permanently, gradually occupying Spain as well. They remained allies of the Empire and helped the Romans repel a dangerous Hun invasion in 451. But as the western Empire weakened, the Goths grew more independent; by 500 they were entirely free from imperial control. The Visigothic king ruled his own realm, and the authority of Rome was only a distant memory.

Other Germanic Migrations

Shortly after the Visigoths started their long march to the west, other Germanic groups pushed across the frontiers. The Romans had neither the troops nor the will to stop the invaders, but they were able, in most cases, to reach an accommodation with them. They granted the Germans the status of allies and al-

A Vandal general in the service of Rome. Although he is a barbarian, he wears Roman clothing (panel of an ivory diptych, *ca.* 400).

Alaric, "King of the Goths," depicted in a seal contemporary with the sack of Rome in 410.

lowed them to set up kingdoms in Roman territory. By thus regularizing the occupation, the Romans avoided much violence. The Germans, who were not very numerous, had no desire to destroy the Romans and their cities; all they wanted was a reasonable share of the land. The Romans, with a declining population, had land to spare; so long as they could keep some of their property, they could tolerate the rule of barbarian kings. Thus in most of the western Empire there was no catastrophic loss of life or property as the Germans moved in. The one great exception was Britain, where the imperial government had collapsed so completely that no peaceful settlement could be worked out with the invading Anglo-Saxons.

One of the longest, and in the end the most unsuccessful, of the Germanic migrations was that of the Vandals. This coalition of peoples moved from north Germany through Gaul into Spain. Attacked by the Visigoths, they abandoned Spain and finally settled in North Africa. Here they built a fleet with which they dominated the western Mediterranean for half a century. They even managed to seize Rome briefly in 455; but although they plundered the city, they were not guilty of the kind of wanton destruction that has become associated with their name. The Vandals did not try to hold Italy, and even in North Africa they grew so weak that they were easily crushed by the Eastern Roman Empire in the sixth century.

More typical of the German migrants were the Franks and the Burgundians. They made a shorter journey and established successful and permanent settlements. Until the death of Theodosius both peoples had been confined to border territories along the Rhine and in northeastern Gaul. The Franks then began to move south and west, while the Burgundians settled in the Rhône valley. Neither people was ever again brought under control of the imperial government.

At about the same time the Angles and the Saxons began to raid Britain from their homes along the North Sea. Rome had withdrawn its army and its officials from Britain, and the invaders,

crossing the sea in small flotillas, were unable to concentrate their forces. With no unified command on either side, negotiations were almost impossible. Small groups of native Britons fought small groups of Anglo-Saxons in a bloody war that lasted for over a century. In the process Roman civilization was wiped out. Cities and villas were destroyed, and the Britons, driven back into Wales or Cornwall, gave up the use of Latin and reverted to their native Celtic. The larger part of Britain became England, a land of Germanic speech and customs.

By the middle of the fifth century all that was left of the Empire in the West was Italy and a fragment of Gaul. Even this remnant was threatened by a new advance of the Huns under their famous king Attila, the "Scourge of God." A first attack on Gaul was defeated in 451 by Aëtius, the "last general of the Empire," with the help of Visigothic and Frankish allies. Attila invaded Italy the next year, but he found the peninsula too barren to support his army. He was persuaded to withdraw by an embassy led by Pope Leo I, an episode that gave great prestige to the papacy. With Attila's death in 453 his empire disintegrated, and the Huns no longer menaced the West.

Aëtius' victory gained him only the jealous suspicion, not the thanks, of the emperor. The general was put to death; his followers retaliated by assassinating the emperor. For a while German army commanders governed Italy behind a façade of puppet emperors. At last, in 476, Odovacar, the leader of a band of German mercenaries, tired of the pretense. He deposed the last emperor and became king of Italy. All Roman territories west of the Adriatic were now under barbarian rulers.

Zeno, the emperor in Constantinople, promptly regularized the situation by naming Odovacar his representative in Italy. Thus the fiction of imperial unity was preserved, though Zeno had no real authority in the West. A decade later the imperial government tried to turn fiction into fact by sending a new group of Germans to attack Odovacar. These Germans were the Ostrogoths, who had finally escaped Hunnish domination after the death of Attila. Like the Visigoths, they had settled in the Balkans; and like the Visigoths, they were so unruly that the emperor was delighted to speed their way to Italy. After several years of fighting, the Ostrogoths defeated and killed Odovacar and by 493 had full control of Italy.

The Ostrogothic king, Theodoric, was one of the ablest of the Germanic rulers. Having lived several years at the court of Constantinople, he made a greater effort than most barbarian kings to preserve the forms of Roman government. He always acknowledged the formal sovereignty of the emperor, but in fact he was just as independent as Odovacar. Theodoric had no intention of restoring imperial rule in the West.

The "Fall of the Roman Empire"

The deposition of the last western emperor in 476 is often referred to as the "Fall of the Roman Empire." Taken literally, this is a meaningless phrase. There was almost nothing left to fall in the West, and in the East the Empire survived as a powerful state. No inhabitant of the Mediterranean world could believe that the Empire had "fallen" in 476, though he might have good reason to feel that the western part of it was decrepit.

Still, the passing of the Latin-speaking part of the Empire under Germanic rule was a watershed in history. Basic ideas of government and law had come from the Latin West; an Empire that was largely Greek could not remain a Roman Empire, even though it kept the name. The Latins became barbarized under Germanic rulers; the Greeks became Orientalized as their contacts with the West decreased. Thus the two halves of the Roman world drifted apart, preparing the way for the later split between eastern and western Europe.

This divergence between the two parts of the Empire raises a question that has puzzled generations of historians. Why did the Empire and the civilization it embodied collapse in the West and survive in the East? The East suffered the same social illnesses as the West; why did they do less damage? About all that can be said is that the East was favored by geography and that it had more eco-

Capella on Geographic Zones

Martianus Capella's *Satyricon*, from which the following was taken, was written in the early fifth century. It was one of the typical encyclopedic digests of the late Empire.

The round world may be divided into five zones or bands of different characteristics. Of these, great excesses of heat or cold force three to be abandoned. The two zones which touch either end of the earth's axis, dominated by terrible cold, are deserted because of frost and snow, while the middle zone, baked by flames and breath-taking heat, scorches all living things that come near. The two other zones, tempered by the breath of life-sustaining air, offer a habitation to living things. These zones, curving around the sphere of the earth, go around both the upper and the lower hemisphere. . . . Those who live opposite us are called "antipodes." . . . For when we roast in summer, they shiver with cold; when spring here begins to cover the fields with flowers, there worn-out summer is passing into sleepy autumn.

From Martianus Capella, *De nuptiis philologiae et Mercurii* (Leipzig: Teubner, 1866), Book VI (on Geometry), p. 252.

nomic and spiritual vitality than the West. As long as Persia remained neutral the rich eastern provinces of Asia Minor, Syria, and Egypt could not be attacked. They were protected by impregnable Constantinople, where the main strength of the defense forces could be concentrated. The Balkan provinces were more exposed, but they did not attract permanent German settlement. In the West it was easy to attack and occupy the rich farmlands of Gaul and the Po Valley. Furthermore, commerce and industry were concentrated in the East; the wealth of eastern cities could be used to hire armies and bribe enemies. The West had no such resources.

Finally, Christianity had cut deeper and spread more widely in the East than in the West, and zeal for the faith often led to support of the state that protected the faith. This identification of religion with patriotism was not universal—nor was it always helpful. Heretics often bitterly opposed the imperial authorities. But at least in the East some people felt strongly enough about their beliefs to fight for them; in the West, Christians were as apathetic as pagans. Western bishops disliked the Arian Goths, but they did not fight them, either to preserve the true faith or to save the eternal Empire. During the fifth century the eastern emperor was able to recruit soldiers from among his subjects, while in the West the Roman population hardly lifted a finger to protect itself.

But these were differences in degree and not in kind. The East was only a little more stable than the West; it saved itself from the Germans but could not repel the next great attack, that of the Arabs (see p. 173). The basic trouble was that very few inhabitants of the Empire believed that the old civilization was worth saving. As we have seen, there never was a time when the Romans did not greatly outnumber the invaders. A reasonably trustworthy source numbers the entire Vandal people—men, women, and children—at about eighty thousand when they crossed the Straits of Gibraltar. Yet this small group overran all North Africa. The "Fall of the Empire" was not a political episode of the year 476; it was a deadly crisis in the history of a civilization.

ART AND LITERATURE DURING THE MIGRATIONS

Secular Art and Literature

Officially sponsored literature, education, and art were as decadent as imperial politics during the time of the Germanic migrations. The blight of imitation lay heavily on all secular thought and literature. Overrefinement of earlier techniques had produced a style that was involved, ornate, and often deliberately obscure. Greek was seldom studied in the West—another sign of the drawing apart of the two halves of the Empire—

and the Greek scientific tradition was scarcely known to men of Latin speech. A final sign of the degeneration of secular studies was the making of digests— handy collections of familiar quotations, one-volume encyclopedias, summaries of the rules of grammar in a few pages. Scholars studied these digests more than the original works from which they were drawn; they were to become the basic textbooks of the Middle Ages.

Official art, like secular literature, was heavy and imitative. Few new buildings or monuments were constructed. Those that were built often were decorated with materials taken from earlier works. For example, on the Arch of Constantine there is a striking contrast between the crude work of the fourth century and the elegant sculptures borrowed from a second-century monument. The same decline is evident in the coins of the period. The Romans had been masters of realism, if not of the higher forms of art, and the coins of the emperors of the first and second centuries carry striking portraits. By the end of the fourth century the coins are less well made and the portrait is becoming a symbol—the emperor as a type rather than as an individual.

Thus wherever one turns in the fourth and early fifth centuries one sees apathy on the part of the multitude and a lack of creativeness among the upper classes. The framework of imperial government held the Roman world together long after Roman civilization was dead, but it could not support a corpse indefinitely. New forms of organization and new beliefs were needed before civilization could revive.

Christian Art and Literature

The new beliefs and many of the new forms of organization were developed by the Christian Church, the only segment of late Roman society that still had any vitality and originality. Christian literature and Christian art of the fourth century stood at the beginning of a new tradition rather than at the end of the old classical tradition. But the old tradition had to die before the new tradition could reveal its full potential. Christians could no more preserve classical literary and

Art of the fourth and fifth centuries declined from the elegant work of the first and second centuries. Contrast the fine modeling of the coin of Tiberius (14–37 A.D.) with the crude portrait of Honorius (395–423) beside it.

artistic forms than they could preserve the political organization of the Empire.

The career of St. Augustine, the greatest Christian theologian of the period, illustrates this point. Augustine (354–430) was born in what is now Tunisia, the only son of a well-to-do family. He received a good classical education and could have had a profitable career as a lawyer or as a member of the imperial bureaucracy. But Augustine, like many of his contemporaries, was concerned about religion and salvation. He was not at first a Christian—one more proof of the slow spread of the faith into the West. As a young man he turned to Neoplatonism and then to Manicheanism to satisfy his spiritual interests. When he finally accepted Christianity he abandoned public life entirely and dedicated his remarkable intellectual gifts to the service of the Church.

Augustine was not greatly concerned by the troubles of the Empire, though at the time of his death the Goths had seized Rome and the Vandals were attacking Hippo, the city where he was bishop. Pagan charges that neglect of their gods had caused the sack of Rome did inspire him to write *The City of God*, but only to prove that the fate of Rome was unimportant compared with the preservation of the holy community of saints and angels. His real concern was with God's ways toward man, and especially with the problems of free will and predestination, of evil and sin. If God is all-wise and all-powerful, does man really have free will? How can such a God allow man to sin and condemn himself to endless suffering? How can a merciful God countenance the existence of evil? These were the questions Augustine wrestled with in his *Confessions*, one of the most remarkable autobiographies of all time. He dealt with them again in *The City of God* and in the innumerable treatises that made him the most influential theologian of the West.

By avoiding extreme answers Augustine found solutions that have appealed to Christian scholars of all times and all sects. Thus he argued that evil is not an independent power (as the Manicheans taught) nor yet the creation of God; it is merely the absence of good. Man has

St. Augustine on the City of God

Accordingly, two cities have been formed by two loves: the earthly by the love of self, even to the contempt of God; the heavenly by the love of God, even to contempt of self. The former glories in itself, the latter in the Lord. For the one seeks glory from men, but the greatest glory of the other is God, the witness of conscience. . . . In the one, the princes and the nations it subdues are ruled by the love of ruling; in the other, the princes and the subjects serve one another in love, the latter obeying, while the former take thought for all. The one delights in its own strength, represented in the persons of its rulers; the other says to its God: "I will love Thee, O Lord, my strength." And therefore the wise men of the one city, living according to man, have sought for profit to their own bodies or souls, or both, and those who have known God "glorified him not as God, neither were thankful, but became vain in their imaginations, and their foolish heart was darkened. . . ." For they were either leaders or followers of the people in adoring images, "and worshipped and served the creature more than the Creator." But in the other city there is no human wisdom, but only godliness, which offers due worship to the true God, and looks for its reward in the society of the saints, of holy angels as well as holy men, that God may be all in all.

From St. Augustine, *City of God*, in *Basic Writings of St. Augustine*, ed. by Whitney J. Oates, Vol. II, p. 274. Copyright 1948 by Random House, Inc. Reprinted by permission.

free will, but this free will is ineffective without the assistance of divine grace. Augustine made his points emphatically, sometimes too emotionally, but he was writing about subjects that were important to him.

The other chief Latin Christian authors of the fourth century were St. Jerome and St. Ambrose. Jerome (335–420) was a better scholar than Augustine; he knew both Greek and Hebrew. He spent much of his life translating the Bible into Latin, a translation on which the Vulgate—the official Catholic text—was based. Ambrose (d. 397) was an administrator and preacher rather than a scholar. He had had a successful career in the imperial civil service before he became bishop of Milan. He was involved in a long quarrel with Arian heretics, and, as we have seen, he forced the emperor Theodosius to do public penance for his sins. During these disputes he encouraged his flock by writing ser-

The church of Santa Sabina, built in 425, incorporates the characteristics of a Roman basilica—a long, rectangular nave divided from two side aisles by rows of pillars.

such as the dove to represent the Holy Spirit. Christian painting and sculpture of the late Empire are sometimes crude, but never flaccid.

It was also during this period that the basic patterns for church architecture were developed. In the West, the model was the Roman law court, or basilica, a long rectangular room with two sets of pillars dividing the room into a central hall, or nave, flanked by two side aisles. The roof over the nave was elevated to admit light through windows set above the side aisles. Eventually the far end of the nave was rounded into an apse that held the altar and seats for the clergy. Later a transept was inserted between nave and apse. This was a hall that crossed the nave at right angles and protruded beyond the aisle walls, thus giving the church the form of a cross. There were basilicas in the East as well, but the most typical form for eastern churches was a round or polygonal structure with a dome over the central portion. This pattern still characterizes churches of the Greek rite.

Christian art and Christian literature were to have their fullest development in later centuries. But even before 500 two things had been demonstrated: first, that under the inspiration of Christian doctrine new styles were arising to replace those that had dominated the Mediterranean world for centuries; second, that the people of the Greco-Roman world, despite all their troubles, were still capable of creative activity.

mons, and even more by writing hymns for them to sing. This was a rather new idea; Ambrose did much to popularize hymn singing in the West, and his hymns are still sung in the Catholic Church.

Christian art of the late Empire showed the same vigor as Christian literature. The trend away from realism to symbolism was entirely appropriate for religious art. During this period some of the most persistent symbols for representing Christian ideas were developed,

Suggestions for Further Reading

Note: Asterisk denotes a book available in paperback edition.

The Late Empire There are many fine histories of the late Roman Empire. One that was used by many later scholars is the synthesis by F. Lot, *The End of the Ancient World** (1931). An excellent survey is A. H. M. Jones, *The Later Roman Empire*, 3 vols. (1964); an abridged version was published in 1966. Both S. Dill, *Roman Society in the Last Century of the Empire** (1910), and M. I. Rostovtzeff, *The Social and Economic History of the Roman Empire,** rev. ed. (1957), discuss the reforms of Diocletian. Rostovtzeff is more thorough and is useful as a reference, but Dill is more readable. P. Brown, *The World of Late Antiquity** (1971), is a brilliant recent study. See also J. Vogt, *The Decline of Rome* (1967), an excellent book. The most recent work is R. MacMullen, *The Roman Government's Response to Crisis* (1976). See also J. Matthews, *Western Aristocracies and the Imperial Court,* A.D. 364–425 (1975).

The Spread of Christianity One of the great problems in European history is that of the conversion of the emperor Constantine. R. MacMullen, *Constantine* (1969), in his good short biography of the emperor, is inclined to see a semimagical, semireligious impulse. The Swiss historian J. Burckhardt, in his influential book *The Age of Constantine the Great,** trans. by M. Hadas (1952), sees Constantine's conversion as completely an act of political expediency. A. H. M. Jones, *Constantine and the Conversion of Europe* (1948), interprets the conversion as religious in motivation. Both Burckhardt and Jones base their arguments on the writings of the court bishop Eusebius and the scholar Lactantius, significant parts of which are in K. Setton and H. R. Winkler, eds., *Great Problems in European Civilization* (1954). This book has excellent source material on the spread of Christianity. J. Lebreton and J. Zeiller, *The Emergence of the Church in the Roman Empire* (1962), discuss the spread of Christianity. The short monograph of E. R. Goodenough, *The Church in the Roman Empire* (1931), presents Christianity as a summation of various religious ideas of the Roman environment. Goodenough is a useful introduction to the study of Christianity in this period. On the persecutions, see W. H. C. Frend, *Martyrdom and Persecution in the Early Church** (1967).

The Goths and the Huns H. Mattingly, *Tacitus on Britain and Germany** (1952), is a rich mine of information about the political, social, and economic conditions of the Germanic peoples at the time when they first came in contact with the Roman Empire. There is a good picture of the Germanic migrations and warlike spirit in Jordanes, *Origins and Deeds of the Goths,* trans. by C. C. Mierow (1908). J. B. Bury's *The Invasions of Europe by the Barbarians** (1928) has valuable material on the barbarian impact on Europe, while L. Halphen, *Les Barbares* (1930), traces the beginnings and spread of the Germanic peoples down to the eleventh century. Halphen has good bibliographic material. Another good book in French is E. Demougeot, *La formation de l'Europe et les invasions barbares* (1969). The old study of P. Villari, *The Barbarian Invasions of Italy,* 2 vols. (1902), is still valuable. See also E. A. Thompson, *The Visigoths in Spain* (1969).

The Fall of the Empire in the West E. Gibbon's monumental work, *The History of the Decline and Fall of the Roman Empire,* ed. by J. B. Bury (1896–1900), presents an answer to this problem in a book that has stood as a classic in English literature since 1776. A leading French medievalist, F. Lot, in *The End of the Ancient World** (1931), attributes the decline largely to economic causes, while C. Dawson, *The Making of Europe** (1934), shows the importance of religious developments. See also W. C. Bark, *Origins of the Medieval World** (1960), a good short account of the transition from the late Empire to the early Middle Ages.

Art and Literature From its beginnings Christianity has inspired art in the pictorial form. C. R. Morey, *Early Christian Art** (1942), is an interesting introduction. W. Lowrie, *Art in the Early Church* (1947), is an excellent study of early Christian art, with fine reproductions and a critical bibliography. The broad survey of W. R. Lethaby, *Medieval Art from the Peace of the Church to the Eve of the Renaissance, 313–1350,* rev. by D. Talbot-Rice (1947), covers all art forms and has considerable material on the early Church.

Perhaps the greatest thinker the western Church produced in the Middle Ages was St. Augustine of Hippo. *The Confessions of St. Augustine** (many editions) is one of the most remarkable accounts of a spiritual pilgrimage ever written. St. Augustine's *City of God** (many editions), which deals with such basic theological questions as the nature of God, free will, sin, and salvation, played a large part in the evolution of Roman Catholic and Protestant thinking. P. Brown, *Augustine of Hippo** (1967), is the best work in English. The writings of most of the early Church Fathers have been collected and translated in *The Fathers of the Church* series, ed. by R. J. Deferrari (1947 ff.).

H. Marrou, *History of Education in Antiquity** (1948), which carries the reader down to 700 A.D., has good material on Christian literature. A. Alföldi, *A Conflict of Ideas in the Later Roman Empire* (1932), is a short and brilliant book.

6 Ancient India and China

The civilizations we have discussed so far were all in direct and constant contact with one another. The peoples of the ancient Middle East had exchanged techniques and ideas from the second millennium B.C.; Greece had drawn heavily on these older civilizations; Rome had received the Greek heritage and had had close relations with all the cultures of western Eurasia, from the Celts in the West to the Persians in the East. The Romans were familiar with the religions, the social and political organization, the agricultural and industrial techniques, the science, the literature, and the art of the vast region that stretched from Spain and Gaul to Egypt and Mesopotamia. They were more interested in some aspects of older civilizations than in others; for example, they accepted Oriental religions but tended to neglect Hellenistic science. Neglect was not the same thing as ignorance, however; the works of Archimedes were available even if few inhabitants of the Roman world chose to study them, and any educated Roman knew who Archimedes was.

The two great civilizations that arose in East Asia had only intermittent contacts with each other and even less with the Middle East and the Mediterranean.

India and China were cut off from each other by jungles and mountains and from the rest of the Eurasian continent by vast deserts and thousands of miles of semiarid steppes. Some trade was carried on in these forbidding regions, even in the third millennium B.C. But on the whole, for many centuries China and India had little influence on each other and cast only vague shadows on the life of Mesopotamia, Egypt, and the Mediterranean. After 500 B.C. merchants; missionaries, and conquering armies brought the peoples of Eurasia into closer association. Trade between China and India grew, and one of the great Indian religions, Buddhism, penetrated the region north of the Himalayas. Greek soldiers of fortune, following Alexander's footsteps, built states in central Asia from which Greek ideas and forms of art were disseminated to both China and India. At the height of the Empire the Romans traded directly by sea with India and Ceylon, and indirectly with China through middlemen who carried silk across Asia to the Black Sea and Syria. The many Roman coins found in India testify to the extent of that trade.

These contacts, however, were tenuous and easily disrupted by political or

Jade statuette of
the head and shoulders
of a horse (Han dynasty).

economic disasters. Even in the second century A.D., the time of Rome's closest contact with East Asia, the Romans knew little of the civilizations of China and India and were scarcely influenced by them. Neither Buddhism nor Confucianism had any impact on the Mediterranean world. The Romans could incorporate the temple-states of Syria and the semidivine monarchies of Asia Minor into their society, but they never understood the caste system of India or the imperial institutions of China. Even in the field of technology, where innovations spread most rapidly because they have no ideological flavor, the Romans ignored such significant Asian innovations as the stirrup and the horse collar. And yet East Asia probably had more influence on the West than the West had on East Asia.

Relations between India and China were closer than those between East Asia and the West, but there was no wholesale borrowing between the two countries. Each region developed its own way of life, very different from the other and equally different from the world the Romans knew.

This relative isolation of India and China from the West makes it hard to describe their civilizations in terms understandable to a western reader. There is bound to be some distortion when English words are used to describe Asian ideas and institutions, for there are no exact parallels in western experience to the intellectual and social patterns that developed in India and China. But it is worth making an effort to understand the early civilizations of East Asia. From time to time events in this region exerted a powerful influence on the peoples of the West. Some of the basic differences between East and West that still cause difficulties in relations between the two areas were already evident in the early history of India and China. Finally, it is well to remind ourselves of the fact that there are other solutions to the perennial problems of mankind than those devised by the peoples of the West. History has shown that the most enduring and successful of these alternative solutions have been formulated by the Indians and the Chinese.

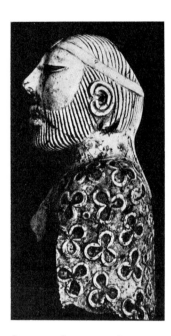

Statuette of a man, perhaps a priest, wearing an ornamental robe, from Mohenjo-Daro (*ca.* 2500 B.C.).

INDIA

As we have seen, India, like the ancient Middle East, had a very early river-valley civilization, centered in the basin of the Indus. This Indus Valley civilization, however, was first weakened and then destroyed by a series of disasters after 2500 B.C. Decline may have begun with climatic changes that led to repeated floods, but the final collapse was probably caused by invasions of northern peoples. Little is known about conditions in India between 2500 and 1500 B.C. When the darkness lifts there has been a great change. The early inhabitants of India—the Dravidians—have been enslaved or driven south by the conquerors from the north, a group who speak an Indo-European language and who seem to be related to the Greeks and even more closely to the Aryans of Persia. These Indo-Aryans were far less advanced than the builders of Mohenjo-Daro in the Indus Valley, who had lived one thousand years earlier. They had no cities; they were herdsmen and farmers living in scattered villages. But they were excellent fighters, and they gradually occupied first the Indus Valley, then the Ganges Valley, and finally the central part of the Indian peninsula. As the dominant race, they established the religious concepts and the social institutions that have persisted in India to the present day.

Early Indo-Aryan Society

The language of the Indo-Aryan invaders, Sanskrit, resembled Greek in many ways, and there is other evidence that the two peoples were related. They worshiped similar gods; they accorded special honor to the warrior class; and they were organized in many small states instead of one unified kingdom. A Heroic Age in northern India, commemorated in Indo-Aryan epics, seems to have been very similar to the Greek heroic age described by Homer. But there were also significant differences between the Greeks and the Indo-Aryans. In the first place, the Indo-Aryans created a literature that gave enduring form to their ideals far earlier than the Greeks. Their oldest works, the Vedas, go back at least to 1400 B.C. The Vedas are religious rituals or hymns to the gods, not accounts of worldly adventures such as the *Iliad* or the *Odyssey*. It was many centuries before the Vedas were written down, but oral transmission through carefully trained priests seems to have preserved much of the original text. This difference in the character of their early literature illustrates another divergence between the two peoples: religion and an organized priesthood were far more important among the Indo-Aryans than among the Greeks. Finally, the Indo-Aryans developed race and class distinctions that were far sharper than those of the Greeks.

These peculiarities of early Indian society tended to reinforce one another. The fact that the language had been fixed for religious purposes at such an early date meant that there was a growing discrepancy between the sacred and the vulgar tongue. In the end the only people who could still understand and interpret the early religious literature were the priests, who thereby assumed added authority. Tendencies toward a caste system were reinforced by the differences between the conquering Aryans and the subjugated Dravidians. Because the Dravidians were shorter and darker than the Aryans, they were readily distinguishable from the ruling group. And because they were obliged to work at the dirtiest jobs, the conquerors had good reason to remain aloof from them. Though differences between conqueror and conquered eventually disappeared in other societies—as in the Roman Empire, for example—in India they were given a religious sanction and so became permanent. And if one caste barrier could be justified by religion, then other barriers could be instituted among the members of the ruling group. Eventually each principal occupation formed a caste, and intermarriage among these castes was forbidden.

Ultimately a society emerged that was dominated by religion, unlike the secular societies of ancient Greece and Rome. Early Indian religion, like that of Greece, was based on carefully formulated rituals. When the Greeks became dissatisfied with the intellectual content of their reli-

Vedic Hymns

ORIGINS OF CASTE

When they [the gods] divided the Man,
   into how many parts did they divide him?
What were his mouth, what were his arms,
   what were his thighs and feet called?

The brahman [priest] was his mouth,
   of his arms were made the warrior.
His thighs became the vaisya [merchants and cultivators],
   of his feet the sudra [servants] was born.

The moon arose from his mind,
   from his eye was born the sun,
from his mouth Indra and Agni [the war god and the fire god],
   from his breath the wind was born. . . .

HYMN OF CREATION

Then even nothingness was not, nor existence,
There was no air then, nor the heavens beyond it.
What covered it? Where was it? In whose keeping?
Was there then cosmic water, in depths unfathomed?

Then there was neither death nor immortality,
nor was there then the torch of night and day.
The One breathed windlessly and self-sustaining.
There was that One then, and there was no other. . . .

But, after all, who knows and who can say
whence it all came, and how creation happened?
The gods themselves are later than creation,
so who knows truly whence it has arisen?

Quoted in A. L. Basham, *The Wonder That Was India* (London: Sidgwick and Jackson, 1954; New York: Macmillan, 1968), pp. 241, 247–48.

gion, they developed philosophies that were completely divorced from their old faith. In India there was also a shift from empty ritual to philosophical speculation, but Indian philosophy always remained closely associated with religious faiths. Philosophy and religion combined to produce pantheism, a belief that all living things were part of a world-soul (Brahma) from which they emanated and to which they returned. A natural result of this doctrine was belief in the transmigration of souls. Each individual soul, before its final absorption in the world-soul, might inhabit many bodies in many lifetimes. But these individual existences and the world of the senses were mere illusion; the one reality was the world-soul. Thus death was not to be feared, and worldly misfortune could be endured in the hope that the next reincarnation would be happier.

These ideas were expressed in the Upanishads, a series of religious treatises written in the eighth and seventh centuries B.C. They also appear in the epic of the Mahabarata, which was probably first written down in the fifth century B.C. and then reedited and expanded until it reached its final form about 200 A.D. The Mahabarata is a story of wars leading to the creation of a vast empire under the hero Krishna, but the narrative is frequently interrupted by discussions of right conduct and proper belief. The best-known section of the epic is a religious poem called the Bhagavadgita, which closes with a strong affirmation of belief in the immortality of the soul through transmigration. "Never was there a time when I was not, nor thou . . . and never will there be a time when we shall cease to be. . . . Just as a person casts off worn-out garments and puts on new, so does the soul cast off worn-out bodies and put on others. . . ." The other great Indian epic, the Ramayana, was written about 200 A.D. It also discusses the relation between religious belief and right conduct, but its principal theme is the devotion of a faithful wife to the hero Rama, who is trying to regain his rightful position as a ruler.

During the Heroic Age (*ca.* 1000–*ca.* 500 B.C.), a split developed between the religious concepts of the leading thinkers and those of the people. The philosophers still saw universal truths behind the bewildering variety of gods and rituals, but the mass of the population became content with external observances. The number of gods increased; ceremonies and offerings were substituted for the inner enlightenment that the great religious leaders had sought; and caste lines became increasingly rigid. The Brahmans, as the priests were called,

The Buddha often was not pictured in human form in early representations; his presence here is indicated by the tree in the upper left corner (detail from a pillar at Sanchi, first century B.C.).

profited from the heightened formalism of religion; since they alone knew what was pleasing to the gods, they became the dominant caste. Next to them in the caste scale were the kings and warriors, while farmers and artisans filled lower ranks. Almost at the bottom were the laborers, who performed humble tasks and whose very shadow would defile a Brahman. Most miserable of all were the outcastes—men who had no caste at all and who could not participate in the religious or social activities of their villages. These unfortunates were to become the untouchables of modern India. Every man was supposed to stay in his caste and to perform the duties appropriate to it, since his fate had been determined by the will of the gods. Social mobility was not completely blocked, especially for men who left their native villages and went to the towns, but the great majority of the people could not change their occupations. This waste of human resources slowed down economic development and explains, to some extent, India's economic backwardness.

The Buddha

Before the sixth century B.C. there were from time to time kings who united most of northern India under a single ruler. But none of their ephemeral empires had much influence on the development of Indian society. The real genius of India lay not in politics but in religion. And about 580 B.C. India produced one of the great religious leaders of all time, Sakyamuni the Buddha. The Buddha, son of a petty Indian king, at first led the normal life of a wealthy aristocrat. He became convinced of the futility of worldly pleasure, but he was repelled by the formalism and superstition that had crept into the official religion. Renouncing the world, he spent many years seeking enlightenment through fasting and self-discipline. Finally he saw the true path. All man's troubles spring from his attachment to the things of this earth. So long as a man craves pleasure, or even merely existence, he is condemned to be reborn again and again, in higher or lower form, depending on his behavior in his last reincarnation. The only escape from this dreary repetition of sorrow and pain is to renounce all worldly desires. Then the individual soul will be freed from the Wheel of Things and can achieve nirvana. The term *nirvana* is hard to define; it means a complete cessation of worldly cares, an end to the cycle of birth and rebirth, and complete absorption into the Universal Soul that is God.

Though the final goal of Buddhism was the loss of individual consciousness, it was an intensely individualistic religion for those who wanted to follow its teachings in this world. No ritual or priesthood could save the individual who was seeking enlightenment; salvation depended on his own thoughts and actions. He must follow the Eightfold Path of right views, thought, and action; he must observe a strict moral code; above all else, he must never relax in his personal quest for salvation.

Buddhism was a reformation rather than a renunciation of the principles of the old Indian religion. The Buddha disdained the elaborate rites and rituals of the Brahmans and the worship of a multiplicity of gods. He also opposed the rigidities of the caste system; according to legend, he had eaten with a poor laborer just before he died. But while the Buddha wanted to purify Indian religion, he accepted its basic doctrines of the one world-soul, the illusory nature of the world of the senses, and transmigration of souls. Unlike most of the Brahmans, however, he held these beliefs with such intensity that he could convince many of his hearers that renunciation of the world was happiness and that beyond illusion was true wisdom. He attracted a devoted group of disciples who lived together in monastic dwellings and helped in turn to convert others. During his lifetime, the Buddha's ideas spread rapidly through the north of India, where he had begun his teaching, and some Buddhists could be found in every part of the peninsula.

In the years that followed, Buddhist monasteries developed into notable cen-

The Basic Doctrines of Buddhism

The following is part of a sermon of the Buddha.

There are two ends not to be served. . . . The pursuit of desires and of the pleasure which springs from desires . . . leading to rebirth, ignoble and unprofitable; and the pursuit of pain and hardship, which is grievous, ignoble and unprofitable. The Middle Way . . . avoids both these ends; it is enlightened, it brings clear vision, it makes for wisdom, and leads to peace, insight, full wisdom and Nirvana. . . .

This is the Noble Truth of Sorrow. Birth is sorrow, age is sorrow, disease is sorrow, death is sorrow, contact with the unpleasant is sorrow, separation from the pleasant is sorrow, every wish unfulfilled is sorrow.

This is the Noble Truth of the Arising of Sorrow. [It arises from] thirst, which leads to rebirth, which brings delight and passion, and seeks pleasure now here—now there—the thirst for sensual pleasure, the thirst for continued life, the thirst for power.

This is the Noble Truth of the Stopping of Sorrow. It is the complete stopping of that thirst, being emancipated from it, being released from it, giving no place to it.

This is the Noble Truth of the [Middle] Way that Leads to the Stopping of Sorrow. It is the Noble Eightfold Path—Right Views, Right Resolve, Right Speech, Right Conduct, Right Livelihood, Right Effort, Right Recollection and Right Meditation.

Quoted in A. L. Basham, *The Wonder That Was India* (London: Sidgwick and Jackson, 1954; New York: Macmillan, 1968), p. 271.

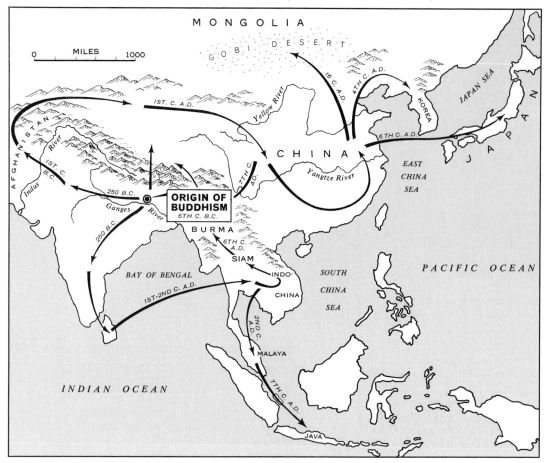

ters of learning and stimulated the growth of the new religion. For a while it seemed that the whole subcontinent might become Buddhist. The future of Buddhism seemed especially bright under the Mauryan dynasty, which lasted from 322 to about 184 B.C. The first king of this dynasty, Chandragupta Maurya (322–298 B.C.), came closer to uniting India than had any earlier ruler; only the extreme south escaped his domination. The third Mauryan king, Asoka (*ca.* 273–*ca.* 232 B.C.), became a Buddhist, and with his support Buddhism developed into the first great missionary religion. The only other faiths that have spread as widely are Christianity and Islam. In Asoka's day Buddhism was accepted in most parts of India and throughout Ceylon. Later it spread to the countries of Southeast Asia and across the mountains into China. And with

Buddhism went Indian art, literature, and philosophy. The influence that India still exercises in eastern Asia began with this cultural expansion under Asoka.

The Mauryan Empire

The Mauryan Empire was a strong state; it had a reasonably advanced civil service and an adequate financial system. Asoka, a more benevolent ruler than most of his predecessors, tried to soften the harsh penalties of earlier laws and to improve the lot of the poor through extensive charities. Though a Buddhist himself, he was tolerant of other faiths and never tried to convert his people by force.

Yet there were two serious weaknesses in the empire, even at the height of its power. The first was economic. Both internal trade and external trade with the Hellenistic states of Egypt and Syria were taxed heavily. But the economy was still based on agricultural villages rather than on trade centers. The government owned most of the land and took large shares of the peasants' income. The resulting hardships meant that there was no real loyalty to strong centralized rule.

The second weakness was that the Mauryan government was a despotism, enlightened at times but always arbitrary. The *Arthasastra*, a manual of statecraft written under the Mauryans, reads very much like an Indian version of Machiavelli:

> With increasing strength, make war; when you have a clear advantage over a neighbor, march against him; do not disturb the customs of a newly conquered people.

But the most revealing statement is this: "Government is the science of punishment." Even the kindly Asoka invoked the death penalty freely, and the other kings of his house devised frightful tortures for rebels and traitors. Fear was a poor means of creating loyalty to the dynasty, as future events demonstrated.

Asoka sought to show his devotion to Buddhism by supporting a magnificent program of religious building. During his reign and the reigns of his immediate successors, Indian art developed some of its most typical forms. Stupas, or burial mounds with elaborately carved stone gateways, were erected over the relics of Buddhist leaders. At Ajanta a series of immense cave temples was built, with gigantic columns and carvings that imitated woodwork. In these cave temples of Ajanta some of the earliest Indian painting is found, though the finest examples there were created a few centuries later. But Indian painting had already acquired some of its chief characteristics—an emphasis on rhythmic, curving lines and the absence of any light–shadow pattern.

Soon after Asoka's death the Mauryan Empire disintegrated, and for several centuries no ruler held more than a fraction of the territories Asoka had controlled. It is curious that India should have split into small states just at the time when Rome was uniting the Medi-terranean world and the Han emperors were building an empire in China. But separatist tendencies were always strong in India, where people felt that cultural unity was far more important than political unity. Governors of outlying provinces threw off the control of Asoka's weaker successors and set themselves up as independent rulers. It is possible that the Buddhist doctrine of nonviolence weakened the military strength that had created the Mauryan Empire. Asoka, after his early conquests, gave up war as an instrument of policy, and his successors, though not going so far, did not show much capacity for organizing military operations.

The collapse of the Mauryan state had serious consequences for Buddhism. Deprived of the support of kings like Asoka, the religion began to decline in India, although the missionary work begun in the Mauryan period enabled it to survive elsewhere in Asia. But the decline of Buddhism in India meant that a gap was opening between northern Buddhists, such as those in the sub-Himalayan kingdoms, and southern Buddhists, such as those of Ceylon. In the second century A.D. the religion split into two branches, Hinayana Buddhism in the south and Mahayana Buddhism in

Capital on a column erected by Asoka to commemorate the Buddha's preaching of the First Sermon in Sarnath.

THE MAURYAN EMPIRE   *ca.* 250 B.C.

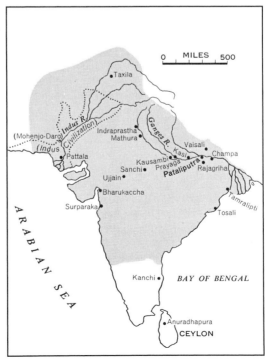

129

The Great Stupa at Sanchi
(first century B.C.).

ments of Greek style into their work. It was also by the land route through western Asia that Indian philosophy and mathematics reached the Greeks and Greek astronomy reached the Indians. The sea route was important for the exchange of goods between India and the West but was far less effective than the land route for the exchange of ideas. The chief Indian ports for western commerce were in the extreme south, a region that lay outside the main centers of Indian culture, and seaborne commerce declined rapidly after 200 A.D., when the Roman Empire was weakened by civil war.

The Kushan and Andhra Dynasties

The Kushan state, established in the first century A.D., was even more effective than the Mauryan Empire in establishing relations with China and with the West. The Kushans, a nomadic people of central Asia, gradually took over the northwestern corner of India. Since they also retained their old holdings in central Asia, their empire provided a channel through which Indian ideas and Indian goods could flow northeast toward China and northwest toward Rome. The most famous example of Kushan influence occurred when their king Kanishka was converted to Buddhism soon after 120 A.D. Kanishka, concerned about disagreements among Buddhist teachers, called a council to clarify and reconcile their statements of belief. This council defined the doctrines that became those of the northern, or Mahayanan, school of Buddhism.

The Andhra dynasty of central India (ca. 225 B.C.–ca. 225 A.D.) began earlier than the Kushan but reached the peak of its power at about the same time. Control of the Ganges Valley gave the Andhras a dominant position in eastern India, where the people were more inclined to preserve ancient traditions than those of the northwest. Though tolerant, the Andhras favored the Brahmans, and Buddhism lost ground under their rule.

The Gupta Period

Both the Andhra state and the Kushan Empire disintegrated during the

the north. The Hinayana version is still the principal religion of Ceylon, Burma, Thailand, Cambodia, and Laos, and in these areas it has remained fairly close to the ideals of its founder. The northern version dominates Tibet and has many followers in China and Japan. This form of Buddhism has become more like other religions; in it Buddha is a savior who renounced nirvana in order to redeem mankind. A cult of saints (bodhisattvas) grew up around him, and emphasis on ritual and ceremony increased.

With the establishment of the Mauryan Empire, a period of close contacts between India and its western and northern neighbors began. The most significant relations were by land, for the Seleucid Empire and certain of its successor states bordered on northern India. From these countries Indian artists learned something about Greek sculpture and thus were able to incorporate ele-

322 B.C.	ca. 225	184	ca. 1 A.D.	ca. 225	ca. 320	ca. 500 A.D.
Mauryan Empire			Kushan Dynasty—Northwestern India	Period of Political Disorder	Gupta Dynasty	

Andhra Dynasty—Central India

first years of the third century. A period of disorder followed, until northern India was finally reunited under the Gupta dynasty, which was founded in 320. The Guptas never held as much of India as the Mauryans had, but the region they controlled prospered under their rule.

During the Gupta period (*ca.* 320–*ca.* 500) Buddhism almost vanished from India. The collapse of the Kushans weakened the religion in the northwest, the last region in which it had had any real strength. The chief centers of Buddhism were now outside India, and the Indians began to feel that a religion taught by outer barbarians was un-Indian and unacceptable. The Guptas themselves were tolerant, but they clearly preferred the old Indian religion, which had now settled into the form known as Hinduism. Buddhism withered away, and Hinduism, with the support of the Gupta kings, became the religion of the vast majority of the inhabitants of India.

The central beliefs of Hinduism—the unity of all life and the need to recognize and feel this unity as the highest good—had come down through the centuries unchanged. Indian philosophers and religious leaders still taught the necessity for meditation, renunciation, and union with the world-soul. But the common people of India could not understand these remote ideals; they needed visible images to worship and fixed rules to obey. They needed gods who watched over human activities and who could be placated by sacrifices. Their chief gods constituted a trinity—Brahma the creator, Vishnu the preserver, and Shiva the destroyer. But the Indians worshiped innumerable other divinities, each with his own special temples and forms of worship. As the gods multiplied, the caste structure also became more complicated: the large, original castes broke up into many subcastes. Growing rigidity in caste

and social structure led to a deterioration in the position of women. Most well-to-do men took many wives, a practice that had been rare in earlier times. It was during the Gupta period that suttee, the custom of widows burning themselves on their husband's funeral pyres, became common, though it was not obligatory.

Indian mathematics probably reached its height under the Guptas. The Indians had long been interested in mathematics and surpassed even the Greeks of the

The Buddha (second century A.D.).

Hellenistic period in some of its branches. For example, the Greeks tried to solve their problems by the visible demonstrations of geometry, but the Indians, using the abstract principles of algebra, could cope with much more difficult concepts. Greek algebra was rudimentary, but the Indians invented the concept of negative quantities, solved quadratic equations, and found the square root of 2. When the Ptolomaic system of astronomy entered India, the Indians tried to explain it in terms of algebra rather than of geometry. Indian astronomy never advanced very far, for lack of careful observation of the stars, but the Indians knew that the earth was round and that it rotated, and they had some understanding of gravitation. Their most famous invention, however, was the system of so-called Arabic numerals, which first appeared in India in the third century B.C. By the time of the Guptas, Indian mathematicians were using a form of decimal system. The final and most important innovation, the zero, may or may not have resulted from the work of Indian mathematicians. But it is significant that the zero first appears in the works of scholars familiar with Indian numerals. It is also significant that Christian Europe did not know of Indian-Arabic numerals until the twelfth century and did not use them extensively until the sixteenth. The two civilizations were too far apart and contacts between them too infrequent for even such obviously useful ideas to travel quickly from one region to the other.

Gupta literature influenced the West somewhat more rapidly than Gupta mathematics. The Gupta age was an age of short stories, fables, and fairy tales, some of which reached the Middle East, and then Europe, in a relatively short time. The Indians, endowed with remarkably fertile imaginations, invented situations and plots that have been borrowed by writers in all other languages. The story of Sinbad the Sailor, for example, is drawn from Indian sources. The best-known collection of Hindu tales—the Panchatantra—has had a direct and continuing effect on other literatures. For example, the basic pattern of many fables—stories of animals acting like

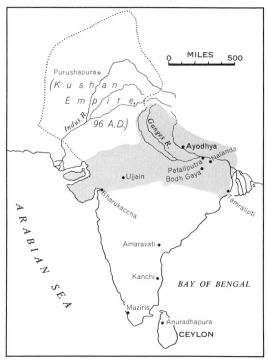

THE GUPTA EMPIRE   ca. 400 A.D.

human beings—comes from this source. Famous poets and playwrights such as Kalidasa (ca. 395–450) remained unknown outside India; their poems and plays were too thoroughly Hindu to be understood elsewhere.

During the Gupta period classical Indian art reached its highest level. Before the Gupta period Greek influence on Indian art had been noticeable, but after 300 that influence declined and Gupta art reverted to the basic Indian patterns that had taken form in the Mauryan period. Indian art was essentially religious in purpose and symbolic in form. Restrained and dignified, it tried to express the eternal truths of the Indian religions. The finest paintings at Ajanta are from this period, as are some of the last great Indian sculptures representing scenes from the life of the Buddha.

The Gupta state, which never controlled more than half of India, was constantly threatened by enemies along the frontiers. Its administrative system was simpler and less bureaucratic than that of either of the great contemporary empires—the Roman and the Chinese. The relative weakness of centralized control may have made life easier for the people, but it made the kingdom vulnerable to internal disorder and attack from aggressive enemies. The Gupta state probably had less income than the Mauryan empire because the peasants now owned their own land and gave less to the state. With the death of Chandragupta II in about 412, the Gupta state began to decline. The Huns, whose depredations had weakened Han China and imperial Rome, also contributed to the fall of the Guptas. The Huns, or a people associated with the Huns, invaded the Punjab late in the fifth century and held northwest India for a time. But the invaders were driven out after a few decades, and an outbreak of rivalry among local princes was probably the chief cause of the disintegration of the state. By the sixth century the Gupta kingdom had collapsed, and it was generations before any large state was to emerge again.

For the next six centuries India suffered an endless succession of internal wars and foreign invasions. Unlike the Chinese, who always managed to build a new empire on the ruins of the old, the Indians seemed unable or unwilling to replace their small, warring states with larger political units. They were more interested in religion than in politics, and the overwhelming influence of the Brahman priests made it difficult for secular rulers to exercise effective political control. When a new Indian Empire finally appeared it was ruled by Moslems, not by Hindus.

CHINA

If Indian civilization was predominantly religious, Chinese civilization was predominantly secular. In the earliest periods of Chinese history this secularism is less noticeable than it is later, but it still can be observed. The early Chinese attached great importance to religious rituals and ceremonies. They worshiped a god of Heaven, an Earth god, and lesser divinities, and they made sacrifices and consulted oracles; but they never brooded over religious problems as did the Indians, nor did they develop a powerful priesthood. True, they long believed that the ruler held his power through the Mandate of Heaven. But when he lost his power it was usually because of a rebel-

A ceremonial vessel in the form of an elephant (Shang dynasty).

Ancient symbol *Yi,* which stands for "changes." One of the five Confucian classics is the *Book of Changes.*

lion led by some political subordinate rather than because of a pronouncement by a group of religious leaders. For the Chinese the most urgent problems were good crops and good government, not salvation and immortality.

Even though some of the oldest human fossils have been found near Peking in northern China, very little is known about the first stages of Chinese civilization. Agricultural settlements certainly existed in the Yellow River region at an early date; it is difficult, however, to determine when the Chinese began to develop more elaborate forms of political organization and economic specialization. It seems likely that the first cities arose somewhat later in China than in Egypt or Mesopotamia—considerably after, rather than before, 3500 B.C.

At any rate, the Shang dynasty (*ca.* 1500–*ca.* 1100 B.C.) presents firmer ground. Early Chinese historians preserved stories about the remarkable accomplishments of the Shang that were once thought legendary but that we now know had a solid basis in fact. It was under the Shang that the Chinese began to use bronze, a development that may

have contributed to the power and splendor of the dynasty. The Chinese rapidly acquired great skill in casting this metal, and some of the sacrificial vessels of this period show remarkably fine workmanship. Another sign of advancing civilization was the appearance of the first specimens of Chinese writing—pictographs, which, like early Egyptian hieroglyphs, represented words, syllables, or ideas rather than sounds. Finally, though most of the people were still peasant farmers, industry and commerce had developed to a point where they could support many artisans and traders, who lived in the walled cities of the Shang rulers.

Soon after 1100 B.C. the Shang dynasty was succeeded by the Chou. The Chou domain stretched from the area around Peking to parts of the lower Yangtze Valley, but the heart of the state was the lower valley of the Yellow River. The Chou did not rule a unified kingdom; they were merely the heads of a confederation of peoples who spoke the same language and lived more or less the same way. The Chou kings did not have the military strength to dominate the local rulers. The relationship between the Chou king and local lords was somewhat like the feudal relationship that later developed in western Europe; each lord was to aid the king in time of war, but he was almost independent in his own region. Eventually the local rulers became less and less submissive to central control; principalities increased in size and power and engaged in incessant war, so that during the third century B.C. the Chinese lands were divided among a group of warring, regional states.

THE CHINESE STATES AT THE TIME OF CONFUCIUS   *ca.* 500 B.C.

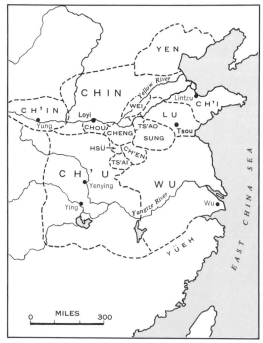

Confucius

It was during the later years of the Chou dynasty that China's great philosopher, Confucius (K'ung Fu-tzu, 551–479 B.C.), was born. A scholar, and for a while an official of one of the local rulers, he eventually retired from public life to teach sons of aristocrats and devote himself to the development of an ethical system. The Chinese, as we have seen, had never been particularly concerned about religion and had developed no systematized theology. Nor had they been especially interested in political theory; they simply accepted the fact that there always had been, and always would be, rulers and subjects. But they were greatly concerned with human conduct, with the problems of how a man should adjust to the world in which he lived and to the society of which he was a member. Such problems became especially acute during the disorders of the late Chou period. Confucius taught respect for authority, for tradition, and for custom. He was rather skeptical about religion. "If you do not know about the living," he asked, "how can you know about the dead?" But he believed that at all levels of society there was a guiding force that should be honored and obeyed: the father guided the family, the ruler the state, and Heaven the universe. By accepting such guidance, man could achieve both harmony with himself and harmony with his environment.

This doctrine, with its emphasis on self-control, conformity, and obedience, created a strongly conservative force in Chinese society. It strengthened existing tendencies toward ancestor worship, the veneration of ancient customs, and the acceptance of authority. This outcome was not wholly contrary to Confucius' own desires; and yet we should remember that Confucius saw himself as a reformer trying to bring stability to a turbulent society and that his teachings were opposed by many rulers of his own time. His ethical principles may have been conservative, but he insisted that they applied to nobles and kings as well as to commoners, and one of his successors, Mencius (*ca.* 372–288 B.C.), logically concluded from this that a bad ruler could be deposed by the people.

Moreover, the conservatism that flowed from Confucius' teaching was neither arrogant nor obscurantist. It was tempered by punctilious respect for good manners, which Confucius felt were as important as good institutions. This emphasis on courteous behavior proved a precious lubricant as the Chinese population grew. It enabled millions of people with limited resources to live close together without developing dangerous social tensions. And with good manners

---

Confucius on Government

Duke Ting [d. 495 B.C.] asked if there were any one phrase that sufficed to save a country. Master K'ung [Confucius] replied, saying, No phrase could ever be like that. But here is one that comes near it. There is a saying among men: "It is hard to be a prince and not easy to be a minister." A ruler who really understood that it was "hard to be a prince" would have come fairly near to saving his country by a single phrase.

Duke Ting said, Is there any one phrase that could ruin a country? Master K'ung said, No phrase could ever be like that. But here is one that comes near to it. There is a saying among men: "What pleasure is there in being a prince, unless one can say whatever one chooses, and no one dares to disagree?"

From *The Analects of Confucius*, trans. by Arthur Waley (London: Allen and Unwin, 1938), p. 175.

---

went an admirable ethical code. The "superior man repays evil with uprightness and kindness with kindness." He treats others as he himself would be treated.* Confucius also stressed the value of education in developing men worthy to rule—a lesson the Chinese upper classes never wholly forgot. True, education in China became highly formalistic and traditional, and the ability to quote extensively from ancient texts came to be regarded as the essence of scholarship. Nevertheless, Chinese education did produce men with disciplined minds trained to think clearly. And during most of China's history this educated class held key positions in the government; periods in which the military enjoyed complete domination were exceptional and brief.

Confucius never claimed divine inspiration, and he had little influence on Chinese society during his lifetime. But his ideas survived and gradually, through the efforts of several generations of disciples, became the philosophy—almost the religion—of the ruling classes. Eventually, sacrifices were offered to the spirit of Confucius, and he was venerated as

*See Charles A. Moore, *Philosophy: East and West* (Princeton, N.J.: Princeton University Press, 1946), p. 28.

Chinese calligraphy. Left: a rubbing from one of the ten "Stone Drums," an example of the Great Seal style of writing, which evolved in the latter part of the Chou dynasty. Right: a rubbing from a stone inscription of the Han dynasty, inscribed in the Official Style.

Divine seal of Lao-Tzu, used in Taoist magic.

Taoist Teaching

The following is ascribed to Chuang Tzu (*ca.* 320 B.C.).

I first learned to consider myself as an external object, then I no longer knew if I were dead or living. . . . After having seen the One [*tao*] he [the disciple] is able to attain a state where there is neither past nor present, and then a further state where he is neither dead nor living. . . . Were the thunder to bring down the mountains or the hurricane to spill the ocean, he would not care. He is borne up by the air and the clouds; he rides on the sun and moon and frolics beyond the limits of space.

How can we know if the self is what we call the self? Once I dreamed that I was a butterfly . . . and I felt happy. I did not know that I was Chuang Tzu. Suddenly I awoke and was myself, the real Chuang Tzu. Then I no longer knew if I were Chuang Tzu dreaming that he was a butterfly or a butterfly dreaming that he was Chuang Tzu.

From René Grousset, *The Rise and Splendour of the Chinese Empire* (London: Bles, 1952; Berkeley: University of California Press, 1953), pp. 32–35.

the chief religious teacher of China. More than any other man, he gave permanent form to ideas that the Chinese people had been working out for many centuries. The early codification of these ideas gave enduring strength to Chinese society. From the time of Confucius down to this century, despite the impact of foreign ideas and the rule of barbarian conquerors, the Chinese were able to maintain their way of life because they had standards to which they could make both foreign ideas and foreign rulers conform.

Taoism

The ethical code of Confucius was based on a rational analysis of Chinese society, but there was another side to Chinese thought. This side was represented by Lao-Tzu, a shadowy figure, who probably lived at about the same time as Confucius. Lao-Tzu's doctrine was intuitive and mystical, and even Chinese scholars are not in full agreement on its meaning. At least this much is clear: while Confucius believed that man could achieve harmony with the world by making an effort to think rightly, act rightly, and organize society properly, Lao-Tzu believed that harmony came from renunciation and passivity. Man should allow the forces of nature to work on him as they do on all other material things; feeling is more important than thinking; harmony with the guiding world-principle is more desirable than action. This philosophy was called Taoism—the Way—and there are obvious resemblances between it and the Way of Buddha. Taoism, in fact, made it easier for Buddhist doctrines to spread into China, and Chinese Buddhism was colored by Taoist thought.

Though Taoism never became the dominant philosophy in China, it was highly influential for centuries. Politicians and scholars tended to be Confucianists, while painters and poets were more likely to have Taoist leanings. By seeking harmony with nature, by allowing the inner essence of things to penetrate their minds, Chinese artists and writers achieved remarkable results with remarkable economy of effort. They avoided direct, literal representations of reality; instead, with a few strokes of the brush, or in a short poem, they evoked the mood occasioned by some event or some natural object.

Chinese Art and Literature

The Chou dynasty was a period of rapid development in Chinese art and literature. Bronze works of high quality continued to be made, and some of the earliest and finest jade carvings were created in this era. The peculiarly Chinese art of calligraphy also became prominent at this time. The Chinese had developed a written language very early that used a separate symbol for each word or idea. By the time of the Chou dynasty there were about four thousand such symbols, many of them very intricate. It was difficult enough to write these characters accurately, especially as a soft brush was the most common implement; it was even harder to write them with style and elegance. Anyone who could do so has always been admired by the Chinese; over the centuries they have regarded fine calligraphy as satisfying as a beautiful painting.

It was also during the Chou period that the Five Classics of Chinese literature were compiled from earlier writings. These books include history, philosophy, poetry, and rules for religious ceremonies. Tradition has always given Confucius credit for these compilations, but he almost certainly did not do the actual editorial work. The books are in harmony with his philosophy, however, and two were quoted in his own teachings. For centuries the Five Classics served as the foundation of Chinese education; all students had to study them thoroughly before attempting anything else.

The First Emperor

The struggle among the states that developed in the late Chou peiod was checked about the middle of the third century B.C., when the rulers of Ch'in, one of these states, undertook the unification of all China. Tough, cruel frontiersmen who measured their victories by the number of enemy heads cut off, they created a strong, disciplined army. About

221 B.C. King Sheng of Ch'in subdued the last of the rival kingdoms and took the title of First Emperor. He was, in fact, the first real emperor in Chinese history. He ruled directly through provincial governors instead of depending on the doubtful cooperation of semi-independent local rulers, and he instituted uniform laws and weights and measures throughout the empire. His authority and income must have been substantial, for he was able to build the Great Wall, stretching fourteen hundred miles across North China, to protect his country from barbarian invaders. This work included sections of earlier fortifications, but its completion required tremendous human suffering. Whole familes were uprooted to work on the wall, and food was scarce in the barren regions through which it was built. Sheng also tried to destroy all copies of the Confucian classics because opponents of his absolutism cited them to support their criticisms. Memories of the harshness of the First Emperor may explain why his heir was quickly overthrown. The general who succeeded the Emperor's heir founded the Han dynasty, which was to rule China from 202 B.C. to 220 A.D.

The Han Period

The Han emperors, who extended the boundaries of their realm to Turkestan in

Bronze wrestlers and a bear tamer (Chou dynasty).

the west and to Canton in the south, strove to understand the ways of foreign peoples and to open up trade with them. A substantial trade in silk with Persia and Rome was developed, though it was carried on almost entirely by middlemen. Far more direct and influential were Chinese contacts with India. Buddhism began to find acceptance in China during the Han period, and with it came a host of intellectual and artistic concepts. The Chinese pagoda, for example, is modeled on Indian Buddhist shrines.

The Han emperors expanded the centralized administrative system that had been instituted by the Ch'in. China was relatively peaceful and prosperous under their rule, and the doctrines of Confucius were nationally honored. All officers of government, including the emperor himself, paid reverence to the philosopher's spirit, and an official Confucian cult was supported by the state. The Han emperors had copies made of all the Confucian texts that could be found, a task that was simplified by the invention of paper making early in the first century A.D. They honored scholars and made scholarship a means of access

to high official positions. The Han also encouraged the writing of history, both of the ancient past and of the Han period itself. This emphasis on history tended to reinforce the Confucian emphasis on tradition and continuity.

During the Han dynasty vast water-control projects were undertaken in an effort to expand the economic resources of the country. The North China plain is subject to flooding in seasons of heavy rainfall and to disastrous droughts at other times of the year. The local princes of the area had made some effort to control the floods and to build irrigation systems, but none of them had controlled enough territory for their programs to be effective. The Han rulers, however, could plan on a larger scale, and their water-control projects added substantially to the productivity of Chinese agriculture. These projects also served to increase the prestige of the imperial government, since they were more successful than those that had been attempted by local lords.

In the Chinese Empire, as in the Roman Empire, a rather narrow economic base supported an elaborate polit-

THE HAN EMPIRE   100 B.C.

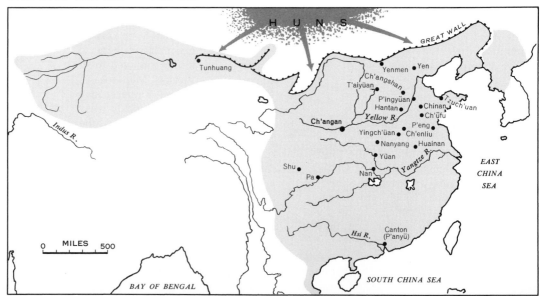

The Great Wall of China, completed in 204 B.C.

Pottery tile rubbing depicting hunters and peasants (Han dynasty).

an agricultural society, had been only temporarily suppressed. It revived in the second century A.D. and began to impair the unity of the Han Empire. Finally, palace intrigues among members of the imperial family weakened the central government. In China, as in Rome, the third century was a period of civil war. The Han dynasty was overthrown in 220 A.D., and for generations no one ruler proved powerful enough to reunite the country.

This period of disintegration was especially dangerous because China, like Rome, had a long, vulnerable northern frontier to defend. Chinese settlement had stopped at a line where diminishing rainfall made agriculture impossible. Beyond that line lay the vast, arid reaches of central Asia. These were the domains of nomad tribes, who were the most dangerous barbarians the civilized world has ever known. In their wide-ranging raids these nomads struck at Europe and India, and they were always an immediate threat to China. In order to protect the border zone where the nomads threatened Chinese outposts, the First Emperor built the Great Wall and the early Han rulers subdued Turkestan. When China was strong, the nomads were content to trade peacefully with the Chinese; but when China was weak, they were quick to renew their assault. Such a period of weakness came at the end of the Han dynasty. The Huns made several attacks on China, but in the end it was a group related to the Tartars who overran North China in the fourth century. For the next three hundred years most of the Chinese were ruled by barbarian dynasties.

These nomad rulers gradually accepted Chinese civilization. In the end they became far more Chinese than their contemporaries, the Germanic kings of western Europe, became Roman. But it was several centuries before they were fully assimilated. Meanwhile, just as a remnant of the Roman Empire survived around Constantinople, so a Chinese state survived to preserve the old traditions in the Yangtze Valley in South China. There were similar parallels in religious developments. In Europe, Christianity spread most rapidly after the

ical structure. The Chinese peasants had to support the governing classes, the scholars, the writers, and the artists. It is not surprising that they became discontented at times. Toward the end of the Han period that discontent manifested itself in a series of peasant revolts. Moreover, localism, which is usually strong in

THE ATTACKS OF THE HUNS   Fourth century

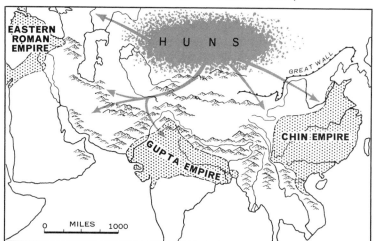

fall of the Roman Empire and during the rise of the early Germanic kingdoms. In China, Buddhism spread most rapidly after the collapse of the Han Empire and during the period of confusion and division that followed. But Buddhism was never as strong and pervasive in China as Christianity became in Europe. Though it was favored by many rulers, other religions were tolerated, and Buddhism never became part of the political structure of Chinese states.

This was a crucial period in Chinese history. There were many forces working for Chinese unity—the relative isolation of the people, the fact that they all spoke dialects of a common language, the existence of a form of writing that represented ideas rather than sounds and hence could be understood whatever the dialect of the speaker, and most of all, a tremendous contempt for the outer barbarian. But the strength of these forces had not been fully tested until the collapse of the Han Empire. The three centuries of barbarian rule of the north might have led to a permanent division of China. The fact that China was finally reunited proclaimed the enduring strength of the Chinese tradition. Never again did China go through such a long period of fragmentation.

Suggestions for Further Reading

Note: Asterisk denotes a book available in paperback edition.

India There are a number of valuable works on the early history of India. P. Masson-Dursel, *Ancient India and Indian Civilization* (1934), in the *History of Civilization* series, treats all facets of early Indian history and culture and is a good starting point for study. Another fine survey is that of the great Indian authority R. C. Majumdar, *Ancient India* (1952), which devotes considerable space to religion and culture and has bibliographic material. A. L. Basham, *The Wonder That Was India** (1954), is particularly good on early Indian art and literature. Majumdar, *An Advanced History of India* (1967), is a more scholarly work with special attention to political history. The same author's *The Military System in Ancient India* (1955) traces the evolution of the military system up through the Moslem conquest of Hindustan. M. Wheeler, *Early India and Pakistan* (1959), is a very readable study based largely on archeological evidence. For an essentially political account, H. Raychaudhuri, *Political History of Ancient India* (1952), is interesting but technical, and P. Mookerjee, *Local Government in Ancient India* (1919), stresses that India's elaborate system of local government preserved the independence and integrity of Hindu culture. H. G. Rawlinson, *India and the Western World* (1916), studies the relations between India and the West up through the fall of the Roman Empire.

China Probably the best introduction to the early history of China is H. G. Creel, *The Birth of China** (1937), which deals with the political, social, and cultural life of China in early times. L. C. Goodrich, *A Short History of the Chinese People** (1943), has very good material on the political history of China through 600 A.D., and W. Eberhard, *A History of China* (1955), is an excellent account of Chinese history with concentration on sociological development. Eberhard includes a good critical bibliography. C. P. Fitzgerald, *China: A Short Cultural History** (1938), a standard work on the subject, stresses the vitality of Chinese culture throughout its history. R. Grousset, *The Rise and Splendour of the Chinese Empire** (1952), is impressionistic but stimulating.

For the economic history of China, see the valuable monograph of E. S. Kirby, *Introduction to the Economic History of China* (1954), which has material on the period before 600 A.D. Liu Wu-chi, *A Short History of Confucian Philosophy** (1955), is a good starting point for the study of Chinese philosophy and the Chinese moral system, and H. G. Creel, *Confucius: The Man and the Myth* (1949), is valuable on the influence of Confucius. Both Wu-chi and Creel are great authorities.

For bibliography on Chinese history, L. C. Goodrich, *A Syllabus of the History of Chinese Civilization and Culture* (1941), is invaluable.

7 The Germanic Kingdoms in the West

The great empires of the Eurasian continent had all been destroyed by internal struggles and foreign invasions during the third, fourth, and fifth centuries. They had all suffered a decline in economic and cultural activity. Everywhere men faced the problems of adapting the remains of an old civilization to new conditions, of rebuilding political organization and stimulating economic growth. The people of western Europe had perhaps the most difficult task of all. Disintegration and barbarization had gone further there than in most other areas, and religious disputes were more divisive. The period during which western Europe slowly rebuilt its civilization is known as the "Middle Ages," and it is to the early centuries of the medieval period that we now turn.

This fragment from the crown of the Lombard king Agilulf shows the king being greeted in the cities he conquered (early seventh century).

During the fifth century all the Roman territories of the West fell under the control of Germanic peoples. The Vandals ruled North Africa; the Visigoths held the Iberian Peninsula; Italy itself was occupied by the Ostrogoths. Gaul was split among the Visigoths in the southwest, the Burgundians and Ostrogoths in the southeast, and the Franks in the north and center. The Angles and Saxons gradually took over most of Britain, although the Celts preserved fiercely independent kingdoms in Scotland and Wales.

THE NORTHERN AND SOUTHERN KINGDOMS

The Germanic kingdoms that emerged from this welter of migration and conquest had very different fates. The Mediterranean group—the Vandals, the Visigoths, the Ostrogoths, and the Burgundians—absorbed Roman civilization readily and preserved much of the Roman way of life. But though they seemed to be more advanced than the northerners, the Germanic kingdoms of the Mediterranean had no staying power. During the sixth century the Vandals and Ostrogoths were crushed by the Eastern Roman Empire, and the Burgundians were conquered by the Franks. The Visigoths weakened and finally, in the eighth century, came under the rule of Moslem invaders. In contrast, the northern invaders—the Franks and the Anglo-Saxons—learned much less from the Romans and at first had a lower level of civilization. But their kingdoms endured and became the strongest states of medieval Europe.

This difference in the history of the northern and southern kingdoms can be

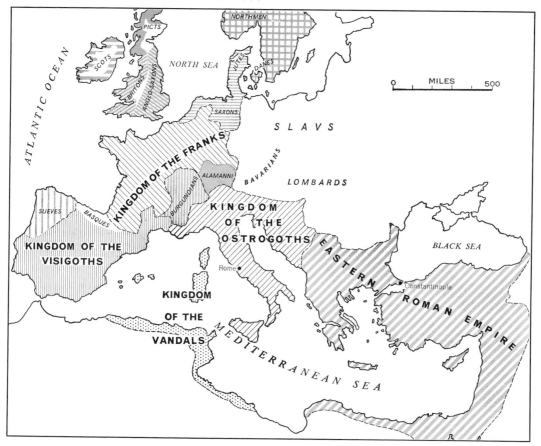

explained largely by geographic and demographic factors. The Germanic groups that reached the Mediterranean were entirely cut off from their old homes and could not be reinforced by new migrants. They found themselves in the most densely populated and most thoroughly Latinized area of the Empire, and they were vulnerable to attack from the strong states of the eastern Mediterranean—first the Eastern Roman Empire and then the Moslem caliphate. The Goths, Vandals, and Burgundians also suffered from having been converted to the heretical Arian form of Christianity. This made it extremely difficult for their rulers to win the loyalty of the orthodox Roman population. Thus the Germanic kingdoms that had the greatest need for strength were actually the weakest. The number of their fighting men dwindled, and the apathetic Roman population gave little support to the new rulers.

The northern invaders, on the other hand, remained in constant contact with their homelands, and for several generations their ranks were strengthened by new bands of migrants. In the sparsely settled lands they entered, they had an opportunity to preserve their old customs and to maintain effective armies. Since they were eventually converted to orthodox Christianity, they gained the support of the Church. The Eastern Roman Empire never touched Gaul, and the Moslems, even at the height of their power, could only send raiding parties toward the Loire. Thus the northern invaders had time to develop new institutions strong enough to enable them to survive during the troubled centuries of the early Middle Ages.

A glance at a modern map will illustrate this difference between the northern and southern Germanic kingdoms. Italy and Spain have retained their old Roman

Gold coin of Theodoric, Ostrogothic king of Italy in the early sixth century.

Religious carving from Niederdollendorf, probably depicting the symbols of Thor.

names; they did not become East Gothia and West Gothia. But the Franks imposed their name on Gaul, which became France, just as the Angles imposed theirs on the largest part of Britain, which became known as England.

And yet the southern kingdoms, even though they were politically short-lived, aided the difficult transition to a new age by making a conscious effort to adapt Roman culture to the needs of a simpler, semibarbaric society. Latin literature and Roman law survived in the south, but not in the north. The Burgundian and Visigothic kings, for example, issued brief codes of Roman law for the use of their Roman subjects. These codes would have seemed crude and incomplete to the great lawyers of the Roman Empire, but they covered most of the cases that were likely to arise and they preserved some of the basic principles of Roman law. Moreover, the existence of Roman law codes encouraged Germanic kings to put some of their own legal customs in writing.

The Ostrogothic Kingdom of Italy

The most important work in assimilating Roman culture was done in Ostrogothic Italy. Theodoric, king of the Ostrogoths, had been closely associated with the court at Constantinople and understood Roman ways very well. During his reign in Italy (493–526) he safeguarded the elements of Roman civilization and ensured the continuation of the Roman administrative system. The fact that the Ostrogothic army had its own law meant no more to the ordinary citizen than does the existence of military law in a modern society. Theodoric also named eminent Roman scholars to the highest official posts. Two of these men, Boethius and Cassiodorus, eager to preserve the learning of the past, made a deliberate effort to put it into a form that could be used by future generations.

Boethius (ca. 480–524) was especially disturbed by the gap that had opened between Greek and Latin learning. Since the fourth century few inhabitants of the West had studied Greek, and even so eminent a writer as St. Augustine was not able to read it easily. This ignorance of Greek was particularly serious in mathematics, science, logic, and philosophy, where Latin scholars had done little original work and where all the advanced texts were in Greek. Boethius hoped to preserve this precious heritage by writing elementary treatises on mathematics and translating the major works of Aristotle and Plato. Unfortunately, Boethius did not live to complete his ambitious project, and some of the translations he did make were neglected by later scholars. But his basic mathematical texts and his translations of two of Aristotle's introductory treatises on logic were used throughout the Middle Ages. Until the twelfth century these treatises supplied medieval scholars with most of their philosophical vocabulary and ideas about logic. By showing, in his theological *Tractates*, how logic could be applied to problems of Christian theology, Boethius ensured the survival of logic as a branch of medieval learning.

Boethius' career was cut short when he fell into political difficulties. Theodoric, in spite of his admiration for Roman culture, was always a little uneasy about the loyalty of the upper-class Romans. The Arianism of the Ostrogoths offended the Catholic Romans, and the emperor at Constantinople, who still claimed authority over the West, encouraged intrigues against Theodoric. It is possible that Boethius entered into these plots against his king; at any rate, he was accused of treason, jailed for a year, and then executed. While he was still in prison he wrote the work for which he is best remembered, the *Consolation of Philosophy*, a long dialogue, partly in prose and partly in verse, between the prisoner and Philosophy. Philosophy argues that all worldly honors and pleasures are vain and that external misfortunes are unimportant. The only thing worth striving for is the good of the soul, expressed in virtue and in reason. This idea was at least as old as Plato, but the conviction with which Boethius stated it made his work a real consolation to many troubled men in years to come.

Cassiodorus (ca. 490–580) was more skillful in riding out political storms. Though he had been secretary to Theo-

Bust of a young German warrior, of the type the Romans fought. The soldier wears a necklace believed to have magic power.

doric, he survived both court intrigues and the long wars between the Eastern Romans and the Goths and died peacefully at the age of ninety in his ancestral home in southern Italy. He was something of a pedant; the letters he wrote for Theodoric are tricked out with far-fetched allusions to classical literature and mythology. But he saw, perhaps more clearly than Boethius, that ancient learning could be saved only with the aid of the Church. In his last years he founded a monastery to preserve the secular learning that he felt was necessary for true understanding of Christian writings. Cassiodorus preserved as many classical texts as he could and, in his *Introduction to Divine and Secular Literature*, outlined the basic reading that was necessary for an educated clergyman.

Digests such as that of Cassiodorus, and elementary treatises such as those of Boethius, made up the basic educational materials of the early Middle Ages. Many classical works had been lost, and those that survived were seldom studied because they were too long or too difficult. The digests and handbooks were no real substitute for the originals, for they stressed what was obvious and omitted or oversimplified what was complicated.

Nevertheless, they preserved useful knowledge. Even more important, they suggested that better sources might be available. A quotation from Vergil might make a reader eager to ferret out the whole *Aeneid;* a reference to Aristotle might encourage a scholar to seek the original work. It was a long time before any large-scale efforts were made to recover and study the basic works of the classical period, but at least the scholars of the early Middle Ages were aware that their knowledge was incomplete.

GERMANIC SOCIETY

The early Germanic kingdoms were not very successful in preserving the intellectual heritage of Rome. They were even less successful in preserving the Roman political and administrative system. Here they ran into a double difficulty: the native population was weary of the old imperial forms of government, and the Germans themselves had no concept of the state and no experience in administration. Consequently, there was a drastic simplification of political institutions in all the countries of the West.

Since the early Germans had lived in rather small groups given over to agriculture and cattle raising, they had felt no need to create elaborate political institutions. The family was their basic social unit—not the small family of father, mother, and children, but the large family that included grandparents, uncles, and cousins out to the second or third degree. The family protected the lives and property of its members, sometimes waging blood-feuds with other families. Above the family was the neighborhood, a group of family heads who cooperated in local defense, in settling disputes, and in performing difficult agricultural tasks. The folk, or people, which was made up of many neighborhoods, was supposedly a blood-group descended from a few common ancestors. It had almost no function except to make war on or defend itself against neighboring peoples.

Early Germanic society was not democratic; it was very conscious of differences in class and rank. Certain families, which claimed descent from the gods,

Compurgation

When Chilperic I was assassinated, he left a young son who was to hold his father's share of the Frankish kingdom under the guardianship of his uncle, King Guntram. There were doubts about the boy's legitimacy, doubts that Guntram apparently shared.

After this King Guntram went to Paris [in 585] and openly addressed all the people, saying, "My brother Chilperic on his death is said to have left a son . . . but the boy is concealed, he is not shown to me. Therefore I feel certain that matters are not as they have been represented, but that the child is, as I believe, the son of one of our nobles. For if it had been of our blood, it would have been brought to me. Know therefore, that I will not acknowledge it until I receive satisfactory proofs of its paternity." When Queen Fredegonda [the mother of the boy] heard this she summoned the chief men of her kingdom, namely three bishops and three hundred nobles, and with them made oath that Chilperic was the father of the child. By this means suspicion was removed from the king's mind.

From Gregory of Tours, *History of the Franks*, trans. by Arthur C. Howland, *Translations and Reprints* (Philadelphia: University of Pennsylvania Press, 1897), Vol. IV, No. 4, p. 3.

had great wealth and supplied leaders in time of war. But these leaders—the kings and the nobles—had little to do in time of peace. Their wealth and ancestry won them respect, and their bands of armed retainers commanded fear. Although their advice was often sought when trouble arose, they did not administer a state or govern a people. Most of the ordinary business of the people was conducted by the family and neighborhood groups.

Germanic Courts

The difference between Germanic and Roman political organization is seen most clearly in the administration of justice. A Roman who had a grievance against a neighbor went to a court established by imperial authority. His case was judged according to laws promulgated by the emperors, and the court's decision was enforced by local administrative officials.

A German who felt that he had been wronged, however, had to rely first and foremost on his own strength and that of his family. The most common remedy was reprisal, which easily developed into the blood-feud. Only if the injured family felt that reprisal and feud were unnecessary or dangerous would the case go to a court. The usual court was an assembly of neighbors that, lacking coercive power, relied largely on public opinion and religious sanctions. It had no power to force a defendant to come to court. If he did appear and denied his deed, the court had no means of establishing the facts in the case. A defendant with a bad reputation was usually sent to the ordeal. This meant that he was obliged to expose himself to a test and let the gods indicate whether or not he was lying. He might, for example, be thrown into a pond to see if he would float or sink. Floating was a sign of guilt, for it meant that the pure element of water had rejected the accused. A man of good reputation, however, could clear himself by compurgation—that is, he would swear that the charge against him was baseless, and a fixed number of friends and relatives would swear that his oath was "clean." These oath-helpers were not giving testimony in behalf of the accused,

An artifact of the migration period. Ostrogothic gilt bronze buckle with jewels (sixth century). The style is Germanic.

for they might know nothing at all about the facts in the case. They were simply swearing that the accused was not a perjurer, and by so doing they automatically cleared him of the charges against him.

If the plaintiff won his case, he received compensation from the defendant, either in money or in kind. This was true even for crimes of violence, such as homicide or mayhem. There was no idea that crime was an offense to the community as a whole, and no attempt was made to inflict physical punishment on the wrongdoer. Tables of compensation made up the largest part of the laws of every Germanic people. It cost more to kill a man of high birth than an ordinary freeman, more to kill a woman of childbearing age than a grandmother. The penalties were substantial; the compensation for killing a man of high birth would ruin a poor family. However, no provision was made for collecting the penalties, other than the threats of the injured family and the pressure of public opinion.

These courts were probably more effective than we might think in dispensing a rough kind of justice. The most common offenses among the early Germans were acts of physical violence, of which no one was ashamed and which no one sought to conceal. To quarrel, fight, wound, and kill was the natural behavior of a self-respecting man. Thus in many cases the facts were not denied, and the sole function of the court was to prevent a feud by determining the compensation to be offered to the injured party. When the facts were in dispute, ordeal and compurgation, though they might not reveal the truth, at least provided quarreling families with an excuse not to launch a feud. Once the gods had spoken, it was unnecessary to prove one's manhood by fighting. Like many other legal systems, the system dictated by Germanic custom was more concerned with stopping fights than with administering abstract justice. Any solution, so long as it was peaceful, was better than a grievous outbreak of blood-feuds.

Nevertheless, this Germanic legal system had serious defects, and no civilized life was possible until they had been remedied. It gave no place to public authority and set loyalty to the family far above loyalty to any larger group. It accepted as natural a state of violence in which no one's life was secure. Effective only in dealing with open wrongdoing, it could not easily be applied to commercial transactions. From the fifth to the twelfth century western European rulers struggled to create effective courts of justice; only when they had succeeded in this difficult task could the people they ruled advance beyond the stage of small, self-sufficient agricultural communities.

Archbishop Hincmar on the Ordeal by Cold Water   Ninth century

Now the one about to be tested is bound by a rope and cast into the water, because, as it is written, each one shall be holden with the cords of his iniquity. And it is evident that he is bound for two reasons; to wit, that he may not be able to practice any fraud in connection with the judgment, and that he may be drawn out at the right time if the water should receive him as innocent, so that he perish not. . . . And in this ordeal of cold water whoever, after the invocation of God, who is the Truth, seeks to hide the truth by a lie, cannot be submerged in the waters above which the voice of the Lord God has thundered; for the pure nature of the water recognizes as impure and therefore rejects . . . such human nature as has once been regenerated by the waters of baptism and is again infected by falsehood.

From Archbishop Hincmar, trans. by Arthur C. Howland, *Translations and Reprints* (Philadelphia: University of Pennsylvania Press, 1897), Vol. IV, No. 4, p. 11.

Germanic Kingship

The loyalties of a German were personal. He was loyal first of all to his family—and understandably so, for he could scarcely hope to exist without family backing. Men who had no families or whose families were weak had to become dependents or even slaves of some strong man. Next, the German showed loyalty to the leaders of the local community. Finally, he might show some loyalty to the king, if that king was known and respected for his prowess in war. But the king could not count on the unanimous support of his peoples; his real strength lay in his bands of armed retainers. These retainers lived with the king, were bound to him by personal oaths of loyalty, shared in the spoils of conquest, and were usually faithful to him unto death. A king seldom had more than a few hundred of these devoted retainers. The rest of his subjects were not ready to die to protect him from usurpers or outside enemies. So long as there was a king to lead them in times of emergency, they cared little who he was.

It was difficult enough for kings to exercise authority when they ruled small groups in limited territories and when they were personally acquainted with most of the fighting men of the folk. The task became far more difficult when they tried to rule large populations, composed of different races, scattered over wide areas of the old Empire. The king could not be present in all parts of his realm, nor could he know more than a few of the leading men in each district. He could neither preserve the old Roman administrative system nor create a new Germanic one. The idea of a civil service was foreign to Germanic custom, and the Germans did not know how to delegate authority. Either they ignored the king's delegate and tried to deal directly with the king, or else they transferred their loyalty to the delegate himself and enabled him to become an almost independent ruler in his administrative district. Until kings were able to delegate authority without losing control—and it took them centuries to find out how—European kingdoms remained loose federations of local communities.

Given the primitive state of the Germanic economy and the structure of Germanic society, the local community was almost self-sufficient. The ordinary German might like to hear stories of adventures in distant lands, but otherwise he was not particularly interested in anything that happened more than a day's journey from his home. He drew almost everything he required from his own land and he produced nothing to sell in distant markets. He relied on the great men of his community for local defense and followed them to war without worrying about causes or objectives. Thus the establishment of a large kingdom did little to aid the ordinary German, nor did the division of a large kingdom into little principalities hurt or shock him.

Although settlement in the Western Empire posed puzzling new problems for the Germanic kings, it also gave them some help in solving those problems. Royal authority was always greatest in time of war, and the period of migration was a period of almost constant war. And, though they did not fully understand the Roman concept of the state and of public authority, the kings learned enough from contact with Romans to make them eager to be more than mere tribal war leaders. Most important, the Church, which had taken over many of the Roman traditions of government, sooner or later gained great influence in all the Germanic kingdoms. Not all churchmen were good administrators or enlightened statesmen; in fact, many were only one degree less barbarous than the flocks they tended. But most of them realized that Christianity could not flourish in an area broken up into isolated small communities and that, bad as the kings might be, there was more to be hoped for from them than from the even less enlightened lords of petty provinces. Many bishops served as advisors to the kings and helped to create a rudimentary central government. Others preserved a certain degree of unity by meeting together in local church councils. Prominent laymen frequently attended these church councils, which often dealt with such secular matters as the suppression of violence or declarations of loyalty to a king.

THE CHURCH IN THE GERMANIC KINGDOMS

Though the Church had a privileged place, it suffered severely during the chaotic years following the Germanic ascendancy. The old Roman population was far from being completely Christian in the fifth century, and the new Germanic population was either pagan or Arian. Even when they had been converted to Catholic Christianity, the Germans often tried to use the Church for their own purposes. A good many bishops of doubtful character, for example, were foisted on the Church by kings anxious to reward their friends and supporters.

The Church at this time was not yet the self-sufficient, highly organized institution it was to become in later centuries. Formerly it had relied on the imperial government for support and protection, and it had not yet perfected its own administrative system or established clear lines of authority. Theoretically, the kingdoms should have been divided into dioceses, each administered by a single bishop. North of the Alps this division was far from complete; many bishops had dioceses that were too large or whose boundaries had not been defined. The division of the dioceses into parishes had gone even less far. This meant that there were no churches at all in many rural areas and that many nominal Christians had little opportunity to attend Christian services. Finally, while the pope's authority to determine questions of faith and morals was generally acknowledged, his power to remove inefficient or corrupt bishops was not yet fully established. Thus the influence of the Church varied from diocese to diocese with the character of the bishop and the amount of aid he could get from his king.

Fortunately for the Church, the growth of monastic communities provided a new, disciplined force at a time when it was badly needed. In the Late Empire many Christians, feeling that they could not live a truly religious life while absorbed in secular activities, had withdrawn from the world to wilderness or desert and had passed their lives in contemplation and prayer. But it was not

A German king (above) and his bishop. From an early manuscript copy of Alaric's code of law.

St. Benedict giving his Rule to his monks. This eighth-century drawing is the oldest known representation of St. Benedict.

lence and instability. Many abbots in Italy and Gaul tried to develop rules suited to western conditions, but none had more than local influence.

St. Benedict and Monasticism

It was St. Benedict of Nursia (480–543) who was most successful in adapting monasticism to the needs of the Western Church. He was born into a well-to-do Roman family, but like many other men of his time he had fled in disgust from a world that seemed hopelessly corrupt. At first he lived as a hermit in the hills near Rome. As his reputation for holiness attracted others to him, he found himself forced to organize a regular monastic community. He built a monastery on the commanding height of Monte Cassino,* near the main route from Naples to Rome, and established a rule that gradually became the basic constitution for all western monks.

The great strength of the Benedictine Rule lay in its combination of firmness and reasonableness. The abbot's authority was absolute. Monks were not to leave their monastery or transfer to another monastery without permission. They were to keep themselves occupied all day. Their first and most important duty was to do the "work of God"—that is, to take part in religious services that filled many hours of the day. But they were also to perform any manual labor that was necessary for the welfare of the house, including such activities as copying manuscripts. The primary purpose of the Rule, however, was not to make the monastery an intellectual center but to keep the monks from extremes of idleness or asceticism. Most monks were neither writers nor scholars, and most monasteries never distinguished themselves by their literary productions. They did, however, distinguish themselves as centers of prayer and worship, as dramatic examples of the Christian way of

easy for the hermit to endure the rigors of an isolated existence; his devotion might falter or he might be unable to provide himself with food and clothing. Thus there was a tendency for hermits to come together in communities in order to obtain spiritual and physical assistance from their fellows. By the end of the third century, some of these communities had become formally organized as monasteries under the headship of abbots.

Monasteries and monastic rules had existed in the East for several generations and were spreading to the West at the time of the Germanic migrations. But the eastern rules were not entirely suitable for western conditions; they were both too harsh and too soft. They were too harsh in physical matters, for the scanty food and clothing that would support life in the Egyptian desert were completely inadequate in the colder northern countries. They were too soft in matters of authority, for many eastern monks were completely undisciplined and wandered about from place to place as they saw fit. Yet the monastic life was becoming steadily more attractive to men in the West; it offered both spiritual and physical security in an age of increasing vio-

*A great battle of the Second World War was fought for the strategic position of Monte Cassino. The mountain had been continuously occupied by a Benedictine monastery ever since the time of St. Benedict, though the buildings destroyed in the battle were not the original ones.

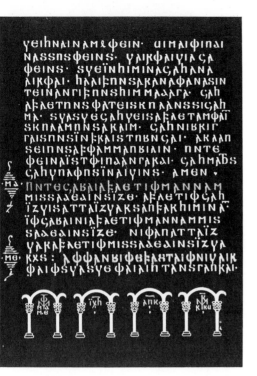

Page from a Gothic Bible (*ca.* 500). This translation, by the Arian bishop Ulfila, helps explain the success of the Arians in converting the Germans. Orthodox Catholics did not translate religious works into German until much later. Ulfila's Bible is one of the earliest specimens of a Germanic dialect and is the basis of most scholarly work on early German. Notice that some new letters, not in the Greek or Latin alphabets, had to be devised to accommodate unusual sounds in the Gothic language.

and lack of discipline. Finally, in many parts of Europe the Benedictines introduced valuable new techniques, such as building in stone and organizing agriculture around the large estate. Benedictine monasteries often served as nuclei for the growth of towns, for they were almost always more prosperous than the neighboring countryside.

In view of these benefits, many kings and wealthy landowners decided that founding a monastery was a good investment. The founder and his family gained both spiritual and material rewards. It was obviously good for the donor's soul to have holy men praying for him; it was also good to know that the monastery might furnish grain in time of famine and lend its gold and silver ornaments when its benefactor ran short of money. By attracting settlers to waste lands, it might increase productivity and enhance the ruler's authority in remote areas. Thus monasteries spread rapidly throughout most of the Germanic kingdoms, often more rapidly than organized dioceses and parishes.

life. Most monasteries also performed certain social services, such as extending hospitality to travelers or giving food to the poor, and a few operated important schools.

A Benedictine monastery in a Germanic kingdom exerted a powerful influence. It offered pure Christian doctrine to people who were pagans, heretics, or at most only nominal Catholics. Very early the monasteries became centers of missionary activity and reform. At the same time, the Benedictine emphasis on obedience to higher authority helped to hold the Church together during a period when any sort of centralization was hard to achieve. The Benedictines emphasized papal authority and a well-organized Church; they opposed local autonomy

St. Benedict on the Authority of the Abbot

This excerpt illustrates the firm yet reasonable discipline that St. Benedict sought to instill in western monasteries.

Whenever any weighty matters have to be transacted in the monastery let the abbot call together all the community and himself propose the matter for discussion. After hearing the advice of the brethren let him consider it in his own mind, and then do what he shall judge most expedient. We ordain that all must be called to council, because the Lord often reveals to a younger member what is best. And let the brethren give their advice with all humble subjection, and presume not stiffly to defend their own opinion. Let them rather leave the matter to the abbot's discretion, so that all submit to what he shall deem best. As it becometh disciples to obey their master, so doth it behove the master to dispose of all things with forethought and justice.

In all things, therefore, every one shall follow the Rule as their master, and let no one rashly depart from it. In the monastery no one is to be led by the desires of his own heart, neither shall any one within or without the monastery presume to argue wantonly with his abbot. If he presume to do so let him be subjected to punishment according to the Rule.

From the *Rule of St. Benedict,* trans. by Cardinal Gasquet (London: Chatto and Windus, 1925), pp. 15–16.

The Conversion of the Anglo-Saxons

England offers a good example of the importance of monasteries under the Germanic kingdoms. The Anglo-Saxon conquest of Britain was slow, piecemeal, and bloody. The Britons put up a stiffer resistance than any other group in the western part of the Empire, and during this long resistance they abandoned many of their Roman ways. Faced with a stubborn enemy, the Angles and Saxons had to be more destructive than, for example, the Franks were in the Seine Valley. Very little of Latin civilization remained in Britain: the language was abandoned, the towns were deserted, and much of the cultivated area sank back into wilderness. Christianity survived only among the native Britons in Wales; from Wales it spread into Ireland. But the conquering Anglo-Saxons were slow to accept the religion of their enemies, and in any case the Christians of Wales and Ireland, cut off from the rest of the western world, were developing peculiar ideas and usages. They celebrated Easter at a different time; they gave abbots authority over bishops; they did not follow the Roman ritual. Irish

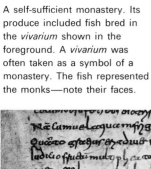

A self-sufficient monastery. Its produce included fish bred in the *vivarium* shown in the foreground. A *vivarium* was often taken as a symbol of a monastery. The fish represented the monks—note their faces.

The helmet (reconstructed from fragments) of a seventh-century Anglian king. From the Sutton Hoo treasure, one of the great archeological discoveries of this century, found under the untouched funeral mound of an early Anglian king.

missionaries had some influence in Scotland and on the Continent, but little in England, except in the north. Thus the basic ingredients that were to produce early medieval civilization—the Latin, Germanic, and Christian traditions—had not yet begun to fuse in Anglo-Saxon England.

The picture began to change during the pontificate of Gregory the Great (590–604). Gregory had been a monk and then an abbot; in fact, he had been most unwilling to leave his monastic life to take on the responsibility of governing the Church. He realized more fully than his predecessors the value of the monks as a disciplined force obedient to the orders of Rome. Gregory also realized how hard it was to maintain unity and decent conduct among the clergy of the Western Church. His correspondence shows how diligently he worked at this task and how difficult it was to make any impression on bishops and priests protected by Germanic kings. Gregory kept some measure of control in Italy, but beyond the Alps he could do little more than register his complaints. And beyond the Frankish area, where at least a form of Christianity existed, though corrupt

THE ANGLO-SAXON KINGDOMS OF ENGLAND   Seventh century

Augustine converted the king of Kent without much difficulty and established the first English bishopric, at Canterbury. But after this promising start the Roman version of Christianity spread only slowly through the island, partly because Augustine was not a very good organizer, partly because Irish missionaries were influential in the north, and partly because the Anglo-Saxons were divided and quarrelsome. It was only late in the seventh century that these obstacles were overcome. Most of the north abandoned Irish forms, and in 669 a great organizer, Theodore of Tarsus, became Archbishop of Canterbury. Theodore gave the Anglo-Saxon Church a firm institutional base by dividing the country into regular dioceses and made the Church an integral part of Anglo-Saxon society.

From this time on the Anglo-Saxons were loyal and energetic supporters of the Roman Church. The most successful missionaries of the eighth century were Anglo-Saxon monks, who not only converted the remaining pockets of heathen Germans on the Continent but even succeeded in reforming and making obedient to the pope the corrupt and anarchical churches of the Frankish kingdom. Gregory's decision to support monasticism and missionary activities produced remarkable results, for the missionary monks both increased the number of Christians and greatly strengthened the pope's authority in western Europe.

THE RISE OF THE FRANKS

During this period of missionary activity, the Franks were rising to political dominance in western Europe. They occupied a favored position. They had penetrated deep enough into the Empire to profit from its wealth but not deep enough to jeopardize the sources of their military power. They held northern Gaul, which was Roman, but they also held the solidly Germanic regions of the middle and lower Rhine. Their first great king, Clovis, a member of the Merovingian* family, came to power in about 480. He was king of only one group of Franks, and at

and unsatisfactory, stretched a great expanse of heathen territory, from the North Cape down to the middle Danube, from England across Frisia and north Germany into the limitless lands of the Slavs.

Gregory probably prepared no master plan for the reform and conversion of the West. But he was quite ready to take advantage of special opportunities, and he turned to the monks for help. Britain seemed to be a promising field for conversion, since the king of Kent, in southern England, had married a Christian Frankish princess. So in 597 Gregory sent a group of monks to Kent, led by an abbot named Augustine.*

*This Augustine also became a saint, but he should not be confused with the great theologian St. Augustine of Hippo, who died more than a century and a half before the mission to England (see p. 119).

*This family was named for an early and almost unknown Frankish king, Meroweg.

A Northumbrian cross (*ca.* 700).

Childeric, father of Clovis and an early king of the Franks, from a signet ring found in his tomb. His long hair and his spear are signs of royal authority.

first he held only a small corner of Gaul. But Clovis was both a good fighter and a skillful intriguer: he rapidly increased the size of his realm by assassinating or defeating his rivals. Clovis had married a Catholic Burgundian princess, and through her he gained the idea that the Christian God might be a powerful help in war. He is supposed to have tested this idea in a battle with the Alamanni (a Germanic people who held lands around the upper Rhine) about 506, in which he gained a hard-fought victory. It is still uncertain how much credit he gave to divine intervention, but soon after the battle, Clovis sought baptism from the Catholic bishop of Reims.

The conversion of Clovis, even more than that of Constantine, which it resembled so closely, was based on expediency. Clovis remained a bloody and treacherous barbarian; all he wanted was to exploit the power of the Christian God and gain the support of Catholic bishops and the old Roman population against Arian Germans. He used his newly acquired orthodoxy as an excuse to attack the Visigoths, who still held southwestern Gaul as well as Spain. Proclaiming that he could not endure the presence of heretics in Gaul, Clovis drove the Visigoths back across the Pyrenees and annexed their territories on the French side of the mountains. This victory almost completed the task of unifying Gaul. Only the Burgundian kingdom in the Rhone Valley escaped Clovis' domination, thanks to the aid it received from the Ostrogoths of Italy.

The Frankish kingdom remained strong for a century after Clovis' death in 511. His sons finally succeeded in conquering the Burgundians and added their territories to the Frankish realm. They also began to extend their authority over the Bavarians and other Germanic peoples east of the Rhine. Although the Frankish kings quarreled bitterly among themselves, the Franks still had the best army in the West, and none of their neighbors could profit from their disunity.

The Frankish kings also profited from the fact that their orthodoxy was seldom questioned, whatever might be said of their morals. Orthodoxy gained them the steady support of the bishops, most of whom came from old aristocratic families and had great influence with both Frankish warriors and Gallo-Roman land holders. Bishops could be very useful to kings, especially as they did not insist on impossibly high standards of conduct. Thus Bishop Gregory of Tours (538–594), who wrote a famous *History of the Franks,* was rather gentle in his judgment of the Frankish kings. Gregory admits that Clovis was treacherous and that on one occasion Clovis bewailed his lack of rela-

The Morals and Faith of the Early Franks

ca. 575

Ragnachar was then king at Cambrai, a man so unrestrained in his wantonness that he scarcely had mercy for his own near relatives. . . . Clovis came and made war on him, and he saw that his army was beaten and prepared to slip away in flight, but was seized by his army, and with his hands tied behind his back, he was taken with Ricchar his brother before Clovis. And Clovis said to him: "Why have you humiliated our family in permitting yourself to be bound? It would have been better for you to die." And raising his ax he dashed it against his head, and he turned to the brother and said: "If you had aided your brother he would not have been bound." And in the same way he smote him with his ax and killed him. . . . These kings were kinsmen of Clovis, and their brother, Rignomer by name, was slain by Clovis's order at the city of Mans. When they were dead Clovis received all their kingdom and treasures. And having killed many other kings and his nearest relatives, of whom he was jealous lest they take the kingdom away from him, he extended his rule over all the Gauls. . . . For God was laying low his enemies every day under his hand, and was increasing his kingdom, because he walked with an upright heart before Him, and did what was pleasing to His eyes.

From Gregory of Tours, *History of the Franks,* trans. and annot. by E. Brehaut (New York: Columbia University Press, 1916), pp. 48–50.

tives "not because he grieved at their death but with the cunning thought that he might perhaps find one still alive whom he could kill." But Gregory could still sum up Clovis' career by saying: "God was laying low his enemies every day under his hand, and was increasing his kingdom, because he walked with an upright heart before Him, and did what was pleasing to His eyes." Gregory was equally favorable to King Guntram (561–593), of whom the best that could be said was that he murdered somewhat fewer people than his rivals did. "One would have taken him," says Gregory, "not only for a king, but for a priest of the Lord."

Nevertheless, the bishops did make an effort to mitigate the cruelty and selfishness of their rulers. They protected men unjustly accused; they did their best to prevent civil wars among members of the royal family. They were aided by the monasteries, which were just beginning to appear in the Frankish realm. Monks who had already abandoned the world were not easily terrified by the threats of kings. St. Columban, the founder of Luxeuil, denounced King Thierry (595–613) to his face as a sinner and predicted that his sons would never be kings. The saint was exiled, but he soon returned and saw Thierry's family wiped out in a civil war. Yet in spite of all the efforts of bishops and monks, the Franks were Christians only in externals; it took a long time for the faith to sink into their hearts.

The Collapse of the Gothic Kingdoms

While the Franks were gaining control of Gaul and western Germany, their only possible rivals were being eliminated. After Theodoric's death, Justinian, the Roman emperor at Constantinople (see pp. 159–65), was determined to conquer the Ostrogothic kingdom in Italy. It took years of hard fighting, but by 552 the desperate resistance of the Ostrogoths had been snuffed out, and a devastated Italy was restored to imperial control. But Italians did not have any great loyalty to an empire that had ruined them, and they were too weak to defend

themselves. As a result, when a new Germanic people, the Lombards, began to push into Italy from the Danube in the latter part of the sixth century, a large part of the peninsula lay open to conquest. The imperial forces held onto the south and some outposts in the north, such as Ravenna and Venice; the Lombards took the rest (although Rome retained some autonomy). The Lombards extended their conquests somewhat during the next century, but they never subdued the whole peninsula; in fact, no one was able to unite Italy again until 1870. The Lombard kingdom—weak, divided, and far less influenced by Roman civilization than the Ostrogothic kingdom had been—posed no threat to the Franks, who conquered it in the eighth century.

The Visigothic kingdom of Spain lasted a little longer than the Ostrogothic. The Visigothic kings strengthened themselves by abandoning their Arian heresy and accepting Catholic Christianity. Justinian struck them only a glancing blow; he regained some of the southeast coast of Spain but never had enough resources to reconquer the whole peninsula. But for more than 150 years the Visigoths suffered all the usual troubles of Germanic kingdoms—disputed successions, quarrels among the great men, and dwindling military strength. Thus when a Moslem army crossed the Straits of Gibraltar in 711 (see p. 175) and crushed the royal army, there was no effective resistance, and the Visigothic kingdom collapsed at once. A few Christians took refuge in the northern hills of Asturias and Galicia and established a petty kingdom there. The rest of the peninsula was drawn into an Arab empire and remained under Moslem control for centuries.

The Decline of the Merovingian Kings

After the sixth century only one power was left in Western Europe—the Frankish kingdom. The Anglo-Saxons were divided into petty kingdoms; the Scandinavian monarchies were just beginning to take form; the Germans of the north and east, such as the Frisians and the Old Saxons, had almost no organization; and

Two Ostrogothic brooches. The one above is made of gold inlaid with emerald and garnet and marks the zenith of the Ostrogothic style; the one below, made after the defeats of 552–553, is poor in quality and crudely decorated.

the Visigoths and the Lombards were weakened by internal quarrels. But the apparent strength and solidity of the Frankish kingdom were deceptive. The Franks soon began to suffer from the same political ills as the other Germanic peoples; their kingdom survived only because it was not seriously threatened by outside enemies. In Frankland, as elsewhere, the kings had found it difficult to establish any sort of central control, and political power was passing rapidly into the hands of the great noble families.

In addition to holding large amounts of land, these families were the local representatives of royal authority. The Frankish kingdom was divided into counties, each ruled by a count who collected the revenues, presided over the courts, and controlled the military forces of his district. The king supposedly could name counts as he saw fit, and in the sixth century men of poor families sometimes achieved the position. But this was always distasteful to the great families, and as the kings weakened, the nobles gained a virtual monopoly of all important offices. By the eighth century counts could be selected only from a small group of aristocrats. Many countships were, if not strictly hereditary, usually held within the same family.

Frequent outbreaks of civil war strengthened aristocratic control over local government. The Frankish kings treated their state as private property and regularly divided the kingdom among their sons. Just as regularly, one or more of the rival kings tried to eliminate his brothers and cousins and acquire their territories and treasuries. To gain support, he rewarded his own men and bribed the retainers of his rivals with grants of land and concessions of governmental power. These grants further weakened royal authority. Whatever central power remained passed more and more into the hands of an official known as the mayor of the palace.

The Mayors of the Palace

Originally the mayor was merely the head of the royal household, the man who managed the king's private affairs. But the Germans made little distinction between public and private affairs and used any official for any business. Thus the mayor of the palace, who was always at court, gradually became a viceroy who acted for the king in all important matters. The mayor was usually a member of one of the great Frankish families, supported by a coalition of local magnates. In order to keep his place, he had to grant favors to these magnates just as the king had done.

To make things worse, by 700 the Frankish lands had been split into an eastern, largely Germanic kingdom called Austrasia, a western, more Latinized kingdom named Neustria, and a much weaker southern kingdom of Burgundy. Southwest Gaul (Aquitaine) and southeast Germany (Bavaria) were practically autonomous. In each of the major kingdoms there was a mayor of the palace who was constantly threatened by rebellion among his own supporters and who constantly threatened his rival mayors with direct attacks and underhanded intrigues. Wars among the mayors were as bad as wars among the kings, and there seemed to be little hope that the Frankish kingdom could survive this turmoil.

Yet by 700 a remarkable family had appeared that was to reunite the Frankish kingdom and strengthen it so that within its shelter a new western European civilization could begin to take shape. This family—called Carolingian, from its most famous member, Charlemagne, or Charles the Great (Carolus Magnus)—came from the eastern Frankish kingdom of Austrasia. It gave strong support to the Church and especially to missionary and reform activities. It also showed remarkable skill in gaining and keeping the loyalty of the counts and great landowners. With their support the head of the family, Pippin, made himself mayor of the palace in both Neustria and Austrasia late in the seventh century. When Pippin died there was a rebellion, but his illegitimate son, Charles Martel (714–741), was eventually accepted as mayor of all the Frankish kingdoms. With Charles Martel all power in the Frankish kingdoms was caught up by the Carolingian family. Although the Merovingian kings kept their empty title a few more years, they had no further influence on the course of events.

The European Kingdoms
ca. 700

Suggestions for Further Reading

Note: Asterisk denotes a book available in paperback edition.

Theodoric, Boethius, and Cassiodorus

The life of one of the striking figures of the early Middle Ages is portrayed by T. Hodgkin, *Theodoric the Goth* (1891). Hodgkin writes in the "grand manner" of the nineteenth-century historian, and the book is still fresh. His *The Letters of Cassiodorus* (1886) contains the extensive correspondence of Cassiodorus and good biographical sketches of Cassiodorus and Boethius. A superior study of Cassiodorus and his monastic writings is *Introduction to Divine and Human Readings*, trans. by L. W. Jones (1946). Boethius' works are available in numerous translations. The most scholarly is in the *Loeb Classical Library*, trans. by E. K. Rand and H. F. Stewart (1918), but the Modern Library edition of Boethius' most famous work, *The Consolation of Philosophy*,* trans. by W. V. Cooper (1942), or R. Green (1962), are more readable. Both E. K. Rand, *Founders of the Middle Ages** (1928), and H. O. Taylor, *The Emergence of Christian Culture in the West** (1901), discuss Cassiodorus and Boethius as "transmitters" of the Greco-Roman legacy. M. L. W. Laistner, *Thought and Letters in Western Europe, 500–900** (1966), combines fine scholarship with good style. Paul the Deacon's *History of the Langobards*, trans. by D. Foulke (1907), is our chief source for the Lombard kingdom of northern Italy.

St. Benedict and the Monasteries

The cornerstone of monasticism in the West is the short *Rule of St. Benedict*, trans. by J. McCann (1952). The best scholarly study of the Rule is P. Delatte, *Commentary on the Rule of St. Benedict* (1908), but the more recent study by H. van Zeller, *The Holy Rule* (1958), is more interesting and more understandable to the modern student. C. Butler, *Benedictine Monachism* (1923), and D. Knowles, *Christian Monasticism* (1969), are valuable for an understanding of the spirit and meaning of the monastic life. J. McCann, *St. Benedict** (1952), gives a good account of St. Benedict and Benedictines through the centuries. A fascinating and provocative picture of monastic life today, in the form of a diary, is T. Merton, *The Sign of Jonas** (1956). The classic work of W. James, *Varieties of Religious Experience** (1902), does a great deal to explain the "phenomenon" of monasticism in the perspective of modern civilization.

The Franks and Gregory of Tours

A shockingly vivid picture of the chaotic society of sixth-century Gaul is presented by the contemporary Gregory of Tours, *History of the Franks*,* trans. by E. Brehaut (1916), or, in a fuller version, by O. M. Dalton (1927). This is our best evidence for the political and social condition of Merovingian Gaul. There is an excellent study of Gregory's language and its reflection of the decline of learning in the West in E. Auerbach, *Mimesis** (1946). *The Life of St. Columban*, trans. by D. C. Munro (1921), reinforces Gregory of Tours' picture of moral decadence. F. Lot, *The End of the Ancient World** (1931), contains a scholarly study of Gaul under the Merovingians, with emphasis on political conditions. The older work of S. Dill, *Roman Society in Gaul in the Merovingian Age* (1926), emphasizes economic and social aspects. A good overall survey is J. M. Wallace-Hadrill, *The Barbarian West: 400–1000** (1966); see also his excellent book on the Franks, *The Long-Haired Kings* (1962).

The Conversion of the Anglo-Saxons

The Venerable Bede of Jarrow's *The Ecclesiastical History of the English Nation** is incomparably the greatest authority we have for the early centuries of the English settlements. For the life and works of Bede, see the scholarly collection of essays edited by A. H. Thompson, *Bede: His Life, Times, and Writings* (1935), and P. H. Blair, *The World of Bede* (1970). The classic poem *Beowulf*,* trans. by D. Wright (1957), is a mine of information about Anglo-Saxon society in the seventh and eighth centuries. D. Whitelock, *The Beginnings of English Society** (1952), is a very good introductory treatment of the period, and G. O. Sayles, *The Medieval Foundations of England*,* Chapters 1–3 (1948), is a "history of ideas in action" with an excellent and detailed critical bibliography. See also S. J. Crawford, *Anglo-Saxon Influence on Western Christendom* (1933).

Gregory the Great

F. H. Dudden, *Gregory the Great*, 2 vols. (1905), the standard study of Gregory's pontificate, gives a good account of conditions in Italy at the time. Dudden pays special attention to the conversion of England. The increasing activities of the papacy under Gregory are shown in his letters in *Library of Nicene and Post Nicene Fathers*, Vols. XII and XIII (1895). *The Dialogues of St. Gregory the Great*, trans. by E. G. Gardner (1911), and, more recently, by M. Uhlfelder (1967), illustrates the religious and intellectual climate of the times. *The Dialogues* is our chief source for the life of St. Benedict.

8 Byzantium and Islam

The East was the first region of the Empire to be threatened by the barbarian inroads of the fourth and fifth centuries. Before moving west, the Visigoths and the Ostrogoths had held the Balkans for a time. But their presence, which was to alter profoundly the political and social pattern of the West, was only a passing episode in the history of the East. By 500 the Roman Empire in the West had vanished, whereas the Empire in the East was beginning a revival that was once more to give it a strong government, a highly developed economy, and an active intellectual and artistic life.

THE EASTERN ROMAN EMPIRE

This contrast shows once more that internal weaknesses rather than external attacks were the real cause of the collapse of the Roman Empire. In the West, where the internal weaknesses were more serious and more pervasive, nothing could be done to save the Empire. But in the East there were strengths as well as weaknesses. There the cities were economic assets rather than parasites, as they were in the West. Christianity was both more widespread and more deeply felt in the East than in the West, and it served as a substitute for patriotism. The excellent defensive positions of the East,

View of the interior of Hagia Sophia in Constantinople (532–537).

especially Constantinople, made it impossible for the Germans to touch the richest cities and provinces. Moreover, the Eastern emperors and their advisers were somewhat more skillful—or at least more successful—politicians than their colleagues in the West. They prevented the Goths from making any permanent settlement in the Balkan Peninsula, and they freed themselves from dependence on Germanic soldiers by recruiting troops in Asia Minor. Because they retained control of the great trading cities of Constantinople, Antioch, and Alexandria, the Eastern emperors could always collect enough taxes to support their administration and their army. With the departure of the Ostrogoths for Italy and the weakening of the Huns, the Eastern Empire was freed from immediate danger. During the sixth century it was able to start the difficult task of recovery.

Justinian

The leader of this first revival of the Eastern Empire was the emperor Justinian (527–565), a man of ambition, energy, and imagination. In spite of his abilities, however, his stubborn determination in pursuing mistaken policies led him to waste resources, miss opportunities, and plunge the Empire into useless wars. He was successful in most of his projects, but a less successful ruler might have done less harm. Every success encour-

Byzantine gold wedding ring (*ca.* fifth century).

aged him to extend his commitments, so that by the time of his death both the loyalty and the resources of his subjects had been nearly exhausted.

Justinian was not the sort of ruler one would expect to find in a state composed largely of Greeks, Syrians, and Egyptians. His family came from the extreme west of what was left of the Empire, from a district near the Adriatic, where Latin was still spoken. This Latin background may explain some of Justinian's policies. Fascinated by the idea of recovering the West, he was willing to sacrifice the people of the East in order to regain the old heart of the Empire. In a sense, Justinian was the last of the Roman emperors. After his death the Latin tradition died out, Greek became the official language of the Empire, and the ties between East and West slackened.

Justinian was lucky in his immediate predecessors, for they had rebuilt the army, set the Empire's finances in order, and repaired its administrative system. He was even luckier in what seemed at first a disastrous marriage. While he was still a young man, he had fallen in love with a woman named Theodora, who had been the sixth-century equivalent of

a stripteaser. She had had many lovers, and to marry her seemed socially impossible and politically unwise. But Justinian insisted on marrying his mistress, and he never had cause to regret it. Theodora was a courageous woman who kept Justinian from fleeing early in his reign when he was threatened by a rebellion of the people of Constantinople. She also understood the people of the East far better than her husband did; after her death he found it hard to retain their loyalty. Theodora secured important positions for many of her friends; through these supporters and through her own personal influence she was able to modify and even to reverse imperial policy, especially in the field of religion.

Nevertheless, the basic objectives of the reign were set by Justinian. He was determined to restore the Empire, to regain its lost territories, and to rebuild its cities. He always aimed high, reaching for the utmost in power and magnificence. Unfortunately, his resources were inadequate, and his plans were often contradictory.

Justinian's determination to reconquer the West was strengthened by the weakness of the Germanic kingdoms on

EXPANSION OF THE BYZANTINE EMPIRE UNDER JUSTINIAN   527–565

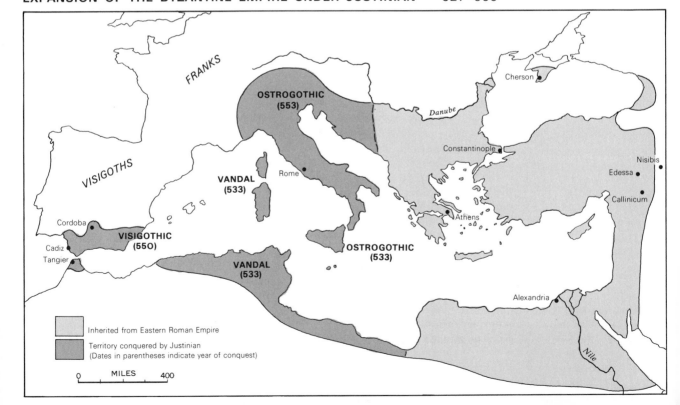

the Mediterranean. His first campaigns were encouragingly successful. The Vandal kingdom of Africa fell after a short war in 533. The Ostrogoths in Italy, left without a capable leader after the death of Theodoric, at first offered little resistance to the imperial army. In the end, the tide of reconquest even reached far-off Spain, where Justinian seized a strip of the southeastern coast with very little difficulty.

But it was easier to gain provinces in the West than to keep them. The Roman population of Italy, Spain, and Africa experienced no patriotic thrill on being reunited with the Empire. In fact, the reintroduction of the imperial tax system made many people long for the easier rule of the barbarians. Justinian tried to gain their loyalty by accepting Roman religious dogmas and rejecting the views of a large part of the clergy of Syria and Egypt. But he succeeded only in alienating many of his eastern subjects without gaining solid support in Italy. Soon the West lapsed into its old apathy. Justinian's rule was based on a small group of soldiers and bureaucrats; the bulk of the population was passive, taking part in neither politics nor war.

The barbarians were quick to take advantage of the situation. The Vandals had been thoroughly crushed, but the Berbers, fierce tribesmen living on the fringes of the civilized area, took up the fight for Roman Africa. After many years of conflict, the Berbers were pushed back from the coastal towns, but they continued to hold most of what is now Morocco and western Algeria.

Justinian had even more trouble in Italy. There the Ostrogoths, who had been defeated but not broken, elected a new king who nearly drove the imperial forces from the peninsula. Justinian never gave his Italian commanders enough troops, partly because so many other demands were being made on his resources and partly because he feared, like many a Roman emperor before him, that a too successful general might seek the throne for himself. As a result, the war dragged on for eighteen years, from 535 to 553. In the end the Goths were almost exterminated, but Italy had been devastated. Although Justinian retained

Procopius on Justinian's Wars

Procopius served for many years on the staff of one of Justinian's generals, and was later an official in Constantinople. He was well informed, but he exaggerated and was spiteful and envious, so that he must be read with caution. Nevertheless, there is much truth in his criticism of Justinian's military policies.

In estimating the territory that he depopulated, I should say that millions perished. For Libya [the Vandal kingdom] . . . was so thoroughly ruined that for a traveller who makes a long journey there it is no easy matter to meet a human being. . . . Immediately after the defeat of the Vandals Justinian did not concern himself with strengthening his dominion over the country nor make provision that its wealth should be safeguarded through the good-will of its inhabitants. . . . He sent out assessors of the land and imposed certain very heavy taxes. . . . As for Italy, it has become everywhere even more empty of men than Libya. Indeed, all the errors that he made in Libya were repeated. . . . By adding to the administrative staff oppressive financial agents he upset and ruined everything. . . . Meanwhile the Arabs were overrunning the Romans of the East . . . and the Persians under Chosroes four times made inroads into the Roman domain . . . leaving the land bare of inhabitants. . . . [Justinian] in time of war would grow lax for no good reason and carried on preparations for military operations too deliberately, all because of his parsimony. . . . [This last criticism is not entirely fair; Justinian often had trouble raising enough money for his armies.]

From Procopius, *The Anecdota or Secret History*, trans. by H. B. Dewing (London, 1954), pp. 215, 217, 219, 221.

Italy for the rest of his reign, it contributed nothing to the strength or wealth of the Empire.

In the long run Justinian's policy of reconquest was a failure. None of the western provinces he regained was secure, either in a political or a military sense; most of them were lost within a generation or two after his death. The Lombards, who had migrated from the north into what is now Austria, pushed through the mountain passes and settled in the Po Valley, to which they gave their name, Lombardy. Then they drove down past Rome, and in the end all that was left of Justinian's Italian conquest was a large part of the south and the districts of Venice, Ravenna, and Rome. The Spanish reconquest proved just as ephemeral; by 624 the Visigoths had regained all the

Mosaic portraits of Justinian and Theodora, San Vitale, Ravenna (*ca.* 547).

coastal territories they had lost. North Africa stayed longer with the Empire, but fell to the Moslems at the end of the seventh century.

Though Justinian waged an offensive campaign in the West, he was kept on the defensive in the East. The Persian kingdom, the ancient enemy of Rome, was once more growing in strength and pressing hard on the eastern frontiers. On several occasions the Persians broke through the Roman defenses and plundered much of Syria and Asia Minor. With a large part of his army tied up in the West, Justinian was never able to defeat the Persians decisively, but through force of arms, diplomacy, and bribery he did manage to retain Syria and western Asia Minor. In the Balkans, Hunnic groups, aided by Slavic allies, staged raids that at times came very close to Constantinople. Justinian held on to most of the Balkan Peninsula, but he had to allow some of the Slavs to settle there. This was the beginning of Slavic predominance in the Balkans.

Justinian's policy in the East was not only cautious, which may have been sensible, it was also expensive. Diplomacy, bribes, and occasional payments of tribute to exceptionally dangerous enemies cost huge sums of money, but they did not end the necessity for maintaining an army and building fortifications. At the same time, many eastern provinces that were devastated by raids and invasions failed to pay their share of taxes.

Burdened though he was by wars of conquest in the West and by wars of defense in the East, Justinian did not spend the Empire's entire income on military operations. Restoration of the Empire meant more to him than territorial expansion; he was determined to recreate the magnificence of Rome at the height of its power. The New Rome of Constantinople was to be even more splendid than Old Rome, and provincial capitals were to reflect this splendor. Justinian put as much energy into this program as he did into his wars, and the results were somewhat more lasting.

They were more lasting because he accepted eastern standards instead of trying to impose his own western, Latin prejudices. Classical Roman art and architecture had simply decayed in the West, but in the East they had been transformed under the joint impact of Christianity and the revival of Oriental cultures. A new style was already emerging when Justinian gained the throne, and he gave it a chance to express itself through his great building program. All through the Empire, from Mount Sinai in the Egyptian desert to Ravenna in reconquered Italy, magnificent churches rose, rich with mosaics, goldsmiths' work, and many-colored marble.

The architects of these churches, so far as we know their names, came from the Asiatic provinces, and the decoration was largely inspired by Oriental examples. The new churches emphasized the interior, which blazed with light and color, rather than the exterior, which was often left rough and unadorned. In the famous church of St. Sophia in Constantinople, Justinian's architects built a great dome pierced with many windows high over the central part of the building. By solving the problem of setting a circular dome firmly atop a rectangular opening, they made the dome a far more effective element than it had been before, both esthetically and as a source of light. Earlier Roman architects had bolstered their domes with high walls that concealed them from view and blocked out much of the light. Even when Justinian's architects did not use the dome, they raised the walls of their churches and enlarged the window spaces in order to admit more light. And everywhere there were brilliant mosaics, gold and silver ornaments, richly woven textiles, polished stones of every hue. The decoration was stylized, symbolic, and not at all realistic; for this very reason it had a greater impact on the beholder. The endless ranks of saints and angels along the walls were clearly not human beings; rigid, solemn, and intense, these figures were unmistakably inhabitants of another world. And with the saints and angels appeared the figures of Justinian and Theodora, humble before their God, but haloed like saints and immeasurably superior to all other human beings. One of the emperor's most cherished titles was "Equal of the Apostles," and his churches gave visible support to this claim.

Religious Disputes

Justinian was certainly a sincere and pious Christian. But he was also something of a scholar with a dangerous taste for theology, and he ruled over subjects who would fight for religious dogmas when they would fight for nothing else. There had already been serious quarrels over basic articles of the faith before Justinian became emperor; he probably could not have avoided interfering in religious matters even if he had so desired. But he did not so desire. Instead, he wanted to use religion to unify the restored Empire. His efforts failed, although he bullied popes, deposed patriarchs, and imprisoned monks and priests. At his death the Empire was still badly divided in its religious beliefs.

The basis of the controversy was the old argument about the union of the human and the divine in Jesus Christ. If Jesus was not fully divine, then the Redemption was impossible; if Christ was not fully human, then he did not suffer for us, and so the Crucifixion lost its meaning. Few people any longer took the extreme positions of "fully divine" or "fully human," but in trying to describe the way in which divine and human were joined together it was easy to overstress one or the other and thus fall into heresy.

When Justinian took over the imperial government the most dangerous heresy was that of the Monophysites, a group that recognized the existence of a human nature in Christ but subordinated it to the divine nature to such an extent that it became meaningless. Those who supported and those who opposed the Monophysites were stirred by something more than a desire for precise theological definitions. Monophysitism had become the national religion of Egypt, and in Syria it probably had more adherents than any other sect. It gave the inhabitants of these lands a chance to voice their long-suppressed desire for cultural and spiritual independence. It was anti-Greek, anti-Roman, antipapal, and anti-West.

Justinian's own beliefs were opposed to Monophysitism, and his political aims intensified his opposition. As we have seen, he wanted to recover the West, and the West, led by the pope, was almost unanimous in its rejection of Monophysite doctrine. Early in his reign, therefore, Justinian persecuted the Monophysites and tried to suppress their teachings.

But in religion as in war, Justinian found that he could not concentrate exclusively on the West. Theodora, always far more understanding of eastern viewpoints than her husband, realized that his flat opposition to Monophysitism was endangering imperial control of Egypt and Syria. She probably had some personal inclinations toward the doctrine as well. Under her influence, Justinian became somewhat more tolerant and finally settled for an interpretation that was technically orthodox but that leaned toward the Monophysite position.

No one was pleased with this solution. Pope Vigilius, who had come to Constantinople against his better judgment to confer with the emperor, refused at first to accept the compromise formula. He yielded only after a long period of house arrest and threats. The orthodox clergy of Constantinople were equally indignant, although easier to deal with; Justinian simply dismissed them from their posts. The Monophysites themselves, whom Justinian was trying to conciliate, found the new orthodox doctrine just as unacceptable as the old. Almost all Egyptians, and many Syrians, seceded from the official Church and formed their own religious organizations, which were bitterly hostile to the government and to the orthodox, Greek-speaking clergy. This sharp division in religion helps explain the ease with which the Arabs took over most of the East in the next century (see p. 173). Syrians and Egyptians saw no reason to fight the Arabs to preserve the rule of intolerant and orthodox Greeks. The Moslems had nothing to gain by forcing religious uniformity on the inhabitants of the lands they conquered, so there was more toleration of different Christian sects under their government than under the Byzantine emperors.

Justinian's Summary of Roman Law

Justinian's love of precise definition, which led him into dangerous religious policies, found happier expression in the field of law. Perhaps his only two completely successful achievements were the building of St. Sophia and the codification of Roman law. The most impressive intellectual achievement of the Romans had been in law, and the keenest minds of the Empire had worked on legal prob-

Gold coin portraying Justinian on horseback. The coin was struck to commemorate the defeat of the Vandals in 535.

lems. But this was the very reason that codification was needed; Roman law had developed over so many centuries that its basic rules had to be sought in the voluminous works of generations of lawyers and officials. There had been earlier attempts to codify and digest Roman law, but no one had had the energy or the determination to survey the entire mass of legal literature and reduce it to manageable proportions.

Justinian attacked the problem of codifying the law with the same energy and ruthlessness with which he planned the reconquest of the West. At the very beginning of his reign he picked a group of capable men, led by the great jurist Tribonian, and gave them a free hand to produce a statement of the law that would be brief, clear, and consistent. He must have put heavy pressure on them, for they completed the task with incredible speed. The essential work was done between 528 and 534, and little was added after 546, the year of Tribonian's death.

The books produced by this effort came to be known collectively as the *Corpus Juris.* The first and most important unit was the *Digest,* a collection of extracts from the works of leading Roman lawyers, especially those of the second century, the golden age of Roman law. These extracts dealt with such basic problems of jurisprudence as the nature of law and justice, and the relation between law and custom. But they also included brief statements on the guiding principles of Roman law in, for example, such matters as property, contract, and inheritance. The next book of the *Corpus Juris* was the *Code*, a restatement and simplification of statute law. These two major works were followed by the *Institutes*, a textbook of Roman law for students, and the *Novels*, laws promulgated after 534 to amend or supplement the *Code*.

The speed with which the *Corpus Juris* was compiled led to some unfortunate results. Important material was omitted, while insignificant and even contradictory statements were included. Moreover, because the *Corpus Juris* was the only authorized version of Roman law, earlier works on the subject were neglected and lost. Almost none of the thousands of volumes on Roman law written under the Empire have survived. On the other hand, judging by what happened to Latin literary works, most of the legal writings would have been lost in any case, and the *Digest* did at least preserve quotations from the ablest Roman lawyers.

Curiously, although the *Corpus Juris* was never applied as actual law in the West, it had a far greater effect on western countries than it did on the East. In the East the emperors continued to revise the laws, treating Justinian's work not as a final summary of legal thinking but only as a foundation for their own efforts. In the West the *Corpus Juris* was regarded as the final and perfect expression of Roman law. For many generations the *Corpus Juris* was neglected in the West, but when the revival of medieval civilization began in the late eleventh century (see Chapter 10), Justinian's work seemed a treasure beyond price. It gave men who were struggling with primitive and confused notions of social relationships the precise concepts of a highly developed legal system. It had a tremendous impact on both the state and the Church, on both private and public institutions. The *Corpus Juris* became an essential part of the western intellectual tradition and affected the law of every western European country. Justinian's real reconquest of the West came many centuries after his death, not through his armies but through his law.

From Eastern Roman to Byzantine Empire

It is well to remember this ultimate triumph of Justinian, for the immediate results of his reign were disastrous. His successors ranged from mediocre to despicable, but even able emperors would have found it difficult to cope with the legacy of bankruptcy, internal discontent, and external enmity that Justinian had left. Repeated rebellions made it impossible to guard the frontiers. The western conquests were lost, while in the East the Persians again attacked the Asian provinces of the Empire. And a new danger arose in the north: the Avars, a nomad people akin to the Huns, pillaged the Balkan provinces and threatened Constantinople itself. The Slavs again assisted the invaders and occupied large areas of the Balkans.

Early in the seventh century the plight of the Eastern Empire seemed hopeless. The Persians had taken Syria and Egypt, and the Avars had set up permanent camps close to Constantinople. But the Eastern Empire clung to life with amazing tenacity and showed marvelous powers of recuperation. Beneath the appearance of luxury and decadence, behind the intrigues and the factional quarrels, was a very hard core of administrative competence, diplomatic skill, military capacity, and a passionate loyalty among the people of Constantinople to their state and their religion. In the seventh century, as it would again and again in the future, the Empire rallied and beat off its enemies.

Heraclius, who became emperor in 610, slowly worked out a policy of avoiding conflict with the Avars through bribes and diplomacy, while throwing the bulk of his army against the Persians. He had little success at first, but he finally ended the war with a raid deep into Persian territory that forced the Persians to make peace in 628.

The half-century of civil and foreign war that followed the death of Justinian wrought profound changes in the character of the Eastern Roman Empire. In the first place, the Latin element in the Empire, which had long been weakening, almost vanished. Early in his reign Justinian had used Latin for the *Corpus Juris*, but by the time of his death Greek was the only language that could be used for administrative and legal purposes. In the second place, religious dissent grew in Syria and Egypt, and the long period of Persian occupation and raiding did nothing to strengthen loyalty to Constantinople. The heart of the Empire was now the Greek-speaking, religiously orthodox region centering around Constantinople. The city itself supplied the wealth, the educated classes supplied the administrative personnel, and the poorer part of the population supplied the politico-religious fervor that kept the Empire going. Only one more thing was needed—an army—and the best recruiting ground for soldiers was Asia Minor. Therefore a successful emperor had to hold Constantinople and enough of Asia Minor to maintain his military strength. If an emperor could keep this core area, the Empire would stand virtually unbeatable. Heraclius seems to have had some understanding of this principle; at least he made little effort to hold the northern

and western Balkans and postponed the reconquest of Syria until he had gained access to the old recruiting grounds in eastern Asia Minor.

But an empire based on Constantinople and Asia Minor was no longer a Roman Empire, even though the name continued in official use. To mark the change, most historians have called the continuation of the Roman Empire in the East the Byzantine Empire. This term, derived from the old Greek name for Constantinople (Byzantium), emphasizes the importance of the capital city and the Greek-speaking element in the Empire. It should not be used, therefore, for the sixth-century Empire, which was still Mediterranean in outlook and largely non-Greek in population. It becomes increasingly appropriate during the seventh century, however, when Syria, Egypt, and North Africa were lost, and when the Empire was restricted to the eastern Balkans, Asia Minor, and a few districts in Italy.

The Byzantine Empire gradually developed patterns of behavior and organization that made it very different from western Europe. In religion, for example, slight differences in creed, organization, and ritual between the Christians of the West and those of Constantinople were magnified by quarreling theologians, ambitious rulers, and subjects who

Greek fire, a mixture of quicklime, petroleum, and sulfur that ignited when it came in contact with water, was introduced into the Byzantine navy after 675. It was a very effective weapon against the Arabs (detail from a fourteenth-century manuscript).

A Byzantine lady of rank (late fifth or early sixth century). Note her elegantly draped mantle and the snoodlike bonnet of the imperial type.

Early Byzantine jewelry contained Hellenistic and Roman features. The clasp of this late-sixth-century necklace, for example, is of a Hellenistic type, while the cylindrical slides between the pendants are a late Roman feature.

feared everything foreign. The Roman Catholic Church and the Greek Orthodox Church slowly drifted apart, a divergence that encouraged divergences in other fields.

But religion alone does not account for all the profound differences between the Byzantine Empire and its neighbors. More than any other state, it preserved the cultural traditions of Greece and the political techniques of the old Roman Empire. Not that the Byzantine Empire was a stagnant society. It showed marvelous skill and flexibility in adapting itself to new conditions, and this is precisely why it was able to preserve so much of its heritage. The Byzantine Empire never had to make an entirely fresh start, for it was always able to modify and thus retain its old ideas and institutions. It always possessed a highly trained bureaucracy, skillful diplomats, and a professional army. Economic activity and church administration were manipulated for the benefit of the government. Art, literature, and scholarship were encouraged, so that there was no break in the Greek literary and artistic tradition.

In short, the Byzantine Empire stood forth as a highly centralized and autocratic state at a time when the very concept of the state had been almost forgotten in western Europe. This state had a great urban center, an active commercial life, and a sophisticated literary and artistic tradition in contrast to the agricultural and largely illiterate society of western Europe. Both Augustus and Louis XIV would have understood and sympathized with many of the ideas and practices of the Byzantine Empire, but few western Europeans between 700 and 1400 could fathom the Byzantine way of life.

The differences between the Byzantines and the Arabs, who conquered Syria, Egypt, Armenia, and Palestine in the seventh century, were not so great as those between Byzantines and western Europeans. The Arabs took over much of the administrative system and many of the intellectual traditions of the old Eastern Empire. But religious hostility hampered intellectual contacts, since the Arabs had accepted the new religion of

Mohammed. Moreover, while both the Greeks and the Arabs revered Plato, Aristotle, and other early philosophers, the Arabs put more emphasis on the Greek scientific tradition than did Byzantine scholars. There were interesting similarities between the Arab Empire and the Byzantine Empire, but these similarities became less apparent when the Arab Empire broke up into warring and short-lived states. No Moslem state endured as long as Byzantium or created such a permanent bureaucracy. Thus the Byzantine Empire gradually became unique, and it soon began to glory in its uniqueness. The Greeks of Constantinople, like their remote ancestors of the fifth century B.C., believed that they were the only civilized people and that their neighbors—especially their European neighbors—were barbarians. Caught between the barbarous West and the infidel East, the Byzantines clung with increasing tenacity to their government, their culture, and their religion.

MOHAMMED AND THE RISE OF THE ARAB EMPIRE

A few years after the death of Justinian in 565, a child was born in Arabia who was to found a religion that spread more rapidly than Christianity and an empire that was larger than that of Rome at the height of its power. Few men have had more impact on history than Mohammed. His religion split the old Mediterranean world and transformed the civilization of the Middle East; his influence is felt today in a broad belt of territory stretching from West Africa to the East Indies. Islam was the last of the three great world religions to emerge, and for many centuries it was more vigorous than either of its rivals—Christianity in the West and Buddhism in the East.

The Early Arabs

Arabia had played no important role in history before the time of Mohammed. The huge peninsula, about one-third the size of the United States, was like an arid wedge driven into the fertile lands of the

Middle East. Most Arabs were nomads, driving their herds from one scanty patch of vegetation to another. A much smaller, but very influential, group was made up of traders who dealt in products from the southern part of the peninsula, notably frankincense, and in goods imported from India and the Far East. Overland trade through Arabia was not extensive, but there was enough to support a few small towns along the southern and western sides of the peninsula.

The early Arabs were thus in touch with all the civilizations of the East and had learned something from all of them. Since they themselves spoke a Semitic language, they had been most influenced by other peoples of this language group who lived in the Fertile Crescent north of the peninsula. The Arabs developed a system of writing related, at least indirectly, to the Phoenician alphabet. They had the usual Semitic interest in religion, although it was expressed in almost indiscriminate polytheism. They had numerous tribal deities, and they had had contacts with the Christians and Jews who inhabited the northern part of the Arabian Peninsula. They honored poets, and the ideal Arab leader was as ready to make verses as he was to make war. They knew a good deal about astronomy, for knowledge of the stars is as helpful in crossing the desert as it is in navigating the seas. At their best, the Arabs were imaginative and eager to absorb new knowledge. They assimilated and profited from Greco-Roman civilization far more rapidly than did the Germans who took over the western part of the Roman Empire.

And yet there were grave defects in the social and political organization of the early Arabs. The nature of the country forced them to live in small, scattered tribes, and each tribe was almost constantly at war with its neighbors. The leading families within each tribe were often jealous of one another, so that blood-feuds were frequent and persistent. Weaker members of each tribe, and indeed of each family, were harshly treated by their stronger relatives. Sickly children were often killed, and orphans had little hope of receiving their parents' property. Women had almost no rights; their fathers or their husbands controlled their lives and their property. Men who could afford it had many wives and could divorce any of them whenever they wished. The divorced woman was usually left without any property or regular income.

In spite of all this disunity, certain strong ties bound the Arabs together. They were great genealogists; the leaders of many tribes could trace their ancestry back to the same ancient families—families that were known and respected throughout Arabia. Most of the tribes accepted a few common religious observances. There was a sacred period in each year, for example, when fighting was suspended and when many Arabs made a pilgrimage to the religious center of Mecca, a trading town near the west coast. In Mecca was the Kaaba, an ancient building full of images, including one of Christ. Here almost every god known to the Arabs could be worshiped. Here, too, was the most venerated object in the Arab world, the sacred Black Stone that had come from heaven. This habit of worshiping together at Mecca was the strongest unifying force in Arabia and one that was carefully preserved by Mohammed.

Mohammed's Teaching

Mohammed was born about 570 in Mecca. We know little about his early years, except that he was a poor orphan. When he reached adolescence he began to work for a woman named Khadija, the widow of a rich merchant. In her service he made many caravan trips, during which he may have accumulated his information about the Jewish and Christian religions and his knowledge of the legends and traditions of other Arab tribes. He eventually married his employer, though she was considerably older than he, and the marriage gave him the wealth and leisure to meditate on religious problems.

Like many other Arabs, Mohammed had a sensitive mind, a deep appreciation of the wonders of nature, and a strong interest in religion. These qualities were enhanced by mysterious seizures, to which he had been subject since childhood. During these attacks he seemed to be struggling to express ideas that were not yet fully formed in his own mind. He gradually came to believe that this was God's way of trying to communicate with him, but until he was about forty he had no clear idea of what he was meant to do. Then he had his first revelation: a vision of the angel Gabriel, who commanded him to speak "in the name of the Lord, the Creator . . . the Lord who taught man what he did not know."

Mohammed was still doubtful about his mission, but as revelation succeeded revelation he became filled with the vision of the one, eternal God, the Lord of the world. He began to appeal to his fellow citizens of Mecca to abandon their host of false deities and to worship the one, true God. These early revelations bear some resemblance to the Psalms, both in their poetic quality and in their

appeal to the wonders of nature as proofs of God's greatness and mercy. The stars in the heavens, sunshine and rain, the fruits of the earth—"all are signs of God's power if you would only understand."

By now Mohammed was convinced that he was a prophet, the last and greatest in the succession of prophets whom God had sent to enlighten and save mankind. He never claimed to be more than a prophet and even denied that he could work miracles, although he admitted that some of his predecessors had had this gift. He also admitted the divine mission of the Jewish prophets and of Jesus, but he claimed that their teachings had been distorted or misinterpreted. He was quite certain that the revelations he received superseded everything that had come before. The earlier prophets had had glimpses of the true religion, but he

The holy Kaaba in modern Mecca is the most sacred Islamic shrine.

An Early Revelation to Mohammed

By the white forenoon
and the brooding night!
Thy Lord has neither forsaken thee nor hates thee
and the Last shall be better for thee than the First.
Thy Lord shall give thee, and thou shalt be satisfied.

Did He not find thee an orphan, and shelter thee?
Did He not find thee erring, and guide thee?
Did He not find thee needy, and suffice thee?

As for the orphan, do not oppress him,
and as for the beggar, scold him not;
and as for thy Lord's blessing, declare it.

From A. J. Arberry, *The Koran Interpreted* (London: George Allen and Unwin, 1955), Vol. II, p. 342, Ch. 93.

alone had received the full message. Their teachings were to be accepted only when they agreed with the final word of God, which had been revealed to him.

Mohammed at first made little progress in converting his countrymen. His wife, Khadija, believed in him and comforted him when he was despondent, and his cousin Ali was one of his first converts. But most Meccans of good family were hostile; most of his early followers were from poor and uninfluential families. Mohammed's attacks on idols angered those who believed that the prosperity of Mecca depended on its being the center of worship of all the known gods. Mohammed's followers were persecuted, and his own life was threatened. Finally he fled with his supporters to the city of Yathrib, some distance north of Mecca. The Mohammedan era begins with this flight, or Hegira, which took place in 622 A.D.*

Mohammed was welcomed as an arbitrator of local disputes in Yathrib. The town was renamed Medinet-en-Nabi (Medina), the City of the Prophet. Jewish

*This does not mean that dates of the Moslem era can be converted to our reckoning simply by adding 622 years. The Moslem year is based on a lunar calendar, and so does not coincide with ours. Our year 1978 was 1398 A.H.

influence was strong there, and the Arabs of Medina found nothing strange in the doctrine of a single, all-powerful God. Mohammed soon gained many converts among the pagan and half-Jewish Arabs and became virtually the ruler of the community. He now became involved in political problems, and the revelations he received during this period dealt largely with law and government. For example, it was at Medina that the rules about marriage, inheritance, and the punishment of criminals were laid down.

During the stay at Medina, Mohammed's reputation and power increased steadily. A desultory war between Medina and Mecca gradually became more serious, and by 630 Mohammed had gained so many supporters that he was able to capture Mecca with little difficulty. He immediately destroyed the idols in the Kaaba, except for the Black Stone, and made the temple the center of his religion. He had long asserted that the Kaaba had been built by Abraham and that Abraham had placed the heavenly Stone there as a sign of God's power. Thus he was able to preserve Mecca as the religious center of Arabia.

The fall of Mecca convinced many Arabs that Mohammed really was a prophet or at least that he was too strong to oppose. During his last years, most of the tribes of the peninsula acknowledged his spiritual and political leadership. Nevertheless, when Mohammed died in 632 Arabia was far from being a unified state, and many Arabs had only vague ideas about the religion they had accepted.

The Koran

Mohammed, however, had left behind the Koran, a collection of his revelations. He had taught that the Koran was God's guide for the human race, that it had always existed in heaven, but that no one had been worthy of receiving it before his own appearance on earth. Although he had received the Koran piece by piece, as circumstances made its teachings applicable, it formed a consistent and coherent whole. It contained all that man needed to know, and it was to be followed without question. Mohammed said: "Let the Koran always be your guide. Do what it commands or permits; shun what it forbids."

From the very start of Mohammed's mission, his followers had carefully written down his revelations on parchment, palm leaves, or whatever else was available. The task of sorting out and arranging this mass of sayings was begun soon after Mohammed's death by Abu-Bekr, but his version was not universally accepted. Othman, who ruled the Arab Empire from 644 to 656, ended the disputes that arose by compiling an authoritative version and banning all other collections. Othman's version has remained almost unchanged down to the present.

In no other major religion was there such early agreement on the official version of the founder's teachings. In fact, the Koran was put together so hurriedly that it seems somewhat confused and illogical to a non-Moslem. The basic rule was to put the longer passages first. Thus the earliest revelation, in which Mohammed was ordered to begin his mission, comes in Chapter 96, after many of the long, prosaic Medina passages. Seemingly repetitious and even contradictory statements were never harmonized. But these flaws are not admitted by orthodox Moslems, who consider the Koran a masterpiece of Arabic literature as well as the ultimate word of God to man.

The religion taught in the Koran was easy to understand and easy to follow. The basic creed was simple: "There is no God but Allah and Mohammed is his prophet." The faithful must also believe in the resurrection and the day of judgment, when every man will be rewarded according to his merits. The Mohammedan hell is very like the Christian one, but the Mohammedan paradise is unmistakably Arabian—a green garden full of running water and fruit trees with beautiful damsels to wait on the souls in bliss. Finally, the Koran teaches predestination: "Every man's fate have We bound around his neck"—that is, all human events have been determined, once and for all, by the will of God. Mohammed's own name for his religion was Islam—"submission to the will of God"—and his followers were called Moslems—"those who submit."

Leaf from a manuscript of the Koran, Egypt (eighth or ninth century).

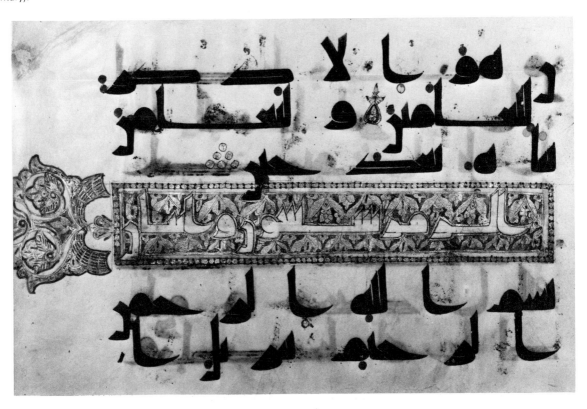

The principal religious practices of Islam were as simple as its theology. Every Moslem was to pray five times a day and to fast during the daylight hours of the month of Ramadan. Alms giving was a religious duty. Finally, every believer was to make a pilgrimage, if possible, to Mecca. But "only he shall visit the Mosque of God who believes in God and the Last Day, and is constant in prayer, and gives alms and fears God alone."

The Koran forbade wine drinking, usury, and gambling, and a dietary law, somewhat like that of the Jews, banned certain foods, especially pork. There was also a rudimentary code of law designed to check the selfishness and violence that had prevailed among the Arabs. Arbitration was to take the place of the blood-feud, infanticide was condemned, and elaborate rules of inheritance safeguarded the rights of orphans and widows. Mohammed also made an effort to limit polygamy by ruling that no man might have more than four wives simultaneously. Divorce was still easy, but the divorced wife could no longer be sent away penniless. These and other provisions were enough to furnish a framework for a judicial system.

There were obvious resemblances between Islam and Christianity, especially between Islam and the Christian heresies that denied or minimized the divinity of Christ. Since Mohammed admitted that Jesus was a major prophet, many heretics could accept Islam without feeling that they had greatly changed their beliefs. Other unorthodox Christians in Asia and Africa were so angered by their persecution by the Greek Church that they turned to Islam as a lesser evil. And in the competition for the loyalty of groups with little knowledge of either religion, Islam had a great advantage. It needed no organized church, for it had neither a priesthood nor a sacramental system. Each individual had to assure his salvation by his own right belief and good conduct. Every essential act of the religion could be accomplished by a man living quite by himself. It was customary for the faithful to meet together for prayers, especially on Friday, and from the earliest period certain men devoted themselves to explaining the Koran. But none of this was essential; anyone could accept Islam without waiting for the organization of a religious community, and any believer could make

THE GROWTH OF THE ISLAMIC CALIPHATE   632–750

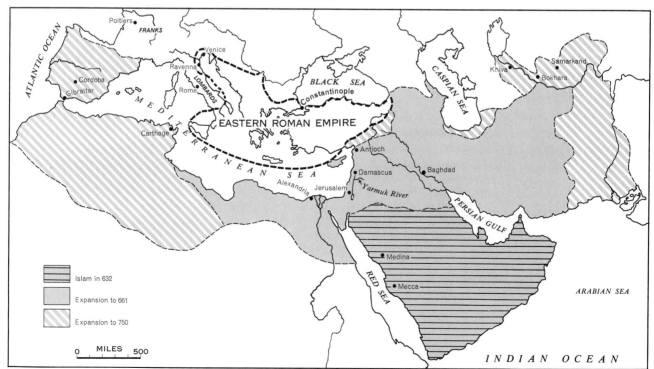

converts without waiting for an ordained priest to come and validate his action. Simple and uncomplicated monotheism was easier to explain than the doctrine of the Trinity.

These advantages often gave Islam the victory in competition with Christianity. On several occasions in the Middle Ages the Moslems were able to move in and convert a pagan people while the Christians were still trying to recruit a troop of missionary priests. And even today Islam is spreading more rapidly among the peoples of Asia and Africa than is Christianity.

The Caliphate

Mohammed left no very clear instructions about how his successor should be chosen. At his death there was confusion in the ranks of his followers and rebellion on the part of recently converted tribes. The faithful finally decided to choose a caliph, or successor to the prophet, who would act as both spiritual and political leader of Islam. The first caliph was Abu-Bekr, one of the earliest and most pious of Mohammed's converts. Though he ruled only two years (632–634), he succeeded in suppressing the revolts and in completing the unification of Arabia. Under his successor, Omar (634–644), the great conquests began. The Arabs had long been in the habit of raiding their wealthier neighbors to the north. Now they found themselves united for the first time, while both the Byzantine and the Persian states had been weakened by disastrous wars. In their first probing attacks, the Arabs met such slight resistance that they soon turned to wars of conquest. Their defeat of a Byzantine army at the Yarmuk River in 636 determined the fate of all the eastern provinces. Some fortified towns held out for a few years, but by 649 the Arabs had conquered Syria, Armenia, Palestine, and Egypt. Persia gave even less trouble and was completely in Arab hands by 642. Only the outbreak of civil war in Arabia slowed this first wave of conquest.

The civil war was caused by bad feeling between the early converts and some of the leading Arab families who had

An Islamic coin (698–699), the first silver coinage struck of purely Islamic type. The inscription in the center of the coin reads: "There is no God but God alone; no one is associated with him." The insistence on God's oneness and the denial of an associate to him is directed against the Christians and their doctrine of the Trinity.

accepted Islam only after Mohammed's triumph was assured. The trouble began under the caliph Othman (644–656), who was an early convert himself but who was not so opposed to the latecomers as were some of the prophet's other companions. He was accused of favoring recent converts and of pushing forward his kinsmen, the Ommiads, who had at one time led the Meccan opposition to Mohammed. The accusation was largely true, but it is hard to see what else Othman could have done. He now had an empire to govern, and he needed the help of every man who displayed qualities of leadership, whatever his past religious behavior had been.

Quarrels between the two factions led to the assassination of Othman in 656. He was succeeded by an old believer, Ali, the son-in-law and adopted son of Mohammed. But since Ali was accused of condoning Othman's murder, the Ommiads soon revolted and secured the nomination of one of their family as caliph. Ali held Persia and Mesopotamia for a while but was assassinated in 661 by a member of a small, fanatical sect that believed the office of caliph was unnecessary. After Ali's death, the Ommiad caliph, who had taken no part in the assassination, was accepted as ruler by the entire Moslem world.

The Ommiad Dynasty

The first Ommiad caliph transferred the capital of the Arab Empire from Mecca to Damascus. This act was typical of the family, which put far more em-

Islamic door with ivory panel (eighth century).

phasis on politics than on religion. Damascus was not the prophet's city, but it had public buildings, a large group of educated and experienced civil servants, and a central location. It was far more satisfactory as a capital than Mecca, and it had the additional advantage of containing few of the prophet's early companions. The Ommiads bestowed key positions on members of the Arab aristocracy rather than on the early converts, and they filled the government bureaus with Christian Syrians and Egyptians. Thus the Arab Empire began to change from a loosely organized tribal theocracy into a centralized state employing many Byzantine administrative techniques. Fi-

The Dome of the Rock in Jerusalem. This mosque was built on the spot from which Mohammed was believed to have ascended to heaven.

nally, the office of caliph ceased to be elective and was made hereditary in the Ommiad family.

The policy of the Ommiads toward conquered peoples was also based on purely political considerations. The Arabs, like most tribal peoples, had never paid taxes, and they had no intention of doing so now that they were lords of a large part of the civilized world. In any case, the Arabs were not in actual possession of farms and businesses; they were administrators, not property owners. Thus the government was financed by tribute exacted from unbelievers, which meant that mass conversions would be a threat to its financial stability. So, instead of forcing Islam on their subjects, the Ommiad caliphs did not encourage conversion. New converts had to pay a heavy land tax, from which Arabs were exempt, and they were seldom given responsible positions in the government.

This policy caused little trouble in Syria, where the Arab aristocracy was satisfied with its special privileges and where Christians were numerous. But in both Persia and Mesopotamia, where Ommiad control was less secure, most of the population became converted to Islam. The new converts resented their inferior position and often revolted against the rule of Ommiad officials. They were encouraged in their resistance by the more pious Arabs, who felt that the Ommiads were far too worldly, and by survivors of the faction that had supported Ali.

In spite of hidden weaknesses in their state, the Ommiad caliphs profited more from the late Roman civilization they had taken over than did the Germanic kings of the West. Syria, the heart of the Ommiad state, had always been more advanced intellectually and economically than Gaul, the heart of the strongest Germanic kingdom. The Ommiads began to draw on their heritage from the older civilization almost as soon as they gained power. They organized their administrative services on Roman and Persian models. They welcomed scholars of all nationalities to their court and urged them to undertake the task of translating philosophical, scientific, and medical works into Arabic. They built impressive mosques at Damascus and Jerusalem, adapting Syrian architecture to the needs of the Mohammedan religion. A new civilization began to grow up around the Ommiad court, a civilization based on Greek, Syrian, Egyptian, and Persian traditions and yet with a style and a spirit of its own. This new civilization reached its peak only after the Ommiads had lost the throne and the capital had been moved from Damascus to Baghdad. Much of the work of the Ommiads was either absorbed in or surpassed by the accomplishments of their successors. But the Ommiads laid the foundations, and they did so at a time when western kings had almost no administrative services, when western scholars had almost no books but compendia and epitomes, and when western architects showed almost no skill in designing large buildings.

New Conquests

The stability and prosperity assured by the early Ommiads soon made it possible for the Arabs to undertake further conquests. In the East the Ommiads took Khiva, Bokhara, and Samarkand, thus gaining control of one of the oldest and most important trade routes in Eurasia—the silk road from China. These conquests in turn opened the way to the occupation of Afghanistan and the valley of the Indus. The strong Moslem position on the northwest frontier was a permanent threat to India, as the invasions of the next thousand years were to demonstrate.

In the West the Arabs advanced steadily along the southern shore of the Mediterranean. North Africa was their first objective, and here, as often before, the invaders profited from the fact that the native population hated Byzantine government. Justinian's reconquest of the Vandal kingdom had been followed by

heavy taxation and persecution of heretics. Many of the Romanized Africans had fled the country; the Berbers, who remained, were neither Romanized nor obedient to the orders of Byzantine officials. When the Arab attack came, both the Roman cities and the Berber countryside resisted bravely, but there was little cooperation between them. The Arabs quickly defeated their divided enemies, taking Carthage in 697 and winning control of the entire North African coast by 708.

Although the Berbers had fought fiercely to preserve their independence, they felt no particular antipathy to Islam. Many of them became converts and joined the victorious army in the hope of sharing in the spoils of the next conquest. This addition to their strength enabled the Arabs to pass over into Spain. The Visigothic rulers of Spain had been weakened by quarrels over the succession and had not been able (or willing) to build up strong local forces. A single victory over the royal army in 711 was enough to open the whole country to Tarik, who commanded the invading forces, and from whom Gibraltar takes its name.* The largest part of his army was probably composed of recently converted Berbers, and now many Visigothic nobles joined the victors—an illustration of the Arabs' ability to gain the cooperation of conquered peoples in a remarkably short time. Only the support of thousands of non-Arabs made possible Islam's rapid conquests.

The Moslem army quickly overran the entire Iberian Peninsula except for the extreme northwest, where a few Christians maintained their independence. The Moslems then pushed on across the Pyrenees into the Frankish kingdom, which was not quite so helpless as Spain. The Franks could not de-

*Gebel Tarik—Tarik's hill.

fend the south, but when the raiders pushed north the Frankish leader, Charles Martel, assembled an effective army that checked the invasion. Charles' victory at Poitiers in 732 was not very decisive, for the Moslems withdrew in good order and held towns in southern Gaul for another thirty years. But they made no more raids on the north.

During the early years of the eighth century the Ommiads reached the height of their power. They had created the largest Moslem state that ever existed, and in less than a hundred years they had built an empire larger than that of Rome. But they had reached their limit; their setback at Poitiers in 732 had its counterpart in an earlier failure to take Constantinople in a great siege in 716 to 717. Although the Byzantine Empire had lost almost all of its outlying provinces, it had preserved the most important part of its territories. Like the Frankish kingdom, Byzantium grew stronger after the early eighth century, and the Moslems were long unable to make any headway against these two bulwarks of Europe.

The Rise of the Abbasids

The Ommiad state had also begun to weaken internally. It was difficult to rule a vast empire that stretched from Spain to India and that embraced dozens of different peoples. Moreover, many Moslems continued to distrust and oppose the Ommiads. There was still a party that honored the memory of Ali and considered the Ommiads usurpers; there were also puritanical Moslems who loathed Ommiad luxury and worldliness; and there were recent converts, especially in Mesopotamia and Persia, who resented the domination of the Arab aristocracy.

All these groups were united by Abu'l Abbas, who was to found the Abbasid dynasty. By claiming one of Mohammed's uncles as an ancestor, he satisfied most of the legitimists; by making himself appear more devout than the Ommiads, he gained the support of most of the inhabitants of Mesopotamia and Persia. By 750 Abu'l Abbas was strong enough to risk rebellion. He decisively defeated the Ommiad caliph and almost exterminated the family. One Ommiad escaped to Spain, where he founded an independent state in 756, but the rest of the Moslem world accepted Abu'l Abbas as caliph.

Since the Abbasid caliph's primary strength was in Mesopotamia and Persia, he moved his capital to Baghdad, a new city built on the banks of the Tigris. This move symbolized a turning point in the history of civilization. The old unity of the Mediterranean world, shaken by earlier events, was now forever destroyed. The Ommiad caliphs at Damascus had drawn heavily on Greco-Roman civilization, but the Abbasids at Baghdad were increasingly influenced by the ancient traditions of Mesopotamia and Persia. The Moslem world on the southern and eastern shores of the Mediterranean became more and more unlike the Christian world on the northern shores. At the same time, Moslem pressure was forcing Byzantium in on itself and accentuating the peculiarities of the Byzantine way of life.

A citizen of the Roman Empire had been equally at home in Rome and Constantinople, in Alexandria and Antioch. Now these centers of civilization were drifting apart and becoming more and more strange to one another. By the tenth century a westerner, merely by crossing the Mediterranean, entered a completely different world. Egypt was as strange as China, and even Christian Byzantium seemed remote and Oriental.

Thus the world of the Romans had broken into three fragments of unequal size and wealth. The largest and richest area was held by the Moslems, who also controlled the key trade routes to India and China and all but one of the great cities of the Middle East. Next came the Byzantine Empire, anchored on impregnable Constantinople, rich from its own industry and from the trade that flowed through its lands to the West. Far behind was western Europe, poverty-stricken and ill-governed, no match for the great civilizations centered in Constantinople and Baghdad. For centuries western Europe had depended on the East in trade and industry, in art and religion. It remained to be seen what the Europeans could do now that they were on their own.

Suggestions for Further Reading

Note: Asterisk denotes a book available in paperback edition.

The Age of Justinian P. N. Ure, *Justinian and His Age** (1951), is lively reading. The contemporary accounts by Procopius, *History of the Wars,* trans. by H. B. Dewing (1935) and *Secret History,** trans. by G. A. Williamson (1969), are also lively, but not entirely trustworthy. For this and the next section, A. H. M. Jones, *The Later Roman Empire,* 3 vols. (1964), is extremely valuable.

Byzantium A wealth of literature is available on the life and thought of Byzantine civilization. P. N. Ure, *Justinian and His Age** (1951), which discusses many facets of Byzantine history and civilization, is a good starting point. J. W. Barker, *Justinian and the Later Roman Empire* (1966), is even better. S. Runciman, *Byzantine Civilization** (1933), combines deep knowledge of the subject with a superb prose style in a very sympathetic treatment. The old theory that the Byzantine Empire was perpetually moribund is severely attacked in N. H. Baynes, *The Byzantine Empire* (1926), which stresses the vitality of the Empire's history. N. H. Baynes and H. L. B. Moss, *Byzantium** (1948), is a collection of essays on Byzantine history and culture written by leading scholars in the field. The most thorough and scholarly treatment of Byzantine history is G. Ostrogorsky, *History of the Byzantine State,* trans. by J. M. Hussey (1956). The older work of A. A. Vasiliev, *History of the Byzantine Empire,* 2 vols. (1928), is more readable than Ostrogorsky but lacks recent bibliographic material. Two works by the French scholar C. Diehl, *History of the Byzantine Empire* (1901) and *Byzantium: Greatness and Decline** (1957), are valuable for the facts but are considerably dated in historical interpretation.

The beauty of Byzantine art has fascinated many who have come in contact with it. C. R. Morey, *Early Christian Art** (1942), which has good plates, describes the influence of Byzantine iconography on western art in the early Middle Ages. But for the magnificence of its reproductions and the general excellence of its text, no survey of Byzantine art can compare with the fine Skira edition, *Byzantine Painting,* ed. by A. Grabar (1953). The brief study of D. Talbot-Rice, *Byzantine Art** (1935), is worthwhile and perhaps more accessible.

Islam The best introduction to the world of Islam is the Koran,* of which there are many translations. Perhaps the best is that of A. J. Arberry, *The Koran Interpreted** (1955). H. A. R. Gibb, *Mohammedanism** (1949), is a good historical survey of the Moslem religion, while B. Lewis, *The Arabs in History** (1966), emphasizes the political and social aspects of Moslem history. See also his *Islam,* 2 vols. (1974). The foremost American historian of Islam, P. K. Hitti, has written a number of fine studies. His *The Arabs** (many editions) is a scholarly treatment of the rise and spread of Mohammedanism; his translation of *The Origins of the Islamic State* (1916) traces the growth of Islam and is excellent for an understanding of the Moslem world view. Even more thorough is M. G. Hodgson, *The Venture of Islam,* 3 vols. (1974). The now classic study by H. Pirenne, *Mohammed and Charlemagne** (1936), advances a significant theory about the impact of Islam on western Europe in the early Middle Ages. H. A. R. Gibb and H. Bowen, *Islamic Society and the West,* 2 vols. (1950), explores the impact of the West on Islam in later times. G. von Grunebaum, *Medieval Islam** (1946), traces the temper and flavor of the Moslem Middle Ages and gives a fine account of the Moslem influence on western Europe in the Middle Ages. Both R. P. A. Dozy, *Spanish Islam* (1913), and S. Lane-Poole, *The Story of the Moors in Spain* (1886), give exciting accounts of the Arabs in Spain. Washington Irving's *The Alhambra** (many editions) gives a vivid and unforgettable picture of Moslem culture in Spain. There is interesting material on the Ommiads in W. Muir, *The Caliphate: Its Rise, Decline and Fall* (1915), and in T. W. Arnold, *The Caliphate* (1963), but neither is so thorough in historical interpretation as is the research of Hitti. D. S. Richards, *Islam and the Trade of Asia* (1971), shows the shift in interest toward the East under the Abbasids.

H. A. R. Gibb, *Arabic Literature* (1926), is a brief survey of Arabic literature with an appendix of Arabic works in English and other modern languages. T. W. Arnold, *Painting in Islam** (1965), is a readable study of the place of art in Moslem culture, with very good reproductions. See also R. Ettinghausen, *Arab Painting* (1962). T. W. Arnold and A. Guillaume, *The Legacy of Islam* (2nd ed. by J. Schacht and C. E. Bosworth, 1972), an account of the elements in European culture that are derived from the Islamic world, is the best one-volume study of Moslem culture and thought.

9 The Emergence of a Western European Civilization

Not all contacts were lost when the Mediterranean world broke into three distinct cultural units—a German-Latin bloc in the West, a Greek-Slavic bloc in the East, and an Arab-Syrian-Persian bloc in the South. Merchants still traveled back and forth across the Mediterranean; ideas, art forms, and scientific and industrial techniques passed from the Byzantine Empire and the Moslem Caliphate to Italy, France, and Germany. And yet contacts among the West, the East, and the South of the Mediterranean world were less frequent and less intimate than they once had been. This was due in part to the endless wars between Byzantium and Islam, which discouraged Mediterranean commerce. It was due even more to the poverty and backwardness of western Europe, whose stocks of precious metals had been seriously depleted, making it difficult for westerners to purchase eastern goods. The western commodities most useful to the Greeks and Arabs were timber, iron, and slaves—all of which could be considered contraband of war in times of conflict. As a result, the West could not earn enough foreign exchange to trade extensively with either Byzantines or Arabs. Nor did the West have adequate intellectual capital for a rewarding exchange of ideas with Greek or Arab scholars. There were relatively few educated men in western Europe, and most of them were painfully at work trying to understand the writings of the Latin Church Fathers and fragments of the Latin classics. Until the West had fully assimilated its Latin heritage, it was to have little interest in the learning of the East.

Thus the people of western Europe were more dependent on their own resources than they had been for centuries. They had to create their own civilization. Several favorable factors allowed them to do so. Although western Europe seemed poor and backward in comparison with the East, it actually possessed great potential for growth. It had plenty of good agricultural land and virtually untouched resources of raw materials. Trade in the Mediterranean had fallen off, but trade in the northern seas was flourishing. The Scandinavians, who traded with the

western kingdoms, were also beginning to import eastern goods through the Russian river system. The Church had preserved the rudiments of an educational system and some ideas about political and social organization. Finally, the new line of Frankish rulers that had emerged in the eighth century brought political stability and laid the foundations for a new civilization.

KING PIPPIN AND THE CHURCH

This new line of rulers descended from Pippin and Charles Martel, the mayors of the palace who had put an end to the disorders of the seventh century. These men had been content with the title of mayor, but the son of Charles Martel, another Pippin, decided in 751 to seek the kingship itself. He won over most of the nobles, and to overcome the scruples of those who were still attached to the old dynasty Pippin asked the pope for an opinion on the legitimacy of his bid. Pope Zacharias declared that the man who bore the responsibilities of the king deserved the title; his successor actually journeyed to France and anointed Pippin in the manner in which the Old Testament kings had been anointed. This was probably the first use of this ritual in the West, and it is hard for us to realize the impression it must have made on public opinion. As God's anointed, Pippin became a semisacred personage, far above all ordinary lay dignitaries. It was God's will that he and his family should rule the Franks.

These acts of the papacy had serious consequences for future European kings. The pope had not initiated the change of dynasty, but the very fact that he had been consulted enabled later pontiffs to claim that Zacharias had deposed an unworthy king and had chosen a suitable successor. Therefore the Church could remove other unworthy rulers. Equally significant was Pippin's consecration, for it was soon believed that a king did not enjoy full authority until he had been anointed by the Church. It could then be claimed that church officials were superior to lay rulers, since no layman could

Charlemagne presents a model of his church at Aix-la-Chapelle to the Virgin (detail from a panel of the shrine at Aix).

consecrate a bishop but a bishop could consecrate a king. The obvious conclusion was that royal power, in some fashion, was dependent on the sanction of the Church.

The Alliance of the Papacy with the Franks

Probably none of this had been foreseen by either Pippin or Zacharias. Their cooperation was based on the realization that each could gain some practical advantage by supporting the other. The pope, who received little support from the Byzantine emperor, was constantly harassed in Italy by Lombard attacks. He was also distressed by the condition of the Church in the Frankish realm. Many of the Frankish clergy were ill educated and corrupt, and the Church had little influence on a large part of the population. A strong Frankish king might be willing to protect the pope against the Lombards and aid in the administrative and moral reform of the Church.

As for Pippin, he had inherited a family tradition of cooperating with the Church. One of his ancestors had been a

An iconoclast whitewashing an image in a Byzantine church (from a ninth-century psalter). In 730 Leo III issued an edict forbidding the veneration of images. For a hundred years thereafter, icons, mosaics, and frescoes in churches were destroyed or whitewashed.

bishop and a saint, and his father, Charles Martel, had had the support of the Church in his struggle with the Frankish aristocracy. In return, Charles had supported the work of missionaries and reformers in the Frankish kingdoms. The family was undoubtedly pious, but it also had political reasons for aiding church reform. Educated and reformed bishops were likely to support strong government and resist aristocratic factionalism, and they would make useful advisers and administrative agents for the king. Moreover, a reformed Church that emphasized the principles of Christian morality could assist the king in his task of preserving public order.

The alliance between Pippin and the pope changed the political fate of western Europe. First, and perhaps most important of all, it removed Italy from the Byzantine sphere of influence and attached it to the Germanic north. The popes had long found the Byzantine emperors unsatisfactory suzerains. It was bad enough when they failed to push back the Lombards; it was even worse when they stirred up an unnecessary theological controversy by forbidding images of sacred personages in churches. It is true that eastern Christians had begun to pay extravagant respect to sacred images and that certain monasteries had gained enormous political influence by possessing images that were especially revered. But excessive devotion to images had not been particularly troublesome in the West, and the popes felt that the drastic remedy of iconoclasm (the destruction of images) was unnecessary. The largely illiterate western population needed images as illustrations of Christian doctrine, and the popes had no intention of abandoning them.

Dislike of iconoclasm, combined with concern over the Lombard threat, prompted the pope to look to the Franks for support. Charles Martel had refused to intervene in Italy, but Pippin was more willing to aid the papacy. In 753 he invaded Italy and forced the Lombards to withdraw from the environs of Rome. The campaign closed with two significant acts: Pippin gave Pope Stephen II a large strip of territory in central Italy which had formerly been held by the Byzantine

Empire. The pope gave Pippin the title of *patricius Romanorum,* which had formerly been held by the chief Byzantine representative in Italy.

To ignore Byzantium's centuries-old claim to Italy was a bold act. It needed justification, which may be why an unknown churchman (probably a Frank) forged the famous *Donation of Constantine* at about this time. According to the forger, Constantine, as an act of gratitude after his conversion, had given all Italy and the western part of the Empire to the pope. After withdrawing to the East, the emperor was supposed to have left the pope as the supreme authority in the West. This was a clumsy falsehood, but no one disproved its authenticity for 700 years. Meanwhile it supported papal claims to lordship over a large part of central Italy and vaguer rights of intervention in the political affairs in the West.

North of the Alps, Pippin and the pope helped each other to gain control over peoples who were only nominally their subjects. Pippin had little authority in such outlying districts as Bavaria and Aquitaine; the backing of the Church aided him in gaining some measure of obedience from the rulers of these provinces. The Church had little influence over the people of Gaul and Germany; Pippin gave full support to the work of one of the greatest missionaries and organizers the Church has ever known, an Anglo-Saxon monk named Boniface.

St. Boniface

Boniface came to Frankland as a young man hoping to convert the still-heathen Germans of Frisia and Saxony. He soon realized that an even graver problem was posed by the state of Christianity among the Frankish people, many of whom were called Christians only because they had no other faith. They seldom saw an orthodox priest, and the visits of wandering Irish monks did little to strengthen their belief. Boniface realized that thorough reform and reorganization of the Frankish Church were essential, and he spent most of his life at this task. In 748 he was made archbishop with full powers over the German clergy.

He used this authority to create the basic structure of the German Church. In Gaul he summoned local councils to improve the morality of Frankish churchmen and to make them more obedient to the pope. As the years passed, the Church north of the Alps became an effective force in the lives of the people, and its increased centralization and improved administration gave the Church strength enough to influence the ruling classes. At the end of his life Boniface returned to missionary work and found the martyrdom he had long desired. He was killed by heathen Frisians in 754.

The Establishment of Parishes and Tithes

Boniface's work was made more effective by the development of rural parishes in the Frankish kingdom—a development that had begun earlier but that received its greatest impetus from the descendants of Charles Martel. So long as churches existed only in the cities, as they did at first, country dwellers found it impossible to maintain regular contact

The Donation of Constantine

Constantine tells how Pope Sylvester I cured him of leprosy. In gratitude Constantine accepts baptism and decrees

that the sacred see of blessed Peter shall be gloriously exalted above our empire and earthly throne. . . . And the pontiff who presides over the most holy Roman Church shall be the highest and chief of all priests . . . and according to his decision shall all matters be settled . . . for the worship of God or the confirmation of the faith.

We convey to the most blessed pontiff, our father Silvester, universal pope, both our palace [the Lateran] and likewise all provinces, places and districts of the City of Rome and Italy and of the regions of the West, . . . bequeathing them to the power and sway of him and his successors.

Wherefore we have perceived that our empire and the power of our government should be transferred to the regions of the East . . . for it is not right that an earthly emperor should have authority . . . where the head of the Christian religion has been established by the Emperor of heaven.

From the Donation of Constantine, as quoted in *Select Documents of European History,* ed. by R. G. D. Laffan (London: Methuen, 1930), Vol. I, pp. 4–5.

with the clergy and hence Christianity had little influence on them. A rural parish with a resident priest was the obvious solution to this problem, but priests were not likely to stay resident until their churches had an adequate income. North of the Alps the landlords and counts were the only men wealthy enough to build and endow rural churches. They began to do so on a large scale only in the eighth century, prompted by Boniface's reforms and by the example and persuasion of the ruling family.

The ultimate step in giving parish churches an adequate income was taken when Pippin's son Charles made tithing compulsory. The clergy had long taught that the faithful should give 10 percent of their income to the Church, but they had permitted tithing to remain a purely voluntary act. By ruling that all Christians had to pay the tithe, the king assured the Church sufficient income to support an extensive network of rural parishes. Not all tithes went to parish priests; in fact, their share tended to diminish as time went on. Nevertheless, they always received enough so that the rural churches could function.

These were revolutionary changes. For the first time the ordinary inhabitant of the Frankish realm was in regular and frequent contact with Christian priests. The rapid growth of the parish system gave the Church more opportunities to impress Christian doctrine and morality on the people. There had always been sincere believers, but in the Merovingian period many men had acted as if Christianity were only a superior form of magic. Although they venerated relics that were alleged to bring good luck, they had no strong convictions about either faith or morals. Now Christianity began to be a matter of internal concern rather than one of exterior behavior. The eighth century is the first period in which one can be sure that all western Europe was hearing and beginning to understand the Christian message.

This improvement in the position of the Church had begun before Pippin's time and continued under his descendants. But Pippin's reign was the crucial period. He accelerated the pace of the reform movement, and he made the binding alliance with the papacy that ensured the cooperation of religious and secular authorities in building a new civilization. Pippin's work was overshadowed by that of his son Charles, but Charles built on the solid foundation left by his father.

CHARLEMAGNE

Pippin died in 768 and was succeeded by his two sons, Charles and Carloman. Fate saved the Franks from the dangerous consequences of divided authority, however, for Carloman died after three years, and Charles assumed sole control of the government.

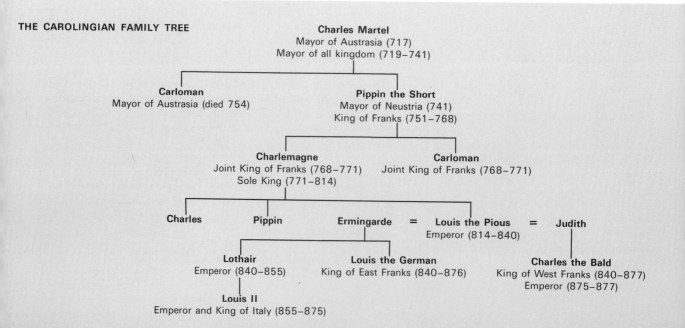

THE CAROLINGIAN FAMILY TREE

Charles Martel
Mayor of Austrasia (717)
Mayor of all kingdom (719–741)

Carloman
Mayor of Austrasia (died 754)

Pippin the Short
Mayor of Neustria (741)
King of Franks (751–768)

Charlemagne
Joint King of Franks (768–771)
Sole King (771–814)

Carloman
Joint King of Franks (768–771)

Charles

Pippin

Ermingarde = **Louis the Pious**
Emperor (814–840)
= **Judith**

Lothair
Emperor (840–855)

Louis the German
King of East Franks (840–876)

Charles the Bald
King of West Franks (840–877)
Emperor (875–877)

Louis II
Emperor and King of Italy (855–875)

in patria pax inuuolata inregno·
&dignitas gloriosa regalis palatii·maxi
mo splendore regiae potestatis· oculis
omnium luce clarissima coruscare
atqȝ splendescere · qua splendidissi
mi fulgoris maximo pfusa lumine

The elegant Carolingian handwriting was characterized by small letters and bold, rounded design. It is the basis of modern type (detail from a ninth-century manuscript).

Charles' reign was so successful that even in his own lifetime he was known as Charlemagne, or Charles the Great. To his contemporaries he was great first and foremost because he was a persistent and victorious warrior. He solved the Lombard problem by defeating the Lombard king and annexing the Lombard lands in northern and central Italy. He eased the Moslem threat by crossing the Pyrenees and annexing a small strip of Spanish territory to the Frankish kingdom. When the nomadic Avars, who had established themselves on the middle Danube, became troublesome, his army almost annihilated them in a single campaign. His longest and hardest war was with the Saxons of northeastern Germany, the last large group of German heathens. The Saxons resisted Frankish domination and Christianity with equal bitterness, and only after thirty years did Charlemagne finally manage to conquer and convert them.

Charlemagne's Educational Reforms

Charlemagne was more than a successful general, as many of his contemporaries realized. He wanted a strong kingdom, but he also wanted it to be a Christian kingdom, and his efforts to make it so left an indelible impression on western civilization. Even more than his father, Charlemagne realized that an uneducated clergy was an unorganized and uninfluential clergy. Both by decree and by his own example he tried to raise the level of learning in the Frankish realm.

He imported scholars from every country of western Europe and either kept them with him in his Palace Academy or gave them high positions in the Frankish Church. The most famous of these scholars was the Anglo-Saxon Alcuin, head of the Palace Academy and eventually abbot of St. Martin's of Tours, but there were also Franks, Lombards, Visigoths, and even newly converted Saxons among them.

The work of these scholars was not very original or imaginative, but originality and imagination were not the chief needs of the eighth century. What was needed were men who could preserve and assimilate the intellectual heritage left by Rome and the early Church. Even preservation was no easy task, for much of Latin literature had already been lost and there were few copies of the works that had survived. The Scriptures and the works of the Church Fathers were in less danger of being lost, but Charlemagne complained that copies of the Bible were full of serious errors. By encouraging the making of new and accurate copies of ancient texts, Charlemagne saved many classical works from oblivion; we have few manuscripts of Latin authors from before his time. The acceleration of manuscript production in turn led to a reform in handwriting, a reform in which Alcuin and his monastery at Tours played a leading role. The scribes of Tours developed a beautiful, clear script that was a notable improvement on earlier handwriting. The Romans had used only capital letters, which were hard to read when they filled a solid line, espe-

56 B.C.	ca. 486 A.D.	751	987	1328

cially since the Romans did not separate words. Later writers separated words and developed small letters, but the letters were badly shaped and easily confused. It was the Carolingians who gave small letters almost the form they have today.

Charlemagne's educational revival gave Europe a common cultural tradition. As we have seen, scholars of all nations mingled at the Frankish court and worked with the same materials—the Bible, the Church Fathers, the encyclopedias of the Late Empire, and some of the Latin classics. When they became bishops or abbots, they carried this common stock of learning to various regions and taught it to their own students. All students used Latin, whatever their native tongue, so there was no problem of translation. Thus scholars everywhere were reading the same books and commenting on them in the same language, and western Europe developed a common stock of ideas and a common vocabulary in which to express them. If western Europe has any unity at all today, that unity lies in its ideas, in its way of looking at the world, and for this unity it owes much to the work of Charles the Great.

Revival of the Empire in the West

By wiping out the Lombard kingdom, Charlemagne had made himself directly responsible for the security of the pope and the government of Rome. He also felt it his personal duty to make Christianity a more effective force in his kingdom. His laws dealt as often with ecclesiastical matters as with secular affairs. He laid down rules of proper conduct for monks and priests; he ordered schools to be established for the training of the clergy; he intervened in theological disputes; and, as we have seen, he gave the Church a solid financial basis by making the payment of tithes compulsory. He was the head of a Christian people, and he expected clergy as well as laity to follow his leadership.

This close relationship between king and Church reached its climax in the year 800. Pope Leo III, driven from Rome by his enemies in the city, had appealed to Charlemagne for aid. Charlemagne reinstated the pope and stayed on in Rome to make sure there would be no further trouble. On Christmas Day, 800, the pope placed the imperial crown on Charlemagne's head and hailed him as Augustus. The West once more had an emperor.

In one sense, the coronation merely symbolized existing facts. As ruler of France, Germany, and most of Italy, Charlemagne already had more power than the last western Roman emperors. The emperor had been the traditional

CHARLEMAGNE'S CONQUESTS AND EMPIRE 814

protector of the Church, and Charles was clearly performing this function. There seems to be no doubt that Charlemagne wanted to be emperor, for the pope was in no position to impose undesired titles on his powerful protector.

Nevertheless, a man who knew Charlemagne well said that the king grumbled that he never would have gone to church that Christmas Day had he known what the pope had in mind. If the report has any substance it may reflect Charlemagne's misgivings about receiving his title from the pope, misgivings that proved well founded. Later popes claimed that Leo III, by his own authority, had transferred imperial power from the Greeks to the Franks, and that Charlemagne's coronation was one more proof of the superiority of ecclesiastical rulers over secular rulers. But whatever his doubts, Charlemagne accepted the situation. He referred to himself as emperor in public documents, and, before his death, he was careful to see that his son was crowned emperor. The pope took no part in this coronation, which suggests again that Charlemagne did not want to admit that the pope could make an emperor.

Charlemagne's Government

The essential unit of government under Charlemagne, as under his Merovingian predecessors, was the county. Each county was headed by a count, who was almost always a member of a noble and wealthy family. The count had to share his power with various subordinates; he had to respect the position of the other noble families of his county and of the neighboring bishops and abbots. Nevertheless, an energetic count could build up a strong position in his county. He presided over the local courts and kept a third of the fines that were collected there. He led the freemen of his district to war; he collected tolls; he built and garrisoned forts. Clearly, the king's chief problem was to keep his counts under control.

Charlemagne tried to meet this problem by two devices. First, in order to keep the counts from abusing their judicial power, he created independent groups of local judges to decide cases. Second, he sent out royal envoys—called *missi dominici*—to see that the counts obeyed his orders and observed reasonable standards of justice and honesty. The *missi* were chosen from men of the highest standing at court and had the full support of the emperor. Their admonitions and reports helped immeasurably

Ninth-century statue of Charlemagne on horseback. He wears a crown and carries an orb, symbol of royal power.

The Coronation of Charlemagne 800

Now when the king upon the most holy day of the Lord's birth was rising to the mass after praying before the tomb of the blessed Peter the Apostle, Leo the Pope, with the consent of all the bishops and priests and of the senate of the Franks and likewise of the Romans, set a golden crown upon his head, the Roman people also shouting aloud. And when the people had made an end of chanting praises, he was adored by the pope after the manner of the emperors of old. For this was also done by the will of God. For while the said Emperor abode at Rome certain men were brought to him who said that the name of Emperor had ceased among the Greeks, and that there the Empire was held by a woman called Irene, who had by guile laid hold on her son the Emperor and put out his eyes and taken the Empire to herself. . . . Which when Leo the Pope and all the assembly of the bishops and priests and abbots heard, and the senate of the Franks and all the elders of the Romans, they took counsel with the rest of the Christian people, that they should name Charles king of the Franks to be Emperor, seeing that he held Rome the mother of empire where the Caesars and Emperors always used to sit.

From *Chronicle of Moissac*, trans. by J. Bryce, *The Holy Roman Empire* (New York: Macmillan and St. Martin's Press, 1911), p. 54.

Gold coin bearing the likeness of Irene, empress in Constantinople from 797 to 802. She was the first woman to assume sole rule over the Empire (and she took the title of emperor, not empress). Her rule provided the pope with an excuse to crown Charlemagne emperor in 800 to fill the allegedly vacant throne.

Louis the Pious, son of Charlemagne. The words in the poem written across the portrait can also be read as a crossword puzzle, so that the letters in the cross and halo also form verses (*ca.* 840).

to improve the conduct of local government. Nevertheless, even the *missi* did not give the emperor full control over his counts. Abuses of power continued, and there were cases of flat disobedience to Charlemagne's orders.

The central government was not well enough organized to direct and coordinate the work of local authorities. The secretarial staff was very small—barely able to handle correspondence and keep records. It is worth noting that under Charlemagne these men were all members of the clergy,* whereas the Merovingians had had no difficulty in finding laymen capable of keeping records and writing letters. This change demonstrates the decline of education among laymen and the political as well as the religious importance of an educated clergy. In addition to the secretaries there were a few lay judges to hear the rare cases that were brought to the emperor's court, and a large and undifferentiated group of household officials and counselors. Any of these men could be used for any task, but no one had permanent responsibility for overseeing local courts or centralizing local revenues.

In directing and controlling local officials Charlemagne issued many capitularies (ordinances made up of various *capitula*, or chapters). Most of these were administrative directives that told the local officials what to do. For example, one capitulary contained rules for the education of the clergy, and another regulations about the powers and behavior of the counts. Charlemagne seldom attempted to make law, since he, like most men of his time, believed that law consisted of eternal and unchanging principles. Nevertheless, some capitularies interpreted, and thus changed, the law. And by laying down rules that were applicable to all subjects, Charlemagne did a good deal to wipe out earlier distinctions between Roman and German, or Frank and Burgundian. There was never complete uniformity of law among his subjects, but the differences that remained were regional rather than racial and were never so great that regions with differing laws could not cooperate.

Charlemagne, working against great obstacles, had united the West and given it common ideals and common institutions. But he had succeeded only because he was a man of boundless energy, unusual perseverance, and strong personal-

*This is reflected in the similarity of the English words *clerk* and *cleric*. From the time of Charlemagne to the end of the Middle Ages, all "clerks" were members of the clergy.

ity, who had impressed himself on his contemporaries. It was too much to expect his descendants to be men of equal stature, and the Carolingian Empire was too large, too loosely administered, and too imperfectly unified for lesser men to hold it together. There were few economic ties among the far-flung regions. Bavarians, for example, had no reason to care about what happened in Aquitaine. Western Europeans could satisfy their common ideals simply by sharing in the life of the Church. Their common institutions, which were most effective at the county level, seemed to work equally well whether there was one empire or many kingdoms. Charlemagne himself apparently was not particularly concerned about preserving the unity of the Empire, for he followed the old Frankish tradition and divided his holdings among his sons. It was only the premature death of two of his heirs that gave an undivided realm to his son Louis.

THE COLLAPSE OF THE CAROLINGIAN EMPIRE

Louis had increasing difficulty in holding the Frankish state together. He was a well-meaning but weak man, easily swayed by his family and friends. In order to gain the aid of the Church, the only institution that was really concerned with western unity, he humbled himself as Charles never would have done. Thus Louis allowed himself to be crowned emperor a second time by ecclesiastical authority and did public penance for mutilating a nephew who had rebelled against him. The greatest danger to the Empire sprang from the jealousies among his three sons, Lothair, the younger Louis, and Charles. Louis drew up several plans for partitioning the Empire, but none of them satisfied all his heirs. They fought with him and they fought with one another. When Louis died in 840, he left the Empire in a state of civil war.

Louis' sons finally settled their quarrels by dividing the Empire (and the imperial estates) in the Treaty of Verdun (843)—a division that had a lasting effect on European history. Charles received the western part of the Empire, a kingdom that corresponded roughly to modern France. Louis took eastern Frankland, including Saxony, Bavaria, and the counties along the Rhine. The eldest son, Lothair, became emperor and received the largest part of the family estates. This gave him a long, narrow strip of territory between the eastern and western kingdoms embracing the Low Countries, Alsace-Lorraine, Switzerland, Savoy, Provence, and northern Italy. Lothair's kingdom turned out to be a buffer state, and like many buffers it was ground to

THE DIVISION OF CHARLEMAGNE'S EMPIRE

Pro dõ amur & pxpian poblo & nro commun saluament. dist di en auant. in quant dr saur & podir me dunat. si saluaraieo. cist meon fradre Karlo. & in ad iudha. & in cad huna cosa. sicu om p dreit son fradra saluar dist. Jno quid il mi altre si fazet. E t ab ludher nul plaid nnqua prindrai qui meon uol cist. meon fradre Karle in damno sit | Quod cu lodhuuic expleffet. karolus teudisca lingua sic ex eade uerba testatus est.

Jn godes minna in duuthes xpanes folches. in dunser bedhero gealtniffi. fon these moda ge frammor desso framso mirgot geuuuzci in dimadh fur gibit sohal dihtes au mnan bruodher soso man mit rehtu sinan bruher scal inthi irtha zer mig soso madno. in dimit luheren in nohein juz hnng nege ganga. zheminan uuillon imo ces cadhen uuerhen.

---

ernments and threw the burden of defense on local leaders.

The most dangerous and persistent of these new invaders were the Scandinavians of the north. Though related to the Germans, and just as fond of fighting, the Scandinavians had taken no part in the early migrations and conquests. By the ninth century, however, many of them had begun to venture overseas. They were expert seamen and traders, and they had perfected a type of long, shallow-draft ship that was very effective for raiding. These vessels used a sail when the wind was astern, but they were usually propelled by oars. Equipped with such craft, the Scandinavians could swoop down from the sea and loot a whole river valley before the local troops, moving slowly over bad roads, could be mobilized to repel them.

No one knows why the Scandinavians became so aggressive during the ninth century. It may be that improved metallurgical techniques enabled them to construct better weapons, such as their famous war axes. It may be that frequent civil wars forced defeated bands of warriors to flee the country. It may be that some families had a surplus of younger sons who sought adventure abroad. In any case, the political weakness of Europe would have tempted anyone. The Frankish Empire was disintegrating; the British Isles were split up into small, warring kingdoms; and the Slavs who now held eastern Europe were politically disorganized. The Continent lay open to any group of determined men bent on marauding, on looting, and even, perhaps, on founding a new state.

Although the Scandinavian raiders called themselves vikings, the rest of Europe usually referred to them as Northmen. In their first serious raids against Ireland early in the ninth century they rapidly occupied the east coast. They met somewhat stiffer resistance from the Anglo-Saxons in England, but by 870 they had subdued all the Anglo-Saxon kingdoms except the southern state of Wessex. They had already begun to attack the Frankish lands. Year after year the Northmen pushed their long ships up the Rhine, the Seine, and the Loire to collect tribute and loot from towns and

pieces in conflicts between its neighbors. After Lothair's death in 855 the kings of West Frankland and East Frankland began to contend for possession of parts of the Middle Kingdom. In the end the Treaty of Mersen (870) gave the king of East Frankland the provinces that lay north of the Alps, but the dispute continued even to our own day. In 1870, 1914, and 1939, France and Germany were still fighting for Alsace and Lorraine, fragments of the old kingdom of Lothair.*

The New Invasions: The Northmen

The Frankish state, gravely weakened by civil wars, now was threatened by a series of new invasions with which the later Carolingians simple could not cope. Attacks from the north, east, and south strained the resources of the central gov-

* *Lorraine* is simply a French form of *Lotharingia*— Lothair's kingdom. The German *Lothringen* shows the connection even more clearly.

monasteries. Finally, an especially strong band of raiders forced the West Frankish king to cede them the land at the mouth of the Seine. This outpost, founded about 911, became the nucleus of Normandy, the most famous of the viking states.

In a show of bravado, the Northmen even sailed their ships into the Mediterranean and plundered a few coastal cities in Spain, southern France, and Italy. Their move west across the Atlantic had more permanent results, for they had settled Iceland by the year 1000, and from Iceland a few adventurous leaders moved on to Greenland. Along the west coast of the island they established colonies that endured to the fourteenth cen-

tury. And from Greenland some ships reached the North American continent, although it is still not known just where the Northmen landed or how long they stayed.

The viking raids and settlements in the West were largely the work of Danes and Norwegians. In the East the Swedes began to push down the Russian river valleys toward Constantinople. They had known this route for a long time; eastern goods and eastern coins had been common in Scandinavia long before the great raids began. In the late ninth and tenth centuries, however, the Swedes began to settle in Russia and to bring the scattered Slavic population under their control. The fortified trading posts where the

INVASIONS OF THE NORTHMEN, THE MOSLEMS, AND THE MAGYARS
Eighth to tenth centuries

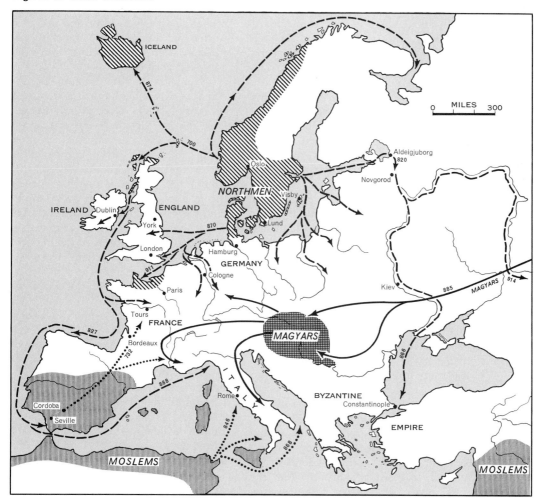

A rune stone (*ca.* ninth century) found in Scandinavia. The carving is distinctly viking: within an elaborate border are two panels, one showing a chieftain on a horse and the other, a viking ship on a voyage.

Swedish drinking horn (*ca.* eighth century).

vikings settled soon burgeoned into towns; the most famous of them was Kiev, which became the capital of a large principality. Once they had gained a footing in Russia, the vikings, with typical boldness, turned their eyes south to Constantinople. Their attacks on the imperial city were unsuccessful, but they did manage to wrest a favorable commercial treaty from the emperor. These early viking princes and warriors gave the eastern Slavs their first effective political organization; in fact, the word *Russia* itself probably comes from *Rus*, the name of a Swedish tribe.

The New Invasions: The Moslems and the Magyars

Compared with the Northmen, who settled from Greenland to the Ukraine and raided from Northumberland to north Italy, the other invaders of the ninth and tenth centuries seem almost provincial. But they covered enough ground to cause suffering in many parts of southern and central Europe. The Moslems, coming up from the south, seized Sicily and the other islands of the western Mediterranean, thus endangering navigation in that part of the sea. They also established fortified outposts near Rome and on the coastal road from France to Italy, from which they molested land travelers as well.

Even worse were the Hungarians, or Magyars, who belonged to the nomadic stock of central Asia that had launched earlier raids against the coastal civilizations of China, India, and Europe. The Magyars were as great horsemen as the vikings were seamen, and their skill gave them the same advantages of surprise and mobility. They drove into the Danube Valley in the ninth century and established headquarters in what is now Hungary. From this base they raided Germany and Italy regularly and eastern France occasionally. The Magyar occupation of the middle Danube basin split the western Slavs into two groups. The Slavs were politically backward in any case, but this division made it even harder for them to form kingdoms strong enough to resist subjugation. And the weakness of the states of the western

Slavs has in its turn tempted their neighbors to fight with and dominate them, as the history of Czechoslovakia in the period from the Thirty Years' War to the invasion by Hitler (1618–1939) demonstrates.

The End of the New Invasions

The people of western Europe suffered grievously at the hands of the new invaders. Large areas were depopulated and impoverished, and the plundering of monasteries dissipated many of the benefits of the Carolingian reforms. Yet western Europe resisted the new invasions far more successfully than Rome had resisted the earlier invasions of the Germans and Huns. Instead of a whole continent, only a few small territories, such as Normandy and Hungary, were permanently relinquished to the invaders. The Northmen and Magyars were converted to Christianity and accepted western traditions fairly quickly; the Moslems were pushed back from their advanced positions.

How was it that western Europe managed to weather these disastrous new invasions? There were several reasons. First, the new invaders were not so numerous as the Germanic and Hunnic groups that had overrun Europe at the end of the Roman Empire. Second, the Church took an active role in opposing the invaders. Finally, and most important, there was effective local resistance. The people of the Roman Empire had depended almost entirely on the imperial government for protection; when its armies failed, they had accepted barbarian rule without protest. But when the Carolingian kings failed to defend Europe during the ninth-century invasions, local leaders appeared who had enough military power to defend their territories.

This growth of new leadership was especially noticeable in England, Germany, and France. In England the collapse of all the other Anglo-Saxon kingdoms had left Wessex alone to face the Danish invaders. The king of Wessex, Alfred the Great (870–899), proved to be a brave and stubborn fighter. Though he was defeated again and again, he never gave up. He eventually forced the Danes to accept a peace that gave him control of about half of England. His son and grandson carried on the fight until they had seized the rest of the Danish-occupied territories. By 950 all England was united under the Wessex dynasty. In Germany, the new Saxon dynasty that replaced the Carolingians first checked and then, in 955, thoroughly defeated the Magyars.

France is the most instructive example of the development of new leadership. So long as the Carolingian kings were able to raise armies to fight the Northmen, they kept the loyalty of most of the country. But when, at the end of the ninth century, they failed completely in their efforts to defend northern France, local leaders took over most of the responsibility for defense. Eventually, in 987, Hugh Capet, the descendant of one of these local leaders, seized the throne from the helpless Carolingians.

In short, the inhabitants of western Europe showed a will to resist that had been lacking in the fourth and fifth centuries. The resistance was strongest at the local level, among the counts who governed local districts and among the professional fighting men whom they controlled. When the kings proved that they could defend their countries, as they did in England and eventually in Germany, the local nobles supported them and a certain degree of unity was preserved. But when the kings failed, as they did in France, the counts became virtually independent rulers and gained the loyalty of most of the people in their districts.

FEUDALISM

Out of the ninth-century invasions emerged a new type of government, which we call feudalism. The invasions were only a contributing factor to this development, however, for the civil wars among the last Carolingians and the lack of strong economic ties among districts also played a part. Nevertheless, the fact that feudalism first appeared in northern France and only gradually spread to other countries suggests that the invasions gave the final push toward the development of this new form of political organization. France had suffered more severely from the invasions than any other country, and its kings had been less successful than other monarchs in coping with the danger.

The Ingredients of Feudalism

Feudalism may be defined by three characteristics: fragmentation of political authority, public power in private hands, and the lord–vassal relationship. The typical feudal state was a county, or a fraction of a county, and the typical feudal lord was a count, or a custodian of a castle, who had turned his office into a private, hereditary possession that he exploited for his own benefit. Rights of government were treated just as if they were rights to land; they could be given away, exchanged, or divided among heirs. The lord kept control over his district through his vassals, or retainers, many of whom lived with him in his fortified dwelling. Other vassals lived on

Twelfth-century seal depicting a vassal giving homage to his lord.

The Ceremony of Becoming a Vassal

1127

This description comes from the period when feudalism was fully developed. It is very full because the leading men of Flanders had just accepted a new count after a disputed succession. Homage (the specific obligation of the vassal) is carefully distinguished from the more general obligation of fidelity. By the twelfth century it was assumed that most vassals had fiefs.

On Thursday, homages were done to the count. First, they did homage in this way. The count asked [the vassal] if he wished to become his man without reserve, and the latter answered: "I do." Then, joining his hands together, he placed them in the hands of the count, and they bound themselves to each other by a kiss. Then the man who had just done homage pledged fidelity . . . to the count in these words: "I promise on my faith to be faithful from now on to count William and to observe [the obligations of] my homage completely, in good faith, and without deceit." This he swore on the relics of the saints. . . . Finally, with a little stick that he held in his hand, the count gave investiture of fiefs to all those who had . . . promised security, done homage, and taken the oath.

From Galbert of Bruges, *De Multro Karoli comitis Flandriarum*, ed. by H. Pirenne (Paris, 1891), p. 89.

their own estates, which the lord had granted them as a reward for faithful service. The lands and rights held by a vassal from a lord were at first called benefices; later, fiefs.* All vassals were bound to help their lord in war and government. Though their chief duty was to fight for their lord, older and wealthier vassals might also be asked to attend law courts or to administer small areas within the county. This was feudalism in its simplest form: a small area ruled by a lord with the aid of a band of military retainers.

Some of the ingredients of feudalism had come into existence during the last years of the Merovingian kingdom, but it was almost two centuries before these ingredients were combined into a consistent pattern. The lord–vassal relationship, for example, first emerged clearly in

*Our word *feudalism* comes from the medieval Latin *feudum,* which meant "fief." No medieval writer ever spoke of "feudalism"; he was more likely to say "vassalage," which stressed the personal relationship between lord and retainer.

The Church and Feudalism

At the height of feudalism, churches needed protection against raiders but feared that they would lose much of their wealth to their protectors. This charter was an attempt to avoid both dangers.

I, Baldwin, by the grace of God count of Flanders, acknowledge and testify before all my barons that the abbey of Marchiennes was always free from obligations to an advocate. . . . However, because of the present evil state of the world, it needs an advocate for its defense. That I may be the faithful advocate and defender of the church, the abbot gave me two mills and two ploughlands in the town of Nesle. I, however, have given the mills and the land with the consent of the abbot to Hugh Havet of Aubigny, so that he may be a ready defender of the church in all things.

And this is what he receives in the abbey's lordship. He shall have one-third of all fines in cases where the church has asked his assistance and has gained something by his justice. If he is not called in he shall have nothing. In time of war he shall have from each plough-team two shillings, from half a team one, and from each laborer three pennies. He shall not give orders to the men of the abbey, nor hold courts of his own, nor take money from peasants. He is not permitted to buy lands of the abbey, or to give its serfs in fiefs to his knights, nor to extort anything from them by violence. . . . Done at Arras in the year of our Lord 1038.

From *Polyptyque de l'Abbé Irminion,* ed. by B. Guerard (Paris, 1844), Vol. II, pp. 356–57.

the eighth century, probably because of a change in military techniques. During the wars with the Moslem invaders, Charles Martel and Pippin discovered that heavy-armed cavalrymen gave them increased striking power. They wanted large numbers of these soldiers, but ordinary freemen, with at best a small farm, could not afford to provide themselves with specially bred horses, mail shirts, and swords and spears. No ordinary horse could carry a fully armed soldier, nor could an ordinary village blacksmith make armor or forge a sword. Only the king or wealthy lords could afford to provide this equipment, and they naturally expected the men who received it to accord them special loyalty in return. The new type of fighting men became vassals of the king or the lords and before long were the most effective element in the army.

The Frankish kings soon sensed that the bond between lord and retainer was far more compelling than the loose tie between king and subject. So they began to use vassalage to strengthen their political authority as well as their military position. Pippin, Charlemagne, and Louis all encouraged fighting men to become vassals of the king. They began the practice of granting public offices, such as countships, as benefices to lords, just as the lords granted estates as benefices to some of their soldiers. But there was a great difference between an ordinary mounted soldier who was completely dependent on his lord for his livelihood and a powerful count who needed no help from the king. The lesser vassals were almost always obedient to their lords and gave them good service. But the great vassals of the king became more and more disobedient during the ninth century and gave him service only when they chose to. The king received a certain amount of deference from and exercised some influence over the lords with whom he had contact. But by the end of the tenth century the real rulers of France were the lords who had succeeded in building little principalities out of the fragments of the old Frankish kingdom.

Feudalism was primarily a political device for assuring a minimum of security to each section of a badly fragmented country. But counts, lords of castles, and their vassals had to have adequate incomes, and the scanty public revenues that remained—mainly tolls, market dues, and fines from courts—were inadequate to meet the needs of the governing class. In the end everyone in authority (including bishops and abbots as well as laymen) was dependent on dues squeezed out of the peasants, who constituted the majority of the population.

The burden on the peasants varied greatly, according to the region in which they lived and the degree of freedom that they enjoyed. In some areas (for example, Normandy) most peasants were free and owed relatively little to their superiors—a few pennies or small amounts of grain per acre for the use and protection of their land, presents (which soon became compulsory) of hens and eggs at Christmas and Easter, three or four days' work a year on the lord's land at harvest time. At the other extreme were the unfree serfs (numerous in eastern France) who owed heavy payments, worked several days a week for the lord, and could not even marry a subject of another lord without buying permission. Economic considerations, however, cut across these lines. A serf with a large holding might be better off than a freeman who had only four or five acres; a man who had oxen was far more prosperous than a man who had no draft animals. But everywhere crop yields per acre were low, and even in a good year the average peasant did not rise far above a subsistence level of living.

From the point of view of the governing classes, the neatest arrangement was to possess a village in which all the peasants were under one lord and in which the lord's land, intermingled with that of the peasants, could be cultivated by the village as a whole. Such villages were relatively easy to exploit and usually produced a fairly regular income. But many villages were divided among several lords, and not all peasants lived in well-organized villages. Dues from scattered holdings and hamlets were difficult to keep track of and to collect.

It is easy to see why the greater lords eventually granted some of their estates, especially their smaller and more remote

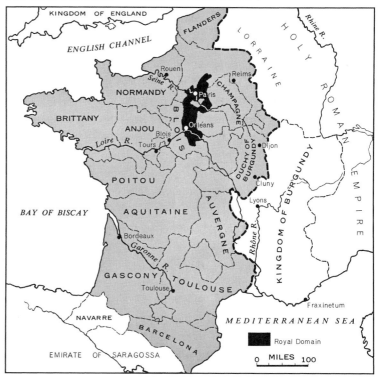

FEUDAL FRANCE Late eleventh century

lands, to their vassals. The vassal had to be supported in any case; by giving him an estate the lord lost little income and saved himself the trouble of collecting peasant dues. The vassal who received and lived on a small estate might exploit it more efficiently than a distant lord. Thus in the long run large numbers of peasants became tenants, or serfs, of lesser vassals.

This did not mean, especially in the ninth and tenth centuries, that the knight or other minor vassal had much political power over the peasants whose dues he received. He had to be given enough authority to force peasants to pay what they owed, and eventually most knights acquired a sort of police-court jurisdiction. They could judge cases of disorderly conduct; they could settle minor squabbles among peasants over the boundaries of fields and the division of family holdings. But they could not judge serious criminal cases or disputes over the possession of fiefs; such matters were reserved to counts and other great lords. In short, the fragmentation of political authority never went down to the lowest

ET SYRIAM SOBAL· ET CONVERTIT·
IOAB· ET PERCVSSIT EDOMINVAL
LE SALINARVM·XII MILIA·

The life of a feudal knight: carrying a standard into battle, feasting, and accompanying a traveling king.

level of the feudal hierarchy. The smallest effective political unit was the area ruled by the lord of a castle, not the estate held by a knight.

A Changing Institution

During the centuries when feudalism was at its height—from about 900 to about 1100—the institution underwent several striking changes. First, some lords succeeded in subduing their neighbors and building up relatively large and powerful states. This was especially true of the Count of Flanders and the Duke of Normandy, who added many counties to their original holdings and kept them under fairly effective control. Other lords in France, west Germany, the Spanish March, and north Italy were almost as successful, and their wars and alliances

determined the political history of the area for two centuries. Second, since these new states were too large to be governed through the informal and personal decisions of their rulers, various new legal and financial institutions were created, which produced a body of feudal law. Third, the benefice, or fief, became more important. In the early years of feudalism many vassals had been primarily household retainers; they had no fiefs and spent most of their time with their lord or in garrisoning his forts. But, as we have seen, lords gradually found it more convenient to assign estates to their vassals, and by 1100 it was customary to give fiefs even to lesser vassals. It also became customary for the vassal to spend most of his time on his fief and to serve his lord only on special occasions or in time of war. Moreover, the fief, which originally had been only a loan to the vassal, gradually became hereditary, to be held by the vassal and his heirs as long as they gave service.

In short, the relationship between vassal and lord was changing, with the vassal becoming more of a country gentleman and less of an armed retainer. He began to begrudge the time spent in his lord's service and tried to reduce it as much as he could. The lord countered by defining the service owed by vassals more and more precisely and by developing legal procedures for confiscating the fiefs of defaulting vassals. What had at first been a close personal relationship began to assume the form of a contractual obligation.

Feudalism was an inadequate and limited form of government; it did little for the mass of the people except to protect them against external and internal enemies. Even this protection was not always effective. In the endemic wars between neighboring lords, a favorite tactic was to ravage the peasants' fields and drive off their animals. Lords held local courts from time to time, but they were more interested in pocketing fines than in administering justice. They made little effort to maintain roads and other public facilities. At its best, feudal government was inefficient paternalism; at its worst, it was pure exploitation of the peasants.

Yet with all its disadvantages, feudalism had vitality and real capability for growth. It spread from France throughout most of western Europe, and the countries that were most thoroughly feudalized, France and England, were the first medieval states to develop effective political institutions. Moreover, many feudal rulers managed to gain the loyalty of their subjects, something that neither the late Roman emperors nor the Germanic kings had achieved. There was personal devotion to the ruling dynasty; there was also a feeling that each man had an interest in preserving the customs and institutions of his little state. With this loyalty it was possible to build stronger states and to give more protection and better justice to the people.

Feudalism was almost perfectly adapted to conditions in early medieval Europe. The working political unit, the area dependent on a castle, matched the working economic unit, the local neighborhood. The struggle to base a large political organization on what was essentially a local economy—a struggle that had weakened both the Roman and the Carolingian empires—was abandoned. The exploitation of the peasants by an aristocracy was nothing new, and at least the feudal aristocracy had duties as well as privileges. Lords had to defend and govern their lands in person—no one else would do it for them—and if they did their job badly they would lose their lands to more efficient neighbors.

Even the fact that feudal government was rudimentary was an advantage. Europe at this time could not support a complex government; it had to concentrate on essentials. And precisely because early feudalism was highly informal and personal, change was easy and experimentation common. In the end the ablest feudal lords devised more effective forms of government than Europe had had for many centuries, and their methods were copied by their less imaginative colleagues.

GERMANY

It took several centuries for feudalism to reveal all its possibilities. At first it seemed to do as much harm in encouraging local wars as it did good in warding off outside raiders. Feudal France was weak and divided. Germany and England, still unfeudalized and united under their kings, were far stronger. Germany, in fact, was the dominant country in Europe from the early tenth century down to the eleventh century.

In the period after the breakup of the Carolingian Empire, Germany had remained more united than France. It had suffered less from invasion and civil war, which meant that the lords had had fewer opportunities to usurp power. Even the transition to a new ruling family was made more easily in Germany than in France. The last able German Carolingian died in 899; by 919 King Henry I had established the new Saxon dynasty firmly on the throne.

In spite of these advantages, however, the German king had lost much of his authority by 919. During the troubles of the ninth century most of the country had come under the control of five great lords, the dukes of Saxony, Franconia, Swabia, Bavaria, and, after its final annexation to Germany in 925, Lorraine. Each of these dukes ruled a wider territory than that of any French feudal lord, and each exercised reasonably effective control over the counts and other nobles of his duchy. The dukes were willing to have a king as a sort of president of their club, but they expected to be virtually independent within their own duchies. Henry I, for example, was strong only in his own duchy of Saxony; elsewhere he had to negotiate with the other dukes to carry out his policies. Sons had begun to succeed their fathers as a matter of course in both duchies and counties.

Nevertheless, Germany was not yet feudalized, although feudal ideas were creeping in through Lorraine, the duchy that lay closest to France. Counts and dukes were not completely independent of the king; they were public officers who could be removed if they failed to show obedience. Lords had not yet gained a monopoly of power; ordinary freemen had a voice in the courts and still served in the armies. Strong regional loyalties, especially in Saxony and Bavaria, held the duchies together. In short, Germany had not fragmented as France had, and the king still had a chance to establish his authority throughout the realm.

Otto the Great
and the German-Roman Empire

Otto the Great (936–973) made the most of this opportunity. He held Saxony in his own right, and he gradually brought the other duchies under control by forcing out disobedient dukes and bestowing their offices on members of his own family. This policy was not wholly successful, for Otto's own sons rebelled against him. But there was still the Church, which had great wealth and cherished the idea of unity. Most of the bishops and abbots owed their positions to Otto; they supplied him with money and troops from their estates, and they provided him with administrative officers. The support of the Church made Otto supreme in central Europe; he was able to put down all rebellions and inflict a crushing defeat on the Magyars in 955.

Otto's position was so strong that he was able to intervene in Italian affairs and eventually to annex northern Italy. He has often been blamed for this action, since in the long run involvement in Italian politics weakened the German monarchy. But, given the situation in the tenth century, it would have been difficult for Otto to avoid involvement. The Italian kingdom was small—it included only the northern half of the penin-

GERMANY AND ITALY AT THE TIME OF OTTO THE GREAT   962

Ivory plaque showing Otto the Great offering a model of Magdeburg Cathedral to Christ (late tenth century).

Detail of an ivory panel showing Otto II, his wife, and their child, the future Otto III, in adoration (ca. 980).

sula—and its kings were weak. Tempted by this weakness, French feudal lords had already tried to establish themselves as kings of Italy, and the Duke of Bavaria also had thoughts of crossing the Alps. Otto, anxious to preserve his position as the strongest ruler in western Europe, could hardly allow Italy to pass to a potential rival, much less to one of his own subjects.

Otto's close relations with the Church in Germany also impelled him to intervene in Italy. He was not a mere exploiter of the Church; he felt, as Charlemagne had, that it was his duty to preserve and strengthen ecclesiastical institutions. The papacy was in miserable condition; deprived of the support of the Carolingians, it had fallen under the control of corrupt and self-seeking Roman nobles. So little authority and prestige did it enjoy that a tenth-century German archbishop actually refused to become pope. Otto may have hoped that intervention in Italy would free the papacy from domination by Roman nobles and that he could ensure his continued use of church resources by gaining a voice in papal elections.

Otto at least had a romantic excuse for his invasion of Italy. Adelaide, widow of an Italian king, was being annoyed by her husband's successor. Otto came to the rescue of the queen, married her, and then claimed the Italian throne. A ruler backed by the German Church and in control of northern Italy could hardly be ignored by the pope, who recognized Otto's position by crowning him emperor in 962.

Since there had been no emperor with real power since Louis, Charlemagne's son, and not even a nominal emperor since 924, Otto's coronation constituted a refounding of the medieval Empire. After Otto there was no break; the imperial title and the German kingship were to remain indissolubly united for the rest of the Middle Ages. This Roman Empire of the German Nation, as it was called by some contemporaries, was the strongest state in Europe until about 1100 and an important force in European politics for two hundred years after that. Especially significant were the relations between the German-Roman Empire and the popes. Otto, as successor to Charlemagne, thought of himself as leader of the Christian West and protector of the papacy. He took this second responsibility so seriously that by the end of his life he dominated papal elections. The Church eventually reacted violently against imperial control, but for almost a hundred years the emperors named and deposed popes. And on the whole they strengthened the Church; popes chosen by the emperors were abler and better men than those selected by Roman nobles.

Gerbert

Having revived the Carolingian tradition of an alliance between emperor and Church, an alliance in which the emperor was unquestionably the dominant partner, Otto proceeded to revive the Carolingian interest in scholarship. One of the most famous of the scholars he encouraged was Gerbert, who was born in southwestern France about the middle of the tenth century but who spent much of his life in the service of Otto's son and grandson. Gerbert had studied in Spain, where contact with the Moslems had revived interest in mathematics and astronomy. He learned what he could of these subjects—very little by later standards but enough to give him a reputation for profound, even magical, knowledge in his own day. He also tried to teach elementary ideas about astronomy and devised some simple apparatus to demonstrate his points.

Although few westerners had paid much attention to mathematics or astronomy during the ninth and tenth centuries, these scientific interests were not unprecedented. What made them significant was the fact that Gerbert was more than a secluded scholar; he was one of the most influential churchmen of his time. The emperors he served made him first the abbot of a great monastery, then Archbishop of Reims, and eventually pope. As Pope Sylvester II (999–1003) he

was the chief adviser of the emperor Otto III (983–1002), whose tutor he had been. The two men dreamed of an empire that would be much more like the old Roman Empire than Charlemagne's had been, an empire in which emperor and pope would act as the joint heads of a unified western state.

This was a hopeless dream, though both pope and emperor died before they realized quite how hopeless it was. But the fact that they could conceive of such a plan shows how strong Roman ideas were in the Ottonian court. And Gerbert might be excused for overestimating imperial power. After all, his spectacular career had been largely due to the emperor's support.

Gerbert's political program was a failure, but his scholarly work marked a turning point in European intellectual history. The fact that such an influential man was interested in mathematics and science attracted younger students who carried on his work. Other scholars took the road to Spain and prepared the way for the intellectual revival of the twelfth century, a revival in which western Europeans, for the first time, took a real interest in science.

Gerbert had also become absorbed in the study of logic, partly because logic and science were closely related in the Greek scientific tradition he was trying to revive, partly because he felt that he needed this tool in order to comprehend

The four provinces of Slavinia, Germania, Gallia, and Roma (left) paying homage to Otto III (right), from the Reichenau Gospels (tenth century). Note that Otto wears a Roman imperial costume, not a Germanic one.

the new knowledge he had acquired. Logic, like Latin, was essential in assimilating ancient knowledge, and Gerbert's use of logic, simple as it was, greatly impressed his contemporaries. Here again his example was not forgotten. The study of logic continued throughout the eleventh century and was one of the most important forces in the intellectual revival that came at the end of that century.

The direct line of Otto I ended in 1002 with the death of Otto III, but collateral branches of the family retained the throne and kept the Ottonian system of government going. Compared with France, which was splitting up into feudal states, Germany seemed to be flourishing. The German emperors stood unchallenged in their realm. They had wealth and prestige, and the greatest scholars of Europe came flocking to their courts. But the German state had serious weaknesses that had been masked by the remarkable ability of the emperors and the relatively slow development of feudal elements in German society. Imperial power depended on the support of the Church, and it was by no means certain that the Church would always be willing to remain subordinate to a secular ruler. The power of the local lord was growing in Germany as it had earlier in France, and there was no assurance that local lords would not some day seek independence. The emperor had to rely on churchmen and nobles to carry out his plans, for he had no bureaucracy. In short, the Ottonian Empire was little more than a slightly modified Carolingian Empire, an empire that had long been out of date. The emperor's position rested on a precarious balance of forces—clergy versus laymen, one group of lords versus another group—and the crises that arose in the last half of the eleventh century were to show just how precarious that balance was.

ANGLO-SAXON ENGLAND

England, like Germany and unlike France, was not feudalized in the tenth century. Like Germany again, it developed a relatively strong monarchy and an active intellectual life during that century. As the descendants of Alfred drove back the Danes, they had to develop new institutions with which to hold and govern the territories they reconquered. These institutions were especially effective at the local level—so effective that they survived the Anglo-Saxon monarchy for centuries and even formed the basic pattern of local government in the United States.

New Institutions

The Anglo-Saxon kings of the tenth century divided the country into shires, or counties, and then subdivided the shires into smaller units called hundreds. Shires and hundreds were judicial as well as administrative units; there was a shire court that met twice a year and a hundred court that met about once a month. Fortified towns, which were both military and trading centers, were called boroughs; the borough also had a court of its own.

This system was not unlike that of the Carolingian Empire and the states that succeeded it. But there was one striking difference: in England the nobles never gained control of shire, hundred, and borough government, whereas in France the count was the ultimate authority within his county. In England the highest royal official was the alderman, later called the earl. The alderman was usually responsible for many shires, and he could not handle all problems of local administration. An official was needed in each shire to collect revenue, muster troops, and preside over the courts. After a long period of experimentation the Anglo-Saxon kings eventually developed a very effective local official, the shire-reeve, or sheriff.

At first the shire-reeve was only one of a group of reeves, or agents, who managed the king's estates. It was logical to ask one of these men in each shire to supervise the others and to see that all the king's revenue in that district was brought together in one place. Eventually the chief reeve became the king's representative in all affairs, with wide administrative and executive powers. Just as the sheriff of a western county in the United

ENGLAND AFTER THE NORMAN CONQUEST
Late eleventh century

States in the nineteenth century was the key official in his district, so the Anglo-Saxon sheriff by the eleventh century was the most important official in his shire.

Powerful as the sheriff was, he never became independent of the king. He ranked beneath the really great men, the aldermen, or earls, and he could always be replaced if he failed to do his job loyally and efficiently. With a few exceptions, the office of sheriff never became hereditary. From 1000 on, the king of England always had a local official in every part of his realm who would carry out his orders with reasonable efficiency and collect his revenues with reasonable honesty. Kings on the Continent grew weak and poor because they had lost control of local government and revenues. But the king of England gained

power and wealth, even though his country was small and thinly populated, because he could use the resources of all his counties.

Law and Literature

The Anglo-Saxon kings of the tenth and eleventh centuries also improved internal security by discouraging blood-feuds and by insisting that certain serious crimes, such as murder, arson, and rape, were offenses against the king. Since he received a substantial fine when a defendant was convicted of such crimes, the king had an added incentive to strengthen and support the courts in which these cases were tried. Much of the legislation of the Anglo-Saxon kings deals with the arrest and punishment of criminals. And it is a sign of their power that they could issue general laws; the great period of Anglo-Saxon legislation was between 950 and 1050, a time when the king of France could hardly make rules even for his own private estates.

Like the German kings, the Anglo-Saxon rulers encouraged ecclesiastical reform and sponsored literature and scholarship. But they were interested in writings in the vernacular as well as in Latin. Alfred the Great had translated Latin works into Anglo-Saxon, and under Alfred's successors, Anglo-Saxon literature reached its peak. The epic of *Beowulf* was put into its final form about 1000; the two great battle poems *Maldon* and *Brunanburh* came about the same time. Even more important for the historian is the *Anglo-Saxon Chronicle*, which was probably begun in the days of Alfred and was continued into the twelfth century. It is mainly a history of kings and bishops, of wars and rebellions, but it tells us much about Anglo-Saxon customs and beliefs.

Military Weakness

With all its achievements, the Anglo-Saxon monarchy was not exempt from the difficulties that had weakened the continental kingdoms. Most of the peasants had put themselves under the protection of lords, and most of the lesser landlords had placed themselves under the patronage of the king or an earl. Everywhere the bond between lord and follower was becoming stronger than the old ties of kinship and community. But, though the followers of the king and the great men had honorable status and were entrusted with important missions, they were not primarily a class of specially trained military retainers. Thus there were weaknesses in England's military posture. As the lords interposed themselves between people and king, the folk-army became less effective, and no one was developing the bands of heavy-armed cavalrymen that were proving so effective on the Continent. King and lords depended largely on their household retainers—good fighters, but probably not as well armed nor as versatile as French vassals.

This military weakness became evident soon after 1000 when the Danes renewed their attacks on England. King Ethelred the Ill-Counseled, after failing to defeat the Danes in battle, resorted to the hopeless expedient of buying them off with the proceeds of a national tax, the Danegeld. This gesture only encouraged the Danes, and by 1016 their king, Canute (or Knut), had completed the conquest of England.

England did not suffer greatly under Danish rule (1016–42), although some Anglo-Saxon lords lost their lands and official positions to Danes. Canute preserved, and even strengthened, Anglo-Saxon institutions; in fact, the last Anglo-Saxon laws were promulgated during his reign. But he did not entirely solve England's military problem. He increased the body of royal house-carls, or retainers, to several thousand; however, they were warriors of the old Germanic type, not mounted knights. A heavy-armed cavalry was essential; England still could not match the new type of force that was developing in France.

Page from the earliest manuscript of *Beowulf* (tenth century).

Edward the Confessor

When Canute's sons died without leaving direct heirs, the Anglo-Saxons had no trouble in restoring the old line of kings descended from the House of Wessex. But Edward the Confessor (1042–66) was strong only in his piety; in all other things he was easily swayed by his relatives and advisers. Having spent long years of exile in Normandy, he wanted to bring Norman ways into England and give Normans high positions in both ecclesiastical and secular administration. At the same time he was influenced by the earl Godwin, who was half Danish and wholly anti-French. Edward married Godwin's daughter and gave earldoms to Godwin's sons. Other Anglo-Saxon earls were naturally jealous of Godwin, and quarrels among the various factions at times reached the level of civil war.

Edward's situation was not unlike that of the last French Carolingians. Like them, he strove to preserve a precarious balance among aristocratic factions. Like them, he had to accept a notable transfer of political power into private hands. Bishops, abbots, and great lay lords assumed control of the courts of many hundreds, and even lesser lords acquired police-court jurisdiction over their men. Moreover, many of the powerful lords built up bodyguards large enough to constitute private armies.

Here we have some of the ingredients of feudalism, and it is possible that even without the Norman Conquest England might have developed its own kind of feudalism. The Anglo-Saxons, however, had not gone very far in this direction. The followers of the lords did not have the special military training of French vassals. Many of them were not even permanently bound to their lord; as the records say, they "could go with their land" to any lord they chose. This meant in turn that there were no fiefs, that the followers of a lord did not hold land and offices in return for service. And this was even truer of the earls than it was of ordinary retainers. They were not vassals of the king, and they owed him no service for the lands they possessed. They expected, of course, to be consulted by the king, and they also expected to receive the chief offices of government, such as the earldoms. On his side, the king expected the earls and their relatives to assist him in the work of governing and defending the realm. But there were no permanent and binding obligations on either king or lord. The king could take an earldom from one lord and give it to another, and a lord who failed to serve the king in an emergency did not thereby forfeit his land.

England, in fact, was facing the same problem that Germany was facing in the eleventh century. In both countries the king still acted on the theory that the great men were his obedient subjects, that he could use them as public officials and dismiss them at will. But in both countries this theory was becoming unrealistic; the great men had acquired independent strength, and it was increasingly difficult for the king to control them. But while in Germany the tendency toward disintegration proved irreversible, in England it was checked at the end of the eleventh century. A disputed succession and quarrels among the earls exposed the Anglo-Saxon kingdom to conquest by a French feudal army. The leader of this army, William the Conqueror, introduced into England the most rigorous type of feudalism that Europe had yet seen. He imposed heavy and precise obligations on the lords and seized their lands if they failed to fulfill them. Thus William corrected the chief weakness of the old Anglo-Saxon state. At the same time, he preserved all the really effective Anglo-Saxon institutions, especially the remarkable Anglo-Saxon system of local government. The work of the Anglo-Saxon kings had not been wasted; the combination of their institutions with Norman feudalism was to make England for many generations the strongest state in Europe.

Suggestions for Further Reading

Note: Asterisk denotes a book available in paperback edition.

Pippin and St. Boniface

"The evolution of monarchical institutions and the idea of kingship during the Dark Ages from 400 to 1000 provides one of the most instructive examples of the complex process by which different social and religious elements became interwoven in a culture," writes C. Dawson in *Religion and the Rise of Western Culture** (1950), a very good introduction to this period. See also his *Making of Europe** (1934). C. H. Talbot, *Anglo-Saxon Missionaries in Germany* (1954), gives the correspondence of Pippin and St. Boniface and provides a cross section of the religious life of the eighth century difficult to parallel elsewhere.

Charlemagne and the Revival of the Empire

The best biography that we have of the man who was at the center of this epoch is the contemporary Einhard's *Life of Charlemagne,** foreword by S. Painter (1960). Another edition, which also includes Notker's account of Charlemagne, was published by L. G. Thorpe (1969). J. H. Robinson, ed., *Readings in European History,* Vol. I (1904), has excellent source material on the administration of the Carolingian Empire. There are several good studies of the man and the age: H. Kleinclausz, *Charlemagne* (1934), is a scholarly work that concentrates on political conditions, while the more recent and very readable study by H. Fichtenau, *The Carolingian Empire** (1957), gives greater attention to social conditions. F. L. Ganshof, *The Imperial Coronation of Charlemagne* (1949), focuses on a problem that has interested many historians. Ganshof's collection of essays, *Frankish Institutions under Charlemagne* (1968), is also useful. The best study of the rise and decline of the Carolingian Empire is L. Halphen, *Charlemagne et l'Empire Carolingien* (1949). Halphen, however, is not as interesting reading as Fichtenau.

The Carolingian Renaissance Most of the general works cited above have material on the Carolingian Renaissance. M. L. W. Laistner, *Thought and Letters in Western Europe, 500–900** (1966), devotes considerable attention to the prose and poetry of the period. E. S. Duckett, *Alcuin, Friend of Charlemagne* (1951), gives a somewhat romantic picture of the Frankish court and the Palace Academy. The influence of political and social factors on Carolingian art is brought out in A. Hauser, *Social History of Art,** Vol. I (1957). W. Levison, *England and the Continent in the Eighth Century* (1948), combines great knowledge of the literature of the age with a fine prose style. J. Boussard, *The Civilization of Charlemagne* (1969), is very helpful.

Collapse of the Empire and the New Invasions For an overall view of this period drawn from the sources, see R. S. Lopez, *The Tenth Century* (1959). P. Sawyer, *The Age of the Vikings,* 2nd ed. (1971), gives a good description of the Northmen. J. Brønsted, *The Vikings** (1960), presents a fascinating account of viking art and civilization. T. D. Kendrick, *A History of the Vikings* (1930), shows the impact of the viking invasions on Britain, western Europe, Russia, and even America. A. Olrik, *Viking Civilization* (1930), and G. Turville-Petre, *The Heroic Age of Scandinavia* (1951), interpret the age of the vikings from the legends and sagas of individual Norsemen; of the two, Turville-Petre is the more readable. The great poem *Beowulf,** trans. by D. Wright (1957), provides information about viking civilization that has been documented by archeological findings. C. A. Macartney, *The Magyars in the Ninth Century* (1930), is a scholarly study of the origins and wanderings of the Magyars.

Feudalism Both *Raoul de Cambrai,* trans. by J. Crosland (1926), and *The Song of Roland,** trans. by D. L. Sayers (1957), present excellent pictures of the ideals and attitudes of the feudal caste in the first age of western feudalism. F. L. Ganshof, *Feudalism,** 3rd English ed. (1964), shows the development of "classical feudalism" from its Carolingian origins. M. Bloch, *Feudal Society** (1961), is an outstanding study from a more social and economic point of view, while J. R. Strayer, *Feudalism** (1965), gives a brief account emphasizing political factors. A. Boutrouche, *Seigneurie et féodalité* (1959), studies the first age of the feudal and manorial systems and compares European feudalism with eastern forms. Boutrouche has a thorough bibliography. F. Kern, *Kingship and Law in the Middle Ages* (1939), is a historical essay that is invaluable for an understanding of the nature and development of the idea of kingship in early medieval Europe.

Otto I and the Saxon Dynasty *Medieval Germany,* Vol. I, articles trans. by G. Barraclough (1938), has as its theme the internal development of the German state in the obscure period from the tenth to the thirteenth century. See also the materials published by B. H. Hill, Jr., *The Rise of the First Reich: Germany in the Tenth Century* (1969). There is information on Otto I and the Saxon dynasty in H. A. L. Fisher, *The Medieval Empire,* Vol. I (1898), but G. Barraclough's chapters in *The Origins of Modern Germany* (1947) are more up-to-date. Luitprand of Cremona, *Chronicle of the Reign of Otto I, Embassy to Constantinople,* trans. by F. A. Wright (1930), presents a picture of Church–state cooperation under the Saxons and an insight into the western attitude toward Byzantium in the eleventh century.

The Anglo-Saxon Monarchy to 1066 *The Anglo-Saxon Chronicle* (Everyman's Library) is the indispensable framework for developments in England before 1066. There is interesting source material in *Six Old English Chronicles,* trans. by J. Giles (1875), and *English Historical Documents,* Vol. I, *500–1042,* ed. by D. Whitelock (1955); Vol. II, *1042–1189,* ed. by D. C. Douglas and G. W. Greenaway (1953–55). F. Barlow, *The Feudal Kingdom of England, 1042–1216* (1953), has a good account of the reign of Edward the Confessor. The best scholarly treatment of the entire period is F. M. Stenton, *Anglo-Saxon England* (1943), but G. O. Sayles, *The Medieval Foundations of England,** Chapters 5–16 (1948), is much more readable and has a good critical bibliography. D. Whitelock, *The Beginnings of English Society** (1952), is a good brief account. P. H. Blair, *An Introduction to Anglo-Saxon England* (1959), is very useful.

Anglo-Saxon Art Most of the works cited above have information on the artistic achievements of the period. T. D. Kendrick, *Anglo-Saxon Art* (1938), is a good survey. D. Talbot-Rice, *English Art, 950–1100* (1952), traces the development of architecture, sculpture, and manuscript illumination. It has good plates and an excellent bibliography. A. W. Clapham, *English Architecture before the Norman Conquest* (1930), is a first-rate introduction to early Anglo-Saxon architecture. A more recent work is H. M. Taylor and J. Taylor, *Anglo-Saxon Architecture,* 2 vols. (1965).

10 Revival and Reform in Western Europe

Battered and torn by invasions and civil wars during the tenth century, western Europe began to recover after 1000. The worst of the invasions were over; France was achieving some degree of stability under its feudal lords; England and Germany were relatively peaceful under their kings. Italy was more turbulent, and Spain was still being devastated by Christian-Moslem wars. But the heart of western Europe, the great stretch of land running from Rome to London and from Bremen to Venice, had survived its worst difficulties.

Although the increase in security in the eleventh century was slight, western Europe had the resources and the vitality to profit from even slight improvement. Beginning in the last half of the eleventh century and continuing throughout the twelfth, there was a surge forward in all forms of human activity. Production and trade increased; political, legal, and religious institutions grew stronger; religious feeling became deeper and more meaningful. Along with these advances, remarkable work was done both in art and in scholarship.

THE ECONOMIC REVIVAL

The first and most obvious result of increased stability was a rise in population. The evidence for this rise—indirect, but convincing—is simply that during the late eleventh and twelfth centuries men could always be found to undertake new occupations and activities. There were enough men to clear forests and drain swamps, to enlarge old towns and build new ones, to establish new farms and villages in the half-deserted Slavic lands beyond the Elbe. There were enough men for conquests and crusades, for William's seizure of England, for the expansion of Christian holdings in Spain, for expeditions overseas to regain the Holy Land. And there were enough men, too, to furnish a striking increase in the number of students and teachers, of writers and artists, of clergymen, lawyers, and doctors.

Agriculture

The increase in population would have been a burden on society, rather than a stimulus, if production had not increased at the same time. The most important, and most difficult, increase to achieve was in the production of food. Clearing new land helped, since soil that had lain uncultivated for centuries was often very fertile. But new land came into production slowly, not nearly fast enough to keep up with the growing population. Production from old land had to be increased by acquiring more and better tools, by better organization of labor, and by better farming techniques.

Where soil and terrain permitted, the peasants developed a tightly integrated village community whose resources they

FBR · MAR · APR · MAI · I · HUS · IUN · AGS · SEPB · OCTB · NOVB DECB · IANR

GIRAVLDVS
FECT ISTSPRTA

used with considerable efficiency. The arable land was divided into large fields, each of which was in turn divided into long, narrow strips. Each peasant held strips in each field, and some strips were cultivated for the benefit of the lord. All the heavy work was done in common; the peasants pooled their work animals to form plow teams, and all joined together to harvest the big fields when the grain was ripe. Since farm animals were few and scrawny and tools were dull-edged and heavy, this was the best way to handle a hard job in a reasonable length of time.

One of the most bothersome problems was to find enough feed for the work animals. The yield of grain was low, at best only about four times the amount of seed sown, and almost all of it had to be saved for human consumption and for seed for the coming year. Since grass grew only in small meadows along the streams, few villages produced enough hay to feed their animals during the winter months. To solve this problem, the peasants reserved the poorer lands exclusively for pasture and allowed the animals to graze on the cultivated fields after the crops had been harvested. Here again, through community organization the peasants saved themselves trouble and time, for a few herdsmen could take care of all the animals of the village.

Finally, the village had to have a common woodland. Wood was needed for fuel, for the frames of peasant huts, and for tools, which were made with as much wood and as little iron as possible. Forests were also used for pasturing large herds of half-wild pigs. These pigs sup-

Tympanum of the church of St. Ursin at Bourges (twelfth century). This tympanum is unusual in its depiction of secular themes—the hunt and the labors of the months.

plied the peasants with most of their meat, since other animals were too scarce to serve as a regular source of food. The wild game of the forests was reserved for the lords, though there was a good deal of poaching.

The agricultural system had obvious advantages and equally obvious drawbacks. It left little room for individual initiative: everyone had to follow customary routines of planting and harvesting, and the work pace was set by the slowest oxen driven by the most stupid villager. Moreover, it provided no chance to improve the breed of animals or the stock of seed, since the animals ran together in common pastures and the seed on one strip was inevitably mixed with that of neighboring strips.

The medieval village, however, was less hostile to innovation than is sometimes believed. In the obscure years between the breakup of the Carolingian Empire and the end of the eleventh century, improved agricultural techniques spread widely throughout much of Europe. The heavy wheeled plow with a moldboard to turn the soil had been used in a few Germanic regions even before the collapse of the Roman Empire. It was far more effective than the light Mediterranean plow in cultivating the heavy, wet clay soils of northern Europe, but it required a large team to draw it. The ordinary peasant had at most one or two oxen, but those who lived in integrated villages could pool their animals to form a plow-team. By 1100 the heavy plow had been adopted in Germany, northern France, and southern and central England. Its use increased food production, for the peasants could now cultivate lands the Romans had never touched.

Another innovation, also closely connected with the integrated village, was the three-field system. Since artifical fertilizers were unknown and manure was scarce, the usual method of preserving the fertility of the soil was to let half the land lie fallow each year. In northern Europe farmers discovered that they could get equally good results by dividing the land into three large blocks (hence the term three-field system) and rotating their crops. During the first year of the cycle, they planted one block in winter wheat, which they harvested in July; then they let the winter-wheat field rest until the following spring, when they sowed it with spring grains. This crop they harvested in the fall, and then let the land rest once more until the following fall, when it was sown with winter wheat. Thus in any year, one-third of the land produced winter wheat, one-third produced spring grain, and one-third was left uncultivated. And yet, over the three-year cycle, each field could lie fallow for at least a year and a half. This system could not be used in the Mediterranean basin, where there is not enough summer rain for spring grain to mature. And it was hard to use in regions where there were no well-organized villages. But where it was used, it increased production by a third.

Only about half of western Europe was organized in integrated villages. Where the soil was thin or the rainfall scant there were only small, loosely organized hamlets and individual farms, as in northern England, Brittany, and Mediterranean France. Except for wine-growing areas, these districts produced less per acre and per man than the integrated villages, though they were normally self-sufficient in food. Overall, western Europe had a food surplus by the middle of the twelfth century. Nevertheless, bad roads, a shortage of draft animals, and

THE THREE-FIELD SYSTEM	Field A	Field B	Field C
First Year	FALLOW until the fall Sow wheat in the fall	Harvest wheat in July FALLOW from July until the spring	Sow oats in the spring Harvest oats in the fall FALLOW until the next fall
Second Year	Harvest wheat in July FALLOW from July until the spring	Sow oats in the spring Harvest oats in the fall FALLOW until the next fall	FALLOW until the fall Sow wheat in the fall
Third Year	Sow oats in the spring Harvest oats in the fall FALLOW until the next fall	FALLOW until the fall Sow wheat in the fall	Harvest wheat in July FALLOW from July until the spring

local wars and brigandage meant that there might be severe local famines even in a year of general surplus.

Commerce and Industry

During this same period, the towns of western Europe were experiencing a striking growth in size and number. They absorbed some of the surplus population and furnished a steadily growing market for agricultural products. They also intensified trade among all parts of Europe and increased the production of textiles and metalware. The growth of towns was especially conspicuous throughout Italy and Flanders.

The Italian towns depended almost entirely on international trade, particularly in Oriental goods such as silk and spices. During the eleventh century, Italian shipping in the Mediterranean increased steadily. With the Byzantine Empire weakening and the Moslem Caliphate breaking up, the Italian merchants had little competition. As if to aid the Italians in their new-found prosperity, nomadic invaders were strangling the alternate trade route from the East along the Russian rivers to the Baltic. Thus the Italians almost monopolized the trade in Oriental goods for western markets. And these markets were becoming steadily more profitable, thanks to the general increase in prosperity and security throughout the West. The great seaports of Venice, Pisa, and Genoa flourished most brilliantly, but the towns of the Po Valley, especially Milan, were not far behind. As the Italian merchants carried their wares north through France and Germany, they stimulated the growth of other trading centers along the routes they traveled.

The towns of Flanders found their nourishment in industry rather than in trade. The flat, marshy lands along the sea seemed to be good only for sheep raising, so that Flanders had a surplus of wool from a very early date. Moreover, since Flanders was one of the first feudal states to achieve a relatively high level of stability and internal security, there was soon a surplus population, both native born and immigrant, that could be used to process the surplus wool. Wool was

the basic clothing material in western Europe, for cotton was scarce (it grew only in Mediterranean regions) and both linen and silk were terribly expensive. But to transform raw wool into good cloth took a great deal of time and energy. The wool had to be cleaned and carded, spun into thread, woven, smoothed by shearing off the knots and rough places, and finally dyed. All these tasks could be performed after a fashion by village workers, but the rough cloth they turned out was neither comfortable nor attractive. Anyone who had an income above the subsistence level wanted better cloth produced by skilled craftsmen. For many people, a good suit of clothes was the only luxury they possessed. This is why, from the early Middle Ages into the nineteenth century, the textile industry was the most important industry in western Europe.

Perhaps as early as the time of Charlemagne, and certainly by the eleventh century, Flanders had become the textile center of Europe. It had the wool, it had the labor, and soon Flemish cloth was famous near and far. It was bought by well-to-do people throughout Europe and even found markets in the Middle East. The first European manufactured product with much appeal for non-Europeans, it helped to balance European trade with the Orient. By the twelfth century the Flemish textile towns of Ghent, Bruges, and Ypres rivaled the flourishing seaports of Italy in wealth and population.

Outside Italy and Flanders the towns were smaller, and the growth of commerce and industry was less spectacular. But everywhere old towns were expanding and new towns were springing up. Some served as distribution centers along the trade routes; others specialized in manufacturing goods for local consumption. Thus western Europe began to enjoy a more rational division of labor and a better use of human resources.

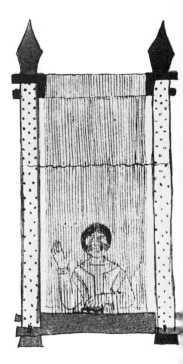

Weaving became an important industry in the eleventh and twelfth centuries. Note that the upright loom was used instead of the horizontal loom, which was developed a century later (detail of a miniature painting from the eleventh-century encyclopedia of Rabanus Maurus).

Illustration from an eleventh-century calendar depicting plowing and sowing.

A peddler offering silver beakers (detail from a twelfth-century manuscript).

Peasants and landlords began to specialize in producing food for the market, while skilled craftsmen in the towns concentrated on manufacturing. This development may seem so elementary that it is hardly worth mentioning. But it was precisely this division of labor between town and country that had been lacking in the late Roman Empire and the early Germanic kingdoms.

The growth of towns stimulated the economy of Europe, but it put serious strains on the social and economic system. The ruling classes, feudal lords and churchmen, knew how to control and exploit peasants, but they were not so sure of themselves in dealing with merchants and artisans. Obviously, townspeople needed personal freedom and some local self-government. A serf could not function as a merchant, and feudal courts were poorly equipped to deal with lawsuits among businessmen. But if the townsmen became too free they might escape completely from the control of the ruling classes. The more intelligent lords granted the towns enough freedom to become prosperous but retained enough control to share in that prosperity, through taxes, tolls, and payments for market rights. It was not always easy to strike this balance, however, and all through the eleventh and twelfth centuries lords and towns haggled over the terms of their relationship. The Church had an especially difficult time. Like all landlords, it hated to surrender any of its rights, and it had little sympathy with the businessman's way of life. In eastern France there were bloody conflicts between bishops and their towns, and Rome itself staged frequent rebellions against the pope throughout the twelfth century.

In the end, the towns gained personal freedom for their people and a separate system of municipal government. But the extent of self-government varied with the strength of the country's kings and nobles. In England and in the feudal states of France, for example, the towns never became independent. Towns in Spain enjoyed considerable liberty at first, but it was gradually whittled away as the kings became stronger. In Germany the process went the other way: so long as the emperors were strong, the towns had little independence; but after the collapse of the Empire in the thirteenth century many, though not all, of the cities became free. In Italy no medieval ruler managed to control the towns for any length of time, and most of them became independent city-states. These differences in the autonomy of towns from one country to another were to have a significant effect on the political structure of Europe. Rulers who could not tap the wealth of their towns found it difficult to build strong centralized states; this is one reason why Italy and Germany remained disunited for so long. Conversely, rulers who could draw on the resources of their towns were able to build powerful administrative and military organizations; this is one reason why France and England had centralized governments at such an early date.

An Early Medieval Merchant

When the boy had passed his childish years quietly at home [in Norfolk, England], he began to follow more prudent ways of life, and to learn carefully and persistently the teachings of worldly forethought. He chose not to follow the life of a husbandman but . . . aspiring to the merchant's trade, he began to follow the peddler's way of life, first learning how to gain in small bargains and things of insignificant price and thence . . . to buy and sell and gain from things of greater expense. For in his beginnings he was wont to wander with small wares around the villages and farmsteads of his own neighborhood, but in process of time he gradually associated himself by compact with city merchants. . . . At first he lived for four years as a peddler in Lincolnshire, going on foot and carrying the cheapest wares; then he traveled abroad, first to St. Andrews in Scotland and then to Rome. On his return . . . he began to launch on bolder courses and to coast frequently by sea to the foreign lands that lay about him. . . . At length his great labors and cares bore much fruit of worldly gain. For he labored not only as a merchant but also as a shipman . . . to Denmark and Flanders and Scotland; in all which lands he found certain rare wares, which he carried to other parts wherein he knew them to be less familiar and coveted by the inhabitants. . . . Hence he made great profit in all his bargains, and gathered much wealth in the sweat of his brow, for he sold dear in one place the wares which he had bought elsewhere at a small price.

From *Life of St. Godric of Finchale*, trans. by G. G. Coulton, *Social Life in Britain from the Conquest to the Reformation* (Cambridge: Cambridge University Press, 1925), pp. 415–17.

THE POLITICAL REVIVAL

The economic revival of Europe was accompanied by a political revival, which was most noticeable in northern France and in England. In northern France the Count of Flanders and the Duke of Normandy had built up relatively well-governed states. The counts of Flanders were fortunate in having neither dangerous neighbors nor powerful vassals. They enlarged the boundaries of their original holdings without ever losing personal control over the county. They named their own men to occupy the fortified castles; they suppressed private wars; and they kept the higher law courts firmly in their own hands. Warfare often broke out along the borders, but the heart of Flanders was relatively peaceful and Flemish industry grew apace.

The vikings had received Normandy in 911, but it took some time for the wild sea rovers to settle down on the land. Only after 950 could the dukes of Normandy begin to organize their government. Given the environment, this had to be a feudal government, but the dukes stressed those elements in the feudal relationship that kept them strong and minimized those that reduced their power. They avoided the fragmentation of political authority that occurred elsewhere and kept full control over barons and lesser vassals. The Duke of Normandy could raise a larger army in proportion to the size of his holdings than could any other French feudal lord. At the same time, to ensure that no vassal became too powerful, he discouraged private war, ordered that no new castle could be built except by special license, and reserved to himself the administration of justice over serious crimes throughout Normandy. His firm control over most of the towns assured him a good income from their growing commerce. And, since he named all the bishops and most of the abbots, he dominated the Norman Church. In order to keep their lands, churchmen had to supply the duke with a large part of his army and much of his administrative staff. Normandy, like Flanders, was a relatively peaceful and prosperous state, and its population soon began to expand.

The energies of Normandy and Flanders were directed into different channels, however. The Flemings concentrated on industry and agriculture. Many of them settled in the towns and became textile workers; others began the centuries-long struggle to reclaim from the sea the flooded land of the coast. They became so skillful in the arts of diking and draining that they were sought by rulers of other provinces. In the twelfth century thousands of Flemish peasants moved across Germany to clear and drain the lands that German lords had won from the Slavs. In Normandy, on the other hand, though some new land was cleared, there was none of the intensive agricultural and industrial activity that marked Flanders. Instead, the Normans turned toward military and political expansion.

The Normans in Italy

The first Norman conquest was in southern Italy, where only the wreckage of earlier political systems survived. The Byzantine Empire held the mainland coasts; the interior was divided among Lombard princes; and the island of Sicily

---

The Duke of Normandy and the Norman Church
1172

Although this document comes from the twelfth century, it repeats obligations laid on the Norman Church in the time of William the Conqueror.

The bishop of Avranches owes 5 knights, and another five from the fief of St. Philibert.

The bishop of Coutances, 5 knights

The bishop of Bayeux, 20 knights

The bishop of Sées, 6 knights

The bishop of Lisieux, the service of 20 knights

The abbot of Fécamp, the service of 10 knights

The abbot of Mont St. Michel, the service of 6 knights in the Avranchin and Cotentin and 1 knight in the Bessin

The abbot of St. Ouen of Rouen, the service of 6 knights [other abbots owe a total of 25 knights].

From Charles H. Haskins, *Norman Institutions* (Cambridge, Mass.: Harvard University Press, 1925), p. 8.

was ruled by rapidly shifting Moslem dynasties. The first Normans came to Italy in the early eleventh century as mercenary soldiers, but soon they were fighting for themselves instead of for their employers. Under Robert Guiscard the Normans had conquered almost all of the mainland by 1071. Meanwhile Robert's younger brother Roger had launched the conquest of Sicily. In this slow and bloody operation, the Moslem strongholds had to be reduced one by one, but by 1091 Sicily was firmly in Roger's possession. His son, Roger II, eventually inherited the mainland conquests as well and in 1130 took the title of King of Sicily.

This conquest of southern Italy and Sicily was in many ways a more remarkable feat than the Norman conquest of England. There were fewer Normans in southern Italy than there were in England, and their first leaders had little authority. But in Italy, as in Normandy earlier and in England later, the Normans showed an uncanny ability to build a strong government out of whatever institutions they found ready at hand. They introduced Norman feudalism in order to guarantee the ruler a strong army, but they preserved much of the Byzantine and Moslem bureaucratic apparatus. The Norman kingdom of Sicily, when it

finally took shape in the twelfth century, was one of the wonders of the medieval world. Norman barons and knights, Greek secretaries, and Moslem financial experts all worked together to make the king strong. He had full control over justice and administration; he regulated the commerce of the entire kingdom; he enjoyed a steady income collected by a centralized financial bureau. Only the king of England could rival him in these matters, and during most of the twelfth century even the king of England probably had less authority.

The Norman Conquest of England

In the long run, however, it was the Norman conquest of England that had the more important consequences. The brilliant Sicilian state fell on evil days in the thirteenth century when it was conquered by a French prince. Only in England did the Norman genius for government have an opportunity to produce lasting results.

As we have seen, in the years just before 1066, Anglo-Saxon England was torn by dissension. King Edward the Confessor could not control his quarreling earls, and he had no direct heir. At one time he had thought of naming his mother's cousin William, Duke of Normandy, to succeed him. But William was not descended from the Anglo-Saxon kings, and the English disliked the Normans. Later Earl Godwin and his son, Earl Harold, became so strong that William's claims were set aside. Harold gained the dominant voice in the government, and when Edward finally died in 1066 Harold was unanimously chosen king by the leading men of the country.

But William was determined not to lose the inheritance to which he thought himself entitled. As Duke of Normandy he already had a powerful army, and he reinforced it by recruiting soldiers from all the neighboring feudal states. The pope was annoyed with the Anglo-Saxons because they had driven out a French Archbishop of Canterbury during one of their anti-Norman demonstrations and had replaced him with a disreputable and unreformed Englishman. He gave his

THE NORMAN CONQUEST OF SOUTHERN ITALY   1130

blessing to William's enterprise, an act that helped William's recruiting efforts. By the summer of 1066 William had assembled an army of over five thousand men.

Harold, aware that the attack was coming, massed his forces in southern England. But just as William was ready to sail, Harold was called north to face the last great invasion of the Northmen. Harold defeated the invaders in a hard battle and hurried back to the south in time to take up a strong position on a hill near Hastings. He might have been better advised to stay back of the Thames and let William's army waste away, as invading armies usually did in the Middle Ages. Forced marches had exhausted the Anglo-Saxon army, and heavy battle casualties had thinned its ranks; moreover, expected support from the northern earls failed to materialize. Harold made a heroic defensive stand, but in the end he was killed and the English shield-wall broke. William marched on London and was accepted as king.

William's victory owed much to chance, but his subsequent consolidation of power in England demonstrated his real ability as a ruler. He had to deal with a bewildered and disoriented native population and with an unreliable group of conquerors, more than half of whom were not Normans. There were some Anglo-Saxon risings; there were even more cases of disobedience and rebellion on the part of his French barons. But he rode them all down: "The rich complained and the poor lamented," says the *Anglo-Saxon Chronicle*, "but he was so sturdy that he cared not for their bitterness; they had to follow his will entirely if they wished to live or to keep their lands."

William's power rested on two basic principles. First, he insisted that he was the lawful heir of Edward the Confessor and so had inherited all the rights of the Anglo-Saxon kings. The Anglo-Saxon aristocracy, by opposing their rightful ruler, had forfeited their lands and rights. This led to the second principle: the new Norman aristocracy now held all lands and rights as fiefs of the king. No lord *owned* anything; he merely had a right to hold it so long as he obeyed and rendered service to the king. This arrangement overcame the chief weakness of the Anglo-Saxon monarchy—namely, its failure to control or discipline the earls and great landlords. A Norman baron who resisted the king knew that he would lose part or all of his land.

William gave his barons and knights extensive powers in local government. He transferred most of the hundred courts to private hands and named Norman barons as sheriffs. This put the peasants at the mercy of the new aristocracy, and many freemen became serfs.

Norman troops on horseback engaging Anglo-Saxon foot soldiers in battle (detail from the Bayeux tapestry, late eleventh century).

The death of Harold, as portrayed in the Bayeux tapestry.

Silver penny bearing the likeness of William the Conqueror.

But men above the peasant level were protected by the king. The county courts were still the king's courts, and any baronial sheriff who showed signs of trying to build up independent power could be summarily removed. The king kept the peace so well that, to quote the *Chronicle* again, "a man might travel through the kingdom unmolested with a bosomful of gold."

Norman Government in England

The most striking result of the Norman conquest was a steady growth in the power of the king's central court. This court had a solid core of household officials and clerks, and a fluctuating population of bishops and barons who happened to be with the king at any given moment. The court assisted the king in any business he laid before it; it could advise on policy, audit accounts, or try cases involving the barons. William kept it very busy, and he himself traveled incessantly up and down England settling local quarrels. When he could not be present himself, he sometimes sent a delegation from his court to represent him. These delegations, with the full authority of the king, could try suits involving land disputes among the king's vassals. They often used a new and very effective procedure that William had imported from Normandy: trial by inquest. In an inquest, neighbors of the litigants were sworn to give true answers to questions concerning the matters in dispute. Procedure by inquest was a much better way of getting at the facts than trial by battle (the procedure favored by the Norman barons), and it enabled the king to settle disputes peacefully and to protect both his own rights and those of his vassals.

The most famous example of the inquest was the Domesday Survey. Faced with the confusion caused by the rapid redistribution of land after the conquest, William wanted to know what each district owed him and what estates were held by his vassals; he probably also wanted to settle a number of boundary disputes among his barons. In 1086 he sent delegations from his court to every county in England with orders to obtain inventories of the possessions of the great landholders. These inventories were checked by swearing in a group of men to make an inquest in each village. The village inquests told the king's men how much land there was in the village, how many men, who had held the land before the conquest, who held it now, and what it owed the king. The results of all these inquiries were summarized by the king's clerks in Domesday Book, a nearly complete survey (London and the northern counties are missing) of the kingdom of England. This amazing feat shows both William's power and his administrative skill. No other eleventh-century king could have done it; no later medieval king had vision enough to attempt it. Domesday stands alone between the tax surveys of the Roman Empire and the censuses of the modern period.

William died in 1087 and was followed by his sons William Rufus (1087–

William the Conqueror

This description of William, in version E of the *Anglo-Saxon Chronicle*, was written by a man, who, as he says, "once lived at his court."

King William was a very wise man and more honored and stronger than any of his predecessors. He was mild to those good men who loved God but severe beyond measure towards those who resisted his will. . . . He kept in prison earls who acted against his pleasure . . . and at length he spared not his own brother Odo. . . . Among other things the good order that William established is not to be forgotten; it was such that any honest man might travel over the kingdom with his bosom full of gold unmolested and no one dared kill another, whatever injury he had received. . . . Being careful of his own interest he surveyed the kingdom so thoroughly that he knew the possessor of every hide* of land and how much it was worth. . . . [Domesday Book]

He caused castles to be built and oppressed the poor. He took from his subjects many marks of gold and many hundred pounds of silver. . . . He made great forests for game and ordered that anyone who killed a deer should be blinded [for] he loved the stags as if he were their father. . . . The rich complained and the poor lamented, but he was so sturdy that he cared not for their bitterness; they had to follow his will entirely if they wished to live or to keep their lands.

*hide: 120 acres.

There are many translations of this passage; this one is adapted from J. A. Giles, *The Anglo-Saxon Chronicle* (London: Bell and Daldy, 1868), pp. 461–63. Easier to find is the version in *English Historical Documents, 1042–1189*, ed. by D. C. Douglas and G. W. Greenaway (London: Eyre and Spottiswoode, 1953), pp. 163–64.

1100) and Henry I (1100–35). Rufus exploited his rights over bishops and barons until he brought them to the point of rebellion, but he made no permanent innovations in government. Henry, on the other hand, made the central government much more efficient. Following earlier precedents, he segregated the financial work of the court in a separate department, the Exchequer, to which the sheriffs had to give an accounting twice a year for every penny of income and expenditure. All these reports were copied out each year in a long document called a Pipe Roll. By consulting earlier Pipe Rolls the Exchequer could make sure that the sheriffs had not overlooked or embezzled royal revenues and that they were paying their arrears. Though England was still thinly inhabited—Domesday figures suggest a population of not much over 1 million—Henry's efficient administration gave him an income larger than that of the king of France, who nominally ruled a much larger country.

Henry also improved the administration of justice. He sent out delegates from his court so often that they came to be more like circuit judges than special commissioners. Few important cases were any longer heard by the sheriffs—a precaution that, added to the strict financial accounting imposed on them, removed any danger of their becoming too independent. Henry also used inquests frequently and kept the peace as his father had done. At his death in 1135 England was a unified kingdom, far more peaceful than most of western Europe, far more powerful than its size and population seemed to warrant.

THE RELIGIOUS REVIVAL

The perfecting of the parish system and the elimination of paganism west of the Elbe during the Carolingian period meant that for generations everyone in western Europe had been exposed to Christianity. By the eleventh century the cumulative effects of this exposure began to make themselves felt. True, the strength of Christian ideals was diluted by the corruption or ignorance of many members of the clergy, but the ideals were powerful enough to survive. Slowly Christianity became less and less a matter of external observance, more and more a matter of strong internal conviction. A great wave of popular piety swept through Europe in the eleventh and twelfth centuries, changing the whole character of European society.

The Peace Movement

The Peace Movement was one of the earliest manifestations of the growing influence of Christian ideals. Feudal warfare was waged largely at the expense of noncombatants; the usual tactic was a raid on enemy lands in which crops were destroyed, cattle driven off, and churches plundered. During the late tenth century,

The Domesday Survey   1086

The monks of Ely added this note to their copy of Domesday returns for their lands.

Here is written down the inquest of the lands [of Ely] as the king's barons inquired about them: namely, by the oaths of the sheriff of the shire and of all the barons and their French soldiers, and of the whole hundred [court], and of the priest, the reeve and six villeins of each vill. Then, how the manor is called, who held it in the time of King Edward [the Confessor] and who holds it now, how many hides, how many plows on the demesne, how many men, how many villeins, how many serfs, how much woods, how much meadow, how much pasture, how many mills . . . how much it was worth altogether and how much now. . . . All this three times over, once for the time of King Edward, once for the time when King William gave it out, and once as it now is—and whether more can be had from it than is now being given.

Translated from W. Stubbs, *Select Charters* (Oxford: Clarendon Press, 1921), p. 101.

bishops in central France tried to protect their people from the horrors of war. Under their leadership peace associations were formed in which each member swore not to attack peasants, merchants, or churchmen. The associations raised armies to punish violators and often levied an annual assessment to support their operations. The movement to protect noncombatants was known as the Peace of God. Leaders of the Peace Movement also tried to forbid fighting on certain holy days, such as Sunday and the Christmas and Easter seasons. This attempt, known as the Truce of God, was far less effective than the Peace of God and did little to curb feudal warfare.

So long as the Peace of God depended on diocesan armies led by churchmen, it had only limited success. But in the eleventh century the idea was taken up by powerful lords in northern France and western Germany as a means of restraining unruly vassals. With no hope of plunder, feudal war seemed less enticing; and with no chance to make war on his neighbors, a minor lord could seldom become strong enough to challenge his lord. The Count of Flanders and the Duke of Normandy, along with many other rulers, enforced the Peace of God in their lands. Thus the Peace Movement gave added security to peasants and merchants and helped increase agricultural production and trade.

Monastic Reform

Another sign of the growing strength of Christian ideals was the movement toward monastic reform. The older monasteries, rich in endowments and resigned to the demands of kings and nobles, were no longer centers of piety or learning. Reform was clearly necessary; the movement began in Germany and France in the tenth century and reached its peak in the eleventh. Reforming abbots, after they had improved the discipline and the administration of their own monastery, were often asked to help reorganize neighboring establishments. Thus groups of monasteries, inspired by the same ideals and governed by the same methods, were formed. The most famous of these groups was the one

headed by Cluny, a monastery in eastern France, and the abbot of Cluny was often as influential as the pope.

Many people were attracted by the opportunity to enter one of the reformed monasteries, so that by the end of the eleventh century there were more monasteries and more monks than ever before. And, without exactly intending it, the reformed monks stirred up such enthusiasm for strict adherence to Christian ideals that it spilled over into other areas and caused drastic changes in the Church.

The Problem of Secular Control

The most dramatic manifestation of popular piety and the desire for reform was a struggle, in the late eleventh century, to free the Church from secular control and to make it the final authority in western society. The early monastic reformers had worried little about this problem. So long as kings and lords let them restore discipline within their orders, they were quite willing to give service to the ruler and even to accept his candidates as abbots. What happened outside the monastery was the king's business, not theirs. But so long as laymen controlled the appointment of bish-

Bronze figure of a monk writing on the tail of a monster, on which he is seated (from a cross or candlestick base, north German or English, *ca.* 1150).

ops and abbots, there was no hope of creating a truly Christian society outside the monasteries. At best, kings and great lords appointed good administrators who spent most of their time on secular affairs. At worst, they sold abbacies and bishoprics or gave them as a sort of pension to incompetent relatives. In either case prelates appointed in this way were likely to be poor spiritual leaders. Some reformers were reluctant to break entirely with the kings, who after all were semisacred personages, but as the eleventh century went on, more and more of them came to believe that the Church could not accomplish its mission until it was independent of lay authority.

They also came to believe that the only way to gain independence and authority for the Church was to strengthen the position of the pope. An isolated bishop or group of clergymen could not resist the pressure of secular rulers. But if the Church were tightly organized under the pope's leadership, then the moral influence of the entire Church could be brought to bear on all the problems of European society. By 1050 the reformers began to proclaim that the pope should be completely independent of all laymen, even the emperor, and that he should have complete administrative jurisdiction over all churchmen, even those who were officials and vassals of kings.

The man who did most to formulate and execute this program was the monk Hildebrand, who later became Pope Gregory VII. He had served in the papal court since the 1040s, and in 1059 he inspired a famous decree that placed the election of the pope in the hands of the cardinals. The cardinals were the leading clergymen of the Roman region—priests of the major Roman churches and bishops of the dioceses around the city. This decree, designed to eliminate the influence of both the Roman nobility and the emperor, proved remarkably successful; after 1059 no pope owed his position to direct lay appointment.

The Investiture Conflict

Hildebrand soon became pope. As Gregory VII (1073–85) he tried to gain the same independence for the Church as a whole that he had already won for the papacy. He concentrated his attack on the appointment of bishops by laymen. Eventually, this controversy became focused on lay investiture, the practice by which a secular ruler bestowed the symbols of spiritual authority, such as the ring and the staff, on the bishops he had appointed. The target was well chosen. A king might legitimately claim that he should have some influence in the choice of bishops, since they had secular as well as religious duties. But he could hardly justify a ceremony that suggested that he was bestowing spiritual authority on officials of the Church. Gregory, however, was seeking more than the abolition of an obnoxious ceremony. He was trying to end all forms of lay control over ecclesiastical appointments and so free the Church to exert its influence directly on all people in western Europe.

The attack on lay interference with ecclesiastical appointments plunged Gregory into a bitter struggle with the

Detail of a manuscript illustration of Gregory VII.

Principles of Gregory VII   ca. 1075

This document was certainly drawn up in Gregory's circle, and probably by the pope himself. It expresses the views of those who were trying to increase papal power in both Church and state.

1. That the Roman church was founded by the Lord alone.
2. That only the Roman pontiff is rightly called universal.
3. That he alone can depose or reestablish bishops.
4. That his legate, even if of inferior rank, is above all bishops in council; and he can give sentence of deposition against them. . . .
12. That it is permitted to him to depose emperors. . . .
18. That his decision ought to be reviewed by no one, and that he alone can review the decisions of everyone.
19. That he ought to be judged by no one.
20. That no one may dare condemn a man who is appealing to the apostolic see.
21. That the greater cases of every church ought to be referred to him.
22. That the Roman church has never erred nor will ever err, as the Scripture bears witness.
23. That the Roman pontiff, if he has been canonically ordained, is indubitably made holy by the merits of the blessed Peter. . . .
24. That by his precept and license subjects are permitted to accuse their lords. . . .
27. That he can absolve the subjects of the unjust from their fealty.

From *Dictatus Papae Gregorii VII*, trans. by E. Lewis, *Medieval Political Ideas* (New York: Knopf, 1954), Vol. II, pp. 380–81.

emperor Henry IV (1056–1106). Henry had had a difficult time asserting his authority in Germany; he had succeeded only because he controlled the resources of most of the bishoprics and abbeys of the country. Thus Gregory, by forbidding lay investiture, was in effect depriving Henry of the only means he had to preserve the unity and strengthen the central government of Germany.

Henry's reaction was violent and ill advised. He had just defeated a dangerous group of rebels in Saxony and was feeling both belligerent and overconfident. He denounced Gregory as an illegally elected pope and summoned a council of German bishops to depose him from the papal see. In a bitter letter announcing this decision to Gregory, Henry ended with the curse: "Down, down, to be damned through all the ages!" Gregory countered by excommunicating Henry and freeing his subjects from their oath of allegiance to him.

"It is right," said Gregory, "that he who attempts to diminish the honor of the Church, shall himself lose the honor which he seems to have."

The issue was fairly joined. Now everything depended on the reaction of the bishops and princes of the Empire. Many of the German princes were delighted to have an excuse to resist Henry; the bishops, who owed their jobs to the king, were more loyal. The religious issue, in the end, brought the waverers over to Gregory's side, and an assembly of bishops and princes at Oppenheim in 1076 decided to depose Henry unless he was absolved by the pope.

Henry, headstrong but no fool, saw that he must make his peace with the pope. In wintry weather, he journeyed to Italy and came to Gregory at the castle of Canossa in 1077. He stood as a penitent outside the castle for three days while Gregory wrestled with the conflict between his political aims and his spiritual duties. If he absolved Henry he would wreck the coalition supporting his German policies, but the head of the Church could scarcely reject a repentant sinner. In the end Gregory admitted Henry, accepted his promise to obey papal orders, and then granted him absolution.

In the short run Henry gained a political victory by his act of submission. As both he and Gregory had foreseen, the German princes felt that the pope had failed them; they could no longer oppose a king who had been reconciled with the Church. Henry regained much of his authority; he even became strong enough to invade Italy and force Gregory to take refuge with the Normans in the south. But in the long run the victory went to the papacy. The pope had demonstrated that he could force the most powerful ruler in the West to yield and that he could stir up rebellion against an anointed king. The lesson was not lost on western rulers; for two hundred years after Canossa few of them were willing to risk prolonged defiance of the pope.

The struggle over lay investiture persisted for a generation after Gregory's death in 1085. Henry was plagued by rebellion for the rest of his reign, and trouble continued under his son, Henry V (1106–25). At last a compromise

Henry IV before journeying to Canossa. Miniature from an early–twelfth-century manuscript of the life of Countess Matilda of Tuscany. Henry, kneeling, asks Abbot Hugh of Cluny and Countess Matilda to intercede for him with Pope Gregory VII.

Rex rogat Abbatem. Mathildim supplicat atq;

was reached at the Concordat of Worms (1122) by which lay investiture in the strict sense was abandoned. The emperor could still nominate bishops, but the pope could refuse approval to men who were clearly unqualified, and he could suspend or even remove bishops who proved unworthy. In practice, this meant that the German bishops had to show a certain amount of obedience to the pope if they wanted to keep their jobs. The German ruler, deprived of full control over the Church in his own country, lost his chief source of power. The independence of the German princes increased accordingly.

Similar but less acute struggles took place in France and England. In neither country was the king as dependent on control over the Church as the German emperor had been, so it was easier to reach a settlement. The outcome was about the same: the pope admitted royal influence over appointments, but he remained the final judge of the qualifications of bishops. No one who offended the pope could hope to become or remain a bishop. Assured of administrative control of the Church, the pope could now insist that his policies be accepted throughout Europe. Acceptance was slow and grudging in some places, but it could never be entirely denied. The Church, far stronger and more independent than it had ever been before, had an unprecedented opportunity to guide and control European society.

The First Crusade

During the Investiture Conflict many barons and knights had supported the pope. The influence of the Church over the military class was further demonstrated by the First Crusade. A crusade was a military expedition organized by the pope to attack enemies of the Church. Earlier expeditions against the western Moslems had been encouraged by the pope, but these campaigns included only small groups of knights and were not fully under the control of the Church. By the end of the eleventh century, however, the papacy was stronger, and the military class was eager to prove its devotion to the faith.

The First Crusade was proclaimed by Pope Urban II at the Council of Clermont in 1095. He had many reasons for his action, and it is impossible to decide which was dominant. Urban had just reaffirmed the principles of the Peace of God, and he certainly believed that Europe would be more tranquil if the military classes turned their weapons against an outside foe instead of fighting one another. Moreover, the investiture struggle was still going on; if the pope could enlist large numbers of fighting men under his banner, it would demonstrate that he and not the emperor was the real leader of the West. Finally, the situation in the Near East seemed ripe for intervention. The Turks, who had come into Mesopotamia as mercenary soldiers of the caliphs, had crushed the Byzantine army at Manzikert (1071) and had occupied most of Asia Minor. The Byzantine Empire, in mortal peril, turned to the West for aid. At the same time Jerusalem had fallen to a fanatical Moslem dynasty that ruled from Cairo. Pilgrimage to the Holy City was now more difficult than it had been when Jerusalem was held by the tolerant Abbasid caliphs. A western army could strengthen Byzantium, and gratitude for its assistance might close the breach that had opened up between the Roman and Greek Churches since the controversy over iconoclasm. The capture of Jerusalem would make it easier

Urban's Speech at Clermont   1095

I exhort you . . . to strive to expel that wicked race [the Turks] from our Christian lands. . . . Christ commands it. Remission of sins will be granted for those going thither. . . . Let those who are accustomed to wage private war wastefully even against believers go forth against the infidels. . . . Let those who have lived by plundering be soldiers of Christ; let those who formerly contended against brothers and relations rightly fight barbarians; let those who were recently hired for a few pieces of silver win their eternal reward. . . . The sorrowful here will be glad there, the poor here will be rich there, and the enemies of the Lord here will be His friends there. Let no delay postpone the journey . . . when winter has ended and spring has come . . . enter the highways courageously with the Lord going on before.

Adapted from Fulcher of Chartres, *History of Jerusalem*, trans. by M. E. McGinty (Philadelphia: University of Pennsylvania Press, 1941), p. 16. Fulcher was at Clermont and went on the First Crusade.

for Christians to accomplish the most salutary of all pilgrimages, the visit to the Holy Sepulchre.

Urban's appeal for an army to fight the Turks and regain Jerusalem met with an astonishing response. The Count of Toulouse was the first to take the Cross, and he was soon joined by the Duke of Lorraine, four great lords from northern France, two Norman princes from southern Italy, and thousands of lesser men. The largest number of crusaders came from France and the German provinces near France, but all the countries of western Europe were represented in the undertaking. Nothing shows more clearly the strength of religious conviction and the effectiveness of the leadership of the Church. Some of the greater nobles may have thought of the crusade as an opportunity to acquire new lands; some knights may merely have been seeking adventure. But the majority of crusaders had purely religious motives. Urban had promised them full absolution for their sins and immediate entrance to heaven if they died fighting the infidels. So numerous were the volunteers that it took a year to organize the main armies; meanwhile thousands of noncombatant pilgrims, escorted by a few knights, set off for the East. Most of them were massacred by the Turks; only a few survived to join the armies that followed.

The crusaders' slogan was "God wills it!" Certainly it was a near miracle that they succeeded. Almost everything was against them: they knew nothing of the geography or politics of the East; they had little money and no supply services; they had no single commanding officer, and bitter feuds broke out among their leaders even before they entered Moslem lands. The Byzantine emperor, as soon as he found that he could not use them as mercenaries, grew suspicious of them; he wanted to reconquer Asia Minor, not go off on a harebrained raid on Jerusalem. That the crusaders overcame all these obstacles was due partly to their enthusiasm, and partly to the fact that the Turks were divided into many small principalities and were disliked by other Moslems. Moreover, the heavy-armed western cavalry was one of the best fighting forces on the Eurasian continent.

The crusaders suffered severely from disease and starvation; they were battered in two hard-fought battles; they were weakened by continuing dissension among their leaders. But somehow they kept going. In 1099 they took Jerusalem and set up a series of crusading states stretching from Antioch in the north down through Tripoli and Jerusalem to the Dead Sea.

The dramatic success of the First Crusade reinforced the influence of the Church and strengthened the self-confidence of the peoples of western Europe. The many chronicles that describe the great campaign, though ascribing victory to God's protection, nevertheless show obvious pride in the crusaders' heroic deeds. But it would be a mistake to overemphasize the effects of the crusade; it was a result, not a cause, of the great medieval revival.

THE "RENAISSANCE OF THE TWELFTH CENTURY"

That revival continued without break into the twelfth century. Few periods in the history of the West have shown as much energy and originality. The men of the twelfth century not only continued the reform of ecclesiastical and secular government but also laid the foundations for a new architecture, a new literature, and a new system of education. All these activities drew on the Church for intellectual inspiration and material support, and in many of them churchmen played a leading role.

St. Bernard

The most powerful churchman of the early twelfth century was St. Bernard of Clairvaux (1090–1153). He was the first outstanding leader produced by the Cistercian Order, one of the very strict monastic groups founded toward the end of the eleventh century. Earlier reformers, such as the monks of Cluny, had aimed only at honest observance of the Benedictine Rule, but this was not enough for the new generation of religious leaders. The strong religious feeling that made possible the First Crusade also found

Capital in the Cathedral of St. Lazarus at Autun showing the flight into Egypt.

expression in more ascetic forms of monastic life. The Cistercians refused to own serfs or revenue-producing properties and insisted on living in the wilderness by the labor of their own hands. In the end this uncompromising attitude gained them considerable wealth, for they had to develop new agricultural techniques, such as large-scale sheep raising, to make up for their lack of serfs. But in the early, heroic days the Cistercians attracted many able and zealous men by the example of their rigorous life.

St. Bernard, who entered the Cistercian order as a young man, was soon sent to found a new monastery at Clairvaux. Under his direction Clairvaux became a center of piety and asceticism. St. Bernard sought only to be a worthy abbot of this model monastery, but while he had no ambitions for himself, he had great zeal for the Church. Whenever he saw its unity threatened by schism or heresy, or its ideals menaced by worldly pressures and interests, he could not rest. Therefore this abbot, who wanted only a narrow cell in a secluded monastery, spent most of his life in public business, advising popes, giving lectures to kings, preaching to crowds, and writing letters to every prominent man in Europe.

From 1125 to the year of his death in 1153, St. Bernard dominated the West through his eloquence, his piety, and his boundless energy. His support saved causes that were tottering to failure; his opposition damned men who seemed born for success. In a disputed papal election in 1130, St. Bernard convinced the rulers of Europe that Innocent II should be recognized as the rightful pope, even though he had received fewer votes in the College of Cardinals than an opposing candidate. Innocent II was naturally influenced by St. Bernard, as was Pope Eugenius III (1145–53), who had been a Cistercian monk himself. When Eugenius inaugurated the Second Crusade in 1147 to regain some lost territories in Syria, he turned to St. Bernard for help in recruiting leaders for the campaign. St. Bernard did not disappoint the pope; he persuaded both the king of France and the emperor of Germany to take the Cross. When the Second Crusade failed, St. Bernard wrote the official apology ascribing the debacle to the sins of the Christians.

St. Bernard was in many ways a conservative man. He disliked the new architecture of the twelfth century; costly churches seemed to him unnecessary for the worship of God and a waste of money that might better be given to the poor. He disliked the new learning, which exalted human reason and led men to think that they could approach God through logic rather than through faith. He worried about the growing bureaucracy at the papal court, even though he realized it was essential to the unity of the Church and the authority of the pope.

But although he was a conservative in worldly matters, St. Bernard was an innovator in religion. He was a leader of the new piety, the movement to humanize Christianity and Christianize human life. He emphasized devotion to the Virgin and dwelt on the life of Jesus on earth. As Dante was to point out, the central theme in St. Bernard's teaching was love, the love of God for man and the love that man should have for God. He talked more of the joys of heaven than of the pains of hell. He was saddened and angered by those who rejected the love and mercy of God, but he always hoped to save the sinners he de-

Cistercian monks shown living by their own labor. Detail from a manuscript of St. Gregory's *Moralia in Job,* written at the motherhouse of Cîteaux in the twelfth century.

St. Bernard on Love

First, then, a man loves his own self for self's sake, since he is flesh, and he cannot have any taste except for things in relation with him; but when he sees that he is not able to subsist by himself, that God is, as it were, necessary to him, he begins to inquire and to love God by faith. Thus he loves God in the second place, but because of his own interest, and not for the sake of God Himself. But when, on account of his own necessity, he has begun to worship Him and to approach Him by meditation, by reading, by prayer, by obedience, he comes little by little to know God with a certain familiarity, and in consequence to find Him sweet and kind; and thus having tasted how sweet the Lord is, he passes to the third stage, and thus loves God no longer on account of his own interest, but for the sake of God himself. Once arrived there, he remains stationary, and I know not if in this life man is truly able to rise to the fourth degree, which is, no longer to love himself except for the sake of God. . . .

From *Some Letters of Saint Bernard*, trans. by S. J. Eales (London: Hodges, 1904), pp. 202–03.

Left: barrel vault, church of St. Savin (eleventh century). Although no light could be admitted in the upper part of the nave, the vault could be covered with fine Romanesque painting. Center: groin vault, formed by the intersection of two barrel vaults, Mont-Saint-Michel (twelfth century). The walls could now be pierced with windows. Right: rib vault, Mont-Saint-Michel (late Romanesque). Ribs reinforce the groin vault, but the effect is still heavy.

nounced. In all this he gave a lead to his contemporaries. The number of churches dedicated to the Virgin increased sharply, more emphasis was placed on the Nativity and the childhood of Jesus, and hope of salvation began to outweigh fear of damnation. In many ways the twelfth century was an age of optimism, an optimism that was reflected in its religion as well as in its secular activities.

Abbot Suger and Gothic Architecture

Another great abbot, second only to St. Bernard in influence, was Suger of St. Denis (*ca.* 1091–1152). The son of poor peasants, he had been given to the monastery by his parents when only a child. Sheer ability carried him to the position of abbot, an outstanding example of the opportunities the Church offered to men of low birth. St. Denis was one of the wealthiest monasteries in France as well as the burial place of the French kings. Suger was thus closely associated with the royal house, and his administrative ability made him a close adviser of two kings, Louis VI and Louis VII. During the absence of Louis VII on the Second Crusade, Suger acted as regent of France; he was remarkably successful in preserving both the stability and the solvency of the realm.

Suger was more than a successful administrator, however. He wrote several books, including an interesting biography of Louis VI. But his overwhelming interest was the rebuilding of the church of St. Denis, which he was determined to make the most beautiful church in France, the "crown of the kingdom." St. Bernard was suspicious of this desire for magnificence, as he was of Suger's involvement in worldly business, but the abbot of St. Denis had tact as well as energy. By giving his full support to the Cistercian's reform policy, he conciliated St. Bernard and gained a free hand for his own activities.

Suger wanted his church to be full of light and color. He had enough money to do as he wished and a remarkable willingness to experiment with new ideas. Workmen flocked to St. Denis from all over France, bringing with them solutions to problems of church architecture that had been worked out in the last half-century. The result was a church that, for the first time, incorporated all the essential elements of the Gothic style.

From 1000 on there had been a great wave of church building in western Europe. The basic plan was still that of the old basilica, a long nave with lower side aisles and a transept crossing the nave before the altar. At first the churches were low and dark, with strong emphasis on horizontal lines. Then experiments were made in raising the walls and enlarging the windows. For example, architects discovered that a pointed arch over a window increased the area that could be glazed. There had also been some use of stained glass.

But the most important innovations had to do with the vaulting of the interior roof of churches. The flat wooden roofs of the early Roman churches were not very satisfactory in the wet, cold climate of the north. A stone vault covered by a steep-sloped roof would be far more satisfactory in keeping out the weather and reducing the danger of fire. But it took generations for architects to devise the best way of covering the great open spaces of a church with a stone vault. The first and easiest solution was the barrel vault, a continuous semicircular arch extending the entire length of the church. But this scheme was not particularly safe when used for very wide areas. Moreover, because the barrel vault put an equal strain on every part of the side walls, it made the use of large windows impossible, since any substantial cutting into the walls would weaken the whole structure. Then architects hit on the idea of designing a roof as if it were the intersection of two barrel vaults, in that way concentrating the downward and outward thrust of the roof at a few points along the wall, which in turn could be strengthened by pillars, or piers, and

Left: early Gothic rib vault, Mont-Saint-Michel. Greater height and light are now being exploited. Right: rib vaulting on a grand scale, the nave of Chartres Cathedral (1194–1220). Great height and light have been achieved; the upper (clerestory) windows are larger and more useful than those at floor level.

buttresses. Now the walls could be pierced with large, high windows, flooding the church with light. The final refinement was to mark the lines of the intersecting vaults with stone ribs, thus both strengthening and improving the appearance of the roof.

The churches of the eleventh and early twelfth centuries were larger and more beautiful than any that had been built before in the north, but no one of them embodied all these innovations. They still adhered more or less to the old, or Romanesque, style. But the massive Romanesque churches, impressive and beautiful as they were, did not satisfy many churchmen of the twelfth century. They wanted a style that reflected their new aspirations, something less practical and earthbound, something that symbolized the mystery and splendor of heaven.

Suger felt these longings with particular keenness, and it was under his direction in the church of St. Denis that the decisive step was taken in the evolution of the new style. Suger used almost all the new ideas: pointed arches, rib vaults, larger and higher windows, and stained glass. He described the result in one of his verses: "Bright is the noble building which is pervaded by the new light." Churches were built near Paris along the same principles, and the new Gothic style soon became the standard for church architecture. Southern France, Germany, and Italy clung for some time to Romanesque, but by the early years of the thirteenth century, Gothic was triumphing in those areas as well.

Abelard

A third great figure of the early twelfth-century revival, Abelard (ca. 1079–1142), was also an abbot, but an unwilling and unhappy one. The son of a minor vassal in Brittany, he had, like many other men of the twelfth century, become inflamed with the love of learning. About 1100, he renounced his inheritance and went to study at Paris.

Paris was full of famous teachers, though there was as yet no formal curriculum. The growing horde of students had overflowed the old cathedral school on the Île de la Cité, and lectures were already being given on the Left Bank in what was to become the Latin Quarter. This new enthusiasm for learning resembled in some ways the new piety; scholars were examining old texts that had been known for centuries and were discovering in them fresh meanings and personal applications. The learning of the Moslem-Byzantine world had not yet entered Europe, but students were finding a new excitement in the old books.

Abelard's first love, like that of many of his contemporaries, was logic. He mastered all the available material in a remarkably short time and immediately set himself up as a teacher, much to the annoyance of some of his former professors. Abelard thoroughly enjoyed teaching logic, but, again like many of his contemporaries, he saw in it more than a formal intellectual exercise. He was convinced that it was a universal tool (somewhat like mathematics today) that could be used to solve old problems and acquire new knowledge. To a man of his time, the most important problems were theological, so he decided to become a master of theology as well as logic. Again he completed his studies in record time and began to steal students from, and contradict, his old teachers.

Abelard was a great teacher and scholar; he was also a very brash young man. For example, he produced an exercise book for his students called *Sic et Non (Yes and No)*, in which he marshaled opinions from the Bible and the Church Fathers on both sides of controversial questions. It took considerable ingenuity to find support for some of his statements—for example, that God is threefold and the contrary; that sin is pleasing to God and the contrary—and his cleverness added to the suspicions of his contemporaries. The prologue to the book made it seem even more dangerous, for here Abelard announced: "The first key to wisdom is this . . . industrious and repeated inquiry. . . . For through doubting we come to inquiry and through inquiry we discover the truth." Abelard also wrote a treatise on the Trinity in which he tried to define the attributes of each Person by a rigorous use of logic. This meddling with the central mystery of the faith annoyed St. Bernard, who in one of his angriest letters denounced Abelard as a writer who sought to place "degrees in the Trinity, modes in the Majesty, numbers in the Eternity." St. Bernard felt that God was too great to be defined by the human mind and that all the virtue went out of faith when it was made to seem too rational.

Abelard's personal life increased his reputation for vanity and presumption. His downfall began when he seduced Héloïse, the niece of a canon of the cathedral of Paris. The affair could not be hushed up, for his love poems had been circulated throughout the city, and Héloïse had a child. The girl's uncle was, naturally, furious and put such pressure on Abelard that he agreed to marry Héloïse, provided that the marriage were kept secret. This was not one of Abelard's most brilliant ideas; there had to be witnesses to the marriage, and the witnesses talked. Héloïse had argued against the marriage because it would block Abelard's chance of promotion in the Church and would lessen his reputation as a philosopher, a man who should be above earthly pleasures and cares. When rumors about the marriage spread, Héloïse denied that they were true. Abelard was even more perturbed, and considerably less self-sacrificing. He persuaded Héloïse to take refuge in a nunnery, an act that looked suspiciously like an attempt to dissolve the marriage. The uncle, angrier than ever, hired a gang of thugs to castrate the scholar. The scandal was so enormous that Abelard temporarily retired from teaching and became a monk in St. Denis.

St. Denis was not a very lively place (this was just before Suger became abbot), but Abelard managed to stir things up. He criticized some of the legends about the monastery's patron saint and denounced the scandalous life of the monks. He was right on both points, as he often was, but he was thoroughly disliked by his companions. At the same time he wrote a treatise on the Trinity that was condemned and burned at the Council of Soissons (1120). It was clearly impossible for Abelard to stay at St. Denis; Suger (now abbot) gave him permission to live elsewhere. He established an oratory in the wilderness (later given to Héloïse as the foundation of a new nunnery), and then became abbot of a remote Breton monastery. He found the monks there brutal (they threatened his life), ignorant and entirely unwilling to follow any monastic rule. Abelard finally abandoned his post and returned to the neighborhood of Paris, where he began to teach again. As usual, he drew crowds of students, but he had changed neither his methods nor his opinions. His ene-

Abelard on Scholarship

. . . Investigation is the first key to wisdom: it is the kind of industrious and repeated inquiry which Aristotle, the wisest of all philosophers recommended to his students in saying: "It is difficult to solve problems with confidence unless they have been frequently discussed. It is not useless to express doubts about some matters." For through doubting we come to inquiry and through inquiry we discover the truth, as Truth Himself said: "Seek and you will find, knock and the door will be opened to you."

St. Bernard on Abelard

We have in France an old teacher turned into a new theologian, who in his early days amused himself with logic and who now gives utterance to wild imaginations upon the Holy Scriptures. . . .

There is nothing in heaven above nor in the earth below which he deigns to confess ignorance of: he raises his eyes to heaven and searches the deep things of God and . . . brings back unspeakable words which it is not lawful for a man to utter. He is ready to give a reason for everything, even for those things that are above reason. Thus he presumes against reason and against faith. For what is more unreasonable than to attempt to go beyond the limits of reason? And what is more against faith than to be unwilling to believe what cannot be proved by reason? . . .

And so he promises understanding to his hearers, even on those most sublime and sacred truths that are hidden in the very bosom of our holy faith. He places degrees in the Trinity, modes in the Majesty, numbers in the Eternity. . . . Who can endure this? . . . Who does not shudder at such new-fangled profanities?

Translated from *Sic et Non*, ed. by V. Cousin, *Ouvrages inédits d'Abélard* (Paris: Imprimerie royale, 1836), p. 104; translated from *Patrologia latina*, Vol. 182, cols. 1055–56.

mies, led by St. Bernard, found his success unendurable. His writings on the Trinity were again condemned by a local council (Sens, 1140). Abelard appealed to the pope, but fell ill on his way to Rome. He took refuge at Cluny, where Peter the Venerable let him live in peace until his death in 1142.

Abelard's real fault was vanity, not impiety; he had sought to make Christian doctrine more precise, but not to contradict it. He was only the most conspicuous of many scholars who were trying to combine logic, philosophy, and theology in an effort to give Christian doctrine a more rigorous intellectual structure. St. Bernard, who was a mystic rather than a scholar, was perhaps right in feeling that excessive rationalism would weaken the appeal of religion. But he was fighting a losing battle; the future belonged to men who followed Abelard's methods. For the rest of the Middle Ages, theology was studied according to the rules of formal logic, and authorities were cited on both sides of every question in order to reach a final, and orthodox, answer. The most popular theological book of the twelfth century, Peter Lombard's *Sentences*, resembled Abelard's work far more than it

did that of St. Bernard. The system used by Abelard, Peter Lombard, and others eventually became known as "scholasticism," and scholastic methods dominated European thought for the next three centuries.

The Beginnings of Universities

Exciting as theology was, it did not monopolize the attention of twelfth-century scholars. A revival of interest in the Latin classics, especially noticeable in the scholars who congregated at Chartres, led to a marked improvement in Latin style. John of Salisbury (d. 1180), who wrote one of the first medieval treatises on political theory, had had some connection with the scholars at Chartres. A growing interest in medicine, centered at Salerno in southern Italy, prompted the study of old Roman textbooks and the new observations of Arab doctors. But theology's real rival was law, and in the long run students of law became far more numerous than students of theology.

Although Roman law had not been completely forgotten during the early Middle Ages, it had been little studied, and most of the copies of Justinian's *Corpus Juris* had disappeared. At the end of the eleventh century there was a revival of interest in Roman law, especially in Italy and southern France. The first great teacher, Irnerius, attracted so many students to his school at Bologna that the city became, and remained for centuries, the chief center of legal studies in Europe. Roman law appealed to students for many reasons: it was a fine example of logical and precise reasoning; it was part of the intellectual legacy of Rome; it gave intelligent answers to problems of human relations that the unsophisticated customary law of medieval Europe had scarcely considered. The Romans had been the most legal-minded people of antiquity, and western Europeans had inherited their fondness for law. The *Corpus Juris*, which summed up the work of generations of Roman lawyers in fairly compact form, could be mastered by students within a reasonable length of time. And a young man soundly trained in Roman law could look forward to a bril-

MEDIEVAL SCHOOLS AND UNIVERSITIES   1100–1250

liant career; by the middle of the century legal training had become the surest route to promotion in the service of popes and kings. The number of law students who flocked to Bologna from the most distant parts of the Continent increased steadily during the twelfth century.

A special branch of legal studies was canon law, the law of the Church. The Church, of course, had relied heavily on Roman law in formulating its basic rules and procedures, but it had to cope with many problems that Roman law had never touched—for example, the forms to be followed in choosing a bishop, or the requirements for a valid Christian marriage. In deciding these questions the Church relied on the writings of the Fathers, decrees of councils, and administrative and judicial rulings of the popes. Some collections of this scattered material had been made, but none of them enjoyed unquestioned authority. Then about 1140 the monk Gratian produced his *Decretum,* or *Concordance of Discordant Canons,* which was rapidly accepted as the definitive treatise on canon law. Gratian, following the pattern already set by earlier students of canon law (and quite compatible with the methods of Abelard and other theologians), quoted the authorities on both sides of each question, and then gave what seemed to him the approved solution. Since Gratian taught at Bologna, students went there to study canon law as well as Roman law, and soon there was a large group of experts in the subject. Canon law, even more than Roman law, opened the road to high office, in this case high office in the Church. Many bishops and almost all the popes from 1159 to the end of the fourteenth century were students of canon law.

These groupings of students and teachers at centers like Paris and Bologna eventually coalesced into universities, one of the most significant institutional legacies of the Middle Ages. The best of the cathedral schools, such as Paris, had some degree of organization before 1150, but not all schools were cathedral schools, and even the cathedral schools needed a stronger structure and more powers of regulation. The many foreign students at Bologna, for example, felt that they were being cheated by the Italian boardinghouse keepers, and sometimes by their professors as well. They formed a union to keep down the price of food and lodging and to make sure that teachers covered an adequate amount of material in their lecture courses. At Paris the chief problem, illustrated by Abelard's career, was to determine at what point a student was entitled to set himself up as a teacher. The bishops, or their chancellors, who were supposed to license teachers, had neither the knowledge nor the time to deal with the growing number of applicants. So in Paris the teachers themselves formed a union, to which they admitted only students who had passed a rigorous examination. It was out of these unions of students and teachers that the university was to emerge.

The intellectual interests that created the first universities were the most striking manifestations of the new vigor of western European society. The people of western Europe had not yet equaled the Romans in the arts of government, and they perhaps had done no more than equal the Romans in total economic production. But they had an intellectual curiosity, an urge to acquire new ideas, that the Romans of the Empire had never possessed. And in the long run this curiosity and drive were to lead to the revival of science and the transformation of European society.

The Revival of Roman Law

Three times has Rome given her laws to the world, three times has she bound different peoples together: first, by the unity of the state, when the Roman people stood at the height of their strength, second, by the unity of the Church after the Empire had fallen, and third, by the unity of law when Roman Law was accepted during the Middle Ages. The first victory was won by force of arms, but the other two by the power of the mind. . . . Roman Law, like Christianity, has become an essential element of modern civilization.

From Rudolph von Jhering, *Geist des römischen Rechts* (Leipzig: Breitkopf und Härtel, 1907), Vol. I, p. 1.

Suggestions for Further Reading

Note: Asterisk denotes a book available in paperback edition.

Economic Revival

The first three volumes of the *Cambridge Economic History of Europe,* ed. by M. M. Postan (1952–66), contain excellent articles on medieval agriculture, commerce, and industry. (Be sure to get the second, much improved, edition of Volume I.) There is good source material on the revival of medieval trade in R. S. Lopez and I. W. Raymond, *Medieval Trade in the Mediterranean World* (1955). A useful short survey is R. Latouche, *The Birth of the Western Economy** (1961). For England, see R. Lennard, *Rural England* (1959). The effect of the Moslem control of the Mediterranean on European economy is discussed by H. Pirenne, *Economic and Social History of Medieval Europe** (1937), with special attention to the economic activity of Italy and the Low Countries. H. F. Brown, *Venice: An Historical Sketch of the Republic* (1895), is the best one-volume study in English of that important commercial center. G. Duby, *Rural Economy and Country Life in the Medieval West* (1968), is the best overall study of rural life. E. Power, *Medieval People** (1954), gives a vivid picture of social and manorial life from the point of view of individuals.

H. Pirenne, *Medieval Cities** (1925), is a fine general study of the beginnings of urban civilization and the part played by the middle class in the development of a modern economic system and modern culture. Both C. Stephenson, *Borough and Town* (1933), and J. Tait, *The Medieval English Borough* (1936), are scholarly studies of town development in England with opposing interpretations on the origins of towns. For source material, see J. H. Mundy and P. Riesenberg, *The Medieval Town* (1958).

Political Revival

There are many valuable works on the political history of this period. C. Petit-Dutaillis, *Feudal Monarchy in France and England * (1936), discusses the preservation and development of the monarchy in France and England from the tenth to the thirteenth century. An excellent brief study of the growth of royal power in France is R. Fawtier, *The Capetian Kings of France,** trans. by L. Butler (1960). The older study of E. Lavisse, ed., *Histoire de France,* Vol. II, Part 2 (1901), which reviews economic, social, and cultural phenomena as well as political, has not been surpassed for comprehensiveness.

Medieval Germany, Vol. I, articles trans. by G. Barraclough (1938), has good material on Germany in this period, and G. Barraclough, *The Origins of Modern Germany* (1947), analyzes the reasons why Germany lagged behind the rest of Europe in the development of political institutions.

We have interesting evidence on England at this time in the contemporary Ordericus Vitalis, *History of England and Normandy,* 3 vols., trans. by T. Forester (1854), which concentrates on religious events, and in William of Malmesbury, *Chronicle,* trans. by J. A. Giles (1847), which gives attention to both political and religious developments. Both histories go up to 1154. F. W. Maitland, *Domesday Book and Beyond** (1897), is a monument in historical prose writing. The best scholarly treatment of the establishment of Norman feudalism in England is F. M. Stenton, *First Century of English Feudalism* (1932). D. C. Douglas, *William the Conqueror* (1964), is an excellent biography.

C. H. Haskins, *The Normans in European History** (1915), shows the Normans as founders and organizers of states. More recent works on this subject are D. C. Douglas, *The Norman Achievement* (1969) and *The Norman Fate* (1976). See also J. Le Patourel, *The Norman Empire* (1976). Political developments in Italy are discussed by P. Villari, *Medieval Italy from Charlemagne to Henry VII* (1910), a broad readable survey. C. Cahen, *Le Régime féodal de l'Italie normande* (1940), is a critical study of Norman institutions in Italy. An older but still useful book is E. Curtis, *Roger of Sicily and the Normans in Italy* (1912).

Religious Revival

Since the impetus for the religious revival of the eleventh century was the monastery at Cluny, J. Evans, *Monastic Life at Cluny* (1931), is a good starting point for study. L. M. Smith, *Cluny in the Eleventh and Twelfth Centuries* (1930), is a valuable if somewhat disjointed study of the influence of Cluny on the religious life of Europe, while D. Knowles, *The Monastic Order in England* (1951), is a thorough and readable study of almost every facet of English monastic life from 900 to 1215.

There is interesting source material on the Investiture Conflict in B. F. Tierney, *The Crisis of Church and State* (1964), and in K. Morrison, *The Investiture Controversy* (1971). A. J. Macdonald,

Hildebrand: A Life of Gregory VII (1932), is a good brief biography, and the *Correspondence of Gregory VII*, trans. by E. Emerton (1932), contains information not only on the problem of investiture but on the increase in papal activities under Gregory. The excellent book by G. Tellenbach, *Church, State, and Christian Society at the Time of the Investiture Controversy* (1940), shows the conflict as a papal attempt to revalue Christian society in the light of canon law. The consequences for the Church and the state are carefully analyzed by N. F. Cantor, *Church, Kingship and Lay Investiture in England, 1089-1135* (1959), a very scholarly study. W. Ullmann, *Growth of Papal Power in the Middle Ages* (1955), treats the effect of the controversy on the growth of the papal government.

The First Crusade

A. C. Krey, *The First Crusade* (1921), gives a very good picture of the crusade from the accounts of eyewitnesses and participants. One of the best chronicles of the crusade is Fulcher of Chartres' *History of the Expedition to Jerusalem,** ed. by H. S. Fink (1973). *The Alexiad of Anna Comnena*, trans. by E. A. S. Dawes (1928), contains the Byzantine attitude toward the crusade, and Usāmah ibn Munqhid, *An Arab-Syrian Gentleman and Warrior in the Period of the Crusades*, trans. by P. K. Hitti (1929), gives the Moslem point of view. The best recent book on the crusade is the fascinating account of S. Runciman, *A History of the Crusades,** Vol. I (1951). Runciman includes a thorough bibliography. M. L. W. Baldwin, ed., *The First Hundred Years* (1955) (Vol. I of *A History of the Crusades*, ed. by K. M. Setton), is a collection of essays by leading historians of the crusades. The establishment of feudalism in the conquered East is treated by J. L. La Monte, *Feudal Monarchy in the Latin Kingdom of Jerusalem* (1932). H. E. Mayer, *The Crusades* (1972), is a good short synthesis of the whole movement.

The Renaissance of the Twelfth Century

The best general study of the revival of learning in the West is C. H. Haskins, *The Renaissance of the Twelfth Century** (1927), which discusses scholarship, Roman law, and philosophy, and has a good critical bibliography. Another excellent book is C. Brooke, *The Twelfth Century Renaissance** (1969). H. O. Taylor, *The Medieval Mind*, Vol. I (1953), has good material on intellectual developments in the twelfth century, and R. W. Southern, *The Making of the Middle Ages** (1953), presents an excellent account of the influence of the new piety on cultural growth. His *Medieval Humanism and Other Studies* (1976) is even more useful. There is a good cross section of the poetry of the period from 900 to 1160 in H. Waddell, *Medieval Latin Lyrics** (1929).

St. Bernard, Suger, and Abelard

There is a wealth of material on these three men, who to a great extent dominated the intellectual life of the first half of the twelfth century. *St. Bernard of Clairvaux*, trans. by G. Webb and A. Walker (1960), is an interesting biography written by Bernard's friend William of St. Thierry. Bernard's relations with political and intellectual leaders of his time are presented in *The Letters of St. Bernard*, trans. by S. J. Eales (1904). E. Gilson, *The Mystical Theology of St. Bernard* (1940), stresses Bernard's thought. B. S. James, *St. Bernard of Clairvaux* (1957), focuses attention on Bernard the man.

Suger on the Abbey of St. Denis, trans. by E. Panofsky (1946), is a mine of information about the beginnings of Gothic architecture and about monastic government and life. Panofsky's introduction has a good brief biography of Suger. K. J. Conant, *Carolingian and Romanesque Architecture** (1959), gives the background out of which the new architecture developed.

The best serious study of Abelard is E. Gilson, *Heloise and Abelard** (1948). H. Waddell's novel *Peter Abelard** (1959) gives a good picture of twelfth-century intellectual activity based on sound scholarship. *Abelard's Letters* were translated by C. K. Scott-Moncrieff (1926). B. Radice, *The Letters of Abelard and Héloïse* (1976), is a more recent and in some ways a more satisfactory version.

11 Medieval Civilization at Its Height

After 1150 western Europe began to cash in on the pioneer work of the tenth and eleventh centuries. The boom in population, production, and trade brought increasing prosperity. The peasants embarked on a great migration to new lands, comparable only to the nineteenth-century movement to the New World. Forests were cleared in England, France, and western Germany; marshes were drained and walled off from the sea in the Netherlands. In the biggest shift of all, migration toward the East, the Germans filled up the land between the Elbe and the Oder and settled large areas of western Poland, eastern Prussia, and Bohemia. This drive to the East almost doubled the size of medieval Germany. It also set the stage for the contending nationalisms of modern times, for the Slavs remained numerous in Bohemia and the lands beyond the Oder, which meant that many German settlements were surrounded by Slavic populations.

TOWNS AND TRADE

Atlantic and Baltic trade grew steadily during the twelfth century. German merchants, who dominated Baltic commerce, pushed their outposts to Riga and to Novgorod in Russia. They dealt in furs, timber, and other bulky commodities that returned only a small profit per ton. Atlantic trade, in wool from England and in salt and wine from ports in the Bay of Biscay, was also only moderately profitable. Most of these goods were carried by German and French vessels; the English had little shipping and could not even move their own wool overseas. This northern trade brought modest prosperity to such towns as Lübeck in Germany and Bordeaux in France.

The really profitable trade, however, was still the trade in Oriental goods. Italian towns, especially Venice, Genoa, and Pisa, had by far the largest share of this lucrative business. Their fleets made regular voyages each year to Constantinople, Alexandria, and Acre to bring back incense, spices, and silk. By the end of the twelfth century these fleets were large enough to move whole armies. Crusaders

no longer had to take the long and dangerous overland route; they simply hired ships.

It was not until the second half of the thirteenth century that the Genoese and the Venetians began to make regular voyages through the Strait of Gibraltar to England and the Netherlands. Even then, most of their goods were sent north across the Alps by pack-train. The steady stream of merchants along this route stimulated the growth of the towns of the Po Valley, southern France, and southern Germany. It also stimulated the development of the fairs of Champagne, which became the central market for all western Europe. Champagne lay across the river valleys leading south to the Mediterranean and north to Paris, the English Channel, and western Germany. The counts of Champagne were wise enough to encourage commerce and strong enough to protect the wandering merchants. At the fairs of Champagne, textiles and wool from the north were exchanged for Oriental goods from the south. Merchants gradually developed the practice of settling their yearly accounts when they met in Champagne, thus making the fairs the money market as well as the commodity market of the West.

By the end of the twelfth century no one could deny any longer that businessmen were entitled to special status. Personal freedom and some degree of local autonomy made the townsmen a privileged class—not so privileged as the clergy and nobels, but still well above the peasants. As a privileged class they began to be accorded a special name— *bürger* in Germany, *burgesses* in England, and *bourgeois* in France, whence the collective term, *bourgeoisie.** Most townsmen were satisfied with this special status; only in the greatest cities could they dream of full independence, and only in Italy did they have much hope of getting it. But the old hostilities still ran deep. The bourgeoisie still distrusted the nobility and criticized the clergy, who in turn still suspected the bourgeoisie of

* All these terms are derived from the German word *burg*, which meant first "fort" and then "walled town." Walls were the symbol of a town's autonomy.

The rose window of Amiens Cathedral (thirteenth century).

GERMAN EXPANSION TO THE EAST   800–1400

GERMAN EXPANSION TO THE EAST 800-1400

MILES 0 200

BALTIC SEA

Reval
ESTONIANS
RUSSIANS
Riga
Düna River
LETTS
Memel
Nieman
Königsberg
River
Lübeck
Rostock
Hamburg
Danzig
PRUSSIA
Bremen
Elbe River
POMERANIA
Vistula River
Berlin
Gnesen
Magdeburg
Brandenburg
Oder River
Posen
Leipzig
Dresden
S L A V S
Mainz
Prague
Cracow
Bamberg
BOHEMIANS
Ratisbon
MORAVIANS
Theiss River
Vienna
Salzburg
M A G Y A R S
Buda
R U M A N I A N S
Danube River

Germanized before 800 A.D.   Germanized between 800 and 1400   German minorities by 1400

harboring dangerous ideas about religion and the social order. A twelfth-century clergyman could still speak of free towns as *tumor plebis, timor regis*—a cancer of the people, a threat to the king.

Bankers and Moneylenders

The growth of banking and money-lending strengthened this hostility. The great international merchants, and the moneychangers who served them, had become expert at transferring funds from one region to another and had also accumulated surplus capital. They gradually began to act as bankers who received deposits, paid out money on order, and made loans. Kings and popes called on them when, for example, they wanted to transfer money to the East to pay for crusades. And bishops and abbots, lords and knights, all borrowed money from the bankers to pay for their steadily rising living standards. But as a result of all

these transactions the bourgeoisie seemed to be profiting at the expense of the clergy and the nobility. Even kings had to pay a high rate of interest on loans—8 to 10 percent for a ruler with as good a reputation for financial integrity as Saint Louis of France—and lesser folk paid more. When the day of reckoning came, the borrowers often had a hard time repaying their loans: kings had to impose new taxes on their subjects; barons had to sell their lands; churches had to melt down their altar vessels. Bankers were generally unpopular, for they seemed to be thriving on the misfortunes of their fellow Christians.

Artisans, Gilds, and the Proletariat

Most townsmen were not bankers or international merchants but small shopkeepers with purely local trade. Butchers, bakers, and the like profited little from the growth of international commerce. The same was true of many artisans in the metal industries. And even artisans who produced goods for a wider market had to rely on international merchants who kept most of the profits in return for their services. Many workers in the textile industry were only subcontractors, dependent on merchants for raw materials and for markets. A Flemish weaver in Ghent, for example, could not import his raw wool directly from England; he had to obtain it from a merchant. When his cloth was finished, he could not carry it to the fairs of Champagne or the ports of Italy; he had to sell it at a low price to a merchant who knew the markets and the trade routes and who was willing to assume the risks of distribution. The position of such workers was precarious and they often suffered prolonged unemployment. For the first time since the fall of the Roman Empire an urban proletariat began to appear in the countries of western Europe.

It was during the twelfth century that townsmen began to organize themselves into occupational groups. The men within each trade or craft naturally saw a good deal of one another and felt that they had common interests to defend against outsiders. They often had a code prescribing standards of good workmanship, and they were determined to see that these standards were maintained. And so they formed associations, called gilds in England, to pursue their common objectives. The gild contributed to the local church that honored its patron saint, and it acted as a mutual benefit society for the families of its members. It also tried to enforce regulations barring strangers and untrained men from the craft and forbidding careless or dishonest production. The gild was usually dominated by its most experienced members, the master workmen, who owned their own shops and equipment. Under them were the journeymen, who worked for daily wages, and under them the apprentices, who were boys learning the trade. In the thirteenth century, when most journeymen could hope to become masters themselves one day, there was little friction among these groups.

Money-changers are portrayed in this stained-glass window at Le Mans Cathedral (thirteenth century).

There was considerably more friction among the gilds themselves, including all the jurisdictional disputes that we find among trade unions today. For example, the harness of a horse contains both metal and leather: should it be made by leather workers, metal workers, or both? There was also a good deal of jockeying for political advantage. Strong gilds tended to take over the control of town governments, and often the larger gilds would line up against the smaller ones, or the wealthy gilds against the poor.

To escape such controversies and to protect themselves from the excessive power of the gilds, many lords refused to allow gilds to be established in their towns. But the advantages of some sort of trade organization were so obvious that the lords usually created similar, but looser, associations under their own control. In the nongild towns as well as the gild towns, there were the same regulations on production and the same division of workers into the three groups of masters, journeymen, and apprentices.

In the long run, the division between the urban rich and the urban poor sharpened into political conflict and even armed rebellion. But during the first part of the thirteenth century the people of most towns remained fairly well united. Still rather insecure in a society that originally had had no place for them, they feared outside oppressors more than internal exploiters. Only when the bourgeoisie began to feel reasonably secure did internal differences break out into open feuds.

LITERATURE AND ART

The general prosperity of the period was reflected in a burst of artistic and literary activity. Wealth does not necessarily produce great art, but it certainly increases the opportunities open to artists. Vast sums of money were needed to build a Gothic cathedral, and more cathedrals were built in the late twelfth and thirteenth centuries than at any other time in European history. This money did not all come from the Church; kings and feudal lords made large contributions, as did the people of cathedral cities. In fact, there seems to have been a good deal of civic rivalry: if one town erected a handsome new cathedral, its neighbors strove to surpass it. The classic example is Beauvais, whose residents decided that they would build the loftiest cathedral in France. The technical difficulties were great—the vaults collapsed twice—and by the time they were overcome, money and enthusiasm were running out. So the cathedral of Beauvais stands today still unfinished, with almost no nave. But it does have the greatest interior height of any church built during the period.

Gothic Art

As the example of Beauvais shows, the architects of the day were trying to exploit all the possibilities of the new Gothic style. They strove for greater height and more light by emphasizing vertical lines and making their windows larger and larger. In a small church like the Sainte-Chapelle in Paris they were able to build the walls almost entirely of magnificent stained glass, supported by a few slender pillars. Even in the larger churches there was far more glass than stone at the upper (clerestory) level.

The portals of Gothic churches were filled with hundreds of statues of Christ, the Virgin, the apostles, and the saints. The windows all had a story to tell or a moral to point. There was a strong tendency toward allegory and symbolism; thus at Chartres the continuity between the Old and New Testaments is illustrated by windows in which a prophet carries an evangelist on his shoulders. But there was also a tendency toward realism in Gothic art, a tendency that appears even in the twelfth century in some of the floral decorations. This tendency grew stronger during the thirteenth century, preparing the way for the very realistic art of northern Europe in the fifteenth century.

Technically, Amiens is perhaps the most perfect Gothic cathedral of all—the cathedral in which all problems were solved successfully. But many critics prefer the massive solidity of Notre Dame of Paris or the less uniform but more interesting cathedral of Chartres,

Two representations of the Visitation. Left: Romanesque façade of the abbey church of St. Pierre at Moissac (twelfth century). Right: Gothic façade of Reims Cathedral (late thirteenth century). The Romanesque work is linear and heavily stylized, like a manuscript illustration. The Gothic sculpture is more naturalistic.

with its glorious stained glass. As the Gothic style spread to England, Germany, and other countries, it produced remarkable buildings, not entirely like the French, but beautiful in their own right. Only in Italy was Gothic a relative failure. The commercially minded Italians were less willing to spend money on their churches, and they were so imbued with Roman traditions that they never really understood the basic principles of the Gothic style.

Histories and Vernacular Literature

The great period of cathedral building was also a period of intense literary activity. We shall return to the work of scholars writing in Latin and mention only one of their activities here—the writing of history. Western Europeans had always been interested in historical narratives, partly because they had inherited this tradition from Rome, partly because the Christian religion puts strong emphasis on the way in which God's plans are worked out through history. There had always been chronicles, but never before had they been as numerous or as well written as they were after 1150. Kings began to patronize writers who would glorify their deeds and justify their policies—writers like Otto of Freising in Germany, Guillaume le Breton in France, and the St. Albans group of historians in England. Counts and bishops also sought to have their acts recorded in local histories. Western Europeans were proud of their recent achievements and wanted them to be remembered.

An even more striking change was the rapid development of vernacular literature. Minstrels had been composing songs and epic poems long before 1100, but very few of their compositions had been written down. During the twelfth century the practice arose of recording their poems in more or less permanent form, and by the early years of the thirteenth century there was a respectable body of literature in French, German, and Provençal (a southern French dialect). Italy lagged somewhat, perhaps because the Italian dialects were still so close to Latin that they were scarcely recognized as separate languages. Eng-

land was even further behind because of the Norman conquest. The upper classes in England spoke French and patronized French poets well into the thirteenth century, and without their support the Anglo-Saxon literary tradition could not survive. Left to the peasants, Anglo-Saxon gradually became what we call Middle English; it was only toward the end of the thirteenth century that the ruling classes began to use this language

William of Poitou: A Song of Nothing

These verses from a poem by William, Count of Poitou and Duke of Aquitaine (1071–1127), are not typical of the lyric poetry that was developing in southern France in the late twelfth century—most troubadours took themselves and their loves more seriously. But it illustrates the emerging modernism of the lyric poem, which dealt with personal and emotional themes that were unknown to the epic tradition. William, who was reputed to have been the first troubadour, was, through Eleanor of Aquitaine, the great-grandfather of Richard Lion-Heart, who also wrote songs.

> I'll make some verses just for fun
> Not about me nor any one,
> Nor deeds that noble knights have done
>   Nor love's ado:
> I made them riding in the sun.
>   (My horse helped, too.)
> When I was born I cannot say.
> I am not sad, I am not gay,
> I am not stiff nor dégagé;
>   What can I do?
> Long since enchanted by a fay
>   Star-touched I grew.
> I have a lady, who or where
> I cannot tell you, but I swear
> She treats me neither ill nor fair.
>   But I'm not blue,
> Just so those Normans stay up there
>   Out of Poitou.
> I have not seen, yet I adore
> This distant love; she sets no store
> By what I think and furthermore
>   ('Tis sad but true)
> Others there are, some three or four,
>   I'm faithful to.

"A Song of Nothing," trans. by T. G. Bergin, in C. W. Jones, ed., *Medieval Literature in Translation* (New York: McKay, 1950), p. 668.

Medieval English minstrels, as depicted in marginal drawings in the Luttrell Psalter (*ca.* 1340).

The Death of Roland

This passage comes from the *Song of Roland.* Roland, commander of the rear guard of Charlemagne's army, has been cut off by a greatly superior Moslem force. He beats off their attacks repeatedly, but finally all his men are killed and he himself is mortally wounded. He hears the horns of Charlemagne's army as it advances to avenge him, and prepares for death.

> Then Roland feels that death is seizing him;
> Down from the head upon the heart it falls.
> Beneath a pine he staggers, lays him down
> On the green grass, and hides beneath his heart
> His famous sword and his great ivory horn.
> He turns his face toward the infidel
> For greatly he desires that Charles should say,
> With all his men: "Roland, the noble count,
> Roland the brave has died a conqueror."
>
> Then Roland feels that his last hour has come.
> Facing toward Spain he lies upon the hill. . . .
> And many memories flood into his mind
> Of all the conquests he, the brave, had made.
> Of gentle France, of heroes of his House,
> Of Charlemagne, his lord, who fostered him. . . .
>
> He cries his Culpe, he prays to God for grace:
> "O God the Father who has never lied,
> Who called the holy Lazarus back to life,
> And Daniel from the lions' jaws preserved,
> Protect my soul, and pardon all my sins!"
>
> His right-hand glove he proffered unto God;
> Saint Gabriel took it from his faltering hand. . . .
> God sent to him his angel cherubim
> And the count's soul they bore to Paradise.

Translated from *La Chanson de Roland,* ed. by T. A. Jenkins (Boston: Heath, 1924), ll. 2355–95.

and that English came to be a literary language.

Most works in the vernacular were written for the aristocracy. The *chansons de geste*, for example, are long narrative poems celebrating the courage and fortitude of feudal warriors. The most famous, the *Song of Roland*, tells of the heroic death of a handful of Charlemagne's knights ambushed by a Moslem army; others describe conflicts between unreasonable lords and long-suffering vassals. Lays, based on Celtic legends about King Arthur and his court, appear a little later. They introduce an element of the marvelous—Merlin and his magic—and also the theme of romantic love. Finally came the short lyric poems, which seem to have originated in southern France but quickly spread to Germany and Italy. Some of these lyrics describe the joys of battle, others are political satires, but many of them are love poems. They show a high degree of skill in versification; the sonnet, for example, was to develop out of this type of poem.

One might say that medieval vernacular literature began with masterpieces, such as the *Song of Roland* (though perhaps only the masterpieces survive). But besides its intrinsic interest, this literature had long-lasting consequences. First, it introduced themes, such as the story of Tristan and Isolde, that are still common in our literature, and in expressing these themes the poets of the day developed most of our traditional poetic forms. Second, it helped to weaken Latin as the universal language. Not all early vernacular literature was written for amusement; portions of the Bible were translated into French in the twelfth century, and several histories had been written in French by the early thirteenth century. If French could be used for these purposes, it could also be used for official documents, and during the thirteenth century an increasing number of royal letters and government records were written in French. This same pattern developed in other countries. The growing use of the vernacular language was one, though only one, of the forces that gave each kingdom a sense of its own identity and contributed to the rise of nationalism.

Finally, the new literature was one of the forces that helped soften the manners of the upper classes. Even the poems about warfare were often a substitute for violence. The lords and knights who listened to the *Song of Roland* were likely to be less belligerent than the heroes they admired. Love poems and religious works were even further removed from the old tradition of violence. The new ideas of courtesy and chivalry were expressed in many romances. It is easy to exaggerate this development; many members of the feudal class were still ignorant and brutal. But in some circles and at some levels ignorance and brutality were being softened by the desire for a little learning and for rudimentary good manners. Vernacular literature both reflected and helped to spread this new pattern of courtly life.

THE WESTERN MONARCHIES

It is in this context of a more prosperous and more peaceful western Europe that political developments must be placed. There was a general desire for more government and better government to help preserve the gains of the last hundred years—a desire that eased the task of the leaders who were reorganizing secular government during the late twelfth and early thirteenth centuries. The greatest progress was made in England and France, but everywhere there was a tendency to create new institutions and to make laws that were more exact and more inclusive.

England Under Henry II

Royal government in England had been weakened by a dispute over the successor to Henry I. But in 1154 Henry II, the grandson of Henry I, came to the throne with a clear title. He was already lord of all western France, for he had inherited Anjou and Normandy from his parents and had acquired Aquitaine by marrying Eleanor, the only child of the last duke. Henry spent more than two-thirds of his reign in France—naturally enough, since he held more land there than the French king. Nevertheless, he made a greater impression on England than many kings who spent their entire lives there. He needed a strong government in England both to keep the country quiet while he was abroad and to obtain men and money to protect his French possessions against jealous neighbors. In his attempts to strengthen the English government, he enlarged the activities of the royal courts and created the English common law.

Henry invented no new procedures; he simply used old devices, such as the circuit judge and the jury, more intensively. But by making regular and habitual procedures that his predecessors had employed only on exceptional occasions, Henry changed the whole nature of royal government. Whereas William the Conqueror had used inquests or juries on a large scale only once in his reign (to obtain the information recorded in Domesday Book), Henry's circuit judges summoned juries in county after county, year after year. These juries were somewhat like our grand juries today, but they not only indicted criminals; they also had to answer questions about the state of the royal domain and the behavior of local officials. Again, William the Conqueror and Henry I had occasionally allowed prelates or barons to use juries to determine disputes over the possession of land and rights annexed to land. Henry II made this procedure available to every free man and threw open his courts to all cases involving land.

The early jury was by no means an ideal instrument of justice, for it based its decisions on common knowledge and neighborhood gossip rather than on the carefully tested evidence of sworn witnesses. But imperfect as it was, it was far better than trial by ordeal or combat. Litigants began to flock to the king's courts, and by the end of Henry's reign all disputes over land were being settled by juries in royal courts. By the middle of the thirteenth century all cases of any importance, both criminal and civil, were decided by juries.

This great increase in the amount of work done by the king's courts naturally strengthened the royal government and weakened the control of feudal lords over their vassals. Important cases no longer came to the courts of the lords, and if the lords tried to resort to extralegal means their vassals could always turn to the king's courts for protection. The circuit judges rode regularly through the counties, and a permanent court at Westminster heard cases that came up when circuit judges were not available. Everyone in the country was subject to the king's justice, and most men, sooner or later, appeared in royal courts as jurors or litigants.

This constant exposure to royal justice enhanced the people's respect for royal power and indoctrinated generation after generation in the principles of English law. By applying the same rules in all parts of the country, the king's judges gradually created a common law for the whole realm. The first textbook on the English common law was written at the end of Henry's reign, and others followed in the thirteenth and fourteenth centuries. A powerful unifying force, the common law eventually became a symbol of English nationalism. Englishmen were proud of it, regarding it as a guarantee of their liberties rather than as a manifestation of royal power. And this pride is one reason that English common law survived when all the other countries of Europe were abandoning their medieval legal systems in favor of codes based on Roman law.

Henry II also increased royal revenue. Following a precedent of his grandfather, he regularly accepted money from his vassals in lieu of military service they owed him. He also imposed a general tax on the country in 1188 in order to pay for a crusade he had promised to join. A tax of this sort was not easy to make stick, for medieval opinion was strongly set against taxation, even for a worthy cause. But, while the king of France had to abandon his efforts to impose a tax for the same crusade, Henry's tax was collected and set a precedent for additional taxes in the years ahead.

Although the English barons offered no effective opposition to Henry's reforms, Henry did have one dangerous

ENGLAND AND FRANCE AT THE TIME OF HENRY II
1154–89

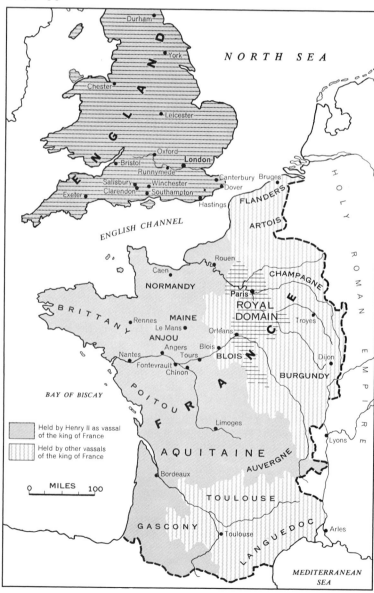

opponent: Thomas Becket, Archbishop of Canterbury, who resisted Henry's efforts to subject clergymen accused of crimes to the jurisdiction of royal courts. The quarrel grew bitter, and at last the archbishop was murdered in his own cathedral by four of Henry's knights, who thought they would please their king by ridding him of a troublesome foe. Henry swore, probably quite truthfully, that he had not planned the assassination, but he abandoned his attempts to bring clergymen under the jurisdiction of royal courts. This concession did little harm in the long run; later kings found ways to control the clergy without trying them in royal courts. But Thomas was canonized and became one of the most popular saints in England. His stand against injustice (as he saw it) was invoked by later opponents of powerful kings.

Magna Carta

Henry's sons, Richard (1189–99) and John (1199–1216), lacked his political ability. Richard was a good general and nothing more; he spent his entire reign either on the Third Crusade or in fighting Philip Augustus of France. Richard was feared for his strength and admired for his bravery, but he gave little attention to the government of England. He spent less than ten months during a reign of ten years in his island kingdom; all he wanted from England was men and money. It says much for Henry II's political institutions that the government continued to function despite Richard's neglect and his repeated demands for taxes to pay for his wars.

John was not even a good general. Richard had been winning the war with the king of France, but John lost it. Intelligent but neurotic, he suspected his most loyal supporters of treason and thus forced them into neutrality or opposition. William Marshal, Earl of Pembroke, was famous throughout Europe as a model of knightly behavior; John exiled him to Ireland because he did not trust him. This kind of behavior explains why, in the long war with Philip Augustus of France, John's vassals either deserted or fought with little enthusiasm. As a result,

John lost Normandy, Anjou, and the northern part of Aquitaine to the French king. He also suffered a serious defeat by the Church; after resisting for five years, John finally was forced to accept an Archbishop of Canterbury he did not want but who had been chosen by the pope.

John had taken large sums of money from his vassals for his wars in France; he had also punished without trial many of

The murder of Archbishop Thomas Becket in his cathedral at Canterbury in 1170. This representation was made shortly before 1200.

Richard I spent much of his reign fighting in the Third Crusade or against Philip Augustus of France (detail from the effigy on his tomb, 1199).

the men he distrusted. These actions might have been tolerated if he had been successful, but his repeated failures made him vulnerable. The barons of England were outraged by the loss of Normandy, where they or their relatives had had extensive holdings. Many of them had been unjustly punished by heavy fines or confiscation of their lands. In 1215 a large group of barons revolted. The Archbishop of Canterbury advised them, and the merchants of London supported them. This coalition was too powerful for John to resist; on June 15 at Runnymede he put his seal to a charter that embodied the barons' demands for reform.

This document, which soon became known as "Magna Carta"—the Great Charter of Liberties—was reasonable and workable. It shows how well John's predecessors had accomplished their task of unifying England and instilling a respect for law even among the feudal lords. The barons made no attempt to break England into autonomous feudal states or to preserve local laws and institutions. They accepted the new legal system and the institutions of central government created by Henry II almost without question. The barons simply wanted to restrain the abuses of the central government, not to destroy it. They insisted that the king, like everyone else, was bound by law and that he was not to tax them without their consent. They demanded that he observe due process of law and forgo punishing an alleged offender before he had been convicted in the king's courts. If the king broke these promises, the barons warned, his subjects were free to rebel against him.

The purpose of Magna Carta was to protect the rights of the barons, not to establish constitutional government. But the English barons were more advanced politically than the feudal lords of other countries, for powerful kings had forced them to work together and to think in terms of laws that affected the whole kingdom. Consequently, they stated the liberties they claimed for themselves in such a way that those liberties could easily be extended to other classes. Thus before the end of the century the right to consent to taxes, originally restricted to the barons, was gained by lesser landholders and merchants, and the right to a fair trial was appropriated even by unpropertied classes. Magna Carta symbolized the supremacy of law, the conviction that even the king was bound by law and must respect the limits it set on his power. Since it was invoked again and again in protests against the arbitrary use of royal power, it served as a foundation stone in the English system of constitutional government.

The Growth of Royal Power in France

In England, which had achieved unity at a very early date, the chief political problem was how to restrain an overpowerful sovereign. In France, which had been divided into autonomous feudal states since the tenth century, the chief political problem was how to build larger and more effective units of government.

Excerpts from Magna Carta   1215

We [John] have conceded to all free men of our kingdom, for us and our heirs forever, all the liberties written below, to be held by them and their heirs from us and our heirs: . . .

12. No scutage [redemption of military service] or aid [grant to the king] shall be taken in our kingdom except by the common counsel of our kingdom. . . .

14. And for obtaining the common counsel of the kingdom, for assessing an aid . . . or a scutage, we will cause to be summoned by our sealed letters the archbishops, bishops, abbots, earls and greater barons, moreover we will cause to be summoned generally by the sheriffs . . . all those who hold of us in chief [the other vassals] for a certain day . . . and place . . . and once the summons has been made the business shall proceed on the assigned day according to the advice of those who are present, even if all those summoned have not come. . . .

39. No free man may be seized, or imprisoned, or dispossessed, or outlawed, or exiled . . . nor will we go against him or send against him except by the legal judgment of his peers and by the law of the land.

40. To no one will we sell, to no one will we deny or delay right and justice.

Translated from W. Stubbs, *Select Charters* (Oxford: Clarendon Press, 1921), pp. 294 ff.

The first solutions to this problem had been reached in the feudal states themselves, and by the end of the twelfth century such provinces as Normandy, Flanders, and Champagne had well-developed legal, financial, and administrative systems. There were as yet no similar institutions for the kingdom as a whole, however. Even in the region stretching from Paris to Orléans, which the king ruled directly, political institutions were less advanced and less specialized than in some of the great feudal states.

As the king of France gained power and prestige during the twelfth century, however, he gradually became master of his own domain; no longer could petty lords defy him from castles only a few miles from Paris. A series of legends grew up about the king that transformed him into a semisacred personage far above any ordinary feudal lord—in the end, far above any other European king. At his coronation he was anointed with holy oil that had miraculously descended from heaven; he healed the sick; he carried the sword and banner of Charlemagne. This increased prestige was reinforced by the growing desire for law and order that appeared everywhere in the twelfth century. More men sought the judgment of the royal law courts, and the king was occasionally able to impose his decisions even on lords outside his own domains. In short, a real opportunity existed for a great expansion of royal power. And at the end of the twelfth century a king appeared who made the most of that opportunity.

This king was Philip Augustus (1180–1223), the first really able ruler of the Capetian dynasty. Because Philip could not be strong so long as the kings of England held all of western France, he spent much of his reign trying to pull them down. Richard withstood his attacks, but John was more vulnerable. John had made himself even more unpopular in France than in England by murdering one of his nephews, who was heir to the county of Brittany. He exposed himself even more by marrying an heiress who was engaged to one of his own most powerful vassals in Aquitaine. This was a clear breach of feudal law.

John had dishonored his vassal, and the aggrieved man promptly appealed to the king of France, from whom John held all his French lands. Philip Augustus seized on this excuse joyfully. He was already planning to attack John; now he could do so in a way that would give him the support of many feudal lords. Philip summoned John to his court, and John, by failing to appear, again put himself in the wrong. Philip ordered all John's French fiefs confiscated for default and carried out the sentence by force of arms. John's English vassals fought badly, and many of his French vassals refused to fight at all. So Philip annexed Normandy, Anjou, and Poitou with little difficulty.

By this conquest of northwestern France, Philip more than tripled the royal domain. For the first time in centuries the king of France was stronger than any of his vassals. And in order to hold and exploit the territory he had gained, Philip went on to devise new institutions that set a pattern for all his successors. Because he created a territorial base from which the king could dominate the rest of the country and provided an institutional base with which to control the enlarged domain, Philip was the real founder of the French monarchy.

Philip seems to have been guided by two principles. One was to use local institutions whenever he could, thus preserving the earlier work of the feudal lords and at the same time conciliating his new subjects. The other was to divide the new provinces into small administrative districts and to give full powers in each district to men sent out from his own court. Thus Normandy, for example, retained its Norman law and its Norman court system and was never subjected to the law and customs of Paris. But it was divided into thirteen districts, in each of which a bailiff appointed by the king presided over the courts, collected the king's revenues, and commanded the castles and the military forces. No Norman was named as bailiff until much later in the century, and even then most of the bailiffs still came from the old royal domain around Paris.

Philip's principles of government served him well. His respect for local institutions and customs induced the

THE EXPANSION OF THE ROYAL DOMAIN IN FRANCE
1180–1314

Royal Domain at the death of Louis VII, 1180

Acquisitions to the death of Philip Augustus, 1223

Acquisitions to the death of Philip III, 1285

Acquisitions to the death of Philip IV, 1314

conquered provinces to accept his control with little protest. The bailiffs, who depended on him for their high office, were loyal and reasonably efficient. Philip made sure that his bailiffs were always strangers to the district they ruled, and he moved them frequently from one district to another to keep them from forming local attachments. He paid them well and made it clear that they could expect better jobs if they gave him faithful service. Some of them were unnecessarily harsh, and some were dishonest. But on the whole their behavior convinced Philip's new subjects that royal government was, for the most part, better than the government of the feudal lords had been.

All Philip's successors followed his practice of permitting local diversity within a centralized bureaucratic framework. They enlarged the administrative districts, reducing the thirteen original districts in Normandy to five, for example, and they sent out more and more officials to help the bailiffs in their work. But they did not alter Philip's basic system. In the end, France became a very different sort of country from England. With no common law, most Frenchmen remained attached to their local rights and customs. This meant, in turn, that local leaders were uninterested in the problems of the central government; their loyalties were primarily to their provinces. France was held together by the king and his officials; it was a much more bureaucratic state than England. Moreover, as France grew into the most powerful state in Europe, its example was followed by others. The bureaucracies of the continental countries today are all descended from the model set by Philip Augustus.

Germany and Italy
Under the Hohenstaufen

Germany and Italy, meanwhile, were still nominally united under the emperor. But the emperor's power, which was based on his control of the Church, had been seriously weakened by the struggle over lay investiture. The German princes, profiting from the emperor's predicament, had seized local rights for themselves and had begun to insist on their right to elect the emperor. The towns in Italy were becoming almost as independent as the German princes. Thus the old institutions of the Empire were falling into decline, and there were no new institutions to replace them.

In spite of these difficulties, Frederick Barbarossa (1152–90) of the new Hohenstaufen dynasty* made a heroic and almost successful effort to unify the Empire once again. Apparently impressed by the achievements of the kings of France and England, he modeled much of his program on their example. Imitating the king of France, he tried to build a secure royal domain in the Hohenstaufen lands in the southwest corner of Germany. Imitating the king of England, he

*The Hohenstaufen descended, in the female line, from Henry V. They took their name from their ancestral castle in Swabia.

tried to make all vassals take an oath of allegiance directly to the king, no matter who their immediate lord was. Most important, however, was his attempt to transform German feudalism into a coherent and all-embracing system of government. Many of the most powerful men in Germany owed him no allegiance, and many of those who did held part of their lands as private property exempt from feudal obligations. Frederick seems to have hoped that by bringing all men and all lands into a feudal system he could check the disintegration of the Empire. Thus by making the leading churchmen vassals of the king, as they were in England, he could regain his control over the resources of the Church; and by making the princes of the Empire his vassals, he could curtail their growing independence and punish them for disobedience by confiscating their fiefs.

Frederick had some success in these attempts, but his own version of feudalism proved inadequate. Both points are illustrated by his conflict with Henry the Lion, Duke of Saxony and Bavaria. Henry was the head of the Welf family, which had long had hopes of gaining the imperial throne, and his two duchies made him the most powerful man in Germany. When Henry failed to give Frederick the military support he owed during an imperial war, Frederick decided to eliminate this dangerous enemy once and for all. He had Henry condemned by a feudal court in 1180, just as Philip Augustus of France was to have John of England condemned by a feudal court some twenty years later. But while Philip was able to seize John's lands and incorporate them into the royal domain, Frederick was immediately obliged to grant Henry's duchies to other princes. Frederick seems to have been seduced by the idea of a perfect feudal pyramid, in which all lesser lords held their lands and powers from the princes, who in turn

held them from the emperor. Thus when one prince was dispossessed, his place had to be filled by another, or else the pyramid would lose its symmetry. For obvious reasons the princes were delighted with this rule, and for reasons of his own the emperor seems to have accepted it as well. In the long run this peculiar form of feudalism tended to build up the power of the princes rather than that of the emperor.

Frederick also tried to reassert his imperial rights in Italy, for he knew that if he could gain control of the Italian towns he would be the richest ruler in western Europe. The incessant quarrels among the Italian towns enabled him to establish himself in the Lombard plain

Late—twelfth-century gilded reliquary bearing the features of Frederick Barbarossa.

and take control of many of its cities. But the Italians, frightened by his success, suddenly called a halt to their feuding and formed a coalition—the Lombard League—to oppose him. Pope Alexander III, who feared that any increase in imperial power in Italy would threaten his independence, supported the League. Frederick tried to overcome this opposition by supporting an antipope and by destroying Milan, the chief Lombard town. But the hostile coalition proved too strong for him. The towns of the Lombard League defeated Frederick at Legnano in 1176 and with the pope's backing forced him to accept a peace that assured them virtual independence.

Frederick, still hoping to make something of his Italian claims, moved his base of operations farther south to Tuscany, where the towns were weaker and less hostile. Though he had some success in Tuscany, his advance there created new problems for himself and his successors. Tuscany was closer to Rome than Lombardy; the imperial base there frightened the pope and involved Frederick even more deeply in Italian affairs.

The involvement increased when Frederick's son married the heiress of the Norman kingdom of Sicily. When Frederick was drowned in 1190 while leading a crusading army through Asia Minor, his son, Henry VI (1190–97), was accepted as emperor by the German princes. But Henry spent almost all his time in Italy, first making good his claim to Sicily and then opening a corridor along the east coast of Italy to connect his south Italian kingdom with Germany. Henry secured his corridor by taking lands claimed by the papacy by virtue of the donations of Pippin and Charlemagne. With Rome now encircled by lands held by the emperor, the popes' old fears of imperial domination became stronger than ever.

THE CHURCH AT THE HEIGHT OF ITS POWER

The late twelfth century was a bad time in which to alarm popes, for they were steadily increasing their power. They were gaining administrative control of the Church, and in a fervently Christian Europe this meant that they could control public opinion. While kings, lords, or local clergy might nominate bishops, the pope had to approve all appointments and could quash those he felt to be irregular. In the event of a dispute over the choice of a bishop, the pope frequently set aside both candidates and imposed a man of his own choice, as he did at Canterbury in 1207. At the same time he kept close watch over the bishops by sending out legates to enforce papal orders and by encouraging appeals from bishops to the papal court. The bishops in turn strengthened their control over the clergy of their dioceses by making frequent tours of inspection and appointing men trained in canon law to preside over the ecclesiastical courts. Thus the Church became a highly centralized organization, with the bishops responsible to the pope and with all lesser clergy responsible in turn to the bishops.

This centralization created new problems. As the popes and bishops spent more and more of their time on administrative and judicial details, they ran the danger of abdicating their role as spiritual leaders. St. Bernard had worried about this problem in the middle of the twelfth century, and later reformers shared his concern. Moreover, papal and episcopal courts had to demand heavy fees from those who did business with them. But these fees were not enough to cover extraordinary expenses, and in 1199 Pope Innocent III imposed an income tax on the clergy, an example that was followed by all his successors. The higher clergy shifted these expenses to the parish priests, who in turn began to exact fixed fees for such services as marriage and burial. Soon the complaint arose that the Church was selling its spiritual benefits.

Innocent III

The Church reached the height of its power at the end of the twelfth century, during the pontificate of Innocent III (1198–1216). Innocent, who felt responsible for the moral and spiritual welfare of all western Europe, once said, "Nothing

Contemporary mosaic portrait of Innocent III, from the old basilica of St. Peter in Rome.

bury. But when John yielded, Innocent granted him papal protection and forbade the French to carry out their planned attack.

Innocent III and the Empire

Innocent's most striking intervention, however, was in the affairs of the Empire. The premature death of Henry VI in 1197 created a complicated problem of succession. Henry's heir, Frederick II, was only three years old, and, though Frederick's claim to Sicily was undeniable, the princes of the Empire had never accepted the rule of hereditary succession. They split into two factions, one supporting Philip of Hohenstaufen, the brother of Henry VI, the other supporting Otto, the son of Henry the Lion and head of the Welf family. Innocent took advantage of this dissension by driving the German troops and governors out of central Italy and resuming control of all the Papal States, including the territory on the east coast. Alleging that since the pope crowned the emperor he had a right to reject unworthy candidates, he postponed the solution of the German problem for ten years. Finally, in 1208, after Philip had been assassinated, Innocent recognized Otto as emperor on condition that Otto renounce all claims to the lands in central Italy that had been seized by Frederick Barbarossa and Henry VI. When Otto broke his agreement, Innocent turned against him and persuaded the German princes to accept Frederick II as their ruler. By 1215 the young Frederick was in full control of Germany, and Innocent felt that he had an emperor who would be a dutiful subordinate of the Church instead of a dangerous rival.

Actually, Innocent had made a series of disastrous mistakes. By prolonging the dispute over the succession in Germany, he had given the German princes a chance to increase their power at home; after 1215 the position of the emperor north of the Alps was very shaky indeed. Frederick II, soon deciding that he could make nothing of Germany, turned his eyes toward Italy, thus reviving the danger of encirclement that Innocent thought he had ended by putting Frederick on the German throne. Instead of showing grat-

in the world should escape the attention and control of the Sovereign Pontiff." The Vicar of Christ, "less than God but more than man," could reprove and punish kings who broke the divine law. A man of remarkable energy (he was only thirty-seven years old when he became pope), Innocent came very close to making the papal court a supreme court for all of Europe. He kept the clergy under tight control and intervened repeatedly in secular affairs whenever he felt a moral issue was involved. Thus he threatened to support a French invasion of England in order to make John accept his own choice as Archbishop of Canter-

Detail from a page of Innocent's Register showing two wolves, one in friar's clothing, probably assisting in a heretical mass. The page deals with the Church's power to punish sinners.

itude for the pope's support, Frederick renewed the old attempt to annex a corridor along the east coast and to assert imperial power in Tuscany and Lombardy. But Innocent had committed the papacy to the propositions that the Papal States must stretch from coast to coast and that the emperor must not gain control of central and northern Italy. The result was a long struggle that badly damaged the prestige of the Church. It also destroyed the last chance of unifying Germany, or of bringing Italy under a single government, leaving two dangerous problems for the nineteenth century.

Innocent III and Heresy

Innocent also found that, for the first time in centuries, the Church was seriously threatened by heresy. Dangerous ideas were creeping in from the East along the busy trade routes; others were being formulated by the leaders of towns in Italy and southern France. Many people charged that priests were ignorant, prelates greedy and immoral. Some of these critics remained Christian but felt that they were as capable as the clergy of interpreting the Bible. Laymen organized themselves into groups to read the Scriptures together and to try to apply Christian standards in their daily life. The Waldensians, who still exist, were typical of these groups; they had adherents throughout the Rhone Valley and in many northern Italian towns. Other groups accepted a new and only partly Christian faith that had originated in the Balkan provinces of the Byzantine Empire. Based on very early Christian heresies, it taught that all material things had been created by an evil god, who was engaged in a constant struggle with the God of good. It rejected the Old Testament as the work of the evil god and thought of Jesus as simply an emanation of the good God and so denied His humanity. The believers in this doctrine called themselves "Cathari" (the purified) because they had rejected the evil world. They organized a church of their own, with a very simple ritual and with leaders who were admired even by Catholics for their piety and goodness. Because they were especially numerous in the region of Albi in southern France, they were often called Albigensians.

By 1200 the heretics had the support of thousands of people and dominated whole communities. Innocent tried at first to convert them by peaceful means, but he soon became convinced that he would have to use force. He proclaimed a crusade against the Albigensians in 1207 and enlisted an army of knights from northern France to invade the south. The conflict was as much a civil war as a religious war; since the northerners aimed at the conquest of the south, many Catholic nobles of the region aided the Albigensians. An old legend reports that at the sack of Béziers the exasperated northerners cried: "Kill them all, God will know his own!" In spite of stubborn resistance, the southerners were crushed, and the lords of northern France now ruled the entire land.

The victory over heresy was still not complete. Repeated revolts against northern domination could be sup-

Thirteenth-Century Arguments About the Crusade

Should the Crusade never be preached against schismatics and the disobedient and rebels? This is not expressly stated in the law and therefore certain people in Germany have doubts about it, saying that it does not seem right or honest to take up the cross against Christians. . . . However, the Son of God did not come into the world, nor did He die on the cross to gain land, but to call sinners to penitence. There is greater danger in permitting sin than in losing land because the soul is more precious than material things. Thus if we consider the degree of the offense, no one can doubt that disobedient and schismatic Christians are greater offenders than the Saracens. . . . And although the overseas Crusade may seem more desirable to the simple, the Crusade against disobedient Christians will seem more just and reasonable to anyone who considers the problem intelligently. . . .

Rome should not, I think, if one of her sons has fallen into error . . . send upon him an elder brother to destroy him. Rather should she summon, talk gently, and admonish him than waste his country. When the French go against the people of Toulouse, whom they consider heretics, and when a papal legate leads and guides them, that is not at all right in my opinion.

The first quotation is from Hostiensis (a cardinal and a famous canon lawyer), *Summa aurea* III, 34 (de voto), 19 (in quo casu). The second is from Guillaume le Clerc (a French poet), as cited by Palmer A. Throop, *Criticism of the Crusade* (Amsterdam, 1940), p. 43.

pressed only by a new crusade led by the king of France himself. He took over all the conquests of the northern lords; thus one unforeseen result of the Albigensian war was a marked increase in the power of the French king. The king's victory ended open manifestations of heresy, but many heretics continued to practice their rites in secret. In order to unearth them the Church had to develop a new court, the Inquisition. Any contact with heretics was ground for suspicion. The court accepted neighborhood rumors as a basis for accusations and used torture to secure confessions. The Church justified this procedure on the grounds that the heretic, who caused the loss of an immortal soul, was far worse than the murderer, who merely killed the body. In the end the Inquisition wiped out the Albigensian heresy, but it had an evil effect on European society. It often corrupted communities by encouraging fanatics and talebearers, and it provided a regrettable example for secular courts to follow. The only major areas to escape the Inquisition were England and Scandinavia, where there were not enough heretics to bother about.

The Revival of Science

By the middle of the twelfth century the scholars of the West had absorbed the Latin classics and the Roman law. Searching about for new materials, they seized on the rich store of learning in the East that had never been translated into Latin. Though Aristotelian logic had greatly stimulated the revival of scholarship, the West had only Aristotle's introductory treatises on logic. Scholars were deeply interested in astronomy and astrology, but they had only a few brief texts on these subjects, while the Greeks and Arabs had scores of volumes. The same problem existed in medicine and biology, in mathematics and physics. All the really advanced works were in the eastern languages; in Latin there were only elementary textbooks.

To correct this deficiency, the scholars of the West began the task of translating into Latin the works of Aristotle and the scientific writings of the Greeks and Arabs. The difficulties were formida-

ble—there were no grammars, no lexicons, none of the scholarly apparatus we take for granted in learning foreign languages. The Romans had never been particularly interested in science and had never developed a scientific vocabulary; consequently, even when a translator knew the meaning of a Greek or an Arabic word he had trouble finding a Latin equivalent. Moreover, many of the important texts had been corrupted by repeated translation.

Nevertheless, western scholars completed the task they had set for themselves. By the middle of the thir-

Illustration from a twelfth-century English manuscript showing a surgical operation (above) and the process of heating the instruments (below).

teenth century they had translated into Latin almost all the works of Aristotle and a great mass of other material. The West had acquired the philosophy and the science of the East—and just in the nick of time, for during the thirteenth century both Byzantium and the Arab world were shattered by civil wars and foreign invasions. Though they made a partial recovery later on, they were never again the intellectual centers they had been in the early Middle Ages. The scientific tradition that the Greeks had originated and the Arabs had preserved might have vanished had it not been for the efforts of the translators of the twelfth and thirteenth centuries.

Medieval science was not the science of our own day. It was based on authority rather than direct observation; it developed its ideas through formal logic rather than through experimentation; and it was contaminated by the wishful thinking of philosophers and magicians.

But at least it was an attempt to explain the physical world, to find ways of summing up seemingly unrelated phenomena in general laws. The important thing was not the accuracy of the results, but the fact that meaningful questions were asked about the nature of the universe. The questioning, once it began in the twelfth century, never stopped, and from that questioning our modern science has developed.

Understandably, the Church was suspicious of this new learning, which had been derived from pagan Greeks and handed on by Moslems and Jews. It carried with it many dangerous ideas—remnants of old religions disguised as magic, and philosophical doctrines that denied basic articles of faith. For example, some of the Arabic commentators on Aristotle had advanced the idea that the world was eternal and by so doing denied the Creation and the Last Judgment. By 1200 western scholars were teaching

A university lecture, as portrayed in a fourteenth-century Italian miniature. Attention to the lecturer is not undivided; several students are talking, and one is certainly asleep.

these ideas to eager young students, especially in the great center of learning at Paris.

The First Organized Universities

The Church wanted to control the new learning, and it found a means of doing so in the universities. As we have seen, twelfth-century professors and students had formed associations to protect their respective interests. Both groups found it to their advantage to insist on prescribed courses of study and examinations as prerequisites to obtaining a license to teach, or, as we would say, a degree. This system enabled the students to know what their obligations were and permitted teachers to bar unqualified men from their profession. It was not unlike the system that prevailed in the gilds, where a journeyman had to demonstrate his knowledge of his craft to a board of masters before he could become a master himself. In fact, the word *university* originally meant an association of any sort and not just an organization of accredited teachers and their students.

But any corporate group had to be recognized by some higher authority, and the natural authority for scholars was the Church. The Church saw obvious advantages in patronizing associations of scholars: it could more easily control the new learning, and it could use the professors as experts to examine suspect doctrines. The University of Paris, for example, began to denounce dangerous ideas derived from Aristotle and the Arabs almost as soon as it received official recognition from the pope.

Innocent III, who had been a student at both Paris and Bologna, favored university organization and bestowed valuable privileges on both his old schools. His patronage was matched by secular rulers, who needed educated men to staff their rapidly growing bureaucracies. By the end of the thirteenth century there were universities at Oxford and Cambridge in England, at Paris, Montpellier, Toulouse, and Orléans in France, at Coïmbra and Salamanca in the Iberian Peninsula, and at Bologna and Padua in Italy. There was no university in Germany until the fourteenth century. Paris remained the unquestioned leader in theology and liberal arts, and Bologna in law, but many men studied at more than one university. The famous scholars of the thirteenth century were university professors, and university graduates filled high offices in the Church and important positions in secular governments. In short, during the thirteenth century the universities took over the intellectual leadership of western Europe.

The idea of the university was one of the most important medieval contributions to modern civilization. Most civilized peoples have had schools of one kind or another, but they have usually concerned themselves with the private instruction of novices by priests, or the private tutoring of wealthy young men by individual teachers. True, the Roman

Church Regulation of the University of Paris

1215

Robert [de Courçon] by the divine mercy cardinal priest . . . and legate of the apostolic see, to all the masters and scholars at Paris, eternal safety in the Lord.

Let all know, that having been especially commanded by the lord pope . . . to better the condition of the students at Paris, and wishing . . . to provide for the tranquility of the students in the future, we have prescribed the following rules:

No one is to lecture at Paris in arts before he is twenty years old. He is to study in arts at least six years before he begins to lecture. . . . He must not be smirched with any infamy. When he is ready to lecture, each one is to be examined according to the form contained in the letter of the bishop of Paris. . . .

The treatises of Aristotle on logic, both the old and the new, are to be read in the schools in the regular and not in the extraordinary courses. The two Priscians [on grammar] . . . are also to be read in the schools in the regular courses. On the feastdays [there were nearly one hundred of these] nothing is to be read except philosophy, rhetoric, books on the *quadrivium* [arithmetic, geometry, music, and astronomy], the Ethics [of Aristotle] and the fourth book of the Topics [of Boethius on logic]. The book of Aristotle on Metaphysics or Natural Philosophy, or the abridgements of these works, are not to be read, nor the doctrines of [certain contemporary teachers accused of heresy].

From Robert de Courçon, *Statutes*, trans. by D. C. Munro, *Translations and Reprints* (Philadelphia: University of Pennsylvania Press, 1899), Vol. II, No. 3, p. 12.

St. Francis strips off the garments he wore as a well-to-do young man and renounces all worldly goods. Painting by Giotto (1266?–1337), in the church of St. Francis at Assisi.

Empire established professorships for scholars to lecture to anyone who cared to listen, but it never developed the university or an examination system. China, during the European Middle Ages, had a prescribed course of study, with an examination system and something very like our system of scholarly degrees, but it lacked an autonomous, self-perpetuating faculty. Only in medieval Europe does one find all the elements that make a modern university—a faculty constituting an organized and privileged community of scholars, a regular course of study, and final examinations leading to the degree as a certificate of scholarly competence. This type of educational organization has its disadvantages—it tends to become overly conservative and tradition-bound—but by and large it has proved the most successful form of higher education ever devised, and it has spread throughout the world.

The Mendicant Orders: Franciscans and Dominicans

The heresies mentioned above were only the most obvious manifestations of a threatened decline in the Church's influence over the population of western Europe. Even those who were not heretics criticized the character of the clergy and the administrative system of the Church. They felt that the Church was not doing its job, that it was failing to meet the challenge of changing times. They feared that it was yielding to the temptations created by a more prosperous and better-organized society—the love of wealth and the love of power—instead of finding ways to combat them. A society that had been oriented toward the future life was now finding far too much satisfaction in the pleasures of this world.

It was in response to these criticisms that the medieval Church, with the establishment of the Franciscan and Dominican Orders, embarked on its last great wave of reform. St. Francis (ca. 1182–1226), the son of a well-to-do Italian merchant, was particularly sensitive to the problem of wealth. His own conversion began with his renunciation of all claim to his family's property, and throughout his career he insisted on absolute poverty for himself and his followers. He also demanded literal and unquestioning observance of the precepts given in the Gospels to the disciples of Christ. Probably no other group of Christians has ever come closer to imitating the life of Jesus and the Apostles than did St. Francis and the early Franciscans. Their example of holy living impressed laymen who had become weary of routine religious services and encouraged them to make a new effort to apply Christian principles in their daily life.

The other leader of the new religious movement was St. Dominic (ca. 1170–1221), a Spanish priest who had begun his career by trying to convert the heretics of southern France. He was primarily concerned with the instruction of the faithful through preaching and teaching. Like St. Francis, he emphasized the ideal of absolute poverty, not only as good in itself but also because the leaders of the heretics he was combating had gained great influence by renouncing all worldly goods. Even more than St. Francis, he wanted his order to be an order of preachers. Realizing that perfunctory sermons and routine services were

scorned by the more sophisticated groups of western Europe, St. Dominic spent his life training men who would be subject to the rigorous discipline of a religious order but who would also be well enough educated to hold their own in arguments with scholars, townsmen, and secular officials. The Dominicans established excellent schools to train

Women and Religious Reform

The impulse toward lay devotion and voluntary poverty was not confined to the Mendicant Orders. It was especially strong among women who founded private associations to satisfy their religious aspirations. These women were called "beguines" in the Low Countries, where they were numerous. Jacques de Vitry, a famous crusade preacher and historian (and later a cardinal), described them in 1213.

You have seen and you have rejoiced to see . . . great crowds of holy women in many places who despising the charms of the flesh for Christ and scorning the riches of this world for the heavenly kingdom . . . seek by the labor of their hands their meager nourishment, although their relatives have an abundance of riches. They abandon their families and the homes of their fathers, preferring to endure poverty rather than to enjoy wealth wrongly acquired or to stay with danger among the proud men of this world.

From Jacques de Vitry, *Vita B. Marae Orgniciacensis* in *Acta sanctorum*, for 4 June (Antwerp, 1717).

St. Francis Gives a Lesson in Poverty

Once when the blessed Francis had visited the Cardinal of Ostia [who was afterward Pope Gregory IX] at the hour of dinner he went as if by stealth from door to door begging food. And when he had returned, the Cardinal had already sat down at table, with many knights and nobles. But blessed Francis placed those alms which he had received on the table beside him. . . . And the Cardinal was a little ashamed . . . but he said nothing. . . . And when blessed Francis had eaten a little he took of his alms and sent a little to each of the knights and chaplains of the Cardinal on behalf of the Lord God. And they all received them with great joy and devotion. . . . [The Cardinal later rebuked him gently, but Francis answered:] "I will not be ashamed to beg alms, nay, I hold this a very great nobility and royal dignity before God and a means of honoring Him Who, when He was Lord of all, wished for our sakes to become servant of all, and when He was rich and glorious in His majesty became poor and despised in our humility."

From "The Mirror of Perfection," *The Little Flowers of St. Francis* (New York and London: Everyman's Library, 1910), Ch. 23, p. 203.

members of the order, and the graduates of these schools soon dominated the faculties of theology of European universities.

Both the Franciscan and the Dominican Orders met with immediate success. Thousands of men joined their ranks during the thirteenth century, and these friars, as they were called, became the most influential group among the clergy. Unlike the monks, who secluded themselves in their cloisters, the friars wandered about as missionaries, preaching and talking to laymen. They brought religion to the very centers of thirteenth-century society—to the courts, the universities, and the towns. At first there was some tendency for the Franciscans to appeal more to emotion and the Dominicans to reason, but by the middle of the century this difference had almost vanished. Each order produced a famous teacher of theology—the Dominicans, St. Thomas Aquinas; the Franciscans, St. Bonaventura. And each order carried on revivals among the people of the towns. The fact that the Church managed to preserve its leadership throughout most of the thirteenth century, in spite of the growing prosperity and worldliness of society, was due largely to the work of the friars.

Suggestions for Further Reading

Note: Asterisk denotes a book available in paperback edition.

Towns and Trade   The articles in the *Cambridge Economic History of Europe* remain the best guide for this period. Older and still useful works are W. Cunningham, *The Growth of English Industry and Commerce* (1910), and P. Boissonade, *Life and Work in Medieval Europe** (1929). R. de Roover, *Money, Banking and Credit in Medieval Bruges* (1948), is a readable study of the operations of the Italian merchant-bankers in Flanders. A. Sapori, *The Italian Merchant in the Middle Ages** (1970), is excellent. L. White, *Medieval Technology and Social Change* (1962), is a good introduction to the fascinating subject of medieval technology.

Gothic Art   There are many beautiful and exciting books on Gothic art. A. Temko, *Notre-Dame of Paris** (1955), is a charming study of this cathedral written as a biography. A. E. M. Katzenellenbogen, *The Sculptural Program of Chartres Cathedral** (1959), is a detailed study of Chartres, with the latest and most plausible historical interpretation. The best treatment of Gothic art in the High Middle Ages is P. Frankl, *Gothic Architecture** (1963), which traces the development of this architecture in all regions of Europe and stresses the slow perfection of the art. Frankl includes the most up-to-date bibliography. O. von Simson, *The Gothic Cathedral* (1956), is another first-rate book. The old work of T. J. Jackson, *Gothic Architecture* (1915), is sound and still valuable. Every student of medieval history should become familiar with one of the great monuments of American scholarship, Henry Adams' *Mont-Saint-Michel and Chartres** (1905). This is a great appreciation not only of the art but of the entirety of medieval civilization. In the same way, E. Mâle, *Religious Art in France in the Thirteenth Century* (1913) (published in paperback edition as *The Gothic Image*), is a study of the thought of the thirteenth century as expressed in art.

Vernacular Literature   Both C. C. Abbott, *Early Medieval French Lyrics* (1932), and J. A. Symonds, *Wine, Women and Song* (1899), have selections of typical lyric poetry of the twelfth century; the translation of Symonds, although somewhat more romantic, is superior. P. Dronke, *Medieval Latin and the Rise of the European Love-lyric* (1968), is very useful. *French Medieval Romances,* trans. by E. Mason (1911), is a collection of short novels probably dating from the reign of Henry II. The best critical study of the vernacular literature of the twelfth and thirteenth centuries is E. Curtius, *European Literature and the Latin Middle Ages** (1963), which has excellent bibliographic materials.

Scholarship and the Rise of the Universities   Perhaps the central figure of the Christian humanism of the twelfth century was John of Salisbury, most of whose works have now been translated. *The Statesman's Book,* trans. by J. Dickinson (1927), a work of political theory, had a great influence on the development of twelfth-century humanism.

John of Salisbury's *Historia Pontificalis,* trans. by M. Chibnall (1956), describes western Europe during and after the Second Crusade as seen through the eyes of an Englishman in the papal Curia. An excellent penetration into John's thought and personality and his close association with Canterbury and Rome is given in *Letters of John of Salisbury,* 2 vols., ed. by W. J. Millor and H. E. Butler (1955). C. J. Webb, *John of Salisbury* (1932), presents him as a great medieval churchman and plays down his role as scholar and humanist.

There is very good source material on university life in L. Thorndike, *University Records and Life in the Middle Ages* (1944). L. Thorndike, *History of Magic and Experimental Science,* Vol. II (1923), traces the origins of modern science in the medieval universities. C. H. Haskins, *The Rise of the Universities** (1923), is a good general survey of the beginnings of the universities. Another useful short account is by H. Wieruszowski, *The Medieval University** (1966). The standard scholarly study is H. Rashdall, *The Universities of Europe in the Middle Ages,* 3 vols., rev. and ed. by F. M. Powicke and A. B. Emden (1936). H. Waddell, *The Wandering Scholars* (1927), gives a good picture of student life in the period of the formation of universities.

Henry II, Richard, The English practice of preserving records has provided us with a vast amount of evidence for this
and John period. Both Roger of Hoveden, *The Annals,* 2 vols., trans. by H. T. Riley (1853), and Roger of Wendover, *Chronicle,* 2 vols., trans. by J. A. Giles (1849), are interesting contemporary histories. There is valuable material in *English Historical Documents,* Vols. II and III, ed. by D. C. Douglas and G. W. Greenaway (1953–55). For the study of the growth of English law there are representative documents in C. Stephenson and F. G. Marcham, *Sources of English Constitutional History* (1937). J. E. A. Jolliffe's *Constitutional History of Medieval England** (1937) is a readable and scholarly study with a good critical bibliography, and F. Pollock and F. W. Maitland, *History of English Law,* Vol. I (1923), is fundamental. J. E. A. Jolliffe's *Angevin Kingship* (1955) traces the character and growth of royal power and the development of the organs of government through the twelfth century. S. Painter, *The Reign of King John** (1949), gives an excellent account of the political and administrative history of this reign. Painter's *William Marshal: Knight-Errant, Baron, and Regent of England** (1933) is an exciting biography that presents a vivid picture of the thoughts and attitudes of the English feudal class. The most thorough treatment of Magna Carta is that of W. S. McKechnie, *Magna Carta* (1914), a chapter-by-chapter analysis. See also J. C. Holt, *Magna Carta* (1965). A. L. Poole, *Domesday Book to Magna Carta* (1951), is the most comprehensive one-volume history of this period; although it is sometimes dull reading (on a fascinating period), there is an excellent critical bibliography.

Philip Augustus Both J. Evans, *Life in Medieval France* (1925), and A. A. Tilley, *Medieval France* (1922), are very good surveys arranged in topical fashion. There is a good account of French society in A. Luchaire, *Social France at the Time of Philip Augustus,** trans. by E. B. Krehbiel (1912). The works by Petit-Dutaillis, Fawtier, and Lavisse listed at the end of Chapter 10, in the second section, also contain material on this subject.

Innocent III The best study of this important pope is that of the great French historian, A. Luchaire, *Innocent III,* 6 vols. (1904–08). *Selected Letters of Innocent III Concerning England,* ed. by C. R. Cheney and W. H. Semple (1953), provides us with considerable information on English–papal relations in the stormy period from 1198 to 1216. There is a very readable interpretation of Innocent's remarkable ascendancy in S. R. Packard, *Europe and the Church under Innocent III* (1927).

Heresy and H. C. Lea, *A History of the Inquisition of the Middle Ages,* 3 vols. (1888), has considerable material on
the Friars the Albigensian heresy, but the reader would do well to take Lea's judgments with some reservations and to read in conjunction with it E. Vacandard, *The Inquisition* (1908), which sees this terrible institution more in the light of its time. S. Runciman, *The Medieval Manichee* (1947), follows the history of the Dualist tradition in Christianity. This is a sound and urbane book. For the crusade against heretics, see J. R. Strayer, *The Albigensian Crusades* (1971).

The best one-volume collection of the lives and writings of St. Francis is in *The Little Flowers of St. Francis** (Everyman's Library). P. Sabatier, *The Life of St. Francis of Assisi* (1894), is a scholarly book with good bibliographic material, but J. Jorgensen, *St. Francis,** trans. by T. O. Sloane (1955), is more interesting. B. Jarrett's *Life of St. Dominic** (1924) gives a good, if adulatory, picture of the man, and P. Mandonnet, *St. Dominic and His Work* (1944), emphasizes the spirit and work of the Order.

super infernu̅ ꝯtutulat̅ ē n̄alde ꝛ
laxate sunt õs aie q̄ erant i̅ i̅ferno ꝛ
clamalãt uoce magna dicẽtes ꝟt
dicimus te ꝟꝛe sili dei iuu̅ q̄ dignat̅

es nob̄ ursurgenu̅ daṛe ꝉ dieꝛ ꝉ noc
tis qua̅ totu̅ teṁp̅ qᷓ uiuimus
tꝛeua̅. bi ꝗ q̅i tucdo duit die dᷓa
q̄i ꝛ ꝓi ḣebit̄. ꝓte au̅ scis i̅ scla sclor̄.

12 The Rise of the Secular State

The popes and the mendicant orders had combined to check the spread of heresy in the thirteenth century. By organizing the Albigensian Crusades and the Inquisition the popes ended the threat of popular heresy. A remarkable group of theologians (mostly Dominicans and Franciscans) succeeded in reconciling the new Greco-Arabic learning with the Christian faith and thus reduced the danger of intellectual heresy. By the middle of the thirteenth century there was little open dissent from orthodox doctrine in western Europe. Most people were honestly and sincerely Catholic in belief; the few who were not found it expedient to pretend that they were.

THE IMPACT OF ECONOMIC CHANGE

Yet the position of the Church was less secure than it seemed. The Church could deal with the heretic, who was an open enemy; dealing with the lukewarm friend was a more difficult problem. Men had to make a living and obey their rulers. But at what point did a normal desire to make a decent living turn into an im-

moderate lust for wealth? At what point did obedience to authority turn into a loyalty that subordinated the interests of the Church to those of the state? It was easier to sense this gradual growth of worldliness than to do anything about it, and the Church itself was infected by the ills it sought to cure. Some clergymen sought to accumulate offices in order to augment their income. Even more of them entered the service of secular rulers. The first group exposed the Church to criticism; the second often failed to defend its interests.

It has always been hard for a religion to deal with the problem of prosperity. Wealth creates pride and self-assurance, neither of which is entirely compatible with devoutness. The thirteenth-century Church strove, with some success, to give the wealthy a sense of social responsibility. It condemned flagrant profiteering and callous neglect of the poor. It accepted the idea that a man who invested in a commercial enterprise was entitled to interest on the money he risked, but it denounced the small moneylenders who charged high rates for personal loans. Many of these loansharks in the end left large sums to charities to atone for their profits from usury. But while the Church

Medieval coins. Top to bottom: Florentine gold florin (thirteenth century); Venetian gold ducat (thirteenth century); obverse and reverse of a silver penny of Henry III of England (thirteenth century); gold agnel of Philip VI of France (fourteenth century). The gold coins were used for large-scale transactions; the silver, for wages and household purchases.

could mitigate some of the consequences, it could not alter the fact that western Europe was shifting to an economic system in which money was becoming more important than inherited status. Concern over money made it hard for men to follow the teachings of the Church or to put the interests of the Church ahead of their own.

The growth of a money economy involved the landed classes, including most churchmen, in an economic squeeze. Increasing demand caused a steady rise in prices, while income from land lagged behind. Ancient custom or fixed agreements determined what peasants paid. On many estates lords had commuted labor services and payments in kind for rents of a few pennies an acre. It was not easy to change customary payments or contractual agreements, for peasants who were pushed too hard could flee to the towns or to the new lands that were still being cleared in the East. Thus the real income of landlords tended to decrease during the thirteenth century.

Some landlords saved themselves by leasing their domain lands for short times. This gave them an income related to the market value of their produce rather than an income tied to a customary rent. In some regions landlords turned as much land as they could into pasture, since wool brought in more profit than grain. But these devices could not satisfy the financial needs of kings and princes, of popes and bishops, who had to govern as well as live comfortably. Sooner or later they had to supplement their ordinary income by taxes and fees. When they did, however, they stirred up bitter resentment among their subjects and conflicts among themselves over who had the right to tax.

The Church was especially vulnerable to criticism of its financial policies. The income tax on the clergy, first imposed by Innocent III, was levied more and more frequently, and at higher rates—10 percent or even 20 percent. Fees were imposed or increased for papal letters, legal documents, and confirmation of appointments to high offices in the Church. Both taxes and fees were derived, in the last analysis, from payments by laymen. As a result the Church was

criticized for being too eager to raise money, too ready to give spiritual benefits in return for cash payments. The more zealous wing of the Franciscans urged that clergymen abandon all their property and lead lives of apostolic poverty, but this solution was hardly realistic. The Franciscan Order itself was acquiring property, even though it tried to disguise the fact by vesting title in trustees. When reformers—Franciscans and others—became bishops and popes, they found that in the existing economic situation they could make no important changes in the Church's financial system. Since not even the most zealous reformers could find inoffensive ways of raising money, there was a loss of respect for the Church as an organization, even among men who were completely orthodox in doctrine.

THE FRENCH AND ENGLISH MONARCHIES

At the very time that respect for the Church was declining, the prestige of secular governments was rising. These governments were not hostile to the Church, but they were consciously or unconsciously competing with the Church for the loyalty of the people. And just as the Church was becoming more worldly and more like a secular government, so secular rulers were reasserting their old claim to be God's lieutenants on earth and were taking on responsibilities hitherto reserved for the Church. Kings claimed to be protectors of the common welfare, agents of divine justice, defenders of the faith. None of the great thirteenth-century popes became a saint, but several kings were canonized. And one of these saintly kings, Louis IX of France, probably exercised greater moral authority over the Europe of his day than did any churchman.

St. Louis

Louis IX (1226–70) was the grandson of Philip Augustus, the first really strong French king. Philip had conquered the northwestern part of France in his war with John, and Philip's son, Louis VIII, had acquired large holdings in the south by his timely participation in the crusade against the Albigensians. As a result, Louis IX was far more powerful than any combination of hostile French lords. He put down a few halfhearted rebellions early in his reign, and for the rest of his life his authority was never challenged. No one could oppose Louis' claim to rights or land. An arrogant man might have abused this power, but Louis was determined to follow the ideals of a Christian ruler. He settled the longstanding dispute with England by a generous treaty that gave the English king many border districts in Aquitaine. He kept faith with all men, even with Moslems. In France he submitted all disputed questions to the decisions of his courts and did his best to restrain the zeal of his administrative agents, who tended to exaggerate the extent of royal rights. No other medieval king had such a reputation for honesty and fair dealing.

Louis was pious and generous, but he was not soft. His loyalty to the faith did not keep him from exercising independent judgment about the policies of the Church. He refused to join Pope Innocent IV in the attack on the emperor Frederick II; he rejected demands of the French bishops that he punish all men who remained excommunicated for more than a year. He felt that, as a Christian king, he knew better than anyone else how to provide for the spiritual and material welfare of his people.

Louis' concern for law and justice led, naturally enough, to a strengthening of the royal judicial system. During his reign one of the great institutions of the French monarchy was created—the Parlement of Paris. This was the king's own court, staffed with his closest advisers. It heard appeals from the decisions of his local administrative agents and, even more important, it heard appeals from the courts of the great feudal lords. By reviewing, and often reversing, the decisions of feudal courts, it established a legal basis for royal claims to supremacy over all subjects.

The king's local courts, headed by bailiffs and other administrative agents, were even more zealous than the Parlement in upholding royal rights. Since

Statue of Louis IX, in the church of Mainville in Normandy.

St. Louis as Described by Joinville

Jean de Joinville, a noble of Champagne, was a friend of St. Louis and went with him on his crusade of 1248.

This holy man loved God with all his heart, and imitated his works. For example, just as God died because he loved his people, so the king risked his life many times for the love of his people. . . . He said once to his eldest son: . . . "I beg you that you make yourself loved by the people of your realm, for truly, I would rather that a Scot came from Scotland and governed the people of the kingdom justly and well than that you should govern them badly. . . ." The holy king loved the truth so much that he kept his promises even to the Saracens.

A friar told the king . . . that he had never read that a kingdom was destroyed or changed rulers except through lack of justice. . . . The king did not forget this lesson but governed his land justly and well, according to the will of God. . . . Often in summer he went to sit down under an oak-tree in the wood of Vincennes, after hearing mass, and made us sit around him. And all those who had suits to bring him came up, without being hindered by ushers or other people. And he would ask them: "Does anyone here have a suit?" And those who had requests would get up. . . . And then he would call Lord Pierre de Fontaines and Lord Geoffroi de Villette [two of his legal experts] and say to one of them: "Settle this affair for me." And if he saw anything to correct in what they said on his behalf, he would do so.

From Jean de Joinville, *Histoire de Saint Louis,* ed. by N. de Wailly (Paris: Firmin Didot, 1874), pp. 11, 34.

earlier kings had been too weak to enforce their theoretical claims, no exact boundary between the privileges of local lords and the rights of the monarch had ever been drawn. Thus on issues for which there were no clear precedents it was only natural that the bailiffs should rule in favor of the king. Louis did not take undue advantage of this situation; in fact, he and his Parlement often modified the more extreme claims of the bailiffs. But the net result was an increase in royal power, an increase that was cheerfully accepted by most of the people in the country. After all, Louis had suppressed disorder, and his courts, though not perfect, dispensed a better brand of justice than those of most feudal lords.

A just and powerful king, Louis was also a zealous crusader. Jerusalem had been lost to the Moslems in 1187, and all efforts to recover it had failed. Armed expeditions had gained nothing, and a treaty arranged by Frederick II of Germany had given the Christians only a few years of occupancy of the city before it fell again to the Moslems. These successive failures had somewhat dampened enthusiasm for overseas expeditions, but Louis felt that his responsibilities as a Christian ruler extended beyond the limits of his realm. In 1248 and again in 1270 he led crusades to recover Jerusalem. The earlier expedition had some chance of success, but after a first victory Louis' army was cut off from its supplies and was forced to surrender. The second expedition was hopeless from the beginning, for Louis let himself be talked into attacking the outlying Moslem state of Tunis. Even if he had conquered the country, it would have done his cause little good; as it was, he and many of his followers died of fever soon after landing.

Louis IX was made a saint within a generation after his death. His canonization was more than a personal tribute to a pious crusader; it completed the work of sanctifying the French monarchy. Louis' long search for justice and order had created an almost inexhaustible reservoir of support for his dynasty. Some of his successors were evil and some were weak, but for centuries loyalty to the king was the strongest political force in France. The king stood as the symbol of unity and good government; he alone could override provincial differences and selfish local ambitions. France remained Catholic, but loyalty to the Church began to take second place to loyalty to the state.

Henry III of England

France was united only through its king and his bureaucracy. The provinces retained their own customs and privileges; no one could have spoken of a

Henry III of England (1216–72) discusses the progress of a building (perhaps Westminster Abbey) with his architects. The workmen are raising materials to the masons with a windlass.

French common law or the "rights of Frenchmen." But in England the monarchy, in its long years of ascendancy, had created a common law and common institutions. The propertied classes in England had become attached to the laws and institutions that protected their rights. Thus the growing loyalty to the English state was loyalty to a system of government as much as it was loyalty to a dynasty. The king could not claim that he alone was working for the common welfare, for his opponents could assert that they too were seeking the good of the "community of the realm." Thus in England even bitter struggles between king and aristocracy could not destroy the unity of the country.

This unusual political situation in England explains certain apparent contradictions in the reign of Henry III (1216–72). On the one hand, royal officials strengthened the administrative and judicial institutions of the country. They created new types of general taxation and devised new writs for bringing more cases into royal courts. Most important of all, trial by jury, already used to settle most land disputes, became the normal procedure in criminal cases. All lawsuits of any significance were now tried by royal judges, and private courts began to die out. These developments were summed up in a remarkable treatise on English law written about 1250 by Henry de Bracton, a royal judge. Bracton gave a clear, logical, and thorough explanation of the common law, citing precedents and stating general principles. He made the common law so coherent and self-sufficient that it was invulnerable to all outside influences for many centuries, and his book became the basic text for the training of English lawyers.

On the other hand, during Henry's reign there was constant friction between the king and his barons. The barons were not trying to destroy the central government; they were trying to use it to protect their status and their views of what English policy should be. And they often found it expedient to claim that they were defending the realm against a foolish and spendthrift monarch.

When Henry came of age in 1225, the barons persuaded him to confirm Magna Carta by granting him a tax. There was no rebellion, as there had been in 1215, but a fair bargain. Henry III gave his consent without coercion, and the 1225 version of the Charter was accepted by everyone as the law of the land. What is more, the king made his officials enforce it, thereby satisfying the barons for some time. But by the 1240s they were once more in open opposition to the king. They could not hate him as they had John—Henry was a likable, honest man, almost as pious as St. Louis—but they did dislike his policies. He wasted money in vain attempts to reconquer lost territories in France. He filled bishoprics and secular offices with his French relatives and friends. Moreover, he allowed the pope to draw large sums of money from England for the papal war against the Hohenstaufen rulers of Italy. Modern nationalism did not exist in the thirteenth century, but we can see the beginnings of nationalism in the attitude of the barons: they were not interested in Henry's French lands; they resented his French friends; they saw no reason for England to help the pope. They wanted English jobs to be filled by Englishmen, and they wanted English money to be spent in England. The barons' opposition to foreign intruders and foreign entanglements were supported by most lesser landholders and by a surprising number of English clergymen.

Henry III's chronic shortage of money enhanced the power of the barons. Ordinary income from the royal domain was barely adequate for peacetime needs, and Magna Carta made it difficult to gain new

The shield of
Simon de Montfort
(1208?–65).

revenues without the consent of the barons. If Henry wanted to wage war he had to levy taxes. But after 1240 the barons steadily refused to grant any taxes. Henry nevertheless went ahead with an ambitious project to help the pope conquer Sicily. The English clergy, under papal pressure, gave him some money but not enough. By 1258 Henry was hopelessly in debt, and his foreign policy was a complete failure. In desperation, he appointed a committee of barons to reform the government.

The baronial committee soon forgot reform and concentrated on making policy and appointing high officials. Naturally, it soon split into factions. The barons had found it easy to agree in their opposition to Henry's policies; they found it more difficult to agree on a positive policy of their own. Though the barons clearly needed someone to act as leader, they felt that they were all equal, and they were jealous of the ablest man in their group, Simon de Montfort. In the end, Simon gained control of the government, but he lost most of his baronial support in doing so. Henry's eldest son, Edward, managed to raise an army with which he defeated and killed Simon in 1265, and Henry's authority was fully restored.

This episode is significant for two reasons. First, it set a pattern that was to be repeated in England many times during the next two centuries. Again and

again the barons, annoyed by royal policy, took over the central government; and again and again factionalism and jealousy kept them from maintaining their position. Second, the struggle between Henry and the barons for control of the central government speeded up the development of a representative assembly in England. The two sides were so evenly matched that they both sought support from men of lesser rank—the knights and other free landholders in the rural areas and the burgesses of the towns. The easiest way to win the support of these men was to invite them to send representatives to the full meetings of the king's court, which, from the 1240s on, were beginning to be given the name Parliaments.

Early Parliaments

A Parliament, in the middle years of the thirteenth century, was a meeting of the king with his chief officials, his bishops, and his barons. *Parliament* was a slang term at first; it meant "talk-fest" and could be used for any sort of discussion. Gradually it came to mean a meeting at which difficult cases were heard that could not be decided by ordinary law courts. The English Parliament, like the French *parlement*, was a high court of justice. Even today the House of Lords is the highest court in England, though cases are actually heard only by specially appointed "law lords." But the English Parliament was also a Great Council that advised the king on matters of policy and granted taxes. It was in Parliament, for example, that the English barons criticized Henry III's plans and refused to give him money. A meeting of parliament, with all the great men of the realm assembled to deliberate and make important decisions, was truly an impressive occasion.

Representatives from the countryside and the towns who were summoned before Parliament were naturally influenced by its authority and prestige, and they in turn influenced their constituents when they went back home to report what had taken place. It was useful to impress these people because local government in England was still largely controlled by local notables. The king of England, unlike the king of France, had never had to establish a provincial bureaucracy. With no conquered provinces to hold down and no strong loyalty to provincial institutions to fear, it was perfectly safe, and much cheaper, for the central government to pass on its orders to local notables, who served without pay. Thus in the counties the sheriffs, the tax collectors, and the custodians of royal property were usually knights of the shire—that is, country gentlemen resident in the district they governed. In the towns the mayors and aldermen were well-to-do businessmen. These local officials proved reasonably loyal, but they found their government jobs burdensome and annoyingly unprofitable. When they did not like government orders they could drag their feet with no fear of reprisal. It was no great punishment to be removed from office, and those removed had to be replaced with men of the same sort. Thus when the king or his barons wanted to introduce any innovation in government, such as a new law or a new tax, it was clearly advisable to gain the goodwill of the knights and burgesses. And a good way of doing so was to invite them to send representatives to Parliament, where they could hear and discuss the reasons for the shift in policy.

Both Henry III and the baronial leader, Simon de Montfort, had tried to justify their policies by asking the counties to send knights to parliament. In 1265 Simon de Montfort, in an effort to compensate for his loss of baronial support, took the additional step of asking the towns to send representatives. These precedents were not forgotten. In 1268 Henry III summoned both knights and burgesses to Parliament, and Edward I called the same groups to the first great assembly of his reign in 1275. These early representatives had little power and always accepted the propositions laid before them by king and barons, but the very fact that they were being summoned at frequent intervals was to be significant in the future.

Parliament was not the first or the only representative assembly. During the Middle Ages most governments found it expedient to summon local leaders to hear explanations of policy. Innocent III, for example, had called representatives of the towns when he was establishing his government in the Papal States, and the Spanish kings held similar assemblies during the reconquest of the peninsula from the Moslems. In the end, the English Parliament was to prove unique, but there was nothing unusual in the experiments conducted by Simon de Montfort and Henry III.

THE PAPAL–HOHENSTAUFEN FEUD

In Germany and Italy the central government was far weaker than in England and France—a situation that Frederick II, whom Innocent III had made emperor, spent his life trying to correct. Though he failed in this effort, he came close enough to success in Italy to precipitate the last great struggle between Empire and papacy.

Frederick II was by birth and education an Italian, although he was de-

Portrait of Emperor Frederick II, from a manuscript of his treatise, *The Art of Hunting with Falcons.*

scended from the Hohenstaufen of Germany. He spent a few years in Germany after becoming emperor, but he never felt at home there and never had much power over the Germans. Apparently deciding that he could do nothing with Germany, at least until he had brought Italy fully under control, he abandoned almost all authority to the princes of the Empire. All he expected from Germany was a supply of soldiers for his Italian wars.

In Italy he followed exactly the opposite course. First he eliminated all opposition in his hereditary kingdom of Sicily, transforming it into a nearly absolute monarchy, and then he began to revive the old imperial claims to central and northern Italy. Thanks to the factional quarrels within and among the Italian towns, he was able to make substantial acquisitions of territory. Some of the

northern Italians became so frightened that they revived the Lombard League, but Frederick crushed them at Cortenuova in 1237. For the moment he seemed to be in control of the entire Italian peninsula.

The papacy, however, was still determined to keep Italy from falling into the hands of one master. The independence of the Church seemed bound up with the independence of the Papal States, and Frederick's victories were threatening that independence. No pope could believe that an emperor who ruled all Italy except the region around Rome would long respect Rome itself. Innocent III had kept the Empire in turmoil for years rather than risk this danger; the precedents he laid down were hard to forget.

Moreover, Frederick II's orthodoxy was somewhat doubtful. No one was ever sure what this brilliant and inquisitive man really believed. He exchanged friendly letters with Moslem rulers; he dabbled in science and magic; he was accused of writing a book called *The Three Impostors: Moses, Jesus, and Mohammed.* This charge was completely false, but the fact that it could be made tells something of Frederick's reputation. He tried hard to convince people that he was an orthodox ruler, even going on a crusade and persecuting heretics, but these actions raised more doubts than they settled. He succeeded in regaining Jerusalem for a few years, not by fighting the Moslems but by making a treaty with the sultan of Egypt, and his persecution of heretics seemed prompted only by a desire to improve his political position.

When it became apparent that Frederick was going to insist on full control of both northern and southern Italy, the pope decided that drastic measures were necessary. Pope Gregory IX tried to hold a council in Rome to discuss the problem, but Frederick intercepted the fleet bearing many of the prelates and captured or drowned most of them. This direct attack on the Church did not improve Frederick's reputation. The next pope, Innocent IV, just as determined and almost as able as his great namesake, Innocent III, called a council at Lyons in 1245. The council declared that Frederick had forfeited all his possessions, and that

GERMANY AND ITALY AT THE TIME OF FREDERICK II
ca. 1250

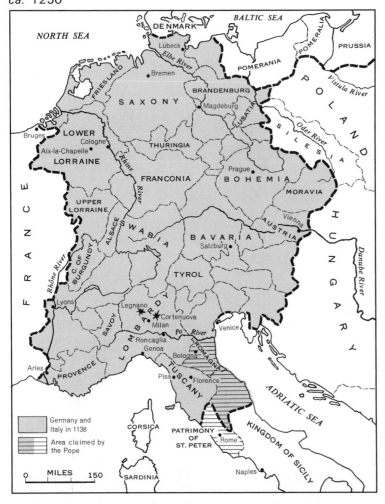

In 1241 Frederick's fleet captured (or drowned) two cardinals and a hundred bishops who were on their way to a council summoned by Gregory IX to depose the emperor. This manuscript illustration shows Frederick in the ship on the left, though actually he was not present. On the right, his soldiers attack the prelates in a ship bearing the papal ensign of the keys of St. Peter.

neither he nor any member of his family should ever be allowed to rule in Germany or Italy. Innocent IV proclaimed a crusade against Frederick and imposed a tax on the clergy to pay for armies to carry it out.

The papal attack destroyed the last remnants of imperial power in Germany. Turning the conflict to their own advantage, the princes refused to obey either Frederick or an opposition line of rulers elected by propapal faction. Germany became a loose confederation of states under the control of princes who were free to accept or reject the policies suggested by the nominal ruler. No German emperor after Frederick exercised any real authority except in his own family possessions.

In Italy the issue was not decided so quickly. Frederick held on to most of the territory he had gained, but he never managed to build up a strong govern-

ment in the north. After his death in 1250 the towns of northern and central Italy became independent, though the Kingdom of Sicily remained loyal to his sons. The papacy might have been satisfied with this state of affairs—after all, the danger of encirclement had been dispelled forever—but it had been too badly frightened by Frederick to take any chances. So the popes carried on the war against the "viper brood" of the Hohenstaufen, refusing to rest until the hated family had been ejected from Sicily and Naples. They preached crusades, collected taxes from the clergy to cover their expenses, and sent cardinals out with armies to do battle with Frederick's heirs. And when all these efforts proved ineffectual, they turned for help to England and France. The attempt to involve England led only to the rebellion of the English barons against Henry III, but the approach to France met with greater success. St. Louis reluctantly permitted his brother, Charles of Anjou, to attempt the conquest of the Kingdom of Sicily. Charles, aided by crusade privileges (including remission of sins for his soldiers) and crusade taxes, defeated the last Hohenstaufen ruler of Sicily in a lightning campaign in 1266. A grandson of Frederick II made a desperate attempt to regain the kingdom, but his forces were crushed in 1268 and the young Hohenstaufen was executed in cold blood. The papacy, aided by the French, had won a complete victory over its enemies.

Loss of Prestige by the Church

But in winning this political victory, the papacy had lost moral prestige. There had been some doubts about the deposition of Frederick II—St. Louis had preserved a careful neutrality in this struggle—although the Church clearly had a case against him. Frederick was threatening the independence of the Papal States, and he was certainly unconventional and possibly unorthodox in his ideas. But Frederick's heirs were much less powerful and much less dangerous to the Church; it seemed pure vindictiveness to harry them for two decades. The Church was using its spiritual authority to gain a political end. The pope was acting very much like a secular prince, assembling armies, making alliances, carrying on political intrigues. The distinction between ecclesiastical government and secular government was no longer clear. One could argue that if it was proper for the pope to tax the clergy for a war in Italy, it was equally proper for a king to tax the clergy to defend his kingdom. This claim was to cause the next great conflict between the papacy and secular rulers.

Moreover, the popes had won their victory over the Hohenstaufen only by creating political instability on both Germany and Italy, and this instability in the long run weakened the Church. No one in Germany was strong enough to protect the bishops, so they had to fight and intrigue to protect themselves. No one in Germany was strong enough to wipe out the heresies that erupted in the fifteenth century and laid a foundation for Luther's revolt. In Italy the absence of any central government encouraged the growth of factionalism and local wars. These disorders spilled over into the Papal States and made the pope's position there almost untenable. He could either flee Italy and lose the prestige that was associated with Rome or stay and play the petty politics of a minor prince. Neither course would strengthen the papacy.

SCHOLARSHIP AND THE ARTS

It took a generation for the Church to feel the full consequences of the new political situation; meanwhile it enjoyed its last years of unquestioned leadership in Europe. The kings of the West were at peace with one another and obedient to the pope. Both the education and the behavior of the clergy had steadily im-

St. Thomas Aquinas, detail from the Crucifixion, by Fra Angelico (1387–1455). Although this representation was made two centuries after Thomas lived, it seems accurately to depict his large head and bearlike appearance.

proved. This last period of Church leadership (1250–75) saw the building of the most perfect Gothic cathedrals and the culmination of medieval Christian philosophy in the work of Thomas Aquinas (1225–74).

It was probably no accident that these two forms of expression reached their peak at about the same time. There was a strong logical element in the perfected Gothic cathedral, just as there was a strong architectonic quality in Thomas Aquinas' thought. In both, the basic structural plan is clearly revealed, uncluttered by architectural or literary embellishment. Just as the cross section of a pillar of a Gothic church shows exactly what the superstructure will be, so the first paragraph of a chapter by Thomas Aquinas reveals exactly how his argument will proceed. But while we still appreciate the qualities of Gothic architecture—the emphasis on height and light, the clean expression of the function of each architectural member—we are less at home with the methods and ideas of medieval scholastic philosophy.

St. Thomas Aquinas

Thomas Aquinas, unlike some other Christian thinkers, feared neither the world nor the new knowledge about the world that scholars had acquired from the Greeks and the Arabs. God had put man in the world not to punish him but to enlighten his feeble understanding through concrete examples. Man could rely on his reason, which was the gift of God; the truths discovered by the ancient philosophers were perfectly valid truths, though they might be incomplete. Thus a pagan philosopher could give an acceptable proof of the existence of God even though he knew nothing of the doctrine of the Trinity. Reason needed to be enlightened by faith, but there was no conflict between the two.

In the same way, there should be no conflict between the Church and secular governments. Secular government was necessary and good in itself, for it gave men an opportunity to manifest social virtues. Even among the pagans, secular governments were divinely established and should be obeyed. Thomas admitted

The Reconciliation of Christian and Classical Philosophy

This extract from the *Summa Contra Gentiles* by St. Thomas Aquinas shows how a thirteenth-century scholar was able to use the ideas of Aristotle.

We have now shown that the effort to demonstrate the existence of God is not a vain one. We shall therefore proceed to set forth the arguments by which both philosophers and Catholic teachers have proved that God exists.

We shall first set forth the arguments by which Aristotle proceeds to prove that God exists. The aim of Aristotle is to do this in two ways, beginning with motion.

Of these ways the first is as follows. Everything that is moved is moved by another. That some things are in motion—for example, the sun—is evident from sense. Therefore, it is moved by something else that moves it. This mover is itself either moved or not moved. If it is not, we have reached our conclusion—namely, that we must posit some unmoved mover. This we call God. If it is moved, it is moved by another mover. We must, consequently, either proceed to infinity, or we must arrive at some unmoved mover. Now, it is not possible to proceed to infinity. Hence we must posit some prime unmoved mover.

From *On the Truth of the Catholic Faith. Summa Contra Gentiles*, trans. by A. C. Pegis (New York: Doubleday, 1955), p. 85.

that it was proper to resist a king who was openly violating the law of God, but he felt that resistance to a secular ruler should be resorted to only after everything else had failed.

As for the new wealth, here again there was no danger if men used their reason properly. God had given man dominion over the world, and it was part of the divine plan to make full use of the world's natural resources. Land did not fulfill its function unless it was cultivated; a tree was of no use unless it was used for construction. Men should remember their Christian duty to the poor, and they should never allow their desire for wealth to become immoderate. But there was nothing wrong in an honest effort to earn a decent living.

Thomas Aquinas believed that in the light of true reason everything made sense, that the world was a harmonious whole. Wisdom was the greatest earthly good, and the felicity of the afterlife consisted in the contemplation of the eternal Wisdom which is God. It was this serene conviction of the unity and rationality of all experience that made Thomas Aquinas' work so persuasive, that led to his early canonization and to his present reputation as the leading philosopher of Catholicism.

Even in his own day, not all scholars shared the views of Thomas Aquinas. Doubtless there was some professional jealousy involved; Aquinas was a Dominican, and scholars in other orders resented the influence the Dominicans had acquired in theological studies. But there was also honest concern, both about the extreme rationalism of his approach and about the reliance he placed on Aristotle and other Greek philosophers. The most eminent Franciscan theologian, St. Bonaventura, emphasized will rather than reason. And a group of Franciscan scholars at Oxford undermined the philosophy of Aquinas by proving that his chief authority, Aristotle, had made certain mistakes about natural phenomena. In correcting these mistakes they helped start a new trend in physics, which, advanced by obscure scholars of the fourteenth and fifteenth centuries, culminated in the work of Galileo. Roger Bacon was a member of this Oxford group, but he has received more credit than he deserves; his vague predictions about automotive vehicles and the like had no scientific basis. The real leader of the Oxford school was Bacon's teacher, Robert Grosseteste. Grosseteste realized that theory needed to be verified and refined by experiment. His own work on optics was not entirely successful, but it led to a better understanding of the field, notably in an explanation of the rainbow (*ca.* 1300) that was almost the one accepted today.

These scholarly disputes shook the confidence of scholars. More important was the fact that Thomas' arguments were too rational to have much influence on laymen. He might see no conflict between reason and faith, no opposition between secular interests and those of the Church, but for most people these contradictions did exist and could not be exorcised by words. They were faced with hard choices between the teachings of the Church and the demands of secular life, and they did not always choose the side of the Church.

Dante's Divine Comedy

THE INSCRIPTION ON THE ENTRANCE TO HELL

Through me you pass into the woeful city
Through me you pass into eternal pain
Through me you go amid those lost forever.
Justice it was that moved my Great Creator;
Power divine and highest wisdom made me
Together with God's own primeval love.
Before me there was nothing save those things
Eternal, and eternal I endure.
All hope abandon, ye who enter here.

THE ATTACK AT ANAGNI

Dante disliked Boniface VIII, whom he consigned to hell, but still felt that the attack at Anagni, which he describes below through the lips of Hugh Capet, was an outrage.

O avarice, what worse canst thou now do
Since thou dost so completely rule my race
That they care nothing for their flesh and blood?
Past wrongs and future they will now compound.
Into Anagni storms the lilied flag;
Christ is a captive in his Vicar's form,
And the old mockery again renewed
With vinegar and gall. I see him bleed
Amid the living robbers; Pilate too,
I see, so cruel that even this dreadful deed,
Is nót enough.

THE FINAL VISION

O grace abundant, through which I presumed
To fix my gaze on the eternal light
Which near consumes who dares to look thereon.
And in those depths I saw, bound up by love
Into one volume, all the universe. . . .
Here vigor failed the lofty vision, but
The will moved ever onward, like a wheel
In even motion, by the love impelled
Which moves the sun in heaven and all the stars.

From Dante, *Inferno,* canto 3; *Purgatory,* canto 20; *Paradise,* canto 33, trans. by H. F. Cary (London: Bell, 1877).

Dante

The greatest medieval poet—one of the greatest poets of all time—was Dante Alighieri (1265–1321). One of the first men to write in the vernacular in Italy, he helped establish the Tuscan dialect as the standard form of the Italian language. He wrote graceful lyrics in Italian and two notable treatises in Latin, one defending his use of the vernacular, the other a strong plea for strengthening and preserving the Empire. But the work for which Dante will always be remembered is the *Divine Comedy*, a vision of Hell, Purgatory, and Heaven written in magnificent Italian verse.

Dante had a troubled and unhappy life. Deeply involved in Florentine politics, he was permanently exiled from the city he loved in 1302. In spite of these troubles Dante, like Thomas Aquinas, remained convinced of the unity and meaningfulness of all human experience. Unlike many of his contemporaries, he did not sink into pessimism or seek out partial truths. He was almost the last representative of the confident, optimistic, all-embracing spirit of the great period of medieval civilization.

Dante was well read in both secular and religious literature. His guide through Hell and Purgatory was the Roman poet Vergil, and this part of his poem is full of allusions to classical mythology. But he also knew scholastic philosophy; the *Paradise* in many places reads like a verse translation of Thomas Aquinas. Like Thomas Aquinas, Dante saw no contradiction between the truths worked out by human reason and the truths revealed to the Church; all knowledge led to God if it was rightly used.

But to Dante knowledge was not enough; even good conduct was not enough. Faith in God and love of God and of one's fellow man were the essentials. In Hell the most lightly punished sins were those against oneself, such as gluttony. The lower depths were reserved for those who hurt others, and the worst sinners were Judas, who betrayed Christ, and Brutus and Cassius, who betrayed Caesar. In Purgatory sins were purged through suffering, and angels sang Beatitudes at each step of the ascent. In Paradise Dante came closer and closer to the eternal Light until he finally had his great vision of God—"the love which moves the sun and all the stars."

The *Divine Comedy* was recognized as a classic almost as soon as it was written, but admiration for the poem did not mean wide acceptance of its point of view. Few of Dante's contemporaries had his serenity or his breadth of vision; few could accept any longer his dream of a harmonious world in which men could seek both happiness on earth and eternal rewards in heaven. By the end of the thirteenth century secular and religious goals were coming into conflict, and more and more attention was being given to the secular.

Dante and his guide, Vergil, visiting the circle of Hell to which usurers have been relegated (illustration from a fourteenth-century Italian manuscript).

P cro scomemmo ala ceftra mamella.
c dicce paffi fammo un fu lostremo.
per ben ceffar larena ela fiamella.

Secularism in Art and Literature

The gradual growth of secular interests may be seen clearly in art and literature. For example, after 1270 there is a striking change in statues of the Virgin. In early Gothic sculpture she is the Queen of Heaven, majestic and dignified. In late Gothic sculpture she is girlish and human, with none of the semidivine characteristics of the earlier period. In literature the break is shown by the difference between the two parts of a famous poem, *Romance of the Rose.* The first part, written by Guillaume de Lorris in the 1230s, is an allegory of courtly love; the second part, written forty years later by Jean de Meung, is a satiric encyclopedia. The first part respects the ethics and conventions of upper-class society; the second part attacks the fickleness of women and the greed of the clergy and gives brief summaries of the knowledge that every educated man was supposed to possess. The discrepancy between the two parts is obvious today, but apparently it was not obvious to men of the late thirteenth century. No other poem was so popular during the later Middle Ages. It was copied and recopied in hundreds of manuscripts, and at the end of the fourteenth century Chaucer began an English translation of it. Nothing illustrates better the rise of a class of educated laymen, eager for wordly knowledge, suspicious of the clergy, and a little cynical about ideals of any kind. Such men could no longer be counted on to support the policies of the Church if those policies interfered with their interests, or even with their convenience.

The Courtly Lover ca. 1237

But be thou careful to possess
Thy soul in gentleness and grace
Kindly of heart and bright of face
Towards all men, be they great or small. . . .
Watch well thy lips, that they may be
Ne'er stained with ill-timed ribaldry. . . .

Have special care
To honor dames as thou dost fare
Thy worldly ways, and shouldst thou hear
Calumnious speech of them, no fear
Have thou to bid men hold their peace. . . .
Above all else beware of pride. . . .
Let him who would in love succeed
To courteous word wed noble deed.

And next remember that, above
All else, gay heart inspireth love.
If thou shouldst know some cheerful play
Or game to wile dull hours away
My counsel is, neglect it not. . . .
And much with ladies 'twill advance
Thy suit, if well thou break a lance
For who in arms his own doth hold
Winneth acceptance manifold.
And if a voice strong, sweet and clear
Thou hast, and dames desire to hear
Thee sing, seek not to make excuse.

From Guillaume de Lorris, *Romance of the Rose*, Part I, trans. by F. S. Ellis (London: Dent, 1900), Vol. I, ll. 2184–2291.

ENGLAND, FRANCE, AND THE PAPACY

In England and France the central government grew stronger than ever in the last quarter of the thirteenth century. Edward I of England (1272–1307) was determined to increase his power but clever enough to retain the support of most members of the propertied classes. He seems to have had two main objectives: first, to restore royal authority after the weak reign of his father, Henry III; and second, to make himself supreme ruler of the British Isles. He achieved his first goal through sheer force of personality, hard work, and intelligent selection of officials. Edward's royal rages were terrifying—the dean of St. Paul's dropped dead of fright during a dispute with him—and few men dared to contradict him openly. There was less reason to contradict him than there had been to oppose his father. Edward's policies were on the whole successful, especially during the first part of his reign. His avoidance of continental entanglements and his concentration on the conquest of Wales and Scotland harmonized with the desires of the aristocracy. As a result, Edward controlled his administration

Scene from a manuscript of *Romance of the Rose*. The lover enters the garden in which he will catch his first glimpse of the Rose.

and, unlike his father, was not dominated by a baronial council.

He was less successful in attaining his second objective. He did complete the conquest of Wales, which had been begun long ago by the barons of William the Conqueror. He replaced the last native prince of Wales with his own infant son, thereby creating a precedent that has endured to the present day. But Scotland proved more troublesome. Edward first tried to install a puppet king, but when his candidate proved less subservient than he had hoped he deposed him and tried to rule the country directly. But Edward could not keep a big enough army in Scotland to suppress all dissent, and the Scots rebelled, first under William Wallace and then under Robert Bruce. The rebellion was still raging when Edward died, and the Scots won their independence at Bannockburn in 1314.

Edward I and Parliament

Outside his own island, Edward had to resist an attempt by the king of France to take over the duchy of Aquitaine, the last French holding of the English royal family. Edward's wars cost huge sums of money and kept him very busy—two reasons why he made greater use of Parliament than any of his predecessors. With all the important men in the kingdom present at meetings of Parliament, Edward could get their advice on policy, settle difficult legal cases, make statutes, and obtain grants of taxes. He could probably have done all this outside Par-

Edward I of England (1272–1307) on his throne (illustration from a fourteenth-century manuscript).

liament, but it was more efficient to take care of everything at one time and in one place. Moreover, Parliament had great prestige; it was the highest court in the kingdom, and it spoke for the community of the realm. England, unlike other countries, was so thoroughly united that decisions made in a single central assembly were accepted as binding on all men. Thus it was clearly advantageous to obtain the sanction of Parliament for as many decisions as possible. Edward lost nothing by following this policy, for he controlled Parliament as effectively as he did every other branch of government. He could not have foreseen that he was building up a powerful institution that might some day develop a will of its own.

Representatives of counties and towns came before the king in 1275, but for the next twenty years Edward summoned such representatives only sporadically. The essential element in Parliament was still the Council, composed of high officials, bishops, and barons. But in 1295 Edward summoned representatives to a very full meeting (the "Model Parliament"), and from that time on they were frequently present. Again, Edward's decision seems to have been prompted by the desire to save time and trouble. Legally, baronial approval was probably enough to validate his new laws and new taxes, but in practice it was necessary to win the support of the knights and burgesses as well. They were the men who, as sheriffs and mayors, would have to enforce the new laws, and they were the men from whose ranks tax collectors would have to be appointed. There were obvious advantages in bringing representatives of all the counties and towns together at a meeting of Parliament where they could listen to the great men of the realm discuss the king's needs.

These representatives had not yet joined together in an organized body, and their role seems to have been largely passive: "to hear and to obey," as some of the early summonses put it. Such opposition as there was in Parliament came from the barons. On one notable occasion in 1297, when Edward had pushed a new tax through at a very small meeting of the Council, the barons protested and forced the king to promise that in the future he would levy taxes only "with the common assent of the whole kingdom." This was not quite an admission that only Parliament could grant taxes, but it certainly implied that the assent of a large number of people was needed; and clearly the easiest way to obtain such assent was in Parliament. The barons hesitated to grant taxes on their own responsibility and were usually anxious to get the endorsement of at least the county representatives. And when, in the last years of the reign, the barons sent petitions to Edward asking for government reform, they invited the representatives of both counties and towns to join them. In these ways the representatives gradually became caught up in the work of Parliament, though their position was still much inferior to that of the barons.

France Under Philip the Fair

In France, which was less unified politically than England, the growth of royal power followed a different course. The French barons were still struggling to preserve their local rights of government and their exemptions from the authority of royal officials. Not particularly interested in controlling the central government in Paris, they simply wanted to keep it from interfering with their lands and their subjects. The chief problem of the French king was not to keep the barons from dominating his council but to see that his orders were enforced in their lands.

This problem came to a head in the reign of Philip the Fair (Philip IV, 1285–1314), the grandson of St. Louis. Like his grandfather, Philip was pious, upright in his private life, and imbued with a sense of the divine mission of the French monarchy. But he was narrow-minded where St. Louis had been magnanimous, and grasping where St. Louis had been merely firm. The number of bureaucrats grew enormously during his reign, and Philip encouraged them in their efforts to expand royal authority. He was willing to condone any expedient to break the power of a local ruler who tried to retain a semi-independent status. Lesser vassals could not resist, but the more powerful men were indignant. It is not surprising that Philip spent a large part of his reign warring with his greatest vassals, including the king of England (as Duke of Aquitaine) and the Count of Flanders. He gained some land from both, but he never took the rich textile cities of Bruges and Ghent from Flanders, or the flourishing port of Bordeaux from Aquitaine.

Philip the Fair had a harder time than Edward I in raising money to pay for his wars. The French had never been subjected to a general tax, whereas the English had been afflicted with national taxes since the end of the twelfth century. Moreover, France was so divided that no central assembly like the English Parliament could impose a uniform tax on the whole country. Instead, royal agents had to negotiate with each region, and often with each lord or each town within each region. This cumbersome system consumed a great deal of time and reduced the yield. France was at least four times larger than England in both area and population, but it is doubtful whether Philip enjoyed any larger tax revenue than did Edward I.

These difficulties in collecting taxes explain some of the military weakness of France during the next hundred years. They also explain why the French representative assembly, the Estates General, never became as powerful as the English Parliament. Philip, as we shall see, was the first French king to call representatives to meetings at Paris. But he never asked them for a grant of taxes, for he knew that the country at large would pay little attention to the decision of a central assembly. This lack of any real power over taxation remained one of the chief weaknesses of the Estates General. Conversely, tax negotiations with local leaders and assemblies, though tedious, in the long run gave the ruler a free hand in imposing levies. It was easy to play one region off against another, or to threaten isolated areas that could not count on outside support. The royal bureaucracy was so persistent and skillful in conducting these negotiations that sooner or later it succeeded in breaking down most of the regional resistance to taxation.

Thus England was a strongly united country in which the king and the propertied classes cooperated in carrying out policies that they both approved. France was united more by the royal bureaucracy than by common interests, but the propertied classes in France were on the whole ready to trust the king on policy matters. And in both England and France some of the ideas that distinguish the modern sovereign state were beginning to appear: the welfare of the state was the greatest good; the defense of the realm was the greatest necessity; opposition to duly constituted authority was the greatest evil. As one of Philip's lawyers put it: "All men, clergy and laity alike, are bound to contribute to the defense of the realm." People who were beginning to think in these terms were not likely to be impressed by papal appeals and exhortations.

The Struggle with Boniface VIII

The pope at this time was Boniface VIII (1294-1303), an able canon lawyer and a veteran of the political conflicts endemic to Italy. Sensing that the new type of secular authority developing in the West would be more dangerous to the Church than the medieval Empire had ever been, he tried to reassert the superiority of ecclesiastical interests and the independence of the Church. He made no claim that had not already been made by his predecessors, but the climate of opinion had changed since the days of Gregory VII and Innocent III. With the shift in basic loyalties from the Church to the state, many people now believed that their chief duty was to support their king rather than to obey the pope. As a result, Boniface was defeated in a head-on clash with the kings of England and France—a blow from which the medieval Church never recovered.

The issue was clear-cut: were the clergy to be treated as ordinary subjects of secular rulers, or were they responsible only to the pope? Specifically, could they be taxed for defense of the realm without the pope's consent? As we have seen, thirteenth-century rulers could not run their governments without taxes, and it was always a temptation to tap the resources of the Church. By imposing taxes on the Church for political cru-

The Issue Between State and Church   1302

Boniface VIII says in the Bull Unam Sanctam:

Both the spiritual sword and the material sword are in the power of the Church. But the latter is to be used for the Church, the former by her; the former by the priest, the latter by kings and captains, but by the assent and permission of the priest. The one sword, then, should be under the other, and temporal authority subject to spiritual power. . . . If, therefore, the earthly power err, it shall be judged by the spiritual power. . . . Finally, we declare, state, define and pronounce that it is altogether necessary to salvation for every human creature to be subject to the Roman pontiff.

◇   ◇   ◇

One of Philip's ministers, speaking for the king, says:

The pope pretends that we are subject to him in the temporal government of our states and that we hold the crown from the Apostolic See. Yes, this kingdom of France which, with the help of God, our ancestors . . . created—this kingdom which they have until now so wisely governed—it appears that it is not from God alone, as everyone has always believed, that we hold it, but from the pope!

From *Select Documents of European History*, ed. by R. G. D. Laffan (London: Methuen, 1930), p. 117; from C. V. Langlois, *St. Louis, Philippe le Bel, et les derniers Capetiens directs* (Paris: Hachette, 1911), pp. 149–50.

sades, the popes had suggested that the clergy might also be taxes for purely secular conflicts. And so, when Edward I and Philip the Fair drifted into a war over Aquitaine in 1294, they both asked their clergy for a grant of taxes. They were outraged when Boniface prohibited these grants in 1296. Both Edward and Philip succeeded in stirring up public opinion against the clergy as disloyal members of the community. Both kings seized ecclesiastical property and forbade the transfer of money to Rome. Edward went further and virtually outlawed the English clergy. In the end, the harassed churchmen of both countries begged the pope to reconsider and remove his ban. Boniface did so, grudgingly but effectively, in 1298.

This was bad enough, but worse was to follow. In 1301 Philip the Fair imprisoned a French bishop on a flimsy charge of treason and refused to obey a papal order to free him immediately. When Boniface threatened to punish the king and his agents, Philip countered by calling a great assembly at Paris in 1302. This assembly contained representatives of the three Estates, or classes, of clergy, nobility, and bourgeoisie; it was the prototype of the French Estates General. The assembly gave its full support to the king and emphatically rejected any papal authority over France. When the dispute continued, Philip, through his minister, Guillaume de Nogaret, accused Boniface of immorality and heresy and appealed to a general council to condemn him. Local assemblies throughout France endorsed Philip's plan—the nobility and townsmen enthusiastically, the clergy reluctantly but almost unanimously. Philp undoubtedly resorted to pressure to ensure this response, but he clearly had the backing of his people, as subsequent events were to show. The people may not have believed all the accusations, but they felt that a worldly Church was probably corrupt and that the pope should not interfere with French internal affairs.

Assured of support at home, Philip now launched a very risky venture. In 1303 he sent Nogaret to Italy with a small force to join some of the pope's Italian enemies. Together they staged a surprise attack on Boniface's summer home at Anagni and succeeded in capturing the pope. They probably hoped to take him back to France as a prisoner to await trial by a church council, but they had no chance to put their plan into effect. The Italians had no great love for the pope, but they cared even less for the French. A counterattack by the people of Anagni and neighboring regions freed Boniface from his captors. He took refuge in Rome and began to prepare bulls of excommunication against the French. But Boniface was an elderly man, and the shock of capture had proved too much for him. He died before he could act.

Force had been used against earlier popes, but for the last two centuries the Church had always been able to retaliate and put the aggressor in a worse position than before. After the assault at Anagni, however, the Church did not dare to react strongly. No one, either inside or outside France, seemed disturbed by what had happened, and Nogaret remained one of Philip's favored ministers. Boniface's successor was not a strong man, and when he died within a year the cardinals surrendered completely. They elected a French archbishop as pope, a man who was not even a member of their group and a man who was clearly agreeable to Philip, if not suggested by him. This new pope, Clement V, yielded at every turn to the king of France. He absolved Nogaret and declared that Philip had been prompted by laudable motives in his attack on Boniface. By failing to defend itself—indeed, by praising the aggressor—the papacy revealed that it had surrendered its leadership and its control over public opinion. From this time on the pope could influence and advise, but he could no longer command as Innocent III had done.

The Popes at Avignon

The pliability of Clement V soon led him to an even more momentous deci-

sion. After he was elected pope, he set off for Rome, but, dismayed by the disorder in Italy, he paused in the Rhône Valley. The papacy was now paying for its stubborn opposition to the establishment of a strong Italian kingdom; the warring city-states had made even the Papal States unsafe. Somehow Clement never got started again. France was pleasant, and Italy was dangerous; moreover, the French king and the French cardinals were urging him to stay on. And so Clement settled down at Avignon on the Rhône, where he and his successors were to reside for over seventy years.

This long period of exile in France (1305–78) is known in church history as the Babylonian Captivity.* The papacy did not lose its independence, for Avignon was papal territory and the surrounding country was technically part of the Empire and not of France. No subse-

*This is an allusion to the exile of the Jews to Babylon under Nebuchadnezzar in the sixth century B.C. The original Babylonian Captivity lasted only fifty years.

Pope Boniface VIII receives St. Louis of Toulouse, a grandnephew of St. Louis of France and son of Charles II of Naples. The representation of the pope corresponds to other pictures of him. Fresco by Ambrogio Lorenzetti, Siena (ca. 1330).

quent Avignonese pope was as subservient to the French king as Clement V had
been; most of them were able, even
forceful, administrators of the affairs of
the Church. And yet, though the papacy
did not lose its independence, it lost its
reputation. Many people, especially the
English, were convinced that the pope
was a servant of the French king, in spite
of evidence to the contrary. Many more
believed that no true successor of Peter
would abandon Rome for the "sinful city
of Avignon." A spiritual leader was not
supposed to be swayed by motives of
expediency or fear of discomfort.
Charges of worldliness and corruption
leveled against the Church seemed more
justified than ever.

Actually, although the Avignonese
popes were not especially corrupt, they
were primarily administrators rather than
religious leaders. Their chief accomplishments were to perfect the Church's
legal system and its financial organization. To men who were already critical,
this very success looked like a proliferation of red tape and a perfection of
methods of extortion. No one could obtain anything from the papacy without
engaging in long and expensive lawsuits
or paying heavy fees to everyone from
doorkeeper to cardinal. So drastically did
the prestige of the pope sink that he was
forced to pay tribute to leaders of mercenary troops. Leadership in Europe had
clearly passed from the papacy to secular
rulers; what they would do with it remained to be seen.

Rome without a pope is pictured as a widow mourning
her past glory. From a eulogy to Rome written before the
return of the papacy.

Suggestions for Further Reading

Note: Asterisk denotes a book available in paperback edition.

St. Louis The royal councilor Joinville's *Life of St. Louis* (Everyman's and other editions) is one of our chief
sources for the life of King Louis IX of France and for an understanding of the spirit of the thirteenth
century. There is excellent material on the growth of monarchical power and the development of
institutions under St. Louis in C. Petit-Dutaillis, *Feudal Monarchy in France and England* (1936), and in
E. Lavisse, ed., *Histoire de France*, Vol. III, Part 2 (1901). J. R. Strayer, *The Administration of Normandy
under St. Louis* (1932), is a study of one of the most important provinces of the French monarchy and
the Norman influence on that monarchy.

Henry III and England

There is a vast amount of significant detail in the contemporary Matthew of Paris, *Chronicle*, trans. by J. A. Giles (1852), a valuable framework for events in the period from 1235 to 1273. F. M. Powicke, *King Henry III and the Lord Edward*, 2 vols. (1947), is an excellent study of the political and social history of England at the time and the best biography of a medieval king. There is documentary material on early representative assemblies in C. Stephenson and F. G. Marcham, *Sources of English Constitutional History* (1937); the best commentary is F. Pollock and F. W. Maitland, *History of English Law*, Vol. II (1923). R. F. Treharne, *The Baronial Plan of Reform, 1258–1263* (1932), has a good account of the aristocratic reaction to royal rule presented as a great constitutional revolution. F. M. Powicke, *The Thirteenth Century* (1953), is a fine study of the period, with a critical bibliography.

The Papal–Hohenstaufen Feud

Philippe of Novara's *The Wars of Frederick II Against the Ibelins*, trans. by J. L. La Monte (1936), has primary material on the career and imperialism of Frederick II and presents a vivid picture of the life and ideas of the thirteenth-century knights who settled in the Latin Orient. E. Kantorowicz, *Frederick II* (1931), encompassing the broad and complex field of papal–Hohenstaufen relations, is a classic study in historical biography. There is a broad survey of politics, religion, literature, and art in H. D. Sedgwick, *Italy in the Thirteenth Century*, 2 vols. (1912). W. F. Butler, *The Lombard Communes* (1906), has information on the Lombard Communes in the Hohenstaufen wars. T. C. Van Cleve, *The Emperor Frederick II* (1972), can also be highly recommended.

Scholasticism: St. Thomas Aquinas

The most useful edition of St. Thomas' writings is *Basic Writings of St. Thomas Aquinas*, ed. by A. C. Pegis (1944), which contains a good selection of the most significant and widely read treatises. F. C. Copleston, *Aquinas** (1955), is a very good introduction to Aquinas' ideas, and G. Leff, *Medieval Thought** (1958), shows the influence of Aquinas' thought on the thirteenth century. M. De Wulf, *Philosophy and Civilization in the Middle Ages** (1922), describes how the thought of the period was intimately connected with the whole of medieval civilization. The best scholarly treatment of scholastic philosophy is in E. Gilson, *History of Christian Philosophy in the Middle Ages* (1954), which has valuable bibliographic material. E. Panofsky brilliantly shows the parallel development of art and philosophy in the thirteenth century in *Gothic Architecture and Scholasticism** (1954).

Edward I and Parliament

T. F. Tout, *Edward the First* (1893), is an old but sound biography of Edward with a good account of the beginnings of legislation and the English Parliament. A good introduction to the development of Parliament is G. L. Haskins, *Growth of English Representative Government** (1948). D. Pasquet, *Essay on the Origins of the House of Commons* (1925), is an excellent study of the evolution of Parliament from the king's court. There is much useful material on Parliament in B. Wilkinson, *Constitutional History of Medieval England*, Vol. III (1958). See also the titles by Stephenson and Marcham, and Pollock and Maitland mentioned above.

Philip the Fair and Boniface VIII

There is valuable material on the reign of Philip the Fair in E. Lavisse, ed., *Histoire de France*, Vol. III, Part 2 (1901). J. R. Strayer and C. H. Taylor, *Studies in Early French Taxation* (1939), explore the relationship between finances and early representative assemblies under Philip the Fair and Philip V. There is material on the reign of Philip the Fair in the books by Fawtier and Petit-Dutaillis cited in the bibliography at the end of Chapter 10. C. T. Wood, *Philip the Fair and Boniface VIII* (1967), has interesting extracts on the conflict between king and pope. See also the articles on Philip the Fair and the development of the French government in J. R. Strayer, *Medieval Statecraft* (1971).

H. K. Mann, *Lives of the Popes in the Middle Ages*, Vol. XVIII (1932), is a lengthy study of Boniface VIII and his pontificate from a Catholic point of view. A. C. Flick, *The Decline of the Medieval Church*, Vol. I (1930), has material on Boniface from a Protestant point of view. Though interesting reading, both are rather provincial in interpretation. The best study of this pope is T. S. R. Boase, *Boniface VIII* (1933), which is a sympathetic but far more critical treatment.

Clement V and the Babylonian Captivity

W. E. Lunt, *Papal Revenues in the Middle Ages*, 2 vols. (1934), contains considerable source material on the bureaucracy and finances of the papal Curia. An amusing, if infuriating, study of the period of the Babylonian Captivity is L. E. Binns, *The Decline and Fall of the Medieval Papacy* (1934), which was written as a supplement to the great history of E. Gibbon. See also G. Mollat, *The Popes at Avignon** (1965). A serious introduction to this period, M. Creighton, *A History of the Papacy from the Great Schism to the Sack of Rome*, Vol. I (1919), traces the reasons for the decline of papal power. G. Barraclough, *The Medieval Papacy** (1968), explores the historical background of the papacy.

13 The End of the
Middle Ages

The fourteenth and early fifteenth centuries were a time of confusion and chaos in the West. Decade after decade everything seemed to go wrong: economic depression, war, rebellion, and plague harried the people, and neither ecclesiastical nor secular governments seemed capable of easing their distress. At times the whole structure of European society seemed to be crumbling, as it had at the end of the Roman Empire. Yet the Europe that emerged from this time of troubles went on to conquer the world. The science and technology, the navies and the armies, the governments and the business organizations that were to give Europe unquestioned supremacy for four centuries—all were taking shape in the fourteenth and fifteenth centuries. The dire stretch of history marked by the Hundred Years' War, the Black Death, and the Great Schism seems an unlikely seedbed for these great accomplishments. We are struck by the decay of the medieval way of life rather than by the almost imperceptible emergence of new ideas and new forms of organization. But we should not forget that the new ideas were there, that the people of western Europe never quite lost faith in their destiny, never quite gave up striving for a more orderly and prosperous society. There was confusion and uncertainty, but not the complete disintegration that had followed the collapse of the Roman Empire.

ECONOMIC WEAKNESS AND POLITICAL FAILURE

The most obvious cause of the troubles of the last medieval centuries was economic depression. Given the techniques then prevalent, by 1300 western Europe had about reached the limit of its capacity to produce food and manufactured goods, and, consequently, its ability to increase its trade. There were no more reserves of fertile land to bring into cultivation; in fact, a good deal of the land that was already being cultivated was marginal or submarginal in quality. For many years there was no significant increase in industrial output; production

might shift from one center to another, but the total output remained about the same. Population ceased to grow; most towns barely held their own, and some, especially in southern France, declined sharply. The Italian towns fared better; they increased their share of Mediterranean trade and of the production of luxury textiles. But even Italy had economic difficulties during the middle years of the fourteenth century when northern rulers, like Edward III of England, repudiated the debts they owed Italian bankers. In short, until Europe found new sources of wealth and new markets both governments and individuals were constantly on the verge of bankruptcy.

Economic stagnation created a climate of opinion hostile to innovation and efforts to cooperate for the common welfare. Each individual, each community, each class was eager to preserve the monopolies and privileges that guaranteed it some share of the limited wealth available. It was during these years that the towns and gilds adopted their most restrictive regulations. Ordinary laborers found it difficult to become master workmen; master workmen were discouraged from devising new methods of production. Fortunately the attempt to preserve the status quo was thwarted by the weakness of government and by the ingenuity of enterprising businessmen. Some new techniques were introduced, and some new industries were established. But capital was limited, and it took many years before new techniques or new products had much impact on the economy.

Economic weakness helps explain the weakness of most governments. Rulers were always short of money, for the old taxes brought in less and less revenue and it was very difficult to impose new taxes. Salaries of government officials were insufficient, because of continuing inflation, and were often years in arrears. Most officials supported themselves by taking fees, gifts, and bribes from private citizens; they began to think of their offices as private possessions. Men with this attitude could keep up the routine, which was an important element of stability in a troubled society. But they showed much less zeal in perfecting their

Manuscript illustration of the crucial point in the meeting of Richard II with the main body of the rebels during the Peasants' Rebellion of 1381. Wat Tyler is being struck down by one of Richard's men.

administrative techniques than had their thirteenth-century predecessors.

Financial difficulties were not the only cause of weakness in government. The assertion of sovereignty by secular rulers at the end of the thirteenth century had been somewhat premature. They had neither the ability to make realistic plans for the welfare of their people nor the authority to impose such remedies as they did devise. Most secular rulers could think only of increasing their revenues by conquering new lands. Such a policy solved no problems; it merely postponed them for the victor and aggravated them for the vanquished. With governments discredited by futile and costly wars, many men lost faith in their political leaders and turned to rebellion and civil war.

The leaders of revolt, however, showed no more ability than the kings and princes against whom they were rebelling. Many of the leaders were members of the landed nobility who still had wealth and influence even though they had lost their old rights of feudal government. But while they found it easy enough to gain power, they did not know how to exercise the power that they gained. Their main purpose was to preserve their own privileges or to direct government revenues to their own pockets—again, policies that solved no basic problems. Impatient with the routine tasks of administration, the aristocracy usually split into quarreling factions. The upper classes sometimes used parliamentary forms to justify their acts, but this only made representative assemblies appear to be vehicles of factionalism and disorder. When the desire for stronger government finally arose once again, the kings found it easy to abolish or suspend assemblies; only in England did representative assemblies retain any vitality.

Other classes performed no better than the nobles. The bourgeoisie thought in terms of local or, at most, regional interests, and they were inept in running their own municipal governments. The townsmen split into factions—old families against new families, international traders against local merchants, rich against poor—and the faction in power tried to ruin its opponents by unequal taxation or discriminatory economic leg-

Lawlessness in Fifteenth-Century England

John Paston was the son of a royal judge and well-to-do landowner in Norfolk. His father had bought the manor of Gresham, but in 1448 Lord Molyns claimed it, though he had no right to it. John Paston tried to settle the claim peacefully, but Molyns' men seized the manor house and Paston moved to another "mansion." While he was seeking help from his friends, Paston's wife was left to defend their home. She wrote her husband this letter late in 1448.

Right worshipful husband, I recommend me to you and pray you to get some cross-bows and windlasses to wind them with and arrows, for your house here is so low that no one could shoot out of it with a long-bow, even if we had great need. I suppose you could get these things from Sir John Falstoff [a friend of the Pastons]. And also I would like you to get two or three short pole-axes to guard the doors and as many jacks [padded leather jackets] as you can.

Partridge [leader of Molyns' men] and his fellows are sore afraid that you will attack them again, and they have made great preparations, as I am told. They have made bars to bar the doors cross-wise, and they have made loop-holes on every side of the house to shoot out of both with bows and with hand-guns. The holes made for hand-guns are scarcely knee-high from the floor and no one can shoot out of them with a hand bow.

[Margaret Paston apparently took all this as a matter of course; she then turned to an ordinary shopping list.] I pray you to buy me a pound of almonds and a pound of sugar and some cloth to make clothes for your children and a yard of black broad-cloth for a hood for me.

The Trinity have you in His keeping and send you Godspeed in all your affairs.

Put into modern English from Norman Davis, ed., *Paston Letters* (Oxford: Clarendon Press, 1958), pp. 9–10.

islation. The result was that local self-government collapsed in town after town. Venice remained powerful and independent under a merchant oligarchy, as did some of the German trading towns. But more often a tyrant seized power, as in certain towns in Italy, or else the officials of a king or a powerful noble took over control of the towns.

As for the peasants, they were far more restive and unhappy than they had been in the thirteenth century. With no new lands to clear and no new jobs to be had in the towns, they had little hope of improving their lot. Some of them managed to ease the burden of taxes and of payments to landlords by renegotiating their leases or by moving from one estate to another, but for most of them this road to advancement was too tedious and uncertain. The peasants rebelled in country after country, killing landlords, burning records, and demanding that payments for their land be lowered or abolished altogether. These rebellions were hopeless; untrained and poorly armed peasants were no match for an aristocracy with a strong military tradition. But the fact that the peasants did rebel reveals the despair and the tendency to violence that marked the end of the Middle Ages.

THE TROUBLES OF THE CHURCH

The failure of secular government would not have been so serious had the Church been able to regain its old leadership. The people of western Europe were still Christians, and they knew that they were not living up to the precepts of their faith. They multiplied religious ceremonies and appeals for the intercession of the saints; they flocked to revival meetings to repent their sins with tears and trembling. But the Church failed to remedy the disorders of western society; in fact, the Church was infected with the same evils that beset secular government. Repentant sinners returned to their careers of violence and fraud because no one could show them any other way to survive.

The Great Schism

The leadership of the Church was further impaired by the Great Schism that followed the Babylonian Captivity. The popes at Avignon, realizing that their exile was impairing their authority, had made several halfhearted efforts to return to Rome. Finally, in 1377, Gregory XI actually moved back to Italy, but he was

Miniature paintings of a fourteenth-century pewterer turning a jug on a lathe (left), and a locksmith (right), from the Guild Book of the Twelve Brothers' Foundation in Nuremberg.

Land giving allegiance to Rome

Land giving allegiance to Avignon

Shifting and divided

Clement VII, set up his court at Avignon, and denounced Urban as a usurper.

Emperors such as Henry IV and Frederick Barbarossa had tried to set up antipopes, but they had never deceived secular and religious leaders. Everyone knew who the true pope was, even if the emperors supported an opponent. But this time there was no such consensus, and most of Europe was honestly bewildered. Both popes had been elected by a majority of duly appointed cardinals; if Urban had the advantage of being the first named, he also had the disadvantage of being repudiated by the very men who had elected him. Rulers could decide which pope to follow only on the basis of political expediency. France, and its ally Scotland, naturally accepted the Avignonese pope; England just as naturally supported Urban at Rome. The Spanish kingdoms backed Clement, while most of Germany and Italy held to the Roman pontiff. Both popes intrigued to gain support in hostile areas, and both created new cardinals. When Urban and Clement died, in 1389 and 1394, respectively, the rival groups of cardinals each elected a new pope, thus prolonging the Great Schism into the next century.

Though the people of western Europe were deeply distressed by the schism, they could see no way out of their troubles. Who could be sure which was the false pope and which the true one? This uncertainty weakened both the organization and the moral influence of the Church. The popes of the Captivity had at least been good administrators, but the schism made effective administration impossible. Reform in the Church's financial system was desperately needed, but a pope who controlled only half the Church could hardly afford to lose revenues or alienate supporters by abolishing profitable abuses. A divided and unreformed Church had little hope of guiding European society.

Reformers and Heretics

The state of the Church during the Captivity and the Great Schism seemed so hopeless that many men began to seek salvation through their own efforts. The mildest, and probably the most numer-

appalled by the disorder in Rome and the Papal States. He was about to return to Avignon when he died, in 1378. The Romans, with the papacy once more within their grasp, had no intention of again losing the income from pilgrims and visitors to the papal court. When the cardinals met to elect Gregory's successor, they were besieged by a howling mob demanding that they choose a Roman, or at least an Italian, pope. It is hard to estimate how effective this pressure was; certainly it had some influence. In the end the cardinals elected an Italian archbishop who took the title of Urban VI.

The cardinals may have hoped that Urban would be a pliant and cooperative pope; instead he bullied them, rejected their advice, and denounced their behavior. The majority of the cardinals were French, but even the non-French were outraged by Urban's behavior. The whole group soon fled from Rome and declared that Urban's election was void because it had taken place under duress. They proceeded to choose a new pope, a French-speaking cardinal of the family of the counts of Geneva. He took the title of

ous, group of reformers did not break openly with the Church; they simply ceased to rely on it. They formed little associations, such as the Brethren of the Common Life, to encourage one another to lead devout Christian lives and to seek direct contact with God through mystical experiences. These groups, which were especially numerous in the Rhineland and the Low Countries, produced some remarkable works of devotion, such as the *Theologia Germanica*, which influenced later reformers. They also founded schools that were to play a great role in the educational revival of the fifteenth and sixteenth centuries; Erasmus (see pp. 376–77) was educated in such a school. These mystical and contemplative reformers were looked on with some suspicion by conservative churchmen, but most of them remained within the bounds of orthodoxy.

A more radical element was not content simply to withdraw into devout groups. These men wanted a thorough-going reform of the Church, and many of them felt that only laymen could do the job. An early example of this attitude can be seen in the *Defensor pacis*, written by Marsilius of Padua about 1324. Marsilius, who like many Italians had a completely secular point of view, believed that the state should control the Church just as it controlled other organizations. If the state could regulate the behavior of doctors, it could also regulate the behavior of priests. Marsilius' book was condemned, but his ideas inspired criticism of the Church throughout the fourteenth and fifteenth centuries.

Another dangerous critic of the Church was an Oxford professor, John Wiclif (*ca.* 1320–84). At first concerned mainly with the problem of private property, including the property of the Church, Wiclif decided that the Church was being corrupted by wealth and that it would be better for everyone if church lands were taken over by kings and nobles. This position naturally pleased influential laymen and may explain why Wiclif was never punished for his unorthodox doctrines. Wiclif went on to cast doubt on the Catholic doctrine that the bread and wine in the communion service are transformed into the Body and Blood of Christ. He wound up by attacking the whole administrative structure of the Church as corrupt and largely unauthorized by the Bible. He taught that the pope could err, that the hierarchy had no absolute authority, and that kings should protect and guide the Church in their own realms.

Though Wiclif had no intention of launching a popular movement, his ideas spread rapidly beyond the scholarly circles for which he had written. By emphasizing scriptural authority, he had encouraged his followers to produce an English translation of the Bible that could be used by wandering preachers. These preachers, taking advantage of social discontent, popularized Wiclif's most radical views and gained a considerable following among the lower and middle classes in England. Some of them became social as well as religious reformers: if the Church had no right to property because it misused it, did the barons and knights

A manuscript illumination showing an antipope receiving his crown from the Devil and in turn crowning an emperor as a pledge of mutual support against the true head of the Church.

The burning of infected clothing during the Black Death (detail from a contemporary manuscript illumination).

after 1400. But the suppression was not wholly effective; the Wiclifite translation of the Bible and memories of Lollard doctrines survived until the time of the English Reformation. And the writings of John Wiclif reached as far as Bohemia, where they influenced John Hus, the great fifteenth-century opponent of the Church (see pp. 360–61).

THE BLACK DEATH

The effects of economic depression, political confusion, and religious uncertainty were intensified by terrible outbursts of plague in the middle years of the fourteenth century. The Black Death (probably bubonic plague) first appeared in Italy in the 1340s and swept through Europe during the next two decades. The worst was over by 1360, but repeated, though less severe, outbreaks throughout the next half-century kept the population from reaching its preplague numbers. Although no accurate estimate can be made of the mortality, it was especially severe in thickly populated areas. Some towns lost more than two-fifths of their inhabitants, and some monasteries almost ceased to function. Since doctors were helpless, the only way to avoid the plague was to take refuge in isolated country districts.

have any more right? Such ideas may have helped to touch off the English Peasant's Rebellion of 1381. Fear of economic radicalism may have induced the English upper classes to join with the king in suppressing the religious radicals—or Lollards, as they were called—

The panic caused by the Black Death drove the sorely tried peoples of western Europe into emotional instability. It is no accident that the bloodiest peasant rebellions and the most senseless civil wars took place after the plague, and that the witchcraft delusion, unknown in the early Middle Ages, then reached its height. This was a double delusion. Innocent men and women were falsely accused of practicing black magic, but there were people, including men of high position, who genuinely believed that they could gain their desires by making a compact with the Devil. More than anything else, the witchcraft delusion demonstrated the state of shock in which western Europe found itself at the end of the fourteenth century. The rationalism and confidence in the future that had been so apparent at the height of medieval civilization had vanished.

The Black Death in England

Then that most grievous pestilence penetrated the coastal regions by way of Southampton and came to Bristol, and people died as if the whole strength of the city were seized by sudden death. For there were few who lay in their beds more than three days or two and a half days; then that savage death snatched them about the second day. In Leicester, in the little parish of St. Leonard, more than three hundred and eighty died; in the parish of the Holy Cross, more than four hundred, and in the parish of St. Margaret, more than seven hundred. . . .

And the price of everything was cheap, because of the fear of death, there were very few who took any care for their wealth, or for anything else. For a man could buy a horse for half a mark [about 7 shillings] which before was worth forty shillings, a large fat ox for four shillings, a cow for twelve pence, a heifer for sixpence, a large fat sheep for four pence. . . . And the sheep and cattle wandered about through the fields and among the crops, and there was no one to go after them or collect them. They perished in countless numbers everywhere, for lack of watching . . . since there was such a lack of serfs and servants, that no one knew what he should do. For there is no memory of a mortality so severe and so savage. . . . In the following autumn, one could not hire a reaper for less than eight pence [per day] with food, or a mower at less than twelve pence with food.

From Henry Knighton, *Chronicle*, in *The Portable Medieval Reader*, ed. by J. B. Ross and M. M. McLaughlin (New York: Viking, 1949), pp. 218–19.

ENGLAND IN THE LATER MIDDLE AGES

Even France and England, the two strongest states in the West, were shaken by the events of the fourteenth century. They had enough momentum and solid enough administrative structures to survive as political units, but there were times when neither country had a government capable of preserving law and order. While the bureaucrats were able to keep the machinery of government running, they could not hold back the rising tide of lawlessness. Under these circumstances, the nobles regained much of the power they had lost in the thirteenth century. They tried to control policy and direct revenues to their own pockets; in England they even deposed their kings.

The expansionist policies of Edward I (see p. 267) had severely strained English resources. A reaction would have taken place in any case; it was made more acute by the character of Edward II (1307–27). So incompetent that no one respected him, Edward turned over the business of government to a series of favorites who were hated by the great lords. The barons tried the old expedient of setting up a committee to control the government, but it worked no better than it had under Henry III. Finally Edward's own wife and her lover, Mortimer, one of the lords of the turbulent lands of the Welsh frontier, led a rebellion against him. Edward was deposed in 1327 and quietly murdered a few weeks later; his young son, Edward III (1327-77), became king.

The Hundred Years' War: The First Phase

Edward III shared his barons' fondness for courtly magnificence and chivalric warfare. More popular with the aris-tocracy than his father had been, he was also more susceptible to their influence. Never quite willing to risk his popularity by forcing a showdown with the barons, he allowed them to retain a strong position in Parliament and in the Council. This is probably why he drifted into the Hundred Years' War with France. War was a policy on which he and his barons could agree, and so long as the war was successful he could avoid domestic controversies.

There were, of course, other reasons for the war. France was still trying to annex the English holdings in Aquitaine and gain full control of Flanders, which was the best market for English wool. France was aiding Scotland, which had regained its independence in the battle of Bannockburn (1314) and was in a state of almost permanent hostility with England. French and English sailors were intermittently plundering each other's ships. These frictions were enough to cause a war, but they do not quite explain why the war lasted for generations. The king persisted because he gained new and valuable territories; the barons, because

The Later Middle Ages

So violent and motley was life, that it bore the mixed smell of blood and of roses. The men of that time always oscillated between the fear of hell and the most naïve joy, between cruelty and tenderness, between harsh asceticism and insane attachment to the delights of this world . . . always running to extremes. . . .

Bad government, the cupidity and violence of the great, wars and brigandage, scarcity, misery, and pestilence—to this is contemporary history nearly reduced in the eyes of the people. The feeling of general insecurity . . . was further aggravated by the fear of hell, of sorcerers and of devils. Everywhere the flames of hatred arise and injustice reigns. Satan covers a gloomy earth with his sombre wings.

From J. Huizinga, *The Waning of the Middle Ages* (London: Arnold, 1924), pp. 18, 21.

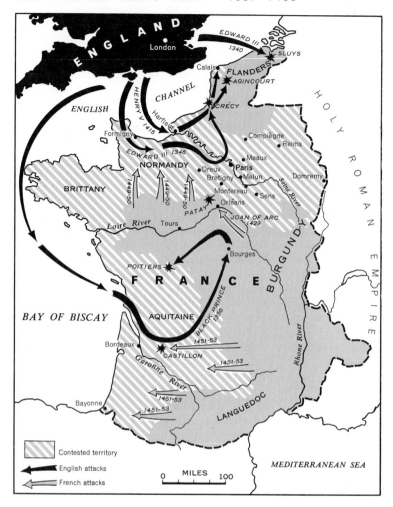

Contested territory
English attacks
French attacks

MILES
0   100

Edward had succeeded because his country was more united than France and gave him more consistent financial support, and also because he had developed new tactics for his army. He mixed companies of archers, armed with the famous English longbow, with companies of dismounted cavalry in heavy armor. A charge, by either mounted or foot soldiers, would be thrown into confusion by showers of arrows. The few men who broke through to the main line could be easily dealt with by the troops in heavy armor. The only weakness in Edward's formation was that it was essentially defensive; it could not be used for a charge. Only when portable firearms were invented at the end of the fifteenth century was it possible to use missile weapons for an attack.

Like many other generals, Edward found it easier to win victories than to profit from them. The French, with no intention of fulfilling the terms of the treaty they had signed, launched a war of attrition that gradually exhausted their enemies. England simply did not have enough men or enough resources to garrison territories larger than Edward's whole kingdom. The French learned to avoid headlong rushes at large English armies and concentrated instead on picking off isolated garrisons and small detachments. As a result, the English had lost a large part of their conquests by the time of Edward III's death in 1377.

Rebellion and Revolution

Military misfortunes abroad led to bickering at home. There was a complete failure of leadership during Edward's last years. The king was sinking into senility, and the Black Prince, crippled by disease, died a year before his father. One of Edward's younger sons, John of Gaunt, Duke of Lancaster, had more authority than anyone else, but he was disliked and distrusted by many members of the aristocracy. He was accused, with some justice, of associating with a group of corrupt officeholders and, with less justice, of coveting the throne. The duke's taste in art and literature was excellent—he gave a government job and a pension to Geoffrey Chaucer—but inter-

they acquired booty and profitable military commands.

After a bad start, caused largely by financial difficulties, Edward came up with an amazing string of victories. He gained control of the Channel in a naval battle at Sluys (1340) and nearly annihilated the French army at Crécy (1346). Then he went on to take Calais, which remained a port of entry for English armies for two centuries. Ten years later, Edward's son, the Black Prince (also named Edward), crushed another French army at Poitiers and took the French king prisoner. In the treaty that followed this victory the French agreed to pay a huge ransom for their king and to cede about two-fifths of their country to the English.

1066	1154	1399	1461	1485
Norman Kings	House of Plantagenet	House of Lancaster	House of York	

1454
Wars of the Roses

est in the arts has seldom added to the stature of a politician in English public opinion.

The new king, Richard II (1377–99), the son of the Black Prince, was only a child when he inherited the throne. During the first part of his reign England was governed by successive groups of barons. These men did nothing to distinguish themselves; their inefficiency and bad judgment led directly to the Peasants' Rebellion of 1381. The war in France was still costing large sums of money, even though the English were now almost entirely on the defensive. Casting about for a new source of revenue, the government hit on the idea of a poll tax, a levy of a few pennies on each English subject. This brought to a peak all the smoldering resentment of the peasants and the poorer inhabitants of the towns. They were already suffering from economic stagnation; now they felt that they were being asked to carry an unfair share of the tax burden. All southern England exploded in rebellion. Peasants and artisans burned tax rolls and manorial records, killed unpopular officials and landlords, and finally marched on London. The barons, taken off guard, scurried about trying to raise an army. Meanwhile Richard had to stand by and watch the rebels occupy London, burn the palace of the Duke of Lancaster, and murder the chancellor and the treasurer of England. Forced into humiliating negotiations with the rebel leaders, he was obliged to promise complete forgiveness for all past offenses, the abolition of serfdom, and the remission of almost all manorial dues.

The rebellion was weakened when its leader, Wat Tyler, was killed during a conference with the king. It was suppressed as soon as the barons could get their troops together, for the poorly armed peasants and townsmen were no match for professional soldiers. The king repudiated his promises and apparently all was as before. Actually, the rebellion had two important results. First, serfdom declined steadily after 1381, and by 1500 there were almost no serfs left in England. Second, Richard had seen a convincing demonstration of the inefficiency and clumsiness of baronial government. It is not surprising that when he came of age in 1386 he tried to increase royal authority and to concentrate all power in his own hands.

Richard showed considerable skill in his efforts to strengthen the monarchy,

Richard II, from the portrait by Beauneven of Valenciennes (1398) in Westminster Abbey.

but he made two fatal mistakes. The barons might have tolerated the loss of political power, but Richard threatened their economic position as well by confiscating the property of those he distrusted. Moreover, Richard failed to build up a powerful army under his own control. Most of the armed forces in the country were private companies paid by the king but recruited and commanded by barons and knights. This system had developed during the early years of the Hundred Years' War, when it had seemed easier to allow members of the aristocracy to raise troops than for the government to deal with the tedious problem of recruiting. Any lord with a taste for fighting could maintain his own little army at government expense, a situation that encouraged disorder and rebellion. The king's personal bodyguard was no match for the combined forces of several great barons. As a result, Richard was helpless when Henry of Lancaster, son of John of Gaunt and cousin of the king, rebelled in 1399. Henry himself had been driven into exile and stripped of his lands, and he was supported by many members of the aristocracy who feared the same fate. Richard was deposed and

died in prison, and Henry of Lancaster mounted the throne as Henry IV (1399–1413).

The Hundred Years' War: The Second Phase

The Lancastrian kings, who ruled from 1399 to 1461, never quite lived down the violence by which they had come to power. Their title was faulty—there were other descendants of Edward III with a better claim—and they seldom had the unanimous support of the great lords. Henry IV had difficulty suppressing two serious rebellions, and Henry V (1413–22) tried to unite the country by the dangerous expedient of reviving the Hundred Years' War. He was a brilliant general, as he revealed in his victory at Agincourt (1415); he was the first commander of a European army to use siege artillery on a large scale. By securing the alliance of the Duke of Burgundy, a disgruntled French prince, he was able to force the French king, Charles VI, to accept a treaty in which Charles disinherited his son, married his daughter to Henry, and agreed that any son born of this union was to be king of France. The

The battle of Formigny, which was fought at the end of the Hundred Years' War. Notice that the English (right) are on foot and are flanked by bowmen, while the French are delivering a cavalry charge. Usually the English won in such circumstances, but this time they were defeated.

next year both Charles and Henry died, and a one-year-old baby, Henry VI, became king of England and France.

Henry V, with all his ability, would have found it hard to control two kingdoms; Henry VI never had a chance. His long minority was disastrous. In England his uncles and cousins, supported by baronial factions, quarreled bitterly. In France, the disinherited son of Charles VI claimed the throne as Charles VII and carried on the war from the unconquered country south of the Loire. The English pressed him hard, but just as his cause seemed hopeless he was saved by the appearance of Joan of Arc. To the English, Joan was "a limb of the devil." But she stirred the French to drive the English back from the Loire and to win an important victory at Patay (1429). After these successes it hardly mattered that Joan fell into English hands and was burned as a witch, for the courage and enthusiasm with which she had inspired the French survived her. The Burgundians abandoned the English alliance, and the English position in France deteriorated steadily. Forts and provinces fell one by one, until by 1453 only Calais was left. And so after twelve decades of fighting and plundering, the war at last came to an end.

The Wars of the Roses

When the English could no longer blame Joan of Arc for their defeats, they began to blame one another. Commanders were accused of treason and incompetence; some were executed and others exiled. Henry VI, even when he came of age, could do nothing to stop the feuds among the great lords. Humble in spirit and weak in mind, he was dominated by a French wife whom most of the aristocracy disliked. The English barons had acquired the habit of violence, and a decade after the end of the Hundred Years' War they plunged England into the series of civil conflicts known as the Wars of the Roses.* The ostensible reason for these wars was an attempt by

*Long after the wars, the legend arose that the Red Rose was the badge of Lancaster and the White Rose, of York. This error led to the name Wars of the Roses.

some of the barons to replace the Lancastrian king with the Duke of York, who represented the oldest line of descent from Edward III. The attempt succeeded, but the Yorkist kings, who ruled from 1461 to 1485, had almost as much trouble with the barons as their Lancastrian predecessors. In fact, the Wars of the Roses were the last uprising of the barons, the last attempt of a small clique to take over the central government and use it for their own purpose. The wars destroyed everyone who took part in them—the House of Lancaster, the House of York, and many of the great noble families. It was left for the half-alien Tudors, indirect and illegitimate descendants of John of Gaunt, to restore order in England.

England made some economic gains toward the end of this period in spite of the failure of political leadership. The kings of the fourteenth and fifteenth centuries were no economists, but they were able to grasp one simple fact—that so long as England produced only raw materials, she would never grow very rich. From Edward III on, they encouraged the migration of textile workers to England and protected the growing English textile industry. They also encouraged the development of English shipping. The results should not be exaggerated, for even at the end of the fifteenth century England could not rival Flanders in textiles or Italy in shipping. But a good start had been made; England had come a long way from being a country whose chief economic function was to raise raw wool to be carried in foreign ships to Flemish looms.

The Development of Parliament

There were also two important institutional developments: the rise of the justices of the peace and the continuing growth of Parliament. The justices of the peace were created by Edward III in the fourteenth century to take over some of the work of local law enforcement that had formerly been the duty of sheriffs and feudal lords. The justices were men of position and leisure, not great lords but well-to-do local landholders of the class that had long carried heavy respon-

The only known contemporary portrait of Joan of Arc.

sibilities in local government. Like the sheriffs and the tax collectors, they served without pay; their reward was leadership in their own community. By the middle of the fifteenth century their powers had grown to a point where they controlled local government. They arrested criminals and tried minor offenses (major cases were reserved for the circuit judges). They were responsible for en-

forcing economic regulations and orders of the central government. They collected information for the Council and were supposed to inform it of plots against the government. In practice, the justices of the peace were often the creatures of the most powerful baron of their region. But when the Tudors reestablished royal authority, the justices of the peace, with their wide local knowledge and influ-

An English court in the later Middle Ages. This miniature is from a law treatise of the reign of Henry IV (early fifteenth century). At the top are the five judges of the Court of King's Bench; below them are the king's coroner and attorney. On the left is the jury, and in front, in the dock, is a prisoner in fetters, flanked by lawyers. In the foreground more prisoners in chains wait their turn. On the center table stand the ushers, one of whom seems to be swearing in the jury.

ence, became the key agents of the crown in the counties.

The century and a half of political instability, stretching from Edward II through Henry VI, gave Parliament a chance to make itself an indispensable part of the government. Weak rulers sought the appearance of public support, and usurpers sought the appearance of legitimacy. Both were eager for parliamentary ratification of important acts, since Parliament represented all the propertied classes of the country. Thus Edward III and Henry IV, after successful revolutions, asked Parliament to accept statements justifying the deposition of their predecessors. Similarly, all taxes and most legislative acts were submitted to Parliament for approval.

Equally important was the union (about 1340) of the county representatives (knights) and the town representatives (burgesses). These groups, which had acted separately under Edward I, now formed the House of Commons and made Parliament a far more effective assembly. Now there were only two houses (Lords and Commons) instead of three, or, as in some countries, even four. And the lower house included an element, the knights, which would have been considered noble in any other country. The knights were landlords, just as the barons were; they could intermarry with baronial families, and some of them became barons themselves. Their presence gave the House of Commons much more influence than a mere assembly of burgesses (such as the French Third Estate) could have. Through the leadership of the knights, cooperation with the lords could be assured. This situation sometimes enabled Parliament to effect significant changes in government, for when both houses attacked a minister of the king they could usually force him out of office.

By the fifteenth century Parliament had become an integral part of the machinery of government, and no important act was valid until it had received parliamentary approval. So well established had Parliament become that it survived even the period of strong kingship that began under the Tudors in 1485. But Parliament only gave legal validity to acts of government; it did not make policy, which was the province of the king or the great lords. For example, Edward II and Richard II were not deposed by the initiative of Parliament; Parliament was merely asked to ratify the results of a revolution engineered by a few great barons. Not until the seventeenth century did Parliament begin to formulate policies of its own.

FRANCE IN THE LATER MIDDLE AGES

The monarchy in France also had its troubles during the fourteenth and fifteenth centuries. The sons of Philip the Fair (see pp. 268–71) died in rapid succession, leaving only daughters to succeed them. The barons, afraid that one of their number might gain excessive power by marrying a reigning queen, invented a rule barring women from the succession. In 1328 they placed Philip of Valois, a cousin of the last king and a nephew of Philip the Fair, on the throne. But since Philip owed his position to the barons, he had to spend most of his reign bestowing favors on his supporters and keeping peace among factions of nobles. The widespread loyalty to the king that had marked the late thirteenth century weakened, and the rebellions and acts of treason plagued the country. These internal disorders help to account for the French defeats in the first few decades of the Hundred Years' War.

Philip's son, John (1350–64), had no better fortune. His capture by the English at Poitiers, with the subsequent loss of territory and the heavy taxes needed to raise his ransom, caused widespread dissatisfaction. In 1358 the peasants rose in a revolt that was no more successful than the English rebellion but much more bloody and destructive. In the same year the Estates General, led by the Paris bourgeoisie, tried to take over the government. The attempt failed, both because the Estates had had little experience in government and because their leaders had no support among the great nobles. John's son, Charles V (1364–80), regained much of the lost ground by suppressing his opponents at home and by driving the English from one stronghold after another. If his successor had been a more capable ruler, the French might have escaped another century of troubles.

Unfortunately, most of the brains and determination in the French royal family went to uncles and cousins of the new king rather than to the king himself. Charles VI (1380–1422) was never strong either in mind or in character, and after 1390 he suffered intermittent spells of insanity. The government was conducted largely by princes of the blood royal who quarreled bitterly among themselves over offices, pensions, and gifts of land. When the Duke of Burgundy was assassinated in 1419 by the followers of the Duke of Orléans, the quarrels turned into a civil war and the new Duke of Burgundy allied himself with the English. Since, in addition to Burgundy, he had acquired Flanders and other provinces of the Low Countries, he was the most powerful prince in France and his defection proved disastrous. It was during this period of civil war that Henry V made his rapid conquests and forced Charles VI to recognize Henry's son as heir to the French throne.

The Defeat of England

Charles VII (1422–61) faced an almost hopeless situation when his father died. He had been officially disinherited; the English and their Burgundian allies held the largest and richest part of France. Charles had little military strength, and he was not using what he did have very effectively. It was at this moment that Joan of Arc, a peasant girl from the extreme eastern frontier, appeared at court and announced that heavenly voices had ordered her to drive the English out of the country. Joan, self-confident and persuasive, shook Charles from his lethargy and talked him into the counterof-

fensive that turned the tide of the war. Joan's execution by the English scarcely checked the reconquest, for Charles soon had another stroke of good fortune. England under Henry VI was as torn by factional strife as France had been under Charles VI, and the leader of one faction, an uncle of the English king, mortally offended the Duke of Burgundy. The duke's return to the French cause in 1435 greatly weakened the English and facilitated Charles' recovery of northern France.

Joan of Arc was not unique in having visions, for in those troubled years many men and women were convinced that they had had divine revelations. But in the content of her visions we can see how deep were the roots that the religion of the French monarchy had struck among the people. Joan was convinced that Charles VII was the only rightful king of France and that it was her religious duty to restore him to his throne. She also believed that "to make war on the holy kingdom of France was to make war on the Lord Jesus." Her beliefs were shared by people of all classes. In spite of the misgovernment of the last century there was still a deep reservoir of loyalty to the French monarchy. And in spite of treachery and factionalism there was at least a beginning of national feeling among the French people. Under all the confusion and disorder of the early fifteenth century they clung to two basic beliefs: faith in the French monarchy and faith in the Christian religion. When the two beliefs were united as they were in Joan of Arc, they were irresistible. Joan foreshadowed that union of religion and monarchy on which the absolute states of the early modern period were to be built.

Restoration of Royal Power

France suffered more severely than England during the Hundred Years' War,

A fifteenth-century Swiss halberd.

since all the fighting took place on French soil. Wide areas were devastated by raiding armies and wandering companies of mercenary soldiers who found plundering more profitable than loyal service. But precisely because the French predicament was so much graver than the English, royal power was restored more rapidly and more completely in France. A king who showed any promise of putting an end to disorder could override most limitations on his power to levy taxes. Charles V began the work of freeing the monarchy from these restraints, and Charles VII finished the job. As soon as he had the English on the run he began to levy taxes at will, without asking consent from the Estates. His task was made easier by the fact that provincial feeling was so strong in France that a central parliamentary assembly was seldom called, and when it was called it had little authority. Real influence lay with the provincial and regional assemblies, with the local Estates of Normandy or of Languedoc rather than with the Estates General. And it was relatively easy for Charles to overcome the fragmented opposition of these local assemblies.

The same overwhelming interest in provincial affairs kept the great French nobles from entrenching themselves in the central government, which remained the preserve of the king and his bureaucrats. Thus in the long run the Hundred Years' War reinforced tendencies that had been apparent in France prior to the end of the thirteenth century—tendencies toward a bureaucratic state in which the king was strong and all other political forces were weak and divided. This French pattern became a model for the rest of Europe during the early modern period.

GERMANY IN THE LATER MIDDLE AGES

The political history of the rest of western Europe during the later Middle Ages resembled that of France and England. Everywhere there were rebellions, civil wars, and attempts to conquer neighboring territories. But all this furor produced surprisingly little change. A political map

of Europe in 1450 looks very like a map of 1300, and the basic characteristics of most of the governments were similarly unchanged.

Certain developments in Germany deserve attention, however. First, during the fifteenth century the dukes of Burgundy gradually gained control over all the provinces of the Low Countries, roughly the equivalent of modern Belgium and the Netherlands. This was one of the richest and most productive regions of Europe. The union of the Low Countries under the House of Burgundy separated their fate from that of the rest of Germany and gradually gave them a distinct national identity. At the same time their wealth made them the object of a long series of European wars that began in the fifteenth century and have continued to our own day.

Second, during the fourteenth century the peasants and townsmen of Switzerland gradually gained their independence from the Habsburg family, which had dominated this part of Germany. In defeating the Habsburgs the Swiss developed well-disciplined infantry formations, armed with long pikes, that could beat off a charge of heavy cavalry. By the fifteenth century companies of Swiss infantry had acquired such a reputation that they were being hired by French kings and Italian princes. The Swiss were also demonstrating the possibility of republican government to a Europe that had had little confidence in this system. The faction-ridden Italian towns were losing their independence, and the German towns proved unable to form a permanent confederation. But the Swiss Confederation, loosely knit though it was, endured. Each district, or canton, had its own institutions, and no canton was under a feudal lord. The towns were ruled by the wealthier burgesses, but the peasant cantons, where the movement for independence had begun, were almost pure democracies.

The third important development in Germany was the rise of a new power center on the middle Danube as a result of the peculiar electoral habits of the German princes. By the fourteenth century the number of princes taking part in imperial elections had been reduced to

seven. These great men feared giving the title to any powerful prince, so for some time they regularly chose as emperors counts with small holdings. Though the title gave no real power, it did confer enough social prestige to enable such counts to marry well-endowed heiresses. Thus the Habsburgs, petty princes in West Germany who had served briefly as emperors around 1300, managed to acquire the duchy of Austria and nearby counties. A little later, the Count of Luxemburg, an equally undistinguished prince, became emperor and arranged a marriage through which his son received the kingdom of Bohemia. Later Luxemburg emperors acquired Silesia and

eventually Hungary. When the last male Luxemburg leader died in 1438, his nearest heir was the Habsburg Duke of Austria. The union of the two sets of holdings marked the beginning of the vast Habsburg Empire, which for five centuries was to be one of the great powers of Europe.

ART, LITERATURE, AND SCIENCE

The art and literature, the scholarship and the technology of western Europe during this period showed the same uneven development as the politics. There was a considerable amount of sterile imitation, or mere elaboration of familiar themes. On the other hand, no essential skills or ideas were lost, and there were some promising innovations. For example, while many late Gothic churches were cold and uninspired copies of earlier work, in other churches some striking results were achieved by making windows higher and wider, by emphasizing perpendicular lines, and by devising intricate patterns of vaulting. Elaboration could be carried too far; one late Gothic style is rightly known as the Flamboyant, because spikes and gables, traceries and canopies concealed the basic lines of the structure. Better results were achieved in manuscript illumination, because the richly ornamented borders did not hide the text or distract attention from the miniature illustrations, which were becoming increasingly realistic.

In literature there were the same contradictions. Many of the old narrative poems became fantastic romances (such as those Cervantes mocked in *Don Quixote*), and the lyrics became society verse. On the other hand, there were significant gains—deeper psychological insights in describing human behavior, and a notable improvement in the writing of prose. It is much harder to write good prose (especially on technical subjects) than to write acceptable poetry, but a high level of prose writing was reached in all western countries in the later Middle Ages. To take only one example, Nicolas Oresme, a French scholar, translated Aristotle's *Politics.* He had to invent or redefine many words in accomplishing this task, and in doing so he greatly enriched the French language.

The scholars of the period could also be accused of thrashing old straw without producing much new intellectual grain. Some of their arguments were overrefined—elaborate games that interested only the players. But there were original thinkers, especially, as we shall see, in the fields of science and mathematics.

These contradictory developments in late medieval culture disgusted the Italians of the Renaissance. They damned most medieval work as "gothic," which

to them meant barbarous. It took many generations to overcome this prejudice, and even now it has not entirely disappeared.

Literature

The medieval authors who are most widely read today all wrote in the fourteenth and fifteenth centuries. The best-known example is Geoffrey Chaucer (*ca.* 1340–1400), who began as a mere translator and adapter of French works and developed into one of England's greatest poets. His most famous work, the Prologue to the *Canterbury Tales,* reveals his skill in describing individual characters and his wit in depicting human foibles.

Chaucer on Good and Bad Churchmen

THE PARSON

There was a good man of religion too,
A country parson, poor, I warrant you
But rich he was in holy thought and work . . .
Who Christ's own gospel truly sought to preach;
Devoutly his parishioners would he teach . . .
He was right loath to curse to get a tithe
But rather would he give, in case of doubt
Unto those poor parishioners all about
Part of his income, even of his goods . . .
He was a shepherd and not mercenary.
And holy though he was, and virtuous,
To sinners he was not impiteous . . .
To lead folk into Heaven but by stress
Of good example was his busyness . . .

THE PARDONER

His wallet lay before him in his lap
Stuffed full of pardons, brought from Rome all hot . . .
And in his bag he had a pillowcase
The which, he said, was our Truly Lady's veil.
He said he had a piece of the very sail
That good Saint Peter had what time he went
Upon the sea, till Jesus changed his bent . . .
But with these relics, when he came upon
Some simple parson, then this paragon
In that one day more money stood to gain
Than his poor dupe in two months could attain.

From Prologue to the *Canterbury Tales,* rendered into modern English by J. U. Nicolson (New York: Corici, Friede, 1934).

own genius. Chaucer was something of a psychologist as well as a poet, but while he saw through pretense and sham, he never became bitter. He rose fast in English society under the patronage of John of Gaunt; he accepted the world as he found it and rather liked what he found.

François Villon (b. 1431) was less fortunate. A friend of the thieves and prostitutes of Paris, and a convicted criminal himself, he shows how close French society came to breaking down under the strains of the early fifteenth century. He used the old poetic forms to describe with gusto life in taverns and thieves' dens. But his poems also express his bitterness over his wasted life and portray the hopes and fears of the poor and the outcast—the simple piety of an old woman, the last thoughts of men condemned to hang. The tendency toward realism, already evident in Chaucer, became even stronger in Villon.

Devotional works written for laymen were far more numerous after 1300 than they had ever been before. There was a tremendous desire among all classes for more intense and personal religious experience to supplement the conventional observances. Writers of the fourteenth and fifteenth centuries produced innumerable meditations, visions, and moral tracts. Some of the finest religious writings of any period were composed at this time, especially the *Imitation of Christ*, ascribed to Thomas à Kempis. In England there was *The Vision of Piers Plow-*

Death was a favorite subject for illustration in the late Middle Ages. Shown here is the Dance of Death from a manuscript of about 1400. Death, playing a trumpet decked with the papal banner of the keys of St. Peter, summons a pope.

A fifteenth-century representation of Chaucer from the Ellesmere manuscript of the *Canterbury Tales*.

His people range from the "perfect, gentle Knight" and the poor parson, who taught Christ's lore, "but first he followed it himself," through the earthy Wife of Bath, who had buried five husbands, down to scoundrels like the Miller and the Summoner. Perhaps his knowledge of all levels of English society was due to the fact that Chaucer worked for years in the customs service in the busy port of London. But his subtle portrayal of human behavior, shown also in *Troilus and Criseyde*, came only from his

man by William Langland, one of the first important works written in English after the long eclipse following the Norman Conquest. We know little of Langland, except that he lived in the middle years of the fourteenth century and that he came of peasant stock. The English of *Piers Plowman* is archaic, but it is recognizably English and not, as Anglo-Saxon was, an early German dialect.

Piers Plowman also illustrates the widespread desire to transform religion into a strong social force. The poet criticizes every class for its worldliness and selfishness; only by a return to the pure principles of the Gospel can the world be saved. There was nothing anti-Catholic in Langland's program, but it did bear testimony to the continuing inability of ecclesiastical authorities to satisfy adequately the aspirations expressed in the poem and in many similar works.

Painting and Sculpture

The same tendency toward realism that we have noted in Chaucer and Villon is also evident in much of the sculpture and painting of the period. This tendency, which had already appeared in some of the details of thirteenth-century works, now began to be expressed in the principal figures. It sometimes took a macabre form: skeletons and corpses were depicted with loving care on funeral monuments and in the Dance of Death, a favorite subject of artists. But we also find at this time the first real portraits painted in western Europe and the first attempts to depict a landscape that is more than a conventional background. There were capable artists everywhere—English, French, and German sculptors, French and German painters. But the most interesting group were those who worked for the dukes of Burgundy. The Flemish school of painting, which developed in the late fourteenth and early fifteenth centuries, was a worthy rival of the Italians of the early Renaissance. In some techniques these painters were ahead of the Italians—the first painting in oils, for example, was done in Flanders. The best-known Flemish painters, such as the van Eycks, van der Weyden, and Memling, combined

Jan van Eyck, *Giovanni Arnolfini and His Bride* (1434).

meticulous attention to detail with genuine religious feeling. And there is nothing in Italy that quite equals the Flemish portraits of this period, such as Jan van Eyck's picture of the Arnolfinis, or his *Léal Souvenir.*

Science

The scholarly work of the period is less well known, and a few years ago it would have been dismissed as unoriginal and unimportant. But even when it was unoriginal it was useful to men with ideas of their own. For example, Columbus based most of his ideas about geography on books written in the fourteenth and early fifteenth centuries. And not all the work was unoriginal. In philosophy there was a sharp attack on the system of Thomas Aquinas that freed scholars, to some extent, from their adherence to the Aristotelian ideas that had been incorporated into Thomas' theology. Once Aristotle's ideas had been challenged, there could be wider speculation on scientific questions, especially on explanations of motion. The problems through which Galileo revolutionized the science of physics had already been raised by fourteenth-century scholars. For example, mathematicians at Oxford came very close to a correct solution of the problem of accelerated motion.

More important than any specific achievement was the very fact that interest in scientific problems persisted. Up to the end of the Middle Ages, western scholars, relying largely on the work of the Greeks and Moslems, had made no outstanding contributions to scientific knowledge. But they were remarkably persistent and kept working on scientific problems after other peoples had given up. The Greeks and Moslems eventually lost interest in science, as did the Chinese, who had had their own independent scientific tradition. But from the twelfth century on, there were always some scholars in the West who were interested in science, and this long devotion led, in the end, to the great discoveries of the early modern period. Men like Copernicus and Galileo were trained in universities that used the methods and the books of the later Middle Ages.

No one has ever given a completely satisfactory explanation of this continuing interest in science. Certainly westerners were paying more attention to the things of this world during the later Middle Ages and less attention to the aims of the Church. But Chinese society was far more secular, and the Chinese, in the long run, fell behind the Europeans. Perhaps more important was the western tendency to be dissatisfied with the status quo, a tendency that was especially evident in the crucial years between 1300 and 1600. In China, a philosopher like Thomas Aquinas would have become an unchallenged authority; in Europe his system was questioned within a generation after his death. Europeans respected authority, but they always felt that authoritative treatises needed to be reinterpreted. Finally, there was a curious patience with details, a willingness and an enthusiasm to work very hard for very small gains.

Technology

These qualities also explain some of the advances in technology that were made in the last medieval centuries. Perhaps the most important was the development of firearms. Here, as in many other cases, the Europeans capitalized on a technique known to other peoples. The Chinese, for example, were probably the first to discover gunpowder, and they had cannon about as early as the Europeans. But Chinese guns were never very efficient, and the Chinese never developed an army that was primarily dependent on firearms. The Europeans carried their experiments with cannon much further than the Chinese. Although the first European guns were not very good—they were as apt to kill the men who fired them as those at whom they were aimed—they had become fairly reliable by the end of the fifteenth century. The military significance of this development is obvious. It reduced the power of local lords by making their castles untenable; conversely, it increased the power of kings and great princes like the Duke of Burgundy, for they were the

An early gun, lighter and more portable than the first cannon. The gun was placed on a forked stand and was braced against the ground by its long tail (illustration from a German manuscript, *ca.* 1405).

only ones who could afford the expensive new weapons.

The development of firearms caused a rapid growth in other branches of technology. In order to make gun barrels that would not burst under the shock of an explosion, much had to be learned about metallurgy. And in order to make gun barrels that were truly round and hence could deliver the full effect of the charge, better metalworking tools and more precise measuring instruments had to be developed. Better techniques in using metals led to greater demands for metals, and this in turn stimulated the mining industry. The miners of Germany (including Bohemia and Austria), who were the chief suppliers of metals for Europe, learned to push their shafts deeper and to devise ways of draining off underground water. Increased use of metals and greater skill in mining in the long run transformed European industry. To take the most famous example, pumps operated by a piston traveling in a cylinder were developed in order to remove water from mines; it was this kind of pump that eventually furnished the model for the first steam engine.

The invention of printing in the fifteenth century (see p. 364) also owed much to developments in metallurgy. The essential element in printing was the use of movable type, and good type in turn depended on the availability of a metal that would take the exact shape of the mold into which it was poured. Thanks to their knowledge of metallurgy, the Germans succeeded in developing an alloy that expanded as it cooled, so that it fitted the mold exactly. Type faces molded from this alloy produced sharp, clear impressions.

Another technical advance of western Europe in the later Middle Ages was in ocean shipping. Here there was at first more patient experimentation than striking discoveries. By the end of the thirteenth century the sailors of western countries had ships that could tack against the wind and were seaworthy enough to survive the storms of the Atlantic. The navigators of the period could find their latitude, though not their longitude, by star and sun sights; they knew that the earth was round, and that the

distance to the rich countries of the East was not impossibly great. Very little more was needed for the great voyages of discovery except practice, and during the fourteenth and fifteenth centuries daring men were mastering the art of oceanic navigation. French and Spanish seamen had reached the Canary Islands at least by the early fourteenth century, and the Portuguese by 1400 had pushed down to the bend in the African coast, claiming Madeira and the Cape Verde Islands along the way.

These voyages illustrate the point that was made earlier: Europeans were no more skillful or intelligent than other peoples; they were simply more persistent or more aggressive. During the same years in which the Europeans were making their first sorties into the Atlantic, the Chinese were sending expeditions into the Indian Ocean. There they found rich kingdoms, ancient civilizations, and profitable sources of trade. In contrast, the Europeans discovered only barren islands and the fever-stricken coast of Africa. Yet the Chinese abandoned their explorations because they, or at least their rulers, were satisfied with what they had at home. The Europeans persisted, though it was almost two centuries before they reached the thriving trading centers of the East or the treasures of Mexico and Peru.

Not as striking as the early voyages, but almost as significant, was the invention of the mechanical clock. The first clocks, which appeared in the fourteenth century, were not very accurate, but they were soon improved by the discovery of the principle of escapement—the system by which the train of gears moves only a precise distance before it is checked and then released to move the same distance again. Crude as the first clocks were, they modified, in the long run, the mental outlook of the western peoples. For several centuries one of the sharpest differences between the West and the rest of the world lay in attitudes toward precise measurement, especially the precise measurement of time. Western civilization has come to be dominated by the clock and the timetable, and westerners have had little sympathy with people who have managed to escape this domination.

Mechanical clock made in 1410. The first clocks had only one movable hand.

Suggestions for Further Reading

Note: Asterisk denotes a book available in paperback edition.

Economic Weakness

H. A. Miskimin, *The Economy of Early Renaissance Europe, 1300–1460** (1969), is a good brief survey of the problem. J. W. Thompson's *Economic and Social History of Europe in the Later Middle Ages* (1931), which has excellent material on almost all aspects of European economic life in this period, is a good starting point for further study. There is a very thorough treatment of the methods for the enforcement of early economic legislation in England in B. H. Putnam, *The Enforcement of the Statutes of Labourers* (1908). B. N. Nelson, *The Idea of Usury* (1949), studies the development of a universal morality conducive to systematic capitalist enterprise. The second edition of Vol. I of the *Cambridge Economic History of Europe* is especially good on this period. See also E. E. Power and M. M. Postan, *Studies in English Trade in the Fifteenth Century* (1933), and S. L. Thrupp, *The Merchant Class of Medieval London* (1948).

Attacks on the Church: Marsilius, Wiclif, and Hus

There is a wealth of material available in English on these men, who revolutionized the political and religious thinking of western Europe. A. Gewirth, *Marsilius of Padua*, Vol. I (1951), is a scholarly and readable treatment of the political philosophy of Marsilius. The great treatise of Marsilius, the *Defensor pacis*, trans. by A. Gewirth (1956), brings out the premises by which Marsilius overthrew the doctrines of the papal plenitude of power and the Gelasian theory of the parallelism between the spiritual and temporal powers.

A good introduction to the political, social, and religious climate on which the thought of Wiclif fell is G. M. Trevelyan, *England in the Age of Wycliff** (1899). Trevelyan was one of the great social historians of his century and a very good writer. H. B. Workman, *John Wyclif*, 2 vols. (1926), is a study of the impact of Wiclif's thought on his times and on the English Church. D. S. Schaff, *John Huss* (1915), is an interesting biography of this Czech nationalist and precursor of reformation. The short monograph of M. Spinka, *John Huss and the Czech Reform* (1941), is a study of the influence of Wiclif on the thought of Hus. There is valuable material on the influence of Marsilius and Wiclif on the evolution of political thought in C. H. McIlwain, *Growth of Political Thought in the West* (1932). For an excellent account of the Hussite movement, see F. G. Heymann, *John Ziska and the Hussite Revolution* (1955) and *George of Bohemia* (1965).

The Great Schism

The best background for understanding the Great Schism of the West is W. Ullmann, *Origins of the Great Schism* (1948). W. E. Lunt, *Papal Revenues in the Middle Ages*, 2 vols. (1934), has source material on the finances of the papacy at this time. There is a full account of the Great Schism in M. Creighton, *A History of the Papacy from the Great Schism to the Sack of Rome*, Vols. I and II (1919), and in L. Pastor, *History of the Popes*, Vol. I (trans. 1891), but the interpretation of Creighton is more balanced.

The Black Death

F. A. Gasquet, *The Black Death* (1893), is a good study of this epidemic, with detailed material on the consequences of the plague for the social and economic life of England in the later Middle Ages. The more recent work of A. E. Levett, *The Black Death on the Estates of the See of Winchester* (1916), rejects the older view that the Black Death seriously disrupted the economic development of England. Differing points of view on this problem are presented by W. M. Bowsky, ed., *The Black Death* (1971). There is material on the Black Death in all political and economic histories of this period.

England from 1307 to 1485

A. R. Myers, *England in the Later Middle Ages** (1952), a broad survey of this period, is a good introduction. There is valuable source material on the reign of Edward II in *The Life of Edward II*, trans. by N. Denholm-Young (1957), which goes into considerable detail on the revival of baronial powers and the civil wars under Edward. T. F. Tout, *The Place of the Reign of Edward II in History* (1936), sees this reign as the period of marked transition from court administration to national administration.

J. Froissart, *Chronicles** (many translations), presents a vivid picture of the life and spirit of fourteenth-century England. Froissart is an invaluable source for the reign of Edward III. There is a wealth of primary information on the reigns of Henry VI, Edward IV, and Richard III in *The Paston Letters*, 3 vols., ed. by J. Gairdner (1895). H. L. Gray, *The Influence of the Commons on Early Legislation* (1932), is a scholarly study of the development of the House of Commons in the fourteenth and fifteenth centuries. S. Armitage-Smith, *John of Gaunt* (1904); A. Steel, *Richard II* (1941); and P. M. Kendall, *Richard the Third** (1955), are all interesting reading and based on sound scholarship.

For material on the development of the English constitution, see B. Wilkinson, *Constitutional History of Medieval England*, Vols. II and III (1958).

E. Perroy, *The Hundred Years' War*, trans. by W. B. Wells (1952), is an excellent account of the military history of this period, with a discussion of the implications of the war on the constitutional growth of England. R. B. Mowat, *The Wars of the Roses* (1914), is an interesting, if somewhat romantic, treatment of this confusing struggle.

France from 1314 to 1461

H. Pirenne et al., *La fin du moyen age* (1931), is a thorough study of this period by outstanding French historians. The broad scholarly work of E. Lavisse, ed., *Histoire de France*, Vol. IV, Part 2 (1902), is invaluable for the political, economic, military, and cultural history of France in this period.

There is a full documentary account of the trials of Joan of Arc in *Jeanne d'Arc*, ed. by T. D. Murray (1920), a very readable translation. L. Fabre, *Joan of Arc*, trans. by G. Hopkins (1954), is a fine biography of Joan and presents a fascinating picture of France in the period of the Hundred Years' War. R. Vaughn in *Philip the Bold* (1962), *John the Fearless* (1966), and *Philip the Good* (1970), gives a good picture of the growth of Burgundian power.

There are two very readable studies of the last Duke of Burgundy: J. F. Kirk, *Charles the Bold, Duke of Burgundy*, 3 vols. (1864–68), is a study of the man in relation to his times; R. Putnam, *Charles the Bold* (1908), concentrates on Charles the man. A good picture of the brilliant life of the Burgundian court is given in O. Cartellieri, *The Court of Burgundy* (1929). The outstanding achievement of J. Huizinga, *The Waning of the Middle Ages** (1924), is a study of the forms of life and thought in France and the Netherlands in the last days of the brilliant court of Burgundy.

Germany in the Later Middle Ages

Both J. Bryce, *The Holy Roman Empire* (many editions), and G. Barraclough, *The Origins of Modern Germany** (1947), contain information on Germany in the later Middle Ages. Barraclough presents a fresher historical interpretation. The old study of H. Zimmer, *The Hansa Towns* (1889), is still valuable.

The origins and development of Switzerland are carefully treated in W. D. McCracken, *Rise of the Swiss Republic* (1901).

The titles by Pirenne and Lavisse in the sixth section above contain information on the rise of the Habsburg dynasty and the Burgundian takeover of the Low Countries.

Art, Literature, Science, and Scholarship in the Later Middle Ages

E. Panofsky, *Early Netherlandish Painting* (1953), is a beautiful study of art in northern Europe at this time, and M. Meiss, *Painting in Florence and Siena after the Black Death** (1951), describes the impact the Black Death had on the art of southern Europe. Both volumes are by outstanding art historians and have good reproductions.

Some of the greatest literature of the western world was produced in the later Middle Ages. Chaucer's *Canterbury Tales** (many editions); Villon's *Poems*, trans. by H. D. Stacpoole (1926); and Dante's *Divine Comedy,** trans. by D. L. Sayers (1949–58), are all masterpieces. Each was written in the vernacular, each reflects the changing world view, and each gives a superb picture of the spirit and thought of the times. J. Gardner, *The Life and Times of Chaucer* (1977), is a lively reconstruction of the poet's career. The great English poem of Langland, *Piers the Ploughman,** trans. by J. E. Goodridge (1959), is a fourteenth-century inquiry into the good life as judged by contemporary criteria. G. Lagarde, *Naissance de l'esprit laïque*, 2 vols. (1956–58), a brilliant treatment of late medieval thought and scholarship, traces the development in western Europe of a distinctly secular spirit. There is interesting material on late medieval science in H. Butterfield, *Origins of Modern Science, 1300–1800** (1949), a broad survey. A. C. Crombie, *Medieval and Early Modern Science,** 2 vols. (1959), gives considerable attention to methods in physics in the late Middle Ages and stresses the continuity of the western scientific tradition from Greek times to the present. Crombie includes a good up-to-date bibliography. The thought of the fourteenth century is lucidly presented in G. Leff, *Medieval Thought** (1958), which discusses Occam, science, and political theories. E. Gilson, *History of Christian Philosophy in the Middle Ages* (1954), has information on Occam and the later Schoolmen. There is a wealth of material on the intellectual and spiritual life of the period from 1216 to 1485 in D. Knowles, *Religious Orders in England*, 2 vols. (1954–55).

14 Western Europe's Neighbors During the Middle Ages

At a time when the governments of western Europe were weak, its cities almost nonexistent, and its scholars limited to the study of encyclopedias and digests, both Byzantium and Islam had well-organized bureaucratic states, large commercial cities, and eminent scholars. Understandably, western Europeans felt awkward in dealing with their more fortunate neighbors, and their sense of inferiority often led them into suspicion and hostility. But neighbors they were, and contacts of some sort were inevitable.

THE BYZANTINE EMPIRE

The Byzantine Empire recovered only slowly from the external shock of the Arab conquests and the internal shock of the long religious controversy over the veneration of images. The Moslems remained a constant threat from the south, and the Bulgars, an Asiatic people who gradually mixed with the southern Slavs, menaced Constantinople from the north. But the Empire still had its wealth, its diplomatic skill, and its professional army, and with them it managed to limp through the eighth and early ninth centuries.

With the accession of Basil I (867–886), who founded the Macedonian dynasty, the Byzantine Empire began one of its marvelous recoveries. For a century and a half most of the emperors were first-rate generals. They took advantage of dissensions among their enemies to drive back the Moslems in the south and the Bulgars in the north. They recovered all of Asia Minor and gained control of the eastern Mediterranean, making possible the reconquest of Crete and Cyprus. The Byzantine Empire was never richer or more powerful than it was about the year 1000.

Byzantine Art and Literature

An intellectual and artistic revival accompanied and outlasted the political revival. The schools at Constantinople reached the peak of their activity soon after 1000, when a faculty of philosophy and a school of law were established. This was not quite a university of the western type, since standardized courses and degrees were lacking, but professors were paid regular salaries and often held

Interior of the mosque at Cordoba (*ca.* 785).

Byzantine art exhibited Christian influence and a love of ornamentation. Above: a tenth-century clasp bearing the image of a saint. Below: a reliquary cross (probably twelfth century).

high positions at the imperial court. Byzantine scholars spent much of their energy copying and commenting on ancient texts, useful though not original work that preserved many books that otherwise would have been lost. Especially important was the Byzantine interest in Plato. The other great group of scholars of this period—those who wrote in Arabic—were much more concerned with Aristotle, and western Europe had inherited only a few fragments of Plato in Latin translation. When the Italians of the fifteenth century became interested in Plato, they had to obtain their texts, and scholars to expound them, from Constantinople.

Not all Byzantine writing, however, was based on ancient materials. The Byzantines produced some notable histories—works that were not impartial, since they were usually written to justify the actions of a ruler or a faction, but that were far superior to contemporary western chronicles. Another interesting genre that flourished during this period was the popular epic. Stories of heroic deeds performed against the enemies of the Empire were written in the language used by the people, and for this reason they were far more widely known than scholarly works written in correct classical Greek. The most famous of these poems, the epic of Digenis Akritas, was still remembered at the time of the Cypriote rebellion of 1957 to 1958.

Under the Macedonian emperors and their immediate successors, Byzantine art entered into its golden age. As in scholarship, so in art there was a revival of classical influence. Byzantine artists were far less imitative, however, than were Byzantine writers. While deriving a certain dignity and sobriety from ancient works, they retained the Byzantine love of color and ornamentation. Unlike the scholars, they had something to say to the people; they portrayed the truths of the Christian faith and the events of recent history. Every church and many private homes had their icons (paintings of sacred personages); every important manuscript was illustrated with miniatures. With hundreds of artists at work, it is not surprising that many of them were competent and a few great.

Byzantium and the West

Byzantine influence was felt throughout western Europe. Italian merchants came regularly to Constantinople and after 1100 took over most of the carrying trade of the Empire. Byzantine influence remained strong in southern Italy, even after the Norman conquest, and in Venice, which had once been a Byzantine protectorate. Popes and German kings exchanged embassies with the emperor at Constantinople, and thousands of western pilgrims passed through the city on their way to the Holy Land. Easy access to the markets of Constantinople speeded up the growth of Italian cities, and the Italian cities in turn led the economic revival of the West. The use of Byzantine artists by Italians—as in the designing of the Venetian Cathedral of St. Mark's—left its mark on Italian art. The first native Italian painters were clearly influenced by Byzantine models.

Western scholars were not greatly interested in the theology or philosophy of the Byzantines. But after 1100 a few westerners journeyed to Constantinople to discover and translate ancient manuscripts. Their work was less appreciated than that of their contemporaries who were working on translations from the Arabic, and sometimes books that had passed from Greek to Syriac to Arabic to Latin were preferred to direct translations from the Greek. Because western translators were primarily interested in Aristotle, they overlooked the opportunity to increase the stock of Platonic works available in Latin. Nevertheless, some important texts, such as the advanced works of Euclid, would have been unknown to western medieval scholars had it not been for the efforts of the translators at Constantinople.

During the eleventh century the Latin and Greek Churches gradually drifted apart. There had long been friction between them, since the patriarch at Constantinople rejected the pope's claims to universal authority and the pope resented the patriarch's claim to independence. There were theological disputes, such as the one over sacred images, and the question raised by Charlemagne about the relationship between the Holy

Ghost and the other two Persons of the Trinity. But the basic reason for the split was that the West and Byzantium were becoming so different in institutions and culture that each was suspicious of the other's motives. Finally, in 1054, pope and patriarch excommunicated each other, and the two Churches broke off relations. The break was not taken too seriously at first; such splits had happened before and had always been repaired. But this time, in spite of repeated efforts, the breach could not be healed. Each Church went its own way, and cooperation between them became more and more difficult.

Byzantium and the Slavs

Byzantine masons at work (miniature from a psalter, 1066).

Byzantium's greatest influence was on the peoples of the Balkans and Russia. In spite of frequent wars and rebellions, there were long periods in which the Serbs and the Bulgars were either subject to, or allied with, the Eastern Empire. Byzantine princesses were frequently married to Slavic rulers in order to gain influence in neighboring courts. These ladies brought with them missionaries and teachers, artists and scholars, thus helping to spread the Greek Orthodox religion and Byzantine culture throughout the regions inhabited by the eastern Slavs. The conversion of the Bulgars began in the ninth century and that of the Russians in the tenth; both peoples were soon thoroughly Christianized. For a long time the leading clergymen in Bulgaria and Russia were appointed by the patriarch of Constantinople. Even with a growing tendency toward autonomy in the Slavic churches, Byzantine influence remained strong. Down to the fifteenth century all but two or three of the metropolitans (heads) of the Russian Church were Greeks.

The fact that the eastern Slavs received their religion and culture from Constantinople had lasting consequences for the history of modern Europe. Byzantine civilization and western European civilization had a common origin, but, as we have seen, they drifted apart during the Middle Ages. Byzantium remembered much that the West forgot, and it was always more strongly influenced by eastern ideas and customs. The West went through experiences, such as the Investiture Conflict, and developed institutions, such as feudalism, that scarcely touched Constantinople. Misunderstandings were inevitable, and they were especially bitter because each region expected better things of a related Christian civilization and because each felt that the other was betraying a common heritage. The eastern Slavs, especially the Russians, shared these tensions. The West both attracted and repulsed them, and the current Russian attitude toward the West is a new and intensified form of an old suspicion.

THE MOSLEM CALIPHATE

The Abbasid Caliphate, established in 750, achieved its golden age before the tenth-century revival set in at Constantinople. It reached its peak of power and wealth under Harun-al-Rashid (786–809). Harun, who exchanged letters and gifts with Charlemagne, ruled a far larger empire than his western contemporary. The lands of the caliph stretched from Morocco to the Indus River, from the steppes of central Asia to the Sudan. After 900, although the Caliphate began to break up into separate states, the Moslem world remained an economic and cultural unit. In this vast territory, which was traversed by all the important East–West trade routes, there were dozens of populous and prosperous cities, but Baghdad was the largest and richest.

Arabic Scholarship

The city of Baghdad attracted books and scholars just as it did merchandise and traders. The Abbasids did even more than the Ommiads to transform their empire into a center of scholarship. Hundreds of Greek works, especially on philosophy, science, and mathematics, were translated into Arabic, and much was learned from Persian and Jewish sources. Chinese scholarship had little influence, but the Abbasids borrowed many ideas from the Indians, notably the system of arithmetic notation that we call Arabic figures. By the ninth century Moslem scholars had assimilated the work of their predecessors and were beginning to make original contributions of their own. From 900 to 1200 the most important work done anywhere in the world in mathematics, astronomy, physics, medicine, and geography was done in Moslem countries.

Much Arabic scholarship merely added details to support established scientific theories—for example, accurate observations of star positions or clinical descriptions of certain diseases. More was done in geography because the Arabs knew more about the world than had the ancient writers. But their most remarkable contribution was in physics and mathematics. In physics they performed interesting experiments in reflection and refraction. In mathematics, besides greatly simplifying arithmetical operations through the use of the new Arabic figures, they carried trigonometry far beyond the Greek accomplishment. And their work in algebra was even more impressive, for they fashioned a whole mathematical discipline out of the few hints provided by their predecessors. Their contribution is recorded in the very word *algebra*, which is Arabic.

Two notable Moslem mathematicians were al-Khwarizmi (d. *ca.* 840) and the poet Omar Khayyám (d. *ca.* 1120). Al-Khwarizmi recognized, more clearly than many of his contemporaries, the value of the new Hindu-Arabic figures, especially the zero. Use of the zero made it possible to reckon by position and simplified all work in arithmetic. Al-Khwarizmi did much to popularize this new arithmetic;

he also wrote a text on algebra that was used in both Moslem and Christian countries for centuries. Omar Khayyám calculated the length of a solar year with great accuracy and devised methods of solving algebraic equations that had been too complicated for his predecessors.

Arabic Influence on the West

Moslem interest in mathematics and the natural sciences had a decisive influence on the course of western civilization. The Byzantines tended to neglect these subjects, and little was known about them in western Europe. The Chinese had great technical skill—for example, they discovered the principle of the compass very early—but they developed few general theories. And the Indians, after a promising start, lost their interest in scientific problems. Thus the Moslem world was the only region that was both actively interested in science and close enough to western Europe to touch off a revival of scientific interest there. Western European scholars made their first attempts to recover ancient scientific texts by going to the Moslems of Spain and Sicily; only after the revival was well under way did they begin to seek manuscripts in Constantinople. Certainly the West would not have developed a scientific tradition of its own as rapidly as it did without the assistance of Moslem scholarship, and quite possibly it never would have developed the tradition at all.

It is somewhat anachronistic, however, to separate science so sharply from other studies. For Moslem scholars, as for medieval Christians, science was merely one aspect of philosophy. Aristotle, the great authority on science for both peoples, was thought of primarily as a philosopher, and one of the chief intellectual problems of the Middle Ages was to reconcile his philosophy with the revealed truths of religion. Here again, Moslem scholars led the way. Avicenna (ibn-Sina, 980–1037), who wrote a famous book in Arabic on medicine, also prepared commentaries on Aristotle that influenced western scholars during the twelfth and thirteenth centuries. Even more important was the Spanish Moslem Averroës (ibn-Rushd, 1126–98), some of whose assertions shocked both Islam and Christendom—for example, that the world is eternal, and that there is no personal immortality. But Averroës was no freethinker; one of his strongest convictions was that there can be no real conflict between the truths of philosophy and the truths of revealed religion. This doctrine, which was taken over by Christian scholars in the thirteenth century, made it easier for them to justify the assimilation of Greco-Arabic philosophy into the Christian tradition. Maimonides (Moses ben Maimon, 1135–1204), a Spanish Jew living under Moslem rule, was thoroughly familiar with the Arabic versions of Aristotelian philosophy and tried to reconcile them with the Jewish faith. His proofs of the existence of God are very like those advanced a half-century later by Thomas Aquinas.

Until the Moslems broke away from the Koran's strict ban on representing living beings, they could do nothing with sculpture and painting. They were, however, great builders and created a distinctive style out of such old forms as the dome, the arcade, and the tower. Moslem architectural styles made a deep impression on every country in which they appeared; their influence may still be seen in Spain and India. Moslem buildings were lavishly decorated with colored tiles and intricate geometric carvings—ideas that were imitated by neighboring countries.

THE DECLINE OF BYZANTIUM AND THE CALIPHATE

The Byzantine Empire and the countries controlled by the Abbasid Caliphate remained important centers of commerce and intellectual and artistic activity throughout the European Middle Ages. But after the tenth century they began to decline as political units. Some problems were common to both states—for example, the lack of a fixed rule of succession to the throne. Neither the emperor nor the caliph was necessarily the eldest son of his predecessor; he might be anyone connected with the ruling family who had been able to win the support of the bureaucracy and the army. Theoretically this practice might have assured the selection of the ablest man; actually it encouraged palace intrigues and civil wars. The western European tendency to insist on the rule of primogeniture was not an ideal way of picking a ruler, but in practice it gave greater stability and continuity to political institutions. Another problem common to both the Byzantine Empire and the Arab Caliphate was that of raising an army. It was easier to hire soldiers from among the neighboring barbarians than to disrupt civilian life by forcing city workers and peasant farmers into the army. But mercenaries were never entirely reliable, and the better they were as fighting men, the greater the danger that they might try to take over the government.

Each state also had problems of its own. In Byzantium there was a growing hostility between the bureaucracy of the capital city and the great landlords of the

A Moslem pharmacist concocting a medicinal wine (from a thirteenth-century manuscript of Dioscorides' *Materia Medica*). The text reads: "The making of a drink (*shirab*) for catarrhs, coughs, swelling of the belly, and loosening of the stomach." The recipe calls for wine mixed with myrrh, roots of licorice, and white pepper.

303

rural districts. The bureaucrats, quite rightly, felt that the landlords were trying to reduce the peasants to a state of serfdom and to make themselves independent rulers in the outlying provinces. The landlords felt, quite rightly in turn, that the bureaucracy was a nest of intrigue and corruption. Attempts to weaken the landlords or reform the bureaucrats merely intensified the bad feelings between the two groups. These disruptive tendencies were held in check during the tenth century, but after the death of the last great Macedonian emperor, Basil II, in 1025, they grew more virulent.

The problems peculiar to the Caliphate sprang from its size and from the peculiar nature of Moslem law, which emphasized ethical and religious duties, but left enforcement to the whims of the ruler. It was almost impossible to establish a centralized administrative system for such widely separated regions, each with its own traditions. Regional viceroys had to be given extensive powers, and there was always the danger that one of them would set himself up as an independent ruler. Moreover, though the caliphs had built up a bureaucracy on Roman and Persian models, and though they had developed a comprehensive legal system, Moslem government was always rather arbitrary and unpredictable. No one wanted to be bound by rules, least of all the caliph and his officials. Since everything depended on the whim of the man in power, it was better to catch his ear than it was to try to win a case at law. This lack of respect for legal principles encouraged intrigue and disobedience. Instability was increased by religious divisions among the Moslems. Minority groups that questioned the Abbasid ruler's claim to be the orthodox successor of Mohammed naturally felt very little respect for his government.

The first crack in the Caliphate showed itself in 756, when a member of the deposed Ommiad dynasty established an independent state in Spain. The loss of this outlying territory did little damage, but the next secessions were more serious, for they cost the Caliphate all of North Africa. In the tenth century much of this area was seized by the new Fatimid dynasty. This family claimed descent from Fatima, the daughter of Mohammed, a claim that gave it the support of the Shi-ites, the largest group of dissenters in Islam. The Shi-ites believed that Islam must always be led by a lineal descendant of Mohammed; they had rejected the Ommiad caliphs and were now ready to turn against the Abbasids. By taking the title of caliph in 909, the founder of the new dynasty directly challenged the claim of the Abbasid ruler to be leader of all the Moslems. In 969 the Fatimids conquered Egypt, thereby gaining one of the wealthiest Moslem provinces; they established their capital in the newly built city of Cairo in 973. The Fatimid domains now stretched from Morocco to the Red Sea and even included Jerusalem. At the height of their power the Fatimid caliphs of Cairo were far stronger than the Abbasid caliphs of Baghdad.

The Coming of the Turks

By the end of the eleventh century the Fatimid Caliphate was beginning to weaken. The Abbasids, however, profited little from the decline of their rivals. In an effort to hold on to their remaining provinces, they had come to rely more and more on mercenary soldiers, especially the Seljuk Turks. A branch of the nomadic stock of central Asia, the Turks had all the toughness, bravery, and love of conquest of their eastern relatives. They became devout Moslems and fought well for their new religion, but they also fought for themselves. Having become the dominant military power in the lands of the Abbasid Caliphate, they soon began to seek political power as well. By the eleventh century the Turkish sultans (kings) had become the real rulers of most of Syria and Mesopotamia. They preserved the caliph as a religious leader, but they did not allow him any real power in government.

The rise of the Turks had serious consequences for the Byzantine emperors as well. Disputes over the succession to the imperial throne and quarrels between the bureaucrats of Constantinople and the great landlords had seriously weakened the Eastern Empire. Suspecting that they would meet with little resistance, the Turks began to push into Asia Minor; when the emperor Romanus IV tried to drive them out he was defeated and captured at the battle of Manzikert in 1071.

The Byzantine Empire never fully recovered from this defeat. After Manzikert the Turks overran almost all of Asia Minor; they even took Nicaea, only fifty miles from Constantinople. Through heroic efforts a new Byzantine dynasty, the Comneni, regained some of the lost territory, but it could never eject the Turks from central and eastern Asia Minor. This was a serious loss to the Empire, for the provinces seized by the Turks had furnished large numbers of fighting men and had protected the wealthy coastal regions. Skillful diplomacy and the wise use of limited resources enabled Byzantium to survive, but the Eastern Empire under the Comneni never had the vigor it had displayed under the Macedonians.

Fortunately for the Byzantines, the first Turkish Empire began to disintegrate almost as soon as it was established. As might have been expected in this part of the world, the lack of a fixed rule of succession did most of the damage. Each sultan established little principalities for junior members of the family, and military commanders began to turn their governorships into independent states. Each ruler fought and intrigued with his neighbors in order to gain more land. In the end the old Abbasid Caliphate dissolved into a welter of petty states, only loosely associated by their theoretical allegiance to caliph and sultan.

The Early Crusades

It was this confusion in the Middle East that made possible the success of the first Crusade and the establishment of the crusader Kingdom of Jerusalem in 1099. The Moslems were too divided to cooperate against the common enemy, and some of them even encouraged the Christians to attack their rivals. Only a part of the Turkish forces could be assembled to fight the crusaders at Antioch; once Antioch had been lost to the Christians, few of the Syrian Moslems cared about the fate of Jerusalem. Jerusalem, after all, was held by the Fatimid heretics, who were little better than the Christian infidels. The Fatimids, on their part, regarded Jerusalem as an outlying possession of little military or political value and made no great effort to regain the Holy City. A dynasty of Christian kings, descended from the crusader Baldwin of Lorraine, held Jerusalem and most of Palestine from 1099 to 1187.

The emperor Alexius Comnenus (1081–1118) must have looked on the First Crusade as a very successful piece of Byzantine diplomacy. He had shown remarkable skill in whisking unruly western armies through his lands with a minimum of friction and looting, and he had used the crusading forces to screen his reoccupation of much of western Asia Minor. The establishment in 1099 of the Kingdom of Jerusalem and the northern

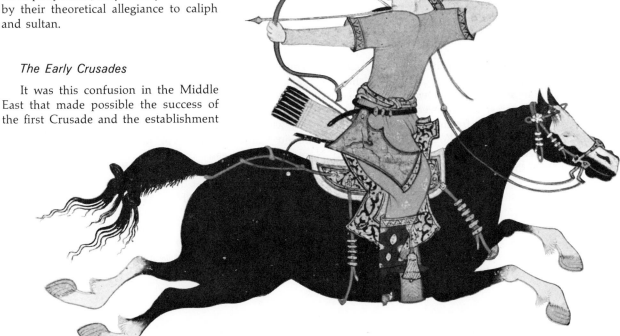

Turkish miniature depicting an Asiatic bowman. Unencumbered by armor, he could move swiftly on his small, strong horse.

CRUSADE ROUTES   1096–1270

Political boundaries are those of the middle of the twelfth century

—·—1— First Crusade, 1096-99   ····4· Fourth Crusade, 1202-04

··—2—·· Second Crusade, 1147-49   L· First Crusade of Louis IX, 1248-54

····3· Third Crusade, 1189-92   --LL- Second Crusade of Louis IX, 1270

0   MILES   300

crusading states of Tripoli, Antioch, and Edessa drove a wedge into the Moslem states of the Middle East and made cooperation among them more difficult than before. Moreover, by posing a threat to Islam, the crusading states also distracted Moslem attention from Byzantine expansion in Asia Minor.

The crusade was not all profit for the Byzantines, however, for it reinforced western suspicions of Byzantine morals and motives. The leaders of the crusade were sure that Alexius' failure to aid them in the siege of Antioch showed that he was more interested in recovering his lost provinces than in freeing the holy places from the Moslems. Western hostility to Byzantium was strengthened by the events of the Second and Third Crusades. The Byzantines were not really interested in fostering these movements; in fact, they twice withdrew into neutrality in return for advantageous treaties with the Turks. The westerners, dismayed by this subtle diplomacy, soon began to think that the Byzantines were

almost as great a threat to Christendom as the Moslems. The sack of Constantinople by a crusading army in 1204 was the price Byzantium paid for arousing these suspicions.

The Moslems recovered only slowly from the shock of the Christian conquest of Jerusalem. Gradually a series of able army commanders began to reunite the scattered Moslem states. The first of these generals, Zangi, took the outlying Christian county of Edessa in 1144 and held it against the badly mismanaged Second Crusade. Even more decisive was the work of Zangi's son, Nureddin (Nūr-al-Dīn), who put an end to the decaying Fatimid Caliphate of Egypt in 1171. Nureddin was already master of most of Syria; by adding Egypt to his domain he became far stronger than the Christian kings of Jerusalem. He was succeeded by his ablest general, Saladin (Salāh-al-Dīn), who overran the Kingdom of Jerusalem and seized the Holy City itself in 1187. The Christians were left with only a few seacoast towns.

306

The loss of Jerusalem sent a shock of horror throughout Latin Christendom. The three greatest kings of the West—Frederick Barbarossa of Germany, Philip Augustus of France, and Richard Lionheart of England—agreed to unite their forces in an attack on Saladin. But this Third Crusade was only partially successful. Frederick was drowned while crossing Asia Minor with his army, and Philip Augustus, after helping to recapture Acre, rushed back to France to look after the affairs of his kingdom. Richard hung on, fighting so bravely that he became a legend among the Moslems, but he never had a large enough army to risk an attack on Jerusalem. He did reconquer a long strip of coastal territory, thus prolonging the life of the Kingdom of Jerusalem for a century. But the revived kingdom was never strong; it played a far less important role in the thirteenth century than it had in the twelfth.

The Later Crusades

Saladin's empire began to dissolve soon after his death in 1193. As so often happened in the Moslem world, his states were divided among members of his family, who promptly began intriguing against one another. The Christians could once more hope to regain Jerusalem, and they staged three major and several minor expeditions to the Middle East in the first half of the thirteenth century. None of these crusades was successful; when Frederick II briefly regained Jerusalem he did it through a treaty with the sultan of Egypt. On the other hand, the thirteenth-century crusades, by weakening both Saladin's dynasty and the Byzantine Empire, aided the rise of new powers in the Middle East.

The Byzantine Empire in 1200 was neither as rich nor as powerful as it once had been. Most of its commerce was in the hands of Italian merchants; the Byzantine navy had almost ceased to exist; and the army, composed largely of mercenaries, was too weak to guard all the frontiers. The Turks were threatening Asia Minor, and a revived Bulgarian kingdom was attacking Thrace. Internal dissension had reached a dangerous point, with many of the great families lined up against the emperor. More or less by accident, the first people to take advantage of this inviting situation were a group of crusaders.

The Fourth Crusade started in 1202 as a routine expedition against the Moslems of the East. But the army was heavily in debt to the Venetians, who had supplied ships to carry it to the East. The Venetians, who cared little about crusades but a great deal about profit, made the army work off part of its debt by capturing Zara, a rival trading town across the Adriatic. Then a pretender to the Byzantine throne turned up with a very tempting proposition: he would pay all the army's debts and augment its forces if the crusaders would make him emperor. The Venetians saw a chance to acquire a monopoly of trade with Byzantium, and under their urging, most, though not all, of the crusaders agreed to attack Constantinople. Aided by Byzantine weakness and disunity, the small western force—probably not more than twenty thousand fighting men—managed to seize one of the most strongly fortified positions in the world (1203).

They soon quarreled with their puppet emperor and took over the city for themselves (1204), sacking churches and stealing relics. Then they elected one of

A Byzantine View of the Crusaders

Anna Comnena, the author of this piece, was the daughter of the Emperor Alexius I.

Now he [the emperor] dreaded the arrival of the Crusaders, for he knew their irresistible manner of attack, their unstable and mobile character, and all the peculiar . . . characteristics which the Frank retains throughout; and he also knew that they were always agape for money, and seemed to disregard their truces readily for any reason that cropped up. . . . The simpler-minded Franks were urged on by the real desire of worshipping at our Lord's Sepulchre, but the more astute, especially men like Bohemund . . . had another secret reason, namely the hope that . . . they might by some means be able to seize the capital itself. . . . For the Frankish race . . . is always very hot-headed and eager, but when it has once espoused a cause, it is uncontrollable.

From Anna Comnena, *The Alexiad*, trans. by E. A. S. Dawes (London: Kegan Paul, 1928), pp. 248, 250.

A Crusader's View of Byzantium

Odo of Deuil, the author of this piece, was a historian of the Second Crusade.

And then the Greeks degenerated entirely into women; putting aside all manly vigor, both of words and of spirit, they lightly swore whatever they thought would please us, but they neither kept faith with us nor maintained respect for themselves. In general they really have the opinion that anything which is done for the holy empire cannot be considered perjury. . . . When the Greeks are afraid they become despicable in their excessive abasement, and when they have the upper hand they are arrogant. . . .

Constantinople itself is squalid and fetid. . . . People live lawlessly in this city, which has as many lords as rich men and almost as many thieves as poor men. . . . In every respect she exceeds moderation, for just as she surpasses other cities in wealth, so too does she surpass them in vice. . . .

[The bishop of Langres] added that Constantinople is Christian only in name and not in fact . . . and that her emperor had ventured a few years ago to attack the [Crusader] prince of Antioch. . . . "Though it was his [the emperor's] duty to ward off the near-by infidels by uniting the Christian forces, with the aid of the infidels he strove to destroy the Christians."

From Odo of Deuil, *De profectione Ludovici VII in orientem,* trans. by V. G. Berry (New York: Columbia University Press, 1948), pp. 57, 65, 69.

their own leaders, Baldwin, Count of Flanders, as emperor, and divided most of Greece and Thrace among the Venetians and western feudal lords. This Latin Empire of Constantinople lasted only a half-century (1204–61), but feudal principalities held by western lords survived in Greece to the end of the fourteenth century, and Venice held some of the Greek islands and ports in the Peloponnesus until the seventeenth century.

Innocent III, who was pope at this time, at first severely condemned the diversion of the Fourth Crusade. After 1204, however, he was seduced by the prospect of ending the schism with the Greek Church and gave full support to the Latin Empire. His first reaction was the sounder one; the capture of Constantinople was a disaster for western Christendom. Instead of healing the breach

between the two Churches, it intensified Byzantine hatred of the Latins and convinced the Greeks that the independence of their Church was synonymous with national survival. Even when they were about to be conquered by the Turks, the Greeks refused to consider union with Rome. As one of them said: "Better the turban of the sultan than the tiara of the pope." Nor did the capture of Constantinople help the Kingdom of Jerusalem; instead, it meant that western money and fighting men had to be diverted to support the Latin Empire and the feudal principalities of Greece. By ruining the Byzantine Empire the crusaders exposed all southeastern Europe to Turkish conquest. Even though the Latins were driven out of Constantinople in 1261, the revived Byzantine Empire was only a shadow of what it had been. It held only a fragment of the Balkans and a small strip of Asia Minor; it could not check the Turkish advance into Europe in the fourteenth century.

Saladin's dynasty would have lost power in any case, but the thirteenth-century crusades speeded up the process. Louis IX of France precipitated a crisis by leading an army against Egypt in 1248. The sultan of Egypt by this time was almost entirely dependent on his household slaves, who formed the core of his army and held many high administrative posts. There were many able men among these slaves, or Mamelukes, as they were called, and they were weary of fighting to keep a decaying dynasty in power. The early successes of the crusading army led them to assassinate the sultan and to replace him with one of their own commanders. For centuries Egypt was to be ruled by Mameluke generals who rose from the ranks of a slave army. Only tough and brutal men could reach the top, and when one of them showed signs of softening, he was apt to be replaced by a younger and more vigorous fighter. But in spite of their internal quarrels, the Mamelukes were a first-rate military power. They were determined to drive the westerners out of the Middle East, and they rapidly accomplished their purpose. By 1271 they had occupied the entire area except for a few coastal towns, and in 1291 Acre, the last stronghold of the crusaders, was taken by the Mameluke sultan.

The fall of Acre did not end the crusades; there were some large-scale expeditions against the Turks in the fourteenth century, and popes talked of crusades as late as 1464. But none of the later crusades gained a permanent foothold in the East or did much to halt the Turkish advance. Whatever influence the crusades had on western civilization had been exerted by the end of the thirteenth century. And that influence was considerable: the crusades had helped to stimulate the growth of the Italian naval power that was to make the Mediterranean a Christian lake for three centuries. The fact that thousands of westerners lived in, or visited, Syria and Palestine encouraged the demand for eastern luxuries and thus changed western standards of living, although there would have been some increase in demand in any case.

On the other hand, the crusaders showed little evidence of intellectual or cultural interests. Armies of occupation are more likely to bring home material objects than ideas. Western scholars learned more from peaceful contacts with the Moors of Spain and the Greeks of Constantinople than they did from the inhabitants of the Kingdom of Jerusalem. In short, the significance of the crusades in East–West relationships was primarily political and economic. The crusades marked the first attempt of western Europe to expand into non-European areas, and they added to the difficulties of both the Byzantine Empire and the Moslem Caliphates. They did little to promote understanding or intellectual contacts among the three civilizations that bordered the shores of the Mediterranean Sea.

THE MONGOL EMPIRE

Far more important than the later crusades was the advance of the Mongols into Russia and the Middle East. The Mongols were another of those nomadic peoples of central Asia who from time to time developed great military power and burst into the lands of their civilized neighbors. The pattern was a familiar one: an able leader would organize his own tribe into an effective striking force and then subjugate other tribes belonging to the same racial stock. Once he had established himself as the predominant power in the vast steppes of central Asia, other nomadic peoples would join him either out of fear or in the hope of sharing in the loot. Finally, the united forces would become strong enough to strike out at China, India, or Europe. This had been the story of the Huns, and it was to be the story of the Mongols.

A small group originally, the Mongols became the dominant element in a great federation of nomadic tribes. But while the Mongols followed the old pattern, they expanded more widely and held their conquests longer than any of their predecessors. The leader who began the expansion of Mongol power, Genghis Khan (ca. 1160–1227), was the ablest of all the nomad rulers, and his immediate descendants were almost as competent. The Mongol khans were not only first-rate generals; they also knew how to organize and administer an empire. As a result, the Mongols became the dominant power in Asia and eastern Europe for a century and a half, and they remained a formidable force well into the fifteenth century.

The Mongols first concentrated their forces against China; they took Peking in 1215 and had occupied most of northern China by the death of Genghis in 1227. The Sung dynasty in the South held out longer, and the Mongols were not able to gain control of the whole country until the 1270s. Meanwhile they found easier conquests to the west. A strong army, under one of the ablest Mongol generals, set out against Persia and Mesopotamia. The Mongols overran Persia quickly, and in 1258 they took Baghdad, plundered the city, and put the caliph to death. This attack ended the Abbasid Caliphate, the last symbol of Moslem unity.

For a time it looked as if the Mongols were going to conquer all the Middle East. But when they attempted to take Syria, they were completely defeated by the Mameluke sultan of Egypt (1260). Since no one else from the Mediterranean to the Yellow Sea could claim to

Genghis Khan (detail from a manuscript illustration, ca. 1310).

have defeated a Mongol army, this victory gave the Mamelukes great prestige. The Mongols made little effort to advance further, and the Mamelukes in Egypt and the Turks in Asia Minor remained independent.

Russia and the Mongols

Meanwhile another Mongol horde had attacked Russia, the chief outpost of Byzantine culture. The viking leaders, who had invaded Russia in the ninth century, had built a strong state around Kiev. This state controlled the trade route between the Black Sea and the Baltic, a route that in the early Middle Ages probably carried as many Oriental wares as the route across the Mediterranean. The princes of Kiev grew rich from their trade and were powerful enough to attack Constantinople itself on several occasions. But after the conversion of the Russians to Greek Orthodox Christianity

at the end of the tenth century, relations between Kiev and Byzantium were generally friendly. The Russians accepted the civilization of the Eastern Empire along with its religion; they built their churches in the Byzantine style, and their scholars translated Byzantine texts into Russian. Although the Russians added ideas of their own, Kiev at the height of its power in the early eleventh century must have resembled Constantinople in many ways. It was certainly larger, wealthier, and more of an intellectual center than either the Paris of the first Capetian kings or the London of William the Conqueror.

In the twelfth century Kiev began to decline. It lost some of its trade to the Italians, who exploited the Mediterranean route and sent their ships into the Black Sea. It suffered even more from the Pechenegs, a nomadic people who pushed through the gap between the Urals and the Caspian and cut the trade

Iron and silver helmet found at the site of a battle between the sons of a Russian prince (1216). The helmet bears the figure of the archangel Michael.

THE MONGOL EMPIRE AND ITS SUCCESSOR STATES   Thirteenth century

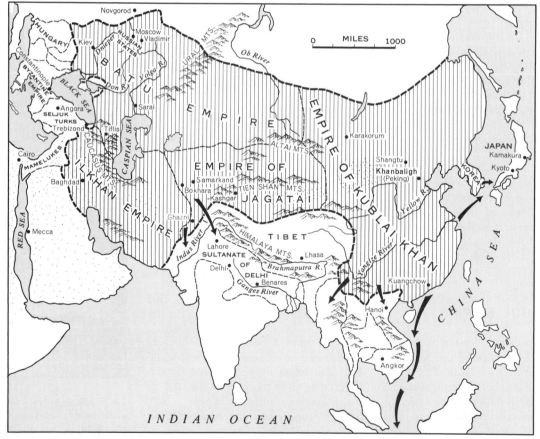

route between Constantinople and Kiev. Meanwhile other centers of power were developing in the upper Volga basin. The princes of Kiev had given outlying towns to younger members of their family to be ruled as dependent principalities. This practice worked well enough at first, but as Kiev declined and family ties weakened, the junior princes became greedy for power. They sacked Kiev itself in 1168, and this disaster, combined with commercial difficulties, put an end to the unity and prosperity of early Russia. The strongest ruler was now the prince of Suzdal, a region that included the newly founded town of Moscow, but his territories were poor and backward compared with Kiev in its great days. Once a land of cities and merchants, Russia was now becoming a land of peasants scratching out a bare living from the thin soils of the north. Declining prosperity, however, did not put an end to feuding among the princes, who found it almost impossible to take combined action against a common enemy such as the Mongols.

It is not surprising, then, that the Mongols conquered Russia so easily. Their first serious attack came in 1237; by 1241 they had overcome all resistance and were pushing across the Carpathians into Hungary. Hungarians resisted no more successfully than Russians—their armies were slaughtered near Budapest—but the death of the Great Khan ended the Mongol threat to central Europe. The commander of the Mongol army rushed home to influence the choice of a new ruler, and he never resumed his attack. The Mongols were at last satiated. They had every right to be, for they had created one of the largest empires the world has ever known.

The Mongols used terror as a means of conquest, wrecking cities and executing entire populations in order to convince their foes of the dangers of resistance. But once they had established their empire, they were willing to profit from the knowledge and skills of their subjects. In China and Persia, where they came in contact with relatively advanced civilizations, they soon became assimilated and carried on the old administrative and cultural traditions. In Russia, where they had less to learn, they held

RUSSIA ABOUT 1200

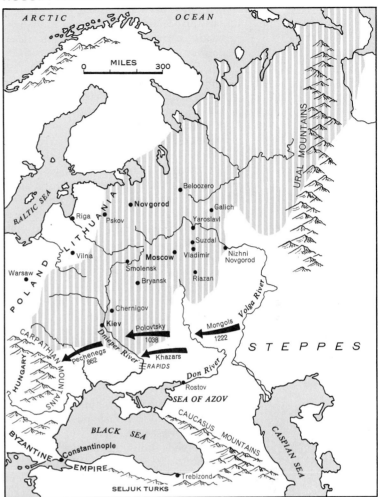

themselves apart and retained more of their own characteristics. They occupied only the steppes north of the Caspian, a region in which there never had been very many Slavs.

Western Europe and the Mongols

The coming of the Mongols might have changed the history of all Europe if western Europeans had been more alert. For several decades the most dangerous opponents of the Mongols were Mamelukes and Turks, and the Mongols repeatedly suggested to Christian rulers that they form an alliance against the common Moslem enemy. None of these suggestions was ever followed up very seriously, however, and an alliance may well have been impossible. Nevertheless, an alliance between Mongols and Christians might have checked the rising power of the Turks.

Europe also missed the opportunity to convert the Mongols. They were not greatly attached to their own primitive beliefs, and at times they seemed attracted to Christianity. The first Mongol viceroy of Persia had a Christian wife and favored her coreligionists, and the Mongol khan of China, Kublai, asked the pope several times to send him missionaries. Unfortunately, the thirteenth-century popes were occupied with matters nearer at hand, such as their feud with the Hohenstaufens and their efforts to preserve the crusading states. They sent a few envoys, but no solid corps of permanent missionaries. The popes of the early fourteenth century made a greater effort, but by that time it was too late. The western Mongols had already been converted to Islam, one more example of the advantage the simpler Moslem faith enjoyed in missionary competition. The Mongols of China were becoming submerged in the sea of Chinese culture and were soon to lose their power. The few missionaries who were sent from the West made thousands of converts, and a Catholic archbishop sat in Peking for a few years. But the whole effort was swept away when the Mongols were overthrown in 1368 and the strongly antiforeign Ming dynasty came to power.

Some Italian merchants took advantage of the opening of the overland route to China. The most famous of them was Marco Polo, who went to China in 1275 and spent many years in the country, part of the time as an official of the Mongol government. After he returned to Italy, Marco wrote a long and fairly accurate account of his travels, and his description of the wealth and splendor of the Far East did much to encourage the great explorations of the fifteenth century. But Marco had less influence on the people of his own time. He was accused of wild exaggeration and nicknamed "Marco Millions"; few other merchants followed in his footsteps. Here was another lost opportunity. At the end of the thirteenth century the European econ-

Kublai Khan (1259–94), a descendant of Genghis Khan and ruler of China at the time of Marco Polo's visit.

omy was grinding toward stagnation; it desperately needed the stimulus of new markets. But fourteenth-century Europe lacked the capital, the energy, and the technical skill needed to open direct trade with the Far East. It was not until the late fifteenth century that western merchants could again dream of reaching China.

RUSSIA: ISOLATION AND AUTOCRACY

During the Mongol occupation, the Russians were allowed to live under their own princes and had little direct contact with the Mongols. So long as the princes paid tribute and sought confirmation of their authority from the khan, they could have whatever laws and religion they pleased.

Loss of Contact with the West

Nevertheless, the period of Mongol domination was a difficult one for Russia. Contacts with the West were sharply reduced, for both in commerce and in diplomacy the Russians had to deal primarily with the Mongols. The Russians were also blocked off from the West by the growing power of Poland and Lithuania.

Poland had received its religion and much of its civilization from the West. It had been converted at the end of the tenth century by Roman Catholic missionaries, and for a long time it was a vassal state of the German Empire. Often weak and divided, the Poles gradually began to grow stronger in the fourteenth century, as the German Empire fell apart. Their trade was largely with the West; their official language, for government as well as for religious affairs, was Latin; and they were rather inclined to look down on the Russians as a backward people.

The Lithuanians were a very ancient people, of the Indo-European language group, who had struggled for centuries to maintain their independence in their home on the south Baltic coast. Both Russians and Germans had tried to convert them, but the bulk of the population remained pagan until well into the fourteenth century. Just as the Poles profited from German weakness, so the Lithuanians gained by the collapse of Kievan Russia. They expanded south and east, acquiring some of the most fertile Russian lands.

In 1386 the Poles and the Lithuanians united. The Poles accepted the Lithuanian grand duke as their king; in return the Lithuanians were supposed to become Latin Christians. Poland-Lithuania was oriented to the West and was usually hostile to the Russians. Down to the sixteenth century, Poland-Lithuania was larger and stronger than all the Russian principalities put together. It intervened again and again in Russian politics, and it acquired so much Russian land that Moscow, at times, was almost a frontier city. Russia was cut off from the Baltic and had few dealings with any western state.

Russia's loss of contact with the West was at first compensated for by increased contacts with the East. As long as the Mongols remained relatively united, the long land route across the Eurasian plain to China was heavily traveled—more heavily than it was to be again until the nineteenth century. But the subordinate khans who governed outlying regions of the Mongol Empire gradually became independent of the Great Khan, who had his headquarters in Mongolia. Thus the Russians had little to do with the relatively civilized Mongols of China and Persia. They dealt primarily with the so-called Golden Horde, the Mongols of the lower Volga region, who were the least advanced of all the Mongol groups.

Thrown back on themselves, the Russians took refuge in their religion. Their faith differentiated them from the Mongols, but it separated them almost as sharply from the West. They became fiercely orthodox and even less willing than the Greeks to compromise with the Roman Church. This stubbornness, added to their fear of the Catholic Poles, made them suspicious of westerners and western influences that might change their way of life and endanger their faith.

The Rise of the Autocratic Russian State

Isolation, poverty, and constant wars were not ideal conditions for the growth of Russian society. Opportunities diminished for all classes, especially for the peasants. The most the peasants could hope for was to keep their freedom and a little piece of land, and often they found even these modest desires thwarted. Almost the only productive group in the country, the peasants had to support the Mongols, the princes, the nobles, and the Church. The easiest way for their overlords to make sure that they would meet all these obligations was to bind them to the soil; thus serfdom grew in Russia at

The Church of the Savior at Novgorod (twelfth century). This is an early example of what became a typical style of ecclesiastical architecture in Russia.

the very time it was declining in the West. In order to escape serfdom, some peasants moved off into the desolate forest regions of the northeast, but even there the princes caught up with them and assigned them as serfs to monasteries and nobles.

The government of the princes became increasingly arbitrary, though its arbitrariness was always tempered by administrative inefficiency. Economic pressure forced the princes into absolutism; their states were small, and the burdens of Mongol tribute and war expenses were great. The princes had inherited a tradition of autocracy from Byzantium,

and Mongol demands encouraged the growth of absolutism. A prince who could not collect his tribute was sure to be in trouble; it did him no good to explain that he could not raise the money without violating the rights of his nobles and peasants.

During the fourteenth century the principality of Moscow became the strongest state in Russia. Its rise was due partly to chance; for several generations only one heir to the principality survived, and thus it was not weakened by constant divisions. Moreover, the metropolitan of Russia moved his seat to Moscow, thus bestowing on the Muscovite princes

THE GROWTH OF THE GRAND PRINCIPALITY OF MOSCOW   1300–1584

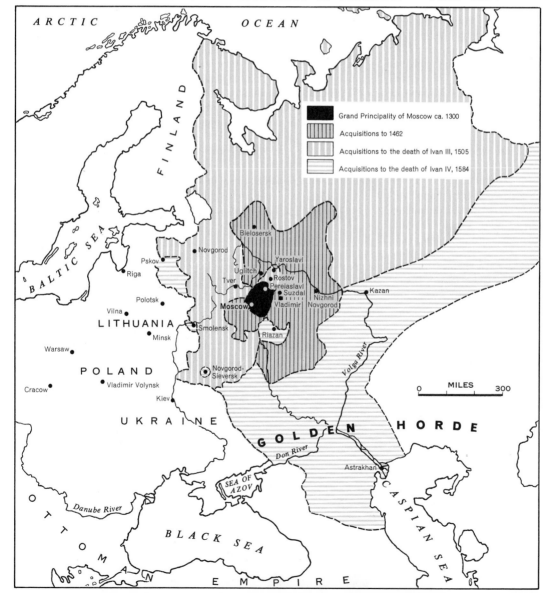

the support of the highest religious authority in the country. Many of the Muscovite princes were men of superior ability, both in diplomacy and in war. They managed to keep on relatively good terms with the Mongols and were given the title of Grand Prince, which meant that they were the chief tribute collectors for the entire country. This position gave them an excuse to intervene in the incessant quarrels of other principalities and an opportunity to annex surrounding territory. As the Mongols weakened, the Grand Princes of Moscow became bolder; one of them actually defeated a Mongol army in 1378. Their assertion of independence was premature, however, for the Mongols still had a strong enough army to defeat the Grand Prince and burn Moscow a few years later. Mongol suzerainty was reestablished and continued into the fifteenth century. Nevertheless, the Grand Prince had established himself as leader of the Russians, and his victory over the Mongols was better remembered than his subsequent submission.

During the fifteenth century a civil war broke out in Moscow, but it served to strengthen the principality. The legitimate heir won the final victory and established the principle that Moscow was not to be divided as other Russian states had been. From this point on, the growth of the Muscovite state was phenomenal. It quickly absorbed neighboring principalities and, under Ivan the Great (Ivan III, 1462–1505), annexed the Republic of Novgorod, which held all northern Russia to the White Sea and the Arctic. Ivan also rejected, once and for all, Mongol suzerainty, and the Russians soon began to annex Mongol lands along the lower Volga. By the end of the sixteenth century the Muscovite state had expanded into a Russian Empire, with territories stretching from the White Sea to the Caspian and from the Lithuanian frontier well into western Siberia. The original principality of Moscow had covered only about five hundred square miles; the Russian Empire of the sixteenth century was the largest state in Europe.

Absolutism grew with the growth of the Muscovite state. The peasants had lost their rights long before; now it was

Russia, the Heir of the Byzantine Empire

Letter of Abbot Philotheus of Pskov to Tsar Vasily III in 1511.

The Church of ancient Rome fell because of the Apollinarian heresy; as for the second Rome, the Church of Constantinople, it has been cut down by the axes of the Hagarenes [Turks]. But in the third, new Rome, the Universal Apostolic Church under thy [Tsar Vasily III] mighty rule sends out the Orthodox Christian faith to the ends of the earth and shines more brightly than the sun. And may thy lordship realize, pious Tsar, that all Christian kingdoms have come together under thy sole empire; thou alone in all the earth art Tsar to the Christians. . . . Two Romes have fallen, but the third stands, and there will be no fourth.

Adapted from Thornton Anderson, *Russian Political Thought* (Ithaca, N.Y.: Cornell University Press, 1967), p. 72.

the turn of the nobles. They were not as independent as the nobles of the West. Most of them had become servants of the princes and held their estates only so long as they performed services for the ruler. They had no permanent power base, such as a duke of Lancaster or a duke of Burgundy had in the West. Soon their very life and property depended on the whim of the prince. By the sixteenth century the greatest men in the land could be put to death on the mere suspicion of disloyalty, and bishops and metropolitans who contradicted the wishes of the sovereign were sent into exile. The old title of Grand Prince no longer seemed sufficient to express this concentration of power. Ivan the Great, who married a niece of the last Byzantine emperor, soon began to think of himself as successor to the Caesars. Moscow was to be the "Third Rome" that would endure forever, and Ivan began to call himself Autocrat and Sovereign of All Russia. He also occasionally used the title of tsar (a Russian form of Caesar), but this did not become official until the reign of Ivan the Dread (Ivan IV, 1533–84). Ivan the Dread was a great conqueror and one of the bloodiest tyrants in history. He massacred nobles and townsmen with little reason and killed his own son in a fit of rage.

Part of the dowry of the marriage of Byzantine Princess Zoe to Ivan the Great (1462–1505) was the right to adopt the Byzantine two-headed eagle as the tsar's royal coat of arms.

Roman Empire
Divided in Half
395 A.D.

Turks Take
Constantinople
1453

Byzantine Empire

In spite of its size and the authority of its ruler, sixteenth-century Muscovy was not yet a powerful state. Still cut off from the main trade routes, its only outlet to the ocean was in the far north, on the White Sea. It was thinly settled; probably there were more people in France than in all the territories of the tsar. It was poor; it had almost no industry, and agriculture was backward. It was still militarily weak, open to attack by Poles from the west and Turks and Tatars from the southeast. The bulk of the peasants were still farming the poor soils of the north by primitive methods, and there were few settlers in the rich black-earth districts of the south. It was far behind its neighbors in all intellectual activities, in science and technology as well as in scholarship and literature. Only after 1600 did the Russians begin to overcome these great handicaps.

THE ADVANCE OF THE TURKS

The problem for much of Europe was not the Mongols but the Turks. As we have seen, the Mongol advance left the Turks of Asia Minor relatively unharmed, and the Byzantine Empire had been fragmented by the Fourth Crusade. The Serbs and Bulgars dominated the back country, western feudal lords ruled most of Greece, and Venice held the islands. The Byzantine Empire, as revived in 1261, possessed only Constantinople and a narrow strip of land on each side of the Straits. The new Turkish dynasty of the Ottomans, founded in 1299, rapidly exploited the weakness of the Christians. As good at war as their predecessors, the Seljuks, the Ottomans showed far more ability in building a permanent state with a strong administrative system. After conquering most of western Asia Minor, they began, in the 1350s, to make permanent settlements on the European side

of the Straits. The Christians offered no concerted resistance, and by 1365 the Turks had established their capital in Adrianople, not far from Constantinople. In 1389 they broke the power of the Serbs, who had the strongest state in the Balkans, at the battle of Kossovo. This victory brought the Turks to the borders of Hungary, and the West at last began to take alarm. The pope proclaimed a crusade, and a large army—mostly German and Hungarian with some French knights—advanced against the Turks. But bad generalship and poor discipline ruined whatever chance of success it had, and the crusaders were thoroughly defeated at the battle of Nicopolis in 1396.

The battle almost destroyed Christian power in the Balkans, but before the Turks could fully exploit their victory they were attacked from the east. Timur the Lame (Tamerlane), who claimed to be a descendant of Genghis Khan, had created a nomad army worthy of his supposed ancestor. The Mongols were once more on the march, and this time the Ottoman Turks were one of their chief enemies. In 1402 the two armies met at Ankara, where Timur won a complete victory. The Mongols captured the Turkish sultan and occupied most of his lands in Asia Minor.

Timur died soon after his victory, and his successors made little effort to hold the remote regions he had taken from the Turks. Nevertheless, the defeat at Ankara, followed by a generation of civil war, was a severe test of the Ottoman political system. The fact that the state was pulled together once again showed that the early sultans had done their work well. They had created a corps of disciplined and capable administrators, and it was with their assistance that one of the Ottoman princes was able to reestablish himself as sole ruler. By the 1440s the Turks were once more advancing in the Balkans. Their chief opponents this time were the Hungarians, commanded by John Hunyadi. Though a first-rate general, Hunyadi lost two major battles to the Turks.

The End of the Byzantine Empire

Now the road lay open to Constantinople. The last Byzantine emperor, Constantine XI, made a desperate appeal to the West for aid. Over the strong opposition of his subjects, he agreed to reunite the Greek and Latin Churches in return for western aid. But the union was never effective, and the popes of the fifteenth century lacked the prestige needed to rouse the West. Constantine received no real help and was left to fight the final battles alone. In 1453 the Turks made an all-out attack on the imperial city. The emperor was killed defending a breach in the walls, and the Turks poured into Constantinople. This was the end of the Byzantine Empire and of the emperors who claimed to be heirs of Caesar and Augustus. For many years there had been nothing Roman about them except their titles, but they were not unworthy of those titles in their last struggle.

Turkish advances in Europe continued after the fall of Constantinople, largely at the expense of Hungary. The Hungarians fought valiantly but were pushed back little by little until the Turks reached their high-water mark of conquest at the unsuccessful siege of Vienna in 1529.

As the Turkish advance slowed down in Europe, it speeded up in Asia and Africa. During the sixteenth century Syria, Mesopotamia, and Arabia were added to the Turkish Empire in Asia, and Egypt, Tunisia, and Algeria in North Africa. With this Turkish conquest of the southern and eastern coasts of the Mediterranean, Moslem naval power began to revive. The Turks never closed the Mediterranean to Christian shipping, but they and the semipiratical fleets of their subjects did interfere seriously with commerce from time to time. It was not until the 1800s that the Mediterranean became as safe for western merchants as it had been in the thirteenth century.

The Decline of Moslem Civilization

The rise of the Turks coincided with a decline in Moslem intellectual activity. Both the Turks and the Mongols have often been blamed for this decline, but neither people seems to have been entirely responsible. It is true that both Turks and Mongols were originally rough warriors from the steppes with little interest in intellectual matters, but both of them absorbed Moslem civilization with great rapidity. Art and literature flourished under the Mongol rulers of Persia. In fact, Persia was the leading cultural center of Islam in the fifteenth century, but its influence was felt more in the East, especially in India, than in the West. The Turks did some remarkable work in architecture and developed a highly literate corps of administrators. Moreover, one of the most eloquent laments over the decline of Moslem learning came from the historian ibn-Khaldun (1332–1406), who spent most of his life in North Africa, a region that was never touched by the Mongols and that fell under Turkish control only in the sixteenth century. There must have been more deep-seated causes, prevalent throughout the Moslem world, of the decline of Moslem civilization.

Ibn-Khaldun, probably the greatest of all Moslem historians, tried to work out a historical theory to explain the decline.

Mohammed II, ruler of the Turks when they took Constantinople in 1453.

His idea was that there had always been antagonism between the educated, open-minded, prosperous city dwellers and the ignorant, narrow-minded, poverty-stricken inhabitants of the desert and the steppes. When the city people became soft and decadent, as they had in his time, power passed to the crude but warlike tribes of the open country. This political shift in turn caused a shift in the climate of opinion. Rigid orthodoxy was favored, and science and philosophy were looked on with contempt and suspicion.

There is some truth in ibn-Khaldun's explanation. The dominant dynasties of the Moslem world in the fourteenth century were all nomad in origin, and some of them did emphasize strict Moslem orthodoxy. But this is only part of the story. Earlier nomadic conquerors, beginning with the Arabs themselves, had absorbed the intellectual heritage of the ancient world without difficulty, and fourteenth-century orthodoxy did not prevent the rise of mysticism in the Moslem world. Some leaders of the mystical movement, who had large followings, advanced ideas that went far beyond the early teachings of Islam, so that we cannot say that a sort of Islamic fundamentalism blocked all forms of speculation. It seems rather that Moslem science and philosophy had reached a dead end, and that the educated classes had become uninterested in them.

Perhaps Moslem learning had reached its peak too early and too rapidly. Few new ideas entered the world of Islam after the tenth century, and all the changes on the old themes had been rung by the thirteenth century. With nothing new to be done, there was naturally a loss of interest in academic sub-jects. In comparison, western scholarship, which was far inferior to that of the Moslem world in the tenth century, received a fresh stimulus every time it was about to reach a dead end. There were the translations from the Arabic in the twelfth century, the revival of Greek studies in the fifteenth, and the great scientific discoveries of the early modern period. Moreover, theology, philosophy, and science were so closely associated in Christian thought that activity in one field prompted activity in the others. Extraordinary interest in theology in the fourteenth century stimulated activity in philosophy and science. The theology of Islam, on the other hand, was much less complicated. Some Moslems took it for granted; others simply memorized the Koran, paying no attention to philosophy. Thus religious education in Moslem countries did not require corresponding activity in philosophy or science. Finally, as we have seen, western scholars were not quite so bound to authoritative, scholarly interpretations; more innovation was possible in fourteenth-century Paris than in fourteenth-century Cairo.

Whatever the value of these explanations, one basic fact is clear: for the first time in history, western Europe was to take the lead in certain types of scholarly investigation. Byzantine scholarship, never very original, was blighted by the Turkish conquest. Moslem scholarship was rapidly decaying in the fourteenth and fifteenth centuries. Of all the peoples who had inherited the great Greek tradition of philosophical and scientific inquiry, only the scholars of western Europe were still active. And their activity was to give the West an incalculable advantage in the next four centuries.

Suggestions for Further Reading

Note: Asterisk denotes a book available in paperback edition.

Byzantium 750–1453 S. Runciman, *Byzantine Civilization** (1933), gives a good general picture of Byzantine institutions and culture and is the best introduction. The most thorough and scholarly study is G. Ostrogorsky, *History of the Byzantine State,* trans. by J. M. Hussey (1956). The older work of A. A. Vasiliev, *History* *of the Byzantine Empire,* 2 vols. (1928), is more readable than Ostrogorsky but not as thorough nor as fresh in historical interpretation. There is valuable material on the commercial activities of the Italian city-states within the Byzantine Empire in E. H. Byrne, *Genoese Shipping in the Twelfth and Thirteenth Centuries* (1930), and in C. Diehl, *Une République patricienne: Venise* (1916). G. Every, *The Byzantine Patriarchate* (1947), compares the liturgical and doctrinal differences between the eastern and western Churches, and J. M. Hussey, *Church and Learning in the Byzantine Empire* (1937), is useful for understanding Byzantine intellectual activity. See also the titles by Baynes, Diehl, Grabar, and Talbot-Rice mentioned after Chapter 8. An interesting survey of Byzantine civilization and its influence on the West is S. Vryonis, *Byzantium and Europe** (1967). The best account of the Latin conquest of Constantinople is *Latin Conquest of Constantinople,* ed. by D. E. Queller (1971).

The Caliphate 750–1258
B. Lewis, *The Arabs in History** (1966), a broad, quick survey, is a good starting point for study. B. Spuler, *The Muslim World,* Vol. I, trans. by F. R. C. Bagley (1960), is an authoritative survey of the entire period and a useful handbook. The old account of T. W. Arnold, *The Caliphate* (1963), is still valuable for the theory and development of the Caliphate. There is considerable material in P. K. Hitti, *A History of the Arabs** (1956), the standard treatment of the subject, invaluable for the facts of the period but quite controversial in historical interpretation. For the Caliphate as an institution, see E. Tyan, *Le Califut* (1954), and E. I. J. Rosenthal, *Political Thought in Medieval Islam* (1958). The growth of Turkish power is well treated by P. Wittek, *The Rise of the Ottoman Empire* (1958).

The Crusades
There are several accounts of the later crusades that give us real insight into the spirit and motivation of the crusaders. Both Geoffrey de Villhardouin, *The Conquest of Constantinople** (Everyman's Library), and Robert of Clari, *The Conquest of Constantinople,* trans. by E. H. McNeal (1936), are fascinating eyewitness accounts of the Fourth Crusade. Philippe of Novara, *The Wars of Frederick II Against the Ibelins,* trans. by J. L. La Monte (1936), contributes a great deal to our knowledge of Frederick II and his crusades. The counselor Joinville's *Life of St. Louis** (Everyman's Library) has exciting material on St. Louis' expeditions to Egypt and Tunis on the Sixth and Seventh Crusades.

E. Barker, *The Crusades* (1923), is old but still valuable. The best recent study is the beautifully written and highly urbane account by S. Runciman, *A History of the Crusades,** 3 vols. (1951–54). Runciman includes a thorough bibliography. There is good material on the crusades in the books by Setton, Hitti, and La Monte listed after Chapter 10, in the fourth section. For crusading efforts after 1300, see A. S. Atiya, *The Crusade in the Later Middle Ages* (1938).

The Mongols in the Arab World and Russia
B. Spuler, *The Muslim World,* Vol. II: *The Mongol Period,* trans. by F. R. C. Bagley (1960), is excellent. G. Le Strange, *The Lands of the Eastern Caliphate* (1905), a study of the historical geography of the Near East and central Asia in the Middle Ages, is an old treatment but very good reading. Juvaynī ʻAlāʼ al-Din ʻutā Malik, *The History of the World Conqueror,* trans. by J. A. Bayle (1952), is an important study, while V. V. Barthold, *Four Studies on the History of Central Asia* (1955), contains the authoritative history of central Asia and the Mongols. Probably the best treatment of the Mongol rule of Russia is G. Vernadsky, *The Monguls and Russia* (1953), a scholarly and readable work by a leading authority on Russian history.

Russia 1100–1600
There are several very good studies of this period of Russian history. M. T. Florinsky, *Russia: A History and Interpretation,* Vol. I (1955), has valuable material on this formative period of the Russian state. The old work of V. O. Kliuchevsky, *A History of Russia,* 2 vols. (1912), is very interesting reading and still important. Undoubtedly the best treatment of Russia from 1100 to 1600 is G. Vernadsky, *Russia at the Dawn of the Modern Age* (1959). Vernadsky includes excellent maps and genealogical tables and up-to-date bibliographic material. *A History of the U.S.S.R.,* ed. by A. M. Pankratova (1947), is a modern Marxist interpretation of the evolution of the Russian state.

The Decline of Arabic Learning
Most of the titles mentioned in the second section above contain information on Arabic learning. R. Landau, *Islam and the Arabs* (1958), devotes considerable attention to Moslem culture. T. W. Arnold and A. Guillaume, *The Legacy of Islam* (2nd ed. by J. Schacht and C. E. Bosworth, 1972), provide a good summary that traces those elements in European culture that have roots in the Islamic world.

15 India, China, and Japan 500–1600 A.D.

The fifth-century invasions of the Huns and related tribes were a disaster from which northern India never fully recovered. Its political system was shattered, and not until the establishment of the Moslem sultanate of Delhi in 1206 did a single state manage to dominate northern India again. The Ganges Valley was divided into small warring kingdoms that were briefly united by the rajah Harsha (606–647). Northern India was fairly prosperous during his reign, and both scholarship and literature flourished. But Harsha was unable to conquer central India, and only his personal ability kept the Ganges Valley united. After his death his kingdom collapsed. During the next two and a half centuries northern India was dominated by the Rajputs, many of whom were descendants of warriors from central Asia who had entered India during the chaotic years following the Hunnic invasion. The Rajputs intermarried with Hindus and adopted Hindu religious beliefs and social practices with great enthusiasm. After a time they began to claim that they were members of the Hindu warrior caste—next to the Brahmans, the highest group in Hindu society—and therefore the rightful lords of the common people.

INDIAN KINGDOMS

The Rajputs created a way of life not unlike that of the nobles of western Europe in the thirteenth and fourteenth centuries. They loved combat and developed a chivalric code that valued fair fighting and mercy to the weak and helpless. They showed more respect to women than was customary in other parts of India; their court poets recited epics commemorating the heroes of the past. The Rajput aristocrats led a brilliant and exciting life, but they showed little political capacity. They used up their qualities of courage, honor, and loyalty in endless internecine wars and left northern India so weak that it was easily overrun by Moslem invaders after the tenth century.

The dynasties established farther south had a somewhat longer life. South-central India, the Deccan, was united for two centuries under the Chalukya kings (*ca. 550–ca. 750*), who were strong enough to repel Harsha and other invaders from the north. Even after the fall of the Chalukyas, the Deccan was less fragmented than the northern region. It broke up into a few fairly large states, which preserved their independence until the fourteenth century. In the ex-

Colossal statue of the Trimurti (Brahma, Vishnu, and Shiva) from a cave temple in western India (eighth century).

treme South were the Tamils, remnants of the original Dravidian inhabitants of India. They too created large kingdoms, first Chola, which lasted from the tenth to the end of the thirteenth century, and then Vijayanagar, which fell to the Moslems only in 1585. At its height Vijayanagar held the whole southern third of the peninsula, carried on an active foreign commerce, and was fabulously wealthy.

The Spread of Indian Culture

The most important events of these centuries were not the rise and fall of dynasties, but the consolidation of Hindu culture and the spread of Indian influence overseas. As we have seen, Buddhism was declining in India during the Gupta period, and it lost even more ground during the invasions and wars that followed the downfall of the Gupta dynasty. By the end of the tenth century Buddhism was almost extinct in India, and the entire population followed some form of the old Hindu beliefs. There were many variants of this religion; each part of the country had its own special rituals and favorite gods. But each sect was usually tolerant of the others, since all divinities were considered manifestations of the same underlying spiritual forces. And the basic elements of the Hindu way of life—the power of the Brahman priesthood, the caste system, and the intellectual and religious tradition—permeated the whole peninsula.

The real strength of Hindu civilization was in its social rather than its political structure. The great majority of the people lived in small agricultural villages that were administered by a council of elders and were advised—often dominated—by a Brahman priest. These villages showed little interest in the changes of dynasties and the rise and fall of kingdoms; they paid tribute to the ruler of the moment and preserved their traditional way of life through all the storms of war and rebellion. Under the caste system every man's place in society and his occupation were clearly marked out, and it took more than a change of rulers to upset such well-established patterns. At a higher level the Brahmans, who served as intellectual and religious leaders, preserved the continuity of tradition. Some kings were more influenced by the Brahmans than others, but between the collapse of Buddhism and the Moslem conquest of northern India there was no rival religious or intellectual leadership. In the long run the ideas of the Brahmans influenced all governments and all classes and gave a basic unity to Indian life in spite of extreme local diversity.

During the centuries of the European Middle Ages the Indians were barred from the West by the growing power of Islam, but they found that the backward and unorganized peoples of Southeast Asia were easily influenced by their civilization. It is still not clear whether Indian emigrants conquered neighboring lands or whether they secured a dominant position by peaceful penetration. Certainly many of the ruling families of the kingdoms to the east of India bore Hindu names, and the art and literature of these countries show strong Indian influence. Imposing Buddhist and Hindu shrines were built, of which the most striking is the enormous temple of Angkor Wat in Cambodia. With its five great towers and its long walls covered with scenes from Hindu epics, Angkor Wat is one of the largest religious centers ever created by man. The complex of buildings covered more ground than most medieval Euro-

The Rajput Code

A widow speaks to the page who witnessed her husband's death.

"Boy, tell me, ere I go, how bore himself my lord?

"As a reaper of the harvest of battle. I followed his steps as a humble gleaner of his sword. On the bed of honor he spread a carpet of the slain, whereon, a barbarian his pillow, he sleeps ringed by his foes."

"Yet once again, boy, tell me how my lord bore himself?"

"Oh mother, who can tell his deeds? He left no foe to dread or to admire him."

She smiled farewell to the boy, and adding, "My lord will chide my delay," sprang into the flames.

As quoted in H. G. Rawlinson, *India: A Short Cultural History* (New York: Appleton-Century, 1938), p. 202.

pean cities, and the individual structures were larger and more richly ornamented than most cathedrals.

Indian influence was strongest and most lasting in Burma, western Siam, and the Malay Peninsula. In Indochina it had to compete with Chinese influence from the north. Tongking and part of Annam (North Vietnam) were always closely connected with China, while South Vietnam, Cambodia, and Laos were more like India—a fact that may help to explain recent political problems in this region. Indonesia received Buddhism and much of its culture from India, and the Sailendra dynasty, which ruled the archipelago from the eighth to the eleventh century, built some of the most magnificent Buddhist shrines the world has ever seen. The Sailendra kings were followed by Hindu rulers, who held the islands until the Moslem conquest of the sixteenth century. Java, the most populous of the islands, became thoroughly Moslem at this time, but the smaller island of Bali to the east preserved a basically Hindu culture.

The Political Weakness of India

During this eastern expansion India was at its best—full of energy, imagination, and understanding in dealing with strange peoples. But by the end of the tenth century the period of expansion was over, and the qualities that had made it possible seem largely to have vanished. This decline was due partly to the Indians' failure to create permanent and stable governments. Every society needs constant rebuilding if it is not to stagnate or disintegrate, and rebuilding is very difficult in the absence of effective political institutions. Individual Indian rulers often had excellent ideas, but their plans died with them and India failed to adapt itself to new conditions.

There was little economic development. Trade remained at its old levels; industry was decentralized, with as many artisans in the countryside as in the towns, and the magnificent royal cities consumed more than they produced. The Indian peasant still carried most of society on his back. He was happiest when there were not too many middlemen (landlords and petty officers) between him and the court that was the ultimate consumer of his taxes, but such good fortune was rare during periods of weak government.

In addition, the prevailing Hindu way of life became more and more conservative, while the leaders of Hindu thought became complacent and self-satisfied. They had little to do with the Moslems to the west, and their contacts with China decreased. The people they knew best were those of Southeast Asia, but they considered these people inferior. As a

Shiva, Hindu god of destruction and reproduction, as Lord of the Dance (India, twelfth or thirteenth century).

A view of the temple of Angkor Wat, built in the twelfth century by the king of Cambodia.

Brahma, Hindu god personifying the essence and creator of the universe (India, tenth or eleventh century).

result, there was a tendency for Indian civilization to freeze in a rigid pattern—to fall back on its past accomplishments rather than to advance to new ground. The caste system became both more complicated and more unchangeable; little new work was done in science. Thinkers such as the great Indian philosopher Sankara, who tried to see one eternal being behind the multiplicity of gods, had little influence. Even the art of war fell into a set pattern in which armies were maneuvered according to the teachings of ancient writers rather than according to the needs of a particular campaign.

THE MOSLEM CONQUEST

All these weaknesses became critical when Moslem pressure on the northwest frontier increased. In the eighth century, during their first wave of expansion, the Moslems had taken over the southern Indus Valley, but this annexation neither influenced Indian culture nor caused much ill will between the Islamic and Hindu religious communities. The situation changed sharply, as it did in so many other regions, with the coming of the Turks in the tenth century. The Turks renewed the conquering tradition of Islam and showed themselves far less tolerant of alien religions than the Arabs. It is true that Hinduism, with its images, its hundreds of gods, and its elaborate ceremonies, contradicted everything for which Mohammed had stood, and that it was far easier for Moslems to be tolerant of Christianity, with which they had some common traditions, than of Hinduism, which was completely alien to them. Nevertheless, the Arab rulers of the lower Indus Valley had not been implacably hostile to the Hindus; it was the Turks who transformed the two religious communities into bitter and persistent enemies.

The Turks and related peoples first established themselves in Afghanistan in the tenth century and immediately began to nibble away at the holdings of the Rajput princes in northwest India. This process was completed by Mahmud of Ghazni, who held most of the northwest by 1022 and pushed his daring raids deep into Hindu territory. Intermittent raiding and fighting continued for a century and a half, until the next great Moslem conqueror appeared. This was Mohammed Ghori, who pushed east toward the Ganges Valley and defeated the allied Hindu kings of the North in a decisive battle at Panipat in 1192. This victory opened the entire region north of the Deccan to the Moslems. Mohammed Ghori was assassinated in 1206, but in

Moslem and Hindu in the Fourteenth Century

Ala-ud-Din [sultan of Delhi, 1296–1316] was a king who had no acquaintance with learning and never associated with the learned. He considered that policy and government were one thing and law another. "I am an unlettered man," he said, "but I have seen a great deal. Be assured that the Hindus will never become submissive and obedient until they are reduced to poverty. I have therefore given orders that just enough shall be left them of grain, milk, and curds from year to year, but that they must not accumulate hoards and property."

From the Moslem historian Barani, as quoted in H. G. Rawlinson, *India: A Short Cultural History* (New York: Appleton-Century, 1938), p. 228.

the same year his chief minister made himself sultan of Delhi. The Delhi sultanate rapidly became the dominant state in India. It controlled all of the North by 1236 and had taken over most of the Deccan by 1320. Only Vijayanagar in the extreme South remained an independent kingdom in which the Hindu tradition and culture could flourish without Moslem interference.

The Moslem Impact on India

The Delhi sultanate lasted nominally until 1526, but it lost most of its power after 1398. Even with its decline the Hindus found no relief, however, for the sultan's provincial governors set themselves up as independent kings and continued to dominate the native population. The Delhi sultanate failed to create stable political institutions and never established a fixed rule of succession. Most sultans acquired the throne by murdering their predecessor, and the art of government consisted largely in collecting taxes from the Hindu peasants. Heavy taxation was not only a means of supporting the government; it was also designed to keep the Hindus weak and powerless. Many of the sultans and their agents were fanatical Moslems who delighted in killing Hindus or in forcing them to accept Islam at the point of a sword. This policy of forced conversion succeeded in making the northwest and the extreme northeast (Bangladesh) largely Moslem. Even in the Deccan some 10 to 15 percent of the population was persuaded to adopt the faith of the conquerors. But in the regions where conversions were most numerous, hostility between Moslem and Hindu was strongest, and it endured to our own day. When India gained its independence in 1947 the country had to be split into two states, Moslem Pakistan (northwest India and east Bengal, now Bangladesh) and Hindu India.

The Moslem conquerors—mostly Turks and Afghans—were the first invaders of India who did not merge fully with the Hindu population. But though they remained a separate community, they had some influence on Hindu civilization. Some of the most bloodthirsty sultans were also the patrons of scholars, writers, and artists. They introduced ideas from Persian and Arabic literature and elements of Moslem architecture, such as the minaret and dome. The conquerors even developed a new language, Urdu,* based on Hindu rules of grammar but with a vocabulary that was largely Persian. This language is still spoken in Pakistan and also in parts of northwestern India. Even in their most intolerant moods, Moslem rulers had to employ some Hindu officials, simply because there were not enough Moslems who knew much about local conditions. In this way, the Moslems had some influence on Indian art, literature, and social customs. For example, the practice of keeping women in seclusion and discouraging them from appearing in public was due largely to the example of the Mohammedan ruling class.

The Delhi sultanate was almost annihilated by an invasion by Tamerlane in 1398—the same Tamerlane who checked the advance of the Ottoman Turks in the

* *Urdu,* which means "camp language," or "army language," comes from the Turkish word for a camp of armed tribesmen. In English the word has become *horde.*

THE MOSLEM CONQUEST OF INDIA
1192–1320

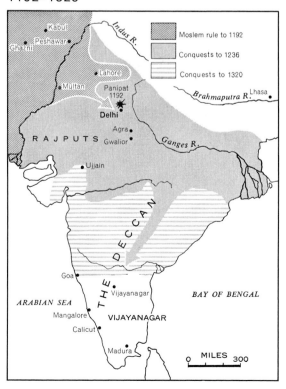

	Moslem rule to 1192
	Conquests to 1236
	Conquests to 1320

Kabul · Peshawar · Ghazni · Indus R. · Lahore · Multan · Panipat 1192 · Delhi · Agra · Gwalior · RAJPUTS · Ujjain · Brahmaputra R. Lhasa · Ganges R. · THE DECCAN · Goa · Vijayanagar · ARABIAN SEA · Mangalore · Calicut · VIJAYANAGAR · BAY OF BENGAL · Madura · MILES 0 300

West. Tamerlane, who wanted only booty from India, looted the northwest, sacked Delhi, and killed tens of thousands of noncombatants and prisoners. But he did not found a government in northern India, and the Delhi sultanate was eventually restored, though with only a fraction of its former territory. Independent Moslem rulers controlled the rest of the country, except for some Rajput strongholds in the North and Vijayanagar in the South. It was during this period that firearms and heavy artillery began to be used in India.

The Moguls

India finally gained some degree of unity and orderly government under the Mogul dynasty in the sixteenth century. The Moguls, who, like so many earlier

THE MOGUL EMPIRE   1605

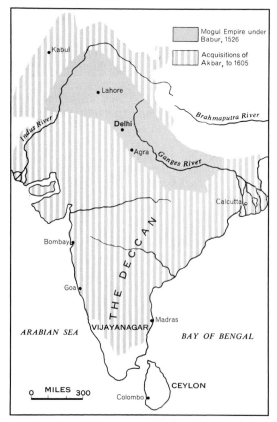

conquerors, came from central Asia, had both Turkish and Mongol ancestry; the first strong Mogul ruler, Babur, claimed descent from both Genghis Khan and Tamerlane. He entered India in 1524 and defeated the sultan of Delhi on the old battlefield of Panipat in 1526, thus winning control of most of the North. Babur secured his position in 1527 by defeating a coalition of Rajput leaders who were trying to establish an independent Hindu state in the northwest.

There was some dissension among the conquerors after Babur's death, but eventually his grandson, Akbar, gained the throne, and under him the Mogul Empire reached the height of its power. Akbar had completed the conquest of the North by 1576 and then turned to the Deccan, which he brought largely under control by 1600. A few more or less independent states survived in the South, but none of them had any importance. Vijayanagar had been destroyed by the Moslem kings of the Deccan shortly before Akbar's conquest, so that for all practical purposes Akbar was master of India.

Akbar

Akbar was a Moslem in religion and a Turko-Mongol in race, but he had far more regard for his Indian subjects than most earlier conquerors with this background. He set up an efficient administrative hierarchy and tried to keep his officials reasonably honest by paying them regular salaries and punishing them severely for accepting bribes. He was determined to see that justice was done and often acted as a judge himself. His more efficient and honest government made it possible to keep taxation at a moderate level. In fact, the assessment of the land tax under the Moguls was equitable enough to be used as the basis for later assessments under British rule.

Akbar realized that religious intolerance and racial quarrels were a threat to the permanence of his empire. He tried to conciliate the Rajputs, who were still resisting at the beginning of his reign, by honoring their bravery and by marrying three Rajput princesses. He appointed Hindus to high government positions, though Moslems still held most of the important posts. Even more significant was his insistence on complete religious toleration. Scholars of all faiths were welcome at his court; he even extended hospitality to a Jesuit mission and allowed them to build a chapel. Toward the end of his life he became convinced that there was some merit in every religion and that claims to exclusive possession of the truth were unjustified. There were earlier precedents for this belief. During the long centuries of conflict, enlightened Hindus and Moslems had suggested that there was only one divine power, which was worshiped under many names. The Hindu poet Kabir (1440–1518) had been especially eloquent on this subject. But none of these earlier religious leaders had the power of an Akbar. He tried to create a universal religion that would include all that was good in earlier faiths and that would end religious controversy in India. But artificial universal religions, like artificial universal languages, have little appeal to most people. While Akbar lived he was able to win some support for his new faith, but on his death India fell back into its old religious disputes.

Akbar's court was a center of art and learning. He collected a large library and wanted to have his books illustrated by the best artists of the country. One of the most brilliant schools of manuscript illumination that has ever existed developed at his court. Akbar was also a great builder, and some of the finest Indian architecture comes from his period. Both manuscript illumination and architecture showed strong Persian influence, but the Hindu tradition continued and many works of art show a mingling of the two styles.

Akbar inspecting building operations at a royal city in the Ganges Valley (illumination from the Akbar-nama manuscript, *ca.* 1590).

Akbar's Religious Beliefs

O God, in every temple I see those who seek thee.
And in every tongue that is spoken Thou art praised.
Polytheism and Islam grope after Thee.
Each religion says, "Thou art One, without equal."
Be it mosque, men murmur holy prayers; or church,
The bells ring for the love of Thee.
Awhile I frequent the Christian cloister, anon the mosque,
But Thee only I seek from fane to fane.
Thine elect know naught of heresy or orthodoxy, whereof
Neither stands behind the screen of Thy truth.

From a poem by Akbar's secretary, Abul Fazl, as quoted in H. G. Rawlinson, *India: A Short Cultural History* (New York: Appleton-Century, 1938), p. 310.

The Collapse of the Mogul Empire

In spite of his ability, Akbar did not succeed in ending the evils of misgovernment and religious controversy that had plagued India for so many centuries. Under Akbar's successors, who were less competent and less broadminded than he, Islam was reestablished as the official religion of the governing class, and discrimination against Hindus again became common. Civil wars among members of the ruling dynasty weakened the government, and provincial viceroys gradually became independent rulers. Hindu leaders began to organize resistance groups to throw off Mogul domination. India, as it had done so often in the past, was dissolving into a welter of conflicting states.

This time, however, there was a new force to be reckoned with—the merchants and soldiers of western Europe. The first European settlements in India had been made by the Portuguese just before the founding of the Mogul Empire. The Portuguese never held more than a few seacoast towns, but they were followed by French and English merchants who were more ambitious and had more powerful governments to back them. The growing disunion of India gave these adventurers from overseas easy opportunities to establish themselves in key positions throughout the country. The battles that determined the fate of modern India were directed by French and English generals and were fought for the profit of their respective nations. The heirs of the Moguls were to be not the Hindu rajahs who struggled so hard to regain their independence, nor the Moslem viceroys who tried to hold together fragments of the old empire, but the directors of the British East India Company.

CHINA
UNDER THE T'ANG DYNASTY

The old center of Chinese civilization, the valley of the Yellow River, fell to the nomads of the steppe only about a century before the western nomads (the Huns) helped to destroy the Western Roman Empire. For almost three centuries, from about 317 to about 589, northern China was ruled by Huns or other nomadic people. There was little political stability; few dynasties lasted for as long as a century, and most of the time China was divided into several warring states.

Yet with all these political difficulties, Chinese civilization made a quicker recovery from the shock of conquest than did the civilization of the Roman West. In the North, the Chinese slowly assimilated the barbarians. In the South, the Chinese remained for the most part independent, and the fertile valley of the Yangtze was fully exploited, for the first time, by refugees from the North. These settlers in the Yangtze Valley preserved and developed all the essential elements of Chinese civilization and began to impress their ideas on the still barbarous peoples who lived even farther south. Contact with all these strange peoples had a stimulating effect on the Chinese; they were more open to foreign influence at this time than they were to be again for centuries. It was during this period that Buddhism made its greatest gains in China. It was also during this period that

Tree of Life and Knowledge (southern India, seventeenth century).

The Chinese of the T'ang and Sung periods were open to contact with foreigners. This silk painting shows barbarian royalty worshiping the serene Chinese Buddha. Note the caricature in the depiction of the dress and expression of the foreigners.

Chinese Buddhists made frequent pilgrimages to India and other countries in Southeast Asia. They brought back information about the history and geography of Asian lands, and some very useful mathematical and scientific lore from India. Thus, instead of decaying, Chinese civilization spread beyond its original limits and was enriched by new ideas from abroad.

Nevertheless, these years of disunity and foreign invasion were hard for the masses, who suffered from war, famine, and exploitation by selfish rulers. There was a great burst of energy and optimism when the country was at last reunited under Chinese rulers. The Sui dynasty (581–618), which accomplished this feat, "ruled without benevolence," as one Chinese writer put it, but at least its harshness had some purpose. The country was reunified. The Sui emperors built huge granaries to help avert famine; even more important, they built roads and a canal system that united North and South and made it easier to move grain from surplus to deficit regions. But these useful tasks could be accomplished only by impressing thousands of laborers, who were harshly treated. Resentment grew, and defeats by the Turks brought open rebellion at home. The Sui dynasty was overthrown and replaced by the T'ang.

The T'ang period (618–906) was one of the most brilliant in Chinese history. The first emperor of the dynasty, an able general, drove the Turks and other nomads from the frontiers and eventually attacked the heart of Turkish power in central Asia. Most of the Turkish leaders acknowledged the suzerainty of the Chinese emperor and paid him tribute. This victory extended Chinese power into Turkestan and ended, for over a century, the threat of invasion from the northwest. Succeeding emperors made Korea a protectorate and, at the southern extremity of the empire, established their authority in northern Indochina. Not until the time of the Manchus in the seventeenth century was China again to control such a vast territory.

Chinese Government and Society Under the T'ang

Early T'ang government was efficient and, on the whole, benevolent. It clearly separated military from civilian offices and revived the professional civil service, going far beyond the rather undeveloped system that had existed in the Han period. By recruiting most civil servants through a system of competitive examinations, it followed the precedent of the Han period, although the Han examinations had been neither as regular nor as uniform as those of the T'ang era. Under the T'ang emperors young men were examined at regular intervals on a fixed body of materials, mainly the classics of Chinese literature and philosophy. There were various levels of difficulty, ranging from the preliminary examination, which admitted a man to an official career, to the highest examination, which qualified him for the top posts in the imperial court. Theoretically the examinations were open to all subjects, regardless of birth and wealth. In practice, few men could take them unless they belonged to the family of an official or a landlord, and recommendations from powerful men still carried much weight. Even if there was no favoritism, it took years of study to qualify for even the preliminary examination, and more years to reach the highest level. No peasant could afford such expensive training for his son.

This flaw in the examination system illustrates one of the enduring characteristics of Chinese society. From at least the T'ang period until the twentieth century, the most influential class in China was the one that has been called the scholar-gentry. This was a landlord class, which owned and leased to the peasants most of the land in the country. It was also the class that furnished most of the officials to the government at both the local and higher levels. And since official position depended on education, it was the class of scholars. Thus a single family might own most of the land in a district, hold most of the government jobs there, and have one or two representatives in high positions at court.

These scholar-gentry families were almost indestructible. If they lost favor at court, they retired to their estates and waited until the ruler or the dynasty changed. If the central government collapsed, they kept local government going until central authority could be reestablished. If nomad invaders conquered the country, they preserved classical learning and Confucian philosophy and taught them to the conquerors. More than any other group, they were responsible for the continuity of the Chinese way of life.

At the same time, the scholar-gentry class was responsible for some of China's social problems. It was supported by the peasants, and it often exploited them. If the central government made unreasonable demands, the gentry sometimes passed them on to the peasants, thus increasing their burden. If the central government was weak, the gentry sometimes used its official position to increase its land holdings and to take illegal payments from peasants and artisans. No government could exist without using the services of the gentry, but it was often difficult to make them behave according to the Confucian principles they professed. And oppression by the gentry often led to peasant rebellions.

Most Chinese dynasties, when they were strong, tried to protect the peasants against the landlords, and the early T'ang rulers were no exception. They broke up some of the large estates and remitted taxes in years of crop failure. They were able to reduce the burden on the peasants because commerce was flourishing, and therefore taxes on merchants and government monopolies on sales of salt and iron more than made up for a decrease in peasant payments.

China seems to have been generally prosperous during the early T'ang period. There was a wide market for silk and porcelain, which were exported to Japan on the east, to India and Indochina on the south, and to the Arab Empire on the west. The population increased notably, an indication that the peasants and artisans were thriving. It was also during the T'ang period that tea became the national drink of China. Formerly tea had been a luxury, but now it could be purchased by all classes. Since it had to be shipped from the South, the only region where it could be grown, its use throughout the country suggests that transportation facilities were good and that even the poorest people had risen a little above a bare subsistence level.

Religion Under the T'ang

The T'ang dynasty's revival of a national government and its emphasis on knowledge of the Chinese classics for admission to the civil service eventually strengthened Confucianism and weakened other faiths. Confucianism, which was the basis for the Chinese political and social system, was highly rational and secular in spirit. A good many T'ang officials were Buddhists, but others looked with suspicion on Buddhism, which, in some of its variants, led to emotional excesses and antisocial behavior. They were also worried by what seemed to them an excessive number of Buddhist priests, monks, and nuns. They used the same arguments against them

Seated court lady, sculpture of the T'ang period (618–906).

that European politicians used against Christian monks in the sixteenth century: they were idle and unproductive; they held too much of the wealth of the country; they encouraged superstition. On several occasions the government seized Buddhist temples and monasteries and compelled the monks and nuns to return to secular life. These attacks were intermittent, and Buddhism continued to influence many inhabitants of China. But Buddhism was gradually weakened by official disfavor, and its influence on Chinese life slowly declined.

A considerable number of middle- and lower-class Chinese had no very clear idea of religious differences. Any manifestation of divine inspiration was to be respected; they gave equal honor to Confucius, the Buddha, and Taoist teachers. Even the upper classes, though officially Confucianist, admitted that other philosophies had some merit. In this lukewarm religious atmosphere, Buddhism had no real power.

T'ang Scholarship

The T'ang period was an age of scholarship during which encyclopedias were compiled, a national academy was established, and dictionaries of foreign languages were prepared. The government established the practice of employing large groups of scholars to write histories of earlier dynasties, a practice that was faithfully followed by later rulers. As a result, China has hundreds of volumes of official histories covering almost its entire past, though the histories are concerned mainly with the affairs of the court and the bureaucracy.

The Buddhist monks, despite their troubles, made important contributions to T'ang scholarship. One spur to their scholarly work was their desire to translate large numbers of Sanskrit texts into Chinese. Since the two languages are very different, the monks came to pay careful attention to problems of syntax, grammar, and vocabulary. Some of the first books to bridge the language gap were the work of Buddhist monks. Hsuan-tsâng, a famous traveler who made a pilgrimage to India from 629 to 644, was one of the leaders in this work.

He wrote a notable account of his travels and translated some of the complexities of Buddhist thought into Chinese.

Chinese Printing

The Buddhists were also probably responsible for the invention of block printing. They wanted to make many copies of their sacred writings, both because the act of multiplying prayers and sacred texts was meritorious in itself, and because they could reach more people by reproducing key passages of their scriptures. They had an ideal material on which to print, for paper had been invented in China in the first century A.D.

An example of Chinese calligraphy. This stone rubbing was made from an inscription in the Regular Style by Ou-Yang Hsün, a scholar and calligrapher of the T'ang period.

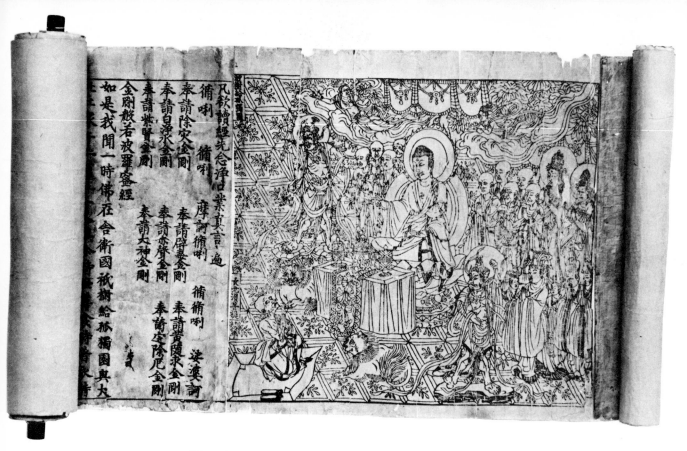

First portion of the oldest printed book, *The Diamond Sutra* (868). It was printed on a scroll from wooden blocks. This page gives discourses of Buddha and shows him teaching.

The Chinese had probably already developed the custom of brushing engraved seals with ink and stamping them on paper, and block printing carried this idea one step further. The text of an entire page was carved out of a single block of wood; the wood was inked; and then a sheet of paper was pressed on it. The first block prints come from the eighth century, and the first printed book (only six sheets of text) was published in 868.

Although preparing these printing blocks required a tremendous amount of labor, once they were ready it was easy to make many copies of a text. Later, Chinese scholars began to experiment with individual, movable type, but this idea was never accepted by Chinese printers. Since there are thousands of Chinese characters, preparing and setting movable type seemed to offer little saving in time and expense. In Korea, however, individual, movable type was used with great success early in the fifteenth century.

The history of the diffusion of paper and printing shows how isolated China was, in spite of superficial commercial contacts, and how slowly ideas and techniques spread from East to West. Paper, invented in China a little before 100 A.D., began to be used in Arab countries only in the eighth and ninth centuries. Western Europeans learned about it from the Arabs, but it was seldom used in Europe until the thirteenth century and did not become common until the fifteenth. Thus it took over a thousand years for a fairly simple and obviously useful technique to travel to Europe from China.

The history of printing is even more curious. Block printing spread rapidly throughout the Chinese cultural area and was used in Japan almost as soon at it was invented in China. But the Moslems, who sat in the middle of every trade route between China and the West, took no interest in block printing and, except for a few early experiments, never used the invention. Eventually Europe obtained a few samples of Chinese printed work, such as playing cards and paper money, and these may have stimulated some early European experiments with block printing. But there is no evidence

332

that Europeans knew that the Chinese had occasionally used movable type. The typical European method of printing with individual pieces of movable type, locked in a form and mounted in a press, seems to have been an independent invention. It is an amazing coincidence that men at the two extremities of the Eurasian continent—Korea and Germany—discovered almost simultaneously how to put movable type to practical use.

T'ang Poetry

The T'ang period was an age of poets as well as an age of scholars. The Chinese believe that this was their greatest period of lyric poetry and have preserved thousands of poems of the T'ang era. In the West, Li Po (*ca.* 700–762) is probably the best known of the T'ang poets, but some Chinese critics would place Tu Fu (712–770) higher. Chinese poetry tries to recreate a mood, brief flashes of intense feeling caused by the sight of a mountain valley, a sudden rainstorm, an empty road, or piercing moments of clarity in which the unity of nature or the impermanence of worldly beauty is realized. It is often indirect and allusive, and always highly subjective. At its best it is very great poetry, and it has been increasingly appreciated by the rest of the world.

There is a gentle melancholy in much of this poetry; rain, loneliness, and autumnal scenes are favorite topics. One of Tu Fu's poems ends:

A few last leaves are falling, blown
    by the breeze;
The sun sets behind the curving hill.
How late the solitary crane returns!
In the twilight the rooks are already
    flocking to the forest.

The same note of sadness appears in many of Li Po's verses:

Before my bed a patch of moonlight
    shone;
I thought there must be frost upon
    the ground,
And raised my head and stared at the
    moon so bright,
Sank back again and longed for my
    native land.

And at times T'ang poetry becomes sardonic, as in this poem of Li Po:

Life is a journey, death is a return to
    the earth.
The universe is like an inn, the passing years are like dust.
We complain when we think of the
    past.
We would complain more if we
    thought of the future!

In criticism of the T'ang wars of conquest, Tu Fu wrote:

Snow is falling, the army makes its
    way through the high mountains;
The track is dangerous; for fear of
    slipping they cling from rock to
    rock,
Their frozen fingers slip on ice. . . .

There they are far distant from the
    land of Han [China].
When will men be satisfied with
    building a wall against the barbarians?
When will the soldiers return to their
    native land? *

The Fall of the T'ang Empire

The T'ang period was one in which China strongly influenced its eastern neighbors. Both Korea and Japan adopted some of the basic elements of Chinese civilization at this time—the Chinese system of writing, Chinese literary and artistic techniques, Chinese ideas about philosophy and religion. Buddhism came to Japan from China and struck even deeper roots in the islands than it had on the continent. Japanese students read the Chinese classics; in fact, the curriculum in Japanese schools was almost the same as that in Chinese schools. Even in government Korean kings and Japanese emperors borrowed many techniques from their Chinese contemporaries.

*All these excerpts are quoted from René Grousset, *The Rise and Splendour of the Chinese Empire* (London: Geoffrey Bles, 1952; Berkeley: University of California Press, 1953), pp. 155, 152, 163.

Marble guardian lion (T'ang period).

The T'ang dynasty flourished for over a century. It then began to suffer from internal weakness and external attacks. As more money was spent on the army, army officers became more influential. Provincial governors gradually gained a considerable degree of autonomy, and they tended to be drawn more from the military than from the civilian group of officials. Under these circumstances, the quality of government declined. Intrigue weakened both central and local institutions, while inefficiency and corruption stirred up unrest among the people. On the frontiers, the subject peoples regained their independence, and the nomads again threatened the northern frontiers. The Turks inflicted a decisive defeat on a Chinese army in 751 and weakened the T'ang position in central Asia. During the ninth century, the T'ang emperors struggled valiantly against popular rebellions and nomad raids, but their position grew steadily weaker. By 900 they had lost control over many provinces either to their own officials or to outside invaders. In 906 the T'ang dynasty came to an end.

Civil Service Examinations Under the Sung Dynasty

The candidates had to get up in the middle of the night and come to the palace at dawn, bringing their cold meals with them, for they would not be able to leave until the examinations were over. During the examinations they were shut up in cubicles under the supervision of palace guards. There was a rigorous system to prevent bribery or favoritism. The candidates' papers were recopied by official clerks before they were submitted to the examiners, to avoid recognition of their identity by their handwriting. In the recopied papers the writers' names were taken out and kept on file. While the candidates were let out after the examinations, the judges themselves were shut up within the palace, usually from late January till early March, until the papers were properly graded and submitted to the emperor. The candidates were examined first on questions of history or principles of government. There was a second examination on the classics, and finally, after the successful ones had been graded, there was one—under the direct supervision of the emperor—on lyrics, descriptive poetry, and again, essays on politics.

From Lin Yu-t'ang, *The Gay Genius* (New York: Day, 1947), p. 38.

THE SUNG DYNASTY AND THE MONGOLS

The fall of the T'ang was followed, as usual, by a period of disunity and internal war. But this time there was no long gap between dynasties. Order was soon restored by the Sung dynasty, which began to reign in the North in 960 and had gained control of the independent southern states by 979. The Sung were never as strong militarily as the T'ang, and they were always threatened by nomads in the North, who held Peking and northeast China, including Manchuria. The dominant group was the Khitan tribe, from whom we get the old English name for China, "Cathay." The Khitan in turn were overcome by the Jurchen nomads. By 1126 the Jurchen had conquered all the lands north of the Yangtze. They established the Chin dynasty, which ruled northern China until the Mongol invasion. South China remained under the Sung until the last decades of the thirteenth century.

In spite of military weakness the Sung period saw some notable advances in Chinese civilization. Block printing was much more extensively used than under the T'ang, and the basic religious and scholarly texts were more widely distributed. A history of China from 400 B.C. to the advent of the Sung was written by Ssu-ma Kuang. Confucianism was reinterpreted and strengthened by the addition of religious and philosophical ideas—many of them borrowed from Buddhism and Taoism. Thus the idea that there was a common moral law governing the entire universe became prominent at this time. There was also a strong belief that human reason, pushed to its limits, could grasp the basic principles behind the workings of the universe. These ideas were brilliantly expressed by Chu Hsi in the twelfth century, and this modernized version of Confucianism gradually became the dominant force in Chinese philosophy and religion.

Two important inventions were made in the Sung period. The exact date of the origin of the compass is uncertain, but it was certainly in use by the end of the eleventh century. It is still not clear whether the compass came to Europe from China, or whether it was independently invented in the West. Gunpowder had long been known to the Chinese but had been used only for fireworks. In the twelfth century it began to be used in warfare in the form of bombs and grenades. It is not certain when cannon were invented, but they were certainly used by the Mongols in the fourteenth century, and it is likely that the Mongols got the idea from the Chinese. However, as we have seen, gunpowder was not very useful until metallurgical techniques had reached a high level of development. Europeans learned of gunpowder later than the Chinese, but they soon surpassed them in the art of making firearms.

Sung Culture and Government

If the T'ang period was the great age of Chinese poetry, the Sung was the great age of Chinese art. Like T'ang poetry, Sung painting tried to recreate a mood—the beauty and vastness, the harmony and inner meaning, of nature. Like poetry again, the paintings are reduced to bare essentials; a few lines suggest the whole. The landscapes of the Sung painters are especially famous; perhaps no other people ever painted so many landscapes or painted them so well.

The Sung period was also a time of rapid growth of population, industry, and trade. A larger percentage of the people lived in cities than ever before, and this massive urbanization had strong repercussions on agriculture. The production of grain—especially rice—had to be increased, and provision had to be made for shipping food over long distances. China became more of an economic unit than before; merchants and moneylenders became more important.

Such changes put a strain on any society. The strain was especially great in Sung China because this was a period of revival of the Confucian tradition. This tradition was hostile to direct intervention by the government; it stressed ethical principles, not imperial legislation. Moreover, the Chinese of the Sung period were under heavy pressure from the hostile nomads who had occupied lands on the northern frontiers, and the government could not both fight wars and remodel society. Some men, such as the statesman Wang An-shih (1021–86), realized the need for extensive reforms—protection of the poorer farmers by regulating and refinancing loans on small holdings, reform of the examination system by putting more emphasis on practical knowledge—but their efforts had only limited results. But in spite of war, the dislocations caused by economic growth, and the misery of marginal producers, Sung China was on the whole prosperous and contented. Especially in the earlier years of the dynasty, almost all government officials were drawn from the intellectual elite of the country through rigorous application of the examination system. The upper and middle classes probably had the most comfort-

THE SUNG AND CHIN EMPIRES
Twelfth century

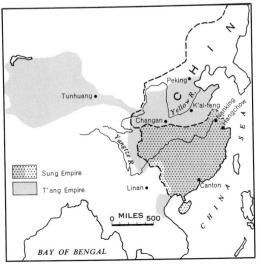

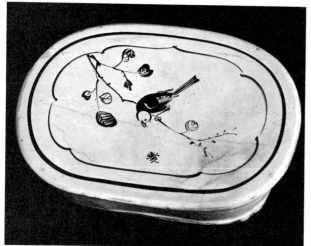

Detail from *Clearing Autumn Skies over Mountains and Valleys,* Sung landscape scroll attributed to Kuo Hsi (*ca.* 1020–90).

Everyday life in the Sung dynasty. Far left top: pillow, Tz'u-Chou stoneware. Far left bottom: porcelain winepot. Left: scroll painting of Buddhist monks laundering, by Lin T'ing-Kuei (twelfth century).

able existence and the highest level of culture of any people in the Eurasian continent.

The Mongols in China

Despite internal strains and losses to the northern nomads, the Sung made a surprisingly strong resistance to the rising Mongol power. At the same time that Genghis Khan united the nomads of the steppes and sent his armies west into Russia, he attacked the Jurchen kingdom of northern China (a nomad state) and took its capital, Peking, in 1215. The successors of Genghis Khan rapidly completed the conquest of the North, but the Sung dynasty in the South held out for almost two more generations. It was only in 1279 that the last Sung ruler was killed—curiously enough, in an attempt to reach Formosa and set up a government-in-exile. China was now ruled by the Mongols, the first time a foreign dynasty had held the entire country.

The vast Mongol Empire was too large to remain unified, however. It was at first divided into subordinate khanates, ruled by members of the royal family under the suzerainty of the Great Khan. But in 1260 the Khan of China, Kublai, became practically independent, and he and his successors ruled China as a separate empire until 1368. Korea was also under the control of this Mongol

dynasty, and Kublai annexed Yunnan (now the southernmost Chinese province) and established his suzerainty over part of Indochina. He failed, however, in his efforts to conquer Japan. The Mongols knew little of naval matters, and their Chinese subjects were not enthusiastic about an attack on the islands. Kublai finally succeeded in sending a fleet against Japan, but it was destroyed by a typhoon. This was the "Divine Wind" (Kamikaze) that the Japanese invoked during their struggle with the United States during the Second World War.

The Mongols were at first greedy and brutal; they pillaged rather than governed the Chinese. They soon found that there were limits to the profits to be obtained by looting and tried to reestablish the old imperial system. But it was some time before they fully trusted the Chinese; Marco Polo, who knew Mongol but no Chinese, was made a district governor in preference to a native. By 1300, however, the Mongols had accepted many aspects of Chinese civilization and were using a good many Chinese officials in their bureaucracy. They soon restored the prosperity of the country. They built a network of roads, with relays of horses every twenty-five or thirty miles to carry official messages. They repaired and extended the canal system and built granaries to store food against famine. Trade by both land and sea increased, and for-

Expulsion of Huns 581	618		906		1126	1234	1368		1644
Sui Dynasty	T'ang Dynasty		Disunity	Sung Dynasty	Chin Empire	Mongol Empire	Ming Dynasty		

960   1279

eign travelers journeyed throughout the empire.

The Mongols and the West

In contrast to the Sung period, China was now in close contact with foreigners from many lands. While the Mongol supremacy lasted, it was easier to travel by land from Europe to China than it had ever been before or than it was ever to be again until the nineteenth century. Ambassadors from the pope and the king of France visited the Mongol court, and dozens of Europeans found employment there. Marco Polo's book shows how easy it was for a European to travel through the Mongol domains and to obtain office in their empire. His account, and those of other travelers, gave Europeans their first real information about China. Stories about the great wealth and strange customs of this distant land made a strong impression on Europe and did much to inspire the voyages of discovery of the fifteenth and sixteenth centuries.

The Mongol emperors were open minded and ready to use good men and new ideas, whatever their origin. The Mongol court was full of officials of every race and religion—Persian Moslems, Russian Christians, Chinese Confucians. And with the men came the ideas, such as a new grain crop, sorghum, and a new instrument for handling problems in arithmetic, the abacus.

The Mongols had no very strong religious convictions and were willing to listen to missionaries of every faith. As we have seen, Kublai asked for Christian priests, but the Church had too many problems in Europe to comply with his request. When missionaries were finally sent in the fourteenth century, it was too late. Although there was a Catholic archbishop of Peking in the 1340s, and some thousands of Chinese converts, the small Chinese Christian organization was not strong enough to survive the downfall of the Mongol dynasty.

THE MING DYNASTY

Like most other Chinese dynasties, the Mongol line of rulers degenerated after the first few generations. They allowed the people to be oppressed by corrupt officials and failed to maintain their military strength. Rebellion broke out in the South, and finally in 1368 an ex-Buddhist monk captured Peking. He founded the Ming dynasty, which ruled China until the coming of the Manchus in the 1600s.

The Ming dynasty has had a bad reputation because, in its efforts to wipe out the memory of Mongol domination, it encouraged a rather imitative culture based on the works of the T'ang and Sung periods. Thus the civil service examinations became more difficult and

---

Marco Polo Describes Chinese Paper Money
ca. 1275

When ready for use, it [a specially prepared paper] is cut into pieces of money of different sizes, nearly square, but somewhat longer than they are wide. . . . The coinage of this paper money is authenticated with as much form and ceremony as if it were actually of pure gold or silver, for to each note a number of officers, specially appointed, not only subscribe their names, but affix their signets also; and when this has been done . . . the principal officer, deputed by his majesty, having dipped into vermilion the royal seal committed to his custody, stamps with it the piece of paper, so that the form of the seal remains impressed upon it, by which it receives full authenticity as current money, and the act of counterfeiting it is punished with death. When thus coined in large quantities, this paper currency is circulated in every part of the grand khan's domains, nor dares any person, at the peril of his life, refuse to accept it in payment. All his subjects receive it without hesitation, because, wherever their business may call them, they can dispose of it again in the purchase of merchandise they may have occasion for, such as pearls, jewels, gold, or silver.

From *The Travels of Marco Polo* (New York and London: Everyman's Library, 1950), p. 203.

THE MING EMPIRE
Fourteenth to seventeenth centuries

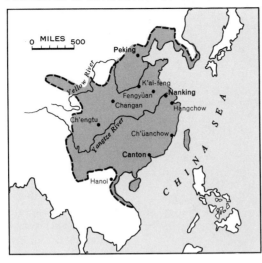

more formalized, demanding an encyclopedic knowledge of Confucian works. The restatement of Confucian doctrine by the Sung philosopher Chu Hsi became the official dogma for all candidates for government posts. In fact, one Ming writer remarked that Chu had discovered everything worth knowing and that no more scholarly books were necessary. In art and in poetry there was the same tendency to imitate or at most to add only a few minor refinements. It is perhaps significant that the most interesting literary works of the Ming period are novels, a form of writing that had not been greatly cultivated before and hence had fewer set standards to follow.

Ming Explorations and Commerce

The early Ming emperors, who were intensely interested in exploration by sea, sent out fleets that surveyed the Indian Ocean and even penetrated the Persian Gulf and the Red Sea. They forced distant rulers, including the king of Ceylon, to pay them tribute and brought back many novelties and luxuries. Chinese shipbuilding and navigation must have been flourishing to make these voyages possible. But they suddenly ceased after 1433, and an imperial edict restricted Chinese shipping to coastal voyages. This decision was probably the

Porcelain jar of the Ming period.

result of Ming suspicion of foreign influences and the jealousy that civil servants felt for military men who commanded the fleets. It was a turning point in world history, for it left the eastern seas open to the Portuguese invaders and their French and English successors.

The Ming dynasty was ruling China when the first Europeans reached the country by sea in the sixteenth century. This was unfortunate, for the Ming period, like several earlier periods, was marked by dislike of foreigners and strong belief in Chinese superiority. It is true that the first Portuguese traders were cruel and arrogant, but the Chinese were almost equally arrogant in their dealings with Europeans. They did not reject the obvious advantages of mutual trade, but they tried to minimize foreign influence on the Chinese way of life. They confined the traders to a few coastal towns and dealt with them through a handful of carefully selected officials. They were suspicious of European ideas and even of European technology. Thus the coming of the Europeans tended to reinforce Ming conservatism rather than to stimulate a reexamination and an enrichment of Chinese culture.

At the end of the dynasty the Ming emperors did begin to take an interest in European learning, thanks to the efforts of Jesuit missionaries such as Matteo Ricci. But by this time it was too late to shake off the effects of generations of hostility to foreign influences. China never assimilated European science and technology; after 1750 it became steadily weaker compared with European powers.

JAPAN

The Japanese islands were inhabited at least as early as 3000 B.C., but very little is known about their early history. The first inhabitants were probably the Ainu, who still exist on the northernmost island, and who are very different physically from the Japanese. The Ainu were overrun by successive waves of Mongoloid invaders who entered the islands by way of the narrow Korean Straits. There is also evidence of invasions by Malay-like peoples coming up from the islands

Japanese tea ceremony,
painting by Kitagawa Utamaro
(eighteenth century).

well suited to Japanese word forms, the written language could not be very precise. Even today the Japanese use Chinese terms for all legal, political, and moral concepts.

Even more important than the beginning of writing was the introduction of Buddhism in 552 A.D. The old native religion, Shinto, was a rather undeveloped form of nature worship, and, though Shintoists made some resistance, Buddhism spread rapidly throughout the islands. By this time there was some degree of political unity on the main island of Honshu, and Buddhism profited from the support of the imperial family. The first great Japanese scholar, Prince Shotoku (d. 621) was especially active in promoting Buddhism, as well as Chinese culture. Dozens of temples with enormous statues of the Buddha were erected, and Buddhist monasteries were founded in many parts of the country.

With Buddhism came a significant increase in Chinese influence. Priests and scholars came over from China, and Japanese Buddhists crossed to the mainland to study with the leaders of Chinese Buddhism. There was great and fully justified admiration in Japan for all aspects of Chinese culture. These close contacts began when China was at the height of the T'ang civilization, and the Japanese borrowed their administrative system, their court ceremonial, their fashions, their art, and their literature from the Chinese.

At the same time, Japan was not a mere imitation of China. It developed its own verse forms, its own drama, and its own style of painting. Tea drinking was learned from China, but the elaborate tea ceremony was a Japanese development. On the other hand, although there were some notable Japanese scholars, learning was never honored in Japan to the extent that it was in China.

Japanese Political Development

The most conspicuous difference between the two countries, however, was in their political development. China had its periods of weak government and civil war, but in general the country remained unified. The emperor and his officials

south of Japan. All these peoples except the Ainu gradually merged and formed one culture.

The Early Japanese

Chinese records begin to mention Japan after 25 A.D., but these early accounts describe it as a very backward and primitive country. Only in the fifth century A.D. did writing become common in Japan, and then the Chinese script was used. Since Chinese characters were not

ruled the country effectively, and military men seldom had much power. When an imperial family produced a series of weak rulers, power was transferred to a new imperial family, but not to the army. In Japan, on the other hand, the emperor was revered as a sacred personage, descended from the Sun Goddess. To remove the imperial family from the throne was unthinkable sacrilege, but most emperors were unable to control the warring Japanese clans. The solution was to retain the emperor as a symbol of unity and as a very remote and formal source of authority and to give real power to the military leaders. Civil wars between the heads of the great military families were frequent, especially in the period from 1200 to 1600. The most honored men in Japan were soldiers, not scholars. While China emphasized civilian virtues, Japan respected, above all else, the military virtues of bravery and loyalty.

During the sixth century A.D. there had been an attempt to make the Japanese emperor the counterpart of a T'ang ruler. The Taikwa reforms (645–650) asserted that he was all-powerful, owner of all the land, and direct ruler of all the people. In practice, however, he had to allow powerful nobles to accumulate great estates, and he tended to lose more and more control over actual government. The leading courtiers intrigued for power and often dominated the emperor by marrying to him ladies of their own families.

Finally, even the appearance of power was transferred from the imperial court. There had long been a custom of appointing an official, known as the shogun (generalissimo), to take full charge of the defense of the country in times of emergency. About the middle of the twelfth century the general Yoritomo succeeded in making the office permanent and the title hereditary in his family for several generations. He established a new government under his control, leaving the emperor and his court with only religious and ceremonial duties.

Japanese Feudalism

Under the permanent shogunate emerged a feudal system not unlike that of western Europe. Beneath the shogun were great lords, the daimyos, and beneath the daimyos were fighting men, or samurai. All these men were immeasurably superior to common peasants and artisans, who had to prostrate themselves whenever a member of the military caste passed by. The whole system was based on the labor of the peasants; a feudal lord was usually given a fief of so many measures of rice, which the peasants had to produce.

The Tokugawa Shogunate

Like feudalism in Europe, Japanese feudalism produced frequent wars. Some shoguns were overthrown, and others had little authority. These shifts in power went on for centuries, and in the fifteenth century Japan seemed ready to disintegrate into a group of petty warring states. It was saved from this fate by two great soldiers of the sixteenth century, Hideyoshi and Iyeyasu. Hideyoshi united the country and brought most of the warring daimyos under his authority. When he died in 1598, Tokugawa Iyeyasu completed his work and reestablished the authority of the shogunate. The Tokugawa shoguns ruled Japan from this time until 1868. The civil wars came to an end, and Japan remained at peace for almost three centuries.

Hideyoshi and Iyeyasu were also responsible for Japan's long isolation from the rest of the world. During the sixteenth century first the Portuguese and then the Dutch had begun to trade with Japan. With the traders came Jesuit missionaries, who converted thousands of Japanese. Hideyoshi felt that the new religion might cause renewed factional quarrels and feared that European soldiers and colonizers would follow the missionaries. Both he and his successor persecuted the Jesuits and the native Christians, and in 1614 Christianity was outlawed. The final step toward isolation was taken in 1639, when foreign ships were forbidden to come to Japan. The Dutch were allowed to keep a small trading post at Nagasaki, but otherwise Japan was closed to foreign contacts until Commodore Perry forced the shogun to accept a commercial treaty in 1853.

Drawing of Hideyoshi, with an inscription by his son (early seventeenth century).

Suggestions for Further Reading

Note: Asterisk denotes a book available in paperback edition.

The Rajputs   There is interesting source material on India in this period in *The History of India,* Vols. I and II, ed. by H. M. Elliott (1867). R. C. Majumdar, *Ancient India* (1952), is probably the best general treatment of political history to 1200 A.D. Majumdar, a leading authority on Indian history, includes a good critical bibliography. The older study of S. Lane-Poole, *Medieval India* (1903), is less scholarly than Majumdar but presents a more exciting account of India under Moslem rule. V. A. Smith, *The Oxford History of India* (1923), is an excellent reference work. There is considerable material on the medieval period in J. C. Powell-Price, *A History of India* (1955), and in I. Prasad, *History of Medieval India* (1928), which stresses military and administrative achievements.

The Spread of Indian Culture   H. G. Rawlinson, *India: A Short Cultural History** (1938), is a thorough account of India's contribution to world culture and a good starting point for study. R. C. Majumdar, *Ancient Indian Colonies in the Far East,* 2 vols. (1955), is a scholarly treatment of the expansion of Indian culture, and F. W. Thomas, *Indianism and Its Expansion* (1917), treats the same subject in a somewhat more lucid fashion. The best recent work is R. Mukerjee, *The Culture and Art of India* (1959), which gives excellent selections of Indian literature and beautiful illustrations of Indian art. Mukerjee includes a good up-to-date bibliography. A. A. MacDonell, *India's Past* (1927), a survey of India's literatures and religions, traces the growth and spread of its culture. For a valuable summary of India's achievement, see *The Legacy of India,* ed. by G. T. Garratt (1937).

The Moslem Conquest   Undoubtedly, the best account is given in the brief monograph of R. C. Majumdar, *The Arab Invasion of India* (1931). The impact of Moslem rule on the political, economic, and cultural life of India is carefully studied in *The Struggle for Empire,* ed. by R. C. Majumdar (1957), a collection of essays by leading scholars of Indian history.

See also the general works cited above for material on the Moslem period.

European Contacts in the Sixteenth Century   There is an exciting eyewitness account of India in early modern times in F. Bernier, *Travels in the Mogul Empire,* trans. by A. Constable (1891). P. Spear, *India, Pakistan, and the West** (1949), traces the relations between India and the West in a good survey. *The Travels of Peter Mundy in Europe and Asia,* ed. by R. Temple (1956–58), describes East–West relations in the sixteenth century.

China Under the T'ang Dynasty   Most of the general works cited after Chapter 6, in the second section, touch on the T'ang period. W. Bingham, *The Founding of the T'ang Dynasty* (1941), is probably the best study of the early history of the dynasty. *The Veritable Record of the T'ang Emperor Shun-Tsung,* trans. by B. Solomon (1955), is a fascinating picture of China in the early ninth century and gives valuable insight into the old Chinese world view. E. O. Reischauer's *Ennin's Travels in T'ang China* (1953) is an absorbing summary of the travels of a ninth-century pilgrim. E. H. Shafer, *The Golden Peaches of Samarkand* (1963), is an excellent description of the material culture of the T'ang period. The standard study of Chinese history is K. S. Latourette, *The Chinese: Their History and Culture* (1946), a scholarly and readable work with excellent bibliographic material. Excellent translations of poems from the T'ang period may be found in A. Waley, *Translations from the Chinese* (1941). See also *China, India and Japan: The Middle Period,* ed. by W. H. McNeill and J. W. Sedlar (1971), which is useful for all three countries and especially good on China.

Buddhism in China   *The Buddhist Scriptures,** trans. by E. Conze (1959), contains a good selection of Buddhist writings drawn from the central tradition of Buddhism. C. Humphreys, *Buddhism** (1951), devotes considerable attention to Buddhism in China and is a very good introductory survey. There is material on the growth of Buddhism in China in both L. Wieger, *History of Religious Beliefs and of Philosophic Opinions in China,* trans. by E. T. C. Werner (1927), and J. Edkins, *Chinese Buddhism** (1893). The most thorough treatment is that of E. Zürcher, *The Buddhist Conquest of China,* 2 vols. (1959). A good short survey is A. F. Wright, *Buddhism in Chinese History* (1959).

| Printing and Scholarship | T. F. Carter and L. C. Goodrich, *The Invention of Printing in China and Its Spread Westward*, 2nd ed. (1955), is very important. There is information on printing and scholarship in C. P. Fitzgerald, *China: A Short Cultural History** (1938), and in H. G. Creel, *Chinese Thought from Confucius to Mao Tsê-tung** (1953), a very interesting work by a leading American authority. |

The Sung Dynasty

The first volume of the monumental study by K. A. Wittfogel and Fêng Chia-shêng, *History of Chinese Society, 907–1125* (1945), includes texts and translations from major Chinese sources on this period. Since the civil service system was the key feature of the Chinese state, E. A. Kracke, *The Civil Service in Early Sung China** (1953), is important for an understanding of the Chinese political system; this work also shows China as a classic example of the managerial state in practice. J. T. C. Liu, *Reform in Sung China* (1959), reveals the "modern" policies of an eleventh-century reformer.

The Mongols

Both R. Grousset's *L'Empire des Steppes* (1939) and his *Conqueror of the World: The Life of Chingis Khan*, trans. by D. Sinor and M. MacKellar (1967), are reliable accounts that give special attention to political history. The famous thirteenth-century Venetian's trip to the Mongol court is presented in H. Yule, *The Book of Ser Marco Polo*, 2 vols., rev. ed. by H. Cordier (1921). L. Olschki, *Marco Polo's Asia* (1960), is a careful analysis of Polo's account. The best account of Christianity in China under the Mongols is A. C. Moule, *Christians in China Before the Year 1550* (1930).

The Ming Dynasty

The most trustworthy general treatment is R. Grousset, *Histoire de l'extrême-orient*, 2 vols. (1929). There is material on the Ming period in two works of O. Lattimore, *China: A Short History* (1944) and *Inner Frontiers of Asia** (1940), which is more detailed but also more interesting. F. Michael, *The Origin of Manchu Rule* (1942), is excellent for the development of the Manchus.

China's First Contacts with Europe in the Sixteenth Century

The best picture that we have of Chinese–European intercourse is *China in the Sixteenth Century: The Journal of Matthew Ricci*, trans. by L. J. Gallager (1953), an account of missionary activity. C. R. Boxer edited three travelers' adventures in *South China in the Sixteenth Century* (1953). K. S. Latourette, *A History of Christian Missions in China* (1932), is a most comprehensive treatment, while C. Cary-Elwes, *China and the Cross* (1957), though not so scholarly, is more readable than Latourette.

Japan from the Beginnings to the Tokugawa Period

K. S. Latourette, *The History of Japan* (1947), is a quick survey of Japanese history and a good introduction. Latourette is mainly concerned with Japanese influence on China. G. B. Sansom covers the period in more detail in *A History of Japan to 1334* (1958) and *A History of Japan, 1334–1615* (1960). There is excellent material on political and social history in F. Brinkley, *A History of the Japanese People* (1915), an invaluable handbook. The standard treatment of the intellectual achievement of Japan is G. B. Sansom, *Japan: A Short Cultural History* (1943). For economic development, see Y. Takekoshi, *The Economic Aspects of the History of the Civilization of Japan*, Vol. I (1930), a scholarly and readable study. A fascinating picture of Japanese civilization in the twelfth century is offered in M. Shinoda, *The Founding of the Kamakura Shogunate* (1960).

The titles by Latourette, Brinkley, and Takekoshi above have information on Japanese feudalism and religion. There is excellent material also in *Feudalism in History*, ed. by R. Coulborn (1956), and in R. Boutrouche, *Seigneurie et féodalité* (1959). For the Tokugawa period, see J. W. Hall and M. B. Jansen, *Studies in the Institutional History of Early Modern Japan* (1968). Probably the best study of anti-foreignism in Japan is J. Murdoch, *A History of Japan*, Vol. II (1964). There is also an interesting study by C. R. Boxer, *The Christian Century in Japan, 1549–1650* (1951).

16 The Revival of Europe

During the course of the fourteenth century economic depression, plague, and war had weakened western Europe. Secular rulers, who in 1300 had seemed close to establishing absolute monarchies, had lost much of their power over the privileged classes and thus much of their ability to maintain law and order. The prestige of the Church had declined during the Babylonian Captivity and the Great Schism. Most men believed in monarchy as the best form of government; almost all believed in the Church as the only source of salvation. But with both these traditional authorities functioning badly, there seemed to be little hope for religious reform or a revival of security and prosperity. Everyone desired peace, a healing of the schism in the Church, better government, and increased production and trade. But there was little agreement on where to begin, and none of the many projects for reform was very successful.

By the end of the fifteenth century, a startling change had taken place. The economic depression had ended; new industries at home and new trade routes overseas had opened up new opportunities and created new wealth. Kings and princes had clearly gained the upper hand over the privileged classes, especially in France, Spain, and England. The papal schism was ended, and Rome was once more the capital of Western Christendom. New forms of learning based on an intensive study of the classics were competing with or modifying older studies. New forms of art were challenging the late Gothic style. Most important, there was a note of optimism and confidence, of excitement and enjoyment. There was talk of a "new age" dawning, a "dark age" past, a rebirth of the best qualities of classical civilization. By 1500 the basic characteristics of our "modern" world were becoming visible: its dynamic economy and fluid society, its sovereign nation-states and international anarchy, its secular ideals, and its intellectual and moral values.

We can now see that the political and economic revival of Europe was led by the north, while intellectual, literary, and artistic innovations were largely the work of Italy. But this sharing of responsibilities was less obvious in the fifteenth century than it was later, and in the transition from the medieval to the modern world the Italians had the great advantage of being the first to realize that a transition was taking place. They were the ones who talked of a new age, of a break with the barbarous past; they were the ones who believed that a new civilization could be created that would be a worthy heir of Greece and Rome. As a result, in the two centuries between the death of Dante (1321) and the sack of Rome by mutinous imperial troops (1527), Italy exerted increasing influence over the rest of Europe. Italians set the style in architecture, sculpture, and painting; they dictated the literary taste that Europe was to follow for generations. By combining the old ideal of the

Donatello, equestrian statue of the Venetian *condottiere* Erasmo di Nardi, who was called Gattamelata (*ca.* 1445–50), in the Piazza del Santo, Padua.

chivalric, courtly knight with their own interest in learning, they developed a genuinely new social ideal, that of "the gentleman," and the educational ideal of a "liberal education." Italy was the school of Europe. Northerners flocked there by the thousands, and Italians, in turn, appeared in every northern court, even in remote Muscovy.

There were several reasons for Italy's leadership in the change from medieval to early modern ways of life. Italy had always been somewhat different from the rest of Europe during the Middle Ages. It was never completely feudalized, and it early rejected most feudal institutions. It rejected a unified monarchy under the German emperor even more decisively.

Scholasticism never dominated Italian thinking, nor did the Gothic style ever dominate Italian art. Since the medieval tradition in Italy was weak, it could easily be rejected. Moreover the Italian cities had great wealth, large populations, and complete independence. When they tried new experiments in art, literature, and politics, they became powerful instruments of social change.

THE CITY-STATES OF NORTHERN ITALY

The northern Italian cities were dominated by international trade. A third of the population of Florence lived by im-

A Renaissance prince and his wife: Giovanni Bentivoglio, lord of Bologna, and Ginevra Bentivoglio (details from paintings by Ercole Roberti, ca. 1480).

porting wool from agricultural countries and selling finished cloth all over Europe and the Levant. Almost all the population of Venice depended directly or indirectly on trade in Oriental goods such as silk and spices. In such communities, capitalists—the banker, the export merchant, the large-scale manufacturer—were the most important figures.

The Italian towns controlled the countryside around them as most northern European towns did not. They had broken the power of the landed nobility and had absorbed the defeated class into their own communities. Peasant villages and small market towns had been annexed by large urban centers. Thus city-states were created—that is, a strong city government controlled not only its own immediate area but hundreds of square miles of rural territory.

There were sharp differences among the people of these city-states. Obviously there were differences in wealth, from the international merchants and bankers—the *popolo grasso*, or "fat people"—through the craftsmen, shopkeepers, and all the lesser bourgeoisie—the *popolo minuto*, or "little people"—down to the growing proletariat of wage workers, and the peasants living outside the city walls. But Italian urban politics cannot be explained in terms of a class struggle. The wealthy men did not stick together. By and large the old rich disliked the new rich, but one old family might dislike another old family even more than it did an upstart neighbor. Men with common interests and ambitions formed political groups that cut across all class lines. The basic rules of the game were to build up the group through alliances among influential families, to gain support among middle and lower income groups through granting protection and political favors, to find a plausible slogan (usually no more complicated than "throw the rascals out!"), and then to stage a *coup d'état* or a revolution. Sometimes there was merely a change in the holders of the principal offices; sometimes there was a fairly drastic revision of the town constitution to ensure the perpetuation of the new dominant oligarchical group; very rarely, as in Florence in 1378, the lower classes demanded, and got, some social

and economic reforms. Such reforms were not only infrequent, they were also short lived.

During the fourteenth century few Italian towns went as long as thirty years without a *coup d'état*. This instability caused material damage and forced many useful citizens into exile (the most eminent example was Dante). Thus when an able man, backed by a strong coalition, seized power and tried to put an end to political turbulence, his advent was usually accepted with some relief. Some of these leaders were not much more than military dictators (for example, the Sforza in Milan). Some of them were primarily very capable political bosses (for example, the Medici in Florence). They allowed no opposition; those who turned against them were eliminated by exile, imprisonment, or execution. On the other hand, these "despots," as they were eventually called, were usually careful to improve the city's public works, strengthen its defenses, devise efficient systems of taxation, and tighten internal security. By and large these programs were helpful to business, but one can hardly say that the despots were principally concerned with the welfare of the business community. They spent much of the money derived from the fruits of restored political stability on "glory" (wars with their neighbors) and "splendor" (buildings and works of art). Venice, the most prosperous Italian town, had no despot.

War and Diplomacy

Oligarchs and despots realized that the merchants and shopkeepers disliked military service and that armed subjects might easily turn against their rulers. Therefore they replaced citizen militias, which had never been very effective, with mercenary troops called *condottieri*. These soldiers were well trained and fairly reliable—as long as they were paid. In a pinch, however, their first loyalty was to their generals rather than to their employers. Moreover, as time went on, the generals sought to preserve their military assets by winning wars through clever maneuvers and negotiations rather than by pitched battles. But while they did not fight very much, they did have a monopoly of military power, and some generals displaced weak despots or divided city governments and became despots themselves.

What distinguished northern Italy most sharply from the rest of Europe was the total independence of its city-states from any central government. From Venice, oldest and proudest of the city-states, on down to towns of a few thousand inhabitants, city governments acted as if they were subject to no superior power. Motivated by economic and political self-interest, each city-state engaged in endless wars, making and breaking alliances, and jealously watching the most powerful state of the moment to make sure that it did not become strong enough to conquer the peninsula. Early in the fifteenth century the Italian city-states began to maintain resident ambassadors at the courts of foreign states to keep rulers in constant touch with governments that might one day become either useful allies or dangerous enemies. In the second half of the century, a kind of "balance of power" began to operate among the five leading states in Italy— Venice, Milan, Florence, the Papal States, and the Kingdom of Naples—in response

to an unwritten understanding that no one of the five must be allowed to gain enough power to threaten the others. When France and Spain intervened in Italy at the close of the fifteenth century, both these practices—the basic machinery of modern diplomacy and the balancing of power among a group of sovereign states—spread to the larger stage of Europe. By the mid-sixteenth century, resident ambassadors were common throughout central and western Europe, and a rough balance of power had been established between the ruling dynasties of the two most powerful states, France and Spain.

Milan, Venice, and Florence

Behind these generalizations lie the striking variety and individuality of the Italian cities of this era. Milan, the largest city of the Po Valley, was perhaps the most typical. It submitted early to a despot, and about 1400 a Milanese ruler, Gian Galeazzo Visconti, came as close as any strong man of the time to eliminating his rivals and uniting northern Italy. He failed, but the fear he inspired persisted, and no other despot managed to come so close to dominating northern Italy.

THE ITALIAN CITY-STATES   1454

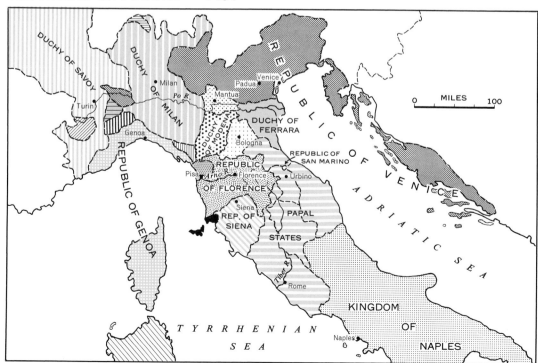

The rise of the Medici: Cosimo de' Medici has the look of the wily businessman, while his grandson Lorenzo appears every inch the prince. Above: Cosimo, detail from a fresco by Gozzoli. Below: Lorenzo, by an unknown artist.

Venice, the greatest commercial power of the peninsula, was absorbed in its widespread Mediterranean interests and was relatively isolated from Italian politics until it began to acquire territory on the mainland in the fifteenth century. Its republican constitution was the oldest and its government the most stable in Italy. There was no despot in Venice—the doge, or duke, was a figurehead—but a tight-knit commercial aristocracy ran the city through a small and tough-minded executive committee, the Council of Ten. Perhaps because the energies of the whole population were so absorbed in commerce, there were no real revolutions and few conspiracies in Venetian history. The constitution of the "most serene republic" (the official title of Venice) stood as a model of republican stability to other Italians.

Florence, like Venice, was proud of being a republic among the welter of despotisms and was especially proud of having helped to frustrate Gian Galeazzo Visconti's attempt to snuff out republican liberties in Italy. But in every other respect Florence and Venice were unalike. Venice lived primarily by commerce; Florence primarily by banking and industry. The most astute bankers and the finest textiles in Europe were both to be found in Florence. The energies of Venetians were directed outward toward the sea; the energies of Florentines were focused on industry and politics within Tuscany. Venetian society and Venetian government exhibited a high degree of stability, whereas nothing seemed stable in Florence. Political intrigues were a constant problem, and changes in the constitution were frequent.

During the fourteenth and early fifteenth centuries the Florentines tried to solve their political problems by riots, by changes in electoral procedures and in governmental structure, and even by calling in outside mediators (who usually did more harm than good). In the end, the Florentines settled for boss rule. In 1434 a new-rich party within the oligarchy, led by one of the city's wealthiest and shrewdest bankers, Cosimo de' Medici, gained power. For almost sixty years Cosimo, his son Piero, and his grandson Lorenzo the Magnificent (d. 1492), ran the city by manipulating elections and tinkering with the republican constitution. Cosimo was a banker who had been forced to play politics in order to save his financial interests. Lorenzo was more of a politician, only incidentally concerned with the family banking business. But each devoted his energy, his money, and his taste to the job of protecting, expanding, and beautifying the city. The most glittering example of Italy's golden age was Florence under the Medici.

ITALIAN URBAN CIVILIZATION

In these busy, crowded cities of northern Italy the structure of society and the ideals of the upper classes had to be modified. There had been a good deal of upward mobility during the fourteenth and early fifteenth centuries, and a new aristocracy was being formed—an aristocracy that included both descendants of old landed families who had prospered in the cities and wealthy merchants and bankers. The Medici, for example, had not been feudal lords, yet they eventually became dukes and married their daughters to kings of France. In the smaller towns, on the other hand, the despot was often a member of the old nobility who had learned how to deal successfully with urban problems. The situation was complicated by the growing prominence of writers, artists, and scholars. Most of these men did not, and never would, belong to the aristocracy, but their services and talents were necessary for the adornment of aristocratic life and their ideas of beauty, good taste, right behavior, and sound learning were accepted by the aristocracy. Finally, the aristocracy had to pay some attention to economic problems—problems far more complicated than those of managing landed estates. Communities dependent on continental markets and faced with sharp competition from their neighbors produced revenues that varied sharply from year to year. Frequent wars could bring even prosperous towns to the edge of bankruptcy. Loans had to be floated and new taxes devised. The oldest and most stable of the Italian aristocracies, that of Venice, was very skillful in managing its economic affairs; others were less successful.

The new ideal of the Italian aristocracies was a combination of old feudal-chivalric values and new urban-cultural values. It might be expressed as the ideal of the cultivated gentleman. A famous sixteenth-century book by Baldassare Castiglione, *The Courtier*, summed up this ideal. The courtier has all the chivalric virtues—physical dexterity, courage, skill in combat, courtesy—and all the new virtues—knowledge of the classics, appreciation of art and literature, eloquence, and good taste.

But besides the aristocrats there were the self-made men—not many, it is true, but just for that reason conspicuous. There was the *condottieri* general Sforza, who made himself ruler of Milan; the low-born artists, such as Leonardo da Vinci; the famous scholars, such as Lorenzo Valla; even a pope (Pius II) who may have had noble ancestors but who made his reputation as a scholar. How could these people be fitted into a common scheme? The answer was that they were men of *virtù*. This was the quality that made a man a free man (Latin, *vir*). It meant more than "virtue" in the modern sense; it also meant "virtuosity," that combination of genius and determination that made for greatness in statesmanship, artistic creation, or literature. In fact, by the time of Machiavelli, the word *virtù* was losing its moral connotation, and simply meant the qualities that led to success.

Individualism

At the upper levels of this society, there was growing individualism. Few of the old authorities carried the weight they had once carried for the aristocrat or highly talented city dweller. If his local government oppressed him, he could always move to another city. Many painters and sculptors were members of gilds, but gild regulations could not control their work. Scholars did not need university appointments in order to concentrate on their work, nor were they dependent on a single patron; a well-known writer could draw subsidies from many sources. And although the Italians considered themselves good Christians, they had little respect for the pronouncements of the clergy and accepted clerical rulings only when they were backed by strong ecclesiastical sanctions.

Thus for the upper classes and the cultural leaders there was a new emphasis on man as a private person, mainly concerned with himself, his family, his friends, and his own self-development. Such individualism sometimes went to extremes, as it did in the case of Benvenuto Cellini (1500–71), a sculptor and goldsmith who described his violent and colorful career in a famous *Autobiography*. Cellini assumed that the ordinary laws of morality were made for ordinary people and that they neither could nor should be enforced in the case of geniuses like himself. He also assumed that autobiography, a literary form that had been very rare in the Middle Ages, was a natural form of expression and one that would find eager readers. He begins his book: "All men of whatsoever quality

A Man of Virtù

Benvenuto Cellini, a Florentine goldsmith and sculptor, had struck medals and coins for Pope Clement VII (1523–34). He claimed that he had been insulted by a jeweler named Pompeo (who also worked for the pope), and after several quarrels, Cellini stabbed Pompeo to death in a street brawl. Clement VII had just died; Cardinal Farnese was elected pope on October 13, 1534, and took the name of Paul III.

After he had put affairs of greater consequence in order, the new Pope sent for me, saying that he did not wish any one else to strike his coins. To these words of his Holiness one of his gentlemen named Latino Juvinale [a Humanist] answered that I [Cellini] was in hiding for the murder of Pompeo of Milan, and set forth what could be argued for my justification in the most favorable terms. The Pope replied: "I know nothing of Pompeo's death but plenty of Benvenuto's provocation, so let a safe-conduct be at once made out for him." A great friend of Pompeo's was there; he was a Milanese called Ambrogio [Ambrogio Recalcati, a papal secretary]. This man said: "In the first days of your papacy it is not well to grant pardons of this kind." The Pope answered: "You know less about such matters than I do. Know then that men like Benvenuto, unique in their profession, stand above the law."

From Benvenuto Cellini, *The Life of Benvenuto Cellini*, trans. by John Addington Symonds (New York: Scribner's, 1926), p. 144.

Minters making silver thalers (from which comes our word *dollar*). A heated metal disk has been placed on top of the die, another die has been placed on top of the disk, and the minter is striking the top die with an iron mallet (detail from the Miners' Altar by Hans Hesse, Church of St. Anne, Annaberg, Saxony).

ines are not exactly irreligious or critical of Christian ideals, but they despise the hypocrisy of priests and monks, and they rejoice in the triumph of clever people of the world over clerical busybodies.

The secularism of Italian society can thus be broken down into two components: preoccupation with worldly pursuits, and contempt for those who professed the ascetic ideal but did not live up to it. There were a few pagans or atheists. But most men simply thought more constantly of this world than of the next, without denying the ultimate importance of the next. There was a latent conflict between the older and the new ideals. This conflict troubled many writers and artists and led to outbreaks of revivalism in the most worldly cities, such as Florence. In fact, tension between worldly and otherworldly ideals was more typical of the period than was the frank and untroubled enjoyment of temporal pleasures.

Humanism

The third mark of Italian urban society was its enthusiasm for classical antiquity. The men most deeply concerned with the classics were called Humanists—from the Latin *humanitas*, as used by Cicero to describe the literary culture proper to a well-bred man. The Middle Ages had always lived in the shadow of Rome, and interest in classical literature was nothing new. John of Salisbury in the twelfth century had a first-rate knowledge of Latin literature, and the greatest medieval poet, Dante, made it his conscious concern to blend the best of both classical and Christian ideals throughout the *Divine Comedy*. However, Francesco Petrarca, or Petrarch (1304–74), is rightly called the father of a new Humanism. His enthusiasm for Cicero, his admiration for Rome (he said he wished he had been born in the ancient world instead of his own), and his feel for the style of classical Latin were contagious. He loved the classics for their own sake, not because they could be used to explain the language of the early Church Fathers. Within a generation or two after his death Petrarch's followers were busily discovering classical manuscripts in

they be, who have done anything of excellence, . . . ought to describe their life with their own hand." Later he remarks, "I make no profession of writing history. It is enough for me to occupy myself with my own affairs." Cellini was obviously interesting to himself, and he was sure he was interesting to others.

Secularism

The second mark of this new society was its predominantly secular tone. This does not mean that it was pagan or anti-Christian. It means that the things of this world increasingly occupied the time and attention of the Italian townspeople—the balance of profit and loss, well-built houses and fine clothes, rich food and drink, and enjoyment of leisure—and that the ascetic and otherworldly ideals of the medieval Church seemed more and more remote to them. Their tastes and attitudes are already evident in the ribald stories of Boccaccio's popular *Decameron* (ca. 1350). The heroes and hero-

monastic libraries, writing letters to one another in impeccable Ciceronian Latin, pouring contempt on the Latin style of medieval scholastic philosophers, and, most important, getting jobs as secretaries at the papal Curia and the courts of the despots, or as teachers of the children of the ruling classes in the cities.

These professional Humanists were something new in European society. Generally they were laymen who made a living by their learning, not clerics or monks devoting spare time to classical study. They were self-made men who were peddling a new type of scholarship to their contemporaries—and who found the market very good. Enthusiasm for the classics was heightened after 1395, when refugee scholars from the Byzantine Empire began to teach Greek to eager students in Florence and elsewhere. And by the end of the fifteenth century a few Italians were even beginning to learn Hebrew and Arabic. Humanism was both a scholarly movement and a social fad. The Humanists revived the study of classical Latin, Greek, and Hebrew, and they got the ruling classes of the Italian cities excited about what they were doing.

The Humanists initiated a revolution in educational theory and practice. Formal education in the Middle Ages had been dominated by the clergy and directed mainly to the production of clerics. Even the students of law were technically members of the clergy, and many of them ended their careers as cathedral canons, as bishops, or even as popes. The nobility had its own program of training knights to hunt and fight and behave properly at court. But neither of these systems of education offered much to the sons of business and professional town dwellers, and by the thirteenth century, if not earlier, there were town schools, primarily for laymen, that taught arithmetic and Latin grammar. The Humanists of the fifteenth century rediscovered what Greco-Roman writers had meant by the "liberal arts": the liberating effect on mind and imagination of the study of great literature and philosophy. To this they added courteous behavior and athletic skill and so formed a new pattern of education. The result was a program designed to produce well-read laymen, able to write classical Latin and perhaps Greek, well mannered and at home in polite society, physically strong, and skillful in the art of war. "We call those studies liberal," wrote one Humanist educator, "which are worthy of a free man . . . that education which calls forth, trains, and develops those highest gifts of body and of mind which ennoble men." In practice this education too often degenerated into a narrowly literary training, floundering in the grammatical details of dead languages. It was available only to a few, and it was consciously aristocratic in its ideals. But at its best it passed on to later generations, including our own, the goal of turning out well-balanced human beings, devoted to both classical and Christian ideals, and able to become better businessmen or lawyers or statesmen because of their liberal education.

Young student reading Cicero (detail from a painting by Vincenzo Foppa).

Historical Self-Consciousness

The fourth and final mark of this urban society was its historical self-consciousness. The historical sense of the Middle Ages was not highly developed.

Petrarch on the Classics and Christianity

You are well aware that from early boyhood of all the writers of all ages and races the one whom I most admire and love is Cicero. You agree with me in this respect as well as in so many others. I am not afraid of being considered a poor Christian by declaring myself so much a Ciceronian. [This is an allusion to a famous vision of St. Jerome in which God told him: "You are a Ciceronian and therefore not a Christian."] To my knowledge, Cicero never wrote one word that would conflict with the principles proclaimed by Christ. If, perchance, his works contained anything contrary to Christ's doctrine, that one fact would be sufficient to destroy my belief in Cicero and in Aristotle and in Plato. . . .

Christ is my God; Cicero is the prince of the language I use. I grant you that these ideas are widely separated, but I deny that they are in conflict with each other. Christ is the Word, and the Virtue and the Wisdom of God the Father. Cicero has written much on the speech of men, on the virtues of men, and on the wisdom of men—statements that are true and therefore surely acceptable to the God of Truth.

From a letter to Neri Morando, 1358, in *Petrarch's Letters to Classical Authors*, trans. by M. E. Cosenza (Chicago: University of Chicago Press, 1910), pp. 18–19.

The crucial events of the Christian drama had already happened, and time now had only to run on and out to its conclusion in the Last Judgment. Caesar and Charlemagne wore the same costume in medieval drawings. Frederick Barbarossa thought it perfectly reasonable to insert his own edicts in the *Corpus Juris* of Justinian. There had been no essential change since the triumph of Christianity. There was no significant difference between Constantine and Otto III, or between St. Peter and Innocent III. The passage of time brought only minor variations in a persisting pattern.

Petrarch and his Humanist successors in the fifteenth century revolutionized this conception of the past. They became more interested in this world and its history. Their enthusiasm for classical antiquity enabled them for the first time to see the ancient world as a civilization that had run its course. It had been born, it had flourished, and it had died. They talked of the "Fall of Rome" and of a "Dark Age" that had followed. Above all, they talked of a "rebirth," or "revival," that was beginning in their age. Rome had had its golden age and had fallen; darkness had succeeded, but now the light was beginning to dawn again. The Humanists and their followers were highly conscious of their position in history and of their historical mission.

THE "RENAISSANCE"

While the Italian Humanists were sure that they lived in an age of rebirth, they were not nearly so sure of the profound implications of their work as were later historians. Chief of these was the Swiss Jacob Burckhardt, who wrote a brilliant book called *The Civilization of the Renaissance in Italy* (1860). Thanks to Burckhardt, western historians accepted the idea that there was a "Renaissance," or rebirth, after the Middle Ages, that it marked a sharp break with medieval ideals and practices, and that it was centered in Italy. There was much truth in Burckhardt's thesis, but he exaggerated both the sharpness of the breach with the medieval past and the uniqueness of Italy compared with the rest of Europe.

The Adimari Wedding, by an anonymous painter (*ca. 1450*). The painting shows the parade of guests at the wedding reception, held under a canopy outside a church in Florence. Such paintings often adorned the bride's *cassone,* a wedding chest designed to hold her trousseau.

The term *Renaissance* is most useful when it is applied to the revolutionary change in the arts, in literature, and in the concept of man that took place in Italy in the fourteenth, fifteenth, and early sixteenth centuries. It is less useful when applied to political and ecclesiastical history because it is hard to say what "rebirth" means in these areas. And it is quite useless when applied to economic and social history, in which changes are always slow and in which the important developments began as far back as the eleventh century. Historians of art and literature are relatively sure of what *Renaissance* means; other historians are unsure in varying degrees to the point of total doubt. This does not mean that artistic and literary developments had no connection with economic and social change. It means simply that the word *Renaissance* is best used to describe the changes in artistic and literary taste and skill that occurred at the close of the Middle Ages.

Literature, Philosophy, and Scholarship

Wherever there were classical models to fall back on, the tendency at first was for both writers and artists to lose themselves in simple imitation, in the first flush of excited rediscovery. It was easy, for instance, for Humanists to imitate the letter writing, the orations, the moral essays, and even the poetry of the Ro-

mans—and they did, relentlessly, in the early fifteenth century. When it became possible for educated Florentines to read Plato in the original Greek, the Medici fostered an informal group of scholars who became known as the Platonic Academy. Their leading members, Marsilio Ficino (1433–99) and Pico della Mirandola (1463–94), tried to reconcile Platonism and Christianity, as Thomas Aquinas had tried to reconcile Aristotelianism and Christianity. It was the one serious attempt at philosophical synthesis during the Renaissance, and it was a failure. But enthusiasm for Plato and Platonism was infectious and had widespread influence on poets and painters throughout Europe in the next century. In fact, Plato dominated the imagination of the Renaissance as Aristotle had earlier dominated the thought of medieval scholars.

All was not mere imitation in Italian thought and writing, however. Modern critical scholarship, in the sense of careful linguistic and historical analysis of the literary remains of the past, dates from the Renaissance, and particularly from one of the keenest minds of the age, Lorenzo Valla (*ca.* 1405–57). Valla analyzed the language and the historical background of the so-called Donation of Constantine, one of the main bulwarks of the popes' claims to temporal power, and proved beyond a shadow of a doubt that the document was a clumsy forgery of the early Middle Ages. He further com-

pared several Greek manuscripts of the New Testament with the accepted Latin translation, the Vulgate, and showed that the translation was full of errors and distortions. The critical spirit and scholarly technique that he inaugurated influenced Erasmus, Pierre Bayle, and Voltaire and resulted in the "scientific" scholarship of the nineteenth century.

Social and Political Thought

Much of Renaissance thought about the relation of man to man simply paraphrased the ethics and political theories of the Greeks and Romans. But sometimes a man wrote freshly from his own experience and spoke directly to the members of his own society. For example, Leon Battista Alberti (1404–72) in his book *On the Family*, described the interests and ideals of the Florentine families he knew: prudence and thrift, strong family feeling and little concern for larger causes outside, appreciation of comfort, planning and foresight, and pride in owning a house in the city and an estate in the country to produce all the family's food. It is one of the earliest idealized portraits of what will later be called the bourgeois virtues.

A social stratum just above that described by Alberti is sketched in the earlier mentioned work of Baldassare Castiglione (1478–1529), *The Courtier*. This book, based on Castiglione's memories of the court of the Duke of Urbino, de-

Machiavelli on Cruelty and Clemency

Is it better to be loved than feared or feared than loved? It may be answered that one should wish to be both, but it is much safer to be feared than loved when one of the two must be chosen. Men on the whole are ungrateful, fickle, false, cowards, covetous. As long as you succeed, they are yours entirely. They will offer you their blood, property, life, and children when the need is distant, but when it approaches they turn against you. And a prince who, relying entirely on their promises, has neglected other precautions, is ruined. . . . Men have fewer scruples in offending one who is beloved than one who is feared, for love is preserved by the link of obligation which, owing to the baseness of men, is broken at every opportunity for their advantage, but fear preserves you by a dread of punishment which never fails.

Nevertheless, a prince should inspire fear in such a way that if he does not win love, he avoids hatred; because he can endure very well being feared while he is not hated, and this will be true as long as he abstains from taking the property of his subjects or their women. But when it is necessary for him to take the life of someone, he must do it with proper justification and for manifest cause, and above everything he must keep his hands off the property of others, because men more quickly forget the death of their father than the loss of their heritage.

From Niccolò Machiavelli, *The Prince*, trans. by W. K. Marriott (London: Dent, n.d.), pp. 134–35.

Machiavelli on the Policy of Princes

You must know, then, that there are two methods of fighting, the one by law, the other by force: the first method is that of men, the second of beasts; but as the first method is often insufficient, one must have recourse to the second. It is therefore necessary for a prince to know well how to use both the beast and the man.

A prince being thus obliged to know well how to act as a beast must imitate the fox and the lion, for the lion cannot protect himself from traps, and the fox cannot defend himself from wolves. One must therefore be a fox to recognise traps, and a lion to frighten wolves. Those that wish to be only lions do not understand this. Therefore, a prudent ruler ought not to keep faith when by so doing it would be against his interest, and when the reasons which made him bind himself no longer exist. If men were all good, this precept would not be a good one; but as they are bad, and would not observe their faith with you, so you are not bound to keep faith with them.

From Niccolò Machiavelli, *The Prince*, in *The Prince and the Discourses*, ed. by Max Lerner (New York: Modern Library, 1940), Ch. 18, p. 64.

scribes the gentleman—graceful, attractive, courteous, liberally educated, noble in spirit if not necessarily in birth, at home either on the field of battle or among cultivated ladies. The concept of "the gentleman" owed much to chivalry and other traditional sources, but Castiglione presented it as a genuinely fresh ideal in the history of European civilization.

In the case of Niccolò Machiavelli (1469–1527), wide reading in the classics illuminated years of practical political experience. Machiavelli's career as ambassador and secretary of the Florentine government helped him to understand the political history of Rome as described by Livy, and Livy helped him to understand the power politics of his own age. Exiled by the Medici to his country home in 1512, he began to read widely and to reflect on what makes states expand and grow, what are the causes of political breakdown, how political leaders get and hold power, what can be learned from the past.

Machiavelli set down his reflections in a long, rambling book, *Discourses on Livy*, and in a briefer and more famous essay, *The Prince*. He made it clear that he was describing things as they were, not as they ought to be. Ideal states he left to others; in the world as it is, power is what counts. The Roman Republic, he thought, was the best example in history of successful state building. Its constitution was a masterly blend of monarchy, aristocracy, and democracy; it had good laws and a good citizen army; its religion supported the civic virtues of justice, prudence, and courage, not those of patience and humility; its rulers knew that the good of the state came before the dictates of individual morality. And so Rome, unlike any Italian city-state of Machiavelli's day, had been able to unite the whole of Italy and to endure for centuries.

But Machiavelli realized that this ideal, real though it once had been, might be too difficult for a corrupt and divided group of Italian city-states to revive. Perhaps a prince of real *virtù*, with the courage of a lion and the cunning of a fox, might be able to learn the laws of politics from history and experience and use them to build a strong state in Italy. He would know that men in their collective relations with one another are bad, and therefore he would not be held back by any moral scruples. If others broke faith with him, as they certainly would, the prince must be prepared to break faith with them for the good of his state. Fortune might frustrate his work, but a man of *virtù* had at least an even chance of overcoming bad luck. If his generation had both the intelligence and the will, Machiavelli believed, something could be done about the helpless state of Italy, which was falling under the heels of France and Spain.

Machiavelli's *Prince* was to become a grammar of political and diplomatic practice to heads of state as remote as Mussolini and Hitler. In its origin it was a perfect example of the fruitful combination in Renaissance thought of classical "rebirth" and contemporary "new birth," of historical example and practical experience. Both Machiavelli's disillusioned analysis of things as they were and his passionate plea for reform were entirely characteristic of the age.

The Arts

The influence of classical examples was strong also in the visual arts, but here original elements were even more noticeable than in social and political thought. Roman buildings survived, of course, all over Italy. Brunelleschi (1377?–1446), the greatest architect of his generation, absorbed their spirit and designed new churches in semiclassical style after 1420, thus inaugurating a return to the classical from the Gothic style in architecture. The late Roman sculpture that was dug up (hardly any of the Greek works of the classical age were yet known) inspired sculptors to imitation. But there were no ancient paintings to look at (Pompeii was not unearthed until the eighteenth century), and so Italian painters had to depend on the inspiration of their medieval predecessors and their own genius in elaborating their art.

Italian Renaissance painting, like that of France and Flanders, tended more and more toward realism. Giotto (1266?–1337), the first Italian to develop the new

A late–sixteenth-century portrait of Niccolò Machiavelli by Santi di Tito. The artist has tried to suggest both the intellectual brilliance and the shrewdness of the man.

style, was little influenced by northern art; later on some ideas were borrowed from the Low Countries (notably the use of oil paint). But north or south, the dominant interest of fourteenth-century writers, artists, and philosophers was in the concrete, individual thing as it actually existed, not in the general idea or eternal truth behind and in all things, which had been the typical concern of earlier medieval thinkers. Late medieval artists and writers tried to represent nature and man more and more realistically—to model a leaf as it actually appeared in nature, to chisel the features of a real man or woman, to sketch the character of a person in concrete detail, as both Boccaccio and Chaucer did with such success in their collections of tales. In fifteenth-century painting, particularly in the Netherlands, this effort resulted in the most astonishing skill in representing the smallest details of visual reality.

It was an Italian painter, however, who first realized that surface realism is not enough, that the artist must conceive the human figure as a whole, place it in three-dimensional perspective, and arrive at a more sophisticated realism that sac-

Donatello's *David* (*ca.* 1430–32). Compare this statue with the *David* by Michelangelo on the opposite page.

rifices minute details to organic unity. This painter was Masaccio (1401–28?), the founder of Renaissance painting and one of the great innovators in the history of the art.

Italian painting of the fifteenth and sixteenth centuries is far too rich in content and varied in technique for us to describe in detail. Some of its general characteristics may be suggested, however. The first thing that strikes the historical observer is the separation of painting and sculpture from architecture. It was as if the sculptured prophets and many-colored saints had stepped down from their niches and stained-glass windows in the great medieval cathedrals to be reincarnated in bronze statues in Italian public squares or painted portraits in Italian palaces. Painting and sculpture were no longer arts subordinate to architecture. Painters began to adorn the walls of monasteries and houses with frescoes. After they had learned from Flemish artists the technique of painting with oils, the Italians went on to develop the easel painting, meant to be hung in a palace or house and to be enjoyed for its own sake. Donatello (1368–1466), in his *David*, was the first sculptor since the ancients to model a free-standing nude figure, and from then on to the great works of Michelangelo (1475–1564) sculptors developed their art with no thought but of its own perfection.

The zest for solving fresh problems infected architects as well as painters and sculptors. Brunelleschi went far beyond classical or medieval models in designing and building his famous dome over the transept of the cathedral in Florence (1420–36). Architecture, sculpture, and painting each went its own way. An individual artist might turn his hand to all three, and a painter might borrow ideas from sculpture. But in each case the artist could create as he pleased without subjecting one art to another.

The second characteristic worth noting was the heightened individuality and social prestige of the artist. A famous passage in Cellini's *Autobiography* describes the unveiling of his bronze statue of Perseus in the central square of Florence in 1554. "Now it pleased God," he wrote, "that on the instant of its exposure to view, a shout of boundless enthusiasm went up in commendation of my work, which consoled me not a little." Such a shout might have greeted the proclamation of a crusade in the eleventh century or the triumphant conclusion of a world war in the twentieth. But the public appreciation of a work of art, the assumption that great art is the product of individual "genius," which is something to be nurtured—these were as characteristic of the Renaissance as they were atypical of ages before and after. Artists and writers felt that they should be to the age of the Renaissance what the saint had been to the Middle Ages. Reality did not always correspond to their expectations; some patrons treated their painters and architects like any other employees. On the other hand, some mediocre men received excessive adulation and high rewards. By and large, Italy's Golden Age was the golden age of the artist and the writer.

In seeking a higher realism, Italian painters studied the laws of spatial perspective about the same time that Humanists were restudying the temporal or historical perspective of their day. As a result, the artists pictured real persons whom they knew, in recognizable space. Some of them spent their lives probing the psychological depths of human beings and trying to put on canvas what they found. The chief of these was the lonely scientific and artistic genius Leonardo da Vinci (1452–1519), whose curiosity about the secrets of nature was as insatiable as his curiosity about the nature of man. In painting *The Last Supper*, he chose not the moment when Christ breaks the bread and remarks, "This is my body . . . ," as a medieval artist might have done, but the more humanly dramatic and startling moment when he announces, "One of you will betray me." The resulting psychological crisis experienced by each disciple is carefully portrayed. The climactic episode of the Creation, as Michelangelo painted it on the ceiling of the Sistine Chapel in St. Peter's, was the creation of Adam—an almost superhuman man at the threshold of self-consciousness, languid, wondering, awakening—almost as if he were a symbol of the man of the Renaissance.

In one of his most famous sculptures, Michelangelo chose to portray Moses at the moment when he has caught sight of his people's idolatrous Golden Calf and is struggling to control himself.

These few examples typify the Renaissance point of view. The central concern is man here in this world, troubled, striving, with unknown possibilities. Thus Renaissance art is humanistic in the broader, more philosophical meaning of the word. Not that the artists rejected God or ignored nature. God is still there, and Renaissance landscapes are charming. But God is seen through man, through man's heroism and his tragedy; and generally nature is of interest only as background or setting to the human drama. The most important question is what is to become of man. Pico della Mirandola, in a famous *Oration* on man's dignity (1486), pictured God as giving man something he had given to no other creature, the unique gift of freedom:

> Thou, constrained by no limits, in accordance with thine own free will, in whose hands We have placed thee, shalt ordain for thyself the limits of thy nature. . . . We have made thee neither of heaven nor of earth, neither mortal nor immortal, so that with freedom of choice and with honor, as though the maker and molder of thyself, thou mayest fashion thyself in whatever shape thou shalt prefer.

Every other creature had its pattern and its limits, but to Pico man's nature and destiny were in his own hands. The men of the Renaissance had not lost belief in God, but they were convinced, in a way their medieval ancestors would not have understood, that man was on his own.

The greatness of Italian art lay in the fact that it reflected all the tensions and contradictions in the prevailing attitudes toward man. There was no party line in Renaissance art; there were no premature solutions of sharp differences, no accepted syntheses. Some artists were realists, others idealists. Donatello modeled despots as he saw them, with hard and observant realism, while Raphael (1483–1520) a generation later idealized the peasant girls he knew as calm and self-

possessed Madonnas of ethereal beauty. Some artists were scientists and psychologists like Leonardo, who tried to peer into the souls of men and women, while others were like the Venetian Titian (1477–1576), who was more interested in the external marks of character and the glorious play of color on the objects about him. Michelangelo, perhaps the most typical as well as the greatest artist of them all, gave his life to attempting the impossible: to reconciling the classical ideal of harmony, balance, and "nothing in excess," with the limitless goals and boundless love of Christian piety. This attempt to reconcile the Greco-Roman and Hebraic-Christian worlds was the central striving of the Renaissance. It failed, but the failure left an imperishable record in the arts.

Michelangelo's *David* (1501–04). Instead of representing David after his victory over Goliath, as Donatello had done, Michelangelo chose to represent him as watchful of the approaching foe, with muscles tensed in gathering strength.

357

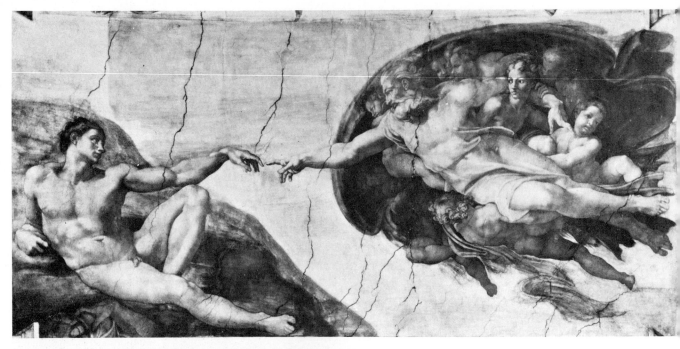

Raphael, detail from *Madonna with the Goldfinch* (1505–06).

Michelangelo, *Creation of Adam* (fresco from the ceiling of the Sistine Chapel of the Vatican, 1508–12).

Leonardo da Vinci, *Ginevra de' Benci* (*ca.* 1481).

Natural Science

The Renaissance contributed relatively little to the progress of natural science, but this little was important. The Humanists in general were more interested in man than in nature and more absorbed in literature than in mathematics and physics. Nevertheless, even at the height of the Renaissance, the Humanists never had full control of higher education. The old medieval curriculum, which included mathematics and physics, drew as many students as the new curriculum based on the classics. And on the practical side, the desire of the upper classes for greater comfort, and the striving of artists for greater realism, led to significant advances.

As craftsmen, mechanics, and engineers, the Italians were the best in Europe. In the science of perspective, their painters worked out the mathematical principles of representing figures in space. Their artists and doctors together advanced the knowledge of human anatomy beyond where it had been left by the Greeks. The *Notebooks* of Leonardo da Vinci, a landmark in the history of both art and science, show how closely the two interests were related in the fifteenth-century mind. His studies of anatomical detail, for instance, are of equal interest to painters and doctors. Furthermore, the medieval interest in science survived in the northern Italian universities, particularly Padua. There the study of mathematics flourished, and the arguments over Aristotelian laws of motion, which had been begun at Paris and Oxford, continued. Padua eventually passed on to Galileo a theory of scientific method in something like its modern form.

THE COUNCILS AND THE PAPACY

Italian energy and enthusiasm did something to dissipate the pessimism of the late fourteenth century. But Europe was still profoundly Christian and could not be entirely satisfied until its religious problems were solved. Of the three difficulties that faced the Church in 1400—the schism, heresy, and administrative reform—only one was completely overcome. By the mid-fifteenth century there was only one pope in Rome, even if the prestige of his office had not regained its thirteenth-century height. The most dangerous heresies had been walled off or driven underground, but the religious atmosphere was still heavy with discontent and revolt. And the more men talked of religious and administrative reforms in the Church, the more impossible it seemed to effect them.

The Great Schism had imposed an almost intolerable psychological burden on Europe. In theory there could not possibly be two true Vicars of Christ, yet there was no way of being sure which of the two claimants was the real successor. Men felt as if they were in a sinking ship: "If we remain in it," a contemporary wrote, "we must perish with it, and if we stray outside, salvation escapes us, since outside the ship there is no salvation." Many Lollards and other heretics had strayed outside. Those who remained on board tried desperately to find some solution.

The stubborn behavior of the two lines of popes at Rome and Avignon, in refusing to resign or to submit to arbitration, had increased antipapal feeling among both clergy and laity throughout Europe. In 1395 the French became so exasperated with their own pope that the French clergy, under pressure from the government, withdrew their obedience from him for five years. This was the first appearance of a policy that was to have an ominous future: secession from papal jurisdiction by the clergy of a large nation under the pressure of the secular government. Even in the fifteenth century there were signs that Christendom might dissolve into independent national churches.

The Conciliar Movement

As early as 1379, the year after the schism developed, scholars at the University of Paris had suggested a more conservative and practical scheme than the withdrawal of obedience. They urged that a general council of the Church be

Mobile bakers, one of the various groups who provided for the delegates to the Council of Constance (1414–18). Notice the "pretzels" in the upper right corner (detail from a manuscript version of Ulrich Richental's *Chronicle,* 1465).

called. The leading advocates of the idea at the university worked out a revolutionary conception of the Church to support their proposal. The Church, they argued, was not centered in the papacy but was made up of the whole body of believers. Thus the final authority in the Church was a council representing all the faithful, and the pope was only a limited monarch responsible to this representative assembly. The so-called fullness of power, which canon lawyers claimed for the pope, was a usurpation. Authority in the Church came from the bottom up, not from the top down. This conciliar theory of the constitution of the Church was to have strong appeal to secular rulers who were looking for a club to hold over the papacy. It was also to have a strong attraction for reformers during the next century.

In 1408 most of the cardinals of both sides deserted their popes and summoned a general council to meet at Pisa the next year. For a moment, a group of cardinals without a pope confronted two popes without any cardinals, but the result was simply the election of a third pope by the council. Unfortunately, neither the Roman nor the Avignonese pope resigned, as had been hoped. After five more years of confused negotiations, the German emperor Sigismund compelled the Pisan pope, John XXIII, to summon a genuinely representative assembly.

This great council, which met at Constance in Switzerland from 1414 to 1418, made a strong impression on the imagination of the age. It healed the schism by bullying John XXIII into resigning, per-

suading the Roman pope to resign after he had gone through the formality of resummoning and approving the council himself, and deposing the Avignonese pope, who by now had fled to Spain and was supported only by Aragon. In 1417 the council elected a new pope, Martin V, who soon commanded the allegiance of all western Christendom. The council was less successful in instituting reform. The English and German delegates worked in vain to have reform considered before the election of a new pope; the Latin nations were more anxious to heal the schism first and let reform come later. Once Martin V was elected, interest flagged in even the mild report of a committee to study abuses, and the council dispersed without ever really facing the complicated malpractices in the hierarchy. On the other hand, the council dealt energetically, though shortsightedly, with the problem of heresy.

John Hus

The danger spot in 1414 was Bohemia. Here during the preceding century the emperor Charles IV had helped to foster a national and cultural awakening among the Czechs. But Czech scholars ran into two obstacles: a corrupt and leaderless Church, and a steady influx of Germans into the cities and into the newly founded University of Prague. Since the Czechs tended to be reformers, while the Germans generally supported the status quo, the gifted group of Czech preachers and teachers who attacked ecclesiastical abuses soon found themselves leading a movement that was as much patriotic as it was religious. In 1402 a brilliant young leader appeared in John Hus (*ca.* 1369–1415). The burden of his preaching was that faith must be based on the Bible as the only source of authority, that Christ, not the pope, was the true Head of the Church, and that a man is saved by God through Christ, not by trusting in ceremonies and in a mediating priesthood that was thoroughly corrupt. Hus knew and used the ideas of Wiclif, whose books had been brought to Bohemia by Czech students returning from England, but he had developed his basic theories independently. By 1414 Hus had been excommunicated by the Roman pope, but he was at liberty and his ideas were accepted by a majority of the Czech people.

Hus eagerly seized the opportunity to journey to Constance to present his case before the council. He was almost immediately imprisoned for heresy. The emperor, who had granted him a safe-conduct, withdrew his protection the moment the dreaded charge of heresy was made. The conciliar leaders would have preferred a public recantation that could have been publicized throughout Bohemia, but Hus stood firm. In the dra-

matic trial that followed, the essential issue was whether the Bible and a man's conscience are the ultimate religious authority, as Hus argued, or whether the Catholic Church represented by the clerical hierarchy is the sole authority, as the council declared. Hus was condemned and burned at the stake outside the walls of Constance in May 1415. His follower, Jerome of Prague, was burned on the same spot the following spring.

Before the council disbanded, civil and religious warfare had broken out in Bohemia. It lasted for almost twenty years. The upshot was an agreement in 1436 between the more conservative Hussites and the Church. This agreement recognized a national church in Bohemia with local control over ecclesiastical appointments and with its own liturgical practices, notably the right to offer the cup as well as the bread to the laity when giving communion. For the first time the Church had made an agreement on equal terms with condemned heretics after excommunicating them and solemnly preaching a crusade against them. Wiclif's Lollards had been driven underground in England, but the Hussite heresy had simply been walled off in Bohemia.

The Papacy's Triumph over the Conciliar Movement

The restored papacy, which owed its existence to the Council of Constance, was more successful in defeating the conciliar movement than it was in extirpating heresy. The fathers had decreed at Constance that general councils must be summoned every ten years. But the superior diplomacy and the more efficient administrative machinery of the Roman papacy soon made this provision a dead letter. The temper of the times was changing; the idea that a ruler should be controlled by an assembly now seemed to lead only to confusion. Just as most European kings weakened their parliaments and humbled their nobles, so the popes weakened the conciliar ideal, stopped holding councils at regular intervals, and humbled the princes of the Church, the cardinals. By the time Nicholas V became pope (1447–55) the threat

John Hus being burned at the stake in 1415. He wears a fool's cap with pictures of the Devil and the word *heresiarch* (leader of heretics).

that the Church might be transformed into a limited monarchy was over. Never again was there a general council of the Church that the pope could not control.

The popes' triumph over the councils left the papacy stronger in some respects but weaker in others. No one within the Church itself could challenge the papal "fullness of power," but the victory had been bought by making wide concessions to secular rulers. In opposing the reforming element in the councils, the popes had isolated themselves from clerical and lay leaders of opinion, particularly in the north of Europe. As a result, the popes depended on the support of lay rulers and could not resist their efforts to control the clergy within their own realms. In 1438 the king of France summoned an assembly of the French clergy and issued a solemn decree known as the Pragmatic Sanction of Bourges. This decree strictly limited the pope's power of appointment and taxation in France and in effect set up a national, or "Gallican," Church, as it was called. In later years the popes were able to persuade the French monarchs to modify this one-sided action by "concordats," or agreements, between the papacy and the French crown. But in these agreements the monarchy always retained its control over appointments to the higher clergy. With some differences, the kings of England and Spain established similar limitations on papal power during the fourteenth and fifteenth centuries. In Germany, where there was no central government strong enough to stand up to the pope, papal rights of appointment, taxation, and jurisdiction were not limited as they were in the stronger monarchies. The popes had eliminated all their clerical rivals for power, only to be faced by much more greedy and formidable lay rivals—the monarchs.

The Renaissance Papacy

The eighty years between the accession of Nicholas V to the papacy (1447) and the sack of Rome (1527) are often called the period of the Renaissance papacy. It was a brilliant but tragic era in the history of the Church. Some of the popes of the period were patrons of Humanism and the arts, notably Nicholas V, founder of the Vatican Library, and Julius II (1503–13), builder of St. Peter's. Pius II (1458–64) had been Aeneas Sylvius, a celebrated Humanist, before his election. Two were particularly noted for their wars: Sixtus IV (1471–84), who was rumored to have died of rage at the conclusion of a peace settlement; and Julius II, who was known to his generation as "the Warrior Pope." More than one was notorious for his nepotism, as favoritism to relatives, including bastard children, was

Aerial view of St. Peter's in Rome. In 1505 Pope Julius II commissioned Bramante to construct a church that would mirror the classical-Christian aspirations of the sixteenth century. The plans were changed several times, and the building was not completed until 1626. Michelangelo designed the dome; the colonnades were designed by Bernini in the 1600s.

called. Roderigo Borgia, Alexander VI (1492–1503), was by far the worst of the lot. His mistresses lived openly with him; his voracious Spanish relatives got whatever they asked for; and his illegitimate son, Cesare Borgia, made a bloody attempt to become the ruler of all central Italy with his father's help.

All the accumulated evils of many years seemed to become intensified in the papal court: simony, nepotism, immorality, involvement in secular politics and warfare. Two centuries before, Innocent III had been immersed in secular diplomacy, but it had been on a Europe-wide scale, and the excuse had always been the advancement of the Church's cause. Now the scale of involvement was limited to the Italian peninsula, and the popes were generally motivated by selfish family interests. As time went on, the papacy became thoroughly Italianized, perhaps out of fear of another schism. (Since the end of the schism in 1417, only one non-Italian pope has been chosen, in 1522.) Most secular rulers came to assume that as ruler of the Papal States the pope would act like any Italian despot, at the dictates of his own personal and family interests—with the unfair competitive advantage, of course, that he was considered to be the Vicar of Christ. But even when the papacy seemed to be simply another Italian principality it was sustained by the basic belief that the office was greater than the man, that the moral character of the pope did not lessen his authority in spiritual matters.

The open corruption of the papal Curia during the fifteenth century had much to do with the Protestant revolt that began in 1517. As one historian has put it, the popes of the Renaissance tried to substitute splendor for reform. In the hands of an intelligent and devoted Humanist like Nicholas V this was not an unworthy idea. To him it meant reconciling Christianity with the best in ancient civilization and rebuilding Rome as the capital of a revived Christendom. But this ideal did not satisfy the mystical and moral strivings of thousands of the faithful, particularly those outside Italy. Significantly, it was under a cultivated son of Lorenzo de' Medici, Pope Leo X

(1513–21), that much of Germany rebelled against the papacy, and under an illegitimate son of Lorenzo's brother, Pope Clement VII (1523–34), that England set up a national Church.

ECONOMIC GROWTH IN THE NORTH

While Italy was building city-states on the wealth derived from its monopoly of Mediterranean trade, northern and western Europe was building nation-states based on new industries and new trade routes. The cumulative effects of technological change began to stimulate the transalpine economy during the fifteenth century. Thus gradual improvements in building and rigging sailing ships made possible the great voyages of Vasco da Gama to India and of Columbus to America. Da Gama's voyages gave the Atlantic countries an increasing share of the lucrative trade in Oriental goods. Columbus gave the same countries a monopoly of the wealth of a New World. Even though Italian trade remained close to its old level, it was dwarfed by the much greater trade of Portugal and Spain, of France, England, and the Netherlands.

In Europe, new and profitable industries began to appear. For example, improved techniques in metallurgy made it possible to take full advantage of the discovery of gunpowder and to make cannon for sieges and naval warfare. Since more metal was needed, mining methods had to be improved and blast furnaces had to be enlarged to enable metal workers to use the increased supply of ore. The Atlantic states were able to gain control of world sea lanes not only because their ships were slightly better than those of their rivals but because they were more powerfully armed with naval cannon. On land the use of siege cannon weakened the noblemen and strengthened the monarchs, and so increased security. The noble's castle was no longer a secure retreat, and no ordinary noble could afford the vast cost of heavy guns. If they were to maintain their military tradition, the nobles had to become officers in the armies of kings

Cesare Borgia, anonymous copy of an authentic portrait.

and princes who could afford to buy the new weapons. They were not always well-disciplined officers, but they were no longer independent war-lords.

As we have seen, the invention of printing from movable type also depended on advances in metallurgy. And that invention, in the middle of the fifteenth century, had even more revolutionary effects than the invention of the cannon. So long as books had to be laboriously copied by hand, only a few men could aspire to higher learning. But as printing presses spread rapidly from the Rhine Valley to Italy, the Netherlands, France, Spain, and England, Europeans had a flood of books available at prices that would have been unbelievable a century earlier. There were "standard editions" of the Bible, the Church Fathers, and the classical writers in both Greek and Latin, scientific works, devotional treatises, and popular manuals in the vernacular languages. Like all mechanical inventions, printing brought

both good and evil in its train. The "standard editions" could multiply errors as well as corrections, and the pamphlets that were now so easy to print and circulate in large numbers could mislead as well as inform. But one thing was clear: learning would never again be the monopoly of a small upper class in European society. Anything human beings had written could now be multiplied and placed quickly and cheaply in the hands of anyone who could read.

Industry and Agriculture

New industries such as cannon founding and printing required large initial investments in plant and machinery. They were organized from the start as capitalistic enterprises—that is, enterprises in which accumulated wealth was deliberately used to produce more wealth. In addition to capital, these industries needed and attracted free laborers from town or country who could be employed for a wage and dismissed when business slacked off.

Even in rural areas capitalistic methods calculated to produce a profit were occasionally being applied to the land. Landlords had long realized that raising sheep for wool might be more profitable than accepting a customary rent. Legally or illegally, many of them, particularly in England, managed to fence off, or "enclose," lands formerly reserved for the common use of villagers, or to convert ploughed land to pasture. Since tending sheep required far fewer man-hours than raising food on the same amount of land, many families were displaced from the soil. Occasionally "improving landlords" turned to more intensive cultivation of the soil in order to produce a larger cash crop of food for the growing urban markets, often riding roughshod over the preference of villagers for timeworn methods.

In short, capitalism was being applied to industry and agriculture wherever individual entrepreneurs saw profit to be made in producing books, weapons, clothing, or food for sale in the open market. For some peasants and workers this meant new opportunity. Many an ambitious peasant was able to better his

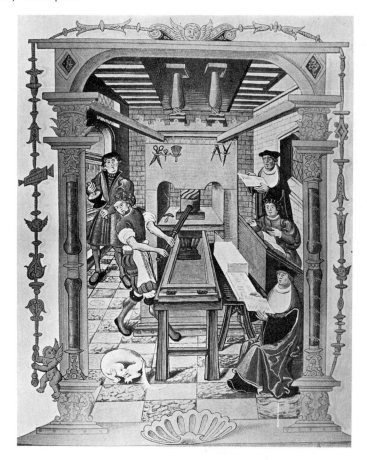

An early printing press, as shown in an early–sixteenth-century French print.

position, as Martin Luther's father did by becoming a miner. But a great deal of misery and unemployment also resulted from the breaking down of customary economic relationships, the eviction of peasants from their holdings, and the movement of population to the new industrial centers. "Sturdy beggars" and "vagabonds" were a constant problem for sixteenth-century town governments.

Wealth derived from the new industries and commerce tended to concentrate in a few hands in a few places. For a brief period the most powerful banking house was that of the Fuggers of Augsburg in south Germany. Jakob Fugger (1459–1525), as banker for the Habsburgs and the pope, could invest in Austrian mines and Spanish colonies and carry on dealings with every part of the Continent. On the whole, however, from about 1476 to 1576 Antwerp was the Wall Street of northern Europe, with Lyons not far behind. Then, for a century after 1576, it was Amsterdam. The wealth that poured in from the Orient and the New World had a way of gravitating to the commercial centers of the Netherlands. Where the investment market was freest, where the largest and most aggressive firms transacted most of their business, here were the nerve centers of European finance. Italy was losing its old place as the banking center of Europe. Financial power was clearly shifting to the north.

POLITICAL CONSOLIDATION AND CENTRALIZATION

The most highly developed monarchies of western Europe—England and France—had undergone a severe crisis in the fourteenth century (see Chapter 13). The successors of Edward I and Philip the Fair allowed their political ambitions to outstrip their financial resources. The Hundred Years' War (1337–1453) exhausted both France and England, and plague and social revolt added their toll of misery to war. The monarchs were not equal to the strain. As the fifteenth century opened, France was ruled by a king who had periods of insanity (Charles VI), and England was ruled by a usurper who owed his throne to his fellow barons and

THE FINANCIAL EMPIRE OF JAKOB FUGGER
ca. 1485–1525

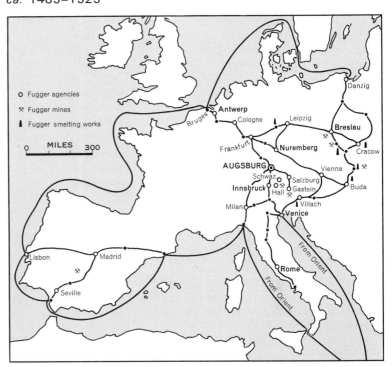

Jakob Fugger with his bookkeeper. The cabinet in the rear lists the names of cities where Fugger had branch offices—Innsbruck, Nuremberg, and Lisbon, among others (detail from a painting by Matthaus Schwartz, 1516).

to Parliament (Henry IV). The future did not seem very bright for the monarchies that had been so painfully built up in the twelfth and thirteenth centuries.

The later fifteenth century, however, saw a remarkable recovery of monarchical institutions in western Europe. As people grew more and more weary of war, violence, and anarchy, the forces striving to restore some semblance of law and order rallied to the support of the monarchs in France, the Spanish kingdoms, and England. Even weak rulers profited from the demand for peace and strong government. And economic growth made it easier to support stronger armies and more effective bureaucracies.

France

At times during the Hundred Years' War the authority of the French king had almost disappeared, but there had been considerable recovery before the war ended in 1453. Charles VII was not a great king, but he was clever enough to find able men to work for him (he was known in his time as Charles the Well-served). He began his reign by using the widespread enthusiasm aroused by Joan of Arc to expel the English and to restore law and order to the French countryside. In 1438, by the Pragmatic Sanction of Bourges, he asserted his authority over the French clergy at the expense of papal power. In the 1440s he solved the financial problem of the crown by obtaining consent from the Estates to a broad-based tax on land called the *taille*; he then continued to levy the tax on his own authority. He organized a small standing army (at most, 25,000 men) under direct royal control, gained the support of wealthy merchants who supplied him with a siege train of heavy artillery, and methodically ousted the English from all their strongholds on the Continent except Calais.

Louis XI (1461–83) carried on his father's work and left the monarchy stronger than it had been since Philip IV. Louis, a slovenly and superstitious man with a morbid fear of death, had none of the majesty of kingship. He was called "the Spider" because he preferred to trap his enemies in diplomatic webs than to fight them. Machiavelli admired him, with reason. The greatest threat to the French monarchy was the powerful state that the dukes of Burgundy had built up on France's eastern frontier, including the wealthy provinces of the Netherlands as well as Burgundy proper. Louis never actually defeated his rival, Charles the Bold, Duke of Burgundy (1467–77), but he shrewdly helped Charles defeat himself. Louis encouraged quarrels between Charles and his eastern neighbors, and in the end the duke was killed in battle against the Swiss. The richest portion of his inheritance, the Netherlands, fell to the Emperor Maximilian (1493–1519) through his marriage with Mary, daughter of Charles the Bold; but the strategically located Duchy of Burgundy went to the king of France. At home, Louis encouraged trade and kept a firm rein on the nobles and higher clergy. His successor Charles VIII (1483–98) married the heiress of Brittany and so brought the last remaining feudal duchy under direct royal control.

With France fully under control, Charles felt strong enough to invade Italy (1494) in order to assert his claims to Naples as the remote heir of Charles of Anjou (see p. 202). Spain, which also had claims in Italy, quickly reacted, and foreign armies fought over the peninsula for half a century. The Italian city-states were helpless; even if they had been united they probably could not have resisted such powers as France and Spain. As it was, Spain gradually gained a dominant position in Italy, and with the loss of independence Italian life lost much of its vigor and excitement. On the other hand, France was not greatly weakened by its losses in the Italian wars, an indication of the monarchy's new strength.

Spain

The Iberian Peninsula had suffered almost as severely as France from war and anarchy in the early fifteenth century. From 1085 to 1252 the Christian kingdoms of northern Spain had fought heroically to reconquer the peninsula from the Moslems in a movement known in Spanish history as the *Reconquista*. By the fifteenth century these kingdoms had

Joint Reign of Ferdinand and Isabella

750		1085	1252	1479 1504
Moslem Rule in Spain		*Reconquista* in the North	Amalgamation of Kingdoms into Portugal, Aragon, and Castile	
		Moslem Rule in Granada		

1481 1492

Reconquest of Granada

Illumination of Ferdinand and Isabella of Spain— known as the "Catholic Kings"—with their daughter Joanna.

coagulated into three monarchies: Portugal in the West, Castile in the center, and Aragon on the Mediterranean coast. The Kingdom of Granada, a small strip in the South, was the last remnant of Moslem rule. In 1469 a momentous marriage took place between Ferdinand of Aragon (1479–1516) and Isabella of Castile (1474–1504). The marriage brought no organic fusion of the political institutions of the two states, but husband and wife followed a common foreign policy and their heir could properly be called king of "Spain." A new national monarchy had been born from a dynastic union.

Isabella reestablished the authority of the crown in Castile and with her husband led a successful eleven-year "crusade" (1481–92) to expel the Moors (as the Moslems in Spain were called) from Granada. The victory touched off a wave of national patriotism and religious intolerance, which had been slowly gathering force during the later fifteenth century. In 1492 all Jews in both kingdoms were ordered either to become Christians or leave the land, and ten years later, in spite of promises of toleration when Granada fell, all Moors in Castile were offered the same choice. In 1478 some Dominicans had persuaded the pope to authorize Ferdinand and Isabella to set up the Spanish Inquisition. This dreaded instrument became a powerful force toward royal absolutism when the monarchs directed it against "converted" Jews and Moors who were suspected of secretly adhering to their old beliefs. There was thus a note of religious fervor and racial hatred, which was lacking elsewhere, in the birth of Spain as a great power.

A second marriage was greatly to affect Spain's European destiny in the sixteenth century. The Emperor Maximilian and his wife, Mary of Burgundy, had a son, Philip, who was heir to Austria through his Habsburg father and to the Netherlands through his mother. Philip married Joanna, the daughter of Ferdinand and Isabella. Their son Charles, born in 1500, eventually became king of Spain (1516–56) and ruler of the Netherlands, Austria, Milan, Naples, and the Spanish possessions in America. In 1519 the German princes elected him emperor as Charles V. Thus Spain was thrust out into the full stream of European politics and world empire by coming under the Habsburg dynasty in 1516.

Spain was not a wealthy country, nor were its two halves, Castile and Aragon, ever thoroughly amalgamated. Even today Catalonia is markedly different from Castile. But the Spanish armies soon proved themselves the best in Europe during campaigns in Italy and the Netherlands, and Columbus' discoveries brought in a stream of gold and silver from the New World that surpassed all European dreams of wealth. As a result, Spain was to become the leading power in Europe in the sixteenth century.

England

The Hundred Years' War had been a heavy burden on England. But the most severe trial followed the end of the war, when a restless nobility and professional soldiery returned from France to plunge into thirty more years of intermittent civil strife in the Wars of the Roses (1454-85). The excuse for the wars was the rivalry between the House of Lancaster and the House of York (both descended from Edward III) for the throne. Actually the wars were contests between shifting factions of nobles for control of the government. When it was all over, the first of the Tudors was on the throne as Henry VII (1485-1509), by right of conquest and a dubious hereditary claim. The bloodshed and violence of the wars had sickened the people, and plots and counterplots had killed off most of the leaders of the nobility. Taking advantage of the opportunity to restore the monarchy, Henry proved himself one of the ablest rulers in English history. He kept England out of foreign wars, encouraged trade, restored the sources of royal revenue, and eliminated all pretenders to the throne. His son, Henry VIII (1509-47), inherited a full treasury, a united nation, and (for its

day) an efficient administration. Henry VIII soon wasted the treasury surplus in war with France, but he and his overbearing minister, Cardinal Wolsey, did manage to concentrate power in their own hands. Henry VIII's England could compare well with either France or Spain in governmental efficiency and potential military strength, even though it had only about half Spain's population and a fourth that of France.

The Monarchs and the Nobility

Louis XI, Ferdinand and Isabella, and Henry VII all had common problems, which they met in strikingly similar ways. The chief obstacle in the path of rebuilding royal authority in the later fifteenth century was the military, political, and economic strength of the great nobles in each country (the kings were wise enough never to attack the social prestige of the nobility). The monarchs used various expedients in their cold war with overmighty subjects. The key to success was to make the royal Council an

Effigies on the tombs of Ferdinand of Aragon and Isabella of Castile, who created a united Spain.

effective agency of central government. Councillors were selected from among nobles who were loyal to the king and from members of the upper middle class who sought power and promotion. Key councillors, often at their own expense, developed groups of agents who kept them informed about internal and external threats to the security of the state. At the same time the Council, or one of its committees, was given supreme judicial power so that it could act quickly in any emergency. Thus in England the Secretaries of State, who were the most influential members of the Council, were well aware of plots against the throne through their close contacts with local authorities, with English ambassadors abroad, and with a network of spies. The Star Chamber, the judicial arm of the Council, could be used to suppress any manifestations of aristocratic independence, and the ordinary courts almost never failed to convict men accused by the Council. In France and Spain the Council was equally well informed and had even greater judicial power.

The Monarchs and the Representative Assemblies

A second possible obstacle to royal absolutism was the representative assembly: the Estates General in France, the Cortes in the Spanish kingdoms, and Parliament in England. These assemblies had reached the peak of their influence in the fourteenth century. In the fifteenth century, they declined everywhere but in England. This was due more to the ineffectiveness of assemblies than to the hostility of monarchs. Except in England, provincial feeling was so strong that it was difficult to reach agreement on any issue. Assemblies were more ready to grumble than to act. In France, for example, the Estates General, in spite of repeated requests, neither supported, nor proposed clear-cut alternatives to, royal policies. It is also true that the kings had weakened the Estates by depriving them of their financial powers; old taxes were continued and new ones imposed by royal authority alone. Thus the Estates General of France were weak and useless and gradually ceased to meet. In Spain,

the monarchs played off class against class by summoning only the representatives of the cities when they needed money, thus depriving the townsmen of the possible aid of the great nobles. Anxious to support royal authority, the town representatives usually consented readily to whatever taxes the king demanded. Deprived of any real power, the Cortes of Castile, like the Estates General of France, met less and less frequently after the end of the fifteenth century.

In England Henry VII apparently had little respect for Parliament and, after the first years of his reign, seldom summoned it. But since the English Parliament could speak for all the privileged classes and all parts of the country, it was more difficult to ignore than the weak and divided assemblies of other countries. In England provincial rivalries scarcely existed; landowners and the bourgeoisie usually cooperated, and no general tax could be levied without Parliamentary consent. When Henry VIII got into trouble with the pope, he summoned Parliament to give him support. This use of Parliament as an accomplice had unanticipated results. By 1600, thanks to the frequent use Henry Tudor and his successors made of it, Parliament had become a more powerful force in English government than ever before. By that time the representative assemblies on the Continent, in states governed by absolute monarchs, had become hollow forms.

The Monarchs and the Church

The final obstacle to the development of monarchical power was the Church. Against this obstacle the kings moved cautiously. Louis XI was proud to be called "Most Christian King" of France; Ferdinand and Isabella were proud to be known as the "Catholic Kings"; and Henry VIII was especially proud of his title "Defender of the Faith," which the pope granted him in 1521. But on the three crucial questions of appointment of the higher clergy, taxation of the clergy, and the appeal of ecclesiastical cases to Rome, not one of the monarchs admitted the full papal claims. The kings of England and France had established their right to tax their own clergy by 1300. The French kings had asserted their right to control clerical appointments in the Pragmatic Sanction of Bourges, and the pope had granted Francis I the right to nominate the higher clergy and to settle the bulk of ecclesiastical disputes in France in the Concordat of Bologna in 1516. Even the "Catholic Kings" of Spain asserted and maintained their right to appoint, to tax, and to reform the clergy within their kingdoms, despite papal objections. Thus long before the Protestant Reformation, kings were trying to build "national churches"—churches that looked to the authority of the secular ruler in matters of appointment, taxation, and even jurisdiction, although not in doctrine.

Consolidation and Centralization Elsewhere in Europe

These tendencies in western Europe toward the consolidation of territory and the centralization of political power also appeared in the kingdoms of Norway and Sweden. They appeared too in Russia, where Ivan the Dread (1533–84) ruthlessly broke the power of the aristocracy. In Italy, however, there was no central government to be strengthened (much to the despair of observers like Machiavelli). In the German Empire the central government was a sham. There was no imperial army and no effective system of imperial taxation. There was an imperial supreme court, but it was so inefficient that it had little authority. An attempt at the close of the fifteenth century to strengthen the imperial government was almost a total failure. When Charles V became emperor in 1519, his real strength lay in the fact that he was duke of Austria, lord of the wealthy towns of the Netherlands, and king of Spain, with its well-equipped armies and overseas treasure. Becoming emperor added something to his prestige, much to his responsibilities, but little to his power. Many German princes expanded their territories at the expense of weaker neighbors and increased their authority within their principalities by methods very similar to those of the kings of western Europe. But in 1500 there was no central authority in Germany strong enough to resist papal exactions, foreign intervention, or the spread of heresy.

This lack of central authority was to be of crucial importance for the future. On the one hand, it meant that the Protestant Reformation, once it started, could not be brought under control. On the other, it meant that the emperor could rely only on his own hereditary domains in meeting a new threat that came from the East. The Turks had advanced steadily after the fall of Constantinople in 1453. The greatest of their sultans, Suleiman the Magnificent (1520–66), captured Belgrade, won most of Hungary in the battle of Mohacs (1526), and almost took Vienna in 1529. With a divided Germany behind him and a dangerous enemy facing him in the Danube Valley, the emperor could not play his old role of defender of Christendom until he had built a new state out of the old Habsburg territories.

Suggestions for Further Reading

Note: Asterisk denotes a book available in paperback edition.

General J. Burckhardt's great "essay," *The Civilization of the Renaissance in Italy* * (1860), is still the starting point for study. W. K. Ferguson, *The Renaissance in Historical Thought* (1948), traces the development of the idea of "rebirth" from the Humanists themselves through Burckhardt to the present. His *Europe in Transition: 1300–1520* (1963) is a good survey of the period. So is L. W. Spitz, *The Renaissance and Reformation Movements,* * 2 vols. (1971). M. P. Gilmore, *The World of Humanism: 1453–1517* * (1952), makes excellent use of recent monographic material and offers a critical bibliography. D. Hay, *The Italian Renaissance* * (1962), is a newer work of considerable value. See also his *Europe in the Fourteenth and Fifteenth Centuries* (1971).

Italian Society and Politics

There is interesting material on Renaissance businessmen and bankers in M. Beard, *A History of the Business Man* (1938), and R. de Roover, *The Rise and Decline of the Medici Bank** (1963). I. Origo, *The Merchant of Prato* (1957), is an enjoyable study of a small-town businessman. G. Mattingly, *Renaissance Diplomacy** (1955), traces the origins of modern diplomacy in Italy in a fascinating way. There are histories of all the major Italian states, but the most important for an understanding of the Renaissance are those on Florence. G. Brucker, *Renaissance Florence* (1969), is the best brief treatment in English. D. Herlihy, *Pisa in the Early Renaissance* (1958), and W. M. Bowsky, *The Finances of the Commune of Siena* (1970), provide the histories of two other leading cities. H. Baron, *The Crisis of the Early Italian Renaissance*,* 2 vols. (1955), is an important study of Florentine politics and culture in the early fifteenth century. Perhaps the best single volume on Machiavelli is F. Chabod, *Machiavelli and the Renaissance** (1958). D. Merejkowski's novel, *The Romance of Leonardo da Vinci** (1902), gives a vivid and unforgettable picture of Italian society based on sound historical scholarship. D. S. Chambers, *The Imperial Age of Venice: 1380–1580** (1970), examines Venice's power as a commercial enterprise. On another kind of enterprise, see M. Mallet, *Mercenaries and Their Masters* (1974), an excellent study of the *condottieri*.

Literature and Art

Most of the general works listed above contain discussions of the literary and artistic achievements of the age. The classic literary history, still well worth reading, is F. de Sanctis, *History of Italian Literature* (1870; trans. 1931). G. Highet, *The Classical Tradition** (1949), traces Greek and Roman influences on western literature. P. O. Kristeller, *Renaissance Thought,** 2 vols. (1961, 1965), is a brief but penetrating analysis. The best introduction to the educational theories of the Humanists is W. H. Woodward, *Vittorino da Feltre and Other Humanist Educators** (1905). Of the many works on Italian Renaissance art, two by masters of their subjects may be mentioned: B. Berenson, *The Italian Painters of the Renaissance,** rev. ed. (1930), and E. Panofsky, *Renaissance and Renascences in Western Art,* 2 vols. (1965). An older handbook, still useful, is H. Wölfflin, *The Art of the Italian Renaissance** (1903; edited as *Classic Art,* 1952). A. C. Krey, *A City That Art Built* (1936), is an interesting brief attempt to relate cultural flowering to economic and political circumstances in Florence. See also A. Smart, *The Renaissance and Mannerism in Italy* (1971), and A. Blunt, *Artistic Theory in Italy, 1450–1600** (1962).

Contemporary Writings

It is easy to become acquainted with the thought of Renaissance writers because of the number of readily available translations. Two source collections are particularly good: *The Renaissance Philosophy of Man,** ed. by E. Cassirer (1948), which includes Pico's *Oration,* and *The Portable Renaissance Reader,** ed. by J. B. Ross and M. M. McLaughlin (1953), which includes a selection from Alberti's *On the Family.* See also W. L. Gundersheimer, *The Italian Renaissance** (1965). There are many editions of Boccaccio's *Decameron,* Cellini's *Autobiography,* and Castiglione's *The Courtier.* N. Machiavelli, *The Prince and the Discourses** (trans. 1940; Modern Library), is the most convenient edition. C. B. Coleman has edited *The Treatise of Lorenzo Valla on the Donation of Constantine* (1922), and E. A. McCurdy has edited *The Notebooks of Leonardo da Vinci,* 2 vols. (1938). *The Vespasiano Memoirs** (trans. 1926) offer contemporary thumbnail sketches of Humanists, artists, and princes. G. Bull has translated Vasari's *Lives of the Artists** (1965).

The Church

There is a full account of the councils of Constance and Basel and of the Renaissance popes in the five-volume work by an Anglican bishop, M. Creighton, *A History of the Papacy from the Great Schism to the Sack of Rome* (1919). The best account, however, based on the Vatican archives, is the still larger work of the Swiss Catholic L. Pastor, *History of the Popes,* 40 vols. (trans. 1891–1953). On conciliar ideas, see B. Tierney, *Foundations of the Conciliar Theory* (1955), and E. F. Jacob, *Essays in the Conciliar Epoch* (1953). H. Jedin, *A History of the Council of Trent,* Vol. I (trans. 1957), gives a good account of the events leading up to the council.

Technological and Economic Growth in the North

On printing, see P. Butler, *The Origin of Printing in Europe* (1940); D. C. McMurtrie, *The Book: The Story of Printing and Bookmaking,* 3rd rev. ed. (1943); E. P. Goldschmidt, *The Printed Book of the Renaissance* (1950); and V. Scholderer, *Johann Gutenberg* (1963). R. Ehrenberg, *Capital and Finance in the Age of the Renaissance* (trans. 1928), is a study of the Fuggers. The Fugger Newsletters of the later sixteenth century are available in *News and Rumor in Renaissance Europe.** On science, see M. Boas, *The Scientific Renaissance, 1450–1630** (1962), and W. Wightman, *Science and the Renaissance,* 2 vols. (1962).

17 Reform and Revolution in Western Christendom

At the opening of the sixteenth century, the Roman Church was in greater danger than it had been at any time since the Great Schism. Suspicion of Church policy and contempt for the leadership of the Church were widespread. Even the peasants were annoyed by the financial demands of the clergy and bored by routine services; many of them were ready to respond to radical evangelical preachers. There had always been some tension between the Church and the bourgeoisie. The Church had never been able to incorporate business ethics into its system of values, and the bourgeoisie had never been happy about the Church's special financial privileges. The better educated the townsmen became, the more clearly they saw the weaknesses of the Church. The nobility either denounced the corruption of the Church or profited from it.

Most dangerous of all were the secular rulers who were limiting the papacy's powers of taxation, jurisdiction, and appointment. Caught in the maelstrom of Italian power politics, the popes of the fifteenth century found themselves threatened by leagues of Italian princes and thus forced to seek help from and make concessions to more distant and more powerful rulers. The popes had no military power of their own. Moreover, by 1500 they were regularly in debt, with little prospect of finding any easy way out of their financial straits.

THE NEED FOR REFORM IN THE WESTERN CHURCH

Even able and devoted Vicars of Christ might have had difficulty defending the independence of the papacy and raising its moral prestige. But this was the era of the Renaissance popes—at best, good administrators and patrons of artists and scholars; at worst, corrupt and immoral men with secular tastes and interests. Some, like Alexander VI, used the contributions of the faithful to carve out principalities for their illegitimate sons. Most of them, under financial pressure, sold justice in their courts and appointments to office in their councils.

Bishops and archbishops throughout Europe were generally of noble blood, and many of them had been nominated by monarchs or by the pope for loyal service rather than for their piety or administrative ability. Some held more than one bishopric, although this was contrary to canon law, and some rarely visited their sees (one bishop visited his only once, when he was buried there). Even conscientious bishops found that their power to appoint the clergy and to reform abuses within their dioceses had diminished. Many powers that properly belonged to the bishop had either fallen into the hands of local laymen or had been "reserved" by the pope. The ignorance and immorality of the parish clergy were bywords among contemporary writers. The parish priest in fact was no better or worse than he had been for centuries, but moral sensitivity to clerical misconduct had been rising. Furthermore, the tithes that the priest levied and the fees that he charged for baptisms, marriages, and burials were burdensome to peasants and small craftsmen. In earlier centuries monks and friars had made up for many of the deficiencies of the parish clergy, but by 1500 the religious orders had little influence on laymen. Monastic life no longer attracted the pious, as it had several centuries earlier, and monasteries now had to search out recruits to keep their numbers up.

The most widespread complaints were caused by practices that could be interpreted as the selling of spiritual benefits. The Church was rich in land but poor in the newer forms of wealth. It cost money to maintain such a large institution, and the clergy had a right to ask for a fair share of the growing wealth of Europe. But the methods used to raise money and the purposes for which the money was spent (such as waging war to regain territory claimed for the Papal States) outraged many believers. Papal demands for money were passed from the bishops to the parish clergy to the people. Thus some priests demanded the best garment of a deceased parishioner as a "mortuary fee" and had regular tables of charges for other religious rites. Even worse were the abuses that the pope allowed to creep into the sale of indulgences.

Lucas Cranach the Younger, *Martin Luther and the Wittenberg Reformers* (*ca.* 1543).

Indulgences

Indulgences, in fact, were the raw nerve of the Church's whole financial system. An indulgence was a remission of the temporal penalty for sin (penances in this life and the pains of Purgatory after death) imposed by a priest in the sacrament of penance. It was granted on condition of true contrition for the sin and in consideration of some pious deed performed, such as going on a crusade or

A pair of woodcuts by Lucas Cranach the Elder contrasting Jesus and the pope. On the left, Jesus is driving the moneychangers from the temple; on the right, the pope is taking money for indulgences.

a pilgrimage. During the Middle Ages a money "contribution" became the normal consideration, and the necessity for contrition was often forgotten by the believer. In the fourteenth century the popes developed the doctrine that Christ and the saints had accumulated a "treasury of merits" from which Christ's Vicars could dispense benefits to the faithful through indulgences. In the fifteenth century Sixtus IV, on the strength of this doctrine, claimed the power to release the souls of the dead from the penance they were undergoing in Purgatory as the temporal penalty for their sins. This claim helped make the indulgence trade even more lucrative. It was hard to withhold a contribution that would release the soul of a dead parent from years of suffering in the next world. In theory, the money was a "contribution" for pious purposes. But many laymen concluded that the Church was selling salvation at a price—and was then wasting the money on petty wars and luxurious living.

The Dangers of Criticism

Criticism of the Church was not new. Though the Church was divinely instituted, everyone knew that it was administered by fallible human beings—that is,

by sinners. The moral state of the clergy was probably better in 1500 than in the year 1000. But the world of 1500 was far different from that of 1000, and it is well to review some of the main differences in order to understand why criticism now constituted a real danger to the Church.

The European world of 1500 was more secular in its interests and ideals, as we have seen. The artist, the despot, the sea captain, and the businessman were pursuing careers that seemed more exciting than sainthood, and the medieval interpretation of life in this world as a pilgrimage to life after death seemed unsatisfying, even though it was not yet openly rejected. Granted that salvation was the goal of mankind, some men began to ask: Was renunciation of the world the only, or even the surest, way to gain that goal?

While the fifteenth century was an age of increasing secular interests for some, it was an age of heightened religious sensitivity and piety for others. Both the worldly minded and the devout were becoming critical of the growing complexity of the Church's sacraments and ceremonies. Popular piety of the late Middle Ages had nurtured a luxuriant growth of religious practices that seemed to verge on superstition and idolatry. The cult of the saints and the veneration of

In the first of this pair of woodcuts, Cranach shows Jesus kissing the feet of his disciples as he washes them. The other woodcut shows the pope offering his foot to be kissed by kings and nobles.

relics became a kind of obsession. For almost every human ill there was a saint, who, if properly approached, could prevent or heal the affliction. And as the number of sacred symbols and ceremonies multiplied, their religious significance almost disappeared. A fifteenth-century French artist painted a sensual, photographic portrait of the French king's mistress as the Virgin Mary, apparently without being conscious of any blasphemy. As a modern historian has put it, the religious atmosphere of the later Middle Ages was "supersaturated," and the most observant church leaders of the fifteenth century grew worried. They saw that the Church was becoming dangerously vulnerable to radicals who might ask: What is the core of Christianity? Is it to venerate an image of St. Anthony, to avoid meat on Fridays, and to go a pilgrimage? Or, rather, is it to love one's neighbor and to live a Christlike life?

A final reason why ecclesiastical abuses were so dangerous to the Church in 1500 was that there were now secular rulers strong enough to use the cry for reform for their own purposes. The monarchs of western Europe were already appointing and taxing the clergy. The upper classes all over Europe coveted the wealth of the Church. Many

secular rulers, should they so decide, now had the power to confiscate the Church's lands, buildings, and revenues in the name of reform. Reform by royal command sometimes had good results. In Spain, Cardinal Jiménez de Cisneros, strongly backed by Ferdinand and Isabella, instituted many reforms in the Spanish clergy at the opening of the sixteenth century. But there was always the danger that reform by a secular power might result in state control of the Church and confiscation of its property.

Failure of Fifteenth-Century Reform Movements

Various schemes for reform had been advanced in the fifteenth century. In the Rhineland, the Brethren of the Common Life, a group of laymen who devoted themselves to communal living and biblical piety, emphasized direct, intimate communion with God in their communities and schools. In Florence between 1494 and 1498 one of the most remarkable preachers of the age, the Dominican monk Girolamo Savonarola, moved multitudes to repentance and for a time had the crowds making bonfires of their wigs, makeup, and other "vanities." These reformers still held to the medieval conception of reform. According to that conception, the Church itself was divinely constituted and so could not be "reformed," but the individuals who composed it could and should be regenerated. The leaders at the councils of Constance and Basel were reformers of a more modern sort. They meant to reform the institution itself by giving more power to representatives of the clergy, thus making the pope a limited monarch. Hus wanted to reform both the individual and the institution by returning to the Bible as the standard of Christian living and ecclesiastical practice.

Each of these differing conceptions of reform was to take root and bear seed in one way or another during the sixteenth century. But before 1500 the impetus of each movement was soon spent, and the institutional abuses remained untouched. The councils failed to make permanent changes in the constitution of the Church, and both Hus and Savonarola were burned as heretics. Whenever attempts at reform threatened to undermine the status of the clergy as mediators between God and man, or the power of the pope as the Vicar of Christ, they were declared heretical and stamped out. It seemed that the strength of vested interest and the dead weight of authority were so strong that the Church would never be roused from its complacency.

Christian Humanism

A new and hopeful type of reform movement emerged in the sixteenth century—Christian Humanism. Under the inspiration of the classical revival in Italy, a number of scholars in northern Europe began to recommend a return to the best of both the classical and the Christian traditions through a study of the classics and the Bible. They argued that if men could appreciate the ethical perfection of Socrates and Jesus, of Plato and Paul, then the absurdities of theological hair splitting and the irrelevance of many ecclesiastical practices would become evident. Reform would inevitably follow from a better understanding of the simplicity of primitive Christianity—and of the noble ideals of the Greeks and Romans, which they felt to be complementary rather than antagonistic to Christi-

anity. Let the Church take for its guides the Bible and the early Fathers rather than the scholastic theologians of the Middle Ages. Abuses would disappear if laymen and clerics alike would recognize that Christianity was an attitude of mind and a way of life, not a complex set of dogmas and ceremonies.

This program was fundamentally conservative, designed to save the Church from itself. Its leaders were almost without exception loyal to Rome. It was obviously optimistic in its estimate of human nature. It rated the power of reason and education very high. It encouraged historical and literary studies in the hope that they would reveal earlier and purer practices. Cardinal Jiménez in Spain set scholars to producing a monumental edition of the Bible that presented the original Hebrew and Greek texts in parallel columns with the Latin. In Germany, Johann Reuchlin defended the study of Hebrew literature as a means of understanding the Old Testament, even though a group of Dominicans wished to destroy all Hebrew books. In France, Lefèvre d'Etaples studied the Epistles of Paul and translated the New Testament into French (1523) in an effort to enlighten his contemporaries and further the cause of reform. For Sir Thomas More in England, study and reform were also closely related. In his famous *Utopia*, More wrote a searching analysis of the most glaring social, political, and ecclesiastical evils of his day from the point of view of a scholar steeped in Humanism and the Gospels as well as in the monastic tradition of the Middle Ages.

Erasmus

The acknowledged leader of these Christian Humanists was Erasmus of Rotterdam (*ca.* 1469–1536). Erasmus' enthusiasm for the Greco-Roman classics matched his enthusiasm for the Bible and early Christian writings. He devoted his life to scholarship in the conviction that sound learning would help save the Church. He edited the New Testament in the original Greek (1516), with a preface urging that it be translated into all the vulgar tongues, and he published editions of the early Church Fathers. His hundreds of letters and his briefer books were even more influential. In them, with lively humor, underlying seriousness, and an unsurpassed command of the Latin language, he argued for what he called "the philosophy of Christ," the love of God and neighbor that he saw as the essence of Christianity. He feared that the Church of his day had obscured this essential truth with useless forms and ceremonies. In a typical passage he ridiculed monkish ideas of religion. When the final reckoning comes, one monk will point to his fastings and ceremonies for credit; "another will boast that for sixty years he never touched money, except when his fingers were protected by two pairs of gloves." Christ will interrupt their boasts and say, "Whence comes this new race of Jews [that is, Pharisees]? I promised the inheritance of my Father, not to cowls, prayers, or fasts, but to works of charity." This device of imagining how Christ himself would judge the world of the 1500s was characteristic of Christian Humanism.

Christian Humanism offered the last chance of peaceful reform. But it was a movement that needed time, patience, and understanding to have any impact on the upper classes, and it never had much appeal for the mass of the population. It influenced every effort, both Protestant and Catholic, to reform the Church, but as a practical program it was doomed to failure. It was too aristocratic and too intellectual. The times were revolutionary, and the remedies that Europe was to adopt were both sterner and simpler than Erasmus' "philosophy of Christ."

LUTHER'S REVOLT FROM ROME

On October 31, 1517, an Augustinian friar serving as Professor of Bible in the little University of Wittenberg in Saxony prepared ninety-five theses, or propositions, for academic debate on the subject of indulgences. The author, Martin Luther (1483–1546), was outraged by the unscrupulous salesmanship of a Dominican friar named Tetzel who had been hawking indulgences in Magdeburg. "So soon as coin in coffer rings," Tetzel was reported as preaching, "the soul from Purgatory springs." The proceeds from this particular sale of indulgences were meant to go toward the building of St. Peter's church in Rome, though half of it actually ended up in the pockets of the Archbishop of Mainz and of the

Portrait of Erasmus by Albrecht Dürer.

Erasmus' Preface to His Edition of the New Testament

I utterly dissent from those who are unwilling that the sacred Scriptures should be read by the unlearned translated into their vulgar tongue, as though Christ had taught such subtleties that they can scarcely be understood even by a few theologians, or, as though the strength of the Christian religion consisted in men's ignorance of it. The mysteries of kings it may be safer to conceal, but Christ wished his mysteries to be published as openly as possible. I wish that even the weakest woman should read the Gospel—should read the epistles of Paul. And I wish these were translated into all languages, so that they might be read and understood, not only by Scots and Irishmen, but also by Turks and Saracens. To make them understood is surely the first step. It may be that they might be ridiculed by many, but some would take them to heart. I long that the husbandman should sing portions of them to himself as he follows the plough, that the weaver should hum them to the tune of his shuttle, that the traveller should beguile with their stories the tedium of his journey.

From Erasmus, "Paraclesis," *Novum Instrumentum*, trans. by Frederic Seebohm, in *The Oxford Reformers* (New York: Dutton, 1914), p. 203.

Ohr deutschen merket mich recht/
Des heiligen Vaters Papstes Knecht/
Bin ich/vnd br ing euch jet allein/
Zehn tausent vnd neun hundert carein/
Gnad vnd Ablaß von einer Sünd/
Vor euch/ewer Eltern/Weib vnd Kind/
Sol ein jeder gewehret sein
So viel ihr legt ins Kästelein/
So bald der Gülden im Becken klingt/
Im huy die Seel im Himel springt/

Contemporary caricature of Johann Tetzel hawking indulgences. The last line of the jingle is: "So soon as coin in coffer rings, the soul from Purgatory springs."

Fugger banking firm. Luther's theses were immediately printed and debated not only in Wittenberg but all over Germany. The sensation they caused marked the start of the Protestant Reformation. Luther's chief propositions were:

> There is no divine authority for preaching that the soul flies out of purgatory immediately the money clinks in the bottom of the chest. . . . It is certainly possible that when the money clinks in the bottom of the chest, avarice and greed increase. . . . All those who believe themselves certain of their own salvation by means of letters of indulgence will be eternally damned, together with their teachers. . . . Any Christian whatsoever, who is truly repentant, enjoys plenary remission from penalty and guilt, and this is given him without letters of indulgence.

At the time, Martin Luther was a strong-willed, keen-minded, high-strung man in his early thirties. He was the son of a prosperous peasant turned miner, who had been able to give his boy a university education. The young Luther had experienced several severe emotional crises; the most acute one led him to become a friar. But in his convent he had become increasingly dissatisfied with the emphasis his teachers laid on good works. He had been a most conscientious friar; he had fasted and prayed and confessed without end. If good works could win a man salvation, surely they should win it for him, he thought. Yet performing the acts commanded by the Church gave him no inner certainty that he was forgiven, only a growing sense of guilt, despair, and deepening spiritual crisis. Peace came to him when he suddenly understood what St. Paul had meant when he said that a man is saved not by doing the works of the Jewish law but by his faith in Christ. The ceremonies and religious practices of the medieval Church seemed to Luther a new Jewish law. Man is too corrupted by sin to meet the demands of such a law by his own efforts, and so he must rely on his faith in God's mercy. It is unthinkable that a man can buy God's favor by doing a good deed or performing some sacramental act. In the matter of saving a man's soul, Luther concluded, God does everything, man can do nothing.

It took Luther some time to work out the revolutionary implications of this thought. If man is saved by faith alone, then ceremonies and sacraments, pilgrimages and indulgences, everything the medieval Church called "good works," are at best irrelevant and at worst dangerous. Indulgences were the first "good work" at which Luther struck. Within a short time after his attack their sales dropped off sharply in Germany. When the Dominicans, chief sellers of the indulgences, persuaded Pope Leo X to condemn his theses, Luther was gradually driven to deny the authority of the pope. Soon afterward, when he came to believe that John Hus had been right on certain matters in spite of his condemnation by the Council of Constance, he denied the authority of general councils as well. By April 1521 Luther was standing before the Emperor Charles V at an imperial diet at Worms and declaring that he was bound by the authority of the Scripture and his own conscience rather than by that of either pope or council. He could not recant any of his writings, he added, because his conscience was "captive to the Word of God" and because it was "neither safe nor right to go against conscience." The

Bible and conscience—these were to be the two chief pillars of Protestant Christianity.

Luther was not burned at Worms, as Hus had been at Constance. His safe-conduct was respected, and he was allowed to return to the protection of his ruler, Frederick, the Elector of Saxony. For twenty-five years, till his death in 1546, he taught, preached, and wrote at Wittenberg. Meanwhile the revolt against the papacy that he had started gathered momentum and spread over northern Europe. In the end, the unity of Western Christendom was permanently destroyed.

Lutheran Principles

In breaking with the papacy, Luther was guided by three main principles: salvation by faith, not by works; the ultimate authority of the Bible; and the priesthood of all believers. The three were closely related. It was through study of the Bible that Luther came to his belief in salvation by faith, and it was to the Bible that he always appealed against the authority of tradition or the papacy. His greatest literary work was a German translation of the Bible (completed in 1534), which he wrote in order that God's Word might be put into the hands of every devout person in Germany who could read. There was no essential difference between a priest and a layman, he insisted. A dedicated layman reverently reading the Scripture was closer to divine truth than a worldly pope proclaiming dogma for the Church. Christ had meant every believer to be a priest to his neighbor; He had not intended a special few to act as mediators between man and God. A Christian can serve God as well by being an honest merchant or a faithful housewife as by becoming a monk or a nun. Thus Luther encouraged the dissolution of the monastic orders, and in order to dramatize his convictions he married a nun and became the happy father of six children.

Luther's original protest had been a purely religious matter, rooted in his own spiritual experience. But to gain support he had to appeal to the nationalistic and financial grievances of his fellow Germans. "What has brought us Germans to such a pass that we have to suffer this robbery and this destruction of our property by the Pope?" he asked in 1520.

Portrait of Martin Luther by Lucas Cranach (1533).

Luther on Justification by Faith

For the word of God cannot be received and honored by any works, but by faith alone. Hence it is clear that, as the soul needs the word alone for life and justification, so it is justified by faith alone and not by any works. For if it could be justified by any other means, it would have no need of the word, nor consequently of faith. . . .

It is evident that by no outward work or labor can the inward man be at all justified, made free and saved, and that no works whatever have any relation to him. And so, on the other hand, it is solely by impiety and incredulity of heart that he becomes guilty and a slave of sin, deserving condemnation; not by any outward sin or work.

Therefore the first care of every Christian ought to be to lay aside all reliance on works, and strengthen his faith alone more and more, and by it grow in the knowledge, not of works, but of Christ Jesus, who has suffered and risen again for him.

From Martin Luther, *On Christian Liberty*, trans. by H. Wace and C. A. Buchheim, in *First Principles of the Reformation* (London: Murray, 1883), pp. 107–08.

"If the kingdom of France has resisted it, why do we Germans suffer ourselves to be fooled and deceived?" Luther appealed to princes eager to confiscate church property, to businessmen unhappy about papal finance, to German patriots resentful of the Italians who dominated the papacy and the College of Cardinals, and to devout laymen and conscientious priests who were shocked by the corruption in the Church. His principles of salvation by faith and of serving God in one's secular calling appealed especially to laymen, who found in them a way of reconciling Christian devotion with an active concern about worldly affairs. High-minded and low-minded motives were inextricably mixed in the minds of those who accepted Luther's arguments.

Luther had no intention of breaking away from the true Church of Christ or of setting up a rival organization. But after 1520 he was convinced that the Church founded by Christ and the Apostles had wandered from the true path somewhere in the Middle Ages, and that the bishop of Rome was not the Vicar of Christ, but rather the Anti-christ. Much of the dogma and ritual of the Church of his day, Luther believed, was the work of men, not of God. Such accretions must be swept away, leaving only the pure faith of the Apostles and the early Church Fathers. In the purified Church there would be only two sacraments (Baptism and Holy Communion) in place of seven, a simplified ritual in German rather than in Latin, and more emphasis on the congregation's participation in the service. But Luther did not want to set up a "new" church; he sought only to reform *the* Church. There could be only one true Church, into which all men were received in baptism. Either Luther was right in defying the pope, or the pope was right in excommunicating Luther. At first there were not two churches, one "Catholic" and one "Lutheran," but an irreconcilable argument over the nature of the one true Church.

The Spread of Lutheranism

Luther's ideas were spread by his students and by the books and pamphlets that poured from the new printing presses. During the early years of the movement, publishers overwhelmingly supported Luther. Leopold Ranke calculated that in 1523 there were almost four hundred books and pamphlets written by Luther and his supporters compared with only twenty or so pro-Catholic works. Many of the younger Humanists supported Luther's ideas and gave his movement intellectual respectability, and even the older Humanists greeted the attack on indulgences with joy. As Luther became more vehement in his criticism of the Church, the older Humanists retreated to the fold of the Catholic Church, but with some reluctance. Even Erasmus, who came to consider Luther a fanatic, broke with him only in 1524, after repeated pleas for moderation had failed.

Many priests and monks, on the other hand, were convinced by Luther's arguments and were among his first converts. These converts were especially numerous in the German cities, and the cities gave Luther his first solid basis of support. The town governments had their own grievances against the Church.

Luther on the Church

Thus it may come to pass that the Pope and his followers are wicked and not true Christians, and not being taught by God, have no true understanding, whereas a common man may have true understanding. Why should we then not follow him? Has not the Pope often erred? Who could help Christianity, in case the Pope errs, if we do not rather believe another who has the Scriptures for him? Therefore it is a wickedly devised fable—and they cannot quote a single letter to confirm it—that it is for the Pope alone to interpret the Scriptures or to confirm the interpretation of them. They have assumed the authority of their own selves. And though they say that this authority was given to St. Peter when the keys were given to him, it is plain enough that the keys were not given to St. Peter alone, but to the whole community. . . . Moreover, if the article of our faith is right, "I believe in the holy Christian Church," the Pope cannot alone be right; else we must say, "I believe in the Pope of Rome," and reduce the Christian Church to one man, which is a devilish and damnable heresy. Besides that, we are all priests, as I have said, and have all one faith, one Gospel, one Sacrament; how then should we not have the power of discerning and judging what is right or wrong in matters of faith?

From Martin Luther, "Address to the Christian Nobility of the German Nation," in *Luther's Primary Works,* ed. by H. Wace and C. A. Buchheim (London: Hodder and Stoughton, 1896), pp. 170–71.

The clergy could avoid most local taxes, and at the same time the financial demands of the Church bore especially heavily on the urban population. The worldly life of the higher clergy and the ignorance of many parish priests were offensive to pious laymen. The towns had already taken over responsibility for most social services (education and charity); why should they not assume responsibility for religion as well? Thus in town after town, with very little violence, the conservative clergy were replaced by followers of Luther. Considering that many towns were in fact independent political entities, they were establishing the first state churches. They did so a decade or more before some of the German princes made Lutheranism a state religion. Luther was not entirely happy about this development (he would have preferred no secular control), but he realized that if the truth, as he saw it, was to prevail, it must be protected by secular rulers.

The peasants were excited by Luther's message at first, but he lost most of them after the Peasants' Rebellion of 1524 to 1525. This was the largest and bloodiest of the many peasant uprisings that resulted from complex economic and social causes during the later Middle Ages. The rebels' chief aim was to abolish serfdom and the burdens of the manorial system. "Therefore do we find in the Scripture that we are free," they argued, "and we will be free." Luther was close enough to his peasant origins to sympathize with their demands, but the freedom he was interested in was an inner religious freedom, freedom from an ecclesiastical system, not from social or political bondage. At last, some reported atrocities committed by the peasants turned him against them, and he wrote a bitter condemnation of the uprising. The rebellion was finally put down with atrocities that went beyond even those of the rebels. The peasants felt that Luther had betrayed them, but the middle and ruling classes welcomed his social conservatism. After 1525 he and his followers fought as hard against radicals, who wanted to carry the religious revolt too far, as they did against the Roman Catholics, who wished to wipe out Lutheranism.

There was at first no effective resistance in Germany to the spread of Luther's ideas. The emperor Charles V never wavered in his orthodoxy, but the task of holding together his scattered dominions proved so difficult that he was unable to bring political or military pressure to bear on cities and states that had turned Lutheran. From 1522 to 1559 Charles and his son Philip were caught up in a series of conflicts with France that absorbed much of their energy and income. Meanwhile Charles and his brother Ferdinand were also trying to stem the tide of Turkish conquest in the Mediterranean and the Danube Valley. The French in the West and the Turks in the East, sometimes in alliance with each other, allowed the emperor only a few intervals of peace in which to turn his attention to the religious division of Germany.

By the time of Luther's death in 1546, the German principalities were about evenly divided between the two faiths, while the majority of the free cities supported the Lutheran movement. In 1547, during a peaceful interlude in his international struggles, Charles V finally found an opportunity to attack the Lutheran states. The confused war that followed proved that neither side could destroy the other, and in 1555 the emperor reluctantly allowed his brother Ferdinand, who was ruler of Austria and later emperor, to conclude the Religious Peace of Augsburg. This peace allowed the city-states and princes of the Empire to choose between Lutheranism and Catholicism and bound them to respect each other's rights. *Cuius regio, eius religio*, as someone later summed up the

Title page of the first German translation of the Bible, by Martin Luther, printed in 1534 with the approval of the Elector of Saxony.

Contemporary engraving depicting a noble lady and her son kneeling before peasant rebels to plead for their lives during the Peasants' Rebellion (1524–25).

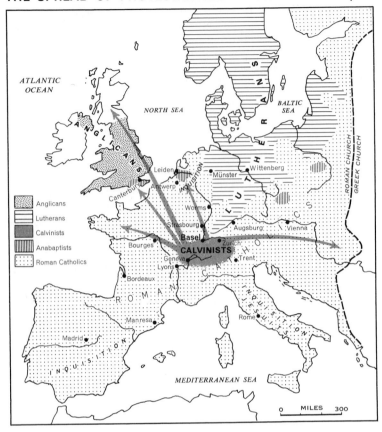

southern Germany remained mostly "Catholic." The division remains today about as it was in 1560. Outside Germany, Lutheran ideas spread widely but took root only in Scandinavia, where Denmark, Norway, and Sweden became Lutheran before mid-century. Perhaps because Luther spoke so forcefully in the German idiom to his follow Germans, his teaching was not so well adapted to export as was the teaching of John Calvin.

CALVINISM

Luther's University of Wittenberg was not the only center from which reform ideas radiated. Other important centers were Zurich, Basel, Strasbourg, and especially Geneva. In these southern German and Swiss cities there developed a type of Protestantism closely related to Lutheranism but different in emphasis—more rational and systematic, more organized and disciplined, laying more stress on moral conduct and political action, less on the inner relation of man to God. The members of this second family of Protestant churches are generally called "Reformed" churches, in contrast with the "Lutheran."

Among the early Swiss and south German reformers were the Humanists Ulrich Zwingli of Zurich (1484–1531) and Martin Bucer of Strasbourg (1491–1551). Neither man agreed entirely with Luther. Zwingli took a more radical position on the sacraments, arguing that Communion was essentially a memorial service commemorating the Last Supper. Bucer tried to reconcile various Protestant groups and was more tolerant than most of the other reformers.

More influential than either Zwingli or Bucer was John Calvin (1509–64). Calvin had been trained as a lawyer and a Humanist in his native France before he became converted to Protestantism and settled down as a pastor in Geneva. He learned much from Luther, as well as from Zwingli and Bucer. Through these influences and through his early training, he became the chief theologian and organizer of second-generation Protestantism. His *Institutes of the Christian Religion* served as the basic handbook of Protes-

Sketch of John Calvin drawn by a student, perhaps during a lecture.

principle: the ruler determines the religion for the region. People who disliked the ruler's choice might migrate to another state. Lutherans were allowed to keep any church lands they had seized before 1552, but it was agreed that every Catholic bishop or abbot who turned Protestant in the future would have to resign his title and leave his lands in Catholic hands. This last clause was difficult to interpret and caused trouble later. The chief flaw in the settlement, however, was the exclusion of Calvinists, whose numbers were growing rapidly, from the benefits of the peace.

The Peace of Augsburg was the first official recognition, however grudging, that Western Christendom had been rent asunder and would have to continue as a house divided. It was not religious toleration, but it was a step along the way. In the end, northern Germany became mostly "Protestant" (as Lutherans had been called since 1529, when they presented a "protest" at an imperial diet);

The more rigid Protestants objected to all religious paintings and sculpture as leading to idolatry. In this engraving of 1579, Calvinists are pulling down statues of saints and destroying stained-glass windows.

tant principles for two centuries. it was a clear, well-organized, well-written book in both its Latin and its French versions, and its argument had all the logic a trained lawyer could bring to it. Calvin's two polar principles were the absolute sovereignty of God and the radical depravity of man. No acts of sinful man can merit salvation; God, through his inscrutable will, has chosen some to be saved and some to be damned. The effect of this doctrine on Calvin's followers was not to induce resignation and despair but to stimulate moral activity and strenuous effort as God's instruments. Good works might not save a Calvinist—but they might be evidence that God was working through him. Good works were a "sign" that a man was probably one of the Elect.

As time went on, Calvin's church in Geneva became the model for Presbyterian or Reformed churches in France, England, Scotland, the Netherlands, the Rhineland, Bohemia, and Hungary—later in North America and Dutch South Africa. Calvin advocated that each local congregation have a ruling body composed of both ministers and laymen (presbyters, or elders) who were to watch carefully over the moral conduct and beliefs of the faithful. These officials then met in synods that linked up the Reformed congregations of a whole district or nation. Thus in place of the Roman Catholic hierarchy of bishops and priests under the pope, and in place of Luther's state churches, Calvin devised a peculiarly tough and flexible system of church government that resisted control by the state, maintained strict discipline, and, in the lay elders, included a potentially democratic element. Unlike Lutheranism, Calvinism met the two conditions for

Calvin on Predestination

Predestination we call the eternal decree of God, by which he has determined in himself, what he would have to become of every individual of mankind. For they are not all created with a similar destiny; but eternal life is foreordained for some, and eternal damnation for others. . . .

In conformity, therefore, to the clear doctrine of the Scripture, we assert, that by an eternal and immutable counsel, God has once for all determined, both whom he would admit to salvation, and whom he would condemn to destruction. We affirm that this counsel, as far as concerns the elect, is founded on his gratuitous mercy, totally irrespective of human merit; but that to those whom he devotes to condemnation, the gate of life is closed by a just and irreprehensible, but incomprehensible, judgment. . . .

How exceedingly presumptuous it is only to inquire into the causes of the Divine will; which is in fact, and is justly entitled to be, the cause of everything that exists. . . . For the will of God is the highest rule of justice; so that what he wills must be considered just, for this very reason, because he wills it.

From John Calvin, *Institutes of the Christian Religion,* trans. by John Allen (Philadelphia: Westminster Press, 1930), Book III, Ch. 21, pars. 5, 7; Ch. 23, par. 2.

Radical Protestantism: The Teaching of Menno Simons

Menno Simons (1496–1561) was one of the ablest leaders of the radical wing of the Reformation. Simons' followers formed the Mennonite Church, which still exists. His ideas also contributed to the development of the Baptist Church. He never summed up his doctrine in a single document; it has to be put together from scattered pamphlets.

We do not find in Scripture a single word by which Christ has ordained the baptism of infants, or that his apostles taught and practiced it. We say that infant baptism is but a human invention. . . . To baptize before that which is required for baptism, namely faith, is to place the cart before the horse.

Never should any commandment be observed which is not contained in God's holy Word, either in letter or in spirit.

The regenerated do not go to war nor fight. . . . How can a Christian, according to Scripture, consistently retaliate, rebel, make war, murder, slay, torture, steal, rob, and burn cities and conquer countries?

Where have you read in the Scriptures, that Christ or the Apostles called upon the power of the magistracy against those who would not hear their doctrine or obey their words? . . . Faith is a gift of God, therefore it cannot be forced on anyone by worldly authorities or by the sword.

We must be born from above, must be changed and renewed in our hearts and thus be transplanted from the unrighteous and evil nature of Adam into the righteous and good nature of Christ, or we cannot be helped in eternity by any means, divine or human.

From "Selections from the Writings of Menno Simons," in *The Medieval World and Its Transformations*, Vol. II, ed. by G. M. Straka (New York: McGraw-Hill, 1967), pp. 463, 466, 467, 468, 470.

---

on the Dutch Netherlands. Calvinist minorities formed a kind of revolutionary international society throughout Europe in the later sixteenth century. Like their chief rivals, the Jesuits, the Reformed ministers were often able to elicit a religious loyalty that transcended loyalty to secular rulers and nations. Calvinism was the militant, international form of Protestantism.

THE RADICALS

Some reformers wanted to move much further and faster along the road of religious revolution than Luther, Zwingli, or Calvin. Throughout Germany workers and peasants had been hard hit by the economic changes of the fourteenth and fifteenth centuries. Often their discontent took on a religious coloring, combining easily with what survived of earlier heresies—Waldensian, Lollard, and Hussite, for example. These uneducated men and women took most of Luther's ideas literally—the Bible as ultimate authority, the priesthood of all believers, the freedom of true Christians from man-made ecclesiastical laws and organizations. During the 1520s in Switzerland and in the upper Rhine Valley particularly, little groups of such people came together proclaiming that a true church of Christians was a voluntary association of converted believers, not an official or established institution like that of the Lutherans or Catholics. Most of them believed that until a man came of age and knew what he was doing, he should not be admitted to the church through baptism. Thus, since they had to rebaptize most of their converts, their enemies called them Anabaptists, or rebaptizers. Their ritual was simple, and generally they took the Bible literally. Most of them would not take an oath in a law court, accept public office, or serve as soldiers; some practiced communism of goods on the model described in the second chapter of Acts.

They were cruelly persecuted by Catholics and conservative Protestants alike as dangerous heretics and social radicals. A small but violent minority gave temporary excuse for such persecution by capturing the city of Münster and

successful export all over Europe: it possessed a systematic theology, and it offered a practical substitute for medieval church organization.

By the 1550s Calvinism was spreading rapidly. Except in a few cities like Geneva, the nerve center of the movement, and in Scotland, Calvinists never became a majority. But the Calvinist minorities were stubborn, well organized, and widely distributed over Europe. Calvinism left a deep imprint on English society in the form of Puritanism, on France through the Huguenots, on Hungary, and

conducting a reign of terror there for over a year (1534–35). But generally they were pacifists and eager to suffer as their models, the Apostles, had done. After the 1530s the Anabaptists were to be found mainly in the Netherlands, Bohemia, Poland, and England, having been stamped out in southern Germany, where they had originated.

In addition to such "evangelical" groups, which tried to return to the first-century Gospel even more literally than Luther, there were other religious radicals. Some, like the Quakers in the seventeenth century, continued the medieval mystical tradition by following an inner voice rather than the letter of the Scripture. Others were more rationalistic, anticipating the doctrine that the nineteenth century was to call Unitarianism, the belief that there is only one God, not a Holy Trinity, and that Jesus was not God but man at his best. No one in the sixteenth century went quite this far, but the Spanish physician Michael Servetus (1511–53) combined an emphasis on the humanity of Christ with mystical and rationalistic ideas. He was imprisoned by the Catholic Inquisition, escaped, and in 1553 was burned at the stake in Geneva as a result of Calvin's influence.

The ideas of these religious radicals, who went too far not only for Roman Catholics but also for Luther and Calvin, were of great importance in the religious history of the Anglo-Saxon peoples. It was in England during the seventeenth century and later in the English colonies in America that Anabaptist ideas were fully realized. There the doctrine that the church should be a voluntary association, "a free church in a free state," organizing itself and electing its pastor, was accepted without any restrictions. Modern Baptists (who believe in adult baptism only), Congregationalists (who emphasize the autonomy of local congregations of Christians), and Quakers (who rely on the "inner light" and tend toward pacifism) all look back to the religious radicals of the sixteenth century as their remote ancestors. American Protestant conceptions of the place of the church in society derive more from the Anabaptists than from either Luther or Calvin.

ANGLICANISM

The peculiarity of the English Reformation is that it was initiated by a king for reasons that had almost nothing to do with religion. Henry VIII cut England off from the papacy much as the king of France had cut his realm off from the papal obedience in 1395. But in England the jurisdictional breach with Rome was followed by a decisive religious change.

In 1527, ten years after Luther had written his ninety-five theses, both England and its king seemed entirely orthodox. Parliament had restricted papal rights of appointment and jurisdiction in England, but England had not gone so far toward developing a national, or "Anglican," Church as France had in "Gallicanism." Lutheran ideas, strongly opposed by the king, had taken only shallow root in England among a few merchants, monks, and university scholars. There was some anticlericalism and opposition to papal taxation among the people, and

Title page of Daniel Featley's *Description* of 1645, known also as "The Dippers Dipt," a satirical view of the Anabaptists.

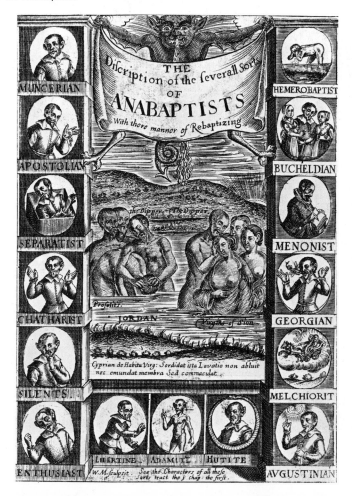

some talk of reform among the intellectuals, but no organized movement of revolt. Henry, however, found himself in a personal quandary that was to lead him into direct conflict with the pope, Clement VII. After eighteen years of married life, Henry's wife, Catherine of Aragon, had given him only one living child, a daughter. He knew that the lack of a male heir might well throw England into a new War of the Roses, and he knew that Catherine could bear him no more children. Furthermore, he was infatuated with a lady of the court named Anne Boleyn. Henry therefore asked the pope to annul his marriage with Catherine so that he might marry Anne. It was not hard to find technical grounds for the annulment. Catherine had been married to Henry's short-lived elder brother, and it was against Church law to marry the widow of one's brother. But it was hard to persuade the pope to grant the annulment because he was in the power of the emperor Charles V, and Charles was the nephew of Catherine.

Henry, a strong-willed man convinced that he was right, was skillful in political manipulation. In 1529 he summoned Parliament, determined to make the nation his accomplice in whatever he might have to do. He and his chief minister, Thomas Cromwell, deftly built up anticlerical sentiment in Parliament and forced the English clergy to acknowledge that the king was "Supreme Head of the Church in England." Then Henry threatened to withdraw all revenue and obedience from the pope. When Clement still refused to grant the annulment, Henry carried out his threat. He had the marriage annulled in England by Thomas Cranmer, whom he had just persuaded the pope to name as Archbishop of Canterbury, married Anne, and then, in 1533 to 1534, had Parliament cut all ties between the Roman papacy and England by a series of statutes. Conscientious monks, priests, and laymen who resisted this separation were executed. The most prominent martyr was Sir Thomas More (1478–1535), author of *Utopia* and chancellor of England from 1529 to 1532, who was proclaimed a saint in the twentieth century. Henry was now a kind of pope of the Church of England, except that as a layman he never claimed the power to administer the sacraments. Between 1535 and 1539 he and his agents demonstrated the extent of his authority by dissolving all English monasteries, turning their inmates out into the world, and confiscating their lands. Because Henry needed ready money to carry on a war with France, most of these lands were eventually sold to nobles, gentry, and merchants. The result, probably unforeseen, was to bind a whole new class of landowners to the English crown and to the new religious settlement.

In breaking with the papacy, Henry had no intention of breaking with orthodox Catholic belief and practice. He made it clear to his people that the breach with Rome meant no letting down of the bars against heresy, whether Lollard, Lutheran, or Anabaptist. It was impossible, however, to seal England off from the influx of Protestant tracts and ideas, and Henry himself approved the

A Catholic, Sir Thomas More, on the Church
1557

The true Church of Christ is the common known church of all Christian people not gone out nor cast out. This whole body both of good and bad is the Catholic Church of Christ, which is in this world very sickly, and hath many sore members, as hath sometime the natural body of a man. . . . The Church was gathered, and the faith believed, before any part of the New Testament was put in writing. And which was or is the true scripture, neither Luther nor Tyndale [translator of the New Testament into English] knoweth but by the credence that they give to the Church. . . . The Church was before the gospel was written; and the faith was taught, and men were baptised and masses said, and the other sacraments ministered among Christian people, before any part of the New Testament was put in writing. . . . As the sea shall never surround and overwhelm the land, and yet it hath eaten many places in, and swallowed whole countries up, and made places now sea that sometime were well-inhabited lands, and hath lost part of his own possession in other parts again; so though the faith of Christ shall never be overflown with heresies, nor the gates of hell prevail against Christ's Church, yet in some places it winneth in a new people, so may there in some places by negligence be lost the old.

From *The Workes of Sir Thomas More*, pp. 527, 852, 853, 921.

distribution to churches of an English translation of the Bible. By the time of Henry's death in 1547, the Protestant wing of the English clergy led by Archbishop Cranmer was growing in power. During the brief reign of Henry's sickly son Edward VI (1547–53), the government moved rapidly toward building a church that was moderately Protestant in doctrine and ritual. Cranmer gathered together the most impressive parts of the ancient liturgies of the Catholic Church and translated them into majestic English in the Book of Common Prayer. This collection served as the rallying point of Anglicanism, as Luther's hymns did for Lutherans and Calvin's *Institutes* for Calvinists.

This new official Protestantism had no time to take root among the people. In 1553 Catherine of Aragon's daughter, Mary, the most honest and least politic of all the Tudors, came to the throne. She tried to vindicate her mother and atone for her father's sins by turning the clock back to 1529, abolishing all antipapal legislation, and restoring England to the papal obedience. But she outraged her people's patriotism by marrying a foreigner, Philip II of Spain, son and heir presumptive of Charles V, and she shocked their humanity by allowing three hundred Protestants to be burned for heresy in about three years. The courage with which Cranmer and more obscure victims went to their deaths, together with the arrogance of Philip's courtiers, left an indelible impression on the English people. Patriotism and Protestantism became identified in the public mind.

When Anne Boleyn's daughter, Elizabeth I (1558–1603), came to the throne, there was little possibility that she would keep England in the Catholic camp. Elizabeth cautiously guided her Parliaments and her bishops into a compromise religious settlement. She accepted the title of "Supreme Governor" of the Church in England, but she saw to it that revised articles of the faith and the Book of Common Prayer could be accepted by both moderate Catholics and Protestants. For the rest, she refused "to make windows into men's souls," as she put it; that is, she persecuted only open opponents of her policies but not those who quietly dissented from them. After the pope excommunicated her in 1570 she was forced to treat zealous Catholics in England as traitors, but she was almost as annoyed with the "Puritans," who wished to go much further than she in purifying the English Church of Catholic

Sir Thomas More, after Hans Holbein (1527).

Henry VIII, after Hans Holbein (*ca.* 1540).

traditions. The Puritans were strong in Parliament, but when they became obstreperous, Elizabeth clapped some of them into jail. The idea that patriotism required independence from Rome became dominant during her reign, and in the end England was the largest single state to secede permanently from the Roman obedience. The secession cost less in bloodshed than it did elsewhere, largely because of the firm control that Henry VIII and Elizabeth exercised over the pace of religious change in England.

England under Elizabeth was clearly Protestant, but it accepted a conservative form of Protestantism, a form that looked on Presbyterians with suspicion and on Baptists with contempt. This conservatism grew during the religious disputes of the seventeenth century. Today many Anglicans would follow Henry VIII in insisting that their church is not "Protestant" at all. According to this theory, it was the Roman papacy that in effect had "seceded" from the Catholic tradition during the Middle Ages, and it was Henry VIII and Cranmer who restored the true continuity between the Church of the Fathers and the Church of the sixteenth century. Elizabeth always took the position that the Church of England occupied a middle ground between a Catholic minority that wished to bring England back to Rome and a Puritan minority that wished to build a more radically Protestant church in England.

THE CATHOLIC REFORMATION

Luther, Calvin, Cranmer, and the radical reformers thought of what they were doing as a "reformation" of the Church, and to this day the movement is generally called the Protestant Reformation. To Roman Catholics, however, the movement was a "revolt" against the divine authority of the Vicar of Christ, a religious revolution. From this point of view the only true "reformation" was the successful effort finally made by the Roman Church to reform itself, partly in response to the Protestant attack, partly as a result of internal pressures. Historians call this movement the Catholic Reformation, or the Counter Reformation.

This movement was both a religious revival and a counterattack on Protestantism. Before Luther appeared on the scene, some distinguished members of the clergy founded the Oratory of Divine Love at Rome in the hope of beginning a spiritual revival among the clergy. They directed their efforts toward the monastic orders and the papal court itself. In the course of the sixteenth century they succeeded in transforming the atmosphere at the Vatican. The bloody sack of Rome in 1527 by undisciplined imperial troops practically ended papal hopes of becoming powerful Italian princes. Italy was now effectively under Spanish control. As dreams of temporal power waned, better popes were chosen, who in turn appointed better cardinals. In the second half of the century, several of the popes were zealous, almost fanatical, men who would have seemed utterly out of place in the Renaissance papacy a century earlier. Politics still influenced religion and certain administrative abuses persisted, but the popes of the later sixteenth century were spiritual leaders, not Italian princes.

The driving forces behind the Catholic Reformation, especially the political forces, originated in Spain. Years of crusading against the Moors had given Spanish Catholicism a peculiarly intense quality lacking in the rest of Europe. King Philip II of Spain (1556–98), the son of Emperor Charles V, was a devoted Catholic who felt that it was Spain's destiny to stand as the bulwark of Roman Catholicism against the Protestants in Europe. He tended to give orders to the popes rather than to take orders from them, but during his reign Spanish armies and navies, Spanish diplomacy, and Spanish saints constituted the hard core of a revived and militant Catholicism all over Europe.

The most powerful single agency in restoring papal power, in rolling back the tide of Protestantism, and in carrying Catholic missions overseas was a new order founded by one of the most single-minded and influential saints in Christian history, a Spaniard of Basque descent named Ignatius of Loyola (1491–1556). While he was fighting the French in the service of his king, Ignatius' leg was fractured by a cannon ball. During a long and painful convalescence, he devoured the lives of the saints, which were the only reading matter at hand, and decided to enlist as a kind of Christian knight in the service of the Virgin Mary. During a lengthy period of trial and temptation he perfected the "spiritual exercises" that he later passed on to generations of followers. These exercises consisted in the believer's concentrating his imagination on the most vivid details of hell and of the life and death of Christ in order to strengthen his will and to direct it toward salvation. While Ignatius was a student at the University of Paris (about the same time as Calvin), he enlisted nine friends, who became the nucleus of a new order. This new order, which was approved by the pope in 1540, was the Society of Jesus. Its members became known as Jesuits.

The rules of the new order were designed to develop a flexible, disciplined, and efficient body of ecclesiastical shock troops for the papacy. The Jesuit wore no distinctive habit; he dressed as his job might require, as priest, teacher, missionary, or secret agent. He swore a special oath of obedience to the pope. He was carefully selected and trained for the most dangerous and difficult tasks the Church might require, from serving as confessor to a king, to venturing into Protestant countries where he might be executed as a traitor, to voyaging to foreign lands as remote as Brazil or India. The Jesuits were spectacularly successful. They strengthened the pope's control over the Church itself; they ran the best schools in Europe; and during the late sixteenth century they won back most of Bohemia, Poland, Hungary, and southern Germany from Protestantism.

The Roman Church strengthened itself against the Protestant attack in other ways as well. A general council was held at Trent in three sessions between 1545 and 1563 to define Catholic dogma and to reform abuses. Since the papal representatives and the Jesuits controlled the deliberations from the beginning, there was no danger of a revolt against the papacy as there had been in the councils of a century before. In reply to the central doctrines of Protestantism, the council declared that salvation is by both faith and works and that final religious authority is in the Bible and tradition as interpreted by the Roman Church. A beginning was made at reforming financial and administrative abuses in the ecclesiastical organization (the final and most drastic changes were made by the pope).

Seminaries were set up for the training of priests. The council defined the Church's teachings much more sharply than they had ever been defined before and recognized the absolute supremacy of the pope over the clerical hierarchy. Rome had lost much in the struggle with heresy, but the Catholic Church of 1563 was far better able to cope with future heresies than it had been in 1500. New forms of the Inquisition had been established in Spain (1480), the Netherlands (1523), and Italy (1542), and a system of censorship of printed books (the Index) was instituted by the pope in 1559 and approved, with some additions, by the Council of Trent in 1563. All the faithful were forbidden to read any book on the Index.

The Roman Church had found a new religious vitality and had closed its ranks against the Protestant threat. By the second half of the sixteenth century a relatively monolithic Catholic Church, reorganized from within and backed by Spain, the strongest military power in

Engraving showing the third session of the Council of Trent (1562–63). An amphitheater was set up in the church of St. Maria Maggio.

Europe, faced the divided Protestants on somewhat better than even terms.

SIGNIFICANCE OF THE REFORMATIONS

It is not easy to sum up the significance of the Protestant and Catholic Reformations. They were religious movements, phrased in theological terms, rooted deep in the religious experience of men like Luther and Loyola, and resulting in a religious fragmentation of western Christendom that has lasted to the present day. But Luther's angry protest against indulgences would not have had such far-reaching results had not the economic, social, and political conditions been just right. The religious upheaval was intermingled with the growth of capitalism, of secularism, of national sentiment, and of absolutism in government. It is difficult to say precisely what was cause and what was effect. While German princes, for example, took advantage of purely religious protests to confiscate church property for their own interests, religious reformers also utilized purely secular events, like Henry VIII's desire to get rid of his wife, to advance the Protestant cause.

One thing is clear. The era of reform and revolution in the Church temporarily arrested the trend toward the secularization of culture that had begun in the last centuries of the Middle Ages. The century that followed Luther's death was a religious age; its most serious arguments were religious arguments; its wars were intensified by religious fanaticism; and most of its leading figures were either men of religion or men considerably affected by religion. Intensified interest in religion introduced a new and intolerant "ideological" element into the economic and political causes of conflict in European society. The hatred among Catholic, Lutheran, Calvinist, and Anabaptist was as profound in the sixteenth century as the hatred among fascist, communist, and democrat in the twentieth, and for somewhat the same reasons. No man could believe that he or his family or his society was safe so long as opposing religious groups were allowed to exist. Only

Luther tweaks the beard of Calvin as both of them pull the hair of the pope. This satirical engraving presents a Catholic view of the Reformation controversy.

in time did it become evident that differing religious beliefs did not necessarily lead to civil war and the collapse of the state. Religious toleration was an eventual result of the Reformation but not of the efforts of the reformers.

For over a century the long-term effects of the Protestant Reformation on the economic, political, and cultural development of Europe have been vigorously debated by historians. It has been argued and denied that Protestantism, with its emphasis on serving God in one's secular calling and with its appreciation of the bourgeois virtues of honesty, thrift, and self-discipline, provided the necessary religious sanction for the development of capitalism. It has been argued and denied that Lutheranism aided the growth of divine-right monarchy, whereas Calvinism provided a spur toward the development of constitutionalism, and Anabaptism toward the development of modern socialism. It has been argued and denied that Protestantism wrecked the development of art by destroying religious sculpture and paintings and by rejecting most religious symbolism. And it has been argued and denied that by dissolving monasteries and thus destroying educational foundations, Protestants set back elementary education many years. Both the good and the bad in modern capitalism, modern nationalism, and modern secularism have been attributed to Protestantism by one historian or another.

The historical data are far too complex for dogmatic judgments in such matters. The permanent schism of western Christendom and the temporary intensification of religious motives in European politics can justly be attributed to the Protestant movement. Beyond this, all that can be said surely is that Protestantism allied itself with developments that had their origins far back, sometimes intensified them and accelerated their growth, occasionally blocked or countered their expansion. Capitalism, democracy, nationalism, and the secularization of culture appeared in Catholic as well as Protestant lands, and none of these phenomena can be explained by a simple chain of causes leading back to Luther and his revolt from Rome.

Suggestions for Further Reading

Note: Asterisk denotes a book available in paperback edition.

Background of the Reformation

For the background of the Reformation, see S. Ozmont, *The Reformation in Medieval Perspective** (1971); G. Strauss, *Pre-Reformation Germany** (1972); and the famous "essay" by J. Huizinga, *The Waning of the Middle Ages** (1924). Huizinga's *Erasmus** (1952), and R. H. Bainton, *Erasmus of Christendom** (1969), are perceptive biographies. Erasmus' best-known writings are available in many modern editions, for example, J. P. Dolan, ed., *The Essential Erasmus* (1964).

The Religious Upheaval

An old, but still useful, work is P. Smith, *The Age of the Reformation** (1920), a lively and opinionated book. H. J. Grimm, *The Reformation Era* (1973), does religious developments fuller justice than Smith and is abreast of recent scholarship, particularly on Luther. H. Holborn, *A History of Modern Germany: The Reformation* (1959), is excellent on Germany. There are briefer treatments of the period in general in R. H. Bainton, *The Reformation of the Sixteenth Century** (1952), and E. H. Harbison, *The Age of Reformation** (1955). The best recent work is L. W. Spitz, *The Renaissance and Reformation Movements*, Vol. II (1971). See also O. Chadwick, *The Reformation** (1964), and H. J. Hillerbrand, *The World of the Reformation** (1973). J. Lortz, *The Reformation in Germany*, 2 vols. (1969), is a fair statement of the Catholic position. A. G. Dickens, *The German Nation and Martin Luther* (1972), stresses the urban nature of the Reformation. F. Wendel, *Calvin, The Origin and Development of His Religious Thought* (1963), is excellent. See also G. Rupp, *Luther's Progress to the Diet of Worms** (1964), and R. H. Fife, *The Revolt of Martin Luther* (1957). There are many translations of the writings of Luther, Calvin, and other reformers, for example in the *Library of Christian Classics*. A good anthology of contemporary writings on the movement is H. J. Hillerbrand, *The Protestant Reformation: A Narrative History* (1964).

For the radicals, see G. H. Williams, *The Radical Reformer* (1962). Good introductions to different aspects of the "left wing" of the Reformation are offered in F. H. Littell, *The Free Church* (1958); R. H. Bainton, *The Travail of Religious Liberty** (1951); and C. L. Clausen, *Anabaptism: A Social History* (1972).

The best work on England is A. G. Dickens, *The English Reformation* (1964). See also the brief and authoritative accounts by F. M. Powicke, *The Reformation in England* (1941), and T. M. Parker, *The English Reformation to 1558** (1950). J. J. Scarisbrick, *Henry VIII** (1968), is a brilliant work. A good Catholic account is by P. Hughes, *The Reformation in England*, 3 vols. (1950–54). For the Puritans, see P. Collinson, *The Elizabethan Puritan Movement* (1967).

An excellent discussion of the Catholic Reformation is H. Daniel-Rops, *The Catholic Reformation,** 2 vols. (1961). The best biography of St. Ignatius is by the Jesuit P. Dudon (1949). For a less favorable treatment, see R. Fülöp-Miller, *The Power and Secret of the Jesuits* (1930). H. Jedin is engaged in writing a definitive *History of the Council of Trent*, the first two volumes of which have appeared in translation (1957). See also A. G. Dickens, *The Counter Reformation** (1969); M. R. O'Connell, *The Counter-Reformation, 1560–1610** (1974); and H. O. Evennett, *The Spirit of the Counter-Reformation** (1968).

Results of the Reformation

On the economic, political, and cultural consequences of the Reformation there are wide differences of opinion. A famous "essay" by M. Weber, *The Protestant Ethic and the Spirit of Capitalism** (1905), became the starting point of a long controversy about the economic significance of Protestantism, which still continues sporadically. *Protestantism and Capitalism: The Weber Thesis and Its Critics,** ed. by R. W. Green (1973), is a convenient collection of selections from the literature of this controversy. Other collections are L. W. Spitz, *The Reformation: Basic Interpretations** (1972), and R. Kingdom and R. Linder, *Calvin and Calvinism: Sources of Democracy** (1972). K. Holl, *The Cultural Significance of the Reformation** (1911), is inclined to view Luther as the prophet of modern Germany and of twentieth-century culture in general. For a readable and perceptive survey of the period, see A. G. Dickens, *Reformation and Society in Sixteenth-Century Europe** (1966).

and the Greatness of Spain

A sixteenth-century sailing ship, with its
navigator (left center) sighting the sun to
determine his latitude. The foremast (right)
is square-rigged for running with the wind.
The mainmast and the mizzenmast astern (left)
are lateen-rigged for better tacking against
the wind.

The Protestant Reformation struck a Europe that was already in the throes of a different sort of revolution. That revolution was launched by Portuguese voyages down the northwest coast of Africa; it quickened with the discovery of America and the sea route to India; and it continued unabated throughout the sixteenth century. For Europeans this was an age of discovery without parallel. For the first time they found themselves in direct contact with all the continents on the globe and with all the civilized peoples who inhabited them. That contact began to have a profoundly disturbing effect on the economy and the politics of Europe just as the Peace of Augsburg was bringing a respite from religious strife.

THE DEVELOPMENT OF OCEANIC COMMERCE

In 1400 Europeans knew scarcely more about the earth than the Romans had. The oceans around the Continent were still impenetrable barriers; the only long voyages ever taken by Europeans were the almost forgotten expeditions of the Northmen to Greenland and America. Franciscan friars and the Polos of Venice had shown that China could be reached by land and that the steppes linked Europe and Asia. But after the collapse of the Mongol Empire in the fourteenth century the routes across the steppes were no longer safe for missionaries or merchants. Arab sailors now became the middlemen between the Orient and Europe. They brought the spices and textiles of India and the East Indies to Alexandria and Beirut, whence the Venetians distributed them to the rest of Europe. The Europeans themselves had no direct contact with the East.

By the end of the sixteenth century an almost incredible geographical revolution had taken place. Arnold J. Toynbee defines it as "the substitution of the Ocean for the Steppe as the principal medium of world-communication." Europeans had mastered both the technological and the psychological problems of making long voyages over the sea. Their ships had crossed and recrossed the Atlantic Ocean, rounded the southern tips of Africa and South America, pushed into the Indian Ocean, and crossed the Pacific. Before this time men had believed that there was far more land than water on the surface of the globe. Now explorers were discovering that there was far more water than land, and that the water could serve as a highway to any coast in the world for men who knew how to use its winds and ride its waves. The Mongol Empire had rested on mastery of the steppes. The empires of the future would rest on mastery of the oceans. When the first ship to circumnavigate the globe finished its voyage in 1522, Europe had begun to cast a web of communication and influence around the earth. During the next four centuries that web was to draw all the civilizations of the world under the influence of Europe.

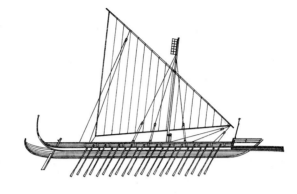

Top: Mediterranean war galley with lateen sail (*ca.* twelfth century); middle: lateen-rigged vessel, much like Columbus' *Niña* (early fifteenth century); bottom: Spanish galleon of sixteenth century, the typical long-distance ship for Spanish commerce.

Conditions
for Maritime Discovery

By the year 1000, Norsemen from Iceland and Greenland had coasted North America in small, open boats. They were too few, however, to make any permanent settlement, and their discoveries were unknown to the rest of Europe. Before Europeans could make a sustained drive to push out across the Atlantic they needed better ships, more reliable aids to navigation, and stronger motivation.

Better ships were long in coming. Oar-propelled galleys had already mastered the Mediterranean, and by the thirteenth century Genoese and Venetian galleys were venturing out into the Atlantic to Morocco and Flanders. But on the open seas mariners needed sails rather than oars and broad, round hulls rather than long, narrow galleys. By the fifteenth century the Portuguese had devised a craft capable of long ocean voyages: the squat, three-masted caravel, with two masts generally square-rigged and one mast lateen-rigged (see the illustration on p. 394). The caravel preserved the advantages of both the northern European square-rig, which was better for running before the wind, and the Arab lateen-rig, which was better for sailing close to the wind. It was slower than the galley, but it had more space for cargo and for supplies on long voyages.

Galleys had generally stayed close to land, hugging the shoreline. Before ships could venture straight out to sea, shipmasters needed some way of determining their direction and their whereabouts. The compass (used in Europe by the thirteenth century) gave them a sense of direction in dark weather; the astrolabe (known since the eleventh century) enabled them to determine their latitude with fair accuracy by measuring the elevation of the sun and stars; and improved charts gave them confidence that they could recognize the approaches to most European ports. (No precise way of determining longitude was known until the eighteenth century.)

City-states were the original bases for long-range navigation. Venetian and Genoese merchants linked the Black Sea and Egypt with Italy and England, and the Germans of the Hanseatic League traded from Russian Novgorod to French Bordeaux. But transoceanic exploration, trade, and colonization required a broader base for support. The new monarchies of western Europe were better situated geographically than the Italian or German city-states to open up the Atlantic. They also had advantages in manpower, resources, and political centralization. After 1400 the larger monarchies gradually replaced the cities as the major centers of commercial enterprise.

It is not easy to determine the motives that prompted Europeans—rather than Chinese or Moslems—to "discover" the rest of the world by taking to the sea. The Moslems had been crossing the Indian Ocean for centuries, and the Chinese regularly sailed up and down the East Asian coast and into the Indian Ocean; but neither people tried to go farther. Certainly the crusade ideal influenced Portuguese and Spanish rulers. To convert the heathen and to weaken Islam by placing Christian allies in the Moslem rear was the goal of many explorers. Crusading zeal was not the main impetus of the great discoveries, but it could be used to inspire enthusiasm for dangerous ventures and to sanctify more worldly motives.

Of those more worldly motives, the need to find precious metals was the most compelling. In an age without refrigeration, the spices that helped preserve meats and make them more palatable—pepper from India, cinnamon from Ceylon, ginger from China, nutmeg and

An illustration from a sailing book, *Art de Naviguer* (1583), demonstrating how to determine latitude by observing the sun's height.

Toynbee on the Age of Discovery

Since A.D. 1500 the map of the civilized world has indeed been transformed out of all recognition. Down to that date it was composed of a belt of civilizations girdling the Old World from the Japanese Isles on the north-east to the British Isles on the north-west. . . . The main line of communication was provided by the chain of steppes and deserts that cut across the belt of civilizations from the Sahara to Mongolia. For human purposes, the Steppe was an inland sea. . . . This waterless sea had its dry-shod ships and its quayless ports. The steppe-galleons were camels, the steppe-galleys horses, and the steppe-ports "caravan cities." . . . The great revolution was a technological revolution by which the West made its fortune, got the better of all the other living civilizations, and forcibly united them into a single society of literally world-wide range. The revolutionary Western invention was the substitution of the Ocean for the Steppe as the principal medium of world-communication. This use of the Ocean, first by sailing ships and then by steamships, enabled the West to unify the whole inhabited and habitable world.

From Arnold J. Toynbee, *Civilization on Trial* (New York: Oxford University Press, 1948), pp. 67–70.

By the late fifteenth century a restless, energetic, and bold seafaring population was scattered along Europe's Atlantic coastline. Resourceful sailors, fishermen, and merchants had developed the techniques and the ships for making long voyages. They had religious and economic motives strong enough to overcome their superstitious fears of what lay beyond known waters, and their governments were often ready to back them. Europe needed direct contact with Asia, and some Europeans believed that it would not be too difficult to reach Asia by sea. Ptolemy in the second century had underestimated the size of the globe and had overestimated the span of Asia, and the geographers of the fifteenth century, accepting his miscalculations, were convinced that Japan and China lay only a few thousand miles west of Europe. The size of Africa was also underestimated, so that an eastern route did not seem to be too difficult. Either an eastern or a western voyage seemed possible, and the material and psychological environment was favorable for an age of discovery.

Portuguese Exploration

Perhaps the most interesting figure of the whole age stands at its very beginning: Prince Henry the Navigator (1394–1460), the younger son of King John I of Portugal. Prince Henry was obsessed with the desire to learn more about Africa; he devoted his life to organizing, equipping, and sending out fleets that pushed farther and farther down the African west coast. In a remarkable observatory at Sagres on Cape St. Vincent, the southwestern tip of Portugal, he brought together the scientific and the seafaring knowledge of his day. He had vague notions of outflanking Islam by reaching lands that the Moslems had never touched, but his main objective was to find gold. When the Portuguese reached the Gold Coast of Africa in the 1450s this objective was achieved.

After Henry's death the impetus of exploration was lost for a time. But Henry's grandnephew, King John II (1481–95), speeded up the effort to find an all-water route to India that would short-

cloves from the East Indies—were luxuries that were almost necessities. The long journey from India or the Moluccas and the Arab-Venetian trade monopoly made such spices expensive. But Europeans needed them (and other luxuries such as cotton and silk cloth) more keenly than Asians needed anything Europe had to offer except gold and silver; so there was a steady flow of precious metals from Europe eastward. This drain limited the supply of specie (hard coins) in Europe at a time when it was increasingly needed as currency. Before credit systems became widely used in the seventeenth and eighteenth centuries, the only practical way to provide the money needed by burgeoning commerce and industry was to increase the supply of bullion. European mines had never been very productive and were nearly exhausted by 1400. Fifteenth-century rulers were acutely aware of their need for gold. They knew that they had to have hard cash in their treasury to hire soldiers, equip navies, and maintain bureaucracies, and they knew that European supplies of precious metals were limited.

circuit the Venetian-Arab monopoly. By 1488 Bartholomew Dias had discovered the Cape of Good Hope, and in 1497 Vasco da Gama rounded the cape with four ships, reached Calicut on the Malabar Coast of India in 1498, and was back in Lisbon with two of his ships in 1499. In 1500 a larger fleet, commanded by Cabral, touched the coast of Brazil and then headed for India in Da Gama's wake.

This first contact by sea with India was to have momentous consequences, but neither side was particularly impressed by the other on first meeting. The Hindus had only contempt for the bedraggled sailors who had spent months aboard Da Gama's ships, and the Europeans soon made it clear that they found nothing to respect in the civilization of India. When the Hindus asked Da Gama what he sought in India, he is said to have replied laconically, "Christians and spices."

During the sixteenth century the Portuguese strove to build a commercial empire in the Indian Ocean. Affonso de Albuquerque, the brutal but able Portuguese governor from 1509 to 1515 and the real founder of that empire, under-

stood the relationship between trade, sea power, and strategic bases. He seized Goa on the western coast of India to serve as his headquarters, Malacca on the Strait of Malacca to control the trade between the Spice Islands and the Indian Ocean, and Ormuz to dominate the Persian Gulf. He failed to capture Aden, a base from which he could have strangled the Arab-Venetian trade through the Red Sea. He was as ruthless in disciplining his own men as he was in terrorizing Hindu princes and fighting Arab seamen. At Albuquerque's death in 1515 the Portuguese had a large share of the spice trade (though not a monopoly) and controlled strategic bases all the way from Africa to the East Indies.

It was easy for the Portuguese and other Europeans to seize footholds in India because the Moslem and Hindu princes of the coastal districts were weak, and the Mogul Empire of the North had little power in the South. The Portuguese, however, established only trading posts, not colonies of settlement, in India, and even the trading posts soon ceased to be very profitable. The early voyages had made large profits for their backers. But the cost to the Portuguese

The Portuguese as others saw them. Above: African bronze sculpture of a Portuguese man. Left: detail from a seventeenth-century Japanese screen painting showing a Portuguese sailor playing a game of *go* with a Japanese friend in a native ship.

THE WORLD OF THE VOYAGERS
1415–1550

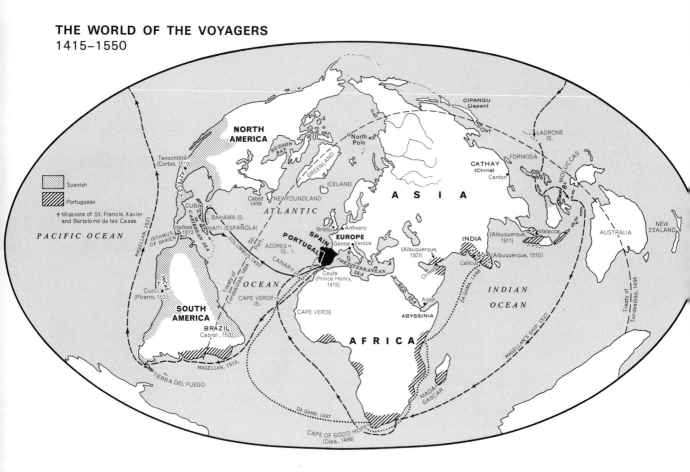

government of equipping fleets and maintaining fighting forces soon ate up the profits. Portugal was a relatively small and poor country, with a small merchant class. Italian, German, and Flemish bankers soon dominated the Portuguese trade, and the spices that arrived at Lisbon were sent on directly to Antwerp, which proved to be a better point from which to distribute them to Europe. The burden of empire was already proving heavy when Portugal fell into the grip of Spain in 1580.

Columbus and Spanish Exploration

In 1484, before the Portuguese had reached the Cape of Good Hope, a Genoese sailor named Christopher Columbus had tried in vain to persuade King John II of Portugal to back him in a voyage of exploration to the west. Columbus was convinced by all the evidence at hand that it would be comparatively easy to

reach Cipangu (Japan) by sailing due west. But for years he was unable to persuade any monarch to back him. At last the rulers of Spain, who had conquered the Moorish Kingdom of Granada in January 1492, were free to turn their attention elsewhere. And so it was under Castilian auspices that Columbus sailed on his famous voyage. It took the Portuguese almost a century of patiently organized effort to reach the Old World eastward, while the Spanish reached the New World westward in one brilliant voyage. There was a large element of luck in the founding of Spain's empire in the New World.

Columbus touched land in the Bahamas on October 12, 1492, thinking he had struck some small islands in the Japanese archipelago. Throughout four voyages and until his death in 1506, he remained convinced, even after touching the mainland, that it was the Old World of Japan and China that he had discovered. And so, although it was Columbus

Christopher Columbus, the Genoese sailor who sailed west in search of Japan and found the New World. This portrait of Columbus is thought to be the closest existing likeness of him. It is a copy, made in about 1525, of an earlier painting that has been lost.

Vasco da Gama.

Magellan plotting his position (detail from an allegorical portrait by De Bry).

Verde Islands was favorable to Spain, at least in the Western Hemisphere. The Portuguese were unhappy, perhaps because most of the unknown regions of the Atlantic were left to Spain, and in 1494 they persuaded the Spanish to sign the Treaty of Tordesillas. By this treaty a line was drawn from pole to pole 370 leagues west of the Cape Verde Islands, separating Portugal's claims to the east from Spain's to the west. The Portuguese assumed that the line applied only to the Atlantic (it gave them Brazil, though they did not know this in 1494). The Spanish preferred to believe that the line extended round the world, cutting it in half as a knife cuts an orange. They hoped that this interpretation might give them the Moluccas, the heart of the Spice Islands, and, in fact, it would have given them part of what is now Indonesia. But Spain was soon too busy in the Americas to concentrate on the East Indies, and in 1527 it sold all its claims to these islands to Portugal.

Magellan

By 1512 the Portuguese were in the Moluccas, and in 1513 the Spaniard Balboa sighted the Pacific from the Isthmus of Darien in Central America. In the years to come, the Spanish, the English, and others tried again and again to discover a strait through the New World by which they might sail westward into the Pacific and reach the Spice Islands. The Portuguese navigator Magellan was convinced that he could do just that by rounding the southern tip of South America. He knew that Portugal would never back him in such an expedition because it would create a Spanish-dominated route to the islands, so in 1519 he sailed with Spanish backing. It was the third of the truly great voyages—along with those of Columbus and Da Gama. Magellan negotiated the straits that are named for him and got across the Pacific after incredible hardships, only to be killed by natives in the Philippines. His navigator, Sebastian del Cano, brought one of the five original ships back to Lisbon by way of the Cape of Good Hope in 1522, the first ship to sail round the world.

who named the "Indians" he found on the shores of Haiti and Cuba, it was the Florentine Amerigo Vespucci who gave his name to the continents Columbus had discovered. Amerigo, director of the Medici branch bank in Seville, sailed on both Spanish and Portuguese voyages and described what he saw in letters that were widely read throughout Europe. In one he referred to the great southern continent in the west as *Mundus Novus*, a New World. Later map makers labeled the two new continents "America," after the man who first realized that it was a new, not an old, world that was opening up to view.

The Treaty
of Tordesillas, 1494

Since both Spain and Portugal were seeking the same lands, they soon had to appeal to the pope for an adjudication of their rival claims to unoccupied and heathen lands around the globe. The pope, Alexander VI, was a Spaniard, and the line of demarcation that he drew in 1493 a hundred leagues west of the Cape

THE SPANISH EMPIRE IN THE AMERICAS

From 1520 to 1550 the conquistadors of Spain carved out an empire in the Americas. As the Spaniards on the Caribbean islands began to hear exciting tales of wealthy, half-civilized empires, they turned from exploration to conquest. The most notable of the conquistadors were Hernando Cortes, who from 1519 to 1521 conquered the formidable Aztec Empire in Mexico with six hundred men, sixteen horses, and a few cannon, and Francisco Pizarro, who from 1533 to 1534 conquered the Inca Empire in Peru with even fewer followers. Their firearms, steel swords, and horses gave the Spaniards an advantage over the more primitively armed groups that faced them, but it was primarily their daring, their discipline, and their fanatical faith that accounted for their fantastic successes.

Within a generation Spanish soldiers, lawyers, and friars unexpectedly found themselves the undisputed rulers of vast stretches of territory and millions of human beings. Often the new ruling class simply stepped into the place of former conquerors like the Aztecs and Incas, living on the tribute from subject populations that had supported their predecessors. But the Spaniards needed labor to exploit the new lands fully, and the upland Indians could not survive in the rich, but unhealthy, lowlands. Thus when sugar became an important crop, Negro slaves were imported from Africa to do the work. Until the seventeenth century, however, the industry most favored by the Spanish government was the mining of gold and silver. After the discovery of enormously rich silver mines in both Mexico and Peru in 1545, the extraction and shipment of silver became the main business of the Spanish Empire as a whole. Every spring after 1564 the plate fleet of twenty to sixty vessels gathered at Havana harbor to be convoyed by warships to Seville. And every year the Spanish government waited anxiously until the bullion, which everyone agreed was the key to national strength, was safely in harbor.

The empire that grew out of these exploits and these economic activities was a kind of compromise between what the Spanish settlers, the Christian friars, and the Spanish government at Madrid would each have liked to see develop in America. The settlers, many of them former conquistadors, would have liked to set themselves up as manorial lords living on the forced labor of the natives, unmolested by any political direction from Madrid. The Franciscans and other friars, particularly the great Dominican, Bartolomé de las Casas, would have liked to see the natives treated as fellow Christians and fellow subjects of the Spanish crown. Las Casas worked tirelessly to protect both the legal and the moral rights of the Indians in the face of relentless pressure from the settlers to exploit them. The government in Spain was determined to centralize all decision making in Seville or Madrid, and to protect the natives so far as possible, as the friars urged.

The policy of the Spanish Empire, as it had unfolded by the end of the sixteenth century, was remarkably sensible

---

Las Casas on the American Indians in the Sixteenth Century

It has been written that these peoples of the Indies, lacking human governance and ordered nations, did not have the power of reason to govern themselves—which was inferred only from their having been found to be gentle, patient and humble. It has been implied that God became careless in creating so immense a number of rational souls and let human nature, which He so largely determined and provided for, go astray in the almost infinitesimal part of the human lineage which they comprise. From this it follows that they have all proven themselves unsocial and therefore monstrous, contrary to the natural bent of all peoples of the world.

... Not only have [the Indians] shown themselves to be very wise peoples and possessed of lively and marked understanding, prudently governing and providing for their nations (as much as they can be nations, without faith in or knowledge of the true God) and making them prosper in justice; but they have equalled many diverse nations of the world, past and present, that have been praised for their governance, politics and customs, and exceed by no small measure the wisest of all these, such as the Greeks and Romans, in adherence to the rules of natural reason.

From Bartolomé de las Casas, *Apologética historia de las Indias,* in *Introduction to Contemporary Civilization in the West,* 3rd ed. (New York: Columbia University Press, 1960), Vol. I, p. 539.

ycpolínhą mexica

Cortes accepting the
surrender of Quauhtemoc,
last king of the Aztecs. The
artist was a Spanish-trained
native from Tlaxcala, who
chronicled Cortes' conquest
of Mexico. Notice the
mixture of European and
Indian styles.

and humane by contemporary standards. The settlers were allowed to command the forced labor of the subject Indians, but this labor was regulated by public authority, not by private right. There were serious abuses, especially in Mexico, and the long arm of the home government was often awkward and exasperatingly slow in dealing with local problems. But as time went on the Spanish came close to accomplishing what the Portuguese failed to accomplish in the East and what the English never attempted in North America: the Christianization and Europeanization of a whole population. The Spaniards took seriously the papal bulls of 1493, which gave them the heathen peoples of the New World to convert and nurture in the Christian faith. In theory, the natives were considered Christians and subjects of the king (unlike the unfortunate Negroes, who had been enslaved by West African rulers and who gained no new rights when they were sold to Europeans). The gulf between Spaniard and native was never entirely closed, in either religion or culture. But Spanish and Portuguese in the end became the languages of all but the most isolated Indians, and Roman Catholicism the dominant religion. Intermarriage was so common that the mestizos, or descendants of mixed marriages, eventually became more numerous than the pure-bred of either race. The Spanish (and the Portuguese in Brazil) made a serious attempt to convert the New World to western civilization.

SPAIN UNDER PHILIP II

In the later sixteenth century Spain was the dominant power in Europe as well as in America. The accession of the Habsburg Charles to the throne of Spain in the early sixteenth century had thrust the Spanish into the full stream of European politics and diplomacy at a moment when the Protestant revolt was beginning to spread, the Turks were expanding up the Danube Valley, and the job of exploring and colonizing America was demanding a huge expenditure of energy. To roll back the threats of heretics and infidels while conquering a new world was a heavy task for a state so recently formed. But for a brief and brilliant time, the Spanish under the Emperor Charles V (1515–56) and his son, King Philip II (1556–98), were almost equal to the challenge. The sixteenth and early seventeenth centuries were the golden age of Spain.

In 1555-56 Charles V divided his family holdings between his brother Ferdinand and his son Philip. To Ferdinand went the Habsburg possessions in Austria and the imperial crown (still elective in theory, but by now always bestowed on a Habsburg). To Philip went the crowns of Castile and Aragon, with Castile's possessions in the New World, the Kingdom of Naples and the Duchy of Milan (which meant control of Italy), and the Netherlands. Thus for a century and a half after 1556 there were "Austrian Habsburgs" and "Spanish Habsburgs," separate ruling houses but houses that cooperated closely in matters of dynastic policy. Except for the Netherlands, which might well have gone to Ferdinand because of the Netherlands' close cultural and geographical ties with the Empire, the possessions of Philip II formed a more tight-knit and centralized state than his father's holdings.

Philip II was thoroughly Spanish in speech, thought, and character. After the conclusion of peace with France in 1559, he returned from the Netherlands to Spain to remain until his death almost forty years later. He caught the imagination of his people as few of their rulers had done. To the Spanish he is still "Philip the Prudent," one of their greatest kings. Distrustful of his advisers, unable to delegate authority even in minor matters, slow in coming to a decision, strongly Catholic in religion (his enemies would have said "bigoted"), convinced of his divine right to govern Spain as an absolute ruler strictly accountable to God but to no one else, Philip devoted his country to the ideal of a restored Catholic Christendom with the Spanish monarchy as its leading power and defender. For centuries the Spanish had fought the Moors. To Philip, the crusade would continue against half-converted Jews and Moors at home and against Turks and Protestants abroad until the Christian Commonwealth of the Middle Ages had been restored. Meanwhile the Catholic faith would be carried to the New World. Since Spain was the divinely chosen agent of this mission, what was in the interest of Spain was naturally in the interest of Christendom as a whole. Or so it appeared to Philip and to most of the Spanish nobility.

If ever there was a monarchy and a ruling class with a sense of destiny, it was the Spanish of the sixteenth century. This spirit was evident in the Spanish Jesuits who guided the Council of Trent and helped to reconvert much of central Europe to Catholicism, in the Spanish

Philip II of Spain, by Titian.

On Philip II of Spain

The pallor of his complexion was remarked on by all observers, and most of them drew the proper conclusion, namely, that it indicated a weak stomach and lack of exercise. Reddened eyes were a penalty of his excessive devotion to the written word both day and night. . . . Reading and writing occupied the major portion of Philip's day. . . . He had taken deeply to heart his father's injunction to direct everything himself, and never to give his full confidence even to the most faithful of his ministers, and the natural result was that his time was completely occupied with receiving and answering reports and letters. . . . Reports, reports, and even more reports; Philip was literally submerged with them in his later years, and moreover he did not stop at reading them; he annotated them, as he went along, with comments on matters as absurdly trifling as the spelling and style of the men who had written them—all in that strange, sprawling hand of his, one of the most illegible hands of an age more than usually replete with chirographical difficulties.

From R. B. Merriman, *The Rise of the Spanish Empire in the Old World and in the New* (New York: Macmillan, 1934), Vol. IV, pp. 21–24.

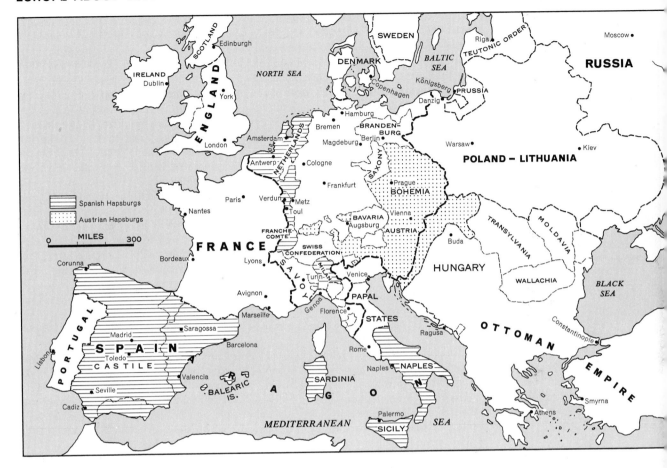

friars who labored to convert the American Indians, in the conquistadors who toppled native empires in the New World, and in the tough Spanish infantry who, for over a century, defeated every organized army they met in Europe, and gained at least a draw in their struggle with the Dutch guerillas. Philip II's Spain was the strongest military power on the Continent, the strongest naval power in the Atlantic (in spite of the defeat of the Armada in 1588), and the wealthiest state in Europe. Spain was the nerve center of the Catholic Reformation. No wonder the terror of the Spanish name lived on into the seventeenth century long after Spanish strength had begun to waste away.

Economic Policy

The economic basis of Spain's predominance was the gold and silver that flowed to Seville in a swelling stream from the New World. Early in the sixteenth century the bullion imported was almost entirely gold. But after the discovery in 1545 of the rich mines in Peru and Mexico, it was mostly silver. The value of the treasure that reached Spain rose enormously between 1500 and 1600. In very round figures the average yearly value of bullion imports at the beginning of the century was something under $300,000; by about 1550 the value had increased fifteen times; and by 1600 over forty times, to about $12,000,000. Then a steady decline set in, until about 1660 the average was down to around $1,200,000. The Spanish crown received about a quarter of the total as its share.

This influx of precious metals, combined with internal financial problems, contributed to a steep rise in prices. At first the rise was slow and generally

Contemporary map showing Spain as the head and crown of sixteenth-century Europe.

stimulating to Spanish industry and commerce. But it had become precipitous by the middle of the century, amounting to a severe inflation that struck first Spain and then the rest of western and central Europe as the metal flowed out of the Iberian peninsula (in spite of all government prohibitions). It has been estimated that prices quadrupled in Spain in the course of the century. Since prices rose faster than taxes could be increased, Philip II was forced to repudiate his government's debts three times, in 1557, 1575, and 1596. (His successors had to follow the same course in 1607, and 1627, and 1647.) The effect of inflation on Spanish industry was eventually disastrous. Since prices always rose faster in Spain than elsewhere, it was relatively more expensive to manufacture goods in Spain than in other countries. This meant that Spanish producers could not sell their goods abroad and that cheaper foreign products captured the Spanish market.

In the short run, Spain's silver enabled it to maintain supremacy in Europe by paying its armies in cash and buying what goods it needed abroad. In the long run, this policy helped to ruin Spain's industry and commerce, and even to undermine its agriculture. There were other reasons for Spain's economic troubles in the seventeenth century, such as the expulsion of its best farmers, the Moriscoes, as the converted Moors were called. But the influx of precious metals was probably the major reason for both the rapid rise and the equally rapid decline of Spain as the leading power in Europe. Spain lived for a century on the windfall of American treasure, but when the supply of bullion dwindled in the seventeenth century Spain found that the real sinews of its national strength—native industry and agriculture—were ruined.

Religious Policy

Philip II's religious policy was the most narrowly intolerant of his time. He abhorred heresy and unbelief with a holy hatred and said he would rather be king in a desert than in a land of heretics. He feared Islam as the ancient enemy both of Christendom and of his people. In his eyes and in those of most of his countrymen, the Moors who had been forcibly Christianized after the conquest of Granada in 1492 were still Moslems at heart. Furthermore, they were more prosperous than most Spanish farmers, and they were reputedly in league with the Moslems of North Africa. In 1566 Philip ordered them to stop using the Arabic language and learn Castilian, to give up their Moorish dress, and to stop taking hot baths, as was their custom. In 1569 the exasperated Moriscoes broke into a revolt, which was savagely suppressed. They were driven out of Andalusia and scattered over Spain. In the years after 1609 they were driven out of the country entirely. Their numbers and importance have sometimes been exaggerated, but there is no doubt that their loss helped to weaken the Spanish economy.

At the height of the revolt of the Moriscoes in 1570, the Turks captured Cyprus from the Venetians. Once again Europe trembled before the threat of Islamic expansion. Philip II immediately allied himself with the pope and the Venetians to counter the danger, and in October 1571 a Spanish and Venetian fleet won a famous victory over a large Turkish fleet at Lepanto in the Gulf of Corinth. Nothing decisive came of the battle because the Christian forces were unable to follow up their victory. But the event had considerable importance for European morale because it was the first time a Turkish fleet had been defeated.

The Apogee of Spanish Prestige

Philip's prestige probably never stood higher in Europe than in the years immediately following Lepanto. He was popular at home, and his defeat of the Turks gave him the undisputed political leadership of Catholic Europe. France, potentially the strongest monarchy in Europe, was torn by civil war during most of Philip's reign and so was unable to contest his leadership. England seemed weak and divided by religious controversies, and its queen had been excommunicated by the pope in 1570. Meanwhile the Empire was safely in the hands of Philip's Habsburg cousins. It seemed as if his dream of a resurgent Catholic Christendom dominated by Spain was about to become a reality.

This dream was shattered during the last quarter of the sixteenth century by the revolt of the Netherlands, the rise of English sea power, and the accession of a former Protestant to the throne of France. In his struggle with the embattled forces of Protestantism in northern Europe, Philip overreached himself, exhausted his resources, and started his nation on its long decline.

THE REVOLT OF THE NETHERLANDS

The Netherlands were the wealthiest and most densely populated of Philip II's dominions. The 3 million people dwelling

The baptism of Moslem women, from a Spanish relief (1520).

beside the mouths of the Rhine and the Meuse had lived by their industry and commerce since the early Middle Ages. The looms of the southern provinces turned out great quantities of linen and woolen cloth, while the fisheries and shipping of the northern provinces steadily increased in value. The comfortable houses of Bruges, Ghent, Antwerp, and Amsterdam were built with the profits of this flourishing industry and trade.

The seventeen provinces of the Netherlands had been united in a personal union by the dukes of Burgundy. But when Charles V inherited the territories in 1519 through his grandmother, Mary of Burgundy, there was little in the way of national feeling or common institutions to bind them together. Charles, who was brought up in Flanders and spoke Flemish as well as French, was the closest thing to a native ruler the united Netherlands had ever had, but he regularly sacrificed their interests to his broader imperial aims. During his reign the faint beginnings of a Netherlandish national consciousness appeared.

The provinces were a crossroads for ideas as well as for commerce. The Humanism of Erasmus as well as the teachings of Luther took early root in the Netherlands, to be followed by Anabaptist ideas. But in the 1550s a militant, disciplined Calvinism spread rapidly and soon became the dominant form of Protestantism. When Philip II took over the rule from his father in the fall of 1555, Calvinists constituted tight-knit minorities in most of the cities of the seventeen provinces.

Within ten years after his accession, Philip had alienated most of the nobility and bourgeoisie of the provinces. Native nobles were displaced in favor of Spaniards in the governing council, a policy that hurt the pride of the upper classes. A threat to enforce the laws against heresy with new efficiency and severity sent a chill of terror through the Calvinist merchants and ministers. Madrid was almost a thousand miles away from Brussels, and Philip's Spanish-Catholic mind was even more remote from the interests and concerns of his busy, prosperous Dutch and Flemish subjects, whether they were Calvinist or Catholic. The revolt that ensued was partly a provincial reaction against centralization, partly a patriotic movement directed against foreign rule, and partly a religious protest against an inquisitorial Catholicism.

In 1566 Calvinist mobs began to break images of the saints and smash the stained-glass windows in Catholic churches throughout the Netherlands. Philip decided to make a frightful example of the iconoclasts. He sent the Duke of Alva and about ten thousand Spanish regulars to the Netherlands with orders to bring the troublemakers either to the block or to the stake. Alva set up what came to be called a "Council of Blood" and boasted (with some exaggeration) that within the six years of his residence in the Netherlands (1567–73) he had executed close to eighteen thousand people. In addition to spilling so much blood, Alva and his council confiscated large amounts of property and imposed a 10 percent sales tax that almost strangled the trade of the country during the year or two it was in force. The Netherlanders never forgot these six years. Instead of crushing the opposition to Philip, Alva's policy solidified the resistance, at least for a time.

William the Silent and Dutch Independence

By 1572 the resistance movement had found a leader in William the Silent, Prince of Orange, the wealthiest landowner in the provinces. William was no military genius—he lost almost every battle he fought against the Spanish—but he had political wisdom, integrity, and patience, a rugged kind of patriotism, and a deep hatred of religious fanaticism, whether Calvinist or Catholic. He tried his best to hold the Calvinists in check, keep all seventeen provinces united against the Spanish, and still find a solution that would leave Philip as titular ruler. For a few years it looked as if he might succeed. In 1576 Calvinist excesses provoked a frightful sack of Antwerp by Spanish troops known as the "Spanish Fury." This was enough to frighten all seventeen provinces into an agreement to

William the Silent, by Anthony Moro.

stick together. The agreement was called the Pacification of Ghent.

Within three years, however, both Protestant and Catholic radicals had got out of hand, moderates had lost influence, and animosity between Catholics and Protestants had begun to undermine the universal hatred of Spain. The almost unanimous opposition to Alva and his successors gradually gave way to a savage civil war in which the Calvinists, the best-disciplined minority, took over leadership of the opposition to Philip. Most of the Catholics rushed back into the arms of Spain for protection. The seventeen provinces split in two as Calvinists fled to the Dutch provinces in the north beyond the great rivers, where they were better able to defend themselves, and Catholics fled to the Walloon provinces in the south, where Spanish troops could be maintained and supplied from the upper Rhine. In 1579 the Dutch provinces in the north formed the Union of Utrecht. This union ultimately became the foundation of the United Provinces, or Dutch Netherlands, which formally declared their independence of Philip II in 1581. And so the unanticipated result of the revolt of 1566 was that the seven northern provinces broke away from Spanish rule, while the ten southern provinces remained under Habsburg control and eventually (in 1830) became the kingdom of Belgium.

The Rise of the United Provinces

The Dutch Netherlands had to fight for their independence for two generations after 1581. They got some help from French and English troops at various times, but the price that the French Duke of Anjou and the English Queen Elizabeth asked for their help was often dangerously high. In the long run it was dogged determination, geography, and the rivalry of their enemies that won the Dutch their independence. William the Silent was assassinated in 1584, but his descendants carried on his tradition of able and disinterested leadership as *stadtholders* (regents) of one or more of the seven provinces. The "United Provinces" never formed more than the loosest sort of political federation, but the Dutch fought with stubbornness when they had to. The Duke of Parma, who became Philip's representative in the Netherlands in 1578, was one of the best military commanders of his day, but he was unable to reconquer the provinces beyond the bend of the Rhine and the Meuse, especially since he lacked control of the sea. The Dutch "Sea Beggars," or privateers, won as many battles against the Spanish on the water as William's armies lost on the land. When Philip's "Invincible Armada" was broken up in 1588 by the English and the weather, reconquest of the northern provinces became impossible. Finally, in 1648, the king of Spain recognized the independence of his former Dutch subjects.

By this time the new Dutch state had become one of the great powers of Europe. Most long wars exhaust even the victors, but the Dutch came out of this war the most powerful commercial nation in Europe. By the early seventeenth century they were building more ships each year than all other nations combined (two thousand, it was said), and they were better ships than any others. During the first half of the seventeenth century the Dutch captured more and more of the carrying trade not only of Europe but of the world. Their rates were cheaper, their business methods more efficient, their handling of cargo more skillful. Antwerp (in the Spanish Netherlands) had been ruined by the Spanish soldiery and blocked off from the sea through the closing of the Scheldt River by the Dutch. Thus Amsterdam (in the United Provinces) took Antwerp's position as the commercial and financial center of Europe. Until their own vulnerability to attack by land became evident after 1660, the Dutch had no rivals who could contest their power.

The sheer geographical extent of Dutch commercial operations was re-

markable. Dutch ships handled much of the grain trade of the Baltic and a large part of the carrying trade of England, France, Italy, and Portugal. When Philip II seized the crown of Portugal in 1580 and stopped the Dutch from visiting Lisbon (whence the Dutch were accustomed to distribute Portuguese spices to the rest of Europe), the Dutch with characteristic daring went out to the source of the spices themselves in the Moluccas. In 1602 the Dutch East India Company was formed and soon established its headquarters at Batavia on the island of Java. By the middle of the century the Dutch had seized the richest part of Portugal's eastern empire—the Moluccas, Malacca, and Ceylon. For over a century the company paid very large dividends, mainly by ruthlessly monopolizing the production of spices and limiting it to keep up

Example of a propaganda badge worn by Dutch "Sea Beggars." The insurgents' hatred of Catholicism is expressed in the inscription: "Better the Turks than the pope."

THE DIVISION OF THE NETHERLANDS 1581

Amsterdam harbor, center of a worldwide trade (detail from an engraving by Pieter Bast, 1597).

prices. In 1652 the Dutch founded a colony at the Cape of Good Hope as a way station to the East. A few decades earlier they had come close to ousting the Portuguese from Brazil. At about the same time (1624) they founded a settlement on Manhattan Island named New Amsterdam that became the center for a large Dutch carrying trade in the New World. When the French and British embarked on overseas trade and colonization, they found not only the Spanish and Portuguese but the Dutch ahead of them all over the world.

So it was an economic giant that Philip II conjured up when he set out to crush his rebellious subjects in the Netherlands. The revolt of the Netherlands may be considered as a kind of dress-rehearsal-in-miniature for those larger popular and patriotic revolts against absolute monarchy, beginning with the Puritan Revolution in England and continuing through the American and French revolutions, that marked the next two centuries. There are many differences among these movements, but there are many similarities in the mixture of economic, patriotic, and religious grievances, the blindness of the absolute monarchs, and the ultimate triumph of "middle-class" interests.

ELIZABETHAN ENGLAND

Philip of Spain was almost as unfortunate in his dealings with England under Queen Elizabeth I as he was in his dealings with the Netherlands. England was crucial to his plans. If he could have added control of England to his control of Spain, Milan, and the Netherlands, France would have been encircled and the vital sea routes between Spain and the Netherlands would have been safer. For a few years (1554–58), while Philip was married to Queen Mary of England, it seemed as if the emperor's dream would be realized: England had been brought within the Habsburg orbit and restored to Roman Catholicism. But Elizabeth's accession to the throne in 1558 changed everything.

Queen Elizabeth I (1558–1603) is generally accounted the greatest of the Tudors and one of England's ablest rulers, though to some critics she was simply a stingy and narrow-minded woman. Whatever the judgment, England was immeasurably stronger at her death than at her accession, and she died beloved by the great majority of her people. At twenty-five, when she came to the throne, she had already lived through disgrace, humiliation, and even danger of execution during her sister Mary's reign. She had seen how Mary had lost the love of her people by marrying a foreigner and by burning heretics. These early experiences left her a strong-willed and shrewd young woman, aware of how precarious both her own situation and that of her nation were, determined to put politics before religion and to follow a purely national policy.

Elizabeth's instinct was always to temporize and compromise. As the daughter of Henry VIII and Anne Boleyn, Elizabeth could never allow England to submit to papal authority. But she wanted a religious settlement that would not alienate patriotic Catholics, and she hoped she could deceive the Catholic powers of Europe for a time into thinking that she could be won back to Rome. On the other hand, she resented the attempt of the left-wing Protestant minority (a group that was gradually gaining the appellation of "Puritan") to dictate a radical religious settlement and a risky, pro-Protestant foreign policy. However, Elizabeth never completely broke with her patriotic Puritan subjects and never lost their loyalty, even when she punished them for advocating radical measures. Elizabeth's policy was nationalist first and Protestant second, but the long-term result was to encourage that fusion of patriotism and Protestantism that became a permanent characteristic of English public opinion.

She compromised and temporized in her foreign policy as well. Her instinct was to avoid clear-cut decisions, to keep a dozen intrigues afoot so that there were always avenues of escape from any policy, and to avoid war at almost any cost. The chief danger at her accession was from French influence in Scotland. The French had long been allies of the Scots, and Mary Stuart, Queen of Scots, was

Elizabeth I of England, and her signature. The silver medal commemorates the defeat of the Spanish Armada (1588).

Mary Stuart, Queen of Scots, and her signature. Lead medal by Jacopo Primavera (*ca.* 1572).

married in 1558 to the heir to the French crown. A year later John Knox, who had become a Calvinist, returned to his native Scotland from Geneva and began a religious revolution. Catholicism and French influence on the Scots were both undermined. Moreover, since Mary Stuart's husband was now king of France, it was clear that France would make every effort to defeat the Calvinists. For once Elizabeth made a rapid decision: to ally with the Calvinist party in Scotland and keep the French out. By 1560 Knox, the Kirk (Scottish Church), and the pro-English party were in control, and the French had lost all influence in Scotland. The way was paved for the union of the English and Scottish crowns in 1603.

Mary, Queen of Scots

Mary Stuart returned to Scotland in 1561 after her husband's death. She was a far more charming and romantic figure than her cousin Elizabeth, but she was no stateswoman. A convinced Catholic, she soon ran head-on into the granitelike opposition of Knox and the Kirk. Her second marriage, to her cousin Lord Darnley, turned out badly, and she became involved in a plot resulting in his murder. In 1567 she was forced to abdicate, and in the following year she fled from Scotland and sought protection in England from Elizabeth. No visitor could have been more unwelcome. Mary, as Henry VII's great-granddaughter, had the best hereditary claim to be Elizabeth's heir, but she was a Catholic and a foreigner. Elizabeth would never formally recognize her as her successor, nor would she marry in order to produce another heir, nor would she do anything to harm her fellow sovereign, except keep a close watch on her through her agents. This policy exasperated Elizabeth's Puritan advisers and left Mary free to become the center of almost every French or Spanish

plot against Elizabeth's life during the next twenty years.

The Anglo-Spanish Conflict

Though there were many sources of friction between them, Elizabeth and Philip of Spain remained on relatively good terms for over twenty years. As time went on, however, it became increasingly difficult to keep the peace. England was a small country with less than half the population of Spain, but during the quarter-century of peace that Elizabeth's cautious temporizing gave her people, English industry, commerce, and shipping expanded considerably. For reasons we have already suggested, the Spanish were unable to produce the goods needed by their colonies. And Spanish shipping was incapable of supplying the insatiable colonial demand for African slaves. An aggressive merchant named Sir John Hawkins was the first Englishman to carry both goods and slaves direct to the Spanish settlements in 1562. It was profitable but dangerous work. In 1569 he and his cousin, Sir Francis Drake, were almost wiped out by a Spanish fleet. In revenge, Drake seized the annual silver shipment from Peru on its way across the Isthmus of Panama. From 1577 to 1580 he followed Magellan's route around the world and demonstrated the vulnerability of the Spanish Empire. Meanwhile English sailors were boldly probing the coasts of North America in a vain search for a Northwest Passage that would short-circuit the Portuguese route to the Indies. Like their fellow Protestants, the Dutch, the English were contesting the Spanish-Portuguese monopoly of overseas trade.

It was the revolt of the Netherlands, however, that finally brought England and Spain to blows. For centuries the economic ties between England and the Low Countries had been close. The Eng-

The Armada

When the Spanish Armada challenged the ancient lords of the English on their own grounds, the impending conflict took on the aspect of a judicial duel in which as was expected in such duels, God would defend the right. . . . So when the two fleets approached their appointed battleground, all Europe watched. For the spectators of both parties, the outcome, reinforced, as everyone believed, by an extraordinary tempest, was indeed decisive. The Protestants of France and the Netherlands, Germany and Scandinavia saw with relief that God was, in truth, as they had always supposed, on their side. The Catholics of France and Italy and Germany saw with almost equal relief that Spain was not, after all, God's chosen champion. From that time forward, though Spain's preponderance was to last for more than another generation, the peak of her prestige had passed. . . . So, in spite of the long, indecisive war which followed, the defeat of the Spanish Armada really was decisive. It decided that religious unity was not to be reimposed by force on the heirs of medieval Christendom, and if, in doing so, it only validated what was already by far the most probable outcome, why, perhaps that is all that any of the battles we call decisive has ever done.

From Garrett Mattingly, *The Armada* (Boston: Houghton Mifflin, 1959), pp. 400–01.

lish people sympathized with Alva's victims, and English Sea Dogs cooperated informally with Dutch Sea Beggars to prey on Spanish shipping and to cut Spanish communications by sea with the Netherlands. Philip's ambassadors in England became deeply involved in one plot after another against Elizabeth's life, usually with the object of setting Mary Stuart on the throne. In 1587 Elizabeth reluctantly consented to Mary's execution when confronted with unmistakable evidence of her complicity in these plots. Philip immediately planned an attack on England. In 1588 he sent his "Invincible Armada" north to hold the Channel while Parma ferried his Spanish veterans across to conquer England for Spain.

The story of the defeat of the Armada has become an allegory of the triumph of a young, vigorous nation over an old and senile nation. The Spanish ships were large and slow, equipped with inferior cannon, and commanded by a landlubber. The fleet was conceived as a means of transporting troops, not of fighting battles at sea. The English ships that put out from Plymouth to harry the Spanish up the Channel were smaller and more maneuverable, trained to fire their cannon at longer range. When the Spanish reached Calais and anchored there, Parma had still not completed his plans. The English sent in fire ships among the Spanish ships as they lay at anchor, drove them northward in panic, and attacked them fiercely off Gravelines. Stormy weather completed what the English had begun. Hardly half the galleons that had left Spain made their way back northward and westward around Scotland and Ireland. The victory gave a lift to the morale of Englishmen and of Protestants everywhere. It ended all further thought of Spanish conquest of England—or reconquest of the Netherlands, for that matter. It did not mean the end of Spanish sea power, which was still greater than that of any other country. But when peace was finally signed in 1604, the English, with the Dutch, stood close to the Spaniards as powers on the sea.

THE FRENCH WARS OF RELIGION

One obvious reason for Spain's ascendancy in the later sixteenth century was the fact that France, traditionally the chief obstacle to Habsburg expansion, was torn by a series of civil and religious wars that prostrated the monarchy and devastated large areas of the country between 1562 and 1593. Almost overnight France was transformed from an aggressive national monarchy into a victim of intervention by neighboring states.

Background of the Civil Wars

France, with a population about double that of Spain, was the largest nation in Christian Europe under a single government. But, impressive as the French monarchy was, it was far from having absolute power. There was still a powerful and turbulent aristocracy in France, and French provinces clung jealously to local customs and privileges. The country was imperfectly unified; there was no body that could speak for the whole realm, as Parliament could for England. Class differences were sharp, and the bureaucracy was overworked, corrupt, and inefficient. Other countries had the same weaknesses; few other countries had to face the same internal and external threats.

Into this half-established absolute monarchy the strong irritant of religious conflict was injected about the middle of the century in the form of militant Calvinism. The rational theology and disciplined organization of Reformed Christianity—not to mention the superb French style of Calvin's writings—appealed widely to many nobles and bourgeois throughout France. The French Calvinists were nicknamed Huguenots. On the eve of the civil wars they boasted about 2500 churches. They probably never numbered more than a sixth of the population (some scholars say as low as a twelfth), but they were an aggressive and well-organized minority, sure of their faith, and confident of the support of a few men, such as Admiral Coligny, at the very top of the social hierarchy. Arrayed against them were strongly Catholic noble families, and, more important, the University of Paris and the Paris *parlement* (High Court). Most important of all was the fact that the Concordat of Bologna had given the kings of France full control over the appointment of the higher clergy as well as considerable indirect control of papal taxation and jurisdiction. In short, the king and his advisers could see no advantage in religious change, and consequently the Huguenots remained a permanent minority in France.

The Course of the Wars

The wars that broke out in France in 1562 were at once social, political, and religious. When Henry II died in 1559, the royal authority fell into the hands of the Queen Mother, Catherine de' Medici, during the reigns of her three weakling sons, Francis II (1559–60), Charles IX (1560–74), and Henry III (1574–89). Catherine was an astute woman who put politics before religion and did her best to keep the feuding factions at court and the religious fanatics throughout the country from flying at one another's throats. But she lacked formal authority, and by now the animosities had become bitter. Calvinists allied themselves with discontented nobles and upholders of local autonomy. On the other side were Catholics, royal agents, and defenders of the status quo. Fanatics on both sides appealed for foreign aid, the Huguenots to the English, the Dutch, and the Germans, the Catholics to Spain. Both England and Spain sent troops, mostly at the beginning and again at the end of the wars.

Fighting was of the savage and bitter kind that characterizes civil wars. The Catholics won most of the pitched battles but were unable to wipe out the Hugue-

Massacre of St. Bartholomew's Day, 1572 (detail from a painting by an eyewitness, François Dubois).

nots. In 1572 Catherine was persuaded by the Catholic fanatics that one sharp blow might end all the trouble. At two o'clock on the morning of St. Bartholomew's Day, Catholic armed bands set upon the Huguenots in Paris, where many of their leaders were gathered for the wedding of the king's sister to the Protestant Henry of Navarre. Coligny and many others were killed. The slaughter spread quickly to other French cities, and before it was over probably ten thousand Protestants had been massacred. This was the most spectacular of innumerable atrocities on both sides. It horrified Protestants throughout Europe and, according to one story, made Philip II laugh aloud for the only time in his life. But it had little effect on the conflict in France.

Catherine de' Medici in 1561, by an unknown artist.

Henry of Navarre

The wars dragged on for twenty more years, becoming more and more confused and purposeless until the Huguenot Henry of Navarre came to the throne in 1589 as Henry IV (1589–1610). Though he was the nearest male heir, he was only remotely related to the previous king. He had a difficult time making good his claim to the crown against a Catholic League that held Paris and against troops of Philip II that intervened from the Spanish Netherlands under Parma. In the end he found that the only way he could capture Paris was to renounce his faith and become a Catholic, which he did in 1593. He did not forget his former fellow Protestants, however. By the Edict of Nantes in 1598 the Huguenots were granted freedom of conscience, freedom of worship in specified places, equal civil rights, and control of some two hundred fortified towns throughout France. In short, the edict simply recognized a religious stalemate, and zealots on both sides of the religious fence considered it only temporary. But it constituted the first formal recognition by a European national monarchy that two religions could be allowed to exist side by side without destroying the state, and growing numbers of Frenchmen who preferred civil peace at any price to the anarchy and fanaticism of the past forty

Henry of Navarre in court dress (seventeenth-century enamel).

years supported it. With the conclusion of peace with Spain and the publication of the Edict of Nantes in 1598, France was ready to resume building a strong monarchy.

THE GENERAL CHARACTER OF THE LATER SIXTEENTH CENTURY

The age of Philip II and of Elizabeth of England has been called the Age of Religious Warfare. It is true that religion was often the spark that set aflame the combustible materials of sixteenth-century society, but early nationalism, economic instability, and social unrest also played their part. A more precise description of the period might be the Age of Religious Politics. Until the Reformation, European politics and diplomacy had slowly grown less religious and more secular. Now for a century, thanks to the religious schism, politics and diplomacy became once more strongly motivated and embittered by religion. The monarchies were faced by religious ideologies that often commanded fiercer loyalties than could the dynasties themselves. A Jesuit might scheme and work and die for an ideal that obviously transcended all state boundaries. In the same way a Scottish Presbyterian, a Dutch Calvinist, and a French Huguenot might have more in common than subjects of the same king. Thus religious differences sometimes undermined the power of monarchs, as they did in France and the Netherlands. And sometimes religious zeal reinforced loyalty to the dynasty, as it did in Spain and among English Protestants. Perhaps the best symbol of this Age of Religious Politics was the Escorial, which Philip II built for his residence near Madrid. The building was half-palace, half-monastery; and the private chamber of the king was connected directly with the chapel of the monastery. A century later a palace would be built at Versailles that would express the spirit of a quite different age.

The European Witch-Craze

The Age of Religious Warfare coincided with a tragic episode of western civilization: the European witch-craze. The witch-craze began in the mid-sixteenth century and continued for over a hundred years; before it ended, thousands of persons had been hanged or burned at the stake as convicted witches. The exact number of victims may never be known, but it is certain that the overwhelming majority of them were completely innocent.

Superstitious beliefs and practices—often dating back to pre-Christian times—had always lurked beneath the surface of European life. It was widely believed that some people had occult powers that could be used to assist neighbors in distress—or to harm them. Almost every community had its wizard or cunning woman, someone who offered cures and consolations when the efforts of priest or doctor had proved to no avail. From time to time throughout the Middle Ages, people had also been convicted of malevolent witchcraft; that is, of attempting to use occult means to inflict death or disease on others.

During the sixteenth century, however, the number of people accused of witchcraft began to increase dramatically. In one community after another a single accusation, which formerly might have led to a single witch-trial, triggered a chain reaction of arrests. Most of the victims were females—since witches were popularly assumed to be reclusive old women who had relieved their loneliness by making a "compact" with the Devil—but some men and even children were also arrested. Under torture, the suspects were forced to confess participation in lurid "witches' sabbaths" and diabolical schemes to harm or kill their neighbors. Having confessed, the suspects were then forced to name "accomplices," who in turn would be arrested and convicted. Dozens, even hundreds, of victims were often led to the stake in a single community. (In England, more humanely, the suspects were spared torture, and executions were by hanging.)

Historians are still puzzled about why the witch-craze exploded in sixteenth-century Europe. Certainly its occurrence reflected a growing interest in the "science" of demonology, which had begun to flourish in the late Middle Ages. It is

The Escorial, Philip II's monastery-palace near Madrid.

no accident, however, that the actual increase in accusations and executions coincided with the Age of Religious Warfare. The religious passions unleashed by the Reformation had generated deep hostilities on a level unprecedented in European history. Protestants regarded the pope as Antichrist; Catholics believed that Luther had been spawned by the Devil. Prominent intellectuals, such as King James I of England, felt obliged to publish extensive treatises about the works of Satan and his minions. In such an atmosphere, people of every class could become suspicious of their friends and neighbors, while judges took even the most unlikely accusations seriously,

Religion and Patriotism

A Spanish ambassador reporting the words of a French Catholic in 1565:

Nowadays Catholic princes must not proceed as they once did. At one time friends and enemies were distinguished by the frontiers of provinces and kingdoms, and were called Italians, Germans, Frenchmen, Spaniards, Englishmen, and the like. Now we must say Catholics and heretics, and a Catholic prince must consider all Catholics of all countries as his friends, just as the heretics consider all heretics as friends and subjects whether they are their own vassals or not.

◊   ◊   ◊

An English Protestant writing in 1589:

All dutiful subjects in this land desire with all their hearts the continuance of God's religion; the preservation of Queen Elizabeth; and the good success of the English navy. These particulars, I grant, are not expressed in flat in the Lord's Prayer; but they are contained within the compass of, and may be deduced from the petitions of that excellent prayer. Whosoever doubteth of this is void of learning.

As quoted in Erich Marks, *Die Zusammenkunft von Bayonne* (Strasburg: K. J. Trübner, 1889), p. 14; as quoted in Benjamin Hanbury, *Historical Memorials Relating to the Independents* (London: Congregational Union of England and Wales, 1839–44), Vol. I, p. 71.

and interrogated suspects in the most ruthless possible fashion.

Why did the witch-craze end? In the first place, religious warfare died out in the mid-seventeenth century, and with its passing came a cooling of the religious passions that had inflamed post-Reformation Europe. Even more importantly, the emergence of a modern scientific outlook (see Chapter 21) made the belief in invisible spirits and occult forces increasingly untenable among serious intellectuals. By 1660 the witch-panics were on the wane; by 1700 they all but disappeared. But the witch-craze, like the religious wars themselves, showed the instability of sixteenth-century society.

"Golden Ages"

It is characteristic of the history of civilization that periods of intense political and social conflict sometimes coincide with great creative achievements. Thus the late sixteenth and early seventeenth centuries witnessed a "golden age" of literature and the arts in three of the nations under consideration. Shakespeare's plays and Spenser's poetry in Elizabethan England, Cervantes' *Don Quixote* and Velasquez' paintings in Spain of the early seventeenth century, and Vondel's poetry and Rembrandt's portraits in Holland of the mid-seventeenth century represent a kind of summit of achievement in the history of the arts in these three nations. Shakespeare (*ca.* 1564–1616), Cervantes (1547–1616), and Vondel (1587–1679) are still the greatest figures in the literary history of their native countries, and, though Eng-

land produced no great painter, Frans Hals (*ca.* 1580–1666) and Rembrandt van Rijn (1606–69) are the towering figures in Dutch painting, as El Greco (*ca.* 1548–1614) and Velasquez (1599–1660) are in Spanish.

In each case the artistic flowering accompanied or, as in Spain, immediately followed a period of heroic national struggle, effort, and achievement. It is tempting to say that ages of national expansion and excitement, times of heroism and "crusade," provide great artists with the stimulation and the receptive audiences they need. On a more mundane level, it is clear that "golden ages" depend on the existence of a class of people with enough education, wealth, and leisure to appreciate luxuries like books and paintings. The historian can record the existence of such classes and the occurrence of heroic national effort in England, Spain, and the Dutch Netherlands during these years. But he cannot account satisfactorily for Shakespeare's extraordinary appreciation of the complexities of human motivation, Cervantes' sympathy for all sorts and conditions of men, or Rembrandt's penetration of the depths of the religious soul. All these are manifestations of purely individual genius. Nor can he account for the appearance in France during a time of troubles of three writers who have profoundly influenced the French mind: Montaigne (1533–92), Descartes (1596–1650), and Pascal (1623–62). The historian can explain something about the conditions and characteristics of "golden ages." He cannot explain the appearance of genius.

Suggestions for Further Reading

Note: Asterisk denotes a book available in paperback edition.

Geographical Discovery Two brief general studies provide a good introduction to the subject: J. H. Parry, *Europe and a Wider World, 1415–1715* (1949), and C. E. Nowell, *The Great Discoveries and the First Colonial Empires** (1954). J. H. Parry gives a more detailed account in *The Age of Reconnaisance* (1963). W. C. Abbott, *The Expansion of Europe,* 2 vols. (1918), is an older but still valuable general account, including consideration of the effect of the discoveries on Europe. P. Sykes, *A History of Exploration* (1934), surveys the whole subject from ancient times on; H. H. Hart, *Sea Road to the Indies* (1950), describes the Portuguese exploits; J. B. Brebner, *The Explorers of North America, 1492–1806** (1933), and A. P. Newton, *The European Nations in the West Indies, 1493–1688* (1933), treat exploration in particular areas. E. Sanceau has written a good modern biography of Henry the Navigator (1947). S. E. Morison, *Admiral of the Ocean Sea,** 2 vols. (1942), is the best account of Columbus. A shorter discussion by Morison is *Christopher Columbus, Mariner* (1955), and he gives an excellent overall view in *The European Discovery of America* (1971). C. M. Parr, *So Noble a Captain* (1953), is a reliable account of Magellan. E. Sanceau, *The Land of Prester John* (1944), traces Portuguese interest in Abyssinia. The best correctives for older Anglo-Saxon notions of Spanish colonizing are C. H. Haring, *The Spanish Empire in America* (1947), and L. Hanke, *The Spanish Struggle for Justice in the Conquest of America* (1949). R. L. Reynolds, *Europe Emerges** (1961), is a good analysis of European expansion in general.

The Late Sixteenth Century

J. H. Elliott, *Europe Divided, 1559–1598** (1968), synthesizes the political history of this era. Volume III of the *New Cambridge Modern History* (1968) is also useful. F. Braudel, *The Mediterranean and the Mediterranean World in the Age of Philip II,** 2 vols. (1972–73), is a magisterial survey. For an introduction to the witch-craze, see H. R. Trevor-Roper, *The European Witch-Craze of the Sixteenth and Seventeenth Centuries and Other Essays** (1969). Among the best treatments of the witch-craze in specific countries are K. Thomas, *Religion and the Decline of Magic** (1971), for England; J. Caro Baroja, *The World of the Witches** (1965), for Spain; and H. C. E. Midelfort, *Witch Hunting in Southwestern Germany, 1562–1684* (1972). For a general social history of the years 1550 to 1650, see H. Kamen, *The Iron Century* (1971).

Spain

R. B. Merriman, *The Rise of the Spanish Empire in the Old World and in the New*, 4 vols. (1918–34), is a superbly written and scholarly account of Spain in Europe and overseas to the death of Philip II. J. H. Elliott, *Imperial Spain, 1469–1716** (1964), is a remarkable book. R. Trevor Davies, *The Golden Century of Spain, 1501–1621** (1937) and *Spain in Decline, 1621–1700** (1956), are well-informed, interesting, sometimes controversial accounts. J. H. Parry, *The Spanish Theory of Empire in the Sixteenth Century* (1940), studies the effect of empire on the Spanish monarchy. E. J. Hamilton, *American Treasure and the Price Revolution in Spain, 1501–1650* (1934), is the starting point for study of sixteenth-century inflation. G. Parker, *The Army of Flanders and the Spanish Road** (1972), discusses Spain's military decline, with emphasis on the actual life and problems of Spanish soldiers.

The Netherlands

The most scholarly brief account of the Dutch rebellion and its consequences is in the two books by P. Geyl, *The Revolt of the Netherlands, 1555–1609** (1932) and *The Netherlands Divided, 1609–1648* (1936). There is a beautifully written popular biography of William the Silent by C. V. Wedgwood* (1944).

Elizabethan England

There is a wealth of well-written, scholarly books on the period. J. Neale, author of three brilliant volumes on the parliamentary history of the reign, has written the best biography of Elizabeth, *Queen Elizabeth I** (1952). E. Jenkins, *Elizabeth the Great** (1959), adds insight on the purely personal side. C. Read's thorough biographies, *Mr. Secretary Walsingham*, 3 vols. (1925) and *Mr. Secretary Cecil* (Lord Burghley), 2 vols. (1955, 1960), provide intimate knowledge of the politics of the period. A. L. Rowse has written with zest on Elizabethan society in *The England of Elizabeth** (1950) and *The Expansion of Elizabethan England** (1955). J. A. Williamson, *The Age of Drake,** 3rd ed. (1952), is by a master of naval history, and G. Mattingly, *The Armada** (1959), is one of those rare books, a definitive treatment of its subject that is at the same time magnificent reading. A good brief survey is S. I. Bindoff, *Tudor England** (1959).

France

It is more difficult to find good reading in English on France than on England in the sixteenth century. L. Batiffol, *The Century of the Renaissance* (trans. 1916), is an older general account of France in the sixteenth century. J. E. Neale, *The Age of Catherine de' Medici** (1943), is very useful, as is H. Pearson, *Henry of Navarre* (1963). There is a brief modern account of the period in F. C. Palm, *Calvinism and the Religious Wars* (1932). J. W. Thompson, *The Wars of Religion in France, 1559–1576* (1909), is older but still useful. A. J. Grant, *The Huguenots* (1934), is both scholarly and brief. W. F. Church, *Constitutional Thought in Sixteenth Century France* (1941), discusses with discernment the conflict of medieval and modern ideas of government during the civil wars. Social aspects of the wars of religion are well portrayed in N. Z. Davis, *Society and Culture in Early Modern France* (1975).

19 Political and Economic Crises of the Seventeenth Century

Rembrandt van Rijn, *Syndics of the Cloth Guild* (1662).

The seventeenth century, much more than the fifteenth or sixteenth, is the century in which modern European civilization took on recognizable form. It was also a century that was afflicted by severe political, social, and economic crises, crises at least as dangerous as those that had shaken the medieval civilization of Europe in the fourteenth century. Everywhere the growing power of the state was challenged, and in the 1640s the three strongest European monarchies—Spain, France, and England—were weakened by outright rebellions. War was endemic— the last of the religious wars merged with wars to preserve the balance of power, and these in turn with the first commercial wars. The ravages of war were compounded by bad weather, famine, and plague. Population growth leveled off, and in some areas, notably Germany, population declined. There was also a prolonged economic depression, running through the middle decades of the century. The flow of silver from the New World, which had stimulated the economy, dropped off sharply, and industrial production in Europe increased only slightly, if at all. Only gradually, after 1670, did growth in commerce and industry start spiraling upward again. Meanwhile, poverty exacerbated social unrest, and inadequate revenues limited the capabilities of governments.

Yet out of this unpromising environment a new Europe emerged. Governments, businessmen, and intellectual leaders were determined not to be deprived of the gains they had made in the last two centuries. Every challenge was met, at different dates and by different means in different countries. But the net result was that Europe was richer, controlled more of the world's commerce, and had more effective governments in 1700 than in 1600. And, as an unexpected bonus, there was an intellectual revolution, a sharp change in ways of thinking about man and the universe, that did more to change the nature of human life than any of the new ideas that had emerged during the Italian Renaissance (see Chapter 21).

Although seventeenth-century statesmen and writers recognized the im-portance of economic problems more clearly than had their predecessors, they still felt that political problems deserved primary consideration. They wanted to complete the process that had begun in the thirteenth century, the building of a sovereign territorial state. This process had been interrupted by the troubles of the fourteenth century and the religious conflicts of the sixteenth century; now it was to be pushed to a conclusion. From a theoretical point of view, this meant defining the concept of sovereignty ever more clearly. From a practical point of view, it meant concentrating supreme power in some organ of the state, either in the monarchy (as in France and most other states) or in the representative assembly (as in England).

FRANCE: IN SEARCH OF ORDER AND AUTHORITY 1598–1661

Seventeenth-century France still felt the effects of the anarchy and violence that had prevailed for almost half a century before the Edict of Nantes in 1598. Three weakling kings had tarnished the prestige of the monarchy, and the great nobles had become powerful and unruly. Merchants and manufacturers had been hard hit by the wars, and the peasants had suffered heavily from the ravages of undisciplined soldiers. The mass of the people were weary of disorder, eager for security, but still somewhat suspicious of any authority that might violate local privileges and increase the burden of taxation.

Jean Bodin, the most penetrating political thinker of the tragic years just past, had seen what was needed. In his book *The Republic*, which he published in 1576, Bodin argued that in any well-ordered state, supreme power or sovereignty must be clearly lodged somewhere in some organ of the state, preferably the monarchy. Sovereignty he defined as the power of "giving laws to the people as a whole without their consent." Bodin did not think of this power as arbitrary or capricious: the sovereign was still subject to the laws of God and of nature. But he insisted that sovereign power must not

Triumphal Entry of Henry IV into Paris,
large sketch by Peter Paul Rubens (*ca.* 1630).

Jean Bodin on Sovereignty

Jean Bodin was a sixteenth-century French lawyer who was interested in political and economic problems. The *fact* of sovereignty had been recognized for some time, but Bodin was the first writer to express the *idea* in clear and uncompromising terms.

Sovereignty is supreme power over citizens and subjects unrestrained by laws. . . . A prince is bound by no law of his predecessor, and much less by his own laws. . . . He may repeal, modify, or replace a law made by himself and without the consent of his subjects. . . . The opinion of those who have written that the king is bound by the popular will must be disregarded; such doctrine furnishes seditious men with material for revolutionary plots. No reasonable ground can be found to claim that subjects should control princes or that power should be attributed to popular assemblies. . . . The highest privilege of sovereignty consists in giving laws to the people as a whole without their consent. . . . Under this supreme power of making and repealing laws it is clear that all other functions of sovereignty are included.

From Jean Bodin, *Six Books Concerning the Republic,* from the Latin version of 1586 [the French version of 1576 is less coherent], trans. by F. W. Coker, in *Readings in Political Philosophy* (New York: Macmillan, 1938), pp. 374, 375, 376, 377, 380.

be limited by any human agency—that is, it must be "absolute" to be effective. He insisted that it could not be divided—for instance, among king, Estates General, and *parlements*. It must be recognized as legitimately residing in one person or one political institution. No one had defined sovereignty so clearly before or argued so persuasively for it as the only remedy for insecurity and civil war. Bodin's prescription for France's ills was fulfilled in the French absolute monarchy that became the model and envy of most of Europe.

Henry IV and Sully

The first steps toward restoring the power of the monarchy and the prosperity of the land were taken by Henry IV and his minister, Sully. Henry, first of the Bourbon dynasty, was a popular king—courageous, vigorous, humorous, tolerant, and sound in his judgment of men. But he spent much of his time in hunting and lovemaking and left the routine business of government to Sully and others. Sully was a puritanical Huguenot with a keen sense of economy and a hatred of dishonesty. He improved the financial condition of the monarchy, partly by avoiding expensive wars and partly by patching up the tax-collecting system. The French taxation system was inefficient, corrupt, and inequitable. Many taxes were "farmed"—that is, the right to collect them was granted to private collectors who paid the government a fixed sum and then collected all they could. The burden fell most heavily on the peasants, since the nobles and the upper bourgeoisie were exempt from major taxes. Sully could do nothing to make the system more just (nor could any French minister down to the Revolution), but he could make it work better by discharging dishonest and inefficient tax farmers. (It has been estimated that as a rule hardly half the taxes collected in France at this time reached the treasury.) Moreover, the reestablishment of internal peace and order, which allowed agriculture and commerce to recover, helped to increase the government's revenues, especially from customs duties. When Henry IV was assassinated by a Catholic fanatic in 1610 there was a sizable surplus in the treasury.

The Estates General of 1614

Within a few years the work of Henry and Sully was in ruins. Under the regency of Henry's widow, Marie de' Medici, the treasury surplus was sopped up by rapacious courtiers, and Spain began once more to intervene in French affairs, sometimes in a strange alliance with the Huguenots. In 1614 the Estates General were summoned to one of their rare meetings, but the deliberations soon turned into a struggle between the First and Second Estates (the clergy and the nobility) and the Third Estate (the bourgeoisie, who were represented largely by provincial royal officers). No group was willing to take responsibility; and no group had the power to demand reform. The assembly dissolved with a strong declaration that "the king is sovereign in France, and holds his crown

from God only." It was not to meet again until 1789, on the eve of the Revolution.

Richelieu

In 1614 Henry IV's son, Louis XIII, was only fourteen years old. He was soon to be married to Anne of Austria, daughter of Philip III of Spain, as a symbol of Habsburg influence on France. There was not much to be hoped for from the monarch himself—except that he might choose and support some able first minister. The man was already in sight—a brilliant young bishop named Richelieu—but it took him several years to become a cardinal (in 1622) and head of the king's council (in 1624). From 1624 to his death in 1642 Richelieu was the real ruler of France. Richelieu, rather than any member of the Bourbon dynasty, founded absolute monarchy in France.

There is no mystery about Richelieu, as there is about many other great figures in history. He had the clearest and most penetrating mind of any statesman of his generation. And he made his purpose perfectly plain: to enhance the power and prestige of the French monarchy beyond any possibility of challenge. He came to his task with a marvelous grasp of political and diplomatic possibilities, an infal-

Three studies of Richelieu by Philippe de Champaigne.

lible memory, and an inflexible will unhampered by moral scruples. Richelieu admired Machiavelli's writings, and the heart of his political creed was *raison d'état*—the doctrine that the good of the state is the supreme good, and that any means may be used to attain it. He would coolly send an innocent man to his death in order to frighten other troublemakers, enhance the authority of the monarchy, and so save bloodshed in the end. "In judging crimes against the state," he argued, "it is essential to banish pity." He was not irreligious, but the workings of his mind were overwhelmingly thisworldly. "Man is immortal; his salvation is hereafter," he once argued against some conscientious scruples of the king, but "the state has no immortality, its salvation is now or never." While his cardinal's robes helped protect him against assassination, his policy was that of an astute secular statesman who put public order before religious zeal. His reputation for diabolical cleverness went even beyond the reality and helped him to bewilder his enemies and gain his ends.

Richelieu had three concrete objectives that had to be carried out more or less simultaneously. First, he meant to break the political and military power of the Huguenots. Second, he meant to crush the political influence of the great nobles. And finally, he meant to destroy the power of the Habsburgs to intervene in French internal affairs.

The Edict of Nantes had allowed the Huguenots to garrison about two hundred towns, the chief of which was La Rochelle on the west coast. Richelieu persuaded Louis XIII that he would never be master in his own house until he had wiped out this "empire within an empire." Rumors that the government had decided to attack provoked the Huguenots to rebel, and Richelieu proceeded to besiege and capture La Rochelle. At the

Peace of Alais in 1629, which settled the dispute, Richelieu was unexpectedly generous in his terms. He had no respect whatever for what he contemptuously called "the allegedly Reformed religion," but he allowed the Huguenots the right to worship as they pleased once he had attained his primary objective of eliminating their political and military autonomy. He did not wish to alienate Protestants abroad who could help him in a war with Spain and Austria, and he hoped he could make loyal and useful citizens out of the Huguenots. In this he was successful. The Huguenots served the crown in the war that followed against the Habsburgs and loyally supported the monarchy in the crisis of the Fronde.

Richelieu's attack on the political power of the nobility was less successful than his attack on the Huguenots, but it was just as determined. Until the very end of his career, he was constantly threatened by aristocratic intrigues. In response to this threat, he developed a network of spies, set up a special tribunal to try noble lawbreakers, and sternly forbade dueling, a privilege that marked the freedom of the aristocracy from ordinary restraints. He gradually weakened the power of the great nobles who were provincial governors and gave more local administrative responsibilities to direct representatives of the crown. These representatives, called *intendants*, were usually drawn from the *noblesse de la robe*, ennobled officeholders of middle-class ancestry. They were therefore more dependent on the monarchy than the older nobility. Richelieu did nothing to lessen the economic or social privileges of the French nobility, but he did curtail its political power.

Richelieu was no financier, nor did he have any interest in bettering the condition of the common people. He spent large sums on rebuilding the armed forces and even more in actual warfare against Spain. He left the government's finances and the nation's peasants in worse condition than he had found them. But through his subtle diplomacy and his well-timed intervention in the Thirty Years' War (discussed below), he made France, instead of Spain, the leading European power.

Mazarin and the Fronde

Richelieu's death in 1642 (Louis XIII died a few months later, in 1643) put his work to a severe test. Louis XIV was a child of five when his father died, and so his mother, Anne of Austria, was appointed regent. However, she left the business of government to the man whom Richelieu had picked and trained to succeed himself, an Italian cardinal named Mazarin. Mazarin had the subtlety and political skill of his master but not his inflexible will; he was both more adaptable and, as a foreigner, less popular than Richelieu. His two main objec-

tives were to continue the war against Spain until the Habsburgs were defeated and to maintain the prestige of the monarchy at the level to which Richelieu had raised it. The nobility hated him as a foreign upstart, however, and the bourgeoisie hated him for the high taxes he imposed to carry on the war. The result was the last serious rebellion to take place against the monarchy until the French Revolution—a complicated and uncoordinated movement of resistance known as the Fronde (1648–52).

The word *Fronde* referred to a game of slinging clods at passing coaches, which was played by the more unruly children of Paris. The rebellion was like the game; it was annoying, but in the end it did not keep the monarchy from driving along the road to absolutism. The leaders did not want to destroy the French monarchy nor did they wish to upset the established social order. They were composed of several groups—the judges of the High Courts and the chief financial officers, who were practically hereditary bureau-

Outbursts during the Fronde in Paris (1648).

crats, and the nobles led by princes of the blood. Each group wanted to modify the structure of government so that it could have more influence. But no group could agree with others on a joint program, with the exception of the purely negative policy of exiling Mazarin. Thus the *parlements*, which began the struggle, stood for the privileges of the corporations of bureaucrats who controlled the courts and the financial bureaus. They wanted the king to rule with their advice, rather than with that of councilors whom he could make or break as it pleased him. They insisted especially that no tax could be imposed without their consent. The nobles, who joined the rebellion later, had no intention of letting the *parlements* become dominant in government; they wanted to get rid of the *intendants* and regain their old powers as provincial governors. In the provinces, many men rebelled to protect or enlarge local privileges, but they often found it hard to decide whether they should support a *parlement* or a noble governor.

The result might have been different if anyone had dared draw on the deep-seated resentment of the lower classes—a resentment that had been expressed during the first half of the century in many local riots against taxation and misgovernment. But while a few theorists talked of liberty and democracy, no one was willing to take the chance of unleashing forces that might not be controllable. Unlike the contemporary English rebellion, in which the middle and lower classes accepted radical doctrines and defeated the king (see p. 426), the Fronde remained dominated by the nobility and the upper bourgeoisie. Each group approached the brink of making unlimited war on the king even at the risk of social revolution, and each drew back in horror. This innate conservatism, combined with lack of unity among the leaders, led to the disintegration of the rebellion. There was very little hard fighting; by the end of 1652, Mazarin, who had had to flee the country, was once more back in the saddle. Most Frenchmen concluded that a strong monarchy was preferable to futile civil war. The young king, Louis XIV, was to profit from this reaction when he came of age. Meanwhile, he remembered with

loathing the violence and instability of the Fronde. He came to hate Paris, from which he had had to flee in 1648, to despise the mob, and to fear the nobles unless they were restrained by a firm royal hand.

In spite of the Fronde and the tax burden that continued to oppress the common people, Mazarin carried on the war with Spain until the Spaniards were forced to ask for terms in 1659. France gained two Pyrenees counties, and Maria Theresa, daughter of Philip IV of Spain, was married to Louis XIV. Both the treaty and the marriage symbolized the humiliation of Spain and the triumph of France as the leading power in Europe. Mazarin died in 1661, and Louis XIV announced to his ministers that he would henceforth be his own prime minister. Now the work of Richelieu had come to full fruition. The French monarchy no longer had anything to fear from Huguenots and nobles at home or from Habsburgs abroad. It was an absolute monarchy, endowed with a fuller sovereignty than any other yet seen in European history.

ENGLAND: IN SEARCH OF CIVIL AND RELIGIOUS LIBERTY, 1603–60

While Richelieu and Mazarin were laying the foundations of absolute monarchy by divine right, leaders in England were slowly developing a constitutional, parliamentary monarchy. Richelieu could see clearly where he was going, but the goal was never clear to English leaders during their century of conflict with the crown. Englishmen groped their way toward a conception of sovereignty as something rooted in law rather than in personal authority, something to be lodged in the hands of an assembly that represented the community, or at least its more wealthy and influential members. England was not alone in its resistance to absolute monarchy, but the result in other countries, such as Poland, was anarchy and confusion. Only in England was a representative assembly able to increase its power without wrecking the state. When Queen Anne came to the throne in 1702 the English government was both a stronger and a more popular government than it had been in 1603 when James I succeeded Elizabeth I. The example of England, particularly as reflected in the writings of John Locke, was to have an enormous influence on western history throughout the following two centuries.

England, on the periphery of European civilization, had always been peculiar in its political development. For instance, although the strong monarchy of the Tudors (1485–1603) was part of a general European trend, the survival and strengthening of Parliament under such a monarchy was without parallel elsewhere. The Tudors continued to use Parliament in legislation and taxation, whereas rulers on the Continent found representative assemblies either useless or obstructive. Parliament, particularly the House of Commons, slowly acquired a corporate feeling and a sense of being an integral part of the national government. The House of Commons, it will be remembered, represented both the mercantile classes in the towns and the landed gentry (knights and squires) in the country. The gentry had been increasing in numbers, wealth, and political influence since the dissolution of the monasteries. They governed England at the local level as justices of the peace (the English monarchy had no paid bureaucrats like the French *intendants*), and they dominated the lower house of Parliament by sitting as representatives not only of the counties but of many boroughs as well. In any other country they would have been considered members of the lesser nobility; in England they sat in the House of Commons with merchants and lawyers. This House had grown steadily in wealth and influence, until one member could boast in 1628 that the lower house could afford to buy the House of Lords three times over.

Thus the English Parliament in the early seventeenth century represented all the politically active classes of the nation in a way no other representative assembly in Europe did. There were no provincial estates or privileges in England as there were in France, and the class lines among peers, gentry, and wealthy burgesses were not so sharply drawn. The rigid English rule of primogeniture meant that younger sons of the nobility, who were commoners, often went into the professions. On the other hand, English merchants were continually buying land and becoming gentry. This meant that if the monarch should ever fall out with Parliament—and with the social groups it represented—he would not be able to play class against class or district against district.

The Tudors

Queen Elizabeth had had arguments with her Parliaments, but the threat from abroad and the political good sense of both the queen and the opposition kept these arguments from becoming dangerous. It was generally recognized that only Parliament could make a law or impose a tax. It was also recognized that making policy, especially foreign policy, lay outside the competence of Parliament and within the sphere of what was called the royal prerogative.

The Tudors felt, however, that it was sometimes wise to confirm royal policy

Formal meeting of Parliament in 1625. The Lords are seated; the Commons stand outside the bar.

by parliamentary statute, particularly in the delicate field of religion. Henry VIII used Parliament to break with Rome; Mary had asked Parliament to restore England to the Roman obedience by statute; and Elizabeth had broken with the pope once more by statute. Elizabeth's Parliaments tried more than once to reform the Anglican Church in a Puritan direction and to nudge the queen on foreign policy—presumptuous acts for which Elizabeth scolded them sharply. But she was too popular for Parliament ever to make a real issue of the conflict and too astute ever to demand a clear definition of her prerogative. Tudor "despotism" was a popular despotism, and Tudor rulers found that they could exercise their sovereign power most effectively by seeking the cooperation of Parliament.

James I and Parliament

James I, by D. Mytens (1621).

The Stuarts, who ruled from 1603 to 1714, either could not or would not cooperate with Parliament. James I (king of Scotland and of England, 1603–25), the son of Mary Queen of Scots, was a well-meaning but pedantic intellectual who never understood the social structure or the political realities of the kingdom he inherited from Elizabeth. He had been raised as a Protestant by the regents who ran Scotland after his mother's exile, but he had not greatly enjoyed his Presbyterian upbringing. His aims were praiseworthy—peace with Spain, toleration of the Catholic minority in England, union of England and Scotland, and a strong but benevolent monarchy—but he did not inspire confidence as a political leader. Moreover, many of his ministers were incompetent. Unlike Elizabeth, who often concealed her imperious will in cloudy and ambiguous language, James liked to have things dangerously clear. He had written a book, *The True Law of*

Free Monarchies, in which he insisted that kings owed their position to God alone, were responsible only to God, and in fact were themselves like gods on earth.

His belief in a monarchy "free" of restraints, free to do as it pleased for the common good, did not appeal to the classes represented in Parliament. Some of James's policies might have really helped the poor; others simply transferred wealth from one privileged group to another. In either case, opposition to the king could not endanger the country. The Tudors had long ago ended the threat of aristocratic violence, and peace with Spain in 1604 removed the danger of foreign conquest. Only their own king could now attack the beliefs or interfere with the property rights of the privileged classes. Parliament, fearing royal tyranny, began to criticize James's acts. James, fearing parliamentary intervention in policy matters, began to scold Parliament. The delicate Tudor balance was destroyed.

Friction rapidly developed over three related issues: religion, finance, and foreign policy. The Puritans and their sympathizers in the House of Commons wished to "purify" the Anglican Church of everything that savored of Catholic practice, from "popish" ritual to the authority of bishops. James was convinced that the Presbyterian system of church government, which he had known in his youth in Scotland, would not only destroy royal control of the church, but would threaten the monarchy itself. "No bishop, no king," he remarked within a year of his arrival in England. Parliament, annoyed by the extravagance of James's court and dubious about his policies, denied him enough money to meet the rising costs of government. James replied by raising money without parliamentary approval—for example, by increasing the customs duties on his own authority. When his right to take such actions was contested, the courts ruled in his favor—probably correctly, since the king controlled foreign trade as part of his control of foreign policy. But the seeming subservience of the courts to the royal will further disturbed Parliament.

Meanwhile James was following a foreign policy that exasperated the Puritan majority in Parliament. He was too friendly with Spain for the Puritan taste, he did little to defend Protestants abroad against the rising tide of Catholicism, and he tried in vain to marry his son Charles to the Spanish Infanta. When James chided the House of Commons in 1621 for even discussing his foreign policy, the House bristled and passed a unanimous Protestation defending its right to discuss "the arduous and urgent affairs concerning the King, State, and defence of the realm, and of the Church of England." This was revolutionary talk. James tore the resolution from the Commons' *Journal*, but he could not undo what had been done. The House of Commons, which Queen Elizabeth had kept under the control of her privy councilors, was now taking the initiative under leaders of its own. An aggressive and powerful element among James's subjects was demanding a voice in politics that he was utterly unwilling to grant.

Charles I
and the English Revolution

The situation rapidly worsened during the early years of the reign of Charles I, who came to the throne in 1625. Charles tried to please Parliament by attacking Catholic countries, but his incompetent favorite, the Duke of Buckingham, failed to capture Cadiz in Spain or to relieve the French Huguenots at La Rochelle. Parliament had urged war but had not granted adequate taxes, so the government tried to pay for the wars by levying a forced loan and by imprisoning those who objected to paying. Parliament in 1628 drew up a formal protest in the form of a Petition of Right, which they finally compelled Charles to approve. Its two main provisions were that no one should henceforth be compelled to pay any tax or loan "without common consent by Act of Parliament," and that

no one should be imprisoned without cause shown.

By the next year the House of Commons was roused to fury by Charles's assertions of his full control of Church and state. It declared that anyone who introduced anything savoring of Catholic practices in the Anglican Church was "a capital enemy to this kingdom and commonwealth," and that anyone who advised or submitted to the levying of taxes without parliamentary consent was "a betrayer of the liberties of England." The issue of "sovereignty" had finally been raised, and the word itself was being debated by lawyers and parliamentary orators. Where did the supreme power in England lie—in the king or in Parliament? The old answer, that it lay in the "king-in-Parliament," would no longer do. The royal prerogative and "the liberties of England" were not reconcilable any longer.

Charles I now took things into his own hands and ruled without Parliament for eleven years (1629–40). He was less intelligent and more stubborn than his father. James had always yielded before conflict became irreconcilable. Rather than yield, Charles was to resort to duplicity and falsehood in the crises ahead of him, and as a result he ended his life on the block, trusted by almost no one. Trying to duplicate Richelieu's brilliant work across the Channel, he chose tough-minded advisers: Thomas Wentworth, Earl of Strafford, in political affairs, and William Laud, Archbishop of Canterbury, in ecclesiastical affairs. With them and others, Charles devised new methods of nonparliamentary taxation that provided enough money to run the government so long as it stayed out of war. Laud began a movement back toward more ritual and formality in the Anglican service, a movement the Puritans regarded as an attempt to restore Catholicism. All opposition, whether to arbitrary taxation or to innovations in worship, was sternly suppressed by the courts. Everything went well until Laud tried to force the Anglican Book of Common Prayer on stubbornly Presbyterian Scotland. Before long an angry and well-led Scottish army was encamped in northern England. Charles and Strafford,

Charles I, by D. Mytens (1631).

ENGLAND DURING
THE ENGLISH REVOLUTION 1642–49

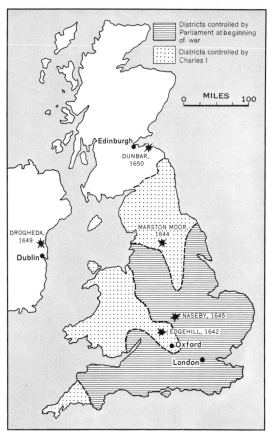

Districts controlled by Parliament at beginning of war

Districts controlled by Charles I

MILES 100

Edinburgh
DUNBAR, 1650
DROGHEDA, 1649
Dublin
MARSTON MOOR, 1644
NASEBY, 1645
EDGEHILL, 1642
Oxford
London

The Dutch view of Cromwell (detail from a print dated April 30, 1653).

ally unanimous. But when the more radical Puritans in Parliament went on to abolish bishops in the Anglican Church and to seek control of the army, a party began to form around Charles in opposition to the parliamentary majority. And thus a civil war broke out in 1642 and lasted until 1649.

Enough has been said to suggest that the English Revolution was primarily a war of ideas, not of classes or of districts or even of interests, although the interests of merchants and gentry who were outraged by nonparliamentary taxation were certainly involved. Generally the towns, the middle class, and the economically advanced southeastern counties of England supported Parliament, while many rural areas, aristocrats, and the backward northwest supported Charles. But nobles, squires, and artisans from all parts of England were to be found on both sides. Unlike the Fronde, in which narrow interest groups failed to work out programs with broad appeal, the English Revolution offered a real alternative to the established order: parliamentary monarchy instead of benevolent absolutism, and a Presbyterian Church governed by elected "presbyters," or elders, instead of an Anglican Church governed by bishops appointed by the crown. Unlike the Fronde again, the English Revolution was able to attract and to accept men with really radical ideas—men who wanted neither a monarchy, nor an established church, nor power in the hands of landlords.

As the civil war intensified, Parliament proved to be more successful than the king in raising money and in building a strong army. A brilliant cavalry officer named Oliver Cromwell formed a "New Model Army" largely from among his fellow Independents, or Congregationalists. These Independents were generally of lower economic status than either Anglicans or Presbyterians. They were unsophisticated, Bible-reading Puritans of strict morals who believed in independent congregations democratically organized, with little or no national organization. Cromwell and his army finally defeated the king's forces in 1645, only to fall out with the Presbyterians, who had dominated Parliament since the Angli-

finding themselves unable to raise an army to fight the Scots, had to summon Parliament to get the money to buy them off.

The Long Parliament, which met in November 1640 and was not dissolved until 1653, became a workshop of revolution. It sent Strafford and Laud to the block. It passed an act stating that a Parliament must be summoned at least every three years. It outlawed all nonparliamentary taxation and abolished the special royal courts (the Court of Star Chamber, which dealt with opposition to the government, and the Court of High Commission, for ecclesiastical affairs), which had been the chief instruments of the "Eleven Years' Tyranny." In other words, in less than a year (1640–41) Parliament had made absolute monarchy impossible in England. This much of its work won unwilling approval from Charles, since sentiment for it was virtu-

cans withdrew in 1642 to join Charles. With Parliament and the army at loggerheads about what to do with the king and about what sort of government to set up in England (many in the army wanted a truly democratic regime), the king was able to escape and make one last bid for victory before being finally defeated by Cromwell in 1648. Cromwell and the Independents in the army were determined now to get at what they considered the root of the trouble. They "purged" Parliament of its Presbyterian members, executed King Charles I in 1649, abolished monarchy and the House of Lords, and set up a republic, or "Commonwealth," with the "rump" of the Long Parliament as its government and Cromwell as its moving spirit.

Cromwell

Cromwell proved to be a revolutionary leader unlike almost any other in western history. He was a deeply religious man who tried in vain to avoid becoming a dictator. Yet he was ruthless and determined when he felt his policies were threatened. He massacred the Catholic Irish when they rebelled, defeated the Scots when they intervened in favor of the son of Charles I, fought a commercial war with the Dutch from 1652 to 1654, and boldly dissolved what was left of the Long Parliament in 1653. In a few short years he had decisively won a civil war, united the British Isles under one government for the first time, made England again the terror of the seas, and apparently wiped the slate clean for any political experiment he wished to try. The rest of his career until his death in 1658, however, was a tragic search for answers to insoluble problems: how to guarantee religious toleration to all kinds of Protestants except determined Anglicans, and at the same time how to develop some constitutional basis for his government. Cromwell tried to rule through a written constitution (the first in the history of any major state) and with the assent of a Parliament. He took the title of Lord Protector instead of king, but he quarreled with his Parliaments as bitterly as the Stuarts had quarreled with theirs. At one point Cromwell had to set

up an open military dictatorship to keep his Parliament from disbanding his army and persecuting his coreligionists. The plain fact was that most Englishmen were not ready for religious toleration, especially toleration of the radical religious minorities that made up a large part of Cromwell's army.

Furthermore, it became more and more evident that it was impossible in England to break utterly with history and to set up a new sort of government simply by writing a constitution. There was already a "constitution" deeply ingrained in the English political tradition, although it was nowhere written down. Soon after Cromwell's death even his own supporters saw that the only possible alternative to military dictatorship was Parliament, and that the only way to restore Parlia-

Oliver Cromwell, painting from the original panel by Samuel Cooper.

Democratic Ideas in the English Revolution

After it was sure of victory, the Parliamentary army began to worry about a proper government for England. A Council of the Army, including representatives of the ordinary soldiers, held a series of debates at Putney in 1647 on a constitution for the country. One of the basic issues was whether all men should be allowed to vote.

Major Rainborough: I think that the poorest he that is in England hath a life to live, as the greatest he, and therefore truly, sir, I think it's clear, that every man that is to live under a government ought first by his own consent to put himself under that government, and I do think that the poorest man in England is not at all bound in a strict sense to that government that he hath not had a voice to put himself under.

General Ireton [Cromwell's son-in-law]: Government is to preserve property. . . . The objection does not lie in the making of the representation more equal but in the introducing of men . . . in this government who have no property in this kingdom. . . .

Sexby [a representative of the soldiers]: I see that though liberty were our end, there is a degeneration from it. We have ventured our lives to recover our birthrights and privileges as Englishmen, and by the arguments urged there is none. There are many thousands of us soldiers that have ventured our lives; we have had little property . . . yet we have had a birthright. But it seems now, except a man hath a fixed estate in this kingdom, he hath no right in this kingdom. I wonder we were so much deceived.

From *Puritanism and Liberty,* ed. by A. S. P. Woodhouse (Chicago: University of Chicago Press, 1951), pp. 53, 62, 69.

The restoration of King Charles II: the crowning in Westminster Abbey (from a contemporary print).

ment was also to restore the monarchy. In 1660 the monarchy, Parliament, and the Anglican Church were all restored when a "Convention Parliament" invited Charles II to return from France and take up the crown.

The Restoration

At first glance nothing more remained in England after twenty years of civil war and revolutionary experiment than had remained in France after the defeat of the Fronde. To this day Englishmen refer to the events just described as the "Puritan Rebellion." They do not call it a revolution because it was succeeded by the "Restoration." But one thing at least had been decided: there was to be no absolute monarchy in England. All acts of the Long Parliament passed before the outbreak of civil war were still valid, and these acts put severe limitations on royal power, even if the balance of power between king and Parliament was still un-

certain. Strafford and Laud had tried to do for Charles I what Richelieu and Mazarin had done for Louis XIV, but all three Englishmen died on the block, while all three Frenchmen died in their beds. The turmoil of the first half of the seventeenth century left most Englishmen with certain half-expressed convictions whose effects can be traced in English history for generations. Among these convictions were a fear of allowing any one individual to acquire too much political power, a deepened respect for government by law rather than by personal command, a reverence for Parliament as the defender of individual rights against arbitrary despotism, and a distaste for standing armies.

The early seventeenth century was a brilliant age in the history of English literature, including Shakespeare's mature work, the Authorized, or King James, Version of the Bible (1611), and Milton's formative years. It was also a brilliant period in political thinking, as statesmen and pamphleteers argued for royalist, parliamentary, or radical principles of government.

Perhaps Thomas Hobbes's *Leviathan* (1651) best represented the political insights and fears, if not the greatest hopes, of these turbulent years. Writing in the midst of civil war, Hobbes pictured the life of man without government as "solitary, poor, nasty, brutish, and short." Without some authority to enforce law, there is no society, no order, only "a war of every man against every man." Men in general are inclined to "a perpetual and restless desire of power after power." So they set up a sovereign power by agreement or contract (it makes no difference whether the sovereign is a king or a Parliament), by which all men agree to obey the sovereign, but only so long as he is able to maintain order. The sovereign is not bound by anything in the contract. No clearer argument for might as the necessary basis of all right had ever been written. Hobbes took Bodin's argument for a legitimate sovereign authority and subtly transformed it into justification of sheer arbitrary power. His book could be used equally well to support Charles I or Cromwell. In a sense the main effort of Englishmen during the seventeenth century was to find some way to refute Hobbes—to subject political power to the restraint of law and to increase its responsibility to the governed. They finally succeeded in 1688.

GERMANY: DISINTEGRATION AND DISASTER, 1618–48

While France was building the strongest monarchy in Europe and England was undergoing a constitutional crisis from which it was to emerge with new strength, the German-speaking peoples were caught up in one of the most futile and destructive wars in the history of Europe. The Thirty Years' War (1618–48) was really four successive wars that began in Bohemia, spread to the rest of the Empire, and finally involved most of the major powers on the Continent. It was a savage and demoralizing conflict that left "Germany" poorer and weaker than the western European states.

The Causes of the Thirty Years' War

The war sprang out of a complicated mixture of religious and political grievances. Lutherans and Catholics had not fought each other since the Peace of Augsburg (1555), but the Catholics were disturbed by the fact that, in spite of the provisions of the peace, most of the Catholic bishoprics in northern Germany had fallen into Lutheran or secular hands. This gave some grounds for creating an ultra-Catholic movement headed by the Jesuits and the German Catholic princes, particularly Maximilian, Duke of Bavaria. The spread of Calvinism introduced a new source of friction because

Title page of Thomas Hobbes's *Leviathan,* a good landmark in the making of the modern state. Hobbes calls the sovereign power of the state, usually conferred on one man, "that great Leviathan, or rather (to speak more reverently) that mortal God, to which we owe under the Immortal God, our peace and defence."

Calvinists had been excluded from the Peace of Augsburg. When Maximilian roughly disciplined the Protestant town of Donauwörth, Frederick V, the Calvinist ruler of the Palatinate, a small state on the middle Rhine, took the lead in forming a Protestant Union among the German princes and cities in 1608. In reply, a Catholic League was organized the next year under the leadership of Maximilian. By 1609 two illegal military alliances faced each other within the Empire, each afraid of the other and each determined to keep the rival religion from making any further gains.

Revolt in Bohemia

As these examples show, each component of the Empire was a virtually independent state. The Habsburgs, who held the imperial title, realized that the only way to rebuild and expand imperial authority was to establish firmer control over what had been their old family domains—Austria, Bohemia, and Hungary. Thus the Austrian Habsburg, Ferdinand of Styria, got himself elected king of Bohemia in 1617.

Bohemia was a flourishing kingdom in which two nationalities (Germans and Czechs) and several religions (Catholicism, Lutheranism, Calvinism, and remnants of the Hussite movement of two centuries earlier) lived fairly peaceably together under earlier Habsburg promises of toleration. Ferdinand, a zealous Catholic, began systematically to undermine this toleration and to re-Catholicize the country. This action provoked rebellion by the Bohemian Estates, which were dominated by a strong Protestant majority. In May 1618 two of Ferdinand's councilors were tossed from a castle

window in Prague, and civil war broke out between the Habsburg ruler and the Estates. The Estates raised an army, deposed Ferdinand, and offered the crown of Bohemia to Frederick V of the Palatinate. When Frederick unwisely accepted, the Protestant Union became involved in defending the Bohemian Estates, while Maximilian of Bavaria brought the Catholic League to the support of Ferdinand. In 1619 Ferdinand was elected emperor. Thus a war that might have remained a local affair soon spread throughout the Empire.

The Bohemian phase of the war was soon ended. The forces of the emperor and the League won an overwhelming victory in 1620. Frederick fled, and the emperor proceeded to work his will on the prostrate Bohemians. Half the property in the country changed hands through confiscation. The Jesuits, with strong secular backing, set out to reconvert the country to Catholicism, and within ten years they had succeeded. The prosperity of the country was ruined, Protestantism was stamped out or driven underground, and Czech nationalism was crushed for two centuries to come. The Habsburgs and their Catholic allies had won the first round decisively.

Danish Intervention

The fall of Bohemia terrified German Protestants and elated the Catholics. The Spanish Habsburgs came to the aid of their fellow Catholics, and the armies of the League were everywhere triumphant. In spite of the common danger, the Protestants could not unite. The Lutherans had been more afraid of a Calvinist victory in Bohemia than of an imperial triumph, and so Lutheran Saxony had ac-

Soldiers and siege artillery of the Thirty Years' War (copper engraving by Merian in ''Theatrum Europeam'').

tually helped Ferdinand put down the revolt. Although Frederick V was the son-in-law of James I, Protestant England gave no help because James and Charles were too involved in difficulties at home.

In 1625 the Protestant king of Denmark intervened, partly to save the cause of his coreligionists but primarily to pick up some territory in northern Germany. Within a year he was beaten in battle by a large army raised by the most inscrutable figure of the war, a wealthy war profiteer and professional soldier named Wallenstein, who had offered the emperor his services. Wallenstein had no serious religious convictions, and his political aims have puzzled generations of historians. His immediate aim seems to have been to build an imperial Habsburg military machine of such strength that it could not only eliminate all Protestant opposition but could operate independently of all other forces in the Empire, including the Catholic League. Before long Wallenstein and the League were as much at loggerheads on one side as Calvinists and Lutherans were on the other. Religion slowly receded in significance as the war became a struggle for the hegemony of Europe.

The high-water mark of Habsburg triumph and Catholic recovery was reached in 1629. Denmark withdrew from the war, leaving Wallenstein's army supreme. The Catholic League and Jesuit advisers persuaded Ferdinand to issue the Edict of Restitution, which restored to Catholic hands all ecclesiastical lands lost to Protestantism since 1552. It was evident that this edict could not be carried out without more bloodshed, because it meant that Catholic bishops were to be restored throughout northern Germany. Such an act would destroy the rough balance between Catholicism and Protestantism in Germany and weaken the northern states for the benefit of Austria and Bavaria. This threat finally roused the Lutherans inside and outside Germany to a sense of their peril.

Swedish Intervention: Gustavus Adolphus

In 1631 growing Habsburg power was blocked by the intervention of Sweden, a country that had not appeared before on the stage of international politics. Gustavus II (Gustavus Adolphus) was the ablest ruler of his generation. His country was sparse in population and resources, but he had cultivated its iron and timber industries, united the nation behind him, and built the best army of the day. It was not large, but it was well

The siege of Magdeburg in 1631 by Habsburg and Catholic forces. This siege resulted in one of the bloodiest massacres of the Thirty Years' War.

The Sack of Magdeburg   1631

Then was there naught but beating and burning, plundering, torture, and murder. Most especially was every one of the enemy bent on securing much booty. When a marauding party entered a house, if its master had anything to give he might thereby purchase respite and protection for himself and his family till the next man, who also wanted something, should come along. It was only when everything had been brought forth and there was nothing left to give that the real trouble commenced. Then, what with blows and threats of shooting, stabbing, and hanging, the poor people were so terrified that if they had had anything left they would have brought it forth if it had been buried in the earth or hidden away in a thousand castles. In this frenzied rage, the great and splendid city that had stood like a fair princess in the land was now, in its hour of direst need and unutterable distress and woe, given over to the flames, and thousands of innocent men, women, and children, in the midst of a horrible din of heartrending shrieks and cries, were tortured and put to death in so cruel and shameful a manner that no words would suffice to describe, nor no tears to bewail it.

From Otto von Guericke, in *Readings in European History*, ed. by James Harvey Robinson (Boston: Ginn, 1906), Vol. II, pp. 211–12.

equipped (with the first uniforms and an improved musket), well disciplined, and inspired by high morale. Gustavus had already come close to making the Baltic a Swedish lake in wars with Denmark and Poland. He now stepped into the fray as the sincere champion of Lutheranism, hoping apparently to set up a federation of Protestant states in Germany under Swedish leadership.

Gustavus arrived too late to save Magdeburg from a terrible sack by the Habsburg Imperialists in May 1631, but in the fall of 1631 he overwhelmed the Imperialist armies at Breitenfeld in Saxony. He then marched triumphantly to the Rhine. Wallenstein, whom the emperor had dismissed under pressure from the Catholic League, was recalled, only to be beaten by Gustavus at Lützen in 1632. Gustavus himself was killed in the battle, however, and by 1634 his army had finally been outnumbered and beaten. Wallenstein had been murdered by one of his staff, and another phase of the war had come to an end. Swedish intervention had saved German Protestantism but had not gained a decision. The most powerful state of all had been watching the course of events closely and was now about to intervene with decisive results.

French Intervention: Richelieu

Since coming to power in 1624, Richelieu had kept in close touch with the progress of the war through his ambassadors and agents. But for ten years he did not feel that the French army was strong enough to intervene in Germany. His major purpose was to crush the Habsburgs, both Austrian and Spanish, and he was ready to ally with anyone, Protestant or Catholic, who was opposed to them. The Dutch, who went back to war with their old enemies the Spanish, were his first allies, and in 1631 he subsidized the invasion by Gustavus Adolphus. When the Swedes were finally defeated in 1634, Richelieu saw that he would have to intervene directly if he was to check Habsburg expansion in, and perhaps control of, Europe. And so in May 1635 he sent a French herald to Brussels to declare war on the king of Spain.

The Thirty Years' War had lasted for seventeen years with no decisive result, and it was to continue for thirteen more dreary years while French, Swedish, and Dutch armies fought against the Spanish and Austrian Habsburgs. Spain was weakened by the successful rebellion of Portugal and the almost successful rebellion of Catalonia (1640). In 1643 the French finally destroyed the legend of Spanish invincibility by crushing a Spanish army at Rocroi in the Netherlands. It was the first time in 150 years that a Spanish army had suffered a major defeat. The emperor's allies deserted him, and by 1648 the Swedes were threatening Vienna and storming Prague. The dream of Emperor Ferdinand II (who had died in 1637) of re-Catholicizing Germany and establishing Habsburg control over the Empire lay in ruins.

The Peace of Westphalia, 1648

A peace was finally worked out at the Congress of Westphalia (1643–48), Europe's first great peace conference and the first international gathering of importance since the Council of Constance (1414–18). But it was a far different gathering from that of two centuries earlier. The atmosphere and the business at hand were now entirely secular, and the communities represented were sovereign territorial states that recognized no earthly superior and only the most shadowy common interests. "Christendom" had dissolved, and the word *civilization* would not be coined till the next century to express in secular terms what *Christendom* had once meant to Europeans in religious terms.

Almost every act of the Congress emphasized the importance of the sovereign state. For example, it recognized the right of each German principality to make alliances and to declare war on its own. This constituted practical recognition of the disintegration of the Empire into over three hundred separate sovereignties. Switzerland and the Dutch Netherlands were finally recognized as sovereign states, independent of all ties to the Empire. France acquired some very ambiguous rights to Alsace, Sweden acquired strips of German territory along the

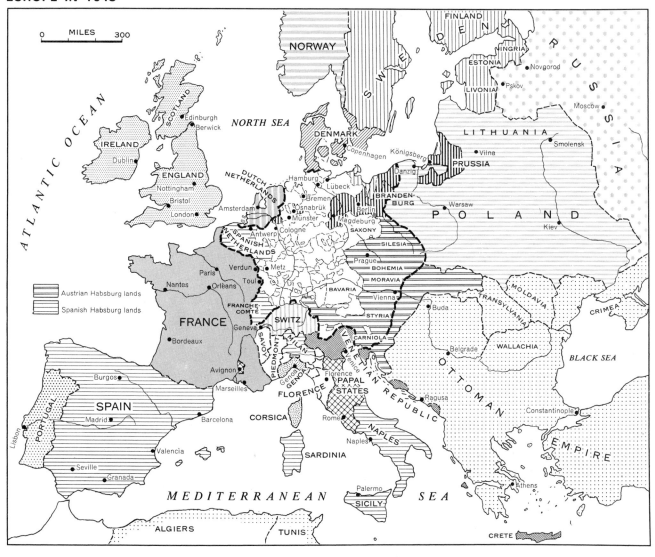

Austrian Habsburg lands
Spanish Habsburg lands

shores of the Baltic and the North Sea, and the two German states of Brandenburg and Bavaria ended up with increased territory and prestige. As for religion, the old principle of *cuius regio, eius religio* was reaffirmed. Calvinism was simply added to Catholicism and Lutheranism as one of the recognized faiths. The ownership of church lands was settled as of 1624, meaning in general that northern Germany remained Protestant and southern Germany, Catholic. France and Spain were unable to reach agreement, so their war continued until French victory was finally recognized in the Peace of the Pyrenees in 1659. France received some territory along the Pyrenees and in Flanders, and the Spanish princess, Maria Theresa, married Louis XIV. In general, the peace settlements of the middle of the century left France the strongest power in Europe, Spain prostrate, the Empire shattered, and a kind of power vacuum in the center of Europe.

The Social Results of the War

The Thirty Years' War was one of the most brutal and destructive wars of which we have record until the twentieth century. Armies robbed, raped, and murdered their way back and forth across Germany. The lack of any modern supply system meant that they had to live off the land. There are gruesome records of towns totally wiped out, cities reduced to a small fraction of their original population, and cultivated land reverting to waste. Starvation and disease killed more than the sword. It is impossible to be sure of the total decline in population, but some historians believe that Germany lost almost a third of its inhabitants. Others insist that the destruction was not so great as contemporary sources would suggest, and that recovery in farming districts was rapid. The social and psychological effects, however, were certainly frightful. A whole generation grew up accepting violence and brutality as normal. The fragmentation of the Empire into practically independent states hampered economic recovery. Cultural and political provincialism were to go hand in hand for the next two centuries in German history. In fact, it is almost impossible to find any good result of the generation of aimless fighting in Germany known as the Thirty Years' War.

DUTCH UNREST AND SPANISH DECLINE

England, France, and Germany were not the only countries to experience political crises in the first half of the seventeenth century. Political upheavals in this era touched every part of Europe. Even faraway Russia underwent an anarchic "Time of Troubles" before settling down uneasily under the rule of the first Romanov tsar in 1613. In the West, there were violent upheavals in the Netherlands and in Spain.

The northern Netherlands had achieved effective independence from Spain by the beginning of the century and were enjoying enormous economic success. Yet the United Provinces were riven by political and religious conflicts. One party, supported by orthodox Calvinists and led by the House of Orange (William the Silent's family), pressed for

an aggressive war against Spain in the southern Netherlands. A second party, supported by the religiously tolerant Arminians (who were unwilling to accept the doctrine of predestination) and led by the mercantile class, favored a policy that might open the way to peaceful trading with Spain. As the Thirty Years' War approached, this tolerant "peace party" was overthrown: war with Spain resumed in 1621 and continued until the Peace of Westphalia. Tensions between the House of Orange and a "regent class" of mercantile interests continued throughout the century. For two decades after 1650 the "regents" dominated Dutch affairs. But when invasion again loomed in 1672—this time France, not Spain, was the enemy—the old conflicts surfaced again. The leading regent, Jan de Witt, was torn to pieces by a mob in The Hague, and the head of the House of Orange—the young Prince William III— was summoned to lead the Dutch war effort.

In Spain, problems that had been building up for decades exploded all at once in 1640. The resumption of warfare in the Netherlands, in Germany, and, finally, with France, put intolerable financial burdens on the Spanish state. Efforts by the leading minister, the Count-Duke of Olivares, to impose a more efficient centralized government and a more effective system of tax collection on the different sections of the Spanish kingdom led to two bitter rebellions in 1640. Portugal (which had been united with Spain since 1580) successfully broke away and regained its independence. And in the same year a revolt broke out in the province of Catalonia. Aided by the French, the Catalans held out for over a decade. Meanwhile unrest also broke out in Spain's Italian provinces.

All of these problems contributed to the decline of Spain and made inevitable its surrender to France in 1659. Yet behind Spain's political troubles lay an even deeper source of trouble: the diminishing strength of Spain's overseas empire. For the decline of Spain was caused largely by changes in the European (and world) economy during the seventeenth century.

THE MERCANTILE ECONOMY OF EARLY MODERN EUROPE

Seventeenth-century kings and ministers were aware that political power depended on economic strength. They sought to increase the wealth of their own countries and to decrease the wealth of rival countries, or at least to prevent its growth. Agriculture, of course, was still the chief occupation in every part of Europe, but very little could be done either to increase home production or to decrease foreign production of food and fibers. Industry was more susceptible to state interference, but none of the major countries was very dependent on industry. On the other hand, the volume and value of European trade had increased enormously. Growth between 1500 and 1600 had been so spectacular that some historians have described it as a "Commercial Revolution." And the countries that were assuming political leadership in Europe were becoming the centers of trade. The main routes now led to Amsterdam, London, and Paris rather than to Venice, Lisbon, and Seville. In the Netherlands, England, and France, the merchant was far more important than the industrialist and far more influential than the farmer.

Therefore, a ruler who wanted to use economic controls as a political weapon thought primarily in terms of altering the patterns of international trade. This policy seemed so natural that no one bothered to give it a name. In 1776, however, Adam Smith, looking at the process with some disapproval, coined the phrase "the mercantile system." This phrase, or its equivalent "mercantilism," has been used ever since.

Problems of Economic Organization

By the end of the sixteenth century it was evident that old forms of economic organization were not able to deal with the vast increase in the volume of trade. The gilds, which controlled production in many towns, could not supply the growing demands of merchants and governments. Most gilds were geared only to local markets and insisted on following traditional, and often inefficient, methods of work. Many governments tried to regulate gilds in order to get uniform, nationwide standards of production, but except for a few luxury articles, this policy proved a failure. It was easier to let the merchants deal with the problem of industrial organization.

One method, already used by the end of the Middle Ages, was called the putting-out system. For example, in the textile industry an entrepreneur might buy wool, pass it out to peasants to be spun into thread, carry the thread to others to be woven into cloth, take the cloth to the dyers, and finally sell the finished product. This system had the double advantage of bypassing the gild restrictions in the towns and of tapping new sources of cheap labor in the countryside. Underemployed peasants with only a few acres were glad to have any extra income; in England they took almost all the work away from the old textile towns. In the same way, English merchants bought Swedish iron, gave it out to Sheffield toolmakers, and sold the product abroad. (The English were the best precision-toolmakers in Europe.) The putting-out system was hard on the laborers, but it increased production and lowered costs.

Another type of organization was the gathering-in system (the factory system). In industries like printing, cannon founding, mining, and shipbuilding, and even in some textile processes such as silk weaving and calico printing, it was more efficient to gather workers together at some central place where their work could be directly supervised and coordinated. There was not much division of labor; each man made a finished or semi-finished article. But transportation costs were cut, and quality could be controlled. In both the putting-out and the gathering-in systems, it was almost invariably a merchant, not the manufacturer or the technician, who did the organizing.

Joint Stock Companies

In commerce an important innovation was the joint stock company. The small partnerships of the Middle Ages (and even the Medici Bank was small by seventeenth-century standards) could not

Page from a pamphlet put out by the London Company in 1609 to persuade investors to support its enterprise in Virginia.

THE CENTER OF EUROPEAN ECONOMY   Early seventeenth century

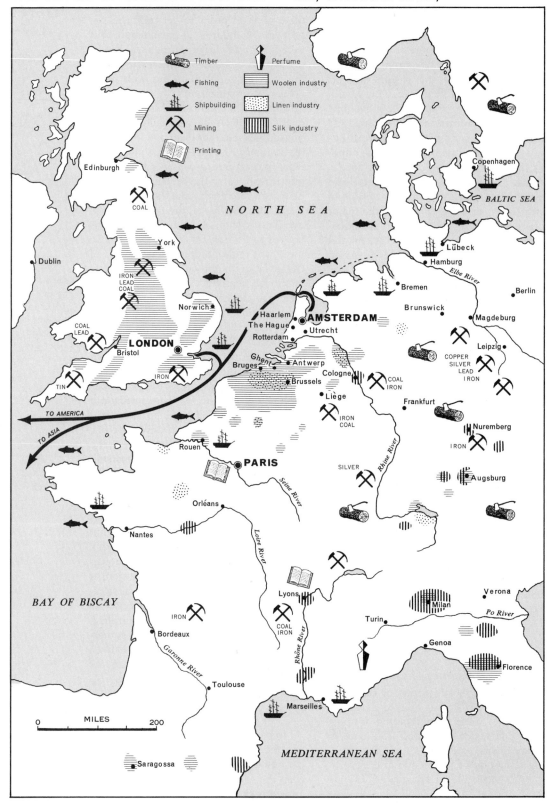

Timber
Fishing
Shipbuilding
Mining
Printing
Perfume
Woolen industry
Linen industry
Silk industry

Edinburgh

COAL

NORTH SEA

Dublin

York

IRON
LEAD
COAL

Norwich

COAL
LEAD

LONDON

Bristol

TIN

IRON

Haarlem
The Hague
Rotterdam

AMSTERDAM

Utrecht

Ghent
Bruges
Antwerp
Brussels
Cologne
Liège

COAL
IRON

IRON
COAL

SILVER

TO AMERICA

TO ASIA

Rouen

PARIS

Seine River

Orléans

Nantes

Loire River

BAY OF BISCAY

IRON

Bordeaux

Garonne River

Toulouse

Lyons

COAL
IRON

Rhône River

0   MILES   200

Saragossa

Marseilles

MEDITERRANEAN SEA

Copenhagen

BALTIC SEA

Lübeck
Hamburg
Elbe River
Berlin
Bremen
Brunswick
Magdeburg

COPPER
SILVER
LEAD
IRON

Leipzig

Frankfurt

Nuremberg

IRON

Augsburg

Rhine River

Verona

Po River

Turin

Milan

Genoa

Florence

raise the capital needed for large-scale, overseas voyages. So merchants formed associations called "regulated companies." Governments gave such groups a monopoly on trade to a given area, but each member of the group, while he helped meet common expenses, traded on his own account. They were associations of men, not of capital. What was needed, however, was a type of association that would attract the investments of men who had neither the desire nor the ability to qualify as active traders in a regulated company. The answer was the joint stock company, an amazingly flexible institution that was to be the parent of many other economic and political institutions on both sides of the Atlantic.

The joint stock company began as an association of investors, not of traders. Individuals bought shares in a venture, such as a trading voyage, and shared in the profits in proportion to their investment. When the association continued beyond a single venture, it became a joint stock company. This device had two advantages: it enabled anyone from a modestly wealthy man to Queen Elizabeth to invest in a business enterprise like Drake's voyages, and it associated businessmen with courtiers and statesmen at a time when both business sense and influence at court were necessary to the success of commercial ventures. The joint stock idea originated in southern Europe, but it was first applied to large-scale overseas enterprise in England in the Russia Company of 1553. The English East India Company, the companies that founded Virginia and Massachusetts, and the Bank of England were all joint stock companies. As these examples show, the first joint stock companies were dependent on government support (usually in the form of a trade monopoly) and were not concerned with industry. The joint stock company rapidly became the dominant form of commercial organization; it developed more slowly in industrial production.

The cumulative effect of these changes was to make the king, not the town, the chief regulator of economic activity. The unit of economic activity in the Middle Ages, apart from agriculture, had been the town or the city-state. As stronger monarchs appeared at the end of the Middle Ages, urban economy was steadily absorbed into the national economy throughout much of Europe, except in Italy and Germany. The monarch stepped into the shoes of medieval town officials and regulated trade and production much as municipal governments had done, but on a larger scale.

Mercantilism

The original aim of economic regulation was to advance the common good, not to increase the wealth of individuals. But a king's definition of the common good was the strength and security of his realm, not a general rise in consumption or standards of living. During the seventeenth century monarchs began to believe that their goals could be attained by following the economic doctrine called mercantilism. This doctrine, as applied in the seventeenth century, assumed that there is only a certain stock of wealth in

An Englishman on the Importance of Trade

ca. 1630

Although a kingdom may be enriched by gifts received, or by purchase taken from some other nations, yet these are things uncertain and of small consideration when they happen. The ordinary means therefore to encrease our wealth and treasure is by foreign trade, wherein we must ever observe this rule; to sell more to strangers yearly than we consume of theirs in value. For suppose that when this kingdom is plentifully served with the cloth, lead, tin, iron, fish and other native commodities, we do yearly export the overplus to foreign countries to the value of twenty-two hundred thousand pounds; by which means we are enabled beyond the seas to buy and bring in foreign wares for our use and consumptions, to the value of twenty hundred thousand pounds; by this order duly kept in our trading, we may rest assured that the kingdom shall be enriched yearly two hundred thousand pounds, which must be brought to us in so much treasure; because that part of our stock which is not returned to us in wares must necesarily be brought home in treasure. . . .

Behold then the true form and worth of foreign trade, which is, the great revenue of the king, the honour of the kingdom, the noble profession of the merchant, the school of our arts, the supply of our wants, the employment of our poor, the improvements of our lands, the nursery of our mariners, the walls of the kingdoms, the means of our treasure, the sinews of our wars, the terror of our enemies.

From Thomas Mun, *England's Treasure by Foreign Trade* (New York: Oxford University Press, 1933), p. 5.

the world at any given time, and if one country gains wealth another loses it. (This is a fairly typical assumption in a period of depression; it had already emerged in the fourteenth century and is not unknown today.) To prevent loss, home industries and shipping should be encouraged and colonies founded to provide raw materials that would otherwise have to be bought from foreigners. By regulating trade in these ways a country's stock of precious metals might be increased and surely would not decrease. This was not an unreasonable precaution in an age when credit devices were in their infancy and when, in case of war, a country had to have a reserve of gold and silver to pay its suppliers and soldiers.

The obvious way to build such a reserve—short of discovering new mines or capturing a Spanish plate fleet—was for a nation to export more than it imported. Foreign buyers would have to settle their balances in precious metals. At the very least there should be a balance of trade, so that more money would not leave the country than stayed in it. And so mercantilism called for tariffs to discourage imports and various benefits to encourage export industries. But it was thought that some exports, such as gold and silver, scarce raw materials, and skilled workmen, would weaken a state and should therefore be forbidden. Logically, mercantilist theory called for the abolition of all internal tariffs and all internal barriers to trade in order to build up the home market, though it was impossible to accomplish this except in England. At the core of mercantilism was the conviction that trade is the most important of all economic activities, that the regulation of trade is the government's most important economic concern, and that regulation should result in self-sufficiency and readiness for war.

As we shall see (p. 440), when new colonial policies were developed during the seventeenth century, mercantilists favored tropical colonies that enhanced the strength of the mother country by furnishing products such as sugar and tea and by buying home manufactures. They had no use for colonies that raised crops or produced manufactured goods that competed with the home country's products, nor for colonies that traded directly with other nations. The integration of colonies into the home economy was a cardinal mercantilist principle.

Mercantilism has necessarily been made to seem more clear-cut and consistent than it actually was in practice. It differed from one country to another, in response to the interests of the ruling group. In France the system was often called *Étatisme*, or state-ism. The hand of the government was very heavy in France: government intervention in commercial enterprise was direct and positive; regulation was intense; and relatively little initiative was left to individual enterprise. In England mercantilism also meant regulation of the economy in the government's interest. But even before the Revolution of 1688, and especially afterward, the English government was more responsive to the pressures of businessmen than was the French. It is often very difficult to tell whether English economic policy represented the interest of the state as a whole or the interests of individual entrepreneurs. In the United Provinces, where the federal government was in effect a government of businessmen, the interest of the state and the interests of the business community practically coincided. Dutch mercantilism was not so much the regulation of trade by the state as it was the control of economic policy by organized business. In the rest of Europe, however—in Spain, Portugal, Austria, Prussia, and Sweden—mercantilism represented primarily the interest of the monarchy and so followed the French model more than the Dutch.

Financial Problems

The rise in prices that had marked the sixteenth century slowed down in the seventeenth, and may even have been reversed for a while. It has been estimated that while prices more than quadrupled between 1500 and 1600, they rose no more than 20 percent during the next hundred years, and most of that gain came during the first two or the last two decades of the century. The problems of inflation had been hard enough to handle. With prices rising faster than government income, bankruptcy was always just around the corner. In Spain, with its heavy military commitments, the government had had to repudiate its debts at frequent intervals (see p. 404). But the problems of deflation were even more serious. Taxes brought in less, while government expenditures (mostly for wars) continued to increase. The optimism that comes with inflation, at least to the classes able to profit from it, decreased. The classes that had profited from the inflation of the sixteenth century—merchants, bankers, men who invested in land (like the English gentry)—found the financial atmosphere of the seventeenth century rather chilling. This is one reason why taxation seemed so oppressive after 1600.

Spain never managed to solve its problems and continued to hang on the edge of bankruptcy until late in the century. France did better, partly because its taxes fell most heavily on the peasants, and agricultural prices remained at a higher level than prices of other commodities, thus giving the peasants enough of a surplus to pay for the extravagances of the court and the waste of war. But the French taxation system was antiquated, and trouble was simply postponed to the eighteenth century. In England the Stuarts were never able to build a sound system of government finance because they lost the confidence of Parliament, which controlled the major part of the royal revenue. But after 1688 a government that had gained the confidence of Parliament as well as the business community was able to construct an exceptionally strong system of public finance that included parliamentary taxation, a national bank, and a permanent public debt. In large measure this system was modeled on Dutch governmental finance, the most successful of the age. Since the rulers of the United Provinces were representatives of the business community, they had little difficulty, at least for a century, in raising the money and credit they needed for their overseas empire building and their wars. In an age dominated by trade, a state that had a flourishing commerce and could command the confidence of its merchants could weather any financial storm. A state that had little commerce, or in which commerce was growing slowly while merchants were discouraged, was likely to find itself in financial difficulties.

EUROPEAN COLONIES IN THE SEVENTEENTH CENTURY

European expansion overseas was checked briefly in the seventeenth century, and picked up again only after some fundamental changes were made in patterns of colonial settlement. The earliest and easiest type of colony to establish was a fortified trading post, to which the natives brought readily salable commodities, such as gold, spices, and slaves. This was the Portuguese pattern, and, as the Dutch gradually ousted the Portuguese from the East Indies, it was the pattern that the Dutch tried to follow. But even the Dutch eventually found that they had to go inland and take over responsibility for governing large numbers of people in order to maintain the flow of commodities, and no other colonizing power found it possible to avoid administrative responsibilities for more than a brief period. The Spaniards, for example, could not exploit the wealth of America without taking over the Aztec and the Inca Empires.

Moreover, it became harder and harder to get riches without effort. There was an apparently inexhaustible supply of slaves in Africa, which is why European colonies there could remain at the trading post level. But the market for spices was soon glutted, and, once the pillaging of the American Indians ended, gold and silver could be acquired only by laborious and expensive mining operations. A new type of colony was needed, a colony that produced goods desired by Europeans with its own labor. The first such colonies were the sugar islands of the Caribbean; later came the tobacco, tea, and coffee colonies.

The East

At first the Dutch, the English, and the French tried to cut in on the Portu-

Miniature by an Indian artist of a foreigner, possibly a merchant of the East India Company (ca. 1600).

guese trade in India, Ceylon, and the East Indies. The English East India Company was founded in 1600, the Dutch in 1602, the French in 1664. The Dutch discouraged English trade with the Spice Islands—they killed ten English merchants in 1623—so the English withdrew to India. There they set up "factories," or trading posts, on the Portuguese model. Until the breakup of the Mogul Empire in central India early in the eighteenth century, it was never possible for Europeans to penetrate very far into the subcontinent of India. Their footholds on the coast depended entirely on sea power for support; and as Portuguese sea power declined in the seventeenth century and as the Dutch busied themselves farther east, the English were able to establish themselves at Bombay, Madras, and Calcutta. Meanwhile, the French at Pondicherry had become their most important potential rivals. The stage was set for a struggle in the next century between the British and the French East India companies over India's commerce and riches.

The Caribbean

In the Caribbean the Dutch, the English, and the French were all searching for footholds around the periphery of the Spanish settlements. After an unsuccessful attempt to take Brazil from the Portuguese, the Dutch seized Curaçao as a base from which to raid Spanish commerce. The English settled Barbados in 1624 and acquired Jamaica in 1655. Meanwhile, the French settled Guadaloupe and Martinique. These acquisi-

tions were made just as the new colonial model—the colony as a producer of tropical goods—became popular. All the West Indian islands rapidly became rich sugar-producing areas, thanks to slave labor. So the English and the French, who came to the Caribbean to trade and buccaneer in the Dutch manner, stayed on to become plantation owners in the Spanish manner. The English and French sugar islands were the darlings of mercantilists at home. The planters cultivated a crop that could not be grown in Europe; they developed no industries to compete with home industries; and they were entirely dependent on their mother countries for shipping. Not surprisingly, the sugar islands were the center of attention among financiers and diplomats for over a century.

The chronic dearth of manufactured goods and slaves in the Spanish colonies meant that foreign smugglers who could slip by the Spanish navy were always welcome. As Portuguese control of the slaving stations on the western coast of Africa relaxed, the Dutch and English stepped in to supply the Spanish West Indies with the slaves needed on their sugar plantations. The brutality of this trade has become a byword, but it aroused no protest whatever in any European nation during the seventeenth and early eighteenth centuries.

North America

In North America a new wave of colonial expansion was beginning that was to have more far-reaching results than

The Javanese port of Batavia, from a Dutch engraving of 1682. Notice the Dutch architecture, entirely inappropriate for the climate.

West Indian sugar planting, though it was long overshadowed by the economic success of the tropical islands. There were many reasons why the Dutch, the English, and the French became interested in North America at the opening of the seventeenth century. For some time their sailors had been searching for a northwest passage to the Indies. Their ships were already engaged in cod fishing on the Newfoundland Banks. It was evident that North America could supply vast quantities of furs and timber. There might be precious metals, and it might turn out that sugar could be grown farther north than the Caribbean. Permanent settlements could support all these economic activities and at the same time help turn the flank of the Spanish in the New World.

Sir Walter Raleigh's unsuccessful attempt to found a colony in Virginia during the 1580s, however, had revealed some of the difficulties of settling the land the Spanish had left unoccupied. Colder climate, poorer soil, and hostile natives discouraged a plantation type of economy. To plant a permanent colony in North America a whole labor force would have to be transported and supported, perhaps for years, until the settlement became self-sufficient. This called for a large investment of capital and a large number of settlers. Furthermore, it called for strong belief and determination.

The Dutch, the French, and the English

It was the English and, to a lesser degree, the French, not the Dutch, whose determination proved strongest. The Dutch explored the Hudson in 1609 and settled New Amsterdam on Manhattan Island by 1624, but their colony of New Netherland never became more than a center for maritime trade and the export

The Indian village of Pomeiock in "Virginia" (actually North Carolina), watercolor by John White, an artist who took part in Raleigh's attempt to establish a colony at Roanoke in 1585. In his text White notes that mats and the bark of trees were used to cover the dwellings; the town was encompassed by poles instead of a wall.

of furs. Unsupported by the company that founded it, it fell to the English in 1664. The French were more successful. From Cartier, who discovered the St. Lawrence in 1535, to La Salle, who coursed the Mississippi in 1682, their explorers were more adventurous, their fur traders better able to adapt to the country, and their Jesuit missionaries more determined, than the representatives of any other European nation in the New World. In 1605 there were French settlers in Acadia, and in 1608 Champlain founded Quebec. By 1640 there were perhaps three thousand Frenchmen in Canada; by the end of the century about ten thousand.

The growth was slow for several reasons. The settlement of French Canada was marked by paternalism and relatively little individual initiative. Only when the French government actively encouraged Frenchmen to emigrate, as it did under Colbert in the 1660s and 1670s, did the colony grow appreciably. Since land was granted in large blocks, or *seigneuries*, to a few proprietors under semifeudal conditions, there was little inducement for peasants to emigrate. The government strictly prohibited the Huguenots, who wanted to emigrate, from going to Canada (they went to the English colonies instead). A fairly solid block of settlements grew up in the St. Lawrence Valley, but the slow-growing colony of *seigneurs* and *habitants* (as the peasants were called) was soon far outdistanced by the English settlements to the south.

The founding of the English colonies in North America was the result of a peculiarly favorable set of historical circumstances in the mother country. The idea that colonization meant wealth had been skillfully sold to ordinary Englishmen by enthusiasts and businessmen before Queen Elizabeth's death. London and Bristol merchants were ready for colonizing ventures and able to organize such ventures by means of joint stock companies. The constitutional and religious conflicts that troubled England through most of the seventeenth century provided many people with both material and idealistic motives for wishing to emigrate. Finally the English government,

whether it was that of the Stuarts or of their revolutionary opponents, encouraged but did not interfere with colonizing projects. In particular, it put no bar in the way of religious minorities that wished to emigrate.

The first successful colony, planted at Jamestown by the Virginia Company in 1607, had a difficult time until the settlers discovered that by concentrating on a single crop, tobacco, they could buy the goods they needed from England. The little band of religious dissenters who landed at Plymouth in 1620 lost half their number during the first winter and survived only by sheer heroism. But the Massachusetts Bay Company, which founded Boston, was able to profit by the Pilgrims' experience. In 1630 it transported nine hundred settlers across the ocean in a large and well-planned operation. Within ten years the population had increased to about fourteen thousand in Massachusetts and within twenty years there were about twenty thousand in New England as a whole. This population had developed a surplus of food for export, and had plenty of fur, fish, and timber to ship back to the mother country. By the end of the century more colonies had been established, either as offshoots of the original settlements or by royal grants to "proprietors," until there were twelve in all (the thirteenth was added in 1732). It has been estimated that by 1700 there were almost two hundred thousand English settlers in North America, as compared with about ten thousand French. It was already clear that most North Americans would someday speak English.

English and French Colonies

The English colonies were more divided and less well controlled by the home government than were the French. New France was under one central administration at Quebec, whereas the English colonies were under twelve separate governments. Each of the twelve eventually elected representative assemblies that controlled local legislation and taxation. The royal governors were not responsible to these assemblies, but, since they were generally dependent on the assemblies for their salaries, their power was effectively limited. In the 1660s Parliament did its best to impose strict mercantilist theories on the colonies—for example, by ruling that certain exports must be sent directly to England in English or colonial ships. These measures caused complaints, and after the Revolution of 1688 the English government gradually became less insistent on asserting its authority. The colonists accepted parliamentary regulation of their trade so long as the regulations were not too strictly enforced, but they became more and more accustomed to running their own affairs to suit themselves.

Without conscious design, the English in the seventeenth century fashioned a new kind of colonial empire in North America, quite different from either the Portuguese or the Spanish. The Portuguese Empire (and, to a large degree, the Dutch) was based on armed trade. The Spanish Empire was based on the efforts of a ruling class of soldiers, planters, and missionaries to convert the natives and exploit their labor. But the Protestant English (and Protestant Dutch) were never particularly interested in converting the natives. They never felt responsible for the Indians as the Spanish did, partly because there was no possibility of exploiting their labor. So they simply displaced the natives from the land on which they settled. The English transferred a whole European population to a new environment and permitted it to blend the traditional institutions it brought from home with the innovations and improvisations evoked by the new surroundings. Not surprisingly, these innovations tended toward economic, political, and religious freedom. The breeze was blowing in this direction in England, and it was blowing even more strongly in the colonies.

The Russians in Siberia

While the French and the British in North America were pushing westward from the Atlantic seaboard toward the

Codfishing in the waters off Newfoundland (ca. 1720).

Pacific, the Russians were pushing eastward from the Ural Mountains across Siberia toward the Pacific. The two movements were strikingly similar in many respects, but the Russians had no ocean to cross at the start and they reached the Pacific first. In 1581, groups of Cossacks—"pioneers," or "frontiersmen," who had earlier pushed back the Tartars and Turks and had settled in the lower valleys of the Dnieper, the Don, and the Volga—began to move eastward from the Urals under a leader, Ermak, who became famed in song and story. Like the French in Canada, the Cossacks were mainly in search of furs, particularly sable, and so they followed the dark pine forest, not the steppe to the south. The great rivers of Siberia—the Obi, the Yenisei, and the Lena—flow north into the Arctic Ocean, but in their upper reaches they branch out so that they almost touch one another. Thus the Cossacks could move easily across the continent by water. The movement was not planned or organized. The settlers simply flowed eastward through the sparsely settled wastes of Siberia in search of furs, occasionally stopping to form widely separated settlements, and reached the Pacific in the early 1640s, barely two generations after the movement began. The distance covered was greater than that across North America, but there were no wide mountain barriers until near the end and no serious resistance from natives until the Cossacks met the Chinese in the Amur Valley. There the Russians were checked by a superior, civilized state, and in 1689, by the first treaty concluded between Russia and China, the Russians withdrew from the Amur basin. They remained behind the Stanovoi Mountains for the next 170 years.

A Cossack warrior.

Like the English, the Cossacks were in search of freedom as well as furs, and their early communities in Siberia were often wild and lawless, like the later towns of the American "Wild West." But the tsar's government soon reached out across the vast distances to establish its administration and to tax the lucrative fur trade—more like the French than the English government in North America. By 1700 there were perhaps half again as many Russian settlers in Siberia as there were French and British in North America. By the end of the century, Russian traders were venturing across the Bering Strait into Alaska and down the North American coastline in search of seals. Thus long before the English colonists in America had reached the Pacific, the Russians, by a combination of individual daring and government backing, had staked out a claim to the northern half of Asia and had even reached out far enough to touch the shores of the Western Hemisphere.

Suggestions for Further Reading

Note: Asterisk denotes a book available in paperback edition.

General Works on the Seventeenth Century

There are several successful attempts at a synthetic treatment of the period. D. Ogg, *Europe in the Seventeenth Century,* 8th ed. (1960), is a sound and interesting narrative of the major developments on the Continent, arranged by country. G. N. Clark, *The Seventeenth Century** (1931), is a more analytical discussion of different aspects of the period: for instance, population, industries, military organization, political thought, science, religion. C. J. Friedrich's volume in the *Rise of Modern Europe* series, *The Age of the Baroque, 1610–1660** (1952), combines narrative and analysis and makes use of recent interpretations of baroque style. C. J. Friedrich and C. Blitzer, *The Age of Power** (1957), is a brief and thoughtful survey of the century, based on Friedrich's larger work. The essays in T. Aston, ed., *Crisis in Europe, 1560–1660** (1965), are uneven, but the best ones are very good.

Mercantilism and Economic Growth

L. B. Packard, *The Commercial Revolution, 1400–1700* (1927), is the briefest reliable treatment of mercantilism. J. W. Horrocks, *Short History of Mercantilism* (1925), and P. W. Buck, *The Politics of Mercantilism* * (1964), are somewhat longer studies. The fullest and best treatment is E. F. Heckscher, *Mercantilism*, 2 vols. (1935). H. Sée, *Modern Capitalism* (trans. 1928), is the best extensive discussion of the subject. F. L. Nussbaum, *History of the Economic Institutions of Modern Europe* (1933), summarizes the work of the great German historian of capitalism, W. Sombart. D. Hannay, *The Great Chartered Companies* (1926), is a good introduction to its subject. J. U. Nef, *Wars and Human Progress* (1950), argues that war is a detriment, not a stimulant, to technological and economic progress, particularly in this period. Up-to-date surveys of economic topics are available in C. Cipolla, ed., *The Fontana Economic History of Europe,* * Vol. II (1974).

Expansion Overseas

In addition to the works cited for Chapter 18 on geographical discovery, the following are useful on special topics: B. H. M. Vlekke, *The Story of the Dutch East Indies* (1945); C. R. Boxer, *The Dutch Seaborne Empire* (1965); C. Gibson, *Spain in America* (1966); and H. A. Wyndham, *The Atlantic and Slavery* (1935). On the rivalry of France and England in America, the many fascinating volumes of F. Parkman dating from the 1860s are still worth reading, especially the earlier ones. G. M. Wrong, *The Rise and Fall of New France*, 2 vols. (1928), is the standard modern account. The *Cambridge History of India*, 5 vols. (1922–37), is useful for reference. Vol. IV of the *Cambridge Economic History of Europe* (1967) emphasizes overseas expansion.

France

J. Boulenger, *The Seventeenth Century* * (trans. 1920), is a standard one-volume account in English. G. Treasure, *Seventeenth Century France* * (1966), is a recent survey. F. C. Palm, *The Establishment of French Absolutism, 1574–1610* (1928), and P. R. Doolin, *The Fronde* (1935), are good special studies. Of the many books on Richelieu, the most trustworthy short account is C. V. Wedgwood, *Richelieu and the French Monarchy* * (1962). C. J. Burckhardt, *Richelieu: His Rise to Power* * (1964), is a solid piece of work. The French social structure is described in P. Goubert, *The Ancien Régime: French Society, 1600–1750* * (1973).

England

The classic one-volume account, Whiggish in sympathy and brilliantly written, is G. M. Trevelyan, *England Under the Stuarts* (1904, 1946). The standard modern account is G. Davies, *The Early Stuarts, 1603–1660,* 2nd ed. (1959), in the *Oxford History of England* series. The detailed narrative history of S. R. Gardiner, published in eighteen volumes (1863–1903) and covering the years 1603 to 1656, is a major achievement of English historical scholarship to which all later accounts are indebted. C. V. Wedgwood has published three volumes of a history of the Puritan rebellion: *The King's Peace* (1955), *The King's War* (1958), and *A Coffin for King Charles* (1964). D. L. Keir, *The Constitutional History of Modern Britain, 1485–1937,* * 4th ed. (1950), and J. R. Tanner, *English Constitutional Conflicts of the Seventeenth Century* * (1928), together constitute a good introduction to some of the more technical constitutional issues of the period. There are many biographies of Cromwell, but the best is still C. H. Firth, *Oliver Cromwell and the Rule of the Puritans in England* (1900, 1925). W. Notestein, *The English People on the Eve of Colonization, 1603–1630* * (1954), is a good introduction to the social history of the period, and B. Willey, *The Seventeenth Century Background* * (1934), a good introduction to its intellectual history. A. S. P. Woodhouse, ed., *Puritanism and Liberty* (1951), is a selection of sources illustrating the ferment of democratic ideas during the rebellion. See also W. Haller, *The Rise of Puritanism* * (1938); M. Walzer, *The Revolution of the Saints* * (1965); and L. Stone, *The Crisis of the Aristocracy, 1558–1642* * (1967). For a vivid introduction to the social history of seventeenth-century England, see P. Laslett, *World We Have Lost,* * 2nd ed. (1971).

Germany

There are good chapters on the Thirty Years' War in Ogg and Friedrich (first section, above), and in H. J. Grimm, *The Reformation Era* (1973), and H. Holborn, *A History of Modern Germany: The Reformation* (1959). Far and away the best general account in English is C. V. Wedgwood, *The Thirty Years War* * (1938). The scholars' argument over how destructive the war was may be followed in S. H. Steinberg's criticism of Wedgwood in *History*, Vol. XXXII (1947), pp. 89–102. T. K. Rabb, ed., *The Thirty Years' War* * (1964), gives readings on the causes and effects of the war. The Swedish phase of the war is well described by M. Roberts, *Gustavus Adolphus* (1953–58). J. Polišenský, *The Thirty Years War* (1971), examines the social effects of the war, especially in Bohemia.

20 Absolutism and Constitutionalism 1660–1715

During the latter half of the seventeenth century France was the leading nation in Europe. Its population was twice that of Spain and over four times that of England. Its land was fertile and its commerce and industry were growing.

FRANCE UNDER LOUIS XIV

There were no disturbing arguments over forms of government; absolute monarchy was accepted by almost all Frenchmen as necessary, reasonable, and right. By the Peace of the Pyrenees (1659) the French army had displaced the Spanish as the strongest military machine on the Continent. As time went on, it seemed as if not only French generals, French military engineers, and French diplomatists but also French architects, painters, dramatists, and philosophers were the best in Europe. French fashions in dress dominated the Continent; the French language became the leading language of diplomacy and polite conversation, and the French court with its elaborate etiquette and ceremonial became the model for countless smaller courts throughout Europe.

As Florence had been the nerve center of the Italian Renaissance and Spain of the Catholic Reformation, so France was the nerve center of late–seventeenth-century politics, diplomacy, and culture.

How much of this predominance is to be attributed to the long reign of Louis XIV is one of those questions that historians can speculate about but never answer. No one doubts that French (and European) history would have run in different channels had Louis never lived—or had he not lived so long. He was born in 1638, became king in 1643, took the reins of power into his own hands in 1661 at twenty-three, and died in 1715 at the age of seventy-seven, leaving the throne to his great-grandson. By temperament and training Louis was the very incarnation of divine-right monarchy—the idea that hereditary monarchy is the only divinely approved form of government, that kings are responsible to God alone for their conduct, and that subjects should obey their kings as the direct representatives of God on earth. In an age that put its trust in absolute rulers, the achievements of the French people at the peak of their greatness cannot be separated from the personality of their ruler, even if it can be proved that many

Louis XIV, by Hyacinthe Rigaud (1701).

The emblem of the Sun King.

of those achievements were unrelated to, or even accomplished in spite of, the ruler.

Louis is said to have remarked, "I am the state." Even if the remark is apocryphal, the words reveal more of the true importance of his reign than anything else he said or wrote. Louis XIV set out early in his reign to personify the concept of sovereignty. He dramatized this aim immediately after Mazarin's death by ordering his ministers thereafter to report to him in person, not to a "first minister."

To be the real head of a large and complicated government required long, hard work, and Louis paid the price. His education was poor, and he had little imagination, no sense of humor, and only a mediocre intelligence. But he had common sense, a knack of picking up information from others, and a willingness to work steadily at the business of governing. "If you let yourself be carried away by your passions," he once said, "don't do it in business hours." Painstakingly he caught up all the threads of power in his own hands. All major decisions were made in four great councils, which he attended regularly. These decisions were then carried out by professional "secretaries" at the head of organized bureaucracies. In the provinces, the *intendants* more and more represented the direct authority of the central government in justice, finance, and general administration. The old French monarchy imposed its authority through judicial decisions and had frequently consulted local and central assemblies. The new monarchy, begun by Richelieu and perfected by Louis XIV, imposed its authority through executive decisions. Louis reduced the importance of the *parlements*, never summoned the Estates General, and, so far as such a thing was humanly possible in his century, built a government that was himself.

Colbert and the Economy

Colbert, Louis XIV's Controller General of Finance, systematically ordered the economic life of the country under royal direction. He was an extreme mercantilist; everything he did was consciously or unconsciously meant to strengthen the country for war. He set up high protective tariffs to help home industry, fostered new export industries, encouraged the French colonies in Canada and the West Indies, and did everything he could to develop a powerful navy and a strong merchant marine. Some historians suspect that his minute regulation of industry and commerce did more to hinder than to help the French economy. But until the burden of foreign wars became heavy in the 1680s, national production and wealth were increasing. Colbert also cut down waste and corruption in the collection of taxes, as Sully had once done, but he was unable to make the burden of taxation much more equitable because of the exemptions held or purchased by members of the nobility

---

Louis XIV on the Duties of a King   1661

During the early period of his direct rule, Louis XIV prepared notes for the instruction of his son in the art of ruling. He had assistance in this task, and the texts do not necessarily give his exact words. They do express his ideas.

I have often wondered how it could be that love for work being a quality so necessary to sovereigns should yet be one that is so rarely found in them. Most princes, because they have a great many servants and subjects, do not feel obliged to go to any trouble and do not consider that if they have an infinite number of people working under their orders, there are infinitely more who rely on their conduct and that it takes a great deal of watching and a great deal of work merely to insure that those who act do only what they should and that those who rely tolerate only what they must. The deference and the respect that we receive from our subjects are not a free gift from them but payment for the justice and the protection that they expect to receive from us. Just as they must honor us, we must protect and defend them, and our debts toward them are even more binding than theirs to us, for indeed, if one of them lacks the skill or the willingness to execute our orders, a thousand others come in a crowd to fill his post, whereas the position of a sovereign can be properly filled only by the sovereign himself.

. . . of all the functions of sovereignty, the one that a prince must guard most jealously is the handling of the finances. It is the most delicate of all because it is the one that is most capable of seducing the one who performs it, and which makes it easiest for him to spread corruption. The prince alone should have sovereign direction over it because he alone has no fortune to establish but that of the state.

From Louis XIV, *Memoires for the Instruction of the Dauphin,* ed. by Paul Sonnino (New York: Free Press, 1970), pp. 63–64.

Henry IV		Louis XIII			Louis XIV			Louis XV		Louis XVI
	Regency		Richelieu	Mazarin			Regency			
		1624		1642		1661		1723		

and the bourgeoisie, the classes best able to pay. During the crisis of Louis' last war an attempt was made to tax these upper classes in order to stave off bankruptcy, but the attempt set no precedent.

The Nobility

The most dangerous potential opponents of royal absolutism, as Louis XIV knew from his own experience during the Fronde, were the members of the nobility. Louis completed Richelieu's work of destroying the political power of the French nobility. He excluded the nobles completely from all responsible positions in government and cheapened their status by increasing their numbers. An army commission came to be almost the only major outlet for a noble's ambition, which meant that the nobles as a class generally constituted a war party at court. All important positions in Louis XIV's government, such as the secretary-ships and intendancies, were filled by men of bourgeois or recently ennobled families.

Louis did not attack the social privileges of the nobility; he used them to make the nobles utterly dependent on him. In 1683 he moved the court and government from the Louvre in Paris to Versailles, fifteen miles away. He had hated Paris since the riots of the Fronde, and now in the formal gardens and ornate chateaux of Versailles, which he had built on waste marsh at considerable cost of human lives and treasure, he felt at home. He also felt safe; Versailles was the first royal residence that was completely unfortified. At Versailles, the king lived in an utterly artificial atmosphere, as far removed from reality as Versailles was physically removed from the bustle of Paris. Here the great nobles were compelled to live. Here a ball seemed as important as a battle, and holding the basin for the king's morning ablutions

was a job as much to be coveted as commanding the king's armies. Instead of competing for political power, nobles squandered their fortunes and exhausted their energies in jockeying for social prestige.

The regular rectangular shapes of the gardens, the balanced classical lines of the baroque architecture, the bright glint of mirrors and chandeliers, all these seemed to symbolize and emphasize the isolation of Versailles from nature, from the French nation, from the real world. Through all this Louis moved with impassive dignity. Years of self-conscious practice in kingship had given him a kind of public personality—cool, courteous, impersonal, imperturbable—which carried out perfectly the artificiality of the little world at Versailles. At his death he left to his successors a privileged nobility shorn of all political power and responsibility, demoralized by the empty pleasures and petty intrigues of court life and uneasily aware of its uselessness. It was a dangerous legacy.

Religious Policy

The only other potential opponents of Louis' absolutism were religious groups. The king had his differences with several popes who disliked his Gallican principles, which stressed royal control over the Church in France. These quarrels, however, never led to a real breach. Louis was always a good Catholic in a formal sense. He disliked and persecuted the Jansenists, an austere group of Catholic "puritans" who emphasized the teachings of St. Augustine on original sin, the depravity of man, and the need for divine grace. They felt that the Jesuits were far too optimistic about man's ability to work out his own salvation, and far too ready to compromise with the world. Louis, whose confessors were Jesuits, thought the Jansenists subversive (they

The medal above, issued in 1661, celebrates Louis' accessibility to his subjects. The medal below was struck in 1685 to commemorate the restoration of military discipline in Louis' reign.

NOVVEAVX MISSIONNERE envoyez
Par ordre de Louis Le Grand pour tout
Le Royaume de France pour Ramener
Les Heretiques a la foy Catholiques de la
Societte de M. De S.t Rut marrechal de Camp
surnommes lemissonnere botter 1686

qui peut me
resister est bien
fort

Raison invincible

La force passe
La Raison

DRAGON
MISSIONNERE

APPEL euangeliques

Heretique finant sa
conuersion

Cartoon of 1686 showing a "missionary" of the king (an armed dragoon) "converting" a Huguenot to Catholicism.

had been condemned by the pope) and impertinent (they disapproved of his numerous mistresses). After 1680, though never a particularly religious man, he seems to have become increasingly concerned about the fate of his own soul. When his queen, Maria Theresa, died in 1683, he gave up his mistresses and secretly married Madame de Maintenon, a pious Catholic whose parents were Huguenots. In 1685 he shocked Protestant Europe by revoking the Edict of Nantes, by which Henry IV had granted religious toleration to the Huguenots.

There were about a million Huguenots out of a total population of perhaps 18 million in France at the opening of Louis XIV's reign. After Richelieu deprived them of their military and political privileges, they had become good citizens and had remained loyal to the crown during the Fronde. Many were successful in industry and the professions, though few had attained the civil and military positions that were theoretically open to them. The French Catholic clergy had long tried to persuade Louis XIV that the continued exercise of the Protestant religion in France was an insult to his dignity and authority, and as the king became more concerned about his salvation the idea of atoning for his sins of the flesh by crushing heresy became more attractive to him. The Edict was "interpreted" more and more strictly. Protestant children were declared of age at seven and converted to Catholicism, and any attempt by their parents to win them back was punished by imprisonment. Money was offered to converts, Protestant chapels were destroyed, and troops were quartered on prominent Huguenots to make life miserable for them. Finally Louis, aided and abetted by his Jesuit advisers, announced that since all the heretics had finally been reconverted to Catholicism there was no further need for the Edict of Nantes, and it was therefore revoked. Protestant churches and schools were closed, and all Protestant children were baptized as Catholics. The Revocation was enforced by imprisonment, torture, and condemnation to the galleys, but many Huguenots continued to practice their faith in secret. Others fled to England, the Dutch Netherlands, Brandenburg, and the New World. The industry and skill of the 200,000 or so Huguenots who escaped contributed appreciably to the economic life of their new homes. To France the Revocation brought both economic and moral loss.

There were only two other examples of such brutal treatment of religious minorities in the seventeenth century: the

Bishop Bossuet on Absolutism

Jacques Bénigne Bossuet was tutor to Louis XIV's son in the 1670s.

The royal power is absolute. With the aim of making this truth hateful and insufferable, many writers have tried to confound absolute government with arbitrary government. But no two things could be more unlike. . . . The prince need render an account of his acts to no one. . . . Without this absolute authority the king could neither do good nor repress evil. . . . God is infinite, God is all. The prince, as prince, is not regarded as a private person: he is a public personage, all the state is in him; the will of all the people is included in his. As all perfection and all strength are united in God, so all the power of individuals is united in the person of the prince. What grandeur that a single man should embody so much! . . . Behold this holy power, paternal and absolute; behold the secret cause which governs the whole body of the state, contained in a single head: you see the image of God in the king, and you have the idea of royal majesty. God is holiness itself, goodness itself, and power itself. In these things lies the majesty of God. In the image of these things lies the majesty of the prince.

From Jacques Bénigne Bossuet, "Politics Drawn from the Very Words of Scripture," in *Readings in European History*, ed. by James Harvey Robinson (Boston: Ginn, 1906), Vol. II, pp. 275–76.

systematic impoverishment and degradation of the Irish Catholics by their English conquerors, and the ruthless suppression of Bohemian Protestantism by the Habsburgs. But in both these cases, unlike that of France, national hatred complicated religious differences. The Revocation of the Edict of Nantes was an anachronistic act of religious intolerance that gained Louis XIV little and lost him much.

Arts and Literature

To dramatize his conception of kingship and to underscore the dependence on the monarch of all other persons and institutions in the state, Louis chose as his emblem Apollo, the sun god. The symbol of the sun, on whose rays all earthly life is dependent, was worked into the architecture and sculpture of the palace of Versailles. The Sun King patronized the arts and gave historians some reason to call his reign the "Augustan Age" of French culture. As befitted such a patron, the prevailing taste was classical, insisting on form, order, balance, and proportion. The ideals of literature and art were "order, neatness, precision, exactitude"—and these were presumed to be the ideals of all reasonable men of all ages.

Pierre Corneille (1606–84) was the father of French classical tragedy. In 1636 he had written *Le Cid*, the first of his powerful dramas that glorified will power and the striving for perfection. Corneille was still writing when Louis XIV began his personal reign, but he was soon eclipsed by his brilliant younger contemporary, Jean Racine (1639–99). Racine wrote more realistically about human beings in the grip of violent and sometimes coarse passions, bringing French tragedy to its highest point of perfection in the years between 1667 and 1677. Then he underwent a religious conversion and renounced playwrighting as an immoral occupation. Some who thrilled to his and Corneille's tragedies had little respect for the comedian Molière (1622–73), but Molière's wit and satire became the unsurpassable model for future French dramatists. From 1659 to his death in 1673 he was the idol of audiences at Versailles. All three playwrights concentrated on portraying types, not individuals—the hero, the man of honor violently in love, the miser, the hypocrite—embodiments of human passions and foibles who belonged to no particular time or place. As a result, French classical drama of the age of Louis XIV could be understood and appreciated by people everywhere, and French taste in writing came to be the dominant taste of other countries as well. So it was with architecture and the other arts. The baroque style, which ruled the design and decoration of the palace of Versailles, was intelligible and exportable. French artistic and literary standards became the standards of cultivated Europeans everywhere.

Caricature of Molière as an actor.

Engraving of a performance of *Le Malade imaginaire*, Molière's last play (1673). Molière died on stage on the fourth night of the performance.

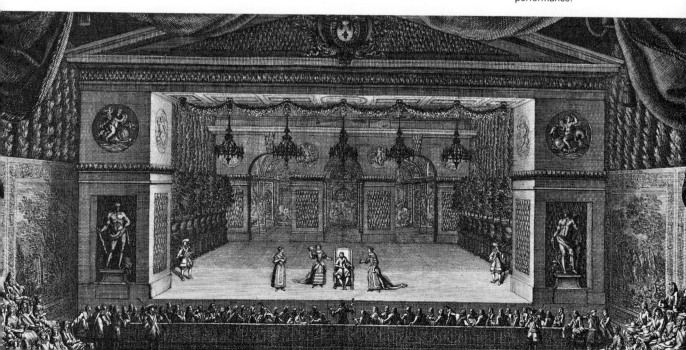

The Wars of Louis XIV

Richelieu and Mazarin had begun the process of strengthening the French army, but French military power reached its peak under Louis XIV. Le Tellier and his son Louvois were the ministers of war for almost fifty years. They subordinated the aristocratic officer class to the royal authority, developed a supply system, coordinated infantry and artillery, and, like Gustavus Adolphus, supplied the soldiers with uniforms. Vauban, one of the great military engineers of history, invented the fixed bayonet and perfected the art of building—and of destroying—fortifications. All in all, Louvois provided his master with the largest and best-equipped army in Europe: one hundred thousand men in peace and up to four hundred thousand in war.

Strengthening the army provided the king with great temptations to use his power in foreign wars. War would please the nobles, who profited by it and who had little outlet for their ambitions at home. War would exercise and justify the enormous standing army. Above all, successful war would enhance the glory of the monarch, raise him still further above his subjects, and perhaps make him the arbiter not only of France but of Europe as well. No one better than Louis XIV exemplified a nineteenth-century historian's dictum, "All power tends to corrupt, and absolute power corrupts absolutely." For half a century Europe was ravaged by wars that were caused by Louis' desire to maintain French prestige and increase French territory. As Louis' thirst for power grew, so did his enemies' fear of him.

The aims of Louis' earlier wars were relatively limited and understandable. With Spain's power broken and the Empire in a state of collapse, he wanted to annex the Spanish Netherlands (later Belgium), Franche-Comté, and bits of western German territories. He fought two wars for these objectives, but each time, after early victories, he found himself thwarted by an alliance of other powers. By 1678 he had gained only Franche-Comté and a few border towns in Flanders.

For a time Louis tried legal chicanery in place of bullets to gain more territory. French courts called Chambers of Reunion were set up to "reunite" to France any land that at any time had been a dependency of a French territory. This process gave Louis control of the independent Protestant republic of Strasbourg in 1681, and it was long before European indignation subsided or Strasbourg became a contented part of France. The Revocation of the Edict of Nantes in 1685 was further evidence to European

The palace at Versailles (1668). Louis XIV is shown arriving in a carriage.

statesmen of Louis' intemperance, and in 1686 the defensive League of Augsburg was formed by the emperor, Spain, Sweden, and several German states. Europe was already at war when William of Orange, ruler of the Dutch Netherlands and Louis' most implacable enemy, became King William III of England in 1689. The circle was closed around France when the English and the Dutch joined the League.

This time France was on the defensive. At the very outset, in 1688, the French united their enemies by perpetrating one of the most senseless atrocities of the century, the systematic devastation of the Palatinate for no good political or military reason just before the occupying French troops withdrew. The War of the League of Augsburg was waged in India and America as well as in Europe, so it may be called the first of the modern world wars. After ten years of fighting, France agreed to the Peace of Ryswick (1697), by which France managed to retain its gains up to 1678 but was forced to renounce nearly all accessions after that date except Strasbourg. England came out of the war considerably stronger as a naval and military power; France came out of it a weaker power than it had been a decade earlier.

The War of the Spanish Succession, 1701–14

At the turn of the century all the fears and hatreds that had been built up during a generation of fighting were concentrated in a fourth struggle, the War of the Spanish Succession (1701–14). This war, like that of 1688 to 1697, was fought in America and India as well as in Europe. In its origins and its course, the older motives of dynastic ambition and preservation of the balance of power were mixed with the newer motives of commercial advantage and national sentiment. Religion now played no important part whatever.

In 1698 Charles II of Spain, who had for thirty years been a kind of walking medical exhibit of half a dozen fatal diseases, was finally dying. He was the last of the Habsburgs who had ruled Spain since 1516, and he had no direct heirs. The question was whether the Spanish

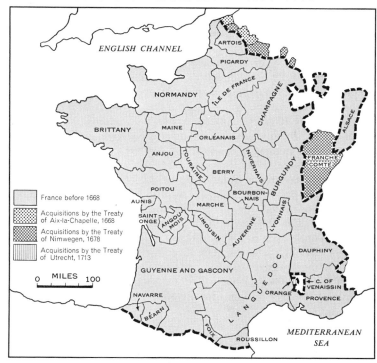

THE CONQUESTS OF LOUIS XIV 1661–1715

France before 1668

Acquisitions by the Treaty of Aix-la-Chapelle, 1668

Acquisitions by the Treaty of Nimwegen, 1678

Acquisitions by the Treaty of Utrecht, 1713

Empire would fall to some member of the Austrian Habsburg family or to some member of the French Bourbon dynasty (both Louis XIV's mother and first wife had been Spanish Habsburg princesses) or would be partitioned or dismembered in some way. The English and the Dutch had obvious reasons for keeping France from gaining control of the Spanish colonial trade or of the Spanish Netherlands. Louis seemed willing to compromise and twice concluded secret treaties with the English and the Dutch to partition the Spanish dominions, but when news of the second treaty reached Madrid the dying king lost his temper. In order to preserve the Spanish Empire intact as a bulwark of Catholicism, he made a will leaving all his dominions to a grandson of Louis XIV. This grandson was proclaimed King Philip V of Spain shortly after the death of Charles II in November 1700.

Louis XIV soon decided to tear up the treaties by which he had accepted a more modest share of the Spanish Empire. He recognized the will of Charles II and sent French troops into the Spanish Nether-

Officer and musketeer of the French Guard (late seventeenth century).

lands. In 1701 William III of England concluded the Grand Alliance of the Hague by which the English, the Dutch, and the Austrian Habsburg emperor bound themselves to fight until they had ended the threat of Bourbon control of Spain and of the Spanish colonies. Louis XIV had made his last and most arrogant bid for the dominance of Europe, but this time he was forced to fight for France's life against enemies who proved as arrogant and unyielding as he. Within a few years the large allied forces under the brilliant command of Prince Eugene of Savoy and the English Duke of Marlborough had beaten the French in four bloody battles (Blenheim, 1704; Ramillies, 1706; Oudenarde, 1708; Malplaquet, 1709). The English navy had trounced the French at sea, and the English had seized Gibraltar. An allied army had even dethroned Philip V in Spain for a time.

Louis XIV, his country exhausted, sued for peace on almost any terms, only to be met by an allied demand that he contribute French troops to expel his own grandson from Madrid. This was too much for even a badly beaten monarch, and he refused, backed by a rising tide of national feeling in France. A similar national reaction in Spain in favor of their new Bourbon monarch, Philip V, resulted in the defeat of English and Austrian troops there. In 1710 a victory of the Tories over the Whigs, who had been the war party in England, brought in a government in London favorable to peace. And finally in 1712 the French won their only important victory of the war. In the end the allies paid the price for asking too much from Louis at the moment when he was almost helpless. The Peace of Utrecht (1713-14), which settled the war, was somewhat more favorable to France than it might have been if it had been signed four years earlier. Here at the very end of his career, the balance of power seemed to work in Louis XIV's favor by preventing the elimination of France from the ranks of the great powers.

The Peace of Utrecht, 1713–14

In theory, the Peace of Utrecht gave the French the prize that they had sought at the beginning of the war. Philip V remained on the throne of Spain, but only on condition that the crowns of Spain and France should never be worn by the same monarch. In every other aim, however, the French were thwarted. They gave up all conquests east of the Rhine, failed to win the Spanish Netherlands, and lost their bid for control of the Spanish colonial trade. England was the chief winner. England took Newfoundland, Acadia (modern New Brunswick and Nova Scotia), and Hudson's Bay Territory from France, and Gibraltar and Minorca from Spain. In addition, the English received the *Asiento*—the right to supply black slaves to the Spanish colonies, a privilege that proved very lucrative and provided an excuse for a large-scale smuggling trade with the Spanish Empire.

England came out of the war rich and powerful, in a position to dominate international commerce and with the strongest navy in Europe. France came out of it still a great nation, but with its people badly exhausted by high taxation and its government bankrupt and unpopular. The Austrian Habsburgs gained by being given the Spanish Netherlands (which now became the Austrian Netherlands), as well as Milan, Naples, and Sicily. Austria thus replaced Spain as the dominant power in Italy. Two new smaller powers, Brandenburg-Prussia and the Duchy of Savoy, came out of the war with increased territories and heightened prestige as a reward for having been on the winning side. A century and a half later Prussia was to unify Germany, and Savoy, as the Kingdom of Sardinia, was to take the lead in the unification of Italy. The Dutch kept the Scheldt River closed, thus blocking the trade of Antwerp, the chief port of the Austrian Netherlands. But they had suffered from the long strain of fighting against the French for half a century and were soon to disappear from the ranks of the great powers.

The Peace of Utrecht ended the first attempt by a European state to establish an overwhelming predominance of power since the days of Philip II of Spain. When Louis XIV died in 1715, rulers outside France breathed a sigh of relief; it was even said that the common people of his own land "openly returned thanks to God." His bid for European hegemony had been defeated by the workings of the balance-of-power principle, but the seeds of future war were unfortunately still deep in the European soil.

ENGLAND: THE EMERGENCE OF A PARLIAMENTARY MONARCHY

While Louis XIV was putting the finishing touches on the institution of absolute monarchy in France, the English, without any very clear idea of where they were headed, were completing the foundation of a constitutional monarchy controlled by Parliament.

The restoration of the king, Parliament, and the Anglican Church in 1660 had established a kind of equilibrium between the crown and Parliament, but it was soon evident that it was a very unstable balance. Who was really to control the government—the king or the wealthy landowners and merchants who dominated Parliament? What was the religious settlement to be, and who was to have the last word in making it? Who was to control foreign policy? These three main questions of the past two generations— the questions of politics, religion, and foreign policy—still awaited final answers. It took almost two more generations of domestic intrigue and foreign war for the answers to be found.

Charles II, 1660–85

Charles II was quite unlike his father—witty, worldly-wise, attractive, a man of easy morals and shrewd political sense. He had lived long in exile in France, and his cousin Louis XIV was his model. He would have liked to restore England to Catholicism and to set up an absolute monarchy on the French model, but he was too intelligent to ignore the difficulties in his way and too cautious to persist in the face of determined opposition. He was resolved not to risk exile or execution. He knew that if his goal was to be reached, it would be by intrigue, manipulation, and compromise, not by force or by open proclamation of his aims. The result was twenty-five years of infinitely complex party politics and secret diplomacy in which the issues were never very clear to the people or to the members of Parliament, or even to the king's ministers.

Cavalier Parliament, 1661–79

Parliament held a commanding position at the beginning of the reign. The "Cavalier Parliament," which met in 1661 and was not dissolved until 1679, was dominated by the landed nobility and gentry, who were now restored to their ancient influence in both local and national government. Both groups were strongly royalist for the moment, both determined to stamp out all remnants of religious and political radicalism. But at the same time they were not willing to see the crown recover any real financial independence of Parliament. In place of the old idea that "the king should live of his own," Parliament now granted Charles a regular income from customs and excise duties, but it was not enough. Charles found that he could not meet even the ordinary expenses of government, let alone the expenses of his extravagant mistresses, from his regular revenue. And there was certainly no money for foreign war unless Parliament approved the objectives. So for a time at least, Charles had to let Parliament have its way under the leadership of his father's adviser, Edward Hyde, Earl of Clarendon.

Parliament also had the last word in the religious settlement. The Cavalier Parliament was as strongly pro-Anglican as it was pro-royalist. In a series of statutes passed between 1661 and 1665 and known as the "Clarendon Code," Puritans who dissented from the established church were excluded from local government and Puritan ministers were rooted out of the Anglican clergy. Later legislation made it illegal for a dissenter to sit in Parliament, to serve in the army or navy, or to attend the universities at Oxford or Cambridge. Behind this attempt to discourage dissent was the fear that Puritans were inevitably political radicals. But

The House of Commons, on the Great Seal of England (1651).

while the Clarendon Code lowered the social position and narrowed opportunities for dissenters, it did not greatly decrease their numbers. Presbyterians, Congregationalists, Baptists, and Quakers (also Methodists a century later) formed permanent but peaceful minority groups. The dissenters remained antagonistic to the ruling Anglican majority, but they were even more bitterly opposed to Catholicism.

Charles did not like the Clarendon Code. He would have preferred a policy that tolerated both Puritans and Catholics, but Parliament would not stand for this. In 1672 Charles issued a "Declaration of Indulgence," which suspended the operation of the laws against both groups. But the next year Parliament forced him to withdraw the declaration and accept a severe Test Act excluding all but Anglicans from civil and military office. To the Anglican gentry in Parliament, Puritans were still radicals and Catholics still traitors.

Foreign Policy

Two natural calamities, an outbreak of plague in 1665 and a fire that destroyed much of London in 1666, contributed to general unrest. Uneasiness increased as king and Parliament drifted apart over foreign policy. In 1665 Parliament forced Charles into a commercial war with the Dutch but did not give him enough money to win it. When victories failed to develop, Clarendon was unfairly held responsible and was exiled. After Louis XIV began his attacks on the Spanish Netherlands in 1667, the ordinary Englishman began to see the military power of Catholic France as more of a threat than the commercial rivalry of the Protestant Dutch. But to Charles II, Louis was still the ideal ally—powerful, wealthy, and an old personal friend.

In 1670 England once more allied itself with France against the Dutch, and Charles negotiated with Louis one of the most notorious deals in the history of English foreign policy, the secret Treaty of Dover. By this agreement Charles promised to declare himself a Catholic and to reconvert England to Catholicism in return for French money and, if necessary, French troops. Probably Charles himself was not sure how far he meant to go, but at the least he was ready to adopt a pro-French foreign policy. Between 1675 and 1681 four more secret agreements were concluded between Charles and Louis in which Charles promised he would thwart Parliament's anti-French moves in return for subsidies from France. The close understanding between Charles and Louis leaked out and gradually built up English fears of Catholicism and French dominance. The landed classes represented in Parliament were suspicious of Charles, increasingly less royalist in sentiment than they had been in 1661, and ready to give way to panic if

Pepys's Account of the Great Fire of London
September 2–6, 1666

The fire started near the river, spread to warehouses full of combustible materials, and destroyed most of the old city of London, including St. Paul's Cathedral. This gave Christopher Wren the opportunity to build his famous churches. Samuel Pepys was an eyewitness to the fire and recorded its events in his diary.

[Pepys heard of the fire and took a boat down the Thames.] Everybody was endeavoring to remove their goods, and flinging them into the river or bringing them into lighters; poor people staying in their houses till the fire touched them, and then running into boats. And the poor pigeons, I perceived, were loth to leave their houses, but hovered about the windows and balconys till they burned their wings and fell down. Nobody, to my sight, endeavoring to quench it, but only to remove their goods and leave all to the fire—the wind mighty high and driving it into the city and everything, after so long a drought, proving combustible, even the very stones of the churches.

[That evening Pepys and his wife went out on the river.] We went as near the fire as we could for smoke and all over the Thames; with one's face in the wind, you were almost burned with a shower of fire-drops. This is very true; so that houses were burned by these drops and flakes of fire [even when] three or four—nay five or six—houses from another. When we could endure no more at the water, we went to a little ale-house on the Bankside and there saw the fire grow . . . as far as we could see up the hill of the city, in a most horrible malicious bloody flame, not like the fine flame of an ordinary fire. We stayed till we saw the fire as only an entire arch of fire from this to the other side of [London] bridge and in a bow up the hill for an arch of above a mile long. It made me weep to see it—the churches, houses and all on fire and flaming at once, and a horrid noise the flames made, and the cracking of houses at their ruin.

From *The Diary of Samuel Pepys* (many editions), entry for September 2, 1666.

any incident should excite their fear of France and popery.

Whigs and Tories

In 1678 these accumulated fears were fanned into flame by a lurid incident known to history as the Popish Plot. A thoroughly disreputable character named Titus Oates concocted a story, accepted by almost the whole country, that there was a Jesuit plot afoot to murder the king and put his Catholic brother James, the Duke of York, on the throne with French help—"a damnable and hellish plot," Parliament called it, "for assassinating and murdering the king and rooting out and destroying the Protestant religion." Civil war seemed about to break out again.

A "Country Party" led by the Earl of Shaftesbury campaigned at the polls and supported a bill to exclude the Duke of York from the succession to the throne. An Anglican and royalist "Court Party" rallied to the support of Charles II and his brother, though at first without very much enthusiasm. Members of the first group were called Whigs (a name hitherto applied to fanatical Scottish Presbyterians); members of the second group were called Tories (a name for Catholic outlaws in Ireland). The Whigs controlled the three brief Parliaments that followed the dissolution of the Cavalier Parliament in 1679, and innocent men went to their deaths for complicity in the Popish Plot. But the Whig leaders soon overplayed their hand; public opinion swung back in favor of the king, and it was now the turn of innocent Whigs to suffer. By 1681 Shaftesbury had fled abroad, the inventors of the Popish Plot were disgraced or executed, and Charles was stronger than ever before. Until his death four years later he ruled without Parliament, thanks to Louis' subsidies, with his brother James by his side.

The origin of political parties in the modern sense—groups organized for the purpose of electioneering and controlling government through a representative assembly—lies in these chaotic years of English history. Instead of civil war, the eventual outcome was the "two-party system," which came to be characteristic

of English and American politics. Whigs and Tories were the remote political heirs of the Parliamentarians and royalists of the 1640s. In turn they became the ancestors of the Liberals and Conservatives, the Democrats and Republicans, of two centuries later.

James II, 1685–88

The Duke of York, who succeeded Charles II as James II in 1685, was a very different sort of person from his brother—a bigoted convert to Catholicism without any of Charles's political shrewdness or tendency to compromise. Within three short years (1685–88) he managed to infuriate almost every group of any importance in English political and religious life, and in the end he provoked the revolution that Charles had succeeded in avoiding. Made overconfident by early successes, he introduced Catholics into the high command of both army and navy and camped a standing army a few miles from London. He surrounded himself with Catholic advisers and attacked Anglican control of the universities. He claimed the power to suspend or dispense with acts of Parliament. In a vain attempt to win the support of Puritans as well as Catholics, he issued a Declaration of Indulgence along the lines of his brother's. By revoking borough charters and browbeating sheriffs he tried to ensure the election of a Parliament favorable to his policies. Louis XIV's Revocation of the Edict of Nantes in 1685 had already terrified Protestants in England. They held back as long as James's immediate heir (his older daughter) was a Protestant, but their fears became unbearable when the hope of a Protestant succession was suddenly destroyed by the unexpected birth of a son to James's Catholic queen.

The "Glorious Revolution" of 1688

In spite of the intense political tension, civil war did not break out in 1688 as it had in 1642. Englishmen still remembered the horrors of civil war, and this time there was only one side. James had literally no support of any signifi-

Engraving of James II, after a painting by Kneller (1688).

cance, except for a handful of personal friends. He had alienated both Anglicans and nonconformists, Tories and Whigs, nobles and common people. The result, therefore, was a bloodless "revolution," a thoroughgoing political overturn that, as historians look back on it, answered all the main questions of the century in favor of a limited, or parliamentary, monarchy and established the constitutional pattern of English public life that has persisted to the present time.

James II had two daughters by his first wife (Clarendon's daughter), both of whom remained Protestants. The elder, Mary, was married in 1677 to the *stadtholder* of the Dutch Republic, William of Orange, who was Louis XIV's outstanding Protestant opponent on the Continent. In June 1688 a group of prominent and representative Englishmen, both Whigs and Tories, invited William to cross the Channel and save the Protestant cause in England. In the following November William landed on the southern coast of England with a Dutch army and marched slowly on London. There was almost no resistance. James II fled to France, and a Convention Parliament (an irregular assembly of men who had had parliamentary seats) declared that James had "abdicated" the throne by his flight. It then invited William and Mary to become joint sovereigns. A "Bill of Rights" was passed and the "Glorious Revolution" was accomplished.

The chief result of the Revolution was the establishment of parliamentary sovereignty over the crown. Parliament had made a king and could regulate the right of succession to the throne. Though William was a strong-willed man, especially in matters of foreign policy, he knew that Parliament had the final say. And though the supporters of James II and his son intrigued and even staged two abortive rebellions in the eighteenth century, there was no second Restoration. Parliament could criticize, influence, and eventually make the government's policy.

The Bill of Rights emphatically denied the king's right to suspend acts of Parliament or to interfere with the ordinary course of justice. It furnished a base for the steady expansion of civil liberties in the generation after 1688. Religious toleration and freedom from arbitrary arrest were established by law; censorship of the press was quietly dropped. The king had to summon Parliament every year because he could not pay or control his armed forces without parliamentary consent. These regular meetings strengthened the parties and made the king dependent on their support. In 1707 the monarch vetoed a parliamentary bill for the last time.

Struggles for control of policy were now no longer between king and Parliament, but between factions in Parliament. The Revolution did not establish democracy, but it did establish control by

Contemporary engraving showing the speaker of the House of Lords offering William and Mary the English crown.

the wealthy landed proprietors and merchants over both the central and local organs of English government. Generally speaking, the greater noble landowners, the bankers and the merchants, and most dissenters were Whigs, while the smaller gentry, the Anglican parish clergy, and some great lords were Tories. But parties were still loosely organized, and small factions with selfish interests often held the balance of power. England was governed by shifting alliances among leaders of the propertied classes.

The Cabinet System

It took over a century for parliamentary leaders to work out a smooth and efficient way to run the government. The ultimate answer was to be the "cabinet system"—that is, government by a committee of leaders of the majority party in Parliament, holding the chief executive offices in the government, acting under the leadership of a "prime minister," and acknowledging primary responsibility to Parliament rather than to the crown for their actions. During the reigns of William and Mary (1689–1702) and of Mary's sister, Queen Anne (1702–14), the first fumbling moves were made that led to such a system, though parliamentary leaders had as yet no sense of their goal, and monarchs still considered ministers to be responsible to them rather than to Parliament. The privy council had long been too large and unwieldy for effective action, so that a "cabinet council," or inner circle of important ministers, had developed under Charles II. The members of this "cabinet" slowly found that it was better to discuss major questions among themselves and to present a united front to the monarch on matters of policy. Sometimes a leading member of the "cabinet" was referred to as "prime minister." In order to gain Parliament's indispensable support in war or peace, both William and Anne occasionally found that it was better to choose their ministers not from both parties but from the majority party. By the time Queen Anne died in 1714 it had become evident that the real government of England was slowly falling into the hands of a cabinet of ministers who controlled a parliamentary majority, often by bribery, and felt themselves ultimately responsible to the political interests of this majority.

Religious Toleration

The Revolution also produced a certain measure of religious toleration. Broad-mindedness was becoming fashionable in educated circles, and both Anglicans and Puritans were now more afraid of Catholic France than they were of each other. Puritans had supported Anglicans against James II, and King William, who came from the most tolerant country in Europe, insisted on a religious truce. The result was the "Toleration Act" of 1689, which allowed dissenters to worship as they pleased and to educate their clergy and laity in schools of their own. Dissenters were still legally excluded from all civil and military offices, however, and there was no repeal of the long series of anti-Catholic statutes, although they were not enforced with any great rigor after 1689. Protestant fear that a Catholic might succeed to the throne was finally quieted by the Act of Settlement of 1701, which provided that the sovereign should always be an Anglican. The act also settled the succession, in case James II's two daughters should die without children, on the descendants of that daughter of James I who had married the ill-fated Elector of the Palatinate before the Thirty Years' War. In this way the elector of Hanover came to the throne in 1714, when Queen Anne died without issue, thus bringing the Stuart dynasty to a close.

Growth of English Power

A third result of the Revolution was to unite crown and Parliament on foreign policy as they had never been united under the first four Stuarts, and thus to turn the energies of a generation of Englishmen from domestic conflict to foreign war. Given English fear of Catholicism, King William had no difficulty bringing England into the Grand Alliance against Louis XIV, who was sheltering James II in exile. Parliamentary monarchy soon demonstrated that it was a more formi-

Medal of Queen Anne (1702–14), and her signature.

dable foe than the absolute monarchy of the Stuarts had been. The English government was able to raise money to fight its wars in a way that was barred to all other European governments except the Dutch. The founding of the Bank of England in 1694 was an important event in the history of English public finance. Within a few days of its founding, it had raised over a million pounds of investors' money that it promptly lent to the government at 8 percent interest. So long as the government continued to pay the interest, the bank made no demand for repayment of this loan. Thus the present permanent, or "funded," national debt began. The merchants and tradesmen, large and small, who invested their money in the bank obviously had confidence in the government, and their investment bound them still more firmly to support the revolutionary settlement.

Throughout the next century English wealth combined with English sea power was to give the island kingdom a striking power out of all proportion to its area and population. During the reigns of William and Mary and of Anne, trade, which was more and more the foundation of English wealth, increased considerably. The Peace of Utrecht (1713) gave English sea power, the guarantor of English trade, an almost unrivaled position. The solution in 1689 of the chief political and religious differences between crown and Parliament touched off an almost explosive release of English energies that by 1763 had rocketed England to the hegemony of Europe.

Ireland and Scotland

The Revolution also did something to further the unification of the British Isles, though indirectly. England, Ireland, and Scotland all had the same king from 1603 on, but union went no further than the common crown. The two smaller kingdoms, especially Ireland, suffered greatly during the seventeenth century through involvement in England's religious and political divisions. The native Irish were Catholic to a man, and the Protestant English both despised them and feared them as potential allies of the Catholic Spanish and French. By settling Protes-

Anti-Catholic woodcuts showing "horrors" of the rebellion by Irish Catholics (1689).

tant colonists in Ulster, James I began the policy of creating a Protestant majority in the northeastern region of Ireland. But the Ulster Protestants were Presbyterians and soon became anti-Stuart, while the rest of the Irish were generally loyal to the Stuart dynasty, and for that reason suffered cruelly under Cromwell. After the Revolution, James II tried to fight his way back to his throne by way of Ireland. He was defeated at the Battle of the Boyne (1689), an event whose memory still stirs up bitter feelings between Catholics and Protestants in Ulster. James's defeat led to a savage and systematic persecution of the Catholic Irish by English (and Irish) Protestant landlords, comparable only to Louis XIV's brutal treatment of the Huguenots. The Irish were exploited and bled white economically, their priests were persecuted, and their Parliament was reserved for Protestants only.

The Scots had somewhat better fortune in the end, although they too suffered by being involved in England's troubles through the century. Scotland had gained little by giving a king to England in 1603. It remained a poor but proud neighbor of a larger kingdom, excluded from the benefits of English trade, jealously guarding its own law and its own Parliament, and firmly defending its Presbyterian Church against Anglican attacks. Although it had been the Scots who touched off the revolution against Charles I, there was strong attachment to the native Stuart dynasty in Scotland, especially among Catholic clansmen of the Highlands. After 1649 and again after 1689 Scotland became a base for risings in support of the Stuarts. The Scots accepted the Revolution of 1688, but they did not accept the Act of Settlement of 1701. They threatened to choose a separate king of their own—possibly the exiled pretender James II—in case James's last daughter, Anne, died without issue. This frightened the English into serious negotiations. In 1707 an organic union between the two kingdoms was finally agreed on and was confirmed by an Act of Union. Scotland retained its own law and its established Presbyterian religion, but it surrendered its separate Parliament in return for representation in the English Parliament. Scottish nationalists were (and still are) angry over their loss of independence, but Scotland gained much in the next century by becoming an integral part of the Kingdom of Great Britain. Scottish merchants, administrators, and philosophers were to play a prominent part during the eighteenth century in building the British Empire and in furthering the Enlightenment.

John Locke

The Revolution of 1640 and the Glorious Revolution of 1688 together constituted the first of those revolutions in modern western states that ended absolute divine-right monarchy and eventually put the middle classes in control of government. English leaders did their best to insist to the outside world in 1688 and 1689 that they were doing nothing new or revolutionary at all, but they never succeeded in persuading foreigners that they were merely conservative supporters of ancient English liberties. Europe was more interested in the interpretation of the Revolution by John Locke (1632–1704), a friend of the Earl of Shaftesbury, the founder of the Whig Party. In *Of Civil Government: Two Treatises* (1690), Locke set down in plain, common-sense fashion the general principles underlying the long English strug-

gle for limited monarchy that culminated in the Revolution of 1688. Even if the logic was not always clear, the reasonableness of the discussion had great influence throughout the eighteenth century.

Locke directed his attack explicitly against the divine-right theory of monarchy, and implicitly against the more pragmatic absolute theory of Thomas Hobbes. He began with the rights to "life, liberty, and property," which he said all men possess naturally, and went on to insist that the sole reason for establishing any government is to preserve these rights. Legislative and executive powers are to be strictly separated; if the executive becomes tyrannical and invades the rights of individuals, the people must curb it through their representative assembly—or if all else fails, they may revolt and set up a new government. In other words, an ultimate right of revolution always resides in the people, and the dissolution of government does not necessarily mean the dissolution of society. Locke's book was probably written before 1688 as a sort of program for revolution, but it was not published until after the Revolution and so naturally became a kind of apology for what had been done. Inalienable rights, government by consent, separation of powers,

John Locke (1632–1704), champion of the "natural" rights of man.

Locke on Government by Consent   1690

Compare "Bishop Bossuet on Absolutism," p. 450.

Men being, as has been said, by nature all free, equal, and independent, no one can be put out of this estate and subjected to the political power of another without his own consent, which is done by agreeing with other men, to join and unite into a community for their comfortable, safe, and peaceful living, one amongst another, in a secure enjoyment of their properties, and a greater security against any that are not of it. . . . When any number of men have so consented to make one community or government, they are thereby presently incorporated, and make one body politic, wherein the majority have the right to act and conclude the rest. . . . Absolute, arbitrary power, or governing without settled standing laws, can neither of them consist with the ends of society and government, which men would not quit the freedom of the state of Nature for, and tie themselves up under, were it not to preserve their lives, liberties, and fortunes, and by stated rules of right and property to secure their peace and quiet.

From John Locke, *Of Civil Government: Two Treatises* (New York: Everyman's Library, 1924), pp. 164–65, 186.

the right of revolution—these were the ideas that Locke implied were at the heart of the Glorious Revolution. These were the ideas that seemed self-evident truths to Americans in 1776 and to Frenchmen in 1789 and that formed a link between the English, the American, and the French revolutions.

CENTRAL AND EASTERN EUROPE 1648–1721

The economy of early modern Europe was divided into two sharply defined halves by an imaginary line running north from the head of the Adriatic Sea, around the Bohemian mountains, and down the Elbe River to the North Sea. West of this line was an area that was increasingly affected by the growth of towns and trade. The majority of the population still lived on the land, but most peasants were free workers and many of them small landowners. Most serfs in the West had become agricultural laborers for pay, and most feudal nobles had become landlords who hired labor for wages (particularly in England) or simply lived on rents. Though still a minority, the bourgeoisie were increasingly influential in society and politics.

East of the line was a society still largely agrarian and feudal, an area of few large towns and an insignificant bourgeoisie. Here in Hungary, Bohemia, Poland, Prussia, and Russia, the landed estates were larger and the landed nobility more powerful politically than in the West. During the sixteenth and seventeenth centuries the nobles of eastern Europe managed to reduce the great majority of the peasants to a state of serfdom in which the peasant was bound to the land and forced to work from two to five days a week for his lord. One reason for this drive to enslave the peasant was that grain prices were rising in western markets, and eastern landlords had every inducement to increase the production of their estates. Another reason was that the governments of eastern Europe were either dominated by nobles, as in Hungary and Poland, or favorable to the growth of serfdom because it supported the nobles

who served the state, as in Prussia and Russia. In western Europe, command of money was increasingly the key to power and influence; in the East, ownership of land and command of compulsory services were still the secrets of power.

Warfare was as common as in the West, and much more dangerous. States with no natural frontiers on the flat plains of central and eastern Europe could easily be wiped out. Modernized armies were needed, but such armies could be created only by strong, centralized administrations and supported only by effective tax systems. Neither centralization nor taxation was easy. Eastern rulers were facing roughly the same obstacles to the growth of centralized government that western rulers had faced two centuries and more earlier: a powerful landed nobility, a church that held itself above dynastic interests and owned a large portion of the wealth of the land, an agrarian economy with limited commerce and infant industries, a bourgeoisie still too small to bear the weight of heavy taxation, and an ignorant and exploited peasantry tied to the land and thus incapable of meeting the need of new industries for labor. To build a "modern" state in the face of these difficulties was beyond the capacities of all but the ablest rulers.

The Holy Roman Empire

The one large political organization bridging eastern and western Europe was the Holy Roman Empire. But although there was still an emperor, and a Diet, which met "perpetually" at Regensburg after 1663, the Empire was a political fiction. It had no central administration, no system of imperial taxation, no standing army, no common law, no tariff union, not even a common calendar. The Peace of Westphalia had recognized the sovereignty of the individual states, as well as the right of France and Sweden to take part in the deliberations of the Diet. In the welter of political units—free cities, ecclesiastical principalities, counties, margravates, and duchies, together with one kingdom (Bohemia)—that made up the Empire, almost every petty princeling fancied himself a Louis XIV and fash-

Division of Eastern and Western Europe

The crown of the Holy Roman Empire of the German Nation, used from 961 to 1792.

ioned a court modeled as closely as possible on Versailles. Already the Empire fitted Voltaire's description a century later as "neither Holy, nor Roman, nor an Empire."

The ruling families of a few of the larger states—Bavaria, Saxony, Hanover, Brandenburg, and Austria—were trying hard to expand their territories by war or marriage and to gain royal titles. Augustus the Strong of Saxony, in addition to fathering (according to legend) more than three hundred children, managed to get himself elected king of Poland in 1696. In 1701 the Elector of Brandenburg obtained the emperor's consent to style himself king in Prussia. And in 1714 the Elector of Hanover became king of England. But only two great powers eventually grew out of the wreck of the Empire. These were Austria and Brandenburg-Prussia.

The Habsburgs and Austria

The attempt of Emperor Ferdinand II (1619–37) to revive and strengthen the Empire under Habsburg control was defeated in the Thirty Years' War. The Habsburgs thereafter turned to a policy that Ferdinand had also furthered: consolidating and expanding the hereditary lands of the family in Austria and the Danube Valley. Thus a centralized Habsburg monarchy might be developed that could hold its own with the states of the West. The Emperor Leopold I (1658–1705) was the chief architect of this policy, aided, and at times prodded, by some capable civil servants and one remarkable general, Prince Eugene of Savoy.

To weld a centralized monarchy together, Leopold had to reduce three separate areas—Austria, Bohemia, and Hungary—to some semblance of unity and obedience. In the Duchy of Austria and neighboring Tyrol, his lawyers were able to establish his ascendancy over a feudal nobility whose economic position was still strong. Bohemia, it will be remembered, had been reduced to obedience to Vienna early in the Thirty Years' War. A new nobility owing its titles to the Habsburg ruler replaced the old, and the crown of Bohemia, previously elec-

tive, was made hereditary in the Habsburg family in 1627.

The real problem was Hungary. Although the Habsburgs had usually been the elected monarchs of the kingdom since early in the sixteenth century, hardly a third of Hungary was actually in Habsburg hands. The rest was either directly or indirectly ruled by the Ottoman Turks. To establish their authority in Hungary, the Habsburg monarchs in Vienna had to deal not only with the powerful Hungarian nobility and the Hungarian Protestants but with the Turks and the French as well. The nobles were wealthy and unruly; the Protestants were numerous and inclined to side with the Turks against the Catholic Habsburgs. The Ottoman Empire was not the power it had been in the sixteenth century, but since 1656 it had been undergoing a revival under a vigorous line of grand viziers of the Kiuprili family, who in the 1660s began a new thrust up the Danube Valley directed at their old enemies, the Habsburgs. Louis XIV, also an inveterate enemy of the Habsburgs, allied himself with the Turks and Hungarian rebels against his Austrian foes. Thus building a monarchy in the Danube Valley was as much a foreign as a domestic problem.

The Siege of Vienna, 1683

The crisis came in 1683. In July of that year a Turkish army of more than one hundred thousand laid siege to Vienna. For two months the fate of Austria seemed to hang in the balance. Then volunteers began to flow in from all over the Continent to help the emperor in his extremity. The greatest pope of the century, Innocent XI, contributed moral and material aid, and King John Sobieski of Poland arrived with an army that helped rout the Turks by September. The retreat continued year after year as the impetus of Europe's last crusade carried on down the Danube Valley, until Eugene of Savoy broke Turkish military power at the battle of Zenta (1697).

The Peace of Carlowitz in 1699 gave the Habsburgs full control of Hungary. The Hungarian Protestants were crushed; many of them were executed for treason.

Emperor Leopold I (above) and Prince Eugene of Savoy, Habsburg commander, detail from a painting by Kupezky.

The landowning nobility was left in full control of its serfs and in possession of many of its old privileges, in return for recognizing the ultimate sovereignty of the chancellery at Vienna. The Habsburgs were thus content with what one historian calls "a loose framework of centralized administration." They left local administration much as they found it, but they had established a strong monarchy in the Danube Valley where none had existed before.

The Treaties of Ryswick (1697) and Carlowitz (1699) marked the appearance on the European stage of two new great powers: England and Austria. Each had risen in response to Louis XIV's bid to make himself the heir of Habsburg power in Spain and Germany. The two illustrated how diverse great powers could be in the seventeenth century: England, a parliamentary monarchy controlled by a commercial and landed aristocracy, its strength based on commerce and sea power; Austria, a bureaucratic monarchy with agriculture and a standing army its most conspicuous sources of strength. At about the same time two more powers were just beginning to appear, each as distinct and different as England and Austria. These were Brandenburg-Prussia and Russia.

The Rise of Brandenburg-Prussia

The story of the rise of the Hohenzollerns in northern Germany is somewhat parallel to that of the Habsburgs in the south, except that the Hohenzollerns started with less and had farther to go. Their achievements owed proportionately more to the genius and patience of one man, Frederick William (1640–88), called the Great Elector.

The Hohenzollerns had been margraves of Brandenburg since 1417 (a margrave was count of a "mark," or frontier province). To this small territory around Berlin they had added by inheritance two other areas: Cleves and some neighboring lands on the Rhine (1614), and the Duchy of Prussia on the Baltic coast to the northeast (1618). When the Thirty Years' War broke out there was nothing to suggest that the ruler of these three scattered territories had any brighter future than a dozen other German princes. He was an Elector—that is, one of the seven princes who (theoretically) chose the emperor—and thus a member of the highest echelon of German princes. But his lands had no natural boundaries, no traditional ties with one another, poor soil, few resources, and sparse population, about a million and a half in all. Furthermore, they were especially hard hit by the Thirty Years' War. Swedish and Imperialist armies tramped back and forth across Brandenburg without hindrance. Berlin lost over half its population. And the Great Elector's dominions as a whole probably lost almost one-third of their people—a loss that took forty years to make up.

The Great Elector, 1640–88

Frederick William was twenty years old when he became Elector in 1640 during the later years of the Thirty Years' War. Though he was a devoted Calvinist, he nevertheless respected the Lutheranism of his subjects and was genuinely tolerant in an age of intolerance and fanaticism. The helplessness of Brandenburg during the war taught him that his first and foremost task must be the development of an army, and to this end he set himself with unrelenting effort.

"A ruler is treated with no consideration if he does not have troops and means of his own," he advised his son in 1667. "It is these, Thank God! which have made me considerable since the time that I began to have them."

In 1640 he had a poorly equipped and ineffective army of twenty-five hundred men. Before the end of the war in 1648 he had increased it to eight thousand and by his death in 1688 he had a peacetime force of thirty thousand which was once expanded in wartime to forty thousand. It was something of a miracle for a state with the meager population and resources of Brandenburg-Prussia to produce such a large, well-equipped, and well-trained standing army in so short a time. In forty years (1648–88) Brandenburg had become the strongest military power in Germany except for Austria. If there was any explanation, it was the

The castle of the Hohenzollerns (detail from a seventeenth-century engraving).

single-minded devotion of the Great Elector to this goal and to any political, social, or economic policy that would help him reach it.

The first thing he had to do was to establish his authority over the Estates of Brandenburg and Prussia, which had almost complete control of taxation. In Brandenburg the Great Elector was strong enough to imitate the practice of the king of France by simply continuing to raise taxes that had once been granted by the Estates, which were never summoned again after 1653. In Prussia the townsmen were more stubborn and the Junkers (or nobles) more unruly. Their leaders turned to Poland for support, and Frederick soon had a fight on his hands. The fight ended only after he had executed the ringleaders of the resistance. In the end Frederick set up a taxation system for the support of his army that was common to all his territories, administered by civil servants of his own choosing, and independent of local control. The nobility were shorn of their power in the Estates and pressed into service to the Hohenzollern state as officers in the army. In return, the power of the Junkers over their serfs on their own estates was left untouched. Military strength, not social betterment, was the Great Elector's objective.

It could be argued, however, that much social betterment came indirectly

Frederick William, the Great Elector, as a young man; painting by his contemporary Mathias Czwiczeic.

from his building of a strong army, even if the Prussian peasants were sinking deeper into serfdom. The devastation of war was even worse than aristocratic oppression, and Frederick William protected a whole generation from invasion. He used his army as a weapon in diplomacy rather than in war by selling his support to one side or another in return for subsidies. The subsidies helped pay for the army, and the alliances seldom required much fighting. By pursuing this policy, the Great Elector and his immediate successors made substantial territorial gains. For example, by playing off Sweden against Russia, the Hohenzollerns gained Stettin and Pomerania in 1720. There was little sentiment and much shrewdness in this foreign policy, which showed its results in the steady growth of the army and the territorial expansion of the state.

Frederick William's economic policy was designed to develop his lands to the point where they could support his army without the need for foreign subsidies. He did much to revive and improve agriculture after 1648, and much to encourage industry and commerce. His tolerant policies made Brandenburg a haven for religious refugees—persecuted Lutherans, German Calvinists, and, above all, French Huguenots after the Revocation of the Edict of Nantes in 1685. These immigrants, together with Dutch, Swiss, and other newcomers, brought new skills in agriculture and industry, helped increase the population, and added considerably to the strength of the state. He welcomed even the more radical Protestant sects and the Jews, drawing the line only at admitting the Jesuits, whom he considered too intolerant.

The recognition of the Great Elector's son as King Frederick I in 1701 symbolized the appearance of a new power in Europe. Prussia (as the Hohenzollern lands came to be known) had devoted relatively more of its population, its resources, and its energies to military purposes than had any other German state during the later seventeenth century. It has been said that in Prussia the army created the state. The army was, in fact, the first institution common to all the Elector's lands, and its bureaus were the models for many organs of the later civil government. But while the needs of the army were especially important in Prussia, they played a significant role in the development of every great power in Europe except England.

Sweden

While Prussia was growing in strength, its neighbors, Sweden and Poland, were declining, for different reasons. Sweden had burst on the European horizon as a military power of first rank during Gustavus Adolphus' invasion of Germany (1631–32). During the latter part of the century the Baltic became a Swedish lake, and a Swedish empire grew up on both sides of the inland sea all the way from the Gulf of Finland to the North Sea. Copper, iron ore, and agriculture were the Swedes' chief resources, a technically superior musket their chief military advantage.

Swedish power, however, rested on shaky foundations. The country had a population of less than 2 million—not much larger than Prussia or the Dutch Republic. Its lines of empire were over-extended, and its enemies—from Russia and Poland to Prussia and Denmark—were hungry for revenge.

When young Charles XII (1697–1718) came to the throne, a coalition of Russia, Poland, and Denmark pounced on his Baltic territories. Charles XII proved to be a military genius and crushed his enemies in a series of lightning campaigns. But he became intoxicated by success and engaged in political adventures that far exceeded his country's resources. He marched deep into Russian territory and was totally defeated at Poltava in 1709. He failed to gain Turkish support, though he spent some years at the Ottoman court seeking an alliance. Finally, he lost his life in a raid on Norway in 1718. In the peace settlements of 1719 to 1721, the Swedish empire outside Sweden was divided among Hanover, Denmark, Prussia, and Russia. Sweden settled down gracefully enough in the eighteenth century to its earlier role of second-class power.

Poland

The case of Poland was quite different, though the results were somewhat similar. Poland, formed in 1386 by the union of the crowns of Poland and Lithuania, was, after Russia, the largest state in Europe. Polish prosperity and culture had reached their peak in the sixteenth century, when the Polish people, linked by their Roman Catholic religion to western Europe, had felt some of the effects of the Renaissance, the Protestant revolt, and the Catholic Reformation. By the beginning of the seventeenth century, however, economic and political decline had set in. The Polish monarchy had always been elective. Until about 1572 the nobles had usually elected the legal heirs of their monarchs, but after this they began to choose anyone whom they believed they could control. By 1700 the real power in Poland lay in the hands of the nobility. The monarchy was almost powerless, although petty German princes still sought election to gain the prestige of a royal title. The peasants were the most depressed in Europe, sunk deep in serfdom. There was almost no bourgeoisie, since the towns had not

THE BALTIC: A SWEDISH LAKE   1621–1721

flourished. Political power was concentrated in the diet, which by now represented only the nobility, since representatives of the towns no longer dared to attend.

The diet was notorious for its futility; one negative vote (the *liberum veto*) could block any action. Moreover, by using the *liberum veto* any member might "explode" the diet—that is, dissolve the diet and wipe out everything it had done up to that moment. Of fifty-seven diets held in the century after 1652, all but nine were so "exploded"—one by a member who simply wanted to see what would happen. If legislation did succeed in running the gauntlet of this national assembly, there was still no way of getting it enforced in the provincial assemblies of lesser nobles or on the private estates of the landed barons. John Sobieski (1674–96), a native Pole of high integrity who made a serious effort to lead the country out of its weakness, was the last great king of Poland. After him the Polish crown became simply the prize of foreign intrigue, and Poland started down the path that led to extinction at the hands of more powerful neighbors at the end of the eighteenth century.

Russia

Throughout the seventeenth century there was no great power east of Sweden, Poland, and the Ottoman Empire. The Grand Duchy of Moscow had fallen on evil days after the death of Ivan the Dread in 1584. Disputes about the succession to the tsar's crown led to a "Time of Troubles," and the accession of the Romanovs, who were to rule Russia from 1613 to 1917, at first did little to strengthen the state. In the 1650s a near revolution was provoked by a reforming patriarch of the Orthodox Church, who ordered that the ritual and liturgy be revised in order to bring them closer to the original Greek text of the Bible. This order exasperated vast numbers of the uneducated masses to whom the Slavonic texts were sacrosanct. For many years after, "Old Believers" resisted the official religious policy of the government in spite of executions and exile.

Russia was a victim state through most of the century, often unable to defend its frontiers against invading Swedes, Poles, and Turks, and still cut off from access to either the Baltic or the Black Sea. English merchants had made contact with Moscow in the 1550s through the White Sea, and German merchants were even more active in the capital. But while Russia absorbed some of the technology (especially the military technology) of the West, it remained relatively untouched by cultural changes in the rest of Europe. The Renaissance, the Reformation, and the scientific revolution, with all the ferment they brought to the West, remained almost unknown to the peoples living east of Catholic Poland.

Peter the Great, 1689–1725

In 1689 one of the most remarkable rulers in all European history came to power in Russia at the age of seventeen. He was a giant of a man, nearly seven feet tall (his enormous boots are still proudly preserved in the Kremlin), with large, skillful hands, inexhaustible energy, insatiable curiosity, and a hot temper. As a boy he had loved to play at war. He had also spent much of his time with the Dutch and Germans who lived in the "German Quarter" of Moscow, listening and learning. In these early years the great passion of his later life seems to have been born: to make Russia a great power by rapidly westernizing its technology, its civil and military institutions, and its popular customs. At his death in 1725 he had aggrandized, upturned, and

Medals celebrating the Treaty of Eternal Peace between Russia and Poland (1686). Above: King John Sobieski; below: personifications of Poland and Russia.

Peter the Great,
by Aert de Gelder.

exhausted his country and had earned the name by which he was to be known to later history: Peter the Great.

Peter's plans at first developed slowly. Using his old-fashioned army, he failed to capture Azov at the mouth of the Don from the Turks in 1695. Next year, after he had built a fleet on the river with Dutch help, Azov fell. Peter had learned a lesson: in order to build a navy and to modernize an archaic army, he would first have to learn a great deal from the West. From 1696 to 1698, thinly disguised as a private citizen, Peter visited Holland, England, and Germany. Here he learned how an utterly different society built its ships, made its munitions, ran its government, and conducted its diplomacy. He alternately shocked and amazed the Dutch and English who came to know him. Direct, spontaneous, and naive in temperament, he always had to try to do things for himself. He

worked in the shipyards, eagerly questioned everyone he met on western technology, and caroused through the night in drunken orgies with his Russian companions. He hired over seven hundred technicians of various sorts to return with him to Russia.

In Vienna word reached him of a revolt of the *streltsi*, the barbarous and undisciplined palace guard, which to Peter represented everything backward and reactionary about Russia. (The *streltsi* were in league with the "Old Believers" and were better at staging palace revolutions than at fighting an enemy.) Peter hastened back to Moscow and made a fearful example of the rebels, executing over a thousand of them and using torture on a scale that shocked even his countrymen, who were used to brutality. At the same time he forbade the wearing of beards and long robes by any Russian, as a sign of his determination to westernize even the personal habits and costumes of his subjects. His subjects wore beards because God was presumed to wear a beard and man was made in His image. But to Peter, beards symbolized the old Russia of reaction, rebellion, and religious fanaticism. The clean-shaven look was western. Typically, the tsar himself took a hand in shaving some of his courtiers.

There was nothing particularly original about what Peter did to reform the military, political, and social institutions of his country. He borrowed his ideas and techniques from what other statesmen were doing at the time in France, England, the Dutch Republic, Brandenburg, and Sweden. But his methods were more casual and informal, more brutal and ruthless, than were those of western countries.

An overwhelming defeat by the Swedes at Narva in 1700 spurred on Peter's efforts to improve his army. With the help of foreign officers and advisers he had trained a formidable force of over one hundred thousand by 1709, the year he annihilated Charles XII's forces at Poltava. At the time of his death the army numbered over two hundred thousand in a population of about 8 million. Years of warfare against the Turks were unsuccessful, and even Azov was lost

Peter the Great Tries to Westernize Russia

The Czar tried to reform fashions, or, to be more exact, dress. Until his time Russians had always worn long beards, which they cherished and preserved with great care. . . . The Czar, to reform that custom, ordered that gentlemen, merchants and all other subjects must each pay a tax of one hundred rubles a year if they wished to keep their beards. . . . Officials were stationed at the gates of the towns to collect that tax, which the Russians considered an enormous sin on the part of the Czar. . . . Many old Russians, after having their beards cut off, saved them to be placed in their coffins, fearing that they would not be allowed to enter heaven without their beards. . . . From the reform in beards, let us pass to that of clothes. Russian garments, like those of [other] Orientals were very long, reaching to the heel. The Czar issued an order abolishing that costume and commanding all the nobles and those who had positions at the court to dress in the French fashion. . . .

As for the rest of the people . . . a suit of clothes cut in the new fashion was hung at the city gates, with an order that everyone except peasants was to have their clothes made on this model. Those who entered the town with clothes in the old style were forced to kneel and have all the part of their garments that fell below the knee cut off. . . . Since the guards at the gates had a good deal of fun in cutting off long garments, the people were amused and readily abandoned their old dress, especially in Moscow. . . .

From Ivan Nestesuranoi, *Memoirs*, 1703, as translated in *Readings in Western Civilization*, ed. by Paul L. Hughes and Robert F. Fries (Paterson, N.J.: Littlefield, Adams, 1960), pp. 130–31.

once again. But decisive victories came in the north. In the Great Northern War Peter gained territory on the Gulf of Finland that had once belonged to Sweden. This gave him the "window on the sea," the direct contact with western Europe through the Baltic, that was his primary aim.

To man his army, Peter developed a conscription system. To pay for it was harder, since he could not borrow money. As expenses increased, he and his advisers taxed anything and everything they could think of: births, marriages, caskets, graves, and beards, among other things. By the end of his reign the combined burdens of heavy taxation, conscription for the army, and forced labor for industry and for building had resulted in a measurable decline in the population.

Political reforms followed military reforms, though more slowly. Peter's method of governing was informal and haphazard. To get something done, he would dash off a hastily written order and set up a commission to carry it out. Slowly, toward the end of his reign, some order was brought out of the resulting chaos. The first provincial governments were set up; the numerous commissions were brought under supervisory "colleges"; and a "senate," or central administrative body, was instituted to interpret the tsar's orders (which were sometimes confusing) and to carry out his will. A secret police also appeared to provide a check on all officials.

In Russia the imperial government did more and individuals or nonofficial groups did less than in any other European country. After 1700 no new patriarch was appointed, and the Orthodox Church was strictly subordinated to the state under a civilian official. When new industries were needed to support the army, government contractors founded them, using forced labor (serfs and criminals) granted by the tsar. One of Peter's most herculean achievements was to compel the ancient hereditary nobility to serve the state. He ordered many of the sons of the nobility to study abroad, them compelled them as well as their parents to serve for life in the army, in the government, or in industry. At the same time he enlisted commoners for the service of the state, giving them land and titles of nobility. He thus created a "service nobility" out of older and newer classes. To support this service nobility, he allowed them a free hand in dealing with the serfs on their lands. A census for tax purposes resulted in greatly increasing the number of serfs in Russia by classifying doubtful cases as servile. Under Catherine the Great, who came to power a generation after Peter's death, the nobles were freed from the obligation of service to the state, but it took another century for the peasants to become free from the galling form of serfdom prevailing in Russia. In central Europe a serf was usually bound to the land, but in Russia he could be sold apart from the land like a slave and was generally at the mercy of his master—a fact that made it easier for new industries to acquire forced labor but degraded the Russian serf to a level even below that of his counterpart in eastern Germany and Austria.

In 1707 Peter moved the seat of his government to a new city that he had built on conquered territory at the eastern end of the Gulf of Finland and had named in honor of his patron saint. St. Petersburg was a perfect symbol of his work as a whole. It was a city unlike Moscow, without roots in the country's past, built new on a marsh by forced labor. The nobles were ordered to build houses in it, and merchants were ordered to settle in it. This seaport city looked westward to Germany, Holland, and western Europe, not to the interior, as landlocked Moscow had for centuries. The nobility and civil servants hated it at first, but in the end it became their capital—the political center of what has been called "a government without a people," and the social center of a westernized aristocracy out of touch with the Russian peasant. As Versailles came to stand for the France of Louis XIV, so St. Petersburg (later called Petrograd and then Leningrad) came to stand for the Russia of Peter the Great—a powerful autocracy with few vital connections with the people.

Historians still differ sharply in estimating the value of Peter's work, but on some things they are fairly well agreed.

Contemporary cartoon of Peter cutting off the beard of a Russian noble. Those who wanted to keep their beards had to pay a tax and carry a license (below).

The older Russian institutions were bankrupt, and western influences were beginning to have their effect even before Peter appeared on the scene. Peter hastened processes of change that were almost certain to have come in any case. He cannot be blamed for all the evil results that followed, since many of them (such as the intensification of serfdom) had their roots deep in the past and owed much of their growth to Peter's successors. Two things he did accomplish: he transformed Russia from a victim state into a great power, and he involved it irrevocably with the future development of Europe. Since his time, Russia has always been a factor in the European balance of power. Peter's westernizing policy ultimately provoked a strong nationalistic and orthodox reaction, leaving Russia divided to the present day between deep suspicion of everything foreign and eager admiration of western technology and culture. But never again was Russia able to turn its back on Europe.

Even more important than Peter's accomplishments were Peter's methods. His example created a tradition of dynamic autocracy. To future tsars and future dictators his reign was to be the classic example of what might be accomplished by a ruthless and demonic will.

CONCLUSION

The half-century between 1660 and 1715 thus saw significant changes in the political and social structure of Europe. Absolute divine-right monarchy reached the apogee of its development in the France of Louis XIV and was imitated from Madrid to St. Petersburg. It is difficult to imagine two more different personalities than Louis XIV of France and Peter of Russia, but their aims were essentially similar. A few smaller peoples like the Swiss had quietly rejected monarchy in favor of republican government, and the Dutch had become wealthy and powerful as a republic. But it took the English Revolution to demonstrate to Europe that there was a practical alternative to absolute monarchy that could serve great powers as well as small. So by 1715 the political alternatives of absolutism and constitutionalism were each embodied in a great power. At the same time there were important shifts of power within the European state system. The French bid for predominance failed, provoking the rise of England and Austria as great powers. Two great empires of the sixteenth century, the Spanish and the Ottoman, were in decline. Two peoples of limited resources and numbers, the Dutch and the Swedes, had bid strongly for great-power status in the mid-seventeenth century, but by 1715 their strength was spent. Two new powers had appeared in the East to join the balance, the small military Kingdom of Prussia and the vast semibarbarous Tsardom of Russia. The rivalries of these states— England versus France, France versus Austria, Austria versus Prussia, Austria and Russia versus the Ottoman Empire— were to become the dynamic elements in eighteenth-century war and diplomacy.

Suggestions for Further Reading

Note: Asterisk denotes a book available in paperback edition.

General   The best general accounts of the period are F. L. Nussbaum, *The Triumph of Science and Reason, 1660–1685** (1953); J. B. Wolf, *The Emergence of the Great Powers, 1685–1715** (1951); and J. Stoye, *Europe Unfolding, 1648–1688** (1969). All three of these books are particularly helpful as introductions to the history of eastern Europe, about which it is hard to find good reading in English.

R. Hatton, *Europe in the Age of Louis XIV** (1969), is excellent on the social history of the period. A general study of an important subject begins with this period: E. Barker, *The Development of Public Services in Western Europe, 1660–1930* (1944). On the general theme of this chapter, see J. N. Figgis, *The Divine Right of Kings** (1896, 1922); C. J. Friedrich and C. Blitzer, *The Age of Power** (1957); and F. D. Wormuth, *The Origins of Modern Constitutionalism* (1949).

France Under Louis XIV There are good chapters on Louis' reign in Ogg and Boulenger, mentioned at the end of Chapter 19. Two excellent short surveys are L. B. Packard, *The Age of Louis XIV** (1914), and M. P. Ashley, *Louis XIV and the Greatness of France** (1946). J. B. Wolf, *Louis XIV** (1968), is a good biography. A. Guérard, *The Life and Death of an Ideal: France in the Classical Age** (1928), is a more thought-provoking and comprehensive discussion, including both politics and culture within its scope. P. Goubert, *Louis XIV and Twenty Million Frenchmen** (1970), relates the career of the king to the social history of France during his reign. J. E. King, *Science and Rationalism in the Government of Louis XIV, 1661–1683* (1949), is an important study. On economic history, the three books of C. W. Cole are the best introduction: *French Mercantilist Doctrines Before Colbert* (1913), *Colbert and a Century of French Mercantilism*, 2 vols. (1939), and *French Mercantilism, 1683–1700* (1943). C. Hill, *Versailles* (1925), is one of many books on the life of the court. W. H. Lewis, *The Splendid Century** (1954), is a popular account of all aspects of the reign, full of fascinating material. The best guides to the literary history of the period are the various works of A. A. Tilley.

England G. N. Clark, *The Later Stuarts, 1660–1714* (1934), in the *Oxford History of England* series, is a particularly fine synthesis. A more detailed narrative history of the period may be found in three books, all more or less Whiggish in sympathy: D. Ogg, *England in the Reign of Charles II,** 2 vols. (1934); the same author's *England in the Reign of James II and William III* (1955); and G. M. Trevelyan, *England under Queen Anne*, 3 vols. (1930–34). A. Bryant, *Charles II* (1931), is more pro-Stuart. The most recent interpretation of the whole period of revolution in England is C. Hill, *The Century of Revolution, 1603–1714** (1961). There is a good modern biography of James II by F. C. Turner (1948), and of William III by S. Baxter (1966). J. Pollock, *The Popish Plot* (1903, 1945), is the standard investigation of a tangled historical problem. On the economic history of the period, there is a good special study, *The Bank of England*, by J. Clapham, 2 vols. (1944), and a masterly brief sketch by G. Clark, *The Wealth of England, 1496–1760* (1947). C. H. Wilson, *England's Apprenticeship, 1603–1763* (1965), is a remarkable study of England's emergence as a great power. Pepys's *Diary* is the most deservedly famous contemporary account of the Restoration period. It is perhaps read best in the abridgment of O. F. Morshead, *Everybody's Pepys* (1926).

Eastern Europe In addition to the general accounts in Nussbaum and Wolf (first section, above), two books are very helpful as an introduction to the problems of eastern Europe: S. H. Cross, *Slavic Civilization Through the Ages* (1948), and O. Halecki, *Borderlands of Western Civilization* (1952). For Germany as a whole, see H. Holborn, *A History of Modern Germany, 1648–1840* (1964). On Habsburg history, P. Frischauer, *The Imperial Crown* (1939), follows the history of the house to 1792 and is mostly concerned with personalities. H. F. Schwarz, *The Imperial Privy Council in the Seventeenth Century* (1943), is concerned with constitutional matters. For the events of 1683, see J. Stoye, *The Siege of Vienna* (1964). On Prussia, S. B. Fay, *The Rise of Brandenburg-Prussia to 1786** (1937), is very brief but also very good. J. A. R. Marriott and C. G. Robertson, *The Evolution of Prussia* (1915), and F. L. Carsten, *The Origins of Prussia* (1954), are more detailed. F. Schevill has written an admiring biography of Frederick William, *The Great Elector* (1947). R. N. Bain, *Scandinavia: A Political History* (1905), and O. Halecki, *History of Poland** (1943), are useful national histories. J. A. R. Marriott, *The Eastern Question* (1917, 1940), is a reliable survey of the slow disintegration of the Ottoman Empire and of the resulting repercussions in Europe. The classic larger history of Russia is by V. O. Kliuchevsky; the standard Marxist account is by M. N. Pokrovsky. There are good one-volume histories by G. Vernadsky, rev. ed. (1944); B. Pares, new ed. (1953); and B. H. Sumner, rev. ed. (1947). B. H. Sumner, *Peter the Great and the Emergence of Russia** (1950), is a well-informed and judicious short account. Kliuchevsky's *Peter the Great* (1958) is an English version of an older but still useful book. R. J. Kerner, *The Urge to the Sea: The Course of Russian History* (1942), contains a valuable account of Russian expansion eastward to the Pacific. J. Blum, "The Rise of Serfdom in Eastern Europe," *American Historical Review*, Vol. LXII (July 1957), is a masterly examination of the differences in the economic development of eastern and western Europe. See also his *Lord and Peasant in Russia from the Ninth to the Nineteenth Century** (1961).

21 The Scientific Revolution and the Enlightenment

Until the seventeenth century the growth of civilized man's knowledge about the natural world around him had been slow, fumbling, and discontinuous. He had made many individual observations of natural phenomena and had derived some useful generalizations from these observations. But many generalizations were poorly stated, and others were entirely erroneous. "Experiments" in the modern sense were all but unheard of, and most people felt that scientific speculation was both unsure and impractical.

THE SCIENTIFIC REVOLUTION

By the eighteenth century a startling change had occurred. A large body of verifiable knowledge about nature had accumulated and has continued to accumulate at an increasing rate down to our own day. This knowledge has had revolutionary effects. Human society today has at its disposal more food, clothing, and shelter, faster ways of moving about the globe, quicker means of communicating across great distances, and more power than anyone could have dreamed of before about 1600. The characteristic mark of our civilization is that it is a "scientific civilization," and this quality began to be noticeable in the seventeenth century.

Discussion of a new method of inquiry—which we call the scientific method—began in the universities in the late thirteenth and fourteenth centuries and came to fruition in western Europe after 1600. The new method was essentially a combination of two elements: careful observation and controlled experimentation, and rational interpretation of the results of this observation and experimentation, preferably by use of mathematics. In Professor Whitehead's words, science is "a vehement and passionate interest in the relation of general principles to irreducible and stubborn facts."

When Galileo and others began to apply this method in physics and astronomy, other brilliant "discoveries" followed. These discoveries fired the imagination and enthusiasm of European thinkers. Scientific societies were organized, scientific journals began to appear, and "chain discoveries," each one resting on the results of the one preceding it, made their appearance. Science, hitherto the pursuit of occasional lonely individuals, became a social enterprise and has continued so to the present. Furthermore, it became fashionable. The Humanists had been little interested in science, but Newton's work made a profound impression on every writer in Europe. Finally, the gap between the theories of the scholar and the practical knowledge of the technician began to close.

The Medieval Universe

Precisely *why* all this took place when and where it did is still a puzzle. The one thing that can be said is that ever since the twelfth century the people of western Europe had been interested in scientific problems. But the medieval answers to these problems were based on deep-rooted, traditional assumptions about the nature of the universe. For example, it was generally believed that the universe was a finite sphere with the earth at the center. Between the center and the outermost limits were nine transparent spheres that carried the stars, the planets, the sun, and the moon in their daily revolutions around the earth, which remained motionless. On earth all was change, corruptibility, and decay. In the heavens all was perfection and incorruptibility—the perfect sphericity of sun and moon, the unvarying circular motion of the heavenly bodies, and the music of the spheres produced by their motion. And so what was the rule on earth was not the rule in the heavens. There was an earthly physics and a heavenly physics, and the laws of the one were not those of the other.

Even in the Middle Ages, however, not all men were satisfied with this relatively simple picture of the universe. In the thirteenth and fourteenth centuries a small but increasing number of scholars began to question existing explanations. Many of them were Franciscans, inspired perhaps by their founder's sensitive feeling for nature. Stimulated by the current study of Greco-Arabic science, a group of

The Danish astronomer Tycho Brahe's underground observatory was the finest of the sixteenth century. Most of his instruments were under the protective domes.

teachers at Oxford and Paris began to apply mathematical reasoning to problems of physics and astronomy, such as accelerated motion. Their speculations were continued by professors at the University of Padua in the fifteenth and sixteenth centuries. At Padua, a center of medical training for three centuries, the proper method of studying nature was vigorously debated in the course of arguments about Aristotle. Medieval universities kept interest in science alive, and the first faint beginnings of the scientific revolution were seen in Oxford, Paris, and Padua.

Most Europeans of 1500, however, did not question the standard Greek authorities. The normal state of everything in the universe was a state of rest: things moved only if they were pushed or pulled by a mover—so said Aristotle. Galen, in the second century, had described the anatomy of the human body so convincingly that doctors still saw the human organs through his eyes. Ptolemy in the same century had worked out such

an ingenious mathematical explanation of the observed irregularities in the movements of the planets that no one in 1500 thought it could be improved on. All motion in the heavens was circular, Ptolemy assumed, but there were smaller circles, or "epicycles," whose centers moved around the circumference of larger circles, and on the circumferences of these smaller circles the planets moved. It took about eighty epicycles to do the job, but the system worked quite well in explaining the observed phenomena. There seemed to be very little reason at the close of the Middle Ages to try to improve on either the observations or the theories of these ancient writers.

The Background of Change

In the fourteenth, fifteenth, and sixteenth centuries, however, certain forces in European society were preparing the way for a change in the general view of nature. Artisans and craftsmen were becoming more skilled in their techniques. The invention of the lens and the development of the glass industry, to take but one example, gave the promise of vastly extending man's powers of observing natural processes. New techniques in shipbuilding led to voyages of discovery, which in turn stimulated interest in nature and turned men's attention to problems of navigation.

The Renaissance, with its emphasis on literature and art and its veneration for the wisdom of the ancients, was in some ways antiscientific. But Humanism stimulated a passionate interest in man. Leonardo's studies of the anatomy of the body and Machiavelli's studies of the anatomy of society owed much indirectly to Humanism. Furthermore, Humanistic study revealed conflicting opinions among the ancients on matters of science, just at the moment when the authority of Galen and Ptolemy was becoming shaky for other reasons. Anatomical studies by artists and the increasing practice of dissection suggested that Galen had made mistakes in observation. Growing skill in mathematics exposed the clumsiness of Ptolemy's explanations. In the opening years of the sixteenth century, conditions were ripe for change.

The medieval cosmos based on the earth-centered Ptolemaic conception. Ptolemy's explanation of the universe as a closed and defined system seemed so perfectly put together that it was not criticized for fourteen centuries—until the discoveries of Copernicus and Galileo.

1543: Vesalius and Copernicus

In 1543 two notable scientific works heralded the end of medieval science and the beginnings of a revolution in western man's conception of nature. Vesalius' *On the Structure of the Human Body* was for its day a marvelously careful description of human anatomy based on direct observation in dissection. Vesalius did not free himself completely from the authority of Galen, nor was there much theory in his book. But it was an influential example of the power of observation. Copernicus' *On the Revolutions of the Heavenly Bodies* was a brilliant mathematical treatise that showed that the number of Ptolemy's epicycles could be reduced to thirty-four if one assumed that the earth turned on its axis once a day and moved around the sun once a year. Unlike Vesalius, Copernicus was no observer. He learned during his study at Padua in the early years of the century that there was an ancient opinion that the earth moved, and he found that this assumption made every-

thing simpler to explain mathematically. Since medieval theory decreed that "nature always acts in the simplest ways," the simpler explanation must be the truer. And so with no experimental or observational proof, Copernicus presented his readers with a theory of a universe in which the earth was no longer the center. The experimental and the theoretical sides of the modern scientific method were perfectly exemplified in Vesalius' and Copernicus' books, but they were not yet conjoined in one man or one work.

In 1600 a monk named Giordano Bruno was burned at the stake for preaching that the universe was not finite but infinite in extent, that it was filled with numberless suns and planets like our own, and that God was equally in every planet or atom in the cosmos. Bruno had been inspired by Copernicus, although Copernicus himself believed in the finite sphere of the fixed stars and the uniqueness of the earth. This intuition of the infinity of the universe spread gradually among scientists.

Bacon and Descartes

Two major prophets of the Scientific Revolution were Francis Bacon (1561–1626) and René Descartes (1596–1650). Bacon, an English lawyer, statesman, and essayist, waged a vigorous battle in his books against the deductive method of Scholasticism, which started from premises usually taken on authority and then deduced all the logical consequences. This method might help men to organize truths already known, he said, but it could never help them to discover new truths. Only inductive reasoning, which starts from direct observations of phenomena and goes on to develop the principles that explain these observations, can produce new truth. Bacon was as interested in controlling nature as in knowing its processes. He pictured an imaginary society of scientists whose end was to benefit mankind by conducting hundreds of experiments and discovering useful facts. Bacon failed to appreciate the importance of mathematical models in theoretical analysis (he was unconvinced by Copernicus), and although he

Scientific revolutionaries of the seventeenth century: Francis Bacon (above) and René Descartes.

praised experimentation, he performed almost no experiments. Nevertheless, his writings did dramatize the importance of empirical research. The founding in 1662 of the Royal Society of London, the first scientific society in England, owed much to Bacon's inspiration, and in a sense he was the remote ancestor of the great research laboratories and research teams of today.

Descartes, a French mathematician and philosopher, was a more important figure than Bacon, but he lacked Bacon's intuitive understanding of the need for careful observations. To Descartes, the excitement of science lay in mathematical analysis and theory. In a famous autobiographical account, he told how the literature and philosophy he studied as a youth left him unsatisfied because they reached no certain conclusions, how mathematics charmed him by its precision and certainty, and how he set out to discover a "method of rightly conducting the reason and discovering truth in the sciences." In November 1619, in a moment of intuition, he saw the exact correspondence between geometry and algebra: the truth that any equation can be translated into a curve on a graph, and that any regular curve can be translated into an equation. This intoxicating vision suggested to him a new way of grasping ultimate truth. If only men would systematically doubt all notions based on authority or custom and start with clear and precise ideas they know to be true, the whole universe might be deduced from a few simple principles and thus comprehended as clearly as the coordinate geometry he had discovered.

Descartes was one of the first to believe that science could save humanity. His enthusiasm was infectious, but he moved too fast. He reduced the universe, including the body of man, to a mathematically intelligible machine. To do this he had to take mind out of the world of matter entirely and define it as a separate substance that comprehended the world of matter but did not exist in it. His generalizations in astronomy, physics, and anatomy were often premature, and his passion for system building went beyond his capacity to check by experiment. But his enthusiasm for scientific "method," his belief that everything could be reduced to mathematical terms, and his insistence on systematic doubt of all earlier theories left a profound mark on the thinking of scientists in the next two centuries. Descartes made it easier for his successors to reject old ideas, and they gradually came to accept his belief that the language of science must be mathematics.

Experiment and Mathematics

Both Bacon and Descartes were overoptimistic. Bacon thought that a generation of determined experimentation would establish a solid structure of knowledge about the universe. Descartes thought that a universal science could be deduced fairly soon from a few basic mathematical axioms. He also believed that the universe was much less complicated than it is; it was one of Descartes' pupils who described the world as a gigantic piece of clockwork.

Meanwhile, experimentation and mathematics were developing slowly and steadily in the hands of a growing host of scientists. William Gilbert used what little was known of the mysterious force of electricity to deduce that the earth itself was a great magnet (1600). William Harvey, who had studied at Padua, proved that the blood must circulate from arteries to veins to heart to lungs and back to heart and then arteries again. He did this by measuring the amount of blood actually pumped out by the heart in a minute and arguing that it must go somewhere (1628). Later in the century the new microscope revealed the tiny capillaries that actually connect arteries to veins. Torricelli, Pascal, and others investigated the ancient proposition that "nature abhors a vacuum," a proposition that had been firmly believed by everyone from Aristotle to Descartes. In order to prove the falseness of the proposition, the new investigators created vacuums in test tubes, invented the barometer, and discovered the pressure of the atmosphere. All these advances evidenced a growing precision in observation and an increasing sophistication both in controlling experiments and in quantifying their results.

At the same time, mathematics was making rapid strides. The invention of decimals and of logarithms early in the century facilitated calculation; Pascal inaugurated the study of probability; and at the end of the century Newton and Leibniz crowned the work of many others by simultaneously inventing the calculus, which provided the first method of analyzing regularly accelerating or decelerating motion.

Kepler

It was in astronomy and physics that observational techniques and mathematical methods found their most fruitful union. The German astronomer Johannes Kepler (1571–1630) was troubled by discrepancies in Copernicus' theory, which he nevertheless believed to be true. He worked from the observations of his master Tycho Brahe, which were far more accurate than those available to Copernicus. Copernicus had clung to the old belief that all heavenly bodies moved in circles. But to Kepler it was obvious that the planets' orbits were not circles. For years he worried about the geometry of these orbits and finally tried the ellipse. The properties of the ellipse had been studied since the time of the Greeks, and Kepler quickly saw that his solution fitted the observations. The planets' orbits, he announced, are elliptical, with the sun in one of the two foci of the ellipse. Further, a line from the sun to a planet sweeps out equal areas of the ellipse in equal times, and the cube of the distance of each planet from the sun is proportional to the square of the time of its revolution. Here was astounding proof of the intuition of Descartes and others that nature in some mysterious sense was mathematical. A geometrical figure, studied for centuries as an abstract form, was found to "fit" the facts of nature. The implication was that nature was perhaps really a machine, intelligible to careful observers equipped with the tools of mathematics.

Galileo

The first fruits of Kepler's work appeared in 1609. During the same year an Italian, Galileo Galilei (1564–1642), professor at Padua and Pisa, turned a newly invented instrument, the telescope, on the heavens and soon afterward published an account of what he saw. The changeless perfection and perfect sphericity of the heavenly bodies had dissolved before his gaze. The moon had craters and mountains; there were moving spots on the sun; there were rings around Saturn; and Jupiter proved to have four moons of its own. A bright new star had already appeared and been noted in 1572, and in 1577 a new comet had cut a path through what should have been crystalline spheres. The finite, spherical universe of the Middle Ages was shattered, and thoughtful men suspected strongly that they were looking out into boundless space, sparsely populated by stars like the sun and possibly by other solar systems as well. The old distinction between terrestrial and celestial physics was apparently dissolving. The moon and sun were not perfect globes, and the stars were not changeless. Perhaps the same forces and laws operated both on earth and in the heavens. Nor was the earth any longer the motionless center of the universe. The earth was a planet circling the sun like Jupiter or any other, and round about the solar system were infinite, silent spaces.

This was too much for obscurantists in the Church. The Copernican theory had been denounced in 1616, and in 1632 Galileo himself was condemned by the Roman Inquisition, threatened with torture, and forced to recant. Nevertheless, his brilliantly written dialogues contributed mightily to the overthrow not only of Ptolemy in favor of Copernicus, but also of Aristotle in favor of a new physics.

Galileo's physics was inspired by the speculations of the fourteenth-century Franciscans, but he went much further and was much more accurate in developing mathematical formulas to describe the laws of motion. He worked out the law of falling bodies. The result was a simple mathematical formula again: the distance covered increases as the square of the time. He saw that the path followed by a projectile is a regular curve, a parabola, produced by the operation of

Two of Galileo's telescopes.

Harvey Discovers the Circulation of the Blood

1628

Since calculations and visual demonstrations have confirmed all my suppositions, to wit, that the blood is passed through the lungs and the heart by the pulsation of the ventricles, is forcibly ejected to all parts of the body, therein steals into the veins . . . flows back everywhere . . . from small veins into larger ones, and thence comes at last into the vena cava and to the auricle of the heart; all this too in such amounts that it cannot be supplied from the ingesta [food] and is also in greater bulk than would suffice for nutrition.

I am obliged to conclude that in all animals the blood is driven around a circuit with an unceasing, circular sort of motion, that this is an activity of the heart which it carries out by virtue of its pulsation, and that in sum it constitutes the sole cause for the heart's pulsatile movement.

From C. C. Gillispie, *The Edge of Objectivity* (Princeton, N.J.: Princeton University Press, 1960), p. 71.

---

two forces on the projectile—the initial impetus and the pull of the earth. He came close to formulating the key concept of modern mechanics, the law of inertia: that all bodies tend to remain at rest or to continue in motion in straight lines unless acted on by outside forces. From this deceptively simple proposition—so fundamentally different from Aristotle's conception of motion as the result of some mover's action—was to spring the law of gravitation. Galileo came within an ace of discovering it, but the honor was to be reserved for one who was born in the year Galileo died, 1642.

Newton

It was the genius of an Englishman, Sir Isaac Newton (1642–1727), that related Kepler's astronomy to Galileo's physics, destroyed all distinction between celestial and terrestrial physics, and accomplished at least part of Descartes' dream of establishing a "universal science." The basic intuition came to Newton while he was still a student in his twenties at Cambridge University. The thought occurred to him that the force that keeps the moon from flying off

at a tangent and bends it into an orbit about the earth must be exactly the same force that pulls an apple from its branch to the ground. There must be a reciprocal force of attraction between every body in the universe, and this force must be calculable—even if we do not know exactly what it is in itself. Newton's earliest calculations came close enough to mathematical proof to persuade him that it was in truth the same force that operated on the moon and the apple, and that this force varied "directly as the product of the masses" involved and "inversely as the square of the distance" separating the bodies. For some time he seems to have lost interest in his "law," but twenty years later a friend, the astronomer Edmund Halley, urged him to work out and publish his theory. Newton developed the necessary mathematics (the calculus) to prove his theory to his own satisfaction and published his conclusions, in Latin, in *The Mathematical Principles of Natural Philosophy* (1687). This proved to be one of the most influential books ever written in the history of science as well as in the history of human thought.

To scientists Newton's law of gravitation provided a single, simple explanation of a growing mass of data in astronomy and physics and laid the foundations of future research in both these sciences. Further, Newton gave scientific method its classic formulation in his "Rules of Reasoning":

In experimental philosophy (i.e., science) we are to look upon propositions collected by general induction from phenomena as accurately or very nearly true, notwithstanding any contrary hypotheses (theories) that may be imagined, till such time as other phenomena occur, by which they may either be made more accurate or liable to exceptions.

Newton's support of the experimental, or inductive, approach was aimed at the premature generalizing of Descartes and his followers. But obviously he did not underestimate the value of mathematical theory, as Bacon had. In Newton the slow growing together of empirical observation and rational interpretation reached full maturity.

The Newtonian Universe

To the layman, who learned about Newton's work through popularizers, a new universe began to open up. It was a far cry from the small and finite medieval universe. It was a universe in which the significant objects were bodies or masses moving about in infinite space in response to regularly operating forces. Mass, force, and motion were the key concepts, and mathematics was the means of understanding them. Medieval man had been obsessed by the question "Why?" and had felt he understood whatever he encountered in nature once he had discovered its end or purpose. Seventeenth-century scientists limited themselves to asking "How?" and were satisfied when they found what appeared to be the regular patterns in natural processes. The world of Kepler, Galileo, and Newton was a vast machine, working according to laws that could be mathematically expressed, laws that were intelligible to anyone who followed the proper experimental and mathematical methods.

What was the place of God and of man in this universe? We shall see what the answers to this question were in the next century. But here it must be observed that no seventeenth-century scientist of prominence thought that he was reading God or man out of the universe. Descartes considered himself a good Catholic and was apparently not troubled by the dangers inherent in his sharp separation of the world of matter from the world of mind. Newton spent most of his energy in his later years in religious speculation. Contradictions between faith and science were not necessarily evident to the first modern scientists and their readers.

Still, the religious view of life was weakening in the later seventeenth century, and the development of science was in part the result of this decline. The charters of the scientific societies and academies that sprang up throughout Europe during the century usually contained clauses stating that purely theological or political discussion would not be tolerated and that "ultimate" or "final" causes were no part of the group's

Newton's design for a reflecting telescope.

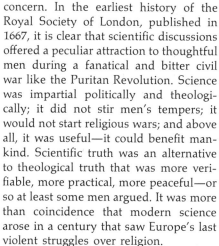

concern. In the earliest history of the Royal Society of London, published in 1667, it is clear that scientific discussions offered a peculiar attraction to thoughtful men during a fanatical and bitter civil war like the Puritan Revolution. Science was impartial politically and theologically; it did not stir men's tempers; it would not start religious wars; and above all, it was useful—it could benefit mankind. Scientific truth was an alternative to theological truth that was more verifiable, more practical, more peaceful—or so at least some men argued. It was more than coincidence that modern science arose in a century that saw Europe's last violent struggles over religion.

One supremely sensitive philosopher felt the religious awe implicit in the new mechanistic picture of the universe. This was an obscure Dutch lens grinder, Baruch Spinoza (1632–77). To Spinoza the new universe of mass, force, and motion, operating in strict obedience to inexorable laws, was God. There was no need, he thought, to consider God as above, behind, or beyond nature. God is not a "free cause" apart from natural law. He is not "Creator" or "Redeemer." He is natural law. "God never can decree, nor ever would have decreed, anything but what is; God did not exist before his decrees, and would not exist without them." Nature is "a fixed and immutable order," with "no particular goal in view." Man, like everything else, is part of this order. So Spinoza could write a book called *Ethics Demonstrated in the Geometrical Manner* and say, "I shall consider human activities and desires in exactly the same manner as though I were concerned with lines, planes, and solids." The wise man contemplates this natural order with serenity and delight. This was Spinoza's religion. Naturally such arguments were called atheistical, and Spinoza was considered a dangerous radical by his contemporaries.

For most men, however, the new science did not destroy the traditional religion. Rather it compelled them to consider the religious significance of a greatly expanded and complicated universe. The telescope was revealing the immense size of the cosmos, displacing the earth and even the sun from the

center of the universe. The microscope was beginning to reveal the wonders of the world's minutiae—the capillaries, the bacteria, the cells, the foundations of life. No one felt the two infinites—the infinitely great and the infinitesimally small—so keenly or speculated so profoundly about their religious significance as Blaise Pascal (1623–62). "The whole visible world is only an imperceptible atom in the ample bosom of nature," he wrote. The universe, he said, is "an infinite sphere, the center of which is everywhere, the circumference nowhere." "The eternal silence of these infinite spaces frightens me." Yet to examine a mite—"with its minute body and parts incomparably more minute, limbs with their joints, veins in the limbs, blood in the veins, humors in the blood, drops in the humors, vapors in the drops"—is equally astonishing. "What is man in nature? A Nothing in comparison with the Infinite, an All in comparison with the Nothing, a mean between nothing and everything." And yet man is greater than anything in the universe because he comprehends all this, and because Christ died on the cross for him. In this way, Pascal related the new universe to Christianity. Other Christians were not so concerned about the new science, and other scientists were not so concerned to articulate a Christian interpretation.

THE CULTURE OF THE SEVENTEENTH CENTURY

The Baroque Style in Art

The age of the scientific revolution was also the age of the "baroque" style in art—a style that sprang up in the later sixteenth century, reached its climax about the middle of the seventeenth, and came to its end around the middle of the eighteenth. The term *baroque* (French for "odd" or "irregular") was invented by eighteenth-century critics who regarded seventeenth-century art as a grotesque corruption of Renaissance art. But modern

View of the baroque interior of the church at Weiss in Germany.

critics consider the baroque a great achievement; one of them has called it "the high-water mark of European creative effort." As a style it is difficult to define because it reflected all the contrasts and contradictions of seventeenth-century culture in general: its religious ecstasy and its sensual worldliness, its credulity and its rationalism, its violence and its respect for order. Baroque painters and sculptors were influenced by all these contradictions. They portrayed voluptuous women in repose, military heroes in battle, and saints in ecstasy with equal skill and zest.

In general, the dominant notes of the baroque were a sense of tension and conflict and a liking for the grandiose and dramatic. The conflicts of man and the universe, of man and man, and of man within himself were conceived on a more heroic, and often a more tragic, scale than they had been in the Renaissance. Renaissance painters and writers had been interested in man himself. Baroque painters and writers were fascinated by man in his environment—typical men torn by conflicting passions, confronted by human and supernatural enemies, buffeted by elemental forces beyond their control.

There were instructive parallels between the thought-worlds of the artists and the thought-worlds of the scientists of the period. To Galileo and Newton, bodies or masses moving through space in response to conflicting forces such as gravitation and centrifugal force were the objects of study. To the great French dramatists of the age—Corneille, Racine, and Molière—the objects of study were typical human beings acting and reacting in response to conflicting passions such as love and duty. Baroque painters were intrigued by space. Vermeer portrayed figures in a space that was bathed and suffused with light; Rembrandt spotlighted them in the midst of darkened space; and others pictured them floating through apparently infinite space (to baroque artists the supernatural was natural). The scientists' concern with "mass, force, and motion" seems closely related to the painters' and poets' concern with men caught in the tension between elemental forces in their whole natural or supernatural environment. The typical hero of baroque literature, it has been said, is Satan in Milton's *Paradise Lost*—swayed by colossal passions, moving through vast three-dimensional spaces, commanding many of the natural forces in the universe, but ultimately checked and frustrated by God.

The most typical product of baroque architecture was the royal palace: Versailles in France, Schönbrunn in Austria, or Blenheim, Marlborough's regal residence in England. The style was fundamentally Renaissance classical, but grander, more ornate, and more complicated. These palaces were designed to be the stage settings of worldly greatness. The vast reception rooms, the halls of mirrors, the great sweeping staircases, and the long vistas of the formal gardens were designed to enhance the drama of royalty and aristocracy. Even the churches of the period—such as Bernini's colonnades framing St. Peter's in Rome—suggested the majesty of God rather than his mercy.

But it was the operas that originated in Italy early in the seventeenth century that were the most original creation of the baroque. The union of dramatic action and a less polyphonic, more direct musical style was a great popular success, and opera continued to grow as a distinct form of art down to the twentieth century. The grandiose and palatial stage settings (sometimes outdoors), the dramatic conflicts of the action, and the emotive power of the music exactly suited the taste of the period. Italian composers led the way until the end of the seventeenth century: Monteverdi, the father of the opera, Frescobaldi, Scarlatti, and Vivaldi. But an Englishman, Henry Purcell, wrote the most moving opera of the century, *Dido and Aeneas* (1687).

Opera singers of the baroque period. Detail from a drawing for an opera setting by Ludovico Burnacinia, Vienna (1674).

SEVENTEENTH-CENTURY THOUGHT ABOUT MAN

The seventeenth century developed conceptions about man that were based on Renaissance views but went beyond them. These conceptions may be conveniently summed up under three heads:

individualism, relativism, and rationalism tempered by empiricism. We are speaking here of the thought of the most adventurous and best-educated minds, not of the many, whose thought-world was still conventional and in many ways "medieval."

Individualism

Radical thinkers of the seventeenth century took an increasingly individualistic view of man in society. The most intense Christian piety of the period—whether it was the Catholic devotion preached by St. François de Sales, the stern conscience of Puritans and Jansenists, or the warm inner conviction of German Pietists—was highly individualistic. The trend was equally evident in political theory. The fashion was to start with the individual and then to ask how society and the state could have originated and how they could be justified. Supporters of the divine right of kings were still numerous, but advanced thinkers were arguing that the state was based on a contract, either explicit or implicit, between the people and the ruler. Some, like Hobbes, argued that this contract, once made, was irrevocable. Others, like Locke, insisted that if the ruler broke the terms of the contract, which were usually thought to provide for good government, the people might depose him and set up a new ruler in his place. This idea of a "political contract" between ruler and people had some basis in the Old Testament and had been reinforced by feudal "contracts" between lords and vassals. It had been revived as a fighting idea by religious minorities when they were resisting the tyranny of rulers.

As time went on, the idea of a "social contract" took its place by the side of the "political contract." This was the idea that society itself was the result of a voluntary agreement among individuals who had been absolutely independent in their original "state of nature." The two ideas were mixed, somewhat confusedly, in Locke and later theorists. In both contracts, the individual with his rights and his natural independence logically came first; then came society or the state. In contrast, the Middle Ages had thought of society as an organism or a "body" in which individuals were mere "members." The more radical thinkers of the seventeenth century were coming to think of society as an artificial organization of independent individuals based on voluntary agreement or consent.

Relativism

The greatest thinkers of the Middle Ages were sure that the people of Christendom were God's chosen people and that the truth had been revealed once and for all to Christians. During the sixteenth and seventeenth centuries, Humanism, the voyages of discovery, and the development of science greatly weakened this assurance.

Humanism had shaken this assurance by revealing Greco-Roman civilization in clearer historical perspective. Here—in a society long since dead, but still alive in its literature, its art, and its historical records—was an alternative to the medieval Christian view of life. Modern historical studies—history, archeology, philology—were born during the Renaissance and were carried on with even greater skill during the seventeenth century. This steady development of the "historical sciences," as they would be called today, slowly impressed on thoughtful Europeans that there had been other societies in other times with values, beliefs, and institutions quite different from those of the present. Thus the idea of relativism in time was born and grew. What had been right behavior for a Roman was perhaps not right behavior in other times.

The idea of relativism in space resulted from the geographical discoveries, as we have seen. The discovery in America of societies far less civilized than Europe and of societies in Asia more civilized in many respects than Europe had the effect of shaking European provincialism. Perhaps the "noble savages" of the New World were happier than the more cultured but more corrupt Christians of Europe. Perhaps Christians had something to learn from Persian sages and Chinese philosophers. Each society had different standards; was any set of standards absolutely right? So at least increasing numbers of Europeans began to think in the seventeenth and eighteenth centuries.

As the temporal and geographical horizons of the European imagination widened, the vision of man's place in nature was complicated by scientific discovery, as we have seen in considering Bruno and Pascal. European Christians were not unique in time and space, as they had once thought; nor, perhaps, was man himself unique.

The intellectual results of historical study, geographical exploration, and scientific discovery are best seen in the work of Pierre Bayle (1647–1706), the great scholarly skeptic of the later seventeenth century. Bayle, originally a Huguenot, was briefly converted to Catholicism, but he renounced all orthodox belief when his brother died in a dungeon during an attempted forced conversion. He took up residence in the relatively tolerant Dutch Netherlands and devoted the latter part of his life to a crusade against superstition, religious intolerance, and dogmatism in general. In 1697 Bayle published a huge rambling book, a *Historical and Critical Dictionary*, which had enormous influence on eighteenth-century thinkers. Into this book he poured all the relativism and skepticism that he had acquired through his extensive historical study, his amateur knowledge of science (he was an admirer of Descartes), and his personal experience. He argued that atheists might be good citizens and that there was no necessary connection between a man's religious beliefs and the way he behaved. Bayle insisted that there is nothing more abominable than to make religious conversions by force. He ridiculed the idea that stars and planets could influence human life and mercilessly attacked superstition on every front. He distrusted all historical authorities, including the writers of the Old Testament, unless he was sure that their account of events was inherently credible. His test of truth was reason—and few if any accounts of miracles met this rigorous test. All in all, Bayle was the most thoroughgoing skeptic and the most destructive critic of his generation.

Rationalism and Empiricism

The leading thinkers of the seventeenth century were predominantly rationalistic. Reason was the faculty that distinguished man from the beast, and the triumphs of seventeenth-century science proved that reason could be trusted. And so the conclusion was drawn that the man of reason could know and understand the world into which he was born if he made the right use of his mind.

This optimistic attitude was reflected in the growing belief in "natural law." The idea of a law of nature that served as a standard of moral behavior for all men at all times in all places originated with the Stoics and was developed by medieval scholars. During the Renaissance and the Reformation this idea went into eclipse, but the discovery of scientific "laws of nature" (like Kepler's laws of planetary motion) helped to revive the belief that natural laws of human behavior also existed. Cicero had given the idea classic formulation: "There is in fact a true law—namely, right reason—which is in accordance with nature, applies to all men, and is unchangeable and eternal. By its commands this law summons men to the performance of their duties; by its prohibitions it restrains them from doing wrong." This law was implanted in the minds of men by God himself. Its content was hazy, but it was understood to include respect for life and property, good faith and fair dealing, giving each man his due. These principles could always be discovered by reason, just as reason could discover the proof of a geometrical proposition. Hugo Grotius, a Dutch jurist and statesman, in his book *On the Law of War and Peace* (1625), turned to the law of nature in an attempt to find some basis for a "law of nations" that would transcend the religious fanaticisms of the Thirty Years' War. And in more general terms, if natural law is the same for all men, then it lessens the contradictions caused by the relativism in time and space that was perplexing seventeenth-century men.

The most influential example of this kind of thinking was John Locke's faith

Title page of John Locke's *Essay Concerning Human Understanding* (1690).

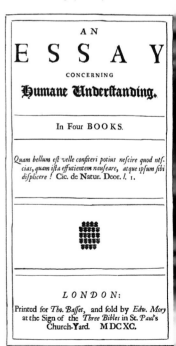

AN

ESSAY

CONCERNING

Humane Understanding.

In Four BOOKS.

Quam bellum est velle confiteri potius nescire quod nescias, quam ista effutientem nauseare, atque ipsum sibi displicere! Cic. de Natur. Deor. l. 1.

LONDON:

Printed for *Tho. Basset*, and sold by *Edw. Mory* at the Sign of the *Three Bibles* in St. *Paul's* Church-Yard. MDCXC.

that there are certain "natural rights" vested in every individual in the "state of nature," notably life, liberty, and property. From this it follows logically, as conclusion from axiom, that men form societies and set up governments mainly to preserve these rights. Descartes had hoped to be able to deduce the universe from a few central mathematical principles; Locke in his *Second Treatise of Government* (1690) assumed that he could deduce society and government from a few simple axioms about man and natural law.

This enthusiastic rationalism in the study of man and society was qualified by an undercurrent of empiricism, of respect for sense-experience. Here again Locke led the way in his *Essay Concerning Human Understanding*. Many of its readers thought that it did for the study of man what Newton had done for the study of nature. Locke argued that all our ideas come from experience. The mind at birth is a *tabula rasa*, a clean slate, on which our sense-experiences gradually imprint conceptions. There are no "innate ideas," and no self-evident axioms (as Descartes had assumed). The mind and its ideas can be explained only by the outside forces that act on it.

This was the purest empiricism. Locke hoped that it would provide a weapon for getting rid of all the superstitions and prejudices that cluttered men's minds, but it could destroy many things besides superstitions, including some of Locke's own doctrines. Logically, Locke's theory of the mind did away with original sin (which was held to be born into all men), with revelation (which did not come through the senses), with mathematical axioms, and with all "natural rights" (which were obviously innate and not based on experience). And so the rationalism of Locke's theory of society clashed with the empiricism of his theory of the mind—as the mathematical tendency clashed with the fact-finding tendency in seventeenth-century study of man in general. The eighteenth century was to inherit both: a strong faith in reason and natural law, together with a firm confidence in the value of sense-experience. Out of these two a new blend was to come in the "Enlightenment."

THE ENLIGHTENMENT

The task that the leading thinkers of the eighteenth century set themselves was to popularize the methods and principles of seventeenth-century natural science and to apply these methods and principles to God, man, and society. Scientific discovery continued, but the work that attracted the most brilliant writers of the age was that of applying the new scientific methods to long-festering human ills—economic, social, political, and ecclesiastical. Their concern was not so much to discover new truth about nature as to use the methods of natural science to reform society.

The eighteenth century's own name for this movement was the "Enlightenment." This term suggested the dawn of an age of light after a long night of darkness—the darkness of ignorance, superstition, intolerance, and slavery to the past. This new light was the light of science, as the poet Alexander Pope suggested:

> Nature and nature's laws lay hid in night;
> God said, "Let Newton be," and all was light.

There were "enlightened" writers and readers in every country of Europe from Russia to Spain and from England to Italy. Correspondence, exchange of publications, and travel linked these men together. Even in far-off America, Franklin and Jefferson were in close touch with and accepted by leaders of the Enlightenment. Nevertheless, this international movement was centered in France, and more particularly in Paris. There were good reasons for this. After the death of Louis XIV (1715) the French government became steadily more inept and ineffective, while the social tension between the privileged aristocracy and the less privileged, but powerful, wealthy bourgeoisie became more acute. Many leaders of the Enlightenment were bourgeois, and their writings often reflected bourgeois interests. These men of letters were angered by bureaucratic stupidity and aristocratic arrogance; they wanted to get rid of privilege and obscurantism. They learned to write with clarity and wit so that they influenced not only their fellow bourgeois but many members of the nobility as well. Government censors were either stupid or secretly in accord with critics of society. They could stop only the most blatant attacks; they were quite incapable of checking the criticism and satire that poured from the presses, particularly in the second half of the century.

For someone interested in ideas, Paris was the most exciting place in Europe during the eighteenth century. Here the intellectuals were in close touch with one another, excited by the feeling that they were helping to guide a revolution of ideas without precedent in European history, and bound together in a crusade to put an end to all the barbarities and absurdities of the old order. Such an intellectual conspiracy could develop only in Paris, capital of the largest and most civilized state in Europe. Other countries were too small or too backward to become major centers of "enlightened" thought and agitation. England, which had had its own Enlightenment or pre-Enlightenment with Hobbes and Locke, was a little too complacent to become a center of the Enlightenment. But the Scots delighted in stirring up their duller neighbors to the south; David Hume and Adam Smith were major Enlightenment figures, and Edinburgh in the eighteenth century was one of the great European intellectual centers.

Voltaire

As a movement the Enlightenment is often dated from Voltaire's visit to England (1726–29). Voltaire (1694–1778)—his real name was François Marie Arouet—became the central figure and moving spirit of the Enlightenment, in part at least as a result of this trip. He already had reason to dislike the old regimé in France, having been imprisoned for a short time in the Bastille. In England he read Newton and Locke, and he sensed the relative freedom of English society compared with his own. After his return to France he published his *Philosophical Letters on the English* (1733), in which he passed on to his readers Newton's main principles in watered-down form, as well as Locke's theories of human nature and

An assembly of *philosophes:* Voltaire (1), Adam (2), Abbé Maure (3), d´Alembert (4), Condorcet (5), Diderot (6), and Laharpe (7). Contemporary engraving by Jean Huber.

Voltaire on Superstition

Almost everything that goes beyond the adoration of a Supreme Being and submission of the heart to his orders is superstition. One of the most dangerous is to believe that certain ceremonies entail the forgiveness of crimes. Do you believe that God will forget a murder you have committed if you bathe in a certain river, sacrifice a black sheep, or if someone says certain words over you? . . . Do better, miserable humans; have neither murders nor sacrifices of black sheep. . . .

Notice that the most superstitious ages have always been those of the most horrible crimes. . . . The superstitious man is ruled by fanatics and he becomes one himself. On the whole, the less superstition, the less fanaticism, and the less fanaticism, the fewer miseries.

Translated from Voltaire, *Dictionnaire philosophique* (Reproduction of edition of 1776. Paris: Editions de Cluny, n.d.), Vol. III, pp. 218–25.

political freedom. He skillfully contrasted the rationality of Newton's method and the reasonableness of the English way of life with the more unreasonable aspects of church, state, and society in France.

These letters set the tone of "enlightened" propaganda in France for the next half-century or so. They were "philosophical"—that is to say, they reflected on the facts of life to discover their meaning, and they searched constantly for general principles that might be useful to mankind as a whole. And so the men of the Enlightenment called themselves *philosophes,* observers of the human scene with breadth of view and a sense of the practical. They were popularizers in the best sense of the word, crusaders for the application of the best intellectual tools of the century to the most vexatious social problems of their own day. Voltaire was the greatest of them—the most prolific, the wittiest, the most readable, and perhaps the angriest. His prime targets were religious intolerance, religious bigotry, and superstition. The close union in France of religious persecution and theological obscurantism with a capricious monarchical despotism exasperated him.

"Ecrasez l'infâme" (crush the infamous thing), he cried, in letters, pamphlets,

stories, and satires. In an essay on "religion" he described a vision he had had of a desert covered with piles of bones, the bones of "Christians slaughtered by each other in metaphysical quarrels." He went on to report a "philosophical" conversation with the shades of Socrates and Jesus, who both deplored the spectacle he had just seen. And he attacked intolerance in his own day as vigorously as the barbarism of the past.

When Voltaire died in 1778, he was the most widely read author in Europe, the first writer to have made a fortune from the sale of his own writings. He was buried in Paris in a ceremony worthy of a king.

Montesquieu

Another leading figure of the Enlightenment, Montesquieu (1689–1755), tried to institute a "social science" by applying the methods of the natural sciences to the study of society. In *The Spirit of the Laws* (1748) he suggested that forms of government were related to climate and other environmental factors, and he tried to discover what form of government best fitted a given set of environmental conditions. The book was not "scientific" by later standards, but it was the first serious attempt to relate a civilization to its environment. (Voltaire later elaborated the concept in his *History of Civilization,* 1754.) Montesquieu, like Voltaire, was impressed by Locke's theories about the English constitution. As a French nobleman he wished to limit the excesses of royal absolutism. He concluded that the ideal political form was a separation and balance of powers within government. This conclusion was to have great influence on the authors of the American Constitution.

Diderot
and the Encyclopaedia

A third major figure of the Enlightenment was Denis Diderot (1713–84), co-editor of a huge *Encyclopaedia* designed to sum up human knowledge and provide a kind of handbook of enlightened philosophy for the educated world. Diderot was an enthusiast for science, and he saw

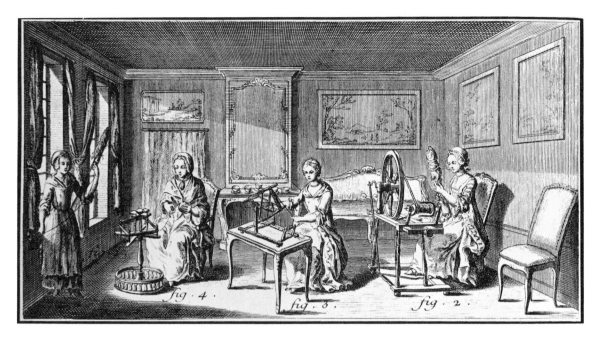

A plate from Diderot's pictorial *Encyclopaedia* illustrating different kinds of domestic spinning devices, from the clumsy spindle and distaff (fig. 1, at left) to the more productive treadle-operated spinning wheel (fig. 2).

the relationship between science and technology more clearly than most of the *philosophes*. The plates showing machinery and industrial processes are one of the most remarkable features of the *Encyclopaedia*. Diderot was also full of confidence in man and his abilities, a kind of prophet of a this-worldly religion of man. His interests were reflected in the titles and content of the *Encyclopaedia*, which appeared in thirty-five volumes over the course of thirty years (1751–80). Much of the most trenchant writing of Diderot, Voltaire, and other *philosophes* (or Encyclopedists) was done in articles for the *Encyclopaedia*. The book succeeded in becoming a bible of the "enlightened" everywhere. Through it ran faith in man's reason, pride in his accomplishments, contempt for his follies, and confidence in his future.

Leading Ideas of the Enlightenment

No intellectual movement is successful unless it has followers as well as

Historical Relativism in Montesquieu: The Effects of Climate and Geography

In Asia they have always had great empires; in Europe these could never exist. Asia has larger plains; it is cut out into much larger divisions by mountains and seas . . . and the rivers being not so large form more contrasted boundaries. Power in Asia, then, should be always despotic; for if their subjugation be not severe they would soon make a division inconsistent with the nature of the country.

In Europe natural divisions form many nations of moderate extent, in which ruling by laws is not incompatible with the maintenance of the state: on the contrary, it is so favorable to it that without this the state would fall into decay. It is this that has formed a genius for liberty that renders each part extremely difficult to be subdued and subjected to a foreign power. . . .

Africa is in a climate like that of the south of Asia and is in the same servitude. America, being lately destroyed and repeopled by the nations of Europe and Africa, can scarcely display its genuine spirit, but what we know of its history is very conformable to our principles. . . .

Monarchy is more frequently found in fertile countries and a republican government in those which are not so, and this is sometimes a sufficient compensation for the inconveniences they suffer by the sterility of the land. Thus the barrenness of the soil of Attica established a democracy there.

From Charles de Secondat de Montesquieu, *The Spirit of the Laws*, Book XVII, Chs. 6, 7; Book XVIII, Ch. 1 (in the Bohn Standard Library edition), Vol. I, pp. 289–91.

leaders, and the Enlightenment, like the Renaissance, produced its full quota of earnest, but dull, disciples and literary hacks who used Enlightenment language to create sensations or to attack their enemies. But the silent supporters of the Enlightenment were even more numerous than the writers who jumped aboard the bandwagon. As Robert Darnton has shown, the sales of the *Encyclopaedia* in tiny, provincial towns were astonishing. The main ideas of the Enlightenment struck root all over Europe and produced a generation that had new ideas about religion and social organization. These ruling ideas may be summed up in five words, each of which bore a heavy freight of meaning in the eighteenth century: reason, nature, happiness, progress, and liberty.

The eighteenth century believed as passionately in reason as the seventeenth, but with a difference. Voltaire's "reason" relied more on experience and less on mathematics than Descartes'. It was a weapon of skeptical inquiry based on observed facts (or what he thought were facts) rather than an instrument of deduction from axioms. To the men of the Enlightenment, reason was the alternative to superstition and prejudice; it

was the only sure guide to the principles that governed man and nature. Man's reason could discover the fundamental rationality of the universe, and it could also make human society more sensible. The *philosophes,* as shown by their writing for the *Encyclopaedia,* were less interested in "pure science" than in its applications, less concerned with system building than with specific reforms. Reason was now a pragmatic instrument, applicable not only to astronomy and physics but to agriculture, government, and social relations as well.

Nature was one of the favorite words of the Enlightenment. It was not always clear just what the *philosophes* meant by it, but it was clear enough that to nearly all of them "nature" or "the natural" were the proper standards for measuring God and man. If a thing was according to "nature," it was reasonable and therefore good. Voltaire and his contemporaries brought the idea of natural law to the peak of its prestige and the beginning of its decline. One of them devised this definition of natural law:

> The regular and constant order of facts by which God rules the universe; the order which his wisdom presents to the sense and reason of men, to serve them as an equal and common rule of conduct, and to guide them, without distinction of race or sect, towards perfection and happiness.

There is order and law, then, throughout the universe—laws of economics, of politics, of morality, as well as of physics and astronomy. These laws can be discovered by reason. Men may ignore or defy them, but they do so at their peril. To the enlightened, the way to happiness lay in conformity to nature and nature's laws. The man who broke nature's laws was looked on by the enlightened of the eighteenth century somewhat as the heretic who broke God's laws was looked on by the clergy in the Middle Ages: as a rebel against the order of the universe.

The end in view now was happiness, not salvation—happiness here in this world, not joy in the next. The Enlightenment was thoroughly secular in its thinking. When Jefferson included "the pursuit of happiness" along with life and

Key Words in History

If we could discover the little backstairs door that for any age serves as the secret entranceway to knowledge, we will do well to look for certain unobtrusive words with uncertain meanings that are permitted to slip off the tongue or the pen without fear and without research; words which, having from constant repetition lost their metaphorical significance, are unconsciously mistaken for objective realities. In the thirteenth century the key words would no doubt be *God, sin, grace, salvation, heaven,* and the like; in the nineteenth century, *matter, fact, matter-of-fact, evolution, progress;* in the twentieth century, *relativity, process, adjustment, function, complex.* In the eighteenth century the words without which no enlightened person could reach a restful conclusion were *nature, natural law, first cause, reason, sentiment, humanity, perfectibility.* In each age these magic words have their entrances and their exits. And how unobtrusively they come in and go out! We should scarcely be aware either of their approach or their departure, except for a slight feeling of discomfort, a shy self-consciousness in the use of them.

From Carl L. Becker, *The Heavenly City of the Eighteenth-Century Philosophers* (New Haven, Conn.: Yale University Press, 1932), p. 47.

liberty as an inalienable human right, he was expressing the general agreement of the enlightened. The tendency of medieval Christianity to ignore misery in this life because it would be compensated for in the next angered the *philosophes*, who insisted that Christian ideals, if they were worth anything at all, must be realized here and now. Voltaire and his fellows were humanitarians. They abominated torture and cruelty, slavery and the callous treatment of the insane. An Italian, Beccaria, was the first to point out that savage penalties do not stop crime and to demand more rational treatment of criminals. The *philosophes* were also cosmopolitan and even pacifist in temper. Some of the bitterest passages ever written about the insanity of war and the absurdity of blind patriotism were penned by Voltaire. The "happiness" that he and others talked about was often materialistic. But it corresponded closely with Christ's injunction to feed the hungry, clothe the naked, and visit the sick and imprisoned. To the enlightened this was far more important than saving anything so vague as one's own soul.

The *philosophes* were the first sizable group of educated Europeans to believe in progress. They took the older Christian idea of the spiritual progression of mankind from the Creation through the Incarnation to the Last Judgment and secularized it. The progress of civilization, they believed, was now out of God's hands and in man's own. Once man had found the clue to discovering and using nature's laws in government, economics, and technology, progress was sure, inevitable, and swift. Both man and society were perfectible. Time was on man's side, they thought, not against him or even indifferent to him.

This was a major revolution in western thought. The Middle Ages could not have conceived of purely secular progress unrelated to God. Men of the Renaissance still felt themselves inferior to the heroic Greeks and Romans. But in a literary battle between "ancients" and "moderns" that began in 1687 the idea appeared that the "moderns" were as good as, and probably better than, the "ancients." By 1750 a French *philosophe* and economist, Turgot, suggested that

the essential element in history was man's slow struggle upward to his crucial discovery of the scientific method. In 1794 Condorcet, a mathematician under sentence of death during the French Revolution, wrote a *Sketch for a Historical Picture of the Progress of the Human Mind*, which summed up all the optimism of his century. He saw "the strongest reasons for believing that nature has set no limit to the realization of our hopes" and foresaw "the abolition of inequality between nations, the progress of equality within nations, and the true perfection of mankind." Progress, he concluded, was now "independent of any power that might wish to halt it" and "will never be reversed." The scientific method cannot be lost, scientific knowledge of natural law will accumulate, and so progress can never cease. It was an intoxicating vision, a vision shared by the vast majority of the enlightened.

All the French *philosophes* were concerned about liberty. They were acutely aware of the limitations on liberty that prevailed inside France: restrictions on freedom of speech, freedom of religion, freedom of trade, freedom to choose a job, and freedom from arbitrary arrest. Looking at England through slightly rose-colored glasses, they envied Englishmen their economic, political, and religious liberty. Their concern about liberty was potentially the most explosive part of their thinking, but almost none of them felt that violence was necessary. Their belief in liberty was tied to their belief in reason. Reason would soon reveal the true natural laws governing everything from trade and government to religion. The artificiality of French society, French government, and French religious practices would become evident, and a benevolent despotism, enlightened by this knowledge, would set things right. Or so at least Voltaire and the majority of the Encyclopedists believed.

The Enlightenment and Religion

These ideas inevitably affected the religious thought of Europe. The fashionable belief among educated persons in the eighteenth century came to be

Deism, the belief in a God who is Creator but not Redeemer. Like a watchmaker who designs and constructs a complicated piece of machinery to keep perfect time, so God created the universe and started it going and then stepped aside to let it run according to its natural laws. God does not concern himself with redeeming men or society. The essence of religion is awe and reverence before the rationality and perfection of the universe—a feeling reflected in the hymns of Isaac Watts, which are still sung in many Protestant churches. To a Deist (Voltaire was a good example) all talk of revelation or miracle, all belief in the special intervention of God in the natural order, was false. All dogma and ritual were superstition, since man needed only his reason to understand God. The heart of natural religion was the morality common to all mankind. "Light is uniform for the star Sirius," Voltaire wrote, "and for us moral philosophy must be uniform." Obviously, Deism tended to undermine orthodox Christianity and to substitute for it a rational belief in God as First Cause and natural law as man's moral guide. A few of the French *philosophes* went further and pushed beyond Deism to atheism. Baron d'Holbach, for example, argued that there is nothing but matter in the universe, that man himself is a conglomeration of atoms, and that everything that happens is determined by natural law. But in the end many Protestants were able to find a compromise between Christian beliefs and the Enlightenment's rationalism, humanitarianism, and tolerance. The result in the nineteenth century was Protestant Liberalism.

Others reacted against Deism in the direction of more intense piety. To the enlightened, religious fervor of any sort savored of the fanaticism that had caused the wars of religion, and so all enthusiasm was frowned on. But Deism could be understood only by the educated, and its cold rationality had no appeal to emotional natures. Hence the wide popularity of two warmly emotional Protestant movements, Pietism in Germany and Methodism in England and America. Both emphasized the importance of inner religious experience, of individual "conversion." Pietism was a second and

John Wesley preaching in a private house.

milder Protestant Reformation, directed this time not against the pope but against both the dogmatically orthodox and those who were inclined to Deism in Germany. Individualistic, tolerant, and unconcerned about creeds or ceremonies, the Pietists attracted followers among both Catholics and Protestants.

John Wesley (1703–91) was the leader of a somewhat parallel revival of a warm, personal Christian piety in England in the years following his conversion in 1738. Finding his efforts resisted by the respectable Anglican clergy, he took his message directly to the people, addressing huge congregations outdoors or in remote chapels, teaching them to sing their way to heaven with the hymns of his brother Charles, and sending out streams of pamphlets from his printing presses to the congregations he had established. In the end Wesley was forced to establish a new denomination outside the Anglican Church—the Methodist (originally a term of derision directed at the "methodical" piety of Wesley's followers). Methodism touched thousands upon thousands of Englishmen at home and in the colonies who cared nothing for the arid intellectualism of many of the Anglican clergy in the eighteenth century. More than one historian has suggested that it was Methodism that kept the English lower classes from turning to revolutionary violence during the first impact of the Industrial Revolution.

Social and Political Thought

The *philosophes* were interested in social and political problems, but they were reformers, not revolutionists. Their formula for reform was simple: discover by reason and experience the natural laws that should operate in any given situation, clear away all artificial obstacles to their operation, and the result will be progress toward happiness and freedom. The first "economists" in the modern sense used this formula to launch an attack on mercantilism. In 1758 François Quesnay published his *Economic Survey*, which argued for the existence of natural economic laws that must be allowed to operate freely. In 1776 the Scot Adam Smith published his *Wealth of Nations*, which argued in parallel fashion that all nations would be wealthier if they removed restrictions on trade and let the natural law of supply and demand govern the exchange of commodities. Quesnay was primarily interested in agriculture and Smith in commerce, but both came to the same conclusion: that economic laws, like other natural laws, should be respected, that interference with these laws is dangerous, and that the greatest happiness and freedom come from allowing these laws to operate freely.

The same line of reasoning in political theory led to the theory of enlightened despotism. The *philosophes* hoped that divine-right monarchy would become benevolent monarchy, that monarchs would gradually become "enlightened" (or perhaps engage enlightened *philosophes* as advisers) and so govern their people according to natural law rather than according to their own caprice. To Voltaire and most of his fellows, government should be for the people but not necessarily by the people. A smaller group believed that reason pointed in the direction of a constitutional monarchy like the English, a government based on natural rights and contract, with a separation of powers as a further guarantee of political liberty. Finally, to enlightened despotism and constitutional government there was added a third theory, the theory of democracy, still too radical to be of much immediate influence but of enormous importance for the future. This was the theory obscurely but excitingly preached in *The Social Contract* (1762) by Jean Jacques Rousseau (1712–78).

Rousseau

Rousseau, a native of Geneva, turned up in Paris after a troubled and wandering youth, came to know Diderot and others of the *philosophes*, and for a time tried to become one of them. He was never easy in their company, however. He trusted reason, but he relied even more on emotion. He trusted nature, but to him nature was the unspoiled simplicity of precivilized man, "the noble savage." In a kind of conversion that he experienced in 1749, he became con-

vinced that mankind had lost more than it had gained by cultivating the arts and sciences, and so he surrendered his faith in progress. He grew more and more irritated by the artificiality of Paris society and finally broke with his former friends. Voltaire thought him mad, and Rousseau was haunted in his miserable later years by the illusion that he was being persecuted by everyone.

Rousseau was the great critic of the Enlightenment. By temperament he was a shy and sensitive misfit who vainly wanted to "belong." Deep down he knew himself to be good, but he felt that he had been corrupted and humiliated by an artificial society to which he did not and could not belong. To what kind of society or state could he give himself, then? Only to a society in which there were no hereditary rulers, no privileged aristocracy, no one with any right to lord it over others, none but those who had freely consented to become members of the society and had given up to the group all their individual rights. Perhaps Rousseau had an idealized Geneva in mind as he wrote *The Social Contract*—a community in which all the citizens knew and trusted one another—in which the minority accepted the majority's view with good grace because both felt themselves part of the same community. At any rate, he developed a theory of liberty as willing obedience to laws that the individual himself had helped to make as an active and loyal citizen, even though he might have been in the minority on any given issue. Locke and Montesquieu had thought that the way to obtain political liberty was to guarantee individual rights and to separate the organs of government so that no one of them could gain unrestricted control. Rousseau thought he would never feel free until he could find a community to which he could give up everything, on condition that all others did the same. In such a community there would be no division between rulers and ruled; the people would rule themselves. What magistrates there were would be mere servants of the community who could be instantly removed if they failed to carry out the people's will. If the people really governed themselves, there should be no checks and balances, no

Jean Jacques Rousseau.

Rousseau on the Social Contract

The problem is to find a form of association . . . in which each, while uniting himself with all, may still obey himself alone, and remain as free as before. This is the fundamental problem of which the Social Contract provides the solution: . . . the total alienation of each associate, together with all his rights, to the whole community. . . . Each man, in giving himself to all, gives himself to nobody. . . . Each of us puts his person and all his power in common under the supreme direction of the general will, and, in our corporate capacity, we receive each member as an indivisible part of the whole. . . . In order that the social compact may not be an empty formula, it tacitly includes the undertaking, which alone can give force to the rest, that whoever refuses to obey the general will shall be compelled to do so by the whole body. This means nothing less than that he will be forced to be free.

From Jean Jacques Rousseau, *The Social Contract* (New York and London: Everyman's Library, 1913), Book I, Chs. 6, 7, pp. 14–18.

separation of powers, no protection of rights.

Rousseau was picturing democracy in its purest and simplest form: a tight-knit community of loyal and active citizens, unhampered by any checks on their collective will because they unreservedly accepted this general will as their own. His book was highly abstract and difficult to understand. But when revolution actually flared up in France after his death, *The Social Contract* came into its own. It was not a work of the Enlightenment; its full force could be felt only in the new age of democratic revolution, nationalism, and Romanticism. And when romantic nationalism reached its peak, Rousseau could be used to justify dictatorship (which after all is supposed to embody the common will) as well as democracy.

So the two centuries that saw the Scientific Revolution and the Enlightenment might well be called the most revolutionary centuries in western intellectual history. The true watershed between what we call "medieval" and "modern" thought about God, man, and nature runs somewhere through these two centuries. The world of Luther and Loyola, of Charles V and Philip II, was still or-

ganically related to the Middle Ages. The world of Newton and Locke, of Voltaire and Rousseau, was unmistakably the father of our own.

ARTS AND LETTERS IN THE EIGHTEENTH CENTURY

The pervasive faith in the rationality, intelligibility, and order of the universe displayed by the scientists and philosophers of the age was reflected in the art and literature of the later seventeenth and early eighteenth centuries. Rationalism blended easily with classicism. The regularity and harmony of Newton's universe seemed to accord with the balance and proportion that Greek architects had admired as artistic ideals and with the rationality and restraint that the leading Greek and Roman writers had held up as literary ideals. The dictators of literary and artistic taste at the close of the seventeenth century were classicists, and when *philosophes* like Voltaire wrote dramas they accepted classical standards as unquestioningly as Corneille and Racine. Architects accepted classical rules of balance and unity with equal zeal in the "Georgian" buildings of England and the beautifully proportioned Place de la Concorde in Paris. Enthusiasm for classical antiquity reached its post-Renaissance climax in 1748, when the remains of the Roman city of Pompeii were discovered in startlingly well-preserved condition under the lava of Mt. Vesuvius.

An Age of Prose

The age of reason was an age of prose. Essays, satirical tales, novels, letters, and histories were the characteristic literary forms of the eighteenth century. Authors bent their energies to description and narrative rather than to suggestion and imagination. The essays of Addison and Steele, which began to appear in 1709, sketched a delightful picture of English rural society, while Jonathan Swift's *Gulliver's Travels* (1726) and Voltaire's *Candide* (1759) were more biting and satirical commentaries on human society. As the century progressed, the novel emerged as the favorite form of literary expression; the most mature example was Henry Fielding's *Tom Jones* (1749). Besides fiction, men read philosophy, economics, and history—of which Edward Gibbon's majestic *History of the Decline and Fall of the Roman Empire* (1776–88) was the most enduring example. Everything that could be done in prose—argument, satire, realistic description, historical narrative—was tried and done well by some French or British writer.

The elegance and aristocratic flavor of eighteenth-century society can be seen in its painting, and especially in the portraits, which were the most characteristic form of the art. The delicate-featured and exquisitely groomed women who look coolly down on the observer, and the worldly, sometimes arrogant, faces of their husbands under their powdered wigs suggest the artificiality of their society and sometimes the hardness of their characters. Furniture, tableware, and the great town and country houses of wealthy merchants and nobles reflect the same elegance and aristocratic spirit.

Not all the books, the arts, and the crafts were meant for the enjoyment of the aristocracy, however. The eighteenth century saw the appearance of the first newspapers, written for a wide audience of educated readers. William Hogarth (1697–1764) made engravings of his realistic satirical sketches of English society and sold them by the thousands. Above all, the novelists, the dramatists, and the musicians began to appeal to a middle-class audience that went far beyond the limits of the aristocracy. After the 1770s the plays and operas in Paris were apt to have a keen, satirical edge and to be directed at bourgeois listeners. The heroes and heroines of the novels were more often of middle-class origins than either upper- or lower-class. Music began to move from the aristocratic salon into the public auditorium.

Music

The greatest cultural achievement of the eighteenth century was its music. The musical world of the early eighteenth century was dominated by two great Germans: Johann Sebastian Bach (1685–1750) and George Frederick Handel (1685–1759) (who spent most of his life in England). Together they realized all the dramatic and emotive possibilities of the baroque style: Handel in his oratorios for chorus and instruments, Bach in his richly varied works for keyboard instruments, chamber groups, orchestras, and choruses. In the latter part of the century the orchestra, which had originated in the seventeenth century, was expanded and strengthened, the pianoforte invented, and music brought more and more into touch with a wider public. Franz Joseph Haydn (1732–1809), who wrote for both chamber groups and orchestras, developed the musical forms known as sonatas and symphonies. The other outstanding musical personality of the latter half of the century, Wolfgang Amadeus Mozart (1756–91), was possibly the most gifted musician who ever lived. A child prodigy, he lived only thirty-five years and died in poverty, but within this short span of time he produced string quartets, concertos, symphonies, and operas that were masterpieces of invention and form.

Wolfgang Amadeus Mozart, unfinished painting by Joseph Lange.

The Beginnings of Romanticism

Beneath the dominant tendency to respect rational structure and classical balance, however, there were countercurrents of revolt. Some evidence of these currents was seen in Pietism and Methodism, and in Rousseau's distrust of an exclusive reliance on reason. More clearly than Rousseau, the Scottish philosopher David Hume (1711–76) criticized reason as a method of knowing truth and defended the validity in human experience of feeling, conscience, and habit. French and English novelists developed sentimentalism to a fine art, putting their heroines through heart-rending misfortune and mistreatment and trying at every turn to arouse the reader's anger, pity, love, or terror. The most influential example was Samuel Richardson's two thousand-page tearjerker, *Clarissa* (1748), which influenced Rousseau in writing his *Nouvelle Héloise* (1761). The strange, the unusual, the offbeat, and the fantastic began to come into fashion. Gothic architecture and literature began to be appreciated once more, and a collection of poems (1762) ostensibly by a medieval poet named Ossian was very popular, though it turned out to be a forgery.

In Germany, which never came totally under the sway of the French Enlightenment, a "Storm and Stress" (*Sturm und Drang*) movement in literature emphasized the great elemental emotions and denied the supremacy of reason. Johann Gottfried von Herder (1744–1803) worked out a philosophy of history that emphasized the uniqueness and peculiarity of each nation or race, the individuality of its genius, and the falsity of any view that denied this uniqueness in the name of universal reason. Johann Wolfgang von Goethe (1749–1832) at the start of his long literary career published *The Sorrows of Young Werther* (1774), a morbid tale ending in a suicide, which appealed to lovers of sentiment and sensibility.

The greatest philosopher of the age, Immanuel Kant (1724–1804), a man who never traveled more than a few miles from Königsberg, his native city in East Prussia, launched a powerful attack on the rationalism of his age as too narrow and too dogmatic. Starting from David Hume's criticism of reason, Kant distinguished carefully between speculative (or scientific) reason and practical (or moral) reason in his very difficult book, *Critique of Pure Reason* (1781). The effect of his work was to enable Christians and idealists to make a new case for religion and morality based on the fact of man's conscience.

Taken together, these various tendencies heralded the beginnings of what was to be called Romanticism. The "Age of Reason" thus contained within itself the seeds of an age that would rely for its artistic, philosophical, and even social insight on emotion and conscience rather than on reason.

Suggestions for Further Reading

Note: Asterisk denotes a book available in paperback edition.

General   J. H. Randall, *The Making of the Modern Mind* (1926, 1940), is the most successful one-volume survey of the course of western thought, by a philosopher with a sense for historical context. To Randall, "the modern mind" is essentially the scientific mind. C. Brinton, *Ideas and Men** (1950)—the material since the Renaissance has been published as *The Shaping of the Modern Mind** (1953)—is a more informally written and engaging narrative by a historian. Both books are particularly good on the seventeenth and eighteenth centuries. G. R. Sabine, *A History of Political Theory* (1938), is the most penetrating one-volume survey, particularly full on English political thought in the seventeenth century and French in the eighteenth. A. O. Lovejoy, *The Great Chain of Being** (1936), is a classic account of the underlying western conception of the universe as a hierarchical structure of being, from the Greeks to the nineteenth century. M. Ashley, *The Golden Century* (1968), is a well-written survey of seventeenth-century social and cultural history.

The Scientific   E. A. Burtt, *The Metaphysical Foundations of Modern Physical Science** (1924, 1955), and A. N. Whitehead,
Revolution   *Science and the Modern World** (1925, 1948), are famous philosophical inquiries into the origins of modern science, not easy reading, but rewarding to the serious student. A. R. Hall, *The Scientific Revolution** (1954), is the best modern account, well informed and critical. H. Butterfield, *Origins of Modern Science, 1300–1800** (1949), is a more readable discussion of the subject for the lay reader written by a general historian. A. Koyré writes absorbingly about the cosmological implications of the "revolution" in *From the Closed World to the Infinite Universe** (1957). C. C. Gillispie, *The Edge of Objectivity**(1960), is a brilliantly written essay on the growth of objectivity in the study of nature from Galileo to Einstein. T. S. Kuhn, *The Copernican Revolution** (1957), describes the transformation of astronomical thought. *The Structure of Scientific Revolutions** (1962), by the same author, is a controversial but brilliant discussion of scientific change in general. R. G. Collingwood traces the

chief western conceptions of the natural order from the Greeks to the present in *The Idea of Nature** (1945). C. J. Singer, *From Magic to Science** (1928), is still valuable for its interpretation of the origins of modern science. On the social background of scientific development, three books are particularly valuable: M. Ornstein, *The Role of Scientific Societies in the Seventeenth Century* (1928); D. Stimson, *Scientists and Amateurs: A History of the Royal Society* (1948); and G. N. Clark, *Science and Social Welfare in the Age of Newton* (1937). There are biographies and special studies, too numerous to list here, of every scientist mentioned in the text. But two studies of a famous case are worth noting: G. de Santillana, *The Crime of Galileo** (1955), and F. S. Taylor, *Galileo and the Freedom of Thought* (1938). The effect of scientific discovery on literature is the theme of M. Nicolson, *Science and Imagination**(1956).

Culture of the Seventeenth and Eighteenth Centuries

There is no full and reliable discussion in English on the baroque style in art, the basic studies being in German. The best introductions are in C. J. Friedrich, *The Age of the Baroque, 1610–1660** (1952) in the *Rise of Modern Europe* series, and Chapter 6 of H. Leichtentritt, *Music, History, and Ideas* (1938). The Pelican *History of Art** has good studies of individual countries for the period from 1600 to 1880. The latter third of G. N. Clark, *The Seventeenth Century* (1931), is devoted to art, literature, and philosophy. B. Willey's two volumes, *The Seventeenth Century Background** (1934) and *The Eighteenth Century Background** (1940), sketch a broad background for the study of English literature in the period. F. Fosca, *The Eighteenth Century* (1953), is probably the best introduction to the painting of the age. In addition to Leichtentritt, M. F. Bukofzer, *Music in the Baroque Era* (1947), is particularly interesting. There is no satisfactory general account of religious developments, but A. C. McGiffert, *Protestant Thought Before Kant* (1911), is a brief reliable account. M. J. Bradshaw, *The Philosophical Foundations of Faith* (1941), is illuminating on the religious attitudes of prominent seventeenth-century figures like Descartes. M. L. Edwards, *John Wesley and the Eighteenth Century* (1933), is one of many books on Methodism.

Contemporary Literature

The best way, as always, to gain a firsthand knowledge of the thought and feeling of the period is through a study of some of the paintings, the buildings, the literary and philosophical writings, and the musical works of the age. This becomes increasingly easy to do after the sixteenth century because of the availability of reproductions, records, and inexpensive reprints. The student will have to make his own selection, but some of the following should be on any reading list (there are many editions of each except where specified): Descartes, *Discourse on Method;** Bacon, *New Atlantis;* Pascal, *Pensées;** Galileo, *Dialogue on the Great World Systems*, ed. by G. de Santillana (1953); John Bunyan, *The Pilgrim's Progress;** John Locke, *Second Treatise of Government** and *Essay Concerning Human Understanding;**Selections from Bayle's Dictionary*, ed. by E. A. Beller and M. D. Lee (1952); Beccaria, *Essay on Crimes and Punishments** (trans. 1953); *The Portable Voltaire,** ed. by B. R. Redman (1949); Rousseau, *Social Contract;** Henry Fielding, *Tom Jones;** Samuel Richardson, *Clarissa* (abridgment, Modern Library, 1950). *The Portable Age of Reason Reader,** ed. by C. Brinton (1956), is an excellent selection of readings from the *philosophes*.

The Enlightenment

The most significant study of the transition from the seventeenth century to the eighteenth, from the Scientific Revolution to the Enlightenment, is P. Hazard, *The European Mind: The Critical Years, 1680–1715** (trans. 1952). There are excellent chapters on the Enlightenment in W. L. Dorn, *Competition for Empire, 1740–1763** (1940), and in the *New Cambridge Modern History*, Vol. VII: A. Cobban, *The Old Régime, 1713–1763* (1957). The most searching interpretation of the movement as a whole is E. Cassirer, *The Philosophy of the Enlightenment** (1932, trans. 1951), which emphasizes the break with older ways of thinking accomplished by the eighteenth century. C. L. Becker's charming lectures, *The Heavenly City of the Eighteenth-Century Philosophers** (1932), emphasize the continuity with the past. G. R. Havens, *The Age of Ideas: From Reaction to Revolution in Eighteenth-Century France** (1955), is a sound study. On the idea of progress, besides Becker, see J. B. Bury, *The Idea of Progress** (1920, 1932); R. F. Jones, *Ancients and Moderns** (1936); and C. Frankel, *The Faith of Reason: The Idea of Progress in the French Enlightenment* (1948). C. R. Cragg, *Reason and Authority in the Eighteenth Century* (1964), is an excellent account of the Enlightenment on the English side of the Channel, and D. Mornet, *French Thought in the Eighteenth Century* (1929), of Enlightenment on the other. P. Gay, *The Enlightenment: An Interpretation** (1966–69), is an attempt to pull all aspects of the movement together. For the political thought of the *philosophes*, see K. Martin, *French Liberal Thought in the Eighteenth Century** (1929); and for the historical thought of Voltaire, Robertson, Hume, and Gibbon, see J. B. Black, *The Art of History* (1926). An unfamiliar aspect of the Enlightenment is brought to light in R. Darnton, "The High Enlightenment and the Low-Life of Literature in Pre-Revolutionary France," *Past and Present*, no. 51 (1971).

22 Aristocracy and Empire, 1715–1789

The seventy-five years between the death of Louis XIV (1715) and the outbreak of the French Revolution (1789) have a character of their own. This was a period of stability and equilibrium. There were no religious wars and no social upheavals (except for an uprising of serfs in far-off Russia), and there appears to have been somewhat less social mobility than in the seventeenth century. Monarchy was the most prevalent form of government, with divine-right monarchy evolving into "enlightened despotism."

Closely examined, however, the governments of the European states in the eighteenth century, both monarchies and republics, are better described as "aristocracies." Everywhere landed or moneyed minorities controlled or strongly influenced the governments of Europe. The Whig nobles and merchants who dominated the English Parliament, the French nobles and lawyers who dominated the royal councils and the law courts of France after the death of Louis XIV, the Junkers who commanded the Prussian armies, the landed nobles who made a farce of the Polish Diet, the "service nobility" that ceased to serve any but its own interests after the reign of Peter the Great in Russia, the wealthy bourgeois who directly controlled the governments of the Dutch Republic and the German free cities—all were rich, well-born, and privileged, and thus fitted the eighteenth-century definition of aristocrats. Everywhere "aristocracy" was resurgent against absolute monarchy, and many of the gains of seventeenth-century monarchies were lost or compromised. Only where the monarch or the chief minister was a man of unusual ability was this revival of aristocratic influence turned to the benefit of the central government.

In this undeclared war between monarch and aristocrat a kind of compromise was generally reached. Eighteenth-century governments maintained an uneasy balance between centralization and decentralization, between absolute monarchy and aristocratic privilege. This might have been illogical, but strict adherence to basic principles had caused the bloody religious and civil wars of the last two centuries. Most men were glad to accept the structure of society and government as they found it after 1715. It was a glorious age to be alive in—if you were an "aristocrat." There was much abject poverty, injustice, and brutality in European society, but these could be forgotten if one centered one's attention on the brilliant "civilization" (the word first appeared in the 1770s) of the Paris salons or the London coffeehouses. To men who remembered the devastation of the Thirty Years' War or the fanaticism of Cromwell's "saints," social stability and political equilibrium were worth a fairly high price in injustice.

INTERNATIONAL RELATIONS

Equilibrium was also the rule in international relations. The defeat of Louis XIV's bid for a preponderance of power in Europe had been bloody and costly, and European statesmen were tacitly agreed that all such attempts to become "top dog" should be stopped at the outset. The balancing of power among the "great powers" of Europe—France, Britain, Austria, Prussia, and Russia (Spain, Holland, Sweden, Poland, and the Ottoman Empire could no longer qualify)—became the chief concern of diplomats.

The balance, of course, seldom remained steady for very long. Every country was constantly on the lookout for additional territory or for new colonies and trading opportunities abroad. In order to avoid large-scale wars like those needed to curb Louis XIV's ambitions, it became the custom for all the great powers to expect "compensation" whenever one of them was fortunate or daring enough to acquire new territory. This was hard on the weaker states, which were carved up to provide the "compensation," but it admittedly preserved the balance and often maintained the peace.

There were wars, and they were fairly frequent. But they were not so bloody or so exhausting as those of the seventeenth century. Generally they were "limited wars"—in two senses. First, they were limited in the numbers of persons who took part in them or were affected by them. Eighteenth-century armies were

Frederick II of Prussia in 1778.

professional armies, often recruited or kidnaped from the dregs of society or composed of foreign mercenaries. Except in Russia, where serfs made up most of the army, there was no general conscription, and the civilian was usually little affected by wars. Warfare consisted of elaborate maneuvering by highly disciplined professional units rather than bloody mass combat. There was little pillaging, even in enemy territory, because it was bad business to devastate a territory that might be annexed.

Wars were limited also in their objectives. There were no wars of annihilation. The enemy of today might be the ally of tomorrow, and it was thought well not to defeat any power too thoroughly because that would disturb the balance. The reli-

gious hatreds of the seventeenth century had cooled, and the passions of revolutionary liberalism and nationalism had not yet sprung into flame. The statesmen and generals fought for comparatively definite and concrete political and economic objectives, not for ideologies. When the objectives were attained—or when it became clear that they could not be attained immediately—the statesmen made peace or arranged a truce. There was no need to fight through to unconditional surrender. In spite of cutthroat competition for "empire"—in the form of land, population, colonies, or trade—the monarchs, bureaucrats, and aristocrats of the eighteenth century felt themselves part of a common civilization. The competition was a jockeying for power

EUROPE IN 1715

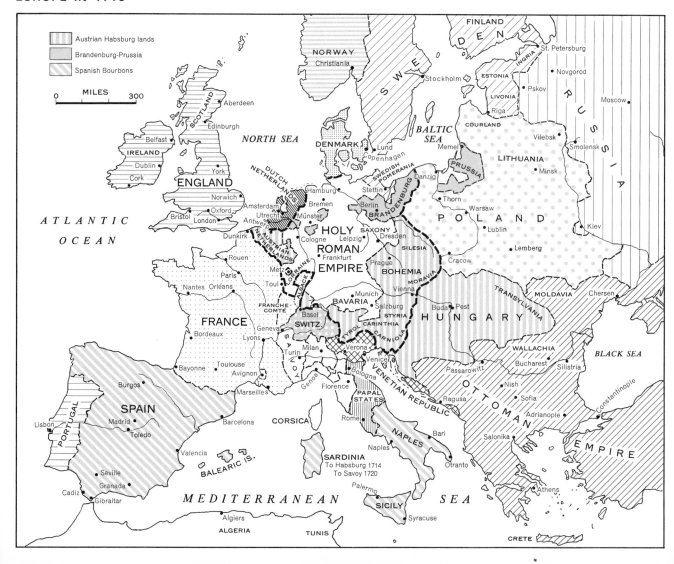

among cousins rather than a fight for survival against deadly enemies.

The picture of a stable, well-balanced eighteenth-century society sketched here could of course be compared to Newton's picture of the universe—a beautifully stable order of perfectly balanced gravitational pushes and pulls in which every mass moved along discoverable lines of force. But this picture must not be exaggerated. The eighteenth century was also a dynamic age. Its precarious equilibrium was an equilibrium among rapidly expanding forces. Wealth and trade were increasing; something like a revolution in agriculture was in the making, and a revolution in industry had begun. European economy and diplomacy were rapidly becoming global rather than continental, and the struggle for empire was reaching the farthest corners of the earth. For the first time, battles fought in America, Africa, and Asia began to tip the balance of power in Europe. And in trying to keep the balance, each country accentuated its own particular sources of strength. England relied more and more on naval power and commerce, Prussia on its army and bureaucracy. Russia intensified its reliance on serfdom, while Austria made up for weakness in Germany by increasing its power in southeastern Europe. France, the one country that did not want to specialize, found itself coming out second-best in most fields—naval power, military power, and industrial growth. Its intellectual and cultural leadership masked, but did not remedy, these weaknesses. In short, differences in the bases of power among European nations increased rather than decreased during the period and made it harder to keep the balance. With growing political rivalry added to rapid social change, it can be seen that the eighteenth century was not all order and stability. It was pregnant with revolution as well.

The years from 1715 to 1789 may conveniently be divided into three periods of about twenty-five years each: (1) a generation of peace and prosperity, 1715–40; (2) a period of worldwide warfare, 1740–63; and (3) an interval of enlightened despotism, aristocratic resurgence, and revolutionary stirrings, 1763–89.

Aristocracy

[By the 1760s] the world had become more aristocratic. Aristocracy in the eighteenth century may even be thought of as a new and recent development, if it be distinguished from the older institution of nobility. In one way it was more exclusive than mere nobility. A king could create nobles, but, as the saying went, it took four generations to make a gentleman. In another way aristocracy was broader than nobility. Countries that had no nobles, like Switzerland or British America, or countries that had few nobles of importance, like the Dutch provinces, might have aristocracies that even nobles recognized as such. . . . Aristocracy was nobility civilized, polished by that "refinement of manners" of which people talked, enjoying not only superiority of birth but a superior mode of life. It was a way of life as pleasing as any that mankind has ever developed, and which the middle classes were to imitate as much and as long as they could, a way of life characterized by dignified homes and by gardens and well-kept lawns, by private tutors and grand tours and sojourns at watering places, by annual migration between town and country and an abundance of respectful and unobtrusive servants.

From R. R. Palmer, *The Age of the Democratic Revolution* (Princeton, N.J.: Princeton University Press, 1959), pp. 29–30.

PEACE AND PROSPERITY 1715–40

After the peace settlements of 1713 in western Europe and of 1719 to 1721 in eastern Europe, both governments and peoples were weary of war. The age that followed was unheroic, unexciting, and corrupt, like many other postwar periods. But peace restored law and order, and order stimulated an enormous expansion of trade, particularly in western Europe.

Increase of Trade and Wealth

Seaborne commerce was the key to wealth in the eighteenth century. Thanks to the enterprise of their merchants and the technical skill of their mariners, the foreign trade of Britain and France increased about five times during the eighteenth century. In the case of Britain the sharpest increase was in colonial trade. This meant that Britain needed a

The Baron, caricature of a member of the French nobility (1785).

larger merchant marine than its rivals and forced the British to build the strongest navy in the world to protect its overseas trade. In the case of France the greatest increase was in trade with other European nations. In both cases the accumulation of wealth in the hands of the upper classes was spectacular. For the first time the wealth of Europe began to eclipse the wealth of Asia. The two preceding centuries of exploration and establishment of overseas trading connections had begun to pay off handsomely in material benefits. The dinner table of a merchant of Liverpool, for instance, was graced by sugar from the West Indies, wine from Portugal, and tobacco from Virginia. His wife might wear calico from India in summer and furs from Canada in winter. Their daughter might be married to the heir of a nobleman whose capacious Georgian house had been built on the combined profits from his land and his mercantile investments.

But many of the commodities on which this thriving trade was based were derived from the labor of slaves or serfs. Only African slaves could be forced to do the kind of work required on the sugar plantations of the West Indies, and even they survived only about seven years, on the average. There was an almost insatiable demand for black slaves in the sugar islands, a demand that was met largely by English slave traders, who procured their victims from the petty kings of the west coast of Africa, exchanged them for sugar in the West Indies, had the sugar converted into rum, then used the rum to debauch native rulers and thus to secure more slaves in Africa. The serfs who toiled without recompense for their noble landlords in the grain-producing regions of eastern Europe were in much the same position in the economic order as the slaves of the West Indies. In short, a large part of the European economy was still based, as the

Engraving from a seventeenth-century history of the West Indies showing the workings of a sugar plantation.

economy of Greece and Rome had been, on servile labor.

There were signs in England, however, of the beginnings of revolutionary changes in both farming and industry. Eventually these changes were to result in an unprecedented expansion in the amount and variety of food, clothing, shelter, and luxuries that Europeans could produce. Historians speak of these changes as the "Agricultural Revolution" and the "Industrial Revolution," but these two revolutions picked up speed very slowly. For example, the first workable, though inefficient, steam engine was in use by 1700; the greatly improved Watts engine appeared three-quarters of a century later but was not widely used until after 1800. Since the results of the Agricultural and Industrial Revolutions were seen most clearly in the nineteenth century, they will be discussed in later chapters.

Mississippi and South Sea Bubbles

European commercial capitalism was still expanding its field of operations in the early eighteenth century. The period of peace after 1713 encouraged both private financial speculation and wildcat commercial ventures. The years 1719 and 1720 saw the first large-scale example of a typically modern phenomenon, a cycle of boom-and-bust, or, as contemporaries called it, a "bubble."

The wars of Louis XIV had burdened both the French and the English governments with large debts. When a Scottish promoter named John Law showed up at the court of France after the death of Louis XIV and offered to solve the government's financial troubles, he was given *carte blanche* to manage the French economy as he saw fit. He set up a bank to issue paper currency and organized a Mississippi Company to trade with France's colony in Louisiana. The company boldly took over the government's debt, accepting government bonds in payment for shares of its own stock. Then it promoted a boom in the price of its stock by spreading tall tales of its commercial prospects. When the price finally reached forty times its original value, investors began to sell in order to cash in on their profits. Before long the price had plummeted, the bubble had burst, and Law had fled the country.

A similar episode occurred across the Channel in London. A South Sea Company had been organized to exploit the trade with the Spanish colonies provided for by the Peace of Utrecht. It too took over much of the government's debt, and it too deliberately promoted a boom in its own stock. In 1720, a few months after Law's failure, the South Sea bubble burst.

The collapse of the Mississippi and South Sea bubbles in 1719 and 1720 hampered the development of joint stock companies and ruined a good many individual investors. But the two companies had shown how to mobilize vast amounts of capital and how to find new sources of support for the public debt. Deliberate encouragement of speculation had tarnished both objectives, but the underlying commercial purposes of the two companies were essentially sound. When they were reorganized, both continued to make money for their investors for many years. French trade, particularly, was stimulated, although investors lost confidence in the French government. In contrast, the English government came to acknowledge the national debt as a public obligation and never again permitted private interests to assume responsibility for it, thus gaining the confidence of investors.

England Under Walpole

During the generation of peace that followed the death of Louis XIV, the English worked out some of their internal political problems. As had been determined by the Act of Settlement, the Elector of Hanover succeeded Anne as ruler of England in 1714. Compared with the Stuarts, the first two Hanoverian monarchs, George I (1714–27) and George II (1727–60), were colorless figures. Both were stupid men who spoke little or no English. They interfered constantly in minor details of government, but neither was capable of grasping the larger issues. As a result, an "inner cabinet" of ministers became more and more responsible

George I of England (1714–27), and his signature. Medal by John Croker.

Caricature of George II drawn by a British officer about 1760.

for policy decisions. Legally, the king was still free to choose his own ministers. Actually, he had to select men who could influence elections and control a majority in Parliament. These leading ministers began to meet at dinner to concert policy. They began to force out of office colleagues who disagreed with the group's majority, and they usually accepted the leadership of the ablest or most powerful among them in presenting their policy to the king. These informal practices vaguely foreshadowed the "cabinet system" and "prime minister" of the nineteenth century.

Robert Walpole, a country squire who had family connections with both the landed and the commercial aristocracies, is generally considered the first prime minister in English history, though he would not have acknowledged the title. For some twenty years, from 1721 to 1742, he was the manager of the Whig party in Parliament and the leading minister in the government. The first two Hanoverians by necessity chose their ministers from Whigs, since the Tories were tainted by affection for the Stuarts and had little strength in Parliament.

Walpole was a good-natured, hard-headed politician who understood the landed and financial "interests" represented in Parliament and knew how to hold a parliamentary majority together by tact, persuasion, and, if necessary, bribery and corruption. The fact that he was addicted to hard drinking and off-color stories helped rather than hurt him in managing the Whig merchants and landed gentry who controlled Parliament and ran local government as justices of the peace. Walpole's motto was, "Let sleeping dogs lie." He took care never to stir up any issue, at home or abroad, that might arouse passion and conflict. In 1733, for instance, he proposed a sensible scheme for raising more revenue from excise taxes and less from customs duties in order to discourage smuggling and encourage legitimate trade. But when his scheme was met by a storm of irrational abuse ("No excise, no popery, no wooden shoes" was one slogan), he dropped it. So far as the colonies were concerned, he followed a policy of "salutary neglect," leaving them to grow in population and wealth by their own efforts. In foreign affairs he preserved the peace until 1739, when the London merchants and their spokesmen in Parliament forced him into a commercial war with Spain. Even then he tried to keep the war as limited as possible.

Sir Robert Walpole (left), leader of the Whig government from 1721 to 1742, talking to the speaker of the House of Commons. Engraving after a painting by Hogarth.

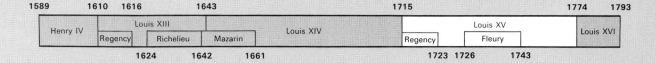
Henry IV	Louis XIII		Louis XIV		Louis XV		Louis XVI
	Regency	Richelieu	Mazarin		Regency	Fleury	
	1624	1642	1661		1723 1726	1743	

On the whole, Walpole's ministry was a fruitful one for England. Both England and its colonies prospered; the credit of the government was never better; and the ruling aristocracy of landed and commercial wealth governed with a loose rein. When Voltaire visited England from 1726 to 1729 he may have idealized English society and government somewhat. But there was without question more equality before the law in England, more personal freedom, more sense of public obligation in the ruling class, more security of property, and more widespread prosperity than anywhere else in Europe.

Louis XV and Cardinal Fleury

The generation of peace that brought strength to Britain brought weakness to France. Louis XIV's great-grandson Louis XV (1715-74) was a child of five when he came to the throne. The Regency that governed in his name for eight years had to make concessions to all the powerful elements in French society that had been kept in leash by the Sun King. The result was an aristocratic reaction in French government. Nobles began to reappear as policymakers on the royal councils, and the *Parlement* of Paris boldly reasserted its ancient claim to register and enforce royal legislation or not, as it saw fit. The French monarchy remained as absolute as ever in theory, but after Louis XIV there was no strong hand to make the theory work. French government became inefficient and inconstant. Aristocratic privilege exasperated the middle classes and in the long run made it impossible for the government to avoid financial insolvency.

For a time the decline was arrested by Cardinal Fleury, the leading minister from 1726 to 1743. Fleury had ability, but he was no Richelieu. He was past seventy when he came to power, and his policy,

much like Walpole's, was to preserve the peace, make cautious compromises, and avoid direct confrontation with the holders of power—in this case the nobility. He dissociated himself from the statesmanlike attempt of another minister to tax the nobility like everyone else, but he stabilized the currency, encouraged trade, and did all he could to make the old system of tax-farming work. His monarch was too debauched and incapable to set a more constructive course.

Fleury lost power in his last years, and when he died at the age of ninety, Louis XV decided that he would govern for himself without a prime minister. This simply meant that France now had a king who could neither govern himself nor let anyone else govern for him. Louis XV's best-known remark, "After me, the deluge," perfectly expressed his attitude. The aristocracy naturally took full advantage of this situation and greatly increased its influence. France remained the largest and potentially the most powerful nation in Europe. French trade and industry were growing at a rapid rate, but the government was run by royal mistresses and favorites (Mme. de Pompadour was the most prominent), and the French state could not make full use of its resources.

Declining Monarchies and Empires

Elsewhere in Europe, with few exceptions, monarchical institutions were in decline as they were in France during the generation after the Peace of Utrecht.

In Spain the Bourbon whom Louis XIV established on the throne, Philip V (1700-46), managed to curb the nobility somewhat and to encourage trade and industry. But the dry rot had eaten too deep into Spanish society and government to allow a real revival of the nation's greatness. Neither the Spanish

Arms of Louis XV, from Diderot's *Encyclopaedia*.

Maria Theresa of Austria with her husband, Emperor Francis I, and eleven of their children.
The future Emperor Joseph II stands in the right center. Painting by Meytens.

economy, nor the army and navy, nor the colonies made any significant gains.

Austria was an imperfectly united empire composed of three separate kingdoms (Austria, Bohemia, and Hungary) and two dependencies of quite different cultures and traditions (northern Italy and the Netherlands). The Habsburg Emperor Charles VI (1711–40) had to spend years in persuading his own subjects and foreign governments to accept a "Pragmatic Sanction" that provided that his daughter Maria Theresa (Charles had no sons) should succeed him as ruler of all his various lands. By the time of his death he had the agreement on paper of everyone concerned, but no one was sure just how long the agreement would be respected by greedy neighboring monarchs or restless Hungarian nobles.

Farther to the east, the Polish and Ottoman empires continued to decline. A desultory and trivial war over the succession to the Polish crown was fought between 1733 and 1738 by France and Spain against Austria and Russia. The Russian candidate for the throne won out, and all the losers were "compensated" by being given scraps of territory elsewhere—Spain in Naples and Sicily, for instance. At the same time Austria and Russia were once more at war with the Ottoman Turks. The Turks were never completely dominated by their neighbors, as were the Poles, but it was evident that neither state counted for much in the European power structure.

In the generation after Peter the Great's death in 1725 a series of palace revolutions placed the Russian crown successively on the heads of half a dozen children or incompetent women. German, particularly Prussian, influence was very strong at the court. As in France, the nobles managed to free themselves from many of the restrictions placed on them by earlier and stronger monarchs. The Russian nobles extended the power that Peter had given them over their own serfs but tried to renounce the obligation to serve the state that he had imposed on them in return. In Russia, as in Hungary and Prussia, the peasant sank deeper and deeper into serfdom during the eighteenth century, while the governments made one concession after another to the hereditary nobles in order to gain their favor. Until the accession of Catherine the Great in 1762 there was no strong hand at the helm of the Russian state, but Peter's work in raising his country to the position of a great power in European war and diplomacy proved to be permanent.

Frederick William I of Prussia

Probably the most successful ruler of his generation apart from Walpole—and for quite different reasons—was King Frederick William I of Brandenburg-Prussia (1713–40). While absolute monarchy seemed to be in decline elsewhere, this strange, uncouth, and furious man, who smoked tobacco and drank beer in Gargantuan quantities, continued the work of transforming one of the smallest and poorest states of Europe into a great military power. Following in the footsteps of the Great Elector, he centralized the administration in a so-called General Directory, pared civil expenditures to the bone, and worked his subordinates remorselessly, all with the object of building the best-disciplined and most formidable army in Europe. "Salvation is from the Lord," he remarked, "but everything else is my affair." When he was through he had increased the size of his army to over eighty thousand men, twice what it

Frederick William I, by Antoine Pesne.

505

had been under his father. But while Frederick William built the fourth largest and the most efficient army on the Continent, he drew back whenever he might have used it. He left his son a full treasury, an efficient civil bureaucracy, and a highly trained army—one that had not fought a battle in over a generation.

He despised his son, Frederick, for his unmilitary habits and his taste for reading Voltaire and playing the flute. On occasion he would break the flute, burn the books, and even have the young man publicly beaten. When Frederick finally tried to flee the country with a friend, his father had the friend beheaded before his son's eyes and put the young man to work in the bureaucracy. Strange to say, the treatment worked. Without losing his taste for literature and music, Frederick grew interested in administration and the army. He succeeded his father in 1740 as Frederick II (1740–86), better known to history as Frederick the Great.

WORLDWIDE WARFARE 1740–63

The peaceful generation just described was followed by a generation dominated by two wars, the War of the Austrian Succession (1740–48) and the Seven Years' War (1756–63), separated by a few years of intensive diplomacy. These wars grew out of two irreconcilable rivalries for power. One was the rivalry between the rising Hohenzollerns of Prussia and the more established Habsburgs of Austria for territory in central Europe. The other was the rivalry between Great Britain and France for trade and colonial empire in North America, the West Indies, Africa, and India. Twice these two rivalries became entangled with each other, although the partnerships changed between the wars. And in the final peace of 1763 England and Prussia gained at the expense of France and Austria.

The British Navy and the Prussian Army

These wars were to demonstrate that the most efficient fighting units in eight-

eenth-century Europe were the British navy and the Prussian army. The most obvious explanation of superiority in each case was the unrivaled excellence of the officers. But behind the two military arms were two sharply different societies and political systems, each well adapted to the particular sort of competition in which the nation found itself.

Great Britain had many advantages in the race for sea power. It was an island, safe from invasion by land, and therefore able to pour into ships the men and money that continental states had to pour into armies. Maritime enterprise was both profitable and patriotic; a seafaring career attracted enterprising younger sons of the nobility and gentry as well as yeomen and artisans. The reservoir of experienced sailors was larger in England than in France, its nearest rival, because the British had the largest merchant marine in the world. Finally, the government and the ruling classes recognized the importance of trade and sea power, and in spite of periods of neglect they supported naval construction and encouraged British shipping.

Britain's rival, France, had almost all the advantages England had—experienced sailors, a large merchant marine, warships superior in design even to the

Figures from recruiting signs for the Prussian army (1740).

506

Ships of the Line: the British
Channel Fleet (1790).

British, and colonial bases overseas. But France had long land frontiers and a tradition of pushing those frontiers to the east and of intervening in the affairs of central Europe. This situation created an impossible dilemma. France could not be both the greatest land power and the greatest sea power, and if the army was favored, as it usually was, then the navy suffered.

The Prussian army was the creation of the Hohenzollerns, who had shaped a society and designed a state to support it. The Prussian bureaucracy and fiscal system had grown out of institutions devised to provide direct support to the army. The Junkers had been taught that their calling was to serve the king, in the army by preference, in the civil service if necessary. In return for their service they were given wide powers over the serfs who supported them. Enterprising members of the small middle class were also enlisted into the civil service, and serfs were conscripted when needed into the army. The proverbial discipline of the Prussian army pervaded to some degree both the society and the government. In England, central government by Parliament, local government by amateurs, and a considerable amount of freedom proved to be a good formula for producing sea power. In Prussia, centralized professional administration with an absolute monarch leading a disciplined aristocracy proved to be a successful formula for producing land power.

The War of the Austrian Succession, 1740–48

In 1740 Maria Theresa, a beautiful but inexperienced young woman, succeeded her father in the Habsburg dominions, to which her right of succession had been guaranteed by the Pragmatic Sanction. Frederick II of Prussia almost immediately threw his army into Silesia, one of her richest provinces, on the northeastern frontier of Bohemia. Frederick had published an anonymous little book against the immorality of Machiavelli, but he had learned some of the Florentine's precepts well. Silesia, with its million inhabitants, its linen industry, and its iron ore, would finally make Brandenburg-Prussia a great power. Both Maria Theresa and the European powers were caught off guard. Frederick seized what he needed and spent the next twenty years defending his gain.

For a time it was not too difficult. Frederick's boldfaced aggression encouraged every enemy of the Habsburgs to join in the attack: Bavaria, Spain, and finally France. Strangely enough, Hungary, which resented Habsburg rule, proved to be Maria Theresa's salvation. When she went to Budapest with her infant son and made an emotional appeal to the Hungarian Parliament, the chivalrous nobility rose tumultuously to her support. During the wars that followed, an able minister, Count Haugwitz, centralized the Habsburg administration and reorganized the army. Austria, a helpless victim state in 1740, was able to revive and become a formidable antagonist to the king of Prussia. Frederick's armies fought brilliantly, however, and the combined pressure of France, Bavaria, and Prussia—shaky though the alliance was—proved to be too much for Maria Theresa to overcome. In 1748, at Aix-la-Chapelle, she agreed to a peace treaty that left Silesia in Frederick's hands.

Meanwhile the Anglo-French rivalry had also broken out into war. When war began between England and Spain in 1739, it was only a question of time before France would be drawn in. France and Spain cooperated closely in the eighteenth century. Both had Bourbon rulers, and France had a large economic stake in the Spanish Empire since France supplied the Spanish colonies with most of their manufactured goods. English and French interests clashed in America and in India. In North America the English felt threatened by the French military hold on Canada and Louisiana, while the French felt threatened by the pressure of the English colonies expanding northward and westward. In the West Indies there was rivalry over the sugar islands. In India the death of the last strong Mogul emperor in 1707 had led to the collapse of all central administration. Both the French and the British East India companies were trying to influence native principalities, particularly around Madras and Pondicherry. From Canada

to the Carnatic Coast of India uneasy Frenchmen and Englishmen were ready to fly to arms.

In 1744 France declared war on Great Britain, and immediately the war in Europe and the war overseas merged into one. In 1745 the American colonists captured Louisbourg in Canada, and in 1746 the French seized Madras. Nothing decisive came of the conflict, however, because the English could not yet make up their minds whether to concentrate their efforts on a land war on the Continent against France or on the war overseas. The former policy was denounced by the "Patriots" in Parliament as "Hanoverianism"—that is, a pandering to the interests of the monarch, George II, who was Elector of Hanover in Germany. The English navy defeated the French; the French army defeated the English on the Continent; but neither side pressed its successes very far, either on sea or on land. A typical "limited" war, the War of the Austrian Succession ended in a stalemate so far as Britain and France were concerned. The French gave up their conquest of Madras, and the English government, much to the disgust of the American colonists, gave back Louisbourg. The French came out of the war with no gains over either Austria or England. The English came out of it with a clearer sense of how they should fight their next war with France.

The Diplomatic Revolution

England had fought in the War of the Austrian Succession in loose agreement with its old ally, Austria. France had fought in a still looser alliance with Prussia (Frederick deserted his ally twice to make truces with Austria). During the years between 1748 and 1756, a "diplomatic revolution" took place in which the chief antagonists in the first general war of mid-century changed partners in preparation for the second. This "revolution" illustrates nicely the main characteristics of eighteenth-century diplomacy.

The chief instigator of the "revolution" was Count Kaunitz, the Austrian chancellor. Burning with desire to crush Frederick and recover Silesia, he decided that the only practical way was to heal the ancient antagonism between Bourbons and Habsburgs and to gain the support of France—and if possible of Russia as well—in a new war against Prussia. Prussia, he was sure, could not last long against the three strongest powers on the Continent. Kaunitz worked carefully to bring the mistress of Louis XV, Mme. de Pompadour, around to his side, but it was a chain of calculations and miscalculations by other statesmen that finally persuaded France to agree to the alliance. The English ministry became worried about whether Austria had the will and ability to help England defend Hanover against France. Prussia was obviously better placed to defend Hanover, but when Frederick agreed to do so in return for British subsidies, the French were irritated. Since Frederick had made an agreement with France's ancient enemy, England, the French were now ready to reach an understanding with Frederick's enemy, Austria. Soon a coalition of France, Austria, and Russia was arranged, and it looked as if Prussia's situation was hopeless. Frederick saw that his only chance was to catch his enemies off guard, and, characteristically, he started the war with an offensive in 1756, almost a year earlier than his opponents had planned.

Conflict Overseas

War had already broken out between the British and the French overseas. In India, Joseph Dupleix had been trying since 1749 to make the French East India Company a political as well as a commercial power. By dominating native states, he hoped to increase the company's revenue and hamper British trade. The English East India Company soon became alarmed, and there were some armed clashes in which Dupleix's forces were defeated. In 1754 the company directors, afraid that Dupleix was leading them into serious conflict with the British, recalled him to France. Ironically, his idea of increasing the company's revenue through domination of native states was adopted by the British East India Company under its brilliant local leader, Robert Clive, and became the foundation of British territorial rule in India.

The situation in America was even more tense than in India. The French in Canada had used the interval of peace to build a chain of forts from the St. Lawrence down the Ohio to the Mississippi, and the British government had countered by sending ships and troops to the American colonies. The time was approaching when the two expanding empires of the North American continent were going to clash, and there were now perhaps a million and a half British subjects (including slaves) in North America and only about sixty thousand French—the ratio had grown to 25 to 1. British troops and colonists began to strike at the French forts. An attempt to capture Fort Duquesne, the most important link in the chain (on the site of modern Pittsburgh), was disastrously defeated in

Bengal miniature of about 1760 showing a British East India Company employee adapting to his Indian environment.

1755, and England and France were at war.

So in 1756 Europe was once more deep in conflict—this time France, Austria, and Russia against England and Prussia. The largest navy in the world had little to fear, but the odds were very great against the best army in Europe. If Prussia were defeated and partitioned, as seemed likely, any British gains overseas might well be wiped out at the peace conference. The Anglo-French and the Austro-Prussian rivalries had become inextricably mingled.

The Seven Years' War*
1756–63

England made no headway in the war until the summer of 1757, when William Pitt became virtual prime minister. Pitt, one of Britain's greatest war ministers, shrewdly focused the nation's war efforts on conquests overseas. His policy repre-

*This war, in its American phase, is known as the French and Indian War.

sented the commercial aims of the London business community, but it also appealed to the pride of the ordinary Englishman in the navy and the growing colonial empire. Pitt concentrated power in his own hands, and his energy and his enthusiasm stimulated his subordinates to unheard-of efforts. The "year of miracles" (1759) demonstrated Pitt's remarkable ability to direct a complex series of operations and to choose first-rate commanders. In this one year Quebec fell, Guadaloupe was taken, French military power in India was broken, and the French fleet was crushed off Quiberon Bay. England's control of the seas enabled it to hold both Canada and India, a classic example of the strategic importance of sea power.

While Britain was destroying the French Empire abroad, Prussia was fighting for its life on the Continent. England's "year of miracles" was a year of near disaster for Prussia. Its army was badly defeated by the Russians at Kunersdorf in 1759; the Prussians now needed a miracle just to survive. Only

View of the taking of Quebec by British forces in 1759. This eighteenth-century engraving is quite accurate in its depiction of military positions.

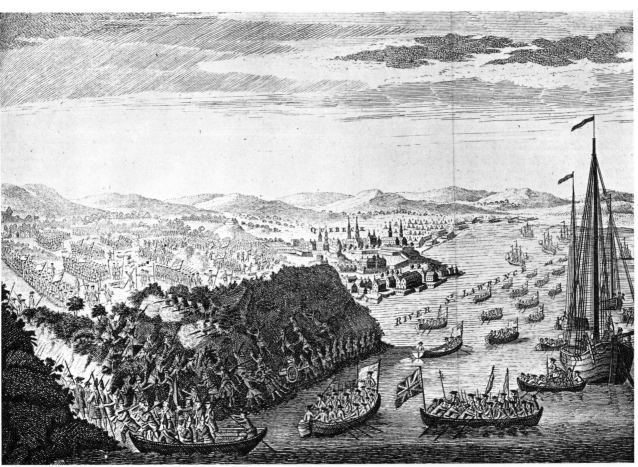

the divisions among his enemies allowed Frederick to prolong the war. Kaunitz had not promised enough of the spoils to France and Russia to stimulate an all-out effort from either country. Pitt's subsidies to German forces were just enough to pin the French down in bloody fighting in Westphalia. The war was unpopular in France and was putting a heavy strain on the already shaky French financial system. Austrian armies were poorly led, and the Austrian government was almost as afraid of the Russian army in the Oder Valley as it was of the Prussian. So Frederick held on, though his resources were almost exhausted, until the "Hohenzollern miracle" occurred. Empress Elizabeth of Russia died in 1762 and was succeeded by her nephew, Peter III, a warm admirer of the king of Prussia. Peter promptly withdrew from the war, and Austria now had only a crippled and sulky France as a major ally. With no hope of winning a decisive victory, Maria Theresa decided to end the war. Peace was made in 1763, leaving Prussia in permanent possession of Silesia. To have preserved the status quo was a moral victory for Frederick. Prussia had clearly established itself as one of the great powers.

The death of an empress saved Frederick the Great from possible defeat. The death of a king indirectly robbed Britain of some of the fruits of victory. When George III succeeded his grandfather in 1760 he wished to prove himself thoroughly English, unlike the first two Georges. This meant withdrawing from all involvement in German affairs, contrary to Pitt's advice. By October 1761, Pitt had been forced out of office. Lord Bute, George's Scottish favorite, deserted Frederick II and set himself to get peace with France at almost any price.

The Peace of Paris, 1763

The peace finally signed at Paris in January 1763 was overwhelmingly favorable to Great Britain, but it was not so severe on the French as Pitt would have wished. France received back from its conqueror most of its purely economic stakes around the world: trading posts in India, slave stations in West Africa, the rich sugar islands in the West Indies, and fishing rights off Canada, together with two tiny islands off Newfoundland, St. Pierre and Miquelon. But in India and in North America the new colonial system required control of large territories to supply the trading posts. Sugar islands could produce great wealth in a few square miles, and the French were happy to retain their possessions in the Caribbean. But in the long run it was the continents that counted. With the collapse of its political and military power in India and on the North American continent, the first French colonial empire was permanently broken. France agreed to maintain no more troops in India and to recognize the native rulers whom the British had set up. France ceded the whole of Canada and everything east of the Mississippi to Britain and handed over Louisiana west of the Mississippi to Spain. Henceforth the British had no serious competitors in North America.

"ENLIGHTENED" DESPOTISM 1763–89

During the twenty-five years that followed the Peace of Paris, the "enlightened" ideas and practices of a number of European monarchs fired the imagination of educated men. The ancient institution of monarchy seemed to take a new lease on life. It looked as if the major ideas of the Enlightenment—reason, natural law, happiness, progress, liberty—were filtering through to the rulers. The later *philosophes* had questioned aristocratic and ecclesiastical privilege, unequal taxation, and the unfair treatment of certain social classes. Was it reasonable? Was it natural? These were the fashionable questions in "enlightened" quarters, and some of the crowned heads of Europe became troubled by them. Further, the mid-century wars had left almost every European state in need of reform and reconstruction. Law and order had to be restored, trade revived, and government treasuries refilled. So the practical needs of a postwar era, added to the ferment of new ideas, produced what was known as "enlightened despotism."

This apparently new kind of monarchy was in many ways a revival of older monarchical ideas, and a reaction against the power that the aristocracy had gained in the eighteenth century. In rooting out irrational customs and vested interests, enlightened despots could curb the power of the nobility and the clergy and attack local and provincial privileges just as monarchs before them had been doing for several centuries. The difference was in the way the enlightened despots justified what they did. They talked little about divine right or hereditary title and a great deal about following reason and serving the public. Frederick the Great called himself "merely the first servant of the state," liable at any moment to render an account of his service to his subjects. But this did not mean that he or any other monarch felt he was really responsible to his people. Monarchs might be "enlightened," but they were still "despots." As one contemporary economist observed, "Whenever old disorders have been eradicated speedily and with success, it will be seen that it was the work of a single enlightened person against many private interests." *

*Quoted in R. R. Palmer, *The Age of the Democratic Revolution* (Princeton, N. J.: Princeton University Press, 1959–64), p. 105.

Few of the rulers who dominated the political horizon in the later eighteenth century measured up to the ideal of an enlightened despot. George III of England (1760–1820) did not even pretend to be "enlightened," and the English would not have been pleased if he had; they were satisfied with the status quo. Louis XV of France (1715–74) was hardly enlightened in any sense of the word, although some of his policies were. Among the minor monarchs, Gustavus III of Sweden (1771–92) and Charles III of Spain (1759–88) had good claims to the title, but the three rulers whom the *philosophes* cited most often as enlightened despots were Catherine the Great of Russia, Frederick the Great of Prussia, and Joseph II of Austria.

Catherine the Great of Russia

Catherine II (1762–96) was a German princess who became empress of Russia through a conspiracy of her friends that led to the assassination of her husband, Tsar Peter III (1762). Uneasily conscious of being a usurper, she tried to make Russia great in an effort to endear herself to her people. She had to make concessions to preserve the support of the nobility, including lavish gifts to a long succession of lovers whom she used as her chief officers of state. She read the books of the French *philosophes*, corresponded with Voltaire, persuaded Diderot to visit her court, and made much of her "enlightenment" for publicity purposes. In 1767 she excited her admirers by summoning a legislative commission to codify the laws of Russia and to give the nation a sort of constitution. The representatives were elected by every class in the land except serfs, and they came armed with statements of grievances. Very little came out of their deliberations, however: some slight religious toleration and some limitation of torture in legal proceedings. The members went home in 1768, and the Russian government was to make no further attempt to summon a representative assembly until the twentieth century.

The net result, in fact, of Catherine's reign was not enlightened government but the strengthening of the nobility and

Catherine the Great, on a gold medal struck to celebrate her accession as empress of Russia.

Map legend:
- Russia in 1462
- Acquisitions to 1689
- Acquisitions of Peter the Great (d. 1725)
- Acquisitions to the death of Catherine II, 1796

MILES 0—300

forces that were making Russia a state built on slavery.

Catherine was called "the Great" not because of her enlightenment—if she had any—but because of her conquests. Peter the Great had pushed his possessions out to the Baltic Sea in the northwest at the expense of Sweden. Catherine expanded the frontiers of her state many hundreds of miles to the west and south at the expense of Poland and the Ottoman Empire. Russians were concerned about the large Orthodox minority in Catholic Poland. Furthermore, during a large part of the seventeenth century, the Poles had threatened Moscow, and the Polish frontier was still only about two hundred miles from the old Russian capital when Catherine came to the throne. The ancient Russian thirst for vengeance on the Poles was to be richly satisfied after 1763 when Catherine put one of her favorites, Stanislaus Poniatowski, on the Polish throne. From that time on, Russia and Prussia made it their business to see that the anarchy and confusion of Polish politics continued and that any suggestion of constitutional reform or revival of the national spirit was snuffed out.

The Partitions of Poland

In 1772 Catherine and Frederick the Great arranged the first partition of Poland. Frederick took West Prussia and so joined Prussia to Brandenburg territorially for the first time. Catherine took a generous slice of northeastern Poland. To preserve the balance of power they thought it wise to give Maria Theresa a share of the loot (Galicia). The pious empress hung back at first, but Frederick remarked that the more she wept for Poland, the more she took. This first partition shocked the Poles into a nationalistic revival. King Stanislaus himself was swept along by the patriotic fervor and forgot that he owed his throne to Catherine. In 1791 after the outbreak of the French Revolution, a remarkable reform constitution was instituted setting up a strong monarchy and abolishing the *liberum veto*. Catherine's answer was swift and ruthless. Early in 1792 she called off the war she was fighting against the Turks, rushed an army into Poland,

the extension of serfdom. From 1773 to 1775 a vast and dangerous uprising of serfs broke out in the valley of the Volga, led by a Cossack named Pugachev. The revolt was directed at the local landlords and officials; and after it was broken and Pugachev had been brought to Moscow in an iron cage to be drawn and quartered, it was these landlords and officials who profited by the reaction. Peter the Great's idea of a service nobility had long been weakening. In 1785 Catherine freed the nobles from both military service and taxation and gave them absolute control over the serfs on their estates. Further, she gave away large tracts of crown land to noble favorites, thus subjecting hordes of relatively free peasants on these estates to serfdom. At the end of her reign it has been estimated that 34 million out of a population of 36 million Russians were in a state of serfdom—a state that was not very different from that of slaves in the American colonies. The net result of Catherine's reign was to encourage the

THE PARTITIONS OF POLAND

abolished the new constitution, restored the old anarchy, and arranged a second partition of Polish territory in 1793, this time with Prussia alone.

These events were followed by a genuinely popular uprising in what was left of Poland, led by a Pole who had fought for the Americans in their revolution, Thaddeus Kosciuszko. The end was inevitable. Kosciuszko was captured by the Russians, the revolt collapsed, and Stanislaus was forced to abdicate. The Kingdom of Poland was wiped off the map in a third partition in 1795 among Russia, Prussia, and Austria. In the three partitions, Russia took almost two-thirds of the original Polish territory, and Prussia and Austria divided the remainder.

Catherine's successes against the crumbling Ottoman Empire were almost as decisive. In a series of wars running from 1768 to 1792 Catherine gained the Crimea and most of the northern shore of the Black Sea. The Treaty of Kuchuk Kainarji (1774) also gave Russia vague rights to protect Orthodox Christians in the Ottoman Empire—rights that were to be used later as excuses for Russian intervention in Turkish affairs. The Ottoman Empire escaped the fate of Poland because it was stronger internally and because its two chief enemies, Austria and Russia, were jealous of each other. But when Catherine died in 1796 there seemed to be little obstacle to a Russian advance to Constantinople and the Mediterranean.

Frederick the Great of Prussia

Frederick II of Prussia (1740–86) had a somewhat better claim than Catherine to be considered "enlightened." He had a first-rate mind and a real grasp of what the *philosophes* were talking about. He invited Voltaire to Potsdam, and although they soon fell to quarreling over the merits of Frederick's poetry, they both agreed that it was the job of a king to combat ignorance and superstition among his people, to enhance their wel-

Maria Theresa on the First Partition of Poland

This letter to a diplomat is doubtless sincere, but as Frederick the Great said, "Maria Theresa wept, but she kept on taking."

This unfortunate partition of Poland is costing me ten years of my life. . . . How many times have I refused to agree to it! But disaster after disaster heaped upon us by the Turks, misery, famine and pestilence at home, no hope of assistance from either France or England, and the prospect of being left isolated and threatened with war both by Prussia and Russia—it was all these considerations that finally forced me to accept that unhappy proposal which will remain a blot on my reign. God grant that I be not held responsible for it in the other world! I confess that I cannot keep from talking about this affair. I have taken it so to heart that it poisons and embitters all my days.

This abbreviated version of the letter is from *Readings in Western Civilization,* ed. by Paul L. Hughes and Robert F. Fries (Paterson, N.J.: Littlefield, Adams, 1960), p. 134.

fare, and to promote religious toleration. Frederick welcomed religious exiles of all sorts—even Jesuits expelled from France and Spain. He treated the Jews badly, but his general tolerance in religion was the best evidence of his enlightenment. He was a mercantilist in his economic policies; he sought national self-sufficiency and used protective tariffs to foster infant industries. Interested in the new scientific agriculture, he tried to encourage new methods by bringing foreign farmers to his kingdom. Some three hundred thousand immigrants entered Prussia during his reign. Finally, he rationalized and simplified the Prussian laws and court procedures—another typical objective of enlightened despotism.

In some respects, however, Frederick was not at all enlightened, though he was always a despot. He believed firmly in social rank and privilege. The Junkers served him well as officers in his army, and the army was the most important organ of the state. In return for their services, he allowed the nobles to keep full control over the peasants on their estates. He strictly defined the ranks of noble, bourgeois, and peasant and made it difficult if not impossible for a man to move from one class to another. Prussian

serfs were not so badly off as Russian and Polish serfs, but those who lived on private estates were almost as much at their lord's mercy. Frederick did something to improve the lot of serfs on his own estates, but otherwise he showed no taste for social reform.

In some respects the discipline, the machinelike efficiency, and the strict centralization of power in the Prussian monarchy were the results of a long Hohenzollern tradition, quite unrelated to the influence of the Enlightenment. The powerful state that Frederick II erected in twenty-three years of war (1740–63) and consolidated in twenty-three years of peace (1763–86) was the most striking political achievement of his time. But twenty years after the strong hand of the despot was removed, Prussia proved to be an easy victim for Napoleon. The weakness of enlightened despotism, as well as its strength, lay in the fact that everything depended on the monarch.

Joseph II of Austria

The monarch with the best claim to be called an enlightened despot was Joseph II of Austria. Although he professed contempt for the *philosophes*, he

THE GROWTH OF BRANDENBURG-PRUSSIA   1640–1795

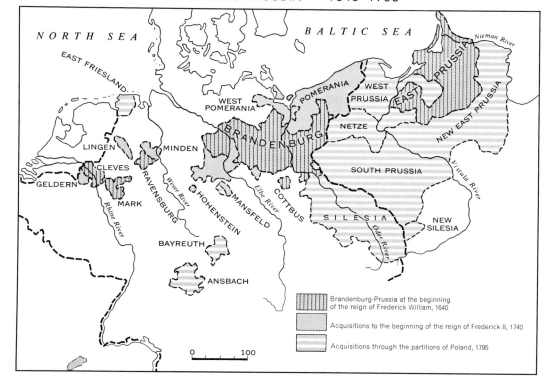

Brandenburg-Prussia at the beginning of the reign of Frederick William, 1640

Acquisitions to the beginning of the reign of Frederick II, 1740

Acquisitions through the partitions of Poland, 1795

was more thoroughly converted to the main tenets of the Enlightenment than any of his fellow monarchs. And he was probably more sincerely devoted to his people's welfare than any of the others.

Frederick II's seizure of Silesia in 1740 was the signal for a reorganization of the Habsburg Empire. During Maria Theresa's long reign (1740–80) an imperial bureaucracy was developed that was able to centralize in Vienna the administration of all the divisions of the empire except Hungary. All parts of the empire but Hungary were brought into a tariff union in 1775. The nobles were compelled to assume at least some of the burden of taxation. Maria Theresa did more for the serfs in her kingdom than any other ruler

of her time by limiting the amount of labor they owed their lords and by curbing the lords' power to abuse them. In much of this she was aided and abetted by her son, Joseph, who became emperor and coregent after the death of her husband in 1765. But Joseph wished to move much further and faster than his mother. Until her death in 1780 he chafed under the compromises and conservatism that characterized Maria Theresa's policies, particularly in religion.

In the ten years of Joseph II's own rule (1780–90), literally thousands of decrees poured out from the imperial chancellery in Vienna. He proclaimed religious toleration for all Christians and Jews. He dissolved monasteries devoted solely to contemplation and turned their revenues over to the hospitals that were to make Vienna the medical center of Europe in the next century. He applied a system of equal taxation in proportion to income to everyone in the Habsburg dominions, regardless of rank or nationality. He imposed one language for official business, German, on all parts of the empire, including Belgium, Italy, and Hungary. Most significant of all, Joseph abolished serfdom. Early in his reign he issued a number of decrees that gave all serfs in the Habsburg dominions personal freedom—freedom to leave the land, to marry whom they pleased, to choose any job they liked. This much of Joseph's work was permanent. In later decrees he tried to relieve peasants who stayed on the land of all forced labor and to turn them into property-owners, but these decrees were repealed by his successors.

Joseph II made more and more enemies by his policy of centralization and reform: the clergy, the landed nobility, non-German parts of his empire like Hungary, even peasants who failed to understand his intentions. In 1789, when revolution broke out in France, peasants in the Austrian Empire began to plunder and to murder landlords to gain the rights Joseph had held out to them. In 1790 both Belgium and Hungary were in revolt against his rule. The Church was bitterly hostile to him. Joseph felt lonely and deserted. "I am the only one holding to the true course," he wrote his brother

Joseph II, an Enlightened Despot

The following two extracts show both sides of enlightened despotism. Joseph wanted to reform the state, but he could do so only by autocratic methods.

I have not confined myself simply to issuing orders; I have expounded and explained them. With enlightenment I have sought to weaken and with arguments I have sought to overcome the abuses which had arisen out of prejudice and deeply rooted customs. I have sought to imbue every official of the state with the love I myself feel for the wellbeing of the whole. . . .

The good of the state can be understood only in general terms, only in terms of the greatest number. Similarly, all the provinces of the monarchy constitute one whole and therefore can have only one aim. It is necessary therefore that there should be an end to all the prejudices and all the jealousies between provinces [and] all races which have caused so much fruitless bickering. [Circular letter of Joseph II, 1783.]

◊　◊　◊

Unity and the end of prejudices, however, were to be achieved by dictates of the monarch. A common language was needed; Joseph II determined what it should be.

The German language is the universal tongue of my empire. I am the emperor of Germany. The states which I possess are provinces that form only one body—the state of which I am the head. If the kingdom of Hungary were the most important of my possessions, I would not hesitate to impose its language on the other countries. [Letter to a Hungarian noble, 1783.]

From T. C. W. Blanning, *Joseph II and Enlightened Despotism* (London: Longman Group, 1970), pp. 131–32; from Louis Léger, *Histoire de l'Autriche Hongrie* (Paris, 1879), p. 373.

Leopold, "and I am left to labor alone. . . . I am without any assistance whatsoever." Worn out, he died in 1790, choosing as his own epitaph: "Here lies Joseph II, who was unfortunate in everything that he undertook."

It is clear why Joseph II has been called "the revolutionary Emperor." Like Peter the Great he had shown what a single determined will could accomplish in the face of stubborn private interests. Unlike Peter, he had been guided by the principles of reason, tolerance, and humanitarianism. But Joseph was a revolutionist without a party. He had to depend on an unimaginative bureaucracy and on the secret police that he found it necessary to set up. Enlightened despotism in his hands might have formed a bridge between divine-right monarchy and democratic revolution. But it also suggested that permanent revolution demanded a broader base of popular understanding and support than he had been able to command.

FRANCE, ENGLAND, AND THE AMERICAN REVOLUTION 1763–89

France and Great Britain were the centers of the Enlightenment, but neither had an enlightened despot as monarch. Perhaps as a result (such large generalizations are very difficult to prove), each suffered a revolution from below. The American colonists won their independence from England in the name of reason and natural rights, and the French bourgeoisie, fired by the same ideals, destroyed aristocratic privilege in France.

Abortive Revolution from Above in France

When the Seven Years' War ended in 1763, both the French and the British governments needed more revenue to carry the burden of their war debts and to meet the rising costs of administration. Louis XV proposed to continue a war tax that fell on nobles and commoners alike and to institute a new tax on officeholders. It was a statesmanlike proposal, but Louis' program was greeted by a storm of

opposition from nobles and wealthy bourgeois alike. The *parlements* resisted the new taxes on the ground that they went against the "fundamental laws" of the kingdom and the "natural rights" of Frenchmen. Louis answered by abolishing the *parlements* and instituting a new system of law courts. It looked like a minor "enlightened" revolution, but it did not last. Louis XV died in 1774, and his son, Louis XVI, was neither strong enough nor determined enough to continue the fight against privilege. The old *parlements* were restored, the new taxes were dropped, and the financial problem was passed on to more cautious ministers. In the end, Louis XV's abortive reforms resulted in a further aristocratic reaction. After 1774 the nobility and the *parlements* came back so strongly from their temporary defeat that the Bourbon monarchy became in effect their prisoner.

The Revolt of the British American Colonies

The political and social situation was different in England, but the course of events was somewhat similar. A reasonable attempt by the government to raise new revenue was met by a storm of opposition in the American colonies. As a result, the attitude of the English governing classes stiffened. Concessions either to the colonists abroad or to reformers at home became impossible, and an irreconcilable conflict broke out that ultimately split the British Empire.

For nearly half a century before the Seven Years' War the policy of the British government toward its American colonies, as we have seen, had been one of "salutary neglect." For all practical purposes, the thirteen colonies governed themselves. Governors were appointed by the ministry in London, but their salaries were paid by colonial legislatures that were in fact quite independent of the British Parliament. These legislatures were also elected more democratically than Parliament or than almost any other representative body in Europe. Before 1763 Parliament never tried to tax the colonies. It did impose customs duties on colonial trade, but the intent of these levies was not to raise revenue but to force trade to flow toward the mother country.

The Seven Years' War, by eliminating French military power from North America, made the colonists feel more confident and less dependent on Great Britain for protection. At the same time it induced Parliament to tax the colonies in order that they might carry a fair share of the financial burden of imperial defense. The colonists had not done much of the actual fighting against the French. English troops had carried the brunt of the war, and after its close it was English troops that had to put down an Indian uprising under the Ottawa chief Pontiac across the Alleghenies. The taxes paid by the average American colonist were less than one-twenty-fifth of those paid by an Englishman. It seemed only fair to ask British Americans to carry some of the cost of maintaining English troops in North America.

In March 1765 Parliament imposed a stamp tax on paper of all sorts, including legal documents, commercial agreements, and newspapers. Familiar to Europeans as such a tax was, it aroused furious opposition in America among lawyers, merchants, and editors—the most articulate groups. A congress of delegates from nine of the colonies urged "that no taxes be imposed on them but with their own consent," and went on to argue that there was no practical way for the British Parliament to get American "consent" to any taxation. A year after its passage, Parliament repealed the Stamp Act but at the same time declared that crown and Parliament had the right to tax the colonies if they wished to. In 1767 Parliament returned to the attack with an act imposing duties on imports into the colonies of tea, paper, paint, lead, and glass. This was met by a determined colonial boycott, and in 1770 all the duties but those on tea were withdrawn.

Up to this point the colonists had shown little appreciation of the financial and military problems of the Empire, and Parliament had shown little appreciation of the factors that made the colonists doubt or fear its authority. But so far there had been no irrevocable break. Beginning in 1773, however, matters came to a head. In that year Parliament took

over political responsibility in India from the East India Company and set up a Governor General, thus founding British rule in India. In order to compensate the company for its loss of political power, it was allowed to sell its surplus tea directly to American retailers. This move would presumably lower prices, increase sales, and thus increase in turn the revenue from the tea duty. The idea that the British government might get more in taxes from the colonies so infuriated a radical minority in Massachusetts that a party of Bostonians disguised as native Indians boarded three East Indiamen in Boston harbor in December 1773 and dumped thousands of pounds' worth of tea into the water. Parliament reacted with a violence out of all proportion to the incident. The port of Boston was closed, and

George Washington at Princeton. Portrait by Charles Willson Peale.

the Massachusetts legislature was deprived of much of its power (1774). This reaction drove the twelve other colonies to rally behind Massachusetts out of fear for their own charters.

To make matters worse, an otherwise statesmanlike measure, the Quebec Act of 1774, was passed at a moment when it appeared to be a further attack on the English-speaking colonies by Parliament. The act guaranteed the preservation of the French language and the Catholic religion in Canada and defined Canada as including all territory north of the Ohio River and west of the Allegheny Mountains. Settlement beyond the mountains was forbidden, an act that annoyed both rich speculators and poor pioneers. By now the breach was irreparable. To George III, to a large majority in

Parliament, and probably to a majority of Englishmen, the American colonists had proved to be thoroughly irresponsible rebels who must be taught a lesson. To a majority of the colonists, the policy of Parliament was leading directly to unbearable tyranny—the kind of tyranny that they now felt it had been their main purpose to escape when they had originally emigrated to America. Fighting broke out at Lexington and Concord in 1775. A Continental Congress was summoned to meet in Philadelphia, and on July 4, 1776, the colonies formally declared their independence of king and Parliament in a declaration whose words rang like a tocsin summoning the people to rebellion throughout the Old World.

The American War of Independence

The American War of Independence was in a certain sense a civil war within the British dominions on both sides of the Atlantic. The colonists had friends in England, and the Irish sympathized with American grievances. The Whig faction to which Edmund Burke belonged tried in vain to induce George III and his prime minister, Lord North (1770–82), to follow a more moderate policy. A group of true "radicals," inspired by a rather unlovable champion of freedom of speech and parliamentary reform named John Wilkes, attacked the king's influence in Parliament, urged the publication of Parliamentary debates, and agitated for more democracy in the election of members. These radicals were too small a minority to carry any weight, but their political faith was that of the Declaration of Independence: that government must be by consent of the governed. Conversely, there were "Tories" in the colonies who agreed with Parliament and deplored the breach with England. In all, sixty thousand of them were to emigrate to Canada, never to return.

The War of Independence (1775–83) was won by the American colonists with French help. Following the principles of balance of power, France wanted compensation for the loss of Canada by depriving Britain of its American colonies. French supplies before the battle of Sar-

George III of England.

atoga (1777) and French troops and ships after the battle were of inestimable help to General Washington in his struggle to wear down the British forces in the colonies. In the peace treaty of 1783 the thirteen colonies gained their independence and won title to all the land east of the Mississippi, north of Florida, and south of the Great Lakes.

During the war most of the colonies had summoned conventions and drafted written constitutions with bills of rights to form the basis of their new governments. In 1787 a constitutional convention of delegates from all the colonies met in Philadelphia and drafted a constitution that bound the colonies in a federal union. This union was so successful that in mid-twentieth century the government founded on it could boast the longest continuous political tradition of any in the world except the British. In the same year, in the Northwest Ordinance, the colonists decided momentously to extend the principles for which they had fought to their still unsettled western territories. When these territories became populated, they would become not colonies or dependencies but "states," equal in status to the thirteen original members of the union.

The Significance of the American Revolution

The success of the American Revolution had profound effects on Europe and eventually on other parts of the world.

As the liberals in Europe saw it, a people had taken its destiny into its own hands, had revolted against its established rulers, and had set up a government and governors of its own choosing. It had gained its liberty without falling into license. John Locke's ideas—natural equality, unalienable rights, government by consent of the governed, and the ultimate right of revolution—had been vindicated. Montesquieu's theory of a separation of powers had been written into both state and federal constitutions across the Atlantic. The constitutional conventions of the former British colonies appeared to demonstrate that a people could create a society and a government by formal contract. Furthermore, events in America seemed to demonstrate that smaller political units could be federated into a larger union without recourse to despotism. In sum, the American Revolution dramatized and passed on to the western world two political ideas of great importance for the future: the idea of limited, or constitutional, government (which had a long history reaching far back into the ancient and medieval worlds), and the idea of popular sovereignty, or democracy (which was relatively new in an age still strongly aristocratic in its thinking).

The quarter-century between the Peace of Paris and the outbreak of revolution in France apparently opened to the western world three possible roads for future development: enlightened despotism, aristocratic domination, and democratic revolution.

Suggestions for Further Reading

Note: Asterisk denotes a book available in paperback edition.

General The best general account of the century in English will be found in the three relevant volumes of the *Rise of Modern Europe* series, each with excellent critical bibliographies: P. Roberts, *The Quest for Security, 1715–1740** (1947); W. L. Dorn, *Competition for Empire, 1740–1763** (1940); and L. Gershoy, *From Despotism to Revolution, 1763–1789** (1944). M. S. Anderson, *Europe in the Eighteenth Century* (1961), is a good recent survey. Volume VII of the *New Cambridge Modern History*, A. Cobban, *The Old Régime, 1713–1763* (1957), has good articles on every major aspect of the period but is not for continuous reading. A. Sorel, *Europe under the Old Régime** (1947), is a translation of the introduction to a famous larger work of 1895 to 1904. R. R. Palmer, *The Age of the Democratic Revolution* (1959–64), is a major work of interpretation that sees the American and French Revolutions, together with the smaller disturbances of the period, as manifestations of a single great "democratic revolution." Another useful study is C. B. A. Behrens, *The Ancien Régime** (1967).

Economic and Social	See the works on mercantilism and economic history noted for Chapters 18 and 19; E. Williams, *Capitalism and Slavery* (1944), argues that mercantilism was compatible with slavery, but that the new industrial capitalism undermined it. On the aristocracy, see *The European Nobility in the Eighteenth Century,** ed. by A. Goodwin (1953), a collection of essays by various authors, and F. Ford, *Robe and Sword: The Regrouping of the French Aristocracy after Louis XIV** (1953), a study of the French aristocracy. For the other end of the social spectrum, see O. Hufton, *The Poor of Eighteenth-Century France* (1974). A. Young, *Tours in England and Wales* (1932), is a selection from the journals of a very keen observer of the eighteenth-century countryside. As brief introductions to the Agricultural and Industrial Revolutions, the general economic histories of Europe by H. Heaton, rev. ed. (1948), and by S. B. Clough and R. T. Rapp (1975) are useful.

Expansion Overseas W. B. Willcox, *Star of Empire: A Study of Britain as a World Power, 1485–1945* (1950), and H. I. Priestley, *France Overseas Through the Old Régime: A Study of European Expansion* (1939), are good general works. J. R. Seeley, *The Expansion of England* (1883), is a very influential older account. C. G. Robertson, *Chatham and the British Empire** (1948), is a brief modern discussion. On India, see H. Dodwell, *Dupleix and Clive* (1920); E. Thompson and G. T. Garratt, *The Rise and Fulfillment of British Rule in India* (1934); and H. Furber, *John Company at Work: A Study of European Expansion in India in the Late Eighteenth Century* (1948). On America, in addition to the books cited for Chapters 19 and 20, see L. B. Wright, *The Atlantic Frontier: Colonial American Civilization, 1607–1763* (1947), and M. Kraus, *The Atlantic Civilization: Eighteenth-Century Origins* (1949). On the economic history of the British colonies, see C. P. Nettels, *The Roots of American Civilization* (1938). On social history, see J. Henretta, *The Evolution of American Society, 1700–1815** (1973).

Political and Diplomatic J. Lough, *Introduction to Eighteenth-Century France* (1960), is a very good starting point for study. The best brief introduction to England is J. H. Plumb, *England in the Eighteenth Century** (1951). B. Williams, *The Whig Supremacy, 1714–1760* (1939), in the *Oxford History of England*, is a more extended topical treatment. Two other books by J. H. Plumb offer interesting reading: *Sir Robert Walpole* (1956) and *The First Four Georges** (1957). The serious student of the English political system and how it operated should examine the various studies of L. B. Namier. On Prussia, there is excellent material in Dorn (first section, above); a first-rate biography of Frederick William I, *The Potsdam Fuehrer*, by R. Ergang (1941); biographies of Frederick the Great by P. Gaxotte (1941) and G. P. Gooch (1947); and an expert general account by W. H. Bruford, *Germany in the Eighteenth Century** (1952). C. L. Morris, *Maria Theresa: The Last Conservative* (1937), is probably the best of several biographies. S. K. Padover, *The Revolutionary Emperor* (1934), and T. C. W. Blanning, *Joseph II and Enlightened Despotism* (1970), are both good on Joseph II. On Joseph's most important reform, see E. M. Link, *The Emancipation of the Austrian Peasant, 1740–1798* (1949). There are many biographies of Catherine the Great, but G. S. Thomson, *Catherine the Great and the Expansion of Russia** (1950), is the most informative from the historian's point of view. On the enlightened despots as a group, G. Bruun, *The Enlightened Despots** (1929), is brief but extremely good. The best accounts of the war and diplomacy of the age will be found in the *Rise of Modern Europe* series, but there is a very brief account in A. H. Buffinton, *The Second Hundred Years' War, 1689–1815* (1929); C. Petrie, *Diplomatic History, 1713–1933* (1946), helps provide the continuity lacking in separate volumes.

The American Revolution Two volumes in the *New American Nation* series provide the best up-to-date introduction: L. H. Gibson, *The Coming of the Revolution, 1763–1775** (1954), and J. R. Alden, *The American Revolution, 1775–1783* (1954). L. Gottschalk, *The Place of the American Revolution in the Causal Pattern of the French Revolution* (1948), and E. S. Morgan, *The Birth of the Republic, 1763–1789** (1956), offer a somewhat broader perspective. On the origins of the Revolution, see C. Andrews, *The Colonial Background of the American Revolution* (1924); B. Bailyn, *Ideological Origins of the American Revolution** (1967); and E. S. Morgan and H. Morgan, *The Stamp Act Crisis* (1953). M. Beloff has selected an interesting set of contemporary sources in *The Debate on the American Revolution, 1761–1783** (1949). On the side of ideas, C. L. Becker's study of the text of *The Declaration of Independence** (1922, 1942) is consistently illuminating. The best recent studies include P. Maier, *From Resistance to Revolution** (1972), and R. M. Calhoon, *Revolutionary America: An Interpretive Overview** (1976).

23

The French Revolution and Napoleon

The French Revolution marked a turning point in European history. The events that began to unfold in 1787 and that terminated with the fall of Napoleon Bonaparte in 1815 unleashed forces that altered not only the political and social structure of states but the map of Europe. Many attempts were made, in France and in other European countries, to undo the work of the Revolution and to repress the ideas of liberty, equality, constitutionalism, democracy, and nationalism that the Revolution had inspired. But the Old Regime was dead, in France at least, and a Europe dominated by monarchy and aristocracy and by a hierarchical social order could never be fully restored. With the coming of the French Revolution, then, we enter into a more modern world—a world of class conflict, middle-class ascendancy, acute national consciousness, and popular democracy. Together with industrialization, the Revolution reshaped the institutions, the societies, and even the mentalities of Europeans.

THE ORIGINS OF THE FRENCH REVOLUTION

By the last half of the eighteenth century, France appeared to have overcome the dismal cycle of famine, plague, and high mortality that, in the preceding century, had inhibited both demographic and economic growth. The vast majority of Frenchmen who lived in the villages and tilled the fields were better off than their counterparts in most of Europe. French peasants, for example, owned some 40 percent of the country's farmlands. The mild inflationary trend that characterized much of the eighteenth century increased the wealth of large landowners and surplus wealth in agriculture served to stimulate the expansion of the French economy as a whole. Modest advances in the textile and metallurgical industries, the construction of new roads and canals, and urban growth were other indications of economic development.

Yet, despite evident signs of prosperity, there was great discontent and restlessness in France in the 1780s. French institutions were obsolete, inefficient, and uncoordinated. They were controlled by the nobility and by self-perpetuating corporations of hereditary officeholders. To anyone touched by the ideas of the Enlightenment they seemed irrational and unjust. The middle classes, especially, were offended by the legal and social distinctions that kept them from attaining high office or exerting political influence. Every bishop in France was of noble birth; only nobles could receive commissions in the army; bourgeois

The First Consul Crossing the Alps, 20 May 1800, by Jacques Louis David (1800).

plans for economic reform were constantly thwarted by the privileged classes. The economy, particularly in agriculture, remained unstable and subject to fluctuations that could drive the peasants and urban poor to starvation. An inefficient and inequitable tax system yielded too small an income to support the state, discouraged economic growth, and fell most heavily on the poor. On the eve of the Revolution, France faced a conjuncture of crises. Three of these crises—agrarian distress, financial chaos, and aristocratic reaction—were particularly acute.

Agrarian Distress

Wretched weather and poor harvests in 1787 and 1788 weakened an agricultural economy that was already somewhat unstable. The poorer peasants lived at a subsistence level at best; with poor crops they starved. The purchasing power of well-to-do peasants declined. Grain shortages led to sharp price increases, particularly in the cost of bread. Moreover, from the late 1770s the long-term growth of the French economy had been interrupted in several important areas, such as the wine trade, and between 1776 and 1787, agricultural profits generally declined, though not to the low levels of the first part of the century. Nevertheless, noblemen and other large landowners, who had become accustomed to high profits, sought to save their own declining fortunes by demanding from their tenant farmers dues and obligations that had long been neglected. The countryside was ripe for revolution.

Financial Chaos

The finances of Louis XVI's government were a shambles. By 1787 one-half of the nation's tax revenues went to service the massive public debt that Louis XIV had left to his successors. France's involvement in the Seven Years' War and in the American War for Independence had driven the government further along the road to bankruptcy. Without a reform of the tax system the king could not meet his obligations. But such a reform would mean an attack on the privileges

of the upper classes, and this Louis could never quite summon the courage to do.

Three ministers in succession struggled with the problem. The first, the Swiss banker Necker, was dismissed by the king in 1781 after he had proposed some modest reforms. Necker's successor, Calonne, thought he could carry on without much change. But as the deficit mounted he grew alarmed, and in 1786 he proposed a much more radical reform program than Necker's. The most striking provision of Calonne's program was a direct tax on all landowners—noble and commoner, lay and clerical. To oversee the assessment of the new tax, Calonne suggested that the king create local and provincial assemblies in which all men of property would be represented regardless of social status. In addition, older taxes, such as the *taille*, which weighed on the lower orders, were to be reduced. Calonne's reforms struck at the very heart of the system of privilege and the social hierarchy of the Old Regime.

Calonne, aware that there would be bitter opposition to his plans, persuaded Louis XVI to call a conference of notables in the hope that they could be induced to back his program. But the members of this assembly, which met in February 1787, were drawn largely from the privileged orders and refused to support Calonne.

The king now dismissed Calonne and put in his place one of Calonne's chief opponents, Lomenie de Brienne, Archbishop of Toulouse. This prelate, though a member of both the higher nobility and the higher clergy, soon came to the same conclusions as Calonne. He tried to enact a similar reform program, but the *Parlement* of Paris, the most privileged of all the corporations of officeholders, refused to register the royal edicts. It declared that only the Estates General could approve such measures. When Brienne tried to break the opposition by exiling the magistrates of the *Parlement* and then by abolishing the high courts, he touched off furious protests by many members of the upper bourgeoisie and the nobility. In the face of attacks by the socially and politically powerful, the government backed away from its reform program. In July 1788, the king yielded to the opposi-

The French peasant supports the clergy and the nobility in this eighteenth-century cartoon. The rabbits and doves eating the peasant's grain were protected by law for the sport of the upper classes.

tion and ordered a meeting of the Estates General for May 1789.

Aristocratic Reaction

During the 1780s, then, aristocratic demands on the peasantry were aggravating the distress of the countryside, and aristocratic resistance to tax reform was hampering the government in its attempts to revamp the nation's financial structure. These were two facets of the aristocratic reaction that was directly responsible for the coming of the French Revolution.

The tremendous strength of the French privileged classes had been built up steadily during the reigns of Louis XV and Louis XVI. At every turn the poor, the aspiring middle class, and enlightened reformers in government confronted the fact of privilege. Some men of the Enlightenment, in particular Voltaire, and such royal ministers as Turgot and Calonne encouraged the king to rationalize state finance and to bring a measure of justice to French society at the expense of the privileged groups. Louis XVI supported several of these plans for reform, but he always backed down when the privileged classes protested. By the 1780s it appeared that the French king was the prisoner of the nobility and that he would do nothing to displease them.

Moreover, the nobles were particularly skillful in confusing the issue. Certain privileges, such as those that protected the laws, institutions, and customs of the provinces from encroachments by the central government, limited the arbitrary power of the king. They could be called liberties rather than privileges. These liberties were compared with the restrictions on royal power in England, and the English were regarded as the freest people in Europe. Thus the nobles could resist royal attacks on any form of privilege by asserting that the king was going to attack all privileges and all liberties and that he was simply trying to get rid of all restrictions on his power. Through this device, the nobility and the *parlements* were able to gain wide support and considerable sympathy when they resisted the arbitrary orders of the king, even when those orders were directed toward desirable ends.

There were those, however, who were not deceived by the rhetoric of the privileged orders. The hesitations of the king and the intransigence of the aristocracy increased the bitterness of large sections of the population. They wanted to put an end to privilege, and they felt that the unreformed monarchy would not help them in this struggle. The attack on privilege and the demand for equality before the law were the driving forces in the Revolution from beginning to end. Aristocratic stubbornness and royal weakness made it impossible to achieve equality through peaceful reform. In the end, privilege could be destroyed only by attacking aristocracy and monarchy.

THE FRENCH REVOLUTION AND THE KING

The Estates General, which had not met since 1614, was convened by the king at Versailles on May 5, 1789. The electoral process by which deputies were selected was a relatively generous one: all adult French males had the right to vote, indirectly, for representatives to the Third Estate, which served the interests of the commoners. Moreover, following some recent examples in provincial assemblies, the Third Estate was given twice as many representatives as those of either the First or the Second Estate. The First and Second Estates (the clergy and the nobility, respectively) represented the privileged orders. The king had asked that all local electoral assemblies draw up *cahiers de doléances*—lists of grievances—to submit to the Estates General when it met. Thus in the months preceding the convening of the Estates General, a great political debate occurred. Almost all politically minded men agreed that the monarchy should yield some of its powers to an assembly and seek consent to taxation and legislation. By 1788 some noblemen were willing to go part way in abolishing privileges and in equalizing taxation. But the early debates in the Estates General revealed that the lawyers and bourgeois who represented the Third Estate were bent on a much more drastic reform.

Caricature of the Abbé Sieyès.

The Estates General and the National Assembly

The mood of the Third Estate was best expressed by one of its deputies, the Abbé Sieyès. In a famous pamphlet, *What Is the Third Estate?*, Sieyès argued that the real French nation was made up of people who were neither clergymen nor noblemen, and that this majority should have the decisive voice in all political matters. This idea, which approached the doctrine of popular sovereignty, was translated into action during the opening debate on voting procedures in the Estates General. Since the Third Estate had as many representatives as the other two combined, it wanted the three Estates to meet and vote together. A few liberal nobles and a somewhat larger number of the lower clergy were sure to support the Third Estate, so joint meetings would give the Third Estate a clear majority. The king and the privileged orders, on the other hand, demanded that the Estates vote separately. This was traditional procedure in meetings of the Estates General, and it assured that the first two Estates would retain control.

The Third Estate not only rejected the king's plan for separate meetings: on June 17 it declared itself the National Assembly of France and invited the other Estates to sit with it. The National Assembly then assumed the right to approve all taxation as well as the right to withhold all taxation if its political demands were not met. In the face of this bold initiative, the king hesitated but finally resorted to a show of force. On June 20 Louis XVI had the Third Estate barred from its usual meeting place. The deputies then convened in a nearby indoor tennis court and took an oath not to disband until they had drafted a constitution. This Tennis Court Oath was the first great act of the bourgeois revolution in France.

In a dreary repetition of the political ineptitude he had shown in previous crises, Louis missed his chance to act as impartial mediator between the hostile Estates. On June 23 he went before the Estates General and offered a program of reform that only partly satisfied the demands of the Third Estate for tax reform and did nothing to abolish the privileges of the nobility. At about the same time, the king began to concentrate troops around Versailles and Paris. His aim was to put down any disturbances that might occur should he decide to dissolve the Assembly. By now, however, neither partial reform nor brute force was a sufficient answer to the political crisis. The revolution had already become a battle between those who desired a more equal and open society and those who wanted to preserve the privileges of the aristocracy.

The Popular Revolt

Most of the deputies in the Third Estate were lawyers, professional men, and lesser officeholders. Their aspirations were those of the French bourgeoisie. In the urban centers and the countryside resided yet another element of the Third Estate—the mass of artisans, shopkeepers, and peasants who lived in poverty or on the edge of it. Their aspirations and needs were not identical with those of the deputies at Versailles. But in the summer of 1789 a series of spontaneous popular disturbances and revolts broke out that linked, for the moment at least, the bourgeoisie and the common people in an uneasy alliance against the aristocracy.

Notable among these uprisings was an attack on July 14 (still France's national holiday) on the Bastille, a royal fortress and prison in Paris. By the end of

The Tennis Court Oath   June 20, 1789

The National Assembly, considering that it has been summoned to establish the constitution of the kingdom, to effect the regeneration of public order, and to maintain the true principles of monarchy; that nothing can prevent it from continuing its deliberations in whatever place it may be forced to establish itself; and finally, that wheresoever its members are assembled, *there* is the National Assembly:

Decrees that all members of this Assembly shall immediately take a solemn oath not to separate, and to reassemble wherever circumstances require, until the constitution of the kingdom is established and consolidated upon firm foundations. . . .

From *A Documentary Survey of the French Revolution*, ed. by John Hall Stewart (New York: Macmillan, 1951), p. 88.

The Oath at the Jeu de Paume, by Jacques Louis David. The deputies of the Third Estate, joined by some of the clergy and nobility, swear not to disband until they have drafted a constitution.

Storming the Bastille (July 14, 1789). The revolutionary leader is accepting the surrender of the prison.

June the city of Paris had grown tense. The economic depression of the 1780s and the poor harvests of 1788 and 1789 had reduced the urban poor to misery, and to misery was now added the fear that the king and the aristocrats were conspiring to dissolve the Estates General. When the king's troops appeared on the outskirts of the city, the Parisians well understood why they were there. The immediate reaction of the citizens was to arm themselves. It was their search for arms that brought the leaders of the Parisian electoral assembly and a crowd of journeymen and workers from the *faubourg* Saint-Antoine to the Bastille on July 14. The commandant at first barred the gates and fired on the crowd. He then lost his nerve, opened the gates, and the crowd stormed in and slaughtered the garrison. This was typical of the royal government's behavior during the first stages of the Revolution; it used just enough force to anger the people but never enough to subdue them.

The fall of the Bastille was an event of small consequence in itself—the crowd had destroyed little more than a building—but its implications were immense. The attack was regarded as a blow against royal depotism. It demonstrated that the Revolution was not simply a debate over a constitution. Of greatest importance, it brought the city of Paris

and the political leaders of Paris to the forefront. A new, insurrectionary municipal government was formed; henceforth Paris would shape the direction of the Revolution. Finally, the events in Paris set off revolts in the provinces.

About the same time that the Parisian crowds were taking the Revolution into their own hands, the French peasants, also disappointed with the slow pace of reform, began to take action of their own. Like the poor of the cities, the peasants had been heartened by the political promise of the winter of 1788/89. They had patiently drawn up their *cahiers* and they had chosen their electoral committees; then they had waited confidently for relief to follow. The Estates General met in May. Spring passed and summer came, but the peasants were still poor; they were still not allowed to till the unused land of the nobles; and they still had to pay their customary dues.

Then, during July 1789, the month of the storming of the Bastille, rumors spread through rural France that there would be no reforms and that the aristocrats were coming with troops to impose reaction on the countryside. The result was panic and rioting throughout the country. During the "Great Fear," as it is called, frightened peasants gathered to defend themselves against the unnamed and unseen enemy. Once assembled and armed, however, they turned against the enemy they knew—the local lord. Though the lords themselves were rarely in residence, peasants burned their châteaux, often tossing the first brand into the countinghouse, where the hated records of their payments were kept.

The Destruction of Privilege

The popular revolts and riots had a profound impact on the king, the aristocracy, and the deputies of the Third Estate alike. Already in June, before the storming of the Bastille, Louis XVI had recognized the National Assembly and ordered the clergy and the nobles to sit with the Third Estate. He also recognized the revolutionary government of Paris and authorized the formation of a national guard composed largely of members of the bourgeoisie. But the king

French Women Become Free. Print from the General Collection of Caricatures about the Revolution (1789).

received no credit for his concessions from the revolutionary leaders, who felt, quite rightly, that his sympathies were still with the nobles. At the same time, Louis' indecision had discouraged many of the strongest supporters of the Old Regime. The most reactionary noblemen, headed by the king's brother, the Count of Artois, began to leave the country. Other members of the aristocracy sought to preserve their property by making dramatic concessions to the call for reform.

On the night of August 4, one nobleman, the Viscount de Noailles, stood before the Assembly and proposed that all feudal levies and obligations be abolished. In a performance at once impressive and bizarre, nobles, clerics, and provincial notables arose to renounce noble privileges, clerical tithes, and provincial liberties. In effect, the Old Regime was dismantled in one night of heated oratory, and the way seemed clear for the Assembly's main business—to provide a

constitution for France. The implementation of the concessions of August 4, however, was somewhat less tidy. The structure of aristocratic privilege was indeed abolished by decree, along with tax exemptions and hereditary officeholding, but peasants were to continue paying customary dues to their lords until they had redeemed them. Only when the Revolution reached a more radical stage was this obligation abolished.

The Declaration of the Rights of Man

On the whole, the National Assembly had succeeded in wiping out the privileges of the upper classes, the corporations of officeholders, and the provinces. Now it faced the task of creating new political, legal, and administrative structures for the country. The ideological framework for this task was set forth by the constitution-makers in the Declaration of the Rights of Man, which they adopted on August 27, 1789.

In this preamble to a constitution yet unformed, the members of the National Constituent Assembly (that is, the National Assembly acting in its constitution-making role) established a set of principles idealistic enough to sustain the enthusiasm of the mass of Frenchmen for the Revolution and sweeping enough to include all humanity. The basic ideas of this document were personal freedom, equality under the law, the sanctity of property rights, and national sovereignty. The first article declared that "men are born and remain free and equal in rights." There were to be no class privileges and no interference with freedom of thought and religion. Liberty, property, security, and resistance to oppression were declared inalienable and natural rights. Laws could be made and taxes levied only by the citizens or their representatives. The nation, not the king, was sovereign, and all power came from and was to be exercised in the name of the nation. Thus was established the framework for a system of liberty under law. The Declaration was a landmark in the fight against privilege and despotism, and it had a great appeal to revolutionary and democratic factions throughout Europe.

The Declaration of the Rights of Man
August 27, 1789

1. Men are born and remain free and equal in rights; social distinctions may be based only upon general usefulness.
2. The aim of every political association is the preservation of the natural and inalienable rights of man; these rights are liberty, property, security, and resistance to oppression.
3. The source of all sovereignty resides essentially in the nation; no group, no individual may exercise authority not emanating expressly therefrom.
6. Law is the expression of the general will; all citizens have the right to concur personally or through their representatives in its formation; it must be the same for all, whether it protects or punishes. All citizens, being equal before it, are equally admissible to all public offices, positions, and employments, according to their capacity, and without other distinction than that of virtues and talents.
10. No one is to be disquieted because of his opinions; even religious, provided their manifestation does not disturb the public order established by law.
11. Free communication of ideas and opinions is one of the most precious of the rights of man. Consequently every citizen may speak, write, and print freely, subject to responsibility for the abuse of such liberty in the cases determined by law. . . .

From *A Documentary Survey of the French Revolution,* ed. by John Hall Stewart (New York: Macmillan, 1951), p. 114.

The October Days

The Declaration of the Rights of Man was not simply a page lifted from John Locke, the *philosophes,* and the Americans. It was a highly political document hammered out in an Assembly that was showing itself to be increasingly divided. There were those among the moderate leaders of the Assembly who found the Declaration too radical and sweeping. These men desired to reconcile Louis XVI with the Revolution and to construct a constitutional system on the English model with a monarch guided by an assembly controlled by the rich and the well-born. The issues that divided the crown and the country could not, however, be compromised. Louis simply refused to give formal approval to the decrees and the Declaration that followed the night of August 4.

The king's recalcitrance, the divisions in the Assembly, and the food shortages combined to produce yet another popular explosion. On October 5, 1789, a crowd of some twenty thousand armed Parisians marched on Versailles, demanding bread and insisting that the royal family return to Paris. The king considered flight, but he was persuaded by Necker, who had been recalled to the government, and by Lafayette, leader of the National Guard, to appease the crowd and leave Versailles. On October 6 the king, Queen Marie Antoinette, and the royal family drove into Paris in their carriage, surrounded by shouting crowds,

The three Estates "hammer out" a new constitution in this contemporary engraving.

and established themselves at their palace in the center of the city. A few days later, the National Constituent Assembly followed.

The Parisians seemed satisfied with the king's capitulation, and the Assembly, together with the king and his ministers, turned to the question of the constitution. Henceforth, however, the deliberations of the Assembly were to take place in the heated atmosphere of Parisian politics. Here in the capital many political clubs were formed to debate the issues and settle on policy. The most famous of these was the Jacobin Club, which included many of the radical members of the Assembly. Here too were political agitators, journalists of all opinions, and, above all, crowds that could be mobilized to bring pressure on the Assembly. From the autumn of 1789 on, the Revolution became more and more a Parisian affair.

The Achievements of the National Constituent Assembly, 1789–91

It took two years to make the constitution. By the end of that time the government had been reorganized, the Church had been dispossessed of its lands, and the rights of Frenchmen had been more clearly defined. Here are the main results of the Assembly's complex and lengthy deliberations:

The Monarchy. By acts passed in September 1789, Louis XVI was reduced from his position as a monarch by divine right to the role of a constitutional officer of the nation. He was given the right of suspensive veto over legislation, a right that allowed him to delay the passage of laws for two years. The monarchy remained a hereditary institution, and the king retained control of military and foreign affairs.

The Legislature. The Constitution of 1791 provided for a unicameral Legislative Assembly, elected for two years. The Assembly had the power to initiate and enact legislation and to control the budget. It also had the exclusive right to declare war. Members of the Constituent Assembly were forbidden to serve in the new legislature, an unfortunate decision that barred experienced men from a body that had few precedents to guide it.

The Electorate. The Constitution did not provide for universal manhood suffrage. It divided Frenchmen into active and passive citizens. Only the former, who met a property qualification, had the right to vote. The active category comprised some 4 million men in a total population of about 25 million. Active citizens voted for electors, who in turn elected the Legislative Assembly. These electors, as well as officeholders in the Assembly, were drawn from some fifty thousand of the country's wealthiest men. Even with these restrictions, a far larger percentage of the population could vote and hold office than in England.

The Administration. The elimination of aristocratic privilege invalidated most of France's local administration, which had been controlled by the nobility or small oligarchies of officeholders and rich bourgeois. The Assembly completed the process of dismantling the administrative apparatus of the Old Regime by abolishing all former provinces, intendancies, and tax farms. On a clean administrative map they drew eighty-three departments, roughly equal in size, with uniform administrative and judicial systems. Administration was decentralized and put in the hands of some forty thousand local and departmental councils, elected by their constituents.

The Church. The reorganization of the French Church was decreed by the Civil Constitution of the Clergy, promulgated in August 1790. It was one of the most important and fateful acts of the Revolution. The Assembly confiscated the lands of the Church and, to relieve the financial distress of the country, issued notes on the security of the confiscated lands. These notes, or *assignats*, circulated as money and temporarily relieved the financial crisis. In addition, clergymen became paid officials of the state, and priests and bishops were to be elected by property-owning citizens.

The Constitution of 1791, together with the Declaration of the Rights of Man, summed up the principles and politics of the men of 1789. In its emphasis on property rights, its restrictive franchise, and its fiscal policy, the Constitu-

tion had a distinctly bourgeois bias. To look upon the document simply as a product of selfish interest, however, would be to underestimate the achievement of the constituents. A new class of peasant proprietors had been created. The framework for a society open to talent had been established. Administrative decentralization, it was thought, had overcome the prevailing fear of despotism. Equality before the law, if not political equality, had been made a fact. These were impressive and revolutionary achievements. But to succeed and mature, the new order established by the Constituent Assembly needed peace, social stability, and the cooperation of the king. None of these was forthcoming. Within a year the Constitution of 1791 had become a dead letter, and the Revolution had entered a new phase.

The Failure of Constitutional Monarchy

The Constitution of 1791 was most certainly an imperfect instrument. The Civil Constitution of the Clergy, for example, offended the pope, who had not been consulted. His disapproval forced a crisis of conscience on French Catholics. Many bishops and priests refused to accept the Civil Constitution, and they found broad support in the country. Schism in the Church became a major factor in the eventual failure of the Assembly to create a stable government for France. Moreover, the restrictive franchise opened the constitution-makers to the charge that they wanted to substitute a wealthy oligarchy for an aristocracy. Such obvious defects, however, were not alone responsible for the failure of constitutional monarchy. The principal culprit was the monarch himself.

At the head of the government stood a king who was thoroughly discredited. In June 1791, Louis XVI tried to escape from France in order to join the forces of counterrevolution outside the country. He very nearly succeeded but was caught at Varennes, near the eastern frontier, and was brought back to Paris. This humiliating episode destroyed what little authority Louis still possessed. In order to keep himself from being completely

Playing cards of the French Revolution. Personifications of Liberty and Equality have taken the place of kings and queens.

displaced, he swore to obey the new constitution; but he was now no more than a figurehead. From the very beginning, the constitutional monarchy was flawed.

At this point the situation was complicated by outside pressures. Louis' fellow monarchs were unhappy over the way in which their royal colleague was being treated. The privileged orders in other countries feared that the leveling principles of the Revolution would spread. The English, many of whom had sympathized with the Revolution so long as it seemed to be following an English model, began to denounce the radicalism and violence of the French. Edmund Burke, in particular, saw clearly the radical nature of the Revolution. In his *Reflections on the Revolution in France* (1790) he insisted on the importance of tradition in preserving an orderly society and declared that it was folly to abandon time-tested institutions in favor of new ones based on abstract ideas. He did not convince radical writers or some of the articulate craftsmen, but he convinced almost everyone in power in England. Hostility to France was an old tradition; Burke gave new reasons for continuing it. And everywhere French refugees spread counterrevolutionary propaganda urging Europe's monarchs to intervene.

The Legislative Assembly
September 1791–September 1792

The Legislative Assembly met in an atmosphere of intrigue, fear, and factional strife. The Assembly, itself bitterly divided, was deprived of the hard-won political experience of the men who had drafted the Constitution.

There were two issues on which it was almost impossible to find a solid majority. The first was the position of the king. He could not be trusted, and he would not commit himself to the principle of equality, on which everyone did agree. Was it worth compromising with the king in order to preserve the constitution and the unity of the country? If not, how far should the Assembly go in restraining or in punishing the king?

The second problem, which caused even sharper divisions of opinion, was

that of defining "equality." Was the emphasis to be on equality before the law, or on equality of opportunity, or on political equality, or on economic equality, or on a mixture of two or more of these ideals? Here there was not only no clear majority, but no consistency within groups and even within individuals.

There were no parties in the Assembly, but there were the "clubs," loosely organized associations with affiliates in the provinces. One of the largest and best-organized groups was the Jacobin Club, with 136 members out of the 745 representatives. The Jacobins were republicans and wanted to get rid of the king. But they were also well-to-do bourgeois; no poor man could afford to pay their membership dues. They were far from agreement on political and economic equality, or on the pace at which change should take place. They were divided into at least two factions. One faction was led by Brissot de Warville, the ablest politician in the Assembly. The other, composed mainly of Parisians, eventually found a leader in Maximilien Robespierre.

As it turned out, the issue that temporarily united the Assembly was that of declaring war on Austria. Stupid diplomacy by European monarchs, even more stupid politics in the French royal court, and a very real threat of counterrevolution convinced millions of patriotic Frenchmen that the forces of reaction were about to destroy all that had been gained since 1789 and that war was the only way to save their country and their freedom. The emperor of Austria and the king of Prussia in the Declaration of Pillnitz (August 1791) proclaimed that European monarchs must unite to restore order and monarchy in France. This was largely bluff, but it sounded ominous. Some conservative ministers thought that a victorious war against Austria would strengthen the king and allow him to end the Revolution. However, Louis XVI and his Austrian queen, Marie Antoinette, apparently hoped for a French defeat that would lead to the restoration of royal authority.

External threats and court plots played into the hands of Brissot's republican faction. Brissot believed that a cru-

Anonymous contemporary portrait of Robespierre.

sade to unseat the monarchs of Europe would rekindle the revolutionary fervor of the French people and rally them around his plan to establish a republic in France. He was opposed in the Jacobin Club by Robespierre, who feared that a war would strengthen the conservatives and lead to dictatorship. But Brissot proved the stronger, and the powerful Jacobin Club passed a resolution advocating a declaration of war. Brissot took the issue before the Assembly, and in April 1792 all but seven deputies voted for war with Austria.

The First War of the Revolution

The declaration of war transformed the Revolution. With war came the end of the monarchy and the constitution. With it also came terror and dictatorship. France became not simply the home of the Revolution but the exporter of revolutionary ideals. Finally, under the stress and emotions of war, France became a modern, unified nation-state.

The war began badly. The French army lacked leadership and discipline. The government was short of money and hampered by factional disputes. The royal family and their supporters encouraged the enemy. It is not surprising that the Austrians and their allies, the Prussians, were soon able to advance along the road to Paris.

Two things saved the Revolution at this moment of crisis. The Austrian and Prussian generals, who were at least as incompetent as the French, delayed and divided their forces. And there was a genuine outburst of patriotic and revolutionary enthusiasm in France. It was during this crisis that the *Marseillaise* was composed, a stirring appeal to save the country from tyranny. The French kept on fighting, despite their failures, and their army did not melt away as the refugee nobles had predicted. As a result, when the Austro-Prussian army was checked at Valmy, one hundred miles from Paris, in September 1792, its cautious commander decided to call off the invasion. The allies had lost their best chance to crush the Revolution before it gathered strength.

THE FRENCH REPUBLIC

During these gloomy months, when everything seemed to be going wrong, the radical politicians of Paris gained a commanding position in the government. These Jacobins—Robespierre and Georges-Jacques Danton were the most important—based their power on national guards summoned to protect the capital, on the Parisian crowds, and, from August 10, 1792, on an insurrectionary Paris Commune that replaced the legal municipal government. The poorer classes were suffering from an economic depression caused by war and political uncertainty, and they were terrified by the thought that the Old Regime might be revived. The bourgeois radicals in the Assembly never fully sympathized with the desire of Paris artisans and workers for economic equality, but they could agree with them on the need for drastic political changes. In August the Jacobins touched off an uprising in Paris that forced the Legislative Assembly to suspend the king from office and to issue a call for a revision of the constitution. A National Convention, elected by universal manhood suffrage, was to determine the new form of the French government. The events of August triggered what is often called the Second French Revolution. This revolution began with the deposition of Louis XVI; it ended in a bloody terror that consumed its own leaders. In many ways it confirmed Edmund Burke's most dire prophecies. And yet the Second French Revolution did not follow inexorably upon the first. War created its own necessities, survival being the most pressing.

The Convention and the Jacobins

The National Convention met in Paris on September 21, 1792, in the wake of a fierce bloodletting earlier in the month—the so-called September massacres. These massacres, which took the lives of some thirteen hundred prisoners in Paris, were part of a pattern of fear, terror, and revolutionary justice that persisted throughout much of the Convention's three-year rule.

The delegates to the Convention were elected by a minority of Frenchmen, despite universal manhood suffrage. Many citizens were repelled by the deposition of the king and the violence of the summer of 1792. Others were intimidated. Some were excluded from the electorate by governmental decree. Thus the most radical elements of the French population had disproportionate strength in the elections. Not surprisingly, many of the delegates were Jacobins.

The Jacobins, however, were divided. The followers of Brissot, now called the Girondists, made up one faction. They dominated the Convention in its early months. In general, the Girondists represented the interests of provincial republicans, and they were bitterly opposed to the Paris Commune. Their foreign policy was aggressive and expansionistic. It was they, for example, who issued a manifesto in November 1792 offering France's aid to all revolutionaries throughout Europe. In domestic affairs, the Girondists were relatively moderate—at least when compared with their Parisian enemies. On the prime issue of 1792, the fate of the king, the Girondists urged that Louis XVI be imprisoned for the duration of the war. There was little doubt then—and less now—that Louis was guilty of treason. But the resolution condemning him to death passed by only one vote. He was guillotined on January 21, 1793. This victory for the so-called Mountain—Robespierre and Danton's faction—was followed by a purge of the Girondists in June 1793. The architects of France's war policy were among the first victims of that policy.

The Jacobins and the War

The Girondists fell before their Jacobin opponents in the wake of crushing French defeats by an overwhelming new coalition of European powers. The execution of Louis XVI, France's designs on Holland, and its annexation of Savoy and Nice prompted England, Spain, Portugal, and several lesser states to join Austria and Prussia in the war against France. In the face of such a formidable combination, the French armies suffered a series of reversals. The victor of Valmy, General

Dumouriez, was badly defeated in Belgium, and, in the spring of 1793, he defected to the enemy.

Now the government, under the direction of a Committee of General Defense (later the Committee of Public Safety), undertook to organize the entire nation for war. It applied conscription on a nationwide scale for the first time in modern European history. It raised huge armies, far larger than those of Louis XIV, far larger than those that could be called up by the old-fashioned monarchies against which France was fighting. And it supported those armies by means of confiscation and heavy taxes. The armies were organized by a military genius, Lazare Carnot, an engineer who made a science out of the service of supply. He also established the division as a tactical unit.

Portrait of Louis XVI during his imprisonment at the time of the Revolution, by Joseph Ducreux.

The Execution of Louis XVI

The carriage proceeded thus in silence to the Place de Louis XV,* and stopped in the middle of a large space that had been left round the scaffold: this space was surrounded with cannon, and beyond, an armed multitude extended as far as the eye could reach. . . . As soon as the King had left the carriage, three guards surrounded him, and would have taken off his clothes, but he repulsed them with haughtiness: he undressed himself, untied his neckcloth, opened his shirt, and arranged it himself. The guards, whom the determined countenance of the King had for a moment disconcerted, seemed to recover their audacity. They surrounded him again, and would have seized his hands. "What are you attempting?" said the King, drawing back his hands. "To bind you," answered the wretches. "To bind *me*," said the King with an indignant air. "No! I shall never consent to that: do what you have been ordered, but you shall never bind me. . . ."

Many voices were at the same time heard encouraging the executioners. They seemed reanimated themselves, in seizing with violence the most virtuous of Kings, they dragged him under the axe of the guillotine, which with one stroke severed his head from his body. All this passed in a moment. The youngest of the guards, who seemed about eighteen, immediately seized the head, and shewed it to the people as he walked round the scaffold; he accompanied this monstrous ceremony with the most atrocious and indecent gestures. At first an awful silence prevailed; at length some cries of "Vive la République!" were heard. By degrees the voices multiplied, and in less than ten minutes this cry, a thousand times repeated, became the universal shout of the multitude, and every hat was in the air. . . .

*Now the Place de la Concorde.

From *English Witnesses of the French Revolution*, ed. by J. M. Thompson (Oxford: Basil Blackwell, 1938), pp. 230–31.

The monarchies of Europe, which were used to fighting limited wars with limited resources for limited gains, were overcome by a French nation organized for war. They could not afford to arm all their people; they still depended on the old officer corps for their leaders. And, much as they despised the Revolution, they were still not prepared to sacrifice all their resources to put it down. Other problems distracted the crowned heads of Europe: England was seeking colonial conquests, and the eastern powers were still concerned with the Polish problem. So the French recovered from the blows of 1793 and by the late spring of 1794 had broken through into the Low Countries. When the Convention ended its work in 1795, France was stronger and held more territory than it had under Louis XIV at the height of his power.

The Instruments of Jacobin Rule

Military success was achieved only through the intensive and often brutal organization of the French people. The Constituent Assembly's program of administrative decentralization had left France without any effective chain of command linking the National Convention in Paris to the provinces. Moreover, the Convention was an ungainly body, incapable of swift action. Into this void moved the radical Jacobins. In the provinces, Jacobin clubs virtually replaced local governing bodies and through their committees of surveillance controlled public life. At the center, executive power was entrusted to two committees—the Committee of Public Safety and the Committee for General Security. The former wielded almost dictatorial power over France from July 1793 until July 1794. It had twelve members, of whom Robespierre was the most prominent.

The genuine achievement of the twelve capable men who composed the Committee of Public Safety, in coping with internal unrest and external war, is often overlooked because of the "Reign of Terror" they imposed on France. The Terror must be put into the context of the problems that confronted Robespierre, Carnot, and their colleagues. From early 1793 there had been a series of internal rebellions against the government. Conservative peasants of the Vendée, a region in the west of France, had revolted against the national conscription and in favor of their priests who opposed the Civil Constitution. Later in the year, the Girondists, who opposed what they thought was excessive centralization, stimulated local uprisings in some large provincial towns. In the heat of war, such rebellions appeared treasonable, and the Terror was used as a political weapon to impose order. Also, during much of the Committee's tenure, Parisian politicians, both to the left and to the right of Robespierre, maneuvered to secure power. Terror, against Danton among others, was a weapon in these internecine conflicts. There was an economic terror directed against war profiteers and hoarders. Finally, there were local terrors, uncontrolled from the center, in which Jacobins and undisciplined representatives of the government took revenge on their enemies. In the end, the Terror gained a certain momentum of its own, and the list of suspects grew. Among the factors in Robespierre's fall was the fear of the Convention that its remaining members would soon become victims of revolutionary justice.

In all, some forty thousand people were killed by the government and its agents. The largest number of victims were peasants; next came rebellious citizens of provincial towns, and politicians. Some hundreds of thousands of suspects were imprisoned and proper judicial

Here Lies All of France. An engraving of Robespierre guillotining the executioner after having guillotined everyone else in France.

procedures, such as the right of the accused to counsel, were undermined. Even the Committee of Public Safety finally divided over the excesses of the Terror. When military successes restored a measure of stability to France, the National Convention reasserted its authority. Among its first acts was the arrest and execution of Robespierre in July 1794.

Jacobinism and French Society

The militant phase of Jacobinism was of relatively short duration. The Committee of Public Safety ruled for a year, and Robespierre had complete authority for only four months. Thus, beyond the brilliant organization of the national defense, the Jacobins made few permanent contributions to French institutions and society. Certain of their acts, however, have remained of symbolic significance to the French Left. Among these were the guarantees of the right to a public education for all and the right of public welfare for the poor; these guarantees were set forth in an abortive constitution drawn up in 1793. In addition, the Jacobins were responsible for decrees establishing price controls and providing for the division of confiscated property among the poor. These decrees, however, were not enforced with much zeal because they were not the product of a conscious social philosophy. They were opportunistic acts designed to win over the disaffected crowds in the cities and the landless peasants at a time of national crisis. The Jacobins were radical democrats who believed deeply in political equality; they were not socialists. With their fall in the summer of 1794, the Revolution fell back into the hands of the propertied bourgeoisie. It was this class that in the end gained most from the Revolution.

The Thermidorian Reaction and the Directory, 1795–99

The demise of Robespierre and the Jacobins touched off a wave of reaction against the excesses of the Terror. This "Thermidorian reaction," named after the month in the revolutionary calendar when Robespierre was executed (Ther-midor/July), turned against the austerity of Jacobin rule and at times took the form of a "white terror" against the radicals in Paris and the provinces.

In 1795 the Convention finally presented France with a constitution, the third since 1789. It provided for a five-man executive board, called the Directory, and a two-house legislature. Even the republican-oriented Convention had been sufficiently sobered by the Terror to abandon its promise of universal suffrage, and the franchise was weighted in favor of the propertied classes. Once in office, the Directory proved both corrupt and incompetent. It maintained a militantly aggressive foreign policy and allowed the French economy to deteriorate disastrously. A more or less communistic movement led by "Gracchus" Babeuf received some support from the poor, but was easily suppressed. The French poor were still largely artisans and peasants—property owners and not wage-

The Thermidorian Reaction

In two days after the execution of Robespierre, the whole Commune of Paris, consisting of about sixty persons, were guillotined in less than one hour and a half, in the Place de la Révolution; and though I was standing above a hundred paces from the place of execution, the blood of the victims streamed under my feet. What surprised me was, as each head fell into the basket, the cry of the people was no other than a repetition of "A bas le Maximum!"* which was caused by the privations imposed on the populace by the vigorous exaction of that law which set certain prices upon all sorts of provisions, and which was attributed to Robespierre. The persons who now suffered were all of different trades; and many of them, indeed, had taken advantage of that law, and had abused it, by forcing the farmers and others who supplied the Paris market, to sell at the maximum price, and they retailed at an enormous advance to those who could afford to pay. I did not see Robespierre going to the guillotine; but have been informed that the crowd which attended the wagon in which he passed on that occasion, went so far as to thrust their umbrellas into the wagon against his body. . . . It now became a measure of personal safety, to be able to declare that one had been imprisoned during Robespierre's tyranny. It was dangerous even to appear like a Jacobin, as several persons were murdered in the streets, by La Jeunesse Parisienne,† merely because they wore long coats and short hair.

*"Down with price controls!"
†"The (gilded, aristocratic) Paris youth."

From *English Witnesses of the French Revolution*, ed. by J. M. Thompson (Oxford: Basil Blackwell, 1938), pp. 248–49.

The interior of the Great Pyramid, as depicted in the *Description of Egypt* (1809–26), published by the scholars who accompanied Napoleon on his campaign in Egypt. They explored ancient monuments and provided the first modern survey of Egypt.

earners. More dangerous was a royalist revival. Elections in 1797 demonstrated such an upsurge in royalist sentiment that the results had to be cancelled. The Directory's single source of strength was the army. With the economy foundering and popular unrest increasing, the Directory was ripe for the *coup d'état* that in 1799 brought one of its most successful generals, Napoleon Bonaparte, to power.

NAPOLEON'S RISE TO POWER

Napoleon Bonaparte was born on the island of Corsica in 1769, shortly after the island had been annexed by France. The Bonapartes were members of the minor nobility of Corsica, and at the age of nine Napoleon was admitted to a military school in France. From that time on, he knew no other life than the army. When most of the aristocratic officer corps left France after the fall of the monarchy, Napoleon stayed on to serve the Republic. He rose to become a brigadier general in 1793 at the age of twenty-four. He helped to reconquer Toulon—one of the towns that rebelled against the Convention in 1793—and he suppressed a royalist riot against the Convention in 1795. By 1797, when the Directory felt its power slipping, Barras, one of the Directors, realized that Napoleon's support could be valuable. He sought Napoleon's friendship first by introducing the young general to one of his cast-off mistresses, Josephine Beauharnais (whom Napoleon married), and then by giving him command of an army that was preparing for an invasion of Lombardy, a province in northern Italy that was then under the control of Austria.

The Italian campaign of 1797 was a success. It removed Austria from the war, gave France control of northern Italy, and established Napoleon's reputation as an outstanding general. After the defeat of the Austrians only England was still at war with France. In 1798 Bonaparte took an army by sea to Egypt, where he hoped to sever England's lifeline to India. He easily defeated the Egyptians, but the English admiral Horatio Nelson sank the French fleet near the mouth of the Nile.

Napoleon's army, trapped in Egypt, was soon decimated by disease and dysentery. In the midst of this crisis, Napoleon heard that the Directory was in danger of falling and that some of the Directors wanted to create a military dictatorship. Leaving his army in Egypt, he made his way secretly back to France to offer his services to the conspirators.

The most important Director was the Abbé Sieyès, and it was with this former leader of the First French Revolution that Napoleon conspired. On November 9, 1799, he used military force to compel the legislators to abolish the Directory and substitute a new government in which a board of three consuls would have almost absolute power. The conspirators asked Napoleon to serve as one of the consuls. Apparently they hoped he would provide the personal popularity and military power needed to support a regime that would be dominated, behind the scenes, by the other two consuls. But when the new constitution was written—at Napoleon's orders—the general emerged as First Consul and virtual dictator of France. When the French people were invited to endorse the constitution in a plebiscite, they voted overwhelmingly to accept it. To Frenchmen exhausted by years of revolution, terror, and economic instability, Napoleon seemed to be the guarantor both of the gains of the Revolution and of order.

NAPOLEON AND DOMESTIC REFORM

Bonaparte was, above all, a military man, and his fortunes always hinged on military success or failure. Yet his domestic reforms were profound and enduring. If the French Revolution gave the country an ideology that, henceforth, would both inspire and divide Frenchmen, Napoleon gave France many of its characteristic institutions. Better than any eighteenth-century monarch, Bonaparte fulfilled the *philosophes'* dream of an enlightened despot.

Between 1799 and 1801 Napoleon led a series of successful campaigns against the coalition that England, Austria, and

Russia had formed to defeat him. He wanted to win a favorable peace so that he could devote himself to consolidating his position in France. Hostilities ended in 1801 and did not break out again on any major scale until 1805. Napoleon used those four years to restore domestic concord and economic stability and to establish a network of administrative institutions that gave coherence and uniformity to the work of his government.

Perhaps Napoleon's most characteristic contribution was the *Code Napoléon.* From the debris of the laws left by the several legal systems of the Old Regime and the succession of revolutionary governments, Napoleon's advisers compiled a uniform legal code that is still the basis of French law. The Code maintained in theory the revolutionary concept of the equality of all men before the law, but it was in fact far less egalitarian than the laws of the revolutionary era. It emphasized, for instance, the authority of the state over the people, of business corporations over their employees, and of male heads of families over their wives and children. Property rights received particularly strong protection under the Code.

Other Napoleonic reforms followed a similar pattern. They often upheld in principle the ideals of the Enlightenment and the Revolution but served in practice to strengthen France's new authoritarian state. Napoleon retained, for instance, the division of France into eighty-three uniformly administered departments. He used the departmental system, however, not to foster local responsibility, as had been intended, but to create a highly centralized administration controlled directly by the First Consul through field administrators called prefects. He also instituted a nationwide system of public schools that not only educated the young—an ideal of the *philosophes*—but imbued them with an exaggerated patriotism and devotion to their ruler.

In reforming France's finances Napoleon followed the British and American examples by chartering a privately owned national bank to provide both a depository for government funds and a source of credit for French businessmen. With government deposits as security, the bank issued paper money as legal tender. Increased currency, a stable franc, and improved credit helped to improve France's shaky economy. Napoleon also resolved that perennial problem of the Old Regime—taxation—by developing uniform taxes collected directly from each individual by paid officials.

Although Napoleon himself was far from religious, he understood better than his republican predecessors that domestic peace could not be achieved until the religious question had been settled. Accordingly, he concluded an agreement with Pope Pius VII, the Concordat of 1801, which regularized the situation created by the Revolution. Although the document recognized that the majority of Frenchmen were Roman Catholics, the Catholic Church was not to be the established church in France. Church proper-

Unfinished portrait of Napoleon by Jacques Louis David, the imperial court painter.

Political Maxims of Napoleon

These extracts from communications to the Council of State (1801–04) come from the period when Napoleon was First Consul and was trying to construct a civilian government.

We have finished the romantic period of the Revolution; we must now start to make it into history, to see only what is real and possible in applying its principles and not what was speculative and hypothetical. To follow any other policy today would be to philosophize and not to govern.

I shall respect public opinion when its judgments are legitimate, but it has whims that must be scorned. It is the duty of the government to enlighten public opinion, not to follow it in its errors.

One can lead a people only by promising it a future; a chief of state is a seller of hopes.

Constitutions should be short and obscure. . . . A constitution should be drafted in such a way that it will not hinder the actions of a government and not force the government to violate it. . . . If there are problems with a government that is too strong, there are many more with a government that is too weak. Things won't work unless you break the law every day.

My system is very simple. I believe that in the circumstances, it is necessary to centralize power and increase the authority of the government in order to build a nation. I am the constitution-making power.

Translated from Edouard Driault, *Napoléon: Pensées pour l'Action* (Paris: Presses Universitaires de France, 1943), pp. 30–34.

ties confiscated during the Revolution were not to be restored. Moreover, the First Consul retained the right to appoint bishops. Through the Concordat of 1801, Napoleon regained the loyalty of French Catholics to the official government and at the same time won the gratitude of owners of former church properties.

Although Napoleon brought a form of enlightened despotism to France, he did so at the expense of much of the individual liberty that had been the first principle of the Enlightenment. The legislative institutions created by the Constitution of 1799 were a sham. Political opposition was punished by police action, and the press was strictly censored. Napoleon's training was military, and too often his solution to political and even social problems was force. Nevertheless, his government in its early years was popular. He preserved the property of those who had gained from the Revolution. He satisfied the social ideal of the Revolution by maintaining equality before the law, equality in taxation, and careers open to all men of talent. In his own administration, he incorporated royalists, constitutionalists, and Jacobins. With such accomplishments to his credit, he easily won popular approval when he declared himself First Consul for life in 1802. And two years later, on December 2, 1804, the nation rejoiced when, in the presence of the pope, he crowned himself Emperor of the French.

THE NAPOLEONIC EMPIRE

Napoleon did not create French imperialism; he inherited, indeed he had been an agent of, a policy of aggressive expansion undertaken by the Convention and the Directory. A satellite republic had already been established in Holland in 1795, and during the victorious campaigns against Austria toward the end of the decade, French armies had brought revolutionary ideals and French power to Switzerland and parts of Italy. This burst of French expansion had come to an end when Napoleon signed separate peace treaties with Austria, in 1801, and England, in 1802. Large-scale hostilities were resumed only in 1805, but from that time

until Napoleon's ultimate defeat ten years later, France was almost constantly at war.

If Napoleon could have avoided war he might have established his empire as the dominant state in Europe. But his own insatiable ambition and the continuing enmity of England made war almost inevitable. England would have looked on France with suspicion in any case; the egalitarian ideas of the Revolution and the early Empire seemed dangerous to the English ruling classes. Napoleon gave the English government other reasons for opposing him by trying to extend his sphere of influence in Germany and Italy. England was determined to keep France from becoming the dominant political and economic power in Europe. French control of the Low Countries had already violated a basic rule of English foreign policy—namely, to keep these invasion bases and commercial centers out of the hands of a strong power. Finally, the British and their ablest statesman of the period, William Pitt the Younger, were convinced that Napoleon was using the peace to ready France for yet another war. Pitt soon was able to persuade other continental states that they must join England to restore the balance of power and resist the spread of French influence in central Europe.

Napoleon was just as ready for war as was England. He felt that his empire could never be secure and that his plans for Europe could never be achieved until England had been thoroughly defeated. The two states drifted into war in 1803, and other continental powers—Austria, Russia, and finally Prussia—joined England.

It was a difficult war for the two major contestants. Napoleon could not gain control of the sea, and without this control he could not subdue England. He made his greatest effort in 1805 when he concentrated his army at Boulogne and tried to pull the English fleet out of the Channel by an elaborate set of naval feints in the Atlantic. But the English were not deceived. While one fleet guarded England against invasion, another, under Nelson, caught the French and their allies off Cape Trafalgar and annihilated them (October 21, 1805). Na-

A cast of the imperial seal of Napoleon, "Emperor of the French, King of Italy, Protector of the Confederation of the Rhine."

1789	1795	1799	Napoleon	1814
Revolutionary Governments	Directory	Consulate	First Empire	

1804

poleon was never again able to threaten England with invasion. The English, on the other hand, could not defeat the French on the Continent and were dependent on the armies of their allies.

By the fall of 1805 the armies of the Russian and Austrian emperors assembled in central Europe for a combined assault on Napoleon. Instead of waiting for the attack, Napoleon marched an army deep into central Europe and took the Austrian and Russian generals by surprise. He defeated the Austrian and Russian forces first at Ulm, and then again in the most spectacular of all his victories, at Austerlitz, on December 2, 1805.

With Austria defeated and Russia in retreat, Napoleon followed up his victory with a complete reorganization of the German states. He helped end the Holy Roman Empire and eliminated many of the small German principalities. Out of these petty states he created a satellite system composed of fourteen larger states that were united in a Confederation of the Rhine; Napoleon served as protector of this German Confederation.

Prussia, which had not at first joined the coalition against Napoleon, entered the fray in 1806 and was soundly defeated at Jena in October of that year. King Frederick William III was forced to accept a humiliating peace and to become an ally of France. The following spring, Emperor Alexander I of Russia again sent an army against Napoleon, only to have it defeated at Friedland in June 1807. In three campaigns in three successive years, Napoleon had defeated the three strongest powers on the Continent and established his position as master of Europe. Russia was too large to occupy, but Napoleon had taught Emperor Alexander the futility of opposition. A few weeks after Friedland, Napoleon and Alexander held a dramatic meeting near Tilsit in eastern Prussia.

Alexander recognized Napoleon's supremacy in the West, and Napoleon agreed not to intervene in Russia's internal affairs or to prevent Alexander from extending Russian influence into the Ottoman-controlled Balkans.

Napoleonic Europe and the Continental System

Napoleon was now at the summit of his power. All Europe, save England, was to some degree under his rule (see color map "Napoleonic Europe"). France, Belgium, Germany west of the Rhine, and parts of Italy and Illyria constituted a French Empire ruled directly by Napoleon as emperor. Holland, Westphalia (a Napoleonic creation in Germany), and southern Italy were theoretically independent kingdoms, over which Napoleon placed three of his brothers as kings. Northern Italy was also a kingdom, with Napoleon himself as king. The Grand Duchy of Warsaw was carved out of Prussia's Polish territories and given to France's ally, the king of Saxony. In 1808, the Bourbon monarch of Spain was overthrown and replaced by Napoleon's brother Joseph.

England alone resisted the tide of French expansion. From 1806 on, Napoleon tried to weaken England by wrecking English trade with the Continent. This so-called Continental System imposed heavy penalties on anyone trading with England and forbade the importation of English goods. Since England produced the cheapest manufactures and was a good market for food and raw materials, this ban put a heavy strain on the economies of the continental countries. England made the strain worse by blockading all countries that subscribed to the French system. The English blockade was harsh enough to drive Denmark into a close alliance with France and to help cause the War of 1812 with the

United States. But on the whole it caused less ill will than Napoleon's decrees. It was simply impossible for the European economy to function properly without English trade.

Napoleon himself had to allow exceptions and grant special licenses, a procedure that irritated everyone who did not receive such favors. Smuggling became a highly organized and profitable business, and attempts to enforce French regulations strengthened the opposition to Napoleon everywhere. Most important of all, it led to a quarrel between Napoleon and Alexander of Russia.

Emperor Alexander had not been entirely happy with the results of his alliance with Napoleon. France had gained vast territories; Russia had acquired only Finland and Bessarabia. Napoleon's creation of the Grand Duchy of Warsaw menaced Russia's control of the Polish lands it had seized in the 1790s. But the great and overwhelming grievance of the Russians was the Continental System. Russia needed English markets for its grain, and Alexander would not and could not enforce the rules against trade with England. Napoleon, bent on the destruction of England, could not tolerate this breach in his system, which was already being weakened by the ill will of other rulers. He requested Alexander to stop the trade; when Alexander refused, Napoleon prepared to invade Russia.

The Weaknesses of the Napoleonic Empire

When Napoleon undertook his Russian campaign in June 1812, his hold on Europe and even on the French had begun to weaken. French expansion had at first been greeted with some enthusiasm by many of the inhabitants of the Low Countries, Germany, and Italy. Enlightenment ideas were strong in these regions, and the existing governments were unpopular. Thus, in the northern Netherlands there was opposition to the domination of the House of Orange and the urban oligarchy. In the Austrian Netherlands (Belgium), nationalist feelings had led to a revolt against Austrian rule as early as 1789. Italy was dominated by Spain and Austria; both growing na-

tionalism and spread of the Enlightenment made the ideas of the French Revolution attractive to many Italians. In Germany the writings of the *philosophes* had been eagerly read, and there was general disgust with the archaic structure of the Holy Roman Empire and the stodgy governments of the petty principalities. French influence and French ideas were especially strong in the Rhineland. In short, there had been serious political unrest in much of Europe in the 1780s and 1790s, and the invading French armies had often been hailed as liberating forces. Napoleon took full advantage of this feeling. He was able to break the archaic political and social structures of many states. Within the Empire, the *Code Napoléon* was established, the privileges of the Church and aristocracies were abolished, and fetters on local industry and commerce were removed. Napoleon saw himself, in other words, as the "revolution on horseback" and sought to impose a new order on Europe—a new order that was enlightened, rational, and French.

This vision of Napoleon's was, at best, only partially achieved, and even those who had most enthusiastically received the invading French armies soon perceived that imperialism was a more important component of the Napoleonic system than was liberation. The Continental System contributed to a general economic crisis in Europe that alienated the commercial and industrial interests. High taxes and conscription were imposed on the tributary states. And the French system was enforced by tight police surveillance. Napoleonic tutelage, even at its most benevolent, appeared incompatible with the libertarian and nationalistic ideals of the French Revolution.

Nationalism had helped the French in their wars in the Low Countries and Italy, but it now became a danger to them. Increasingly, Napoleon was beset by the growth of nationalistic feelings and national resistance to his rule. In Germany, Italy, and Spain, national awakening was intimately linked to the opposition to French hegemony. This opposition took many forms. In Italy and Germany cultural movements gained momentum that

Contemporary engravings of French soldiers of Napoleon's era. Above: a sharpshooter of the Imperial Guard; below: a cannoneer.

emphasized the common history, language, and literature shared by the fragmented parts of these countries. In Spain resistance was expressed in a more violent manner when rebellions broke out in 1808 against the regime of Joseph Bonaparte. It was in Spain that Napoleon first confronted guerrilla warfare and first encountered serious failure. A Spanish victory at Baylen in 1808 was the initial break in the emperor's record of invincibility. By 1813, the Spanish rebels, with the help of an English army under Wellington, had driven the French from Madrid and had organized a constitutional government that controlled more than half the country.

The appearance of a well-organized English army on the Continent was one indication that the balance of power in Europe was beginning to shift against Napoleon. There were other signs, the most important of which was the recovery of France's nominal ally and potential enemy, Prussia. After the humiliating defeat of the Prussians at Jena, the process of reconstructing the kingdom was begun. Under Generals Gneisenau and Scharnhorst, the Prussian army was modernized and a form of universal military training for young men was introduced. To revitalize the country, another reformer, the Baron vom Stein, persuaded the king to abolish serfdom and to grant a large measure of liberty to Prussian municipalities. Stein's social legislation was limited in its effects, but the military reforms allowed Prussia to play a significant role in the final defeat of Napoleon.

At the same time that his enemies were strengthening themselves and challenging the French monopoly of force on the Continent, Napoleon began to lose his grip on the French people. French economic domination of Europe, which had been one of the goals of the Continental System, failed to materialize, and France, like the rest of the Continent, suffered from the economic crisis that marked the last years of Napoleon's reign. Internally, the regime grew more repressive, and Napoleon became increasingly intolerant of criticism and even of his ministers' advice. After his divorce from Josephine and his marriage to an Austrian princess, Marie Louise, Napoleon more and more took on the airs of an Old Regime monarch. In the end, those Frenchmen who had provided him with his magnificent and spirited army were exhausted by the burdens of empire.

The Invasion of Russia and the Fall of Napoleon

In June 1812 Napoleon marched into Russia with six hundred thousand men, the largest army ever assembled up to that time. Only about a third were French. Most had been recruited in the German states or in other dependencies. Napoleon expected to deliver a fast and decisive blow, but the Russians, so greatly outnumbered, did not give battle. Instead they retreated, drawing Napoleon behind them. After one costly but inconclusive engagement at Borodino, Napoleon occupied Moscow in September and waited for Alexander to offer peace terms. But no message came.

After five weeks Napoleon realized that he could not keep so large a force in Russia through the winter, and on October 19 he began the long march westward. Almost immediately he encountered difficulties. Since the land through which he passed had already been burned by both armies, he lost thou-

Napoleon I: A Self-Assessment   1817

In spite of all the libels, I have no fear whatever about my fame. Posterity will do me justice. The truth will be known; and the good I have done will be compared with the faults I have committed. I am not uneasy as to the result. Had I succeeded, I would have died with the reputation of the greatest man that ever existed. As it is, although I have failed, I shall be considered as an extraordinary man: my elevation was unparalleled, because unaccompanied by crime. I have fought fifty pitched battles, almost all of which I have won. I have framed and carried into effect a code of laws that will bear my name to the most distant posterity. I raised myself from nothing to be the most powerful monarch in the world. Europe was at my feet. I have always been of opinion that the sovereignty lay in the people. In fact, the imperial government was a kind of republic. Called to the head of it by the voice of the nation, my maxim was, *la carrière est ouverte aux talents* without distinction of birth or fortune. . . .

From *The Corsican*, ed. by R. M. Johnston (Boston: Houghton Mifflin, 1910), p. 492.

Retreat of Napoleon's army across the Beresina River (1812), by an anonymous painter.

sands of men to disease and starvation. When the cold weather came, the weakened soldiers were no match for the elements. As the remnants of Napoleon's army stumbled closer to the frontier, Polish and German soldiers deserted and headed homeward. When Napoleon reached the German border in December, he could not muster one hundred thousand men. If Austria or Prussia had chosen to launch an attack at this time, the war could have been ended. But the allies as yet had no clue to the vastness of the disaster.

Once in German territory, Napoleon fled in disguise to Paris and organized a new army that he marched toward the Russian border in the spring of 1813. But defeat had deflated the Napoleonic image, and Napoleon was badly beaten at Leipzig in October by the combined armies of Austria, Prussia, and Russia. Napoleon lost about two-fifths of his men and retreated back across the Rhine. Meanwhile, the British general Wellington defeated another French army in Spain and crossed the border into southern France. On March 31, 1814, the combined armies entered Paris, and one week later Napoleon abdicated. After some debate, the allies restored the Bourbons to the throne of France and then called a peace conference in Vienna to settle the fate of the rest of Europe.

Napoleon was exiled to the island of Elba, off the Italian coast. But he still had one battle to fight. In March 1815 he escaped and landed in the south of France. The army proved loyal to the deposed leader, and Napoleon was soon in control of France once again.* But the allies were prepared. Napoleon was conclusively defeated at Waterloo on June 18, 1815, and three days later he abdicated for the second time. The allies now exiled him to St. Helena, a small and remote island off the Atlantic coast of Africa. The era of the Revolution and Napoleon had ended.

The era had ended, but it could not be effaced. The allies could restore a Bourbon to the throne of France, but the new king, Louis XVIII, could not restore the Old Regime. He had to keep many of Napoleon's officials. He had to preserve the Napoleonic administrative system and the Concordat with the Church. He had to accept both the revolutionary principle of equality under the law and the revolutionary land settlement. He had to grant a constitution to his people. It was a conservative constitution with a very limited electorate, but it meant that the king's rule was not absolute. And throughout Europe the great ideas of the Revolution—liberty, equality, and nationalism—lived on, and with them the new and dangerous concept of revolution as a means of attaining social and political goals. These ideas were only partially recognized in some countries and totally suppressed in others, but they persisted everywhere—smoldering coals that were to burst into flame again and again during the nineteenth century.

The political balance of power in Europe had been permanently altered. No one could restore the petty states of Germany or the feeble republics of Italy. No one could ignore the claims of Russia to have, for the first time, a voice in the affairs of western Europe. No one could fail to recognize the tremendous strides that England had made in industry and commerce during the wars. Conversely, for the first time in two centuries, France was no longer the richest and strongest European state. These were some of the new political facts with which the diplomats at Vienna had to deal.

*The three months spanning Napoleon's escape from Elba, resumption of power, and second abdication following his defeat at the battle of Waterloo are known as the Hundred Days.

Suggestions for Further Reading

Note: Asterisk denotes a book available in paperback edition.

General

The best general work on the French Revolution is the authoritative study by G. Lefebvre, *The French Revolution* (1962–64). A somewhat different interpretation may be found in F. Furet and D. Richet, *The French Revolution* (1970). C. Brinton, *A Decade of Revolution, 1789–1799** (1934), in the *Rise of Modern Europe* series, is still a fine introductory summary. See also A. Soboul, *The French Revolution: 1787–1799** (1975), and M. J. Sydenham, *The French Revolution** (1966). Valuable source material may be found in J. H. Stewart, ed., *A Documentary Survey of the French Revolution* (1951), and P. Dawson, *The French Revolution* (1967). J. M. Thompson, *The French Revolution** (1943), is a solid standard work. R. R. Palmer, *The Age of the Democratic Revolutions*, 2 vols. (1959–64), places the French Revolution in its broad European perspective. He published a revised and shortened version as *The World of the French Revolution* (1971). The same is done more briefly in N. Hampson, *The First European Revolution: 1776–1815** (1969), and, with a neo-Marxian approach, in E. J. Hobsbawm, *The Age of Revolution: 1789–1848** (1962).

The Social History of the Revolution

An excellent brief introduction to the social history of the Revolution is N. Hampson, *Social History of the French Revolution* (1962). The essays in J. Kaplow, ed., *New Perspectives on the French Revolution** (1965), are indispensable for an understanding of the social movement. A. Cobban, *The Social Interpretation of the French Revolution* (1964), is an important revisionary statement. On the role of the masses, see G. F. E. Rudé, *The Crowd in the French Revolution** (1959). E. Barber, *The Bourgeoisie in XVIIth Century France** (1955), discusses the background of bourgeois discontent.

Major French Interpretations of the Revolution

Alexis de Tocqueville's *The Old Regime and the French Revolution** (1956) presents the classic view of the Revolution as the continuation of the centralizing tendencies of the Old Regime. G. Lefebvre, *The Coming of the French Revolution* (1947), gives an excellent picture of France in the first year of the Revolution and states precisely and clearly the nature and problem of the French Revolution as a whole. For a treatment from the republican side, see F. V. A. Aulard, *The French Revolution*, 4 vols. (1901, 1910). A. Mathiez, *The French Revolution** (1928), is a sympathetic leftist interpretation of the Revolution.

Special Topics

Perhaps the best introduction to the Convention and the Reign of Terror is the brief study by J. M. Thompson, *Robespierre and the French Revolution** (1953). R. R. Palmer, *Twelve Who Ruled** (1941), is a fascinating account of the Reign of Terror written from a biographical approach. D. M. Greer, *The Incidence of Terror During the French Revolution* (1935), is a statistical account of who was actually executed and how. The role of Paris in the Revolution is the subject of A. Soboul, *The Parisian Sans-Culottes and the French Revolution* (1964). On party politics during the Legislative Assembly and the Convention, see M. J. Sydenham, *The Girondins* (1961) and *The First French Republic, 1792–1804* (1973). The fall of the Jacobins and the period of the Directory are dealt with authoritatively in G. Lefebvre's *The Thermidorians** (1937) and *The Directory** (1946). For a more recent treatment, see M. Lyons, *France under the Directory* (1975).

Napoleon and the Napoleonic Empire

G. Bruun, *Europe and the French Imperium** (1938), in the *Rise of Modern Europe* series, is a good general introduction. Among the many biographies of Napoleon are those of J. M. Thompson, *Napoleon Bonaparte* (1952), and F. Markham, *Napoleon** (1966). The best guide to interpretations of the period and perhaps the best book on Napoleon in English is P. Geyl, *Napoleon: For and Against** (1949). The best treatment in any language are the two volumes by G. Lefebvre, *Napoléon* (trans. 1969). On Napoleon's domestic policy, see R. Holtman, *The Napoleonic Revolution** (1967). Both R. B. Mowat, *The Diplomacy of Napoleon* (1924), and H. C. Deutsch, *The Genesis of Napoleonic Imperialism, 1801–1805* (1938), remain standard works on foreign policy. The best recent treatment of Napoleon's military career is D. Chandler, *The Campaigns of Napoleon* (1966). O. Connelly, *Napoleon's Satellite Kingdoms* (1965), deals with the rule of Napoleon and his relatives over most of Europe. G. H. Lovett, *Napoleon and the Birth of Modern Spain*, 2 vols. (1965), tells a dramatic story. Napoleon's relations with the two peripheral powers of Europe are treated in C. Oman, *Britain Against Napoleon* (1944), and in A. Palmer, *Napoleon in Russia* (1967).

24 The Search for
Stability, 1815–1850

The July Revolution of 1830 at Pont Neuf.

The unrest that had prevailed in Europe since the French Revolution did not end with the defeat of Napoleon. Many of Europe's troubles, of course, stemmed from the long and costly series of recent wars. But there were other causes of unrest. Politically, Europe continued to feel the effects of the issues first raised by the French Revolution—notably liberalism and nationalism. Intellectually, the years after Napoleon saw the flowering of the Age of Romanticism, with its protest against the rationalism of the Enlightenment. Economically and socially, the Continent in the first half of the nineteenth century began to feel in earnest the effects of the "Industrial Revolution," which had already begun in England in the eighteenth century (see Chapter 25). This chapter concentrates mainly on political and intellectual developments. But we must keep in mind that political tension was often the manifestation of underlying economic and social unrest. The rapid increase of Europe's population alone—from 192 million in 1800 to 274 million in 1850—could not help but have unsettling economic and political results. And the fact that more and more people now lived in cities did much to change the everyday lives of many Europeans.

Europe's search for stability after 1815 was marked by a contest between the forces of the past and the forces of the future. For a while it seemed as though the traditional agencies of power—the monarchs, the aristocracy, and the Church—might once again resume full control. But potent new forces were ready to oppose this relapse into the past. With the quickening of industrialization, there was now not only a middle class of growing size and significance but a wholly new class, the urban workers. Each class came to have its own political and economic philosophy—liberalism and socialism, respectively—which stood opposed to each other as well as to the traditional conservatism of the old order. It was inevitable that these rival classes and ideologies should clash. The resulting revolutions did not end until 1850. By that time the forces of the past were still not defeated, but they were everywhere on the defensive.

Economic growth and ideological unrest were not the only causes of revolution in the early nineteenth century. There was also the force of nationalism, which made itself increasingly felt among Europeans everywhere. Nationalism as an awareness of belonging to a particular nationality was nothing new. What was new was the intensity that this awareness now assumed. There were still some signs of eighteenth-century cosmopolitanism, especially among the aristocracy. But for the mass of the people, nationalism became their most ardent emotion, and national unification or independence their most cherished aim.

Generally speaking, the early nineteenth century was a major phase in the slow change from an essentially hierarchical and agrarian order into an increasingly democratic and industrial society. The problem before responsible leaders everywhere was to give political expression to the economic and social changes resulting from the industrial transformation of Europe. In trying to do this, they hoped to bring some degree of stability to their deeply unsettled world.

THE RESTORATION OF THE OLD ORDER

The first task facing the allies after defeating Napoleon was to bring order to a continent that had been disrupted by two decades of war. Europe's statesmen in the main tried to restore conditions as they had been before the French Revolution. In domestic affairs they adopted the principle of "legitimacy"—that is, they brought back the families of the rulers who had been ousted by revolution or war. In international affairs they tried to reconstruct the balance of power that had been upset by France. In retrospect this preoccupation with the past may seem shortsighted. But experience shows that most peace settlements are made with a view to the past rather than a vision of the future.

The Congress of Vienna

Peace conferences are usually dominated by a few leading statesmen. In

1814 and 1815 the decisive figures were Austria's chancellor, Prince Metternich; Britain's foreign minister, Lord Castlereagh; Tsar Alexander I of Russia; the Prussian King Frederick William III; and France's foreign minister, Prince Talleyrand. The fact that the vanquished French were thus able to make their voice heard shows the moderation and common sense of the victors.

The final peace with France was concluded at Paris in November 1815. France was the first to experience the principle of legitimacy. The new French king, Louis XVIII, was the brother of Louis XVI and the uncle of the dauphin, Louis XVII, who had died. Considering the many hardships the French had inflicted on Europe, the peace settlement was re-

markably lenient. France was reduced to its frontiers of 1790; it had to pay an indemnity; and it had to submit to an allied army of occupation.

The settlement with France, however, was only part of the work of restoration. A far more difficult task was to reorder the affairs of the rest of Europe. This was done at a separate conference in Vienna. The Congress of Vienna aroused high hopes among those Europeans who desired a stronger voice in the government of their respective countries or who, like the Germans and the Italians, longed for national unification. Their hopes were to be disappointed. The statesmen at Vienna, notably Metternich, had been deeply disturbed by the excesses of revolution and war and thus were firmly

EUROPE IN 1815

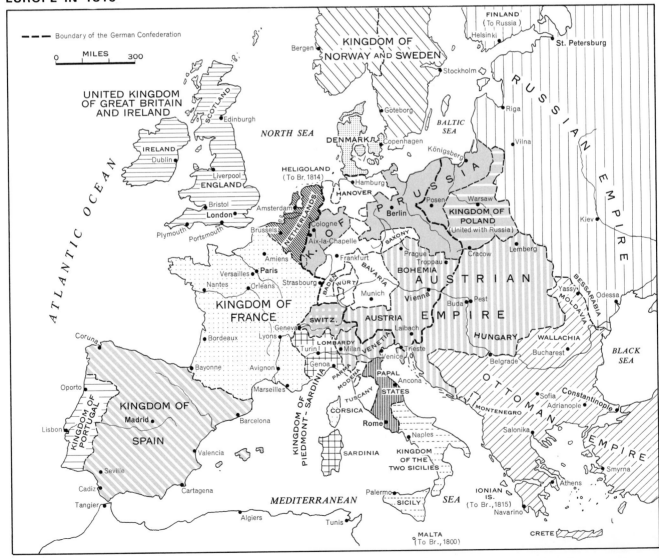

opposed to the forces of liberalism and nationalism in whose name these excesses had been committed.

Considering the conflicting aims of the powers, it is surprising how much was actually achieved at Vienna. Following the principle of legitimacy, the Bourbons were restored in Spain and Naples, and other legitimate rulers were put back on their thrones in the smaller Italian states. Yet the idea of legitimacy was frequently ignored, especially in the case of republics like Genoa and Venice, neither of which regained its independence. To maintain the balance of power and to keep France from repeating its recent aggression, the countries along its eastern frontier were either enlarged or otherwise strengthened. In the north, the Republic of Holland was given a king and was joined with the former Austrian Netherlands (Belgium). In place of the defunct Holy Roman Empire, a loosely joined confederation of thirty-nine states was set up in Germany. This was a far cry from the united nation that many Germans had hoped for. To provide an effective barrier to French expansion in the southeast, Switzerland was reestablished as an independent confederation and was declared perpetually neutral. The protective belt against France was completed by strengthening the Kingdom of Piedmont in northern Italy. In compensation for relinquishing Belgium, Austria received the Italian provinces of Lombardy and Venetia as well as the Illyrian provinces and the Tyrol (some of which Austria had ruled before 1789). This made Austria the leading power in Italy and the leading opponent of Italian unification.

Most of these changes caused no major difficulties, chiefly because the great powers saw eye-to-eye on them. One issue, however, caused much disagreement and at one point threatened to plunge the powers into war. That issue was Poland. A favorite scheme of Tsar Alexander I at Vienna was to pose as the "liberator" of Poland by setting up a Polish kingdom under Russian tutelage. The other powers objected to this: Prussia and Austria because they expected the return of those parts of Poland they had held before Napoleon, and England

because it had no desire to see Russia grow too powerful. To gain his end, Alexander promised the Prussians compensations elsewhere if they would support his Polish scheme. The result was a deadlock at Vienna, with England and Austria facing Russia and Prussia. An armed conflict was narrowly avoided when Talleyrand threw the weight of France behind England and Austria. The compromise that was reached was more advantageous to Prussia than to Russia. Russia received part of Poland, though less than hoped for, while Prussia got compensations in northern and western Germany that made it a powerful contender for leadership within the newly

Two contemporary views of the Congress of Vienna. The caricature portrays Talleyrand and Castlereagh (left) deliberating whether to join the merry dance of England's allies, Frederick William III, Metternich, and Alexander I. The king of Saxony fears the loss of his crown, while the Republic of Genoa (right) plays up to the powers in the hope of keeping its independence. The other view, a group portrait of the peacemakers by Isabey, dignifies the occasion.

Prince Metternich (1773–1859), by Sir Thomas Lawrence.

formed German Confederation and the guardian of Germany's interests along the Rhine.

While most of the decisions reached at Vienna were on specific territorial issues, the Congress also addressed itself to some general questions. Among them was the slave trade. There had been agitation against this scandalous practice since the late eighteenth century, and it had been outlawed in Britain in 1808. At Vienna, Lord Castlereagh succeeded in having the traffic in slaves condemned, but France, Spain, and Portugal did not comply until 1820. Even then it was only the trade, not slavery itself, that was outlawed. The British Empire abolished slavery in 1833, the United States not until a generation later.

Metternich

PRO

He was a statesman of unusual proportions: the greatest foreign minister that Austria ever had, and one of the greatest masters of international politics in the history of the modern European states. . . . He lifted Austria from its deepest downfall to a proud height. . . . He had the greatest part in bringing it about that for thirty years Europe enjoyed comparative international peace, and that during this time, in the center of the continent, learning and art could have a period of the most salutary, quiet cultivation, capital and the spirit of enterprise could undergo a strong increase, and religion and religious communities could experience intensification and consolidation.

CON

The question has often been raised whether he was not rather a good diplomat than a statesman. The question appears to be thoroughly justified: he lacked virtually all the characteristics necessary to a real and great statesman—courage, resolution, strength, seriousness, the gift of breadth of vision, the correct evaluation of the fruitful forces of the future, in brief, everything creative. . . . All revolutions, he held, came not from economic misery or dissatisfaction with bad political conditions, but arose from the secret societies, visionaries and doctrinaires. The new, world-moving force, the idea of national self-determination, counted for nothing with him. Peoples, in his eyes, were "children or nervous women," "simpletons." Liberalism to him was a "spectre" which must be banished by forceful action, a mere fog, which would disappear of its own accord.

From Heinrich von Srbik, *Metternich, der Staatsmann und der Mensch* (Munich, 1925); from Viktor Bibl, *Metternich, der Dämon Oesterreichs* (Vienna, 1936), as quoted in Henry F. Schwarz, ed., *Metternich, the "Coachman of Europe"* (Boston: Heath, 1962), pp. 15–16, 22–23.

The Congress of Vienna had accomplished a great deal, even though it had not lived up to everyone's hopes. In particular, the Vienna settlement ignored the stirrings of nationalism and the hopes for more popular government that the French Revolution had awakened. But more widespread than the middle-class dreams of nationalism and liberalism in 1815 was the hope for peace and order. It was in fulfilling this hope that the statesmen of Vienna scored their major success. There was no war among the great powers for forty years, and no war of worldwide dimensions for a whole century.

The "Holy Alliance" and the "Concert of Europe"

An indication of how sincerely the framers of the Vienna settlement sought peace may be seen in the arrangements they made to maintain it. The most famous of these, though the least important, was the "Holy Alliance" of Alexander I. The tsar had long shown signs that he thought of himself as a savior of the world. In this role he proposed to his fellow monarchs that they should conduct their relations with one another and with their subjects in a spirit of Christian love. To humor the tsar, most European rulers signed his "Holy Alliance"; but it never achieved any practical significance.

Of far greater importance than this "piece of sublime mysticism and nonsense" (as Castlereagh called it) was the Quadruple Alliance signed by England, Austria, Russia, and Prussia at the time of the final peace treaty with France in 1815. Its primary purpose was to prevent any further French violation of the peace settlement. But the powers also agreed to hold periodic conferences (ultimately to include France as well) to discuss matters of general European concern. This was an important innovation. For the first time statesmen seemed to realize that peace might be preserved by dealing with crises before they led to general war. The "Concert of Europe" was thus born.

As it turned out, however, this congress system was not a great success. At the very first meeting, at Aix-la-Chapelle in 1818, it became clear that the powers did not really see eye-to-eye on the fundamental purpose of their system of international government. To Castlereagh, the Quadruple Alliance was mainly an instrument for keeping France in its place and for maintaining international peace. To Alexander I, on the other hand, the Alliance seemed a convenient means of maintaining domestic peace as well. This difference was clearly revealed when Alexander proposed a new alliance that would guarantee not only the territorial status quo in Europe but also the existing form of government in every European country. This latter proposal met with determined opposition from Castlereagh, who did not want to extend the alliance "to include all objects, present and future."

The problem of whether to aid legitimate governments against revolution became acute shortly after Aix-la-Chapelle when a whole series of revolutions suddenly broke out over most of southern Europe. Here was a welcome opportunity for Alexander to repeat his plea for joint intervention. But Britain again voiced its opposition. And to underline his determination not to meddle in the affairs of other nations, Castlereagh refused to attend the Congress of Troppau (1820), at which such intervention was to be discussed.

With England absent, the other powers were able to adopt the "Troppau Protocol," which promised military aid to any government threatened by revolution at home. The effects of the Protocol became clear in 1821. In that year a third congress, at Laibach, commissioned Austria to send its forces into the Italian peninsula to put down the liberal insurrections there. Britain protested, but in vain. Similar action was taken at the next and last congress, which met at Verona in 1822. Again the continental powers, against England's objections, sanctioned the dispatch of a French force to put down a Spanish revolution in 1823.

Diplomacy by congress, so promising at first, had thus failed. It had failed because of a fundamental divergence among the victors over the issue of political change, with Britain opposing and the rest of the powers supporting inter-

Detail from a print showing British troops charging protesters at the Peterloo Massacre.

vention in the domestic affairs of other states to prevent liberal or national uprisings. There were other efforts to hold congresses, but England refused to attend.

A Wave of Reaction

The revolutions of the early 1820s, which are discussed below, were caused by the wave of reaction that followed the peace settlements of 1815. Wherever a legitimate monarch returned, he attempted to restore conditions exactly as they had been before he was ousted. In Spain and Naples the returning Bourbons abolished the liberal reforms that had been granted in 1812. In the Papal States, Pope Pius VII abolished French legal reforms, reestablished the Jesuits, revived the Inquisition, and put the Jews back into ghettos. In Piedmont, Victor Emmanuel I had the French botanical gardens torn up by the roots and the French furniture thrown out of the windows of his palace.

Elsewhere in Italy and over much of Europe the picture was the same. Both Frederick William III of Prussia and Francis I of Austria favored rigorous measures of repression in their respective countries. By tradition as well as actual power, Austria dominated the Diet of the new German Confederation at Frankfurt. Here it was Metternich who used his influence to suppress liberal or national stirrings wherever they appeared in Germany. As protests against this repressive "Metternich System" grew more vociferous, Austria and Prussia in 1819 pressured the Frankfurt Diet into adopting the so-called Carlsbad Decrees, which strictly limited intellectual freedom, especially at the universities.

There were very few exceptions to this general rule of reaction. It was felt even in England, whose foreign policy at least was more enlightened than that of the continental powers. There was much unrest in postwar Britain, chiefly due to economic causes. Overproduction during the war caused prices to fall, which in turn led to lower wages and growing unemployment. To remedy Britain's ills, a number of middle-class radicals advocated that the government be liberalized through parliamentary reform. But any agitation for reform was met by stern repression. In 1819, after the so-called Peterloo Massacre—when the constabulary of Manchester charged into a peaceful public meeting on parliamentary reform, causing many casualties—Parliament passed the repressive "Six Acts," which was England's version of the Carlsbad Decrees.

THE ROMANTIC PROTEST

Before considering the several waves of revolution that swept over Europe between 1820 and 1850, we must examine the intellectual climate in which these events took place. Much of the political turmoil of the generation after Napoleon had its counterpart and its cause in the spiritual ferment associated with the Age of Romanticism.

The Main Characteristics of Romanticism

The term *Romanticism* defies clear definition. It differed not only from country to country but from Romanticist to Romanticist. It inspired reactionaries as well as revolutionaries. It made conservatives look longingly to the past and

liberals look hopefully to the future. It meant escapism for some and a call to action for others. But with all these contradictions, there were certain characteristics that most Romanticists shared. Most prominent among these was their protest against the rationalism of the eighteenth century. The Enlightenment, with its emphasis on the rational nature of man and the rational order of the universe, had largely ignored irrational forces. It had been a brilliantly civilized but overly intellectual age. We have already seen some earlier reactions to this narrow rationalism. The French Revolution and the age of Napoleon had given further impetus to this protest. Reason, it seemed, was not the solution to man's problems that the *philosophes* had promised it to be. If reason had failed, what was there left to turn to but its opposite—faith? As the French writer Madame de Staël wrote in 1815: "I do not know exactly *what* we must believe, but I believe *that* we must believe! The eighteenth century did nothing but deny. The human spirit lives by its beliefs. Acquire faith through Christianity, or through German philosophy, or merely through enthusiasm, but believe in something!"

The desire "to believe in something" was characteristic of Romanticists everywhere. Romanticism was an international movement or trend that actually went back into the late eighteenth century. The typical Romantic followed his heart rather than his head. As the hero of Goethe's romantic novel *The Sorrows of Young Werther* exclaimed: "What I know, anyone can know—but my heart is my own, peculiar to myself." The Romantic was an individualist. The *philosophe* of the Enlightenment had spoken of Man, as though he were the same everywhere. The Romanticist stressed differences among men and felt that each should be a law unto himself. Much of Romantic writing was devoted to the strong personality, the hero, both in history and in fiction. One manifestation of Romanticism's interest in the individual was the growing vogue of autobiographies. One of the most revealing of these was Rousseau's famous *Confessions*. It was Rousseau also who regarded education as a means of realizing a person's individual-

Johann Wolfgang von Goethe (1749–1832), from a medal stamped by the French sculptor David d'Angers in 1829.

Illustration by Daniel Chodowiecki (1726–1801) from Goethe's *The Sorrows of Young Werther.*

ity. The Enlightenment, with its belief in the essential sameness of human minds, had been interested in formal rather than individualized education. Rousseau held that the best education was practically no education at all. Children should be left to develop their own abilities and potentialities.

While many Romanticists took a lively interest in the world about them, others used their imagination as a means of escape. To the eighteenth-century *philosophe* the world had appeared as a well-ordered mechanism; to the Romanticist, on the other hand, nature was a mysterious force whose moods expressed his innermost feelings. The Enlightenment had liked landscapes that showed the civilizing influence of man; Romanticism, by contrast, preferred its nature wild—waterfalls, the roaring sea, majestic mountains—or dreamlike—veiled in mist or bathed in mellow moonlight, the kind of landscape painted by Constable and Turner in England or Caspar David Friedrich in Germany.

This Romantic love of the unusual or the unreal in nature was frankly escapist. As factories began to disfigure the landscape and cities began to encroach on their surrounding countryside, the Romanticists longed to return to an unspoiled and simple life. They abhorred the ugliness and artificiality of city life and extolled the virtues of country folk, whose customs, tales, and songs they hoped to preserve. The escapism of the Romanticists took other forms as well. Some Romantic writers let their imagination roam in faraway, exotic places; others preferred to dwell in the realm of the supernatural. Still others escaped into the realm of religious emotion.

Romanticism and Religion

The close relationship between Romanticism and religion is obvious, since both stressed the emotional, irrational side of man. Catholicism in particular answered the Romanticist's need to "believe in something." The mystery of Catholic theology and the splendor of its ritual provided just the kind of emotional experience the Romanticist craved. As a result, many Romanticists returned or were converted to Catholicism, and the Catholic Church, which had been on the defensive since the French Revolution, was able to reassert itself. In 1814, the Jesuit Order was officially restored. In 1816, divorce, which had been permitted

Cloister Graveyard in the Snow, Romantic painting by Caspar David Friedrich (1810).

in France since the Revolution, was once again abolished. In Spain and parts of Italy, the Inquisition returned. And almost everywhere on the Continent, education once again became a monopoly of the clergy.

Veneration of the Past

The revival of religious interest was closely allied to the general veneration the Romanticists showed for the past. The Enlightenment had derived much of its inspiration from the ancient Greeks and Romans. To the eighteenth century their civilizations had appeared particularly reasonable and attractive. The intervening period, from about 400 to 1300 A.D., had been merely "Dark Ages" of ignorance and superstition. It was to these hitherto neglected centuries that the Romanticists now turned, attracted by the mystery, the glamor, and the grandeur that had survived in medieval castles and Gothic cathedrals.

The Romantic interest in the Middle Ages, by arousing an interest in the past, also awakened a general interest in the study of history. The eighteenth century had viewed the world as a well-ordered, static mechanism that had been set in motion at some specific time in the past. To the Romanticist, on the other hand, the world was an organism that had grown slowly, changed constantly, and was still growing and changing. In an effort to retrace this gradual change, historians in the early nineteenth century developed a careful method of inquiry, using historical sources—documents and other remains—to gain a truer understanding of the past. Historical scholarship, as we know it today, originated in the Age of Romanticism.

Nationalism and Conservatism

One of the things a study of the past teaches us is that mankind has gradually come to be divided into separate groups, most of which are defined by geographic area, language, and historic experiences. In time, all these elements together create a common feeling that may be called "national consciousness." Some such feeling had existed in countries like England, France, and even Germany since medieval or early modern times. To transform this national consciousness into nationalism, however, something more was needed—a sense not only of being different from, but also of being superior to, other national groups. This pride in one's nationality is largely a state of mind. Its first modern manifestations may be seen in the French Revolution and the Napoleonic wars. With its appeal to the emotions, this new nationalism fitted quite naturally into the climate of Romanticism. To the Romanticist, na-

---

The Ingredients of Nationalism

1. A certain defined (often vaguely) unit of territory (whether possessed or coveted).
2. Some common cultural characteristics such as language (or widely understood languages), customs, manners, and literature (folk tales and lore are a beginning). If an individual believes he shares these, and wishes to continue sharing them, he is usually said to be a member of the nationality.
3. Some common dominant social (as Christian) and economic (as capitalistic or, recently, communistic) institutions.
4. A common independent or sovereign government (type does not matter) or the desire for one. The "principle" that each nationality should be separate and independent is involved here.
5. A belief in a common history (it can be invented) and in a common origin (often mistakenly conceived to be racial in nature).
6. A love or esteem for fellow nationals (not necessarily as individuals).
7. A devotion to the entity (however little comprehended) called the nation, which embodies the common territory, culture, social and economic institutions, government, and the fellow nationals, and which is at the same time (whether organism or not) more than their sum.
8. A common pride in the achievements (often the military more than the cultural) of this nation and a common sorrow in its tragedies (particularly its defeats).
9. A disregard for or hostility to other (not necessarily all) like groups, especially if these prevent or seem to threaten the separate national existence.
10. A hope that the nation will have a great and glorious future (usually in territorial expansion) and become supreme in some way (in world power if the nation is already large).

From Boyd C. Shafer, *Nationalism: Myth and Reality* (New York: Harcourt Brace Jovanovich, 1955), pp. 7–8.

tionalism, like religion, provided something in which he could believe. Unfortunately, however, with the memories of the recent wars still fresh in their minds, some Romanticists, notably in Germany, tended to express their nationalism in unpleasantly strident tones.

Nationalism in the early nineteenth century was a revolutionary creed. Since it aimed at the liberation of peoples from foreign domination or their unification into a common state, it posed a threat to the established order. In defense of that order, a new political philosophy had already appeared during the French Revolution, the philosophy of conservatism. Its leading proponent was the Englishman Edmund Burke. We have seen how Burke, in his *Reflections on the Revolution in France*, had warned against the ultimate consequences of that upheaval. He had in particular attacked the revolutionaries for their eighteenth-century belief that man was innately good and endowed with certain natural rights. Far from having any natural rights, man, according to Burke, merely inherited the rights and duties that existed within his society. Since these rights and duties had developed through the ages, they constituted an inheritance that no single generation had the right to destroy. Burke also rebuked the eighteenth-century idea that government was the result of a contract among its citizens. Instead, he held that the state was an organism, a mystic community, to which the individual must submit.

Burke's conservatism, with its veneration for the past, its organic view of society, and its prediction of many of the dire consequences of the French Revolution, had great appeal to the generation after 1815. Like nationalism, conservatism greatly attracted the Romanticists, and Burke found ardent proponents and imitators on the Continent. Initially, conservatism and nationalism were often in conflict. Nationalism, to achieve its ends, was not averse to revolution, the very thing most conservatives abhorred. Conservatism, on the other hand, in its opposition to radical change, often became indistinguishable from outright reaction, which opposed change of any kind. Only gradually did it become clear that na-

tionalism, once it had reached its goals, tended to become conservative in order to defend its gains.

There was one point, however, on which conservatives and nationalists agreed from the beginning, and that was their admiration of the state as the highest social organism. The leading advocate of the supreme importance of the state was the German philosopher Georg Wilhelm Friedrich Hegel. Like the conservatives, Hegel viewed the state as an organism that had evolved historically. Only in submission to a powerful state, Hegel held, could the individual achieve his true freedom. To be strong, a state must be unified, preferably under the authority of a monarch. Each state, according to Hegel, had its own particular spirit, and by developing that spirit it contributed to the World-Spirit. "The State," Hegel wrote, "is the Divine Idea as it exists on earth." As such it is not bound by the usual laws of morality; its only judge is history. The course of history had evolved in three stages: the Oriental, in which only a despot was free; the Greek and the Roman, in which a few were free; and finally the Germanic, in which all would be free. It was his stress on the unique position of Germany and of Prussia that endeared Hegel to German nationalists.

The Impact of Romanticism

Romanticism, as this brief analysis shows, was a bundle of contradictions. It helps us understand the conservatives who made the Vienna settlement, as well as the liberals who tried to overthrow it. It was a movement affecting all provinces of human life and thought. It was particularly strong in the arts, not only in literature but in all forms of artistic expression, especially music. The influence of Romanticism was deep and widespread. All the nations of Europe contributed to it, and it also was a vital force in the United States. Politically, America during the nineteenth century continued its emancipation from Europe. But culturally there were not two worlds—the New World continued to be influenced by, and continued to influence, the Old.

A German peasant girl in her native costume; painting by Ludwig Emil Grimm (1828).

The Romantic protest, or at least the Romantic attitude, did not, of course, end with the Romantic era. Its influence is felt to the present day. Romanticism has been criticized as a rebellion against reason, against measure, against discipline, and as a surrender to the murky passions and emotions of the human heart. The old Goethe, himself a Romantic in his youth, looked back with nostalgia to the reasonableness and clarity of eighteenth-century classicism. "Classic," he said, "is that which is healthy; romantic that which is sick." Romanticism, it is true, did destroy the clear simplicity and unity of thought that had prevailed during the Enlightenment. There was no longer one dominant philosophy that expressed all the aims and ideals of western civilization as rationalism had done during the eighteenth century. But then rationalism had provided a narrow, one-sided view of the world, ignoring whole provinces of human experience. Romanticism did much to correct that unbalance. By insisting that the world was not the simple machine it had seemed since Newton and that man was not a mere cog in that machine, Romanticism provided a more complex but also a truer view of the world. With its emphasis on evolution throughout the universe, and its stress on the creativity and uniqueness of the individual, Romanticism came as a breath of fresh air after the formalism of the Enlightenment. This was its major and lasting contribution.

THE FIRST WAVE OF REVOLUTIONS, 1820–29

The restoration of the old order saved Europe from major international wars, but it was also responsible for the almost unbroken series of domestic wars and revolutions that lasted for more than a generation. We have already noted the unrest in Germany and England shortly after 1815. In France, the assassination in 1820 of the Duke of Berri, who was in line to be Louis XVIII's successor, was the signal for abandoning the moderate course Louis had tried to steer. More serious, however, than these sporadic acts of violence was the whole wave of revolutions that swept through southern Europe in the 1820s.

Revolt in Southern Europe

The first of these revolutions broke out in 1820 in Spain, where the army rebelled against being sent to South America to put down the revolutions in the Spanish colonies. From Spain revolution spread to Portugal and somewhat later to Italy. In every case it was the army that took the initiative, forcing reactionary monarchs to grant liberal constitutions. The situation in Italy was particularly complicated. The Italian peninsula was still divided into a number of sovereign states of varying size, the most important being the Kingdom of the Two Sicilies in the south, the Papal States in the center, and the Kingdom of Piedmont in the north. In addition, Austria ruled directly over the northern provinces of Lombardy and Venetia and exerted influence over the rest of Italy indirectly through Austrian or pro-Austrian rulers in many of the smaller Italian states. The revolutions in Italy, therefore, were directed not merely against the reactionary policy of the various local rulers but against the alien influence of Austria in Italian affairs; the motives of the Italian revolutionaries were national as well as liberal.

As a result of these upheavals, the old order in much of southern Europe seemed to be on the way out. But the initial success of the revolutions did not last. The revolutionaries everywhere constituted only a small minority, finding

Simón Bolívar (1783–1830), outstanding leader of the South American revolution against Spain and the greatest of Latin American heroes.

little support among the apathetic mass of illiterate peasants. In addition, there was much disagreement among the leaders when it came to establishing more liberal regimes. But more harmful than the lack of popular following and the inexperience of the revolutionaries was the intervention of outside forces. Austria, with the blessing of Prussia and Russia, intervened in Italy in 1821, and France intervened in Spain in 1823. Only in Portugal was a semblance of parliamentary government maintained, thanks to the support of Great Britain.

The Monroe Doctrine

With reaction triumphant, there was now a possibility that the powers might try to help Spain recover its colonies in Latin America. Largely under the impact of the French Revolution and the Napoleonic conquest of their mother country, the Spanish colonies, beginning in 1810, had followed the example of the United States and declared their independence. In this they had the sympathy of both the United States and Great Britain, whose commercial interests were eager to gain access to the South American market. In 1822, Britain's new foreign secretary, George Canning, proposed a joint declaration by England and the United States to oppose any European intervention against the Spanish colonies.

But the United States was concerned not only about South America but also about the possible extension of Russian influence southward from Alaska and about England's designs on Cuba. President Monroe, therefore, decided to act on his own. In a message to Congress in December 1823, he warned that any attempt by the powers of Europe to extend their influence over the Western Hemisphere would be considered a "manifestation of an unfriendly disposition toward the United States." The immediate effectiveness of the Monroe Doctrine, of course, depended on the backing of the British navy rather than on the insignificant power of the United States. For that reason, Canning was justified in his famous boast that he "called the New World into existence to redress the balance of the Old."

The Monroe Doctrine

In the wars of the European powers in matters relating to themselves we have never taken any part, nor does it comport with our policy so to do. It is only when our rights are invaded or seriously menaced that we resent injuries or make preparation for our defense. With the movements in this hemisphere we are of necessity more immediately connected, and by causes which must be obvious to all enlightened and impartial observers. The political system of the allied powers is essentially different in this respect from that of America. . . . We owe it, therefore, to candor and to the amicable relations existing between the United States and those powers to declare that we should consider any attempt on their part to extend their system to any portion of this hemisphere as dangerous to our peace and safety. With the existing colonies or dependencies of any European power we have not interfered and shall not interfere. But with the governments who have declared their independence and maintained it, and whose independence we have, on great consideration and on just principles, acknowledged, we could not view any interposition for the purpose of oppressing them, or controlling in any other manner their destiny, by any European power in any other light than as the manifestation of an unfriendly disposition toward the United States.

From President James Monroe, message to Congress, December 2, 1823.

The Greek War of Independence

The revolutions in the Iberian and Italian peninsulas, in their aims as well as their failures, had all been quite similar. But the most important revolution of the 1820s, the Greek War of Independence, was quite a different matter. That war was almost entirely motivated by nationalism. And while the other revolutions failed largely because of outside intervention, the Greek revolt succeeded because the powers helped rather than hindered it. The Greek revolt against the Ottoman Empire was merely the latest chapter in the slow disintegration of that sprawling state. The Serbs had already staged a successful revolt after 1815. Greek nationalism had been gathering force for some time, especially among the "Island" Greeks, whose far-flung commercial contacts had put them in touch with western ideas. The Island Greeks had founded a secret society, the *Hetàiria Philikē*, and it was this society that in-

James Monroe (1758–1831), by Gilbert Stuart.

Mahmoud II (1784–1839), sultan of Turkey at the time of the Greek revolts.

Nicholas I, tsar of Russia, (1825–55); sketch by Sir Edwin Henry Landseer (1802–73).

spired the uprising in early 1821 that started the war against Turkey.

The Greeks, however, were no match for the Turks, especially after the sultan called in his Egyptian vassal, Mehemet Ali, to help him. The great powers, though they watched events in Greece closely, at first were kept from intervention through mutual jealousies. But when the very existence of the Greeks seemed at stake they realized that something had to be done.

Public opinion in the West had favored the Greek cause all along, and the pressure of this "Philhellenism" was partly responsible for the intervention of the powers. In 1827, British, French, and Russian squadrons destroyed the combined Turkish and Egyptian navies in the battle of Navarino. The following year, Russia declared war on Turkey. After brief fighting, the Turks had to submit to the Treaty of Adrianople (1829). Its terms were moderate, except that Russia was given a protectorate over the Danubian principalities of Moldavia and Wallachia, which later became Rumania. After some further negotiations, Greece was set up as an independent kingdom.

The Decembrist Revolt in Russia

While the Greek uprising was still going on, there had been one other attempt at revolution, this time against the most powerful stronghold of reaction, the tsarist regime in Russia. Like the Spanish and Italian revolts, it failed. The enigmatic Alexander I, who liked to pose as a liberal while actually becoming more and more reactionary, left the direction of Russian affairs largely in the hands of his efficient but equally reactionary adviser, Alexis Arakcheiev, who used Alexander's fear of revolution to build a regime of ruthless political oppression.

This policy of oppression naturally aroused the opposition of the few liberal elements in Russia. Many members of the upper class had come in contact with western liberal ideas during the wars against Napoleon and the subsequent allied occupation of France. These officers founded several secret societies. An opportunity for the conspirators to act

came in December 1825, when Alexander suddenly died and there was some doubt about which of his brothers would succeed him. The revolt failed, however, because it was mostly confined to the army, and its leaders were disunited and lacked popular following. Even so, this so-called Decembrist Revolt was significant. Earlier uprisings in Russia had been entirely spontaneous. Here, for the first time, was a revolt that had been planned by a small minority with a definite program. The Decembrist uprising served as an inspiration to all later revolutionary movements in Russia. Meanwhile, the December events inspired in Alexander's successor, Nicholas I, an almost pathological fear of revolution. For thirty years he remained the leading proponent of reaction abroad and repression at home.

THE SECOND WAVE OF REVOLUTIONS, 1830–33

The first wave of revolutions after 1815, far from upsetting the old order, merely seemed to have strengthened its hold. The uprisings had been too sporadic, the work of small army cliques with no following among the mass of the people. The second wave of revolutions was different. It started among the people of Paris, and from there it spread over most of Europe, leaving behind some important political changes.

The French Revolution of 1830

The first years of the restored Bourbon monarchy in France had been peaceful ones. Louis XVIII had tried sincerely to rally his deeply divided country. But he found it increasingly difficult to do so. To the liberals, led by Lafayette, the new constitution, the Charter, with its limited franchise did not go far enough. To the royalists, or "Ultras," led by the king's brother, the Count of Artois, the Charter was the source of all France's ills. Up to 1820, Louis had been able to maintain a moderate, middle-of-the-road course. But after the assassination of the Duke of Berri, the royalist faction gained the upper hand and moderation came to an end.

Louis XVIII, by F. Gerard (1823).

Charles X of France portrayed as a reactionary lobster moving backward; anonymous caricature (1830).

Louis XVIII died in 1824 and was succeeded by the Count of Artois, as Charles X. Reaction now went into full force. While liberal opposition became more outspoken, the government's policy became more repressive. In 1829 Charles appointed as his first minister one of the most notorious reactionaries, the Prince de Polignac. In the past the king had always been careful to enlist parliamentary backing, but this situation now changed. In the spring of 1830, when the Chamber turned against the government, Charles simply dismissed it. And when new elections brought in another liberal majority, Polignac had the king promulgate the July Ordinances, which dissolved the Chamber, imposed strict censorship, and changed the electoral law so that the government in the future would be sure of a favorable majority.

Discontent with this arbitrary policy came to a head in the July revolution of 1830. The hope of the men who fought on the barricades—workers, students, some members of the middle class—was for a republic. But this was not what the more moderate liberals wanted. Much as they hated the high-handed government of Charles X, they were equally opposed to a republic, which recalled the violent phase of the earlier French Revolution. It was due to the careful machinations of these moderates that France emerged from its July revolution as a constitutional monarchy rather than a republic.

The new king was Louis Philippe, Duke of Orléans. Though a relative of the Bourbons, he had stayed clear of the royalists and had affected a thoroughly bourgeois mode of life. Events in France, of course, violated the status quo established in 1814 and 1815. But the other powers had been taken too much by surprise and were too little united to take any action. Their attention, furthermore, was soon caught by events elsewhere, as the French example set off a whole series of revolutions in other countries.

Revolution in Belgium

The first to follow the lead of France was Belgium. Its union with Holland at Vienna had not proved very successful. The only area in which the two countries

got along was in economic matters, and even there the Belgians in time developed grievances. Still, there had been hardly any popular agitation for Belgian nationalism prior to 1830; seldom has nationalism arisen so suddenly and found such quick fulfillment. In August 1830, in part inspired by events in Paris, rioting broke out in Brussels. King William I tried to save the situation by granting a separate administration for Belgium, but he was too late. The Dutch troops sent to quell the uprising were quickly defeated; but the ultimate fate of Belgium depended on the attitude of the great powers. Although France and England looked favorably upon the new state, the three eastern powers were hostile. Since Austria and Russia were preoccupied with disturbances in Italy and Poland, however, any aid to Holland was out of the question. In December 1830 the five powers agreed to recognize the independence of Belgium. The new state was to remain perpetually neutral.

Europe in Revolt

France and Belgium were the only nations in which the revolutions of 1830 achieved any lasting success. But there was hardly a country that did not feel the tremors of revolution. Across the Rhine the events in Paris caused wild excitement among German intellectuals, though there was little echo among the people. Some of the smaller states rid themselves of rulers who were particularly corrupt and vicious, and others won moderately liberal constitutions.

Southern Europe, the scene of revolution a decade earlier, was also aroused by the news from Paris. Struggles among rival claimants to the thrones in Spain and Portugal, together with disturbances fostered by liberals, created widespread confusion. Both nations finally emerged, at least nominally, as constitutional monarchies. In Italy, where secret societies such as the *Carbonari*, or "charcoal burners," were flourishing, revolutions broke out in several states. The revolutionaries hoped to receive aid from France, and had they done so they might have won. But Louis Philippe could not afford to antagonize Austria, and Metternich had a free hand. Again Austrian troops restored the legitimate rulers, who then took revenge against the insurgents.

The Polish Insurrection of 1830

The bloodiest struggle of all in 1830 took place in Poland. The Kingdom of Poland already had been a source of trouble to Alexander I. Under Nicholas I tension mounted further. Like revolutionaries elsewhere, the Polish insurgents had founded a number of secret societies to propagate nationalism and to prepare for revolution. When rumors reached Poland in 1830 that Nicholas was planning to use Polish forces to help put down the revolutions in France and Belgium, the conspirators decided to act. Had the Polish people stood united, the revolt might have succeeded. But the revolutionaries were split into moderates and radicals, with neither faction having much following among the mass of the peasants. The hope, furthermore, that England and France would come to their aid proved vain. Even so, it took almost a year before Russia was able to subdue the rebellious Poles and impose a regime of severe repression. For the next generation Russian Poland remained a sad and silent land.

Reform in Great Britain

There was one other country besides France and Belgium where unrest in 1830 and after led to major political changes. More than any other nation, Great Britain had been feeling the effects of rapid industrialization. The change from an agrarian to an industrial society could not help but have political repercussions. That England was able to make this adjustment without a revolution was due to its long parliamentary tradition and able political leadership. Britain did share in the initial wave of reaction after 1815. With George IV, the worst of George III's sons, succeeding his father in 1820, and with the Tories in control of Parliament, little relief was in sight.

Beginning in 1822, however, a new and more enlightened element within the Tory Party became aware of the political implications of economic change. The first sign that some relief from repression was imminent came with the reform of Britain's criminal code after 1822, which drastically reduced the number of capital crimes. In 1824 the Combination Acts, forbidding workers to organize, were repealed. In 1828 a new Corn Law modified the duties on foreign grain, thus lowering the price of bread. The most important reform of the 1820s, however, was the establishment of religious equality. In 1828 the Test and Corporations Acts, which barred Protestant dissenters from holding state offices, were repealed; and in 1829 the Emancipation Bill permitted Catholics to sit in Parliament.

In most of these reforms the liberal element among the Tories had the support of the Whigs. The leaders of the Whig Party differed little from their Tory rivals in social background and outlook. But while the main backing of the Tory Party continued to come from the landed gentry and the established church, the Whigs were supported by the rising merchant and manufacturing class. For that reason they became the main advo-

The Great Reform Bill of 1832 is the subject of this contemporary cartoon. Political corruption is put through the "reform mill" to emerge as a triumphant Britannia.

THE REFORM BILL.

cates of parliamentary reform. To the Whigs, parliamentary reform meant giving a fairer share of representation in Parliament to the well-to-do middle class. This they were finally able to achieve in 1832.

The Great Reform Bill of 1832 was passed only after domestic unrest had at times brought England to the verge of revolution. Under the new bill, the franchise was extended to about half again as many voters, and proper representation was given to the new industrial towns. As a result, one in five adult males was now able to vote. The workers and the poor were still left without a vote, but this was no different from the situation that prevailed elsewhere in Europe. Even though there was no change in Britain's form of government in 1832, the Reform Bill was every bit as much a revolution as the overthrow of Charles X had been in France. Both were significant stages in the rise to power of the middle, or upper middle, class.

East and West

Because the revolutions in the early 1830s were successful only in western Europe, they helped widen the already existing gap between the powers of the East and the West. France and England, constitutional monarchies both, had seen to it that the revolution in Belgium succeeded. Austria, Russia, and Prussia, still essentially autocratic, had suppressed the uprisings in Germany, Italy, and Poland. The main reason for the success of revolutions in the West had been their popular support. The middle class had taken the lead, but it had been aided by the urban lower class. East of the Rhine, revolutions had found little popular backing and had failed. Industrialization, which had bolstered the ranks of the middle and lower classes in the West, had as yet made little headway in the East. But while the revolutions in western Europe had been successful, they had chiefly benefited the middle class. The workers, who had done much of the rioting and fighting, were left with empty hands. In the West as in the East, therefore, the revolutions of 1830 left much unfinished. Here is the main cause for

the third and largest wave of revolutions, which swept across Europe in 1848 and 1849.

THE THIRD WAVE OF REVOLUTIONS, 1848–49

The third wave of revolutions lasted for over a year and affected most of Europe. Among the major powers, only England and Russia were spared, though England came close to revolt. There were, of course, countless differences among all these upheavals, but there were also some notable similarities. Generally speaking, the revolutions of 1848 were a further attempt to undo the settlement of 1815. In Italy, Germany, Austria, and Hungary the fundamental grievance was still the lack of national freedom and unity. There was also the desire for more representative governments and for the abolition of the many vestiges of feudalism that still remained. But these were secondary aims. Nationalism was the dominant concern of the revolutionaries in central Europe. In western Europe, neither nationalism nor feudalism was any longer an issue. There the chief aim of revolution was the extension of political power beyond the upper middle class. The revolutionaries did not always agree on how far this liberalization should go. The middle class wanted merely to widen the franchise to include the more substantial citizens, whereas the working class wanted political democracy for everyone and some measure of social and economic democracy as well. With the revolutions of 1848, socialism for the first time became an issue in modern politics (see p. 585).

Aside from these political causes, there were also economic reasons for the outbreak of revolutions. Despite, or because of, the unprecedented economic growth of Europe since 1815, there had been several severe economic crises, the latest in 1846 and 1847. These upsets particularly affected the lower classes. The small artisan was fighting against the competition of large-scale industry, which threatened to deprive him of his livelihood. At the same time, the industrial workers in the new factories were eking out a marginal existence on a minimum wage. There were also periodic crises in agriculture, primarily as a result of crop failures. Economic hardship, then, in many cases preceded and helped precipitate political action.

There were other common features among the revolutions of 1848. They were all essentially urban. The leaders came from the middle class, with lawyers, journalists, and professors especially prominent. Much of the actual fighting was done by the urban lower classes, by artisans and workers. Students also played an important part. None of the revolutions had any agrarian program beyond the abolition of feudal dues and services. Once these had been abolished, the conservative peasants withdrew what little initial support they had provided the revolutions.

Europe, in the spring of 1848, was discontented and restless. The causes of discontent differed from middle class to workers to peasants. But so long as these three groups stood united, it was easy for them to overthrow the old order. When it came to building something new, however, all the differences among the revolutionaries asserted themselves. The history of revolution in 1848 is a frustrating tale of missed opportunities.

The "July Monarchy" in France

The key nation in the events of 1848 was again France. The reasons for the failure of Louis Philippe's government are not too obvious. France under the "July Monarchy" (so-called after the month of its birth in 1830) was prosperous and progressive, with a liberal constitution, a free press, and a competent king. Louis Philippe had all the bourgeois virtues—he was thrifty, kindly, and industrious. He was served by capable ministers, and until about 1846 trade and industry flourished. France, which had fallen behind England economically as a result of the French Revolution, had started to regain some lost ground. Yet with all these advantages, the July Monarchy was far from popular. The French, it has been said, were bored. They were bored by a colorless king, bored by a dull domestic policy that favored the wealthy,

Above: a French cartoon showing Louis Philippe courting the public; it was captioned, "Well, good people, do you want some? Here it is." Left: a British cartoon, from *Punch* in 1848, shows Liberty extinguishing Louis Philippe's candle.

and bored by a foreign policy of peace and compromise. Most Frenchmen still smarted from the defeat of Napoleon. Only a glorious foreign policy could wipe out that humiliation. But no sooner was there an opportunity for such a policy than the genuine pacifism of Louis Philippe spoiled it.

In time the opposition against Louis Philippe became crystallized in three groups: the Liberals, the Bonapartists, and the Republicans. The Liberals wanted a further extension of the franchise. The Bonapartists hoped to overthrow Louis Philippe in favor of Prince Louis Napoleon, the emperor's nephew, who promised to restore to France some of the glories associated with his uncle's name. As for Republicanism, it had its roots in the failure of the radicals to assert themselves in 1830. As the number of workers increased, Republican feeling became more widespread. And since the workers also began to make economic demands, Republicanism gradually became tinged with socialism.

Discontent in France mounted after 1846, primarily for economic reasons. In the fall of that year, Europe was hit by a serious depression. In France, as elsewhere, rising prices and growing unemployment particularly affected the workers. Yet the government made no effort to help them, and the lower classes became more and more restive. To ease the situation, Liberals and Republicans joined forces in the summer of 1847 to hold a series of political meetings to discuss parliamentary reform. In February 1848 the government's ban against such meetings brought on a peaceful popular demonstration. As a precaution, the king called out the army, and in the ensuing confrontation several of the demonstrators were killed. Blood had been spilled, and the revolution was on. Major bloodshed was avoided by Louis Philippe's decision to abdicate and go to England. On February 25 a republic was proclaimed.

The Second French Republic

In a very short time and with little loss of life, a tremendous change had been brought about. The people who had been cheated out of the fruits of revolution in 1830 now had reached their goal; the days of upper-middle-class predominance seemed to be over. But this radical phase of the revolution did not last. The new provisional government was faced with tremendous difficulties. Paris was in a constant state of turmoil, with several political factions jockeying for position. Some wanted to concentrate all efforts on domestic reforms; others were more concerned with carrying the revolution beyond the French borders. The socialists in the government proclaimed the right to work and introduced a system of "national workshops," which had been advocated by the socialist Louis Blanc (see p. 586).

In this period of confusion, the elections to the new National Assembly came as a severe shock to the radicals. Of some nine hundred delegates elected, fewer than one hundred supported the radical Republicans. The main reason for this sudden shift lay with the French peasantry, whose aims had been largely met by the first French Revolution and who had subsequently become staunchly conservative.

But the radical element did not intend to give up without a fight. There now followed a series of clashes between the

The February Days in Paris

I spent the whole afternoon in walking about Paris. Two things in particular struck me: the first was, I will not say the mainly, but the uniquely and exclusively popular character of the revolution that had just taken place; the omnipotence it had given to the people properly so-called—that is to say, the classes who work with their hands—over all others. . . . Although the working classes had often played the leading part in the events of the First Revolution, they had never been the sole leaders and masters of the State. . . . The Revolution of July [1830] was effected by the people, but the middle class had stirred it up and led it, and secured the principal fruits of it. The Revolution of February, on the contrary, seemed to be made entirely outside the bourgeoisie and against it. . . .

Throughout this day, I did not see in Paris a single one of the former agents of the public authority; not a soldier, not a gendarme, not a policeman; the National Guard itself had disappeared. The people alone bore arms, guarded the public buildings, watched, gave orders, punished; it was an extraordinary and terrible thing to see in the sole hands of those who possessed nothing, all this immense town, so full of riches, or rather this great nation: for, thanks to centralization, he who reigns in Paris governs France. Hence the terror of all the other classes was extreme; I doubt whether at any period of the revolution it had been so great, and I should say that it was only to be compared to that which the civilized cities of the Roman Empire must have experienced when they suddenly found themselves in the power of the Goths and Vandals.

From *The Recollections of Alexis de Tocqueville*, trans. by Alexander Teixeira de Mattos, ed. by J. P. Mayer (New York: Columbia University Press, 1949), pp. 72–75.

radicals in the provisional government and the moderate National Assembly. Tension came to a head in the bloody "June Days," when the Assembly dissolved the workshops, which it considered breeding-grounds of discontent. The workers again took to the barricades, and the resulting street fighting was the most savage ever, causing thousands of casualties. By the end of June 1848 the back of lower-class resistance had been broken, and the middle class once again could make its wishes prevail. The Constitution of the Second French Republic set up a single legislative Chamber of Representatives, to be elected by universal male suffrage. Executive power was vested in a powerful president, to be elected by the people.

The first presidential election took place in December 1848. There were five candidates, among them Prince Louis Napoleon. The French middle class and the French peasants wanted a strong man as president, a man who would banish the "red peril" of socialism. Such a man, they felt, was Louis Napoleon. The first Napoleon had taken over the reins of government after a similar revolution fifty years ago, and he had brought order at home and glory abroad. Why should history not repeat itself? The victory of Louis Napoleon by an overwhelming majority was thus due chiefly to the glamor of his name. A sign that he was ready to live up to that name came four years later, in 1852, when he proclaimed himself Emperor Napoleon III.* History seemed about to repeat itself.

The Italian Revolution of 1848

History seemed also to be repeating itself in Italy. Revolution had broken out in Sicily as early as January 1848. From there it had spread north. By the middle of March, most of the Italian states except Lombardy and Venetia had won liberal constitutions.

The origins of the Italian *Risorgimento* (meaning "resurrection") can be traced

*Napoleon I's son, known as Napoleon II, had never assumed the throne and had died in 1832.

back to the eighteenth century. The agitation for national liberation and unification had gained momentum during the Napoleonic period. But the hopes of Italian patriots and reformers, as we have seen, had been dashed repeatedly since 1815. Despite the failure of the uprisings of 1830, however, Italian intellectuals had continued making plans for the future of their country. Out of the maze of their projects, three main schemes had emerged: Giuseppe Mazzini, a noted Liberal and an ardent Italian nationalist, advocated the formation of a free, united, and republican Italy. Vincenzo Gioberti, a moderate Liberal and a priest, objected to the republican and centralizing tendencies of Mazzini and instead proposed a federated monarchy with a liberal constitution, headed by the pope. The election of a reputedly liberal pope, Pius IX, in 1846 gave special emphasis to Gioberti's proposals. A third scheme for the future of Italy looked forward to Italian unification under the leadership of the house of Piedmont-Sardinia. Here, then, were three different schemes for the liberation and unification of Italy. Each was tried, and each failed. The fact that there were several plans, rather than one, in part accounts for that failure.

With Austria the main obstacle to Italian unification, the outbreak of revolution in Vienna (see p. 563) naturally aided the Italian cause. As insurrections broke out in the Austrian provinces of Lombardy and Venetia, Charles Albert of Piedmont, in March 1848, gave way to popular pressure and declared war on Austria. Contingents from other Italian states joined the Piedmontese. Pius IX, however, could ill afford to support a war against Austria, the leading Catholic power of Europe. His neutrality and subsequent flight from Rome dashed the hopes of those who had looked to the pope as the leader of Italian liberation.

The war of Piedmont against Austria likewise ended in failure. The forces of Charles Albert were no match for the seasoned troops of the Austrian general Radetzky, especially after the Austrian government had succeeded in putting down its revolution at home. The final defeat of Charles Albert at Novara in March 1849 ended, for the time being,

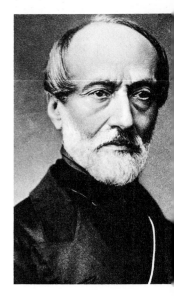

Giuseppe Mazzini (1805–72), Italian nationalist.

Detail of a Dutch caricature of 1852 showing Pope Pius IX removing his "savior's" mask and revealing his true face when he resumed power in 1849.

the chance of uniting Italy under the leadership of Piedmont-Sardinia.

Mazzini's alternative for the unification of Italy, the creation of a republic, also was given a brief chance. With Pius IX away from Rome, radicalism had a free hand. In February 1849 a constituent assembly proclaimed the Roman Republic, under the leadership of Mazzini, and with an army led by another hero of Italian unification, Giuseppe Garibaldi. But as Austria regained its position in northern Italy and as the troops of the ousted King Ferdinand II regained control of the Kingdom of the Two Sicilies, the Roman Republic became a liberal island in a sea of reaction. To make matters worse, Louis Napoleon, newly elected president of France, tried to ingratiate himself with his Catholic subjects by sending an expeditionary force against Rome. It defeated the forces of Garibaldi and thus ended the dream of a republican Italy.

The revolution in Italy had failed. It had done so chiefly because the Austrians had once again proved too strong and because the Italians had proved too little united. Piedmont, having been the only state to put up any fight, earned the leadership in Italian affairs. To rally the rest of Italy behind the national cause, the people had to be promised not only unification but political liberty as well. This the government of Piedmont, now under Victor Emmanuel II, realized. Alone among Italian states, Piedmont kept the liberal constitution that had been adopted during the revolution. It thus became the hope of Italian nationalists and liberals alike.

Revolutions
in the Habsburg Empire

In Italy, revolution had erupted before it did in France. But the outbreaks in Austria were directly touched off by the events in Paris. The Habsburg Empire had long been ripe for revolution. Its government was cumbersome and corrupt, and Metternich's efforts at reform had been of no avail. The main problem facing the Austrian Empire was its conglomeration of nationalities. Besides the Germans in Austria proper, there were

the Magyars in Hungary, the Czechs and Slovaks in Bohemia and Moravia, the Poles in Galicia, and the Italians in Lombardy and Venetia. None of these regions, moreover, was entirely inhabited by one nationality; almost everywhere the peoples just mentioned, together with Slovenes, Croats, Serbs, Ruthenians, and Rumanians, created a situation of utmost ethnic confusion. With the advent of nationalism, this situation endangered the very existence of the Habsburg Empire.

In addition to the demands of these subject peoples for some measure of autonomy, there was also a growing demand for governmental reforms in Austria proper. Industrial progress had swelled the ranks of the middle class and had created an urban proletariat, both of which now added their voices to the liberal protests of university professors and other intellectuals.

The news of the revolution in Paris, however, caused much more excitement among the subject nationalities than it did in Austria. There were some student demonstrations and some violence in Vienna, and a deputation of citizens asked for the resignation of Metternich. But he resigned under pressure from the imperial family rather than from the populace. With Metternich gone, events moved swiftly and smoothly. The emperor removed himself to Innsbruck, and the citizens of Vienna elected a National Assembly to draft a constitution. One of the Assembly's first acts was to lift the last feudal burdens from Austria's peasants, completing a process begun by Joseph II two generations earlier.

From Vienna, revolution spread to other parts of the Empire. The uprisings in Lombardy and Venetia have already been discussed (see p. 562). In Bohemia, except for some local unrest, things remained quiet until early in June of 1848. At that time, disturbances broke out in connection with the first Pan-Slav Congress in Prague, which proclaimed the solidarity of the Slavic peoples against the Germans. Popular demonstrations were quelled when Austria's military governor ordered the bombardment of Prague. This was a significant event, for it was the first major setback of revolution

Prince Metternich (*ca.* 1858). This photograph of the Austrian statesman was taken shortly before his death.

anywhere in Europe. In Hungary, meanwhile, the Austrian government had agreed to the March Laws, which guaranteed a large measure of self-government. Hungary also followed the Austrian example in abolishing the remains of feudalism. But while the Hungarians thus secured freedom for themselves, they refused to grant the same freedom to the Croats within their own borders. Austria could thus play one nationality against the other. In September 1848, Croatian forces with Austrian backing invaded Hungary.

With imperial armies scoring successes against the revolutionaries in Bohemia, Hungary, and Lombardy, the tide of revolution in the Austrian Empire was definitely turning. A second, more radical outbreak in Vienna in October 1848 was soon put down. The Austrian government was now entrusted to Prince Felix Schwarzenberg, a strong-willed reactionary who urged the emperor, Ferdinand I, to resign in favor of his nephew, Francis Joseph. In March 1849 Schwarzenberg dissolved the National Assembly and imposed his own centralized constitution on the whole Empire.

By early spring of 1849 the Austrian government was again in control everywhere except in Hungary. At this point Francis Joseph accepted the offer of Nicholas I of Russia to help put down the Hungarians. The tsar was motivated by feelings of monarchical solidarity and by the fear that revolution might spread to the Danubian principalities and Poland. Hungarian resistance was finally crushed by the joint invasion of Russian and Austrian forces and by simultaneous uprisings among the Slavic peoples of southern Hungary. By mid-August of 1849 Austria was once again in control of its own house.

The "Germanies" in Revolt

The victory of reaction in Austria, as we have seen, affected the fate of revolution in Italy. It had a similar effect in Germany. There the chances for the success of revolution actually seemed most favorable. Unlike Austria, Germany did not suffer from ethnic disunity, nor was there any need to expel a foreign power, as there was in Italy. The failure of the revolution was due to many causes, most important among them the division of the country into many separate states and the general apathy of the population. The majority of Germans seemed content to lead a life of modest comfort and to pursue cultural rather than political interests.

Still, there was enough ferment among German intellectuals to keep alive the agitation for a united and liberal Germany. These aims also found support among the growing industrial middle class. The formation of a German customs union, or *Zollverein*, had eased the movement of goods throughout Germany and thus aided both commerce and industry. But industrialization had also brought many hardships, especially to the artisans. Another discontented group were the peasants in eastern Germany. Since their liberation from serfdom, they were often unable to make a living on their small holdings and instead had to become agricultural or industrial laborers. This economic discontent, which became especially strong during the 1840s, added a new dimension to the liberal and national aims of the German intellectuals. Had the revolutionary leaders understood and utilized this discontent, the results of the revolutions might have been different.

The first German uprising occurred in Bavaria before the events in France. But only with the news from Paris did the revolutions become general. Because Prussia, next to Austria, played the leading role in the German Confederation, events in Berlin were watched with particular interest. Prussia, since 1840, had

been ruled by the brilliant but unstable Frederick William IV. The new king started out with a series of liberal reforms, but his liberalism, like that of Alexander I, was largely a pose. When the revolution came to Berlin in March 1848, Frederick William was easily frightened into appointing a liberal ministry and agreeing to a constituent assembly. But the old regime in Prussia was not really beaten, especially since the Prussian army had remained intact. While middle-class delegates were drawing up a liberal constitution, the lower classes were agitating for more drastic changes—including universal

Carl Schurz's Recollections of 1848

One morning toward the end of February, 1848, I sat quietly in my attic chamber, working hard at the tragedy of "Ulrich von Hutten," when suddenly a friend rushed breathlessly into the room, exclaiming: "What, you sitting here! Do you not know what has happened?"

"No; what?"

"The French have driven away Louis Philippe and proclaimed the Republic."

I threw down my pen—and that was the end of "Ulrich von Hutten." I never touched the manuscript again. We tore down the stairs, into the street, to the market-square, the accustomed meeting-place for all the student societies after their midday dinner. Although it was still forenoon, the market was already crowded with young men talking excitedly. . . . In these conversations . . . certain ideas and catchwords worked themselves to the surface, which expressed more or less the feelings of the people. Now had arrived in Germany the day for the establishment of "German Unity" and the founding of a great, powerful national German Empire. First in line the convocation of a national parliament; then the demands for civil rights and liberties, free speech, free press, the right of free assembly, equality before the law, a freely elected representation of the people with legislative power, responsibility of ministers, self-government of the communes, the right of the people to carry arms, the formation of a civic guard with elective officers, and so on—in short, that which was called a "constitutional form of government on a broad democratic basis." Republican ideas were at first only sparingly expressed. But the word "democracy" was soon on all tongues, and many, too, thought it a matter of course that if the princes should try to withhold from the people the rights and liberties demanded, force would take the place of mere petition. . . . We were profoundly, solemnly in earnest.

From *The Reminiscences of Carl Schurz*, 3 vols. (New York: McClure, 1907-08), Vol. I, pp. 111-13, as quoted in Geoffrey Bruun, *Revolution and Reaction, 1848-1852* (New York: Van Nostrand, 1958), pp. 125-27.

The Chartist Petition of 1848

The Committee on Public Petitions [of the House of Commons] strongly feel the right of petition; consider the exercise of it as one of the most important privileges of the subjects of the realm; and feel the necessity of preserving the exercise of such privilege from abuse.

And, having also a due regard to the importance of the very numerously signed petition forming the subject of the present report, they feel bound to represent to the House, that in the matter of signatures there has been, in their opinion, a gross abuse of that privilege.

The honorable Member for Nottingham stated, on presenting the petition in question to the House, that 5,706,000 signatures were attached to it. Upon a most careful examination, . . . the number of signatures has been ascertained to be 1,975,496. It is further evident to your Committee, that on numerous consecutive sheets the signatures are in one and the same handwriting. Your Committee have also observed the names of distinguished individuals attached to the petition, who cannot be supposed to have concurred in its prayer, and as little to have subscribed it: amongst such occur the names of Her Majesty in one place, as Victoria Rex, April 1; the Duke of Wellington, K. G.; Sir Robert Peel, etc., etc., etc.

In addition to this species of abuse, your Committee have observed another equally in derogation of the just value of petitions—namely, the insertion of names which are obviously altogether fictitious, such as "No Cheese," "Pugnose," "Flatnose," etc. . . .

From *The Annual Register for 1848* (London, 1849), pp. 126–27, as quoted in Geoffrey Bruun, *Revolution and Reaction, 1848–1852* (New York: Van Nostrand, 1958), pp. 184–85.

---

people. The majority were professional people, including many professors. Deliberations dragged on for almost a year. The main argument developed over the question of whether or not the new German state should be under the leadership of and include Austria. The *grossdeutsch* (greater-German) faction, which favored this solution, was opposed by the *kleindeutsch* (small-German) group, which advocated the exclusion of Austria and the leadership of Prussia. The issue resolved itself when the victory of reaction in Vienna disqualified Austria in the eyes of German liberals.

The Frankfurt Constitution, which was finally adopted in March 1849, called for a constitutional monarchy with a parliament elected by universal male suffrage. The Frankfurt Parliament elected Frederick William IV as "Emperor of the Germans." But the king of Prussia refused a crown that was offered him by the people. He would accept it only from his fellow princes. With reaction everywhere triumphant, Frederick William's refusal all but finished the revolution in Germany. There were some last flashes of violence in the smaller states, but Prussian troops soon restored order. The attempt of the German people to build a unified nation under a government of their own choosing had failed.

England in the Age of Reform

The one country in Europe where many people had expected revolution to strike first was Great Britain. And yet, except for a brief flare-up in Ireland, the British Isles proved the major exception to the rule of revolution in western Europe. The Reform Bill of 1832 had been merely the most prominent of a large series of reforms. Most important among these was the establishment of free trade. Britain's merchants and industrialists had long agitated against import duties, but tariffs had been defended on the grounds that the government needed the income. With the reintroduction of the income tax in 1842, however, that argument lost ground, and protective tariffs were gradually abolished. Only in agriculture did they survive. To fight for the abolition of

---

suffrage, socialism, and even a republic. These radical demands drove the middle class, including the well-to-do peasants, back into the arms of reaction. When news reached Berlin in the fall of 1848 that the Austrian government was successfully moving against the revolution in Vienna, Frederick William dissolved the Constituent Assembly and later imposed his own constitution. By the end of 1848, the revolution in Prussia had been defeated.

But German liberals did not give up hope. Since spring, another assembly had been in session in Frankfurt to draft a constitution for all of Germany, including Austria, rather than for Prussia alone. Its delegates had been elected by the

agricultural tariffs, the Anti-Corn Law League had been formed in 1839. In 1846 its relentless pressure succeeded, and the Corn Laws were repealed.

Along with this agitation for economic freedom, there also arose during the 1830s a movement for greater political freedom. The Reform Bill of 1832 had been a disappointment to the lower classes, among whom the so-called Chartist Movement gained its major support. The movement took its name from the "People's Charter" of 1838, drawn up by a group of radical reformers and calling for a further democratization of Parliament. But this radical program met heavy opposition, and Parliament repeatedly turned down petitions based on the Charter. By 1848 discontent had mounted to such a pitch that there seemed to be a real threat of revolution. The Chartists prepared a "monster petition" demanding universal manhood suffrage and other political reforms, with some 6 million signatures (many of them false), and started a demonstration to present it to Parliament. When it began to rain, however, the demonstrators let themselves be dispersed peacefully. The truth of the matter is that a good deal of the discontent in the Chartist Movement was economic, and had disappeared with the repeal of the Corn Laws and a general increase in prosperity. Henceforth workers were turning more and more to trade unionism as a means of improving their status. England thus remained a quiet haven of refuge in the upheavals of 1848, giving asylum to refugees from revolution and reaction alike, including Metternich as well as Marx. Many of the revolutionaries, however, preferred to leave Europe altogether; the United States received them with open arms.

Why Did the Revolutions of 1848 Fail?

The revolutions of 1848 thus had failed everywhere. They had done so because of weaknesses in the revolutionary camp, because of the continued strength of the forces of reaction, and because the economic conditions that helped bring on the revolutions did not last. The economic picture in many countries improved, despite the unsettling effect of revolution.

The weakness of the revolutionaries was due partly to the lack of well-defined programs or else the existence of too many different programs and to the indecision of their leaders. This indecision led to waste of valuable time, which the reactionaries used to prepare for counterrevolution. But the primary weakness of the revolutionaries was lack of widespread popular support outside the cities. The middle class, in most countries, did not really want a revolution. It preferred to achieve its aims through reform, as had been done in England. But once revolution came, sometimes by spontaneous combustion, the middle class tried to reap its benefits. Much of the actual fighting in the revolutions was done by the workers, and the workers wanted more than limited democracy for the well-to-do. They wanted complete democracy, political and, in some cases, economic as well. To the middle class, these demands, especially the socialist ones, not only threatened its political predominance but its very existence. This bourgeois fear of a "red peril" was exaggerated. Despite the incendiary language of *The Communist Manifesto* (which appeared in 1848; see p. 587), the majority of the lower class were perfectly ready

Barricade in Milan, from the *Leipziger Illustrierte Zeitung* (1848).

to follow the leadership of the middle class if that would improve their condition. But the middle class did not live up to these lower-class expectations; as a result the lower class more and more came to distrust the men it had helped gain power.

Not only was there disunity among the revolutionary forces within each country, there was no attempt to coordinate the revolutions in different countries. While the forces of reaction worked together, there was little collaboration among the revolutionaries. On the contrary, almost everywhere their programs showed traces of a selfish nationalism. There was nationalism behind France's talk of spreading the blessings of revolution. The Germans wanted to unite all German-speaking peoples, but they also wanted to lord it over the Poles, and they actually carried on a brief war against the Danes. The Poles wanted to be liberated and united, but they did not want to see the Ukrainians win the same benefits. And the Hungarians behaved every bit as selfishly toward the Croats as the Austrians did toward the Hungarians.

Yet, though reaction won a full victory in 1849, the revolutions of 1848 had not been entirely in vain. Some changes for the better were preserved. In France political power had been somewhat broadened. In Italy some leaders had learned useful lessons of how to go about achieving unification. In Austria the abolition of serfdom during the revolution could not be undone, and Metternich did not return to power. Even in Germany, where the failure of revolution probably had more tragic long-range consequences than anywhere else, a few lasting gains were made.

The mid-century revolutions came at a turning point in European history. Up to this time, the economy of the Continent had still been largely agrarian. From now on, industrialization was really to take hold. Metternich, the dominant figure after 1815, had in many ways been a relic of the eighteenth century. The future was to belong to a different, more modern, type of politician. Two forces emerged from the revolutions that henceforth were to dominate the history of Europe—nationalism and socialism. Neither was new, but both had lost much of their earlier idealism and utopianism. Nationalism and socialism respectively became the main issues in the struggle of nation against nation and class against class.

Suggestions for Further Reading

Note: Asterisk denotes a book available in paperback edition.

General The most stimulating introduction to the half-century following the French Revolution is E. J. Hobsbawm, *The Age of Revolution, 1789–1848** (1962). G. F. E. Rudé, *Debate on Europe, 1815–1850** (1972), is a critical discussion of the period's historiography. J. L. Talmon, *Romanticism and Revolt: Europe 1815–1848** (1967), emphasizes ideas rather than social and economic forces. Good detailed treatments are F. A. Artz, *Reaction and Revolution, 1814–1832** (1934), and W. L. Langer, *Political and Social Upheaval, 1832–1852** (1969). The book by J. Droz, *Europe between Revolutions, 1815–1848* (1968), is a new appraisal by a noted French social historian; see also P. Stearns, *European Society in Upheaval: Social History since 1800** (1967). Among national histories, the following stand out: É. Halévy, *History of the English People in the Nineteenth Century,** Vols. II and III (1926); T. S. Hamerow, *Restoration, Revolution, Reaction: Economics and Politics in Germany, 1815–1871** (1958); A. J. P. Taylor, *The Hapsburg Monarchy, 1809–1918** (1948); A. Cobban, *A History of Modern France,** Vol. II (1957); A. J. Whyte, *The Evolution of Modern Italy, 1715–1920** (1944); and R. Pipes, *Russia under the Old Regime** (1975). The emergence of liberalism is traced in G. Ruggiero, *History of European Liberalism** (1927), and H. J. Laski, *The Rise of European Liberalism* (1936). Some standard works on nationalism are C. J. H. Hayes, *The Historical Evolution of Modern Nationalism* (1931), H. Kohn, *The Idea of Nationalism** (1944), and by the same author, *Prophets and Peoples: Studies in Nineteenth-Century Nationalism* (1946). More recent studies are B. C. Shafer, *Nationalism: Myth and Reality** (1955), and L. L. Snyder, *Varieties of Nationalism: A Comparative Study* (1976).

The Restoration of the Old Order

The standard works on the diplomatic settlements after Napoleon are C. K. Webster, *The Foreign Policy of Castlereagh, 1812–1822,* 2 vols. (1931) and *The Congress of Vienna, 1814–1815** (1934). H. Nicolson, *The Congress of Vienna: A Study in Allied Unity, 1812–1822** (1946), is briefer and makes delightful reading. Good biographies of the leading figures at Vienna are: G. de Bertier de Sauvigny, *Metternich and His Times* (1962); C. Brinton, *The Lives of Talleyrand** (1936); A. Palmer, *Alexander I, Tsar of War and Peace* (1974); and J. C. Bartlett, *Castlereagh* (1967). See also P. K. Grimsted, *The Foreign Ministers of Alexander I* (1969). On Castlereagh's successors, see H. W. V. Temperley, *The Foreign Policy of Canning, 1822–1827* (1925), and C. K. Webster, *The Foreign Policy of Palmerston, 1830–1841,* 2 vols. (1951). The diplomatic aftermath of the Congress of Vienna is discussed in H. G. Schenk, *The Aftermath of the Napoleonic Wars: The Concert of Europe* (1947); P. W. Schroeder, *Metternich's Diplomacy at Its Zenith, 1820–1823* (1962); and H. A. Kissinger, *A World Restored** (1957). The situation arising from the revolutions in Latin America is summed up in D. Perkins, *Hands Off! A History of the Monroe Doctrine** (1941). See also B. Perkins, *Castlereagh and Adams: England and the United States, 1812–1823* (1964).

Romanticism

A good introduction to the complexities of Romanticism is J. B. Halsted, ed., *Romanticism** (1965). Another useful collection is H. E. Hugo, ed., *The Romantic Reader* (1957). I. Babbitt, *Rousseau and Romanticism** (1919), is a classic indictment. See also W. J. Bate, *From Classic to Romantic** (1946), and J. Barzun, *Classic, Romantic and Modern** (1961). The impact of Romanticism on political thought is treated in the works on nationalism cited above, as well as in H. S. Reiss, *The Political Thought of the German Romantics* (1955); C. Brinton, *The Political Ideas of the English Romanticists** (1926); and R. H. Soltau, *French Political Thought of the Nineteenth Century* (1931). See also G. D. O'Brien, *Hegel on Reason and History* (1975). On conservatism, see R. J. S. Hoffman and P. Levack, eds., *Burke's Politics* (1949); E. L. Woodward, *Three Studies in European Conservatism* (1929); and K. Epstein, *The Genesis of German Conservatism** (1966).

Revolutions Before 1848

Good accounts of the numerous upheavals in the 1820s and 1830s may be found in the general histories cited above. For events in France, see also J. Plamenatz, *The Revolutionary Movement in France, 1815–1871* (1952); R. J. Bezucha, *The Lyon Uprising of 1834: Social and Political Conflict in the Early July Monarchy* (1974); and G. de Bertier de Sauvigny's proroyalist *The Bourbon Restoration* (1966). Biographies of leading figures include D. W. Johnson's *Guizot* (1963), and T. E. B. Howarth's *Citizen King* (1961), on Louis Philippe. For the Greek revolution, see C. M. Woodhouse, *The Greek War of Independence* (1952). Russia's Decembrist Revolt is the subject of A. G. Mazour, *The First Russian Revolution, 1825** (1937). On events in Belgium and Poland, see J. A. Betley, *Belgium and Poland in International Relations, 1830–1831* (1960). The general subject of the disintegrating Ottoman Empire is admirably summarized in M. S. Anderson, *The Eastern Question, 1774–1923** (1966). Much has been written on parliamentary and social reforms in Great Britain. Especially recommended are N. Gash, *Politics in the Age of Peel* (1953); M. Brock, *The Great Reform Act** (1973); A. Briggs, ed., *Chartist Studies* (1960); J. T. Ward, *Chartism* (1973); and D. Owen, *English Philanthropy, 1660–1960* (1964). On social unrest, see R. J. White, *Waterloo to Peterloo* (1957), and G. F. E. Rudé, *The Crowd in History 1730–1848** (1964), which deals with both England and France.

The Revolutions of 1848

Among several attempts to present a comprehensive picture of these confusing events, the most successful are P. Robertson, *Revolutions of 1848: A Social History** (1952), and, more recently, P. N. Stearns, *1848: The Revolutionary Tide in Europe** (1974). G. Bruun, *Revolution and Reaction, 1848–1852** (1958), gives a brief introduction, supplemented by documents. R. Postgate, *Story of a Year: 1848** (1955), describes vividly the revolutions as seen from England. A. Whitridge, *Men in Crisis: The Revolutions of 1848* (1949), concentrates on a few leading figures in various countries. V. Valentin, *1848: Chapters in German History* (1940), is learned but fragmentary. On France, see R. Price, ed., *Revolution and Reaction: 1848 and the Second French Republic* (1976). Among specialized works on various aspects of the revolutions, the following deserve mention: D. C. McKay, *The National Workshops: A Study in the French Revolution of 1848* (1933); J. Blum, *Noble Landowners and Agriculture in Austria, 1814–1848** (1948); A. J. P. Taylor, *The Italian Problem in European Diplomacy, 1847–1849* (1939); L. B. Namier, *1848: The Revolution of the Intellectuals** (1947); and L. C. Jennings, *France and Europe in 1848: A Study of French Foreign Affairs in Time of Crisis* (1973).

25 The Coming of the Industrial Age

Much of the political tension in Europe during the first half of the nineteenth century was a manifestation of underlying economic unrest caused by the gradual transformation of Europe's economy from agriculture to industry. This change is usually dated from the middle of the eighteenth century, but it did not become pronounced until after 1815. From then on it gathered momentum, first in England and later on the Continent, until by the end of the nineteenth century most of western Europe had become industrialized.

This industrialization of society is often referred to as the "Industrial Revolution." But this term has come in for some criticism. The change from agriculture to industry, it seems, was a gradual process of evolution rather than the sudden change implied in the term *revolution*. When one considers the total effect of this transformation from agriculture to industry, however, the term *revolution* seems more than justified. By vastly improving the means of communication, industrialization has made the world seem much smaller; by enabling more people to make a living, it has made the world much more crowded; and by raising the standard of living, it has made life infinitely more comfortable. Industrialization has elevated some nations that heretofore were insignificant and has demoted others that did not have the manpower or the raw materials that industry requires. Industrialization has dissolved a rigid and hierarchical order of society and has substituted a fluid and egalitarian mass society.

Not all these changes have necessarily been for the better. While industry created wealth for some, it merely emphasized the poverty of others. While it made nations and individuals more dependent on one another, it also increased their rivalry for a share of the riches the world has to offer. The preoccupation of modern industrial society with material well-being has diverted mankind from more spiritual concerns. But while one may wonder how beneficial the change from agriculture to industry has been in some areas, about the magnitude of that change there can be no doubt.

Coke smelting on the coal-fields of Upper Silesia in Germany, lithograph made in 1841.

THE ROOTS OF MODERN INDUSTRIALISM

Modern industrialism, quite simply, is the mass production of goods by means of machines driven by generated power and set up in factories. There had been few mechanical inventions before the eighteenth century. During the Middle Ages, consumer goods had been produced by hand and for local consumption. With the Age of Discovery and the "Commercial Revolution" in the sixteenth century, the rate of production had increased to provide goods for export. Since the small artisan did not have the capital to buy large quantities of raw materials, to produce a large stock, and to sell it in a distant market, a class of wealthy capitalists and merchants began to inject themselves into the production process. They supplied the artisan with raw materials and sometimes with tools, and they took over the finished product to sell at a profit. This "domestic," or "putting-out," system had become quite common by the seventeenth century. There were even a few simple machines, but they still had to be operated by humans or animals, or by the natural power of wind or water. During the eighteenth century the trend toward large-scale production was accelerated by numerous mechanical inventions that increased the speed and thus the volume of production. The most important step came with the application of steam power to these new machines. This step brought the decline of the domestic system and the gradual shift of production from home to factory.

It was no accident that modern industrialism should have had its start in the eighteenth century. The intellectual climate of the Enlightenment, its interest in science, and its emphasis on progress and the good life were particularly favorable to such a development. The beginnings of modern industrialism fall into the period after 1760, and the acceleration of industrialism was most pronounced in England. England's parliamentary government gave some voice to the rising commercial and industrial classes; it had large colonial holdings and far-flung commercial interests; it had a sound financial system and sufficient surplus capital; and it had an ample supply of basic raw materials and manpower. The manpower had been made available in part by drastic changes in British agriculture—an "Agricultural Revolution"—which converted farmers into laborers and materially increased Britain's food supply.

THE AGRICULTURAL REVOLUTION

Most of the land in Britain before the eighteenth century was still worked under the open-field system, which meant that the holdings of individual owners were scattered about in many strips, separated from those of other landholders by a double furrow. In addition, each landholder shared in the common pastures and woodlands of his community. This arrangement was of particular advantage to the small farmers and cottagers, who participated in the grazing and fueling rights of the "commons." But the open-field system was both inefficient and wasteful. The prevailing method of cultivation was still the medieval system of three-field rotation, under which one-third of the land remained fallow each year. Any attempt to change this routine by experimenting with new crops was impossible, since all strips in a given field had to be cultivated at the same time and planted with the same crop.

The "Enclosure Movement"

Beginning at the time of the Tudors in the sixteenth century, an "enclosure movement" had started in England, under which the scattered strips of individual owners were consolidated into compact holdings surrounded by fences or hedges. Enclosure meant a gain of usable land because it did away with the double furrows, and it made cultivation much easier. But since enclosure also entailed a division of the commons, it worked to the detriment of the small farmer, who thereby lost part of his livelihood. As the population of England increased, agricultural production for the general market rather than for local consumption became more profitable. The trend toward more efficient large-scale farming, and especially sheep raising, through enclosures therefore gained momentum. It reached its climax in the eighteenth century. Between 1702 and 1797, Parliament passed some 1776 enclosure acts affecting 3 million acres. In each case the larger landowner profited at the expense of the smaller farmer. Left with too little land of his own and deprived of his share in the commons, the small farmer had no choice but to become a tenant farmer or move to the cities. Many took the latter course, providing some of the manpower without which the rapid growth of Britain's industry could not have taken place.

The enclosure movement brought hardships to many people, but it brought a dramatic improvement in agriculture. Freed from the restrictions of collective cultivation, landowners were now able to try new methods and new crops. This enabled them to grow more food on the same amount of land. The improvement was such as to give substance to the term "Agricultural Revolution." Like its industrial counterpart, the Agricultural

The Age of Revolution, 1789–1848

Words are witnesses which often speak louder than documents. Let us consider a few English words which were invented, or gained their modern meanings, substantially in the period of sixty years with which this volume deals. They are such words as "industry," "industrialist," "factory," "middle class," "working class," "capitalism," and "socialism." They include "aristocracy" as well as "railway," "liberal" and "conservative" as political terms, "nationality," "scientist," and "engineer," "proletariat" and (economic) "crisis." "Utilitarian" and "statistics," "sociology," and several other names of modern sciences, "journalism" and "ideology," are all coinages or adaptations of this period. So are "strike" and "pauperism."

To imagine the modern world without these words (i.e., without the things and concepts for which they provide names) is to measure the profundity of the revolution which broke out between 1789 and 1848 and forms the greatest transformation in human history since the remote times when men invented agriculture and metallurgy, writing, the city and the state. This revolution has transformed, and continues to transform, the entire world.

From E. J. Hobsbawm, *The Age of Revolution, 1789–1848,* Mentor edition (New York: World, 1962), pp. 17–18.

Revolution at first was almost entirely restricted to Britain. Only with the advent of industrialization did the larger landholders on the Continent seriously begin to experiment with British methods. The small peasants, on the other hand, continued in their backward ways. As new industrial centers developed, new markets for agricultural produce opened up. Improvements in transportation, furthermore, facilitated marketing; and new scientific discoveries and the use of fertilizers brought larger crop yields. These and other developments brought renewed hope for western Europe's farmers, who were gradually being pushed to the wall by the rising industries and were beginning to feel the competition of the fertile agrarian lands of eastern Europe and America.

A result of the Agricultural Revolution: a German threshing machine of the 1850s.

THE BEGINNINGS OF INDUSTRIALIZATION

Inventions and the Rise of the Factory System

The early history of industrialization is related to the rise of mechanical inventions. There were few of these at first, but they multiplied as one discovery created the need for another. When John Kay invented his flying shuttle in 1733, enabling one weaver to do the work of two, the need arose for some new device that would speed up spinning. This demand was met in 1764 by James Hargreaves and his spinning jenny, which permitted the simultaneous spinning of eight or more threads. A few years later, Richard Arkwright devised the water frame, and in 1779 Samuel Crompton perfected the "mule," a hybrid that combined features of both Hargreaves' and Arkwright's inventions. These improvements in spinning in turn called for further improvements in weaving. In 1787 Edmund Cartwright patented a new power loom. After it was perfected, the demand for cotton increased. Cotton production received a boost when an American, Eli Whitney, in 1793 developed the cotton "gin," which speeded up and cut the cost of removing the cotton fiber from its boll. Almost all the early inventions were made in the cotton industry: it was a new industry, it had a large overseas market, and cotton lent itself particularly well to mechanical treatment.

Since most of the earlier devices were small, relatively inexpensive, and hand-operated, they could be used as part of the domestic system in the workers' cottages. Arkwright's water frame, however, was large and expensive, and it needed water power to operate. Arkwright, therefore, moved into the heart of the English textile region of Nottingham, where he opened the first spinning mill in 1771. By 1779 he was employing some three hundred workers who operated several thousand spindles. With this important innovation, the modern factory system had been born. Arkwright's example was soon followed by other manufacturers, especially as the steam engine became the major source of power for newer and larger machines.

The Steam Engine

Of all the inventions in the early years of industrialism, the steam engine was the most important. Until the advent of electricity it remained the chief source of power, and even in our atomic age its usefulness has not entirely ended. The development of the steam engine is

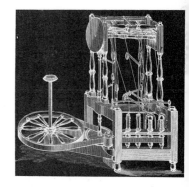

Arkwright's water frame, patented in 1769. It was the first self-acting machine to spin threads fine and hard enough for a weaver to use as the cloth warp.

closely related to the two industries that ultimately proved basic to all modern economic progress—coal and iron. At the beginning of the eighteenth century the smelting of iron was still done by charcoal. The depletion of Britain's wood supply, however, and the discovery, shortly after 1700, of a process for smelting iron with coke, shifted the emphasis to coal. The mining of coal was made considerably easier by a primitive steam engine, developed by Thomas Newcomen, that was used to pump water from the coal mines. This early eighteenth-century engine was a long way from the kind of steam engine that could be used to run other machines. The credit for developing such an engine belongs to the Scotsman James Watt, who patented his first steam engine in 1769. By 1800 some three hundred steam engines were at work in England, mostly in the cotton industry. The use of steam engines, of course, further increased the need for coal and iron. Improvements in iron production, on the other hand, in turn led to improvements in the making of steam engines. The interaction of one discovery with another continued to be a major characteristic of industrial development.

Early Industry on the Continent

Prior to 1815 the "Industrial Revolution," for reasons already stated, was chiefly a British phenomenon. An economic revival in France after 1763, helping to make up for the loss of the French colonies to Britain, had been interrupted by the French Revolution. But the Continental System of Napoleon, which excluded British goods from the Continent, had proved most beneficial to French industry.

In the rest of Europe there were not even the beginnings of modern industrialization. Economic development in Germany was retarded by political disunity. The rich coal fields of the Ruhr and Silesia were hardly worked before 1815, and what little industry there was, especially in textiles, still operated under the "putting-out" system. Russia, Italy, and Austria were almost wholly agrarian. Even

after 1815, continental industries were slow to assert themselves against British competition. It was only after the advent of the railroad in the 1830s that the situation began to improve.

THE RAILWAY AGE

Transportation in the Eighteenth Century

Industrial development was closely related to the improvement of transportation. England again had a special advantage in being able to use coastal shipping for the movement of bulky goods. But like any other country it depended on roads and canals for inland transportation. As industrialization increased the need for transport and travel, the construction of toll roads and canals became a profitable business. England added thousands of miles to its system of roads and canals during the eighteenth century, and France before the Revolution had the finest highway system in Europe. Napoleon improved the situation further by pushing highways far into Germany and the Netherlands. In eastern Europe, however, paved roads were rare. Prussia's kings constructed canals and improved riverways, but the movement of goods was hampered by innumerable tolls and tariffs. Farther east, dirt roads that regularly turned to mud and rivers that ran shallow during the summer and froze during the winter were the only arteries of communication.

The Advent of the Railroad

The railroad, which was to change all this, again had its start in England. Well before 1800, horse-drawn carts, moving first on wooden and later on iron rails, had been used to haul coal and iron. During the 1820s there were several hundred miles of such "rail ways." The problem of providing a faster means of locomotion was solved by putting the steam engine on wheels. The first commercial steam railroad was opened between Stockton and Darlington in 1825. By 1840 Britain had some eight hundred miles of track, and by 1850 it had more

The Railway King, a Victorian caricature.

The opening of the Stockton–Darlington Railway on September 27, 1825; drawing by J. R. Brown.

than six thousand. On the Continent, the railroad was slower in taking hold. The first railroad in France was opened in 1837, and by the middle of the century there were two thousand miles of track. Germany then had three thousand miles, Austria one thousand miles, and Italy and Russia had merely a few fragmentary lines.

The economic impact of the railroad, of course, was overwhelming. Here was an entirely new industry, answering a universal need, employing thousands of people, offering unprecedented opportunities for investment, and introducing greater speed into all industrial and commercial transactions. England, already far ahead of the Continent in economic development, took the Railway Age pretty much in stride. England had been the workshop of the world for some time, and there seemed to be no prospect that it would cease to be. Railroad construction vastly increased the demand for coal and iron, and England continued to lead the world in the production of both.

England also maintained its lead in shipping. The shipping industry was slow to feel the impact of steam. Even though Robert Fulton's steamboat had

made its first successful trip on the Hudson River in 1807, it was not until 1840 that Samuel Cunard established the first transatlantic steamer line. Even then the inefficiency of marine engines and the large amounts of coal needed for long voyages retarded the development of steamship service. Well into the second half of the nineteenth century the fast clipper ship remained the chief means of ocean transport.

There were other important innovations and inventions in the early nineteenth century, with England again leading the way. The introduction of the penny post in 1840 helped business and private individuals alike. The telegraph, invented by the American Samuel Morse, was first used extensively by Julius Reuter's news agency, which was established in 1851, the same year in which the first submarine cable was laid under the English Channel. A reduction in the stamp tax in 1836 substantially lowered the price of newspapers, and by the middle of the century the circulation of the British press had risen more than threefold. The communication of news and ideas kept pace with the faster movements of goods and persons.

The "Crystal Palace" in London, which housed the Great Exhibition of 1851.

The Railway Age on the Continent

In May 1851 the "Great Exhibition of the Works of Industry of All Nations" opened in London's "Crystal Palace." This first "world's fair" was dramatic proof of Britain's industrial world leadership, but it also showed that other nations were beginning to profit from its example. The country in which industrialization made the most rapid progress was little Belgium. An ample supply of coal and a skilled labor force were the chief reasons, but technical aid by British engineers and investment of British capital also helped.

In France, economic development was much slower. The French had lost some of their best coal mines to Belgium in 1815; and while European populations were increasing, the French birth rate, by the middle of the century, had actually begun to decline. Still, with all the encouragement given to commerce and industry by the July Monarchy, the middle class could not help but prosper. Pig iron production, generally considered an index of industrial development, increased fourfold in France during the thirty years after 1825; but it was still only one-quarter that of Great Britain. While England's population by the middle of the century was more than half urban, France remained predominantly rural. This made large imports of food unnecessary and accounted for a self-contained domestic market.

In both Italy and Germany political disunity slowed down economic growth. Industry in northern Italy remained insignificant until later in the century. In Germany, the *Zollverein* (see p. 565) did much to aid industrial development. Machines, imported from England, were being used more and more in the textile industry. With the sinking of the first deep pit in the Ruhr in 1841, coal production began in earnest. Even so, France, despite much slimmer resources, still produced more coal than Germany. As for pig iron, the total German output in 1855 was only half that of France. Railroad construction in Germany made rapid progress during the 1840s. The absence of natural obstacles kept construction costs far below those of Great Britain. It was the progress in railroad building that gave some inkling of the tremendous economic vitality of the German people, which was merely awaiting political unification to assert itself.

Beyond western and central Europe, industrialization had made hardly any headway by 1850. Austria and Russia were still predominantly agrarian. Industrial development depended first and foremost on an abundant supply of free labor. This supply did not exist in Austria until after the last feudal restrictions were abolished in 1849, and in Russia it had to wait until the abolition of serfdom in 1861. Outside Europe only the United States was showing signs of industrialization. By 1850 New England had become largely industrialized, but the total output of American industry was still behind that of France and far behind that of Britain. Like Germany, America was to become a leading industrial power only toward the end of the century.

THE SOCIAL EFFECTS OF INDUSTRIALIZATION

The beginnings of modern industrialization in the eighteenth century appeared to bear out the belief of the Enlightenment that human reason and ingenuity had the power to perfect the world. The invention of labor-saving machines promised to transform man from a beast of burden into a creature of leisure. But that promise soon began to fade. The "Industrial Revolution," in the beginning at least, benefited only a minority, the middle class, while it brought utmost misery and destitution to the growing urban working class. It was only after industrialization had outgrown its infancy that its blessings came to be shared by more and more people.

Population Growth

Many of the early difficulties of industrialization were due to the unsettling effects that the tremendous population growth had on European society. Between 1815 and 1914, the population of Europe increased more than twofold, from 200 million to 460 million. Another 40 million Europeans during this time emigrated to other parts of the world, especially the United States. The rate of growth differed from country to country. It was largest in Russia, less in England and Germany, and least in France. Population growth was probably due less to an increase in the birth rate than to a decrease in the death rate. This decrease had many causes: improvements in medicine and public sanitation, absence of major wars, greater efficiency in government and administration, the revolution in agriculture leading to better diets and more ample food supplies, and, most important, the acceleration of industrial development. Industry provided the means whereby more people could live, and the increase of population, in turn, supplied the necessary industrial labor force and swelled the ranks of consumers. The growth of population and the increasing industrialization of society thus acted on and served to stimulate each other.

Urbanization and Working-Class Misery

With the increase in population and the growth of industry there came a further important change in European society—the movement of people from the country to the city. Large-scale urbanization had been virtually unknown before the early nineteenth century. But as

Life in the Slums

It is impossible to give a proper representation of the wretched state of many of the inhabitants of the indigent class, situated in the confined streets . . . where each small, ill ventilated apartment of the house contained a family with lodgers in number from seven to nine, and seldom more than two beds for the whole. The want of convenient offices in the neighborhood is attended with many very unpleasant circumstances, as it induces the lazy inmates to make use of chamber utensils, which are suffered to remain in the most offensive state for several days, and are then emptied out of the windows. The writer had occasion a short time ago to visit a person ill of the cholera; his lodgings were in a room of a miserable house situated in the very filthiest part of Pipewellgate, divided into six apartments, and occupied by different families to the number of 26 persons in all. The room contained three wretched beds with two persons sleeping in each; it measured about 12 feet in length and 7 in breadth, and its greatest height would not admit of a person's standing erect; it received light from a small window, the sash of which was fixed. Two of the number lay ill of the cholera, and the rest appeared afraid of the admission of pure air, having carefully closed up the broken panes with plugs of old linen.

From "Report . . . from the Poor Law Commissioners on . . . the Sanitary Conditions of the Labouring Population of Great Britain," 1842, pp. 21–22.

Close, No. 118 High Street, Glasgow (1868–77).

Children working in a coal mine, illustration from the Shaftesbury Report (1842). The evidence presented in this report brought about the Coal Mines Act of 1842 and subsequent measures to alleviate industrial abuse.

Child Labor

PRO

I have visited many factories, both in Manchester and in the surrounding districts, during a period of several months, entering the spinning rooms unexpectedly, and often alone, at different times of the day, and I never saw a single instance of corporal chastisement inflicted on a child, nor indeed did I ever see children in ill-humor. They seemed to be always cheerful and alert, taking pleasure in the light play of their muscles—enjoying the mobility natural to their age. The scene of industry, so far from exciting sad emotions in my mind, was always exhilarating. . . . The work of these lively elves seemed to resemble a sport, in which habit gave them a pleasing dexterity. . . . As to exhaustion by the day's work, they evinced no trace of it on emerging from the mill in the evening; for they immediately began to skip about any neighboring playground, and to commence their little amusements with the same alacrity as boys issuing from a school.

CON

The report of the Central Commission relates that the manufacturers began to employ children rarely of five years, often of six, very often of seven, usually of eight to nine years; that the working-day often lasted fourteen to sixteen hours, exclusive of meals and intervals; that the manufacturers permitted overlookers to flog and maltreat children, and often took an active part in so doing themselves. One case is related of a Scotch manufacturer who rode after a sixteen years old runaway, forced him to return running before the employer as fast as the master's horse trotted, and beat him the whole way with a long whip.

From Andrew Ure, *The Philosophy of Manufactures,* 3rd ed. (London: Bohn, 1961), p. 301; from Friedrich Engels, *The Condition of the Working Class in England in 1844* (New York: Lovell, 1887), p. 101.

workers began to flock to the mills, small villages grew into crowded towns and quiet towns into noisy cities. This sudden influx of people brought on wretched housing conditions. Teeming slums lacking in sanitation facilities turned into breeding places of disease, vice, and crime. There was as yet no effective municipal administration to cope with these novel problems, and the workers themselves were too poor to improve their condition.

Poor housing was not the only hardship afflicting the early workingman. Since mechanized industry required little skill, there was always an abundance of manpower, and wages were kept at a minimum. The average working day was between twelve and sixteen hours. But even this rarely yielded sufficient pay to support a worker's family, so that women and children had to work as well. Since they were more easily controlled and received less pay, they were much in demand. But women and children also suffered more than men did from the harsh conditions in factories and mines. No provisions were made for the workers' safety, and accidents resulting from machines to which they were not accustomed were frequent. There was no insurance against accidents, sickness, or old age. Furthermore, as more machines were used and as more efficient machines were invented, unemployment added to the workers' hardships. As industrialization spread to the Continent, so did the abuses that accompanied it. Conditions in Belgium and France were almost as bad as those in England.

Middle-Class Indifference

The attitude of much of the middle class toward the misery of the working class was one of indifference. The pioneers of modern industrialization, the new "captains of industry," were tough and ruthless men. They had to be if they wanted to survive, because competition was keen and risks were great. For every one of them who made good, there were several who fell by the wayside; the path of early industrialism was lined with bankruptcies. Economic booms burst;

wars closed markets; machinery broke down or became obsolete; and the agrarian supporters of the old order fought stubbornly against middle-class efforts to gain economic and political influence.

In order to understand the seemingly callous attitude of the middle class toward the hardships of the workers, we must consider briefly the middle-class philosophy of liberalism, which helped justify such selfish behavior. It was the belief in economic liberalism that prevented any drastic measures of social reform in the early part of the nineteenth century. The absence of such reform, in turn, led to various protests on behalf of the workers, of which Marxian socialism became the most effective.

MIDDLE-CLASS LIBERALISM

The term *liberalism* has assumed so many different meanings that it defies clear definition. In the early nineteenth century, however, liberalism had definite meaning and aims. A liberal was a person who believed in freedom—freedom of thought, freedom of religion, freedom from economic restrictions, freedom of trade, and freedom from the political injustices of the old regime. Most of these freedoms had already been demanded by the leaders of the Enlightenment. The *philosophes* held that every man had certain natural rights—life, liberty, and property. These rights the middle class had already demanded before and during the French Revolution, and it continued to demand them. But as time went on, its claims were based not on natural law, as they had been during the eighteenth century, but on the grounds that they were the most sensible and useful way of bringing about the "greatest happiness of the greatest number." This attitude of applying utility to political and social institutions is called "utilitarianism."

"Utilitarianism"

The key figure in the transformation of liberal thought from the Enlightenment to the nineteenth century was the English philosopher and reformer Jeremy Bentham (1748–1832), the founder of utilitarianism. Bentham was a rationalist, but the reasonableness of an institution for him did not depend on its conformity with natural law; it depended on its utility. How was this utility to be determined? Bentham wrote: "For everyone, his own pleasure and his own freedom from pain is the sole good, his own pain and his own unfreedom the sole evil. Man's happiness and welfare consist exclusively of pleasurable feelings and of freedom from pain." Translated into politics, this meant that the best government was the one that ensured the most pleasure and gave the least pain to the largest number of people. The type of government most likely to produce that effect, according to Bentham, was a democracy.

Bentham's philosophy found many disciples, especially in England. Many of the British reforms in the 1820s and 1830s were due to the agitation of the "Utilitarians," or "Philosophical Radicals." The most influential follower of Bentham was John Stuart Mill (1806–73). Mill was an active public servant, a leading reformer, and a prolific writer on a wide range of subjects. Among his most famous books was the essay *On Liberty* (1859). Its purpose, according to Mill, was to set forth the basic principle according to which relations between the individual and society, between the citizen and his government, should be regulated. That principle, Mill said, is "that the sole end for which mankind may interfere with the liberty of action of the individual is self-protection. The only purpose for which power can be rightfully exercised over any member of a civilized community, against his will, is to prevent harm to others." Here we have a categorical statement in favor of individual liberty. Mill based his plea not on natural law, as earlier advocates of individual freedom had done, but on utility. "I regard utility," he said, "as the ultimate appeal on all ethical questions."

Mill's emphasis on individual freedom, on the right of everyone to do as he saw fit as long as his actions did not conflict with society, had tremendous appeal to the middle-class industrialist and businessman of the nineteenth century. Here was a philosophy that

Jeremy Bentham (1748–1832), detail from a painting by J. Watts.

John Stuart Mill (1806–73).

frowned on any but the most necessary interference by the government in the affairs of the individual. "That government is best that governs least," and leaves the individual free to develop his own abilities. In another essay, *Considerations on Representative Government* (1861), Mill discussed the purpose of government in terms that sounded familiar to businessmen. "Government," he said, "is a problem to be worked like any other question of business. The first step is to define the purpose which governments are required to promote. The next is to inquire what form of government is best fitted to fulfill these purposes." In answer to the first question, what is the purpose of good government, Mill held that it was "to promote the virtue and intelligence of its people"; and in answer to the second question, what form of government is best, Mill, like Bentham, decided in favor of democracy.

Mill's belief in democracy was not shared by most members of the middle class. Nor were his proposals that the government should intervene to protect working children and improve housing and working conditions. Mill was highly critical of the economic injustices and inequities he found in his own society. He was especially concerned about the inequality that women still suffered in Victorian England. His essay *The Subjection of Women* (1869) was a ringing indictment of male chauvinism, and it became the bible of the women's suffrage movement. It remains as meaningful today as it was more than a century ago. There were already in Mill signs of a new type of liberalism that was ultimately to replace the dogmatic liberalism of the early nineteenth century (see p. 652). But even though Mill showed compassion for the fate of the underprivileged, his demand that the government leave the individual alone as much as possible clearly expressed the sentiments held by the majority of the middle class throughout the nineteenth century.

Liberalism in Politics

The middle class was primarily concerned with economic matters. (We shall see presently how liberalism developed

its own economic doctrine.) But the industrialists, merchants, and bankers also realized that economic freedom was of no value unless it was supplemented by political rights. The main guarantee of such rights in the early nineteenth century was seen in a written constitution, like that of the United States. The first document of this kind in recent European history had been the French Constitution of 1791. There were many others between 1812 and 1849. Most of these constitutions favored limited constitutional monarchy rather than true democracy. To ensure the predominance of the middle class, property qualifications for voting and for holding government office were part of all liberal constitutions. Anyone who found this restriction unjust was told that he needed only to work hard and improve his economic status in order to gain a share in the government. Only in their guarantee of individual liberty did these constitutions make some concession to the masses as well as to the classes. Freedom of the press, freedom of conscience, freedom of association, and freedom from arbitrary arrest—these were shared by rich and poor alike, at least theoretically. Workers who organized in order to improve their condition through collective bargaining, or socialists who used the press to call attention to existing injustices, would soon find out that the individual liberties guaranteed in the constitutions of the early nineteenth century did not apply to them.

The political ideal of early nineteenth-century liberalism was limited democracy. It has been aptly characterized as government of the wealthy, for the wealthy, by the wealthy. It was this ideal that motivated the middle class in the various revolutions discussed previously and that accounted for the widening rift between the middle and lower classes in these revolutions.

The "Classical Economists"

As for the economic philosophy of liberalism, its roots, too, went back to the eighteenth century. Its basic elements were already contained in the writings of Adam Smith (1723–90). This Glasgow

Portrait medal of Adam Smith (1797). The reverse side shows symbols of Smith's *Wealth of Nations*.

professor, in his *Wealth of Nations* (1776), had argued for a policy of individual self-interest, free from any government interference, as the surest road to economic prosperity for society as a whole. Smith had proposed this policy of laissez faire, of leaving things alone, in order to liberate the individual from the many governmental restrictions that had hampered economic progress under mercantilism. He was the first of several writers who are usually called the classical economists. These men, for the first time, formulated certain general economic laws that seemed to apply at all times and in all societies. The most prominent members of the group were Smith, Thomas Robert Malthus (1766–1834), and David Ricardo (1772–1823).

Malthus wrote his famous *Essay on the Principle of Population* in 1798. The book grew out of an argument he had with his father. The elder Malthus, a typical product of the eighteenth century, believed that if the world were reformed along rational lines there would be no end to human progress. Young Malthus did not agree. He pointed to the rapidly increasing population of western Europe in the late eighteenth and early nineteenth centuries as an insurmountable obstacle to progress. "The power of population," he wrote, "is indefinitely greater than the power in earth to produce subsistence for man. Population, when unchecked, increases in a geometrical ratio. Subsistence only increases in an arithmetical ratio." Here was the basic hypothesis of Malthusianism: people multiplied much more rapidly than the supply of food that was needed to keep them alive. Human misery, it seemed, was unavoidable. Poverty rather than progress was the normal state of human society.

Many objections have been raised to the dire prophecies of Malthus. Even in his own day, improvements in agriculture and the opening to cultivation of vast new regions in America and elsewhere were increasing the world's food supply. Since then there have been further changes, especially with scientific farming and the development of birth control, to help maintain the balance between population growth and food supply. In our own day, however, the threat of overpopulation has once again taken on a fearful reality, and the current "population explosion" seems to confirm Malthus' most dire predictions.

To the majority of people in the early nineteenth century, the warnings of Malthus also came as a shock. The future, which only recently had held such promise, now suddenly looked bleak; no wonder the new science of political economy was soon called the "dismal science." Yet it was not dismal to everyone—certainly not to the middle class. As industrialists were growing rich while workers were sinking into misery, some voices now favored a more equitable distribution of profits. Such proposals, however, could not stand up against Malthus' assertion that poverty was inevitable. The poor were already increasing much faster than the rich. Giving them more wages or charity, the middle class could argue, would only result in their having more children. The best solution was to keep the poor as poor as possible. Adam Smith had asked government to keep its hands off business; Malthus advocated a similar attitude of laissez faire in regard to social reform.

The pessimistic note that characterizes the teachings of Malthus is also found in the writings of David Ricardo. His basic work, *On the Principles of Politi-*

Thomas Robert Malthus (1766–1834).

Adam Smith on the Limitations of Government   1776

According to the system of natural liberty, the sovereign has only three duties to attend to; three duties of great importance, indeed, but plain and intelligible to common understandings: first, the duty of protecting the society from the violence and invasion of other independent societies; secondly, the duty of protecting, as far as possible, every member of the society from the injustice or oppression of every other member of it, or the duty of establishing an exact administration of justice; and, thirdly, the duty of erecting and maintaining certain public works and certain public institutions, which it can never be for the interest of the individual, or small number of individuals, to erect and maintain; because the profit could never repay the expense to any individual or small number of individuals, though it may frequently do much than repay it to a great society.

From Adam Smith, *An Inquiry into the Nature and Causes of the Wealth of Nations*, ed. by Edwin Cannan (New York: Random House, 1937), p. 651.

H. W. Egley, *In the Omnibus* (1859), captures the tone of the British nineteenth-century middle class.

wages were low and children had to work sixteen hours a day, that was unfortunate; but it was also, as Malthus and Ricardo had shown, inevitable. Attempts to change the situation through charity or legislation designed to improve wages and hours were opposed by middle-class liberals as interference with the beneficent principle of laissez faire.

Liberalism on the Continent

All the intellectual figures mentioned so far in this discussion of liberalism were British. Since England had a larger and more influential middle class than most continental countries, this is not surprising. But the writings of these men had a deep effect on continental liberalism as well. Adam Smith's *Wealth of Nations*, in particular, supplied most of the ammunition for the attacks of continental liberals on the economic restrictions and regulations of their governments. There were some differences in the direction or emphasis of these attacks. French liberalism, for instance, was more concerned with economic matters than was liberalism in Germany, where the problem of national unification overshadowed all other issues. Outside England, France, and Germany, the philosophy of liberalism had few contributors. Liberalism, after all, was the credo of a class that had as yet made little headway outside western Europe.

SOCIAL REFORM

Given the laissez-faire attitude of liberalism, it is not surprising that efforts to solve social problems through government action found little support among the middle class. What social reforms were introduced owed much to the agitation of a few individuals, who were motivated either by humanitarianism or, as in the case of Britain's "Philosophical Radicals," by a desire to be utilitarian and efficient.

Factory Acts

Some of the most effective opposition to early nineteenth-century liberalism

cal Economy and Taxation (1817), was the first real textbook on economics. One of Ricardo's major contributions to the economic theory of early nineteenth-century liberalism was what his disciples called the "iron law of wages." Labor, to Ricardo, was very much like any other commodity. When it was plentiful, it was cheap; when it was scarce, it was expensive. As long as there is an ample supply of workers, wages will inevitably sink to the lowest possible level of subsistence, just above starvation. To try to remedy this situation by lowering profits and raising wages would be futile, since it would merely increase the number of workers' children and, by limiting the supply of capital, cut down production. "Like all other contracts," Ricardo said, "wages should be left to the fair and free competition of the market, and should never be controlled by the interference of the legislature."

Here was another economic law as dismal in its prospects for the lower classes as Malthus' predictions on the increase of population. If there were people living on the verge of starvation, if

came from among the representatives of the old order. For political and economic but also humanitarian reasons, some Tories attacked the new industrial system in its most vulnerable spot, the terrible conditions in the mines and factories. As far back as 1802, Parliament had passed an act that cut down the working hours of apprentices. The first real factory act, passed in 1819, forbade the employment in cotton mills of children under nine years of age and limited the daily labor of children over nine to twelve hours. In 1831 night work was abolished for persons under twenty-one. In 1847 the maximum working day for women and children was set at ten hours. Two acts in 1842 and 1855 made it illegal to employ women and children in the mining industry.

Despite the best intentions on the part of their sponsors, however, these early factory acts were not very effective. They were not strictly enforced, and they applied chiefly to the cotton industry. Not until 1833 was their scope extended to include other industries, and only then was some system of inspection set up to enforce the new provisions.

Social Legislation

There were other reforms in England besides factory acts. The Municipal Corporations Act of 1835 enabled municipalities to cope more effectively with problems arising from rapid urbanization. To ensure some degree of uniformity in matters of public health, Parliament in 1848 set up a system of local boards of health. One of the most pressing social problems was the care of the poor. The New Poor Law of 1834 for the first time brought some order into the complicated system of poor relief. It was, however, a mixed blessing to the poor. The law abolished the traditional practice of "outdoor relief," under which the wages of the poorest workers had been supplemented from public funds. Henceforth, to be eligible for relief, the poor had to report to workhouses; and by making conditions in these establishments as unpleasant as possible, all but those who could not possibly make a living otherwise were discouraged from

going on relief. Here was a measure, clearly utilitarian, that delighted the middle class. It discouraged idleness and cut the expense of poor relief.

On the Continent, little was done to reform the abuses of early industrialism. A French law in 1803 prohibited work in factories before 3:00 A.M. Under the reign of Louis Philippe, the employment of children under eight was prohibited, and the work of children under twelve was limited to eight hours a day. But enforcement of these laws, in France as in England, was very lax. In Belgium, nothing at all was being done to improve the lot of the workers. The only state with any industry in Germany was Prussia, and the Prussian government, in 1839, introduced a factory law that forbade the employment of children under nine and limited the working hours of older children to ten hours.

Liberalism and Education

The only field of social reform in which the Continent was ahead of Great Britain was education. Here, for once, liberalism was a great help. Like the *philosophe* of the eighteenth century, the nineteenth-century liberal was a firm believer in education as a means of improving the world and of helping children get ahead. Any governmental

An early photograph of a classroom in an English school (1856).

measure in favor of education, therefore, had liberal support. Both France and Prussia had a long tradition of public education, which they maintained during the nineteenth century. There was a brief reaction in favor of religious education under the Bourbons, but the Education Act passed under Louis Philippe again asserted the state's role in education. Britain's first provision of public funds for education was not until 1833. It was increased in subsequent years, but even so the amount set aside for education in 1839 was still only half of what it cost to maintain Queen Victoria's horses. Not until 1870 was the first general education act adopted in England. In the meantime, education depended on private initiative, in which the middle class played a leading and beneficial role.

As this discussion has shown, some genuine attempts were made in the first half of the nineteenth century to cope with the ills of early industrialism through social reform. But such attempts ran counter to the laissez-faire philosophy of liberalism. Economic liberalism was, to some extent, a mere rationalization of selfish interests by the middle class. But there was also in it much of the eighteenth-century belief that the world operated according to certain basic laws that could not be altered and that ultimately made for the greater happiness of the greatest number.

This passive acquiescence in things as they were, however, could not possibly satisfy the workers. They refused to believe that the only solution to their troubles was to do nothing, to let matters take their course. They demanded that remedial action be taken on their behalf, else they were prepared to act for themselves.

WORKING-CLASS PROTEST

The protest of the working class took various forms. Some of the discontent expressed itself in political action, as in the revolutions of 1830 and 1848. In another form of protest, workers vented their anger and frustration on the very instruments that to them seemed primarily responsible for their plight—the machines. There were sporadic instances of such "machine-breaking" during the early phase of industrialization, both in England and on the Continent. But these acts of despair could not halt the advance of the machine age. Instead of waging war against mechanization, workers increasingly tried to escape industrialization altogether by emigrating to the United States, where virgin lands offered them the opportunity of making a better living.

Early Labor Unions

There was another, more effective way in which the working class tried to fight the injustices of industrialism. As the workers grew in number, they became aware that they constituted a new and separate class whose interests conflicted with those of their employers. This growing class consciousness among the workers led them to organize their forces in an effort to gain better treatment for themselves.

The first country in which this trend toward labor unions made any headway was again Great Britain. The British government, impressed by the radicalism of the French Revolution, watched with apprehension labor's early efforts to organize. In 1799 and 1800 Parliament passed the Combination Acts, which prohibited workers from organizing to improve their condition. Labor's continued activities, however, together with the agitation of some middle-class reformers, finally made the government relent. In 1824 and 1825, as we have seen, the Combination Acts were repealed. Henceforth, trade unions in England were no longer illegal, though it was still impossible under the law of conspiracy to engage in strikes and other forms of protest. Even so, under the new dispensation local unions arose throughout Britain. The next logical step was the formation of a large labor organization. This step was taken first in 1834, but more successfully in 1845, with the organization of the "National Association for the Protection of Labour." In 1859 the Association was instrumental in having Parliament allow peaceful picketing. In 1868 a Trades Union Congress representing more than one hundred

Slitting room of a pen factory in Birmingham (1851).

thousand members met in Manchester. By 1875, trade unions in Britain had won full legal status, including the right to strike and to picket peacefully. The British labor movement had at last come into its own.

On the Continent, labor's efforts at self-help were much less successful. Labor unions were forbidden in Belgium until 1866, and there was no labor movement in Germany to speak of until after 1870. In France, the right of workers to organize had been forbidden even during the Revolution. This ban was reiterated in the *Code Napoléon* of 1803. Some French workers organized secret societies that fomented strikes and local uprisings; but these only made the government more determined in its repressive policy. The French banker Casimir Périer expressed the feelings of the government and the middle class when he said, "The workers must realize that their only salvation lies in patient resignation to their lot." Others in France, however, took a less passive view of the workers' fate. If England was prominent in defining the middle-class philosophy of liberalism, France was equally prominent in producing its counterpart, the working-class philosophy of socialism.

THE BEGINNINGS OF MODERN SOCIALISM

Socialism as a mode of life is nothing new. It always existed, and still does, in primitive communities where people work together and share the proceeds of their common labor. Socialism as an economic and social philosophy, on the other hand, is a relatively recent development, closely connected with the rise of modern industrialism. The term *socialism* did not come into common use until the 1830s. Like liberalism, it has assumed a wide variety of meanings. Today almost any kind of government interference with the free play of economic forces is called socialism, whether it be the communist system of Russia or the "welfare state" of the United States.

While there are many varieties of socialism, all share certain fundamental principles. All socialists think that the

existing distribution of wealth is unjust, since it gives a few people far more than they possibly need and leaves large numbers of people with barely enough to exist. To close the gap between the haves and the have-nots, socialists advocate common ownership of the resources and means of production that constitute and create society's wealth. The fruits of production—that is, the profits of human labor—socialists propose to distribute in such a way that every member of society receives an equal or at least an equitable share. All schools of socialism agree that there should be far-reaching changes in society in the direction of economic and social as well as political equality.

The Utopian Socialists

Historically, modern socialism is usually divided into pre-Marxian and post-Marxian socialism or, in terms introduced by the Marxists, into "Utopian" and "scientific" socialism. The Utopian socialists earned their epithet because of the unrealistic nature of their schemes. Most of the Utopians were French, and they all came from the middle or upper class. In view of the poverty and lack of education of the working class, this is hardly surprising.

The first Utopian socialist to achieve any prominence was a French nobleman, Count Henri de Saint-Simon (1760–1825). Concerned by the social and economic injustices of a laissez-faire economy, Saint-Simon suggested that the state take a hand in organizing society in such a way that people, instead of exploiting one another, join forces to exploit nature. "The whole society," he held, "ought to strive toward the amelioration of the moral and physical existence of the most numerous and poorest class." Saint-Simon defined the principle according to which this amelioration should operate as: "From each according to his capacity, to each according to his work." In time this became one of the basic slogans of socialism.

Another prominent Utopian was Charles Fourier (1772–1837). Most of the ills of society, Fourier held, were due to the improper social and physical environment in which most people lived. To provide a more favorable environment, Fourier proposed the creation of so-called *phalanges*, or phalanxes. These were to be pleasant communities of some sixteen hundred to eighteen hundred people, living on five thousand acres of land, and forming a self-sufficient economic unit. Fourier's plans never got very far in Europe. But in the United States, where land was cheap and pioneering more common, a number of cooperative establishments were tried. None of them, however, was a lasting success.

The only one among the French Utopians to play an active role in politics was Louis Blanc (1811–82). His reform proposals were a good deal more realistic than those of the other Utopians. Blanc realized that economic reform, to be effective, must be preceded by political reform. Once true democracy had been achieved, the state could initiate the new type of industrial organizations that Blanc proposed. These consisted of social or national workshops—that is, self-supporting units of production, owned and operated by the workers on a cooperative, profit-sharing basis. Workshops of this sort were given a brief try by the revolutionary government of 1848, of which Louis Blanc was a member. The experiment failed, however, largely because the original purpose of the workshops was subordinated to the needs of the moment. Instead of self-supporting industrial enterprises, the workshops of 1848 were used for the temporary relief of unemployment.

The most prominent Utopian socialist outside France was the British industrialist Robert Owen (1771–1858). Appalled by conditions he found when he took

over the cotton mills at New Lanark in Scotland, Owen gave his workers decent housing, increased their pay, and shortened their working hours. In the model community he created, both productivity and profits increased, thus bearing out Owen's contention that satisfied workers were also better workers. Owen was less fortunate with a project he attempted on this side of the Atlantic. The community of New Harmony in Indiana, conceived along the lines of Fourier's phalanxes, turned out to be a fiasco.

Utopian socialism, in fact, had little to show for its manifold efforts. Like the *philosophes*, the Utopians believed in the natural goodness of man and the perfectibility of the world. They soon discovered that most men were not naturally good and reasonable. But even the failure of the Utopians contained a useful lesson. It showed that idealism and the best intentions are not sufficient to reform society. A more realistic and more militant type of socialism was needed that would use the workers' potential economic and political power to wrest concessions from the middle class. This new kind of socialism was first presented in the writings of Karl Marx (1818–83) and Friedrich Engels (1820–95).

Contemporary drawing of Robert Owen.

MARXIAN SOCIALISM

One of the reasons for the failure of the Utopian socialists was that they never sparked any substantial movement among the workers. There were some political working-class organizations during the 1830s and 1840s, but they had to operate as secret conspiracies rather than as open political parties. In France, Auguste Blanqui founded the "Society of Families" and the "Society of Seasons," both of them socialistic or communistic. Another such society, founded by German exiles, was the "League of the Just." Its program was originally supplied by Wilhelm Weitling, a German tailor who in 1842 published his *Guarantee of Harmony and Freedom*. These various underground organizations were all influenced by the writings of the Utopian socialists, but in their demands for complete economic equality, or communism, they went considerably beyond the demands of the middle-class Utopians.

Communism—that is, the abolition of all private property—ultimately became the basis of most socialist programs. A century ago, of course, the term *communism* did not have the connotations it has assumed since the Bolshevik Revolution. The number of communist socialists in the first half of the nineteenth century was extremely small, and very few people realized the ultimate implications of their aims. In 1844 two young Germans, Karl Marx and Friedrich Engels, established contact with the "League of the Just." Soon thereafter its name was changed to the "Communist League," and from secret revolutionary conspiracy it now shifted to open propaganda. From 1847 to 1848 Marx and Engels supplied the League with its new program, which they called *The Communist Manifesto*.

Karl Marx and Friedrich Engels

Both Marx and Engels came from the middle class that they spent most of their lives attacking. Even as a university student in Germany, Marx had shown a lively interest in social issues and socialism. His early writings brought him into disfavor with the police and in 1843 led to his first exile in Paris. There he met Engels, the son of a wealthy German industrialist with industrial holdings in England. Engels was already a communist, and there developed between the two men a close intellectual partnership. Engels is usually overshadowed by Marx, but his contributions to Marxian doctrine were considerable; besides, Engels through most of his life supported Marx financially.

The first result of the collaboration between Marx and Engels was *The Communist Manifesto*, which appeared during the revolutions of 1848. Marx and his fellow exiles welcomed the revolutions, and Marx himself was present during the upheavals in Paris. When the revolutions failed, he went to England. There he remained until his death in 1883, leading a none-too-happy life, constantly beset by financial worries and ill health. It was while in England that Marx wrote most of his basic works, notably *Das Kapital*, the first volume of which appeared in 1867.

The Communist Manifesto

The basic elements of Marx's social philosophy were contained in the brief and persuasive *Communist Manifesto*. Its fundamental proposition, as restated by Engels in his introduction to a later edition of the *Manifesto*, was

> that in every historical epoch the prevailing mode of economic production and exchange, and the social organization necessarily following from it, form the basis upon which is built up, and from which alone can be explained, the political and intellectual history of that epoch; that consequently the whole history of mankind (since the dissolution of primitive tribal society, holding land in common ownership) has been a history of class struggles, contests between exploiting and exploited, ruling and oppressed classes; that the history of these struggles forms a series of evolutions in which, nowadays, a stage has been reached where the exploited and oppressed class—the proletariat—cannot

Family photograph of Karl Marx (right), his wife, and two daughters in the 1860s. Friedrich Engels is at left.

attain its emancipation from the sway of the exploiting and ruling class—the bourgeoisie—without, at the same time and once and for all, emancipating society at large from all exploitation, oppression, class distinctions, and class struggles.

Here are the two things for which Marx is most famous: his economic, or materialistic, interpretation of history, and his theory of the class struggle. Other thinkers before Marx had recognized the influence of material circumstances and of the environment upon history. But Marx focused his attention on one particular aspect of environment that he considered fundamental: the means of production, the way in which people make a living. It is the economic structure of society, according to Marx, that determines its social, political, legal, and even cultural aspects. Historians before Marx, especially after the eighteenth century, had viewed history as an intellectually determined process. Marx took a diametrically opposite view, recognizing material, economic, nonintellectual forces as the sole determining factors.

To illustrate his economic interpretation of history as well as his theory of the class struggle, in *The Communist Manifesto*

Marx gave a brief survey of the history of western civilization as he saw it:

> The history of all hitherto existing society is the history of class struggles. Freeman and slave, patrician and plebeian, lord and serf, guildmaster and journeyman, in a word, oppressor and oppressed, stood in constant opposition to one another, carried on an uninterrupted, now hidden, now open fight, a fight that each time ended either in a revolutionary reconstitution of society at large, or in the common ruin of the contending classes.

Marx then examined the history of western society more closely, beginning with the Middle Ages. At that time, the economy of Europe was predominantly agrarian, with a large class of serfs supporting a small class of feudal nobles. Upon this society, material changes began to work: money, trade, the beginnings of a commercial, capitalist economy. As these changes took hold, a new class, a trading or bourgeois class, was formed. And between the old feudal nobility and the new middle class a struggle arose, which led to some preliminary victories of the bourgeoisie in England and Holland and culminated in the American War of Independence and the French Revolution.

The final victory of the middle class came in the nineteenth century. But this did not end the struggle. Because now a new struggle began, this time between the bourgeoisie and the proletariat. It was brought about by another change in the mode of production, the introduction of the factory system and the rise of industrial capitalism. The workers in this new struggle, which Marx saw going on around him, were now herded together in large factories, under the eyes of their "oppressors." They were held down by the iron laws of capitalist economics to a bare subsistence level. But there was one thing these workers could do, according to Marx: they could organize, they could become class conscious.

Marx felt certain that the bourgeoisie and the workers were already locked in their death struggle. And the victory of the proletariat in this struggle, Marx held, could be predicted with the cer-

On Understanding Marx

Rigorous examination is one thing Marx's ideas will not stand because they were not rigorously formulated. To do justice to his intent they must often be reinterpreted and qualified. They constitute a mixture of the true, the vague, and the false.

It should be apparent to any sensitive reader that Marx writes primarily as a critic of capitalism, as a man fired with a passionate ideal to eliminate the social inequalities, the poverty, and injustices of his time. Much of what he said makes sense and good sense considered as a description of the capitalist society of his time and as a prediction of the probable historical development of any capitalist system *on the assumption* that nothing outside that system, especially political influences, interferes with its development. Marx's fundamental errors arise from an uncritical extrapolation of what he observed in capitalist societies to all class societies, and from a disregard of the enormous influence which political, national, and moral forces have exerted on the development of capitalism as an economic system.

From Sidney Hook, *Marx and the Marxists: The Ambiguous Legacy* (Princeton, N.J.: Van Nostrand, 1955), p. 35.

tainty of a scientific experiment—hence the term *scientific socialism.* By the laws of capitalist competition there were bound to be periodic crises, caused by "epidemics of overproduction." As a result of these crises, the poor would get poorer and the rich would get richer. And there would finally come a time when "it becomes evident, that the bourgeoisie is unfit any longer to be the ruling class in society . . . because it is incompetent to assure an existence to its slave within his slavery. . . . Society can no longer live under this bourgeoisie. . . . Its fall and the victory of the proletariat are equally inevitable."

So much for the collapse of capitalism. What then? What will the world be like after the proletariat has won? On that subject Marx is not too clear. At one point he envisages a kind of transition period—the dictatorship of the proletariat, as he calls it—in which the proletariat by revolution will destroy the existing political machinery of the state, will convert the means of production into public property, and will gradually bring about a classless society. The state, as Engels put it, will gradually "wither away." Then what? "In place of the old bourgeois society, with its classes and class antagonisms," Marx concludes, "we shall have an association in which the free development of each is the condition for the free development of all." This is an idyllic picture, but also rather vague, and not very different from the kind of society certain eighteenth-century writers had envisaged. There was, in fact, a good deal of the eighteenth century in Marxism. It shared the later *philosophes'* belief in progress, in the good life here on earth, and in the natural goodness of man.

The Errors and Contributions of Marx

What about Marx's concept of classes, and of history as a series of class struggles? The concept of class certainly was a useful contribution; and if Marx did not make us class conscious, he helped our understanding of past and present society by making us aware of classes. But his definition of classes en-

tirely in economic terms is much too narrow; and by denying any influence to the individual, it runs counter to the widely held belief in individualism. As for Marx's view of the past as a series of class struggles, it does not really fit the facts of history, nor does his emphasis on merely two opposing classes. Marx rec-

What If Marx Had Never Lived?

No one can read the story of Karl Marx or ponder the somber prognostications of Marx the historian or the economist without asking, "Would history have been significantly different if Marx had not lived?"

It is a surprisingly difficult question to answer. To be sure, the trend of world capitalism would not have been deflected by so much as an inch if it had been deprived of the insights of Marx's masterwork, *Das Kapital.* Marxism as a system of thought has exerted virtually no direct influence on the internal economic evolution of American or European capitalism as such. But the influence of Marxism is not so easily summed up when we look at the revolutionary countries: at Russia or China or Cuba or at the bubbling cauldron of the underdeveloped world. And its effects on these countries has, in turn, affected the West.

A first glance would tell us that in these lands Marx was of the greatest importance. Whole political catechisms and, more than that, crucial political guidance have been wrested from the writings of Marx and his collaborator Friedrich Engels, writings which have on many occasions assumed the role of Biblical literature in a fundamentalist community. Even so relatively liberated a Marxist as the Yugoslav spokesman Edvard Kardelj wrote a polemic against the Chinese position on the question of coexistence in 1960 by leaning not so much on facts and empirical evidence as on what Marx or Engels said. If Marx said (or if one can "interpret" Marx to have said) that coexistence was possible, then it is possible; if he said not, it is not.

Thus Marx and Marxism have indubitably left their imprint on the vocabulary, the thought pattern and the discourse of the revolutionary nations. Yet it is difficult to believe that the revolutions themselves would not have occurred or that Communism (by whatever name) would not be a great world presence today had Marx not lived. The forces which finally burst through the crusts of tired and corrupt societies in Russia, China and Cuba—and which treaten to do so again in Latin America and Asia and Africa—may have been guided by Marxism, but they were not generated by Marxism alone. Had Marx never lived or written, old and incapable regimes would have given way to new and vigorous ones, no doubt with all the agonies by which such changes in history are usually accompanied. The world would have been different surely, but not perhaps all that different.

From Robert L. Heilbroner, in Isaiah Berlin, *Karl Marx: His Life and Environment* (New York: Time-Life, 1963), pp. xviii–xix.

ognized the existence of other classes, but he believed that they would ultimately be absorbed by one or the other of the two contending groups—the bourgeoisie and the proletariat. This prediction, like so many others Marx made, thus far has failed to materialize.

There were, then, a good many blind spots in Marx's socialist theories. While the rich were getting richer, the poor did not necessarily get poorer. The general standard of living in the world's industrial nations was to reach heights undreamed of by Marx. Man, furthermore, does not seem to be motivated exclusively, or even primarily, by economic concerns. Despite Marx's attacks on religion, the established churches have continued to play an important part even in the lives of the lower classes. Another force that increasingly came to command the allegiance of rich and poor alike was nationalism. The great wars of the last century have been fought not between the "oppressed" and their "oppressors," but between the citizens of different nations, including the workers, for the defense or the greater glory of their own country.

Despite errors and shortcomings in his teachings, however, Marx's contributions to modern thought have been considerable. By bridging the gap between politics and economics, he enriched our understanding of the past. We may not accept the dominant role he assigned to economic factors, but we have come to realize the importance of these factors. Prior to Marx, the division of society into rich and poor, haves and have-nots, was accepted as a natural, unchangeable fact. It was chiefly due to Marx that society was jolted out of such complacent acceptance of the status quo. By predicting far-reaching changes, he made people aware that changes were possible. The threat of revolutionary change conjured up in Marx's writings did much to hasten the peaceful evolution that has so markedly improved the condition of the lower classes in industrial societies. Marxian socialism offered its followers a seemingly logical, scientifically certain answer to the many perplexities of modern society. This explains its appeal to workers and intellectuals alike. The ultimate success of Marxism lay in the almost religious fervor it inspired among its disciples.

OTHER FORMS OF SOCIAL CRITICISM

Marxian socialism, in its ultimate effects on society, turned out to be the most important attack on the capitalist philosophy of laissez faire. Other critics of this philosophy, however, tried in various ways to awaken their contemporaries to the social problems created by the industrialization of society.

Humanitarianism

Writers like Victor Hugo and Honoré de Balzac in France and Charles Dickens in England, by dwelling in their novels on the more sordid aspects of the new industrialism, played on human sympathy in the hope of creating a climate favorable to reform. The historian Thomas Carlyle, in his *Past and Present* (1843), showed deep concern over the growing division between the working classes on the one hand and the wealthy classes on the other. He turned against the "mammonism" and the "mechanism" of his age and admonished the new captains of industry to be aware of their responsibilities as successors to the old aristocracy. Benjamin Disraeli, one of the rising young Tories, in his social novel *Sybil* (1845), deplored the wide gap that industrialization had opened between the rich and the poor. It was, he said, as though England had split into two nations "between whom there was no intercourse and no sympathy."

Christian Socialism

Another body of social criticism arose within the Christian churches, first in England and later on the Continent. For centuries past, organized Christianity had been the chief dispenser of charity to the poor and the aged. The beginnings of modern Christian Socialism go back to a small group of English clergymen who felt that the best way to attack the evils of industrialism was to reaffirm the gospel of charity and brotherly love. The leader

Charles Dickens (1812–70), at age forty-seven.

of the Christian Socialist movement was the Anglican theologian Frederick Denison Maurice. Its best-known propagandist was the clergyman and novelist Charles Kingsley. In his famous tract, *Cheap Clothes and Nasty* (1850), written under the pseudonym of "Parson Lot," Kingsley attacked the condition of "ever-increasing darkness and despair" in the British clothing industry, whose sweatshops were "rank with human blood." To remedy a situation in which men were like "beasts of prey, eating one another up by competition, as in some confined pike-pond, where the great pike, having dispatched the little ones, begin to devour each other," Kingsley proposed the formation of cooperative enterprises in which everyone would be "working together for common profit in the spirit of mutual self-sacrifice." Christian Socialism, in appealing to the social consciousness of "every gentleman and every Christian," helped to modify the belief in laissez faire and to prepare the soil for the movement of social reform that gained momentum in the second half of the nineteenth century.

Anarchism

One other form of social protest of quite a different nature deserves mention here, even though its effects were not felt until later in the century. Anarchism, like socialism, was intended to overthrow capitalism. But while the socialists were ready to use the state as a steppingstone for the realization of their aims, the anarchists were deeply opposed to any kind of governmental authority and organization. One of the earliest theorists of anarchism was the French publicist Pierre-Joseph Proudhon (1809–65). In his pamphlet *First Memoir on Property* (1840) he asked the question, "What is property?" and replied with the well-known slogan, "Property is theft!" This seeming opposition to private property appeared to align Proudhon with communism and endeared him to Marx. The latter's admiration cooled, however, when he discovered that Proudhon was less interested in overthrowing the middle class than in raising the worker to the level of that class. Proudhon was against any

kind of government, be it by one man, a party, or a democratic majority. "Society," he wrote, "finds its highest perfection in the union of order with anarchy."

The most famous proponent of anarchism was a Russian nobleman, Mikhail Bakunin (1814–76). A theorist of anarchism, he also practiced what he preached. Bakunin was involved in several revolutions, was three times condemned to death, and spent long years in prison and Siberian exile. Bakunin attributed most of the evils of his day to two agencies—the state and the Church. He objected to both institutions because of the restrictions they impose on human freedom. His ideal society was a loose federation of local communities, each with a maximum of autonomy. In each of these communities the means of production were to be held in common. The way to achieve this governmentless state of affairs, Bakunin held, was not by waiting patiently for the state to wither away, as Marx had held, but by helping matters along, if necessary by means of terrorism, assassination, and insurrection. The last decade of the nineteenth century, as we shall see, witnessed a whole series of assassinations attributed to anarchists. But anarchism never developed into a well-defined movement, partly because of Bakunin's death in 1876, partly because of the impracticable nature of its doctrine. Traces of it, however, survived into the twentieth century and contributed to another type of social protest, syndicalism (see p. 662).

By the middle of the nineteenth century, the coming of the Industrial Age, with its revolutionary political, social, and economic effects, had made itself felt over most of Europe. It also extended to other parts of the world (see Chapter 27). For the next two decades, people's attention in Europe and the United States became absorbed by momentous political developments. A series of wars radically changed the existing order and overshadowed economic developments. Once the political situation had become stabilized, however, shortly after 1870, a second wave of economic development swept over Europe and the world, a wave of such magnitude that it is often called a "Second Industrial Revolution."

The Reverend Charles Kingsley (1819–75), English author and noted Christian Socialist.

Mikhail Bakunin (1814–76).

Suggestions for Further Reading

Note: Asterisk denotes a book available in paperback edition.

General Historians' views of the Industrial Revolution have changed over the years, as is shown in E. E. Lampard's perceptive essay, *Industrial Revolution: Interpretations and Perspectives* (1957), and in D. Landes, *The Unbound Prometheus: Technological Change and Industrial Development in Western Europe from 1750 to the Present* (1969). A good account of early industrialization is P. Deane, *The First Industrial Revolution** (1965). H. J. Habbakuk and M. M. Postan, eds., *The Industrial Revolutions and After* (1965) (Vol. VI of the *Cambridge Economic History of Europe*), contains essays by noted specialists. W. W. Rostow's influential book, *The Stages of Economic Growth** (1960), introduced novel concepts like "take-off" into the debate on industrialization. The widening scope of industrialization is stressed in W. O. Henderson, *The Industrial Revolution on the Continent* (1961). A. P. Usher, *A History of Mechanical Inventions* (1929), and G. Fussell, *The Farmer's Tools, 1500–1900* (1952), discuss the importance of technological change; and T. McKeown, *The Modern Rise of Population* (1972), and W. D. Borrie, *The Growth and Control of World Population* (1970), deal with the beginnings of the current "population explosion." On urbanization, see L. Mumford, *The City in History* (1961). The same author's *Technics and Civilization* (1934), and S. Chase, *Men and Machines* (1929), view with some alarm the impact of technology on man.

Economic Changes in Britain Because England was the first country to undergo the transition to modern industrialism, its Agricultural and Industrial revolutions have been studied most intensively. Both P. Mantoux, *The Industrial Revolution in the Eighteenth Century* (1929), and T. S. Ashton, *An Economic History of England: The Eighteenth Century* (1955), deal with the roots of these developments, although with different emphases. A small volume by T. S. Ashton, *The Industrial Revolution, 1760–1830** (1948), corrects many misconceptions about early industrialism. J. H. Clapham, *An Economic History of Modern Britain,* Vol. I (1926), covers the period between 1820 and 1850. Briefer treatments are W. H. B. Court, *A Concise Economic History of Britain from 1750 to Recent Times* (1954), and A. Redford, *An Economic History of England, 1760–1860* (1947). The changes in British agriculture are the subject of G. Slater, *The English Peasantry and the Enclosure of the Common Fields* (1907); Lord Ernle, *English Farming, Past and Present* (1936); J. L. Hammond and B. Hammond, *The Village Labourer, 1760–1832* (1918); and J. P. D. Dunbabin, *Rural Discontent in Nineteenth-Century Britain* (1975). The following are detailed studies on special aspects of the Industrial Revolution in England: T. S. Ashton, *Iron and Steel in the Industrial Revolution* (1951); W. H. B. Court, *The Rise of the Midland Industries, 1600–1838* (1938); and A. Redford, *Manchester Merchants and Foreign Trade, 1794–1858* (1934). The most important single invention of early industrialism is the subject of H. W. Dickinson, *A Short History of the Steam Engine* (1939), and of J. Lord, *Capital and Steam Power, 1750–1800* (1923).

The Spread of Industrialism Besides England, only France experienced any noticeable industrial development during the eighteenth century. These beginnings are discussed in H. E. Sée, *Economic and Social Conditions in France During the Eighteenth Century* (1927), and S. T. McCloy, *French Inventions of the Eighteenth Century* (1954). Later developments in France are treated in A. L. Dunham, *The Industrial Revolution in France, 1815–1848* (1955), and R. E. Cameron, *France and the Economic Development of Europe, 1800–1914** (1961). British influence on economic developments abroad is traced by W. O. Henderson, *Britain and Industrial Europe, 1750–1870* (1954); E. J. Hobsbawm, *Industry and Empire* (1970); and L. C. A. Knowles, *Economic Development in the Nineteenth Century: France, Germany, Russia, and the United States* (1932). Other useful economic histories are: J. H. Clapham, *Economic Development of France and Germany, 1815–1914** (1936); S. B. Clough, *France: A History of Natural Economics* (1939); W. O. Henderson, *The Zollverein* (1939) and *The Rise of German Industrial Power, 1834–1914** (1976); P. I. Lyashchenko, *History of the National Economy of Russia to 1917* (1949); and J. Blum, *Lord and Peasant in Russia from the Ninth to the Nineteenth Century** (1961).

The Social Effects of Industrialization The traditional emphasis on the negative effects of early industrialism is evident in J. L. Hammond and B. Hammond, *The Town Labourer, 1760–1832* (1917), *The Skilled Labourer, 1760–1832* (1919), and *The Bleak Age** (1947). That emphasis has found confirmation in E. P. Thompson, *The Making of the English Working Class** (1963). A more neutral picture is drawn in A. Briggs, *The Age of Improvement,*

1783–1867 (1959); S. G. Checkland, *The Rise of Industrial Society in England, 1815–1885* (1964); and G. Kitson-Clark, *The Making of Victorian England* (1962). See also M. I. Thomis, *The Town Labourer and the Industrial Revolution* (1975). On urban growth, see A. Redford, *Labour Migration in England, 1800–1850* (1929), and E. Gauldie, *Cruel Habitation: A History of Working-Class Housing, 1780–1918* (1974); and on landed interests, see F. M. Thompson, *English Landed Society in the Nineteenth Century* (1963). The situation in France is dealt with in L. Chevalier, *Working Classes and Dangerous Classes in Paris During the First Part of the Nineteenth Century* (1971); V. R. Lorwin, *The French Labor Movement* (1954); and B. Moss, *The Origins of the French Labor Movement* (1976).

Economic Liberalism	The best way to study the utilitarians and classical economists is through their writings. The most important of these—J. S. Mill, *Autobiography** and *On Liberty;** T. R. Malthus, *An Essay on Population;** and D. Ricardo, *Principles of Political Economy and Taxation**—are available in several editions. The general development of modern economic thought is presented in C. Gide and C. Rist, *History of Economic Doctrines from the Physiocrats to the Present Day* (1913, 1948), and E. Roll, *A History of Economic Thought* (1942). The standard work on Bentham and the utilitarians is É. Halévy, *The Growth of Philosophic Radicalism** (1955). More recent treatments are J. Hamburger, *Intellectuals in Politics: John Stuart Mill and the Philosophic Radicals* (1965), and S. H. Letwin, *The Pursuit of Certainty: David Hume; Jeremy Bentham; John Stuart Mill; Beatrice Webb* (1965). Among the latest works on Mill are the psychohistorical B. Mazlish, *James and John Stuart Mill* (1975), and the more traditional A. Ryan, *J. S. Mill** (1975).
Social Reform	Social reform in the first half of the nineteenth century was almost entirely restricted to Great Britain. W. M. Thomas, *The Early Factory Legislation* (1948), deals with the period between 1802 and 1853. Other notable reform efforts are dealt with in E. L. Woodward, *The Age of Reform, 1815–1870* (1938); L. Radzinowitz, *A History of English Criminal Law: The Movement for Reform, 1750–1833* (1948); and S. Webb and B. Webb, *English Local Government: English Poor Law History*, 3 vols. (1927–29). For accounts of early attempts by the working class to organize itself politically and economically, see G. D. H. Cole, *British Working Class Politics, 1832–1914* (1941); S. Webb and B. Webb, *History of Trade Unionism* (1920); and H. M. Pelling, *History of Trade Unionism* (1963). A good introduction to social reform is through the biographies of some of the leading reformers: G. D. H. Cole, *The Life of William Cobbett* (1942); G. Wallas, *Life of Francis Place* (1925); G. F. A. Best, *Shaftesbury* (1964); and G. M. Trevelyan, *Lord Grey and the Reform Bill* (1929).
Socialism	Good surveys of the subject are G. D. H. Cole, *Socialist Thought: The Forerunners, 1789–1850* (1962), and H. W. Laidler, *Social-Economic Movements* (1949). Less systematic but more readable is E. Wilson, *To The Finland Station** (1953). G. Lichtheim, *The Origins of Socialism* (1969), is brilliant. R. Owen, *The Life of Robert Owen, by Himself* (1920), gives insights into the thought of this leading Utopian reformer. Among several books on Owen, J. F. C. Harrison, *Robert Owen and the Owenites in Britain and America* (1969), is one of the best. F. Manuel, *The Prophets of Paris** (1962), deals with the French Utopian socialists. The literature on Marxian socialism is vast. A convenient collection of basic sources is available in *Karl Marx and Frederick Engels; Selected Works*, 2 vols. (1951). The easiest way for the layman to become acquainted with Marx's basic concepts is still K. Marx and F. Engels, *The Communist Manifesto** (1848), available in countless editions. G. D. H. Cole, *The Meaning of Marxism** (1948), offers one of many keys to an understanding of Marxist theory. G. Lichtheim, *Marxism** (1961), is an important contribution. See also B. D. Wolfe, *Marxism: One Hundred Years in the Life of a Doctrine* (1965), and M. M. Drachkovitch, ed., *Marxism in the Modern World* (1965). There are numerous biographies of Marx, some favorable, like F. Mehring, *Karl Marx: The Story of His Life* (1936), and others hostile, like L. Schwarzschild, *The Red Prussian: The Life and Legend of Karl Marx** (1947). A balanced treatment is I. Berlin, *Karl Marx: His Life and Environment** (1963). The role of Engels in the genesis of Marxian socialism is emphasized by G. Mayer, *Friedrich Engels* (1935). For a discussion of anarchism, see two excellent biographies of its founders: D. W. Brogan, *Proudhon* (1934), and E. H. Carr, *Michael Bakunin** (1937). J. Joll, *The Anarchists** (1965), deals mainly with the later activities of the anarchists.

26 A New Balance of Power, 1850–1871

Napoleon III and Bismarck on the Morning after the Surrender of the French Army at Sedan, by W. Camphausen.

The keynote of European history during the first half of the nineteenth century had been revolution. In a long series of upheavals that reached its climax in 1848, Europe had tried to find some adjustment between the traditional claims of the old monarchical and aristocratic order and the democratic demands of the rising middle and lower classes. By 1850 the middle class had won some notable victories, and parliamentary government had gained a hold in most of western Europe. East of the Rhine, however, the old regime had stood its ground, and the conflict between the claims of monarchical and popular sovereignty continued.

The nature of this conflict, however, changed during the next few decades. In the past, the issues dividing the defenders of the old order and the advocates of the new had been largely drawn along ideological lines. There had been little common ground between the conservatism of men like Metternich and Nicholas I and the liberal and national aspirations of the middle class. The men who rose to leadership after 1850 were less committed to ideology. They were realists, ready to forgo some of their principles in order to achieve some of their aims. It was in realistic appraisal of the new social and political forces brought to the fore by industrialization that Bismarck gave the German middle class some of the concessions for which it had vainly fought in the past. By the same token, the middle class was ready to give up some of its political aims in order to protect and advance its economic interests. Demands for political reform continued. But the unprecedented economic growth of Europe, especially after 1870, helped to divert the attention of the middle class from politics to economics.

Besides economic growth, there was nationalism to absorb people's attention. Before 1850, domestic upheavals and international peace had been the order of the day; after 1850, the reverse was true. Five wars involving great powers were fought between 1854 and 1871, all of them prompted by nationalist aims and interests. In the past, whenever the status quo reached at Vienna had been threatened or actually changed, the "Concert of Europe" had collaborated to see that peace was speedily restored and that the balance of power was maintained. With the rise of nationalism, however, the European concert became more and more difficult to maintain. Even before 1850 the powers had failed to see eye-to-eye on certain international issues. But it was not until after 1850 that the first major showdown occurred. The Crimean War of 1854 to 1855 was the first in a whole series of conflicts that put at least a temporary end to the Concert of Europe. By 1871, a new balance of power had emerged on the Continent, significantly different from the balance that had existed twenty years earlier.

THE EASTERN QUESTION

The Crimean War was the culmination of the latent crisis caused by the slow disintegration of Turkish rule in the Balkans. The "Eastern Question" had already caused one brief war between Russia and Turkey in 1828–29. To ensure year-round navigation, Russia depended on free access to the Black Sea through the Turkish Straits. This it had gained for its merchant ships in 1774, and again in the Treaty of Adrianople (1829). Attempts to gain exclusive passage for Russian warships, however, had run into opposition from the rest of the powers, since such an arrangement would have guaranteed Russian predominance in the Black Sea and the passage of Russian warships into the Mediterranean. Instead the Straits Convention of 1841 affirmed the closure of the Straits to *all* foreign warships.

The Straits were not the only issue involved in the Eastern Question. Both France and Great Britain had considerable commercial interests in the Near East, and the British regarded the eastern Mediterranean as the chief approach to India. These interests, the western powers felt, were threatened by Russia's gradual encroachment on Turkey, as evidenced in its occupation of the Danubian principalities of Moldavia and Wallachia after 1829. While Russia was thus threatening to change the status quo in the Ottoman Empire, France and England hoped to maintain it.

A Consultation About the State of Turkey, a mid–nineteenth-century cartoon. The ''Sick Man of Europe'' (Turkey) is threatened by Death (Russia), while the physicians (France and England) hold their consultation.

Turkey, trusting in British and French support, declared war on Russia. Pressure of public opinion, especially in England, and concern over the expansion of Russian influence later brought the western powers into the war on Turkey's side. For the first time in forty years, the great powers had become involved in war with one another.

The Crimean War and the Peace of Paris

The major action of the Crimean War was a year-long siege against the Russian stronghold of Sebastopol on the Crimean Peninsula. It was one of history's costliest operations, with most of the casualties caused by disease. One of its few positive effects was the creation of the first modern nursing and medical services under the direction of Florence Nightingale, from which ultimately arose the International Red Cross.

The Crimean War lined up most of the European powers against the Russians. As the war progressed, Austria drew closer to the western powers and finally concluded an alliance with them. Austria never did any actual fighting, but even so the Russians resented its ''ingratitude'' for the aid Nicholas I had given the Austrians during the Hungarian uprising in 1849. Prussia outwardly followed Austria's lead but actually maintained a friendly neutrality and secretly aided the Russian cause. The small kingdom of Piedmont-Sardinia also entered the war on the side of the western powers, hoping to gain as a reward their support of Italian unification.

Another source of friction, which ultimately served as the immediate cause for the Crimean War, concerned the so-called Holy Places—that is, those sections of Jerusalem and Palestine that were closely associated with the life of Christ. Christians within the Ottoman Empire had long been guaranteed certain rights by their Turkish masters, and foreign pilgrims had been granted access to the Holy Land. The interests of the western Christians were traditionally championed by France, while Russia considered itself the guardian of eastern, Greek Orthodox rights. Shortly after 1850, conflicts between the two religious groups led to a number of incidents. As a result, the tsar tried to pressure Turkey into officially recognizing Russia's role as protector of Greek Orthodox rights in Turkey. In order to emphasize their interest in the negotiations taking place between Turkey and Russia, Britain and France sent naval contingents to the entrance of the Straits in 1853. Russia replied by reoccupying the Danubian principalities that it had evacuated two years earlier. The Concert of Europe, acting on Austrian initiative, vainly tried to keep tension from mounting. In October 1853

Florence Nightingale (1820–1910).

After eleven months of siege, the fortress of Sebastopol fell in September 1855. Nicholas I had died in March, and his successor, Alexander II, was now ready to talk peace. The Paris Peace Conference met in the spring of 1856. To curtail Russian influence over the area adjacent to the Ottoman Empire, the Black Sea was neutralized, which meant that Russia could not have any warships or fortifications there. In addition, navigation on the Danube River was declared free and open to all powers, and Russia had to surrender part of Bessarabia at the mouth of the Danube to the Turkish principality of Moldavia.

The Paris Conference also discussed the future of the Danubian principalities. Moldavia and Wallachia, it was decided, were to be under the temporary supervision of the great powers. Each principal-

Participants in the Paris Peace Conference (1856). Seated: Baron Hübner (Austria), Ali Pasha (Turkey), Lord Clarendon (Britain), Count Walewski (France), Count Orlov (Russia), Baron de Bourqueney (France), and Lord Cowley (Britain). Standing: Count Cavour (Sardinia), De Villamarina (Sardinia), Count Hatzfeldt (Prussia), Count Vincent Benedetti (France), Mohammed Jemil Bey (Turkey), Baron Brunnov (Russia), Baron Manteuffel (Prussia), and Count Buol (Austria).

Crimean Casualties

In assessing the Crimean War and the armies that fought there, the public mind has been greatly influenced by the highly dramatized accounts of the sufferings that took place. Much of the criticism has been focused on the medical services, which were quite unable to cope with the strain put on them. . . . The 'hospital' in Scutari, an old Turkish barracks, was of course appalling. Whether the smell there was worse than from the Thames at the same time might be debatable. . . . Although bad smells—with the exception of that from farmyard manure—were thought to be unhealthy there was no understanding why this might be so. Only after the Crimean War was over did Pasteur and Lister prove that microbes and bacteria existed. . . . Surgery, as far as the battlefield was concerned, consisted mainly of amputation. . . . There were, of course, no facilities for anything, no proper anaesthetics, antiseptics, dressings, bandages, nor any means even for sharpening the few and inadequate instruments. . . . Surgeon-General Longmore, who conducted an inquiry into the medical service in the Crimea, produced some surprising information. His, and other reports, showed that many of the deaths could have been prevented had the administration been better. The total number of British deaths in the Crimea was 18,058. Of these 1,761 died from enemy action, the remaining 16,297 from disease. . . . As the average strength of the British forces in the first nine months was thirty one thousand the mortality rate in the Crimea during this period was therefore sixty per cent. This was greater than the mortality rate had been in England during the great plagues.

From Philip Warner, *The Crimean War: A Reappraisal* (New York: Taplinger, 1973), pp. 211–13.

ity was given a separate government. This, however, failed to satisfy the national aspirations of the Rumanians, who made up most of the population of the two regions. In 1858, therefore, both principalities elected the same man, Prince Alexander Cuza, as their ruler. After further consolidation of their common institutions, the principalities were finally recognized by the great powers in 1862 as the single and autonomous state of Rumania. The principle of nationality had triumphed once again.

Among the other decisions of the Paris Conference was the formal admission of Turkey to the family of powers, upon promise that it would introduce a number of much-needed reforms. The Paris Conference also issued a declaration against privateering and limited the rights of blockade by specifying that, to be effective, a blockade had to be backed by force. This principle of the "freedom of the seas" was intended to safeguard the rights of neutral countries in time of war. Finally, the Conference took notice, at least, of the "Italian Question" by permitting Cavour, the prime minister of Piedmont, to plead the cause of Italian unification before the assembled dignitaries. This was only a gesture, but it was a significant one.

The Peace of Paris, like the Vienna settlement forty years earlier, was an effort by the great powers to remove the sources of tension that had led to war and to restore the balance of power that had been threatened by one of them. But while the Vienna settlement had succeeded in restoring international stability, the Paris settlement left a legacy of unresolved tensions. The Russians, in particular, felt humiliated, and henceforth would try to recoup the losses they had suffered in the Crimean War. The French, having won an important victory, took pride in the fact that their emperor had emerged as the leading figure at the Paris Peace Conference. But Napoleon III's role as arbiter of Europe merely whetted his appetite for further foreign ventures, and he was soon to come up with new plans for revising the map of Europe. Furthermore, the fact that Cavour had been permitted to raise the question of Italy's future at the conference gave fresh hope to Italian nationalists, whose aspirations could be fulfilled only by war against Austria.

Other than Russia, the country to be most seriously affected by the Crimean War was Austria. Whether it realized it or not, Austria had been seriously weakened not only by its estrangement from Russia but by the coolness that had developed with Prussia. The latter, already restive under the domination that Austria had resumed in German affairs after 1850, was further alienated by Austria's attempts to involve the two leading German powers in the Crimean War. This isolation of Austria from its two traditional friends, Russia and Prussia, was perhaps the most significant result of the war. It was the more ominous because England, having learned a bitter lesson at Sebastopol, once more withdrew from continental affairs. Austria was thus left entirely at the mercy of Italian and German nationalism. The stage had been set for one of the most dramatic periods in European history. The tragic hero of this drama was the French Emperor, Napoleon III.

THE SECOND FRENCH EMPIRE

Louis Napoleon was to guide the destiny of France for the two fateful decades after 1850. To this day, however, he remains very much an enigma. Was he a dictator, as some people have claimed, or was he a genuine democrat, as he himself claimed? After his fall from power in 1870, there was little doubt in anyone's mind that he was a fraud and a failure. More recently, however, historians have become somewhat more charitable in their judgment. In his domestic policy, Napoleon III gave France some of the best years in its history. And if in his foreign policy he showed an unerring instinct for doing the wrong thing, his motives were idealistic, and many of his reverses were due to forces over which he had no control.

Louis Napoleon became emperor by a cleverly managed *coup d'état*. Like most countries after 1848, the Second French Republic experienced a wave of reaction.

Napoleon III, in the uniform of a major general (*ca.* 1860).

Socialists were ejected from the legislature, the right to vote was curtailed, public meetings were restricted, and the freedom of the press was curbed. At the same time, however, France's new president, Louis Napoleon, was eager to gain the support of the French masses. In pursuit of this aim, he dissolved the Assembly in December 1851 and called for new presidential elections. There was some street fighting, but his *coup* succeeded. The French people once again endorsed the name Napoleon by a vast majority. A year later, the president finished his overthrow of the Republic by proclaiming himself Emperor of the French, thus pursuing further the historical parallel between himself and his uncle.

The analogy was carried still further in the Empire's political institutions, which closely followed those of the first Napoleon. There were two parliamentary bodies—an appointive senate and a legislature elected by universal male suffrage—both of which could merely discuss what the emperor saw fit to put before them. By carefully managing elections, furthermore, Napoleon was always in a position to command a parliamentary majority. Most major decisions were reached by the emperor himself in consultation with a Council of State made up of experts with purely advisory functions. The Second Empire, at least during its first ten years, was little more than a thinly disguised dictatorship.

The "Authoritarian Empire"

Despite the absence of political freedom, the authoritarian phase of Napoleon's rule was a period of relative content. The emperor gave his countrymen what they wanted most—prosperity at home and glory abroad. Like many a dictator since, Napoleon III tried to do something for everyone. The peasants, who had voted him into office and who continued to endorse his policy in numerous plebiscites, were helped by large-scale public works and improved credit facilities. The workers, who continued to remain cool to the new regime, were aided by far-reaching social legislation and public housing. But the class with which Napoleon's relations were most harmonious, at least in times of prosperity, was the industrial and commercial middle class.

More than any other statesman of his time, the Emperor of the French realized the importance and implications of modern industrialization, and he did his best to create conditions favorable to industrial growth. As a result, French railway mileage during the 1850s alone increased more than fivefold. A French law of 1863 permitted the formation of "limited liability" companies. By limiting the liability of stockholders to the stock they

Napoleon III

Napoleon III was, to borrow Gamaliel Bradford's phrase, a "damaged soul"; and, after 1860, a damaged soul imprisoned in a damaged body. Grave, thoughtful, kind, devoted to noble causes, determined withal, fearless, and surprisingly practical, he had in him also the tortuousness of the eternal plotter, the vagueness of the Utopian, the weakened fiber of the sensualist, the fatalism of the gambler. Some characters in history are obvious in their greatness, mediocrity, or turpitude: even though our sympathies may widely differ, we feel we can focus Washington, Victoria, Gladstone, and even Napoleon I. Napoleon III is not one of these. His elusive physiognomy changes altogether with the light that is turned upon it. At one moment, he appears impressive: the only political leader in the nineteenth century whose thought could still be a guide for us today. At other times, the caricature drawn by Kinglake and Victor Hugo seems almost convincing: the middle-aged rake in imperial trappings, sinister even in his futility. The most searching, the most persistent light of all, the one in which he was seen by every one who approached him, reveals him as gentle, not merely in speech and smile, but to the very depths of his being.

From Albert Guérard, *Napoleon III* (Cambridge, Mass.: Harvard University Press, 1943), p. 290.

owned, investment was made less risky and the savings of the proverbially thrifty Frenchman were now attracted to industry. In a series of farsighted commercial agreements, notably the Cobden-Chevalier treaty (1860) with England, Napoleon abandoned the traditional protectionism of France in favor of moderate free trade. As a result, French exports soon exceeded imports. France in 1870 was still the chief industrial competitor of Great Britain. French industrial expansion had some negative aspects as well. There was an air of gaudiness and vulgarity about the newly enriched middle class. Speculation and overexpansion led to periodic crises and depressions. But on the whole the new prosperity was sound and was shared by all classes of the population.

As a symbol of the Empire's prosperity and splendor, Napoleon was instrumental in having the city of Paris transformed into the beautiful work of art it remains to the present day. The center of the city was completely rebuilt, with wide boulevards, stately squares, and lovely parks. Like so many of Napoleon's projects, this "urban renewal program" served a dual purpose. By providing employment and eradicating ugly slums, it aided the workers; but at the same time it

did away with the breeding-grounds of radicalism and revolution. The wide avenues of the new city were unsuitable for erecting barricades, and they permitted the use of cavalry and artillery in case there should ever be another popular uprising.

The Second Empire came to an end on the battlefield in war against Prussia in 1870. Before that time, however, domestic discontent had already forced Napoleon to abandon many of the authoritarian practices of his earlier years. Most of this discontent was provoked by his blundering foreign policy. The French people, still smarting from the defeat they had suffered forty years earlier, were not opposed to war, so long as they won. France's involvement in the Crimean War had been popular, and the same was true of a number of small colonial ventures. The occupation of Algeria was completed; new French settlements were established in West Africa; New Caledonia was occupied in 1853; and during the 1860s protectorates were secured over Cambodia and the region later called French Indochina. The French participation in the wars of Italian unification, on the other hand, while it brought some military glory and new

A Paris boulevard (1860). Detail of one part of a stereographic pair on glass, showing the results of Napoleon III's "urban renewal" program.

territory, was deeply resented by French Catholics, since it deprived the papacy of its territorial holdings. Still more disastrous in French eyes were Napoleon's futile efforts, between 1862 and 1867, to establish a French protectorate over Mexico (see p. 628). The crowning blow to Napoleon's prestige, however, came when he failed to secure territorial compensations for France during Prussia's unification of Germany (see p. 609).

The "Liberal Empire"

To pacify the growing domestic opposition, Napoleon, during the 1860s, attempted a gradual liberalization of French political life. The "Liberal Empire" was initiated in 1860, when restrictions on debate in the legislative body were lifted and parliamentary proceedings were made public. Subsequent decrees extended the powers of the legislature and relaxed the restrictions on public meetings and the press that had existed since 1852. But these concessions only helped to swell the ranks of the opposition. By 1869 the government had so lost its grip that the parliamentary elections of that year returned ninety-three opposition candidates, thirty of whom were republicans. With labor unrest prompting a growing epidemic of strikes, and with the republican program of Léon Gambetta gaining more and more adherents, the government made some sweeping last-minute efforts to save its life. In their totality, these reforms amounted to the establishment of a parliamentary regime. In May 1870 the French electorate endorsed these constitutional changes with a rousing majority. But it was too late. Two months later the war with Prussia broke out, sweeping away the Empire and bringing in the Third Republic.

THE UNIFICATION OF ITALY

The domestic events in France must be viewed against the background of Napoleon's foreign policy. He had two main motives: to gain glory for France and to win freedom for suppressed nationalities. It was the conflict between the selfishness and the altruism, the realism and the idealism, inherent in these aims that accounts for much of the fateful vacillation in Napoleon's policy. The vacillation first manifested itself in his dealings with Italy.

Italy After 1848

Italy before 1848 had been an unhappy country, ridden by many factions, each hoping to bring about political unification according to its own plans (see p. 562). As a result of the abortive revolutions of 1848, however, unification under the leadership of the kingdom of Piedmont-Sardinia had emerged as the most feasible scheme. The king of Piedmont, Victor Emmanuel II, had been unique in not revoking the liberal constitution granted during the revolution. He did not relent, furthermore, in his hostile policy toward Austria. Turin, the capital of Piedmont, soon became a haven for Italian patriots from all over the peninsula trying to escape the persecutions of their reactionary, pro-Austrian rulers.

The man who realized the unique position of Piedmont and used it to bring about the unification of Italy was Count Camillo di Cavour. At the age of forty, in 1850, Cavour was appointed minister of agriculture and commerce, and in 1852 he became prime minister. Cavour at first was not so much interested in uniting the whole of Italy as he was in extending the power of Piedmont in the north. This, he realized, could be done only against the opposition and at the expense of Austria. To prepare for a showdown with Austria thus became one of his major concerns.

Before Austria could be tackled, however, several things were needed. The first was to create sympathy for the "Italian Question" outside Italy. This was done by having Piedmontese troops participate in the Crimean War and by having the Italian problem discussed by the powers at the Paris Peace Conference. A second prerequisite for a successful war against Austria was the military and economic strengthening of Piedmont. Cavour did his best to improve the armed forces and to further the building of railroads, of whose strategic importance he was very much aware. In a

Count Camillo di Cavour (1810–61).

number of commercial treaties, Cavour integrated the economy of Piedmont with that of western Europe. He also fostered legislation improving the structure of business corporations, credit institutions, and cooperative societies. These economic measures alone entitle Cavour to a place of honor in his country's history.

Cavour and Napoleon III

The third requirement for Piedmont to be able to move against Austria was outside military aid. To get such aid, Cavour looked to France and Napoleon III. The French emperor had always held a lingering affection for Italy. To aid Italian unification not only appealed to his idealism but it also might strengthen the prestige of France and of himself. It was considerations like these that led to a super-secret meeting at Plombières in 1858 at which Napoleon promised Cavour his aid if Piedmont should become involved in a war with Austria. Once the war was won, Piedmont would form an enlarged kingdom of Upper Italy, and the whole peninsula was then to be united in a loose federation with the pope as president. France was to be rewarded for its help with the Piedmontese regions of Nice and Savoy. It is important to note that the Plombières agreement did not call for an Italy united under Piedmont.

The main difficulty was finding a pretext for war with Austria. While waiting for an opportunity, the two conspirators continued their preparations. As rumors of an impending war in Italy grew more persistent, the other powers began to show concern. Austria was the least worried. The Austrians were used to recurrent rumors of an Italian war and refused to take them seriously. England and Prussia, on the other hand, were less confident. The former, in the spring of 1859, came out with a plan for the evacuation of Austrian troops from the peninsula and the creation of an Italian federation. This was such an appealing scheme that Napoleon began to show signs of trying to back out of his agreement with Piedmont. At this point, when Cavour's carefully laid plans seemed about to fail, the Austrian emperor, Francis Joseph, forced a showdown by demanding that Piedmont refrain from any further preparations for war. When Piedmont turned down this ultimatum, Austrian troops, on April 29, 1859, invaded Piedmont. France thereupon joined its ally in the war against Austria.

The War of 1859

Had the Austrians moved quickly, they might have won the war. But by wasting time, they allowed the French to move their forces into Italy. After six weeks of bloody fighting, the French and Italian armies had won two indecisive victories at Magenta and Solferino and had driven the Austrians out of Lombardy. The next obvious step was the liberation of Venetia.

At this point, in July 1859, Napoleon surprised his ally and the world by concluding an armistice with Francis Joseph at Villafranca. There were several reasons for Napoleon's sudden defection: he apparently had been shocked by the bloodshed at Magenta and Solferino; the

THE UNIFICATION OF ITALY   1859–70

Piedmont-Sardinia on the eve of war in 1859

Acquired in 1859 through war with Austria

Additions in 1860

Addition in 1866

Addition in 1870

Austrian army was by no means beaten; there was dissatisfaction among many Frenchmen with a war against another Catholic power; and there was some fear that Prussia might come to Austria's aid. Under the terms of the Villafranca agreement, Napoleon broke his promise that Piedmont should get both Lombardy and Venetia. Austria merely surrendered Lombardy, which Napoleon then offered to Victor Emmanuel. The king, much to Cavour's consternation, accepted.

The First Phase of Italian Unification

Villafranca, however, turned out to be a blessing in disguise for the Italians. Up to this point the war had been waged chiefly for the enlargement of Piedmont. Now suddenly it became a national war for Italian unification. At the start of the war, some of the small states in northern and central Italy had revolted and driven out their rulers. The prospect of their return now led the populace of these regions to raise an army and to proclaim their union with Piedmont. Cavour, in January 1860, asked Napoleon's consent to Piedmont's annexation of the central Italian states. Napoleon agreed, in return for the surrender of Nice and Savoy, which he had been promised at Plombières but which he had forfeited at Villafranca. In March 1860, plebiscites in Parma, Modena, Romagna, and Tuscany confirmed the union of central Italy with Piedmont.

The next act in the drama of unification was dominated not by Cavour but by a man who was his opposite in all respects—a romantic, a republican, an effective leader of men, but a complete political amateur—Giuseppe Garibaldi. The role of this colorful figure in the brief fiasco of the Roman republic in 1849 has already been discussed (see p. 563). In May 1860, Garibaldi assembled an expeditionary force at Genoa. Its task was to help complete the liberation of the Kingdom of the Two Sicilies, where an uprising against the reactionary Bourbon regime had taken place. Garibaldi's expedition was a huge success. Aided by the local population, his small force of "Redshirts" defeated an army twenty times its size. By August Sicily was in Garibaldi's hands, and he was ready to cross to the mainland.

Garibaldi's success, however, raised a number of problems. His growing popularity threatened to displace Victor Emmanuel as the leader of a united Italy. Garibaldi might give in to the urgings of Mazzini and surrender the southern half of the peninsula to republicanism; or else he might move against Rome, to complete the unification of Italy. Such a move might lead to a conflict with France, which still considered itself the protector of the papacy. To avert such a crisis, Cavour convinced Napoleon that the only way to stop Garibaldi was for Victor Emmanuel to meet him on the way. Promising to respect the independence of Rome itself, the Piedmontese army now invaded the Papal States, defeated the papal forces, and after bypassing Rome came face to face with Garibaldi's band not far from Naples. The situation was tense. But Garibaldi was too much of a patriot to let selfish ambitions interfere with his hope for a united Italy. Instead, he voluntarily submitted to Victor Emmanuel, thus completing the first phase of Italian unification.

The Kingdom of Italy

The Kingdom of Italy was proclaimed in March 1861. Two months later, Cavour succumbed to an attack of typhoid fever and died, just as his country needed him most. The unification of Italy was by no means completed. Venetia did not become part of the kingdom until after another Austrian defeat, this time by Prussia in 1866; and Rome remained in papal hands until 1870. Other difficulties beset the new state. Not all Italians were happy with the results of unification. The followers of Mazzini would have preferred a republic to a monarchy, and even many monarchists would rather have seen a loosely federated union than the centralized monarchy that resulted from the "conquest" of the peninsula by Piedmont. Regionalism and particularism also interfered with the integration of the eight or more separate states. Tensions between the prosperous north and the poverty-ridden south were especially

Giuseppe Garibaldi (1807–82).

Victor Emmanuel II, king of Italy (1849–78).

marked. The illiteracy of the Italian masses, furthermore, made the extension of democracy a slow process, and Italy's parliamentary regime soon became known for its corruption. The wars of unification imposed staggering financial burdens, and taxes now were higher than ever before. At the same time, lack of coal and iron prevented large-scale industrialization, which might have relieved Italy's economic plight. Yet despite these shortcomings, the new Italy considered itself one of the great powers and tried to imitate the wealthier nations by maintaining an army and navy far beyond its means.

Much of the discontent and disillusionment in Italy after unification was blamed on Cavour's hurried policy. But we must remember that the unification of Italy had not really been his goal at the start. Much of his policy was determined by the other two makers of Italy, Napoleon III and Garibaldi, and by the forces of nationalism, which he could not control. Where we may find fault with Cavour is in the devious methods he employed to achieve his aims. But such *Realpolitik*, as it came to be called, was not considered out of place by an age that gloried in nationalism and worshiped success. Much the same spirit that animated Cavour was to guide Bismarck in his German policy. And just as Cavour had started out in the hope of enlarging Piedmont but ended by creating the Kingdom of Italy, so Bismarck began working for a greater Prussia and wound up with a German Reich.

AUSTRO-PRUSSIAN RIVALRY

The most striking similarity between the unification of Italy and that of Germany was Austria's involvement in both. Austria's defeats in 1859 and 1866 were due in large measure to internal weakness caused by political disunity. Nationalism, which proved a boon to Cavour and Bismarck, was a source of infinite trouble to Francis Joseph and the many capable Austrian ministers who tried to find some way of keeping their empire from falling to pieces.

Nationalism in the Austrian Empire

Prince Schwarzenberg, who had succeeded Metternich in 1848, had given Austria a constitution early in 1849. While calling for a high degree of centralization, it had recognized at least some local and provincial privileges. These mild concessions to the spirit of nationalism, however, were only temporary. Beginning in 1850, all but the centralizing tendencies of the constitution were ignored. Schwarzenberg died in 1852, but his policies were continued. Petty officials, most of them German, directed the affairs of provinces whose language they did not speak and whose customs they ignored. Yet instead of counteracting the centrifugal tendencies of nationalism, this system merely increased the tension between the German ruling caste and the subject peoples.

Austria's defeat at the hands of France and Piedmont in 1859 once again brought home the need for reform. As a result, the excessive centralization of the preceding decade now gave way to some degree of provincial autonomy. In 1861 a new constitution established a central legislature, the *Reichsrat*, made up of delegates from the various regional diets. But the new system, like all earlier ones, had serious flaws. Since the German element was still guaranteed a majority, some of the other nationalities, especially the Hungarians (or Magyars), refused to attend the meetings of the *Reichsrat*. It soon became clear that another effort at solving the nationalities problem had failed. In September 1865 Francis Joseph suspended the constitution of 1861.

At this point the war with Prussia intervened (see pp. 607–08), leaving Austria still weaker and less able to resist the demands of the Hungarian nationalists. As a result of extended negotiations between Austrian and Hungarian leaders, a compromise, or *Ausgleich*, was finally reached in 1867. Under the new arrangement a Dual Monarchy was established, with Francis Joseph serving both as emperor of Austria and king of Hungary. Except in such fields as finance, foreign affairs, and war, where joint ministries were set up, the two parts of the mon-

Francis Joseph I (1830–1916), emperor of Austria and king of Hungary.

archy now were entirely autonomous. Yet since neither the Germans nor the Hungarians held a majority in either half of the Dual Monarchy, the *Ausgleich* did not solve the nationalities problem. Subsequent efforts to recognize the Slavic regions by establishing a Triple Monarchy were defeated by opposition from Germans and Hungarians alike. This continued oppression of Slavic nationalism constituted a major threat to the existence of Austria-Hungary and to the peace of Europe.

Prussia After 1850

Prussia presented quite a different picture from Austria. In administrative efficiency, financial soundness, and military strength, Prussia after 1850 was far superior to its Austrian rival. Except for a small Polish minority in the eastern provinces, its population was homogeneous. And while in Austria industrialization had hardly begun, Prussia during the 1850s began to take its place among the leading industrial powers of the Continent.

Like Austria, Prussia had been granted a constitution in 1849. Since it provided for universal suffrage, it had a deceptively democratic appearance. But by dividing the electorate into three classes, according to the taxes each voter paid, the Prussian constitution made certain that the wealthiest citizens controlled a majority in the lower house of the *Landtag*. With this constitutional arrangement it was not surprising that Prussia continued to be one of the most reactionary states in Germany. In 1857 King Frederick William IV was succeeded by his brother, Prince William, first as regent and in 1861 as king. William was sixty-two years old and an arch-conservative. Having spent most of his life in the army, he had little experience in government. It was due to William's concern over the shortcomings of Prussia's military establishment that Prussia, in 1860, entered upon one of the most serious domestic crises in its history.

Despite a considerable increase in population, Prussia's armed forces in 1860 were still essentially what they had been in 1814. When William tried to correct this situation, however, he ran into opposition from the liberal majority in the *Landtag*, which, under the constitution, had to authorize the necessary funds and which objected to some of the details of the government's reform proposals. By 1862 king and parliament had become deadlocked over the issue. At this point William decided to recall his ambassador to Paris, Otto von Bismarck, and charge him with carrying on the fight with the *Landtag*.

Bismarck and the Constitutional Conflict

The man who was soon to direct the affairs of Germany as first chancellor of the German Reich was then forty-seven years old. He came from an old Prussian family of noble landowners, or Junkers. During the revolution of 1848 he had proved himself a devoted royalist. As a reward he had been appointed Prussia's representative to the Frankfurt Diet during the 1850s and later ambassador to St. Petersburg and Paris. In these various assignments he had shown outstanding ability as a diplomat and as a manipulator of men. But he was also known as a fighter. It was this combination that had recommended him to William I.

Bismarck first tried to mediate the conflict between king and parliament. When this proved impossible, however, he did not give in but carried out the proposed army reforms without parliamentary approval, using funds earmarked for other purposes. The conflict was never resolved but was ultimately overshadowed by more spectacular events. Two wars, in 1864 and 1866, not only gave proof of the excellence of Prussia's reformed army but so aroused the patriotism of the *Landtag* delegates that they were ready to forget their liberal principles. When, during the war with Austria in 1866, Bismarck asked parliament for retroactive assent to the unauthorized expenditures of the previous years, the majority of delegates supported him.

The Prussian constitutional conflict had thus been "solved." But in the process, Prussian and German liberalism had

Prince Otto von Bismarck (1815–98).

suffered a serious defeat. Liberals in Germany henceforth were split in two factions—a larger one that continued to support Bismarck, putting nationalism above liberalism, and a smaller faction that stuck to its liberal principles. This split within German liberalism was never healed. It was the most fateful legacy of the period of German unification.

Rivalry Between Austria and Prussia

Bismarck did not really plan the unification of Germany; it developed more or less accidentally out of Prussia's desire to assert itself against Austria's claims for supremacy in German affairs. The rivalry between Austria and Prussia was of long standing—it went back at least to the days of Frederick the Great and Maria Theresa in the eighteenth century (see p. 507). During most of the intervening period, Prussia had been quite ready to recognize Austria's traditional leadership. The most recent manifestation of Prussia's subjection to Austria had occurred in 1850, when Austria had prevented a scheme advanced by Frederick William IV for a union of German princes under Prussian leadership. Instead, Austria had insisted that the diet of the German Confederation under the presidency of Austria be reconstituted at Frankfurt.

Bismarck, as Prussia's delegate to the Frankfurt Diet, did not object to Austria's leadership in German affairs so long as Austria, in return, recognized Prussia's preeminence in northern Germany. Only after Bismarck realized Austria's unwillingness to cooperate did he decide that the interest of Prussia demanded that Austria be excluded from Germany. Before Prussia could assume leadership in Germany, however, it had to make sure of the good will, or at least the acquiescence, of the great powers. The Italian national movement had enjoyed the sympathy of almost everyone outside Austria, but few people in western Europe wanted to see a Germany united under Prussian auspices. During the Crimean War, Austria had tried to induce Prussia to join in aiding the western powers, but Prussia had remained friendly toward Russia. This was the basis for a close friendship between Prussia and Russia that was to remain a constant element in international affairs for the next few decades.

The first outward sign of Prussia's emancipation from Austrian tutelage came during the Italian war of 1859. Austria at the time fully expected Prussia to be its ally against Piedmont and France. Prussia was ready to comply, but asked to be put in charge of its own and whatever other German forces might be raised. Austria, still filled with its own importance, refused this understandable request. Prussia's neutrality during the

Principles of "Realpolitik"

The state is by nature a realistic politician, if only by virtue of the conditions of its existence, and has therefore always had to suffer being treated as a criminal by political idealists and visionaries. . . . In contrast to the politics of the state, the politics of the people is most susceptible to idealism and fantastication. The causes of this difference are obvious. On the one hand we have the school of political life and the consciousness of responsibility, on the other hand inexperience and yielding to intellectual or emotional whim with little or no thought for the consequences. . . .

For the state, in contrast to the individual, self-preservation is the supreme law. The state must survive at any price; it cannot go into the poorhouse, it cannot beg, it cannot commit suicide; in short, it must take wherever it can find the essentials of life.

Politics, in so far as they are not in the hands of the community, are a mandate which carries responsibility toward the constituency as well as toward the moral law, two responsibilities which need to be weighed against one another.

The right of the politician to sacrifice the welfare of the state to his personal scruples of conscience may be undeniable in simple matters or those of secondary significance, but it may be extremely doubtful in difficult and important cases.

The clash of duties, which the individual can as a rule easily avoid, occurs so often, so unavoidably, and so fatefully in the life of the state that politics is often a matter of choice between two moral evils.

Finally, there occur historic necessities and political acts of nature before which the state and the people resign themselves irresistibly and passively, and to which, therefore, the ethical criterion of human conduct is quite inapplicable. . . .

From A. L. von Rochau, *Grundsätze der Realpolitik* (1869), as quoted in W. M. Simon, *Germany in the Age of Bismarck* (New York: Barnes and Noble, 1968), pp. 133–34.

A cartoon depicting the nature of the European balance of power.

war won the gratitude of both France and Italy. Austria's defeat, on the other hand, clearly showed how much its claim to leadership was based on past prestige rather than present power.

By the end of the 1850s most German liberals were expecting Prussia to take the lead in unifying Germany. The constitutional struggle over the reform of the Prussian army, however, put a temporary damper on their enthusiasm. At the same time, the Austrian constitution of 1861 seemed to indicate more liberal tendencies in the Habsburg Empire. It thus encouraged the Catholic and traditionalist forces, especially in southern Germany, who hoped for a united Germany under Austrian leadership. To take advantage of this shift in opinion, Austria convened a congress in 1863 to consider the reform of the German Confederation in the direction of greater national unity. But Bismarck urged his king to boycott the congress. Without Prussia, the Frankfurt meeting was doomed to failure.

The Schleswig-Holstein Question and the War with Denmark

The final showdown between Austria and Prussia grew out of their involvement in the affairs of the two northern German duchies of Schleswig and Holstein. The Schleswig-Holstein question is famous for its intricacy, and its details need not concern us here. The duchies, largely German but partly Danish, had long been held in personal union by the king of Denmark. In an age of rising nationalism, however, this indeterminate status became increasingly difficult to maintain. The issue had already led to a brief war between Danes and Germans in 1848, in which Denmark had been defeated. The issue became acute again in 1863, when Denmark tried to annex Schleswig. This time both Austria and Prussia rushed to the defense. Their motives for intervention were complex. Both wanted to pose as defenders of German unity, but Prussia also wanted to expand its power in northern Germany.

The war itself was brief. The Danes suffered a crushing defeat. Under the Peace of Vienna in 1864 Denmark surrendered Schleswig and Holstein to Austria and Prussia. In this joint possession of the duchies lay the seeds of the war that broke out between Austria and Prussia two years later. Although Austria and most of the German states wanted the duchies to go to a German claimant, the Duke of Augustenburg, Bismarck wanted the duchies for Prussia. The question was how to bring about such annexation. In 1865 the victors reached a temporary compromise in the Convention of Gastein, under which Prussia was to administer Schleswig and Austria Holstein, while the future of the duchies was to remain a joint responsibility. But this arrangement solved nothing. As Austria continued to encourage the aspirations of the Duke of Augustenburg, and as Prussia proceeded to make itself at home in Schleswig, it became clear that force might be needed to decide the fate of both duchies.

The War of 1866

In the fall of 1865, Bismarck met Napoleon III at Biarritz to sound him out on France's attitude toward a possible war between Prussia and Austria. The meeting suggests a certain parallel to the Plombières meeting of Cavour and Napoleon, except that Bismarck was not asking for French aid; all he wanted was a promise of neutrality. This Napoleon gave, hinting at some unspecified compensations for France. Bismarck agreed. In the spring of 1866, Prussia concluded an alliance with Italy, to which Napoleon also gave his blessing. The remaining great powers did not present much of a problem. Since England had stood by while Denmark was defeated, Bismarck felt that it would not intervene to save Austria. And Russia's friendship for Prussia and its antagonism toward Austria left little doubt where it would stand.

With the diplomatic spadework done, Bismarck's next task was to find a cause for war with Austria that would rally the rest of Germany to Prussia's side. This was not easy, since most of the German princes sided with Austria on the future of Schleswig-Holstein. When Bismarck finally used Prussia's differences with Austria over the duchies as an excuse to order Prussian troops into Holstein, the

Area where Bismarck promised to hold a plebiscite. It did not take place until 1920, when part of the region reverted to Denmark.

remaining members of the German Confederation joined the Austrian side. The war of 1866 was thus not only a war of Prussia against Austria but against most of the rest of Germany as well.

There was little enthusiasm in either camp at the start of the war. Austria was deeply divided and poorly prepared. The Austrians were further handicapped by having to fight on two fronts, Italy and Germany. The Prussians, on the other hand, were in excellent military form, equipped with the latest weapons and led by a master-strategist, Count Helmuth von Moltke. As the first news of victory arrived, moreover, the attitude of the Prussian people changed from apathy to enthusiasm. The war was over in a few weeks. It was decided almost entirely by one major battle, near Königgrätz and Sadowa, in Bohemia, in which the Austrians were defeated, though not annihilated.

The final peace treaty was signed at Prague in August 1866. Chiefly because of Bismarck's insistence, the settlement was remarkably lenient. Bismarck realized that the rest of the powers, especially France, would not stand for a punitive peace. Austria consented to the

dissolution of the German Confederation and recognized the various territorial gains Prussia had made in the north, including Schleswig-Holstein. In a separate settlement Austria surrendered Venetia, which went to Italy. As for Austria's German allies, most of the northern ones were annexed by Prussia, while the southern ones had to pay indemnities and conclude military alliances with Prussia. Prussia thus consolidated its holdings in the north and assumed indirect control over the rest of Germany.

THE UNIFICATION OF GERMANY

The war of 1866 had been waged for the aggrandizement of Prussia. But in the minds of most Germans it soon appeared as a deliberate stage in the unification of Germany. During the winter of 1866/67, delegates from the states that were left in northern Germany after the peace settlement met in Berlin to form a North German Confederation. The plan had originated with Bismarck, whose aim was to establish Prussia's preponderance over the whole region north of the Main River.

THE UNIFICATION OF GERMANY   1866–71

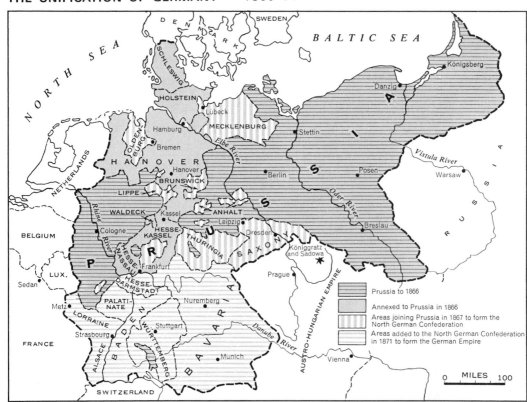

The North German Confederation

The constitution of the North German Confederation established a federal system under which the central government controlled foreign and military affairs. The executive was vested in the king of Prussia as president, assisted by a chancellor—Bismarck. An upper house, or *Bundesrat*, consisted of delegates from the various member states. The lower house, or *Reichstag*, was made up of deputies elected by universal manhood suffrage. Most of the power was vested in the upper house, in which Prussian influence prevailed. There was no ministerial responsibility, since the only minister was the chancellor, and he was responsible only to the president, or king.

The main significance of the North German Confederation's constitution was that it served as a basis for the constitution of the German Empire after 1871. Just as it assured the domination of Prussia in northern Germany after 1867, so after 1871 it perpetuated Prussia's domination over the rest of Germany. How far Bismarck actually foresaw developments beyond 1867 is hard to say. He never was a German nationalist—his major concern was with the power and security of Prussia. Nor was there much desire among the rulers of southern Germany to submit to the king of Prussia. The state of affairs that existed in 1867, therefore, could have lasted for a long time had it not been for the unfortunate machinations of Napoleon III. Like his uncle, Napoleon served as the involuntary agent of German nationalism.

Bismarck and Napoleon III

Napoleon's readiness at Biarritz to let Prussia settle accounts with Austria had been due to his underestimation of Prussian strength. Thinking Prussia and Austria pretty evenly matched, he had expected to throw French power into the balance at the crucial moment. Austria's defeat at Sadowa, therefore, had come as a shock. Together with France's fiasco in Mexico (see p. 628), the defeat of Austria was built up by Napoleon's domestic opponents as a major French defeat. The only way to save French prestige was through some kind of territorial compensations such as France had received during the unification of Italy.

Napoleon should have pressed his demands for compensations while the fate of Austria still hung in the balance. Once Prussia had won the war, Bismarck was no longer in any mood to make concessions. On the contrary, Napoleon's demands served Bismarck to good effect in furthering his own policy. He used Napoleon's bid for territories in the west or south of Germany to cement ties with the southern German states as the best possible protection against French designs; and he later used Napoleon's request for Prussian support in the acquisition of Belgium to incriminate France in the eyes of Great Britain. In a third attempt to gain territorial compensation, Napoleon tried to buy the Duchy of Luxembourg. Bismarck at first approved of the deal but later changed his mind.

Napoleon III, faced with mounting criticism at home and frustrated in his efforts to gather laurels abroad, gradually realized that an armed showdown with Prussia might be inevitable. To prepare himself, he began casting about for allies. But neither Austria nor Italy, whom he approached, had any desire to become involved in a war between France and Prussia. Even so, Napoleon assumed that in case of a war with Prussia he could count on the aid of one or both of the Catholic powers.

The War of 1870

The immediate cause of the war between France and Prussia was the offer of the Spanish throne, temporarily vacated by revolution, to a Hohenzollern prince, distantly related to the king of Prussia. Bismarck was instrumental in having the prince accept the Spanish offer; yet there is no clear evidence that he intended to use the affair to provoke a war with France. Moreover, when France protested the Spanish candidacy, the Prussian government urged the prince to abandon the project. But this did not satisfy the French, who demanded an apology from King William and a promise that the candidacy would not be renewed. This unreasonable demand was made in a famous interview between the French ambassador and the king at the watering place of Ems, an interview that William cut short. When news of this incident reached Berlin, Bismarck edited the report in such a way to make it look as though France had suffered a major diplomatic defeat. It was this edited "Ems dispatch" that led France to declare war on Prussia. In this case Bismarck had foreseen the results, and to that extent he may be held responsible for the war of 1870. Yet his action was merely the latest in a whole series of mutual recriminations, and most historians now agree that responsibility for the war must be shared by both sides.

Events in the early summer of 1870 had moved so quickly that all of Europe was taken by surprise. France's precipitate action lost whatever sympathy it had enjoyed among the other powers. England maintained the aloofness it had shown ever since the Crimean War. Russia continued its policy of benevolent neutrality toward Prussia. Italy was preoccupied with completing its unification by taking the city of Rome. And Austria would prove dangerous only if Prussia ran into difficulties. But there was little chance of that. In numbers, leadership, and morale, Prussia's forces were far superior to those of France. The participation of southern German contingents made this a national German war. The French army fought valiantly, but the quality and morale of its leadership was low. The fact that Napoleon III, worn out by a lingering illness, assumed personal command did not help matters.

The war itself was decided in a series of bloody battles. The climax came on September 2, with Napoleon's capitulation at Sedan. But the fighting continued for several more months, and the city of Paris, where a republic had been proclaimed, did not surrender until the end of January 1871. A temporary armistice was concluded on January 28, pending the election of a representative assembly. The National Assembly chose the liberal monarchist Adolphe Thiers as chief executive. The first task of the new government was to negotiate a final settlement with Bismarck.

The Results of the War

The peace signed at Frankfurt on May 10, 1871, was a harsh one. France had to pay an indemnity of 5 billion francs, and the country was to remain occupied until the indemnity had been paid. In addition, France had to cede Alsace and part of Lorraine, which, for the most part, it had taken from the Holy Roman Empire in the seventeenth century. The inhabitants of Alsace spoke German, but they were pro-French and anti-Prussian in feeling. To take so large a slice of territory in an age of ardent nationalism was a dangerous move. The issue of France's "lost provinces" remained an insuperable obstacle to closer Franco-German relations.

Napoleon III Surrenders at Sedan

September 2, 1870

[Napoleon's aide-de-camp] approached His Majesty and, with a few words, handed him Napoleon's letter. The King opened it and read the short message written by the Emperor himself: "My dear Brother, not having been able to die amidst my troops, nothing remains for me but to surrender my sword into Your Majesty's hands. I remain, Your Majesty's good Brother, Napoleon. Sedan, 1 Sept. 1870." . . . Then the King first discussed with Count Bismarck, General Moltke, and myself the content of the letter he wished to send to Napoleon. . . . The letter, then written by His Majesty himself, ran as follows: "My dear Brother. While regretting the circumstances in which we meet, I accept Your Majesty's sword, and I ask that you would kindly appoint one of your officers, provided with your full powers, to negotiate the conditions for the capitulation of the army which has fought so bravely under your orders. For my part, I have designated General von Moltke for this purpose. I remain, Your Majesty's good Brother, William.—In front of Sedan, 1 September 1870." . . . [Next day, the two men met.] . . . The interview may have lasted for a good quarter of an hour, after which the King and Napoleon by his side stepped back into the reception hall, where the tall, commanding figure of our King appeared wonderfully exalted beside the small, very thick-set figure of the Emperor. When Napoleon saw me, he shook hands with me; heavy tears ran down his cheeks, which he wiped away with his hand, as he mentioned, with the utmost gratitude for both the words and the manner, the way in which His Majesty had just expressed himself. I told him that it was only natural to meet the unfortunate above all with compassion.

From the War Diary of the Prussian Crown Prince, as quoted in H. N. Weill, *European Diplomatic History, 1815–1914* (Jericho, N.Y.: Exposition Press, 1972), pp. 204–05.

The signing of the peace did not end France's troubles. The new National Assembly had a majority of monarchists, so that the survival of the republic depended on the continued split among the three monarchist factions—Bourbon, Orléanist, and Bonapartist. The republican minority had its main support in the city of Paris. It was here, in March 1871, that fear of a monarchist revival, indignation over a humiliating peace, and general misery resulting from the recent siege of the city led to a violent uprising. The Paris Commune, as the government of the insurgents was called, lasted until the end of May. Its aims, on the whole, were moderate. But the Commune also included some socialists. This fact, plus some of the excesses committed during the fighting against the troops of the National Assembly, did much to reawaken middle-class fear of a "red peril," of which the Commune remained the symbol. After their defeat in the final "Bloody Week" of May, thousands of Communards were executed, imprisoned, or deported. The issue of republic against monarchy continued to hang in the balance for some time.

While the siege of Paris was still under way, another important event had taken place. On January 18, 1871, in the Hall of Mirrors in the palace at Versailles,

King William of Prussia was proclaimed German emperor. This ceremony was the climax of long negotiations between Bismarck and the rulers of southern Germany. There had been much hesitation among these Catholic and more liberal states to submit to a confederation dominated by Protestant and reactionary Prussia. Many conservative Prussians were equally hesitant, fearing that Prussia might lose its identity in the larger empire. Even Bismarck, the architect of unification, was not motivated by national enthusiasm. But by fulfilling the German people's dream for unity, he hoped to increase the power and prestige of his beloved Prussia.

The Franco-German War not only completed the unification of Germany; it ended the long struggle for Italian unity. After a plebiscite in October 1870, Rome was annexed to Italy and became Italy's capital. A subsequent effort to mollify the papacy by a generous Law of Papal Guarantees was turned down by the pope, who henceforth considered himself "the prisoner of the Vatican." This state of affairs remained unchanged until 1929, when the signing of the Lateran Treaty put an end to the feud.

The year 1871, like the year 1815, was a landmark in European history. Both years saw the end of a major war, and

French battery in front of Belfort (Alsace), which capitulated to the Germans on February 13, 1871, after a siege of 108 days.

Animated French map of Europe in 1870. A caption with it explains: "England, isolated, swears with rage and almost forgets Ireland, whom she holds on a leash. Spain frets, propped up by Portugal. France repulses the invasion of Prussia, who reaches with one hand for Holland and the other for Austria. Italy, also, says to Bismarck: 'Take your feet away from there.' Corsica and Sardinia, a regular urchin who laughs at it all. Denmark, who has lost his legs in Holstein, hopes to regain them. European Turkey yawns and wakes up. Asiatic Turkey inhales the smoke of her water pipe. Sweden leaps like a panther, and Russia resembles a bugbear out to fill his basket."

both initiated a long period of peace among the major powers. But this is about as far as the parallel goes. Relations among states in 1815 and after had still been conducted according to certain general rules. But the cynical diplomacy of Cavour, Napoleon III, and Bismarck had changed this. From now on, suspicion rather than trust characterized international dealings, and, though there was to be no major war for forty-three years, the threat of war was almost always present.

In 1815 the balance of power had been revived along traditional lines, but by 1871 an entirely new balance had emerged. Austria, Russia, Great Britain, and France had been the leading powers at Vienna, with Prussia lagging far behind and with Italy a mere "geographical expression." By 1871 that order had been thoroughly revised. Both Austria and France now were overshadowed by a Prussianized Germany, and even Italy demanded recognition as a great power. England and Russia continued in their former status; but while at Vienna they had taken an active part in shaping the affairs of the Continent, the balance of 1871 had been brought about without their participation. Here, perhaps, lies the major difference between 1815 and

1871. When Napoleon I had upset the balance of power, the Concert of Europe met at the Congress of Vienna to restore it. There was no such concert in 1871, and hence there was no congress. The Concert of Europe had gone to pieces over the Crimean War. Both Great Britain and Russia had kept out of the subsequent wars of Italian and German unification. It was the passivity of these peripheral powers, as much as the activities of Cavour, Bismarck, and Napoleon III, that helped to bring about the changed European balance of 1871.

ENGLAND'S "VICTORIAN COMPROMISE"

England had always maintained a certain isolation from the Continent, and it had added reason to do so after the middle of the nineteenth century. The British people did not remain immune from the virus of nationalism. But the Crimean War had brought home the futility of military involvement. And besides, it had brought defeat to Russia, whose advances in the eastern Mediterranean had presented the only real threat to British commerce.

The "Workshop of the World"

The twenty years after 1850 were the most prosperous in British history. While wars elsewhere helped retard economic development, Britain's industry and commerce experienced an unprecedented boom. This was the heyday of free trade, a policy from which Britain, as the most advanced industrial nation, profited most. The change in shipbuilding from wood to iron, furthermore, opened up a wholly new field for expansion. By 1870, Britain's carrying trade enjoyed a virtual monopoly. While British engineers were building railroads the world over, Britain's surplus capital sought outlets for investment on the Continent and overseas. Between 1854 and 1870, England's foreign holdings more than doubled.

Though Britain was reluctant to become involved in European politics, it showed no such hesitation overseas. (The next chapter has more to say on British colonial policy.) While in some parts of the British Empire, such as Canada and Australia, the basis for self-government was being laid, elsewhere, notably in India, Britain tightened its reins. In 1859 the rule of the East India Company was taken over by the British government. Commercial expansion in China, begun in the 1840s, made rapid advances in the late 1850s. The new Suez Canal, built by French interests, soon became a major artery for British commerce.

The Second Reform Bill

Britain's prosperity did not do away with political discontent. There had been no major political reforms since 1832. The Tories, now officially called Conservatives, had reluctantly acquiesced in the new conditions created by the Great Reform Bill; and the Whigs, now called Liberals, while favoring reforms in other fields, also considered the Reform Bill

EUROPE IN 1871

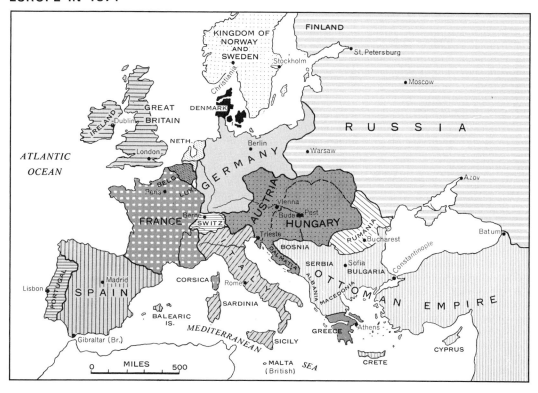

final. The aims of the two parties had thus become almost indistinguishable. Neither the aristocracy nor the middle class was dominant. Government proceeded by compromise.

Meanwhile, as a result of advancing industrialization, Britain's middle and working classes were growing rapidly. This growth could not help but create a demand for further extension of the franchise. By the 1860s the need for reform could no longer be ignored. Both parties at the time had leaders ready to take charge of the contest over parliamentary reform. Since 1852 the Conservative Benjamin Disraeli and the Liberal William Gladstone had played important roles in cabinets of their respective parties. In 1866 Gladstone introduced a moderate reform bill that was promptly defeated by the Conservatives. An even more radical bill introduced the next year by Disraeli was passed, largely with Liberal support. The Second Reform Bill of 1867, by giving the vote to urban workers, doubled the number of voters. It did not introduce universal suffrage, but it did provide the majority of adult British males with a voice in their government.

Gladstone's First "Great Ministry"

The agitation surrounding the Second Reform Bill had ended the Victorian Compromise. Both Conservatives and Liberals now tightened their organiza-

Caricature of William Gladstone in 1869, by "Ape" (Carlo Pellegrini).

tions and became parties in the modern sense. When the elections of 1868 returned a Liberal majority, Gladstone formed his first "great ministry." Just as the Bill of 1832 had been followed by a long series of domestic reforms, so the years after 1867 saw many overdue measures enacted. Notable among them was the Education Act of 1870, which, at long last, relieved a situation in which almost half of Britain's children had received no schooling.

One problem concerned Gladstone above all others—the problem of Ireland. That unhappy country, vastly overpopulated, had long been on the verge of starvation. Migration to the United States relieved some of the pressure but also added to unrest. The Fenian Brotherhood, founded in New York in 1858, was responsible for many acts of violence in England and Ireland. Gladstone considered the solution of the Irish problem his major mission. Its roots were partly religious, partly economic. To solve Ireland's religious grievances, the Disestablishment Act of 1869 freed Irish Catholics from having to support the Anglican

French satirical drawing of England's Irish problem. Queen Victoria, touring the island, is shielded from seeing unpleasant sights.

Church. To improve land tenure, the Land Act of 1870 curtailed the power of absentee landlords to evict their tenants without compensation. But since the Land Act did not heed Ireland's demands for the "three F's"—fair rent, fixity of tenure, and free sale—it was only a half-measure.

Like most of Gladstone's reforms, his Irish policy violated many vested interests and contributed to his defeat in 1874. There were other causes of discontent. Though elected by working-class votes, Gladstone had done little to improve the status of the laborer. Prosperity, meanwhile, had begun to level off, and from 1873 on depression elsewhere made itself felt in Britain as well. Finally, Gladstone's foreign policy—peaceful, sensible, but unexciting—lacked popular support. With Disraeli, who succeeded him in 1874 and who combined social legislation at home with an active imperial policy abroad, a new chapter in British history began.

RUSSIA: REACTION AND REFORM

The second great power on the periphery of Europe, tsarist Russia, pursued its own peculiar course through most of the nineteenth century. The westernization of Russia that had begun during the eighteenth century continued, but very slowly. Because of its vast size and the multiplicity of its backward peoples, Russia faced a number of problems not shared by any of the other great powers. To establish political control in the face of such obstacles required a regime of strict autocracy. The will of the tsar was law. His decrees were translated into action by a huge bureaucracy whose openness to bribery helped somewhat to soften the harshness of tsarist rule. Russia's government has been aptly described as "despotism tempered by corruption."

Aside from autocracy, there were other institutions peculiar to the tsarist empire. Although in western Europe the nobility had lost much of its power, Russia's aristocracy continued to enjoy its traditional privileges. Besides owning al-

most all the land, the nobles were exempt from taxation and from military service. There was as yet no middle class to speak of, except in the few larger towns. The majority of the tsar's subjects, more than 95 percent, were peasants, and most of them were still serfs. Serfdom in Russia was much more burdensome than it had been in western Europe. Even the legally free peasants, who by 1833 constituted about a third of the population, were kept in a decidedly inferior position. Occasionally, when the misery of the Russian masses became too much to bear, they sought relief in local uprisings. There had been more than five hundred such mutinies during the rule of Nicholas I (1825–55). Nicholas actually had introduced some measures aimed at alleviating the worst abuses of serfdom, but to go to the root of the evil and to liberate the serfs would have meant taking land away from the nobility; even the autocratic tsars did not dare do that. Instead, Nicholas continued to preach the principles dearest to his reactionary heart—obedience to autocracy, adherence to the traditional Orthodox religion, and patriotic faith in the virtues of Russian nationality.

"Westerners" versus "Slavophils"

The obstacles that the tsarist government put in the way of education and the restriction it imposed on western ideas helped to keep down the numbers of the Russian "intelligentsia"—that is, those few people whose intellectual interests set them apart from the majority of the people. Still, by the middle of the nineteenth century this group had grown numerous enough to make its influence felt. There were two clearly defined factions among Russian intellectuals—the "Westerners" and the "Slavophils." The Westerners saw their country as essentially a part of western civilization, merely lagging behind but able eventually to catch up. The Slavophils, on the other hand, held that the difference between Russia and the West was not one of degree but of kind. They pointed to the peculiar foundations of Russian civilization—Byzantine, Slavic, and Greek-Orthodox as compared with the Roman, Germanic, and Catholic roots of western civilization. And they believed that each nation should live according to its own traditions rather than try to imitate the institutions and practices of other countries. These theoretical differences between Westerners and Slavophils also determined their attitudes toward current problems. While the Westerners favored constitutional government, rationalism, and industrial progress, the Slavophils saw the salvation of Russia in benevolent autocracy, Orthodox Christianity, and the reform of Russia's predominantly agrarian society. This eastern-versus-western orientation henceforth remained a permanent characteristic of Russian political and social philosophy.

The most important political developments during the regime of Nicholas I were in foreign affairs. One of the main aims of Russian policy continued to be the domination, direct or indirect, over the disintegrating Ottoman Empire.

Western opposition to Russia's Turkish aspirations had finally led to the Crimean War. More than any previous event, this conflict had shown the inefficiency, corruption, and poor leadership of the tsarist regime. Nicholas had died during the war. His successor, Alexander II (1855–81), was far less reactionary. Though he had little understanding of social and economic problems, he was impressed by the clamor for reform that had set in after the Crimean defeat. The most widespread demand of the reformers was for the emancipation of the serfs.

The Emancipation of the Serfs

Alexander II realized that the alternative to abolishing serfdom from above might ultimately be revolution from below. He therefore initiated a careful study of the situation that finally, in March 1861, led to the Emancipation Edict. Its immediate effects, however, were far from happy. It was of little use for the Russian serf to gain his freedom without at the same time obtaining sufficient land to make a living. Yet to deprive the nobility of its labor force and most of its land would have placed the burden of emancipation entirely on that class. The solution finally arrived at was a compromise that satisfied no one. The peasants were given almost half the land, not in direct ownership but in large holdings administered by the village community, the *mir.* The *mir* in turn apportioned land use among the village households. The landowners were compensated by the government; but the redemption money that the government paid to the nobles had to be repaid over a period of forty-nine years by each village community.

Emancipation thus freed the individual peasant from servitude to his noble master but subjected him to the communal control of his village. It substituted a new "peasant problem" for the old problem of serfdom. To be freed from the redemption payments and the tutelage of the *mir,* and to get hold of the land still in the hands of the nobility—these remained burning issues for the Russian peasantry into the twentieth century.

Serfdom

Few realize what serfdom was in reality. There is a dim conception that the conditions which it created were very bad; but those conditions, as they affected human beings bodily and mentally, are not generally understood. It is amazing, indeed, to see how quickly an institution and its social consequences are forgotten when the institution has ceased to exist, and with what rapidity men and things change. I will try to recall the conditions of serfdom by telling, not what I heard but what I saw . . . :

Father . . . calls in Makár, the piano-tuner and sub-butler, and reminds him of all his recent sins. . . . Of a sudden there is a lull in the storm. My father takes a seat at the table and writes a note. "Take Makár with this note to the police station, and let a hundred lashes with the birch rod be given him."

Terror and absolute muteness reign in the house. The clock strikes four, and we all go down to dinner. . . . "Where is Makár?" our stepmother asks. "Call him in." Makár does not appear, and the order is repeated. He enters at last, pale, with a distorted face, ashamed, his eyes cast down. . . . Tears suffocate me, and immediately after dinner is over I run out, catch Makár in the dark passage, and try to kiss his hand; but he tears it away, and says, either as a reproach or as a question, "Let me alone; you, too, when you are grown up, will you not be just the same?"

From Prince Peter Kropotkin, *Memoirs of a Revolutionist* (Boston: Houghton Mifflin, 1899), pp. 49–51.

Alexander II (*ca.* 1876).

Reform, Radicalism, and Reaction

The liberation of the serfs, while the most spectacular of Alexander's acts, was not the only effort he made to strengthen his regime through timely reforms. In 1863 he granted universities a greater degree of academic freedom. In 1864 he reformed the Russian judicial system along western lines. The same year Alexander introduced a measure of local and regional self-government through elected assemblies, or *zemstvos*. The hope of the reformers that this development might eventually culminate in a national assembly was disappointed. But even so, the *zemstvos* provided some opportunity for public discussion and the development of civic responsibility, both hitherto unknown in Russia.

The more changes Alexander introduced, the more hopes he aroused. One of the results of his policy had been to give an impetus to various reform movements among the intelligentsia, whose aims and agitation became ever more radical. Western socialism had been slow to gain a hold in Russia, where industry was still in its infancy. Consequently, Russian socialists like Alexander Herzen tried to appeal to the Russian peasant, whose village community already exhibited many of the collective features cherished by socialists. In the 1860s it became the fashion for members of the intelligentsia to go out and live among the peasants in the hope of arousing them from their apathy and urging them into starting a revolution. This "go-to-the-people" movement (*Narodniki*), however, failed because the peasants were too backward and the authorities too vigilant. In their opposition to everything their government stood for, the younger members of the intelligentsia now began to refer to themselves as "nihilists," believers in nothing. Most of them vented their anger over the existing system merely by expounding radical ideas and by disregarding conventional manners and mores. During the 1870s, however, some of the nihilists fell under the influence of Mikhail Bakunin and his philosophy of anarchism (see p. 591). In 1879

this terrorist faction formed a secret society, "The Will of the People," whose aim was to overthrow the government by direct action and assassination.

Frightened by these manifestations of radicalism, Alexander II reverted to a policy of renewed reaction. Yet by reverting to repression, he merely helped to strengthen the revolutionary forces he hoped to combat. This fact was brought home to him in several attempts on his life, and in 1880 he tried once again to return to his initial policy of reform. But by then it was too late. Alexander II was killed by a terrorist bomb in 1881.

THE PRIMACY OF FOREIGN POLICY

During the two decades after 1850 foreign policy in most of Europe overshadowed domestic policy. There were few discernible trends in domestic affairs. Industrialization continued, but its progress was still uneven. Democracy made gains in some countries (notably England), but it suffered reversals in others (notably Germany). Some important reforms helped ease tension—the Emancipation Edict in Russia, the *Ausgleich* between Austria and Hungary, the Second Reform Bill in England. But for each issue resolved, others arose elsewhere—the conflict between monarchism and republicanism in France, the defeat of

Alexander Herzen (1812–70), Russian writer and socialist whose journal, *Kolokol* (the *Bell*), published in exile, was widely read in Russia, even though it had been banned.

liberalism in Germany, the tension between north and south in Italy, to mention but a few.

The most significant event in the "era of unification" was the emergence of Germany as a great power. From 1871 to 1945 the influence of that belatedly unified nation made itself felt in every major international crisis and in the history of every country. Compared with German unification, the unification of Italy today seems of minor importance, though it did not appear so at the time. Of much greater consequence was the tragic fate of the Second French Empire. Its defeat at the hands of Prussia sowed some of the seeds that brought forth the great wars of our century. But these events were far off in 1871. At the time it seemed as though the Continent at long last had found the stability that statesmen before 1850 had tried so hard to achieve. The future was to show the precariousness of the new balance of power.

Suggestions for Further Reading

Note: Asterisk denotes a book available in paperback edition.

General Most of the general works cited after Chapter 24 also cover this later period. An admirably comprehensive view may be gained from R. C. Binkley, *Realism and Nationalism, 1852–1871** (1935), and, more recently, from E. J. Hobsbawm, *The Age of Capitalism, 1848–1875* (1976). The international affairs of Europe are covered in A. J. P. Taylor, *The Struggle for Mastery in Europe, 1848–1918** (1954).

The Eastern Question The disintegration of the Ottoman Empire is treated authoritatively in J. A. R. Marriott, *The Eastern Question in European Diplomacy* (1926), and more briefly in M. S. Anderson, *The Eastern Question** (1966). On the background of the Crimean War, see E. Horvath, *Origins of the Crimean War* (1937); H. W. V. Temperley, *England and the Near East: The Crimea* (1936); G. B. Henderson, *Crimean War Diplomacy and Other Historical Essays* (1947); D. Hopwood, *The Russian Presence in Syria and Palestine, 1843–1914* (1969); and P. W. Schröder, *Austria, Great Britain, and the Crimean War: The Destruction of the European Concert* (1973). W. E. Mosse, *The Rise and Fall of the Crimean System, 1855–1871* (1967), takes a new look at the larger issues connected with the war. The war itself is vividly portrayed in N. Bentley, ed., *William H. Russell's Despatches from the Crimea, 1854–1856* (1967). The Crimean War also provides a somber background for two fine books by C. Woodham-Smith: *Florence Nightingale, 1820–1910** (1951) and *The Reason Why** (1953).

The Second French Empire The most thorough studies of Napoleon III's early career are both by F. A. Simpson, *The Rise of Louis Napoleon* (1950) and *Louis Napoleon and the Recovery of France, 1848–1856*, 3rd ed. (1951). The political history of the Empire is covered in O. Aubry, *The Second Empire* (1940), and in J. M. Thompson, *Louis Napoleon and the Second Empire* (1955). A. Guérard, *Reflections on the Napoleonic Legend* (1924), traces the Napoleonic heritage of the emperor. The same author, in his *Napoleon III** (1943), draws a sympathetic picture of a man whom others have called a "herald of fascism." A collection of contrasting interpretations of Napoleon III may be found in B. D. Gooch, ed., *Napoleon III: Man of Destiny— Enlightened Statesman or Proto-Fascist?** (1963). N. N. Barker, *Distaff Diplomacy: The Empress Eugénie and the Foreign Policy of the Second Empire* (1967), deals with the influence of the wife of Napoleon III. Among more specialized studies of the Empire, the following are of interest: T. Zeldin, *The Political System of Napoleon III* (1958); F. C. Palm, *England and Napoleon III: A Study in the Rise of a Utopian Dictator* (1948); L. M. Case, *French Opinion on War and Diplomacy During the Second Empire* (1953); L. M. Case and W. F. Spencer, *The United States and France: Civil War Diplomacy* (1970); C. W. Hallberg, *Franz Joseph and Napoleon III, 1852–1864: A Study of Austro-French Relations* (1955); and D. S. Pinckney, *Napoleon III and the Reconstruction of Paris* (1958). R. L. Williams, *Gaslight and Shadow: The World of Napoleon III** (1957), conveys some of the glamour and excitement of one of the most brilliant periods in French history. The same author's *The French Revolution of 1870–1871** (1969), deals with the end of the Empire. E. S. Mason, *The Paris Commune* (1968), is a balanced account. The best books in English on Gambetta are J. P. T. Bury, *Gambetta and the National Defense* (1936) and *Gambetta and the Making of the Third Republic* (1973).

The Unification of Italy The dramatic events of these crucial years are best studied through the lives of the main participants, including Napoleon III. A. J. Whyte, *The Political Life and Letters of Cavour, 1848–1861* (1930), and W. R. Thayer, *The Life and Times of Cavour*, 2 vols. (1914), are standard works. The same holds true for the classic accounts of Garibaldi's colorful exploits in G. M. Trevelyan, *Garibaldi and the Thousand* (1911) and *Garibaldi and the Making of Italy* (1911). More recent are the excellent studies by D. Mack Smith: *Cavour and Garibaldi, 1860: A Study in Political Conflict* (1954); *Garibaldi* (1956); and *Victor Emmanuel, Cavour, and the Risorgimento* (1971). For a good brief account, see D. Beales, *The Risorgimento and the Unification of Italy* (1971). The best biographies of Mazzini are B. King, *The Life of Mazzini* (1902), and G. O. Griffith, *Mazzini: Prophet of Modern Europe* (1932). The role of Napoleon III in the unification of Italy is treated in most of the works on the Second Empire cited above, as well as in L. M. Case, *Franco-Italian Relations, 1860–1865* (1932), and in J. W. Bush, *Venetia Redeemed: Franco-Italian Relations, 1864–1866* (1967). On British policy, see D. E. D. Beales, *England and Italy, 1859–1860* (1961).

The Unification of Germany The most recent comprehensive account in English of the events culminating in 1871 is O. Pflanze, *Bismarck and the Development of Germany: The Period of Unification, 1815–1871* (1963). T. S. Hamerow, *The Social Foundation of German Unification, 1858–1871* (1969), supplies the domestic background. The Prussian constitutional conflict is the subject of E. N. Anderson, *The Social and Political Conflict in Prussia* (1954). On the war with Denmark, L. D. Steefel, *The Schleswig-Holstein Question* (1932), remains standard. For an understanding of Austro-Prussian rivalry, H. Friedjung, *The Struggle for Supremacy in Germany, 1859–1866* (1897, 1935), is still important. See also C. W. Clark, *Franz Joseph and Bismarck: The Diplomacy of Austria Before the War of 1866* (1934), and E. A. Pottinger, *Napoleon III and the German Crisis, 1865–1866* (1966). Subsequent Austrian developments are covered in A. J. May, *The Hapsburg Monarchy, 1867–1914* (1951), and in R. A. Kann, *The Habsburg Empire* (1957). On the war of 1866, see G. Craig, *The Battle of Königgrätz: Prussia's Victory over Austria, 1866* (1964). On the outbreak of the Franco-Prussian War, see L. D. Steefel, *Bismarck, the Hohenzollern Candidacy, and the Origins of the Franco-Prussian War* (1962). R. Millman, *British Foreign Policy and the Coming of the Franco-Prussian War* (1965), is useful. There are many biographies of Bismarck, none of them wholly satisfactory. E. Eyck, *Bismarck and the German Empire** (1950), is an abbreviation of a much longer German work; A. J. P. Taylor, *Bismarck: The Man and the Statesman** (1955), is more readable but less sound. A. Palmer, *Bismarck* (1976), makes pleasant and profitable reading. The international repercussions of German unification are admirably clarified in W. E. Mosse, *The European Powers and the German Question, 1848–1871* (1958). On the war between France and Prussia, see M. E. Howard, *The Franco-Prussian War** (1961).

England Both A. Briggs, *The Age of Improvement, 1783–1867* (1959), and G. Kitson-Clark, *The Making of Victorian England* (1962), contain authoritative accounts of the mid-Victorian era. E. Longford, *Victoria R. I.** (1964), is based on the queen's personal archives. British foreign policy and its chief maker are vividly presented in D. Southgate, *"The Most English Minister": The Policies and Politics of Palmerston* (1966). H. C. F. Bell, *Lord Palmerston*, 2 vols. (1936), is the best biography. For a brilliant survey of social and intellectual life, see G. M. Young, *Victorian England: Portrait of an Age** (1936). Good monographs on important domestic developments are J. H. Hanham, *Elections and Party Management: Politics in the Time of Disraeli and Gladstone* (1959), and F. B. Smith, *The Making of the Second Reform Bill* (1966). On the Irish question, see the excellent book by G. Dangerfield, *The Damnable Question* (1976).

Russia The history of Russia is covered in M. T. Florinsky, *Russia: A History and an Interpretation*, Vol. II (1953); H. Seton-Watson, *The Russian Empire, 1801–1917* (1967); and R. Pipes, *Russia under the Old Regime* (1975). J. H. Billington, *The Icon and the Axe* (1966), is a comprehensive synthesis of Russian culture. A. Herzen, *My Past and Thoughts*, 6 vols. (1924–27), is a graphic contemporary account by one of Russia's leading intellectuals. On the crucial problem of serfdom, see G. T. Robinson, *Rural Russia Under the Old Regime* (1949), and T. Emmons, *The Russian Landed Gentry and the Peasant Emancipation of 1861* (1968). D. M. Wallace, *Russia** (1912), is still valuable for an understanding of the Russian people. The following discuss two basic trends of Russian life and thought: H. Kohn, *Pan-Slavism: Its History and Ideology** (1953), and N. V. Riasinovsky, *Russia and the West in the Teaching of the Slavophiles* (1953). On the latter, see also the pioneering study by A. Walicki, *The Slavophile Controversy* (1975). D. R. Brower, *Training the Nihilists* (1975), dissects the intelligentsia. S. Graham, *Tsar of Freedom: The Life and Reign of Alexander II* (1935), deals sympathetically with a tragic figure. W. E. Mosse, *Alexander II and the Modernization of Russia** (1958), is a brief survey.

27 Europe and the World in the Nineteenth Century

The reception held on the occasion of the arrival of a new British governor in East Africa as depicted by an African artist.

From the Age of Discovery until the nineteenth century the world leadership of Europe had remained virtually unchallenged. As European nations established overseas commercial or colonial contacts, the ultimate conquest of the globe by western civilization appeared inevitable. But there had also been signs of a reverse trend, as some regions seemed to grow restive under European tutelage. The United States had been the first European overseas possession to gain independence, and there were soon to be similar movements for independence in the other regions where Europeans had settled. In time this unrest also affected some of the native peoples. Only the Japanese managed to become sufficiently westernized to escape foreign control. But other potentially great powers, notably India and China, wanted to emulate the Japanese. Despite the continued ascendancy of Europe during the nineteenth century, therefore, there were indications that the day of European supremacy was drawing to a close.

This chapter deals only with the major spheres of European expansion—North and South America, the British Empire, and Asia. The African continent was not opened up to European penetration until the end of the nineteenth century, and the resulting rivalry among the powers there will be more profitably discussed in a later chapter. The United States will command far more attention than any of the other regions, mainly because America remains to this day the most important overseas extension of European civilization.

THE UNITED STATES BECOMES A GREAT POWER

In 1815 America was of little concern to most Europeans. A century later, it had emerged as the decisive arbiter in the greatest war Europe had ever fought. The advent of this newcomer on the international stage was long delayed. Through most of the nineteenth century, America was politically isolated from the rest of the world, so much so that "isolationism" remained a strong trend in American foreign policy.

America and Europe

In the Monroe Doctrine of 1823, America had warned Europe to desist from any further colonization in the Western Hemisphere (see p. 555). On several occasions during the nineteenth century, notably during the 1830s and 1840s, the United States became involved with its neighbors to the north and south over territorial issues. But these localized conflicts had no effect on the European balance of power. Even the international repercussions of the American Civil War did not lead to European intervention. It was only at the close of the nineteenth century, in the war with Spain, that America once again went to war with a European power.

Despite the political isolation in which the United States shaped its destiny, cultural relations between the new republic and the old continent remained close, though America at first was a recipient rather than a contributor in this cultural exchange. In the 1830s and 1840s, foreign travelers still commented on the backwardness and boorishness of American manners and customs. But there were also some friendlier critics, like the young Frenchman Alexis de Tocqueville, whose *Democracy in America* (1835–40) predicted correctly the leading role that the United States would some day play in world affairs.

America had shared the European vogue of Romanticism, and some of Europe's early socialists had tried out their utopian experiments on American soil. By the middle of the nineteenth century, American writers like Irving, Cooper, Longfellow, and Poe drew foreign attention to American literature, and the monumental works of the historians Prescott, Parkman, Bancroft, and Motley did the same for American historiography. There were other fields in which American influence made itself felt. The pioneering efforts of American reformers in advocating women's rights, pacifism, and temperance evoked responses overseas; and the gradual adoption in Europe of universal male suffrage and free public education profited greatly from the American example. In technical inventions America already showed signs of the genius that was ultimately to make it

America led the way in invention of better means of communication. Above: the tape on which the first telegraph message was received in Baltimore on May 24, 1844. Samuel F. B. Morse had tapped out ''What hath God wrought?'' from Washington. Below: Alexander Graham Bell's invention—the telephone (1876).

the leading industrial nation of the world. The cultural exchange between Europe and the United States thus became less one-sided as time went on. Better means of communication also played their part. By the 1860s, the steamship had begun to compete successfully with the sailing vessel, and the laying of a transatlantic cable in 1858 speeded the exchange of news and ideas.

The Westward Movement

In its domestic development the United States faced many of the same social and economic problems that confronted the nations of Europe. But since America was a new nation, unencumbered by feudal traditions and endowed with a rich and virtually empty continent, it grew into something radically different from Europe. Within one century the territory of the United States increased

more than fourfold. To assimilate and integrate these new lands proved to be America's foremost political problem, and its final accomplishment contributed to the origins of a bloody civil war. Yet the abundance of fertile lands also helped to relieve economic and social pressures that might have had similarly violent repercussions. The result of America's territorial expansion was a superpower marked by vast size, advantageous location, wide variety of climate, and great wealth of natural resources.

Immigration

The territorial growth of the United States was closely related to the phenomenal growth of its population. From less than 4 million in 1790, the population shot up to over 60 million in the course of a hundred years. Much of this increase was due to the ceaseless stream of European immigrants, totaling more than 35 million between 1815 and 1914. Many of them still came to escape political or religious persecution, but there was also the attraction of the seemingly unlimited economic opportunities of the New World. The constant supply of cheap labor provided by immigration was a boon to America's growing economy. The rapid Americanization of these new citizens was aided by the fact that the United States had no privileged classes, no established church, and no military caste. American society had its sectional and occupational groupings, but they were not as rigid as the European hierarchies. Economic opportunity for all, an open society in which ability and hard work brought success—these were the ingredients of the "American dream," if not always the American reality.

Early Industrialization

Like most European countries, the United States in the first part of the nineteenth century remained predomi-

De Tocqueville on Russia and America

1835

There are at the present time two great nations in the world, which started from different points, but seem to tend towards the same end. I allude to the Russians and the Americans. . . . All other nations seem to have nearly reached their natural limits, and they have only to maintain their power; but these are still in the act of growth. . . . These alone are proceeding with ease and celerity along a path to which no limit can be perceived. The American struggles against the obstacles that nature opposes to him; the adversaries of the Russian are men. The former combats the wilderness and savage life; the latter, civilization with all its arms. The conquests of the American are therefore gained by the plowshare; those of the Russian by the sword. The Anglo-American relies upon personal interest to accomplish his ends and gives free scope to the unguided strength and common sense of the people; the Russian centers all the authority of society in a single arm. The principal instrument of the former is freedom; of the latter, servitude. Their starting-point is different and their courses are not the same; yet each of them seems marked out by the will of Heaven to sway the destinies of half the globe.

From Alexis de Tocqueville, *Democracy in America* (New York: Knopf, 1953), Vol. I, p. 434.

Immigrants at Ellis Island, New York City (ca. 1912).

nantly agrarian. It was the abundance of land that attracted land-hungry Europeans. But as in Europe, the vast increase of population required additional economic outlets, and these were provided by industry. By the middle of the nineteenth century the eastern states had thriving industries. At the same time, the opening up of western territories provided an ever-expanding market. Full-scale industrialization did not take hold until after the Civil War. Prior to 1860, however, many of the social effects of industrialization that were seen in Europe had already made themselves felt. Labor conditions in American factories on the whole were better than those in Europe. During the first half of the nineteenth century there were the beginnings of American labor unions, but a labor movement in the modern sense, in America as in Europe, did not develop until later.

In its economic philosophy, America shared the faith of European liberals in freedom from state control. The American Revolution had been fought against the mercantilist restrictions imposed by the mother country. Once these restrictions had been removed, there remained few obstacles to free enterprise. A philosophy of laissez faire thus came to permeate the economic life of the United States. There was only one field in which American industry not only tolerated but demanded government control, and that was tariff legislation. With the world's largest free-trade area within their own borders, American manufacturers were eager to keep foreign competitors out.

America After 1815

The revolutionary turmoil in Europe after 1815 had its parallel in the unrest that prevailed in the United States during the 1820s. The source of this unrest was economic and social. As America's population increased, and as the new territories acquired with the purchase of Louisiana (1803) and Florida (1819) filled up with new settlers, a number of differences arose between the established interests in the East and the new forces on the frontier. Another source of unrest arose among the new workers of the East, most of them recent immigrants with little bargaining power and no social standing. Thanks to the growth of the democratic process after the Revolution, this discontent was able to express itself at the ballot box.

Democracy in the United States had been slow to reach all levels of society, and it was not until the late 1820s that male suffrage had been adopted in the majority of states. Largely as a result of this increased democratization, Andrew Jackson was elected president in 1828. More than any of his predecessors, Jackson could claim to be the people's choice. He was the first westerner to win the highest office, a popular hero of the War of 1812, and, most important, a man who had risen from poverty by his own efforts. The road from log cabin to White House henceforth became part of the American dream.

The "Age of Jackson"

The "Age of Jackson" was a period of major change in American life, more so even than the 1830s were in western Europe. The democratization of political life continued with the adoption of the patronage, or spoils, "system," and with the practice of having presidential candidates nominated by national conventions rather than by a handful of party leaders. Closest to Jackson's heart was the further development of the West. In a number of treaties concluded with Indian tribes, the federal government won title to millions of acres of virgin land. These were sold at auction at low cost, after free land for schools, roads, a state university, and other public purposes had been set aside. Jackson's opposition to eastern financial interests, furthermore, made him the advocate of state banks, whose lavish granting of credit helped develop the West.

With the opening of the West, sectional rivalry became one of the major issues in American politics. Not only the West, but the South as well, found itself at odds with the North, especially over

Jackson Forever!
The Hero of Two Wars and of Or'eans!
The Man of the People!
HE WHO COULD NOT BARTER NOR BARGAIN FOR THE
PRESIDENCY!
Who, although "A Military Chieftain," valued the purity of Elections and of the Electors, MORE than the Office of PRESIDENT itself! Although the greatest in the gift of his countrymen, and the highest in point of dignity of any in the world,
BECAUSE
It should be derived from the
PEOPLE!
No Gag Laws! No Black Cockades! No Reign of Terror! No Standing Army or Navy Officers, when under the pay of Government, to browbeat, or
KNOCK DOWN
Old Revolutionary Characters, or our Representatives while in the discharge of their duty.   To the Polls then, and vote for those who will support
OLD HICKORY
AND THE ELECTORAL LAW.

Above: Andrew Jackson (1767–1845), by Thomas Sully. Left: Jackson's campaign poster in 1828.

tariffs. The South, depending on cotton exports, favored free trade, while the North demanded high tariffs to protect its infant industries. Finding itself more and more overshadowed by the North, the South used the proposal of a high tariff in 1828 as an occasion for raising the vital question of "states' rights." The relationship between state and federal governments had been an issue in American politics since the early days of the Republic. The Constitution of 1787 had considerably widened the power of the central government over what it had been under the Articles of Confederation, and the policy since then had been to carry this centralization further.

But there was also strong sentiment against this tendency. Critics of centralization took the view that the Constitution was primarily a compact among sovereign states, and that the states had the right to nullify an act of Congress if it violated the terms of that compact. It was this idea of nullification that was used by Jackson's vice president, John C. Calhoun, a southerner, to fight the "tariff of abominations." In the ensuing crisis Jackson broke with Calhoun and defended the sovereignty of the Union against the advocates of states' rights. A final showdown was averted by the compromise tariff of 1833. But this did not remove the underlying conflict between federal power and state sovereignty.

John C. Calhoun (1782–1850), by Charles Bird King.

Expansionism of the 1840s

In foreign affairs the Jacksonian period was uneventful. As more and more settlers began moving westward, however, it was inevitable that tensions would develop with the British in the north and the Mexicans in the south over rival claims to western territories. These intermittent conflicts came to a head and were settled during the 1840s. American-British economic relations were so advantageous that it was in the interest of both to avoid a major crisis over the American-Canadian frontier. By the Webster-Ashburton Treaty (1842), therefore, the northeastern boundary was adjusted to mutual satisfaction. A similar compromise was reached for the Northwest in the Oregon Treaty (1846), which fixed Oregon's northern boundary along the forty-ninth parallel.

Relations with America's southern neighbor, Mexico, were considerably more stormy. The main controversy here arose over Texas. The influx of American settlers into this Mexican border region had begun in 1821. Because of constant difficulties with Mexican authorities, the American settlers first demanded autonomy and then, in 1836, proclaimed their independence. The next logical step, admission of Texas to the Union in 1845, led to war with Mexico. As a result of the Mexican War (1846–48), Mexico relinquished its claims to Texas. Mexico also ceded California and New Mexico in return for $15 million. Six years later, with the Gadsden Purchase, America acquired another slice of Mexican territory.

The settlement with Mexico, together with the Oregon Treaty, gave the United States an extended frontage on the Pacific. The implications of this development for American foreign policy were to become evident only gradually. For the time being, the most pressing need of the vast regions of the new West was for settlers to substantiate America's claims. In a fitting climax to a decade of expansion, gold was discovered in the Sacramento Valley in 1848. The resulting gold rush profited only a few of the many thousands who streamed to California from all over the world. But these "forty-niners" helped to increase the population of California more than four-fold in a single decade.

The Slavery Issue

The expansionism of the 1840s also aggravated the long-standing sectional conflict between proslavery and antislavery forces. What has been said about the democratic nature of American society did not apply to the large number of black slaves in the South or even to free blacks in the North. While almost everywhere in the world slavery was being

Slavery

AN APOLOGIST'S VIEW

The negro slaves of the South are the happiest, and, in some sense, the freest people in the world. The children and the aged and infirm work not at all, and yet have all the comforts and necessaries of life provided for them. They enjoy liberty, because they are oppressed neither by care nor labor. The women do little hard work, and are protected from the despotism of their husbands by their masters. The negro men and stout boys work, on the average, in good weather, not more than nine hours a day. . . . Besides, they have their Sabbaths and holidays. White men, with so much of license and liberty, would die of ennui; but negroes luxuriate in corporeal and mental repose. With their faces upturned to the sun, they can sleep at any hour; and quiet sleep is the greatest of human enjoyments. . . . The free laborer must work or starve. He is more of a slave than the negro, because he works longer and harder for less allowance than the slave, and has no holiday, because the cares of life with him begin when its labors end. He has no liberty, and not a single right.

AN ABOLITIONIST'S VIEW

The slaves in the United States are treated with barbarous inhumanity . . . they are overworked, underfed, wretchedly clad and lodged, and have insufficient sleep . . . they are often made to wear round their necks iron collars armed with prongs, to drag heavy chains and weights at their feet while working in the field . . . they are often kept confined in the stocks day and night for weeks together, made to wear gags in their mouths for hours or days, have some of their front teeth torn out or broken off, that they may be easily detected when they run away . . . they are frequently flogged with terrible severity, have red pepper rubbed into their lacerated flesh, and hot brine, spirits of turpentine, etc., poured over the gashes to increase the torture . . . they are often stripped naked, their backs and limbs cut with knives, bruised and mangled by scores and hundreds of blows with the paddle, and terribly torn by the claws of cats, drawn over them by their tormentors.

From George Fitzhugh, *Cannibals All!* (1857); from Theodore Dwight Weld, *Slavery As It Is* (1839).

Insignia of the Third United
States Colored Troops.

abolished, it was gaining a new lease on life in the American South. In a nation dedicated to a belief in equality, there now arose an aristocracy of wealthy plantation owners whose belief in their own superiority and the inferiority of the black race was not unlike the racist ideologies that already existed in Europe and became more widespread during the later nineteenth century.

The main concern of southern politicians in the first half of the nineteenth century was to prevent antislavery legislation. This could be done only if an even balance between slave and free states was maintained. Such a balance in the past had been maintained by compromise. But compromise became increasingly difficult as more and more territories were added to the Union. With the petition of California in 1849 for admission as a free state, the issue reached a critical stage. If granted, the admission would upset the existing balance between slave and free states. After prolonged debates, differences were once more patched up. The Compromise of 1850 called for the admission of California as a free state, but it left the question of whether the two new territories of New Mexico and Utah were ultimately to be admitted as free or slave states up to

their own decisions. It was this introduction of state option, or popular sovereignty, that injected a new and disturbing element into the slavery controversy.

Beginning in the mid-1850s a series of tragic events and incidents drove the opposing factions on the issue of the expansion of slavery still further apart. The rivalry between proslavery and antislavery forces over whether Kansas was to be a free or slave state soon plunged that territory into a miniature civil war. The Supreme Court's Dred Scott decision (1857), which ruled that slaves were property and thus could not become free by moving to a free state, deeply antagonized the North. On the other hand, an attempt by the abolitionist John Brown to lead slaves on a raid of the arsenal at Harper's Ferry (1859) aroused the specter of a slave revolt in the South. The presidential campaign of 1860 was dominated by the slavery issue. The Democrats were divided into a southern, proslavery wing and a northern faction holding to the compromising policy of popular sovereignty. The Republicans, on the other hand, stood united against any further extension of slavery.

The Republican candidate, Abraham Lincoln, was chosen as president by an electorate divided along sectional lines.

THE SLAVERY ISSUE 1861

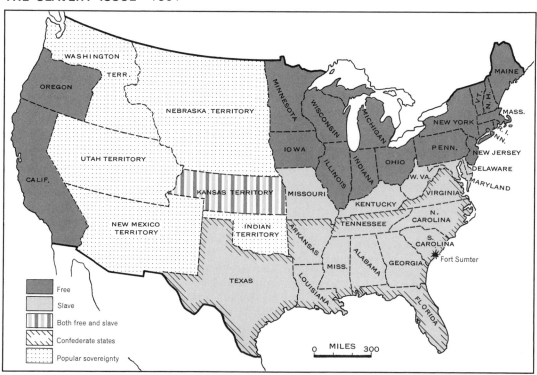

Repeatedly in previous years the South had talked of secession as a last resort in defending its way of life. Calhoun, the defender of states' rights, had suggested that if compromise proved impossible the states should "agree to separate and part in peace." It was South Carolina, the home of the "great nullifier," that now replied to Lincoln's election by passing its Ordinance of Secession. One after another, most of the slave states seceded from the Union and formed the Confederate States of America. In his inaugural address Lincoln strongly rejected the right of secession and vowed to maintain the Union. But he also left the door open for possible reconciliation. The issue of peace or war hung in the balance for a while longer. It was decided on April 12, 1861, when Confederate forces opened fire on the federal garrison at Fort Sumter in Charleston Harbor.

The American Civil War

The American Civil War was fought initially to preserve and protect the Union. To that extent it belongs among the great wars of national unification that were being waged in Europe at the same time. The Civil War was expected to be a brief conflict in which the immense advantages of the North would prove decisive. But the South put up a valiant fight, and in the early part of the war won some brilliant victories. Nobody would have predicted that the war would last four years and would turn into one of the most costly military ventures known up to that time.

Union troops in the Civil War stringing telegraph wires on the battlefield.

Garrison of South Carolina Confederate troops (1861).

Among the political developments of the war the most important was Lincoln's Emancipation Proclamation, a promise of freedom to come. The extension of northern war aims to include the abolition of slavery changed the war from a mere political struggle to an ideological crusade. This change was brought about more by the pressure of circumstances than by actual design. Lincoln himself would have preferred a more gradual and voluntary process of emancipation.

The granting of freedom to black Americans inevitably raised the closely related question of granting them equality as well. The abolitionist minority had never made any distinction between the two. But it took endless debates and several years before the country as a whole was ready to implement the gift of freedom with the guarantee of equality. This was done in several constitutional amendments and civil-rights acts. Beginning in the 1870s, however, the United States Supreme Court interpreted this postwar legislation in a way that violated its spirit, if not its letter, and that kept America's blacks in a position of inferiority for decades to come.

Europe and the Civil War

The Emancipation Proclamation made a very strong impression in Europe. The European powers had watched America's westward movement in the early part of the century with disapproval. During the Mexican War, Great Britain actually considered joint intervention with France on behalf of Mexico, and during the 1850s these two powers helped to discourage American plans for the acquisition of Cuba from Spain. The outbreak of the Civil War led official European circles to hope that America would be permanently weakened by the secession of the southern states. Both the British and the French governments were decidedly cool toward the North. As far as Britain was concerned, the fact that its industry depended on southern cotton played its part. When a northern warship removed two Confederate commissioners from the British steamer *Trent* in 1861, a major crisis was averted only by America's readiness to give in to British pro-

Archduke Maximilian of Austria, emperor of Mexico (1864–67).

tests and release the commissioners. Great Britain, on the other hand, had to heed the protests of the North against permitting southern privateers to be outfitted and to operate from British ports.

American relations with France became strained when Napoleon III tried to bolster his position at home by establishing a puppet regime in Mexico. In 1863 French troops occupied Mexico City, and the following year Archduke Maximilian of Austria was proclaimed Emperor of Mexico. This was in open violation of the Monroe Doctrine, but the United States was too preoccupied to make any protest. Once the Civil War was over, however, it demanded the withdrawal of French troops (1866). Left without support, Maximilian could not last long. He was executed by a Mexican firing squad in 1867.

Not all the governments of Europe hoped to profit from America's domestic tragedy. The Prussian government was favorably disposed toward the North and wished to see the Union preserved as a counterweight to Britain's maritime supremacy. Russia took a similar attitude. The Russians had given up their settlements in California in 1844, and American fears that the tsarist government would take advantage of the Civil War to extend its sphere of influence southward from Alaska proved groundless. Russia sold Alaska, its last remaining colony in North America, to the United States in 1867 for a mere $7.2 million. The same year America also occupied the Midway Islands, thus signifying its new interest in the Pacific area.

The most wholehearted support of the northern cause during the Civil War came from the rank and file of Europe's population. To the Germans and Italians the war appeared as a struggle for national unity, and to people everywhere the Civil War was another phase in the universal fight for freedom and independence that had been waged in Europe ever since the French Revolution. Even before Lincoln's Emancipation Proclamation, most Europeans saw the American war entirely in terms of liberating the southern slaves. The victory of the North was widely hailed as a triumph of democracy, and some historians feel that it contributed to the liberalization of the British and French governments after 1865.

Reconstruction in the South

America's reputation for liberalism and tolerance, however, was considerably tarnished by the Reconstruction period following the Civil War. The assassination of Lincoln had aroused worldwide indignation and sorrow, and the absence of his moderating influence was keenly felt in the American government's efforts to deal with a recalcitrant South. In an attempt to overcome southern resistance to the political and social emancipation of southern blacks, the Reconstruction Acts of 1867 and 1868 placed the South under military rule, from which it could escape only after drafting new constitutions that accepted the constitutional amendments and civil rights legislation passed since the end of the war.

Added to the political tension were economic problems. The South emerged from the war with many of its cities destroyed, its economy disrupted, and one of its major economic assets, slavery, gone. The influx of northern "carpetbaggers," intent on making personal or political profit out of southern misfortune, kept alive the bitterness generated by war. The distinctive way of life on which southerners had prided themselves was gone forever; but the ideals on which it had rested remained alive. The slow process by which southern blacks were once again disenfranchised and, by a series of "Jim Crow" laws, segregated as well, did not really gain momentum until the 1890s. Its cumulative effect was to perpetuate sectionalism by creating a "solid South" dominated by the Democratic Party and dedicated to keeping the black "in his place."

Economic Growth

While America was trying to heal the wounds of war during the last decades of the nineteenth century, it was also trying to fill in its remaining "open spaces" and to realize its great industrial potentialities. Both these developments were aided

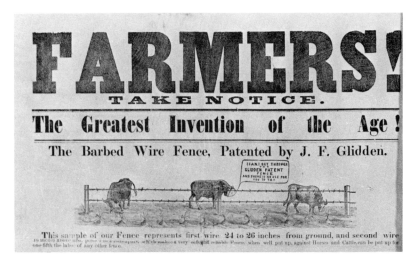

A poster of 1874 advising farmers of "the greatest invention of the age"— barbed wire.

by the continued influx of millions of immigrants. Of considerable help in attracting new citizens and in aiding American farmers were the Homestead Act of 1862 and successive land laws, as well as the easy access provided to the West by the construction of transcontinental railroads. The first such line was completed in 1869. American agriculture already had profited from mechanization. The invention of barbed wire in 1873 made possible the fencing in of vast areas for cattle-raising, and the introduction of the refrigerator car proved a boon to the meat-packing industry. As a result of these and other improvements, western farming took on some of the characteristics of an industry, producing on a large scale for distant markets.

Even more important than the growth of America's agriculture after the Civil War was the expansion of its industries. Government procurement of war materials even at the cost of heavy federal deficits had caused an industrial boom, which continued once the war was over. Between 1860 and 1900 the amount of capital invested in American industry increased more than tenfold, and the export of manufactured articles by 1900 was four times what it had been in 1860. By 1890 the United States had emerged as the world's leader in the production of steel and pig iron, and with close to two hundred thousand miles of railroads in 1900 America had more mileage than the whole of Europe. America also excelled in mass-production methods based on standardization, interchangeable parts, and, ultimately, the assembly line.

Government Regulation of Business

As often happens in rapidly expanding economies, America suffered a series of economic crises, of which the Panics of 1873 and 1893 were the most significant. Both had their parallels overseas, and the withdrawal of European capital from American industry in each case precipitated matters. To modify the effects of competition, American heavy industry after 1873 began to combine its resources in order to meliorate the cost of competition, to fix prices, and to control markets. The first of these "trusts" was the Standard Oil Company of John D. Rockefeller (1879). But since these large organizations evoked strong public protests, Congress in 1890 enacted the Sherman Antitrust Law, a gesture, at least, toward remedy. Its enforcement was sufficiently lax, however, to permit the continued concentration of control in industry and banking.

There were other occasions when the federal government had to intervene in order to curb the excesses of unrestricted competition. Contrary to the practice in Europe, where governments had taken an active hand in the construction and operation of railroads, American lines were built through private initiative, aided by lavish grants of public lands. To realize maximum profits, American railroads charged exorbitant rates where there was no competing carrier. There had been various earlier proposals for federal regulation of the railroads, but not until 1887 was the Interstate Commerce Act passed. The new law was chiefly concerned with rates, and to enforce its provisions it created an Interstate Commerce Commission that at first, however, was not very effective.

There was one field in which American business did not mind governmental intervention. Protective tariffs had been a major concern of industrialists during the early nineteenth century. Southern opposition to protectionism, together with Britain's abolition of the Corn Laws in 1846, had brought a brief interval of free trade. But the economic and financial demands of the Civil War reversed the trend. Beginning in 1861 America entered upon a new era of protectionism. Its high point came with the Dingley Tariff Act of 1897, which made the United States the most protectionist country in the world.

The unprecedented industrial expansion of the years after the Civil War gave an air of opulence and optimism to the "Gilded Age." Not all Americans, however, shared in the rise from rags to riches. The South in particular was slow to recover from its defeat and adjust to a world in which cotton was no longer king. The Panic of 1873, moreover, by causing price cuts among farmers and wage cuts among workers, bred widespread discontent. As a result, the 1870s saw the first serious efforts among these potentially powerful groups to assert their influence in national affairs.

Labor and Farm Unrest

There had been a growing awareness among American workers that they might improve their status by combining their small local unions into a more powerful national organization. The first such body to wield any real influence, the Knights of Labor, was founded in 1869. At its height, it had more than seven hundred thousand members. In 1886 a wave of strikes culminated in the Haymarket Square riot in Chicago, in which several policemen were killed. The Knights of Labor, though not directly involved, were nevertheless blamed. There were other reasons for their decline, notably the growing strength of a new national movement, the American Federation of Labor. The A. F. of L. was to be the spearhead of the American labor movement for the next half-century.

Workers' attempts at organization, however, did not at first improve their condition very much. With large numbers of impoverished immigrants swelling the labor market, working conditions continued to be harsh, hours long, and wages low. Repeated strikes, in which hired strikebreakers fought vicious battles with strikers, further widened the gap between capital and labor. After the

Poster announcing the opening of the Union Pacific Railroad after the railroad had been joined from the Atlantic to the Pacific.

Pullman strike of 1894, the Supreme Court ruled that the Sherman Antitrust Act applied to labor unions if they obstructed interstate commerce. It was only after the turn of the century that American workers began to get a "square deal," in large part because of the efforts of their own unions, but also because of the intervention of a more sympathetic government.

Another large body of Americans who felt their interests neglected in a nation that was becoming rapidly industrialized were the farmers. In 1867 the National Grange of the Patrons of Husbandry had been formed, chiefly as a social organization, but also as a platform for agrarian discontent. The main grievance of farmers was the unfair practices of railways. The Interstate Commerce Act (1887) sought to improve the situation, but its initial effectiveness was limited. Suffering increasingly from protectionism abroad and falling prices at home, America's farmers during the 1880s formed regional groupings that ultimately grew into the National Farmers' Alliance and Industrial Union. Its purpose was to aid farmers by cooperative ventures and by bringing pressure against eastern industrial and banking interests who were held responsible for much of the farmer's plight. The climax of the farmers' discontent came with the formation of the People's Party in 1891. The Populists, profiting from the unrest among workers as well, soon emerged as a powerful third force in national politics. Their demands included currency reform, a graduated income tax, and government ownership of the railroads. A particular issue long close to farmers' hearts was the free and unlimited coinage of silver, from which they expected an upturn of farm prices. When the Democratic Party in 1896 adopted some of the Populist platform, including "free silver," the new party joined forces with the Democrats, thus making the latter the spokesmen of agrarian and labor interests.

Foreign Policy After the Civil War

There were few noteworthy events in American foreign policy between the Civil War and the end of the century. In 1889 America signed a treaty with Germany and Great Britain that established tripartite control over the island of Samoa in the South Pacific. The following year Congress adopted a sweeping naval program, calling for a fleet that would place the United States among the world's leading naval powers. Various plans during the 1890s for an American-controlled canal across Central America failed to materialize, as did attempts to annex Hawaii. The islands did not become American until the Spanish-American War in 1898.

Closer to home, the United States improved relations with the nations of the Western Hemisphere. In 1889 the first Pan-American Conference was held in Washington. In 1895, during a border dispute between Venezuela and British Guiana, Secretary of State Olney reaffirmed the principles of the Monroe Doctrine in strong and belligerent tones. A few years later, in 1898, the United States caught the expansionist fever that was driving the European powers into imperialist ventures. From then on American foreign policy became more and more involved with the rivalries of the other great powers. The days of American isolation were almost over.

American Culture

In cultural matters the United States during the second half of the nineteenth century continued to share in the leading trends of Europe. American painters still went to study in Paris; American scholars were trained at foreign universities; and America's symphony orchestras and opera companies depended almost entirely on European talent. But there was some evidence of a native American culture, making up in freshness and originality for what it lacked in refinement. The writings of Walt Whitman and Mark Twain, the paintings of Winslow Homer and Thomas Eakins, the compositions of Edward MacDowell, and the functional architecture of Louis Sullivan all had an unmistakably American flavor. The most original and influential of America's intellectual contributions during the late nineteenth century was the philosophy

Mark Twain (1835–1910), American humorist of the "Gilded Age" in front of his boyhood home in Hannibal, Missouri.

Walt Whitman: The American Genius

The genius of the United States is not best or most in its executives or legislatures, nor in its ambassadors or authors or colleges or churches or parlors, nor even in its newspapers or inventors . . . but always most in the common people. Their manners, speech, dress, friendships—the freshness and candor of their physiognomy—the picturesque looseness of their carriage . . . their deathless attachment to freedom—their aversion to anything indecorous or soft or mean—the practical acknowledgment of the citizens of one state by the citizens of all other states—the fierceness of their roused resentment—their curiosity and welcome of novelty—their self-esteem and wonderful sympathy—their susceptibility to a slight—the air they have of persons who never knew how it felt to stand in the presence of superiors—the fluency of their speech—their delight in music, the sure symptom of manly tenderness and native elegance of soul . . . their good temper and openhandedness—the terrible significance of their elections—the President's taking off his hat to them not they to him—these too are unrhymed poetry. It awaits the gigantic and generous treatment worthy of it.

From Walt Whitman, Preface to *Leaves of Grass*, 1855.

of pragmatism. Its beginnings went back to the early 1870s, but it only attracted general attention with the writing of William James at the turn of the century. In the popular mind pragmatism justified America's preoccupation with practical pursuits and gave moral sanction to the fierce struggle for material success.

Most Americans were proud of this success. Yet there were some critical voices. In a period of progress and prosperity, both seemingly the result of laissez faire, the American journalist Henry George wrote his *Progress and Poverty* (1879), which challenged the free-enterprise system. Thorstein Veblen, in *The Theory of the Leisure Class* (1899), examined the role of the consumer in the economy of his day and found that such materialistic considerations as "conspicuous consumption" and "conspicuous waste" were exerting an unhealthy influence on the existing price structure. Social criticism also found expression in the novels of Edward Bellamy, Theodore Dreiser, and Frank Norris. All these writers had considerable influence in Europe, where concern over the effects of

unrestrained economic liberalism had long agitated socialists and social critics.

In the realm of ideas, as in politics and economics, America at the end of the nineteenth century was making its influence felt far beyond its frontiers. Viewed with a mixture of awe and envy, hope and uneasiness, admiration and condescension, the United States appeared to most Europeans as the black sheep of their family that had struck out on its own and had made good.

LATIN AMERICA: AN AGE OF DICTATORS

When Latin America won its independence from Spain and Portugal in the early nineteenth century, the region comprised nine sovereign states, most important among them Argentina, Brazil, Chile, Mexico, and Peru. By 1850 several of these states had divided, and their number had grown to seventeen; on the eve of the First World War there were twenty independent Latin American nations. These countries had certain things in common. With the exception of Brazil (where Portuguese was spoken), they were Spanish in culture and language; they were all predominantly Catholic; and the majority of their people were Indians, with white minorities that grew larger as more and more immigrants arrived from the Latin countries of Europe. Economically, Latin America throughout the nineteenth century remained predominantly agrarian and backward. Industrialization did not take hold until after the turn of the century, and then only slowly.

One other characteristic all Latin American countries shared was political instability. Lack of political experience, together with economic difficulties and sectional conflicts, brought an endless succession of dictators. Few countries produced any outstanding leaders comparable to Simón Bolívar (1783–1830), hero of the wars of liberation against Spain. Mexico was an exception, with Santa Anna (1828–55), Benito Juárez (1855–72), and Porfirio Díaz (1877–1911) all gaining fame chiefly through their efforts to resist foreign encroachment.

The weakness and confusion of Latin America seemed to invite such encroachment. The United States, through its Monroe Doctrine, tried to forestall outside intervention. But it was chiefly Britain's support of American policy, combined with a temporary lull in overseas expansion, that kept Europe from challenging the Monroe Doctrine during the first half of the nineteenth century. When the first such challenge was delivered, during the Mexican venture of Napoleon III, the United States was strong enough to take a firm stand. Meanwhile Washington had embarked on its own course of expansion at the expense of Mexico in the 1840s. This first phase of American imperialism was followed by a second round fifty years later (see p. 685). Except for this transitory intervention on the part of the United States, however, Latin America remained free from outside interference. Isolation had its political advantages, but it retarded the economic development of a potentially prosperous region.

THE BRITISH EMPIRE: FROM COLONIES TO DOMINIONS

Prior to 1800 only the American continents had attracted any substantial number of European settlers. Elsewhere, European influence had remained chiefly commercial. It was only during the course of the nineteenth century that Asia, Africa, Australia, and New Zealand were colonized by Europeans. In this process of Europeanization, Great Britain led the way. As the nineteenth century opened, it still had vast holdings on the North American continent and in India. In addition, it had taken the first steps toward opening up Australia and had established claims to New Zealand.

The Empire After 1815

Despite these large possessions, England's colonial enthusiasm after 1815 was at a low ebb. The loss of the American colonies was partly responsible. With the decline of mercantilism, furthermore, the possession of colonies as sources of raw materials and possible markets had lost much of its meaning, since free trade enabled every nation to trade wherever it chose. By 1830 a number of British people were advocating the release of most of the remaining colonies from the control of the mother country. These proposals never got very far, however, mainly because of the agitation of a handful of men usually called the Colonial Reformers. Chief among them were Edward Gibbon Wakefield and the Earl of Durham. Wakefield, in his *Letter from Sidney* (1829), had laid down a plan for the systematic colonization of regions suitable for white settlement. Many of his ideas were subsequently carried out in Australia and New Zealand.

Canada: The First Dominion

Of still greater significance than Wakefield's activities were the proposals made by Lord Durham in his *Report on the Affairs of British North America* in 1839. Canada had been a source of trouble ever since it was taken over from the French in 1763. Its original French settlers resented the influx of large numbers of Britishers, especially after the American Revolution, and efforts to separate the two nationalities by the Canada Act of 1791 had not eased tensions. Discontent with British rule in both Upper and Lower Canada after 1815 had culminated in a brief uprising in 1837. To restore order, Lord Durham was made governor of Canada, and it was on the basis of his first-hand experience that he wrote his famous *Report*. In it he suggested that Upper Canada (Ontario) and Lower Canada (Quebec) be reunited and given responsible self-government. Durham's proposals were incorporated in the Union Act of 1840.

This new arrangement, noted for its granting of self-government, still did not solve the differences between French and British settlers. After long debates among the provincial leaders of Canada, a new federal constitution, the British North America Act, was finally adopted by Britain's Parliament in 1867. Ontario and Quebec were once more separated, and together with the provinces of New Brunswick and Nova Scotia were united

Lord Durham (1792–1840), governor of Canada from 1837 to 1840.

in the Dominion of Canada. From the start the Dominion had complete control over its internal affairs, and as time went on it became more and more independent in external matters as well.

Australia, New Zealand, and the Union of South Africa

The evolution of dominion status for Canada was a landmark in the history of the British Empire. A former colony had been set free and yet had remained loyal to the mother country. The first step had thus been taken on the road toward what later came to be known as the British Commonwealth. The practice followed in Canada was in time applied to other British settlements overseas. Australia's various states were granted self-government beginning in 1850 and were given dominion status as the Commonwealth of Australia in 1901. In New Zealand, self-government began in 1876 and dominion status was achieved in 1907. Finally, in South Africa various of the smaller territories were joined together in the Union of South Africa in 1910. This completed the list of Britain's original dominions.

The four self-governing dominions thus established were not by any means fully sovereign and independent states. In their foreign affairs in particular, they were still under the control of Great Britain. But such dependence was not felt as a burden. When war broke out in 1914, England did not have to bring pressure to bear on its dominions to join the fight against the Central Powers. The bond of common ideals and institutions had created a community of interest that stood the test of war.

India Under the East India Company

The change from colonies to dominions happened only in those regions that had substantial numbers of white settlers. Elsewhere traditional colonialism continued. This was particularly true in the most valuable of England's possessions, India. As a result of the Seven Years' War, England in 1763 had become the dominant European power in that part of the world. Britain's interests in India, since 1600, had been represented by the East India Company. This was a joint stock company that enjoyed a monopoly of trade and operated with little interference from the British government. Primarily concerned with making profits for its investors, the company systematically exploited the natives.

In time the East India Company's policy began to run into criticism at home, forcing the government to impose restrictions on the company's activities. The Regulation Act of 1773 provided for a governor general appointed by the crown, and the India Act of 1784 placed the company's political activities under the supervision of a Board of Control in London. Later measures restricted and ultimately abolished the East India Company's trade monopoly. The general tendency before the middle of the nineteenth century was to transfer more and more of the company's functions and powers to the British government.

The event that brought the company's rule in India to an end was the In-

Walter Bagehot on the Superiority of Englishmen
1869

Let us consider in what a village of English colonists is superior to a tribe of Australian natives who roam about them. Indisputably in one, and that a main sense, they are superior. They can beat the Australians in war when they like; they can take from them anything they like, and kill any of them they choose. . . . Nor is this all. Indisputably in the English village there are more means of happiness, a greater accumulation of the instruments of enjoyment, than in the Australian tribe. The English have all manner of books, utensils, and machines which the others do not use, value, or understand. . . . I think that the plainer and agreed-on superiorities of the Englishmen are these: first, that they have a greater command over the powers of nature upon the whole. . . . Secondly, that this power is not external only; it is also internal. The English not only possess better machines for moving nature, but are themselves better machines. . . . Thirdly, civilized man not only has greater powers over nature, but knows better how to use them, and by better I here mean better for the health and comfort of his present body and mind. . . . No doubt there will remain people like the aged savage who in his old age went back to his savage tribe and said that he had "tried civilization for forty years, and it was not worth the trouble." But we need not take account of the mistaken ideas of unfit men and beaten races.

From Walter Bagehot, *Physics and Politics* (New York: Knopf, 1948), pp. 214–16.

dian Mutiny of 1857. Britain's policy in India during the first half of the nineteenth century, especially under such able governor generals as Lord William Bentinck and the Earl of Dalhousie, had begun to be much more beneficial. India's finances had been overhauled, a system of western education had been introduced, and Indians had been given some participation in their government. Despite these and other improvements, however, there remained a great deal of discontent and unrest. Princes and landlords who had lost their former influence, orthodox Moslems and Hindus who feared the spread of Christianity, intellectuals who objected to the westernization of Indian culture, and the people at large who lived in acute misery—all

these elements combined to bring about the "Great Mutiny" that was staged in 1857.

The revolt started over a minor incident among the sepoys—the native soldiers who made up the bulk of England's armed forces in India. The mutiny was poorly organized and short-lived, but its violence cast a long shadow on Anglo-Indian relations. The British public blamed the East India Company for most of the conditions that helped bring on the rebellion. In 1858, therefore, Parliament took over all the company's duties and obligations. The governor general now became a viceroy, and the place of the old Board of Control was taken by a secretary of state for India within the British cabinet.

THE BRITISH EMPIRE   Nineteenth century

HER MOST GRACIOUS MAJESTY.

Our Queen and our Empress
Is greater and wiser
Than all foreign monarchs,
Including "der Kaiser."

British imperialism: cartoon and verse from *Pictures for Little Englanders,* a children's book published in the late nineteenth century.

British Rule in India

With the assumption of full control by the British government, the history of India entered a new phase. Under the Indian Councils Act of 1861, the viceroy was assisted by legislative and executive councils that included some Indian representation. But the viceroy retained the veto power. It was thus native participation rather than self-government that prevailed in India. Britain's efforts, moreover, to cope with the major problems of a rapidly growing population living in dismal poverty were only partly successful. The Indian farmer, paying exorbitant rents to his landlord and working small plots of exhausted soil, was subject to periodic famines. Industrialization, which might have absorbed much of the surplus population, was discouraged for fear that it might compete with industry back home.

Despite these shortcomings, British rule of India proved a vast improvement over what had existed under the East India Company. With the growth of a native middle class, demands for political and social reforms became more vociferous. In 1886 the most important native political party, the National Congress, held its first meeting. At the start the Congress demanded only moderate reforms. But as time went on it became more radical, and by 1907 there was a faction asking for complete independence. To encourage the moderates within the Congress, the British in 1909 made further concessions toward representative government. For the time being these improvements seemed to satisfy India's demands. When war broke out in 1914, India, like the dominions, rallied to the side of the mother country.

The "New Imperialism"

The lack of interest in colonial expansion, which had prevailed in England during the first half of the nineteenth century, came to an end after 1870. The man who helped rekindle the interest of his countrymen in the far-flung possessions of their empire was Benjamin Disraeli. In 1875 he quietly bought a substantial interest in the Suez Canal Company, thus starting Britain's involvement in Egypt. The following year Disraeli had Parliament confer the title of Empress of India on Queen Victoria, an honor that pleased most of her subjects.

The revival of imperialist sentiment was not confined to England. Almost all the major and some of the minor powers of Europe now started competing for the still unclaimed regions of the world. The reasons for this sudden wave of "new imperialism" were partly political and largely economic (see p. 643). The rivalries resulting from this scramble for overseas possessions were a major factor in the mounting international tension leading up to the First World War. The main spheres of expansion were the newly explored continent of Africa and the ancient empire of China.

CHINA AND THE GREAT POWERS

Contacts between China and the western world in the past had been limited. Some commercial relations had developed with Dutch, Portuguese, and British traders, and in the eighteenth century Jesuit missionaries had been welcomed at the court of the Manchu dynasty. Beginning in 1757, however, the Chinese government, antagonized by the conduct of some of the European traders, had closed all its ports except Canton. Henceforth all business had to be transacted there and under narrowly prescribed rules. These irksome restrictions generated most of the tension that ultimately led to the Opium War of 1839.

The Opium War

Various efforts in the early nineteenth century, especially on the part of the British government, to have additional ports opened to foreign trade were unsuccessful. An added source of trouble between Britain and China was the flourishing trade in opium that had developed during the eighteenth century. There were few commodities China was ready to buy from the outside world, and opium was one of them. The Chinese government had long been alarmed by the flourishing trade in opium and had vainly tried to stop it. In 1839 it moved to confiscate and destroy the vast quantities of the drug stored in Canton. It was this action that started the Opium War with Great Britain.

After three years of intermittent fighting, the Chinese were forced to agree to Britain's terms as laid down in the Treaty of Nanking (1842). Under its provisions, four ports in addition to Canton were opened to British traders, and Britain was given the island of Hong Kong as a base. In subsequent treaties, France and the United States received additional concessions that came to be shared by all powers alike. Most important among these was the principle of "extraterritoriality," which placed all foreigners in China under the jurisdiction of their own consular courts.

The "first treaty settlement," as these various Chinese concessions came to be called, was a landmark in that country's history. As more and more "treaty ports" were added in the course of the century, many of them inland cities, the Chinese Empire was gradually opened up by foreign traders and missionaries, with far-reaching effects on China's economy and society. The first effects of this sudden contact between two very different civilizations were felt in one of the most violent crises in China's history, the Taiping Rebellion (1850–64).

The Taiping Rebellion

The underlying cause of the rebellion was the inefficiency and corruption of the Manchu government and the weakness it had shown in its dealings with the western powers. There had been mounting discontent with a system that exploited the masses of the people for the good of a small ruling clique. With the death of the emperor in 1850, various local manifestations of unrest came together in a general rebellion. In its ideology, the Taiping Rebellion was influenced by Christianity. Its leader was a religious mystic, Hung Hsiu-ch'üan. Its main appeal to the Chinese peasant lay in its abolition of the high land rent.

The Taiping rebels, though antiforeign, nevertheless hoped to gain the support of the European powers in their struggle against the Manchu regime. Tensions between China and the western powers had continued into the 1850s; and as the British and French continued to insist on their treaty rights, a new series of conflicts broke out. The Chinese government thus found itself at war with domestic as well as foreign elements. Had these two opponents joined forces, they could easily have overthrown the Manchu dynasty. As it turned out, however, the European powers, aided by the Taiping rebels, first defeated the Chinese government and then helped the government defeat the Taiping rebels.

After the fall of Canton and the occupation of Tientsin in 1858, Peking was once more ready to come to terms with the powers. Under the Treaties of Tientsin, China opened several more treaty ports, agreed to the establishment of foreign legations at Peking, and permitted foreigners to move freely throughout the country. In addition, the Yangtze River was opened to foreign navigation and the opium trade was legalized. When the Chinese failed to honor these obligations, the French and British briefly resumed

A French caricature of the causes of the Opium War. The Englishman, backed by troops, is telling China: "You must buy our poison. We want you to deaden yourself so completely that we'll be able to take all the tea we want to drink with our beefsteak."

IMPERIALISM IN CHINA   1842–1901

hostilities. The climax came with the storming of Peking and the burning of the emperor's summer palace. Under a new convention signed in 1860, China had to make further concessions. Simultaneously the Russians, taking advantage of China's embarrassment, secured for themselves a large slice of territory north of the Amur River, as well as along the Pacific. Here they founded the port of Vladivostok (1860), thus gaining a long-desired naval outlet.

Once peace had been made, the Manchu government could turn its full force against the Taiping rebels. In this it had the support of the foreign powers.

This western attitude has been rightly criticized. The Taiping rebels certainly were far more enlightened and progressive than the reactionary clique that surrounded the Manchu court. Yet the powers were mainly concerned with the preservation of their privileges, which the rebels intended to abolish. Western policy was motivated by self-interest rather than a desire to reform China.

The suppression of the Taiping Rebellion ushered in a period of comparative peace in Chinese affairs. Some efforts were made by the government to modernize China while maintaining its Confucian tradition, but these were not very successful. Beginning in 1877 China established its first diplomatic missions abroad. The telegraph meanwhile helped to bridge the country's vast distances, but the first railroad was not opened until 1888. The great powers did little to further China's reforming efforts. Some Chinese students studied abroad, and Protestant missionaries continued to bring western ideas to China. But frequent incidents in which Chinese crowds attacked foreigners served as convenient excuses for further foreign encroachment. France strengthened its influence over Indochina in 1884, and Britain's protectorate in Burma was recognized by China in 1886. These regions in the past had been tributaries of China.

The Sino-Japanese War

China's first major international conflict after 1860, however, was not with a western power but with an eastern rival, the empire of Japan. Japan had been far more successful than China in adapting to western ways. And the Japanese did not overlook the revelation of China's weakness in its dealings with the European powers. The area over which the two came to blows in 1894 was Korea, the section of the mainland closest to Japan. Korea had long been a tributary of China, but it had also seen gradual encroachment by Japan. It was this encroachment that finally led to war.

The Sino-Japanese War (1894–95) was won by Japan despite Chinese superiority in manpower and naval strength. Under the Treaty of Shimonoseki (1895), China had to recognize the independence of Korea and had to cede to Japan the island of Formosa, the Pescadores Islands, and the Liaotung Peninsula. The European powers, with the exception of England, were much alarmed by Japan's obtaining a foothold on the Chinese mainland. Russia in particular did not want the Japanese in the Liaotung Peninsula. Russia was joined by France, with whom it had recently concluded an alliance, and by Germany, who was eager to get on better terms with Russia, in putting pressure on Japan to forgo annexation of the peninsula. Japan had little choice but to give in. The Japanese got

even with Russia ten years later (see p. 642).

German cartoon showing the western nations lining up to take their slice of China (1900).

The Scramble for Foreign Concessions

China's defeat by Japan came just when the rivalry among the great powers for overseas territory had reached a new height. The weakness of China now served as the occasion for an imperialist feast the likes of which the world had rarely seen. Between 1896 and 1898, all the major European powers received from China spheres of influence, trading rights, railway concessions, naval stations, mining rights, and whatever other forms of direct and indirect control western imperialists could devise. Russia got Port Arthur on the very same Liaotung Peninsula from which it had just ousted Japan; Germany acquired special rights on the Shantung Peninsula; the British secured a naval base at Weihaiwei; and the French obtained a lease of Kwangchow Bay. The United States, preoccupied with its own venture into imperialism during the Spanish-American War, merely issued a warning to the powers not to interfere with existing treaty ports and other interests in China. This "Open Door" (that is, equal economic opportunity for everyone) note of 1899 had little immediate effect, but it expressed an important principle of future American foreign policy for the Far East.

Reform and Reaction

At the height of the foreign encroachments in 1898, the imperial government made a belated attempt at reform. The short-lived "hundred days

Tz'ŭ Hsi (1854–1908), the dowager empress of China who resisted foreign encroachment by encouraging the abortive Boxer Rebellion. Shortly after her death the Manchu dynasty came to an end.

of reform," as this effort was called, was inspired and directed by K'ang Yu-wei, China's last great Confucian scholar. He hoped to create a constitutional monarchy, improve the civil service, reform the educational system, and introduce some western technology. The reformers had the support of the emperor, Kuang-hsü, but they were opposed by the established political and military hierarchy, which looked for leadership to the dowager empress, Tz'ŭ Hsi. This remarkable woman had long been the center of resistance to all reforms. Discovering in the fall of 1898 that she was about to be arrested, she decided to strike first. She imprisoned the emperor and suppressed the reform movement. Until her death in 1908, the dowager empress ruled supreme.

The victory of reaction in China was aided by a military uprising at the turn of the century, directed primarily against foreigners. The "Fists of Righteous Harmony," or "Boxers," as these antiforeign elements were called, were chiefly active in the north of China. As more and more foreigners were attacked and the foreign legations in Peking put under siege, the great powers decided to strike back. An international expeditionary force descended on China, took Tientsin, and sacked Peking. Only the rivalry among the powers prevented the outright partitioning of the country. Instead, China had to pay a huge indemnity.

China's repeated defeats at the hands of the West had given ample proof that western civilization, at least in its material aspects, was superior to that of the East. As demands for reform within China became stronger, the Manchu dynasty was forced into some half-hearted attempts to liberalize the government. In 1908 a draft constitution was published, calling for the election of a national parliament after nine years. Before it could go into effect, however, the Manchu regime was overthrown.

The Revolution of 1911

The leader of the revolution was a Chinese doctor, Sun Yat-sen, generally considered the founder of modern China. His movement—the Kuomintang, or National People's Party, as it was ultimately called—aimed to reform China and to free it from foreign encroachment. Its program consisted of three main points: national independence, democracy, and social justice. Prior to 1911 Sun's organization engineered some abortive local uprisings. To overthrow the Manchu dynasty, however, added support was needed. This was supplied by some of the provincial governors and military leaders who had long been at odds with the central government. Outstanding among these military figures was Yüan Shih-k'ai, a follower of the dowager empress, who had lost his position when the empress died in 1908. In 1911 the government asked Yüan to help put down a local uprising of Sun Yat-sen's followers at Hankow. Instead, Yüan helped depose the last Manchu emperor. It was this combination of forces that brought about the initial victory of the Revolution. In return for his support, Yüan was made president of the new Chinese Republic.

The main problem facing China after 1911 was how to reconcile the diverse elements in its government. In 1912 a provisional constitution called for a parliamentary government. But meanwhile Yüan Shih-k'ai was trying to extend his own power in the hope of ultimately founding a new dynasty. In 1914 Yüan embarked on a brief period of personal government. He died in 1916. With him China lost a leader who might have prevented the general anarchy and civil war that prevailed throughout the country for the next ten years. China's efforts to set its own house in order had failed.

THE EMERGENCE OF MODERN JAPAN

China's contacts with the West had proved disastrous; Japan's experience was far more fortunate. In the first half of the seventeenth century, Japan had been virtually closed to western influence. It was not until the middle of the nineteenth century that internal weakness and outside pressure brought about the reopening of the island empire. Japan at the time was still being ruled—as it had been for centuries—by the emperor's commander in chief, or shogun. This essentially feudal system, however, was proving increasingly inefficient, and there was fear that unless Japan modernized its ways, it might suffer the fate of China and become a victim of western exploitation.

The Opening Up of Japan

Japan was reopened to the outside world, suddenly and dramatically, through the efforts of the American commodore Matthew Perry. His request in 1853, backed by an imposing fleet of steam warships, that commercial relations be established between the United States and Japan could not be refused, given Japan's military backwardness. In the resulting Treaty of Kanagawa (1854) the first Japanese ports were opened to foreign trade. Commercial and other agreements followed, not only with America but with other nations as well. The long period of Japan's seclusion, thanks to American initiative, had been ended.

Japan, however, did not become a victim but rather a competitor of the western powers in the colonization of the Far East. This it did by a policy of determined modernization and westernization. Japan's rapid transition from feudalism to industrialism did not come about without a major domestic upheaval. The sudden influx of foreigners caused deep resentment among many Japanese. While the shogun was forced by circumstances to collaborate with the western powers, the emperor and his advisers advocated resistance. The struggle between these two factions was decided in 1867, with the victory of the imperial supporters and the resignation of the last shogun. In 1868 the Meiji emperor assumed direct control over the nation, moving his capital from Kyoto to Edo, now renamed Tokyo.

The Meiji Period

The Meiji period (1868–1912) saw the emergence of Japan as a modern great power. The outstanding developments during the last decades of the nineteenth century were the abolition of feudalism and the industrialization of Japan. In 1871 an imperial decree abolished the large feudal fiefs and inaugurated a more highly centralized government along western lines. As the power of the old privileged families declined, so did the importance of their retainers, the samurai. When in 1876, the members of this traditional warrior class were forbidden to wear their two swords, the sign of their privileged status, they revolted. The Satsuma Rebellion (1877), involving some two hundred thousand men, was crushed by troops armed with modern weapons. With it the last resistance of feudal forces came to an end.

The modernization of Japan was most rapid and thorough in the industrial field. Industrialization had to start virtually from scratch, but the imperial government from the beginning took a hand in founding and running essential industries. When financial difficulties after 1880 forced the government to sell its enterprises, they were bought by a few wealthy families, the *zaibatsu*, who from then on dominated the economic life of Japan. The influence of the state over economic affairs, however, continued to be close, and the spirit of laissez faire, so prominent in the West, never gained a comparable hold in Japan.

The modernization of Japan affected every aspect of its life. Together with universal military service, universal education helped to transform illiterate peasants into trained and obedient workers. Buddhism was deemphasized and Christianity was tolerated. There was also renewed interest in the ancient native religion of Japan, the cult of Shinto.

Two views of Commodore Matthew Perry. Above: Japanese representation printed shortly after his mission to Japan in 1853. Below: daguerrotype by Mathew Brady.

With its veneration of the emperor as the Son of Heaven, Shintoism provided a religious basis for Japan's new nationalism. In its efforts to catch up with the West, Japan borrowed freely wherever it could find the institutions best suited to its needs. Its legal system was modernized along French lines, and its financial organization was borrowed from the United States. British officers helped build a new navy, and the new Japanese constitution followed a Prussian model.

One of the main concerns of the Meiji period was the creation of some form of representative government. The emperor had promised a deliberative assembly in his "Charter Oath" of 1868. But it was not until 1884 that the drafting of a Japanese constitution was begun. As promulgated in 1889, the constitution established an Imperial Diet of two houses. The lower house was elected under a restricted franchise that gave the vote to less than half a million Japanese. There was no ministerial responsibility. The emperor could issue decrees with the force of laws, and he could declare war. The Japanese constitution thus did not really affect the traditional power structure. Still, the introduction of parliamentary practices gave some voice and

experience to the rising middle class, and the Japanese people gained more political influence than they had ever had before.

Despite its preoccupation with domestic reform, Japan also was able to carry on an active and successful foreign policy. Industrialization called for raw materials and markets, and a growing population called for living space. As early as 1874 Japan sent an expedition to Formosa. In 1876 Japan started the long rivalry with China over Korea that led to the Sino-Japanese War (1894–95). Japan's victory in that war, as we have seen, caused the tension with Russia that in turn led to a still more important war ten years later.

The Russo-Japanese War

The rivalry between Japan and Russia in the Far East went back to the middle of the nineteenth century. At that time Russia began extending its influence over the portion of China facing the Sea of Japan. By the end of the century, the only region opposite Japan still free from Russian domination was Korea. Japan continued to assert its interests in Korea after its victory over China in 1895. At the same time, however, the tsarist empire was stepping up its activities there. In 1902 Japan concluded an alliance with Great Britain, which had long opposed Russia's expansion in Asia. Japan thus was assured of the friendship of another major power with interests in the Far East.

The Russo-Japanese War, long in the making, broke out in 1904. Japan had definite strategic advantages, but even so the world was little prepared for the resounding defeat inflicted on the Russians. After eighteen months of fighting, the mediation of President Theodore Roosevelt ended the war. The treaty of peace signed at Portsmouth, New Hampshire (1905), completed the emergence of Japan as a major power. Its interests in Korea were now recognized. In addition, Japan received control over the Liaotung Peninsula, together with some Russian railroad concessions in southern Manchuria. Russia also ceded to Japan the southern half of the island of Sakhalin.

Theodore Roosevelt with the Russian and Japanese representatives to the peace negotiations in Portsmouth, New Hampshire, that ended the Russo-Japanese War (1905). Left to right: Sergius Witte, Baron Rosen, Roosevelt, Baron Komura, and Baron Takahira.

Japan's victory over Russia marked a turning point in relations between Europe and Asia. For the first time in modern history, one of the so-called backward nations had defeated one of the major powers of the West. The effects of this event were felt in an upsurge of nationalism among the nations of Asia, the ultimate repercussions of which have lasted into our own day.

AN EVALUATION OF WESTERN IMPERIALISM

The growth of the United States into a major power, the transformation of the British Empire into a worldwide Commonwealth, the opening up of China, and the westernization of Japan—all these were manifestations of the vast influence that western civilization had gained in the course of a single century. One region became almost wholly subservient to western domination during the latter part of the nineteenth century—the continent of Africa (see p. 679).

Much of this expansion of western civilization had taken place in the last decades of the nineteenth century. In an age of ardent nationalism, it was considered a point of honor for any great power to raise its flag over as large an area of the globe as possible. At a time, furthermore, when unprecedented industrial growth created an urgent need for raw materials, markets, and outlets for surplus capital and population, colonies and foreign concessions seemed to provide a ready solution to economic problems. Finally, a civilization that considered itself superior to all others could easily convince itself that its members had a civilizing mission and should assume what Rudyard Kipling called "the white man's burden."

The various motives for imperialist expansion have come in for a good deal of criticism. There can be no doubt about the sincerity with which most western imperialists believed in the advantages that the spread of their civilization would bring to the rest of the world. It was only after the bitter experiences of the twentieth century, when the cause of western imperialism suffered one reversal after another, that this belief began to be shaken. Politically, western domination of colonial regions merely seemed to awaken among the subjected peoples a consciousness of their own national interests and a desire for independence. While this in itself may be a positive achievement, it certainly was not what the imperialists of the last century had envisaged. Economically, the advantages derived from imperialism were limited to small groups within the mother countries. As time went on it became clear that the most advantageous policy in the long run was the economic development rather than the exploitation of backward areas. Such development, however, was slow and expensive, and its ultimate effect was to emancipate rather than subdue colonial areas.

About the civilizing effects of the spread of western civilization, there are divided opinions. There is no need to point out the many advantages that have

Christian missionary in India (*ca.* 1900).

J. A. Hobson on Imperialism   1902

Thus do the industrial and financial forces of Imperialism, operating through the party, the press, the church, the school, mould public opinion and public policy by the false idealization of those primitive lusts of struggle, domination and acquisitiveness, which have survived throughout the eras of peaceful industrial order, and whose stimulation is needed once again for the work of imperial aggression, expansion, and the forceful exploitation of lower races. For these business politicians biology and sociology weave thin convenient theories of a race struggle for the subjugation of the inferior peoples, in order that we, the Anglo-Saxon, may take their lands and live upon their labours; while economics buttresses the argument by representing our work in conquering and ruling them as our share in the division of labour among nations, and history devises reasons why the lessons of past empire do not apply to ours, while social ethics paints the motive of "imperialism" as the desire to bear the "burden" of educating and elevating races of "children." Thus are the "cultured" or semi-cultured classes indoctrinated with the intellectual and moral grandeur of Imperialism. For the masses there is a cruder appeal to hero-worship and sensational glory, adventure and the sporting spirit: current history falsified in coarse flaring colours, for the direct stimulation of the combative instincts. . . . Imperialism is a depraved choice of national life, imposed by self-seeking interests which appeal to the lusts of quantitative acquisitiveness and of forceful domination surviving in a nation from early centuries of animal struggle for existence.

From J. A. Hobson, *Imperialism: A Study* (Ann Arbor, Mich.: Ann Arbor Paperbacks, 1965), pp. 221–22, 368.

come to the rest of the world from its contacts with the West. In the field of medicine alone, the lives of millions of people have been saved by western scientists, and the slow but steady rise in the living standards of even the most backward regions would have been impossible without western aid and examples. The fault that has been found with the westernization of the world has been chiefly in the methods employed by western imperialists. Until quite recently the advantages that western civilization brought to many parts of the world were largely incidental to the primarily selfish aims and ambitions of the more advanced nations. The white man's burden, it has been said, has rested heavily on the shoulders of the black, brown, and yellow men who were subjugated by him. Only in our own day have we come to recognize and to correct some of the mistakes made by western imperialism in the past.

Suggestions for Further Reading

Note: Asterisk denotes a book available in paperback edition.

General Because of its wide range, there are no general works covering the whole subject matter of this chapter. D. K. Fieldhouse, *The Colonial Empires* (1966), is a useful survey, as is S. L. Easton, *The Rise and Fall of Western Colonialism** (1964). P. T. Moon, *Imperialism and World Politics* (1926), is still a standard work on the expansion of Europe. K. S. Latourette, *A History of the Expansion of Christianity*, Vols. V and VI (1945), deals with an important aspect of Europe's spreading influence. Good general works on the Far East are E. O. Reischauer and A. M. Craig, *A History of East Asian Civilization*, Vol. II: *East Asia: The Modern Transformation* (1965), and G. M. Beckmann, *The Modernization of China and Japan* (1962). C. E. Carrington, *The British Overseas* (1950), deals with British colonization. The motives of modern imperialism are treated in numerous books, among them the classics by J. A. Hobson, *Imperialism: A Study** (1902), and N. Lenin, *Imperialism: The Highest State of Capitalism** (1916). More recent studies and critiques of imperialism are J. A. Schumpeter, *Imperialism and Social Classes** (1955), and E. M. Winslow, *The Pattern of Imperialism* (1948). See also A. P. Thornton, *Doctrines of Imperialism** (1965), and R. Koebner and H. D. Smith, *Imperialism: The Story and Significance of a Political Word, 1840–1960* (1964). The effect of imperialism on the colonial peoples is the subject of F. Fanon, *The Wretched of the Earth** (1969). D. O. Mannoni, *Prospero and Caliban: The Psychology of Colonization* (1956), is unique and provocative. On the spread of Europe's economic influence, see W. Woodruff, *Impact of Western Man: A Study of Europe's Role in the World Economy, 1750–1960* (1967).

The United States The vast literature on American history during the nineteenth century makes any selection of representative titles difficult. An excellent introduction to the subject are the relevant chapters in J. M. Blum et al., *The National Experience: A History of the United States*, 4th ed. (1977), written by experts and containing detailed bibliographies. S. E. Morison, *History of the United States* (1965), is considered the master's masterpiece. On the pre-Jacksonian period, see G. Dangerfield, *The Era of Good Feelings** (1952) and *The Awakening of American Nationalism** (1965). The westward movement is discussed in R. G. Athearn, *America Moves West* (1964), and R. A. Billington, *Westward Expansion* (1967). W. E. Washburn, *The Indian in America* (1975), is the best survey of a controversial subject. Among studies on slavery, K. M. Stampp, *The Peculiar Institution** (1956), and E. D. Genovese, *The Political Economy of Slavery* (1965) and *Roll, Jordan, Roll: The World the Slaves Made* (1974), stand out. Industrial development is treated in D. C. North, *The Economic Growth of the United States, 1790–1860** (1961). On the Age of Jackson, see J. C. Curtis, *Andrew Jackson and the Search for Vindication* (1976), and C. M. Wiltse, *The New Nation, 1800–1845** (1961). A. Nevins, *Ordeal of the Union*, 2 vols. (1947), and J. G. Randall and D. Donald, *The Civil War and Reconstruction* (1961), are representative works on the Civil War and its background. The aftermath of the war is treated in K. M. Stampp, *The Era of Reconstruction* (1965), and in C. V. Woodward, *Origins of the New South, 1877–1913** (1951). The following are recommended for their insights into various phases of American thought and society: R. Hofstadter, *The American Political Tradition** (1955); L. Hartz, *The Liberal Tradition in America** (1955); and C. Rossiter, *Conservatism in America** (1955). On relations between the United States and Europe, see J. B. Brebner, *North Atlantic Triangle: The Interplay of Canada, the United States, and Great Britian* (1945), and H. Koht, *The American Spirit in Europe: A Survey of Transatlantic Influences* (1949).

America's search for overseas territory is comprehensively covered in C. S. Campbell, *The Transformation of American Foreign Relations, 1865-1900* (1976).

Latin America

One of the best recent histories of Latin America is J. F. Rippy, *Latin America: A Modern History* (1958). Other good standard works are D. G. Munro, *The Latin American Republics* (1950); H. Herring, *A History of Latin America* (1955); and W. L. Schurz, *The New World: The Civilization of Latin America* (1954). F. Tannenbaum, *Ten Keys to Latin America* (1962), deals with the broader aspects and issues of Latin American life. The following cover specific subjects: J. L. Mecham, *Church and State in Latin America* (1934); G. Plaza, *Problems of Democracy in Latin America* (1950); W. C. Gordon, *The Economy of Latin America* (1950); R. Crawford, *A Century of Latin American Thought*, rev. ed. (1966); and G. Arciniegas, *Latin America: A Cultural History* (1967). On hemispheric relations, see D. Perkins, *A History of the Monroe Doctrine*, rev. ed. (1955); S. F. Bemis, *The Latin American Policy of the United States* (1943); J. L. Mecham, *A Survey of United States-Latin American Relations* (1965); and W. H. Calcott, *The Western Hemisphere: Its Influence on United States Policies to the End of World War II* (1968).

The British Empire

The most comprehensive work on the subject is J. H. Rose et al., eds., *The Cambridge History of the British Empire*, 7 vols. (1929-40). For the period of the "new imperialism," see C. J. Lowe, *The Reluctant Imperialists: British Foreign Policy, 1878-1902* (1967). Two good recent books are B. Porter, *The Lion's Share: A Short History of British Imperialism, 1850-1970* (1976), and R. Hyam, *Britain's Imperial Century, 1815-1914* (1976). The four original dominions are treated individually in J. M. S. Careless, *Canada: A Story of Challenge* (1953); M. Clark, *A Short History of Australia*, rev. ed. (1969); K. Sinclair, *A Short History of New Zealand* (1961); and C. W. de Kiewiet, *A History of South Africa: Social and Economic* (1941). Good brief histories of India are W. H. Moreland and A. C. Chatterjee, *A Short History of India* (1957), and P. Spear, *India: A Modern History* (1961). Britain's role in India is evaluated in P. Woodruff, *The Men Who Ruled India*, 2 vols. (1954); R. P. Mansani, *Britain in India* (1961); M. Bearce, *British Attitudes Towards India* (1961); and E. J. Thompson and G. T. Garratt, *Rise and Fulfilment of British Rule in India* (1934). A key event in Indian history is the subject of T. R. Metcalf, *The Aftermath of Revolt: India, 1857-1870* (1964).

China

Good histories of China are K. S. Latourette, *The Chinese: Their History and Culture*, rev. ed. (1964); W. Eberhard, *A History of China* (1950); and J. A. Harrison, *China Since 1800** (1968). P. W. Fay, *The Opium War, 1840-1842* (1975), is a good book. On the later phase of Chinese history, see V. Purcell, *The Boxer Uprising* (1963); M. C. Wright, ed., *China in Revolution: The First Phase, 1900-1913** (1968); and A. M. Sharman, *Sun Yat-sen* (1934). Chinese views of their country's history may be found in Li Chien-nung, *The Political History of China, 1840-1928* (1956), and I. C. Y. Hsü, *China's Entrance into the Family of Nations: The Diplomatic Phase, 1858-1880* (1960). A useful introduction to Chinese philosophy is H. G. Creel, *Chinese Thought from Confucius to Mao Tse-tung** (1953). F. Michael, *The Taiping Rebellion* (1966), and J. K. Fairbank, *Trade and Diplomacy on the China Coast: The Opening of the Treaty Ports, 1842-1854*, 2 vols. (1953), are pioneering works. Other works dealing with the impact of the West on China are Ssu-yu Teng and J. K. Fairbank, *China's Response to the West: A Documentary Survey, 1839-1923* (1954); R. Dawson, *The Chinese Chameleon: An Analysis of European Conceptions of Chinese Civilization* (1967); A. Iriye, *Across the Pacific: An Inner History of American-East Asian Relations* (1967); J. K. Fairbank, *The United States and China** (1963); and M. Gasster, *China's Struggle to Modernize* (1972).

Japan

E. O. Reischauer, *Japan: Past and Present* (1956), and J. W. Hall, *Japan from Pre-History to Modern Times* (1970), are good introductions. One of the best brief histories of the last hundred years is H. Borton, *Japan's Modern Century* (1955). See also A. Tiedemann, *Modern Japan: A Brief History** (1955). Special aspects of Japanese history and culture are treated in W. W. Lockwood, *The Economic Development of Japan* (1954); M. B. Jansen, ed., *Changing Japanese Attitudes Toward Modernization* (1965); H. Passin, *Society and Education in Japan* (1965); D. M. Brown, *Nationalism in Japan: An Introductory Historical Analysis* (1955); N. Ike, *The Beginnings of Political Democracy in Japan* (1950); and W. T. De Bary, ed., *Sources of the Japanese Tradition* (1958). G. B. Sansom, *The Western World and Japan: A Study in the Interaction of European and Asiatic Cultures* (1950), discusses the rest of Asia as well as Japan. Japanese relations with the United States are treated in P. J. Treat, *Diplomatic Relations Between the United States and Japan, 1853-1905*, 3 vols. (1938-63); R. A. Esthus, *Theodore Roosevelt and Japan** (1967); and R. S. Schwantes, *Japanese and Americans: A Century of Cultural Relations* (1955). Important, though not always accurate, is R. Benedict, *The Chrysanthemum and the Sword: Patterns of Japanese Culture* (1946).

28 The Period of Promise
1870–1914

Eastman Johnson, *The Hatch Family* (1871).

The last decades of the nineteenth century in Europe were optimistic years. With economic prosperity at home, with peace abroad, and with rapid advances in all fields of scientific research, the belief in unlimited progress that had prevailed since the Enlightenment seemed happily confirmed. But from a later vantage point and with the knowledge of what happened in 1914, the period looks different. We now realize that despite rising prosperity, many Europeans continued to live in poverty. Peace on the European continent was bought at the price of subjugating colonial peoples overseas and suppressing national minorities at home. And the preeminence of science, with its stress on material values, makes the pre-1914 period in retrospect appear as a crass and materialistic age.

This chapter is primarily concerned with domestic affairs. Developments in various parts of Europe differed, but certain political, economic, and social trends were common to most countries. In politics, Europe after 1870 witnessed the growth of democracy, that is, the gradual spread of constitutional and democratic government. In economics, most countries shared in the unprecedented industrial development that is sometimes referred to as the "Second Industrial Revolution." In the social sphere, the labor movement and its doctrine of socialism came to play an increasingly important role in the affairs of almost all nations.

THE GROWTH OF DEMOCRACY

To have true democracy, all adult citizens must have a voice in deciding how they are to be governed. In this sense, no country in 1870, and only two or three in 1914, could be called democratic. The main concern during the intervening period was with winning democracy for men only; and here much progress was made. By 1914 almost all the countries of Europe had universal manhood suffrage and several had parliamentary government, a system under which the executive is responsible to an elected legislature.

The degree and effectiveness of this male democracy varied, however. In England some 20 percent of the male electorate still could not vote in 1914. In France and Italy universal manhood suffrage existed, but the smooth functioning of democracy was prevented by weaknesses in those countries' respective parliamentary systems. Germany, too, had universal manhood suffrage; but since the chancellor was not responsible to parliament, democracy hardly existed. In Austria-Hungary the main obstacle to democratic government was the perennial problem of nationalities. In Russia the franchise in 1914 was still limited, and the National Assembly, or *Duma*, had merely advisory functions.

Women's Rights

The only countries in 1914 where women were allowed to vote were Norway, New Zealand, and Australia. Woman suffrage also existed in some parts of the American West, and it was in the United States that agitation for women's rights had its earliest start. In Europe the main efforts were centered in England and to a lesser extent in Germany. We have already seen John Stuart Mill's pioneering agitation on behalf of equality for women (see p. 579). By the end of the century, various local suffrage societies had grown up in England and on the Continent, and in 1903 Emmeline Pankhurst launched her activist Women's Social and Political Union. The efforts of these determined "suffragettes" to gain political rights for women were met by staunch male and also some female opposition. Queen Victoria, herself an example of the equal, if not superior, ability of women, was highly critical of "this mad, wicked folly of 'women's rights' with all its attendant horrors." Outside the political arena, women were gradually freed from the legal restrictions that had kept them the virtual wards of their husbands or fathers. As more and more women started careers of their own, they also gained economic independence. But most of the professions were still closed to women in an age that disapproved and made fun of the "emancipated woman" and adhered to the male slogan that

Women's labor parade, New York City (1912).

"woman's place is in the home," be it as mother or as domestic servant.

Democracy and Education

One profession in which women did gain considerable influence was elementary education. The success of democracy depended to no small extent on the existence of an informed electorate. Consequently the spread of democracy was accompanied almost everywhere by determined efforts to improve education. In England the Education Act of 1870, which introduced general education, was extended by subsequent acts that made instruction free and compulsory. In Germany, already known for its advanced school system, further progress was made, especially in technical training. The main concern of the French Third Republic was to make instruction compulsory and to exclude the Catholic Church from public education. Both aims were accomplished by the so-called "Ferry Laws" (after Jules Ferry) in the early 1880s.

The need for popular education was especially acute in countries with high illiteracy rates. To improve the status of some 68 percent of its population who could not read or write, the Italian government passed legislation in 1877 making education compulsory. But this act became effective only after 1911, when the central government took over the financial support of local schools. While all other countries, including the smaller ones, made deliberate efforts to stamp out ignorance, the tsarist government of

Evidence of the growth of advertising—a London bus at the turn of the century.

Russia tried to discourage lower-class education on the grounds that it would "draw people away from the environment to which they belong."

The growth of democracy and general education between 1870 and 1914 did not necessarily bring the many blessings that liberals in particular had expected. Some earlier writers on democracy, like de Tocqueville and Mill, had already warned against imposing the standards of the majority on society as a whole. Such criticism continued in the late nineteenth century. To Henry Adams, democracy was one of the lower forms of government. The Englishman Walter Bagehot warned that the voice of the people might easily turn out to be the voice of the Devil. And the German philosopher Friedrich Nietzsche criticized parliamentary government as a means "whereby cattle become masters." How justified these warnings would turn out to be in some countries was not realized until after the First World War.

THE "SECOND INDUSTRIAL REVOLUTION"

The second general trend shared by most of Europe in the late nineteenth century was an unparalleled increase in the rate of industrial growth. In some respects this "Second Industrial Revolution" was merely a continuation of the first, but it had certain unique characteristics. New sources of power—electricity and oil—competed with steam in driving more intricate machinery. Refined techniques of steel production and the discovery of methods to use lower-grade ores made steel available in greater quantities and at a much lower price. Synthetic products, notably dyes produced from coal tars, became the foundation of whole new industries; and the introduction of dynamite by the Swedish chemist Alfred Nobel in 1867 had repercussions in the military as well as the industrial field.

There were many other novel features of industrialism at the end of the century. New means of communication and transportation helped to speed up business transactions; new methods of promotion boosted sales; a vast increase in the supply of liquid capital aided economic growth; and the rapid expansion of many enterprises led to new forms of industrial organization. All these innovations had one thing in common: they helped to increase the industrial output of Europe beyond anything ever known. The Second Industrial Revolution was mainly a quantitative phenomenon. The total production of the western world, including the United States, more than tripled between 1870 and 1914.

Social Effects

This increased industrialization accentuated earlier trends in society. The population of Europe, except in France, continued to grow by leaps and bounds. With this growth of population, the shift from rural to urban life continued. While in 1800 most Europeans were still living in the country or in small towns, by 1900 from one-third to one-half of the population in the more highly industrialized countries lived in large cities. As industries expanded, agriculture declined. Through mechanization and chemical fertilizers, farmers were able to achieve remarkable increases in crop yields. But even so, Europe would have gone hungry had it not been for the expanding agricultural economies of Russia, the Americas, and Australia.

Industrialization continued to affect people's lives in many other ways. The invention of labor-saving devices and the mass production of consumer goods helped to make life easier and more comfortable. Central heating, the use of gas and electricity, the low-cost production of ready-made clothing, and the perfection of canning and refrigeration were only a few of the conveniences now enjoyed by most of the population.

But mechanization and mass production also had their negative sides. Sociologists began to worry that the influence that machines gained over man might in time make him the slave rather than the master of his inventions. Mass production tended to standardize and cheapen public taste. Closely related to mass production was the problem of overproduction. To stimulate sales, advertising steadily gained in importance. The pro-

duction of cheap paper from wood pulp in the 1880s and the resulting growth of popular journalism proved a boon to advertisers. Yet some people deplored the money spent by manufacturers to make people buy at higher cost goods that they did not really need or want.

"Big Business"

One of the characteristics of industrial development since 1870 has been the substitution of "big business" for the smaller factories that had prevailed earlier. As enterprises became fewer, larger, and more competitive, producers found it desirable to form combinations to control production, distribution, and price levels. The "trusts" of the United States, the "amalgamations" of Great Britain, the "cartels" of Germany, and the "syndicates" of Russia differed in specifics but were alike in their efforts to establish some control over the production and distribution of goods. Opponents of this industrial concentration claimed that it tended to create monopolies that kept prices at artificially high levels. In response to such criticism, the United States in 1890 prohibited the formation of trusts, but it was the only major country to do so.

The period of "monopolistic capitalism," as the decades after 1870 are called, was also the heyday of the great industrialists—the Carnegies, Rockefellers, Krupps, Nobels, and others. The huge economic power of these "tycoons" could not help but give them political influence as well. But business leaders did not use their wealth only for their own ends. The ruthlessness that had characterized business during the early days of industrialization was gradually mitigated by signs of social consciousness on the part of some leading capitalists. One of the best examples of this humanitarian attitude was the steel magnate Andrew Carnegie. In his book *The Gospel of Wealth* (1900), Carnegie insisted that wealth was a public trust, not to be handed on within a single family but to be returned to the community from which it had been derived. To practice what he preached, Carnegie gave more than $300 million to worthy causes in the

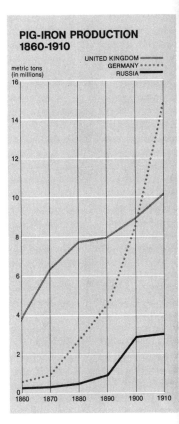

PIG-IRON PRODUCTION 1860-1910

UNITED KINGDOM
GERMANY
RUSSIA

metric tons (in millions)

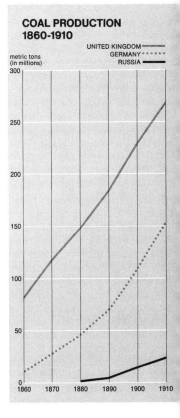

COAL PRODUCTION 1860-1910

UNITED KINGDOM
GERMANY
RUSSIA

metric tons (in millions)

Sidney (1859–1947) and Beatrice Webb (1858–1943), English Fabian socialists.

United States and Great Britain. There were also humanitarian capitalists in Europe, where the Nobel Prizes and the Rhodes Scholarships commemorate two highly successful businessmen.

THE RISE OF THE WORKING CLASS

A third general trend prevalent in Europe during the period after 1870 was the increasing influence of the working class and its socialist philosophy. Much of the improvement in the worker's condition was due to the political power he came to wield through various socialist parties and to the economic power of his labor unions. As a result of the many efforts on his behalf, the status of the European worker by 1914 had been raised far above what it had been in 1870.

New Varieties of Socialism

The basic aims and ideas of modern socialism as derived from Karl Marx and Friedrich Engels have been discussed (see pp. 586–90). Marx had predicted an increasing concentration of capital, balanced by a growing impoverishment of the masses, leading eventually to the col-

lapse of capitalism. Events during the late nineteenth century, however, failed to bear out Marx's predictions. While much capital was concentrated in a few hands, there was a corresponding diffusion of ownership by means of joint stock companies. And while in recently industrialized countries workers suffered from many of the hardships that had marked the First Industrial Revolution, once industrialization had taken hold their condition improved. By the end of the century it became clear that Marx's prediction had to be adjusted to changed circumstances. The result of this adjustment in Marxian doctrine is called "revisionist," or "evolutionary," socialism.

The leading theorist of revisionism was the German socialist Eduard Bernstein. Bernstein had spent some time in England, where he came in contact with a non-Marxian brand of socialism advocated by a group of intellectuals, among them Sidney and Beatrice Webb, H. G. Wells, and George Bernard Shaw. Their socialism was called "Fabianism" after the Roman general Fabius, who preferred to defeat his enemies by gradually wearing them down rather than by directly attacking them. In this same manner the Fabian Socialists opposed violent revolution and sought instead to achieve socialization by way of gradual reform. Bernstein, on his return to Germany in the 1890s, began to expound his own revised version of Marxian socialism. One of its chief characteristics was the denial of Marx's concept of the class struggle. In his *Evolutionary Socialism* (1899), Bernstein advocated that instead of waging a revolutionary struggle against the middle class, the working class should collaborate with any group, proletarian or bourgeois, that would help to bring about a gradual improvement in the workers' condition.

The revisionist ideas of Bernstein caused a major stir in Marxist circles. Orthodox Marxists denounced revisionism and reaffirmed their faith in the validity of all Marx's teachings. One of the most determined defenders of pure Marxism, the Russian Vladimir Ilyich Ulyanov, better known by his pseudonym, N. Lenin, held that collaboration with capitalism would help to perpetuate a system that would become more and more oppressive to the working class. Only a revolution could overthrow this system, and it was up to a minority within the proletariat, organized into a well-disciplined workers' party, to prepare the way for revolution by keeping alive the idea of class struggle. Except in eastern Europe, this revolutionary brand of "Leninism" found few followers before the First World War.

Another form of violent protest arising at the turn of the century was syndicalism. Its main exponent was the Frenchman Georges Sorel, whose *Reflections on Violence* (1908) popularized his social philosophy. Like anarchism (see p. 591), syndicalism saw the state as an instrument of oppression and advocated its abolition. Instead, the trade unions (*syndicat* is the French word for "union"), as the basic units of production, should seize control of a socialist society. To achieve their aim, the syndicalists advocated various means of industrial sabotage, culminating in a general strike. Syndicalism flourished most in Italy, Spain, and France; it also influenced the Industrial Workers of the World (IWW) in the United States.

International Socialism

Marxism as a political force was envisaged by its founder as an international movement. Marx had believed that the best way to combat capitalism was for the workers of the world to unite their efforts. He had been instrumental, therefore, in founding the International Workingmen's Association in 1864. But the First International, as it was called, was not very successful. Marx's domineering manner, his controversy with Bakunin, who was among the leaders of the International, and the excesses of the Paris Commune in 1871, which were falsely blamed on the socialists, combined to bring about the gradual decline of the First International and its demise in 1876.

With the rise of socialist parties in most major countries during the next decade, however, there was again a need for some kind of international organization, and a Second International was

formed in 1889. From the start it was beset by grave internal differences, especially on the issue of revisionism. As time went on, moreover, it became obvious that the national loyalties of most socialists were stronger than their feelings of international solidarity. The Second International opposed war as a means of settling international disputes; but when the test came in 1914 the ideals of international socialism quickly gave way to the stronger appeal of national patriotism.

The Growth of Labor Unions

In addition to setting up their own political parties, workers tried to improve their lot through the formation of labor unions. In the early part of the nineteenth century, unions had made little progress anywhere except in Great Britain, and even there their activities remained restricted. This situation improved markedly after 1870. In England, in a series of legislative acts in 1874 and 1875, unions were given permission to strike and to engage in peaceful picketing. The most important advance in the history of British organized labor came as a result of the famous London dock strike of 1889. The first major strike among unskilled workers, this event marked the extension of union activity

Headquarters of the First International, in a Paris back street.

Leninism

1902

I assert: [(1)] That no movement can be durable without a stable organization of leaders to maintain continuity; (2) that the more widely the masses are spontaneously drawn into the struggle and form the basis of the movement, the more necessary it is to have such an organization and the more stable must it be (for it is much easier then for demagogues to sidetrack the more backward sections of the masses); (3) that the organization must consist chiefly of persons engaged in revolutionary activities as a profession; (4) that in a country with an autocratic government, the more we *restrict* the membership of this organization to persons who are engaged in revolution as a profession and who have been professionally trained in the art of combating the political police, the more difficult will it be to catch the organization; and (5) the *wider* will be the circle of men and women of the working class or of other classes of society able to join the movement and perform active work in it.

From N. Lenin, "What Is to Be Done?" in *Selected Works* (London: Lawrence and Wishart, 1936), Vol. II, pp. 138–39.

beyond the skilled groups that in the past had made up union membership.

On the Continent the labor movement was slower in gaining momentum. In France labor unions had made little headway by 1870. The bloody events of the Paris Commune of 1871 (see p. 611) cast a shadow on any kind of labor activity, and it was not until 1884 that the Waldeck-Rousseau Law granted full legal status to unions and allowed them to form larger federations. The decisive step in this direction came in 1895, when the General Confederation of Labor (CGT) was organized along syndicalist lines.

Germany, too, witnessed little union activity before 1870. Since the German labor movement was closely allied with socialism from the start, it was adversely affected by the antisocialist measures of Bismarck. It thus did not really gain momentum until after 1890. Under the Imperial Industrial Code, German workers were permitted to strike, but an unfriendly government and hostile courts restricted the activities of organized labor wherever possible. Even so, the labor movement in Germany, by exerting pressure on government and employers, helped to improve the condition of German workers.

In the less industrialized countries of Italy, Austria-Hungary, and Russia, trade unionism played a minor role. In Italy the labor movement was split into several factions, the largest of which, the socialist General Italian Federation of Labor, was founded in 1907. Socialist unions also predominated in Austria, though there was hardly any organized labor in agrarian Hungary. Russia had no real labor unions until after 1905, and even then they did not gain much influence.

The "Welfare State"

The agitation of European workers for political, economic, and social reforms did much to make their governments adopt programs of social legislation designed to help the lower classes. Such intervention by the state in the affairs of the individual was a radical departure from the laissez-faire philosophy of early–nineteenth-century liberalism. The idea that the state should con- cern itself with the well-being of its citizens and become, as we would say today, a "welfare state," found acceptance among politicians both in England and on the Continent. The social legislation resulting from this new attitude was so far-reaching that it has been referred to as "state socialism." Its chief purpose was to satisfy the reasonable grievances of the working class and by so doing to preserve the capitalist system.

Similar motives were behind various appeals of the Christian churches, notably the Catholic Church, for collaboration rather than conflict between employers and workers. Christian Socialism was nothing new, but it gained significance as the teachings of Marx began to compete with and to undermine the influence of Christianity among workers. The leading pronouncement on Christian social policy was made by Pope Leo XIII in his encyclical *Rerum novarum* in 1891, in which he condemned socialist attacks on private property and the Marxian concept of class struggle and suggested that the state aid its poorer citizens and that employers and workers settle their differences in a spirit of Christian brotherhood.

So much for the general trends— political, economic, and social—that prevailed in Europe between 1870 and 1914. As we now turn to a discussion of the domestic affairs of the major powers, we shall find these trends much in evidence.

ENGLAND: "MOTHER OF DEMOCRACY"

England after 1870 continued along the road of gradual political and social reform that it had followed since the early nineteenth century. The long reign of Queen Victoria reached its halfway mark in 1869. Gladstone's "great ministry" came to an end in 1874. For the next six years Disraeli, Earl of Beaconsfield from 1876, conducted a policy noted chiefly for its successes abroad. Between 1880 and 1895, Liberal and Conservative governments alternated, with Gladstone heading three more ministries and Lord Salisbury serving as his Conservative counterpart. The last two decades before

Benjamin Disraeli, British Conservative prime minister, shown around 1870, before his first ministry.

1914 were equally divided between the two major parties, the Conservatives remaining in power until 1905 and the Liberals leading thereafter. Generally speaking, the Liberals were more active in domestic affairs, where Gladstone's reforming zeal found its successor after the turn of the century in the dynamic David Lloyd George. The Conservatives, on the other hand, were more concerned with foreign affairs, especially England's overseas interests. Lord Salisbury personally assumed the post of foreign minister in his three cabinets, and he was ably seconded by Joseph Chamberlain as colonial secretary.

The British problem that overshadowed all others was the question of Ireland. Gladstone, who had long been working to improve that country's unhappy condition, sought once again to remedy some of the worst abuses of Irish land tenure in the Land Act of 1881. He failed, however, chiefly because of resistance from Ireland's Nationalists. Under the leadership of Charles Parnell, the Nationalists demanded political rather than economic reforms. Gladstone hoped to satisfy Irish demands by two Home Rule Bills, but he was defeated both times by a coalition of Conservatives and dissident Liberals. Subsequent Land Purchase Acts, under Conservative sponsorship and aimed at helping Irish tenants buy their land, somewhat counteracted the agitation of Irish nationalism. The Irish question became acute once more in 1912, when the Liberals introduced a third Home Rule Bill, which did not become law until September 1914. By that time war had broken out, and home rule had to be postponed.

England's ability to resist any really serious crises, except for the perennial Irish question, was largely due to the peaceful adjustments it continued to make to the demands of an increasingly democratic age. The franchise that had been granted to urban workers in the Reform Act of 1867 was extended to rural laborers under the Franchise Act of 1884. A Redistribution Bill in 1885 established uniform electoral districts, and the Parliament Bill of 1911 abolished the veto power of the House of Lords over money bills. Democracy (for men only) had

Gladstone giving a "whistle-stop" speech (1885). His practice of making political speeches from trains was said to have horrified Queen Victoria.

Victoria's "Golden Jubilee"

Queen Victoria made her historic progress through London on June 22nd, 1887, in brilliant sunshine. As if to put a seal on the legend of "Queen's Weather," the sun came out from a dull sky as the first guns in Hyde Park announced that she had left the Palace, having previously touched an electric button which telegraphed her Jubilee Message round the Empire: "From my heart I thank my beloved people. May God bless them!"

Queen Victoria's account of her reception by London was by no means exaggerated. "No one ever, I believe, has met with such an ovation as was given me, passing through those six miles of streets . . . the crowds were quite indescribable, and their enthusiasm truly marvellous and deeply touching. The cheering was quite deafening, and every face seemed to be filled with real joy."

London's sense of its own greatness, as the metropolis of a far-flung Empire, vied with a poignantly personal affection for the venerable figure who was both a living and a symbolic mother. "Our Hearts Thy Throne," declared a triumphal arch at Paddington; the Bank of England declaimed: "She Wrought Her People Lasting Good." "Go it, old girl!" called an ecstatic voice from the crowd. . . .

Nothing went wrong. Gradually she relaxed in her carriage . . . tears of happiness filled her eyes and sometimes rolled down her cheeks, whereupon the Princess of Wales would lean forward and gently press her hand. . . . She was incomparably the best Queen the world had got and more than one foreign nation, still struggling under the rule of tyranny, self-indulgence or fatuity, wished she were theirs.

From Elizabeth Longford, *Victoria R. I.* (London: Weidenfeld and Nicolson, 1964), pp. 688–90.

made considerable progress in Britain by 1914, leaving only some 20 percent of the male population—domestic servants, bachelors living with their parents, and men with no fixed abode—without a vote.

Economic Developments

As we turn from politics to economics, the picture in England looks somewhat less bright. Prior to 1870, British industry had enjoyed undisputed leadership, and despite the repeal of the Corn Laws in 1846 British agriculture had been able to hold its own. This situation gradually changed as Germany and the United States became England's chief industrial rivals, and as the influx of cheap agricultural products from overseas caused a rapid decline in British farming.

Germany and America overtook England in the basic iron and steel industries by 1914, and England's share of the world's total trade fell from 23 percent in 1876 to 15 percent in 1913.

Much of this relative decline in England's economic leadership was inevitable, of course, as nations that had once been Britain's customers began to supply their own needs and claim their own share of world trade. But there were other causes for the slowdown in England's economic growth. Scientific and technical education lagged behind that of other nations, notably Germany. England was slow in modernizing its industrial equipment and adopting new methods, and it failed to realize the importance of effective salesmanship. Furthermore, while tariff walls were being erected everywhere else to protect industry and agriculture, Britain clung to its policy of free trade, despite efforts, notably by Joseph Chamberlain at the turn of the century, to change to protectionism.

Labor and Social Reform

Even though its economic leadership was declining, Britain was still the most prosperous nation of the world. This prosperity was shared by the British worker, who was far better off than the workers in most continental countries.

Great Britain was the only major European country in which Marxian socialism did not gain any large following. In 1881 an organization advocating Marxist principles was founded, but its advocacy of violence had little attraction for the British workingman. The Fabian Society, founded in 1883, appealed chiefly to middle-class intellectuals. What political influence the British working class exerted before 1914 came chiefly from the British Labour Party. Its origins went back to the early 1890s, but its official beginning dates from 1900, when several groups, including trade unions and Fabians, joined forces behind the Labour Representation Committee. In the general election of 1906, the Labour Party won twenty-nine seats in Parliament. Its program called for the gradual socialization of key industries and utilities, very much along Fabian lines.

Another avenue through which British labor improved its status was union activity. The London dock strike of 1889 was successful, but there were occasional reverses, such as the Taff Vale decision of 1901 and the Osborne Judgment of 1909, both handed down by the House of Lords. Under the Taff Vale decision, labor unions were to be liable for damages resulting from strikes, while the Osborne Judgment made it illegal for unions to pay stipends to Labour members of Parliament. Both restrictions were subsequently removed under the influence of the Labour Party.

While the worker was helping himself, the government also did its share to help him through welfare legislation. There had already been examples of such legislation earlier in the century, especially the several factory acts. Factory legislation was now extended by other acts—in 1878, 1901, and 1908—and a minimum-wage law was passed in 1912. Social insurance was initiated, first against accidents (1880), then against old age (1909), and finally against sickness and unemployment (1911). To finance these expensive measures, which Conservatives and some old-time Liberals termed "socialist," the Liberal government of Lloyd George in 1909 introduced a "People's Budget," which shifted the main tax burden to the rich. It was passed only over the stiff opposition of the House of Lords, whose powers, as we have seen, were subsequently curtailed.

As the result of an enlightened policy at home and a strong position abroad, England in 1914 was at the height of its power. There were some danger signals—in Ireland and India. Britain's economy was going "soft," and its political system needed further reforms. But there was no reason to assume that it would not be able to cope with these issues in the future as it had in the past. Britain, on the eve of the First World War, was contented and confident.

FRANCE: REPUBLIC IN CRISIS

Britain's steady progress toward political and social democracy had no parallel on the Continent. The French Third Republic, after stormy beginnings, developed a system of government that in some ways was more democratic, though far less stable, than that of Great Britain. The French presidency was largely a ceremonial office. The cabinet was responsible to a bicameral legislature, the lower body of which, the Chamber of Deputies, was elected by universal male suffrage. Instead of clearly defined political parties, France had a large number of loosely organized factions, each headed by some outstanding political figure. This feature made the formation of workable majorities in the Chamber of Deputies extremely difficult and led to a long series of coalition cabinets, more than fifty during the forty years before the First World War.

Republicans versus Monarchists

One of the main reasons for the erratic course of French politics after 1870 was the antirepublican sentiment of many Frenchmen. On several occasions in the early years of the Republic, the various royalist factions had come dangerously close to resurrecting the monarchy. But the Third Republic survived, partly because of the lack of unity among its enemies. It was not until 1879 that the French government became wholly republican in its legislative and executive branches.

But the republican elements were no more united than their enemies. A radical faction, led since Gambetta's death in 1882 by Georges Clemenceau, was deeply anticlerical and interested chiefly in revenge against Germany. The moderate republicans, on the other hand, were willing to compromise on domestic and foreign issues. Their chief figure, Jules Ferry, emerged as France's leading statesman in the last decades of the century. During most of the 1880s, radicals and moderates managed to cooperate in launching the Republic on a successful course at home and abroad. Despite their many achievements, however, widespread opposition persisted. Beginning in 1886 this opposition rallied around the recently appointed minister of war, General Georges Boulanger. By early 1889 the popularity of the dashing general was such that he might easily have led a successful *coup* against the Republic, had not his courage failed him at the crucial moment. Nevertheless, the Republic had come dangerously close to being overthrown.

As it turned out, the Boulanger affair helped to strengthen the Republic by drawing the radical and moderate republicans more closely together. But this gain was soon lost again in the so-called Panama Scandal, in which a number of radical republican deputies were found to have accepted large bribes from the corrupt and bankrupt Panama Canal Company. The dust of this affair had still not quite settled when the Third Republic

English cartoon of General Georges Boulanger as Napoleon Bonaparte (1889), a parody of the famous painting of Napoleon by Jacques Louis David, *The First Consul Crossing the Alps*.

was shaken by an even more serious crisis, the Dreyfus case.

In the fall of 1894, Captain Alfred Dreyfus, a Jew, was accused of having betrayed military secrets to the Germans and was condemned to life imprisonment on Devil's Island. Despite clear evidence of his innocence, it took five years before he was fully vindicated. During this time, the reactionary right—monarchists, Catholics, and the army, together with a handful of anti-Semites—denounced any attempt to clear Dreyfus as an attack on the honor of the nation and the discipline of the army. The radical left, spearheading the defense of Dreyfus, cleared its reputation of the blemish incurred in the Panama Scandal. The Dreyfus case was an extended duel between the two factions that had fought each other since the founding of the Third Republic. While its outcome was a victory of republicanism, the struggle itself testified to the continued strength of the forces of reaction.

The most immediate result of the Dreyfus affair was a shift from moderate to radical republicanism. After winning the elections of 1902, the Radicals formed their first ministry and at long last were able to carry out their own program. Their most drastic measures were directed against the Catholic Church. A bill for the separation of church and state brought to an end the Concordat of 1801, whereby the state had paid the salaries of the clergy and had participated in the selection of priests. The Church, henceforth, was to be entirely on its own. In social reform the Radicals were less successful. With the emergence of socialism in France at the turn of the century, radicalism found a powerful rival with far more sweeping social and economic aims.

Economic Developments

France, which had enjoyed considerable prosperity before 1870, was set back by the Franco-Prussian War and was slow to profit from the Second Industrial Revolution. The losses in manpower and material, Germany's demand for a heavy indemnity, and especially the surrender of the valuable industrial region of Alsace-Lorraine, severely retarded French industrial growth. The majority of the French, moreover, were still engaged in agriculture, and protective tariffs, such as the Méline Tariff of 1892, mainly aided the farmers. What industry there was consisted largely of small establishments, and only a few industries were affected by the trend toward industrial concentration. French foreign trade almost doubled between 1870 and 1914. But since the commerce of its competitors increased at a much greater rate, France found itself demoted from second to fourth place in world trade. There was one activity in which France led the rest of the world: the amount of French money invested abroad during the thirty years before 1914 rose from 13 to 44 billion francs. These foreign loans were a valuable source of national income, and they were used as an effective instrument to facilitate French foreign policy.

Socialism and Social Reform

Since France was less industrialized than some other nations, its working class was smaller and French socialism never gained the influence it did elsewhere, especially in Germany. Socialism in France, furthermore, had received a serious setback in the disastrous Paris Commune, a setback from which it did not recover until the late 1870s. Like socialists in most other countries, the

Captain Alfred Dreyfus in 1899 passing between a "guard of dishonor," soldiers whose backs are turned to him. The reactionary military faction arranged for this practice in order to discredit and humiliate Dreyfus.

French were split into moderate and radical factions. The revolutionary group, led by Jules Guesde, and the moderates, led by Jean Jaurès, did not join forces until 1905, when they formed the United Socialist Party. Again like most other socialist parties, the French socialist party was revolutionary in theory but evolutionary in practice. Between 1906 and 1914, its membership in the Chamber of Deputies nearly doubled.

In the realm of social reform, France lagged behind England. A factory law of 1874, amended by subsequent acts, fixed the minimum working age for children at thirteen, restricted working hours for adults to twelve hours, and introduced various other health and sanitation measures. Social insurance did not begin until the end of the century. Accident insurance was introduced in 1898, and old-age pensions were started in 1910. There was no protection against unemployment, and health insurance was left to private initiative under state supervision.

Even though the French working class was not as numerous as its counterparts in England and Germany, the government's failure to solve some of the economic and social problems of the worker caused constant domestic unrest during the years just before 1914. At the same time, the Third Republic continued to be attacked from the right. Royalism and an intense brand of nationalism were kept alive by a few wealthy reactionaries in the *Action Française* of Charles Maurras and Léon Daudet. Yet the majority of the French seemed to approve the programs of reform at home and peace abroad, which brought resounding victory for the Radicals and Socialists in the elections of 1914. French pacifism, while admirable, came at a most inopportune time, just when Europe was getting ready for a major war. France, on the eve of the First World War, was still a nation divided on many vital issues.

GERMANY: EMPIRE TRIUMPHANT

The new German *Reich* presented a spectacle of wealth, success, and supreme self-confidence. Had its unprecedented industrial growth been paralleled by political changes in the direction of a more liberal parliamentary government, Germany might easily have rivaled England as the most progressive nation in Europe.

We have already discussed the constitutional framework of Germany and of its largest member state, Prussia (see p. 605). Repeated demands of liberals and socialists for the reform of the Prussian three-class franchise and for the introduction of parliamentary government in the Empire were of no avail. The *Reichstag*, to be sure, was elected by manhood suffrage. But the main direction of policy continued to rest with the chancellor (who was appointed by and responsible to the emperor) and the Federal Council, or *Bundesrat*, in which Prussia held a controlling position. Even so, the German electorate might have made its influence felt more decisively had it not been split into five or six major parties, each of which differed in political and economic aims and none of which ever won a majority.

Repression at Home— Aggression Abroad

During its first twenty years, the German Empire was ruled by the strong hand of Bismarck. The "iron chancellor's" claim to fame rests on his foreign rather than his domestic policy. During the 1870s Bismarck antagonized large sections of the German people by his fierce struggle against the Catholic Church. The so-called *Kulturkampf* (conflict of cultures; that is, German and Catholic), while appealing to liberal anticlericalism, failed in its major objective—to prevent the rise of political Catholicism. The Catholic Center Party emerged from its persecution as a potent factor in German politics. Bismarck's attempt, during the 1880s, to prevent the rise of a strong Socialist Party was equally unsuccessful. By enlisting liberal support in his fight against Catholics and socialists, Bismarck perpetuated the political disunity of the German people and contributed further to the decline of German liberalism.

Jean Jaurès (1859–1914) at a socialist party rally in 1913.

William II, emperor of Germany and king of Prussia (1888–1918), in the uniform of the Death's Head Hussars.

Bismarck had no worthy successor. The unceremonious manner in which the great chancellor was dismissed by William II in 1890 was indicative of the young emperor's desire to be his own chancellor. But William II was utterly unsuited for such a role. Erratic, unstable, and given to rash utterances, especially on matters of foreign policy, the kaiser launched Germany on an expansionist *Weltpolitik* (world policy) that soon lost it the international trust it had gained under Bismarck. More than in any other country, issues of foreign policy played a dominant role in Germany. The army, long powerful in Prussian affairs, remained one of the cornerstones of the empire. Except for its budget, which the *Reichstag* had to grant for several years in advance, it remained entirely free from civilian control.

Within the *Reichstag* there was very little chance for any effective opposition to the government's aggressive policy abroad and its backward policy at home. The alliance between prominent industrialists and landowners, initiated under Bismarck, assured the government of a workable parliamentary majority. Both groups profited from tariff protectionism, and both were united in their opposition to lower-class demands for political and social democracy. Against this coalition between the industrialist National Liberals and the agrarian Conservatives, the Socialist opposition and the occasionally critical Center and Progressive parties could do very little, especially as they were rarely united among themselves. On a few occasions, notably during the "Daily Telegraph Affair" in 1908, when William II, in an interview to the British press, made some irresponsible statements on Anglo-German relations, it seemed as though public indignation might check the kaiser's erratic rule. But the discipline so deeply instilled in every German, and the economic prosperity the nation enjoyed, kept the public from taking any drastic steps.

Economic Developments

The immediate effect of Germany's unification in 1871 had been a short-lived economic boom, which had come to a sudden halt in the worldwide depression of 1873. It was only during the last two decades of the century that Germany began to show its great economic power, a power based on ample resources of coal and iron and a well-trained and disciplined labor force. Much of Germany's economic success can be attributed to the protective policy that Bismarck initiated in 1879. Germany was not the first nation to abandon free trade, but it was Germany's step that ushered in a period of tariff rivalry among the major powers and thus injected a strong element of nationalism into economic relations.

Germany's rapid economic growth was due in large measure to the development of its domestic market—its population increased from 41 million to 67 million between 1871 and 1914—but German competition was also felt abroad. The main pillars of German prosperity were coal and iron, concentrated in Alsace-Lorraine, the Saar, Upper Silesia, and particularly the Ruhr area, where the firms of Krupp, Thyssen,

Kaiser Wilhelm II

Every society, it is sometimes said, gets the ruler it deserves. This is true in part, but only in part, for Wilhelmine Germany. Kaiser Wilhelm II was certainly more representative of his age than Bismarck or Hitler were of theirs. And yet the Second Reich was unlucky in the man fate chose to rule it. He was deformed from birth, his left arm hanging six inches shorter than his right and incapable of movement. . . . His upbringing at the hands of the Calvinist Hinzpeter was severe. He hated his English Liberal mother, and despised his father for permitting her to dominate him. Although inwardly he may have been plagued by a sense of insecurity, his public utterances and actions stressed his own importance to a disturbing degree. He intervened in ship-design, archaeology, music, painting and theatre production with the same self-assurance that characterized his military and political moves. Much of his thinking was tinged with a brutal racialism which most people would now associate with a later period in German history. . . . He warned new recruits that they would have to shoot down their own fathers and brothers if he ordered them to. . . . His strongest language he reserved for the deputies of the Reichstag. They were "scoundrels without a fatherland" who were behaving "more and more like pigs.". . . It is no exaggeration to say that contending with the Kaiser was a major preoccupation of Germany's leading statesmen from Bismarck's fall until the outbreak of the First World War.

From J. C. G. Röhl, *Germany Without Bismarck: The Crisis of Government in the Second Reich, 1890–1900* (London: Batsford, 1967), pp. 27–29.

and Stinnes built their huge industrial empires. Germans took the lead in other pursuits as well, especially the electrical and chemical industries. By 1914 Germany's merchant marine was second only to that of Great Britain, although the British commercial fleet was still more than three times as large as that of Germany.

Socialism and Social Reform

The main critics of German domestic and foreign policy were the Social Democrats. Theirs was the largest and most influential socialist party in Europe. The origins of the party went back to the 1860s, but it did not become a political force until 1875. At that time a non-Marxian faction, organized by Ferdinand Lassalle in 1864, and a Marxian faction, led by Wilhelm Liebknecht and August Bebel, united to form the Social Democratic Party (SPD). Despite severe restrictions and the persecution of its members by the Bismarckian government, the numbers of the SPD steadily increased, until by 1912 it had become the largest party in the *Reichstag*. Its program, first formulated at Gotha in 1875 and revised at Erfurt in 1891, while strictly "orthodox" in tone, nevertheless included a number of "revisionist" demands for specific reforms.

The agitation of the SPD was directed against the political and social rather than the economic inequities of the empire. The phenomenal economic growth of the country could not help but be reflected in a rising standard of living for the workers. The German government, furthermore, through extensive programs of social reform, tried to alleviate the hardships inherent in massive industrialization. In 1878 factory inspection was made compulsory, and in 1891 an Imperial Industrial Code introduced the usual sanitary and safety provisions and regulated working hours for women and children. Germany's pioneering efforts were in the field of social legislation. In a calculated effort to divert German workers from socialism, Bismarck, between 1883 and 1889, introduced far-reaching measures for health, accident, and old-age insurance. These served as models for similar legislation in other countries, notably England.

The German Empire in 1914 was an anomaly among European powers—economically one of the most advanced, yet politically one of the most backward. The majority of Germans, though not happy about their political impotence, took comfort in their economic achievements. They might criticize their government's domestic policy—its opposition to parliamentary rule, its refusal to curb the influence of the military, its favoring of the few at the expense of the rest of the population. But most Germans saw little wrong with a foreign policy that demanded "a place in the sun" for Germany. Germany in 1914 was rich, powerful, and self-assertive.

AUSTRIA-HUNGARY: THE RAMSHACKLE EMPIRE

The Austro-Hungarian Empire, ever since the *Ausgleich* of 1867, had been virtually divided into two separate states. Both Austria and Hungary were constitutional monarchies, but their governments were far from democratic. Various attempts before 1914 to improve this situation were complicated by the perennial problem of nationalities. After 1873 the Austrian lower house, or *Reichsrat*, was elected by a complicated four-class franchise, which gave disproportionate influence to the upper classes and the German minority among the population. This system, with some minor changes, lasted until 1907. By that time agitation among the various subject nationalities had become so strong that electoral reform could no longer be put off. The electoral law of 1907 at long last granted universal manhood suffrage. But the return in subsequent elections of a large majority of non-German delegates led to such constant wrangling in the *Reichsrat* that the orderly conduct of democratic government became impossible and rule by decree remained the order of the day. In Hungary the situation was still more hopeless. Here the upper crust of Magyar landowners completely dominated both houses of parliament. The rising protest of Hungary's various subject nationalities

Bertha von Suttner (1843–1914), Austrian writer, whose pacifist novel, *Lay Down Your Arms* (1892), inspired Alfred Nobel to establish the Nobel Peace Prize. In 1905 she became the first woman recipient of the prize.

brought some slight electoral reforms, but Hungary in 1914 remained essentially a feudal state dominated by a Magyar aristocracy.

Conflict of Nationalities

The overriding problem of Austria-Hungary continued to be the conflicts among its many nationalities. In Austria the Czechs were the main problem. The Poles of Galicia formed a compact group that was relatively well treated and enjoyed cultural autonomy. The Czechs, on the other hand, were closely intermingled with Germans. Attempts to introduce Czech, together with German, as the official languages of Bohemia were met by German opposition. German nationalism found a mouthpiece in the German *Schulverein* of Georg von Schönerer. Meanwhile, the "Young Czechs," led by Thomas Masaryk, fought for the rights of their own people.

While Austria made at least some concessions to its minorities, Hungary followed a strict policy of Magyarization, trying to eradicate rather than appease opposition. The major problem in Hungary was created by the Croats, who looked to Serbia for the lead in forming a Yugoslav—that is, South Slav—federation. The situation was complicated by

the fact that the region of Bosnia-Herzegovina, since 1878 under Austrian administration, was also inhabited by Southern Slavs. The heir to the Austro-Hungarian crowns, Archduke Francis Ferdinand, was known to favor reforms that would give the Slavic element within the Dual Monarchy equal rights with Germans and Magyars. Neither Hungary nor Serbia liked such schemes. The Hungarians wanted to continue lording it over their Slavs, and the Serbs hoped to attract the Southern Slavs away from Austria-Hungary.

Thus the existing state of affairs in Austria-Hungary had few real supporters. Emperor Francis Joseph, eighty years old in 1910 and the most respected monarch in Europe, tried his best to meet the rising tide of nationalism by appealing to the traditional loyalty to the House of Habsburg. But his efforts were in vain.

Economic Developments

Even though there was considerable industrialization in the Austrian half of the empire, the country as a whole remained predominantly agrarian. As such it suffered increasingly from the competition of the larger agrarian economies of Russia, the United States, and Australia. A high tariff policy, though it protected agriculture, kept living costs high, which in turn made for high wages and prevented Austrian industries from successfully competing abroad. Even so, there was some industrial progress. It would have been greater had the economic interdependence between Austria and Hungary been better utilized. As it was, industrial Austria and agrarian Hungary pursued separate and often contradictory economic policies.

Socialism and Social Reform

Socialism in Austria did not become a factor to be reckoned with until the end of the century. In 1889, Victor Adler, the most prominent Austrian socialist, unified various socialist factions behind the Austrian Social Democratic Party. Socialist agitation, in part, was responsible for the introduction of universal male suffrage in Austria in 1907. This development, in turn, helped the party to

Emperor Francis Joseph (center) relaxing with guests at the wedding party of his grandnephew and eventual successor, Archduke Karl Franz Joseph (1911).

grow. The program of the Austrian socialists was revisionist, and their main support came from the working-class population of Vienna. Their major weakness was national diversity: by 1911 the party had split into German, Czech, and Polish factions. There was no socialist movement to speak of in Hungary.

The Austrian government, like governments elsewhere, took a hand in improving the workers' lot. A system of factory inspection was set up in 1883, and an Industrial Code in 1907 set the minimum working age at twelve, provided for an eleven-hour working day, and introduced safety and sanitation standards for factories.

The economic and social problems of the Austro-Hungarian Empire in 1914 were still overshadowed by its nationalities problem. Every possible solution to this problem had been proposed, and a few had been tried. Since each proposal left one or another of the many nationality groups dissatisfied, a policy of repression always prevailed. The result of this negative policy was the assassination of Francis Ferdinand at Sarajevo on June 28, 1914.

ITALY: GREAT POWER BY COURTESY

In Italy, economic backwardness and widespread illiteracy retarded the growth of democracy, although some superficial progress was made. The Italian constitution, the *Statuto*, which Piedmont had adopted in 1848, still limited the franchise in 1870 to a mere 2.5 percent of the population. Property qualifications and the voting age were gradually lowered, however, and virtually all adult males were permitted to vote by 1914. But this extension of the franchise was a mixed blessing. By giving the vote to the illiterate poor, it enabled a handful of ambitious politicians to manipulate elections and to make Italy's parliament a pliable instrument of their policy. The practice of "transformism"—that is, of avoiding parliamentary opposition by giving the most powerful critics a share in the government—avoided difficulties, but in the long run it proved a serious obstacle to the growth of democracy in Italy.

Political Instability

Despite marked economic improvements, Italy remained a poor and struggling country. A great power by courtesy more than through actual strength, Italy's frantic efforts to live up to a glorious past led it into military ventures it could ill afford. The conservative forces that had brought about the country's unification remained in power until 1876. Regional opposition to extreme centralization and widespread discontent with heavy taxation then shifted the power to the more liberal factions. From 1887 to 1891 and from 1893 to 1896, the experienced Francesco Crispi as prime minister provided firm leadership. His attempts to divert the people's attention from discontent at home through colonial ventures abroad suffered a dismal defeat at the hands of Ethiopia in the battle of Adua (1896). The end of the century saw a rising tide of labor unrest, bread riots, and street fighting. In 1900 King Humbert fell victim to an anarchist assassin and was succeeded by the more liberal Victor Emmanuel III.

During the last years before the war, Italy, under the capable but unprincipled Giovanni Giolitti (1842–1928) at long last made some headway in the solution of its worst economic difficulties. Giolitti also managed to effect a partial reconciliation between the Italian government and the Catholic Church. The pope continued to consider himself "the prisoner of the Vatican," but in 1905 he did lift the ban against the participation of Catholics in political affairs.

Economic Developments

Most of Italy's troubles were due to its poverty. Even more so than France, Italy was still primarily an agrarian nation. But while France was able to produce the bulk of its own food, Italy's soil was too poor and its agricultural methods too backward to support its rapidly growing population. The mounting population pressure could be relieved only through large-scale emigration and increased industrialization. The latter was hampered, however, by lack of essential raw materials and shortage of capital. Attempts at protectionism, furthermore,

Francesco Crispi (1819–1901), prime minister of Italy (1887–91, 1893–96).

Giovanni Giolitti (1842–1928). Five times prime minister of Italy (1892–93, 1903–05, 1906–09, 1911–14, 1920–21).

tended to affect Italy's own exports, and it was only with the conclusion of a series of commercial treaties in the 1890s that Italian exports picked up. With the help of hydroelectric power to make up for its coal shortage, Italy gradually developed its own textile industry and gained world leadership in the production of silk. But despite these improvements, and despite almost a doubling of its foreign commerce between 1900 and 1910, Italy's balance of trade continued to be unfavorable and Italy depended heavily on foreign loans.

Socialism and Social Reform

As it did almost everywhere else in Europe, industrialization in Italy brought in its wake the rise of socialism. The first socialist party in Italy was organized in 1891. It, too, had its initial difficulties over revisionism, and it was not until 1911 that the radical, "orthodox" element won the upper hand. The Italian socialist party did not gain any mass following until after 1900. Many Italian workers were attracted by the more violent programs of anarchism and syndicalism. Syndicalism applied the anarchist principle of direct action to economic affairs through sabotage and strikes. The first major general strike in Italy took place in 1904. It failed for lack of popular support.

The Italian government tried to cope with the social effects of industrialization by factory acts and social legislation. Accident and old-age insurance were introduced in 1898. But the basic causes of trouble—poverty and illiteracy—could not be erased overnight. Meanwhile the Italian people, inexperienced in the ways of democracy, fell more and more under the influence of extremists of the right or left—the right calling for glorious ventures abroad, the left opposing war and demanding reforms at home. Thus divided, Italy was in no condition to enter a major war in 1914.

RUSSIA: STRONGHOLD OF AUTOCRACY

Tsarist Russia, to the bitter end in 1917, remained the most autocratic among European states. The brief flurry of reforms under Alexander II during the 1860s had soon given way again to Russia's traditional policy of repression. The reign of Alexander II came to a violent end in 1881, when he was assassinated by members of the terrorist "Will of the People." His son, Alexander III (1881-94), was a reactionary and a Slavophile, not unlike Nicholas I. For well over a quarter-century Alexander III and his son and successor, Nicholas II (1894-1917), followed a policy of darkest reaction. Aided by Vyacheslav Plehve, director of the state police and later minister of the interior, and by Constantine Pobedonostsev, who as "Procurator of the Holy Synod" was the highest official in the Russian Orthodox Church and one of the most powerful men in Russia, the principles of orthodoxy, autocracy, and nationality once again became the watchwords of Russian policy. Catholics in Poland and Protestants in the Baltic provinces were persecuted; the powers of local and provincial zemstvos (councils), established under Alexander II, were curtailed; popular education was discouraged; and nationalism in Finland, Poland, the Ukraine, and elsewhere was suppressed. A particularly shocking feature of Russian policy was its persecution of the Jews. There were hardly any positive achievements during this period of unrelieved repression, except the economic reforms of Count Witte.

Economic Developments

Russia was the last major European power to feel the impact of industrialization. The government's main concern prior to 1890 had been the improvement of farming methods and the cultivation of new lands. Russia's agricultural exports between 1860 and 1900 increased almost fourfold, despite rising tariff barriers. Beginning in the 1890s, Russia also embarked on a program of industrialization, chiefly under the direction of its minister of finance and commerce, Count Sergei Witte (1849-1915). By introducing the gold standard in 1897, Witte stimulated economic activity and made investment in Russian industry more attractive to outsiders. The construction of the

Trans-Siberian Railway, begun in 1891, helped open up the country's rich mineral resources and furthered the iron industry in the Ural Mountains. As a result Russia by 1900 held fourth place among the world's iron producers and second place in the production of oil. The opposition of agrarian interests to Witte's industrial policy, however, led to his retirement in 1903. Together with an economic depression and the Russian defeat in the war with Japan (1904–05), Witte's departure helped to slow down Russia's industrial development. Lack of capital, the educational backwardness of the Russian worker, and his continued subjection to the village community were chiefly responsible for Russia's failure to realize its tremendous economic potentialities.

Socialism and Social Reform

Because of the government's vigilance toward all manifestations of social and political protest, socialism in Russia was slow to take hold. It was not until 1891 that the first Marxian socialist party was organized by Georgi V. Plekhanov. The activity of the Social Democratic Party was largely confined to underground agitation. At a party congress in London in 1903, Russia's socialists split into two groups. The Mensheviks (or minority), under Julius Martov, advocated a gradual evolution to democracy and socialism, while the Bolsheviks (or majority), under Lenin, followed the more radical, "Leninist" line. The two factions (despite their name, the Bolsheviks were actually in the minority) also differed on the question of how their party should be organized. Besides Marxian socialism, which appealed to the rising industrial proletariat, there was also an organization of agrarian socialists in Russia, the Socialist Revolutionaries. Their program harked back to the ideas of Alexander Herzen and to the populist "go-to-the-people" movement (see p. 617). To achieve their goals, the Socialist Revolutionaries advocated terrorism and assassination.

Increased industrialization in Russia brought the usual hardships for the working class. With an ample supply of manpower from landless peasants, wages remained low and the Russian worker had to slave long hours to eke out a meager existence. The government, in time, did regulate the employment of women and children and introduced maximum working-hours. But without a corresponding increase in wages, these restrictions merely tended to lower the total income of workers' families. Moreover, to voice discontent through labor unions was prohibited by law. Even so, unrest among the workers gave rise to frequent strikes of increasing violence.

The Revolution of 1905

The workers were not the only class that was restless at the turn of the century. There were the masses of landless peasants, whose grievances were kept alive by the Socialist Revolutionaries; there was opposition among national minorities against the government's policy of Russification; and there was growing agitation among liberal members of the middle class, who demanded a change to constitutional government. As economic depression was worsening the lot of the workers, the Russo-Japanese War upset the rural economy by requiring that peasants be drafted. With the tide of war turning against Russia, tension mounted

"Bloody Sunday" (January 22, 1905). A procession of workers is fired on by tsarist troops on its way to the Winter Palace; 70 people were killed and 240 wounded.

The march on the Winter Palace on "Bloody Sunday" in 1905 was organized by the priest Georgy Gapon.

and finally erupted in revolution. The Revolution of 1905 began on January 22, "Bloody Sunday," when a peaceful protest march was fired on by tsarist troops. A general strike soon crippled the major industrial centers, peasants rose against their landlords, and mutinies broke out in the army and navy. In October the Social Democrats and the Socialist Revolutionaries set up a Soviet (or Council) of Workers' Delegates in St. Petersburg.

By that time, however, the revolution had run its course. Tsar Nicholas, after first intending to meet force by force, finally gave in and made a number of political concessions. The "October Manifesto" of 1905 guaranteed individual freedoms and called for the election of a National Assembly, or *Duma*, by almost universal male suffrage. But the promises made by Nicholas under duress were soon forgotten. It took three elections, each under a more restrictive franchise, before a *Duma* was finally elected that satisfied the tsar's wish for an advisory rather than a legislative body. Meanwhile the government had taken savage reprisals against the rank and file of the revolutionaries, executing an estimated fifteen thousand and arresting many times that number. Even so, Russia for the first time in its history now had an elected national assembly that could at least serve as a training-ground in parliamentary procedures. The democratic spirit thus penetrated, if ever so slightly, the last stronghold of autocracy.

Repression and Reform

The outstanding figure of the last decade before the war was Peter Stolypin, chief minister until 1911. A conservative monarchist, he nevertheless believed in a limited degree of representative government. He worked harmoniously with the moderate faction within the third *Duma*, the "Octobrists," who in contrast to the more liberal "Cadets" (constitutional democrats) were satisfied with a mere consultative role. Stolypin's policy combined repression with reform. On the one hand, he bore down hard on all revolutionary activities by Social Democrats and Socialist Revolutionaries. Their leaders were arrested, driven into

exile (as were Lenin and Trotsky), or sent to Siberia (as was Stalin). These negative measures, however, were supplemented by far-reaching reforms. Realizing the desire of Russia's peasants for land of their own, and aware of the support that could be gained from a large class of small farmers, Stolypin started to divide the communal holdings of the villages, distributing the land among the individual members of the *mir*. This was a slow and complicated process, and by 1917 only about one-tenth of Russia's peasants had become independent farmers. Nevertheless, it was a farsighted move, and it might have saved the tsarist regime if land reform had been completed in time.

Stolypin's reformist policy was opposed not only by the advocates of revolution, for whom it did not go far and fast enough, but also by the forces of reaction. The latter again gained the upper hand when Stolypin was assassinated in 1911. Nicholas II was a weak and vacillating monarch, firmly committed to the autocratic beliefs of his father and deeply under the influence of his German wife. The Tsarina Alexandra had fallen under the spell of an evil and ignorant "holy man," Gregory Rasputin. This power-hungry Siberian peasant gained such influence over the imperial family that he became the real power in Russia. Reaction coupled with corruption and inefficiency led to a gradual paralysis of Russia's government, making it doubly vulnerable to any major crisis. Such a crisis arose with the First World War.

THE "CULT OF SCIENCE"

This discussion of the domestic affairs of the major powers between 1870 and 1914 thus far has dealt entirely with political, social, and economic events. Now it is necessary to outline the intellectual climate in which these developments took place. The title of this chapter—"The Period of Promise"—fits particularly well the intellectual and cultural trends of these years. Their outstanding characteristic may be described as an overriding interest and a deep belief in science. Man had been interested in science before.

A Russian political cartoon, "The Russian Ruling House," shows Nicholas II and Alexandra manipulated by the dominating Rasputin.

But it was only in the second half of the nineteenth century that a veritable "cult of science" developed. Science offered a positive alternative to the seemingly futile idealism and Romanticism of the early nineteenth century. Scientific research, in the past the domain of a few scientists and gentleman scholars, now became the concern of large numbers of people, especially as the application of science to industry gave an incentive for new inventions. "Pure" science continued to be of fundamental importance. But "applied" science—the "marriage of science and technology" so characteristic of the Second Industrial Revolution—now took precedence in the minds of most people. A virtually endless series of scientific inventions seemed to provide tangible evidence of man's ability to unlock the secrets of nature. If support was needed for the optimistic belief in unlimited progress, science provided it.

Materialism and Positivism

The growing concern of modern man with the material aspects of his civilization was also reflected in late-nineteenth-century thought. A few basic scientific discoveries served as a foundation for an essentially materialistic philosophy that appealed to the educated middle class. Chemists and physicists earlier in the century had found matter and energy to be constant and indestructible. These scientific findings were translated by certain "popularizers of science"—writers who interpreted the discoveries of scientists to the average layman—into a philosophy of materialism. An early exponent of this philosophy was the German philosopher Ludwig Feuerbach (1804–72). More influential, however, was the German physician Ludwig Büchner (1824–99), whose book *Force and Matter* (1855) went through twenty-one editions and was translated into all major languages. Proclaiming the eternity of force (that is, energy) and matter, Büchner concluded that it was "impossible that the world can have been created. How could anything be created that cannot be annihilated?" Another influential scientific writer was the German biologist Ernst Haeckel (1834–1919), whose most famous book, *The Riddle of the Universe at the Close of the Nineteenth Century* (1899), became an international best-seller. Haeckel's "monistic philosophy" was entirely concerned with the material world, emphasizing not merely the eternity of matter and energy but insisting that even the human mind and soul had their material, physical substance. As for the riddles of the universe, Haeckel declared with the optimism typical of his age that all but one of them had been solved; and the remaining one, "what the pious believer called Creator or God," was not worth troubling with, since there was no means of investigating it.

More lasting in its effect on western thought than materialism was another philosophy concerned with the impact of modern science on society—positivism. This philosophy had been worked out in the first half of the nineteenth century by the Frenchman Auguste Comte (1798–1857), but its influence was not felt until later. According to Comte, man in his development had passed through two well-defined phases, the theological and the metaphysical, and had now entered a third phase, the scientific, or positive. In this last phase man no longer concerned himself with ultimate causes, as he had during the metaphysical stage, but was satisfied with the material world and with whatever he might learn from observing it. Here was a philosophy that accepted science as its only guide and authority and which for that reason was eminently suited to the late nineteenth century.

THE DARWINIAN REVOLUTION

The scientific development that had the most revolutionary impact on almost every facet of western thought and society in the second half of the nineteenth century occurred in biology. It is concerned with the theory of evolution, and its major exponent was the British scientist Charles Darwin (1809–82).

The idea of evolution was nothing new. Both in the general sense of a gradual development of human society from simple to more complex institutions, and in the more narrow biological sense that all organisms had evolved out of more elementary forms, the concept of evolution had earlier roots in western thought. Darwin's major contribution was to provide a scientific basis for what had previously been a mere hypothesis.

Darwinism

Darwin was influenced in the formulation of his theory by the writings of the geologist Charles Lyell (1797–1875) and by Thomas Robert Malthus' *Essay on the Principle of Population.* Lyell, in his *Principles of Geology* (1830), had restated the thesis advanced some fifty years earlier by James Hutton that the earth's physical appearance was the result of the same type of geological processes that are still active today. This idea of vast changes brought about by natural causes, which Lyell had applied to the inorganic world, Darwin applied to the world of organisms. In searching for an explanation of organic evolution, Darwin was impressed by Malthus' account of the intense competition among mankind for the means of subsistence.

The essence of Darwinism is stated in the full title of his basic work: *On the Origin of Species by Means of Natural Selection, or the Preservation of Favoured Races in the Struggle for Life* (1859). His theory was subsequently elaborated and applied to the human species in *The Descent of Man* (1871). According to Darwin, life among all organisms is a constant "struggle for existence." In this struggle only the fittest survive. This survival of the fittest, Darwin held, was due to certain favorable variations within the given organism that proved of particular advantage in its competitive struggle with other organisms. These lucky variations, handed on to subsequent generations and enhanced by further variations, would in time evolve an entirely new organism, so radically different from its ancestor as to be considered a new species. This "natural selection," Darwin suggested, was further aided by "sexual selection"—that is, the mutual attraction and consequent mating of the fittest members of a species to bring forth the fittest offspring. Darwin also accepted the notion that certain "acquired characteristics"—the long neck of the giraffe, for example—may be inherited.

Many contemporary scientists accepted Darwin's theories only reluctantly. Yet his main idea—that all existing forms of life have evolved out of earlier and simpler forms—remains valid to this day. Only his explanation of the actual process of evolution has been challenged. The idea of the inheritance of acquired characteristics had been pretty well shaken by the end of the nineteenth century. Darwin's concept of evolution as a cumulative result of many minute changes, furthermore, has gradually given way to the view that evolution proceeds by way of larger and more sudden changes, or "mutations." These modifications came later, however, and thus could not affect the revolutionary impact of Darwin's theories when they were first announced. More than any other single idea of the nineteenth century, the concept of evolution has left its mark on modern thought and society.

The Impact of Darwinism

By applying the idea of evolution to all living organisms, including man, Darwin destroyed many of the most cherished beliefs of his contemporaries. Yet to an age that worshiped science, the thought that man was just as much subject to the logic of science as was everything else in nature also held a great fascination. Underlying much of Darwin's work was the idea of progress, an idea dear to the nineteenth century. History, the study of man's past, suddenly appeared in a new light—as a march toward some far-off, lofty goal. The gentle and retiring scientist himself took little part in the excitement and controversy stirred up by the doctrine that bore his name. The popularization of Darwin's thought was due chiefly to the efforts of other men, especially his friend Thomas Huxley (1825–95). The application of the evolutionary concept to every aspect of human society, from physics to ethics, was carried out by another admirer of Darwin, Herbert Spencer (1820–1903). Spencer's ten-volume *Synthetic Philosophy*, published between 1860 and 1896, was hailed at the time as a

Charles Darwin (1809–82) at the age of forty-five, five years before the publication of *Origin of Species.*

brilliant synthesis of all existing scientific knowledge. Today it has been practically forgotten.

Of all Darwin's new ideas, the concept of life as a struggle for existence in which the fittest would survive had particular appeal to his contemporaries. The philosophy of laissez faire, with its emphasis on competition, had long been hailed as the root of economic success. Darwinism seemed to give scientific sanction to this belief in laissez faire. Big business, according to John D. Rockefeller, was "merely a survival of the fittest . . . the working out of a law of nature and a law of God." But not only the capitalists derived great comfort from Darwin. His emphasis on the importance of environment for the improvement of man also gave hope to the socialists in their demands for social and economic reform. More than ten years before Darwin published his *Origin of Species*, Karl Marx, the "Darwin of the social sciences," had already sketched the evolution of society through a series of struggles among social classes.

The emphasis on struggle as a necessary condition for progress, however, was a narrow and one-sided interpretation of Darwinism, not shared by its author. In his *Descent of Man*, Darwin had emphasized that a feeling of sympathy and coherence, social and moral qualities, were needed for the advancement of society. But to the majority of people the struggle for existence assumed the validity of a natural law, a law, moreover, that applied not just to relations among individuals but to relations among groups.

"Social Darwinism"

Herbert Spencer was one of the first to apply the theory of evolution to groups and states. History to Spencer was a struggle for existence among social organisms leading, as in the case of the struggle among individuals, to the "survival of the fittest." The classical statement of what came to be called "Social Darwinism" was made by the English banker and political scientist Walter Bagehot (1826–77) in his book *Physics and Politics: Thoughts on the Application of the*

Darwin testing the speed of an elephant tortoise in the Galápagos Islands during his voyage on the surveying ship *Beagle* (1831–36). This journey provided most of the observations for his theory of evolution. Drawing by Meredith Nugent.

Principles of Natural Selection and Inheritance to Political Science (1872). According to Bagehot, the struggle for existence had always applied to groups as well as individuals, and in this struggle "the majority of the groups which win and conquer are better than the majority of those which fail and perish." In other words, among nations as among individuals, the strongest survive and the strongest, for that reason, are the best. Needless to say, this restatement of the well-known maxim that "might makes right" had little to do with Darwin's original theory.

Social Darwinism has been described as a blending of evolutionary and nationalist elements. To a generation that had recently experienced several major wars and that was actively engaged in numerous expeditions against colonial peoples overseas, Social Darwinism, with its glorification of war, came as a welcome rationalization. "The grandeur of war," Heinrich von Treitschke, one of Germany's most popular historians, told his students, "lies in the utter annihilation of puny man in the great conception of the state. . . . In war the chaff is winnowed from the wheat." It is not surprising to find such views in a country that owed so much to war. But war also found advocates elsewhere. The Frenchman Ernest Renan praised it as "one of the conditions of progress, the sting which prevents a country from going to sleep"; and President Theodore Roosevelt held that war alone enabled man to "acquire those virile qualities necessary to win in the stern strife of actual life."

Darwin on Man's Moral Qualities

The development of the moral qualities is a more interesting problem. The foundation lies in the social instincts. . . . A moral being is one who is capable of reflecting on his past actions and their motives— approving of some and disapproving of others; and the fact that man is the one being who certainly deserves this designation, is the greatest of all distinctions between him and the lower animals. But in the fourth chapter I have endeavoured to show that the moral sense follows, firstly, from the enduring and ever-present nature of the social instincts; secondly, from man's appreciation of the approbation and disapprobation of his fellows; and thirdly, from the high activity of his mental faculties, with past impressions extremely vivid; and in these latter respects he differs from the lower animals. . . .

Social animals are impelled partly by a wish to aid the members of their community in a general manner, but more commonly to perform certain definite actions. Man is impelled by the same general wish to aid his fellows. . . . The moral nature of man has reached its present standard, partly through the advancement of his reasoning powers and consequently of a just public opinion, but especially from his sympathies having been rendered more tender and widely diffused through the effects of habit, example, instruction, and reflection. It is not improbable that after long practice virtuous tendencies may be inherited. With the more civilized races, the conviction of the existence of an all-seeing Deity has had a potent influence on the advance of morality. . . . Nevertheless the first foundation or origin of the moral sense lies in the social instincts, including sympathy; and these instincts no doubt were primarily gained, as in the case of the lower animals, through natural selection.

From Charles Darwin, *The Descent of Man*, rev. ed. (New York: Appleton, 1886), pp. 610–12.

The influence of Social Darwinism may also be seen in the injection of racialism into nationalism. If being victorious meant being better, what was more natural than to view the triumph of one nation or race over another as a sign of the victor's inherent superiority? Among the earliest writers on racialism was the French count Arthur de Gobineau (1816–82). His *Essay on the Inequality of the Human Races* (1853–55) proclaimed the superiority of the white race and distinguished within that race between the superior Germanic "Aryans" and the inferior Slavs and Jews. Gobineau's racial doctrine, wholly unscientific, found its main echo in Germany. But the idea of white, specifically Anglo-Saxon, superiority was also popular in England and America. It provided an ideological justification for the imperialist expansion of the late nineteenth century.

The "Warfare of Science with Theology"

The most violent repercussions of Darwinism were felt in the religious field. The controversy between Darwinism and religion was part of a larger conflict that has been described as the "warfare of science with theology." The religious revival during the Age of Romanticism had soon given way to a noticeable decline in religious interest. As the state took over the functions of the churches in social welfare and education, and as some of the material benefits of industrialization spread among the lower classes, the need for the aid and comfort that religion had given in the past was no longer so acute. The tendency of the churches, furthermore, to favor the political status quo antagonized many liberals, and political anticlericalism became an important issue in most countries. Finally, there was the appeal that nationalism, socialism, and materialism came to have for many people. Both socialism and materialism were avowed enemies of religion.

Although these causes go far to explain the decline in religious interest in the second half of the nineteenth century, the most important reason was the effect modern science had on Christianity. Many scientific discoveries, especially in geology and biology, contradicted Christian beliefs, and the methods of scientific inquiry, when applied to Christianity itself, produced some disturbing results. In biblical, or "higher," criticism, for instance, scholars studying the origins of the Bible discovered that most of its books had been written long after the events they described, and that few biblical writings existed exactly as they had originally been written. Other scholars, concerned with the study of comparative religion, detected striking similarities between Christianity and other religions. They found that there were few differences in dogma and ritual between early Christianity and some of the many mystery cults that had flourished in the eastern Mediterranean at the time of Christ. Christianity, it seemed, was merely the one among many similar religions that had survived.

These discoveries concerning the origins of Christianity became more widely known when they were used in modern accounts of the life of Christ. A German scholar, David Friedrich Strauss (1808–74), as early as 1835 had written a *Life of Jesus* that denied the divinity of Christ. Less scholarly and more popular was the *Life of Jesus* (1863) by the French writer Ernest Renan (1823–92). Both works recognized Christ as a superior human being, but they denied that he had performed miracles or had risen from the dead.

Darwinism and Religion

Far more drastic in their effect on the faithful than these attempts to humanize Christ were the findings of Darwin. Not only did Darwin and Lyell challenge the biblical view of creation, but by making man a part of general evolution, Darwin dethroned the lords of the creation from the unique position they had hitherto occupied. Why, one might ask, should man alone of all creatures possess an immortal soul, and at what stage of his evolution was he endowed with it?

The Catholic Church, because it was more tightly organized and in its doctrine placed less exclusive emphasis on the Bible, was able to take a firmer and more consistent stand in this controversy than the various Protestant churches. In 1864 Pope Pius IX issued "A Syllabus of the Principal Errors of Our Times," which condemned most of the new political, economic, and scientific tendencies. Six years later a general Church council, in an effort to strengthen the pope's position, proclaimed the dogma of papal infallibility. The pope henceforth was to be infallible in all statements he made *ex cathedra*—that is, officially—on matters of faith and morals. The new dogma ran into some opposition among Catholics, and it also contributed to the struggle between Church and state in Germany, Italy, and France.

The succession of the more conciliatory Leo XIII to the papacy in 1878 helped pacify matters. Leo was able to make peace with the German and, to a lesser extent, the French governments, and in the social and economic sphere, he tried to steer a middle course between capitalism and socialism. In science, Leo did not oppose discoveries that did not affect Catholic doctrine. Only on the subject of evolution did the papacy persist in its rigid opposition. Some Catholics had begun searching for ways to reconcile the contradictions between science and theology. This "modernism," as such attempted compromise was called, was considered a heresy by the Church. Only after the First World War did the Church gradually take a more tolerant view.

In contrast to Catholicism, Protestant (and to some extent Jewish) doctrine and ritual were almost entirely based on the Bible. The effect of scientific discoveries at variance with biblical statements, therefore, was felt more deeply. The fact, furthermore, that Protestantism was split into almost three hundred sects made any uniform stand in the warfare between science and theology very difficult. At the same time, however, Protestant emphasis on the freedom of the individual to work out his own relations with God made it possible for many Protestants to reach their own compromise between faith and reason. A minority of Protestants, called "Fundamentalists," less influential in Europe than in the United States, continued to cling to a literal interpretation of the Bible and insisted on the validity of the account of creation as given in the Book of Genesis.

Despite the confusion it caused not only among Christians but among Jews, the conflict between science and theology did not seriously interfere with the progress of science. The world in 1914 was still viewed as the intricate mechanism that Newton had supposedly shown it to be, a mechanism whose secrets would gradually yield to scientific inquiry. Only a handful of scientists realized that new developments—the discovery of X-rays (1895), the isolation of radium (1898), and, most important, the formulation of the theory of relativity (1905)—had opened up an infinite number of new mysteries and had brought the world to the threshold of another scientific revolution.

ART IN THE AGE OF SCIENCE

The cult of science that dominated the intellectual climate at the end of the nineteenth century also had its devotees in art and literature. It is difficult in dealing with any period, especially one as diverse as the one described in this chapter, to single out those artistic trends that most clearly reflect the spirit of the age. To call the early nineteenth century an Age of Romanticism and the late nineteenth century an Age of Realism is very much an oversimplification. There were Romanticists and Realists in both these "ages," and some artists combined the characteristics of both periods in their work.

The Romantic artist, as we have seen, had preferred an ideal world of his imagination to the real world in which he lived. He had set his concept of natural beauty against the ugliness of early industrialism. And he had escaped from a harsh present to a more rosy past. Before the middle of the nineteenth century, however, some artists had already begun to be interested in the world as it was, not as they felt it ought to be. This shift from Romanticism to Realism was most evident in literature; it was less pronounced in painting, and there were hardly any signs of it in music.

Realism and Naturalism

The novel now became the favorite medium in literature. Most of the great novels of the nineteenth century—from those of Dickens and Thackeray in England to those of Balzac and Flaubert in France, Fontane in Germany, and Turgenev and Tolstoy in Russia—fall into the category of social novels. Not only did these authors describe the society in which they lived; they dwelled on the problems of that society. Literature was becoming increasingly a form of social criticism.

Henri de Toulouse Lautrec (1864–1901) at work in the garden of his Montmartre studio in Paris.

The shift toward Realism reached its climax in the late nineteenth century in a literary movement called Naturalism. Naturalism represented the conscious effort of some writers to apply scientific principles to art. Naturalistic writers like Émile Zola in France, Henrik Ibsen in Norway, and Gerhart Hauptmann in Germany were not interested so much in beauty as they were in truth. To get at truth they discarded subjective intuition and strove to describe objectively what they had learned from study and observation. The Naturalist was much impressed with the discoveries of modern science, especially in biology and such new fields as sociology and psychology, and he made use of this new knowledge in his writing. The Naturalist felt it was one of his chief functions to call attention to existing evils and abuses. If this meant focusing his artistic efforts on the seamy side of life, he did so, hoping that by serving as diagnostician of society's illness he might help cure it.

Impressionism

The change from Romanticism to Realism was far less pronounced in painting than in literature, though some new trends did appear. In the past artists had been concerned with the unusual and beautiful, but now they turned more to ordinary and often ugly everyday subjects heretofore considered unworthy of their attention—farmers, laborers, and urban scenes.

The real innovation in nineteenth-century painting, however, was not so much in subject matter as in technique. As Naturalism did to literature, so Impressionism applied scientific principles to painting. Influenced by scientific discoveries about the composition of light, painters like Camille Pissarro (1830–1903), Claude Monet (1840–1926), and Auguste Renoir (1841–1919) used short strokes of pure color to depict nature in its ever-changing moods, not as it appeared to the logical mind but as it "impressed" the eye in viewing a whole scene rather than a series of specific objects. An Impressionist painting, examined at close range, thus appears as a maze of colored dabs that, viewed from a distance, merge into recognizable objects with the vibrant quality imparted by light.

In trying to find the scientific temper of the late nineteenth century reflected in literature and art, however, one must guard against oversimplification. A relationship between art and science certainly existed. But it would be wrong to assume that the majority of people at the time were aware of this relationship. The average European probably had little use for Naturalistic novels or plays or Impressionist paintings. He liked pictures that "told a story," preferably a sentimental one. And he liked second-rate novels of love and adventure by authors long since forgotten.

Symbolism

If these cultural interests of the average man expressed an unconscious desire to escape the realities of the present, a similar tendency may be noted among a few highly sensitive writers. They deplored their generation's preoccupation with material values, and far from singing the praises of the industrial age, they spoke out against its dirt and vulgarity. Earlier in the century, the Englishmen Matthew Arnold (1822–88) and John Ruskin (1819–1900) had lamented the materialism and the loss of esthetic values resulting from industrialization. Their complaints were echoed later by their compatriot William Morris (1834–96), who would have preferred to withdraw from the machine age with its cheapening of taste and return to the simplicity and dignity of the Middle Ages.

There was a note of romanticism and escapism in this longing for beauty in an age of slums and soot. Naturalism had little use for beauty; to the Naturalist, art had to serve a purpose and preach a message. In protest against this arid view, a group of French writers at the end of the century proclaimed that art was sufficient unto itself—"art for art's sake." Art to these neo-Romantic, or Symbolist, poets—Stéphane Mallarmé (1842–98), Paul Verlaine (1844–96), and others—was not for everyone but only for the select few to whom it spoke in "symbols," using words not so much for their meaning but for the images and analogies they conveyed, often by sound alone. Symbolism, like Romanticism before, was deeply subjective and thus difficult to define. It is significant as an indication that there were people before 1914 who did not find all things perfect in a society that gloried in its material achievements and accepted the struggle for wealth as a sign of progress.

The Symbolists were not alone in their criticism. The most outspoken critic of the generation before 1914 was the German philosopher Friedrich Nietzsche (1844–1900). In a series of beautifully written, epigrammatic books in the 1880s, Nietzsche attacked almost everything his age held sacred—democracy, socialism, nationalism, racialism, imperialism, militarism, materialism, intellectualism, and especially Christianity. Little understood by his contemporaries and much misunderstood since, Nietzsche's influence was felt more after than before the First World War. Few people today would agree with his wholesale condemnation of his age. Yet in striking out, Nietzsche could not help but hit on many of the weaknesses we have since come to recognize in an age characterized above all by smugness and misplaced self-confidence.

Friedrich Nietzsche (1844–1900).

Suggestions for Further Reading

Note: Asterisk denotes a book available in paperback edition.

General Two good broadly conceived works that treat European civilization as an entity are C. J. H. Hayes, *A Generation of Materialism, 1871–1900** (1941), and O. J. Hale, *The Great Illusion, 1900–1914** (1971). National events are well covered in R. C. K. Ensor, *England, 1870–1914* (1936); D. W. Brogan, *The Development of Modern France, 1870–1939*, Vol. I, rev. ed. (1966); K. S. Pinson, *Modern Germany, Its History and Civilization*, 2nd ed. (1966); D. Mack Smith, *Italy: A Modern History* (1959); A. J. May, *The Hapsburg Monarchy, 1867–1914* (1951); and H. Seton-Watson, *The Decline of Imperial Russia, 1855–1914** (1952).

The Growth of Democracy The progress of political and social democracy is treated in A. Rosenberg, *Democracy and Socialism* (1939). On social thought, see G. Masur, *Prophets of Yesterday: Studies in European Culture, 1890–1914** (1961), and H. S. Hughes, *Consciousness and Society: The Reorientation of Social Thought, 1850–1930** (1958). Other relevant works are J. Bowle, *Politics and Opinion in the Nineteenth Century** (1954); C. Moraze, *The Triumph of the Middle Classes* (1966); and C. Cipolla, *Literacy and Development in the West** (1969). Problems of parliamentary government in western Europe are discussed in É. Halévy, *History of the English People in the Nineteenth Century,** Vols. V and VI (1936), and D. Thomson, *Democracy in France Since 1870,** 4th ed. (1964). The peculiar situation in Germany is analyzed in two valuable studies: A. Rosenberg, *The Birth of the German Republic, 1871–1918** (1931), and A. Gerschenkron, *Bread and Democracy in Germany* (1943). Habsburg attempts to cope with the nationalities problem are disentangled in O. Jászi, *The Dissolution of the Habsburg Monarchy** (1929), and with emphasis on individual national groups in R. A. Kann, *The Multinational Empire*, 2 vols. (1950). The halfhearted efforts at political reform in Russia are discussed in G. Fischer, *Russian Liberalism from Gentry to Intelligentsia* (1958), and B. Pares, *The Fall of the Russian Monarchy* (1939). Women's efforts for equal rights are the subject of W. L. O'Neill, *Woman Movement: Feminism in the United States and in England* (1969), and D. Mitchell, *The Fighting Pankhursts: A Study in Tenacity* (1967).

The "Second Industrial Revolution" Several of the books mentioned in the reading list for Chapter 25 also cover this later period. D. Landes, *The Unbound Prometheus: Technological Change and Industrial Development in Western Europe from 1750 to the Present* (1969), is a major recent contribution. Additional treatments for the leading industrial countries are A. L. Levine, *Industrial Retardation in Britain, 1880–1914* (1967); W. W. Rostow, *The British Economy in the Nineteenth Century* (1948); G. Palmade, *French Capitalism in the Nineteenth Century* (1972); and G. Stolper, K. Häuser, and K. Borchardt, *The German Economy—1870 to the Present* (1967). M. S. Miller, *The Economic Development of Russia, 1905–1914* (1926), is more detailed, and W. L. Blackwell, *The Industrialization of Russia: An Historical Perspective** (1970), covers a longer period. On European economic expansion overseas, see H. Feis, *Europe, the World's Banker, 1870–1914** (1930).

The Rise of the Working Class A brief introduction to European radicalism is D. Caute, *The Left in Europe Since 1789** (1966). On evolutionary socialism, see P. Gay, *The Dilemma of Democratic Socialism: Eduard Bernstein's Challenge to Marx** (1952), and A. M. McBriar, *Fabian Socialism and English Politics, 1884–1918** (1962). The best book on socialism in Germany is C. Schorske, *German Social Democracy, 1905–1917** (1955). For France, see A. Noland, *The Founding of the French Socialist Party, 1893–1905* (1956), and H. Goldberg, *Life of Jean Jaurès* (1962). Good surveys of international socialism are J. Joll, *The Second International, 1889–1914** (1955), and M. Beer, *Fifty Years of International Socialism* (1937). On the growth of organized labor, see W. A. McConagha, *The Development of the Labor Movement in Great Britain, France, and Germany* (1942); H. Pelling, *The Origins of the Labour Party, 1880–1900*, 2nd ed. (1964); and J. W. Scott, *The Glassworkers of Carmaux* (1974). Social legislation before 1914 is covered in K. de Schweinitz, *England's Road to Social Security* (1943), and W. H. Dawson, *Social Insurance in Germany, 1883–1911* (1912). The influence of individual reformers in England is discussed in H. Ausubel, *In Hard Times: Reformers Among the Late Victorians* (1960), and M. Richter, *The Politics of Conscience: T. H. Green and His Age* (1964). On the role of the churches in the field of social reform, see D. O. W. Wagner, *Church of England and Social Reform Since 1854* (1930); J. N. Moody, ed., *Church and Society: Catholic Social and Political Thought and Movements, 1789–1950* (1953); K. S. Inglis, *Churches and the Working Class in Victorian England* (1963); and J. McManners, *Church and State in France, 1870–1914* (1972).

Domestic Affairs of the Major Powers

Much of this subject is covered in the works already cited. An interesting way of supplementing the more general accounts is through biographies. Among the standard lives of the great, L. Strachey, *Queen Victoria** (1921), is a classic, though E. Longford, *Victoria R. I.** (1964), is more reliable. R. Blake, *Disraeli* (1967), and E. J. Feuchtwanger, *Gladstone* (1975), are more readable than earlier standard accounts. Two great French leaders are commemorated in G. Bruun, *Clemenceau** (1943), and G. Wright, *Raymond Poincaré and the French Presidency* (1942). There are no really satisfactory works on the continental monarchs. M. Balfour, *The Kaiser and His Times* (1964), is entertaining but not definitive. J. Redlich, *Emperor Francis Joseph* (1929), lacks color; and neither Nicholas II of Russia nor the kings of Italy have been found worthy of major scholarly biographies.

B. D. Wolfe, *Three Who Made a Revolution** (1955), tells about the future rulers of Russia—Lenin, Trotsky, and Stalin—before their rise to power. The nineteenth-century background of Russia's revolutionary movement is described in E. Lampert, *Studies in Rebellion* (1957) and *Sons Against Fathers* (1965). See also A. Yarmolinsky, *Road to Revolution* (1957). T. H. von Laue, *Sergei Witte and the Industrialization of Russia* (1963), is important for Russian economic history.

Significant monographs on German history include P. G. J. Pulzer, *The Rise of Political Anti-Semitism in Germany and Austria** (1964); J. C. G. Röhl, *Germany Without Bismarck: The Crisis of Government in the Second Reich, 1890–1900* (1967); M. Kitchen, *The German Officer Corps, 1890–1914* (1968); G. Roth, *Social Democrats in Imperial Germany* (1963); and F. Stern, *The Politics of Cultural Despair** (1965). For a balanced view of the most crucial event in French politics, see D. Johnson, *France and the Dreyfus Affair* (1967). Other phases of French politics are treated in E. Weber, *Action Française* (1962) and *Peasants into Frenchmen: The Modernization of Rural France, 1870–1914* (1976); M. Curtis, *Three Against the Third Republic* (1959), which deals with Sorel, Barrès, and Maurras; and R. Byrnes, *Anti-Semitism in Modern France* (1950). R. D. Anderson, *France, 1870–1914: Politics and Society* (1977), is brief and has an excellent bibliography. Britain on the eve of the First World War is the subject of C. Cross, *The Liberals in Power, 1905–1914* (1963), and G. Dangerfield, *The Strange Death of Liberal England** (1961). The Italian scene is described in J. A. Thayer, *Italy and the Great War: Politics and Culture, 1890–1915* (1964), and in C. Seton-Watson, *Italy from Liberalism to Fascism, 1870–1925* (1967).

Intellectual History

The general works by J. H. Randall, *The Making of the Modern Mind* (1926, 1940), and C. Brinton, *Ideas and Men** (1950), have good chapters on the intellectual life of the late nineteenth century. E. Weber, *Paths to the Present: Aspects of European Thought from Romanticism to Existentialism** (1960), contains unusual selections of readings. See also O. Chadwick, *The Secularization of the European Mind in the Nineteenth Century* (1976). On the history of science, see A. E. E. McKenzie, *The Major Achievements of Science*, 2 vols. (1960), and W. C. Dampier, *A Shorter History of Science** (1957). The all-pervasive influence of Darwin is shown in P. B. Sears, *Charles Darwin: The Naturalist as a Cultural Force* (1950), and J. C. Greene, *The Death of Adam: Evolution and Its Impact on Western Thought* (1959). On the contemporary impact of Darwinism, see W. Irvine, *Apes, Angels, and Victorians* (1955). J. Barzun, *Darwin, Marx, Wagner** (1958), stresses similarities in three outwardly different contemporaries. W. Bagehot, *Physics and Politics** (1956), the work of a leading Social Darwinist, is still important. The wide appeal of Social Darwinism is shown in R. Hofstadter, *Social Darwinism in American Thought** (1955). W. Kaufmann, *Nietzsche: Philosopher, Psychologist, Antichrist** (1956), is a leading interpretation of the most influential philosopher of the period. See also D. B. Allison, ed., *The New Nietzsche: Contemporary Styles of Interpretation* (1976).

The classic study on the literature of the nineteenth century is G. Brandes, *Main Currents in Nineteenth-Century Literature*, 6 vols. (1923). Briefer and more pertinent is E. Wilson, *Axel's Castle: A Study in the Imaginative Literature of 1870–1930** (1958). For the impact of science on literature, see M. Nicolson, *Science and Imagination* (1956). The beautifully illustrated volume by R. Raynal, *The Nineteenth Century: New Sources of Emotion from Goya to Gauguin* (1951), shows the transition from traditional to modern art. T. Shapiro, *Painters and Politics: The European Avante-Garde and Society, 1900–1925* (1976), is a pioneering work. See also F. Mathey, *The World of the Impressionists* (1961). H. Leichtentritt, *Music, History, and Ideas* (1938), and C. Gray, *History of Music* (1947), discuss musical trends. On "popular culture," see R. Williams, *Culture and Society, 1780–1950** (1958), and B. Rosenberg and D. M. White, eds., *Mass Culture** (1959).

29

The Struggle for a European Equilibrium 1871–1914

The diplomatic history of Europe and the world between 1871 and 1914 must be viewed in the context of the political, economic, and cultural trends noted in the preceding chapter. The spirit of competition that pervaded relations among individuals and classes had its parallel in the political and economic rivalry among nations. Many international crises arose directly out of domestic tensions. Had the internal affairs of the powers before 1914 been more harmonious, international affairs might possibly have been more peaceful.

Our view of international relations after 1870 is conditioned by knowledge of what happened in 1914. Most historians agree that, while some of the immediate causes that brought about war in 1914 could have been avoided, its real causes were deeply rooted. To understand how deeply, we must remember the far-reaching effects that the unification of Italy and Germany had had on the European balance of power. Two regions that heretofore had been mere pawns in international affairs suddenly emerged as great powers. The political and territorial framework of the Continent thus lost much of its former elasticity. The only region in Europe where major changes

were still possible was the Balkan Peninsula. Austria-Hungary, now excluded from German and Italian affairs, claimed the Balkans as its natural sphere of influence. Since Russia and, less strongly, Italy made the same claim, the Balkans became the scene of recurrent international crises.

Another source of international tension was the growing colonial rivalry among the powers. With opportunities for territorial expansion on the Continent restricted, and with expanding economies clamoring for markets and raw materials, colonial conflicts injected an element of perennial friction into international affairs. An added cause for tension was nationalism. As long as members of one nationality were subjected to domination by another, as was the case in Austria-Hungary, Turkey, Russia, and, to a lesser extent, Germany and Great Britain, the peace of Europe remained precarious at best.

THE AGE OF BISMARCK, 1871–90

Despite the unsettling effects of Italian and German unification, Europe at first managed to adjust peacefully to the

674

changed situation. The chief credit for the relative stability that prevailed for the two decades after 1871 belongs to Prince Bismarck. The fundamental aim of the German chancellor was the consolidation of the new German *Reich*. For this he needed peace. Bismarck considered Germany a "satiated" power, with no further territorial ambitions. The main threat to its security was France's desire for revenge. To keep France isolated, therefore, became the guiding principle of Bismarck's foreign policy.

The basic moderation of the German chancellor's aims and the consummate skill of his diplomacy rightly command respect. They show that *Realpolitik* need not necessarily rely on "blood and iron" but can use with equal effect peaceful pressure and persuasion. Yet in merely trying to maintain existing conditions and ignoring those forces that were straining against the status quo—notably nationalism and imperialism—Bismarck showed the same blindness that had characterized Metternich before him.

William II and George V at Potsdam (1913); this was the last meeting of the cousins before the outbreak of the First World War.

Admirable as the Bismarckian system was, it was to fall to pieces as soon as the masterful guidance of its creator was removed.

The "Three Emperors' League"

The first of Bismarck's many international agreements was concluded in 1872 among Germany, Austria, and Russia. The *Dreikaiserbund* tried to revive the collaboration that had existed in the days of the "Holy Alliance." But the feeling of solidarity that had animated the three conservative powers in the days of Metternich had since given way to mutual rivalries. Russia, in particular, had never forgiven Austria its "ingratitude" during the Crimean War, and it now resented the leadership that Germany assumed within the new Three Emperors' League. A first sign of disagreement between Germany and Russia appeared during the so-called "war-in-sight" crisis of 1875, when rumors that Germany was planning a preventive war against France brought protests from England and Russia. Bismarck's role in fomenting the crisis is not quite clear, though there is no evidence that he was seriously considering war against France. Russia's action, therefore, seemed unnecessarily meddlesome, especially in view of its traditional friendship with Prussia. The monarchical front had shown itself far from solid.

The Russo-Turkish War and the Congress of Berlin

A far more serious rift within the Three Emperors' League developed out of Russia's ambitions in the Balkans. The inefficiency and corruption of the disintegrating Ottoman Empire had invited intervention several times before, most recently during the Crimean War. In 1875 new revolts against Turkish misrule broke out in the Balkans. The Turks acted with their usual ferocity in putting down these nationalist uprisings and would have held the upper hand if Russia, in the spring of 1877, had not joined the insurgents. It did so after making sure of Austrian neutrality and recognizing in return Austria's right to occupy the Turkish provinces of Bosnia and Herzegovina. In addition, Russia promised not to support the formation of any large Balkan state.

The Russo-Turkish War, after some reversals, ended in Russian victory. In a treaty signed at San Stefano in March 1878, several of Turkey's subject nationalities were granted independence. Among them was to be a large Bulgarian state, which Russia was to occupy for several years. In addition, Russia was to get some territorial compensations. This startling increase of Russian influence in the Balkans deeply alarmed the other great powers. Their pressure induced Russia finally to agree to submit the settlement to an international conference at Berlin in June 1878.

Most of the important decisions of the Congress of Berlin were actually reached in preliminary agreements, which the Congress then confirmed. The proposed Greater Bulgaria was divided into three parts, leaving only a small Bulgarian state; Serbia, Montenegro, and Rumania were granted full independence; Austria was given the right to occupy and administer Bosnia and Her-

---

Bismarck

PRO

Bismarck is generally described in the textbooks as the first *Realpolitiker*; but unfortunately so much has been written about *Realpolitik* that its meaning has become obscure and mixed up with blood and iron and incitement to war by the malicious revision of royal telegrams. . . . It may be permissible to suggest that the essence of Bismarck's realism was his recognition of the limitations of his craft, and that it was this, coupled with the passion and the responsibility that he brought to his vocation, that made him a great statesman.

CON

Himself always plotting combinations against others, Bismarck was convinced that all the world was plotting combinations against him and lived in a half-mad imaginary world in which every statesman was as subtle and calculating, as ruthless and assiduous as he was himself. . . . At bottom he was a barbarian of genius, mastering in the highest degree the mechanical and intellectual side of civilization, altogether untouched by its spirit.

From Gordon A. Craig, *From Bismarck to Adenauer: Aspects of German Statecraft* (Baltimore: Johns Hopkins University Press, 1958), p. 28; from A. J. P. Taylor, *The Course of German History* (New York: Coward-McCann, 1946), pp. 95–96.

zegovina; and England was given control over the island of Cyprus. Russia rightly felt that it had been cheated out of its victory. While England and Austria made substantial gains, Russia had to be satisfied with a small addition to Bessarabia and some gains in the Caucasus. The Russians blamed their defeat on Bismarck, who, they held, had violated his self-styled role as "honest broker" by favoring the interests of Russia's adversaries. The Congress of Berlin provoked a serious crisis in the relations between Germany and Russia and ended the Three Emperors' League.

The Austro-German Alliance

The breakup of the Three Emperors' League forced Bismarck to find a substitute. This he did in a secret alliance with Austria. The Dual Alliance of 1879 was the climax of Germany's *rapprochement* with Austria that had been Bismarck's concern since 1866. The alliance was renewed periodically and remained in force until 1918. Its provisions were purely defensive, calling for mutual aid if either member was attacked by Russia. Bismarck has been criticized for tying Germany's fate to the ramshackle Dual Monarchy. But he did not necessarily envisage the alliance as permanent, and he thought Germany strong enough to keep Austria's ambitions in the Balkans in check so as to avoid a showdown with Russia. Nor did the union with Austria mean that Germany was ready to sever relations with Russia altogether. Bismarck expected that Russia, unable for ideological reasons to draw closer to republican France, and separated from England by rivalries in Asia, would feel sufficiently isolated to desire a renewal of its former ties with Germany. Bismarck's assumption proved correct.

The Second "Three Emperors' League"

Russia would have preferred a treaty with Germany alone, but Bismarck insisted that Austria be included as well. A new Three Emperors' League was finally concluded in 1881. It provided that in case one of the members became in-

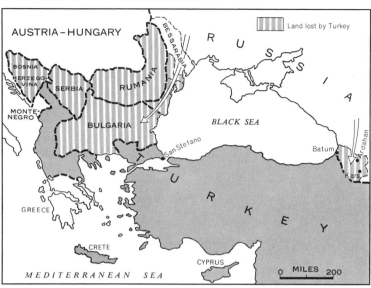

THE TREATY OF SAN STEFANO   1878

THE CONGRESS OF BERLIN   1878

volved in war with a fourth power, the other two would remain neutral. In this way Bismarck relieved his fear that Russia might join France in a war against Germany. The most important provisions of the treaty dealt with the Balkans: any territorial changes in that region henceforth were to require the consent of all three powers; Austria reserved its right to annex Bosnia and Herzegovina at a time of its own choosing; and Russia's wish for the eventual union of Bulgaria and

Eastern Roumelia (one of the regions separated from Greater Bulgaria at Berlin) was recognized. By dividing the Balkans into spheres of influence, the three powers seemed finally to have brought the Balkan problem under control. The new arrangement, however, overlooked the national aspirations of the Balkan peoples themselves.

The Triple Alliance

Before the Balkan question became acute once more in 1885, Bismarck had further extended his diplomatic network with the Triple Alliance of Germany, Austria, and Italy in 1882. The initiative this time came from the Italians. Italy for some time had hoped to enhance its status as a great power by occupying the Turkish region of Tunis in North Africa. It was deeply distressed, therefore, when the French took Tunis in 1881. To strengthen its diplomatic position for the future, Italy sought closer ties with Austria and Germany. Like the rest of Bismarck's treaties, the Triple Alliance was primarily defensive. Bismarck never took it very seriously, except for the fact that it contributed to the diplomatic isolation of France.

The years immediately after 1882 mark the high point of Bismarck's influence in Europe. French nationalism appeared to have been successfully diverted into colonial channels in North Africa; the situation in the Balkans appeared under control; and Austria's position had been strengthened by a secret treaty with Serbia in 1881 that made Austria the protector of its small neighbor. In 1883 Rumania concluded an alliance with Austria, to which Germany adhered later. The treaty was chiefly directed against Russian ambitions in the Balkans, where a new crisis flared up in 1885.

The Reinsurance Treaty

This latest Balkan crisis was touched off by an upsurge of Bulgarian nationalism in Eastern Roumelia, leading to the reunion of that region with Bulgaria. During the ensuing wrangle the Three Emperors' League met its final fate. For some time Russian nationalists, resenting German support of Austria in the Balkans, had demanded that Russia seek the friendship of France. Bismarck's worst fears seemed about to come true. But the tsarist government was reluctant to cut its connections with Berlin. Russia, therefore, proposed to the Germans that they enter into an agreement without Austria. The upshot was the so-called Reinsurance Treaty of 1887, which provided for benevolent neutrality in case either partner became involved in war, unless Germany attacked France or Russia attacked Austria. The Reinsurance Treaty also recognized Russia's interests in Bulgaria and the Turkish Straits.

This last of Bismarck's major treaties has been both hailed as a diplomatic masterpiece and condemned as an act of duplicity. It certainly did run counter to the spirit, if not the letter, of the Dual Alliance. But while Bismarck encouraged Russia's Balkan ambitions, he at the same time put an obstacle in the way of these ambitions by sponsoring the so-called Mediterranean Agreements between England, Italy, and Austria. Signed also in 1887, these agreements called for the maintenance of the status quo in the Mediterranean, including the Balkans. Any assurances Bismarck had given to Russia about Bulgaria and the Straits were thus successfully neutralized.

In making a fair appraisal of Bismarck's diplomacy, it is necessary to go beyond a mere comparison of treaty texts and consider the motives behind his treaties. These invariably were to maintain peace. Bismarck hoped to achieve this aim by isolating France and balancing the rest of the powers so that any unilateral disturbance of the peace would automatically result in a hostile coalition against the aggressor. Seen in this light, Bismarck's policy was less crafty than it appeared when the world first learned about the Reinsurance Treaty after the chancellor's retirement. A valid criticism of Bismarck's policy is that it was far too complicated to be successful in the long run and that it rested more on the attitudes of Europe's statesmen than on the sentiments of their peoples. Such disregard of public opinion became increasingly difficult in an age of democracy and nationalism.

FROM EUROPEAN
TO WORLD POLITICS

One of the most important trends in international affairs after Bismarck has been the growing involvement of Europe in world affairs. This development, as we have seen, had started much earlier, of course; but it was only at the end of the nineteenth century that events in Europe and overseas became so intricately interwoven that the histories of Europe and the world could no longer be treated separately.

The "New Imperialism"

The expansion of European influence in the late nineteenth century is often called the "new imperialism," to distinguish it from earlier phases of overseas expansion. Its motives were similar to those found earlier in the century, although they now operated with far greater intensity. Imperialism in the past had been chiefly limited in its appeal to the upper classes. Now suddenly it became of vital concern to everyone. More than any other movement, the new imperialism expressed the general climate of the period before 1914. Aggressive nationalism, ruthless economic competition, the restless struggle for success, all found an outlet in the scramble for overseas colonies and concessions, protectorates and spheres of influence. Here was an opportunity for men of daring and initiative to suffer hardships in distant lands not merely to advance their own fortunes but also, as they never tired telling the world, to undertake a "civilizing mission" for the good of mankind. Of the many driving forces behind the new imperialism, this "aggressive altruism" was one of the most potent.

England continued to lead in the new imperialism as it had in the old. After a period of declining interest in overseas expansion, Britain resumed its imperialist course after 1870. By 1914 it controlled one-fifth of the world's land and one-fourth of its population. The second largest colonial empire in 1914, that of France, had been acquired almost entirely during the nineteenth century. In its expansion into North Africa, France became involved first with Italy over Tunis, then with England over Egypt and the Sudan, and finally, after the turn of the century, with Germany over Morocco. Germany, prior to 1880, had no overseas possessions, and Bismarck was slow to enter the colonial race. When he finally did, beginning in 1884, it was in part to enhance Germany's bargaining position in Europe. It was William II who launched Germany in earnest on a course of *Weltpolitik*, in pursuit of which it provoked several international crises. Similar friction was caused by Italy's belated claims to colonies. Russia, as in the past, confined its expansion to adjacent areas in Asia. The only major power refraining from colonial expansion was Austria.

THE CONQUEST OF AFRICA

The most spectacular expansion of European influence after 1870 took place in Africa. In order to simplify the involved story of the scramble for African territory, events in the northern, central, and southern regions will be discussed separately. But it must be remembered that many of these developments actually happened simultaneously.

North Africa

The Mediterranean coast of Africa, since the seventh century, had been under the influence of Moslem civilization; since the early sixteenth century, it had been under the direct or indirect rule of the Ottoman Empire. France gained its first foothold in North Africa with the acquisition of Algiers in 1830. In the course of the century France extended its sphere of influence inland, and in time Algeria became an integral part of France. The next major move came with the establishment of a French protectorate over Algeria's eastern neighbor, Tunis, in 1881. Subsequently France began extending its influence westward over the sultanate of Morocco. The situation here was complicated by the fact that several other powers, notably Germany, also had economic interests in that region. A French protectorate over Morocco was thus not won until 1911, and

Algerian officer in the French army (1886).

The Sphinx is neck-high in sand and British soldiers in this photograph taken in 1882, after the bombardment of Alexandria.

The influence of African art on European art. Above: wood doll from Ghana (late nineteenth century); below: Amedeo Modigliani, *Head* (ca. 1913).

then only after two major international crises (see pp. 689, 691).

Egypt, the Sudan, and Tripoli

While France was establishing itself in the western half of North Africa, Britain was doing the same in Egypt and the Sudan. Egypt in 1870 was still nominally part of the Turkish Empire. Its gradual subjugation to foreign control was due to reckless borrowing of foreign money at prohibitive interest rates. When, in 1876, the Egyptian government suspended interest payments on some of its foreign obligations, Britain and France, the leading creditors, established a dual control over Egypt's finances. The subsequent rise in taxes infuriated the Egyptian taxpayer. To counteract a rising tide of Egyptian nationalism, Britain occupied Egypt in 1882. As a result, Anglo-French dual control over Egypt came to an end.

France, needless to say, resented its exclusion from Egypt and on every occasion tried to put obstacles in England's way. Tension between the two powers was aggravated by their rivalry over the Sudan. This Egyptian dependency had won temporary independence in 1885. But when France and Belgium began advancing toward the Sudan from central Africa, British and Egyptian forces in 1896 started to retake the region. The climax of their expedition came in 1898, when British and French forces met at Fashoda on the Upper Nile. As both Britain and France laid claim to the

Sudan, war seemed imminent. But the French government, troubled by the Dreyfus affair at home and inferior in naval strength, finally gave in and left England in control. In 1899 Egypt and England established joint control over what came to be known as the Anglo-Egyptian Sudan.

One stretch of land along the Mediterranean had not as yet come under foreign control—the region of Tripoli between Egypt and Tunis. It was of little value, consisting largely of desert. But in an age when overseas expansion was a matter of prestige, even so poor a prize seemed worth taking. After making certain of French support by recognizing France's claims in Morocco, Italy in 1911 and 1912 waged war against Turkey and annexed Tripoli. The Italian colony of Libya, as it was called, was one of the least lucrative of imperialist ventures. But it was a source of great pride to the Italians.

Central Africa

Very little of central Africa had been explored before the second half of the nineteenth century. Among the most famous explorers of the region were David Livingstone and Henry Morton Stanley. Livingstone, a Scottish missionary, spent almost thirty years in Africa. When he failed to return from his third and last major expedition in 1871, Stanley, a British-born American journalist, was sent to find him. Stanley's successful search for Livingstone gave him a taste for exploration that made him the leading explorer of the Congo region. After vainly seeking to interest the British in his plans for opening up the Congo, Stanley found a sponsor in King Leopold II of Belgium. Leopold's claims to the Congo Free State were recognized by an international conference at Berlin in 1885. For the next twenty years a policy of the most ruthless colonial exploitation made a vast fortune for Leopold's various personal enterprises in the Congo. Only after these brutal methods were revealed was control over the region transferred to the Belgian state in 1908.

The practice whereby enterprising individuals staked out claims that were later protected by their governments was also used to great advantage by the Germans. Beginning in 1884 the German government took over the rights that various German merchants and explorers had staked out over large parts of southwest, central, and east Africa. The British tried to discourage these German moves. When this attempt proved fruitless, they moved quickly to stake out their own claims for the interior of the continent. France, meanwhile, extended its holdings in central and west Africa and in 1896 proclaimed possession of the island of Madagascar. Italy acquired Eritrea and Somaliland at the southern end of the Red Sea in 1890. Italy's attempts to extend its holdings inland into Abyssinia were stopped by Ethiopian forces in the battle of Adua (1896).

South Africa

Some of the most valuable colonial prizes were to be found in the southern part of the African continent. Britain had acquired the Dutch Cape Colony there in 1806. As a result of tension between the

IMPERIALISM IN AFRICA   1884 and 1914

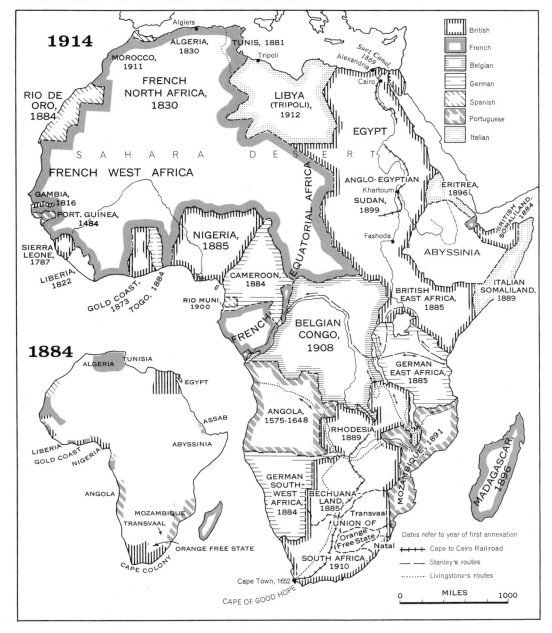

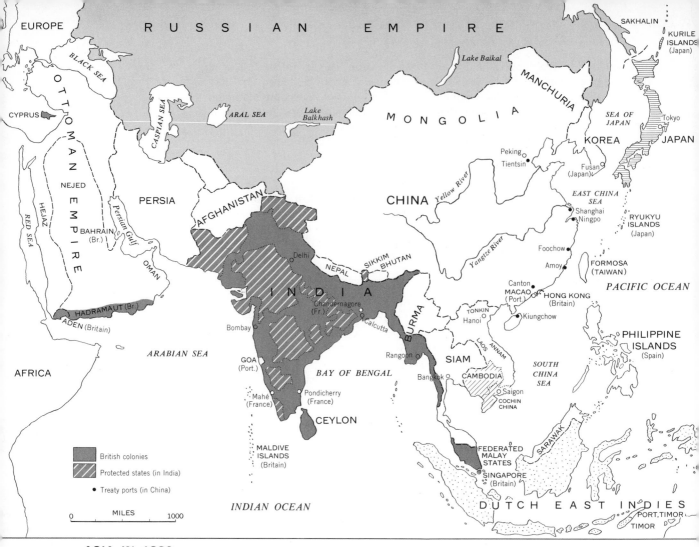

ASIA IN 1880

new British immigrants and the original Dutch settlers, or Boers, the latter, beginning in the 1830s, had moved northward and founded two new Dutch colonies, the Orange Free State and the Transvaal. Britain recognized the independence of these republics in 1852. With the subsequent discovery of diamonds and gold in these regions, however, the inhabitants of the Cape Colony began to call for an extension of British sovereignty over the Orange Free State and the Transvaal.

The leading advocate of Britain's South African interests in the late nineteenth century was Cecil Rhodes. A typical "empire builder," Rhodes owned extensive interests in South Africa's diamond and gold fields. He became prime minister of the Cape Colony in

1890. Meanwhile a new discovery of gold in the Transvaal in 1886 had touched off a veritable British invasion into the region. To discourage this foreign influx, the president of the Transvaal, Paul Krüger, placed heavy restrictions on British immigrants. One of the more spectacular incidents in the growing tension between Britons and Boers was the abortive Jameson Raid at the turn of the year 1895/96, an attempt by one of Rhodes's associates to start a revolution among the British minority in the Transvaal. An ill-advised and well-publicized telegram from the German kaiser congratulating Krüger on his defeat of the plot cast a deep shadow on Anglo-German relations at the time.

Finally, in 1899, tension between the Boers and the British led to war. It took

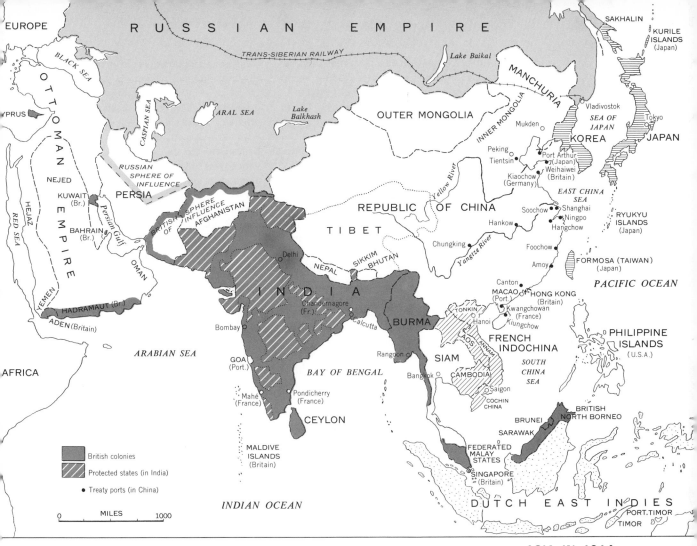

ASIA IN 1914

THE NEW IMPERIALISM IN ASIA AND THE PACIFIC

Britain two and a half years to defeat the tenacious Boers. Not until 1902 did the Boers lay down their arms, and then only on the promise of very lenient peace terms. As a result of this leniency, the issues of the past were quickly forgotten. When the Union of South Africa was formed in 1910, a former Boer general became the first prime minister of this newest self-governing dominion.

The sudden outburst of imperialism after 1880 also affected Asia and the Pacific. In contrast to Africa, large parts of this region had been under European domination for some time. Developments in India and China have already been discussed (see pp. 634–40); we shall now turn to the rest of the Asian continent and to the Pacific islands.

Russia in Asia

One of the principal powers with interests in Asia was Russia. Its advances there took three main directions: to the southwest into the Near East—the Ottoman Empire and especially the region around the entrance to the Black Sea; to the Far East—Siberia and the adjacent coastal regions of China; and to the Middle East—Afghanistan and Persia. Foremost among Russia's aims in the Near and Far East was to find outlets to the sea and ice-free harbors that would enable it to escape its landlocked position. Attempts to do so in the Near East, as we have seen, were met by resistance from the other great powers, notably England. Whenever it met with a setback, as in 1878, Russia shifted its attention from west to east, from Europe to Asia.

Russian expansion into Siberia had proceeded slowly but steadily for more than three centuries. It was greatly facilitated by the acquisition of a section of China's coast along the Sea of Japan in 1860 and the founding of the Pacific port of Vladivostok. Russia's aim was to expand southward across the Amur River into Manchuria and then into Korea. But its plans were foiled by the conflicting interests of Japan. As a result of the Russo-Japanese War, Russia's territorial position in the Far East in 1905 was substantially what it had been fifty years earlier. Its failures in the Far East in part explain Russia's renewed interest in the affairs of Europe and the Near East during the last decade before the First World War.

Anglo-Russian Rivalry

In the third sphere of Russian expansion, the Middle East and central Asia,

Russia made considerable progress during the nineteenth century. By 1880 the whole region north of Persia and Afghanistan had become Russian. This extension of Russian power was watched with growing apprehension by Great Britain, which feared that Russia's advance was ultimately directed at India. The mountainous country of Afghanistan served as a buffer against a possible invasion of India from the northwest. In 1879 England had overthrown the pro-Russian ruler of Afghanistan and had occupied most of the country. But British-Russian rivalry continued. It was not resolved until 1907, when Russia finally recognized England's predominant position in Afghanistan.

Another scene of Anglo-Russian rivalry was Persia. The contest here was primarily economic, with both Russian and British interests seeking concessions. But England also feared that Persia might serve as another approach to India. Differences in Persia, as in Afghanistan, were negotiated by the Anglo-Russian Entente in 1907 (see p. 689).

This encroachment of the great powers on hitherto sovereign states was typical of much of European imperialism in Asia. The gradual subjection of China to foreign tutelage during the second half of the nineteenth century was an example. Another example was Siam. The French, after extending their protectorate over Indochina during the 1880s, turned their attention westward. Here they came in conflict with the English, who were interested in Siam because it bordered on Burma, which Britain had taken in 1852. After a certain amount of controversy, Siam in 1896 was made into a neutral buffer state between Burma and Indochina.

The Pacific

The most valuable islands of the Pacific were taken long before 1870. The rivalry of the powers over the few remaining small islands was a sign of how intense the imperialist urge had become. The main contestants in the Pacific were England and Germany, with the United States and France intervening occasionally. It is unnecessary to enumerate all

President McKinley and the Philippines

I have been criticized a good deal about the Philippines, but I don't deserve it. The truth is, I didn't want the Philippines, and when they came to us, as a gift from the gods, I did not know what to do with them. . . . I walked the floor of the White House night after night until midnight; and I am not ashamed to tell you, gentlemen, that I went down on my knees and prayed Almighty God for light and guidance. And one night late it came to me this way—I don't know how it was, but it came: (1) That we could not give them back to Spain—that would be cowardly and dishonorable; (2) that we could not turn them over to France or Germany—that would be bad business and discreditable; (3) that we could not leave them to govern themselves—they were unfit for self-government . . . and (4) that there was nothing left for us to do but to take them all, and to educate the Philippinos, and uplift and civilize and Christianize them, and, by God's grace, do the very best we could by them, as our fellow men for whom Christ also died. And then I went to bed, and went to sleep, and slept soundly, and next morning I sent for the chief engineer of the War Department (our map-maker), and told him to put the Philippines on the map of the United States.

William McKinley, as quoted in G. A. Malcolm and M. M. Kalaw, *Philippine Government* (Manila: Associated Publishers, 1923), pp. 65–66.

the bits and pieces of land picked up by these powers. The most important, besides America's annexation of the Philippines, was the acquisition of eastern New Guinea by England and Germany in 1884. The most serious crisis arose over the Samoan Islands, which were claimed by Britain, Germany, and the United States. After ten years of intermittent dispute, the islands were divided in 1899 between the United States and Germany, with England receiving compensations in the Solomons.

THE UNITED STATES AS A WORLD POWER

Developments in the United States during the period before 1914 were remarkably similar to developments in Europe. In the purely political sphere, there was less need for further democratization than there was in some European countries, although the agitation of the Populists in the 1890s and of the Progressive Party in 1912 showed that many Americans felt their interests were neglected under the two-party system. In the economic sphere, the United States shared fully in the industrial expansion that took place in Europe, and by 1914 America led the world in the production of coal, iron, and petroleum.

In trying to cope with the social and economic problems resulting from rapid industrialization, the activities of both the labor unions and the government, in America as in Europe, brought a marked improvement of the worker's status. The efforts of Theodore Roosevelt, after the turn of the century, to secure a "square deal" for the workingman, and his attempts at "trust busting," helped to bridge the gap between capital and labor. Despite the opposition of many Americans to governmental intervention in economic affairs, the United States showed the same tendency toward becoming a "welfare state" that prevailed in most European countries. In the one field in which American business had welcomed government interference—tariff legislation—the trend by 1914 was in the direction of lower tariffs. This was seen by some as a sign that American industry had come of age and was ready to compete with foreign imports on the home market.

The Spanish-American War

America at the end of the nineteenth century thus shared most of the major trends of Europe. This was nowhere more evident than in foreign affairs. Agitation during the 1890s to annex Hawaii and to construct a canal across Central America ran parallel to European expansionism during the same period. Under the administration of Grover Cleveland, such expansionist sentiments were kept under control. His successor, William McKinley, however, was less able to resist the pressures of American nationalism. One of the main subjects of agitation at the time was Cuba, where a revolt against Spanish rule had started in 1895. American sentiment sided with the Cuban rebels and demanded that the United States go to their aid. When the U.S.S. *Maine* mysteriously exploded in Havana harbor in early 1898, the clamor for war became too strong to be resisted any longer.

The Spanish-American War was the first war between the United States and a European power since 1814. The United

American forces landing at a Cuban port in 1898, during the Spanish-American War.

States had little difficulty winning the "splendid little war" against Spain. In the peace treaty signed at Paris in December 1898, the United States obtained Puerto Rico, the Philippines, and Guam. Cuba received its independence, though the Platt Amendment, adopted by Congress in 1901, made it a virtual American protectorate.

America made its influence felt in the Far East and elsewhere in other ways as well. In 1898 the United States finally annexed Hawaii and in the following year divided the Samoan Islands with Germany. Also in 1899, Secretary of State John Hay proclaimed the "Open Door" policy, which called for equal opportunity in China for all powers, and in 1900 an American contingent participated in a joint expedition of the powers to put down the Boxer Rebellion in China (see p. 640). The United States also sent delegates to the First Hague Peace Conference in 1899, at which a Permanent Court of International Arbitration was created; and in 1905 President Roosevelt helped settle the Russo-Japanese War in the Treaty of Portsmouth.

The United States and Latin America

America's first and foremost concern, however, was with affairs closer to home. Theodore Roosevelt in particular had long favored an active American policy in Central America. The Hay-Pauncefote Treaty of 1901 secured British consent for the construction of an American canal across the isthmus. In 1903 Panama, in a revolt sponsored by American interests, seceded from Colombia, and the United States was able to acquire the necessary land for its canal. The Panama Canal was opened shortly after the outbreak of war in 1914.

One of the chief dangers to peace in Latin America came from the loans that European investors in search of large profits had granted to the dictators of that region. Failures to meet payments invariably led to foreign intervention and threatened violations of the Monroe Doctrine. In 1902, Germany, Italy, and Great Britain sent warships to force Venezuela to pay its debts. Two years later

Cartoon of Theodore Roosevelt "walking softly and carrying a big stick" as he tows American ships through the Caribbean.

another group of powers moved against the Dominican Republic. As a warning, and to forestall European intervention, President Roosevelt, in 1904, proclaimed a Corollary to the Monroe Doctrine. It gave the United States the exclusive right to exercise international police power in the Western Hemisphere. In line with its new policy, America sent marines to Cuba in 1906 and to Nicaragua in 1912.

The motive for America's intervention on these occasions was not merely to maintain order but also to protect its own financial interests. This "dollar diplomacy," as its opponents called it, caused much resentment in the countries concerned and among the other great powers. America's policy, its Latin American neighbors charged, despite idealistic pronouncements, was every bit as imperialistic as that of the European powers.

THE FORMATION OF THE TRIPLE ENTENTE 1890–1907

The events outside Europe discussed in the preceding pages provide the background for the diplomatic realignment of Europe after 1890 and the succession of international crises that culminated in the First World War.

The Franco-Russian Alliance

When Bismarck was dismissed in 1890, his complicated diplomatic system did not long survive. To start with, William II followed the advice of some of Bismarck's more timid underlings and refused to renew the Reinsurance Treaty with Russia. The cutting of Bismarck's "wire to St. Petersburg" did not by itself make the subsequent *rapprochement* between Russia and France inevitable. Only when Germany continued to show deliberate coolness toward its former friend while drawing closer to England did Russia begin to listen to French suggestions for a better understanding. The Anglo-German Heligoland Treaty of 1890, by which Germany surrendered large claims in East Africa to England in return for the small strategic island of Heligoland in the North Sea, was generally interpreted as a sign of German eagerness to oblige England. At the same time, a tariff war was impairing Russo-German commercial relations, and an increase in Germany's armed forces was seen as preparation for a possible war on two fronts. Germany's policy toward Russia, it seemed, was undergoing a complete reorientation.

Even so, Russia was slow to respond to France's overtures. The main obstacle was the differences between their autocratic and republican systems of government. It took four years of deliberations before a final agreement was reached. On January 4, 1894, France and Russia signed a secret military convention that amounted to an alliance. It was designed as a counterpart to the Triple Alliance between Germany, Austria, and Italy. Like the latter, the Franco-Russian alliance was defensive. It protected France against an attack by Germany, or by Italy supported by Germany; and it protected Russia against an attack by Germany, or by Austria supported by Germany.

By the middle of the 1890s, therefore, two sets of European alliances existed. This did not mean, however, that the Continent had been split in two. There were many subsequent occasions when Russia cooperated with Germany and Austria, or when Germany cooperated with Russia and France. International rivalries for the next decade shifted almost entirely to regions outside Europe. Both French and Russian interests in many parts of the world conflicted with those of Great Britain; and Germany, unable to tie England as closely to its side as it wished, now frequently joined the two in opposing British aims. Faced by the discomforting possibility of a continental alliance against it, Britain, rather than Germany, had cause to be alarmed by the new alignment of powers.

Britain's Colonial Rivalries

The regions over which Britain came into conflict with one or several of the continental powers during the 1890s were chiefly the Near and Far East, the Sudan, and South Africa. In the Near East the source of trouble, as usual, was the disintegrating Ottoman Empire. Beginning in 1894 a series of Armenian uprisings against Turkish repression were put down with the massacre of thousands of Armenians. England tried repeatedly to intervene, and Lord Salisbury on two occasions suggested plans for partitioning the Ottoman Empire. But rival interests among the powers and suspicion of British motives prevented what might have been a final solution of the troubles of the Near East. The situation was further complicated in 1897 by an insurrection against Turkey on Crete in favor of union with Greece. In the resulting war between Greece and Turkey, the British supported Greece, but the rest of the powers prevented any aid from reaching Greece. The Turks were victorious, although the powers succeeded in obtaining autonomy for Crete.

While Britain thus found itself at cross-purposes with the rest of Europe in the Near East, Germany took advantage of the various crises in that region to advance its own economic interests. The main instrument of its push to the southeast was to be a Berlin-to-Baghdad railway, for which the sultan granted a concession in 1899. In 1898, Emperor William, on a visit to Damascus, proclaimed himself the friend of the world's 300 million Moslems. Germany appeared well on the way toward replacing England as the protector of Turkey.

In this German cartoon, Queen Victoria is flattened by the Boer leader, Paul Krüger, as the South African imperialist Cecil Rhodes looks on with dismay.

In the Far East the first serious differences between England and the three continental powers came as a result of the Sino-Japanese War in 1895 (see p. 639). When Russia, Germany, and France asked British participation in forcing Japan to give up most of the territory it had taken from China, Britain refused. In the subsequent scramble for concessions from China, France, Germany, and especially Russia gained at the expense of England's hitherto unchallenged dominance there.

All the time that Britain was losing ground in the Near and Far East, its situation in Africa was even more serious. First there was the trouble with Germany over the kaiser's "Krüger telegram" (see p. 682); then came the showdown with France over the Sudan; and finally, in 1899 the Boer War broke out. During that war Britain was without a single friend, and it is surprising that Russian proposals for a continental coalition in favor of the Boers did not materialize. The plan failed because of Germany's insistence that the three powers first guarantee one another's own territories in Europe. This would have meant French renunciation of Alsace-Lorraine.

In view of England's many predicaments, it is understandable that it should look for some way out of its no longer splendid isolation. The obvious choice for a possible ally, considering Britain's many points of friction with France and Russia, was Germany. So in 1898 England began to sound out Germany on a closer understanding.

Britain Abandons Isolation

The Anglo-German negotiations failed. And the main reason for the failure was the reluctance of the Germans to abandon what they considered an unusually favorable position between the Franco-Russian and British camps. Overestimating Britain's eagerness to come to an understanding and underestimating Britain's ability to find friends elsewhere, Germany's foreign secretary, Bernhard von Bülow, and his chief adviser, Baron Holstein, made demands on England that it was unwilling to meet. Britain was primarily interested in enlisting German support against further Russian encroachment in the Far East. Germany, on the other hand, was chiefly worried about a war between Russia and Austria in which Germany might become involved and for which it wanted British aid. Britain, however, refused to extend its commitments to eastern Europe, where, as a naval power, it could not be of much use.

When Anglo-German negotiations finally broke down in 1901, England turned elsewhere. In 1902 it concluded an alliance with Japan. This did nothing to end England's isolation in Europe, but it fulfilled a main purpose—to stop Russia's advance in the Far East. Two years later Japan took advantage of this situation and in the Russo-Japanese War destroyed Russian sea power in the Pacific (see p. 642). In this way Japan emerged as the dominant power in the Far East.

Before the showdown between Russia and Japan, England had already taken a step in Europe to escape its isolation—*rapprochement* with France. England had long been irked by its dependence on Germany, which the latter used on every possible occasion to wring concessions from the British. By settling its longstanding differences with France, Britain not only hoped to find support against Germany but also to allay once and for all its fear of a continental alliance against it. France also felt a need for new friends. Its alliance with Russia had proved disappointing, especially during the Fashoda crisis, when the Russians had refused to back up their ally (see p. 680). After Fashoda, France had turned its attention once more to the Continent. The aim of its nationalistic foreign minister, Théophile Delcassé, was to strengthen France's position by improving its relations with powers other than Germany. He had taken a first step in this direction in 1902 by concluding a secret agreement with Italy. In return for French support of Italian ambitions in North Africa, the Italians promised to support French aims in Morocco, and to remain neutral in case France became involved in a defensive war, even if France "as the result of a direct provocation" should find it necessary to declare such a war itself.

A far greater achievement of Delcassé, however, was the Entente Cordiale between France and England. The Anglo-French agreement of 1904 settled the main colonial differences that had disturbed relations between the two countries, especially in Africa. Most important was France's recognition of British interests in Egypt and Britain's recognition of French interests in Morocco. The agreement was merely a "friendly understanding." It was not an alliance, and it need never have assumed the character of one had it not been for the careless actions of Germany.

The First Moroccan Crisis

Germany, which was understandably alarmed by the agreement between France and Britain, decided to test the strength of the Entente. In March 1905 William II, on a visit to Tangier in Spanish Morocco, proclaimed Germany's continued support of Moroccan independence and served notice that Germany, too, had an interest in Morocco. The ensuing crisis forced the resignation of Delcassé, and Germany seemed ready to go to war. Franco-German differences were finally brought before an international conference at Algeciras (1906). Here the independence of Morocco was reaffirmed; but in settling specific questions of Moroccan internal administration, the majority of the powers supported the French. Only Austria-Hungary stood by its German ally. Germany's attempt to split the Anglo-French Entente had backfired.

Actually, the first Moroccan crisis brought the French and British still closer together by inaugurating conversations between French and British military and naval authorities concerning possible cooperation in case of war. These conversations continued intermittently until 1914. Beginning in 1912, furthermore, the British navy concentrated its forces in the North Sea, permitting the French to shift their own warships to the Mediterranean. England thus assumed at least a moral obligation for protecting France's northern coast in case of war. The Entente Cordiale, in spirit if not in fact, had been transformed into a virtual alliance.

PRE-FIRST WORLD WAR ALLIANCES AND ALIGNMENTS

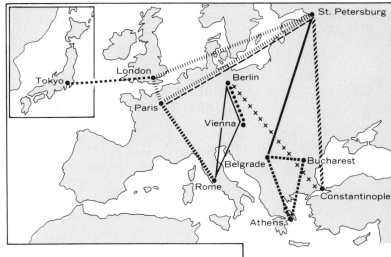

●●●●●	Austro-German Alliance, 1879
——	Triple Alliance, 1882
– – –	Franco-Russian Alliance, 1894
ııııııııı	Triple Entente, 1904/07
▮▮▮▮▮▮	Franco-Italian Agreement, 1902
——	Russian-Serbian Friendship
＼＼＼＼＼	Russian Push to Constantinople
+ + +	Turkish-German Alliance, 1914
●●●●●●	Anglo-Japanese Alliance, 1902
▪▪▪▪▪▪	Balkan League

The Triple Entente

England's close affiliation with France quite naturally raised the question of its relations with France's ally Russia. As a result of Russia's war with Japan, the threat of Russian predominance in China had been removed, and there was now no reason why England should not try to settle its colonial differences with Russia as it had with France. This was done in the Anglo-Russian Entente of 1907, which settled the long-standing rivalries of the two powers in Afghanistan, Persia, and Tibet.

The formation of the Triple Entente, as the agreements of 1904 and 1907 together are called, amounted to a diplomatic revolution. A situation that only a few years earlier Germany had considered impossible had now come to pass: England had settled its differences with France and Russia, and the Triple Alliance had found its match in the Triple Entente. The latter was no more aggressive in its initial intent than the Triple Alliance had originally been. But as areas for compromise outside Europe became fewer with the annexation of the remaining colonial spoils, the scene of international rivalries once more shifted to Europe and especially to the Balkans. In the past, Russia's ambitions in this area had been held in check by the rest of the powers. Now it could count on French and British support against Germany and Austria. Germany, on the other hand, left with only Austria as a reliable friend, could no longer restrain Austria's Balkan policy as it had in the past. Any change in the status quo of the Balkans, therefore, was sure to lead to a major crisis.

THE MOUNTING CRISIS 1908–13

This brings us to the last fateful years before 1914, when growing international tension, at least in retrospect, appears as a fitting prelude to an inevitable showdown.

Revolution in Turkey and the Bosnian Crisis

Abdul-Hamid II, known as "Abdul the Damned" for his cunning and cruelty, was chiefly responsible for the continued backwardness and corruption of the Ottoman Empire during his long rule (1876–1909).

The Balkans once again became the scene of international complications in 1908 when a revolution broke out in the Ottoman Empire. Turkey's ruler since 1876, Abdul-Hamid II, had never lived up to his repeated promises of reform. Opposition to the sultan's corrupt and decadent regime centered in a group of liberal patriots, the "Young Turks." Their aim was to reform Turkey along the lines of a liberal constitution that had been granted in 1876 but had been completely disregarded afterward. The revolutionaries had a large following among the Turkish army, and the government's resistance to the uprising in 1908 soon collapsed. The Young Turks, however, though liberal in some respects, were extremely nationalistic in their dealings with Turkey's many national and religious minorities. Persecution of Greek Orthodox Christians and efforts to assimilate Turkey's subject peoples soon led to further disruption of the empire: Bulgaria proclaimed its independence in 1908; Crete completed its union with Greece in 1912; and Albania, after a series of bloody uprisings, finally gained its independence from the Ottoman Empire in 1913.

The most important event connected with the Turkish revolution, in its effects on relations among the great powers, was Austria's annexation of Bosnia and Herzegovina in 1908. There had been no serious tension between Austria and Russia over the Balkans for some twenty years. But this peaceful situation changed after 1905, as Russia once again turned its attention from the Far to the Near East. Russia's foreign minister, Alexander Izvolsky, was an unusually ambitious man, and he found a kindred spirit in his Austrian colleague, Count Aehrenthal. Russia had long hoped to lift the closure of the Turkish Straits to Russian warships; Austria, for its part, had been looking forward to annexing Bosnia and Herzegovina, which it had been administering since 1878. Encouraged by the Turkish revolution, Izvolsky and Aehrenthal met at the latter's castle of Buchlau in September 1908 and there pledged mutual support for their respective aims.

The Bosnian crisis was precipitated when shortly after the Buchlau Agreement Austria went ahead and proclaimed the annexation of Bosnia and Herzegovina without waiting for Russia to act in the Straits. Russia, thereupon, backed by France and England, demanded that Austria's action be brought before an international conference. Germany, on the other hand, supported Austria in opposing a conference unless the annexation of Bosnia-Herzegovina was recognized beforehand. The situation was made more serious because Serbia also had hoped one day to take Bosnia-Herzegovina. Encouraged by Pan-Slav propaganda emanating from Russia, Serbia now demanded compensation from Austria. Since Russia, however, was in no position to fight a war at this time, it had to bring pressure on Serbia to recognize the *fait accompli* in Bosnia and Herzegovina. This the Serbs did under protest.

The Bosnian crisis left a legacy of tension that lasted until the First World War. Both Russia and Serbia had been humiliated. To prevent the recurrence of such a defeat, Russia now began to prepare in earnest for the showdown that seemed inevitable, while Serbia stepped up its agitation among Austria's southern Slavs. Austria had been the real culprit in the affair. But even it would have had to back down if it had not had the support of Germany. The fact that such support had been given only reluctantly was not known to the rest of the world. Italy, finally, was hurt not to have been consulted by Austria about the annexation of Bosnia and Herzegovina and not to have received compensations, both of which it felt entitled to under the Triple Alliance. In October 1909 Italy entered into a secret understanding with Russia, the Racconigi Agreement, in which it promised to support Russia's interests in the Straits, while Russia agreed to back Italy's designs in Tripoli. Italy thus had taken another step away from the Triple Alliance.

The Second Moroccan Crisis

Europe had barely recovered from the Bosnian affair when another crisis arose, this time in North Africa. Despite the Act of Algeciras of 1906, friction in Morocco between French and German interests had continued. When native disturbances in Morocco in 1911 led to the intervention of French troops, Germany protested against what it considered a violation of Moroccan independence. To make up for France's increased influence in Morocco, Germany now claimed compensations elsewhere. And to give weight to its demands, it sent a German gunboat, the *Panther*, to the Moroccan port of Agadir, ostensibly to protect German lives and interests. For the most part it was British intervention that finally forced Germany to modify its claims and settle the crisis. But meanwhile Europe

had once again been brought to the brink of war.

Anglo-German Naval Rivalry

England, throughout the crisis, suspected that Germany's real aim was to secure a naval base in Morocco, which would have posed a threat to Britain's base at Gibraltar. Anglo-German naval rivalry had by now become a matter of deep concern to the British. Naval expansion was closely related to imperialism. A powerful fleet was considered necessary to protect overseas possessions, and overseas possessions in turn were needed as naval bases and coaling stations. The most influential exponent of this new "navalism" was an American, Captain Alfred T. Mahan, whose writings, especially *The Influence of Sea Power upon History* (1890), were carefully studied in England and Germany.

As a precaution against the naval increases of the rest of the world, England in 1889 had adopted a "two-power standard," which called for a British fleet 10 percent stronger than the combined naval forces of the two next-strongest powers. The most serious challenge to Britain's naval power came from Germany. Beginning in 1898, Germany entered on a course of naval expansion that, by 1914, had made it the second-strongest naval power in the world. Germany's

THE DISSOLUTION OF THE OTTOMAN EMPIRE to 1914

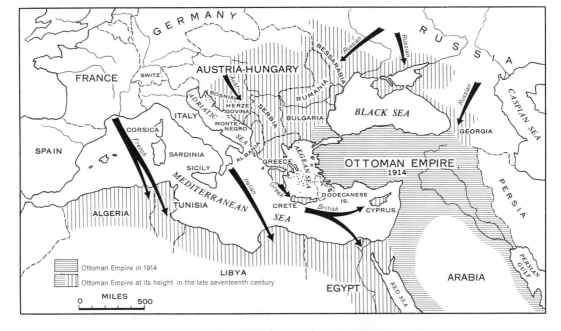

secretary of the navy, Admiral Alfred von Tirpitz, knew that he could not possibly expect to catch up with the British. He tried to build a navy strong enough that no other country would dare risk getting into a fight with Germany. The German navy was built not so much for a possible showdown with England as for reasons of prestige.

It was difficult for England to see matters in quite the same light. The British felt that Germany, primarily a land power, did not really need a navy, especially since it already had a powerful army. If the Germans went to the great expense of building a navy, this could only mean that they expected some day to challenge Britain's naval supremacy. Again and again, notably in 1908 and 1912, Great Britain urged Germany to slow down its naval construction, offering in return to support German colonial aspirations. But William II and Tirpitz saw these efforts merely as a confirmation of their "risk theory" and looked forward to the day when England would be forced to seek an agreement on Germany's terms. More than any other issue, this naval race was responsible for the growing tension between Germany and England during the last decade before the war.

The Balkan Wars

The Moroccan crisis of 1911—besides further strengthening the Anglo-French Entente—also helped to start a series of small wars aimed at the further disruption of the Ottoman Empire. The first of these broke out in the fall of 1911, when Italy, encouraged by France's success in Morocco, decided to embark on the annexation of Tripoli. Since Italy had carefully secured the prior consent of all the great powers, its war with Turkey of 1911 to 1912 did not by itself cause any major crisis. As we have seen, it brought Italy its long-coveted North African colony. The Tripolitanian War, however, encouraged several small Balkan states to move against Turkey and thus to reopen the Balkan question.

The chief motive behind the First Balkan War (1912) was the desire of Bulgaria, Serbia, and Greece to gain further concessions at the expense of Turkey. Together with Montenegro, these countries had formed a Balkan League in early 1912. Taking advantage of the war over Tripoli, they invaded the Ottoman Empire in October of that year. Turkey was decisively defeated, and under the Treaty of London (May 1913) it lost all its European possessions except the region adjacent to the Straits.

The peace was less than a month old when a Second Balkan War broke out, this time among the victors over the distribution of the spoils. Under arrangements made before the first war, Serbia was to receive an outlet to the Adriatic in Albania. This met with Austrian and Italian protests, however. As compensation for its loss, Serbia now demanded some of the territory that Bulgaria had received in Macedonia; and when the Bulgarians refused, war ensued between Bulgaria on the one hand and Serbia, Greece, Montenegro, Rumania, and Turkey on the other. Against such an overwhelming coalition, the Bulgarians proved powerless. In the Treaty of Bucharest (August 1913), Bulgaria kept only a small part of Macedonia, the Greeks and Serbs taking the rest.

The Balkan Wars caused deep anxiety among the great powers. A Conference of Ambassadors was convened in London to deal with the Balkan problem, notably the controversy between Austria and Serbia over the latter's aspirations in Albania. As in the past, Russia backed Serbia. Germany, on the other hand, served as a brake on Austria's desire to intervene against Serbia. Since England and

Turkish infantry during the First Balkan War (1912).

Italy also favored the independence of Albania, Russia finally withdrew its support from Serbia and peace was preserved. In the course of events, however, Austria and Russia, together with their allies, had again come close to war. Serbia had suffered another defeat, for which it blamed Austria and for which even its gains in Macedonia could not be consolation enough. Serbia's outraged nationalism sought revenge a year later in the assassination of the Austrian Archduke Francis Ferdinand at Sarajevo.

THE OUTBREAK OF THE GREAT WAR

In discussing the origins of the First World War, historians distinguish between underlying and immediate causes. In the first category belong all those factors that contributed to the acute state of international tension before 1914: nationalism, territorial disputes, economic competition, and imperialist rivalries. Some of the tension has also been blamed on the secret diplomacy of the powers, which led to secret alliances that involved nations in conflicts not of their making. But it has also been held that there was not enough secret diplomacy, that a "summit" meeting of Europe's leading statesmen in the summer of 1914, away from the clamor of their nationalistic press, might have resolved the differences that instead led to war. There had been many instances in the past when such joint action on the part of the Concert of Europe had proved effective. By 1914, however, the feeling of European solidarity that had animated the great powers in the days of Metternich and even Bismarck had everywhere given way to the powerful and divisive force of nationalism. The absence of any effective international agency to preserve peace did much to bring about the catastrophe of 1914.

The story of why and how the war came about has been told many times and in great detail. But to this day information is missing on some important points, and there are still wide differences among historians in the evaluation of the available evidence. It is quite pos-

sible that a different action by one or another of the statesmen in the summer of 1914 might have once more prevented a general war. Yet it seems unlikely that such a war could have been postponed much longer. If ever there was a time that seemed ripe for war, it was the summer of 1914.

Sarajevo

As we turn from the underlying to the immediate causes of the war, the most important was the assassination of Austrian Archduke Francis Ferdinand at the Bosnian capital of Sarajevo, on June 28, 1914.

The assassination of the archduke and his wife was carried out by an Austro-Bosnian citizen of Serb nationality, Gavrilo Princip. The crime had been planned and its execution aided by a secret society of Serb nationalists, the "Black Hand." The archduke had been chosen as victim because he was known to favor reconciling the southern Slav element in the Dual Monarchy, a policy that interfered with the aspirations of Serb nationalism, which hoped for the ultimate union of all southern Slavs under Serbian rule. There is no evidence that the Serbian government had any hand in the plot itself; but Serbia's prime minister, Nicholas Pashitch, had general knowledge of it. Austria, taking for granted that the Serbian government was involved, decided once and for all to settle accounts with Serbia. This it hoped to do in a localized war. But Austria's

Archduke Francis Ferdinand of Austria and his wife at Sarajevo on June 28, 1914, about to enter the automobile that carried them to their deaths.

The arrest of the assassin.

foreign minister, Count Berchtold, did not seem averse to a larger war if it was necessary to achieve Austria's aim.

European reaction to the assassination at first was one of deep shock and genuine sympathy for Austria. In indignation over the horrible crime, Germany gave Austria that fateful promise to "stand behind it as an ally and friend" in anything the Austrian government should decide to do. As it became clear, however, that Austria intended to use the Sarajevo incident to punish Serbia, the powers became alarmed. Russia warned the Austrians that it "would not be indifferent to any effort to humiliate Serbia." At the same time, France's president, Raymond Poincaré, assured the Russians of French support in any action they took on behalf of Serbia. By the middle of July, it was clear that Austria, backed by Germany, was ready to move against Serbia, and that Russia, backed by France, was equally ready to protect Serbia.

The Eve of War

The situation thus far was serious, but it was not as yet critical. It became so when Austria, on July 23, presented a stiff ultimatum to Serbia. The latter's reply, while not wholly complying, nevertheless was favorable enough to justify further negotiations. Instead, Austria broke off diplomatic relations and on July 28 declared war on Serbia. Germany had little choice but to live up to its earlier "blank check" and to support Austria. By doing so, the Germans hoped to discourage Russia from helping Serbia and thus to localize the Austro-Serbian conflict. But the Germans were also ready to stand by Austria if the conflict should develop into a general war.

The decision whether the war was to be a local or a general one rested primarily with Russia. Germany's action throughout the crisis had given the impression, not unjustifiably, that far from trying to discourage Austria, the German government was actually urging it on into the showdown with Serbia. Since an Austrian victory over Serbia would be tantamount to a Russian defeat, Russian military authorities now began calling for mobilization. The question was: should such mobilization be partial, against Austria-Hungary only, or should it be general, against Germany as well? Plans for a partial mobilization had been abandoned some time ago and in any case would have entailed considerable disadvantages in case general mobilization should become necessary later on. But a general mobilization, it was understood, would make a European war inevitable. The internal debate over this issue went on for several days. Only when the tsar finally became convinced, on July 30, that efforts to restrain Austria were futile, was the decision made to go ahead with a general mobilization.

The Outbreak of War

Germany's chief of staff, General Helmuth von Moltke, nephew of the great Moltke of Bismarckian times, was worried by reports from Russia. He therefore urged Austria, behind his government's back, to mobilize against Russia, promising unconditional German support. Austria ordered general mobilization on July 31, thus killing any chance for last-minute peace efforts. The same day Germany sent Russia an ultimatum demanding that the latter cease its preparations for war. When the tsar's government replied that this was impossible, Germany, on August 1, mobilized its own forces and a few hours later declared war on Russia. France, meanwhile, had also begun military preparations. To a German inquiry about its attitude in a Russo-German war, France replied that it would "act in accordance with its interests." On August 3, Germany declared war on France.

The reason for Germany's haste in declaring war lay in the plans that its general staff had worked out for a war on two fronts. The basic idea of the "Schlieffen Plan"—named after its originator, Count Schlieffen, who had been chief of the general staff from 1891 to 1906—was for Germany's main forces to turn west, deliver an annihilating blow against France, and then turn east against the slowly mobilizing Russians. To succeed with its plan, Germany not only needed to mobilize as quickly as possible, but it also had to invade France at its most vulnerable spot, the northeastern frontier between France and Belgium. The Schlieffen Plan, in other words, called for German violation of Belgian neutrality, which, together with the rest of Europe, the Germans had guaranteed in 1839.

Germany's invasion of Belgium on August 3 brought England into the war the next day. Great Britain has subsequently been reproached for not making its position in the crisis clear enough from the start, the argument being that if it had come off the fence earlier, it would have deterred the Austrians from going to war against Serbia. Through the Entente Cordiale, especially its secret military and naval understandings, England was deeply committed to France. On the other hand, there had been a marked improvement in Anglo-German relations in the early months of 1914; and England's Entente with Russia had never been very popular. For reasons of its own security, Britain could not possibly afford to stand idly by while Germany won victories over France and Russia that would make it the dominant power on the Continent. But to get the British public to approve involvement in the war, some event was needed to dramatize the German danger. Such an event was Germany's violation of Belgian neutrality. Almost overnight it helped to convert Britain's indecisive neutrality into determined belligerency.

"War Guilt"

A word remains to be said about the question of "war guilt," a subject of controversy to the present day. Most historians agree that Germany, Austria, and Russia bear a major share of the responsibility. England clearly belongs at the other extreme, its errors being chiefly of omission; and France stands somewhere in between. This much is certain: no one power alone was responsible for the war, and none of the great powers was entirely free from responsibility. Many Europeans actually welcomed the war as a

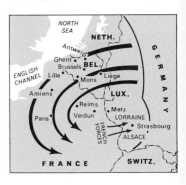

THE UNEXECUTED SCHLIEFFEN PLAN Pre-1914

The Schlieffen Plan: A Critique

It was a conception of Napoleonic boldness, and there were encouraging precedents in Napoleon's early career for counting on the decisive effect of arriving in the enemy's rear with the bulk of one's forces. . . . But Schlieffen failed to take due account of a great difference between the conditions of Napoleonic times and his own—the advent of the railway. While his troops would have to march on their own feet round the circumference of the circle, the French would be able to switch troops by rail across the chord of the circle. That was all the worse handicap because his prospects mainly depended on the time factor. The handicap was further increased because his troops would be likely to find their advance hampered by a succession of demolished bridges, while their food and ammunition supply would be restricted until they could rebuild the rail tracks and rail bridges through Belgium and Northern France. The great scythe-sweep which Schlieffen planned was a manoeuvre that had been possible in Napoleonic times. It would again become possible in the next generation—when air-power could paralyze the defending side's attempt to switch its forces, while the development of mechanized forces greatly accelerated the speed of encircling moves, and extended their range. But Schlieffen's plan had a very poor chance of decisive success at the time it was conceived.

B. H. Liddell Hart, from Foreword to G. Ritter, *The Schlieffen Plan: Critique of a Myth* (Horsham, Eng.: Riband Books, 1956), pp. 6–7.

relief from the almost unbearable tension that had preceded it. Yet most of the leading statesmen, when faced with the certainty of war, were overcome by fear and desperation. It was as though they had a foreboding that the war they had failed to avert would be far more terrible than they could imagine, and that the world they had known would never be the same again.

Suggestions for Further Reading

Note: Asterisk denotes a book available in paperback edition.

General

Among the major studies on the diplomatic background of the First World War, L. Albertini, *The Origins of the War of 1914*, 3 vols. (1952–57), is generally considered the best. A. J. P. Taylor, *The Struggle for Mastery in Europe, 1848–1918** (1954), is shorter and less objective. J. Remak, *The Origins of World War I, 1871–1914** (1967), is the briefest and most readable account. L. Lafore, *The Long Fuse** (1965), emphasizes the disintegration of Austria-Hungary as a cause of war. Monographs on the foreign policy of individual powers are F. R. Bridge, *Great Britain and Austria-Hungary, 1906–1914* (1972); M. Foot, *British Foreign Policy since 1898* (1956); J. A. S. Grenville, *Lord Salisbury and Foreign Policy: The Close of the Nineteenth Century* (1964); C. Howard, *Splendid Isolation* (1967); C. J. Lowe and F. Marzari, *Italian Foreign Policy 1870–1914* (1975); and I. Geiss, *German Foreign Policy 1871–1914** (1976).

The Age of Bismarck

The leading book in English is still W. L. Langer, *European Alliances and Alignments*, 2nd ed. (1950). The Near Eastern crisis of the 1870s is discussed in B. H. Sumner, *Russia and the Balkans, 1870–1880* (1937), and its outcome in W. N. Medlicott, *The Congress of Berlin and After* (1938). For the formation of Bismarck's system of alliances, see A. C. Coolidge, *The Origins of the Triple Alliance* (1926), and N. D. Bagdasarian, *The Austro-German Rapprochement, 1870–1879* (1976). P. B. Mitchell, *The Bismarckian Policy of Conciliation with France* (1935), rounds out the picture in the West. Germany's first colonial ventures are described in M. E. Townsend, *The Origins of Modern German Colonization, 1871–1885* (1921), and in A. J. P. Taylor, *Germany's First Bid for Colonies** (1938). The closing years of Bismarck's career are studied critically in J. V. Fuller, *Bismarck's Diplomacy at Its Zenith* (1922). The chancellor's dismissal is dealt with in K. F. Nowak, *Kaiser and Chancellor* (1930). G. A. Craig, *From Bismarck to Adenauer: Aspects of German Statecraft** (1958), offers a sympathetic appraisal of Bismarck the diplomat.

Imperialism in Africa and Asia

Some of the works cited in the suggested reading list in Chapter 27 are also relevant here. The authoritative work on the imperialist rivalries of the great powers is W. L. Langer, *The Diplomacy of Imperialism, 1890–1902,* 2nd ed., 2 vols. (1951). The colonization of Africa is covered in R. Robinson and J. Gallagher, *Africa and the Victorians** (1961); E. A. Walker, *A History of Southern Africa* (1957); R. L. Tignor, *Modernization and British Colonial Rule in Egypt, 1882–1914* (1966); P. Gifford and W. R. Louis, eds., *Britain and Germany in Africa* (1967); and H. R. Rudin, *Germans in the Cameroons, 1884–1914* (1938). See also N. Ascherson, *The King Incorporated: Leopold II of the Belgians* (1963), and J. Duffy, *Portuguese Africa* (1959). On the Far East, G. P. Hudson, *The Far East in World Politics* (1939), is the best brief book. See also J. T. Pratt, *The Expansion of Europe in the Far East* (1947); P. Joseph, *Foreign Diplomacy in China, 1894–1900* (1928); and B. H. Sumner, *Tsardom and Imperialism in the Far East and Middle East* (1942). For the economic penetration of the Middle East, see S. N. Fisher, *The Middle East* (1959), and W. I. Shorrock, *French Imperialism in the Middle East* (1976). Financial imperialism is treated in H. Feis, *Europe, the World's Banker, 1870–1914** (1930), and E. Staley, *War and the Private Investor* (1935). Good general treatments of the colonial policy of some of the great powers include M. Beloff, *Imperial Sunset: Britain's Liberal Empire, 1897–1921* (1969); H. Brunschwig, *Myths and Realities of French Colonialism, 1871–1914* (1966); and R. F. Betts, *Europe Overseas: Phases of Imperialism* (1968). The following monographs are based on fresh archival sources: A. White, *The Diplomacy of the Russo-Japanese War* (1964); G. N. Sanderson, *England, Europe and the Upper Nile, 1882–1899* (1965); C. C. Eldridge, *England's Mission: The Imperial Idea in the Age of Gladstone and Disraeli, 1868–1880* (1974); R. G. Brown, *Fashoda Reconsidered* (1970); and I. H. Nish, *The Anglo-Japanese Alliance: The Diplomacy of Two Island Empires, 1894–1907* (1966).

The United States as a World Power   America's share in the scramble for overseas possessions is treated in A. K. Weinberg, *Manifest Destiny* (1935); J. W. Pratt, *America's Colonial Experiment* (1950); and H. K. Beale, *Theodore Roosevelt and the Rise of America to World Power** (1956). The best books on the Spanish-American War are J. W. Pratt, *Expansionists of 1898** (1936); F. B. Freidel, *Splendid Little War** (1958); and H. W. Morgan, *America's Road to Empire: The War with Spain and Overseas Expansion** (1965). Other phases of American foreign policy are dealt with in E. H. Zabriskie, *American-Russian Rivalry in the Far East* (1946); P. M. Kennedy, *The Samoan Tangle: A Study in Anglo-German-American Relations, 1878–1900* (1974); H. Sprout and M. Sprout, *The Rise of American Naval Power, 1776–1918* (1939); C. D. Davis, *The United States and the Second Hague Peace Conference* (1976); and R. H. Heindel, *The American Impact on Great Britain, 1898–1914* (1940). The influence of the military is treated in R. D. Challener, *Admirals, Generals, and American Foreign Policy, 1898–1914* (1973). For a seasoned diplomat's analysis of America's involvement in world affairs since 1898, see G. F. Kennan, *American Diplomacy, 1900–1950** (1951).

The Formation of the Triple Entente   W. L. Langer, *The Franco-Russian Alliance, 1890–1894* (1929), is another authoritative study by this distinguished diplomatic historian. On the formation of the Entente, see J. J. Mathews, *Egypt and the Formation of the Anglo-French Entente of 1904* (1939); P. J. V. Rolo, *The Entente Cordiale* (1969); G. Monger, *The End of Isolation: British Foreign Policy, 1900–1907* (1963); C. Andrew, *Théophile Delcassé and the Making of the Entente Cordiale* (1969); and R. P. Churchill, *The Anglo-Russian Convention of 1907* (1939). Also still relevant is E. N. Anderson, *The First Moroccan Crisis* (1930). S. R. Williamson, *The Politics of Grand Strategy: Britain and France Prepare for War, 1904–1914* (1969), deals with the military conversations growing out of the Entente Cordiale. There is no satisfactory general work on Anglo-German relations during this period, but the following discuss various aspects of the problem: R. J. Sontag, *Germany and England: Background of Conflict, 1848–1894** (1938); R. J. S. Hoffman, *Great Britain and the German Trade Rivalry, 1875–1914* (1933); and P. R. Anderson, *The Background of Anti-English Feeling in Germany, 1890–1902* (1939). The influence of sea power on diplomacy is treated in E. L. Woodward, *Great Britain and the German Navy* (1935), and A. J. Marder, *The Anatomy of British Sea Power* (1940) and *From the Dreadnought to Scapa Flow: The Royal Navy in the Fisher Era, 1904–1919*, 3 vols. (1961–66). See also P. G. Halpern, *The Mediterranean Naval Situation, 1908–1914* (1971). A good deal of diplomatic history can be found in N. Rich, *Friedrich von Holstein: Politics and Diplomacy in the Era of Bismarck and William II*, 2 vols. (1965).

The Mounting Crisis   The events of the last decade before the war are summarized in D. E. Lee, *Europe's Crucial Years: The Diplomatic Background of World War I, 1902–1914* (1974). The policy of two of the major powers is brilliantly discussed in V. R. Berghahn, *Germany and the Approach of War in 1914* (1973), and Z. Steiner, *Britain and the Origins of the First World War* (1977). On individual phases of the mounting crisis, see B. E. Schmitt, *The Annexation of Bosnia* (1937); I. Barlow, *The Agadir Crisis* (1940); W. C. Askew, *Europe and Italy's Acquisition of Libya, 1911–1912* (1942); E. C. Helmreich, *The Diplomacy of the Balkan Wars* (1938); P. Padfield, *The Great Naval Race: The Anglo-German Naval Rivalry, 1900–1914* (1974); and E. C. Thaden, *Russia and the Balkan Alliance of 1912* (1965). The influence of public opinion on foreign policy during the prewar era is explored in O. J. Hale, *Publicity and Diplomacy* (1940), and E. M. Carroll, *Germany and the Great Powers, 1866–1914: A Study in Public Opinion and Foreign Policy* (1939) and *French Public Opinion and Foreign Affairs, 1870–1914* (1930).

The Outbreak of War   V. Dedijer, *The Road to Sarajevo* (1966), is the last word on this subject. The assassination of the Austrian archduke is dramatically told in J. Remak, *Sarajevo** (1959). Although the crisis thus set in motion has been more carefully studied than any comparable event in history, historians still do not agree on who was responsible for the war. S. B. Fay, *The Origins of the World War,** 2 vols. (1932), puts the major blame on Serbia and Russia. B. E. Schmitt, *The Coming of the War, 1914*, 2 vols. (1930), is more severe toward Germany and Austria. The German case is presented in E. Brandenburg, *From Bismarck to the World War: A History of German Foreign Policy, 1870–1914* (1927), and the French position is stated in P. Renouvin, *The Immediate Origins of the War* (1928). More recently, two German historians have placed the major blame on their own nation: F. Fischer, *Germany's Aims in the First World War** (1967) and *War of Illusions* (1974), and I. Geiss, ed., *July 1914: The Outbreak of the First World War** (1968). Their works have touched off a major controversy among historians, which is summarized in F. Fischer, *World Power or Decline** (1974).

30 War, Revolution, and Peace, 1914–1929

British soldiers blinded by poison gas during the German spring offensive (1918).

The "Great War," as it was called at the time, only gradually turned into a "World War." It was not the first worldwide conflict, but it was the largest. Before the war ended in November 1918, 49 million men had been mobilized in the "Allied" camp, against 25 million among the "Central Powers." It was truly war on an unprecedented scale. Also, more than any previous conflict, this war involved everyone, not only soldiers. The First World War was a truly "total war." The war lasted much longer than anyone had thought a modern war could, and it brought far more sweeping changes than anyone would have thought possible. Traditional empires collapsed and new nations arose from the wreckage. The New World, hitherto of little significance in European affairs, suddenly emerged as decisive to an Allied victory. Europe, which in the past had always settled its own affairs, apparently was unable to do so any longer.

The Great War was part of a transitional phase in modern history and will be treated as such here. There was no clear-cut end to the war—certainly not the peace settlements of 1919 to 1920. The problems that the statesmen at Paris wrestled with then continued to plague Europe and the world for at least a decade thereafter. The ways in which these problems were tackled were still very much reminiscent of the nineteenth century. It took a new series of crises, touched off by the Great Depression of 1929 and culminating in another World War, to complete the transition from nineteenth to twentieth century.

THE COMPARATIVE STRENGTH OF THE POWERS

Despite differences in numbers, the actual military strength of the Allies and the Central Powers at the start of the war was quite evenly balanced. The impressive size of the Allied armies was due chiefly to the ill-trained and poorly equipped Russian army. Germany's forces, on the other hand, were the best in the world. France and Britain matched the Germans in numbers, but the Germans excelled in the quality and quantity of their equipment. The Austrian army was inferior to that of Germany and was weakened by its large Slav contingent. But since the main showdown was expected in the West, this handicap did not seem serious.

The Central Powers had other advantages, aside from their superior strength on land. Command of the interior lines of communication enabled them to shift their forces rapidly from one theater of war to another. The Allies, on the other hand, were widely separated; Russia in particular, with the closing of the Baltic and Black Seas, was cut off from much-needed aid. German industry, furthermore, was more readily converted to war production than the industries of its opponents. The Central Powers had more than enough coal and iron, and territories seized on the western front increased their resources. In their supplies of foodstuffs, however, Austria and Germany fell seriously short of their needs.

Had the war been as brief as most wars of the nineteenth century, Germany and Austria might have won it. But as the fighting dragged on, Allied inherent superiority made itself felt. Their manpower was greater; their industrial potential was superior; and, thanks to Great Britain, the Allies enjoyed naval supremacy. By keeping the sea lanes open, the British navy assured the uninterrupted flow of men and material; and by clamping a tight blockade on Central Europe, Britain aggravated Germany's and Austria's food problems.

Each side tried to strengthen its position further by seeking additional partners. Since the Allies usually had more to offer, they were more successful in this contest. At the end of the war, thirty "Allied and Associated Powers" were ranged against the Central Powers—Germany, Austria-Hungary, Turkey, and Bulgaria.

The most important additions to the Allied camp, aside from the United States, were Japan, Italy, Rumania, and Greece. Japan's entry into the war in August 1914 proved to be a most profitable move. Without delay the Japanese seized Germany's holdings in China's Shantung Province and occupied Germany's Pacific islands north of the equa-

British soldiers "go over the top" to attack German lines.

German Zeppelin attacking Antwerp in 1914. Painting by W. Moralt.

THE GREAT STALEMATE 1914–16

Both sides had prepared plans for a brief offensive war. In its grand simplicity, however, the German Schlieffen Plan promised a far quicker decision than France's Plan XVII, which called for an invasion of Alsace-Lorraine.

1914: The Allies Ahead

From the start of hostilities on the western front, Germany held the initiative. After one month of fighting, German forces had advanced to within twenty-five miles of Paris. In early September 1914, however, the German drive was halted at the river Marne. The battle of the Marne was one of the decisive events of the war, since it dashed Germany's hope for an early victory. There were many reasons for Germany's disappointment. Belgium had put up more resistance than had been expected. Germany, furthermore, had failed to concentrate sufficient forces on the right wing of its invading armies to make possible the gigantic enveloping move that was to strike at the rear of France's forces southeast of Paris. The Schlieffen Plan depended on the closest possible communications between field commanders and the high command, and on rapid lines of supply; neither of these had been provided for.

The battle of the Marne was followed by a series of engagements in which each side hoped to outflank the other, and in the course of which the front was gradually extended to the sea. By November 1914 the fighting in the West had changed from a war of movement to a war of position. Until the spring of 1918 the western front, except for an occasional thrust of a few miles in one direction or the other, remained unchanged.

With the bulk of Germany's forces tied down in the West, Russia was able to score some unexpected successes in the East. In mid-August 1914 two Russian armies invaded East Prussia and within a few days overran almost half of Germany's easternmost province. At the height of danger, the kaiser recalled from retirement General Paul von Hinden-

tor. Italy did not join the war until 1915. It had refused to honor its obligations under the Triple Alliance, claiming that its terms did not apply. To balance possible Austrian gains in the Balkans, moreover, the Italians had demanded territorial concessions from Austria. The Austrians agreed to some of Italy's demands, but the Allies were able to offer more. By the secret Treaty of London in April 1915, England, France, and Russia promised Italy not only the Austrian regions inhabited by Italians but also considerable territory along the eastern Adriatic and in Asia Minor and Africa. Having received these promises, the Italians declared war against Austria-Hungary in May 1915, and against Germany in August 1916. At that time, Rumania also joined the Allies, and Greece followed in June 1917. In both these cases the pressure of military events and the hope for territorial gains were decisive.

The only two countries that joined the Central Powers were Turkey and Bulgaria. The Ottoman Empire had long maintained close economic ties with Germany, and its army had been trained by German officers. In August 1914 Turkey concluded an alliance with Germany; three months later a Turkish naval squadron bombarded Russia's Black Sea ports; and in early November 1914 the Allies declared war on the Ottoman Empire. As for Bulgaria, it had been wooed by both sides. But the Central Powers were able to promise more, and in October 1915 Bulgaria joined the Germans and Austrians in a major drive against Serbia.

burg, a specialist on conditions in the East, and appointed as Hindenburg's chief of staff the younger and more capable Erich Ludendorff. These men soon reversed the situation on the eastern front. In two major battles, at Tannenberg and the Masurian Lakes, Russia lost close to 250,000 men. Russia's reversals in the north were balanced by successes in the southeast against Austria. In a sweeping campaign under Russia's commander in chief, Grand Duke Nicholas, Russian forces in September took most of Galicia and advanced to the Carpathian frontier of Hungary.

In the East, as in the West, the end of 1914 found the Allied and Central Powers locked in a stalemate. But since Ger-

many had failed to deliver a knockout blow in the West and appeared to be stalled in the East, the advantage was felt to lie with the Allies. In addition, British naval superiority had been responsible for the sinking of a German naval squadron off the coast of South America and for the seizure of most of the colonies that had belonged to Germany.

1915: Allied Reverses

But Allied dreams of victory were premature. The new Italian ally they gained in the spring of 1915 proved to be of little use. Furthermore, a British attack against the Gallipoli Peninsula and the Turkish Straits failed. Had it succeeded,

THE FIRST WORLD WAR   1914–18

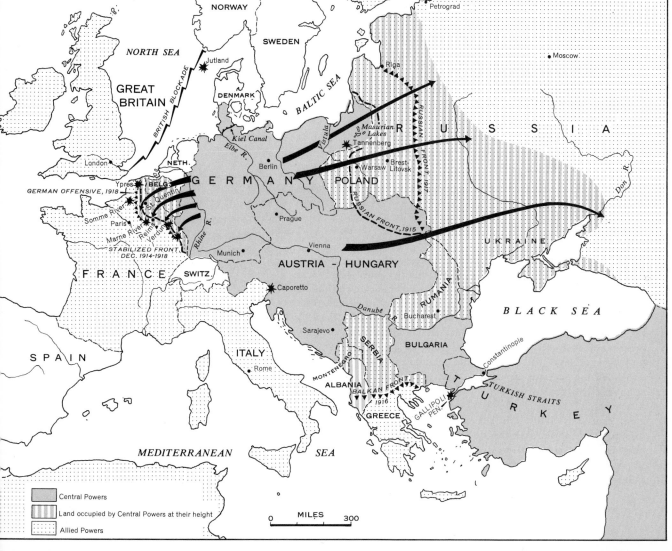

Central Powers

Land occupied by Central Powers at their height

Allied Powers

MILES 0 — 300

Advertisement placed by
Germany in American
newspapers to warn neutral
travelers of the risks of
crossing the Atlantic in the
British vessel *Lusitania*.

Turkey would have been seriously weakened and the Black Sea opened to Allied shipping. Instead, the Straits remained closed for the rest of the war.

The most serious Allied reverses during 1915 were on the eastern front and in the Balkans. In the spring and summer, German forces in the north and combined Austro-German forces in the south advanced in a series of offensives that cost the Russians Poland, Lithuania, and Courland, drove them out of Galicia, and lost them almost a million men. All of central and eastern Europe was now in German and Austrian hands. In October the Central Powers turned against Serbia; and in November they moved into Montenegro and Albania.

By the beginning of 1916 the tide of war on land seemed definitely to have turned against the Allies. Even on the high seas the Germans were able to make some gains. To counteract Britain's blockade, the German government, in early 1915, imposed a submarine blockade against the British Isles. The first phase of German submarine warfare came to a head with the sinking of the British liner *Lusitania* in May 1915. The loss of 139 American passengers caused a serious crisis in American-German relations. It was settled only after Germany promised to restrict its submarine tactics in the future.

The Sinking of the *Lusitania*

The full horror of the sinking of the *Lusitania* has now been revealed; and it has stirred the people of this country more deeply than even the poison clouds, or any other of the wanton and murderous acts committed by the Germans. . . . By thousands of dastardly crimes the Germans have demonstrated that they are determined to wage this war under conditions of cold-blooded and deliberate murder and outrage, of destruction and brutality, such as the world has never known. . . . Never before, since the world began, has there been witnessed the spectacle of a whole race, numbering many millions, scientifically organised for the objects of wholesale murder and devastation. . . . It is universally seen now that the Germans are a nation apart, that their civilisation is a mere veneer, that they have fallen immeasurably lower than their tribal forbears, and that their calculated and organised barbarity is without precedent in history. Nations, we perceive, can sink to unprecedented depths. No nation has ever fallen so low in infamy. . . .

From an editorial in *The Times* (London), May 10, 1915.

1916: Stalemate

Since time was clearly on the side of the Allies, it seemed imperative to the Germans to force a major showdown. In February 1916, therefore, they launched an all-out offensive against the French stronghold of Verdun. The battle of Verdun was the most famous battle of the war. It lasted more than four months and caused more than seven hundred thousand casualties; yet it ended undecided. Its chief hero on the French side was General Henri Philippe Pétain. Like Hindenburg after the battle of Tannenberg, Pétain became the idol of his people. Both men were to play fateful roles in later years. The battle of Verdun was followed by an Allied counteroffensive along the Somme River. But the battle of the Somme, like that of Verdun, failed to force a final decision in the West.

Events elsewhere during 1916 were equally indecisive. In June, Russian forces under General Brusilov started a major drive against the Austrian lines and within a few weeks had taken most of eastern Galicia. These successes brought Rumania into the war. But its participation only made matters worse for the Allies. In late September, Austro-German forces invaded Rumania, and by January 1917 most of that country's rich resources were in the hands of the Central Powers. In the East as in the West, the outcome of the war continued to hang in the balance.

The year 1916 also saw the one great naval battle of the war between Germany and Britain. The German navy, to have a chance of success, had to fight in its home waters. But the British refused to venture forth that far. On several occasions the Germans went out into the North Sea, hoping to entice the British into battle. It was on one of these sallies that the two fleets made contact off the coast of Jutland in May 1916. The battle of Jutland was costly and indecisive. The British lost more naval tonnage than the Germans, but they could better afford to. The German fleet henceforth remained safely at home.

By the end of 1916 a stalemate had been reached on all fronts, and victory for either side seemed far away. Meanwhile losses and material costs of the war had been staggering, and the strain of war had begun to tell on the home fronts as well as on the battlefields.

THE HOME FRONTS

People everywhere had greeted the outbreak of war with enthusiastic demonstrations of national unity. Each side believed that it was fighting a "just war." In addition, the war was expected to be short. The Germans hoped to be in Paris before the summer of 1914 was over, and the French were looking forward to Christmas in Berlin. When instead the war dragged on for two years, with no end in sight, enthusiasm gave way to deep depression.

One of the important conditions for victory was effective leadership. Both England and France found outstanding civilian leaders—the British in David Lloyd George, and the French in Georges Clemenceau. In Germany, Austria, and Russia, on the other hand, where the monarch was both chief executive and symbol of national unity, much depended on the leadership he provided. In none of the three countries did the ruler measure up to expectations. William II had neither the ability nor the energy to cope with the problems of a total war. As he gradually faded into the background, his role was taken over by Hindenburg and Ludendorff. In Austria, Francis Joseph was too old and his grandnephew Charles, who succeeded him in 1916, was too inexperienced to keep the crumbling empire together. The saddest figure among Europe's conservative monarchs was Nicholas II of Russia. In 1915 he assumed personal command of his armed forces, leaving the government in the hands of his wife and her sinister adviser, Rasputin.

Total War

The demands of total war presented many new and difficult problems. All the powers experienced periodic munitions shortages. Labor was scarce. Women were employed in growing numbers, and Germany "recruited" workers from Bel-

Nicholas II with Grand Duke Nicholas, commander in chief of the Russian armies until 1915.

gium and France. Except for the Russians, who were almost completely isolated, the Allies were able to supplement their domestic production of food and war materials with overseas imports. The Central Powers, on the other hand, cut off by the blockade, were chiefly dependent on their own resources. The Germans tackled the problem with customary efficiency, devising scores of ersatz, or substitute, products and perfecting new processes to obtain scarce materials. Austria-Hungary was far less successful in these respects. Its difficulties were made worse by continuous economic feuds between Austria and Hungary.

The most serious shortages of the Central Powers were in food and clothing. Germany began rationing in 1915, but rationing did not increase available supplies. Shortages of labor and transportation reduced the coal supply, adding the misery of cold to hunger. Faced with these hardships, many Germans, especially among the working class, hoped for a speedy end to the war, even without victory.

War Aims and Peace Proposals

Neither side ever stated its war aims openly, except in the most general terms.

German women working in a government munitions factory during the war.

Secretly, however, the Allies had agreed on the following distribution of spoils: Russia was to get most of the Polish regions under German and Austrian rule, as well as control over the Turkish Straits; France was promised the whole left bank of the Rhine; England was allotted the German colonies; and Italy was to have parts of Austria and territories elsewhere. In supplementary agreements most of the Ottoman Empire was divided into Russian, Italian, French, and British spheres of interest.

The war aims of the Central Powers called for the "liberation" of the Poles and the Baltic peoples from Russian domination, the setting up of small satellite states under German and Austrian control, and the annexation of some regions outright. In the West, Germany hoped for additional regions rich in iron ore from France and political and economic control over Belgium. There were also ambitious schemes for a central European federation under German leadership, a *Mitteleuropa*, and for a compact central African colony.

In view of these far-reaching Allied and German war aims, it is not surprising that efforts to reach a compromise peace proved fruitless. The Central Powers took the first official step in December 1916, informing President Wilson that they were ready to enter into peace negotiations. Wilson thereupon asked both sides to state their terms. But this the Germans refused to do. There were other peace moves, notably one inaugurated by Pope Benedict XV in August 1917. All these efforts failed. Both sides wanted peace, but neither side wanted it badly enough to make any real concessions.

Women in Wartime

In industry as a whole the total employment of women and girls over ten as between 1914 and 1918 increased by about 800,000, from 2,179,000 to 2,971,000. . . . It is in these arid statistics that we traverse a central theme in the sociology of women's employment in the twentieth century. . . . The growth of large-scale industry and bureaucracy would undoubtedly have brought this development eventually, but it was the war, in creating simultaneously a proliferation of Government committees and departments *and* a shortage of men, which brought a sudden and irreversible advance in the economic and social power of a category of women employees which extended from sprigs of the aristocracy to daughters of the proletariat. . . .

Given the rigidities of the Edwardian class structure, there are difficulties in the way of summing up the consequences of the war for women as an entire sex. In the business, medical and military functions . . . the women concerned were very largely women of the middle and upper classes. Yet the major section of these women had been in pre-war years a depressed class, tied to the apron-strings of their mothers or chaperons, or to the purse-strings of their fathers or husbands. Now that they were earning on their own account, they had economic independence; now that they were working away from home, in some cases far from home, they had social independence.

Obviously, then, women of all classes shared in a similar kind of emancipation. The suffragette movement before the war had . . . aimed simply at the same limited franchise for some women as was enjoyed by some men. The Women's Movement from 1915 onwards is a more unified movement than ever it had been previously.

From A. Marwick, *The Deluge: British Society and the First World War* (New York: Norton, 1970), pp. 91–94.

THE UNITED STATES ENTERS THE WAR

The United States at first had made every effort to remain neutral. Isolationism was still a strong force; and although there were many Anglophiles in the East, there were also large numbers of German-Americans in the Middle West. America's abandonment of neutrality had several causes. Effective Allied propaganda was one. Another was the growing financial involvement of many Americans in the Allied cause. But more important than either of these factors was Germany's resumption of unrestricted submarine warfare early in 1917.

Unrestricted Submarine Warfare

Germany reached its decision to step up the submarine campaign after its peace move of December 1916 had failed. Germany's civilian authorities opposed unrestricted submarine warfare, fearing that it might bring America into the war. But the real power now lay with the military. With time on the Allied side, Hindenburg and Ludendorff felt that only drastic submarine action could still win the war. They realized that this might lead to American intervention, but they thought England would be defeated long before such intervention would become effective.

Unrestricted submarine war began on February 1, 1917. America broke off diplomatic relations with Germany on February 3. As German submarines began sinking American ships, public opinion became more and more interventionist. The publication of the intercepted "Zimmermann Telegram," a note sent by Germany's foreign secretary urging Mexico to make war on the United States, did the rest. On April 6, 1917, Congress declared war on Germany.

THE RUSSIAN REVOLUTION

America's entrance into the war was made more urgent by changes in Russia that weakened the Allied cause. Events there had long been pointing toward a major domestic upheaval. At first the Russian people had loyally supported their government's war effort. But the sufferings of war soon dampened their spirit. With insufficient arms and a chronic shortage of munitions, the army lost more than a million men during the first year of the war. While the armies lacked essential materials, the civilian population suffered from food shortages, despite the fact that Russia's economy was primarily agrarian. The blame for all these ills was rightly placed on the inefficiency and corruption of the government. The elected assembly, the *Duma*, repeatedly urged the adoption of reforms; but the tsar continued to meet discontent with repression.

The Background of the Revolution

Repression alternating with reform had been the policy for decades. There had been an earlier revolution in 1905, but it had brought few changes (see pp. 663–64). To understand the sudden and complete collapse of the tsarist regime in 1917, we must go back still further, to 1861 and the emancipation of the serfs by Alexander II (see p. 616). The peasants liberated at the time provided the manpower for the belated industrialization of Russia. The resulting proletariat,

uprooted and subject to all the hardships of too rapid industrialization, provided a particularly fertile breeding ground for revolution. By 1914 industrial workers made up less than 20 percent of the total population, but they were concentrated in the larger cities. It was here that the revolution started; but it found a ready echo in the countryside, where the mass of the peasants were leading a marginal existence, only a few of the more enterprising among them, the *kulaks*, having profited from the emancipation.

The "February Revolution" and Provisional Government

The Russian Revolution had not been planned. According to Marx, a country, to be "ripe" for revolution, first had to pass through an industrial-capitalist phase. In Russia, that phase had only begun. The overthrow of the tsarist regime was the climax of a gradually mounting wave of popular protest. By 1917 more than a million soldiers had deserted the armed forces; in the cities, food shortages led to repeated strikes and riots; and in the countryside, landless peasants began to seize the land of their noble landlords. In early March street demonstrations broke out in Petrograd (the name given to St. Petersburg at the beginning of the war). In the past the government had always been able to use the army against such disturbances. But the troops now fraternized with the rioters. From the capital, insurrection spread to the provinces. On March 12—or February 27 in the Russian calendar, hence the term "February Revolution"—the *Duma* established a Provisional Government under the premiership of a liberal aristocrat, Prince George Lvov. Three days later, Nicholas II abdicated. He and his family were later moved to Siberia, where they were murdered by the Bolsheviks in the summer of 1918.

The new Provisional Government was faced with problems for which it was completely unprepared. To meet the discontent of the masses some immediate reforms were introduced, but these did not go far enough. The situation was complicated by the existence of a rival for political power, the Petrograd Soviet (Council) of Workers' and Soldiers' Deputies, consisting of Socialist Revolutionaries, Mensheviks, and some Bolsheviks. Because of its popular support, the Soviet was the more powerful of the two groups.

The Provisional Government's main difficulty arose from its desire to continue the war. In July the new minister of war, Alexander Kerensky, launched a futile offensive against the Austrians in Galicia. Its failure led to further riots in Petrograd. To restore order, Kerensky, on July 25, replaced Prince Lvov as prime minister. To strengthen his position, Kerensky appointed as commander in chief General Lavr Kornilov, who was popular with the army's rank and file. Kornilov succeeded in restoring some discipline but was unable to halt a German offensive against Riga. When there were signs that Kornilov wanted to make himself military dictator, he was arrested, and on September 14 Kerensky himself assumed supreme command of the army.

The revolution, meanwhile, which thus far had been free from terrorism, became increasingly violent, as workers sacked stores, peasants burned manor houses, and soldiers killed their officers. Revolution among the non-Russian nationalities in the borderlands, furthermore, threatened the unity of the country. Finally, the Petrograd Soviet, which until then had tolerated the Provisional Government, was gradually falling under the control of its most radical faction, the Bolsheviks.

The "October Revolution"

The exiled Bolshevik leaders—Lenin, Trotsky, Stalin, and others—had returned from abroad or from Siberia after the February Revolution. Their immediate aim was to gain control of the soviets in Petrograd and elsewhere. At first they only commanded a small minority within the Petrograd Soviet. Lenin advanced his radical program—immediate peace, seizure of land by the peasants and of factories by the workers—against the do-nothing policy of the Mensheviks and the Socialist Revolutionaries. Constantly reiterating this program, the Bolsheviks

Alexander Kerensky studying a map (November 1917). Kerensky took over the supreme command of the Russian forces.

gradually increased their following within the Soviet and without. As a result, the balance slowly shifted. By September the Bolsheviks controlled the soviets in Petrograd, Moscow, and several other cities.

The only way for the Bolsheviks to gain control of the government was to use force. When Kerensky got wind of the Bolshevik plot and ordered the arrest of their leaders, Bolshevik forces began occupying strategic points in Petrograd on November 6. The main fighting took place around the Winter Palace, seat of the Provisional Government. On November 7 Kerensky took flight, first to the front and later abroad. The same afternoon an All-Russian Congress of Soviets convened. The majority of its delegates were Bolsheviks. As a first move they formed a new executive, the Council of People's Commissars, with Lenin as Chairman, Trotsky as Foreign Commissar, and Stalin as Commissar for National Minorities.

The "October Revolution"—so named because November 7 was October 25 old-style—was only the first stage on the road to a Bolshevik victory; a long drawn-out civil war was yet to follow. The followers of Lenin still numbered only a small percentage of the Russian people. When the constituent assembly was elected in late November, less than

Bolshevik propaganda poster: the tired Russian soldier.

one-fourth of the delegates were Bolsheviks. But this was to be the first and last free election in Russia. When the assembly met for the first time in January 1918, it was dispersed by Bolshevik forces.

The Treaty of Brest-Litovsk

The most important immediate result of the October Revolution was to end the war on the eastern front. On December 5, 1917, the Bolsheviks concluded an armistice with Germany, and on December 22 peace negotiations began at Brest-Litovsk. The Bolsheviks wanted "a just, democratic peace without annexations or indemnities." But the Germans were in no mood to forgo their advantages. At one point the Russians broke off negotiations, whereupon the Germans resumed their advance. On March 3, 1918, the Russians gave in and accepted Germany's terms.

Under the Treaty of Brest-Litovsk, Russia was to lose a quarter of its European territory, a third of its population, more than half of its coal and iron, and a third of its industry. The treaty was later invalidated because of the Allied victory in the West. But, for the moment, the Central Powers were freed from the burden of a two-front war and won access to the vast economic resources of eastern Europe. Their position was further strengthened by a peace treaty forced on Rumania at Bucharest on March 5, 1918, under which Germany received a ninety-year lease on that country's oil wells. The triumph of German expansionist aims served to warn the Allies of what to expect in the event of a German victory.

CONTINUED STALEMATE IN THE WEST, 1917

With the Central Powers victorious in the East, the Allies more than ever depended on aid from the United States. A first small contingent of American troops under General John J. Pershing had landed in France as early as June 1917. But it was not until spring of 1918 that American units took any real part in the fighting. America's main contribution

was material aid. To meet the submarine danger, a vast shipbuilding program was initiated. Unrestricted submarine warfare at first was a serious threat to the Allied cause. But in time various ways of countering the submarine menace were devised, notably the convoy system.

While the Allies were holding their own at sea, the Central Powers were successfully resisting Allied attempts to force a decision on land. The campaigns on the western front in 1917 were among the bloodiest in the whole war. Yet the lessons of Verdun and the Somme still seemed to hold true—a decision on the western front was impossible. The Central Powers, meanwhile, scored one of their greatest victories on the Italian front. The battle of Caporetto in October 1917 cost Italy close to half a million men in casualties, prisoners, and deserters. Only French and British reinforcements averted a still greater disaster.

The Decline of Civilian Morale

Continuous heavy losses at the front and deprivations at home caused a serious decline in civilian morale. The British, suffering least among Europeans, bore up best. The French, on the other hand, experienced a major military and political crisis. In May 1917 the senseless bloodshed in the West led to open mutiny among troops at the front. The French home front, too, was becoming

Lenin in 1919.

Lenin

November 7, 1917

It was just 8:40 when a thundering wave of cheers announced the entrance of the presidium, with Lenin—great Lenin—among them. A short, stocky figure, with a big head set down in his shoulders, bald and bulging. Little eyes, a snubbish nose, wide, generous mouth, and heavy chin; clean-shaven now, but already beginning to bristle with the well-known beard of his past and future. Dressed in shabby clothes, his trousers much too long for him. Unimpressive, to be the idol of a mob, loved and revered as perhaps few leaders in history have been. A strange popular leader—a leader purely by virtue of intellect; colourless, humourless, uncompromising and detached, without picturesque idiosyncrasies—but with the power of explaining profound ideas in simple terms, of analysing a concrete situation. And combined with shrewdness, the greatest intellectual audacity.

From John Reed, *Ten Days That Shook the World* (New York: International Publishers, 1919), p. 125.

more and more defeatist. In Italy, where a strong faction had opposed the war from the start, shortages of food and coal brought on a series of strikes. It was only the disaster of Caporetto that made people rally to the support of the government, realizing that the future of their country was at stake.

The Central Powers underwent similar crises. In Germany, differences between civilian and military leaders caused the resignation of Chancellor Theobald von Bethmann Hollweg and the assumption of virtually dictatorial control by Hindenburg and Ludendorff. In Austria the war gave new momentum to the separatist tendencies of the empire's many nationalities. The Czechs and the Yugoslavs set up organizations abroad to work for Allied recognition of their cause, and Polish, Czech, and Yugoslav prisoners in Allied hands were formed into national legions to fight against their homeland.

The general weariness that affected all the belligerents after three years of war quite naturally gave rise to further peace efforts. Like all the earlier attempts, however, they failed, since neither side was ready to make the necessary concessions. The Bolsheviks published the secret treaties revealing Allied war aims, and western statesmen made highly idealistic pronouncements to counteract these revelations. In January 1918 President Wilson, in an effort to dissociate America from agreements to which it had not been a party, stated his famous Fourteen Points as the basis for a just peace. Briefly stated, they were:

(1) "Open covenants of peace" and an end to secret diplomacy; (2) freedom of the seas in peace and war; (3) "the removal . . . of all economic barriers and the establishment of an equality of trade conditions"; (4) the reduction of armaments "to the lowest point consistent with domestic safety"; (5) the "impartial adjustment of all colonial claims"; (6) the "evacuation of all Russian territory" and an attitude of "intelligent and unselfish sympathy" toward Russia; (7) the evacuation and restoration of Belgium; (8) the freeing of the invaded portions of France and the restoration to it of Alsace-Lorraine; (9) the "readjustment of the frontier of Italy . . . along clearly recognizable lines of nationality"; (10) "the freest opportunity of autonomous development" for the peoples of Austria-Hungary; (11) the evacuation and restoration of Rumania, Serbia, and Montenegro; (12) autonomy for the non-Turkish nationalities of the Ottoman Empire and the permanent opening of the Dardanelles to all nations; (13) the creation of an independent Poland, including "the territories inhabited by indisputably Polish populations," and assurance to Poland of "a free and secure access to the sea"; and (14) the formation of "a general association of nations . . . for the purpose of affording mutual guarantees of political independence and territorial integrity to great and small states alike."

The Fourteen Points were to play an important role in the later negotiations for an armistice and peace, but for the time being they had little effect. The only way to get a satisfactory peace, leaders on both sides felt, was to win the war. With time running against it, Germany, in the spring of 1918, decided to make an all-out bid for victory.

THE COLLAPSE OF THE CENTRAL POWERS

Ludendorff's plan for a large-scale spring offensive had some chance of success. The Germans were able to move large numbers of troops from the East. The Allies, on the other hand, were still suffering from the heavy losses of their 1917 offensives, and reinforcements from America were only just beginning to arrive in sufficient numbers.

The Last Offensives

The gigantic "Emperor's Battle" was launched in March 1918. At first it was overwhelmingly successful. Within three months the Germans once again stood on the Marne, only fifty miles from Paris. But despite brilliant victories, they failed to breach the Allied front. On July 15, when the Germans mounted their last major drive, in the vicinity of Reims, the Allied front was held largely with the aid of American forces.

British tanks at Amiens in 1918. In the final months of the war the Allies effectively used large numbers of tanks under a smoke screen as a cover for advancing infantry.

On July 18, the Allies began their counteroffensive. Ludendorff at first was able to withdraw his forces in good order. But on August 8, the German army suffered its "black day." Using for the first time large numbers of tanks, the British advanced almost eight miles. From here on the Allies never gave the Germans a moment's rest. By the end of September the German army had lost a million men in six months. Morale was low and desertions mounted. Germany's allies, moreover, were showing signs of imminent collapse. On October 4, finally, Germany and Austria appealed to President Wilson for an armistice based on the Fourteen Points.

Chaos in Central Europe

By the time prearmistice negotiations were completed a month later, all the Central Powers had collapsed. The first to give up was Bulgaria. The Bulgarian lines were broken in late September, and before the month was out the government had sued for an armistice. Next came Turkey. During the last year of the war, British forces had steadily advanced from the Persian Gulf into Mesopotamia and from Egypt into Palestine and Syria. With Bulgaria out of the war, Turkey was threatened from the north as well. On October 30 it concluded an armistice.

The Austro-Hungarian Empire, meanwhile, was falling to pieces. On October 21, 1918, the Czechoslovaks declared their independence, and a week later the Yugoslavs followed suit. On November 1, Hungary established an independent government. Ten days later, Emperor Charles renounced his throne, and by the middle of November both Austria and Hungary had proclaimed themselves republics.

In Germany the government had reformed itself, in the hope of obtaining more favorable armistice terms. But the Allies would have no dealings with the kaiser. On November 3 mutiny broke out among German sailors at Kiel. Within days the revolt spread through most of northern Germany. On November 7 revolution broke out in Munich and the king of Bavaria abdicated. On November 9, finally, revolution in Berlin overthrew the monarchy and a German Republic was proclaimed.

The Allies, meanwhile, had agreed to accept the Fourteen Points as a basis for an armistice. Under its provisions Germany had to withdraw its forces beyond the Rhine; it had to renounce the treaties of Brest-Litovsk and Bucharest; and it had to surrender large quantities of strategic materials. The terms were so designed as to make any resumption of hostilities impossible. Fighting was officially ended on November 11, at 11 A.M.

The war that was to have been over in four months had lasted more than four years. At its height it had involved some thirty-four nations. It had killed close to 10 million soldiers, wounded twice that number, and caused close to a million civilian deaths. Its total cost has been estimated at over $350 billion. It had brought revolution to central and eastern Europe and had swept away the last remnants of autocratic monarchism. The war's initial purpose—to determine the future of Serbia—had long since given way to far bigger aims. Germany had dreamed of hegemony in Europe and perhaps the world. The Allies had hoped to avert that German threat and in the process to round out their own possessions. Only the United States was seeking nothing. The Peace Conference was to show whether America's idealism would prevail against the hardheaded nationalism of its European allies.

THE PARIS PEACE CONFERENCE

The Peace Conference opened on January 18, 1919. All the belligerents were present, except the Central Powers and Russia; this was to be a peace dictated by the victors. As in most major peace conferences, the important decisions were made by the great powers who had contributed most to winning the war. The peace was thus made by a handful of men, the "Big Four": Wilson, Lloyd George, Clemenceau, and Orlando.

The star of the conference was Woodrow Wilson, a figure of hope to Europeans. The favorite aim of the American president was to set up a League of Nations. But his position had been weakened by the return of a Republican majority in the recent congressional elections. Great Britain was represented by its prime minister, David Lloyd George, the mercurial Welsh politician. Although his views on the peace were fairly moderate, he had recently won an election on the promise of a harsh peace—a promise that was to haunt him throughout the peace negotiations. The most impressive figure of the conference was France's premier, Georges Clemenceau. He hated the Germans, and his foremost aim was to protect France by weakening its former enemy in every possible way. Italy's representative, Prime Minister Vittorio Orlando, played only a minor role. Far more important was his foreign minister, Sidney Sonnino, who was determined to hold Italy's allies to the far-reaching promises they had made in 1915.

Problems of Peacemaking

The problems before the Paris conference were without precedent. The last comparable meeting had been held at Vienna a century earlier. But while the Congress of Vienna had been concerned only with reordering the affairs of Europe, the problems before the Paris conference ranged over the whole world. The Allies as well as the Central Powers had accepted the Fourteen Points as a basis for peace, but many of Wilson's principles differed from the provisions of the Allies' secret treaties. Other complications arose from the many foreign and domestic disturbances that occurred while the conference was in session, the popular clamor in the Allied countries for a speedy settlement, and the physical and nervous strain under which the delegates labored. It is not surprising that the peace they made was not perfect.

So long as the victors agreed among themselves, negotiations at Paris went smoothly. But there were several questions on which they did not see eye to eye. The most important were Germany's colonies, the Rhineland, reparations, Fiume, and the Shantung Peninsula.

The Allies agreed that Germany's colonies should not be returned, but they did not agree on what to do with them. France, Japan, and Great Britain and its dominions wanted to annex Germany's holdings. President Wilson, on the other hand, felt that this would violate his Fourteen Points. The impasse was finally resolved by the adoption of the "Mandate Principle," which provided that the German colonies as well as a large part of the Ottoman Empire were to be placed under foreign control, subject to supervision by the League of Nations. Germany later attacked this solution as "veiled annexation" and a violation of the fifth of Wilson's Fourteen Points.

The crisis over the future of the Rhineland almost broke up the conference. The French, having been invaded by the Germans twice within the last half-century, demanded that the left bank of the Rhine be made into an autonomous buffer state for reasons of security. Such an arrangement, however, ran counter to Wilson's principles. The compromise arrived at after long and acrimonious debate called for the permanent demilitarization of the Rhineland and its occupation by Allied forces for

Woodrow Wilson and French President Raymond Poincaré wave to Parisians on Wilson's arrival in Paris for the Peace Conference.

fifteen years. In addition, the territory of the Saar was to remain under League administration for fifteen years, and France was given the region's coal mines. Finally, Great Britain and the United States promised France an alliance against possible German aggression.

In the discussion of reparations, an argument arose over the extent to which Germany was to make good damages done to the civilian population of the Allies. Wilson finally gave way to the pressure of his European colleagues and agreed that this should include pensions to victims of war and allowances to their families. To justify so vast a claim, the Allies affirmed that German aggression had been responsible for starting the war. The controversial issue of "war guilt" was thus injected into the peace treaty.

The crisis over Fiume arose from Italy's demand that it be given the Adriatic port in place of the Dalmation coast, which it had been promised in the Treaty of London but which had been incorporated into Yugoslavia. The Yugoslavs, on the other hand, claimed Fiume as an essential outlet to the sea, and in this they found Allied and American support. When Prime Minister Orlando finally left Paris in protest, the united Allied front showed its first open rift. Italy felt that it had been cheated out of its just reward.

The issue of Shantung involved Japan and China. China had entered the war on the Allied side in 1917. Japan's claim to succeed to Germany's former rights in the Shantung Peninsula clearly conflicted with China's own rights and with Wilson's principles. But the president had only just managed to resist French demands in the Rhineland, and the Fiume crisis was still at its height. So he gave in to Japan's demands, for fear that the Japanese might otherwise refuse to join the League of Nations. The Shantung solution was a serious defeat for the American president, and it lost the United States the traditional friendship of China.

While the negotiations at Paris were in their final stages, the German delegation arrived at Versailles. The Germans were handed a draft of the treaty on May

---

Germany Unrepentant — May 7, 1919

Germany's foreign minister, Count Brockdorff-Rantzau, denied Allied charges of German "war guilt" in a speech at the Peace Conference at Versailles.

Gentlemen, we are deeply impressed with the great mission that has brought us here to give to the world forthwith a lasting peace. . . . We know the intensity of the hatred which meets us, and we have heard the victors' passionate demand that as the vanquished we shall be made to pay, and as the guilty we shall be punished.

The demand is made that we shall acknowledge that we alone are guilty of having caused the war. Such a confession in my mouth would be a lie. We are far from seeking to escape from any responsibility for this World War, and for its having been waged as it has . . . but we with all emphasis deny that the people of Germany, who were convinced that they were waging a war of defense, should be burdened with the sole guilt of that war. . . .

Public opinion in every enemy country is echoing the crimes Germany is said to have committed in the war. Here, too, we are ready to admit that unjust things have been done. . . . But in the manner of waging war, Germany was not the only one that erred. . . . Crimes in war may not be excusable, but they are committed in the struggle for victory, when we think only of maintaining our national existence, and are in such passion as makes the conscience of peoples blunt. The hundreds of thousands of noncombatants who have perished since November 11, because of the blockade, were destroyed coolly and deliberately after our opponents had won a certain and assured victory. Remember that, when you speak of guilt and atonement. . . .

From A. Luckau, *The German Delegation at the Paris Peace Conference* (New York: Columbia University Press, 1941), pp. 220–21.

---

7 and were given fifteen days in which to present their written observations. These resulted in only a few minor changes. The Germans, therefore, charged that this was a dictated settlement. The signing of the treaty took place on June 28, 1919, at Versailles, five years to the day after the assassination of the Austrian archduke at Sarajevo.

THE TREATY OF VERSAILLES

The peace treaty with Germany contained territorial, military, and economic clauses. It also called for the punishment

The Disillusionment of Peace

We came to Paris confident that the new order was about to be established; we left it convinced that the new order had merely fouled the old. We arrived as fervent apprentices in the school of President Wilson: we left as renegades. I wish to suggest in this chapter (and without bitterness), that this unhappy diminution of standard was very largely the fault (or one might say with greater fairness 'the misfortune') of democratic diplomacy.

We arrived determined that a Peace of justice and wisdom should be negotiated: we left it, conscious that the Treaties imposed upon our enemies were neither just nor wise. To those who desire to measure for themselves the width of the gulf which sundered intention from practice I should recommend a perusal of the several Notes addressed to the Supreme Council by the German Delegation at Versailles. . . . It is impossible to read the German criticism without deriving the impression that the Paris Peace Conference was guilty of disguising an Imperialistic peace under the surplice of Wilsonism, that seldom in the history of man has such vindictiveness cloaked itself in such unctuous sophistry. Hypocrisy was the predominant and unescapable result. Yet was this hypocrisy wholly conscious, wholly deliberate? I do not think so. . . . We did not realise what we were doing. We did not realise how far we were drifting from our original basis. We were exhausted and overworked.

From Harold Nicolson, *Peacemaking, 1919* (New York: Harcourt Brace Jovanovich, 1933), pp. 187–88.

Clemenceau, Wilson, and Lloyd George leaving the palace at Versailles after signing the peace treaty with Germany.

of "war criminals," including the kaiser. Under the territorial terms of the treaty, Germany had to surrender 13 percent of its prewar area and population. This meant a loss of more than 15 percent of its coal, close to 50 percent of its iron, and 19 percent of its iron and steel industry. Besides giving up its colonies, Germany also had to recognize the independence of Austria. This last provision was to prevent a possible *Anschluss*, or union, for which there was much sentiment in both countries.

The military clauses of the treaty called for the reduction of Germany's army to one hundred thousand volunteers. The German navy was limited to six battleships of ten thousand tons and a few smaller ships. Germany was to have no offensive weapons—submarines, aircraft, tanks, or heavy artillery—and its general staff was to be dissolved. To supervise German disarmament, an Allied Military Control Commission was appointed.

In the economic field, the precise amount of reparations to be paid by Germany was left for a Reparations Commission to decide. In the meantime Germany was to pay $5 billion in cash or in kind. France was to receive large amounts of coal to make up for the wanton destruction of its coal mines by Germany's retreating armies. Britain was given quantities of ships to compensate for the losses suffered from submarine warfare. German foreign assets of some $7 billion were confiscated; most of its rivers were internationalized; many of its patents were seized; and it was prohibited from raising tariffs above their prewar level. In short, everything possible was done to avert the threat of a renascent and vengeful Germany. The treaty was no worse than the treaties of Brest-Litovsk and Bucharest, which Germany had imposed on Russia and Rumania. Nor was it much better.

THE TREATIES
WITH GERMANY'S ALLIES

The supplementary treaties with the smaller Central Powers were signed in 1919 and 1920. The Treaty of St. Germain

Mustapha Kemal Pasha "Atatürk" (1881–1938), the first president of Turkey (1923–38).

with Austria was almost as harsh as that of Versailles. It called for the surrender of large territories to Czechoslovakia, Poland, Yugoslavia, and Italy. Not counting Hungary, the prewar area of the former empire was cut to less than one-third and its population to one-fifth. In addition, Austria's army was limited to thirty thousand men. It also had to pay large reparations and agree not to become part of Germany.

Hungary, now separated from Austria, signed its own treaty. Because of a brief communist interregnum under Bela Kun, Hungary did not sign the Treaty of Trianon until the middle of 1920. Its territorial provisions were the most severe of all the postwar treaties. After ceding lands to all its neighbors, including Aus-

tria, Hungary was left with little more than a quarter of its former territory and a third of its population. It also had to pay reparations and reduce its army.

Bulgaria, in the Treaty of Neuilly, lost the outlet to the Aegean it had gained in 1913, agreed to reparations, and had to cut its armed forces.

Turkey concluded two peace treaties, one at Sèvres in 1920 and a later one at Lausanne in 1923. The first, which called for a virtual partition of the country, was superseded by the later agreement. In the interim, a revolution of Turkish nationalists under Mustapha Kemal Pasha had completed the revolution begun by the Young Turks in 1908 and overthrown the regime of the sultan. The Allies had favored the dismemberment of Turkey and in 1919 supported the invasion of Asia Minor by Greek forces. But Turkish resistance under Mustapha Kemal finally convinced the powers that their aim was unattainable. The Allies, therefore, revised the earlier peace settlement. Under the Treaty of Lausanne, signed in July 1923, Turkey gave up everything except Asia Minor and a small foothold in Europe. It did not have to pay any reparations, and the "capitulations"—rights and privileges granted centuries ago to foreign powers—were abolished. The Straits were demilitarized and opened to ships of all nations in time of peace, but they could be closed if Turkey itself was at war. Alone among all the defeated countries, Turkey had thus been able to enforce a radical change in an initially harsh peace settlement. In October 1923 it was proclaimed a republic, with Mustapha Kemal "Atatürk" as first president.

THE AFTERMATH OF WAR

Events in Europe after 1919 were a prolonged effort on the part of all nations to overcome the effects of the war. As might be expected, the defeated countries, foremost among them Germany, were deeply opposed to the postwar settlement. They attacked it not only as too harsh but also as unjust, since it violated most of Wilson's Fourteen Points. In its attempt to sort out the hopelessly inter-

THE PEACE SETTLEMENTS IN EUROPE 1919–20

Territories lost by:

Germany

Bulgaria

Austria-Hungary

Russia

Plebiscite areas

Demilitarized Rhineland zone of Allied occupation

NATIONAL MINORITIES IN CENTRAL EUROPE   1919

Polish
German
Russian
Serbian
Croatian
Slovenian
Bosnian
Macedonian
Bulgarian
Hungarian
Rumanian
Albanian
Czechoslovakian

0   MILES   200

ians. The problem of national minorities, a source of much unrest before 1914, had not been solved by the war.

The situation looked more hopeful with respect to another prewar problem: the war, outwardly at least, had brought the victory of democracy. Popular governments replaced autocratic monarchies in central and eastern Europe and Turkey. But since the political changes in countries like Germany, Austria, and Hungary were closely associated with military defeat, democracy in these countries carried a blemish that only time and success could erase. The tense and tumultuous atmosphere of postwar Europe, however, was not conducive to the peaceful consolidation of democracy. The chaos left behind by war and revolution soon proved too much for the new and inexperienced parliamentary governments of central and eastern Europe. In their place there emerged new kinds of dictatorial and totalitarian regimes, better suited, it seemed, to cope with the emergencies of a world in crisis (see Chapter 31).

The first of these authoritarian systems arose in Russia during the 1920s. The victory of communism in that powerful Eurasian country brought an entirely new and disturbing element into international affairs. The founding of the Third Communist International ("Comintern") in 1919 by Lenin's lieutenant, Grigori Zinoviev, seemed to confirm the western fear that communism was not content to confine its influence to one country. Short-lived communist regimes in Hungary and Bavaria at the end of the war showed that communism thrived on domestic disorder. After several other attempts to engineer communist risings in Germany, Lenin finally decided to concentrate his efforts first on the communization of his own country. But the threat of communist Russia continued to frighten the statesmen of Europe until it was overshadowed in the 1930s by the more immediate threat posed by Nazi Germany.

The tripartite division of Europe into victors, vanquished, and the Soviet Union was the cause of much international unrest. To remedy this situation the Allies had created the League of Na-

Revolutionaries drive through the streets of Budapest, January 1919, in a demonstration preceding the Communist takeover in March.

mingled peoples of central Europe, for instance, the principle of self-determination was as often ignored as adhered to. In countries like Poland, Czechoslovakia, and Rumania, from one-fourth to one-third of the population consisted of alien minorities, mostly Germans or Hungar-

tions. Here was something entirely new in European history, a parliament of nations in which international problems could be discussed and solved. That was how the founders of the League had envisaged its mission. But events soon proved otherwise. When the League opened its first session at Geneva in 1921, several of the great powers were missing: Germany was not admitted until 1926, the Soviet Union became a member eight years later, and the United States never joined.

The failure of the United States to ratify the Treaty of Versailles, which also embraced the Covenant of the League of Nations, showed that Americans were not yet ready to assume the role they were destined to play as the world's most powerful nation. America's absence from the League could not help but have unfortunate results. In an assembly dominated by the European victors, the United States would have served as an impartial arbiter. The League of Nations had many shortcomings; but none was as crucial as the void left by America's refusal to become a member.

THE LEAGUE OF NATIONS AND COLLECTIVE SECURITY

The general purpose of the League was "to promote international cooperation and to achieve international peace and security." It was founded on the concept of collective security, under which peace was to be maintained by an organized community of nations rather than by an uncertain "Concert of Europe." The specific tasks of the League were: to work for international disarmament; to prevent war by arbitration of international disputes; to apply sanctions against aggressors; and to register and revise international agreements. In very few of these tasks was the League successful.

Disarmament

The Treaty of Versailles had stated that the disarmament of Germany was intended "to render possible the initiation of a general limitation of the armaments of all nations." But despite this implied promise, general disarmament was tackled most hesitantly. Only in 1926 did a Preparatory Commission begin discussions of a Disarmament Conference, and the Conference itself did not meet until 1932. Its deliberations at that time proved entirely fruitless.

There were several causes for this failure. Shortly after the war, the Allied Military Control Commission began to report a long series of German violations of the Versailles disarmament provisions. Most important were secret contacts between the new German *Reichswehr* and the Russian Red Army. The evidence of these German violations was sketchy, but it was alarming enough to keep the Allies from reducing their own military forces. Another reason for Allied failure to disarm was the difficulty of finding a valid basis for determining a nation's military power. Geographic location, manpower, industrial development, and raw materials, it was felt, were far more significant factors than the actual size of armies. In most of these factors Germany and the Soviet Union excelled, and any general disarmament would have been greatly to their advantage.

Arbitration of International Disputes

The second task of the League was to arbitrate international disputes. Members promised to bring any dispute "suitable for submission to arbitration" before the League Council. Any decision by the Council had to be "unanimously agreed to by the members thereof." If the Council's decision was not unanimous, League members were free to take whatever action they deemed appropriate. Despite the vagueness of these provisions, the League was able to settle a number of international conflicts. Of some thirty cases submitted during the 1920s, the majority were arbitrated. The League was most effective in settling disputes between small powers. As soon as a major power was involved, however, the League proved quite powerless. In the "Corfu incident" of 1923, for instance, when Italy bombarded and occupied the Greek island of Corfu in retaliation for the murder of some Italians, the

Italian government refused to acknowledge the League's competency.

Sanctions Against Aggression

The League's procedure for dealing with military aggression was laid down in Article 16 of the Covenant. As major punishment it provided for economic sanctions against the guilty party. To be effective, this policy needed the cooperation of all the great powers. But since two or more of them usually were outside the League, the application of strict economic sanctions proved impossible. This became evident at the time of Japan's invasion of China in 1931 and Italy's war against Abyssinia in 1935. Article 16 also provided for military sanctions, but these were left entirely to individual members. The League itself maintained no armed forces.

Treaty Revision

The registration and publication of international agreements, called for under Article 18 of the Covenant, was intended to prevent the "secret diplomacy" that Wilson had blamed for helping to start the war. Even so, most serious diplomatic negotiations after the war still went on behind closed doors, and the fear of secret treaties persisted. More significant than the publication of treaties was the provision made in Article 19 of the Covenant for the revision of existing treaties. Here was a possibility for peaceful changes in the peace treaties, once the hatreds of war had cooled down. Had the

Will it work?—a cartoon portraying League of Nations sanctions against Italy as a robotlike contraption constructed by League members. The sanctions against Italy for its invasion of Ethiopia in 1935 did not work.

Will It Work?

powers availed themselves of this opportunity, Europe and the world might have been spared the Second World War.

Clearly the League of Nations suffered from many weaknesses. Most of these could have been eliminated had the great powers been ready to do so. But since each of them was primarily concerned with its own selfish aims, the hopeful experiment of the League turned out a failure. Only in fields that involved none of the vital interests of the great powers did the League score any gains. The League's Mandate Commission was able to improve the standard of colonial administration. The International Labor Organization, affiliated with the League, did much to raise the status of workers everywhere. Various other League agencies concerned themselves with matters of health, the illicit drug traffic, the international arms trade, and so forth. These agencies set important precedents for the far-reaching activities of the United Nations today.

THE "WAR AFTER THE WAR," 1919–23

For several years after the Peace Conference, Europe underwent so many major and minor international crises that people sometimes wondered if the war had really come to an end. Until the fall of 1919, the Allies intervened against the Bolshevik regime in Russia. Poland fought with Lithuania over the town of Vilna, with Czechoslovakia over the region of Teschen, and with Russia over its eastern frontiers. Polish and German irregular forces fought bloody battles over Upper Silesia in 1922. Intermittent conflicts between Italy and Yugoslavia over Fiume lasted until 1924. The Greeks invaded Turkey between 1919 and 1922 and almost came to blows with Italy in 1923. Austria and Hungary clashed over the Burgenland region in 1921. And in 1923 Germany's default in reparation payments led to the invasion of its key industrial region, the Ruhr district, by French and Belgian troops. These were only the more noteworthy among an unending series of international incidents during the early postwar period.

The French Search for Security

The greatest danger to peace was Germany's desire to escape the restrictions of Versailles. This worried the French in particular. The alliance between France and the Anglo-Saxon powers that had been envisaged at the Peace Conference failed to materialize when America withdrew from the peace settlement. Since Germany was still far superior in human and industrial resources, the French felt that their security demanded the strictest fulfillment of the peace terms. But this insistence on fulfillment caused a growing rift between France and Great Britain. The British now were trying to dissociate themselves from continental affairs and to devote their attention to overseas interests. Germany was no longer a serious economic and naval rival; and since Germany had been one of England's best customers before the war, Britain wanted it to get back on its feet. Moreover, England felt that a healthy Germany was the best protection against the westward spread of communism. When France invaded the Ruhr in 1923, therefore, Britain expressed its disapproval. It had no desire to see the French assume hegemony over the Continent.

The loss of British support forced France to look elsewhere for security. With Russia disqualified by communism and Italy dissatisfied with the peace settlement, only the smaller "succession states" of central Europe were left. In 1921 France concluded an alliance with Poland, in 1926 with Rumania, and in 1927 with Yugoslavia. In addition, Rumania, Yugoslavia, and Czechoslovakia began to organize the "Little Entente" in 1921. All these countries were interested in maintaining the status quo, which was being threatened by the revisionist agitation not only of Germany but of Hungary and Russia as well. Outwardly this French alliance system looked quite impressive. But the total military strength of these small powers was less than a million men, and they required a great deal of French financial aid. As an attempt, furthermore, to isolate Germany, the French system was doomed from the start, for the two outcasts of Europe— Germany and Russia—began to draw together in 1922.

The Russo-German Rapprochement

Russo-German relations after the war at first were strained. The Russians still remembered Brest-Litovsk, and the Germans resented Russia's repeated attempts to stir up revolutions in Germany. Common economic and military interests, however, gradually led to a political *rapprochement*. The first outward sign of this understanding was a treaty of friendship concluded at Rapallo in April 1922. The world was startled and disturbed by what it suspected of being a military alliance. But the Treaty of Rapallo was merely a promise of cooperation between the two partners, important chiefly because it helped Germany escape its diplomatic isolation. There were people in both Germany and Russia who hoped that the treaty would some day develop into something more. But this hope was never fulfilled. Economically the two countries were quite complementary, and both stood to gain from mutual trade. But differences in their economic systems made such an exchange difficult. Despite some later economic and neutrality agreements, Russo-German relations throughout the 1920s remained decidedly cool.

The Ruhr Occupation

The French occupation of the Ruhr in 1923 marked a turning point in the history of postwar Europe. Deprived of its major industrial region, Germany was thrown into an economic crisis, which was made more serious by the passive resistance the people of the Ruhr put up against the French. The German government, faced with paying the Ruhr workers' wages, ran the printing presses overtime to "make money," thereby escalating an already severe inflation. By cutting the coal France hoped to get from the Ruhr, the resisters in the Ruhr contributed to French economic difficulties as well. The German government, which feared for the nation's existence, finally

A trainload of coal on its way to France during the occupation of the Ruhr in 1923.

called off the passive resistance and so ended the Ruhr struggle. There were communist disturbances in central Germany and separatist uprisings in the Rhineland. In the south an unknown ex-corporal, Adolf Hitler, was getting ready to make his first try for power.

The Ruhr episode taught an important lesson to both French and Germans. It showed that rigid insistence on the fulfillment of the Versailles Treaty on the one hand, and stubborn resistance against such fulfillment on the other, helped neither side. Both, it seemed, had to give way if Europe was to be saved from chaos. For the next six years a group of dedicated statesmen devoted their efforts to bringing about such a compromise.

THE "ERA OF LOCARNO" 1924–29

The year 1924 saw important political changes in both France and England. In France the rightist cabinet of Raymond Poincaré, known for his vengeful attitude toward Germany, was replaced after the Ruhr fiasco by a left-wing coalition in which Aristide Briand was foreign minis-

ter. In England the Labour Party had a brief inning in 1924 but soon gave way to a Conservative government with Austen Chamberlain as foreign secretary. In Germany the direction of foreign policy after the Ruhr crisis was in the hands of Gustav Stresemann. Together, Briand, Chamberlain, and Stresemann brought Europe a brief respite from fear and uncertainty.

The Locarno Pact

Europe's brief return to stability after 1924 was chiefly due to a more efficient handling of the reparations problem. Without these economic developments, the *rapprochement* between Germany and the western powers would hardly have come about. The first political result of this *rapprochement* was the Locarno Pact.

Under the terms of the Treaty of Versailles, the Allies were to end their occupation of the Rhineland in three phases, beginning in 1925. But since the Allied Military Control Commission had found Germany guilty of disarmament violations, the Allies refused to leave. Stresemann realized that the basic reason for this refusal was France's fear of Germany. To dispel this fear once and for all, he now proposed a treaty by which not only France and Germany, but also England, Italy, and Belgium would guarantee the status quo in western Europe. Such a treaty was signed at Locarno in October 1925.

To a world torn by international strife for more than a decade, the Locarno Pact came as a harbinger of a new age in which peace and good will rather than war and suspicion would prevail. "We are citizens each of his own country," Stresemann said at Locarno, "but we are also citizens of Europe and are joined together by a great concept of civilization." This seeming conversion of Stresemann from a rabid German na-

German Foreign Minister Dr. Gustav Stresemann addressing the League of Nations for the last time, September 9, 1929, shortly before his death.

tionalist into a "good European" commanded the admiration of his contemporaries. But Stresemann was less of an idealist than people thought. He was every bit as eager to abolish the restrictions of Versailles as were his nationalist compatriots. Where Stresemann differed was in his realization that the revision of Versailles could not be achieved by force but only through patient negotiation, once Germany had regained the confidence of the world.

The *rapprochement* between Germany and the West, meanwhile, was causing growing apprehension in the Soviet Union. Despite Russia's resumption of diplomatic relations with France and England in 1924, it had remained an outsider in international affairs. England in particular resented the propagandist activities of the Comintern, and in 1927 once again severed its connections with the Soviets. What Russia feared most was that Germany, as a member of the League, might some day be forced to participate in sanctions against the Soviet Union. To quiet these Russian fears Stresemann, at Locarno, had obtained a modification of Article 16 of the League Covenant, allowing Germany to abstain from participating in any sanctions that endangered its own security. When this still did not satisfy the Russians, Stresemann in April 1926 signed a treaty of neutrality with them. Some saw this Treaty of Berlin as an attempt on Germany's part to play a double game between the East and the West. But there is no doubt that Stresemann's foremost concern was always for closer and stronger relations between Germany and the West.

The Kellogg-Briand Pact

The efforts of the powers to guarantee Europe's security by treaties that would bolster the collective security system of the League climaxed in the signing of the Pact of Paris, or Kellogg-Briand Pact, in August 1928. Its sixty-two signatories, which included the United States, promised "to renounce war as an instrument of national policy." Nothing was more characteristic of the spirit of hopefulness that pervaded the world after

Locarno than this attempt to banish war simply by signing a treaty. The Soviet Union was the only major power not present in Paris, but it joined the pact soon thereafter. If security depended on treaties, the world had nothing more to fear.

THE ECONOMIC CONSEQUENCES OF THE WAR

The economic consequences of the war were even more serious than its political aftermath. The territorial losses of Germany and the dismemberment of Aus-

---

The Kellogg-Briand Pact

Secretary of State Frank B. Kellogg came to Paris with a bouquet of white lilies in one hand and in the other a pen to sign a pact. He was a little old man who looked like a little old woman who resembles a little old man. . . . Stresemann came too; this was the first time a German foreign minister had visited Paris since the Franco-Prussian War of 1871. But he was gravely ill, and when he went to pay his respects to Prime Minister Poincaré, a doctor waited in the anteroom. After an hour the doctor sent a written message to Poincaré beseeching him to order Stresemann home to bed.

The Kellogg-Briand Pact was signed on August 27, 1928, at the Quai d'Orsay in the Salle de l'Horloge, amid an orgy of marbles, velvets, silks, all exquisitely blended, spiced with silver and gold. . . . The scenery must have been pleasing to Richelieu's ghost; but this was an American affair. . . . Now for the first time I saw Hollywood intrude into the plush-carpeted sanctum of a Foreign Office . . . platoons of sweating technicians in shirtsleeves installed 35-millimeter film howitzers that spied down upon the horseshoe table where "those guys" (as I learned engineers refer to ministers) would perform. As the statesmen entered the room (Poincaré stumbling over the cables), the klieg lights exploded in a pink glow, and all the eighteenth-century Venetian luster of crystal and candles was snuffed out by the crude and sober floodlight of twentieth-century technology.

The pact was signed by fifteen nations, with a heavy gold fountain pen especially manufactured for the occasion. It bore the inscription: "If you want peace, prepare for peace." Kellogg took up the pen with trembling hand, but it was too heavy for the old man, and a French secretary had to help him affix his name.

The Kellogg-Briand Pact has been ineffective in practice every time it has been invoked. . . . It was not a pact, after all, so much as a declaration against sin.

From Emerey Kelen, *Peace in Their Time* (New York: Knopf, 1963), pp. 168–69.

Runaway inflation in Germany. Above: a 2 billion mark note; below: marks being baled as waste paper.

tria-Hungary by themselves caused a major economic shock among the defeated powers. The Allies added to their distress by making seemingly limitless demands for reparations. But the victors, too, found the going far from easy. In the West, France and Belgium suffered from the devastation of their industrial regions. In eastern Europe, lack of seed, fertilizers, and agricultural implements resulted in a marked decline of farm production. All the powers, England in particular, had lost important foreign markets. And a general return to protective tariffs retarded recovery everywhere.

The effects of the postwar economic crisis were felt in many ways. Five years after the war Europe's total industrial production was still at only two-thirds of its prewar level. Unemployment, never much of a problem in the past, now assumed alarming proportions. Another repercussion of the crisis was felt in financial matters. All the major countries of Europe suffered from severe inflation. In Germany, Austria, and Russia, this inflation led to total devaluation of the currency.

The Reparations Problem

Much of the responsibility for Europe's economic difficulties rested with the peacemakers of 1919. In their efforts to solve the Continent's political problems, they often ignored the economic effects of their decisions. They carved new states out of old empires without regard to economic consequences. They even failed to examine the probable effects of the purely economic terms of the peace. A member of the British peace delegation, the economist John Maynard Keynes, called attention to these oversights in his book *The Economic Consequences of the Peace* (1920), a sweeping indictment of the Versailles settlement on economic grounds. The most troublesome part of the treaty, as Keynes foresaw, turned out to be the reparations provisions. In order to pay the large sums called for, the defeated nations needed surplus capital. This they could gain only through increased exports. But such exports competed with the products of the

very nations who hoped to profit from reparations. The transfer of large amounts of capital, furthermore, had unsettling effects on the economies of debtors and creditors alike. It was easy, in other words, to ask for huge reparations, but it was difficult to devise sound, workable methods of paying them.

The reparations problem was further complicated by the mutual indebtedness of the victors. The easiest way out would have been the cancellation of all inter-Allied debts. This solution was proposed by Britain and France but was rejected by the United States, who would have ended up paying for the whole war. America's refusal made the European Allies more than ever dependent on reparations.

The main source of reparations was Germany. The total amount of Germany's obligations had been left open at the Peace Conference. It was later settled at $32 billion in 1921. From the start Germany fell behind in its payments. The French, who were to receive more than half of the reparations, were adamant in their demands for prompt payment. The climax of France's insistence on fulfillment came with the invasion of the Ruhr in 1923.

The Dawes Plan and the Young Plan

Prior to this time, America had suggested that the whole reparations issue be studied by an international committee of experts. With the failure of the Ruhr venture, such a committee was appointed late in 1923. It worked out a plan, named after its chairman, the American financier Charles G. Dawes, which went into effect in September 1924. Under the Dawes Plan, Germany was to pay gradually rising amounts that were to reach a "standard annuity" in 1929. The Dawes Plan worked well. But, more than was generally realized, Germany's ability to pay depended on the influx of foreign loans. With the return of general confidence in its economic stability, Germany began to attract large amounts of capital, especially from the United States. This flow continued until 1929, when American investors began to speculate at home.

Since at the same time Germany's yearly payments under the Dawes Plan were about to reach the "standard annuity," and since no time limit had been set on such payments, it seemed a good time to reconsider the whole reparations question.

A series of meetings between German and foreign experts during 1929 finally led to the Young Plan, named after the American expert Owen D. Young. It fixed Germany's total obligations at $29 billion, to be paid over fifty-nine years. But the Young Plan never went into effect. As the Great Depression spread from the United States to Europe, Germany ceased its payments altogether. At a final conference in Lausanne in 1932, Germany was relieved of any future obligations. Opinions differ widely on the total amount of reparations actually paid by Germany. A likely estimate puts it at $6 billion. This was not only far less than originally demanded, but in return Germany had received a far larger amount in foreign loans. The history of reparations has been compared to a merry-go-round: Germany borrowed American funds to pay reparations to the Allies, who used the money to repay their debts to the United States, who lent the money back to Germany.

EUROPEAN RECOVERY

American capital played an important role in the economic life of Europe. Most of America's loans were private and short-term. Their repayment was made even more difficult by the American government's tariff policy. Instead of helping foreign debtors to meet their obligations through increased exports, the United States surrounded itself with high tariff walls. This policy soon provoked a worldwide wave of protectionism. Insistent warnings by European economists against such shortsightedness finally led the League of Nations to call a World Economic Conference in 1927. In their final report, the delegates of the more than fifty participating nations urged their governments to lower tariffs as soon and as much as possible. Before this advice was taken, the Great Depression

began. Not least among its causes was the protectionist policy of the postwar years.

Except for its warning on tariffs, however, the World Economic Conference was quite optimistic. Europe's economy after 1925 seemed to justify such optimism. France had rebuilt its destroyed regions, had modernized its industry, and had stabilized its currency. Germany had recovered from the shock of inflation and with the aid of foreign loans had improved its industries so that once again it was the industrial leader of Europe. England's recovery was made much slower by its adherence to the gold standard, its antiquated production methods, and the high living standard of its workers. In Italy, the Fascist government of Benito Mussolini successfully raised the nation's food production. Even in Russia the "New Economic Policy," with its partial return to capitalist practices, brought gradual economic recovery and some relief from the aftermath of war and revolution.

But this apparent economic recovery also had its weak points. It was chiefly restricted to industry. Agriculture continued to suffer from overproduction and foreign competition. The resulting decline of rural buying power reacted upon industry. Some producers, tempted by American loans and the example of American mass-production methods, expanded far beyond the need of their markets. When, after the crash of the American stock market in October 1929, American loans to Europe ceased and old loans were recalled, Europe's economy, deprived of this financial infusion, collapsed.

Within one decade, Europe had thus come full cycle from despair through hope and back to despair. In the early 1920s it had seemed that the German Oswald Spengler had been right in his best seller *The Decline of the West* (1918), which predicted the impending doom of European civilization. But then in the mid-1920s a "silver lining" had appeared on the horizon. The optimism of the "Era of Locarno" may appear unjustified in retrospect. But to contemporaries the decrease of international tension, the economic recovery, and the general air of

Unemployment in Britain in 1930 afflicted all levels of society.

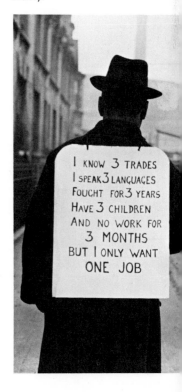

I KNOW 3 TRADES
I SPEAK 3 LANGUAGES
FOUGHT FOR 3 YEARS
HAVE 3 CHILDREN
AND NO WORK FOR
3 MONTHS
BUT I ONLY WANT
ONE JOB

well-being and stability seemed quite real. They were seen as proof that Europe at long last had found the peace it had so long been looking for. One may rightly wonder what would have happened if the recovery of Europe had lasted for another decade. In any attempt to find the causes of the unhappy events of the 1930s and 1940s, the Great Depression will always loom large.

Suggestions for Further Reading

Note: Asterisk denotes a book available in paperback edition.

General There are many volumes covering world history since 1914. One of the most interesting and original is C. Quigley, *Tragedy and Hope: A History of the World in Our Time* (1966). Other recommended books are F. P. Chambers, *This Age of Conflict: The Western World—1914 to the Present*, 3rd ed. (1962), and, for the years between the two World Wars, R. J. Sontag, *A Broken World, 1919–1939** (1971). D. Thomson, ed., *The Era of Violence, 1898–1945* (1960), Vol. XII in the *New Cambridge Modern History* series, includes contributions by noted specialists on every facet of European and world history. The declining influence of Europe in world affairs is the theme of a small volume by H. Holborn, *The Political Collapse of Europe** (1954). R. Aron, *The Century of Total War** (1955), is a thoughtful analysis of world events in the twentieth century, and G. Barraclough, *An Introduction to Contemporary History** (1964), presents a stimulating discussion of modern issues.

The First World War The military side of the war is told in B. H. Liddell Hart, *The War in Outline** (1936), and C. Falls, *The Great War, 1914–1918** (1936). M. Ferro, *The Great War, 1914–1918* (1973), and G. P. Hayes, *World War I: A Compact History* (1972), are more recent treatments. On the home fronts, see J. Williams, *The Other Battleground: The Home Fronts—Britain, France and Germany, 1914–1918* (1972); G. D. Feldman, *Army, Industry, and Labor, 1914–1918* (1966), which deals with Germany; A. J. May, *The Passing of the Hapsburg Monarchy*, 2 vols. (1966); A. Fontaine, *French Industry During the War* (1962); E. L. Woodward, *Great Britain and the War of 1914–1918** (1967); and A. Marwick, *The Deluge: British Society and the First World War** (1970). The diplomatic history of the war years is covered in Z. A. B. Zeman, *The Gentlemen Negotiators: A Diplomatic History of the First World War* (1971). The problem of war aims is treated in F. Fischer, *Germany's Aims in the First World War** (1967); H. W. Gatzke, *Germany's Drive to the West** (1950); and W. R. Louis, *Great Britain and Germany's Lost Colonies, 1914–1919* (1967). America's involvement in the war is discussed in A. S. Link, *Wilson the Diplomatist** (1957), and E. R. May, *The World War and American Isolation* (1959). For a briefer assessment, see D. M. Smith, *The Great Departure: The United States and World War I** (1964). The following are important monographs on various aspects of the war: J. C. King, *Generals and Politicians: Conflict Between France's High Command, Parliament and Government, 1914–1918* (1951); P. Guinn, *British Strategy and Politics, 1914 to 1918* (1965); M. C. Siney, *The Allied Blockade of Germany, 1914–1916* (1957); and J. M. Read, *Atrocity Propaganda, 1914–1919* (1941). For a more vivid impression of the war, the following are highly recommended: B. W. Tuchman, *The Guns of August** (1962); L. Wolff, *In Flanders Fields: The 1917 Campaign** (1958); and A. J. P. Taylor, *The First World War: An Illustrated History* (1963).

The Russian Revolution W. H. Chamberlain, *The Russian Revolution, 1917–1921*, 2 vols. (1952), is a standard work. E. H. Carr, *A History of Soviet Russia: The Bolshevik Revolution, 1917–1923,** 3 vols. (1950–53), is scholarly but controversial. G. Katkov, *Russia 1917: The February Revolution* (1967), is an important study. Other recent studies include R. V. Daniels, *The Russian Revolution** (1972); A. Rabinowitch, *The Bolsheviks Come to Power* (1976); and J. L. H. Keep, *The Russian Revolution: A Study in Mass Mobilization* (1976). The background of the Revolution is treated authoritatively in A. B. Ulam, *The Bolsheviks: The Intellectual and Political History of the Triumph of Communism in Russia* (1965). The peace negotiations between Russia and the Central Powers are described by J. W. Wheeler-Bennett, *Brest-Litovsk: The Forgotten Peace, March 1918** (1939). Allied intervention is dealt with in G. F. Kennan, *Russia Leaves the War** (1956) and *The Decision to Intervene** (1958), and R. H. Ullman, *Anglo-Soviet Relations, 1917–1921,** 2 vols. (1961, 1968). On developments among Russia's national minorities, see R. Pipes, *The Formation of the Soviet Union: Communism and Nationalism, 1917–1923* (1954). O. H. Radkey, *Agrarian Foes of Bolshevism* (1958), deals with the Socialist Revolutionaries during the Revolution.

Several participants have provided their own version of events: L. Trotsky, *The History of the Russian Revolution*, 3 vols. (1932); V. M. Chernov, *The Great Russian Revolution* (1936); N. N. Sukhanov, *The Russian Revolution 1917: A Personal Record* (1955); A. F. Kerensky, *The Kerensky Memoirs* (1966); and P. T. Wrangel, *The Memoirs of General Wrangel* (1929). A vivid eyewitness account by a young American communist is J. Reed, *Ten Days That Shook the World** (1919).

Revolution in Central Europe

The last days of the war are treated in H. R. Rudin, *Armistice, 1918* (1944); F. Maurice, *The Armistices of 1918* (1943); and K. F. Nowak, *The Collapse of Central Europe* (1924). On the overthrow of the Hohenzollern and Habsburg dynasties, see A. J. Ryder, *The German Revolution of 1918* (1967); Z. A. B. Zeman, *The Break-Up of the Habsburg Empire, 1914–1918* (1961); and F. L. Carsten, *Revolution in Central Europe, 1918–1919* (1972). Both A. Rosenberg, *The Birth of the German Republic, 1871–1918** (1931), and O. Jászi, *The Dissolution of the Habsburg Monarchy** (1929), put events in their respective countries into historical perspective. H. Seton-Watson, *Eastern Europe Between the Wars, 1918–1941,** rev. ed. (1962); J. Rothschild, *East Central Europe Between the Two World Wars* (1974); and S. Borsody, *The Tragedy of Central Europe** (1960), deal with the problems of the small succession states.

The Peace Treaties

The standard history of the Peace Conference is H. W. V. Temperley, *A History of the Peace Conference of Paris*, 6 vols. (1920–24). A. J. Mayer, *Politics and Diplomacy of Peacemaking** (1967), emphasizes the peacemakers' fear of communism, as does J. M. Thompson, *Russia, Bolshevism, and the Versailles Peace* (1966). H. Nicolson, *Peacemaking, 1919** (1933), vividly captures the atmosphere of the negotiations. See also A. Headlam-Morley, *Sir James Headlam-Morley: A Memoir of the Paris Peace Conference, 1919* (1972). The following deal with inter-Allied relations before and during the Peace Conference: H. I. Nelson, *Land and Power: British and Allied Policy on Germany's Frontiers, 1916–1919* (1963); S. P. Tillman, *Anglo-American Relations at the Paris Peace Conference of 1919* (1961); and A. J. Mayer, *Political Origins of the New Diplomacy, 1917–1918** (1959). The classic indictment of the Versailles settlement is J. M. Keynes, *The Economic Consequences of the Peace* (1920). It is challenged in E. Mantoux, *The Carthaginian Peace, or the Economic Consequences of Mr. Keynes** (1946). P. Birdsall, *Versailles Twenty Years After* (1941), is a judicious reappraisal of the treaty. See also R. B. McCallum, *Public Opinion and the Last Peace* (1944). On the peace settlements with Austria, Hungary, and Turkey, see N. Almond and R. H. Lutz, *The Treaty of St. Germain* (1939); F. Deak, *Hungary at the Paris Peace Conference* (1942); and P. C. Helmreich, *From Paris to Sèvres: The Partition of the Ottoman Empire at the Peace Conference of 1919–1920* (1974). America's part in the negotiations is reassessed in T. A. Bailey, *Wilson and the Peacemakers* (1947). See also V. S. Mamatey, *The United States and East Central Europe, 1914–1918* (1957).

The Aftermath of War

There is no satisfactory general work in English on international relations between the two wars, although E. H. Carr, *International Relations Between the Two World Wars, 1919–1939** (1947), is an admirable summary. It should be supplemented by the same author's thoughtful analysis of international politics in *The Twenty Years' Crisis, 1919–1939** (1946). S. Marks, *The Illusion of Peace: International Relations, 1918–1933** (1976), covers a shorter period. W. W. Gatzke, ed., *European Diplomacy Between Two Wars, 1919–1939** (1972), is a collection of articles on various aspects of postwar European diplomacy. On British foreign policy, see F. S. Northedge, *The Troubled Giant: Britain Among the Great Powers, 1916–1939* (1946), and W. N. Medlicott, *British Foreign Policy Since Versailles, 1919–1963,** rev. ed. (1968). Differences between the western powers are treated in A. Wolfers, *Britain and France Between Two Wars** (1940), and W. M. Jordan, *Great Britain, France, and the German Problem, 1918–1939* (1943). See also K. L. Nelson, *Victors Divided: America and the Allies in Germany, 1918–1923* (1976), and L. Kochan, *The Struggle for Germany** (1963). Russo-German relations are covered in K. Rosenbaum, *Community of Fate: German-Soviet Relations, 1922–1928* (1965), and H. Dyck, *Weimar Germany and Soviet Russia, 1926–1933* (1966). Germany's relations with the western powers are the subject of J. Jacobson, *Locarno Diplomacy: Germany and the West, 1925–1929* (1972). German agitation over "war guilt" is criticized by L. Fraser, *Germany Between Two Wars: A Study of Propaganda and War Guilt* (1944). On Germany's attempts to evade the disarmament restrictions of Versailles, see H. W. Gatzke, *Stresemann and the Rearmament of Germany** (1954). The reparations problem is surveyed in the book by E. Mantoux cited in the section above, and in K. Bergmann, *The History of Reparations* (1927). See also D. H. Aldcroft, *From Versailles to Wall Street: The International Economy in the 1920's* (1976). S. A. Schuker, *The End of French Predominance in Europe: The Financial Crisis of 1924 and the Adoption of the Dawes Plan* (1976), is an admirable book. The standard history of the League of Nations is F. P. Walters, *A History of the League of Nations*, 2 vols. (1952). See also G. Scott, *The Rise and Fall of the League of Nations* (1973). G. A. Craig and F. Gilbert, eds., *The Diplomats, 1919–1939** (1953), is a collection of lively essays on the making and makers of interwar diplomacy.

Delegates to the Second Hague Conference were caught napping by Erich Salomon, whom Aristide Briand called "the king of the indiscreets."

31 Democracy in Crisis

As in international affairs, the Great War also brought about deep changes in the domestic affairs of the major powers during the "long armistice" between 1919 and 1939. Before 1914 the countries of Europe, despite national differences, still had much in common. What feeling of European unity there had been then was gone by 1919. The Continent was divided into victors and vanquished, "have" and "have-not" nations. Among the latter were not only the countries that had lost the war but countries, like Italy and Russia, that felt dissatisfied with the peace settlements. It was in these "revisionist" powers that a new type of totalitarian government arose, which, more than anything else, helped to destroy the traditional unity of Europe (see Chapter 32).

The Continent's unique role in world affairs was also beginning to be challenged. As the United States gradually emerged from its isolation, and as regions that hitherto had been firmly dominated by Europe began to play a role of their own, Europe's longstanding predominance faded. World politics gradually overshadowed European politics.

THE AFTERMATH OF WAR 1919–29

One of the major war aims of the western powers had been the triumph of democracy over autocracy. This aim seemed to have been achieved with the rise of democratic governments everywhere east of the Rhine. But the war left so many unsolved problems that even countries with a democratic tradition, like France and England, found it difficult to return from the semiauthoritarian and efficient conduct of war to the more democratic and less efficient pursuits of peace. It is not surprising, therefore, that some of the new democratic nations found it hard to cope with the aftermath of war and that their new democracy in many cases turned out to be short-lived.

Stability in Great Britain

Among the western powers, Great Britain enjoyed by far the most stable domestic development. Democracy scored a success when Britain's franchise was extended to all adults in two further reform acts in 1918 and 1928. But while women were thus at long last granted the political rights they deserved, the economic advantages they had gained during the war were soon again curtailed. Transition from war to peace was made easier by the reelection of Lloyd George's coalition cabinet in 1918 and by a brief industrial boom. Beginning in 1920, however, England underwent an extended economic crisis. Its political effect was to shift power away from the Liberals, first toward the Conservatives and later to Labour.

During most of the 1920s Britain was ruled by the Conservatives, who tried valiantly but vainly to tackle the perennial problems of a large deficit and widespread unemployment. In the elections of 1929 Labour finally won its first major victory. But even this did not give it sufficient strength to introduce decisive economic reforms. The solution of England's economic difficulties had to wait until after the Great Depression.

Despite its unsettled economy, Britain had no serious domestic disturbances. There was some unrest among the workers, and in 1926 trouble in the coal mines led to a general strike. But there was no violence. A certain innate moderation seemed to make the average Englishman poor material for radical agitation from either right or left. The Labour Party, though accused of being "soft" on communism, was always moderate in its program and policy; and the Conservatives, though eager to curb the power of the labor unions, were sincerely concerned about the workingman's welfare. The government's policy of maintaining a stable currency was detrimental to British trade, since it hampered competition on the world market. But it also saved Britain's middle class from the de-

British Women in Industry

During the War women passed rapidly into trades hitherto considered unsuitable for them. . . . Because of this increase in numbers, as well as owing to the efficiency shown by women in every type of occupation, the Women's Employment Committee foresaw an extension of openings for women not only in industry, but in the higher branches of commerce, and believed that employers would gladly continue to use them after the War in the work formerly done by men in shops, such as managing, buying and travelling. . . . These sanguine hopes were doomed to disappointment. The War had certainly given the world an object lesson in woman's achievement, but men in general showed a disturbing tendency to be appalled rather than encouraged by this demonstration of unexpected ability. . . . While employers were quite ready to offer "equal pay by results" in trades to which women were not well adapted, they were most opposed to it in such industries as engineering and aircraft wood-working, in the light processes of which women notoriously excelled men. . . . By the autumn of 1919 three-quarters of a million of the women employed at the time of the Armistice had been dismissed, and the position of women in general could "certainly not be described as enviable."

From V. Brittain, *Women's Work in Modern England* (London: Noel Douglas, 1928), pp. 8–15, as quoted in W. C. Langsam, ed., *Documents and Readings in the History of Europe Since 1918* (New York: Lippincott, 1951), pp. 275–77.

moralizing effects of inflation that were felt in most continental countries.

Instability in France

France led a far more hectic existence after the war. It was worse off economically, having suffered greater losses in money and in manpower than Britain. Moreover, the French electoral system of proportional representation, introduced after the First World War, aggravated the excessive factionalism of French politics and caused great instability. There were more than forty different cabinets during the interwar period. For the first five years after the war France was governed by a "national bloc" of rightist and center parties, with Raymond Poincaré as the leading figure. In 1924 reversals in foreign policy, notably the Ruhr fiasco, brought to power a "Cartel of the Left," in which Édouard Herriot and Aristide Briand were prominent.

The most urgent task before the French government was the reconstruction of the devastated regions along the northeastern frontiers. Since Germany, until 1924, remained behind in its reparations payments, France had to pay for this reconstruction. Attempts to raise the necessary funds through increased taxation ran into opposition from the parties of the right. Only the threat of runaway inflation and the pressure of public demonstrations finally led to drastic action. In 1926 a cabinet of "national union" under Poincaré was able to stabilize the currency and put France on the road to recovery. With reconstruction completed and German reparations coming in regularly, France's economy improved rapidly. By 1928 the budget began to show a surplus, unemployment had vanished, and increased wages together with benefits from social legislation gave the lower classes a greater share than before in the nation's economy. France seemed well on the way toward resolving the longstanding conflicts between its rich and its poor.

The Weimar Republic

The new German republic was from the beginning plagued by disunity and disorder. Early in 1919 a constituent assembly at Weimar had drawn up an admirably democratic constitution. One of its less happy features, however, was the adoption of proportional representation. As in France, this scheme contributed greatly to political instability. During the fourteen years of its existence, the Weimar Republic saw more than twenty different cabinets. The heavy legacy of war required a government that had the full support of its citizens. Throughout most of its brief life, the Weimar Republic failed to win such support.

The most loyal friends of the republic were the workers who had suffered most from political discrimination under the empire. The German working class, however, was no longer united. It had been split before and during the revolution of 1918 into a moderate majority of Social Democrats and a radical minority that later formed the German Communist Party. The latter openly threatened to overthrow the republic and on several occasions between 1919 and 1923 tried to carry out its threat.

Most of the bourgeois parties of the Weimar Republic professed loyalty to the new regime, although the parties of the right were known to be hostile to it. This hostility was nourished by nationalist propaganda, which blamed the republic both for Germany's defeat and for the signing of the *Diktat* of Versailles. Soon after the war, rabidly nationalistic groups of "free corps" and veterans' organizations embarked on a series of uprisings against the hated republic.

Considering the many attacks from every direction, it is surprising that the Weimar Republic was able to survive. But even though most Germans were not very enthusiastic about the new state, they were even less enthusiastic about the extremists who threatened to overthrow it. In the early 1920s the moderate antirepublican parties of the right were able to attract almost 30 percent of the vote. The most critical year in the postwar decade was 1923, when the French invasion of the Ruhr, antirepublican risings on the right and left, and the total devaluation of the currency threatened the country's very existence. But as Germany's economy improved after 1924, the prorepublican parties made signifi-

A Nazi coalition poster of 1924 addressing an anti-Semitic appeal to the "exploited" working class in Germany.

cant gains at the expense of the opposition. Had this recovery lasted longer, the Germans might yet have become reconciled to their new republic.

The New Nations of Eastern Europe

If democracy found the going rough in Germany, it faced even greater difficulties in eastern Europe. Most of the states in this area had gained their independence as a result of the war, and most of them faced similar problems. With the exception of Austria and Czechoslovakia, their economy was predominantly agrarian, and the division of large estates among the peasantry had long been a major issue. Where such land reform was carried out successfully, as in the Baltic states, the rise of independent small proprietors contributed greatly to political stability. In Poland and Hungary, on the other hand, where reform was obstructed by the landed aristocracy, domestic peace remained precarious.

Economic recovery in most of eastern Europe was slow. Widespread illiteracy, antiquated agricultural methods, and lack of capital funds for industrialization were the main obstacles. Efforts at economic collaboration, especially among the Austrian succession states, ran into strong nationalist opposition. Nationalism in eastern Europe was intensified by the problem of minorities. Almost all the new nations included large numbers of foreign nationals.

All the new states started out with modern constitutions and parliamentary governments. But this democratic trend was soon reversed. The first to change was Hungary. After a brief communist interlude under Bela Kun in 1919, conservative forces restored order under Admiral Nicholas Horthy, who founded Europe's first postwar dictatorship of the right. In Poland the rise of authoritarian rule came with Marshal Joseph Pilsudski's seizure of power in 1926. Elsewhere "strong men" suspended constitutions and silenced political opposition. With no democratic experience and hopeless economic conditions, firm rule seemed to be the only alternative. None of these regimes was as totalitarian as the communist dictatorship in Russia or the fascist dictatorship in Italy. It was only after Hitler's rise in the 1930s, when fascism gained control over most of central Europe, that the rule of these small dictators became increasingly arbitrary (see Chapter 32).

Of the few countries in eastern Europe where democracy took hold after

German Inflation

The prewar value of the German mark was twenty-five cents. When I first went to Munich at the end of 1921, I already could get about a hundred marks for a dollar. A year later I was getting about sixty-five hundred marks for the dollar. Then, in January 1923, French armies marched into Germany's richest industrial region, the Ruhr, and the German Government decided to finance passive resistance to such foreign military occupation. . . . and for this purpose printed enormous additional amounts of paper money. A month after the occupation of the Ruhr, I was getting more than forty thousand marks for a dollar, and the bottom of the money market began to drop out completely. By August a dollar was buying millions, in September billions, in October trillions of marks. A sad cartoon appeared in a Munich paper showing a little girl sitting beside two huge bundles of paper money, crying pitifully. A passerby was saying: "Why are you crying, little girl?" She answered: "someone stole the leather straps off my money!" I occasionally played a dollar limit poker game for German marks. When we began that game, the limit was one hundred marks; in October 1923, one trillion marks. It was quite a thrill to raise a trillion.

Finally, that month, the German Government virtually repudiated its enormous public debt by introducing a new unit of value called the rentenmark. . . . This meant that every German who had sacrificed and saved to provide for his old age and for his family was ruined.

From Robert Murphy, *Diplomat Among Warriors* (New York: Doubleday, 1964), pp. 37–38.

New members (kneeling in front) being sworn into the Ku Klux Klan in Maryland (1922).

the war, the most important were Czechoslovakia and Austria. Czechoslovakia, ably led by Thomas Masaryk and Eduard Beneš, was generally considered the model among the new democracies. Here land reform was carried out successfully, and with almost half of Austria's former industry under Czech control, the country enjoyed a balanced economy. Czechoslovakia's major problem was the desire for greater autonomy among its numerous minorities, which amounted to almost one-third of its population. Especially troublesome were the 3 million Germans living in the Sudeten region.

Austria, since the war, had only Germans within its borders. But even so the new republic was deeply divided along social and economic lines between the urban, industrialized, and radical workers of Vienna, and the rural, agrarian, and conservative peasants of the provinces. Economically, Austria suffered greatly from the consequences of partition. In 1922 the situation became so serious that the League had to step in and grant substantial loans for Austrian reconstruction. By 1926 Austria seemed to be out of danger. But the real cause of Austria's difficulties—the loss of its economic hinterland—had not been removed. As the least viable among the new states of Europe, Austria was to be the first to feel the effects of the Great Depression that spread from the United States to Europe during the early 1930s.

THE UNITED STATES AND EUROPE

The recovery of Europe, though uneven, seemed well under way by 1929. It would have been still further advanced had the United States been more aware of its new responsibilities as the world's leading economic power. But America preferred to keep aloof from European affairs.

Isolationism and Nationalism

Most Europeans considered this policy of isolationism extremely selfish. America, after all, had suffered much less from the war than Europe had. As a matter of fact, the United States had gained from the war economically, not merely by supplying the Allies but by penetrating into regions formerly controlled by European commerce. The least America could do, or so many Europeans felt, was to forget the loans it had made to its allies during the war. But this the United States refused to do.

There were other sources of friction between the United States and its wartime friends. The French resented America's refusal to honor President Wilson's promise for a joint guarantee, together with Britain, of French security; the British were alarmed by America's growing commercial and naval competition; and neither France nor Britain welcomed the evident *rapprochement* between the United States and Germany. A further cause for concern among Europeans was America's obvious intent of isolating itself not only politically but economically. In an effort to protect American industry against the competition of cheap foreign labor, America during the 1920s introduced some of the highest tariffs in its history.

America's isolationism had its domestic roots in a growing opposition to "foreign" and "radical" influences. This American nationalism manifested itself in several ways. The Ku Klux Klan soon after the war claimed wide support for its persecution of racial and religious minorities; fear of radical elements in the early 1920s caused a "red scare" that led to the arrest of several thousand suspects; and, most important, restrictions on foreign immigration severely restricted the flow of immigrants from backward and hence less desirable regions.

American Involvement in Europe

But no matter how much the United States tried to isolate itself, its humanitarian conscience and its economic interests could not help but lead to renewed involvement in international affairs. Americans had already proved themselves far from isolationist as far as charity was concerned. Various relief organizations right after the war had dispensed millions of dollars' worth of supplies wherever they were most needed, even in the Soviet Union. Beginning in 1924 American experts also took the lead in tackling the reparations problem. With the return of economic stability, American investors during the next five years lent vast amounts to various European countries, especially Germany, Italy, and the smaller nations of central Europe.

In the political sphere America shared the hope of the rest of the world for peace and security. The warm reception that the American people gave the Pact of Paris for the "outlawry of war" was seen by some as a hopeful sign that America had outgrown its isolationism. But in other respects the country remained aloof. Even though many Americans had come to favor the League of Nations, the government refused to participate in any except the League's cultural and social work.

America was also concerned about disarmament, not so much on land as on sea. The rising influence of Japan in the Pacific posed a threat to American interests, and the large increase in Japanese naval expenditure made some limitation of naval forces seem highly desirable. Agreement on this point was reached at a naval conference in Washington in 1921 and 1922. It called for a ten-year naval holiday, the scrapping of large numbers of ships, and a fixed ratio of 5:5:3 respectively for the capital ships of the United States, Britain, and Japan. Simultaneous political agreements guaranteed the status quo in the Pacific, reaffirmed the "Open Door" policy for China, and ended the Anglo-Japanese alliance of 1902. Subsequent efforts at Geneva in 1927 to extend the naval agreement to small ships failed because the British refused to recognize America's claim to parity for all categories. The issue was finally settled to American satisfaction at a third conference in London three years later. But because Japan, France, and Italy remained dissatisfied with the results, these attempts at naval limitation were only partly successful.

AMERICA DURING THE "ROARING TWENTIES"

Although the United States had come out of the war unscathed, it found adjustment to peacetime conditions far from easy. American industry had expanded far beyond its prewar capacity, and the sudden cancellation of government contracts deeply upset the economy. As European industries resumed production, furthermore, United States exports declined. Attempts to cut production costs by lowering wages met with strong opposition from the workers, and once the wartime ban on strikes was lifted, labor unrest revived.

Return to "Normalcy"

In domestic as in foreign affairs, the American people were looking back with nostalgia to the peace and prosperity they had known before the war. The man who promised a return to such "normalcy" was the Republican Warren G. Harding, who was elected president by a large majority in 1920. It was under Harding's administration that America entered on the era of hectic prosperity for which the 1920s are best remembered. The heyday of the "Roaring Twenties" came under Calvin Coolidge.

The Republican administration's overriding concern was with aiding the American business community. High tariffs, the repeal of the excess-profits tax, the lowering of taxes on corporations and on high incomes, injunctions against strikes, and even the persecution of "radicals" and the restriction of foreign immigration—all these measures directly or indirectly benefited big business. America's phenomenal business expansion was also due to the ample capital resources and growing investments that were available from a broader segment of

President Calvin Coolidge at work on his Vermont farm (*ca.* 1925).

society. Big business, so it seemed, was becoming everybody's business.

It was not quite everybody's, though. Neither the worker nor the farmer was getting his due share of prosperity. Labor had suffered from the postwar depression and from the popular hysteria that equated union protest with communism. As a result, union membership during the 1920s declined from its wartime high. The American Federation of Labor held its own among skilled workers, but there was no similar organization for the mass of unskilled labor. Even so, most workers in time benefited from the nation's rising economy through almost full employment and better wages.

The stepchild of the American boom was the farmer. He, too, had expanded his operations during the war, borrowing large funds to buy additional land and equipment. As a result, America's farm output by 1919 had more than doubled. Then, as foreign demand decreased and surpluses accumulated, prices dropped and never regained their former level. The government tried to help farmers by creating additional credit facilities and encouraging cooperatives, but the Republican administration shrank away from anything that smacked of direct subsidies. Protective tariffs, furthermore, raised the price of industrial products needed by the farmer and led foreign countries to retaliate by cutting down their imports of American grain.

The "Jazz Age"

There was an air of restlessness about America's frantic pursuit of business and pleasure during the "Jazz Age" of the 1920s. As is common in periods of rapid economic expansion, America had its share of private and public corruption. The Eighteenth Amendment of 1920, by its rigorous prohibition of alcoholic beverages, almost invited violation of the law by the average citizen. The "speakeasy" and the "bootlegger" became part of American life, and "racketeering" was a common form of crime.

These, unfortunately, were the features that made the deepest impression abroad. Europeans professed to be shocked by the "materialism" of their *nouveau riche* American cousins. But Europe did not remain entirely immune to American influences. American products and production methods found ready imitators abroad, and American styles and American jazz had their admirers among the young. For the first time in history Europe showed signs of becoming Americanized.

The American people themselves seemed well satisfied with their country's apparently endless progress. In 1928 they

Cab Calloway with his band (1936).

voted overwhelmingly for another Republican president, Herbert Hoover. Some developments, however, should have caused alarm. Already before 1929 expansion in some basic areas had begun to slow down. Commodity prices had declined steadily from their peak in 1925, and agricultural prices continued to fall. These signs of recession were obscured by a continuing boom on the American stock market. Here prices were bid up by speculators, mostly with borrowed funds, to levels far out of proportion to dividends and earnings. The first danger signals came in mid-September 1929, when stock prices showed some decline. Failures of speculative companies in London later in the month caused some tremors on Wall Street, but still no panic. The collapse of the American stock market came suddenly, on October 23. The next day, "Black Thursday," American investors sold close to 20 million shares at a total loss of $40 billion. The Great Depression was on its way.

THE GREAT DEPRESSION

With the rise of industrialization, "business cycles"—that is, alternating phases of prosperity and depression—had become a recognized feature of modern capitalism. But there had never been a depression quite so severe as the one following the American stock market crash. The basic cause of the depression was the world's failure to solve the economic problems inherited from the First World War. Neither at the Peace Conference nor afterward was there any real awareness of how interdependent the world had become economically. Industrial expansion continued full force after the war and soon led to overproduction. Beginning in 1924 a brief period of recovery set in. But that recovery was artificial. As neither farmers nor workers really shared in the economic rise, purchasing power failed to keep up with production. In countries like Germany and Austria, furthermore, industrial expansion was largely stimulated by foreign credits. As these credits dried up, recovery ceased and the economy of these nations collapsed.

Soup kitchen in New York City during the Great Depression (1931).

This, however, did not happen until the spring of 1931. In the meantime the situation in central Europe had become serious enough to demand radical remedies. One solution proposed in early 1931 was for an Austro-German customs union. But this proposal met with strong opposition from the French, who regarded it as a first step toward an eventual political *Anschluss.* To put pressure on the Austrians, France began to withdraw some of its short-term credits. In May 1931 Austria's largest private bank collapsed. This is generally seen as the beginning of the European phase of the Great Depression. In July the first German bank suspended payments. In September the British government abandoned the gold standard. As other nations followed Britain's example, the only major European power to cling to the gold standard was France. Here the depression was not seriously felt until 1932.

Effects of the Depression

It is difficult to convey the staggering economic blow that the world suffered in the brief span of three or four years after 1929. World industrial production declined more than one-third, prices

President-elect Roosevelt greets
President Hoover on the way to
the Inauguration (March 4,
1933).

bilize currencies. It failed when America refused to adopt its proposals.

International efforts to pull the world out of its economic slump thus turned out to be either too little or too late. In the meantime governments everywhere reverted to the same practices that had helped to bring on the depression in the first place. As America raised its tariffs to unprecedented heights, the rest of the powers followed suit, with even Britain abandoning its traditional policy of free trade in 1932. These and other measures of economic nationalism hindered the revival of international trade.

THE DEMOCRACIES ON THE EVE OF THE SECOND WORLD WAR

The Great Depression belonged to both world wars—its roots went back to the First, and its effects contributed to the Second. While governments were still trying to repair the damages of the upheaval of 1929, clouds were already gathering for the far greater catastrophe of 1939. In this mounting crisis, resolute political leadership was imperative. In countries like Germany and the succession states of central Europe, democratic governments were no longer able to provide such leadership. As authoritarian regimes gained the upper hand, these nations were lost to the democratic cause. But even among the western democracies the crisis of the 1930s called for firm guidance of political and economic affairs. The need for such guidance was felt particularly strongly in the United States.

The United States: The "New Deal"

The Hoover administration, unwilling to interfere with free enterprise, had done too little to help relieve the economic crisis. Discontent with Republican half-measures was chiefly responsible for the Democratic sweep in the elections of 1932. For more than twelve years thereafter, the United States was guided by Franklin D. Roosevelt. The new president was a superb politician and an inveterate optimist, who met the most

dropped more than one-half, and more than 30 million people lost their jobs. Some countries were harder hit than others. Germany's industrial production declined by almost 40 percent, and at the height of the depression only one-third of Germany's workers were fully employed. In the United States, industrial production and national income by 1933 had decreased more than one-half, and the unemployment figure was estimated at 14 million.

Because of the worldwide scope of the depression, any attempt to counteract it demanded cooperation among all the major powers. As debtor nations began to default on their obligations, President Hoover in 1931 initiated a year's moratorium on all reparations and war debts. But this proved to be only a stopgap. A year later an economic conference at Lausanne all but buried the troublesome problem of intergovernmental debts. To save Germany from complete chaos, "standstill agreements" in 1931 temporarily stopped the panicky withdrawal of short-term loans from that country; but this did not halt the country's economic decline. Finally, a World Economic Conference in London in 1933 sought to sta-

difficult domestic and foreign emergencies with a boldness and confidence that earned him the admiration of the majority of Americans.

Many of Roosevelt's measures were intended for immediate relief and were thus of passing significance, but many others remain in effect to the present day. Republicans at the time charged that government interference with free enterprise, together with vast "give-away programs," tended to corrupt America's pioneering spirit of self-reliance and would ultimately lead to socialism and bankruptcy. In taxing the rich and aiding the poor, America certainly went far toward repudiating its traditional faith in laissez faire. But the rising standard of living of the masses tended to hasten rather than retard the growth of American business; and if the "New Deal" entailed staggering financial burdens, the nation as a whole seemed willing and able to bear them. The unanimity with which the American people supported the country's war efforts during the Second World War was certainly due in large part to the peaceful social and economic revolution of the preceding decade.

Great Britain: Slow Recovery

The most successful holding action against the depression in Europe was waged in Great Britain. In the hope of rallying parliamentary support, Ramsay MacDonald in 1931 transformed his Labour cabinet into a national coalition government. Subsequent elections, however, returned overwhelming Conservative majorities, and in 1935 Stanley Baldwin took over as prime minister. He was succeeded two years later by Neville Chamberlain. As might be expected from a predominantly Conservative regime, Britain sought to solve its economic problems by retrenchment rather than reform. Taxes were raised, government expenditures were cut, and interest rates were lowered. The devaluation of the pound stimulated exports. By the Imperial Duties Bill of 1932 the Conservatives at long last won their battle for protectionism. Subsequent trade agreements with Germany, the Scandinavian countries, and Russia improved British sales

---

Roosevelt's New Deal

In our day these economic truths have become accepted as self-evident. . . . :

The right to a useful and remunerative job in the industries or shops or farms or mines of the nation;

The right to earn enough to provide adequate food and clothing and recreation;

The right of every farmer to raise and sell his products at a return which will give him and his family a decent living;

The right of every businessman, large or small, to trade in an atmosphere of freedom from unfair competition and domination by monopolies at home or abroad;

The right of every family to a decent home;

The right to adequate protection from the economic fears of old age, sickness, accident and unemployment;

The right to a good education.

All of these rights spell security. . . . For unless there is security here at home there cannot be lasting peace in the world.

From President Franklin D. Roosevelt, message to Congress, January 11, 1944.

---

abroad. The overall effect of these measures was a modest but steady recovery. This was due more to the strength of the nation's capital reserves, however, than to any farsighted government policy. The Conservatives were deeply opposed to governmental economic planning. Instead, they preferred to have industry help itself. National income, to be sure, increased; but the basis of Britain's economy, its export trade, did not increase commeasurably.

There were few important events in British politics during the 1930s. King Edward VIII abdicated in 1936 to marry an untitled divorcée. By catering to the average Briton's innate conservatism, his abdication seemed to strengthen the monarchy rather than weaken it. Economic improvement helped to keep labor unrest at a minimum. Britain's main concern was with developments abroad, where Italy and Germany had started on the course of aggression that was to culminate in the Second World War.

Ramsay MacDonald and Stanley Baldwin at a press conference in 1931, during their national coalition government.

France: A House Divided

In contrast to England and the United States, where democracy successfully withstood the severe test of depression, the French Third Republic during the 1930s was shaken to its very foundations. With a high degree of self-sufficiency, a huge gold reserve, and no unemployment to speak of, France until 1932 was an island of prosperity in a sea of economic misery. But when disaster came it struck swiftly. By 1935 French industrial production had fallen almost one-third, exports were declining rapidly, and capital was fleeing the country at an alarming rate. Things looked up briefly after the government devalued the franc in 1936, but the rise in domestic prices soon neutralized any advantage.

It was not so much the severity of the economic crisis as the inability of the French government to cope with it that accounts for the political chaos that ended with the fall of France in 1940. The Third Republic had been deeply divided from the start. As time went on and France became more and more industrialized, economic differences accentuated political divisions. Workers and petty employees were virtual outcasts from French society, while the right-leaning wealthy classes and peasants had little enthusiasm for the Republic. The war had temporarily drawn the nation together, and once the difficult postwar transition had been made, French domestic tensions at long last seemed to have eased. But at this most critical point, the depression intervened, reopening wounds that had only just begun to heal.

Discontent with the government's handling of the economic crisis flared up with sudden violence during the Stavisky scandal in early 1934. Rumors that the machinations of an unsavory promoter, Alexander Stavisky, had enjoyed support from persons high in the government touched off a major riot among rightists in Paris. Many of the rioters were members of various fascist leagues, right-wing and royalist organizations, which in aims and tactics were similar to Hitler's storm troopers and Mussolini's Black Shirts. Fascism, like communism, was apt to strike any country weakened by internal discord.

The government's efforts to meet the emergency by rallying the country behind a cabinet of national union, such as Poincaré had formed in 1926, proved fruitless. In 1936 the parties of the left— Radical Socialists, Socialists, and Communists—became sufficiently alarmed over the fascist threat, both at home and abroad, to bury their longstanding differences. Their "Popular Front" won a decisive popular victory in the subsequent elections.

For almost two years various leftist coalitions, in which the Socialist Léon Blum was the leading figure, tried their best to halt the disintegration of the Republic. Blum introduced more far-reaching reforms, especially for the workers, than any government since the war. But to succeed, Blum's program of social reform needed the cooperation of French businessmen and bankers. And that cooperation was not forthcoming. There were other obstacles to recovery, notably the unsettled state of international affairs, which called for costly rearmament. But the basic reason for Blum's failure was that he was too radical for the right and not radical enough for the left.

While the Germans were preparing to fight the world, the French were fighting one another. Successive waves of "sit-down" strikes—a French innovation— and a rigidly enforced forty-hour week slowed down industry when it should have been working overtime. In April 1938 a slight shift to the right brought Édouard Daladier to the premiership, with far-reaching powers to rule by de-

The Stavisky riots of early February 1934, in which thousands of persons were injured and a number killed.

cree. But Daladier could not do what many abler men before him had failed to do: heal the breach between right and left, bourgeoisie and workers, capitalists and socialists, rich and poor. It was a deeply divided France that went to war in September 1939, and that Hitler found in the spring of 1940.

THE TWILIGHT OF IMPERIALISM

This discussion of events between the two world wars has dealt thus far only with Europe and the United States. But there were important developments elsewhere in the world that affected especially those countries that had colonial possessions. Beginning with the First World War, western imperialism entered a period of slow but steady decline. Economists had long questioned the advantages of colonies to the mother country, and historians had claimed that colonial rivalry had been one of the major causes of the war. The war itself had weakened the great powers and had aroused a feeling of nationalism among the colonial peoples. Just as the desire for independence among European nations had made for international unrest during the nineteenth century, so colonial nationalism was a major cause of international tension in the twentieth.

The Mandate System

The powers had shown signs of a more enlightened attitude toward colonies at the Paris Peace Conference, when they made the mandate system part of the League of Nations Covenant. The former German colonies and certain territories taken from Turkey were to be administered by mandatory powers responsible to the League. In theory this first experiment in international supervision over backward regions was a worthy innovation. But in practice the former German colonies became almost indistinguishable from the mandatory powers' own colonies; and of the more advanced Turkish regions that were promised ultimate independence, only Iraq became a sovereign state. Transjordan, under British tutelage like Iraq, was considered too weak to stand on its own feet. The French mandates, Syria and Lebanon, made some progress toward self-government, but the constitutions granted these countries assured French control.

A special case among Turkey's former possessions was the British mandate of Palestine. The root of the trouble in that area was the conflicting national aspirations of Arabs and Jews. Nationalism among the Jews went back to the Zionist Organization, founded by Theodor Herzl in 1897 to provide a home for the Jews in Palestine. In 1917 the British government, in the so-called Balfour Declaration, had backed these Zionist aspirations. Both Arabs and Jews at first seemed ready to cooperate in joint plans for the future of Palestine. But as more and more Jews migrated to Palestine, the Arabs feared that the Jews would emerge as the dominant faction. In 1929 the first major riots broke out among Arabs and Jews. With the advent of Hitler in 1933, Palestine became a refuge for thousands of Jews and immigration increased manyfold. The result was further tension and intermittent violence between Arabs and Jews. On the eve of the Second World War, the future of Palestine was still far from settled.

Theodor Herzl in 1904.

The Balfour Declaration   November 2, 1917

Foreign Office
November 2nd, 1917

Dear Lord Rothschild,

I have much pleasure in conveying to you, on behalf of His Majesty's Government, the following declaration of sympathy with Jewish Zionist aspirations which has been submitted to, and approved by, the Cabinet.

"His Majesty's Government view with favour the establishment in Palestine of a National Home for the Jewish people, and will use their best endeavours to facilitate the achievement of this object, it being clearly understood that nothing shall be done which may prejudice the civil and religious rights of existing non-Jewish communities in Palestine, or the rights and political status enjoyed by Jews in any other country."

I should be grateful if you would bring this declaration to the knowledge of the Zionist Federation.

Yours sincerely,
(Signed) ARTHUR JAMES BALFOUR.

Quoted in L. Stein, *Zionism* (London: Ernest Benn, 1925), p. 377.

The British Commonwealth

The mandate system was not the only innovation in colonial administration after the First World War. There were also important changes within the British Empire. During the nineteenth century those regions of the empire inhabited chiefly by white settlers had gradually changed from colonies into self-governing dominions. This emancipation from British influence continued after the war. The dominions had served loyally at the side of the mother country during the war. But at the Peace Conference, on matters concerning their own interests, they had shown considerable independence. When the dominions refused to follow Britain's lead on several other occasions during the 1920s, it became clear that the relationship needed clarification. This was achieved at the Imperial Conference of 1926. The formula agreed on at that time stated that Great Britain and the dominions were to be completely equal in status, united only through common allegiance to the crown. The British Commonwealth of Nations thus established was officially launched by the Statute of Westminster in 1931. The dominions became fully sovereign states, bound to the mother country merely by ties of blood, sentiment, and economic self-interest.

Even so tenuous a relationship, however, was too much for one member of the Commonwealth—Ireland. Efforts to extend home rule to that unhappy island had been interrupted by the outbreak of war in 1914. During the war, the anti-British Easter Rebellion of 1916, spearheaded by the Republican Sinn Fein movement, had been put down with undue severity. From that point on, Sinn Fein became the most dynamic force in Irish politics. In 1921 Britain set up the Irish Free State, which held dominion status and thus shared in the transition from Empire to Commonwealth. Yet in the midst of this hopeful development the depression came, and with it a resurgence of radicalism. In the elections of 1932 the Republicans gained a majority, and their leader, Eamon De Valera, became president. During the next few years Ireland severed most of its connections with Great Britain. A new constitution in 1937 completely ignored crown and Commonwealth.

India

Another part of the British Empire that was clamoring for independence was India. Like the dominions, India had stood by Great Britain during the war. As a reward for this support, India expected to be given self-government. A new Government of India Act in 1919, however, still fell far short of home rule. The extremists in the National Congress Party, therefore, refused to cooperate. The new leader of the Congress Party was Mohandas K. Gandhi. A lawyer educated in England, Gandhi had supported the British during the First World War, only to become their most persistent foe thereafter. The keynote of his policy was "noncooperation," an attempt to bring about the breakdown of British rule through passive resistance.

England entered into many fruitless conferences and proposals to try to solve the Indian problem. Since all of them fell short of granting at least dominion status, the National Congress turned them down. The claim of the Congress Party that it represented all of India was denied by the Moslem League of Mohammed Ali Jinnah. This religious split was India's most burning problem. But there were others—economic crises, natural catastrophes, riots, strikes, and famines—all of them adding to the country's extreme instability. When war began in 1939, India's entrance into the family of Commonwealth nations seemed as far away as it had been twenty years earlier.

Colonial Nationalism

The colonial nationalism that caused so much trouble in India was felt elsewhere in the British Empire and in the overseas possessions of the other powers. Britain's protectorate over Egypt was officially terminated in 1922, but continued British control over the Sudan and the Suez Canal gave the Egyptian nationalist "Wafd" party ample cause for agitation. France, in theory at least, had for some time granted French citizenship

Mohandas Gandhi arriving at an Indian conference in London (1931).

and representation in the French parliament to some of its colonies. But the French method of centralized rule discouraged the growth of colonial self-government. In advanced regions like North Africa and Indochina, native nationalists rebelled against Frenchification and demanded a voice in running their own affairs. Similarly, in the Netherlands East Indies a swiftly growing nationalist movement opposed the enlightened but paternalistic rule of the Dutch.

The End of American Colonialism

One country that was in earnest about abandoning its imperialist practices was the United States. America had only one real colony, the Philippines. After repeatedly promising independence to the islands, Congress in 1934 provided for American withdrawal after a transition period of ten years. In 1946 the Philippines became a sovereign nation. In Latin America, American "dollar diplomacy" continued briefly after the First World War. But in time the United States adopted a more benevolent "good neighbor policy," especially in economic matters. In 1930 the Clark Memorandum abandoned the Roosevelt Corollary to the Monroe Doctrine, which had been used in the past to excuse United States intervention in Latin America.

THE FAR EAST: PRELUDE TO WAR

Almost everywhere in the world, colonialism after the First World War found itself on the defensive against native nationalism. The only region where imperialism still thrived was in the Far East. There Japan, between the two world wars, embarked on a wholly new phase of expansion, mainly at the expense of China. During the war the Chinese Republic had already felt the threat of its powerful neighbor: the Twenty-one Demands of 1915 had established a Japanese sphere of influence over the mainland opposite Japan; and Chinese efforts at the Peace Conference to enlist Allied support in regaining the Shantung Pe-

ninsula had proved in vain. Only when the powers realized that Japanese expansion might threaten their own interests did they become alarmed. The Washington Conference of 1921 to 1922, while dealing primarily with naval disarmament, had also discussed the future of China. The powers at Washington reaffirmed the "Open Door" principle and promised to respect China's integrity and independence. In effect, things after the war were where they had been before 1914.

China Under the Kuomintang

China's domestic affairs, since the death of General Yüan in 1916, had been chaotic, with powerful warlords ruling various provinces. The only group that held any promise for the future was the Chinese Nationalist Party, or Kuomintang. But although its leader, Sun Yat-sen, was elected president in 1921, his influence was restricted to a small region around Canton. His program of freeing China from outside influences needed foreign help. Since he had been rebuffed by the West in the past, Sun Yat-sen in 1923 turned to the Russians for aid.

The Soviet Union welcomed the Chinese Republic not only as an ally against Japan but also as a possible convert to communism. A small Chinese Communist Party had been founded in 1921. As a result of its collaboration with the Soviet Union, the Kuomintang, hitherto a small organization, now became a mass movement. To provide the trained military forces necessary to unite China, a military academy was founded under the direction of an able young officer and ardent follower of Sun Yat-sen, Chiang Kai-shek. Sun Yat-sen himself did not live to see the initial success of his movement for unification. He died in 1925 and to this day remains the saint and symbol of the struggle for Chinese unity.

The campaign against the northern warlords was led by Chiang Kai-shek. It began in 1926 and was successful. By 1929 the Nationalist government controlled the whole country from its headquarters at Nanking. But except for the lower Yangtze region, its control was at best nominal. In the west and north the

Chiang Kai-shek (above) succeeded Sun Yat-sen to the leadership of the Kuomintang in 1925 and led the Nationalist government in Nanking. Mao Tse-tung (below) led the Communist faction in southern China in opposition to the Nationalists.

provincial warlords maintained their power; and to the south, in Kiangsi and Fukien provinces, the Chinese Communists under Mao Tse-tung and Chu Teh were busy organizing the landless peasants in opposition to the Nanking regime. The breach between Chiang Kai-shek and the Communists had come in 1927 when Chiang, in a sudden purge, had freed himself from Russian and Communist influence. Here were the seeds of the domestic conflict that was to have such serious consequences after the Second World War.

In the meantime the Nationalist regime had begun to tackle the many problems it had inherited from the past. The western powers assisted by making a few concessions, although most of these did not go far enough. In 1929 Chiang Kai-shek terminated unilaterally the obnoxious treaties granting extraterritoriality to western nations. Railroad construction, a uniform currency, legal reform, and an income tax all tried to help overcome the country's regionalism and backwardness. But the failure of the Nationalist government to introduce an effective agrarian program left the Chinese masses discontented and open to communist agitation. Added to domestic discord and disunity was the constant threat of Japanese intervention.

Moderation in Japan

Japan, in contrast to China, had fared well during the First World War. The country had profited economically from the increased demand for Japanese goods; it had gained territorially from the seizure of German colonies; and it had established a veiled protectorate over part of China. Any desire for further expansion among Japan's militarists was checked by Allied resistance at the Washington Conference of 1921 to 1922. A terrible earthquake in 1923, furthermore, tied down the nation's energies at home. The 1920s were taken up chiefly with domestic developments. The outward westernization of Japan continued, especially among the middle class. In 1925 universal manhood suffrage was introduced. Apathy among the voters, however, together with the limited powers of the Diet, retarded further democratic growth.

The comparative moderation of Japan's policy was especially apparent in the country's relations with China. In 1922 Shantung was returned to China, with Japan retaining only its commercial privileges. A number of moderate Japanese premiers recognized China's right to organize its own affairs and did not hinder the Kuomintang's policies so long as they did not affect Japan's interests. Only when Chiang Kai-shek's move into northern China threatened Japan's sphere of interest in Manchuria were Japanese troops once more sent to Shantung. As late as 1930, however, Japan still recognized China's tariff autonomy; and in October of that year the government, over the violent protests of Japanese patriots, ratified the London Naval Treaty, which further limited naval construction. But this was the end of the era of moderation. The depression began to hit Japan with disastrous results. The need for cuts in military spending particularly alarmed the militarists, who now came to the fore again, advocating their own brand of totalitarianism. In 1931 they urged Japan into the invasion of Manchuria, which touched off a sequence of events that ended in the Second World War.

AN AGE OF UNCERTAINTY

The years from 1919 to 1939 in retrospect appear as a succession of political and economic crises that were almost bound to lead to another major war. There had been a brief return to calm and stability during the mid-1920s, but even then the world had not regained the feeling of optimism that had characterized the period before 1914. The war and its aftermath had shaken many traditional beliefs and had disappointed many expectations. National self-determination and democracy, it seemed, did not necessarily solve Europe's political problems; nor did rugged individualism and laissez faire provide the answer to the world's economic ills. The hope that human reason would solve the few remaining "riddles of the universe" was being undermined by new scientific dis-

A "miracle" of the 1920s: a radio broadcast (featuring operatic soprano Dame Nellie Melba).

coveries, and the widely held belief in unlimited progress seemed open to serious question. As a result of growing doubts about hitherto accepted values, the intellectual climate during the postwar era changed from its prewar feeling of confidence to one of uneasiness and uncertainty.

Material Progress

Not everyone, of course, was equally sensitive to these changes. The majority of people, once they had overcome the hardships of war, were ready to enjoy the spectacular achievements that engineering science had in store for them. Material progress certainly seemed as promising as ever. Not only were there such new "miracles" as the radio and the talking picture, but constant improvements in production and marketing made these and earlier inventions, like the automobile, available to the average person. The veritable avalanche of labor-saving devices and gadgets that combined to make up a "high standard of living" did not necessarily make life richer, but they certainly made things more comfortable.

Other technological and scientific achievements changed man's everyday life. Improvements in the field of transportation virtually eliminated distance as a barrier. The Old World and the New, up to then days apart, became separated only by hours. Some of the most spectacular developments took place in medicine. A concentrated attack—through research, public hygiene, and improvements in nutrition—brought some of the most deadly diseases under control. This accomplishment in turn led to a lengthening of the average lifespan in the more advanced countries from less than fifty years at the beginning of the century to almost sixty-five years by 1939. Modern science and industry thus continued to fulfill their promise of enabling people to live both better and longer than at any earlier time in history.

Critics of Mass Culture

But material progress was not without its drawbacks, as a few social critics were pointing out. The growth of population

prior to the Second World War now was seen as a threat to cultural values more than to the world's food supply. The Spanish philosopher José Ortega y Gasset, in his book *The Revolt of the Masses* (1932), warned that the increase in human beings was so rapid that it was no longer possible to educate modern man in the traditions of his civilization. As a result, the gap between the cultured few and the superficially educated many was wider than ever and becoming more so. And since it was the masses who really exerted political and economic power, their low standards would henceforth be imposed on society as a whole.

Other voices were raised against the dangers of a civilization that envisaged progress entirely in material terms. One of the most perceptive critics was the British novelist Aldous Huxley, who, in his satirical novel *Brave New World* (1932), predicted with uncanny foresight many later "triumphs" of human ingenuity, from tranquillizer pills to brainwashing. The picture Huxley painted was of a well-adjusted society whose members were scientifically conditioned to whatever status they occupied, existing like animals or vegetables on a well-tended experimental farm. Man as a slave to his technological inventions, as a mere cipher in a collectivist society, as a rootless, lonely, and lost being in a world of bewildering complexity—such were the subjects that increasingly occupied social critics, novelists, and poets.

The "Behavioral Sciences"

The study of man, both as an individual and as a member of society, had for some time past been the task of the social sciences. This term had at first been used only for the traditional subjects: history, political science, and economics. But in time the field had been widened to include the new "behavioral

Other "miracles" of the 1900s: a 1932 Ford motor car; an automatic two-slice toaster, manufactured in 1928, that rang a bell when the toast was ready and automatically turned off the current; and an "easily wheeled" Vortex vacuum cleaner, *ca.* 1920.

Sigmund Freud on the occasion of his only trip to the United States (September 1909).

sciences": psychology, sociology, and cultural anthropology.

The beginnings of modern psychology are associated with the name of Sigmund Freud, a Viennese doctor who began formulating his theories at the turn of the century. There had been psychologists before him. True to the spirit of materialism that prevailed at the end of the nineteenth century, men like the German Wilhelm Wundt and the American William James had tried to discover the organic roots of human behavior, assuming that the brain, like any other organ, performed purely biological functions. Freud's approach was radically different. Basic to his teachings was the idea that human behavior is directed by subconscious instincts, or "drives," of which the most repressed is the sexual impulse. These drives are inhibited, usually in early childhood, and such inhibition leads to various degrees of frustration, which in turn may cause serious neuroses. In an effort to cure his patients, Freud developed a technique called "psychoanalysis," which consisted of an extended and deep probing of the patient's mind to get at the subconscious layers ordinarily revealed only in dreams. The purpose of such probing was to make the patient understand the conflicts that caused his abnormal behavior and by such understanding remove the causes of his mental disturbance.

Freud was not the only pioneer in modern psychology; there were others, notably the Russian Ivan Pavlov. All of them tried to discover at long last what made people act the way they did. The knowledge they gained should have been a source of great satisfaction. But actually, in the beginning at least, the opposite was true. Ever since the Age of Enlightenment man had gloried in the belief that he was a wholly intelligent and rational being. Now suddenly he was faced with the realization that he was subject to dark instincts and drives, and that it was these forces rather than his intellect that determined his behavior. Far from increasing man's self-confidence, modern psychology merely added to his feeling of bewilderment and uncertainty.

The second of the behavioral sciences, sociology, had its beginnings in the nineteenth century with men like Auguste Comte, Karl Marx, and Herbert Spencer. But here, too, the twentieth century introduced new methods and provided many new insights. One of the most important modern sociologists was the Italian Vilfredo Pareto, whose *Mind and Society* was published in English in 1935. Pareto accepted the findings of the psychologists that men were swayed by emotion rather than guided by reason. The ideals or rationalizations that social groups set up were to him mere fronts, or "derivations," that screened the basic irrational motives, or "residues," that really moved people to act. Pareto held that any clever leader or any elite capable of seeing through this human self-deception could use the basic aims of their fellow men to gain supremacy and to establish an authoritarian system in which the masses would obey slogans that appealed to their inner instincts. Pareto thus seemed to provide a "scientific" explanation of fascist totalitarianism. His analysis, if correct, certainly held little hope for a rationally ordered, democratic society.

The Freudian Revolution

Freud's extraordinary achievement was to show us, in scientific terms, the primacy of natural desire, the secret wishes we proclaim in our dreams, the mixture of love and shame and jealousy in our relations to our parents, the child as father to the man, the deeply buried instincts that make us natural beings and that go back to the forgotten struggles of the human race. Until Freud, novelists and dramatists had never dared to think that science would back up their belief that personal passion is a stronger force in people's lives than socially accepted morality. Thanks to Freud, these insights now form a widely shared body of knowledge.

In short, Freud had the ability, such as is given to very few individuals, to introduce a wholly new factor into human knowledge; to impress it upon people's minds as something for which there was evidence. He revealed a part of reality that many people before him had guessed at, but which no one before him was able to describe as systematically and convincingly as he did. In the same way that one associates the discovery of certain fundamentals with Copernicus, Newton, Darwin, Einstein, so one identifies many of one's deepest motivations with Freud. His name is no longer the name of a man; like "Darwin," it is now synonymous with a part of nature.

From Alfred Kazin, "The Freudian Revolution Analyzed," *The New York Times Magazine*, May 6, 1956.

Margaret Mead visiting a school in New Guinea.

The third behavioral science, cultural anthropology, likewise tried to find answers to the question of what determined human behavior. By carefully studying primitive tribes, chiefly American Indians and the natives of Pacific islands, anthropologists like Ruth Benedict and Margaret Mead hoped to determine what role environment played in shaping a given culture. One of their discoveries was that differences between cultures were due chiefly to environmental influences rather than to inherent biological factors and that there was no basis for the belief—so dear to many people before 1914—in "superior" and "inferior" races. It was one thing, however, to study a small primitive tribe and another to apply the same research techniques to larger and more complex cultures. But some promising beginnings were made. Students in the field of "human relations," through detailed case studies, were able to gather valuable data on small segments of their own society, in the hope of determining what motivated its members.

Spengler and Toynbee

Most social scientists were concerned with the present rather than the past. Even historians dealing with past events often did so to gain a better understanding of the present. Some of them, notably the German Oswald Spengler and the Englishman Arnold Toynbee, studied the rise and fall of past civilizations in order to predict the future of their own civilization. In the past, history had usually been viewed as a linear process, moving onward and upward toward some faraway goal. These historians presented a different view, according to which history seemed to repeat itself. Civilizations, they held, had always risen and fallen in cycles or curves—from birth to death, from spring to winter, from morning to night. These grandiose views of history tried to supply at least some answer to men's anxious questions about where their civilization was going. The answer that they supplied was far from hopeful.

Oswald Spengler's *The Decline of the West* (1918) was written during the First World War. With an immense display of erudition the author compared some twenty past "cultures," tracing each through identical phases down to a final phase that Spengler called "civilization." Europe, according to Spengler, was in the midst of this final phase. And like all other cultures before it, European culture would soon disintegrate and collapse. This prophecy of impending doom held a morbid fascination for the generation between the two wars. Historical scholars, to be sure, warned that this "morphology of cultures" was far too sweeping, based on evidence that was often incomplete or incorrect. Yet it could not be denied that in his comparative study of "cultures," Spengler had uncovered many suggestive parallels, and in his predictions of things to come he seemed to be remarkably correct.

It was largely due to Spengler's inspiration that the historian Arnold Toynbee embarked on his own monumental work, *A Study of History* (1934–54). Like Spengler, Toynbee assumed that there are parallel phases in the development of major civilizations. The birth of a civilization Toynbee saw in man's successful "response" to a "challenge," usually supplied by geography or climate. The growth of a civilization consists in man's gradually solving his physical problems, thus freeing his energies for more elevated intellectual and spiritual pursuits. Not every member of society shares in this process. It is, rather, a creative minority that takes the lead and makes its views prevail over the passive majority. The breakdown of a civilization, according to Toynbee, occurs when this minority can no longer muster enough creative force to meet a particular challenge. Europe, Toynbee said, was in the midst of this final phase, which he called the "Time of Troubles." He thus arrived at substantially the same prognosis as Spengler of what the future held in store. But unlike Spengler, Toynbee held out some hope for western civilization, if it learned from the mistakes of the past.

The "New Physics"

While the social sciences were giving little comfort in an age of uncertainty, the natural sciences for some time past had

Marie Curie in her
laboratory (1906).

Albert Einstein in Berlin
(1920).

been demolishing the simple, rational, and mechanistic view of nature that had prevailed since the days of Newton. Physical science in the late nineteenth century still viewed the universe substantially in Newtonian terms. Before the end of the century, however, the findings of scientists like Wilhelm Konrad Roentgen, Pierre and Marie Curie, Ernest Rutherford, and Max Planck had already raised doubts concerning those hypotheses. They made it clear that a major new explanation, a whole new system of physics and mathematics, was needed to supply the answers to questions on which Newton had been silent. Such a new system appeared in 1905 when the young German physicist Albert Einstein advanced his "theory of relativity."

According to Einstein's theory, time and space were not absolute, as Newton had assumed, but relative to the observer. Later he included gravitation and motion in his calculations. Mass in Einstein's universe was thus a variable. The mass of a body depended on its rate of motion; its mass increased as its velocity increased, with the speed of light as the theoretical limit. It was the velocity of light, therefore, rather than time and space, that now emerged as absolute in the "new physics."

A further radical departure from accepted theory was Einstein's assumption of the equivalence of mass and energy. Experiments in nuclear physics already had shown that the dividing line between mass and energy was far from clear, and that matter slowly disintegrated into energy by way of radiation. The amount of matter thus lost was infinitesimal compared with the resulting energy. Einstein expressed this relationship between mass and energy in his famous formula $E = mc^2$, in which E is energy, m is mass, and c is the velocity of light. This formula implied that if a process could be devised by which matter could suddenly be transformed into energy, only a small amount of matter would be required to produce a vast quantity of energy. A practical demonstration of the validity of Einstein's formula came with the first atomic explosion in 1945.

These and other revolutionary developments in science did not imme-

diately affect the outlook of the average person. But as scientists began speaking of the "limitations of science," admitting that they no longer knew all the answers, some of their feeling of uncertainty could not help but enter general consciousness. Instead of living in a rational world with few remaining riddles, man, in the words of the British astronomer Sir Arthur Eddington, was faced by a universe in which "something unknown is doing, we don't know what." A mysterious world (as the physicists said it was), inhabited by irrational man (as the psychologists said he was), caught in a civilization predestined for decay and disintegration (as Spengler and Toynbee said our civilization was)—this was a far cry from the happy and confident prospect that had existed only a short time before.

New Cultural Trends

The uncertainty of the age was also reflected in its literature and art. Social criticism among writers was nothing new. But while the Naturalists of the late nineteenth century had hoped to bring about much-needed reforms by their attacks upon society, there was little such hope behind the criticism of the postwar era. Its common denominator was disillusionment—as seen in T. S. Eliot's *The Waste Land* (1922), Thomas Mann's *Magic Mountain* (1924), Theodore Dreiser's *An American Tragedy* (1925), and Sinclair Lewis' *Main Street* (1920). Some of the greatest literature of the years between the wars was escapist—the poetry of Rainer Maria Rilke, the tales of Joseph Conrad, and even the stories of Ernest Hemingway, whose romanticism was concealed behind a tough exterior. The French novelist Marcel Proust, in his *Remembrance of Things Past* (1913–27), looked back with nostalgia on a French society long since gone. And Thomas Wolfe, in *Look Homeward, Angel* (1929), escaped into a less glamorous past.

Though deeply tinged with disillusionment, postwar literature was also immensely creative. The insights of modern psychology into the hidden motives of human behavior proved a boon to writers in their age-old quest for an understanding of human nature. There had been psychological novels before, but it was only in this century that almost every writer, consciously or unconsciously, came under the influence of modern psychology, and especially of Freud. The Irishman James Joyce, in his novel *Ulysses* (1922), introduced a method known as "stream-of-consciousness." The search into the subconscious, so typical of Joyce, also motivated dramatists like the Italian Luigi Pirandello and the American Eugene O'Neill. One of the effects of Freudian psychology was to call attention to the role of sex as a force in man's life. As a result, sexual matters were now written about with far more candor than earlier generations would have thought permissible. Still, a book as outspoken on the subject as *Lady Chatterley's Lover* (1928), by the Englishman D. H. Lawrence, could not be published, except in expurgated form, until over thirty years later.

The mixture of uncertainty and creativity that characterized literature between the two wars also prevailed in painting. Some artists still dealt with recognizable subjects, but more and more of them rebelled against the Realism and Impressionism of the prewar era. Instead, painters like Paul Klee, Vassily Kandinsky, Pablo Picasso, and Ernst Ludwig Kirchner expressed on canvas their inner feelings and impulses, often in styles that reflected the chaotic world in which they lived. These "Expressionists," as they were called, in time became so nonobjective and abstract that it was impossible any longer to recognize in them common aims and interests. Each artist had become a law unto himself.

This same creative uncertainty, this search for new means of expression, had its parallel in modern music. Some composers—Jan Sibelius, Sergei Rachmaninoff, Richard Strauss, and Ralph Vaughan Williams—continued to use traditional methods, inspired by the heritage of their various cultural backgrounds. But others—Arnold Schönberg, Arthur Honegger, Béla Bartók, and Paul Hindemith—departed from familiar forms and in some cases, by adopting new scales and chords, developed a wholly new musical idiom, which

sounded dissonant to most of their contemporaries.

Because so much modern art and music was highly individualistic, it appealed to only a few. Modern architecture had a somewhat wider following. Most architecture in the nineteenth century had been a mere imitation or a mixture of earlier styles. New building materials, steel and concrete, had been developed; but the inherent possibilities of these materials had been ignored by all but a few pioneers, such as the Americans Louis Sullivan and Frank Lloyd Wright. All this changed after the First World War. Architects became increasingly concerned with the function as well as the appearance of their buildings and by striving for simplicity and utility were able to produce structures of great beauty. The doctrine of "functionalism" found its European exponents in Le Corbusier, Walter Gropius, and Ludwig Mies van der Rohe. It took some time, however, before the general public abandoned its preference for traditional and more ornate styles in favor of contemporary simplicity.

Pablo Picasso, *Woman* (study for *Guernica*, 1937).

Anti-Intellectualism

It is difficult to gauge correctly the temper of a period as brief as the twenty years between the two world wars. Many of its accomplishments, especially in science, were impressive. But there was a puzzling paradox behind this extension of human knowledge. The more man found out about the world, the more he realized how little he had known before. From a feeling of supreme self-importance at the end of the nineteenth century, man's view of himself was pushed to the opposite extreme: he felt uncertain and insignificant, a creature of instinct, no longer able to shape his own destiny.

It is not surprising that this uncertainty should turn many people against the rationalist philosophy that had prevailed for the past two hundred years. There had been a similar revolt against reason a century before. And like Romanticism then, antirationalism now sprang from the disillusionment that followed a seemingly futile war. Modern anti-intellectualism, as it is called, took several forms. It brought a revived interest in religion, even among scientists, who had not long ago been ardent defenders of materialism. But far larger numbers turned elsewhere for guidance.

There were many reasons for the sudden rise of totalitarianism after the First World War. Not the least among them was that it provided its followers with simple beliefs in an age of bewildering uncertainty.

Suggestions for Further Reading

Note: Asterisk denotes a book available in paperback edition.

Great Britain and France A. J. P. Taylor, *English History, 1914–1945* (1965), and C. L. Mowat, *Britain Between the Wars* (1955), are the best general books on the subject. R. Graves and A. Hodge, *The Long Weekend: A Social History of Great Britain, 1918–1939** (1940), re-creates the moods and manners of British society during the period. The same is done for the British "establishment" in H. Nicolson, *Diaries and Letters*, 3 vols. (1966–68). There are some excellent biographies of the leading political figures: K. Morgan, *David Lloyd George: Welsh Radical as World Statesman* (1963); R. Blake, *The Unknown Prime Minister: The Life and Times of Andrew Bonar Law* (1955); G. M. Young, *Stanley Baldwin* (1952); G. E. Elton, *The Life of James Ramsay MacDonald* (1939); K. Feiling, *The Life of Neville Chamberlain* (1946); and H. Nicolson, *King George V* (1952). C. R. Attlee, *The Labour Party in Perspective* (1949), is a review of the party's development between the wars by its leader. C. F. Brand, *The British Labour Party: A Short History* (1964), is a useful survey. The best introduction to French postwar history is D. W. Brogan, *France Under the Republic** (1940). E. J. Knapton, *France Since Versailles** (1952), is a brief survey, and A. Werth, *The Twilight of France, 1933–1940* (1942), describes the mounting crisis on the eve of the Second World War. D. Thomson, *Democracy in France** (1964), is helpful for understanding French politics. For biographies of major politicians, see: G. Bruun, *Clemenceau** (1943); G. Wright, *Raymond Poincaré and the French Presidency* (1942); V. Thompson, *Briand: Man of Peace* (1930); and J. Colton, *Léon Blum: Humanist in Politics* (1966). An excellent comparative study is C. S. Maier, *Recasting Bourgeois Europe: Stabilization in France, Germany, and Italy in the Decade after World War I* (1975).

Germany The best political history of the Weimar Republic in English is E. Eyck, *A History of the Weimar Republic,** 2 vols. (1962). A Rosenberg, *A History of the German Republic* (1936), combines insight with criticism. On the dissolution of the Republic, see A. Brecht, *Prelude to Silence: The End of the German Republic* (1944), and the collection of essays by German scholars entitled *Path to Dictatorship, 1918–1933** (1966). The two leading personalities of the period are discussed in H. Turner, *Stresemann and the Politics of the Weimar Republic* (1963), and A. Dorpalen, *Hindenburg and the Weimar Republic* (1964). F. L. Carsten, *The Reichswehr and Politics, 1918 to 1933* (1966), and G. Post, *The Civil-Military Fabric of Weimar Foreign Policy* (1973), deal with a significant phase of the Republic's history.

The Small Powers Good general surveys are: H. Seton-Watson, *Eastern Europe Between the Wars, 1918–1941,** rev. ed. (1962); R. L. Wolff, *The Balkans in Our Times* (1956); and B. A. Arneson, *The Democratic Monarchies of Scandinavia* (1939). On individual countries, see M. MacDonald, *The Republic of Austria, 1918–1934* (1946); H. Roos, *A History of Modern Poland* (1966); C. A. Macartney, *October Fifteenth: A History of Modern Hungary, 1929–1945*, 2 vols. (1957); and R. W. Seton-Watson, *A History of the Czechs and Slovaks* (1943).

The United States The very good studies of the pre-Roosevelt era are A. M. Schlesinger, Jr., *The Crisis of the Old Order, 1919–1933* (1957), and W. E. Leuchtenburg, *The Perils of Prosperity, 1914–1932** (1958); see also E. A. Rosen, *Hoover, Roosevelt, and the Brains Trust: From Depression to New Deal* (1977). The Roosevelt years are covered in several excellent works: A. M. Schlesinger, Jr., *The Coming of the New Deal** (1959) and *The Politics of Upheaval* (1960); D. W. Brogan, *The Era of Franklin D. Roosevelt* (1951); W. E. Leuchtenburg, *Franklin D. Roosevelt and the New Deal, 1932–1940* (1936); and J. M. Burns, *Roosevelt: The Lion and the Fox** (1956). E. F. Goldman, *Rendevous with Destiny: A History of American Reform** (1952), and R. Hofstadter, *The Age of Reform** (1955), deal with the American liberal and progressive movements. F. L. Allen, *Only Yesterday** (1940) and *The Big Change** (1952), are lively social histories of the period.

Among memoirs and biographies of New Dealers, the following stand out: R. E. Sherwood, *Roosevelt and Hopkins** (1948); J. M. Blum, *From the Morgenthau Diaries,* 3 vols. (1959-67); R. G. Tugwell, *The Democratic Roosevelt* (1957); and E. Roosevelt, *This I Remember** (1949).

The Great Depression J. S. Davis, *The World Between the Wars, 1919-1939: An Economist's View* (1975), puts the world economic crisis in its long-range perspective. The crisis itself is studied in J. K. Galbraith, *The Great Crash, 1929** (1955). See also D. A. Shannon, ed., *The Great Depression** (1960), and M. J. Bonn, *The Crumbling of Empire: The Disintegration of World Economy* (1938). H. W. Arndt, *The Economic Lessons of the Nineteen-Thirties* (1944), is an attempt to learn from the past. A major aspect of the international repercussions of the financial crisis is the subject of E. W. Bennett, *Germany and the Diplomacy of the Financial Crisis, 1931* (1962).

The Twilight of Imperialism Typical of western disillusionment with imperialism are the books by G. Clark, *The Balance Sheets of Imperialism* (1936) and *A Place in the Sun* (1936). The changes in the British Empire and Commonwealth are discussed in K. Robinson, *The Dilemma of Trusteeship: Aspects of British Colonial Policy Between the Wars* (1965). H. Mukerjee, *India Struggles for Freedom* (1948), traces the long road to Indian independence. Earlier stages on this road are related in M. K. Gandhi, *Autobiography** (1948), and in two autobiographical works by J. Nehru, *Toward Freedom** (1941) and *Glimpses of World History** (1942). On events in the Far East, see A. Iriye, *After Imperialism: The Search for a New Order in the Far East, 1921-1931** (1965); R. Gould, *China in the Sun* (1946); and S. Chen and P. S. R. Payne, *Sun Yat-sen: A Portrait* (1946). The situation in the Middle East is discussed in G. Antonius, *The Arab Awakening: The Story of the Arab National Movement* (1939); and the first stirrings of unrest in Africa are treated in R. L. Buell, *The Native Problem in Africa* (1928). See also W. E. B. DuBois, *The World and Africa* (1947).

Intellectual History Books dealing with the intellectual ferment of the "age of uncertainty" are legion. H. S. Hughes, *Consciousness and Society: The Reorientation of European Social Thought, 1890-1930** (1958), is a fine general study. J. Barzun, *The House of Intellect** (1959), covers the more recent period. P. Gay, *Weimar Culture* (1968), is excellent on Germany. Other attempts to see the crisis of our civilization in historical perspective are R. Niebuhr, *The Irony of American History** (1952), and R. Williams, *Culture and Society* (1958). J. Ortega y Gassett, *The Revolt of the Masses** (1932), is a classic criticism of our mass society. The modern trend toward conformity is analyzed in W. H. Whyte, *The Organization Man** (1956); V. O. Packard, *The Status Seekers** (1959); and A. C. Valentine, *The Age of Conformity* (1954). Other dangers to democratic freedom are pointed out by F. A. Hayek, *The Road to Serfdom** (1944), and K. R. Popper, *The Open Society and Its Enemies** (1950).

The basic work on Freud and psychoanalysis is E. Jones, *The Life and Work of Sigmund Freud,** 3 vols. (1953-57). See also G. Costigan, *Sigmund Freud: A Short Biography* (1965). The wide impact of Freudianism is treated in P. Reiff, *Freud: The Mind of the Moralist** (1959), and F. J. Hoffmann, *Freudianism and the Literary Mind** (1957).

New trends in the social and behavioral sciences are exemplified in T. Parsons, *The Structure of Social Action* (1949); E. Fromm, *Escape from Freedom** (1941); C. Kluckhohn, *Mirror for Man** (1949); B. L. Cline, *The Questioners* (1965); and in the studies of American society by D. Riesman, *The Lonely Crowd** (1953) and *Individualism Reconsidered** (1955). See also the essays by noted social scientists in R. Linton, ed., *The Science of Man in the World Crisis* (1945). For the influence of science on society, see B. Barber, *Science and the Social Order** (1952); B. F. Skinner, *Science and Social Behavior** (1956); J. Russell, *Science and Modern Life* (1955); and W. Esslinger, *Politics and Science* (1955).

The "prophets of doom" are evaluated in H. S. Hughes, *Oswald Spengler: A Critical Estimate** (1952), and K. Winetrout, *Arnold Toynbee: The Ecumenical Vision* (1975). On the scientific revolution of our century, see L. Infeld, *Albert Einstein** (1950); L. Barnett, *The Universe and Dr. Einstein** (1952); W. Heisenberg, *The Physicist's Conception of Nature* (1958); and M. Planck, *Scientific Autobiography and Other Papers* (1949).

Modern literature is covered in M. Colum, *From These Roots: The Ideas That Have Made Modern Literature* (1944), and C. Mauriac, *The New Literature* (1959). On modern art, see E. Langui, ed., *Fifty Years of Modern Art** (1959); W. Haftmann, *Painting in the Twentieth Century,* 2 vols. (1965); and J. Joedicke, *A History of Modern Architecture* (1959). P. Collaer, *A History of Modern Music** (1961), is an introduction to the subject.

32 The Rise of Totalitarianism

The Communist and Fascist regimes that arose in Europe and Asia during the years between the two world wars have been variously described as autocratic, authoritarian, dictatorial, and totalitarian. These terms do not all mean the same thing. There had been autocratic and authoritarian regimes in the past, most recently in tsarist Russia and imperial Germany; and there have been dictatorships from ancient times to the present. But none of these deserved to be called totalitarian. What we mean by a totalitarian regime is a regime in which a determined minority, by use of threat or force, imposes its will on the total life of a society. The aims of this ruling clique are usually rooted in some all-embracing ideology. The origins of these totalitarian ideologies go back at least to the nineteenth century, with the appearance of the two creeds that contributed most to totalitarianism: socialism and nationalism. Their growth and spread were aided by industrialism, which gave birth to the mass society in which totalitarianism thrives, and which provided the technical means whereby total domination by a ruling clique was made possible.

There were many ideological differences between the totalitarianism of the right and the left—fascism and communism. Communism owed much of its success to the fervor that Marxian socialism inspired among its followers. There was no room for nationalism in Marxism, although nationalism in time became an ingredient of communism. Fascist ideology, by comparison, was less coherent. A mixture of warmed-over nineteenth-century "isms"—Romanticism, Social Darwinism, racialism, militarism, and so forth—its outstanding characteristic was nationalism. Fascism, too, professed a belief in socialism, but it was an extreme form of state socialism from above rather than the Marxian concept of popular socialism from below.

Despite these ideological differences, fascism and communism were alike in many ways. Both exercised the most minute control over the life of every individual; both ruled through a mixture of propaganda and terror; both segregated and persecuted their opponents in concentration and slave-labor camps; and both sought to extend their power abroad through force or subversion. Why should totalitarian regimes have arisen at the time and in the countries they did? As we shall see, the circumstances differed considerably from country to country, but there were also certain similarities. Totalitarianism arose only in nations with little or no democratic tradition. Most of these countries had undergone lengthy domestic crises caused by the First World War or the Great Depression. In all cases a resolute minority, posing as saviors, initiated changes amounting to a revolution. And as a rule this minority was headed by a leader with great demagogic gifts.

COMMUNISM IN CRISIS 1917–28

As we have seen, a Bolshevik minority under Lenin had seized power in the "October Revolution" of 1917 (see p. 706). It took several years for communism to gain full control in Russia. The initial difficulties faced by the new Soviet Republic were so severe that its survival seems almost miraculous. What the Bolsheviks lacked in numbers they made up in revolutionary zeal. To create a new world they tried to make a clean sweep of the old.

"War Communism" and Civil War

In a series of measures usually referred to as "War Communism," the tsarist past was totally eradicated. The nation's economy was socialized, where necessary through terror. From its very start the new secret police, or *Cheka*, was a deadly, efficient instrument of Bolshevik rule. The revolutionary fervor of bolshevism was also reflected in its foreign policy. To Lenin, revolution in Russia was but the prelude to world revolution; and the success of the latter was seen as necessary to guarantee the survival of bolshevism at home. Sporadic Communist uprisings in Budapest, Vienna, Munich, and Berlin led to the founding, in March 1919, of the Soviet-controlled

Hitler and Mussolini in Rome in May 1938, following the firm establishment of the Rome-Berlin Axis and Hitler's Austrian *Anschluss*.

Third Communist International (Comintern) as a permanent agency dedicated to inciting world revolution.

But these Bolshevik attempts to conquer Russia and the world simultaneously turned out to be premature. "War Communism," instead of bringing relief, actually brought further economic misery leading to unrest and civil war. Opposition to the new regime was helped by Allied intervention. Its chief motive was to revive Russian resistance against Germany. During the spring and early summer of 1918, Allied forces landed at various points along Russia's periphery. A Czech legion, made up of Austrian soldiers captured during the war, simultaneously fought Communist forces along the Siberian railroad. The Germans, still in control of much of Russia, encouraged separatist movements in the Ukraine and along the Baltic. And to complete the troubles of the Bolsheviks, the Allies imposed a tight naval blockade.

As the antirevolutionary White armies converged on the Soviet heart of Russia, the sphere of Bolshevik influence shrank to the region around Moscow and Petrograd. Yet despite hopeless odds, the Bolsheviks were able to hold their own. The main reason for their survival was the disunity and dispersion of their opponents. Allied intervention was at best half-hearted. The White armies were suspected of trying to restore the old order and therefore lacked popular support. The fact that the Whites enjoyed Allied help further weakened their cause, since it enabled the Bolsheviks, or Reds, to pose as champions of national resistance against foreign intervention. The White armies, finally, operated on widely separated fronts and under divided leadership. For all these various reasons, the White armies were no match for the newly created Red army. By the beginning of 1920, the Bolsheviks had defeated all the White forces except those in southern Russia under General Wrangel.

At this point a new danger arose. The Poles, who wanted to extend their frontier eastward beyond the Curzon Line, the boundary assigned to them at the Peace Conference, now joined forces with Wrangel in a concerted drive against the Red army. This was no longer a civil but a national war, and in an upsurge of patriotism the Russian people rushed to the defense. In a brilliant counterattack, the Polish army was driven out of Russia and pushed back to the gates of Warsaw. Poland was saved in part by French aid. In the "Miracle of the Vistula," in August 1920, the Red army was halted and thrown back. Under the subsequent Peace of Riga, Poland advanced its borders some 150 miles eastward into regions inhabited chiefly by Russians. Another "minorities problem" had been created.

Lenin's "New Economic Policy"

The end of civil and foreign war did not relieve Russia's misery. To add to the nation's calamities, droughts and crop failures in 1920 and 1921 brought one of the worst famines in Russian history. The desperate situation called for drastic measures. In March 1921, therefore, Lenin initiated his "New Economic Policy," or NEP, which called for a radical departure from "War Communism" and a partial return to prewar, capitalist practices. Lenin's more orthodox comrades, notably Trotsky, were against such a retreat from Marxian doctrine. But as it turned out, Lenin's policy was justified by its results. In the seven years during which NEP was in effect, agriculture and industry returned to their 1913 levels. As a result, most Russians were able to get at least the food and clothing they needed and to enjoy a slight rise in wages and standard of living.

The moderation of Soviet policy at home had repercussions abroad. The failure of Communist uprisings in central Europe had shown that world revolution was not as imminent as the Communists had hoped. And with Russia's economic recovery depending heavily on foreign trade and capital, the Soviet Republic was eager to resume normal relations with the rest of the world. In this aim the New Economic Policy proved helpful, since it was interpreted abroad as a sign that the Bolsheviks had begun to see the error of their ways and in time would abandon their Communist "experiment." There was no reason, therefore, why foreign interests should not avail themselves

Russian poster published around 1920. It illustrates suffering during the grain famine; the caption reads: "HELP."

Leon Trotsky in France after his expulsion from the Soviet Union in 1929 by Stalin.

of the opportunities offered by Russia's vast market and resources. Economic *rapprochement* between Russia and the West began in 1921. By 1925 diplomatic recognition had been granted the Soviet Union by all major powers except the United States.

But despite such hopeful beginnings, relations between Russia and other countries never became really close. The major obstacle to Russia's reintegration into the international community was the well-founded suspicion that the Soviets had not really abandoned their aim of world revolution. As repeated incidents during the 1920s showed, the Comintern was merely marking time.

Lenin did not live to see the results of his New Economic Policy. In 1922 he suffered a paralytic stroke, and in 1924, at the age of fifty-three, he died. He had been a remarkable man, with a great mind and superior talents as an agitator and organizer. His unaffected manner set him apart from most other dictators. With a rare mixture of fanaticism and realism, he had always known how to adjust his policy to changed circumstances. Without his leadership it is doubtful that Russia's revolution would have succeeded.

Stalin versus Trotsky

The death of Lenin brought into the open a struggle for power that had been going on behind the scenes for some time. The two chief contenders were Trotsky and Stalin. In their aims they were not unlike: both looked forward to the ultimate victory of world communism. Where they differed was in the policy they advocated. Trotsky believed that Bolshevik Russia could not survive unless the rest of the world became communist too. Russia, therefore, should concentrate on fomenting and supporting revolutions elsewhere. Stalin, on the other hand, felt that communism should first gain a firm hold in Russia—"socialism in one country"—and only then should pursue its goal of aiding Communist movements elsewhere.

In the struggle that developed between Trotsky and Stalin, the personalities and tactics of the two turned out to

be decisive. Both men had served the revolution well. But while Trotsky's importance as Commissar of War declined once victory had been won, Stalin's influence continued to grow. He won his most important position in 1922, when he became general secretary of the Communist Party. This gave him control over the entire party apparatus. Trotsky's doctrine of "permanent revolution," meanwhile, found little response in a nation exhausted by foreign and civil war. Most Russians preferred recovery at home to revolution abroad. And while Trotsky's often aloof manner offended his comrades, Stalin was careful to make friends with such "Old Bolsheviks" as Leo Kamenev, the party's chief ideologist, and Grigori Zinoviev, the head of the Comintern.

In 1925 Stalin's policy of conciliation and cunning succeeded in forcing Trotsky to resign from the Ministry of War. Soon thereafter, Kamenev and Zinoviev quarreled with Stalin and joined Trotsky in opposition. But Stalin proved the stronger. Allying himself with two other Old Bolsheviks, Alexei Rykov and Nikolai Bukharin, he had the "Trotskyites" expelled from the leadership of the party

Joseph Stalin (1879–1953) in 1919.

Lenin's Testament   1922–23

Comrade Stalin, having become general secretary, has concentrated enormous power in his hands, and I am not sure that he always knows how to use that power with sufficient caution. On the other hand, Comrade Trotsky . . . is distinguished not only by his exceptional ability—personally, he is, to be sure, the most able man in the present Central Committee—but also by his too far-reaching self-confidence and a disposition to be far too much attracted by the purely administrative side of affairs. . . . Stalin is too rude, and this fault, entirely supportable in relation to us Communists, becomes insupportable in the office of general secretary. Therefore I propose to the comrades to find a way to remove Stalin from that position and appoint to it another man who in all respects differs from Stalin only in superiority—namely, more patient, more loyal, more polite, and more attentive to comrades, less capricious, et cetera. This circumstance may seem an insignificant trifle, but I think that from the point of view of preventing a split and from the point of view of the relations between Stalin and Trotsky, which I discussed above, it is not a trifle, or it is such a trifle as may acquire a decisive significance.

N. Lenin, as quoted in David Shub, *Lenin* (New York: Doubleday, 1966), pp. 434–35.

A Soviet poster, "Knowledge breaks the chains of slavery," used in a campaign against illiteracy.

Harvest time on a collective farm in the Ukraine in the 1920s. A propaganda newspaper, *The Collective Farmer,* is being printed on the back of the truck for distribution to the peasants.

and ultimately from the party itself. Trotsky was banished, first to Siberia and after 1929 abroad. He was assassinated in Mexico in 1940. In the meantime Stalin, in 1929, had ousted Rykov and Bukharin, whose gradualist approach to socialization no longer fitted into his schemes. With the last of his potential rivals out of the way, Stalin had emerged supreme.

COMMUNISM TRIUMPHANT 1928–41

The Soviet government in 1928 already was a highly complex system. It received its final form under the "Stalin Constitution" of 1936. The Soviet Union was a federation of states, whose number increased from four in 1922 to sixteen in 1941. Each state at first retained a large measure of cultural autonomy but was under the strict political control of the Supreme Soviet in Moscow. The Supreme Soviet consisted of two chambers, the Soviet of the Union and the Soviet of Nationalities. When they were not in session, their functions were exercised by a Presidium of some twenty-seven members. More important, however, in directing national affairs was the Council of People's Commissars, appointed by the Supreme Soviet.

Actual power rested in the hands of only a few people. But a multiplicity of local, regional, and provincial soviets, together with the Supreme Soviet, gave at least an appearance of representative government. Other features of the Russian constitution were also intended to make it appear democratic. Franchise was universal, and a bill of rights guaranteed all kinds of rights and freedoms. The only trouble was that these rights had to be exercised "in the interests of the working people." And the agency that interpreted what these interests were was the Communist Party.

The Communist Party

The membership of the Russian Communist Party in 1918 was estimated at two hundred thousand. Ten years later, it had increased to over 1 million. But while it continued to grow, it never became a mass party. Its function was rather to serve as an elite, "the vanguard of the working class." Undeviating faith in Marxian doctrine as interpreted by the party's leaders, together with blind obedience to orders from above—these were the basic demands made of all party members. Party organization resembled the structure of the Soviet state, from "cells" at the bottom to the All-Union Party Congress at the top. The Congress selected the Central Committee as the chief policy-making organ, and the Central Committee in turn delegated power to the Politburo, the party's highest authority.

The obedience and self-abnegation demanded by party membership was highly rewarded by the Soviet state. All the leading positions in the bureaucracy went to party members, and they alone could hold political office. The upshot of this system was the growth of a new ruling caste of Communist functionaries. With the Communist Party as the dominant force in Soviet life, control of the party ensured domination of the state. Stalin owed his absolute power to his leading role in the Communist Party rather than to any governmental position. And beginning in 1928 he used this absolute power to carry the Communist revolution to its final triumph.

The Five-Year Plans

In order to survive in a hostile world of capitalist powers, Stalin felt the Soviet Union had to realize as rapidly as possible its inherent economic power. Stalin hoped to achieve this goal in three Five-Year Plans. Their aim was the large-scale development of basic industries and the increase of agricultural production through collective farming.

The first Five-Year Plan was launched in 1928. Even if one discounts the exaggerations of Communist propaganda, the achievements of Stalin's policy were most impressive. Between 1928 and 1940 Russia's industrial output grew more than sevenfold. On the eve of the Second World War, the Soviet Union had become one of the leading industrial powers of the world.

Collectivization was less successful. Agriculture in Russia was hampered by small holdings and antiquated methods. The solution to the problem was seen in large-scale farming and mechanization. But the conservative Russian peasant was opposed to any drastic changes and resorted to passive resistance. To break this opposition, the authorities used force. Executions and deportations, added to the severe famine of 1932 to 1933, caused the death of some 4 million people. But even strong-arm methods did not bring the desired results. While by 1940 most of Russia's land had been converted into collective farms, the problems of Russian agriculture had by no means been solved.

Stalin's Five-Year Plans completed the victory of communism in Russia. But that victory was won at the price of untold sacrifices on the part of the Russian people. Millions perished, others languished in labor camps, and the rest led a regimented and drab existence, spurred by alternate waves of propaganda and terror.

The lot of the average Russian gradually improved before the war. Free medical care and other social services, together with full employment, provided the Russian worker with security at the expense of freedom. At the same time, some of the changes introduced shortly after the revolution were now abandoned. The family, at first deemphasized, now again became the basic unit of society. Education became less progressive but more universal. Religion, once persecuted, was at least tolerated. One of the most surprising reversals of the Stalinist era was the renewed veneration of Russia's past. During the Second World War in particular this new Russian nationalism turned for inspiration to the great events of Russian history, thus ignoring

Collectivization

Hot dry winds had blighted some of the crops in 1932, and there had been a good deal of neglect in cultivation, as a result of apathy and discouragement. The huge weed crop choked out much of the grain, and in some cases a considerable part of the crop remained unharvested. Still it was the general testimony of the peasants that they could have pulled through if the local authorities had not swooped down with heavy requisitions. The last reserves of grain, which had been buried in the ground by the desperate peasants, were dug up and confiscated. A man named Sheboldaev, with a reputation in "liquidating" kulaks in the lower Volga district, was made President of the North Caucasus, where the passive resistance was doubtless stiffer than in other sections of the country, because a considerable part of the population consisted of Cossacks, who had enjoyed a higher standard of living than the mass of the peasants before the Revolution and who had mostly fought on the side of the Whites during the civil war. Under Sheboldaev's orders whole communities, such as Poltavskaya, in the Western Kuban, were deported *en masse* to the frozen regions of the north in the dead of winter. Other villages which did not fill out the grain quotas that were demanded from them were "blockaded," in the sense that no city products were allowed to reach them. Local officials who protested against the pitiless repression were deposed, arrested, in a few cases shot.

From W. H. Chamberlin, *Russia's Iron Age* (Boston: Little, Brown, 1934), pp. 85–86.

Marx's admonition that the proletariat had no fatherland. Stalin's motive in blending the old with the new was to strengthen his regime by rooting it more firmly in the past.

The Sabotage and Treason Trials

Although communism under Stalin gained a firm hold in Russia, there were nevertheless frequent signs of internal unrest. Among the manifestations of such unrest were the so-called sabotage trials of 1928 to 1933 and the treason trials of 1934 to 1938. The sabotage trials involved several groups of Russian and foreign engineers who were accused of sabotaging Russia's industrial efforts. The foreigners in each case denied these charges, but the Russian defendants readily confessed their guilt. Opinion outside Russia was that these trials were staged by the government to try to hide or excuse the many instances of waste and inefficiency revealed during the early years of the Five-Year Plans.

The same explanation, however, did not hold for the treason trials. These amounted to a major purge of thousands of leading figures of the Soviet regime. The reason given for the Great Purge was an alleged conspiracy, instigated by Hit-ler and Trotsky and ultimately directed at Stalin. The purge was touched off by the assassination of Sergei Kirov, party chief of Leningrad, in December 1934. In January 1935 Zinoviev and Kamenev were accused of conspiracy in the murder and were sentenced to imprisonment. They were condemned to death, together with fourteen other "Trotskyites," in 1936. Many others followed, including Rykov and Bukharin. In 1937 the purge spread to the Red army and throughout the entire Soviet hierarchy. Tens of thousands were arrested, executed, or exiled.

Foreign observers were bewildered and horrified by this spectacle of the revolution "devouring its children." The Great Purge was generally seen as a sign of Russian weakness. The significance of the fact that the Soviet state was strong enough to survive so tremendous a bloodletting was overlooked at the time. That there was opposition in Russia cannot be doubted. In spreading his net as wide as he did, some historians feel, Stalin destroyed any possible danger of a future conspiracy. Such drastic action may well have assured the survival of the Soviet Union in the Second World War.

Russia and the West

Prominent in Stalin's repressive policy at home was the fear of possible intervention from abroad. The memory of such intervention during the revolution was never forgotten. Outwardly, Russia's relations with the West improved markedly during the 1930s. The Soviet Union was the only major power not affected by the Great Depression, and the Russian market offered commercial opportunities that existed nowhere else. The rising threats of Nazi Germany in Europe and of Japan in Asia established a further bond of interest between the Soviet Union and the democracies. In 1933 the United States finally recognized the Soviet Union; the following year Russia was admitted to the League of Nations; and in 1935 the Soviets joined France and Czechoslovakia in military agreements against Germany. But despite this apparent *rapprochement*, Russia continued to distrust the West and the West continued to distrust Russia. This mutual suspicion

Khrushchev on the Great Purge

Stalin originated the concept "enemy of the people." This term automatically rendered it unnecessary that the ideological errors of a man or men engaged in a controversy be proven; this term made possible the usage of the most cruel repression, violating all norms of revolutionary legality, against anyone who in any way disagreed with Stalin, against those who had bad reputations. This concept "enemy of the people" actually eliminated the possibility of any kind of ideological fight or the making of one's views known on this or that issue, even those of a practical character. In the main, and in actuality, the one proof of guilt used, against all norms of current legal science, was the "confession" of the accused himself, and, as subsequent probing proved, "confessions" were acquired through physical pressures against the accused. This led to glaring violations of revolutionary legality and to the fact that many entirely innocent persons, who in the past had defended the party line, became victims.

From *The Crimes of the Stalin Era: Special Report to the 20th Congress of the Communist Party of the Soviet Union* by Nikita S. Khrushchev, ed. by Boris I. Nicolaevsky (New York: The New Leader, 1956).

had tragic consequences on the eve of the Second World War.

THE FASCIST REVOLUTION IN ITALY

The rise of fascism, first in Italy and later in Germany, was in part a reaction to the real or imaginary threat of communism. But even without such a threat, conditions in Italy after the First World War made major changes imperative. The Italian people had been divided about intervention in the war. But once the nation joined the Allies, hopes for territorial rewards ran high. Such expectations were bitterly disappointed at the Peace Conference. Popular discontent was heightened by postwar economic problems. Riots and strikes, together with a sharp increase in the Socialist vote, made Italy's propertied elements fear that a communist revolution was at hand. Various democratic governments tried to cope with this hopeless situation but with little success. Parliamentary democracy had never worked well in Italy. Here, then, was a situation in which some able and unscrupulous demagogue could come along and promise a solution to Italy's problems. The man who saw and seized this opportunity was Benito Mussolini.

Benito Mussolini

It has been said that Mussolini was Italian fascism personified, and the movement certainly would have been unthinkable without him. Born in 1883, son of a Socialist blacksmith, Mussolini himself had become a Socialist in his youth. He had worked abroad as an agitator, had been jailed in 1911 for opposing Italy's war with Turkey, and in 1912 had become editor of *Avanti*, Italy's leading Socialist newspaper. When war broke out in 1914, Mussolini was still a pacifist. But he soon changed and advocated Italian intervention on the Allied side. This was the first of many radical reversals in the life of this accomplished opportunist.

Mussolini's first *Fasci di Combattimento*, or "groups of combat," were formed in the spring of 1919. Their name was derived from the old Roman fasces, a bundle of rods bound around the handle of an ax that symbolized unity and authority. These groups were initially made up chiefly of discontented veterans. But the number of these "Black Shirts" rapidly increased from a few hundred to many thousands. Their aims were mostly negative: they were against the monarchy, the Church, the Socialists, and the capitalists. In the elections of 1919 the Fascists failed to get a single seat. But two years later they won thirty-five. Capitalizing on the fears of the middle class by posing as the defender of law, order, and property, Mussolini was able to seize power in the fall of 1922.

The "March on Rome"

Mussolini's boast of having saved Italy from the danger of a Communist revolution was false. That danger, if it ever existed, had run its course by 1922. In the meantime, the Black Shirts were waging a virtual civil war against Socialists and labor unions, and Mussolini was mending his fences in preparation for his *coup*. First he changed his revolutionary movement into a regular political party. Then he proclaimed his loyalty to the monarchy and the Church. And finally he made certain that the army would not oppose him. When everything was ready, in October 1922, Mussolini mobilized his Black Shirts for a dramatic "March on Rome." But King Victor Emmanuel had been well prepared and gave way easily. On October 29, 1922, Mus-

Mussolini (in suit in center) with Fascist followers in 1922 during the famous "March on Rome."

solini was invited to form a new government, and the following day he made his triumphal entry into Rome by train.

The change from democratic to totalitarian rule in Italy took several years. At the start, Mussolini was given full emergency powers for only one year. He used these powers to tighten Fascist control. To make certain of Fascist victories in future elections, a new electoral law in 1923 provided that any party that gained a plurality of votes would automatically receive two-thirds of the parliamentary seats. Even so, opposition in the Chamber continued. In June 1924 one of Mussolini's most fearless critics, the Socialist leader Giacomo Matteotti, was kidnapped, "taken for a ride," and murdered. At first it seemed as though popular indignation would sweep the Fascists from power. Mussolini, pretending to be deeply shocked by the crime, promised severe punishment of the guilty. But when he realized how little united his opponents were, he reversed his course. A new secret police, the OVRA, was founded, and in a wave of persecution, enemies of the state were brought before a special tribunal and sentenced to prison or exile. Non-Fascist members of the cabinet were dismissed, and Mussolini was once again given power to rule by decree. In 1926 all opposition parties were outlawed. The Matteotti affair, far from bringing about the fall of Fascism, served to cap its victory.

The Fascist State

Like communism, Italian fascism created its own system of government. Political power, in Mussolini's "corporative state," was vested in some thirteen "syndicates." These confederations, which included both workers and employers, were initially organized to regulate labor conditions. Strikes and lockouts were declared illegal, and the final word in labor disputes rested with the government. Beginning in 1928 this corporate system was made the basis of Italy's political organization. Under a new electoral law, the syndicates drew up a list of candidates for the Chamber of Deputies. Their final selection, however, rested with the Fascist Grand Council, a body of some twenty party leaders appointed by Mussolini. As under communism, the party thus wielded complete political control. Parliament, under this new system, lost most of its former functions. In 1938 even the outward forms of democracy disappeared when the Chamber of Deputies was replaced by a new Chamber of Fasces and Corporations. Since all its members were appointed, there was no longer any need for elections.

The Fascist Party, again like its Communist counterpart, considered itself an elite. Its membership in 1934 was about 1.5 million. Its leader, or *Duce*, was Mussolini. Fascist youth organizations took care of indoctrinating the young. The press, radio, and movies were under strict censorship, and every facet of intellectual and artistic life was made to fit in with party propaganda. Only in his relations with the Church did Mussolini show a certain leniency. One of the major achievements of his regime was the Lateran Treaty of 1929, which settled the long-standing feud between the Italian government and the papacy.

The major efforts of Mussolini's policy at home were aimed at improving Italy's economic position. Reduction of government spending, suppression of

The Fascist Decalogue   1938

1. Remember that those who fell for the revolution and for the empire march at the head of your columns.
2. Your comrade is your brother. He lives with you, thinks with you, and is at your side in the battle.
3. Service to Italy can be rendered at all times, in all places, and by every means. It can be paid with toil and also with blood.
4. The enemy of Fascism is your enemy. Give him no quarter.
5. Discipline is the sunshine of armies. It prepares and illuminates the victory.
6. He who advances to the attack with decision has victory already in his grasp.
7. Conscious and complete obedience is the virtue of the Legionary.
8. There do not exist things important and things unimportant. There is only duty.
9. The Fascist revolution has depended in the past and still depends on the bayonets of its Legionaries.
10. Mussolini is always right.

From M. Oakeshott, *The Social and Political Doctrines of Contemporary Europe* (Cambridge: Cambridge University Press, 1949), pp. 180–81.

strikes, and increased taxation brought some financial stability. Italy also shared in the general economic recovery of the late 1920s. The Great Depression, however, undid these gains. Even though the Italian government by then had assumed far-reaching control over economic affairs, its policy was far less successful than Russia's planned economy under the Five-Year Plans. Not only was Mussolini less ruthless than Stalin, but Italy lacked the Soviet Union's vast natural resources. Beginning in 1935, furthermore, Mussolini embarked on a costly war, the burden of which had to be borne by the Italian people.

One sure way of diverting domestic discontent is through a strong and successful foreign policy. Mussolini first tried this remedy in 1923, when he ordered the Italian navy to bombard the Greek island of Corfu. But his ardor had been somewhat dampened by the protest of the great powers. For the next ten years, therefore, Mussolini was careful not to appear too aggressive. Italy concluded treaties of friendship with a number of countries, especially those that, like Austria and Hungary, shared its opposition to the peace treaties. In 1924 Yugoslavia, in return for concessions elsewhere, agreed to Italy's annexation of Fiume. Relations with Germany, even after Hitler's rise to power, remained cool, chiefly because of Germany's desire for *Anschluss* with Austria. Mussolini's restoration of domestic order, meanwhile, endeared him to foreign visitors; his opposition to communism made him appear the ally of anti-Communists everywhere; and his improved relations with the Church won him Catholic support. As a result, the new Italy and its leader commanded considerable respect abroad, at least until 1935. Only then did the world begin to realize the danger that fascism posed to world peace.

Fascist Ideology

When Mussolini founded his movement in 1919 he had, by his own admission, "no specific doctrinal plan." He was, as has been said, a born opportunist. In his formative years, Mussolini had come under the influence of a variety of writers, from Machiavelli to Pareto, including Nietzsche, Sorel, and even Marx. Fascism also had its own philosophers, men like Giovanni Gentile and Alfredo Rocco. But one looks in vain for an exposition of fascist doctrine as clear as that provided for communism by Marx or even as rambling as that provided for nazism by Hitler. Fascism was a dynamic movement, devoted to action rather than thought. Its motto was "Believe, Obey, Fight." "Believe" covered a wide range of romantic ideals, from the glories of Rome to the irrational creed of modern nationalism. "Obey" meant subjection to the authority of the state and its leader, the *Duce*. To "fight" was the noblest aim of all. War alone, Mussolini said, "puts the stamp of nobility upon the people who have the courage to meet it." This belief in war for war's sake was the essence of Italian fascism.

THE RISE OF NATIONAL SOCIALISM IN GERMANY

Mussolini's success in Italy was observed with keen interest in Germany, where a movement akin to Italian fascism had been active since the early 1920s. Its leader was an obscure Austrian rabble-rouser, Adolf Hitler, the moving spirit behind the National Socialist German Workers' Party (NSDAP). The brown-shirted members of the party—or "Nazis," as their opponents called them—were similar to Mussolini's first Black Shirts. Most of them were disgruntled war veterans. Like their Italian counterparts, they hoped to seize power by a *coup d'état*. But their Munich *Putsch* in November 1923 had failed. For the next few years Adolf Hitler all but disappeared from the public eye.

Adolf Hitler and His Aims

The man who was soon to determine the fate of the whole world was still not taken very seriously outside the Nazi movement. Born in 1889, the son of an Austrian customs official, Hitler had gone into politics after the First World War, in which he had fought as a German soldier. Considering his humble background and haphazard education, his subsequent rise to power was remarkable. Circumstances played their part, but even they needed a master. The *Führer*, or leader, of the Nazi Party was neither physically nor intellectually impressive. Yet he had certain qualities and abilities that enabled him to subject to his power first a whole people and ultimately a whole continent. One hesitates to call someone "great" who was at the same time so evil. But there was a certain diabolical greatness about this monstrous man. Rarely has anyone inspired such extremes of hatred and adulation as did Adolf Hitler.

As far as Hitler's aims were concerned, National Socialism, in contrast to Italian fascism, had a detailed, though internally contradictory, program. Its twenty-five points offered something to everyone. The worker was promised a share in the profits of industry and the nationalization of the big trusts; the peasant was tempted by land reform and the scrapping of mortgages; and the rest of the people were told to look forward to "the creation and preservation of a healthy middle class." German national honor was to be avenged by breaking the fetters of Versailles. The country was to be strengthened by the union of all Germans in a Greater Germany. The Jews were to be excluded from political life. The parliamentary system was to be abolished. And "positive Christianity" was to replace religious diversity. This program, of course, was never completely implemented, and provisions that might scare off prospective supporters were soon explained away. Yet with its pan-German nationalism, its anti-Semitism, and its opposition to democracy, it clearly foreshadowed future Nazi policy. A still more important prediction of things to come was given in Hitler's autobiography, *Mein Kampf* (*My Battle*), which he began in 1924. Besides Judaism and Marxism, bolshevism now emerged as a major target, and Russia was singled out as the chief victim of future German expansion.

Much of Hitler's ideology, especially its racism and pan-Germanism, had its roots in nineteenth-century Austrian and German thought. Because of such antecedents, and because Hitler's policy, notably in eastern Europe, seemed like a continuation of earlier trends in German history, the rise of National Socialism has been seen as a natural, almost inevitable, and peculiarly German development. There can be no doubt that Germany's past and the characteristics of its people help to explain the rise of Hitler. But of equal if not greater significance were the evil genius of Hitler himself and the specific circumstances in the early 1930s that made his victory possible.

Hitler's Rise to Power

Before Germany had found time to recover from the results of a lost war and a runaway inflation, it was plunged once more into a major economic crisis—the Great Depression. With millions of un-

---

Adolf Hitler

Hitler cannot be confined within a simple formula. For my part I knew three facets of his personality, each corresponding to a like facet in his nature.

His first aspect was one of pallor; his jumbled complexion and vague globular eyes, lost in a dream, lent him an absent, faraway air, the troubled and troubling face of a medium or somnambulist.

The second aspect was animated, colored, swept away by passion. His nostrils would twitch, his eyes dart lightning; he was all violence, impatience of control, lust for domination, abomination of his antagonists, cynical boldness, with a fierce energy ready at no provocation to pull down the universe about his ears. Then his "storm and assault" face was the face of a lunatic.

Hitler's third aspect was that of a naïve, rustic man, dull, vulgar, easily amused, laughing boisterously as he slapped his thigh; a commonplace face without any distinguishing mark, a face like thousands of other faces spread over the face of the earth. . . .

These alternate states of excitement and depression, these fits mentioned by his familiars, ranged from the most devastating fury to the plaintive moanings of a wounded beast. Because of them, psychiatrists have considered him a "cyclothimic"; others see in him the typical paranoiac. This much is certain: he was no normal being. He was, rather, a morbid personality, a quasi-madman, a character out of the pages of Dostoevski, a man "possessed."

From André François-Poncet, *The Fateful Years: Memoirs of a French Ambassador in Berlin, 1931–1938*, trans. by J. LeClerq (New York: Harcourt Brace Jovanovich, 1949), pp. 289–91.

employed barely existing on a meager dole, political extremism flourished. Between 1928 and 1932 the number of Nazi delegates in the *Reichstag* rose from 12 to 230, and Communist strength increased from 54 to 89. This radicalization made the orderly conduct of government by moderate parties impossible. Democracy, which never had taken firm hold in Germany, broke down. Economic and political chaos, the threat of communism, and constant nationalist agitation against the Peace Treaty—these were the elements that helped prepare the ground for the rise of dictatorship in Germany, just as they had done ten years earlier in Italy.

Hitler's actual assumption of power was through perfectly legal means. Like Mussolini before him, he was asked—on January 30, 1933—to form a coalition government. The men who helped Hitler gain power—the aged President von Hindenburg and his political advisers—felt confident that they would be able to use the Nazi movement to achieve their own ends: the establishment of a conservative and authoritarian regime. They failed to realize that Hitler was not a man to let himself be used.

To strengthen his position, Hitler first held new elections for the *Reichstag*. Shortly before the elections, the *Reichstag* building went up in flames, an event Hitler blamed on the Communists. But despite the intimidation of political opponents, only 44 percent of the German people voted National Socialist. As a next step, Hitler manipulated the *Reichstag* into passing an Enabling Act that gave the government dictatorial powers for four years. These powers were then used to prohibit those political parties that did not dissolve themselves. By July 1933 the National Socialists had become the only legal party in Germany. The following November a solidly Nazi *Reichstag* was elected. In the meantime, Hitler had changed his cabinet to include mostly National Socialists. President von Hindenburg, who became increasingly senile toward the end, died in August 1934. Hitler now combined the office of president with that of chancellor, assuming the title of *Führer und Reichskanzler*, leader and chancellor. The transition from democracy to dictatorship was complete.

President von Hindenburg in 1933. Visible directly behind him is Adolf Hitler next to a heavily decorated Hermann Göring.

NATIONAL SOCIALISM IN POWER

Unlike Communist Russia and Fascist Italy, Nazi Germany did not introduce any sweeping constitutional changes. The *Reichstag* continued to meet, though infrequently, to endorse all measures put before it. There were no more elections, but occasionally the German people were asked in a plebiscite to support an act of the *Führer's*. Needless to say, they always did so by a rousing majority. The organization of the civil service was maintained, though it was purged of Jews and political opponents. The legal system was overhauled, and traditional concepts of law were abandoned in favor of a new kind of justice that elevated the welfare of the people and the state above the rights of the individual. To ferret out enemies of the state, a secret police, the Gestapo, was given sweeping powers of arrest and investigation.

Hitler speaks.

Nazism at Home

As was the case in other totalitarian states, the Nazi Party in Germany controlled every aspect of national life. In his struggle for power Hitler had been aided by a number of capable lieutenants. These were now rewarded with leading positions in the government. But some of Hitler's old comrades failed to get what they expected. And others felt that Hitler had broken his word by not carrying out the more radical promises of the early Nazi program. To forestall any "second revolution" on the part of these malcontents, Hitler, on June 30, 1934, instituted a major "Blood Purge." In a lightening move the *Führer* had several hundred of his possible opponents arrested and many of them executed.

With the government and the party now under his firm control, there remained only one sphere in which the *Führer* did not wield complete authority, and that was the military. The armed forces had sworn personal allegiance to him after Hindenburg's death, and Hitler's renunciation of the disarmament clauses of the Peace Treaty in March 1935 had further enhanced his standing with the army. But it was not until 1938, after a thorough-going purge of the army's top echelons had removed the generals about whose loyalty Hitler felt uncertain, that the *Führer* felt he had a force on which he could fully rely. Henceforth Hitler himself was to wield personal command of all Germany's armed forces.

The same process of *Gleichschaltung*, or "coordination," that was carried out in government, party, and army, was extended to every other phase of German life. In many of his innovations, Hitler consciously imitated Mussolini. This was true not only of the symbols and ceremonies of the "Third Reich" but of many of its policies. Like Mussolini, Hitler tried to make his country's economy as strong and self-sufficient as possible. The most spectacular sign of German recovery was the reduction of unemployment. Public works, rearmament, and military conscription ultimately created an actual labor shortage. In 1934 the *Führer* launched the first of two Four-Year Plans

to prepare Germany's economy for war. To finance such costly ventures, huge funds were needed. These funds were raised through increased taxation, special levies, and rigid control of prices and profits.

The main sufferer of this policy of "guns instead of butter" was the German worker. His wages were low, his hours long, and his movements restricted. A German "Labor Front" took the place of the former unions. Like the Italian "syndicates" it included both workers and employers. Strikes were forbidden, and all labor relations were controlled by the state. The farmer fared somewhat better. He was given various kinds of subsidies and was protected against foreclosure. Food production increased, although Germany did not become self-sufficient. One of Hitler's aims was a large and healthy rural population. In Nazi mythology "blood and soil" were considered the source of a nation's strength. Artists and writers, regimented like everyone else in Germany's totalitarian society, were called upon to glorify the "nobility of labor," and Nazi propaganda urged each and every German to place the welfare of the community before the good of the individual.

The majority of Germans readily complied with this appeal to make personal sacrifices and to work hard. Not that the German people were all ardent Nazis. The Nazi Party, like its counterparts in Russia and Italy, considered itself an elite, and its membership was restricted. The average German was, in his own words, *unpolitisch* (nonpolitical). He welcomed what he considered the "positive" features of the Nazi regime, and he secretly grumbled about the things he did not like. There were even some active opposition—the thousands of prisoners in the concentration camps testified to that. Hitler's efforts to force all Protestants under the control of a "German Christian" church, and his evasion of the concordat he had concluded with the Catholic Church in 1933, brought strong and courageous protests from religious leaders of both confessions. There were other circles of resistance. But these groups were only a minority. Before the outbreak of the Second

World War, Hitler's many admirers abroad praised him, like Mussolini, for the miraculous improvements he had brought about, and in particular for the firm stand he had taken against communism at home and abroad.

Anti-Semitism

One aspect of Nazi policy, however, from the start stirred deep concern among observers abroad, and that was the persecution of the Jews. Anti-Semitism had been one of Hitler's earliest obsessions, and it was the aim that he pursued most persistently and ruthlessly to the bitter end. The first measures against Germany's Jews—fewer than six hundred thousand, or 1 percent of the population—were taken shortly after the Nazis came to power. In April 1933 all Jews were excluded from the civil service, and a national boycott was imposed on Jewish businesses. Soon thereafter the Jews were excluded from universities, and lawyers and doctors were barred from practice. The next major step came with the "Nuremberg Laws" of 1935, which deprived all Jews of their citizenship and forbade their marriage to non-Jews. As a result of this "cold pogrom," many Jews went into exile. But worse was yet to come. In November 1938 the assassination of a German diplomat in Paris by a young Polish Jew was made the occasion for a "spontaneous" demonstration against the Jews. Synagogues were burned, shops looted, Jewish homes invaded and their occupants beaten or killed. Jews henceforth had to wear a yellow Star of David and had to live in ghettos.

The intensification of Jewish persecution in 1938 was merely another sign that Hitler was getting ready for war. Most of Germany's domestic policies since 1933 had been geared to that purpose, no matter how ardently the *Führer* might proclaim his peaceful intentions. Hitler's ultimate aim was a "New Order" for Europe, under which the German people would expand into the unlimited *Lebensraum* (living space) of the East and rule over the "inferior" Slavic peoples of that region. The unbounded ambition of Hitler's megalomania plunged the world into the most frightful war it had ever seen.

THE SPREAD OF AUTHORITARIANISM

One of the dangers of totalitarianism, in the eyes of the free world, was its tendency to spread to nations that had been weakened by economic crises and political unrest. The rise of communism was generally considered the greater threat, and many a dictatorship of the right gained power in order to prevent a dictatorship of the left. The Soviet Union tried its best, with the aid of the Comintern, to help Communist parties abroad. But its numerous attempts at fomenting leftist plots in central Europe and in the Far East remained unsuccessful. Nowhere outside the Soviet Union did communism gain a decisive victory during the interwar period.

Authoritarianism in Europe

Efforts to set up rightist dictatorships, on the other hand, proved more successful. We have already seen the rise of strong men in most of the smaller nations of central Europe during the aftermath of the First World War. Similar regimes arose in Spain and Portugal. In some countries—Yugoslavia, Albania, Bulgaria, Greece, and Rumania—kings turned into dictators. In others—Hungary, Poland, and Spain—power was wielded by an alliance of military and agrarian groups. In still others—Austria and Portugal—authority rested with parties supported by the Catholic Church. As in the case of Russia, Italy, and Germany, all these small nations lacked a strong democratic tradition. Their new regimes were authoritarian rather than totalitarian. In some instances Germany and Italy tried to aid the rise of such authoritarian regimes. In Austria a Nazi *Putsch* in July 1934 failed, and Nazi victory was postponed until the *Anschluss* four years later. In Spain, on the other hand, General Francisco Franco defeated the republican government with the help of Italy and Germany. Like communism, fascism had

Nazi picket during the boycott of Jewish-owned shops in 1933. The placard reads: "Germans! Strike back! Don't buy from Jews!"

followers in the democracies as well. But with the exception of France, these native Fascist parties never posed a serious threat. It was only during the Second World War that the Fascist "Fifth Column" became a real danger.

Japanese Fascism

In one nation outside Europe—Japan—economic crisis, rabid nationalism, and the failure of democracy gave rise to a totalitarian regime. The impact of the Great Depression on that heavily industrialized nation had increased the smoldering discontent with the government's inefficiency at home and moderation abroad. The opposition in Japan was centered in the army, particularly among its junior officers. Their aims were expressed in the writings of a young radical, Ikki Kita, who opposed the big industrialists and their political allies and advocated an almost socialist program: restriction of private property, nationalization of industries, and virtual abolition of parliamentary government. With the empire thus revolutionized, he envisaged Japan taking the lead in a crusade against western imperialism and ultimately extending its influence throughout Asia.

The military clique itself had no clear program of action other than to gain control of the government. This they hoped to achieve through pressure, mainly by assassinating moderate politicians. Early in 1936 these activities culminated in a mutiny and the murder of several high officials. The army high command took energetic countermeasures and executed the ringleaders. But at the same time the government made a number of concessions that assured the domination of the military in national affairs. In November 1936 Japan joined Germany and Italy in a treaty against communism, the Anti-Comintern Pact. Fascism had thus founded its own "International."

Japanese fascism differed in several respects from its European counterparts. It was not a well-organized movement under a single leader but rather a small pressure group; and it did not attempt to change the existing system of government but rather to dominate it. Yet in its demands for the submission of the individual to the state, and in its veneration of tradition as embodied in the person of the emperor, Japan's militarism showed definite fascist traits. Most pronounced was the similarity of the foreign policies of the three Fascist powers. Each sought solution of domestic difficulties through foreign expansion; each based the right to such expansion on claims of inherent superiority; and each looked to a special sphere of influence beyond its frontiers. In the case of Japan that sphere was the mainland of China.

THE MARCH OF FASCIST AGGRESSION, 1931–37

The series of international crises that culminated in the outbreak of the Second World War began as far back as 1931 in the Far East.

Japan Against China

Japan, for some time past, had been trying to gain control over Manchuria, China's border province in the northeast. The region was rich in iron and coal; it adjoined Korea, where a Japanese protectorate had been established in 1907; and it was not under the direct control of Nationalist China. In September 1931 the Japanese army, using a minor incident along the South Manchurian Railway as an excuse, seized the Manchurian city of Kirin and surrounding territory. Local Chinese forces proved no match for the aggressors, and within a few months most of Manchuria had come under Japanese domination. In 1932 the victorious Japanese renamed their conquest Manchukuo and declared it a protectorate of Japan.

The Chinese government meanwhile protested to the League of Nations and to the United States against this Japanese act of force. The League appointed a special commission of inquiry under Lord Lytton, onetime viceroy of India. Its report condemned Japan's aggression and proposed the establishment of an autonomous Manchuria under Chinese sovereignty. The United States, in its "Stimson Doctrine," declared that it would not recognize any changes made by force of arms. This was as far as the powers were prepared to go. Under the League Covenant they could and should have taken more drastic action. But China seemed far away and sanctions might prove costly at a time when most of the world was in the throes of depression. So nothing was done. Japan, to have the last word, withdrew from the League of Nations in 1933.

Hitler Against Versailles

The moral of the Manchurian story was that if an aggressor acted quickly enough, nobody would dare stop him. This lesson was not lost on Adolf Hitler. In a series of dramatic moves between 1933 and 1936, he freed Germany from the most onerous restrictions of the Peace Treaty. In October 1933 the Germans withdrew from the Disarmament Conference and the League of Nations. In January 1935 the Saar region voted to return to Germany. Two months later Hitler denounced the disarmament clauses of the Versailles Treaty, and Germany openly began a program of full-scale rearmament.

In order to forestall any opposition to his unilateral policy, Hitler was careful at every step to stress Germany's peaceful intentions. In January 1934 he signed a nonaggression pact with Poland. This was seen as a sign that the Germans had become reconciled to their eastern frontiers. In the spring of 1935 Hitler quieted Britain's fears of German rearmament by concluding an Anglo-German naval agreement. The British thereby acquiesced in the *Führer*'s violation of the Treaty of Versailles and added considerably to France's feeling of insecurity. It is hardly surprising, then, that France should have sought help elsewhere. In May 1935 it concluded an alliance with the Soviet Union. But this merely gave Hitler the pretext he needed for his next major *coup*.

On March 7, 1936, Hitler ordered the German army to march into the demilitarized zone of the Rhineland. It was the *Führer*'s most daring move to date. Had he been forced to back down at this crucial point, the future would doubtless

Former British Prime Minister David Lloyd George visiting Hitler at Berchtesgaden.

Hitler's Visitors

Lloyd George visited Hitler in September 1936, discussed world affairs, and came away convinced that Hitler was a reasonable man with acceptable aims and no desire whatsoever to plunge Europe into war. Conservatives, Liberals, and Socialists alike sought out the Führer, and were mesmerized by him. Even Arnold Toynbee was reported to have been won over at his interview to a belief in Hitler's genuine desire for peace in Europe "and close friendship with England." George Lansbury, a pacifist, and earlier leader of the Labour Party, was convinced after their personal encounter that Hitler "will *not* go to war unless pushed into it by others." Lord Allen of Hurwood told the *Daily Telegraph* on his return from Germany that "I watched him with the utmost vigilance throughout our lengthy conversation, and I am convinced he genuinely desires peace." Halifax recorded after his own visit to Berchtesgaden: "He struck me as very sincere, and as believing everything he said." But all Hitler did at these meetings was to repeat to each visitor the same dreary monologue about the insults of Versailles, the need for German unity on an ethnic basis, the evils of communism which he as a German could appreciate more than they could, the stubbornness of the Czechs, the pugnacity of the Poles, and the long-suffering innocence of the Germans. . . . But . . . when Lord Allen of Hurwood, with greater courage than most of his fellow-visitors, raised the issue of Jewish persecution, Hitler had nothing to say.

From Martin Gilbert, *The Roots of Appeasement* (London: Weidenfeld and Nicolson, 1966), pp. 164–65.

Ethiopian chiefs in the Ethiopian War (1935–36).

ETHIOPIA (ABYSSINIA) 1934

EGYPT

British territories

Italian territories

Mecca

Port Sudan

ASIR

RED SEA

ARABIA

Nile River

Khartoum

Massaua

Asmara

ERITREA

YEMEN

HADHRAMAUT

ANGLO-EGYPTIAN

SUDAN

Aksum · Adua

· Makale

Assab

ADEN

Aden (Br.)

GULF OF ADEN

FRENCH

SOMALILAND

Djibouti

Blue Nile

· L. Tana

Dessye ·

Berhera

BRITISH

SOMALILAND

White Nile

· Addis Ababa

ETHIOPIA (ABYSSINIA)

· Walwal

ITALIAN SOMALILAND

BELGIAN CONGO

· L. Rudolf

UGANDA

KENYA

· Mogadishu

INDIAN OCEAN

L. Victoria

· Kismayu

0   MILES   300

have been far different. But again nothing happened. The French were afraid to act without the British. The British government officially criticized Germany's act. But the general feeling in England was that the Germans merely did what any people would have done under the circumstances—namely, to establish mastery over their own territory. The far-reaching implications of Germany's action were overlooked. Should Germany want to move quickly, as it had done in 1914 and was to do again in 1940, there was no longer any protective zone to save the Lowlands from German invasion.

Mussolini Against Ethiopia

One reason why Hitler was able to get away with his daring move in the Rhineland was that it coincided with a serious international crisis elsewhere. On October 3, 1935, an Italian army had invaded the Kingdom of Ethiopia, or Abyssinia, in northeastern Africa. The isolated and backward region had somehow escaped the scramble for colonies among the European powers before 1914. Once before, in 1896, Italy had tried to invade Ethiopia but had been repulsed. This humiliation was never forgotten. In his desire to increase his nation's power and glory, Mussolini now hoped to join Ethiopia with the existing Italian colonies of Eritrea and Somaliland into a sizable imperium. It was for reasons of prestige, therefore, that the Italian Fascist dictator embarked on his anachronistic venture into colonial imperialism.

The Ethiopian War did not last long. Italy's forces were too powerful for the antiquated forces of Emperor Haile Selassie. On May 9, 1936, Mussolini proclaimed the annexation of Ethiopia to Italy. Meanwhile the League of Nations, for once, had not been idle. After declaring Italy an aggressor, it had instituted a program of economic sanctions. But such a program, to be effective, had to be airtight. With several major powers remaining outside the League, it could not be. Still, it might have been possible to stop the Italians if oil had been included in the list of embargoes. But the fear that a ban on oil might lead to a general war made both France and England hesitate to take such a step. The French, who looked on Italy as a possible ally against Germany, did not wish to endanger their friendly relations with Mussolini. The British feared that their navy would have to bear the major brunt of a possible conflict, and such a risk seemed "unrealistic" over an issue as insignificant as Ethiopia. Without the support of its two most powerful members, the League was powerless to act.

The results of the Ethiopian War were of the greatest significance for the future. Once again the western powers, instead of supporting collective security, had preferred to buy peace by making concessions at someone else's expense. But such concessions, as the next few years were to show, merely whetted the appetites of the dictators. Prior to this time, relations between Hitler and Mussolini had not been very close. Hitler's designs on Austria worried Mussolini, who was himself interested in the Danube region. But with the conquest of Ethiopia, Italy's energies had found an outlet elsewhere, and Germany's friendly attitude during the conflict had further paved the way for closer collaboration. On October 25, 1936, the two powers concluded a formal agreement to coordinate their foreign policies. This "Rome-Berlin Axis" was later joined by Japan.

War in Spain

The fateful significance of the "Rome-Berlin Axis" became evident in connection with the Spanish Civil War. Spain had long been a deeply divided country. Although a republic since 1931, the traditionally promonarchist forces—clergy, army, and aristocracy—still wielded considerable power. The Republican regime had been unable to cope with the economic consequences of the Great Depression. In contrast to the

right-wing opposition, the Republican left was far from solid. In the elections of 1936 Republicans, Socialists, Syndicalists, and Communists buried their differences long enough to form a "Popular Front," and as a result they won a majority. But this Republican victory merely hastened the inevitable clash between Nationalists and Republicans. In July 1936 army units in Spanish Morocco, led by General Francisco Franco, rebelled against the Republic. The Spanish Civil War had begun.

Had the Spaniards been left alone, the war would hardly have become the major tragedy it turned out to be. But the

Barcelona after bombardment by Franco's forces (July 1936).

Emblem of the International Brigades, which served in the Republican army in the Spanish Civil War.

war was not to remain a purely Spanish affair. Both Hitler and Mussolini were quick to recognize General Franco and to send men and materials to the Nationalists. The Russians in turn gave material and ideological support to the Republican, or Loyalist, side. But the Communists alone were incapable of matching the aid supplied by the Fascists. To assure the survival of the Republicans, the wholehearted cooperation of the democracies was needed.

The democracies were no more willing to risk a general war over Spain than they had been to become involved in a war over Manchuria or Ethiopia. Public opinion in general supported the Republicans, and foreign volunteers fought in the International Brigades on the Republican side. But the governments were more cautious. In September 1936 a Nonintervention Committee of some twenty-seven nations—including Germany, Italy, and the Soviet Union—met in London. But the committee could not prevent German and Italian "volunteers" from fighting on Franco's side. In an effort at neutrality, President Roosevelt invoked the Neutrality Act of 1935, prohibiting the export of arms and munitions to both sides in the conflict. But this move hurt mainly the Loyalists, since Franco continued to receive supplies from Germany and Italy.

The Spanish Civil War lasted for almost three years and caused more than seven hundred thousand deaths. By the time the last Republican forces surrendered in Madrid on March 28, 1939, events in Spain had long been overshadowed by more important developments elsewhere. But Hitler's policy of bloodless expansion in central Europe was doubtless aided by the diversion provided by the slow death of democracy in Spain.

THE ROAD TO WAR

Except for the Civil War in Spain, the international situation at the beginning of 1937 seemed quite hopeful. But this impression was mistaken. The preceding years had been a crucial time of preparation for the new German *Wehrmacht*, when determined outside resistance might still have put a stop to Hitler's plans for aggression. From now on the balance of military power began to turn more and more in Germany's favor. In June 1937 Hitler's Minister of Defense issued the first specific directive to prepare for a future war. Five months later Hitler met with his top advisers to present an outline of his strategy. First Germany would seek control over Austria and Czechoslovakia. Then it would be ready to pursue its major aim of eastward expansion to win the living space that the German people were entitled to.

War in the Far East

While Hitler was making his plans in Europe, warfare had already broken out in the Far East. In July 1937 a minor incident near Peking touched off an undeclared war between China and Japan that lasted until 1945. By the end of 1938 the Japanese were in control of most of northern China as far west as the Yellow River and as far south as the Yangtze and Hangchow. Still farther south, Japan had seized the city of Canton and surrounding territory. In March 1938 the Japanese set up a "Reformed Government of the Republic of China" at Nanking.

The government of Chiang Kai-shek, meanwhile, had taken refuge in the inte-

Japanese troops breaking through the Great Wall in northern China (1937).

rior province of Szechwan, with its capital at Chungking. The Chinese armies, while superior in numbers, were woefully short of equipment. To fight the invaders more effectively, Chiang Kaishek and the Chinese Communists agreed to bury their differences. A "scorched earth" policy and constant guerrilla warfare on the part of the Chinese kept the Japanese from consolidating their gains. But despite the determined resistance of the Chinese, their ultimate survival depended on outside aid.

Chinese protests to the League of Nations brought little more than verbal condemnation of Japanese aggression. The French feared that resistance to Japan might lead to a Japanese attack on the French colony of Indochina. And Britain hoped that by appeasing Japan it might keep its commercial interests in China. The United States, too, was careful at first not to antagonize Japan. Only when it became clear that the "Open Door" policy in China was being threatened did the United States begin to aid the Chinese. Of all the major powers, only the Soviet Union supported the Chinese from the beginning of the war. But the aid that reached China was not sufficient to halt the Japanese advance. Beginning in the spring of 1938, furthermore, attention was diverted from Asia to Europe, where Hitler was embarking on his systematic policy of eastward expansion.

The Austrian Anschluss

Hitler's first victim was the small Republic of Austria. Austria's *Anschluss* (joining-together with Germany) had always been a major Nazi aim. The failure of a Nazi *Putsch* in 1934 did not end the Nazi conspiracy. In January 1938 the Austrian government uncovered evidence of another Nazi plot. In the hope of removing the tension resulting from this latest incident, Austria's chancellor,

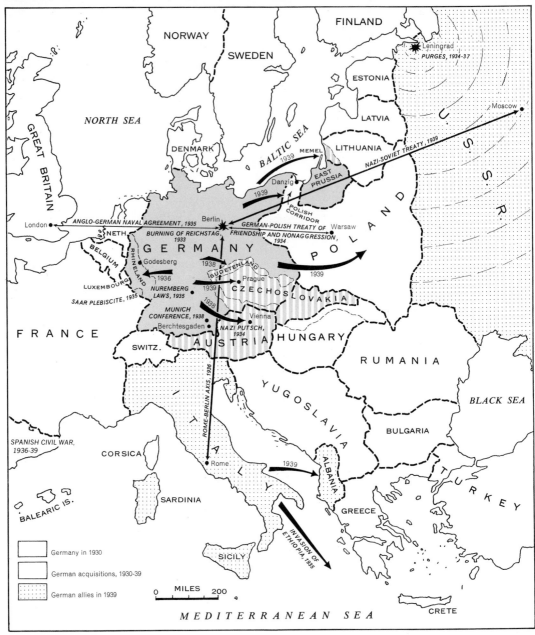

Kurt von Schuschnigg, accepted Hitler's invitation to come to the *Führer*'s retreat in Berchtesgaden in early February. Here he was presented with a set of demands that, if fulfilled, would have made Austria a virtual German protectorate. Refusal to accept, Hitler made clear, would result in a German invasion of Austria.

Faced with these alternatives, Schuschnigg had little choice but to give in. But in March he decided to make one final attempt to save his country by appealing directly to the Austrian people in a plebiscite. Hitler's reaction was swift. Once more threatening invasion, he forced Schuschnigg to call off the plebiscite and to resign. On March 11, an Austrian Nazi, Artur Seyss-Inquart, was made chancellor. On March 12, German troops crossed the Austrian frontier "to help maintain order." On March 13, Austria was incorporated into the Greater German Reich.

The ultimate success of this latest act of aggression again depended on the attitude of the great powers. As on all earlier occasions, there were loud protests but no action. The French were in the midst of one of their innumerable governmental crises and looked to the British to take the lead. But Britain, while deploring Hitler's methods, saw nothing wrong with an Austro-German *Anschluss*, so long as both peoples wanted it. And Italy, although long a champion of Austrian independence, was by now in the German camp. There was also the hope, of course, that Hitler would be satisfied, now that his dearest wish had been fulfilled. And the *Führer* did his best to confirm that hope by making his usual promises of peaceful intentions. The Soviet Union came forth with suggestions for a collective stand, warning that Czechoslovakia was next on Hitler's list; but the western powers considered these proposals premature.

The Conquest of Czechoslovakia

The pretext for Germany's intervention in Czechoslovakia was provided by the German minority in the Czech border regions. The 3 million Sudeten Germans, as they were called, had long been a source of trouble to the Czech government, especially since Hitler's rise to power. Beginning in 1936 their leader, Konrad Henlein, had begun to collaborate secretly with the Nazis; and as Germany's power in Europe increased, the demands of the Sudeten Germans became louder. In April 1938, after the fall of Austria, Henlein demanded complete autonomy for the Sudetenland. Nazi propaganda immediately took up this demand. The climax of Germany's campaign against the Czech government of President Eduard Beneš came with Hitler's address to the annual party congress at Nuremberg on September 12, 1938, in which he threatened German intervention on behalf of the Sudeten Germans.

Hitler's threat was no empty boast. The German army had been spending the summer of 1938 in feverish preparation for the invasion of Czechoslovakia. The French and British, meanwhile, had been trying desperately to effect a compromise solution of the Sudeten problem. But the Czechs proved adamant, trusting in their own military strength and the support of their French and Russian allies. When Hitler's speech intensified riots in the Sudetenland, the Czech government proclaimed martial law. War, it seemed, was imminent. It was narrowly averted by the action of Britain's prime minister, Neville Chamberlain, who now initiated a series of last-minute conferences with Hitler that sealed the fate of Czechoslovakia.

Chamberlain on His Trip to Munich

The events of the next 48 hours entailed terrific physical and mental exertions. I was up the night before till after 2 A.M. preparing my speech. Then came the early rising and the scenes at the aerodrome, and the long flight to Munich. The rest of that day, till after 2 o'clock next morning, was one prolonged nightmare, and I have only gradually been able since then to sort out my impressions.

Hitler's appearance and manner when I saw him appeared to show that the storm signals were up, though he gave me the double handshake that he reserves for specially friendly demonstration. Yet these appearances were deceptive. His opening sentences, when we gathered round for our conference, were so moderate and reasonable, that I felt instant relief.

Mussolini's attitude all through was extremely quiet and reserved. He seemed to be cowed by Hitler, but undoubtedly he was most anxious for a peaceful settlement. . . . His manner to me was more than friendly; he listened with the utmost attention to all I said, and expressed the strong hope that I would visit him early in Italy, where I should receive a very warm welcome. . . .

I asked Hitler about 1 in the morning, while we were waiting for the draftsmen, whether he would care to see me for another talk. He jumped at the idea, and asked me to come to his private flat . . . I had a very friendly and pleasant talk. . . . At the end I pulled out the declaration, which I had prepared beforehand, and asked if he would sign it. As the interpreter translated the words into German, Hitler frequently ejaculated "ja, ja," and at the end he said "yes, I will certainly sign it; when shall we do it?" I said "now," and we went at once to the writing-table, and put our signatures to the two copies which I had brought with me.

From a letter from Neville Chamberlain to his sisters, October 2, 1938, as quoted in Sir Keith Feiling, *The Life of Neville Chamberlain* (London: Macmillan, 1946), pp. 375–77.

Prime Minister Neville Chamberlain signs the Munich Pact (September 30, 1938).

Sullen Czechs watch German troops enter Prague (March 15, 1939).

At their first meeting in Berchtesgaden, Hitler seemed to be satisfied with "self-determination" for the Sudeten region. But when Chamberlain returned to Germany a week later for a second meeting, at Godesberg, the *Führer* upped his demands. He now asked for the immediate surrender of the Sudetenland. This the Czechs declared unacceptable. But their protests were ignored at the final meeting in Munich on September 29–30. Hitler and Chamberlain, together with Mussolini and French Premier Édouard Daladier, now agreed on the Godesberg terms. In a separate agreement, Great Britain and Germany promised to renounce war in settling their national differences. "Peace for our time," as Chamberlain hopefully put it, seemed to have been assured.

The first reaction of the world, when the Munich decisions were announced, was one of relief that war had been averted. But it was not long before criticism started. Deprived of its fortifications and most of its heavy industries, which were located in the Sudetenland, Czechoslovakia, the last outpost of democracy in central Europe, was now at Germany's mercy. The Russians, to be sure, had insisted to the end that they would stand by their treaty obligations. But the strength of the Red army was not rated very high, and there was always the fear that the Soviet Union might try to embroil the West in a war with Hitler. The French, in betraying their faithful Czech ally, had assumed a major share of the responsibility for Czechoslovakia's defeat. But how could they have acted differently without the support of Great Britain? And the British, government and people alike, were neither morally nor materially ready for war. Appeasement, ever since Munich, has been an ugly word. But the purchase of peace at the expense of smaller or weaker nations had been going on for some time. The basic cause of the Czech disaster was the failure of the democracies all through the 1930s to understand the true aims of Fascist aggression. Even at Munich these aims were not yet fully understood. It took one more of Hitler's moves to bring home once and for all the futility of appeasement.

On the eve of Munich Hitler had promised that the Sudetenland would be his last territorial claim in Europe. But even before the year was out he issued directives for the final liquidation of Czechoslovakia. On March 15, 1939, German army units crossed the Czech border, and the next day Hitler proclaimed a German protectorate over the Czech regions of Bohemia and Moravia. Slovakia was to become an "independent" German satellite.

This final dismemberment of Czechoslovakia was an important turning point. Up to then, "Pan-Germanism," that is, the desire to unite all German-speaking peoples, had seemed to be the motive of Hitler's expansionist policy. Now suddenly the world recognized his real aim: to gain living space and to subjugate foreign peoples. It was this latest act of Hitler's that brought about a decisive change in the attitude of the western democracies. On March 31, 1939, Great Britain promised the Poles all possible support in resisting any threat to their independence. And in April both England and France gave similar assurances to Rumania and Greece. What the western powers did not know was that on April 3, 1939, a secret directive had been issued to the German army ordering preparations for war against Poland so that operations could start any time after September 1, 1939.

The Eve of the Second World War

That Hitler should turn against Poland next should have been hardly surprising. Of all the territorial provisions of Versailles, the loss of the Polish corridor and the city of Danzig had been the most resented by Germany.

The world had still not recovered from the dismemberment of Czechoslovakia when the Fascist powers made two more quick moves. On March 21, 1939, Lithuania, in compliance with Hitler's demands, returned to Germany the small territory of Memel; and on April 8, 1939, Mussolini sent his troops to occupy the Kingdom of Albania, which since 1927 had been a virtual Italian protectorate. A month later, Germany and Italy converted their Axis into a full-fledged alliance, the "Pact of Steel."

In late May 1939 Hitler informed his generals that war with Poland was inevitable. The fact that France and Great Britain had promised to protect Poland's independence was denounced by Hitler as an incitement to violence against the German minority in the Polish corridor. On August 22 Hitler held another of his briefing conferences. The *Führer* expressed the hope that France and Britain might decide not to fight. Not that he feared their intervention. The western powers, he said, were completely unprepared. As a final surprise, Hitler then told his generals: "A few weeks from now I shall, on the common German-Russian border, shake hands with Stalin and carry out with him a redistribution of the world."

The Nazi-Soviet Pact

What the *Führer* was referring to was an agreement between Germany and the Soviet Union to which the finishing touches were then being put in Moscow. The role of Russia in a future war, needless to say, was of major importance and had concerned Germany and the western powers for some time. Since April 1939 Russia had been engaged in negotiations with both sides. But France and Britain were unable to overcome their fundamental distrust of the Russians; and they had little faith in the Red army, especially after the recent purges. Still more significant, the western powers were unwilling to concede to Russia the predominance in eastern Europe that Stalin demanded. The Germans, on the other hand, had no hesitation in making concessions in the East if it meant gaining a free hand in the West. The Russo-German talks did not enter their decisive phase until mid-August. From then on events moved swiftly. On August 23 the two powers signed a nonaggression pact. Its most weighty part was a secret protocol that divided eastern and southeastern Europe into respective spheres of Russian and German influence.

The Nazi-Soviet treaty came as a terrible blow to the West. Two powers who, because of their rival ideologies, had heretofore appeared as irreconcilable enemies, now had suddenly buried their differences and established a common front. The advantages of the Russian pact for Germany were obvious: it saved the *Wehrmacht*, once Poland had been disposed of, from having to fight a war on two fronts. Russia's motives in making a deal with Hitler were less clear. According to Stalin, the Soviet Union had long been afraid that the West was trying to turn Nazi aggression against communism. But it has also been argued that Stalin, by supporting Hitler, hoped to embroil Germany in a war with the western powers. Such a conflict might so weaken both sides that Russia would emerge as the decisive factor in the international balance of power.

With the signing of the Nazi-Soviet pact, the stage was set for the outbreak of war. It was still not clear whether the French and British would keep their word and come to Poland's aid. Negotiations for a last-minute compromise continued, and Hitler at one point postponed the start of hostilities to allow the West one more try at appeasement. But the lessons of the last few years had at long last been learned. On September 3, 1939, two days after the German invasion of Poland, England and France declared war on Germany. The Second World War had begun.

Reading of the proclamation of war at the Royal Exchange in London.

Suggestions for Further Reading

Note: Asterisk denotes a book available in paperback edition.

General H. Arendt, *The Origins of Totalitarianism** (1951), and E. Fromm, *Escape from Freedom** (1941), are seminal works on the subject of totalitarianism. C. J. Friedrich and Z. K. Brzezinski, *Totalitarian Dictatorship and Autocracy,* rev. ed. (1965), provides a general theory of the phenomenon. See also C. W. Cassinelli, *Total Revolution: A Comparative Study of Germany under Hitler, the Soviet Union under Stalin, and China under Mao* (1976). The development of communist thought from Marx to Stalin is surveyed in R. N. Carew-Hunt, *The Theory and Practice of Communism** (1963), and B. D. Wolfe, *Marxism: One Hundred Years in the Life of a Doctrine* (1965). Other important books on communism are J. Braunthal, *History of the International,* 2 vols. (1967); R. V. Daniels, *The Nature of Communism** (1962); and M. M. Drachkovitch, ed., *Marxism in the Modern World* (1965). Life under communism is described from personal experience by W. Leonhard, *Child of the Revolution** (1967), and C. Milosz, *The Captive Mind** (1953). M. Fainsod, *Smolensk under Soviet Rule** (1963), is based on unique Russian sources. G. Orwell, *1984** (1949), presents a perceptive fictionalized account. The Fascist brand of totalitarianism is dealt with historically in F. L. Carsten, *The Rise of Fascism** (1967), and ideologically in E. Nolte, *Three Faces of Fascism** (1966). See also H. A. Turner, ed., *Reappraisals of Fascism** (1975), and S. J. Woolf, ed., *European Fascism** (1968). On life in Nazi Germany, see B. Bielenberg, *The Past Is Myself* (1971), and F. P. Reck-Malleczewen, *Diary of a Man in Despair** (1972).

Communist Russia The most comprehensive history of the Soviet Union is E. H. Carr, *A History of Soviet Russia* (1950–69), of which eight volumes have appeared thus far. A good brief history is D. W. Treadgold, *Twentieth Century Russia* (1959). F. B. Randall, *Stalin's Russia: An Historical Reconsideration* (1965), is factual and objective. H. Schwartz, *Russia's Soviet Economy* (1954), is a good introduction. S. Swianiewicz, *Forced Labor and Economic Development: An Enquiry into the Experience of Soviet Industrialization* (1965), is more specialized. M. Fainsod, *How Russia Is Ruled* (1963), discusses the constitution and functioning of Soviet government. L. B. Schapiro, *The Communist Party of the Soviet Union** (1960), is the standard work on the subject. Soviet foreign policy before the Second World War is treated in L. Fischer's two books, *The Soviets in World Affairs** (1951) and *Russia's Road from Peace to War* (1969), as well as in M. Beloff, *The Foreign Policy of Soviet Russia, 1929–1941,* 2 vols. (1947–49). The best and most recent general account is A. B. Ulam, *Expansion and Coexistence: The History of Soviet Foreign Policy, 1917–1973** (1974). The following are good monographs on various aspects of Soviet history and society: J. Erickson, *The Soviet High Command* (1962); L. D. Gerson, *The Secret Police in Lenin's Russia* (1976); R. Conquest, *The Great Terror: Stalin's Purge of the Thirties* (1968); C. Brandt, *Stalin's Failure in China, 1924–1927* (1958); D. J. Dallin and B. I. Nicolaevsky, *Forced Labor in the Soviet Union* (1947); L. B. Schapiro, *The Origins of the Communist Autocracy** (1955); and L. Kochan, ed., *The Jews in Soviet Russia since 1917* (1970). The best biographies of the Communist leaders are L. Fischer, *Lenin* (1965), and I. Deutscher, *Trotsky,* 3 vols. (1954–65) and *Stalin: A Political Biography** (1949). See also R. Hingley, *Joseph Stalin: Man and Legend* (1974).

Fascist Italy E. Wiskemann, *Fascism in Italy: Its Development and Influence** (1969), is a good brief introduction. The early years of Fascist rule are discussed in A. Rossi, *The Rise of Italian Fascism, 1918–1922* (1938). G. Salvemini, *Under the Axe of Fascism* (1936) and *Prelude to World War II* (1954), are authoritative studies of Italian domestic and foreign policy by a leading anti-Fascist Italian historian. Other good accounts are H. Finer, *Mussolini's Italy** (1935); E. R. Tannenbaum, *The Fascist Experience: Italian Society and Culture, 1922–1945* (1972); and C. Seton-Watson, *Italy from Liberalism to Fascism* (1967). The structure of Mussolini's government is treated in H. Steiner, *Government in Fascist Italy* (1938), and W. Ebenstein, *Fascist Italy* (1939). On foreign policy, see A. Cassels, *Mussolini's Early Diplomacy* (1970), and D. Mack Smith, *Mussolini's Roman Empire* (1976). Biographies of Mussolini are I. Kirkpatrick, *Mussolini: Study of a Demagogue* (1964), and L. Fermi, *Mussolini* (1961). The resistance to Mussolini is dealt with in C. F. Delzell, *Mussolini's Enemies* (1961).

Nazi Germany The best general work on the subject is K. D. Bracher, *The German Dictatorship: The Origins, Structure, and Effects of National Socialism** (1970). Among the many books dealing with the roots of nazism, G. L. Mosse, *The Crisis of German Ideology: Intellectual Origins of the Third Reich** (1964); F. Stern, *The Politics of Cultural Despair** (1961); and H. Rauschning, *The Revolution of Nihilism* (1939), are the most revealing. W. L. Shirer, *The Rise and Fall of the Third Reich** (1960), is by a noted journalist. For a briefer and more balanced account, see H. Mau and H. Krausnick, *German History, 1933–1945** (1953). The best biography of Hitler is still A. Bullock, *Hitler: A Study in Tyranny** (1964). For a more recent treatment, see J. C. Fest, *Hitler** (1974). On Hitler's early years, B. F. Smith, *Adolph Hitler: His Family, Childhood and Youth** (1967), sheds much new light. Hitler's aims are stated in A. Hitler, *Mein Kampf** (1939), and more openly in *Hitler's Secret Conversations, 1941–1944* (1953). See also *Hitler's Secret Book** (1961). The early events of Nazi Germany are examined in W. S. Allen, *The Nazi Seizure of Power** (1965).

The domestic affairs of Germany under Hitler are treated in R. Grunberger, *A Social History of the Third Reich* (1971), and its government is discussed in W. Ebenstein, *The Nazi State* (1943). The fateful role of the army in German politics before and during the Hitler years is described in J. W. Wheeler-Bennett, *The Nemesis of Power: The German Army in Politics, 1918–1945** (1953), and R. J. O'Neill, *The German Army and the Nazi Party* (1966). The best books on the SS are H. Höhne, *The Order of the Death's Head* (1969), and H. Buchheim et al., *Anatomy of the SS-State* (1968). On the treatment of the Jews, see G. Reitlinger, *The Final Solution** (1953), and R. Hilberg, *The Destruction of the European Jews* (1961). E. Kogon, *The Theory and Practice of Hell** (1958), is the best book on the concentration camps. Other important works on various phases of Nazi rule are: D. Schoenbaum, *Hitler's Social Revolution, 1933–1939** (1967); E. K. Bramsted, *Goebbels and National Socialist Propaganda, 1925–1945* (1965); G. Lewy, *The Catholic Church and Nazi Germany** (1964); P. H. Merke, *Political Violence Under the Swastika** (1975); J. Stephenson, *Women in Nazi Society* (1976); B. A. Carroll, *Design for Total War: Arms and Economics in the Third Reich* (1968); and A. Schweitzer, *Big Business in the Third Reich* (1964). J. C. Fest, *The Face of the Third Reich** (1969), presents vivid portraits of some of Hitler's lieutenants. On the various resistance efforts against Hitler, see P. Hoffmann, *The History of the German Resistance, 1933–1945* (1976), and G. van Roon, *German Resistance to Hitler* (1971). The final act of the Nazi nightmare is dramatically told in H. R. Trevor-Roper, *The Last Days of Hitler** (1947).

The Road to War

A detailed history of the diplomatic background of the Second World War remains to be written. A. J. P. Taylor, *The Origins of the Second World War** (1961), is stimulating but totally unreliable. G. Weinberg, *The Foreign Policy of Hitler's Germany: Diplomatic Revolution in Europe, 1933–1936* (1971), with a second volume to come, is excellent. Several books discuss Germany's relations with individual countries during the Nazi era: M. Toscano, *The Origins of the Pact of Steel* (1967); E. Wiskemann, *Czechs and Germans* (1938); C. A. Micaud, *The French Right and Nazi Germany, 1933–1939* (1943); J. E. McSherry, *Stalin, Hitler, and Europe* (1968); and E. Presseisen, *Germany and Japan* (1958). Relations between military planning and foreign policy are the subject of E. M. Robertson, *Hitler's Pre-War Policy and Military Plans, 1933–1939* (1963), and D. C. Watt, *Too Serious a Business: European Armed Forces and the Approach to the Second World War* (1975). The following works dealing with British foreign policy in the 1930s are all severely critical of appeasement: M. Gilbert, *The Roots of Appeasement** (1966); M. George, *The Hollow Men: An Examination of British Foreign Policy between the Years 1933 and 1939* (1967); and W. R. Rock, *Appeasement on Trial: British Foreign Policy and Its Critics* (1966). Britain's military power and its effects on foreign policy are treated in D. Wood and D. Dempster, *The Narrow Margin* (1961). American diplomacy in the late 1930s is analyzed in detail by W. L. Langer and S. E. Gleason, *The Challenge to Isolation, 1937–1940** (1952). On United States–German relations, see A. A. Offner, *American Appeasement: United States Foreign Policy and Germany** (1969), and J. V. Compton, *The Swastika and the Eagle: Hitler, the United States, and the Origins of World War II* (1967). The major crises fomented by Hitler are discussed in L. Radomir, *Austro-German Relations in the Anschluss Era* (1975); J. Gehl, *Austria, Germany, and the Anschluss, 1931–1938* (1963); J. W. Wheeler-Bennett, *Munich** (1964); and H. Noguères, *Munich: "Peace for Our Time"* (1965). The best books on the Civil War in Spain are G. Jackson, *The Spanish Republic and the Civil War, 1931–1939* (1965), and H. Thomas, *The Spanish Civil War** (1961). The diplomacy of the Ethiopian War is covered in G. W. Baer, *The Coming of the Italian-Ethiopian War* (1967), and A. Del Boca, *The Ethiopian War, 1935–1941* (1969). The best brief account of the events preceding the outbreak of the Second World War is C. Thorne, *The Approach of War, 1938–1939** (1967). S. Aster, *1939: The Making of the Second World War* (1973), deals with the last few months of peace, chiefly from the British side.

33 The Second World War and Its Aftermath 1939–1950

The Second World War, in its origins and events, was quite different from the First. While the question of responsibility for the First World War has caused much controversy, there can be no doubt that the major responsibility for the Second rests heavily on one country, Germany, and on one man, Adolf Hitler. Still, it might be argued that Hitler would never have been able to go to war if the western Allies had stopped him in time. To that extent England and France, too, may bear some responsibility. As for the Soviet Union, its pact with Hitler made the war well-nigh inevitable.

The war of 1939, far more than the war of 1914, was a world war. Japan had been fighting China intermittently for more than eight years, and before long the conflict was to spread to other parts of Asia and to Africa. The earlier war had been largely a war of position. The Second World War was one of almost constant movement. New weapons, already known but little used in the First World War, were chiefly responsible for the greater speed and mobility of the Second. The airplane in particular revolutionized warfare on land and sea. Its use against civilian targets, furthermore, eradicated all differences between the fighting and the home fronts. The Second World War was a truly total war.

THE AXIS TRIUMPHANT 1939–42

Since he had prepared his war for some time, Hitler at first enjoyed all the advantages of the aggressor. He expected the war to be short. Even though England and France had promised to honor their pledges to Poland, he did not believe they would fight.

Blitzkrieg *in Poland*

Germany's forces crossed the Polish border on September 1, 1939. Everything went according to plan. The Poles were no match for the crack Nazi troops, and the main fighting lasted less than four weeks. During that time the *Wehrmacht* took more than seven hundred thousand

prisoners at the cost of only ten thousand German dead. The Germans obviously had lost none of their skill at making war.

The world was stunned by Germany's rapid success. Even the Russians were hardly ready to avail themselves of the spoils that had fallen to them as a result of their recent deal with Hitler. At the end of September 1939 a treaty of partition was signed between the Reich and the Soviet Union. Under its provisions Poland was wiped off the map, Germany taking the western and Russia the eastern half. This operation completed, Germany and Russia announced to the world that there was no longer any reason for Britain and France to continue the war.

War at Sea

This appeal for ending the war was directed primarily at France. The French, as Hitler gauged correctly, were neither enthusiastic nor confident about the war. The French army had dutifully occupied the fortified Maginot Line along France's eastern frontier, but there it sat and waited in the "phony war," as the war in the West came to be called. For their part the British expected a German air attack at any minute. But so long as Hitler thought that his friend Chamberlain might be made to give up the fight, the German air force remained grounded. It was at sea that England felt the first effects of the war. On September 17 the aircraft carrier *Courageous* was torpedoed off the southeastern coast of Ireland, and in mid-October a German submarine sank the battleship *Royal Oak* at its home base of Scapa Flow. It was not until December 1939 that the British scored their first naval victory, against the German battleship *Admiral Graf Spee* off the coast of South America.

The Russo-Finnish War

The next aggressive act on the European continent did not come, as was generally expected, in the West, but in the East. And this time it was the Russians who took the initiative. No sooner had the Soviets shared in the Polish loot

Four-engine United States Air Force heavy bombers overpower the single-engine German fighter planes.

than they pressured the small republics of Estonia, Latvia, and Lithuania to sign "mutual assistance" pacts that allowed the Red army to occupy strategic bases along the Baltic coast and brought these states within the Soviet orbit. In June 1940 they officially became members of the Soviet Union. The only country to resist Russian pressure was Finland. So on November 30, 1939, Russia renounced a seven-year nonaggression pact with Finland and crossed the Finnish border at eight points. But this was to be no *Blitzkrieg*. The Finns were finally beaten, in March 1940. In the meantime the Russian armies suffered serious losses and showed themselves woefully unprepared. In protest against Russia's attack on Finland, the League of Nations expelled the Soviet Union from membership, the first major power to be thus censured. But attention was soon diverted away from Finland as the Germans embarked on a second round of aggression against the small nations on their periphery.

Germany Turns North and West

Both Norway and the Low Countries were of great strategic importance to Germany. Possession of Norway would extend Germany's narrow coastline, giving its submarines a wider radius of action. The Low Countries—besides providing a protective glacis for Germany's industrial heart, the Ruhr—would offer the necessary base for operations against France and England. Reports in the fall of 1939 that Britain might occupy Norway made Hitler decide to move. In mid-December he ordered preparations for the northern war. Operations began on April 9, 1940. Simultaneously with their invasion of Norway, the Germans occupied Denmark. The British had been forewarned of the German move against Norway but failed to intercept the German invasion fleet. The main fighting in Norway took only a few days. Some pockets of resistance held out until early June, but by that time the Germans had already turned their attention elsewhere.

The war in the West was launched on May 10, 1940. It was one of the most breathtaking and frightening military performances ever witnessed. As spearheads of tanks and armored vehicles drove relentlessly forward, German parachute troops seized bridges and airfields behind the Allied lines, air raids gutted civilian objectives, and dive bombers strafed the endless columns of helpless refugees. It took the Germans less than a week to overrun the Netherlands and little over two weeks to defeat the Belgian, French, and British forces in Belgium. The remains of the Allied armies, more than three hundred thousand men, were evacuated to England from Dunkirk on the Channel coast. The Allied cause had suffered a resounding defeat.

On the day the Lowlands were invaded, Chamberlain resigned. He was succeeded by Winston Churchill, sixty-five years old and already famous, although his greatest contributions still lay ahead. It was Churchill who inspired the British people to their heroic resistance during the "Battle of Britain."

The Fall of France

There was no one to do for France what Churchill did for England. The man who was pushed into the limelight in the hope that he would unite the French people was Marshal Henri Philippe Pétain. Once before, in 1916, he had been the symbol of his country's resistance in time of national emergency (see p. 702). But in 1940 the old marshal was less concerned with continuing the war than with making peace. France, he felt, had been betrayed by its radical left and deserted by its British allies. Why not try and save from the wreckage what could be saved by collaborating with Hitler?

As the German armies reached the Channel coast in late May 1940, Hitler was faced with a major decision: should he invade England, or should he complete the conquest of France? He decided to do the latter, perhaps because he was still hoping to reach a compromise with the British and so did not want to antagonize them unnecessarily. There is no need to go into the melancholy details of the "Fall of France." It was no longer a war, since there was hardly any resistance. When the French were at their lowest and German victory was beyond a

Hitler's delight after learning of the fall of France in 1940.

doubt, Italian troops invaded southeastern France. Mussolini had stayed out of the war thus far, claiming that he was not ready for it. But the collapse of France was too good an opportunity to miss.

The official French surrender to Germany took place on June 22, 1940, at Compiègne. Under the terms of the armistice Germany occupied three-fifths of France, including its entire Atlantic coast. The French also had to pay occupation costs of 400 million francs per day. There were no final territorial provisions; these were to await a later peace conference. The unoccupied, southern part of France chose as its capital the town of Vichy. Besides Pétain, the leaders of the Vichy government included Pierre Laval and Admiral Jean Darlan. The United States recognized the new regime and used its influence to bolster Vichy efforts to keep the French fleet and overseas possessions out of German hands.

The Battle of Britain

With France out of the war, Great Britain now stood alone. Its most immediate fear was of a German invasion. But Hitler lacked the necessary naval power to launch his "Operation Sea Lion," and besides, he never gave up hope that England would capitulate without fighting to the finish. To break down British resistance, the German *Luftwaffe*, in July 1940, embarked on an all-out air offensive. The Battle of Britain lasted through the rest of the year. Several times the British reached the limits of their reserves in planes and pilots. But they did not give in. Meanwhile, halfhearted preparations for "Operation Sea Lion" continued. But Hitler assumed that a successful invasion of England required control of the sea and air, which the Germans never achieved. In the fall of 1940, invasion plans were postponed and Hitler decided to strike elsewhere.

War in North Africa and the Balkans

An empire as large as that of Britain was vulnerable in many places. The British possession most coveted by Hitler was Gibraltar. To take this strongly forti-

fied gateway to the Mediterranean, however, the *Führer* needed the support of Franco's Spain, which he failed to get. Another important British region was Egypt. The task of ousting the British from there was given to the Italians. In September 1940 an Italian army invaded Egypt from Libya. It was stopped almost immediately by a far smaller British force, which then drove the Italians back into Libya. A major Axis defeat was avoided only by the timely intervention of the German *Afrikakorps* under General Erwin Rommel. By early April 1941 the Axis forces had regained the initiative and were once again on Egyptian soil.

The Italians, meanwhile, had become involved in another venture, this time without even consulting the Germans. In October 1940 Italian troops crossed from Albania into Greece. After some minor gains, they were soon pushed back again into Albania. Once more the Germans had to intervene and thus open another major front. Bulgaria and Hungary were already on the side of the Axis. Yugo-

Prime Minister Winston Churchill inspecting ruins of the House of Commons following bombing by the German *Luftwaffe* in 1940.

A policeman cycles through London to warn of an air raid.

There were some other hopeful developments in the spring of 1941, while Britain was still fighting with its back to the wall. The United States was constantly increasing its aid to Great Britain, and ultimate American involvement in the war appeared a definite possibility. The British navy, meanwhile, won a major victory when it sank the German superbattleship *Bismarck* on May 27. And, most important, there were persistent rumors that relations between Germany and Russia were rapidly deteriorating.

HITLER'S RUSSIAN GAMBLE

Russo-German relations since the outbreak of the Second World War had been far from smooth. Two totalitarian countries, each bent on expansion, could not possibly avoid for long getting in each other's way. To be sure, the two partners maintained a mutually beneficial economic exchange. But on the diplomatic front Russo-German interests were far less complementary. Hitler was disturbed by Russia's expansion along the Baltic, and Stalin was taken aback by Hitler's unexpected successes in the West. More serious still were the differences between Russia and Germany over the Balkans, where no clear line of demarcation had been worked out. Efforts to clarify these and other matters were made in November 1940 at a conference in Berlin. But the attempt failed, partly because of Russia's far-reaching demands for the control of eastern and southeastern Europe, partly because Hitler had already decided to attack the Soviet Union.

The German Invasion of Russia

There were obvious reasons for Hitler's Russian gamble: he wanted *Lebensraum*, and he hated communism. But there was still another reason why he decided to strike at Russia. The stubborn resistance of the British, he felt, was due chiefly to their hope that Germany might ultimately become involved in a war with the Soviet Union. To attack and defeat Russia while it was still weak from the

slavia was quickly overrun by German, Bulgarian, and Hungarian troops. Greece was defeated and occupied, and a German airborne invasion took the island of Crete. In the spring of 1941 it seemed that Germany was looking still farther afield, beyond the Balkans, toward the Middle East. But before the *Führer's* schemes went very far, he became occupied with more important objectives in eastern Europe. Combined British and Free French forces were able, therefore, to keep the upper hand in the strategically vital eastern Mediterranean.

Russo-Finnish War, therefore, was the best way of inducing Britain to surrender. The first preparations for the invasion of Russia were made as early as July 1940. The final directives were issued the following December. The *Wehrmacht* struck on June 22, 1941.

The German armies at the start were disastrously successful. During the first weeks of fighting, hundreds of thousands of Russian soldiers were killed, wounded, or captured. But the Russians seemed to have inexhaustible manpower. What was surprising was how the Russian people rallied to their country's defense. Stalin emerged as a strong national leader, and opposition to his ruthless regime disappeared in the face of foreign aggression. One of Hitler's gravest errors, next to invading Russia in the first place, was not to have posed to the Russian people as a liberator from communist oppression. Instead, the *Führer* ordered Russian prisoners to be herded into vast camps where they died of starvation, or else had them transported to Germany as slave labor.

The Russian war helped close overnight the gap between the East and the West. Great Britain now offered Stalin a military alliance, and the Americans included the Soviets in their program of lend-lease. While the East and West were thus joining forces, the Germans were encountering unforeseen difficulties. Winter came unusually early in 1941,

and the German army was not prepared for it. When Germany's commanders wanted to halt their advance, Hitler relieved them and took charge himself. The Germans suffered terrible hardships, but they continued their advance. In the fall of 1942 Hitler's generals once again urged him to shorten his lines to more defensible proportions. But the *Führer* remained unyielding. Since August, large German forces had been engaged in the siege of Stalingrad on the lower Volga. The battle of Stalingrad has been compared to the battle of Verdun in the First World War. Both were fought with unusual ferocity, and both entailed terrific losses. A German victory at Stalingrad would have given Germany control over the rich oil fields of the Caucasus. But instead of ejecting the Russians from Stalingrad, the Germans were caught in the pincers of a Russian counteroffensive and suffered a major defeat by February 1943.

The battle of Stalingrad was not the first Nazi defeat. The western allies were simultaneously advancing and winning in North Africa. But the disaster in Russia was a decisive event. In a gradually mounting offensive, the Russians began to push Hitler's armies back across the plains of eastern Europe. It took almost two more years before the fighting reached German soil. Meanwhile the expansion of Japan in the Far East had also been halted in the winter of 1942/43, and

German soldier in battle.

Russian soldiers pursuing remnants of the German Sixth Army in the battle of Stalingrad (1943).

The New Order

The following is from a confidential address given by Heinrich Himmler to his SS officers on October 4, 1943.

What happens to a Russian, to a Czech, does not interest me in the slightest. What the nations can offer in the way of good blood of our type we will take, if necessary by kidnaping their children and raising them here with us. Whether nations live in prosperity or starve to death like cattle interests me only in so far as we need them as slaves to our *Kultur*; otherwise it is of no interest to me. Whether 10,000 Russian females fall down from exhaustion while digging an antitank ditch interests me only in so far as the antitank ditch for Germany is finished.

From *Nazi Conspiracy and Aggression* (Washington, D.C.: Government Printing Office, 1946), Vol. IV, p. 559.

The "Final Solution"

The first train arrived . . . 45 freightcars with 6,700 people, of which 1,450 were already dead on arrival. . . . A large loudspeaker blares instructions: Undress completely, take off artificial limbs, glasses, etc. Hand in all valuables. Shoes to be tied together (for the clothing collection) . . . Women and girls to the barber, who cuts off their hair in two or three strokes and stuffs it into potato sacks. . . .

Then the line starts moving. . . . At the corner a strapping SS-man announces in a pastoral voice: Nothing will happen to you! Just breathe deeply inside the chambers, that stretches the lungs; this inhalation is necessary against the illnesses and epidemics. When asked what would happen to them, he replies: Well, of course the men will have to work, build houses and roads, but the women won't have to work. If they want to they can help in the household or the kitchen. For a few of these unfortunates a small glimmer of hope which suffices to have them take the few steps to the chambers without resistance—the majority knows what is ahead, the stench tells their fate. . . .

The wooden doors are opened. . . . Inside the chambers, the dead stand closely pressed together, like pillars of stone. . . . Even in death one recognizes the families. They still hold hands, so they have to be torn apart to get the chambers ready for their next occupants. The corpses are thrown out—wet with sweat and urine, covered with excrement, menstrual blood. Children's bodies fly through the air. . . . Two dozen workers use hooks to pry open mouths to look for gold. . . . Others search genitals and anuses for gold, diamonds and valuables. Wirth [an SS-guard] motions to me: Just lift this can of gold teeth, this is only from yesterday and the day before! . . .

From an eyewitness account of mass gassings, in *Vierteljahrshefte für Zeitgeschichte* (1953), Vol. I, pp. 190–91.

the Japanese were being driven back to their home bases. By the spring of 1943, fascist aggression had overextended itself, and the tide of the war began to turn.

HITLER'S "NEW ORDER"

What was the fate of those areas that for several years suffered under German occupation? There was never any master plan for Hitler's "New Order," since the future depended on the final outcome of the war. Few of the territories under German domination were annexed outright, although the degree to which some of them were being Germanized left no doubt about their ultimate fate. The war had done its share in decreasing the population of eastern Europe. In addition, more than 7 million foreign workers were forced to work in German factories. Into the areas thus vacated, ethnic Germans, mostly from outside the Reich, were sent as pioneers of Hitler's Germanization policy.

But Hitler was not content merely with taking land away from other peoples. The most frightful deed committed in the name of his "New Order" was the willful extermination of from 6 to 8 million people, most of them Jews. Wherever the German armies went, Hitler's private army, the elite SS (*Schutzstaffel*, protective force), followed to see that the party's racial policies were carried out. At first there was merely persecution of the Jews, and in this the local populations often participated. But in time more drastic measures were adopted. Hitler's "Final Solution" called for nothing less than the complete extermination of all Jews. This was carried out by means of gas chambers in special extermination camps, such as Auschwitz. There were several such camps, not only for the extermination of Jews but for the "mercy killing" of the incurably ill and insane, and for the liquidation of political prisoners.

These were only the more gruesome acts committed by the Nazis. Additional millions were kept in concentration, slave-labor, and prisoner-of-war camps, where many died more "normal" deaths of starvation. A great many Germans were involved in these crimes; yet after the war almost no one would admit having known of what went on behind the barbed wire of these camps.

AMERICA ENTERS THE WAR

America's involvement in the war was a gradual process. The United States government had followed a policy of strict neutrality during the various acts of German and Italian aggression prior to the Second World War. The question was whether this attitude of aloofness could be maintained in a war among the major European powers. As one country after another fell victim to the Axis powers, America's role in the war became of crucial importance. Axis domination of western Europe and North Africa, once firmly established, would have posed a serious threat to the United States. It was for its self-preservation that America was forced to travel the road from neutrality to belligerency.

Benevolent Neutrality

As early as November 4, 1939, congress had passed a revised Neutrality Act that lifted the embargo on all implements of war and put all maritime trade on a "cash and carry" basis. This move tended to favor the country with the largest funds and the strongest navy, Great Britain. But Britain's enormous need for material aid made its dollar credits dwindle rapidly. The two governments tried to overcome this difficulty in several ways. One was the "destroyer deal" of 1940, when the United States gave Britain some fifty ships in return for a lease of certain British-held naval bases in the Western Hemisphere. Another way for America to help its future allies was through the Lend-Lease Act of 1941. It gave the president power to provide goods and services to any nation whose defense was considered vital to the United States.

The Lend-Lease Act was an important step away from neutrality. There were other signs that America was getting off the fence. But in August 1941, when Congress was asked to extend the Selective Service Act of the preceding September, which established the draft, the measure was passed only by the slimmest margin. The American people, it seemed, were perfectly willing to go to any limit in helping the antifascist cause so long as they did not become involved in the war themselves. It took the Japanese attack on Pearl Harbor to push the United States across the line from nonintervention to belligerency.

War with Japan

The United States, for some forty years past, had stood in the way of Japan's major aim: to dominate China and extend its power over the trading area of southeastern Asia and the neighboring Pacific. Especially since the start of the Sino-Japanese War in 1937, Washington had been concerned about Japan's violations of the "Open Door" policy in China. To put pressure on the Japanese, the United States, in July 1939, ended its thirty-year-old commercial treaty with Japan and subsequently imposed an embargo on certain strategic goods. By the middle of 1941 the embargo was seriously affecting the Japanese. Tokyo's demand for the cessation of United States restrictions were met with American counterdemands for Japan's withdrawal from China. As far back as January 1941 the Japanese government had begun to prepare for an armed showdown. The final decision to strike was made on December 1.

When the Japanese air force staged its sneak attack against Pearl Harbor, on December 7, 1941, it caught the American forces entirely unprepared. The United States suffered more than three thousand casualties and heavy material losses, one of the greatest defeats in its history. Yet terrible as the catastrophe of Pearl Harbor was, it had one good effect—it cut short the debate between isolationists and interventionists. As Italy and Germany declared war on the United States, the American people rallied behind the war effort of their government. With the world's mightiest nation thus fully committed, the outcome of the war looked decidedly more favorable for the British and their Russian allies.

Pearl Harbor, December 7, 1941.

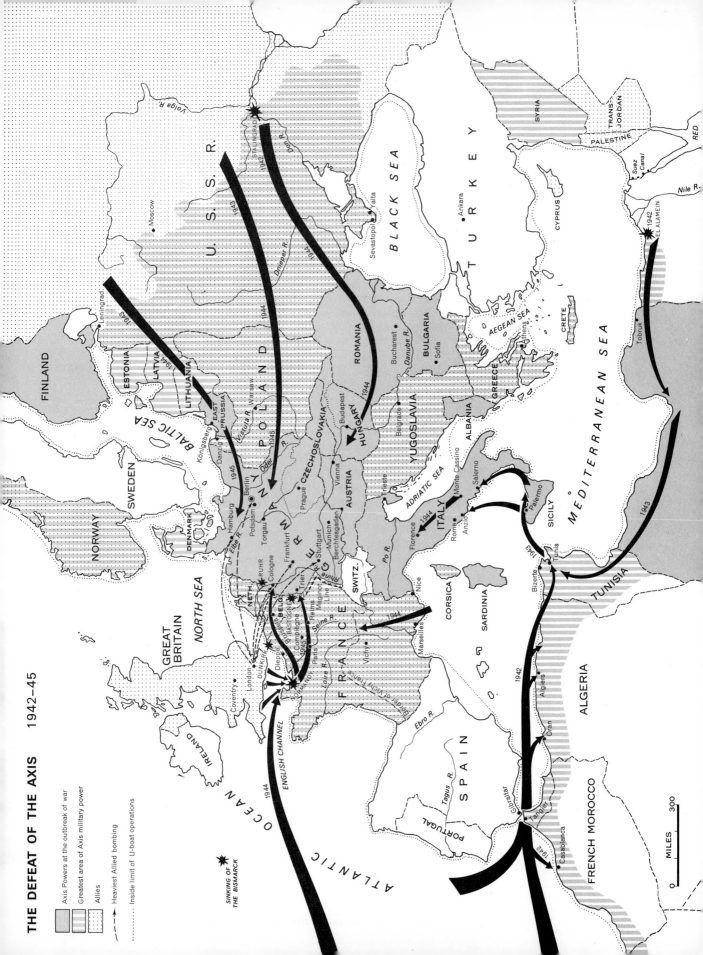

THE DEFEAT OF THE AXIS   1942–45

Axis Powers at the outbreak of war

Greatest area of Axis military power

Allies

Heaviest Allied bombing

Inside limit of U-boat operations

✴ SINKING OF THE BISMARCK

0   MILES   300

ATLANTIC OCEAN

GREAT BRITAIN

IRELAND

NORTH SEA

ENGLISH CHANNEL

Coventry

London

DUNKIRK

Dieppe

NORMANDY

Paris

Loire R.

FRANCE

Vichy

Border of Vichy France

Ebro R.

Tagus R.

SPAIN

PORTUGAL

Gibraltar

Tangier

Casablanca

FRENCH MOROCCO

ALGERIA

Oran

Algiers

TUNISIA

Bizerte

Tunis

SARDINIA

CORSICA

Nice

Marseilles

SWITZ.

Maginot Line

Rhine R.

Reims

Compiègne

BELG.

BASTOGNE

Brussels

NETH.

Cologne

RUHR

Frankfurt

Trier

Stuttgart

Munich

Berchtesgaden

AUSTRIA

Vienna

Prague

CZECHOSLOVAKIA

Hamburg

Elbe R.

Potsdam

Berlin

Torgau

Oder R.

G   E   R   M   A   N   Y

Danzig

Königsberg

EAST PRUSSIA

Vistula R.

Warsaw

P   O   L   A   N   D

LITHUANIA

LATVIA

ESTONIA

Leningrad

FINLAND

SWEDEN

NORWAY

DENMARK

BALTIC SEA

Dnieper R.

U.   S.   S.   R.

Moscow

Volga R.

STALINGRAD

Don R.

BLACK SEA

Sevastopol

Yalta

TURKEY

Ankara

CYPRUS

SYRIA

PALESTINE

TRANS-JORDAN

RED

Suez Canal

Nile R.

EL ALAMEIN

Tobruk

MEDITERRANEAN SEA

CRETE

AEGEAN SEA

Athens

GREECE

ALBANIA

YUGOSLAVIA

Belgrade

Trieste

ADRIATIC SEA

Monte Cassino

Salerno

Anzio

Rome

Florence

Po R.

ITALY

Palermo

SICILY

Bizerte

Tunis

Budapest

HUNGARY

ROMANIA

Bucharest

Danube R.

BULGARIA

Sofia

THE DEFEAT OF THE AXIS

In discussing the defeat of the fascist aggressors, it is simpler to deal with each major field of operation separately. But it should be kept in mind that the war was being fought on a global scale. The European Allies were worried at first that America's involvement in the Pacific would prevent it from continuing its aid to Europe. The Russians in particular kept up a nagging insistence on the immediate opening of a second front on the Continent. Before such an operation could be thought of, however, large numbers of American troops had to be shipped overseas, and that was possible only after the threat of Germany's submarine fleet had been overcome.

On the eve of the war total Allied merchant tonnage amounted to about 25 million. Of this amount, 21 million tons were lost, mostly to submarine action. The final victory over the submarine menace was due in part to the convoy system, by which naval transports were escorted by warships, and to improved methods of detecting submarines. But the victory at sea could not have been won without the "battle of the shipyards," in which American workers built ships faster than the Germans could sink them. By the middle of 1943 Allied shipping had regained its prewar level and the worst of the danger was past.

The Invasion of North Africa

The first involvement of American ground forces in the war against the European Axis took place in North Africa. On November 8, 1942, an Anglo-American invasion force, commanded by General Dwight D. Eisenhower, landed at Casablanca in French Morocco and at various points in Algeria. Allied intervention in North Africa was made easier by the collaboration of the French forces stationed there. The leading French representative in Morocco and Algeria at the time was Admiral Darlan. His cooperation helped keep Allied losses during the landing to a minimum, although the fact that Darlan had in the past been decidedly profascist caused some embarrass-

ment. The admiral was subsequently assassinated by a follower of General de Gaulle. The North African campaign ended on May 13, 1943, with the Allied capture of Tunis and Bizerte. The total losses of the Axis in three years of North African fighting had come close to 1 million men.

In the meantime, the German people were also feeling the effects of American intervention nearer home. Almost daily, large fleets of United States and British planes penetrated the antiaircraft defenses of the Reich, bombing industrial centers and strategic objectives. The much-advertised *Luftwaffe* of Reichsmarshal Göring, which had earlier failed to bomb the British into submission, now proved equally ineffective in defending German soil.

The Allied Invasion of Italy

Having won North Africa, the Allies next aimed for control of the rest of the Mediterranean. The invasion of Sicily and southern Italy was launched in the summer of 1943. Resistance in Sicily collapsed in mid-August, and on September 2 British and American troops landed on the Italian mainland. The campaign in Italy lasted until the end of the war, slowing down as the emphasis shifted to the northern theater of war. Nevertheless, the war in Italy played a vital part in the final victory, since it helped tie down large German forces that might otherwise have been used on Hitler's two other fronts. But the Italian war also caused one of the first major crises between the Anglo-Saxon powers and their Russian ally.

Stalin had long been annoyed with the West for not opening what he considered a real second front. The invasion of Italy gave new cause for such annoyance. During the Sicilian campaign in July 1943, a number of high officials within the Italian Fascist Party staged a *coup d'état* and forced Mussolini to resign. The new Italian government under Marshal Pietro Badoglio asked the Allies for an armistice. While this made the subsequent invasion of the mainland much easier, the agreement with Badoglio further aroused the suspicion of Stalin.

The end of Mussolini. He and his mistress were executed by Italian partisans in Milan (April 29, 1945).

What he feared was that the West might conclude a separate peace without the Russians.

"Operation Overlord"

The delay in opening a second front in the north was partly due to differences within the western camp on where the attack against Hitler's "Fortress Europe" should be launched. Some British experts favored the Balkans, expecting fewer losses from striking at the "soft underbelly of Europe." President Roosevelt and his advisers, on the other hand, saw France as the more suitable terrain for a second front, mainly for strategic reasons. The American view prevailed.

The final decision for "Operation Overlord," the code name for the liberation of France, was made at a conference of the "Big Three" at Teheran in December 1943. The supreme command was entrusted to General Eisenhower; the scene of the landing was to be the coast of Normandy; and D-Day was set for early June 1944. Since the Germans had expected the invasion nearer Calais, the Allies were able to establish a firm beachhead. Within three weeks more than 2 million men had been landed on the Continent. After three months of fighting, the Allies had driven the Germans out of northwestern France. On August 15 a second amphibious operation landed on the French Mediterranean coast and within a month made contact with the main invasion forces in the north. In mid-September the first American forces crossed the German frontier. Here they were halted by the fortified German "Siegfried Line."

The German *Wehrmacht*, although on the run, was still far from beaten. During the week before Christmas 1944, Hitler staged his last big offensive of the war. Under cover of fog and snow in the difficult terrain of the Ardennes, eight German armored divisions drove a deep salient into the Allied lines. This "Battle of the Bulge" proved to be a costly failure for the Germans, but for a brief moment it seemed to threaten the Allied victory in the West.

Germany Invaded from East and West

The Russians, meanwhile, had been pressing slowly but steadily westward. By the end of January 1945 the Red army stood on the Oder River, less than a hundred miles from Berlin. These were terrible months for the Germans, who now felt what it was like to be the victims of invasion. Since the fortunes of war had begun to turn following the German defeat at Stalingrad and the beginning of the Russian movement westward in early 1943, sporadic German opposition to Hitler had gathered sufficient strength for a final attempt to rid the country of its tyrant. But the plot of July 20, 1944, miscarried, and the *Führer* took horrible vengeance. Thousands of decent men and women, who might have played a leading role in the postwar reconstruction of Germany, were put to death. The rest of the German people were urged on into suicidal resistance, especially since the Allied demand for "unconditional surrender" seemed to leave no alternative.

Early in 1945 the Allies stood poised along the western borders of the Reich, ready for the final phase of the European war. The invasion of the Rhineland was launched on February 8, 1945. From here on events happened with lightning speed. By the end of March the Rhine had been crossed; by the middle of April the Ruhr district had been taken; and on April 25 the first American and Russian patrols met on the Elbe River. On April 30, while the Russians were fighting their way into the center of Berlin, Adolf Hitler committed suicide. On May 7, 1945, at the headquarters of General Eisen-

D-Day: the invasion of Normandy, June 6, 1944.

hower at Reims, a German military delegation signed the terms of Germany's unconditional surrender. May 8, 1945, was officially proclaimed V-E Day, victory day in Europe.

THE WAR IN THE PACIFIC

The war against Japan was primarily a naval war in which the United States carried the major burden. Considering America's losses at Pearl Harbor and its heavy commitment of men and material in Europe, the victory in the Pacific was a magnificent achievement. This was particularly true considering the extent of Japanese expansion. A few days after Pearl Harbor, the Japanese overran America's outposts at Guam and Wake Island. Early in 1942, they invaded the Philippines. The Dutch East Indies, the Malay Peninsula, and Burma went next. By May 1942 the whole area east of India and north of Australia, except for the southern part of New Guinea, had fallen into Japanese hands.

American Naval Victories

It was the Japanese attempt to force the Allies out of New Guinea and to gain a base for the invasion of Australia that triggered the first major naval battle between United States and Japanese forces. The battle of the Coral Sea in May 1942 inflicted heavy American losses, but it kept the Japanese from their objective. A still more decisive naval battle took place a month later at Midway Island, northwest of Hawaii. The engagement was deliberately sought by the Japanese, who hoped to annihilate the smaller United States fleet and thus open the way to Hawaii. But the Americans anticipated the enemy's move, and the battle of Midway brought a resounding Japanese defeat. For the first time America held a slight naval edge in the Pacific. The Japanese achieved some last successes when they occupied Attu and Kiska in the Aleutian Islands. But with the landing of United States marines in the Solomon Islands in August 1942, Japanese expansion was halted, and soon the tide began to turn.

The Naming of the Second World War

10 September 1945

The President
The White House

Dear Mr. President:

President Wilson, under date of July 31, 1919, addressed a letter to Secretary of War Baker which read, in part, as follows: "It is hard to find a satisfactory 'official' name for the war, but the best, I think, that has been suggested is 'The World War,' and I hope that your judgment will concur. . . ."

As a matter of simplicity and to insure uniform terminology, it is recommended that "World War II" be the officially designated name for the present war covering all theaters and the entire period of hostilities.

The term "World War II" has been used in at least seven public laws to designate this period of hostilities. Analysis of publications and radio programs indicates that this term has been accepted by common usage.

If this recommendation is approved it is further recommended that the title "World War II" be published in the *Federal Register* as the official name of the present war.

Respectfully yours,
Henry L. Stimson
Secretary of War

James Forrestal
Secretary of the Navy
Approved: September 11, 1945
Harry S. Truman

From U.S., Department of State, *Bulletin*, Vol. XIII (Washington, D.C.: Government Printing Office, 1945), pp. 427–28.

The Turn of the Tide

In 1942 United States naval supremacy was established in the Pacific; the next year brought the first breaks through the outer perimeter of Japan's defenses. Beginning with the battle of Guadalcanal, one after another of Japan's island outposts were retaken in some of the war's bloodiest fighting. Places most Americans had never heard of—Tarawa, Makin, Eniwetok, Iwo Jima, Okinawa—

now suddenly became headlines. Meanwhile, United States submarines were taking a heavy toll of Japanese shipping, and the Japanese islands were put under a blockade. In June 1944 American Superfortresses began their first bombing raids on Japan. In October 1944 United States forces under General Douglas MacArthur began their reconquest of the Philippines. And in Burma, British imperial forces under Lord Louis Mountbatten, supported by Americans and Chinese, were rounding up the Japanese invaders.

The End of the War

The climax of the war in the Pacific came on October 21–22, 1944, with the battle of Leyte Gulf in the Philippine Sea, one of the biggest naval battles ever fought. Japanese losses were such that their navy, henceforth, was no longer a factor in the war. As Allied successes in Europe mounted, more and more strength could be diverted to the Pacific theater. In the spring of 1945 America's commanders in the Pacific were asked to prepare plans for the invasion of Japan. But while these preparations were still under way, on July 16, 1945, the first

atomic bomb was successfully exploded at Los Alamos, New Mexico. The atomic bombing of Hiroshima and Nagasaki on August 6 and 9 led to the surrender of Japan on August 14, 1945, and to the end of the Second World War.

The decision to use this terrible new weapon was not an easy one. Should not efforts be made to lay siege to Japan first? But President Truman and his advisers felt that an early surrender of Japan without invasion was most unlikely. And an invasion of Japan, it was estimated, would cost more than a million Allied casualties and at least again that many Japanese. It was thought preferable, therefore, to bring the war to a quick, though horrible, end: 78,000 people were killed at Hiroshima and 50,000 at Nagasaki. The Atomic Age had begun.

THE SEARCH FOR PEACE

Considering the tremendous political upheaval resulting from the Second World War, it is surprising how little advance thought had been given to the problem of peace. There had been some general pronouncements, especially the Atlantic Charter, which President Roosevelt and Prime Minister Churchill had issued in August 1941. But this idealistic blueprint for the future, which aimed at a world free from want and fear, was drawn up before the harsh realities of the postwar situation were known. Several conferences during the war—between Roosevelt and Churchill at Casablanca and Quebec, and among the two western leaders and Stalin at Teheran—had dealt primarily with immediate military matters and only incidentally with long-range political questions. Only in the final months of the war did the larger issues of the future become the subject of top-level discussions. These took place at two conferences at Yalta and Potsdam, in February and July 1945.

The Yalta Conference

To understand the concessions made at Yalta to the Soviet Union, we must remember that Russia was still an ally of the West and that the expansionist aims

---

Hiroshima

At about 0815 there was a blinding flash. Some described it as brighter than the sun, others likened it to a magnesium flash. Following the flash there was a blast of heat and wind. The large majority of people within 3000 feet of ground zero were killed immediately. Within a radius of about 7000 feet almost every Japanese house collapsed. Beyond this range and up to 15,000-20,000 feet many of them collapsed and others received serious structural damage. Persons in the open were burned on exposed surfaces, and within 3000–5000 feet many were burned to death while others received severe burns through their clothes. . . . The people appeared stunned by the catastrophe and rushed about as jungle animals suddenly released from a cage. Some few apparently attempted to help others from the wreckage, particularly members of their family or friends. Others assisted those who were unable to walk alone. However, many of the injured were left trapped beneath collapsed buildings as people fled by them in the streets. Pandemonium reigned as the uninjured and slightly injured fled the city in fearful panic.

From "The Effects of Atomic Bombs on Health and Medical Services in Hiroshima and Nagasaki," *The United States Strategic Bombing Survey* (Washington, D.C.: Government Printing Office, 1947), p. 3.

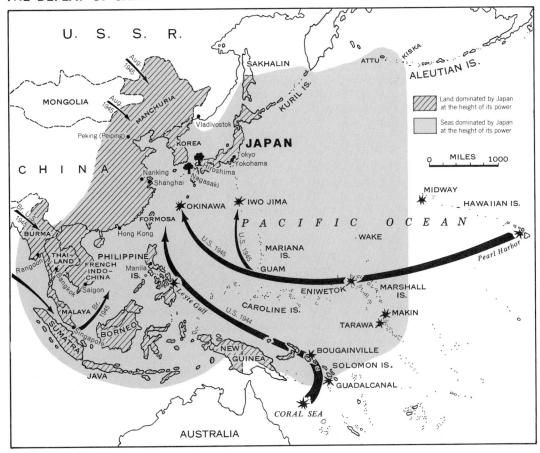

of communism were not yet fully understood. Some of Stalin's claims, furthermore, especially in the Baltic, in Poland, and in the Balkans, had already been recognized, at least by implication. And the fact that all these regions were already occupied by Red armies gave added strength to Soviet arguments. Most important, finally, was the conviction of western military leaders that Russia's continued contribution to the common war effort was essential to ensure an early victory.

The main issues discussed at Yalta dealt with the future of Germany, Poland, the Far East, and the United Nations. So far as Germany was concerned, the meeting achieved very little. The only firm agreement dealt with the postwar division of the country into four occupation zones, including a French one, administered by an Allied Control Council.

The city of Berlin, likewise, was to be divided into separate occupation zones.

A great deal of time at Yalta was spent in trying to determine the future frontiers of Poland and to agree on the composition of its government. On both points the Russians scored a major success. Poland's border was moved westward to the Curzon Line, where it had been fixed briefly after the First World War. Russia thus received almost 47 percent of Poland's prewar territory. The powers agreed, however, that in return for its losses in the east, Poland should receive compensations in the north and west. The new provisional government of Poland, meanwhile, was to be drawn chiefly from the Soviet-sponsored Committee of National Liberation rather than from the Polish government-in-exile, which the western powers had favored; but to make sure that Poland was ruled democratically, "free and unfettered elections" were to be held.

The Far Eastern decisions made at Yalta caused little difficulty at the time, although they have come in for a great deal of criticism since. In return for Stalin's promise to participate in the Pacific war, the Soviet Union was granted large concessions at the expense of both China and Japan. Most of these made up for Russia's losses in the Russo-Japanese War of 1904 to 1905 (see p. 642).

The problem that most concerned the American delegation at Yalta was to get Russian and British agreement to final plans for a United Nations organization. Most of the details for such an organization had already been worked out, except for two important points: the extent of the great powers' veto in the Security Council and the number of seats each was to hold in the UN Assembly. Both points were satisfactorily settled, a fact that greatly contributed to the success of the conference in American eyes. There was some hard bargaining at Yalta, but on the whole the atmosphere had been

friendly. It remained to be seen whether the powers could carry over their wartime unity of purpose into their postwar search for peace.

The United Nations

The first problem tackled after Yalta was the drafting of a charter for the United Nations. This was done at the San Francisco Conference in the spring of 1945. The main purposes of the United Nations are: to maintain peace; to develop friendly relations among nations; and to help solve economic, social, and cultural problems. Any peace-loving nation may become a member if sponsored by the Security Council and a two-thirds vote of the Assembly, and a state may be expelled for violating the provisions of the charter.

As these provisions suggest, the United Nations owes much to its predecessor, the League of Nations. Like the League, the UN, at least at the start, was entirely dominated by the great powers among its members. The most important agency of the UN is the Security Council, five of whose seats were assigned to the United States, Great Britain, the Soviet Union, France, and Nationalist China. (The latter's place was taken by Communist China in 1972.) Since each of these powers has an absolute veto, the effectiveness of the UN has been seriously hampered. The chief task of the Council is to maintain peace and security. Like the Council of the League of Nations, it can recommend peaceful arbitration or measures short of war, such as economic sanctions. But unlike the League, the Security Council may also take "such actions by air, sea, or land forces as may be necessary to maintain or restore international peace."

The Potsdam Conference

While the San Francisco Conference was still in session, the end of the war in Europe called for another top-level meeting to settle the future of Germany. Russia's unilateral actions in eastern Europe, notably in Rumania and Poland, had already called forth repeated western protests. When the powers assembled at

The Yalta Conference. Churchill, Roosevelt, and Stalin sit for a formal picture-taking session with their advisers. Roosevelt clearly shows the strain of their meeting. He was to die two months later, on April 12, 1945.

The launching of the United Nations, as seen by the British magazine *Punch*.

The official symbol of the United Nations.

Potsdam in July 1945, therefore, the cordiality that had prevailed at Yalta had given way to coldness. The United States, after President Roosevelt's death in April 1945, was represented by President Harry S Truman; and Great Britain, after Churchill's defeat at the polls, was represented by Prime Minister Clement Attlee. This left Stalin as the only original member of the Big Three.

The main differences between the East and the West at Potsdam arose over the eastern borders of Germany and over German reparations. As compensation for the territories it had lost to Russia at Yalta, Poland had occupied about one-fifth of Germany, east of the Oder and Neisse rivers. Against Stalin's insistence that these lands become permanently Polish, the western powers at Potsdam won a postponement of any final decision until a later peace conference. As for German reparations, the Soviet Union held on to the high demands it had made at Yalta. But the West got Stalin to agree that Germany was to be left with sufficient resources to support itself and that the country was to be treated "as a single economic unit." Here were several causes for subsequent friction among the victors.

During the closing days of the Potsdam Conference attention shifted to the Far East, where the war with Japan was

drawing to a close. The Soviet Union entered the war at the last minute by invading Manchuria. As soon as the fighting had stopped, Russia took possession of the rights and territories it had been promised at Yalta—special rights on the Chinese mainland in Port Arthur and Darien, and annexation of the Kurile Islands and southern Sakhalin from Japan. The United States claimed control over Japan itself. Korea was divided into Russian and American zones. Here was another potential source of conflict.

Peace with the Axis Satellites

With the war finally over, peace negotiations could begin. The peace conference of the twenty-one nations that had fought against the Axis met in Paris in July 1946. Many of its decisions had been made beforehand by the foreign ministers of the great powers. The peace treaties with Italy, Rumania, Hungary, Bulgaria, and Finland were signed in February 1947. Italy, in spite of its Fascist past, was let off remarkably easily. It lost some territory to France, Yugoslavia, and Greece; its colonies were put under the trusteeship of the UN; and Italy had to pay reparations. The settlements with the rest of the powers were similar. Since, with the exception of Finland, these countries were already under Russian domination, the details of the peace terms are not very important. The Soviet Union in each case was the main beneficiary, getting the major share of reparations and extensive territories. Some of these territories—the Baltic states, eastern Poland, and Bessarabia—had formerly belonged to tsarist Russia; but the Baltic states between the wars had been independent, and Bessarabia had belonged to Rumania. Stalin's aim, it seemed, was to restore Russia's borders as they had been before the advent of communism.

THE PROBLEM OF GERMANY

The signing of the Paris treaties ended peacemaking for the time being. Treaties with Japan and Austria were not signed until several years later, and there has as yet been no peace treaty with Germany. It was over the issue of Germany that the East and West had their first real falling-out.

Germany, at Potsdam, lost about one-fourth of the territory it had held in 1937, before Hitler embarked on his eastward expansion. But Germany still had almost 70 million people, and its industrial resources were considerable. There could be little doubt, therefore, that the former Reich would continue to be a vital factor in world affairs. Beginning in 1946, Russia and the western powers tried to reach an agreement on the future of Germany. But it soon became clear that they did not see eye to eye on many crucial points. What each side hoped was to create a united Germany in its own image. And when this proved impossible, the East and West reorganized their respective zones, eventually creating a divided Germany.

The Division of Germany

The first disagreements arose over economic matters. The division of Germany into occupation zones proved a serious obstacle to economic recovery. But western proposals for economic unification were met by Russian counterproposals for political unity first. Since it had been agreed at Potsdam that Germany was to be treated "as a single economic unit," the western powers, in December 1946, merged their zones economically. West Germany's economy was then given considerable American aid. The result was a miraculous turn for the better. By 1950 the industrial output of West Germany had again reached its 1936 level.

While the West was integrating its two-thirds of Germany into the economy of western Europe, the Russians began the thoroughgoing "sovietization" of their eastern zone. In time these diverging policies could not help but lead to partition. At one point, from 1948 to 1949, the Soviet Union tried to force the West out of the former German capital by imposing a blockade on the Allied sectors of Berlin. But a gigantic western airlift of some three hundred thousand flights foiled Russia's scheme. In May 1949 a West German Parliamentary Council adopted a constitution for the Federal Republic of Germany, with Bonn as capital and with Konrad Adenauer as its first chancellor. In East Germany a Communist-dominated German Democratic Republic was founded in October 1949. By 1950 the struggle between East and West over Germany had resulted in the political division of the country, each part refusing to recognize the other and claiming to speak for the whole.

TERRITORIAL ADJUSTMENTS
AFTER THE SECOND WORLD WAR   1945

The boundaries shown on this map date from the beginning of Second World War

0   MILES   200

Axis nations after Second World War

Lands that changed hands after Second World War

The Berlin airlift (June 1948–May 1949).

THE BEGINNING OF THE COLD WAR

The increasing tension between the western Allies and the Soviet Union is usually called the "Cold War." As with most other wars, its origins and causes have been a subject of controversy. Most western historians still agree that the major responsibility for the Cold War lay with the Soviet Union's attempt to use the chaos of the postwar world to further its own expansionist and ideological aims. In the late 1960s, however, some "revisionist" historians in the United States began to see their own country's desire for economic predominance as having caused the Cold War by forcing the Soviets into communizing eastern Europe for reasons of self-protection.

The Spread of Communism

The communization of eastern Europe was a gradual process. The region had been "liberated" by the Red army, which had then stayed on. At first some outward show of democracy was maintained, with "popular front" governments and "free" elections. But gradually the non-Communist members were ousted and coalition governments were transformed into "people's democracies." By 1947 this policy was causing deep concern in the West. Poland, Ru-

mania, Yugoslavia, Albania, and Bulgaria all had either Communist or pro-Communist regimes, and the trend in Czechoslovakia and Hungary was in the same direction. The only way to halt this creeping expansion of communism, it was felt, was to meet force with force. The occasion to proclaim such a policy of "containment" came in the spring of 1947, when Russia tried to extend its influence near the entrance to the Black Sea.

The Truman Doctrine and the Marshall Plan

In Greece, a small Communist minority, supported by Communists in neighboring countries, was waging a civil war against the government. The British, after the war, had supplied the Greek monarchy with financial and military aid. But Britain had serious economic problems at home, and it was also supporting Turkey's resistance to Soviet demands for concessions. In the spring of 1947, Great Britain announced that it could no longer give aid to Greece and Turkey. It was at this point that the United States took over. In a message to Congress on March 12, 1947, President Truman called for American support to "free peoples who are resisting attempted subjugation by armed minorities or by outside pressures." Such support, the president added, was to be primarily economic. A comprehensive scheme for American aid to Europe was announced three months later by Secretary of State George C. Marshall. By fighting the economic and social conditions that gave rise to communism, the United States hoped to contain it.

The Cominform and the Molotov Plan

The Truman Doctrine and the Marshall Plan opened a wholly new phase in United States foreign policy. America had broken with its isolationist past and had assumed the leadership of the free world. The significance of this break was not lost on the Soviet Union. Secretary Marshall had included all European nations in his European Recovery Program, but any country in the Russian orbit that tried to participate was prevented from doing so by the Soviets. To tighten its control over eastern Europe, the Soviet Union had already concluded mutual assistance pacts with most of its satellites. In order to coordinate the efforts of European communism, the Russians, in 1947, founded the Communist Information Bureau (Cominform), as successor to the Comintern, which had been dissolved in 1943. In the economic field, finally, the Russians announced their "Molotov Plan" as counterpart to the Marshall Plan.

The *Coup d'État* in Prague

Letter from President Beneš to the Presidium of the Communist Party:

. . . **You know my sincerely democratic creed. I cannot but stay faithful to that creed even at this moment because democracy, according to my belief, is the only reliable and durable basis for a decent and dignified human life.**

I insist on parliamentary democracy and parliamentary government as it limits democracy. I state I know very well it is necessary to social and economic content. I built my political work on these principles and cannot—without betraying myself—act otherwise. . . .

◊ ◊ ◊

Reply by the Presidium of the Communist Party:

The Presidium of the Central Committee of the Communist Party acknowledged your letter dated February 24 and states again that it cannot enter into negotiations with the present leadership of the National Socialist, People's and Slovak Democratic Parties. . . .

Massive people's manifestations during the last few days clearly have shown our working people denounce, with complete unity and with indignation, the policy of these parties and ask the creation of a government in which all honest progressive patriots devoted to the republic and the people are represented. . . .

Being convinced that only such a highly constitutional and parliamentary process can guarantee the peaceful development of the republic and [that] at the same time it corresponds to the ideas of a complete majority of the working people, the Presidium of the Central Committee hopes firmly after careful considerations that you will recognize the correctness of its conclusions and will agree with its proposals.

From H. L. Trefousse, *The Cold War—A Book of Documents* (New York: Putnam, 1965), pp. 109–12.

The Communist Coup in Czechoslovakia

While East and West were consolidating their positions, the Russians scored another victory in the Cold War. Among the occupied nations of eastern Europe, Czechoslovakia alone had been able to maintain some of its democratic freedoms. But these were gradually undermined by the usual infiltration tactics of native Communists with Russian backing. By February 1948 the country was ripe for a *coup d'état.* In March, Foreign Minister Jan Masaryk, a friend of the West, was killed in a fall from his office window; and in June, President Beneš gave way to Communist leader Klement Gottwald. Except for Finland, all the countries of eastern Europe were now under Communist rule.

The North Atlantic Treaty

The Communist seizure of Czechoslovakia dramatized the need for military as well as economic integration of western resources. Great Britain and France had already concluded a treaty of alliance at Dunkirk in 1947. As an additional safeguard, in 1948 they asked the Benelux countries—Belgium, the Netherlands, and Luxembourg—to join them in the Brussels Treaty. But the nations of western Europe realized that effective resistance to Russia required the help of the United States. There were still isolationists in America who warned against a military alliance, but the majority of Americans agreed with their government that the only language Russia seemed to understand was the language of force. So on April 4, 1949, the United States joined the members of the Brussels Treaty, together with Italy, Portugal, Denmark, Iceland, Norway, and Canada, in the North Atlantic Treaty. These twelve powers were joined later by Greece and Turkey (1951) and by West Germany (1955). The gist of the treaty was contained in Article 5, which stated that "an armed attack against one or more" of its signatories "shall be considered an attack against them all." A North Atlantic Council was set up to direct the formation of the North Atlantic Treaty Organization (NATO).

THE UNITED NATIONS IN THE COLD WAR

The growing tension between the East and West was also felt within the United Nations. As long as one of the major powers, through its veto in the Security Council, could prevent joint action, the effectiveness of the UN was limited. Only when international disputes did not involve the interests of a major power could the United Nations make its influence felt. It was thus possible to stop the fighting between Dutch and native forces in Indonesia and between India and Pakistan over Kashmir. In trying to keep Russia from meddling in the affairs of Iran, however, or in calling a halt to the civil war in Greece, United States aid was more important than UN pressure. The United Nations did score one major success before 1950: the founding of the state of Israel. But this was possible only because both the Soviet Union and the United States supported it.

The Founding of Israel

There had already been intermittent clashes between Arabs and Jews in Palestine before the Second World War (see p. 735). When the British after the war found it increasingly difficult to keep peace within their mandate, they decided to withdraw. At this point, in 1948, the UN stepped in, hoping to bring about a peaceful partition of Palestine. The Jews proclaimed the independent state of Israel, which was immediately recognized by the United States and the Soviet Union. But the Arabs, who opposed this solution, resisted. In the ensuing war the Israeli forces proved superior. UN efforts for an armistice finally succeeded in 1949. But peace remained precarious and full-scale war was resumed in 1956.

Other UN Activities

The United Nations had other tasks besides settling international disputes. In some of these economic, social, and cultural activities carried on by special agencies, the UN was highly successful. In December 1948 the General Assembly adopted an ambitious program of technical assistance for underdeveloped areas. The United States made available much of the necessary money and personnel under the Point Four program proclaimed by President Truman in January 1949.

Far more important than these economic and social problems, however, was the need for some regulation of international armaments. And here the United Nations made little headway. The main concern was over the control of atomic weapons. In 1946 America proposed to the United Nations Atomic Energy Commission the establishment of an International Atomic Development Authority to which the United States would transfer its atomic knowledge and facilities. The Authority was to be given the right of inspection to prevent the secret manufacture of atomic bombs. Since America still had a monopoly in the atomic field, this proposal was most generous and it was endorsed by an overwhelming majority of the General Assembly. But the Soviet Union vetoed the American proposal, objecting in particular to its provisions for inspection. In July 1949, after three years of fruitless debate, the

Celebrating the partition of Palestine and waving the flag of their new nation, happy Israelis crowd onto an armored British patrol car in Jerusalem.

Atomic Energy Commission adjourned. Two months later, Russia announced the first successful explosion of its own atomic bomb.

THE COLD WAR IN THE FAR EAST

The most momentous changes after 1945 occurred outside Europe. The emancipation of former colonial regions from foreign rule transformed the hitherto passive masses of Asia and Africa into active participants in international affairs. The most important change of the postwar period was the emergence of Red China as a major force in the world's balance of power.

Postwar Japan

Because of its leading role in the occupation of Japan, the United States after the Second World War was more deeply involved in Far Eastern affairs than at any other time in its history. Since there was no rivalry among occupying powers, and since Japan's governmental machinery was left intact, the transition from war to peace went more smoothly in Japan than in Germany. A democratic constitution, in May 1947, transferred sovereignty from the emperor to the people. The Japanese army and navy had already been dissolved, patriotic organizations were banned, and education was reformed along democratic lines. In the economic sphere, the changes were less drastic. Plans to break up the large industrial and financial combinations of the *zaibatsu*, the great family trusts of Japan, were abandoned when such dismantling was found to interfere with Japan's recovery. Most of the large holdings of absentee landlords, on the other hand, were divided among tenant farmers. Despite these and other reforms, economic revival was slow. Only the war in Korea provided the stimulus for Japan's economic recovery during the 1950s.

By 1951 the occupation of Japan had accomplished most of its aims and the time had come for a peace settlement.

THE FAR EAST SINCE THE SECOND WORLD WAR

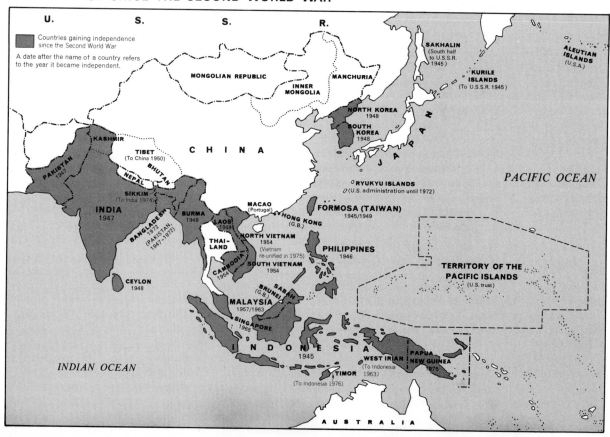

					First Communist Republic Set Up			Communist Victory
Revolution 1911	1916	1921	1929	1931			1945	1949

Rule of General Yüan	Chaos	China United by the Nationalists	Nationalists Nominally in Control		Civil War

The rift between the United States and Russia, however, made a peace conference impracticable. America therefore assumed the chief responsibility for drafting the treaty. Peace with Japan was signed at San Francisco on September 8, 1951. The treaty was generous, restoring full Japanese sovereignty but permitting the United States to maintain military bases in Japan. America and Japan also concluded a defense agreement that ultimately became an alliance.

Communist Victory in China

While events in Japan were going largely according to American wishes, developments on the Chinese mainland were taking a different turn. The end of the war found most of China still divided between the government forces of Chiang Kai-shek and the Communist armies of Mao Tse-tung. Chiang had the backing of Chinese business and banking interests, while Mao's program of land reform brought him the support of the landless masses. Both sides now began a fight for the regions held until recently by Japan. In this contest the Communists proved more successful. By the end of 1948 most of northern China was in Communist hands.

The United States had given large amounts of financial and military aid to Chiang Kai-shek. But as the Nationalist government failed to introduce much-needed reforms, United States aid was curtailed and finally cut off. In the spring of 1949, Chiang Kai-shek began to withdraw his forces to the island of Formosa. By early 1950 the whole Chinese mainland was in Communist hands. On October 1, 1949, the People's Republic of China was officially proclaimed at Peking, with Mao Tse-tung as president. The Soviet Union immediately recognized the new regime, whereas the United States continued to recognize the Nationalist government of Chiang Kai-shek.

The East–West Conflict over Korea

The victory of communism in China radically changed the balance of power between East and West. The effects of this change were felt almost immediately, as events in Korea transformed the Cold War in that country into an armed conflict. The Korean peninsula, at the end of the Second World War, had been divided into American and Russian zones of occupation. Just as in Germany, this temporary partition gradually brought about two quite different regimes. In 1948, elections in the United States-occupied southern part of Korea resulted in the founding of the Republic of Korea, with Dr. Syngman Rhee as president. The Russians thereupon sponsored their own Communist-dominated northern People's Democratic Republic, under the presidency of veteran Communist Kim Il Sung.

Late in 1948 the Soviet Union and the United States began to withdraw their troops from North and South Korea. A UN commission remained behind, trying to prevent a possible conflict between the two parts of Korea. Its efforts, however, proved in vain. On June 25, 1950, North Korean forces crossed the thirty-eighth parallel to "liberate" South Korea. Since Russia at the time was boycotting the Security Council, the United Nations was able to act without being hindered by a Soviet veto. When North Korea refused to halt its aggression, the Security Council asked the members of the UN to go to the aid of South Korea. The United States had already decided to intervene and was soon joined by small contingents from other countries. For the first time, the United Nations had gone to war. The Cold War had turned hot.

Suggestions for Further Reading

Note: Asterisk denotes a book available in paperback edition.

General The most vivid and monumental account of the Second World War is W. S. Churchill, *The Second World War,** 6 vols. (1948–53). An admirably comprehensive treatment is G. Wright, *The Ordeal of Total War, 1939–1945** (1968). Among general military accounts, the following stand out: J. F. C. Fuller, *The Second World War, 1939–45* (1949); P. Young, *World War, 1939–1945* (1966); and B. H. Liddell Hart, *History of the Second World War** (1970). D. Flower and J. Reeves, eds., *The Taste of Courage: The War, 1939–1945* (1966), successfully recaptures the atmosphere of the war at the fronts and at home. This is done even better for the war's early phase in J. Lukacs, *The Last European War: September 1939/December 1941* (1976).

The War: Military and Naval The most detailed coverage of the major engagements may be found in the multivolume series dealing with America's armed forces in the Second World War: Office of the Chief of Military History, *United States Army in World War II,* 70 vols. (1947–69); S. E. Morison, *History of United States Naval Operations in World War II,* 14 vols. (1947–60); and W. F. Craven and J. L. Cate, *The Army Air Forces in World War II,* 7 vols. (1948–53). Phases of the war not covered in the above are treated in M. Bloch, *Strange Defeat* (1949), on the fall of France; A. Johnson, *Norway: Her Invasion and Occupation* (1948); M. Cervi, *The Hollow Legions: Mussolini's Blunder in Greece* (1971); A. Clark, *Barbarossa: The Russian-German Conflict, 1941–1945** (1965); and K. Wierzynski, *The Forgotten Battlefield: The Story of Finland* (1944). On the maritime war, J. Creswell, *Sea Warfare, 1939–1945,* rev. ed. (1967), and S. W. Roskill, *The War at Sea, 1939–1945,* 3 vols. (1954–61), are excellent. For some of the war's more dramatic stories, see R. Grenfell, *The Bismarck Episode* (1949); D. Young, *Rommel: The Desert Fox** (1950); C. V. Woodward, *The Battle for Leyte Gulf** (1947); W. Ansel, *Hitler Confronts England* (1960); C. Ryan, *The Longest Day** (1959), on the Allied invasion of Normandy; and J. Hersey, *Hiroshima** (1946). Most of the war's leading military figures have written their memoirs. Of special interest are D. D. Eisenhower, *Crusade in Europe** (1948); Viscount Montgomery, *Memoirs* (1958); C. de Gaulle, *War Memoirs,** 3 vols. (1960); M. Weygand, *Recalled to Service* (1952); J. Stilwell, *The Stilwell Papers* (1948); and J. Wainwright, *General Wainwright's Story* (1946). For the German side, see H. R. Trevor-Roper, ed., *Blitzkrieg to Defeat: Hitler's War Directives, 1939–1945* (1964); B. H. Liddell Hart, *The German Generals Talk** (1948); H. Guderian, *Panzer Leader* (1952); and E. von Manstein, *Lost Victories* (1958).

The War: Political and Economic J. L. Snell, *Illusion and Necessity: The Diplomacy of Global War** (1963), is a concise and readable introduction. The gradual involvement of the United States in the war is treated in W. L. Langer and S. E. Gleason, *The Undeclared War, 1940–1941** (1953), and more briefly in R. A. Divine, *The Reluctant Belligerent: American Entry into World War II** (1965). The best account of the diplomatic background of the war with Japan is H. Feis, *The Road to Pearl Harbor** (1950). For highly critical views of Roosevelt's foreign policy, see C. C. Tansill, *Back Door to War* (1952); G. Kolko, *The Politics of War: The World and United States Foreign Policy, 1943–1945* (1968); and B. M. Russett, *No Clear and Present Danger: A Skeptical View of the United States Entry into World War II* (1972). Other aspects of American foreign policy are discussed in H. Feis, *The China Tangle** (1953), and W. L. Langer, *Our Vichy Gamble** (1947).

R. E. Sherwood, *Roosevelt and Hopkins** (1948); E. L. Stimson, *On Active Service in Peace and War* (1948); R. Murphy, *Diplomat Among Warriors** (1964); and W. D. Leahy, *I Was There* (1950), give valuable insights into American policy making.

The controversial story of the Vichy regime is brilliantly told in R. O. Paxton, *Vichy France: Old Guard and New Order, 1940–1944* (1973). E. L. Woodward, *British Foreign Policy in the Second World War* (1962), is the standard work on that subject. The relations among the Allies are reviewed in H. Feis, *Churchill, Roosevelt, Stalin** (1957), and M. Viorst, *Hostile Allies: FDR and Charles de Gaulle* (1965). See also A. W. De Porte, *De Gaulle's Foreign Policy, 1944–1946* (1968). On Russia's foreign policy, see L. Fischer, *The Road to Yalta: Soviet Foreign Relations, 1941–1945* (1972). The Soviet Union's harsh wartime experiences are related in A. Werth, *Russia at War** (1964), and H. Salisbury, *900 Days: The Siege of Leningrad** (1969).

Explanations of Hitler's fateful decision to invade Russia are provided in A. Rossi, *The Russo-German Alliance* (1951), and G. L. Weinberg, *Germany and the Soviet Union, 1939–1941* (1954). Hitler's attitude toward the United States is analyzed in A. Frye, *Nazi Germany and the American Hemisphere, 1933–1941* (1967); S. Friedländer, *Prelude to.Downfall: Hitler and the United States, 1939–1941* (1967); and J. V. Compton, *The Swastika and the Eagle* (1967). Relations within the Axis are the subject of an excellent study by F. W. Deakin, *The Brutal Friendship: Mussolini, Hitler, and the Fall of Italian Fascism,** 2 vols. (1966). J. M. Meskill, *Hitler and Japan: The Hollow Alliance* (1966), tells a story of failure. See also M. D. Fenyo, *Hitler, Horthy, and Hungary: German-Hungarian Relations, 1941–1944* (1972). Spain's role in the war is the subject of H. Feis, *The Spanish Story: Franco and the Nations at War** (1948), and C. B. Burdick, *Germany's Military Strategy and Spain in World War II* (1968). On Japan's wartime policy, see F. C. Jones, *Japan's New Order in East Asia: Its Rise and Fall, 1937–1945* (1954).

On the economic aspects of the war, see D. M. Nelson, *Arsenal for Democracy* (1946), and D. L. Gordon and R. Dangerfield, *The Hidden Weapon: The Story of Economic Warfare* (1947). Germany's economic war effort is treated in A. S. Milward, *The German Economy at War* (1965), and B. A. Carroll, *Design for Total War: Arms and Economics in the Third Reich* (1968).

Hitler's "New Order" N. Rich, *Hitler's War Aims,* 2 vols. (1973–74), deals competently with a complicated subject. See also A. Toynbee, ed., *Hitler's Europe* (1954). A. S. Milward, *The New Order and the French Economy* (1971), is an able monograph. A. Dallin, *German Rule in Russia, 1941–1945* (1957), is excellent. The large-scale popular migrations during the war are treated in E. M. Kulischer, *Europe on the Move: War and Population Changes, 1917–1947* (1948). On German use of slave labor, see E. M. Homze, *Foreign Labor in Nazi Germany* (1967). The more horrible aspects of Hitler's tyranny are told in L. Poliakov, *Harvest of Hate* (1954), and G. Reitlinger, *The Final Solution** (1953), which deal with the extermination of the European Jews. On the concentration camps, see R. Hoess, *Commandant of Auschwitz** (1959); B. Naumann, *Auschwitz* (1966); and Lord Russell of Liverpool, *The Scourge of the Swastika: A Short History of Nazi War Crimes** (1954). Resistance to the "New Order" is ably surveyed in H. Michel, *The Shadow War: European Resistance, 1939–1945* (1972).

The Search for Peace The plans made during the war for a postwar settlement are discussed in R. Opie et al., *The Search for Peace Settlements* (1951), and more briefly in W. L. Neumann, *Making the Peace, 1941–1945* (1950). Separate phases of the problem are treated in T. A. Wilson, *The First Summit: Roosevelt and Churchill at Placentia Bay, 1941* (1970), which deals with the "Atlantic Charter"; J. L. Snell, *Wartime Origins of the East–West Dilemma over Germany* (1956); and E. F. Penrose, *Economic Planning for the Peace* (1953). See also L. W. Holborn, *War and Peace Aims of the United Nations,* 2 vols. (1948). The conferences at Yalta and Potsdam are described by some of the leading participants: E. R. Stettinius, *Roosevelt and the Russians* (1949); H. S Truman, *Memoirs, Vol. I: Year of Decisions** (1955); J. F. Byrnes, *Speaking Frankly* (1947); and W. S. Churchill, *Triumph and Tragedy** (1953). The best studies of the two conferences are D. S. Clemens, *Yalta* (1970), and H. Feis, *Between War and Peace: The Potsdam Conference** (1960). On the peace with Japan, see F. S. Dunn, *Peace-Making and the Settlement with Japan* (1963).

The Cold War The best general account of the early postwar years is D. Yergin, *Shattered Peace: The Origins of the Cold War and the National Security State* (1977). See also H. Feis, *From Trust to Terror: The Onset of the Cold War, 1945–1950* (1970); L. E. Davis, *The Cold War Begins: Soviet-American Conflict over Eastern Europe* (1974); and J. L. Gaddis, *The United States and the Origins of the Cold War, 1941–1947* (1972). G. F. Kennan, *American Diplomacy, 1900–1950** (1951), contains Kennan's famous articles on the sources of Soviet behavior and the need for an American policy of "containment." The "revisionist" position is stated in G. Kolko and J. Kolko, *The Limits of Power: The World and United States Foreign Policy, 1945–1954** (1972); W. A. Williams, *The Tragedy of American Diplomacy** (1972); and D. Horowitz, *The Free World Colossus* (1971). Their findings are criticized by R. J. Maddox, *The New Left and the Origins of the Cold War* (1973). On events in Germany, see A. Grosser, *The Colossus Again: Western Germany from Defeat to Rearmament* (1955); H. Zink, *The United States in Germany, 1944–1955* (1957); L. D. Clay, *Decision in Germany* (1950); and J. P. Nettl, *The Eastern Zone and Soviet Policy in Germany, 1945–1950* (1951). Austria is treated in W. B. Bader, *Austria Between East and West, 1945–1955* (1966). H. Seton-Watson, *The East European Revolution* (1951), treats the victory of communism in that area. The Communist seizure of individual countries is told in S. Mikolajczyk, *The Rape of Poland* (1950); H. Ripka, *Czechoslovakia Enslaved* (1950); and for Hungary in F. Nagy, *The Struggle Behind the Iron Curtain* (1948). Developments in the Far East are analyzed by H. Feis, *The China Tangle** (1953); A. S. Whiting, *China Crosses the Yalu: The Decision to Enter the Korean War* (1960); and H. Feis, *Contest over Japan* (1967). S. E. Ambrose, *The Rise to Globalism: American Foreign Policy since 1938** (1971), is a first-rate survey. For the early years of the United Nations, see C. M. Eichelberger, *UN: The First Ten Years* (1955), and T. Lie, *In the Cause of Peace: Seven Years with the United Nations* (1954). J. Kimche and D. Kimche, *A Clash of Destinies: The Arab-Jewish War and the Founding of the State of Israel* (1960), and E. Berger, *The Covenant and the Sword: Arab-Israeli Relations, 1946–1956* (1965), deal with postwar events in the Middle East.

34 From Cold War to Coexistence

In the past a war like the one in Korea might easily have sparked a third world war. That the conflict remained localized was in large measure due to the deterrent effect of the atomic bomb. With both the United States and Russia accumulating large stockpiles of nuclear weapons, the fear that some incident or accident might upset the precarious "balance of terror" between the East and West became a dominant factor in world affairs. Gradually the perennial crises of the Cold War gave way to a state of coexistence, and ultimately watchful *détente*, between the Communist and non-Communist worlds.

The years since 1950 have seen other significant changes. In its early phases, the Cold War was primarily a conflict between two superpowers, the United States and the Soviet Union. Europe, which in the past had occupied the center of the stage, seemed to have been relegated to a mere supporting role. More recently, however, the Continent has staged a remarkable comeback. At the same time, the rise of the former colonial and underdeveloped regions, especially China, to independence and influence has injected a wholly new element into the international balance of power. Most present-day international problems are worldwide in their repercussions, involving more than the two superpowers of the Cold War era.

Other, nonpolitical, issues today, while not new, have suddenly become far more urgent than they were in the past. Foremost among them is the "population explosion." Demographers estimate that by the end of this century 7 billion people will be alive, almost twice as many as in 1975. Scientists claim that the development of existing resources, especially atomic energy, could provide ample livelihood for these vast masses. But even in an age of coexistence, much wealth and energy continue to be diverted to nonproductive military uses. It seems that the alternatives faced by mankind today are either to risk, through a nuclear arms race, the possible extermination of all life on earth, or to ensure, through peaceful effort, a good life for all.

THE DECLINE AND RISE OF WESTERN EUROPE

The decline of Europe's role in world affairs had already set in during the First World War, when only the intervention of the United States had enabled the Allies to win. For a brief span between the two wars, a semblance of the old European system of great powers was resurrected. But the Second World War brought the preeminence of Europe definitely to an end.

The postwar problems facing the nations of Europe were alike in many ways. All the major powers of western Europe suffered territorial losses, either in Europe or overseas, and several of them

were threatened by communism from without or within. The one concern shared by all countries, big and small alike, was to recover from the economic effects of the war. In trying to cope with these problems, the nations of free Europe were forced to modify somewhat their economic and political nationalism and to attempt some measure of economic, if not political, union. European recovery was retarded by the fact that the Continent continued to be divided into Communist and non-Communist spheres. But in time the gulf that the Cold War had created between the two halves of Europe grew narrower. As both eastern and western Europe recovered from the war and as relations between the two improved, the reunion of the European continent again appeared possible.

Great Britain: From World Empire to European Power

Great Britain after the Second World War had to cope with two related problems: the need for economic recovery and the loss of most of its empire. In 1945 the British electorate for the first time returned a Labour majority. Under the leadership of Clement Attlee, the government embarked on a program that

President Richard Nixon and Premier Chou En-lai exchange toasts in Peking in 1972.

was denounced as socialist by the Conservatives under Winston Churchill. Most of the enterprises that were nationalized, however—railroads, airlines, utilities, coal mines, and the Bank of England—remained so even after the Conservatives returned to power in 1951. The most far-reaching measures introduced by the Labour government were the various Social Welfare Acts that aimed at equality of opportunity for all citizens.

The tendency of these measures to make British society more egalitarian was enhanced by the drastic program of austerity by which the government hoped to balance the budget and regain Britain's former position in world trade. Under Conservative rule from 1951 to 1964, the country experienced a temporary economic recovery. In 1964, however, dissatisfaction with a weak foreign policy and renewed economic stagnation once more brought a Labour victory. The second Labour cabinet was no more successful in overcoming Britain's economic paralysis than the first had been. When foreign loans, heavy taxation, and reduced government spending failed to improve matters, the government of Prime Minister Harold Wilson in 1967 finally devalued the pound, in the hope of thus solving Britain's perennial trade deficit. But this and other drastic measures failed to improve the country's economic malaise. In 1970 the Conservatives under Edward Heath won another chance to cope with the nation's rising inflation and unemployment. To economic unrest and strikes now were added bloody riots and bombings in Northern Ireland. In 1974 it became

Labour's turn again, first under Wilson and then under James Callaghan. But neither party was able to halt the spiraling inflation, chiefly caused by union demands. In 1977 the British pound reached its lowest level since the Second World War.

One of the initial causes of Britain's depression was the rapid shrinking of its empire after the war. Wherever colonial peoples became restive and demanded independence, British interests were almost always involved. Most of the resulting new states remained within the Commonwealth of Nations (as the former British Commonwealth was now called). But the ties of this elusive organization grew weaker over the years, partly because of the racial policies pursued by countries like South Africa and Rhodesia. Within less than a generation, the once mighty British Empire virtually melted away.

One possible way of improving its position was for Britain to draw closer to the continental nations that had joined forces in the European Economic Community, or Common Market. But the island kingdom was reluctant to do so, for fear that such economic *rapprochement* might conflict with its Commonwealth obligations. It was not until 1963 that Britain applied for membership in the Common Market. At that time it was barred by the veto of France's president, Charles de Gaulle, who asserted that the British were not ready to assume the full obligations of membership. Ten years later Britain finally joined the European Economic Community, hoping to share in that organization's economic prosperity. That hope was only partly fulfilled.

Queen Elizabeth II with heads of state and representatives of the Commonwealth nations at Buckingham Palace in 1977.

Fall of France
1940

Provisional Government
Under de Gaulle

1958

| Vichy Government | | Fourth Republic | Fifth Republic |

1945 1946

France:
Search for Lost Grandeur

In France political instability at home and continued colonial wars abroad retarded postwar economic recovery. To make a clear break with the past, the French in 1946 gave themselves a new constitution. But the Fourth Republic was little different from the Third. As old enmities persisted and new ones arose, the traditional bickering among numerous small parties and interest groups again dominated the political scene. The chief beneficiaries of this confusion were the French Communists, who until 1958 made up the leading party in the National Assembly. Only in foreign policy did the new republic show some consistency, chiefly as a result of the efforts of foreign ministers Georges Bidault and Robert Schuman.

France, like Great Britain, found it difficult at first to regain its economic health. French financial problems were staggering, and their solution required heavy taxation and a stable currency. But reluctant taxpayers, creeping inflation, and incessant strikes counteracted the beneficent effects of American Marshall Plan aid. In 1954 an end came to the war in Indochina, which had caused a steady financial drain back home despite American aid; but at the same time fighting in Algeria gained momentum. It was not until President de Gaulle began to dominate the national scene in the late 1950s that a broad austerity program, combined with careful economic planning, put France back on the road to prosperity.

France, again like Britain, also faced the rapid dissolution of its colonial empire. In 1946 the Fourth Republic tried to maintain some control over its overseas holdings by founding the French Union. This federation, however, was far too centralized to satisfy the more developed territories, and a number of them—Syria, Lebanon, Morocco, and Tunisia—demanded, and were given, their independence. Indochina and Algeria won independence only after drawn-out and costly fighting. In 1958 the French Union was transformed into the French Community, which included France proper, its few remaining overseas possessions, and most of the new African nations that formerly made up French Equatorial and West Africa. The Community was a loose federation whose main significance lay in whatever prestige it held for the former mother country of a once great empire.

Prestige was the main concern of the man who assumed direction of French affairs in 1958. Charles de Gaulle, leader of the Free French forces in the Second World War, had served briefly as provisional president in 1945 but had retired before the domestic confusion that reigned at that time. He was recalled in 1958 at the height of the national crisis caused by the war in Algeria. Under de Gaulle's direction a new constitution was adopted that, in an attempt to ensure greater political stability, vastly increased the power of the president. In December 1958 General de Gaulle was elected first president of the Fifth Republic.

From 1958 until his forced retirement in 1969, the general's towering figure dominated the French scene. De Gaulle's most important achievement was the solution of the Algerian problem. In 1962 an agreement between French and Arab representatives, endorsed by the French electorate, gave Algeria its independence. Elsewhere, in Europe and overseas, de Gaulle's main ambition was to recapture some of France's past "grandeur." To strengthen his country's position in Europe, de Gaulle maintained close ties with West Germany and cemented relations with the communist powers, notably the Soviet Union. To counteract Anglo-Saxon influence, he took France

Charles de Gaulle, then prime minister of France, campaigning in overseas France on behalf of his constitutional proposals in 1958. In December of that year he was elected president.

out of NATO, preferring instead to rely on an independent French nuclear striking force, and he barred Britain from membership in the Common Market. Along similar lines, de Gaulle drew closer to Communist China, criticized American involvement in Vietnam, and even encouraged separatist sentiment among French Canadians. Supporters of the French president defended his obstructionist policies as a reassertion not merely of French influence but of European influence as well against the growing power of the United States. His critics, on the other hand, charged that when the general said Europe, he meant France; and when he said France, he meant de Gaulle.

In France itself, moreover, de Gaulle's preoccupation with foreign concerns at the expense of domestic ones gave rise to a wave of discontent, especially among workers and students, that almost led to revolution in May 1968. When some of his reform proposals were defeated in a national referendum the following year, de Gaulle resigned, and died soon thereafter.

De Gaulle's successor was one of his close associates, Georges Pompidou. The new president's major concern was with domestic affairs; he tried to improve France's economy by overcoming its antiquated production methods and to ease France's rapid transition into a highly industrialized and urban society. In foreign affairs, Pompidou at long last welcomed Great Britain into the Common Market. When Pompidou died in 1974, Valéry Giscard d'Estaing continued along a road of domestic reforms, fiscal austerity, and long-range economic planning. Meanwhile the gains in local elections by parties of the left showed that many Frenchmen remained critical of their government's policy and raised the possibility of a Socialist–Communist alliance.

West Germany: The "Second Republic"

The most spectacular rise from rubble to riches in postwar Europe occurred in West Germany. The partition of the former Reich in 1949 as a result of the Cold War has already been discussed (see p. 788). During the 1950s the western Federal Republic experienced a veritable "economic miracle." In contrast to the nationalization measures adopted by Great Britain and, to a lesser extent, France, Germany followed a more traditional policy of laissez faire. With a favorable balance of trade, a freely convertible currency, and hardly any unemployment, Germany's "free-market economy" aroused the admiration and envy of its neighbors.

Politically, developments in West Germany were remarkably steady, especially compared with the turbulent years after the First World War. The constitution of the Federal Republic was framed to avoid some of the mistakes of the Weimar Republic. The country was fortunate in having as its first chancellor Konrad Adenauer, a conservative opponent of nazism and a sincere friend of the West. The "old man" virtually dominated German politics from 1949 until his retirement in 1963 at age eighty-seven. His successor, Ludwig Erhard, popular as the author of the "economic miracle," was a man of lesser political stature. In 1966 the middle-of-the-road Christian Democratic Union (CDU), which hitherto had dominated the government, had to share power with the moderately leftist Social Democratic Party (SPD), with Kurt Georg Kiesinger of the CDU as chancellor and Willy Brandt of the SPD as foreign minister. The shift toward the Social Democrats continued in 1969, when Willy Brandt became chancellor in a coalition of the SPD with the small, liberal Free Democratic Party (FDP). Brandt resigned the chancellorship over a domestic issue in 1973 and was succeeded by the equally able Helmut Schmidt.

Next to economic development, the two most vital issues before the West German government were reunification and rearmament. To reunite not only East and West Germany but also the region beyond the Oder-Neisse line (occupied by Poland in 1945) was the fervent wish of every German. Repeated proposals of the western powers to achieve German unity through free general elections invariably met with Soviet opposition. Meanwhile the West German

Konrad Adenauer (1876–1967), in 1959.

Federal Republic refused to recognize the East German Democratic Republic, in order to keep alive the idea of a united Germany. But as time went on, and as each section of Germany developed along widely divergent lines, a growing number of Germans became reconciled to the thought that they might not live to see their country reunited. As long as Adenauer was in control, however, any open acquiescence in the partition of Germany was out of the question.

This situation changed with the advent of Willy Brandt. As foreign minister, Brandt had stated his intention of bringing about a *détente* with the communist world, while at the same time maintaining close relations with the West. Once he was chancellor, he proceeded to carry out his design. As first steps he signed treaties with the Soviet Union and Poland in 1970 that called for mutual renunciation of the use of force and the establishment of normal relations. The agreement with Poland also included West Germany's recognition of the Oder-Neisse line as the German-Polish frontier. Of equal, if not greater, significance was a treaty in 1972 between East and West Germany that recognized the existence of two sovereign German states and provided for closer collaboration between them. To round out this policy of *rapprochement* with the communist world, the Brandt government also resumed economic relations with a number of East European states and established diplomatic ties with Communist China. Despite much criticism from his political opponents, Brandt's *Ostpolitik* (eastern policy) had the support of the majority of West Germans, as was shown by his clear election victory in 1972.

Brandt's policy also helped to dispel whatever apprehension had arisen over German rearmament. The creation of a West German army caused considerable debate in the 1950s. As the Russians at the time began training a German military force in East Germany, the western powers decided to permit the limited rearmament of West Germany. Under an agreement ratified in 1955, West Germany was to contribute a maximum of five hundred thousand men to the common defense of the West under NATO.

In return, the Federal Republic was granted complete sovereignty in domestic and foreign affairs.

There was some fear, both in Germany and outside, that rearmament would cause a revival of German militarism and nationalism. But such fears proved groundless. Relations between Germany and its "traditional enemy" France were better than they had ever been, leading to a treaty of friendship in 1963. Collaboration with the Anglo-Saxon powers was close, and Brandt's *Ostpolitik* gave further proof of West Germany's peaceful intentions. In its domestic policy, furthermore, West Germany showed that it had made a clean break with the Nazi past. There were a few incidents of neonazism, and in the late 1960s a right-wing group, the National Democratic Party, gained some ground in local elections; but the majority of Germans disapproved of these activities. In the mid-1970s, a new type of leftist radicalism emerged in Germany, spearheaded by a small terrorist group whose anarchist violence was reminiscent of the "nihilists" of tsarist Russia (see p. 617). Their acts of terror against government and business leaders led the government to curtail the generous civil rights guaranteed by the Bonn constitution. The fear that such measures would lead to a revival of authoritarianism, however, proved groundless.

Italy: From Poverty to Riches

Italy emerged from the Second World War with its already backward economy in a dismal state. After a slow start, however, the nation staged a remarkable recovery. By 1965 Italy's industrial production had increased fourfold, and the nation's per capita income had doubled. With economic improvement came a period of political stability. The new Italian republic was launched successfully in 1946 under the capable leadership of Alcide de Gasperi and his Christian Democratic Party. But with the onset of the Cold War, the government came under increasing attacks from a strong Communist Party on the left and a growing neofascist movement on the right. Only when the Christian Democrats, be-

France and West Germany united in the opening of a new waterway on the Moselle River in 1962. Among the dignitaries on board were Charles de Gaulle, Heinrich Lübke, president of the Federal Republic of Germany, and the Grand Duchess Charlotte of Luxembourg.

ginning in 1962, started to ally themselves with the moderate Socialists on their left did some measure of political calm return.

Even so, the fact that one out of every three Italians continued to vote Communist showed that all was far from well. While there was prosperity, poverty persisted, especially in the agricultural south. Even in the north real wages did not keep up with the general rise in the economy, and the distribution of income remained uneven. In the late 1960s, economic discontent led to numerous strikes, which, in turn, aggravated an already existing economic crisis. In addition, the center-left coalition broke apart, as Christian Democrats and Socialists differed over the controversial divorce law of 1970 and other issues. Meanwhile, the Communists remained the country's second-largest party, and the neofascist Italian Social movement doubled its forces in the elections of 1972. From here on, Italy was governed by frequently changing minority coalitions that were still dominated by the Christian Democrats. The elections of 1976 brought further Communist gains, and Italy, like France, faced the possibility of having to let the Communists share in its government. In 1978 a wave of attacks by a small band of terrorists, the Red Brigade, against prominent political and business leaders was climaxed by the abduction and murder of a former Christian Democratic premier, Aldo Moro. The resulting grief and anger, shared even by the Communists, did much to reunite the deeply divided Italian nation.

The Quest for European Unity

Given the similarity of their problems, especially in the economic field, it was only natural that western European nations should try to devise means for common action. The Marshall Plan had shown that lasting recovery could be won only through economic cooperation; and the Brussels Pact, besides calling for a military alliance, had also stressed the need for collaboration in economic, social, and cultural affairs (see p. 790). The first major instance of such collaboration was the Schuman Plan, which established the European Coal and Steel Community (ECSC). In 1952 France, Germany, the Benelux countries, and Italy agreed to merge their resources of coal and steel in a common western European market. By 1957 enough progress had been achieved to make it possible to extend the common market to other goods through the European Economic Community (EEC). In a further attempt at integration, the six members of ECSC and EEC founded the European Atomic Energy Community (Euratom) to promote peaceful atomic research and development.

The European Economic Community is not a closed organization; any country can apply for membership. The admission of Great Britain was delayed until 1973, at which time Ireland and Denmark also joined. The next candidates—Greece, Spain, and Portugal—applied in 1977. Representing more than 270 million people, the EEC is the most important and powerful trade area in the world.

Toward a "European Consciousness"?

The adjective "European," which a century ago was understood only by a small minority, and which even in the early twentieth century was accepted perhaps only by the aristocracy, by the high bourgeoisie and by certain intellectuals, today has become an accepted adjective, a designation, a self-ascribed characteristic for the majority of the populations even in Central and Eastern Europe. To many a peasant in the Danube Valley the adjective "European" even twenty or thirty years ago meant either nothing at all or something that was vaguely and suspiciously alien. This is no longer so. Despite Communist political rule and regimentation, life for large masses of people in Warsaw and Belgrade and Budapest and Bucharest has now more in common with life in Berne and Brussels and Paris than it had fifty or one hundred years ago, and this is true of people in Lisbon, Madrid, Palermo, Athens. It is, let me repeat, by no means clear whether the increasing standardization of certain forms of life will, within Europe, lead to a further, and decisive, phase in the development of a European consciousness. That ten thousand Bulgarians watch television or that tens of thousands in Budapest experience their first traffic jam is unimportant. What is important, for our purposes, is to recognize that the collapse of the European state system did not mean the end of European history; that, indeed, we are facing two countervailing historical developments: decline—definite decline—of the European state system on the one hand; rise—vague rise—of a European consciousness on the other.

From John Lukacs, *Decline and Rise of Europe* (Garden City, N.Y.: Doubleday, 1965), pp. 169–70.

Plans for European political union were less successful. Prospects looked bright in 1949, when the Council of Europe was founded at Strasbourg. But it remained a purely consultative body, and the hope for a United States of Europe did not materialize. As Europe recovered economically and as the threat of Soviet expansion subsided, national differences once again came to the fore. Yet despite these disappointments, the general trend toward European unity was unmistakable. The European powers realized that the only way they could wield any real influence was by joining forces and forgetting the divisive issues of the past.

THE AMERICAS

To the rest of the world the United States in 1945 appeared as a country of unbelievable wealth, untouched by the hardships of war. But to Americans themselves the picture looked quite different. Price controls, wage controls, real or artificially induced shortages of essential goods, incessant waves of strikes, and signs of widespread corruption—these were some of the problems faced by the American people. The Democratic administration's attempts to deal with the situation by means of further legislation found little public or congressional support. It seemed that the country was tired of government controls and of a social service state that to most Republicans smacked of socialism.

The Truman Era

President Truman was reelected in 1948 chiefly because of his foreign policy: the Truman Doctrine, the Marshall Plan, and the Berlin airlift. At the time, these measures were applauded by a majority of Americans. Isolationism, of course, did not vanish overnight. But the fact that a Republican administration after 1952 continued substantially the same foreign policy showed that the shift from isolationism was a matter not so much of choice as of necessity.

One aspect of American involvement abroad that was not universally popular was the foreign-aid program. During the first fifteen years after the war, United States economic and military aid amounted to more than $75 billion. Much of it was given in a spirit of genuine helpfulness. But foreign aid was also an important weapon in the Cold War, especially after 1955, when the Soviet Union began stepping up its own foreign-aid program.

In American domestic affairs, one of the major issues at the time was the fear of Communist infiltration. This fear arose shortly after the war, gained momentum as the Communists scored more and more triumphs in Europe and Asia, and reached its climax during the Korean War. Chiefly because of the agitation of Wisconsin's Senator Joseph McCarthy, the American public in the early 1950s was led to believe that its government had allowed Communists to get into key positions in the State Department and the army. These largely unfounded accusations created a climate of fear and suspicion and did much to harm the reputations of innocent people.

The reality of the Communist threat abroad, meanwhile, was brought home by events in Korea. As the war there bogged down in a bloody stalemate, critics of the administration demanded an escalation of the war, including the bombing of Communist bases in China. Foremost among these critics was America's commander in chief in Korea, General Douglas MacArthur. When efforts to silence him failed, President Truman, in April 1951, relieved the general of his command. The ensuing crisis was the most serious the United States had faced since 1945. Together with a mounting wave of government scandals and continued suspicion of Communist influence

A unique photograph of the four men who occupied the American presidency between 1945 and 1968—Kennedy, Johnson, Eisenhower, and Truman. The occasion was the funeral of House Speaker Sam Rayburn in 1961.

in the government, the Korean War was a major cause of the defeat of the Democrats in the election of 1952.

The Eisenhower Years

The victories of the Republican candidate, Dwight D. Eisenhower, in 1952 and 1956 were as much personal as partisan. He enhanced his popularity by concluding a Korean armistice in 1953. During his two administrations, bipartisan majorities in Congress collaborated to produce much valuable social legislation. The nation's economy continued to flourish, except in the agricultural sector, where overproduction posed a serious problem. The administration's attempts to reduce price supports and to return to a free market in agricultural products incurred the opposition of farm groups; this opposition was one of the reasons for the overwhelming congressional victory of the Democrats in 1958. Other reasons were the temporary economic recession of that year and the antagonism that the Republican administration had aroused among organized labor.

A major issue that came to the fore during the Eisenhower administration was desegregation. In *Brown v. Board of Education of Topeka* (1954), the United States Supreme Court ruled that American blacks had the right to attend the same schools as whites. Desegregation proceeded smoothly in most states, but in the Deep South every possible means was used to prevent it. From 1957 to 1958 President Eisenhower had to send federal troops to enforce desegregation in Little Rock, Arkansas. This was only the beginning of a drawn-out crisis, as blacks began to demand that desegregation be extended to other fields. The resistance of die-hard "white supremacists" to these demands did much to tarnish America's image abroad.

From Kennedy to Johnson

The victory of John F. Kennedy in 1960 injected a fresh and youthful note into American politics. His administration got off to a promising start when Congress approved a series of social-service measures chiefly designed to aid the poor. When the president began to tackle the touchy subject of civil rights, however, he lost the support of southern Democrats and his domestic program came to a halt. Some improvement in the status of blacks was made under pressure of nonviolent protests directed by able black leaders. But as police in the South met peaceful demonstrations with violence, the situation became increasingly explosive. Much of President Kennedy's attention was taken up with crises in foreign affairs. In his efforts to stand up to Communist threats in Southeast Asia, Cuba, and Berlin, the president generally found the support that Congress withheld from his domestic program.

President Kennedy was assassinated in Dallas, Texas, on November 22, 1963. A major political crisis was avoided chiefly because of the firm manner in which his successor, Lyndon B. Johnson, took charge. Where Kennedy had labored in vain against congressional opposition, Johnson, a former majority leader in the Senate, was able to achieve some notable successes. By 1964 the new president had gained sufficient popular support to win a landslide victory.

From then on, however, President Johnson found the going more and more difficult. Civil rights had become the key issue in American politics. The Civil Rights Act of 1964 was the most sweeping legislation of its kind ever enacted. But its provisions were still disregarded in many parts of the South. Meanwhile black protests spread to the North, where the demand was for greater equality in employment, housing, and education. Demonstrations that hitherto had been orderly now became increasingly violent, as bloody riots swept through major American cities and as advocates of "black power" preached the use of force. To cope with the economic roots of black discontent, the Johnson administration stepped up the antipoverty programs initiated under Kennedy. But while the "war on poverty" called for vast amounts of money, more and more funds were being diverted to another kind of war.

The war in Vietnam, in which the United States had become increasingly involved since 1961, proved the most

John F. Kennedy (1917–63) brought a vigorous approach to the presidency.

American versus Vietcong: a struggle that lasted more than a decade.

divisive issue in American politics during the last two years of the Johnson administration. As "hawks" (advocating victory through war) ranged against "doves" (favoring American withdrawal), many young Americans chose to go to prison or abroad rather than to fight an "unjust" war. The cause of reform suffered a major loss with the assassination, in June 1968, of Senator Robert F. Kennedy, a leading Democratic contender for the presidency. Racial unrest, meanwhile, had flared up anew after the murder that April of the Reverend Dr. Martin Luther King, Jr., an outstanding figure in the nonviolent civil-rights movement. It was a deeply disturbed and divided nation that gave the Republican candidate, Richard M. Nixon, a narrow victory in November 1968.

The Nixon Administrations

The war in Vietnam continued to be the major cause of tension in American politics. The withdrawal of American forces beginning in 1972 and the subsequent start of armistice negotiations were largely responsible for President Nixon's reelection the same year by an overwhelming majority. An uneasy armistice was finally concluded in early 1973. Meanwhile the president and his dynamic secretary of state, Henry Kissinger, had embarked on new ventures elsewhere by paying visits to the Soviet Union and Communist China, thus easing tensions with the Russians and establishing first contacts with the mainland Chinese.

In his domestic affairs, President Nixon had a less fortunate hand. Most problems had already plagued previous administrations; but some of them worsened as time went on. One of these was crime. "Law and order," a key issue in the 1972 elections, was part of a larger question—the rapid decay of American cities into breeding grounds of crime, often connected with drug addiction. Another growing concern was protection of the environment against pollution by individuals and industries. Unrest among blacks decreased somewhat, as some of their demands were being met. There remained, however, the controversial

issue of "busing" white or black students outside their school districts to achieve a better racial balance. Many of these problems called for official intervention. But such intervention was opposed by an administration that tried to halt the increasing role of government in the life of the individual.

Intervention could not be avoided, however, in the economic sphere. To slow the country's rising inflation, the Nixon administration, beginning in 1971, imposed wage and price controls, measures never before adopted in time of peace. To improve America's growing trade deficit, the dollar was officially devalued by a total of 17 percent in 1972 and 1973. And to curtail government spending at home, President Nixon refused to spend some funds appropriated by Congress for purposes he considered wasteful. This action did not endear him to the legislature, and confrontations between the White House and Capitol Hill were frequent. The Nixon administration was also accused of showing less concern than its predecessors for minority groups; certainly, its support among blacks was minimal.

Far more disquieting than any of these issues, however, was the "Watergate Affair," in which leading members of the president's staff were found to have been involved in illegal acts against the Democratic Party during the 1972 campaign. As judicial and Senate hearings uncovered a sordid story of intrigue and attempted cover-up, the question arose as to whether President Nixon had any part in these events. The president denied any such involvement. As more and more incriminating evidence came to light, however, much of it from the tapes of presidential conversations, and as Congressional impeachment hearings got under way in early 1974, Nixon, on August 9, decided to resign rather than face further charges and revelations. He was the first president ever thus to leave office.

From Ford to Carter

The new president, Gerald Ford, had been appointed vice president by Nixon when Spiro Agnew had resigned after

A beleaguered president tries to regain the nation's confidence in 1973 in a televised address concerning the events of the Watergate Affair.

Andrew Young, United States ambassador to the United Nations.

being found guilty of income tax evasion. The fact that Ford had not been elected was a disadvantage, though his amicable and open manner made him many friends. His popularity suffered, however, when he first granted a general pardon to Nixon and somewhat later a limited amnesty to men who had evaded the draft during the Vietnam War. To ensure continuity in foreign policy, Ford retained Secretary of State Kissinger, who tended to overshadow the president. In domestic affairs, economic issues and the effects of the energy crisis continued to loom large. The elections of 1974 increased the Democratic majorities in both houses of Congress, and the trend continued in 1976. The nightmare of Watergate was not easily forgotten.

The race for the presidency in 1976 was the closest in recent times. The winner, Democrat James Earl ("Jimmy") Carter, was a dark horse, who owed most of his victory to his own untiring efforts. President Carter's proposals for tax reform, reduced government spending, and legislation to deal with the country's long-term energy requirements were innovative and were addressed to the nation's most urgent needs. In an effort to correct the "imperial" image of the presidency, Carter affected a more folksy style, which did not always enhance his popularity. To many Americans, the peanut farmer from Plains, Georgia, seemed to lack sufficient experience for his high office, especially in military and foreign affairs, where the Panama Canal Treaty and the decision to halt development of the neutron bomb met with widespread criticism.

The United States and Its Neighbors

Since the contest between communism and capitalism was a global one, the maintenance of harmony within the Western Hemisphere was of major concern to every administration after 1945. Relations with America's northern neighbor were, on the whole, cordial. Because of its tremendous economic growth, Canada ranked as one of the world's leading industrial and commercial powers. United States capital played

an important part in this expansion, and the resulting American influence caused some resentment among Canadian nationalists. Military relations between the two countries were close, both within NATO and without. Continued membership in the (British) Commonwealth saved Canada from becoming too dependent on its powerful neighbor, although ties with Great Britain grew noticeably weaker.

Relations between the United States and its southern neighbors were far more complicated. The twenty republics of Latin America differed widely in size and significance, and the absence of a strong democratic tradition made many of them prone to authoritarian regimes of the right or left. The most pressing problem of the whole area was its alarming rise in population. Latin America had great economic potentialities, but financial and technical assistance were needed to develop them. The United States was expected to supply this aid. Prior to 1960 little such aid found its way to Latin America. Subsequently, a number of ambitious development schemes were launched, notably the Alliance for Progress, proclaimed by President Kennedy in 1961. But the results of such schemes were disappointing. Besides looking to the United States for help, the nations of Latin America increasingly looked to one another. The Latin American Free Trade Association (LAFTA), set up in 1960, called for the creation of a common market for all of Latin America by 1980; but its progress has been slow. More successful in fostering economic cooperation were various subregional groups, especially the Central American Common Market. Latin America also turned to Europe and the Soviet Union to improve its economic plight.

The United States was concerned with building a united military front against the threat of communism in the Western Hemisphere. In 1947 the Latin American nations and the United States signed the Rio Treaty, which called for mutual assistance in case of war. Subsequent agreements arranged for the exchange of United States arms against strategic raw materials. The most important agency of inter-American coopera-

1928		1953	1957	1964	1977
Stalin		Collective Leadership	Khrushchev	Collective Leadership	

Brezhnev

tion was the Organization of American States (OAS), founded in 1948. It originally included all nations of the Western Hemisphere except Canada, but Cuba was excluded (though not formally expelled) in 1962. The Charter of the OAS proclaimed the equality of its members and laid down the principle of nonintervention in their external and internal affairs. The OAS proved of great value as a stabilizing influence, especially against Castro's Cuba and against recurrent instances of guerrilla uprisings, urban terrorism, and political kidnapings.

The overthrow of Cuban dictator Fulgencio Batista by Fidel Castro's rebel forces in 1959 at first was hailed in the United States and elsewhere as a victory of democracy. But when Castro's regime revealed itself as an outpost of communism the United States broke off relations with Cuba and then, in 1961, supported an ill-fated invasion attempt at the Bay of Pigs by anti-Castro forces. Meanwhile Castro had established close ties with Communist China and the Soviet Union. The latter's attempt, in 1962, to use Cuba as a base for ballistic missiles clearly directed against the United States led to a major showdown between the Soviet Union and the United States in which the Russians had to give way. As time went on, the threat of Castro to the security of the Western Hemisphere subsided and relations between Cuba and the United States improved.

The United States was also involved in a number of other Latin American crises, notably in Chile and Panama. In Chile, the United States was accused of having engineered the violent overthrow of President Salvador Allende Gossens, a Marxist, by a military junta in 1973, a charge that subsequently was proved correct. In Panama, perennial demonstrations against American control of the Panama Canal finally led to the signing of a treaty by Presidents Carter and

Torrijos in 1977, by which the waterway would come under Panamanian control by the end of the century. The agreement ran into considerable opposition in Congress, but was finally approved in 1978.

THE COMMUNIST WORLD

For almost two decades after 1945, while the Cold War lasted, the Communist world appeared to be a monolithic bloc dominated by Moscow. It took the rest of the world some time to realize how much this Soviet predominance depended on one man. In retrospect, the death of Joseph Stalin on March 5, 1953, was a major event in world history. It spelled the end of an era, not only for Russian communism but for world communism as well.

Russia Under Khrushchev

The main features of the Stalinist era, which reached its high point during the years after 1945, have already been discussed (see pp. 749–52). To repair the staggering damages of the war, two Five-Year Plans called for a new round of industrialization and collectivization. Simultaneously, strictest orthodoxy remained the keynote of Soviet political and cultural life. The slightest deviation from Stalinist-Marxist theory brought imprisonment, slave labor, or death. In a famous speech before the twentieth Party Congress in 1956, Khrushchev charged that Stalin, "a very distrustful man, sickly suspicious," had planned even to liquidate his most intimate political associates.

Stalin's reign of terror came to a sudden end with his death. For the first four years or so after Stalin's death, "collective leadership" was instituted. But it was only a matter of time before one of the most determined members of the group,

Nikita Khrushchev delivers an angry diatribe during a United Nations debate in 1960.

Leonid Brezhnev showing journalists in Moscow his official portrait.

Nikita S. Khrushchev, emerged as the recognized leader of the Soviet Union. As Stalin had done a generation earlier, Khrushchev used his key position as Secretary of the Central Committee of the Communist Party to rid himself of his associates. The only novelty was that his rivals were not killed but merely ousted—an example of the "new look" in Soviet policy.

Khrushchev, a career party functionary, never really achieved the absolute power that Stalin had wielded before him. Russia under Stalin had undergone not only an economic but a social revolution. From a nation of illiterate peasants, the Soviet Union had become a nation of educated workers. Although the basic Marxist concept of state ownership of the means of production remained in force, the concept of a classless society had been far from realized. Instead, a substantial upper class had grown up: the party elite, the top echelons of the vast political and economic bureaucracy, managerial personnel, technical experts, scientists, and the like. The Soviet Union, in other words, had become a far more complex society than it had been at the start. To run such a nation by regimentation based on terror was no longer possible. Nor was it even desirable, since blind obedience in the long run killed initiative and made for inefficiency.

The most dramatic change in the life of the average Russian came with the retreat from terror after Stalin's death. This did not mean that there were no longer any political prisoners. But it did mean that the number of punishable political crimes became smaller than it had been under Stalin. Henceforth it became possible to criticize certain aspects of the regime without risking execution.

The liberalization of Soviet life was felt in other ways. In factories and on collective farms the strict discipline of the past was relaxed. Consumer goods became more plentiful, and the housing shortage was reduced. Education was broadened to admit more students to secondary schools and universities. With the easing of travel restrictions, the Russian people for the first time came in contact with the outside world. In Rus-

sian art and literature, the orthodox emphasis on "socialist realism" gave way to tolerance of some modern trends. Initially, outside observers saw these changes as signs that Russia had abandoned its unbending opposition to the West. But Soviet leaders made no secret of the fact that the "new look" was merely a change in methods and that their aim remained what it had always been: the overthrow of capitalism.

Russia Under Brezhnev

The return to virtual one-man rule under Khrushchev was suddenly reversed in 1964, when the Russian leader was purged by his party's Central Committee and his double role as premier and party secretary was divided between Alexei N. Kosygin and Leonid I. Brezhnev. The main reasons for Khrushchev's dismissal appeared to be domestic, notably his failure to live up to his boastful economic promises, although foreign reversals, such as the Cuban missile crisis, also played their part. For a while the trend seemed once again to be toward collective leadership. But like Khrushchev (and Stalin) before him, Brezhnev, as General Secretary of the Communist Party, gradually emerged as the key figure in Soviet affairs. Continuity in foreign policy was assured by the presence of veteran Foreign Minister Andrei A. Gromyko, who continued the policy of *détente* initiated by Khrushchev. In 1977 Brezhnev assumed the additional position of President of the Supreme Soviet, or head of state, replacing Nikolai V. Podgorny and making one-man rule still more visible. A new constitution, meanwhile, attempted to project a more liberal image of the Soviet state by stressing individual rights; but like Stalin's effort in 1936, it was seen by western observers as mere window dressing.

Economic growth in the Soviet Union continued during the 1960s and 1970s, though at a slower rate than predicted, especially in the agrarian sector. With increased material gain came signs of spiritual unrest. The younger generation in particular, the "grandchildren of the revolution," seemed less and less willing to accept the intellectual restrictions of a totalitarian regime. The reaction of the post-Khrushchev regime to manifestations of dissent was twofold. On the one hand, critical writers like Alexander Solzhenitsyn and Andrei Sinyavsky, advocates of civil liberties like Yosif Brodsky and Andrei Sakharov, and various national dissidents in the Ukraine and Lithuania were arrested and in some cases forced to emigrate. But at the same time the government also tried to counter discontent by economic concessions, raising the living standard of the average Soviet citizen. The general tendency, however, was in the direction of repression rather than reform, leading some foreign observers to speak of a return to Stalinism.

Unrest Among the Satellites

The effects of the post-Stalin "thaw" were also felt among the satellite nations of eastern Europe. The first defection from the Soviet bloc had occurred as early as 1948, when Marshal Tito of Yugoslavia, preferring "Titoism" to "Stalinism," had struck out on his own. By 1956, Stalin's successors had made peace with Tito and had acknowledged that there were "various roads to socialism." But the satellites were not satisfied with mere promises of greater independence. In the fall of 1956, revolts against Soviet domination broke out first in Poland and later in Hungary. Both revolts were motivated by ardent nationalist sentiments. In addition, the Hungarian uprising was strongly anti-Communist. For that reason the Hungarian revolution was brutally suppressed by Russian intervention, while Poland's Communists, under Wladyslaw Gomulka, were given greater autonomy from Russian control.

For the next ten or twelve years, there were no further attempts to resist Russian domination forcefully. The nations of eastern Europe were enjoying far greater freedom of action than they had ever had under Stalin. From mere satellites they were gradually becoming junior partners of the Soviet Union. In 1961 growing tension between Russia and Albania over the latter's continued adherence to Stalinism led to an open break. In 1964 Rumania declared its virtual independence from Soviet influence and, like Yugoslavia before, drew closer to the West. Intermittent unrest in Poland came to a head early in 1968 and brought some easing of restrictions. The most dramatic change, however, occurred in Czechoslovakia, where, as a result of a peaceful revolution in the spring of 1968, the country briefly regained many democratic freedoms. The Soviet Union's armed intervention in Czechoslovakia in August against the regime of Alexander Dubček emphasized the threat that these liberalizing tendencies posed to Russia's leadership in the Communist world. It also underlined Russia's determination to meet that threat.

"Socialist Pluralism"

Despite Russia's efforts to maintain its leadership over world communism, the unity that once had prevailed among Communist states and parties had given way to diversity. A Communist world conference in 1968 was attended by only half the world's ruling Communist parties, and even among those present there were wide differences on many key issues. At another conference in 1976, the Communist parties of western Europe proclaimed their own brand of "Eurocommunism," asserting their allegiance to democratic principles and their readiness to join in parliamentary governments. Instead of a monolithic Communist bloc directed from Moscow, there now existed a plurality of socialist states divided into several factions.

The most important split within the Communist camp developed between Moscow and Peking. While Stalin was alive, the potentially powerful People's Republic of China had not contested Russia's claim to leadership. But after 1953 the Chinese gradually began to as-

Hungarians burning Communist books during the uprising in 1956.

sert themselves. At first it seemed as though China's influence was to be on the side of moderation. Beginning in 1957, however, and especially after 1963, Peking showed signs of a new, "hard" line. The Sino-Soviet dispute was first and foremost ideological, each side accusing the other of deviating from true "Marxism-Leninism." Following the principles of Mao Tse-tung's "great proletarian cultural revolution," China's radical ideologists preached "liberation" of peoples everywhere through "armed struggle" rather than through peaceful competition, as advocated by Moscow. In time there arose also a number of specific differences: the Soviets withheld the economic aid that the Chinese expected, and Moscow refused to share its nuclear know-how with Peking. There were occasional clashes along the Sino-Soviet frontier, especially in 1969; and there was constant rivalry between the two countries for the allegiance of the rest of the world's Communist parties. As the debate between the two contestants became more and more vituperative, Communist China asserted that the center of world revolution and the leadership of world communism had shifted from Moscow to Peking.

THE END OF COLONIALISM IN ASIA

One of the most revolutionary developments since the Second World War was the liberation of virtually all the world's former colonial territories. This independence movement had already begun in the years between the two world wars. It was hastened by the weakening of the mother countries in the Second World War and the subsequent rivalry between the free and Communist worlds. Although the various native revolts differed from country to country, they all had one thing in common: intense opposition to any form of colonialism. Some of the new nations took sides in the Cold War, but most of them preferred a "neutralist" stand. The most urgent need for all was economic and technical assistance. At first, most of this aid came from the United States. But in time the Soviet

Union, and even Communist China, began to set up foreign aid and compete for the allegiance of these uncommitted regions.

India, Pakistan, and Bangladesh

The first major additions to the community of free nations came with the partition of the subcontinent of India in 1947 into the independent states of India and Pakistan. Although both were republics, they continued as members of the (British) Commonwealth. India was predominantly Hindu and Pakistan mostly Moslem. In the process of separating the two religions, many bloody riots broke out. India and Pakistan also clashed repeatedly over the northern state of Kashmir, to which both laid claim. In addition, there were intermittent border incidents between India and Red China.

The Union of India was by far the more important of the two states. The new nation suffered a tragic loss in 1948, when its political leader, Mohandas K. Gandhi, was assassinated by a religious fanatic. The task of guiding India through its formative years fell to Gandhi's disciple, Jawaharlal Nehru, leader of the ruling Congress Party. India's main problems were economic. The only way to support its huge population was through long-range development of the country's abundant natural resources with outside aid. India's dependence on such aid from all sides, together with its closeness to the centers of communism and its recent experience with western imperialism, led to a neutralist stand on most international issues. With Nehru's death in 1964, domestic affairs became less stable, especially under his daughter, Indira Gandhi, who became prime minister in 1966. Whatever economic growth the country experienced was neutralized by its high birthrate, despite costly birth-control programs. Periodic famines, epidemics, and riots between Hindus and Moslems, together with a renewed Indo-Pakistani clash in 1971, led to a permanent state of crisis. Matters came to a head in 1975, when Prime Minister Gandhi, who had been accused of illegal

Indira Gandhi, prime minister of India from 1966 to 1977, in 1972.

Morarji Desai, who was elected prime minister of India in 1977.

activities in connection with her reelection, declared a state of emergency, arresting political opponents and suspending civil liberties. With Mrs. Gandhi's electoral defeat in 1977, constitutional government was restored, but India's economic difficulties remained unresolved and its political future uncertain.

In contrast, popular government in Pakistan was much slower in taking root. Like India, Pakistan suffered a serious loss in 1948, when its outstanding leader, Mohammed Ali Jinnah, died. The country's economy was mainly agricultural, and trade with India, its natural market, suffered from political tensions. Economic difficulties in turn led to political instability. When democracy was no longer able to cope with bureaucratic inefficiency and corruption, the head of Pakistan's armed forces, General Ayub Khan, took over and ruled as virtual dictator from 1958 to 1969. Pakistan's foreign policy, at first firmly prowestern, during the 1960s became increasingly neutralist in an effort to attract aid and trade from both sides.

One of Pakistan's major difficulties derived from the fact that it consisted of two parts, separated by a thousand miles of Indian territory. Relations between the two regions were far from smooth; the more numerous and poverty-stricken Bengalis of East Pakistan felt exploited by the affluent and influential Punjabis of West Pakistan. The only bond between the two peoples was their common Moslem religion. Differences between East and West Pakistan came to a head in 1971, when civil war broke out between Bengali and government forces, leading first to the defeat of the Bengalis and then, after intervention by India, to the defeat of West Pakistan. East Pakistan now seceded, taking the name of Bangladesh. In 1972 the new nation signed a treaty of friendship with India, and in 1974 it was recognized by (West) Pakistan. The latter was now headed by Prime Minister Zulfikar Ali Bhutto, who valiantly tried to cope with Pakistan's economic backwardness under a new democratic constitution. In 1977, Bhutto was ousted by the army, whose chief of staff, General Mohammad Zia ul-Haq, proclaimed martial law to cope with the

Colonial Nationalism

The West, having sown its own national wild oats in the past, is now sometimes inclined to look with a combination of dismay and superior wisdom on the upstart countries which assert an allegedly anachronistic desire to follow the same course. . . . However great the disenchantment of Europe with nationalism, the colonial nationalist is little likely to be persuaded by an argument so easily identifiable with the interest of the West in maintaining some facsimile of its older relationships in a world swiftly sliding out of its grasp. . . . Even if it be conceded that nationalism fails to furnish the foundations for an acceptable world order and has outlived its usefulness for the advanced, thoroughly "nationalized," countries of the West . . . it has by no means exhausted its contribution to the development of the non-Western peoples. Nationalism . . . has a chronology of its own derived not from the calendar but from the stages of the gradually spreading impact of the revolution which originated in Western Europe. . . . One can plausibly argue that in the different but related stages of the cycle in which Asia and Africa are now engaged nationalism intrudes itself not only with an aura of inevitability but also as the bearer of positive goods.

From Rupert Emerson, *From Empire to Nation: The Rise to Self-Assertion of Asian and African Peoples* (Cambridge, Mass.: Harvard University Press, 1960), p. 379.

country's continued political and economic problems.

Communist China

The most significant development in Asia after 1950 was the emergence of Communist China as a great power. The People's Republic of China was founded in 1949 (see p. 793). Its government was closely modeled on that of the Soviet Union. As in Russia, all power in China rested with the Communist Party and its leader, Mao Tse-tung. Under the constitution of 1954, the main task of the state was "to bring about, step by step, the socialist industrialization of the country," a goal that was to be achieved in several Five-Year Plans. As was the case in other backward nations, the rapid increase in China's production resulted in some impressive achievements. Symbolic of the country's scientific and technical advances was the detonation of its first atomic bomb in 1964, followed by a hydrogen bomb in 1967.

Celebration of National Day in China, October 2, 1966. The statue of Mao Tse-tung is being carried by the paraders.

In the long run it was only through industrialization that China could solve its most pressing problem of too many people and too little land. With an estimated yearly population growth of more than 16 million, the 1-billion mark would be reached by 1990. Yet the backbone of the Chinese economy was still agriculture, and the government tried by every possible means to boost agricultural production. The second Five-Year Plan of 1958 called for a "great leap forward" in both agriculture and industry. The population was organized in gigantic "people's communes" including as many as one hundred thousand persons and embracing farms and factories.

But the "great leap" not only failed to reach its goals, it actually brought a decline of production. The cause for this failure was seen in the continued moderation of many leading officials. To purge Chinese communism of these "revisionist" elements, another sweeping revolutionary movement was initiated in the 1960s, the "great proletarian cultural revolution." Spearheaded by younger members of the party, the "Maoist" revolution repudiated traditional cultural values, emphasized collectivization and austerity, and elevated the figure of Mao Tse-tung to unprecedented heights of personal adulation. Through indoctrination, brainwashing, and terror China hoped to produce the most regimented society the world had ever seen. At first, these drastic measures aggravated rather than solved China's economic problems. But eventually the discipline and industry of the Chinese people did achieve new high levels of production and make China a major economic power.

As a result of these achievements, the pace of China's development became less hectic as time went on. In 1976 Mao Tse-tung died, and his more radical followers, including his widow, were purged in favor of a more moderate faction, headed by the new Chairman of the Communist Party, Hua Kuo-feng.

In foreign affairs, Red China was at first deeply anti-American. The two countries were on opposite sides in the Korean War and in most other conflicts in Asia. Washington's support of the Chinese Nationalists on Taiwan, its alliance with Japan, and its refusal to recognize Peking were major targets for Communist attacks. This situation changed dramatically in 1972, when the United States, having abandoned its opposition to Communist China's membership in the United Nations the year before, reciprocated Chinese feelers for normalization of relations and President Nixon visited Peking. In 1975 President Ford paid a similar visit, and *rapprochement* between the two countries continued during the Carter administration. In contrast, relations between China and the Soviet Union, initially very close, became more and more hostile as time went on, and on occasion the two appeared on the verge of open conflict.

Chinese contacts with the other communist nations of Asia were close and cordial. In its dealings with neutralist Asian countries, China alternated between kindness and threats. There were repeated clashes along the borders of India, Burma, and Nepal, and Tibetan resistance to communization was ruthlessly suppressed in 1959. If Communist China could spread its influence beyond North Korea and North Vietnam, its position within the Communist world would be greatly strengthened and its population pressure relieved. The most promising outlet for Chinese expansion was Southeast Asia, and it was here that the Chinese Communists concentrated their efforts.

Southeast Asia

The region east of India and south of China saw more political changes after the Second World War than any other part of Asia. Prior to 1945 only Thailand (Siam) was fully independent. In the years that followed, the Philippines, Burma, Indonesia, Vietnam, Laos, Cambodia, and Malaysia gained their sovereignty. Southeast Asia was a wealthy region, producing five-sixths of the world's natural rubber, more than half of its tin, and 60 percent of its rice. Like all underdeveloped areas, Southeast Asia was predominantly agricultural; but, except for Indonesia, it did not suffer from overpopulation. Despite its rich natural resources, the living standard of the re-

Poster of Hua Kuo-feng in Canton urges the Chinese to "March Victoriously Forward Under the Leadership of Chairman Hua."

gion was very low. What Southeast Asia needed most was a better-balanced regional economy with more varied commodities and increased industrialization.

With the exception of Thailand, every country of Southeast Asia experienced communist revolts of varying severity. In the countries that formerly made up French Indochina—Vietnam, Laos, and Cambodia—Communist takeovers were finally successful after drawn-out and bloody civil wars. Burma, Malaysia, Indonesia, Singapore, and the Philippines, on the other hand, were able to crush Communist rebellions that flared up in the 1950s and 1960s. The menace of communism and the general backwardness of the whole area seriously retarded the growth of democracy and encouraged the emergence of strong-man governments.

Asia and the West

The free world, under American leadership, did its best to contain the spread of communism in Southeast Asia and the Far East by providing massive military and economic aid and by encouraging cooperation among the Asian nations themselves. A start was made in 1950 with the Colombo Plan for Cooperative Development in South and Southeast Asia. In 1961 Malaysia, the Philippines, and Thailand formed the Association of Southeast Asia, which was later joined by Indonesia and Singapore. In 1966, another organization, the Asian and Pacific Council, made up of non-Communist countries in the area, called for economic, social, and political cooperation.

In the military field, the United States, Australia, and New Zealand in 1951 signed the ANZUS treaty, a loose military alliance. The Southeast Asia Treaty Organization (SEATO), of which the United States was a member, was established in 1954 for mutual defense against aggression and subversion. It did not prove very effective and was dissolved in 1977. In addition to these multilateral agreements, the United States signed bilateral defense pacts with Taiwan, the Philippines, South Korea, and Japan.

Korea and Japan were the main strongholds of American influence in the Far East. The South Korean army was one of the largest in the world. It was hoped that the forced resignation of Dr. Syngman Rhee's authoritarian government in 1960 would bring the country closer to democracy; but the presidency of General Park Chung Hee, if anything, was still more repressive. In Japan, American influence decreased after the signing of the peace treaty in 1951 (see p. 793). The renewal of the United States–Japanese security treaty in 1960 ran into considerable leftist opposition in Japan, but its extension in 1970 was accomplished without incident. In the postwar years Japan staged a remarkable economic comeback that made it once again one of the world's leading industrial powers. Much of Japan's trade was with the United States, and this fact, together with the return of the island of Okinawa by the United States in 1972, helped cement the political and military ties between the two nations. As the United States in the 1970s reduced its troops and bases in Japan, the country had to assume responsibility for its own security. A "treaty of peace and friendship" concluded between Japan and Communist China in 1972 did much to ease tension in the Far East.

NATIONALISM IN THE ARAB WORLD

One of the most turbulent scenes of rebellion against western influence after the Second World War was the Arab Middle East, the area bridging Asia and Africa, from Iran in the east to Morocco in the west. Most of the region was extremely backward and desperately poor. But it was also of great strategic importance: it contained about half the world's oil resources, and it was the religious center of hundreds of millions of Arab and non-Arab Moslems living as far away as Southeast Asia. Outwardly, the Arab world was united by its opposition to foreign domination and its hatred of Israel. But below the surface there were many divisive forces, chiefly due to rivalries among Arab leaders.

The Suez Crisis

Before the Second World War the only independent Arab states were Egypt, Saudi Arabia, Yemen, and Iraq. After 1945 all the rest won their freedom. The most vociferous proponent of Arab nationalism, until his death in 1970, was President Gamal Abdel Nasser of Egypt. His successor, Anwar el-Sadat, has been more moderate and conciliatory. Following a neutralist course, Nasser's Egypt accepted large-scale aid from the West and East alike. When the western powers in 1956 withdrew their support for the Aswan Dam, a gigantic power project on the Nile, Nasser retaliated by nationalizing the Suez Canal. The ensuing invasion of Egypt by England, France, and Israel might have resulted in a major war had not the United Nations insisted on the withdrawal of foreign troops. Meanwhile Egypt was left in control of the Canal.

To present a united front to the outside world, the Arab nations in 1945 organized the Arab League. Behind this front, however, Arab differences persisted, especially between Egypt on the one hand and Jordan, Lebanon, and Iraq on the other. To meet the threat posed by Communist support of Arab nationalism, Great Britain, Turkey, Iran, Iraq, and Pakistan in 1955 signed a mutual assistance treaty, the Baghdad Pact. When Iraq dropped out of the alliance in 1958, a new Central Treaty Organization (CENTO) was formed. It included the United States, which, under the "Eisenhower Doctrine" of 1957, had already promised armed assistance against Communist aggression to any nation in the Middle East that requested it.

Arabs Against Israel

The main danger to peace in the Middle East was the intermittent war between the Arabs and Israel. The war started in 1948–49, when Israel's neighbors invaded the newly independent country, only to be beaten and evicted. From here on an uneasy armistice prevailed. The Arabs refused to recognize Israel, and hundreds of thousands of Arab refugees, made homeless by the partition of Palestine, helped keep the conflict alive. Full-scale fighting was briefly resumed during the Suez crisis in 1956, when Israeli forces made a quick dash for the Suez Canal. In 1967, in a furious six-day war, Israel took the Sinai Peninsula and some other territory. Arab attempts to regain these lands led to another bloody war in 1973.

The Israelis vowed to retain their conquests until a final and stable peace could be agreed on; they believed that they were fighting for the very survival of their nation. Yet the occupation and possible annexation of Arab lands only exacerbated the Arab-Israeli conflict. Beginning in 1972, a rash of bombings, airplane hijackings, and assassinations by Palestinian Arab terrorists and retaliations by Israeli commandos intensified the crisis. The demand of the Palestine Liberation Organization (PLO) under Yasir Arafat was for return of the Arab lands occupied by Israel and the creation of a separate Palestinian state. In recent years the Arabs have used oil embargoes to deter western nations, particularly the United States, from supporting Israel. In 1977 President Sadat of Egypt approached Israel with a series of peace proposals, aimed at easing Middle Eastern tension. But Israel's refusal to relinquish some of its recent conquests and to agree to a separate Palestinian state continued to be major obstacles to a settlement.

Although most of the unrest in the region stemmed from nationalism, its roots lay in the serious domestic problems of the Arab states, in its age-old poverty and illiteracy. Almost everywhere, Arab society was still sharply divided into tiny minorities of extremely wealthy merchants, landowners and oil sheiks, and huge masses of the poorest peasants. To change this system, a complete social revolution and sweeping reforms were needed. It would also require the aid of the very same foreigners whom Arab nationalists hated.

THE EMERGENCE OF AFRICA

The continent of Africa was the last to be swept by the tide of nationalism. From only four sovereign states in 1950, the number by 1978 had grown to forty-

President Nasser greets fellow Egyptians after having nationalized the Suez Canal (1956).

Prime Minister Menachem Begin of Israel and President Anwar el-Sadat of Egypt at a press conference following their historic meeting in Jerusalem in 1977.

seven. The most recent victories of African nationalism occurred in the most backward part of the continent, south of the Sahara Desert, in areas inhabited by poor, primitive, and illiterate native tribes. The former colonial powers had virtually eradicated tropical diseases, but the resultant population growth had not been matched by a similar increase in food supplies. Most of Africa, therefore, remained underfed. Added to poverty was extreme diversity, with no tradition of political unity and with some seven hundred different native dialects. The one sentiment common to all Africans was anticolonialism. Just as it did every-where else in the world, nationalism in Africa demanded immediate independence, whether people were ready for it or not. This rush into freedom caused severe growing pains for most of the new nations.

Crises in the Congo and Nigeria

All African states were founded as democracies. But lack of political experience and tribal disunity soon gave rise to one-party systems and strong-man rule.

The nation that had more trouble than any other was the Democratic Republic of the Congo. The Belgians had

AFRICA AND THE MIDDLE EAST IN 1978

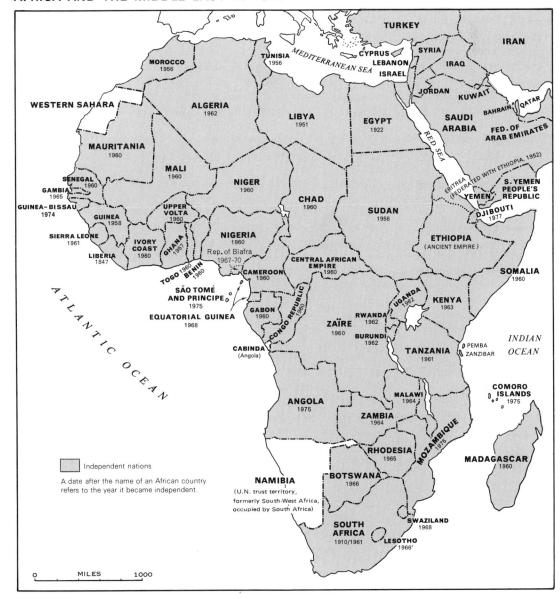

done little to prepare their colony for the independence they were forced to grant it in 1960. As a result, order broke down completely. There were popular riots, mutinies in the army, and threats of secession in some of the Congo's provinces, notably Katanga. The first premier of the new republic, Patrice Lumumba, allegedly pro-Communist, was removed by the Congolese president and army in 1960. His subsequent murder by hostile tribesmen made him a martyr to anticolonialists everywhere. United Nations troops were able to maintain a measure of order and to prevent the secession of Katanga. In 1964 the leader of that province, Moise Tshombe, was given the premiership in the hope that he might prove a unifying force. But he was overthrown in 1965 by General Joseph Mobutu, whose pro-Lumumba and anti-Belgian stand made him popular. In spite of continued mutinies in the outlying provinces, Mobutu proved to be a stabilizing factor. In 1971, as part of an Africanization campaign, the country was renamed Republic of Zaïre, and the Congo River became the Zaïre River.

Another African country troubled by internal unrest was Nigeria. From the beginning of its independence in 1960, Nigeria was beset by festering disputes among its many tribes, especially between the poor and backward Hausa-Fulanis in the north and the more highly educated and advanced, but less numerous, Ibos in the south. As time went on and tensions mounted, persecution of the Ibos led to some ghastly massacres. In 1967 the coastal Eastern Region, inhabited mostly by Ibos, declared itself independent as the Republic of Biafra. The new republic had little chance of survival unless it could obtain outside aid. Yet for the rest of the world to recognize one more African nation might encourage secessions from some of the other new states in which hostile tribal groups were living in uneasy coexistence. By 1970, Biafran independence was extinguished.

Southern Africa: Whites Against Blacks

There was one region in Africa where the black quest for political power con-

tinued to be suppressed. In the Republic of South Africa, as in Rhodesia and in the Portuguese colonies of Angola and Mozambique, small white minorities controlled their country's political and economic affairs. Increasingly, however, this white power came under attack from black nationalism.

In South Africa, where the white minority constituted only 18 percent of the total population, the government in 1948 introduced a policy of strict racial segregation, or *apartheid.* The program provided for complete separation of the races, restricted franchise for nonwhites, forced resettlement of Africans, and separate schools with lower educational standards for black children. The result of this policy was mounting unrest and bloodshed. In 1966 Prime Minister Henrik F. Verwoerd, a leading advocate of *apartheid,* was assassinated; but his successor, Balthazar J. Vorster, continued the policy of segregation. South Africa's racist policies, meanwhile, earned the country the censure of most of the civilized world, including the other members of the Commonwealth. In a show of resentment of such criticism, South Africa withdrew from the Commonwealth in 1961.

In the British dependency of Southern Rhodesia, the ruling white minority amounted to little more than 3 percent of the total population. When the British government insisted on political equality for the black majority as a condition for granting independence to its former colony, the white regime of Ian Smith in 1965 declared the secession of Rhodesia from the mother country. Subsequent efforts to bring Rhodesia into line through economic sanctions failed, as South Africa and the neighboring Portuguese colony of Mozambique rallied to Rhodesia's support. In 1978 Smith broadened his government by including some moderate blacks in his cabinet. But this token measure did not go far enough for the country's radical guerilla faction, which continued its agitation for black majority rule.

Mozambique, together with Angola and Portuguese Guinea, did achieve independence from Portugal in 1975, after bloody fighting. With most of the whites

Whites versus nonwhites in South Africa.

A Ghanian man whose shirt is printed with the portrait of Kwame Nkrumah, the first president of Ghana.

returning to the mother country, the new states faced great initial difficulties. By 1978, black nationalism in Africa had triumphed everywhere except in Rhodesia and South Africa, and here the days of white supremacy clearly were numbered.

The "Third World"

The political emergence of the non-white peoples was a worldwide movement. While the details of their liberation differed, there were still sufficient similarities to suggest possible collaboration among the many nations that so recently had gained their freedom. As a result, several conferences were held, both among the nations of Asia and Africa and among the nations of Africa alone.

The first Asian-African conference met at Bandung, Indonesia, in 1955. It was attended by delegates from twenty-nine countries, representing about half the world's population. There were few tangible results, but the meeting registered common attitudes on such basic issues as anticolonialism and censure of racial discrimination. The next meeting, at Cairo in 1957, was less successful, largely because it was used by Communist nations, including the Soviet Union, to advocate a strongly antiwestern line. The same held true for some of the subsequent meetings. It was only when the Soviet Union was excluded from the proceedings and when the deliberations shifted to economic problems that these meetings became more useful and businesslike.

As time went on and most peoples gained their independence, anticolonialism as a unifying issue lost its importance. Instead, there now were growing differences among the various new nations themselves, as radical and moderate ones clashed. Beginning in 1961, periodic conferences brought together not only the nations of Asia and Africa, but underdeveloped countries from other regions as well, especially Latin America. The participants claimed to represent a nonaligned "third world" that, despite immense resources in essential raw materials, was not receiving a fair share of the world's riches. When the countries of

the Organization of Petroleum Exporting Countries (OPEC), under Arab leadership, doubled the price of oil in late 1973, the subsequent oil crisis in the industrial nations suggested that similar measures might be adopted by the "third world" countries for other raw materials in order to make their influence felt. However, in the ensuing debates between the rich industrial powers of the north and the poor underdeveloped nations of the south, the latter showed little solidarity, as each country pursued its own individual interests.

The Organization of African Unity

The African nations, meanwhile, had founded their own Conference of Independent African States in 1958. As more and more African countries became independent, a need for closer cooperation arose, especially in economic matters. In the early 1960s a number of regional groupings developed. The next step was some wider union of all nonwhite Africa. In 1963 an all-African conference at Addis Ababa, Ethiopia, created the Organization of African Unity (OAU) as a permanent instrument for political and economic cooperation and for the common defense of each member's independence.

Progress toward political cooperation was hampered by the large size and great diversity of the continent. In the economic sphere the trend toward regional groupings, such as the East African Community, founded in 1968, was seen as the surest way to overcome Africa's problems. More helpful than economic cooperation among backward countries in Africa and elsewhere, however, was continued aid from the more advanced nations. It was in aiding underdeveloped regions that the free world and the Communist nations found their most fruitful field for competition.

FROM COLD WAR TO COEXISTENCE

The most clearly discernible trend in international relations during the 1960s was the gradual shift away from the

General Douglas MacArthur waves to New York City crowds during a ticker-tape parade in his honor after he had returned from Korea in 1951.

angry confrontation of East and West in the Cold War to an equally competitive but more peaceful state of coexistence. The Cold War had developed as the result of a gradually mounting crisis; the state of peaceful coexistence came only after a decade of intermittent sparring during the 1950s, in which each side felt out the strength of the other. The avoidance of a major showdown between the East and West was due mainly to the nuclear balance of power that was accomplished during the 1950s.

The Korean War

The years immediately after 1950 brought to a climax the international tension that had been building up since 1945. In the fall of 1950, United Nations forces fought their way into North Korea, close to the borders of Red China. But when victory seemed almost in sight, the Chinese Communists intervened and drove the UN armies back into South Korea. By the spring of 1951, the front had become stabilized once more along the thirty-eighth parallel, and there it substantially remained during the stalemate that lasted for two years. Armistice negotiations were begun in 1951 but were not completed until 1953. By that time the war had cost the United States more than 150,000 casualties. The Korean armistice, moreover, merely established an uneasy truce in which North Korean troops continued to face South Korean and American forces across a demilitarized zone.

Escalation in Both Camps

One of the lasting effects of the Korean conflict was a substantial buildup of western military strength. The United States increased its military expenditures fivefold, doubled its armed forces, and extended its network of military bases abroad, and most of America's allies followed suit. It was during the Korean War that NATO perfected its organization and increased its membership by adding Greece and Turkey. At the same time plans were laid for including West Germany in the western alliance. In 1952, furthermore, the United States exploded

its first hydrogen bomb, thus regaining the nuclear lead it had held before the Soviet atomic explosion in 1949.

The change from a Democratic to a Republican administration in Washington in 1953 brought to the fore a man who seemed determined to use America's military strength not merely to contain but to challenge communism. Until his death in 1959, the new secretary of state, John Foster Dulles, was the leading political strategist in the western camp. But his policy of "massive retaliation" and "brinkmanship" did not always have the support of America's friends, nor did it have the desired effect of scaring the Russians into making political concessions.

More decisive than the changing of the guard in Washington were the events touched off by Stalin's death in 1953. While the new Soviet rulers were consolidating their position at home, they adopted a more conciliatory policy abroad. At the same time, however, the Russian government announced its first successful testing of a hydrogen bomb. And while the West was rallying its forces behind NATO, the Soviets were lining up their eastern satellites behind the Warsaw Pact of 1955.

The Search for Coexistence

The first sign that Russia might be willing to negotiate East–West differences was seen in the Korean armistice, which would have been impossible without Soviet aquiescence. In January 1954 the foreign ministers of the Big Four nations (United States, Britain, France, and the Soviet Union) resumed their talks in Berlin after an interval of several years. In April the Geneva Conference on Far Eastern Affairs, with Communist China attending, temporarily divided Vietnam, where the French had recently been defeated by the Vietminh Communist insurgents. Elections for the whole of Vietnam were to be held in 1956, but these never took place.

The culmination of the initial search for coexistence came with the Geneva Summit conference of 1955. This was the first time since Potsdam, ten years earlier, that the Big Four heads of state had assembled. On the eve of the meeting, the Russians agreed to an Austrian peace treaty on reasonable terms, another hopeful sign of growing Soviet moderation. Relations at Geneva were cordial, especially between President Eisenhower and Soviet Premier Nikolai Bulganin, though the results of the conference were disappointing. On none of the major issues—German reunification, European security, and disarmament—was any understanding reached. The only positive achievement was an agreement on cultural exchanges between East and West.

Continuation of the Cold War

While the "spirit of Geneva" appeared to have dissipated some of the suspicions of the Cold War, events in the Middle East soon showed that war to be far from over. The crisis resulting from President Nasser's nationalization of the Suez Canal in the summer of 1956 and the subsequent attack on Egypt by British, French, and Israeli forces has already been discussed (p. 814). The withdrawal of these forces under pressure from the UN and the United States was seen as a victory for Nasser and his backers in the Communist camp. The Soviet Union's reputation as a champion of anticolonialism, however, was immediately tarnished by its brutal intervention against the uprising in Hungary. Both the Suez crisis and the Hungarian revolution might easily have led to a major showdown had it not been for the fear of a nuclear war.

The year 1957 was relatively peaceful. America's proclamation of the Eisenhower Doctrine served notice that the nation was ready to oppose the spread of Soviet influence in the Middle East. In the Soviet Union, meanwhile, Khrushchev emerged as the supreme leader of communism. The most spectacular event of the year, however, was the successful launching of Russia's first earth satellite, *Sputnik I*, on October 4, 1957. This development proved that the Russians possessed rockets powerful enough to launch a nuclear attack on the United States. The balance of power in the Cold War had apparently shifted in Russia's favor.

To the Brink of War

For the next five years the initiative in international affairs largely rested with the Soviet Union. The United States launched its first satellite, *Explorer I*, in January 1958. But the Russians maintained their lead by placing heavier satellites in orbit. Continued Communist attempts to stir up trouble in the Middle East were foiled by American and British landings of troops in Lebanon and Jordan in 1958. Next came a crisis in the Far East, where Chinese Communist attacks on the offshore islands of Quemoy and Matsu were halted only because America stood firmly by its Nationalist Chinese ally. In November 1958 the Soviet Union reopened the German question by once again challenging the western position in Berlin and insisting that the former German capital be made a "free city" within the East German Democratic Republic.

While East–West relations were thus being kept in a state of latent tension, there were feelers from both sides for a second try at summit diplomacy. But the conference finally scheduled for 1960 never materialized. On the eve of the Paris meeting the Russians shot down an American U-2 intelligence plane flying over the Soviet Union. Eisenhower's refusal to make amends for this incident led to Khrushchev's withdrawal from the conference before it started.

There was much concern in the West over the increasingly aggressive Soviet stance in foreign affairs. Aside from trying to scare the United States into making concessions, Russia's policy was also influenced by the growing rift between Moscow and Peking. The beginnings of this rift went back to 1957, when the Chinese Communists began to criticize Khrushchev's policy of de-Stalinization and his proposed strategy of defeating capitalism through peaceful competition rather than revolution or war. In time, outward signs of the Sino-Soviet split began to appear. Russia failed to back the Chinese in their attack on the offshore islands and withdrew its material and technical aid, which was essential to China's industrial development. Much of the conflict between Peking and Moscow was over the allegiance of the underdeveloped and unaligned countries. It was to reassert his claim to leadership over world communism that Khrushchev delivered his boastful threats of "burying capitalism."

The advent of the Kennedy administration in 1961 at first seemed to bring a slight lessening of East–West tension. The new president was faced by a perplexing array of foreign problems. In April 1961 the ill-fated Bay of Pigs invasion of Cuba—undertaken by anti-Castro refugees with American backing—was quickly suppressed by Castro's forces. In South Vietnam, meanwhile, Vietcong guerrillas, supported by Communist North Vietnam, were stepping up their "war of liberation." A similar war was going on between the Communist Pathet Lao and the government forces in Laos. The most serious problem Kennedy inherited, however, was the continued Russian demand for western withdrawal from Berlin.

Kennedy and Khrushchev had a brief impromptu meeting at Vienna in June 1961. Khrushchev already had made some cordial gestures toward the president, and the encounter was courteous. But shortly after the Vienna meeting the Russians increased their agitation over Berlin, threatening to sign a peace treaty with the East Germans that would give the latter control over access to West Berlin. Only Kennedy's obvious determination to stand firm and go to war rather than give in made Khrushchev finally back down. To stop the stream of refugees from East Germany into West Berlin, the Communists built the Berlin Wall, which henceforth made East Germany a virtual prison. In October 1961 Khrushchev withdrew his ultimatum on Berlin, and the Berlin crisis ended the following year.

There were other signs that negotiations might replace confrontations in East–West relations. In July 1962 a foreign ministers' conference in Geneva agreed on the formal neutralization of Laos. This, it was hoped, would calm the situation in Southeast Asia. But at the same time the Russians were involved in secret activities in Cuba that soon brought the United States and the Soviet Union to the very brink of war.

The Cuban crisis gained momentum during the summer of 1962 as Washington learned about Russia's stepped-up military support for Castro. In September a Soviet-Cuban security treaty was announced. In October the United States gained proof that the Soviets had supplied Cuba with missiles capable of delivering nuclear warheads and that launching sites were under construction in Cuba. President Kennedy immediately imposed a strict blockade on further arms shipments to Cuba and demanded that all Soviet offensive weapons be withdrawn and all missile bases dismantled. Faced with pressure from the United Nations and American threats of retaliation, Premier Khrushchev backed down, after receiving America's promise not to invade Cuba. The most serious confrontation of the Cold War was over.

East–West Détente

The Cuban crisis, surprisingly, ushered in the first genuine *détente* in the

---

On the Brink of War   1962

Sunday, October 28, was a shining autumn day. At nine in the morning Khrushchev's answer began to come in. By the fifth sentence it was clear that he had thrown in his hand. Work would stop on the sites; the arms "which you described as offensive" would be crated and returned to the Soviet Union; negotiations would start at the UN. Then, no doubt to placate Castro, Khrushchev asked the United States to discontinue flights over Cuba. . . . Looking ahead, he said, "We should like to continue the exchange of views on the prohibition of atomic and thermonuclear weapons, general disarmament, and other problems relating to the relaxation of international tension." It was all over, and barely in time. If word had not come that Sunday, if work had continued on the bases, the United States would have had no real choice but to take action against Cuba the next week. No one could discern what lay darkly beyond an air strike or invasion, what measures and countermeasures, actions and reactions, might have driven the hapless world to the ghastly consummation. The President saw more penetratingly into the mists and terrors of the future than anyone else. A few weeks later he said, "If we had invaded Cuba . . . I am sure the Soviets would have acted. They would have to, just as we would have to. I think there are certain compulsions on any major power." . . . When Kennedy received Khrushchev's reply that golden October morning, he showed profound relief. Later he said, "This is the night to go to the theater, like Abraham Lincoln."

From Arthur M. Schlesinger, Jr., *A Thousand Days: John F. Kennedy in the White House* (Boston: Houghton Mifflin, 1965), p. 830.

Citizens of West Berlin wave to friends and relatives on the other side of the Berlin Wall.

East–West conflict. To reduce the risk of accidental war, Washington and Moscow in early 1963 established a "hot line" of direct communication. In early July 1963 the two powers, together with Great Britain, signed a Nuclear Test Ban Treaty outlawing all but underground tests. There were other agreements on minor issues—East–West trade, increased consular service, a Moscow–New York air link. The relaxation of tension, moreover, did not end with Kennedy's death and Khrushchev's fall from power. In the summer of 1967, at the height of the Middle Eastern crisis, President Johnson and Premier Kosygin held a businesslike conference at Glassboro, New Jersey, which helped lessen the international strain.

The *détente* between Moscow and Washington did not at first resolve any of the major issues of the Cold War. The most serious crisis in the late 1960s was the drawn-out war in Vietnam. In an effort to contain the spread of communism in Southeast Asia, the United States poured several hundred thousand men and billions of dollars into a conflict that was in many ways similar to the war in Korea. Just as in that earlier war, the United States perceived Red China as the ultimate threat. But while at the time of Korea the Soviet Union, in its role as leader of world communism, had been instrumental in helping end the war, such mediation was difficult now that Moscow's leadership was being challenged by Peking.

But even the Vietnam War did not seriously alter the climate of coexistence. One of the more hopeful results of that climate was the Nuclear Non-Proliferation Treaty of 1968, which tried to halt the spread of nuclear weapons. It was not only the fear of nuclear war that made peaceful coexistence appear preferable to warlike confrontation. Another factor working for coexistence was the loosening of ties within the eastern and western camps and the emergence of the uncommitted and underdeveloped nations as a "third force" in world affairs. The dissolution of the formerly monolithic communist bloc has already been noted. Similar changes took place within the western camp. The trend toward "poly-

centrism," or many-centeredness, was also evident in the United Nations, where the new countries of Asia and Africa increasingly challenged the predominance of the superpowers.

As a result of these various changes and realignments, neither the United States nor Russia could any longer count on unquestioning support from their friends or satellites in every crisis. The days of bipolar, East–West, Communist–capitalist confrontations were over.

The most dramatic moves toward a more pragmatic, nonideological foreign policy came in the 1970s. Most of the important events have already been noted: West Germany's improved relations with eastern Europe, notably the Soviet Union and Poland; Japan's first contacts with Communist China; President Nixon's historic visits to Moscow and Peking; and the many instances of improved relations between other Communist and non-Communist countries. In 1972, a treaty on Berlin, signed by the four major Second World War allies, including the Soviet Union, removed another perennial source of friction by guaranteeing access to and easing communications within the city. American withdrawal from South Vietnam, while not ending the troubles, at least helped to ease the tensions in that part of the world.

But while an improved international climate thus helped solve or at least defuse some explosive issues, others continued and new ones arose. Arab–Israeli differences in the Near East and black–white confrontations in southern Africa remained a constant threat to peace in both areas, though neither led to major East–West confrontations, as earlier such crises had done. In an effort to limit the arms race, the United States and the Soviet Union in 1972 had concluded a first Strategic Arms Limitation Treaty (SALT); but efforts at further SALT-talks in 1977 and 1978 made slow progress. By that time a new issue had arisen in American–Russian relations, as President Carter began to criticize the Soviet Union and other regimes for violating the basic human rights guaranteed by the Helsinki Accords of 1975. Some Americans, pointing to the continued buildup of

Russia's military forces, criticized *détente* for letting down America's guard; but others welcomed the feeling of relief that normalization of East–West relations had brought. With more and more nations gaining nuclear capability, the United States and the Soviet Union may be the only powers able to prevent a nuclear catastrophe—if they act together. Judging by their actions in recent years, that lesson has been understood in both countries.

Suggestions for Further Reading

Note: Asterisk denotes a book available in paperback edition.

General

The events of the last two decades are put in their wider perspective in G. Lichtheim, *Europe in the Twentieth Century* (1972). One of the best works on the Cold War is D. Yergin, *Shattered Peace: The Origins of the Cold War and the National Security State* (1977). A. Fontaine, *History of the Cold War,** 2 vols. (1968–69), by a leading French journalist, is lively and informative. The works by D. F. Fleming, *The Cold War and Its Origins, 1917–1960,* 2 vols. (1961), and by G. Kolko and J. Kolko, *The Limits of Power: The World and United States Foreign Policy, 1945–1954** (1972), are "revisionist," that is, highly critical of American foreign policy. See also P. Seabury, *The Rise and Decline of the Cold War* (1967). H. L. Trefousse, ed., *The Cold War: A Book of Documents** (1965), is excellent. The best books on Soviet foreign policy are A. B. Ulam, *Expansion and Coexistence: The History of Soviet Foreign Policy, 1917–1973** (1974) and *The Rivals: America and Russia Since World War II** (1972). The effect of the nuclear revolution on foreign affairs is weighed by H. M. Kissinger, *Nuclear Weapons and Foreign Policy** (1957). Russian thinking on military matters is discussed in H. S. Dinerstein, *War and the Soviet Union* (1962), and R. L. Garthoff, *Soviet Military Policy: A Historical Analysis* (1962). For the American side, see H. Kahn's controversial *On Thermonuclear War* (1960), and the thoughtful essay by K. E. Knorr, *On the Uses of Military Power in the Nuclear Age* (1966). R. Aron, *The Great Debate: Theories of Nuclear Strategy* (1965), is a judicious synopsis by a noted French political scientist.

The Decline and Rise of Europe

The most reflective book on this theme is J. L. Lukacs, *Decline and Rise of Europe** (1965). W. Laqueur, *Europe Since Hitler** (1970), is admirably comprehensive. M. Crouzet, *The European Renaissance since 1945** (1971), presents a French view. On Europe's economic recovery, see C. P. Kindleberger, *Europe's Postwar Growth* (1967), and M. M. Postan, *An Economic History of Western Europe* (1967). The following are among the many books dealing with individual countries: F. Boyd, *British Politics in Transition** (1964); P. Williams, *French Politicians and Elections, 1951–1968* (1970); A. Grosser, *Germany in Our Time* (1971); and N. Kogan, *A Political History of Postwar Italy* (1966). On the quest for European unity and its obstacles, see R. Mayne, *The Community of Europe* (1963); J. Pinder, *Europe Against De Gaulle* (1963); and S. Serfaty, *France, De Gaulle, and Europe* (1967). The perennial "German Problem" is treated in J. L. Richardson, *Germany and the Atlantic Alliance* (1966); F. A. Vali, *The Quest for a United Germany* (1967); and R. McGeehan, *The German Rearmament Question: American Diplomacy and European Defense After World War II* (1971). W. F. Hanrieder, *West German Foreign Policy, 1949–1963* (1967), is a helpful book.

The Americas

The difficulties of postwar adjustment in the United States are portrayed in E. F. Goldman, *The Crucial Decade: America, 1945–1955** (1956). C. Phillips, *The Truman Presidency* (1966), and R. H. Rovere, *Affairs of State: The Eisenhower Years* (1956), deal with the Democratic and Republican periods respectively. On the Kennedy administration, see A. M. Schlesinger, Jr., *A Thousand Days: John F. Kennedy in the White House** (1965); on Johnson, see E. F. Goldman, *The Tragedy of Lyndon Johnson* (1969); and on events since then, see J. Witcover, *Marathon: The Pursuit of the Presidency, 1972–1976* (1977). See also G. Hodgson, *America in Our Time* (1976). The economic scene is the subject of J. K. Galbraith, *The Affluent Society,** 2nd ed. (1969), and W. H. Heller, *New Dimensions of Political Economy* (1966). See also H. H. Landsberg et al., *Resources in America's Future: Patterns of Requirements and Availabilities, 1960–2000* (1963). The problems of blacks and of poverty are discussed in A. Lewis, *Portrait of a Decade** (1964); I. E. Lomax, *The Negro Revolt** (1963); J. W. Silver, *Mississippi: The Closed Society** (1966); M. Harrington, *The Other America: Poverty in the United States* (1963); and L. Fishman, ed., *Poverty Amid Affluence* (1966).

The growing importance of Canada is pointed out in N. L. Nicolson, *Canada in the American Community** (1963), and G. M. Craig, *The United States and Canada* (1968). J. Crispo, *International Unionism: A Study in Canadian–American Relations* (1967), deals with the economic impact of the United States on Canada. On Latin America, S. Clissold, *Latin America: New World, Third World* (1972), is a good survey. E. R. Wolf and E. C. Hansen, *The Human Condition in Latin America* (1972), deals with various aspects of Latin American society past and present. D. A. Chalmers, ed., *Changing Latin America: New Interpretations of Its Politics and Society* (1972), is a collection of essays by Latin American specialists. One of the best books on the changes in Cuba is T. Draper, *Castroism: Theory and Practice* (1965). R. P. Fagen, *The Transformation of Political Culture in Cuba* (1969), is a solid and serious book.

The Communist World

Many of the books cited for Chapter 32 are also relevant to this later phase of communism. For works on more recent events, see E. Crankshaw, *Khrushchev** (1966); R. Conquest, *Russia After Khrushchev* (1965); and A. B. Ulam, *The New Face of Soviet Totalitarianism* (1965). On special phases of Soviet life, see H. Schwartz, *The Soviet Economy since Stalin* (1965); W. W. Kulski, *The Soviet Regime: Communism in Practice** (1963); H. Inkeles and R. A. Bauer, *The Soviet Citizen: Daily Life in a Totalitarian Society* (1959); and P. Reddaway, ed., *Uncensored Russia: Protest and Dissent in the Soviet Union* (1972). There are several general studies of Russia's satellites: Z. K. Brzezinski, *The Soviet Bloc: Unity and Conflict** (1967); J. F. Brown, *The New Eastern Europe* (1967); and S. Fischer-Galati, *Eastern Europe in the Sixties** (1963). On Yugoslavia, see D. Rusinow, *The Yugoslav Experiment, 1948–1974* (1976). On communism in the West, see F. Fetjö, *The French Communist Party and the Crisis of International Communism* (1967), and D. L. M. Blackmer, *Unity in Diversity: Italian Communism and the Communist World* (1968). On the split between the Soviet Union and Red China, J. Gittings, *Survey of the Sino-Soviet Dispute* (1968), and D. W. Treadgold, *Soviet and Chinese Communism: Similarities and Differences* (1967), provide good introductions.

The End of Colonialism

R. Strausz-Hupé and W. H. Hazard, *The Idea of Colonialism* (1958), corrects some misconceptions about colonial rule. See also S. C. Easton, *The Twilight of European Colonialism: A Political Analysis* (1960), and R. Emerson, *From Empire to Nation: The Rise to Self-Assertion of Asian and African Peoples** (1960). Changes in the commonwealth are discussed in Z. Cowen, *The British Commonwealth of Nations in a Changing World* (1965). For the major countries of Asia, old and new, see L. Blinkenberg, *India–Pakistan: The History of Unsolved Conflicts* (1972); V. S. Naipaul, *India: A Wounded Civilization* (1977); O. E. Clubb, *Twentieth Century China*, 2nd ed. (1972); G. C. Allen, *Japan's Economic Recovery* (1958); N. A. Tarling, *A Concise History of Southeast Asia* (1966); and B. Higgins and J. Higgins, *Indonesia: The Crisis of the Millstones* (1963). G. Myrdal, *Asian Drama: An Inquiry into Poverty* (1968), covers important ground. On the Middle East, the following are significant: J. M. Landau, ed., *Man, State and Society in the Contemporary Middle East* (1972); T. C. Bose, *The Superpowers and the Middle East* (1972); and T. Little, *Modern Egypt* (1967). African developments are covered in I. Wallerstein, *Africa: The Politics of Independence* (1962) and *Africa: The Politics of Unity* (1967). See also D. G. Morrison et al., *Black Africa: A Comparative Handbook* (1972); R. Emerson and M. Kilson, eds., *The Political Awakening of Africa** (1965); and C. E. Welch, *Dream of Unity: Pan-Africanism and Political Unification* (1966). On continued racial inequality in Africa, see N. Phillips, *The Tragedy of Apartheid* (1960), and R. Gibson, *African Liberation Movements: Contemporary Struggles Against White Minority Rule* (1972). On the attitudes of the two superpowers toward Africa, see R. Emerson, *Africa and United States Policy** (1967), and D. Morison, *The U.S.S.R. and Africa* (1964). B. P. Kiernan, *The United States, Communism, and the Emergent World* (1972), is critical of American policy.

From Cold War to Coexistence

Most of the general works mentioned above also cover this subject. The following is a selection of individual studies on the major international crises of the last two decades. Each of these crises was a potential cause for a major war: D. Rees, *Korea: The Limited War* (1964); H. Thomas, *The Suez Affair* (1967); J. Radvány, *Hungary and the Superpowers* (1972); J. E. Smith, *The Defense of Berlin* (1963); C. Young, *Politics in the Congo: Decolonization and Independence* (1965); A. J. Dommen, *Conflict in Laos: The Politics of Neutralisation* (1964); A. Abel, *The Missile Crisis* (1966); E. R. F. Sheehan, *The Arabs, Israelis, and Kissinger: A Secret History of American Diplomacy in the Middle East* (1976); and F. FitzGerald, *Fire in the Lake: The Vietnamese and the Americans in Vietnam* (1972). On the more peaceful aspects of international relations, see G. Bluhm, *Détente and Military Relations in Europe* (1967), and J. Laloy, *Western and Eastern Europe* (1967). American foreign policy is the subject of R. Hilsman, *To Move a Nation* (1967), on Kennedy's foreign policy, and P. L. Geyelin, *Lyndon B. Johnson and the World* (1966). Among "futurist" literature, attempting to predict the shape of things to come, H. Kahn and B. Bruce-Briggs, *Things to Come: Thinking about the 70's and 80's* (1972), and T. Geiger, *The Fortunes of the West: The Future of the Atlantic Nations* (1973), are thoughtful contributions.

Epilogue:
The Problems We Face

A vivid example of the pollution of our environment.

Looking back over the events of the last forty years, it appears that the Second World War ushered in a wholly new era of world history. Historians do not agree on what to call this new age. Terms like Age of Anxiety, Age of Anarchy, or Age of Uncertainty merely reflect a sense of bewilderment in the face of ceaseless change. All events, of course, even seemingly sudden ones, have their roots in the past. The "population explosion," the nuclear revolution, world communism, "third world" nationalism—they all have their history. But rarely before have so many crucial developments reached crisis proportions so rapidly; and rarely has a generation been confronted with so many changes and challenges.

THE "POPULATION EXPLOSION"

It is difficult to decide which is the most pressing current problem. The one that has existed longest is the relentless growth of population. People first became alarmed by the increase of population in the late eighteenth century, when Thomas Robert Malthus wrote his pioneering *Essay on the Principle of Population* (see p. 581). For almost a century and a half, Malthus' prognosis, that population in time would outgrow the supply of food, appeared overly alarmist. World population increased as never before, but so did the necessary food supply. So long as there were open spaces in moderate climates ready to absorb Europe's surplus millions, and so long as human ingenuity found ways of boosting nature's yield, there seemed no cause for alarm.

All this suddenly changed in this century (see the "World Population" chart in the color map supplement). Before the Second World War, improvements in medicine and public health in the more highly developed countries had substantially lowered the death rate and prolonged the average life span. Since then, these advances have spread to the rest of the world. The results have been a dramatic increase in population. While it took a whole century before 1930 to double the world's population from 1 to 2 billion, present estimates are that the number of people at the end of this century will exceed 6 billion.

The possible consequences of this "population explosion" are alarming indeed, though not to everyone. Some scientists assure us that there will always be enough food for everyone, as agriculture will become ever more scientific and intensive. Deserts will bloom, irrigated by water distilled from the sea, and the oceans will yield their riches of food and raw materials to the inhabitants of man-made islands. The power of our planet to produce subsistence, these optimists claim, is as unlimited as the power of mankind to reproduce itself. The problem is not so much in the production of food as in its distribution.

The Decay of the Environment

Despite such sanguine predictions, there have already been severe famines

Starving Biafran children, rationed to two cups of milk a week.

in some parts of the world, notably in India and Africa. Some of these calamities have been due to climate, chiefly to lack of rainfall leading to "desertification," or the spreading of deserts. Present estimates are that over the next twenty-five years, one-third of the earth's arable land may be lost as a result of natural causes or human mismanagement. This decay of our environment is rooted in population growth. As more and more people come to live in industrial and urban areas, many of life's traditional amenities—clean air, pure water, peace and quiet—are rapidly becoming things of the past.

The awareness of pollution as a threat to our environment is of quite recent origin. While governments are trying to save society from suffocating in smog or being buried in refuse, the voracious appetites of growing populations for the luxuries and conveniences of modern technology make any remedial efforts holding actions at best. And while some of the world's underdeveloped regions are existing on the brink of starvation, the more advanced countries are facing a different crisis, resulting from their consumer-oriented economies and their thoughtless waste of the world's dwindling supplies of energy. The conservation of energy and the discovery of new energy sources is one of the foremost problems we face.

Population Control

The most sensible way to stem the rapid decay of the environment and the depletion of natural resources would be to curb the uncontrolled increase of population. Modern methods of birth control make large-scale population planning possible. In general, the more affluent industrialized societies have been more successful in slowing their population growth than the less affluent nonindustrialized regions. Aside from contraception, population control can be effected by abortion, which has by now been legalized in nearly two-thirds of the world. But age-old prejudices and religious scruples still work against the general acceptance of either method of control. Still, demographers now predict that

there will be a gradual leveling-off of population growth in the next century, resulting in a stable world population of some 11 billion. The world then will be almost three times as crowded as it is at present.

THE CONQUEST OF OUTER SPACE

Some optimists believe that the conquest of outer space may be the answer to the "population explosion." Man's first probes into extraterrestrial regions are still so recent that they are hardly a subject for the historian. Yet the year 1957, when the first man-made object went into orbit around the earth, may some day take its place alongside that other memorable date, 1492, when Europe discovered a whole new world beyond the horizon of the old.

The conquest of outer space began in earnest on October 4, 1957, when the Soviet Union sent its first *Sputnik* into orbit. The United States launched its first *Explorer* on January 31, 1958. Russia's most spectacular feat came on April 12, 1961, when history's first "cosmonaut," Yuri Gagarin, went into orbit around the earth. America did not put its first "astronaut," John H. Glenn, into orbit until February 20, 1962. From then on the two superpowers engaged in a veritable race for outer space (see color map "Exploration in Space"). While bigger and more sophisticated space vehicles were carrying teams of astronauts on more extended orbital flights, unmanned satellites made their first landings on the moon. America's greatest triumph came on July 20, 1969, when astronaut Neil A. Armstrong became the first man to set foot on the moon. Subsequent lunar landings brought back a wealth of scientific information. Meanwhile, the United States and the Soviet Union were extending their unmanned space probes to Mercury, Venus, Mars, Jupiter, and beyond. In 1975 two Soviet spacecraft soft-landed on Venus, and in 1976 America's *Viking I* set down on Mars, sending back remarkably clear photographs. Prediction is that by the year 2000, man will have visited that planet in person.

An *Apollo XV* astronaut and his lunar rover on the moon in 1973.

The implications of these extraordinary advances are far-reaching indeed. Within the foreseeable future, we are told, large numbers of satellites will be orbiting the earth, serving as way-stations to the moon and the planets. America's development of a reusable manned rocket-plane, the "space shuttle" *Enterprise*, will make the transport of men and materials to outer space easier and cheaper. The next step will be the development of large "sailing ships," spacecraft powered by radiation from the sun, to carry man on his three-year round-trip to Mars. To the layman, these and other fantastic schemes, such as giant space ships accommodating thousands of people and relieving population pressure on earth, still seem to belong in the realm of science fiction. But they are being seriously advanced by leading scientists, who claim that the only obstacle to their realization is their truly astronomical cost.

For the time being, the main concern is with developments closer to home, in the space immediately surrounding the earth. It is here that space research has yielded important scientific, economic, and military advantages. Satellites are now being used for communication, meteorology, large-scale surveying, and reconnaissance. The military potential and danger of satellites are obvious. The nation that controls outer space will control the world. In 1966 the United States and the Soviet Union agreed to limit their space exploration to peaceful uses and to ban weapons of mass destruction from outer space. But as each side suspects the other of developing military space vehicles and "hunter-killer" satellites to interfere with communications, the fear of an arms race in space persists.

The 1952 test of the hydrogen bomb in the Pacific left a depression on the ocean floor a mile in diameter and nearly two hundred feet deep.

THE NUCLEAR REVOLUTION

The race for outer space had two aspects. It spurred the leading contenders on to revolutionary scientific advances, but at the same time it created a potential hazard in international relations. The same potential for good and evil prevailed in another phase of competition, the nuclear race. Here the immediate stakes were higher, and the alternatives more fearful. Thanks to atomic energy, man today has within his power the final perfection or the total obliteration of his civilization.

The Nuclear Arms Race

The nuclear revolution burst upon the world on August 6, 1945, when the first atomic bomb—equivalent to twenty thousand tons of TNT—was exploded over the Japanese city of Hiroshima. Seven years later, in 1952, the United States exploded the first hydrogen bomb over the Bikini Atoll in the Pacific. Its power was a thousand times greater than that of the first atomic bomb. In addition, the methods of delivering these frightful weapons have been perfected to the point that intercontinental ballistic missiles, armed with nuclear warheads and traveling at supersonic speeds, can drop their lethal cargoes on targets thousands of miles from the area where they were launched.

For a short time after 1945, the United States held an atomic monopoly. But as the Soviet Union developed its own atomic bomb in 1949 and its hydrogen bomb in 1953, America lost its lead. Since then, the "nuclear club" has grown to include Britain, France, Communist China, and India. It is estimated that twenty-nine additional nations will have the technical ability to produce nuclear weapons within the next decade. As a result, a nuclear attack might be launched from any part of the world at any time.

The only sure way of avoiding such disaster is through disarmament. But here achievements thus far have been minimal. A nuclear test ban treaty in 1963 and a nonproliferation treaty in 1968 tried to put limits on the indiscriminate testing and spread of nuclear weapons. But since some potential nuclear powers would not sign the treaties, their effectiveness was limited at best. More promising were the Strategic Arms Limitation Talks (SALT), initiated between the United States and the Soviet Union in 1969 and leading in 1972 to a first set of SALT agreements, which limited offensive and defensive strategic weapons. Efforts to reach a second set of SALT agreements, however, soon became bogged down in differences between the two superpowers. In an address to the United Nations in 1977, President Carter stated that the United States would be ready to reduce its nuclear arsenal on a reciprocal basis and to work toward "a world truly free of nuclear weapons." But such sweeping promises are more easily made than carried out.

Atoms for Peace

With efforts being concentrated on nuclear armaments, much less has been done to develop the peaceful possibilities of the atom. America's Atoms for Peace Program of 1953 was helpful in sponsoring atomic research among friendly nations, and Russia gave similar support to its allies. In 1957 an International Atomic Energy Agency was established at Vienna. Its purpose was to aid atomic projects in less developed countries by contributing fissionable materials and nuclear equipment. In the same year, the nations of the European Economic Community set up their own European Atomic Energy Community (Euratom) to promote peaceful atomic research and development.

The greatest progress in peaceful atomic development has been in the generation of electric power and the desalinization of seawater. By 1979, the United States was still leading the rest of the world in nuclear power capacity, far in advance of its nearest competitors—Great Britain, the Soviet Union, West Germany, Japan, and France. By then some twenty-five countries possessed nuclear power plants. This spread of peaceful uses of the atom was hampered, however, by fears on the part of the leading nuclear powers that atomic equipment supplied by them might ultimately be used to produce nuclear weapons. Another retarding factor, felt especially by the larger nuclear powers, were the often violent protests by environmentalist groups against possible dangers from radiation. It may be some time before atomic power is generally accepted as a fact of everyday life.

Competitive Coexistence

Because of its great potential as the leading energy source, nuclear power is a major factor not only in the military but in the economic competition between capitalism and communism. In the years since the Second World War, the economic predominance of the United States, western Europe, and Japan has been generally recognized. But in time the communist world came to challenge this lead. In the 1960s the Soviet Union began to boast that before long it would outproduce the United States and that world communism would defeat capitalism without a war, by peaceful competition alone. Russia's boast, in the opinion of some experts, is not an empty one. The Soviet Union has greater mineral

resources than the United States; it has a well-trained and disciplined work force; and it is fully capable of major scientific and technological advances.

The economic achievements of communism will be welcomed by anyone concerned with the eradication of poverty the world over. But the victory of communism, as history has shown, can only be achieved at the price of some or all of the individual freedoms that most of us value so highly. The danger is that communist successes may appeal to the world's underdeveloped regions. If communism should provide an answer to their economic problems, these countries may never miss these freedoms, especially since few of them have ever known them. There have been several instances since 1945 when the spread of communism owed as much to economic as to political or ideological causes.

THE REVOLUTION OF RISING EXPECTATIONS

It has become customary to divide the nations of the world into four categories, or "worlds": industrialized democracies; communist countries; developing nations; and economically troubled states. It is with the third and fourth worlds—developing and troubled economies—that we are here chiefly concerned. In 1975, more than 50 percent of the world's population, in sixty-nine countries, had an annual per capita income of less than five hundred dollars, and 25 percent, in twenty-eight countries, lived on less than two hundred dollars. At the other extreme, 10 percent of the world's population, in nineteen countries, had a per capita income of more than five thousand dollars. To bridge this gap between poor and rich nations is one of the greatest challenges facing the world today.

The expectation of the masses everywhere is to share in the many benefits modern technology has to offer. In order to succeed, this revolution of rising expectations needs outside help. The major assistance to underdeveloped lands thus far has come from the United States. The western European nations, Japan, and, recently, the oil-rich countries of the

César Chávez led a boycott of grapes in 1968 in order to obtain better working conditions for Mexican-American migrant farm workers.

Middle East, also have joined in helping backward areas. In comparison, communist economic aid, as distinct from military aid, has been slight. Most of it has taken the form of long-term credits for "trade not aid," a form of assistance preferred by most recipients.

Foreign aid, initially carried on by a few countries, in time became a multinational concern. The United Nations, in particular, sponsored several agencies and programs devoted to aiding underdeveloped regions. In 1976 the leading western industrial nations initiated periodic economic summits to discuss common problems, including their relations with the third world; and in 1977 the industrial nations of the north and the developing nations of the south held their first Conference on International Cooperation. By now it had become clear that the developing countries, because their control of essential natural resources gave them the power to upset the world's economic order, could demand a voice in determining their economic future. The resulting "north–south dialogue," while bringing few tangible results, clearly pointed a new way toward resolving the world's economic inequities.

The War on Poverty

The revolution of rising expectations, at first confined to the world's backward regions, in time also made itself felt in the United States. While the government was feeding people in faraway lands, millions of its own citizens went hungry; and while America was helping to improve housing conditions abroad, millions of Americans lived in slums and ghettos. It was primarily among minorities—black, Spanish-, Mexican-, and Indian-Americans—that these economic and social injustices prevailed. In response to the growing militancy of the black community, war was finally declared on poverty. Such a war had to be fought on several fronts—from health and housing to education and employment—in order to ensure a decent living for all. Some progress was made on all fronts during the 1960s and 1970s, but much still remains to be done. While black Americans constitute more than 11 percent of the population, their share of the national income is only 5 percent, and unemployment among blacks is twice as high as among whites.

The struggle for racial equality was not restricted to the United States, but had its counterparts in other industrialized countries, notably Great Britain. The most glaring examples of political as well as economic inequality were still found in southern Africa, where white minorities were vainly trying to stem the tide toward equal rights for all (see p. 816).

Women's Liberation

Ethnic groups were not the only ones fighting against economic and social in-

---

The Unwon War

The plight of the underprivileged, bad as it is, is not as bad as it was a generation ago or five generations ago—or as bad as it is in other countries. An impoverished man or woman in the United States today usually owns a television set, a refrigerator, sometimes an auto, and other amenities the poor of yesterday did not enjoy. He or she is certainly at a higher living standard than the poor countries like India or Brazil. Moreover, the percentage of people in poverty in the United States is smaller than in the 1930's or in 1893 or 1837, when there were major depressions. In absolute terms, although far, far too many are still hungry, the conditions of the poor are better than they used to be.

Poverty, however, is something relative; a person is judged to be poor by comparison with other people, as well as by his inability to satisfy elementary needs. In that relative sense the situation is bleak. The gap between those in want and those at the top of the ladder is still as great as—or greater than—it was generations ago.

The impoverished live in a climate of hopelessness. They do not see themselves rising to a higher status. They lack the opportunity for an adequate education. They are unable to find jobs, in part because the educational requirements are now higher. They are poorly housed, poorly fed—millions are still only a step removed from actual starvation. Worse still, there are large numbers of families who have lived in poverty for generations and do not imagine any prospect of climbing out of that poverty in the foreseeable future.

This is America's unwon war—the war against poverty. If it is to be won in the years to come, it will only be because the poor themselves, and people of conscience who sympathize with them, will make a much more sustained effort to abolish poverty than anything known in the past.

From Sidney Lens, *Poverty Yesterday and Today* (New York: Crowell, 1973), pp. 198–99.

Women began to speak out in the women's liberation movement of the 1970s.

justices. Other protests came from women and homosexuals. Of the two groups, the movement for women's rights was the more successful. Women's liberation gained momentum in the early 1970s. In the economic sphere, jobs traditionally reserved for men began to be opened to women, although still rarely at equal pay. To provide a constitutional basis for women's rights, Congress in 1972 passed an Equal Rights Amendment (ERA), but many state legislatures refused to ratify it. The federal government, through its Department of Health, Education, and Welfare (HEW), introduced a program of "affirmative action" to enforce equal opportunity regardless of sex or race. But progress toward full equality for women remains an uphill struggle.

Human Rights

By the mid-1970s, the fight for political and economic equality had turned into a worldwide concern for human rights. At a conference in Helsinki, Fin- land, in 1975, thirty-five communist and noncommunist nations affirmed such basic rights as free speech and freedom

Soviet Women

There are things about our country that a Soviet woman just wouldn't believe. Things so contrary to the commonplace rights she enjoys, and so obviously the due of any woman in a civilized country, that she takes them for granted.

She would be shocked, for instance, to learn that under the U.S. Supreme Court decision of 1974 a woman is not entitled to sick benefits when she has to quit work due to normal pregnancy.

"Then I'd have an abortion!" Maria Ivanovna might say, with appropriate indignation.

"But what if your husband wouldn't let you?" Mary Jones replies.

"My *husband*? Whose body is it?"

When Mary explains that there are eighteen states in this country in which a woman must have her husband's or parents' permission for an abortion, Maria would probably suggest: "Then just go to another state."

"Lots of women don't earn very much," Mary replies. "They couldn't afford it."

"They can't afford transportation and an abortion? Tell me, how much would it be for the abortion? Not in money—yours is different from ours—but in terms of days' pay?"

Mary sighs. "Not days. A couple of weeks' pay, or a month's, depending on—"

"Oh my God! (Russians use religious exclamations as much as we do). With us it's free if the doctor says you have to have an abortion, or about one day's pay if you just decide that you want it yourself." Maria pauses and gropes for solutions. "Couldn't you borrow the money?"

"That depends," Mary says. "In twenty-eight states the husband has to approve if the wife takes out a loan."

"The husband! What does *he* have to do with that?"

"Well, most women in the United States don't have their own money; they don't work at paying jobs. Even if they do, banks too often are afraid they'll quit the jobs or lose them. Women are considered bad risks."

At this point, if not before, Maria Ivanovna would probably change the subject, because Russian notions of hospitality regard it as very impolite to talk about anything that makes a guest or host feel inferior. But if the conversation was turned to other areas pertaining to women, she'd be even more embarrassed. For the simple fact is that Soviet women, in terms of rights, benefits, opportunities, and general treatment, are far ahead of American women. . . .

From William M. Mandel, *Soviet Women* (Garden City, N.Y.: Doubleday/Anchor, 1975), pp. 1–2.

of movement. This Helsinki accord encouraged dissidents in several communist states, including the Soviet Union, to criticize the shortcomings of their regimes. In 1977 a conference at Belgrade, Yugoslavia, reviewed the status of human rights in the participating countries; at the same time, President Carter made human rights one of the main issues of his foreign policy. Respect for personal liberties henceforth was to be a precondition for receiving American aid. A moral note had thus been injected into the revolution of rising expectations.

THE INDIVIDUAL
IN THE NUCLEAR AGE

The major challenges of our time—population explosion, conquest of outer space, nuclear revolution, and revolution of rising expectations—if met imaginatively and courageously, could easily help make the better world that people have dreamed of for so long. So far, however, rather than increasing happiness, these revolutionary changes and challenges seem to have aggravated many tensions and fears.

Foremost among these fears is the dread of war. Ever since the Second World War, political leaders have tried to banish this fear by finding ways of abolishing armaments. They are still trying. Meanwhile, some psychologists and anthropologists claim that the ultimate cause of war does not lie in political and ideological rivalries but in the human tendency toward aggression. Recent discoveries in the study of human relations, however, seem to hold some cause for hope. According to some social scientists, within the next century people will learn more about themselves than they have in their whole previous history. They will discover not only the causes and cures of sickness and pain, but the causes and cures of hate and aggression. They will at long last learn how to live in peace with one another.

The Biological Revolution

While people are learning more about their inner lives and motivations, they are also learning more about their physical being. Biology is making discoveries that may deeply affect and alter human existence. Some of these discoveries—artificial insemination, the transplantation of human organs, and the use of drugs to control moods—are already being put to use. Other research—test-tube babies, the postponement of death, mind control, even the creation of life from inert matter—is still in the experimental stage. In their sum total, the discoveries that biology holds in store amount to a veritable Biological Revolution.

Discoveries and practices that so completely change the traditional pattern of human existence raise staggering ethical questions. They have led some biologists to question whether man is ready to tamper with his heredity. But meanwhile the experiments in the laboratories continue.

The Mind Perplexed

An avalanche of unprecedented changes crowded into the span of a single generation has left most people bewildered. In their search for understanding, they have turned to a variety of old and new doctrines, none of which seems to provide the inner security they are looking for. The temper of our time is a mixture of anticipation and apprehension, optimism and pessimism, confidence and anxiety.

The philosophy of Existentialism well illustrates this blend of hope and despair. Its antecedents go back to the nineteenth century, but its vogue dates from the Second World War. The Existentialists, men like Jean-Paul Sartre in France or Karl Jaspers in Germany, maintain that the individual, rather than the abstract concept of humanity, constitutes true reality. They affirm the loneliness of man in a strange and hostile world. Such loneliness, far from leading to desperation, is seen as a challenge, a call to action, since "man's destiny is within himself."

While some people are searching for a new philosophy to fit a new age, others find existing doctrines sufficient to their needs. To the true communist believer,

Marxist doctrine still supplies ready-made answers to most problems. He has nothing to fear, his leaders tell him, since history is on his side. There was a time when communism had a large following in the West, especially among intellectuals. But most of these people have long since become disillusioned, and new converts to communism in the free world are few. Instead, a modified form of humane socialism has gained ground among the so-called New Left. Its adherents are equally opposed to American capitalism and the bureaucratized communism of the Soviet Union.

Communism's one-time rival, fascism, also has lost most of the following it once had. One of its ingredients, nationalism, is still a potent force, especially in the newly independent nations of Asia and Africa. Where it is used by unscrupulous leaders for selfish ends, nationalism rivals communism as a danger to world peace.

Some of the ground lost by communism and fascism has been reclaimed by religion. There are many reasons for this revived interest in religion, foremost among them the widely felt need for some central belief, some principle of authority, in a time of great intellectual uncertainty and emotional stress. The return to religion has taken many different forms and has involved not only a revival of interest in the traditional faiths of the West, but a new interest on the part of many westerners in the religions of the East. A noteworthy trend among western religions in recent years has been ecumenicalism; that is, the effort to overcome age-old differences and to work toward religious unity.

The Revolt of Youth

These are some of the ways in which people are trying to cope with their feelings of uncertainty and anxiety. There are others. One large segment of society—the younger generation—has been particularly shaken by the vicissitudes of a world they had no part in making. During the 1950s, young people everywhere were reproached by their elders for the passivity with which they faced the turmoil of the times. There were

some "beatniks" and "angry young men," but they were exceptions in an otherwise "quiet generation."

All this changed during the 1960s. As students began to rebel against society, not only in the United States but the world over, the older generation was faced with a new cause for concern in an already deeply troubled world. Most of the unrest was centered in the world's large universities, where huge enrollments, combined with antiquated regulations, tended to dehumanize education. But from the campuses of the "multiversities" the revolt spread to the schools and into the streets. Although the aims of the youthful rebels differed from place to place, the young people were united in their opposition to what they thought their elders stood for—meaningless discipline, social injustice, and senseless wars. Some of the young expressed their protest by withdrawal rather than action, by ignoring traditional manners and mores and becoming "hippies." Others believed that only by attacking the existing "establishment" could they find a way to realize the better world of which they dreamed.

The revolt of youth ended as suddenly as it had begun. In the early 1970s, the academic climate became peaceful again. Yet the confrontation between the old and the young had not been wholly in vain. The youthful rebels could point to some achievements. Not only had their agitation brought about many lasting changes within the universities, but youth's openness to new ideas, its freedom from prejudices, and its advocacy of a less inhibited life style had jolted the older generation out of many of its traditional and outworn habits and attitudes. "Youth culture" had left its imprint on culture as a whole.

An Age of Violence or An Age of Compassion?

Unrest among students was only one manifestation of discontent with the existing order. During the late 1970s another, more violent, form of protest erupted, as terrorists launched a campaign of bombings, arson, and murder against the forces in political and eco-

Confrontation at the 1968 Democratic Convention in Chicago.

nomic control. Like the student revolt, terrorism struck almost everywhere, except in the communist world. Seen in conjunction with other forms of violence—airplane highjackings, killing of hostages, and a steadily rising crime rate—the world seemed to have entered upon an age of violence, uncontrolled any longer by the forces of law and order. It may be that the constant bloodletting of a half-century of virtually uninterrupted warfare has inured mankind to the terror of death. More people have been killed by their fellow men in this century than during any other time in history.

But balanced against this seeming disregard for human life must be the growing awareness of the interdepend-ence of the family of man and the growing compassion and responsibility among the more privileged for the less fortunate members of that family. In the long-range perspective of human development, the present generation is only a mere incident. But in retrospect this age may some day appear as one of the most creative phases of history. Hopefully, it will stand out as an age in which the threat of a nuclear holocaust forced man to learn from his past mistakes; an age in which peaceful competition between rival ideologies brought forth un-dreamed-of economic and cultural progress; and an age in which fruitful debate and cooperation among peoples and races helped create a society in which such progress was shared by all.

Suggestions for Further Reading

Note: Asterisk denotes a book available in paperback edition.

General   The literature on the contemporary world is vast, and it is growing with every passing day. The following is only a small selection from the thousands of books dealing with the issues discussed in the Epilogue. There is no satisfactory general treatment of all these issues, but T. H. von Laue, *Freedom, Power and Necessity in the Age of World Revolutions* (1969), deals with most of them. The reports of the Club of Rome, an international group of renowned intellectuals and scholars, paint a rather pessimistic picture: M. D. Mesarovic and E. Pestel, *Mankind at the Turning Point: The Second Report to the Club of Rome** (1974), and E. Laszlo et al., *Goals for Mankind: A Report to the Club of Rome on the New Horizons of Global Community** (1977). Many authors look beyond the present in an attempt to forecast the future: A. Berry, *The Next Ten Thousand Years: A Vision of Man's Future in the Universe** (1974); D. Bell, *The Coming of Post-Industrial Society: A Venture in Social Forecasting* (1973); and W. W. Harman, *An Incomplete Guide to the Future** (1976).

The "Population Explosion"   The problems caused by population growth is a subject of much concern. The following are good general introductions: P. R. Ehrlich, *The Population Bomb*, rev. ed. (1975); L. B. Young, ed., *Population in Perspective** (1968); N. W. Chamberlain, *Beyond Malthus: Population and Power** (1970); W. D. Borrie, *The Growth and Control of World Population* (1970); and T. McKeown, *The Modern Rise of Population* (1976). On the continuing debate surrounding Malthus' predictions, see J. Oser, *Must Men Starve? The Malthusian Controversy* (1957), and W. W. Cochrane, *The World Food Problem: A Guardedly Optimistic View** (1969). The question of birth control is discussed in G. J. Hardin, ed., *Population, Evolution and Birth Control,** 2nd. ed. (1969), and A. F. Zimmerman, *Catholic Viewpoint on Overpopulation* (1961). The effect of population growth on the environment is treated in P. R. Ehrlich and A. H. Ehrlich, *Population, Resources, Environment: Issues in Human Ecology*, 2nd ed. (1972); W. F. Longgood, *The Darkening Land* (1972); H. W. Helfrich, ed., *Agenda for Survival: The Environmental Crises** (1970); and K. Montague and P. Montague, *No World Without End: The New Threats to Our Biosphere* (1976).

The Conquest of Outer Space   L. B. Taylor, *For All Mankind: America's Space Programs of the 1970's and Beyond* (1974), is a good general introduction. The more distant space probes are treated in M. R. Sharpe, *Satellites and Probes: The Development of Unmanned Space Flight* (1970), and J. Strong, *Search for the Solar System: The Role of Unmanned Interplanetary Probes* (1973). Y. Gagarin and V. Lebedev, *Survival in Space* (1969), relates the experiences of Russia's first cosmonaut. America's major achievements in space are the subject of D. Thomas, ed., *Moon: Man's Greatest Adventure* (1970), and M. Caidin, *Destination Mars* (1972). M. Kinsley, *Outer Space and Inner Sanctums: Government, Business, and Satellite Communication* (1976), deals with the commercial uses of space satellites. The possibility of human residence in space is discussed in T. A. Heppenheimer, *Colonies in Space** (1977), and G. K. O'Neill, *The High Frontier: Human Colonies in Space* (1977). See also W. S. Bainbridge, *The Spaceflight Revolution: A Sociological Study* (1976).

The Nuclear Revolution   R. Calder, *Living with the Atom* (1962), and H. P. Metzger, *The Atomic Establishment* (1972), are general treatments. There has been much concern and debate over the dangers of atomic energy: R. E. Webb, *The Accident Hazards of Nuclear Power Plants** (1976); R. Nader and J. Abbotts, *The Menace of Atomic Energy* (1977); and R. S. Lewis, *The Nuclear-Power Rebellion: Citizens vs. the Atomic Industrial Establishment* (1972). See also M. C. Olson, *Unacceptable Risk: The Nuclear Power Controversy** (1976); S. Novick, *The Electric War: The Fight over Nuclear Power* (1976); and D. Hayes, *Rays of Hope: The Transition to a Post-Petroleum World** (1977). The military results of the nuclear revolution have given rise to a large literature. E. L. M. Burns, *Megamurder* (1967), paints a fearful picture. R. Rapoport, *The Great American Bomb Machine* (1971), deals with America's nuclear arsenal. Nuclear disarmament is discussed by A. Myrdal, *The Game of Disarmament: How the United States and Russia Run the Arms Race* (1977); and its urgency is stressed in W. Epstein, *The Last Chance: Nuclear Proliferation and Arms Control* (1976). See also J. H. Barton and L. D. Weiler, eds., *International Arms Control: Issues and Agreements** (1976). On the SALT agreements, see J. Newhouse, *Cold Dawn: The Story of SALT* (1973), and M. Willrich and J. B. Rhinelander, eds., *SALT: The Moscow Agreements and Beyond** (1974).

The Revolution of Rising Expectations   The depressing subject of world poverty is dealt with in M. Harrington, *The Vast Majority: A Journey to the World's Poor* (1977); and possible remedies are discussed in O. Schachter, *Sharing the World's Resources* (1976). See also G. Chaliand, *Revolution in the Third World* (1977). America's poor are the subject of S. Lens, *Poverty: Yesterday and Today* (1973), a historical approach, and M. N. Danielson, *The Politics of Exclusion** (1976), treated topically. See also C. B. Carson, *The War on the Poor* (1969). On the women's liberation movement, W. H. Chafe, *The American Woman: Her Changing Social, Economic, and Political Roles, 1920–1970** (1974), and G. G. Yates, *What Women Want: The Ideologies of the Movement* (1975), are historical treatments. See also B. A. Babcock et al., *Sex Discrimination and the Law: Causes and Remedies* (1975). B. Friedan, *The Feminine Mystique** (1963), is by a leading figure of the women's movement.

The Individual in the Nuclear Age   Two good general books are K. Allsop, *The Angry Decade: A Survey of the Cultural Revolt of the 1950's* (1969), and M. Dickstein, *Gates of Eden: American Culture in the Sixties* (1977). The best introduction to the Biological Revolution is P. B. Medawar and J. S. Medawar, *The Life Science: Current Ideas in Biology* (1977). Other, more alarmist, works are J. Goodfield, *Playing God: Genetic Engineering and the Manipulation of Life* (1977); M. Rogers, *Biohazard* (1977); and N. Wade, *The Ultimate Experiment: Man-made Evolution* (1977). A good introduction to Existentialism is W. A. Kaufmann, ed., *Existentialism, from Dostoevsky to Sartre*, rev. ed. (1975). See also G. Brée, *Camus and Sartre: Crisis and Commitment* (1972). D. Vree, *On Synthesizing Marxism and Christianity* (1976), and R. Aron, *Marxism and the Existentialists* (1969), are comparative studies. There are several interesting books on religion in our day, old and new. M. E. Marty, *A Nation of Believers* (1976), covers the whole range. P. Rowley, *New Gods in America: An Informal Investigation into the New Religions of American Youth Today* (1971), and C. Y. Glock and R. N. Bellah, eds., *The New Religious Consciousness** (1976), stress recent developments. See also D. F. Wells and J. D. Woodbridge, *The Evangelicals: What They Believe, Who They Are, Where They Are Changing* (1976). On the causes of the student revolts, M. Crozier, *The Stalled Society** (1973), is informative, and L. S. Feuer, *The Conflict of Generations* (1969), presents an inside view. B. R. Wilson, *The Youth Culture and the Universities* (1970), is a general work, and A. Touraine, *The May Movement: Revolt and Reform** (1971), deals with the French "revolution" of May 1968. The best general book on terrorism is W. Laqueur, *Terrorism* (1977). See also F. J. Hacker, *Crusaders, Criminals, Crazies: Terror and Terrorism in Our Time* (1977); J. F. Bell, *A Time of Terror: How Democratic Societies Respond to Revolutionary Violence* (1978); and J. Schreiber, *The Ultimate Weapon: Terrorists and World Order* (1978).

Source of Illustrations

836

118: Courtesy of The American Numismatic Society, New York
120: Alinari/Editorial Photocolor Archives

Chapter 6
123: Victoria and Albert Museum, London
124: From Zimmer, Heinrich, *The Art of Indian Asia: Its Mythology and Transformations,* ed. Joseph Campbell, Bollingen Series XXXIX, Vol. 2. Copyright © 1955, 1960 by Princeton University Press. Reproduced by permission
126: Raghubir Singh, Woodfin Camp and Associates
129: Museum of Archaeology, Sarnath
130: Government of India, Archaeological Survey of India
131: Courtesy of the Smithsonian Institution, Freer Gallery of Art, Washington, D.C.
133: Courtesy of the Smithsonian Institution, Freer Gallery of Art, Washington, D.C.
136: From Chiang Yee's *Chinese Calligraphy: An Introduction to its Aesthetic and Technique,* 3rd Ed., Revised and Enlarged, Copyright © 1973 by the President and Fellows of Harvard College
137: Reproduced by Courtesy of the Trustees of the British Museum
139: Rene Burri, Magnum Photos, Inc.
140: Richard C. Rudolph Collection, Los Angeles

Chapter 7
142: Museo Nazionale, Florence
145: *t* Deutsches Archäologisches Institut, Rome; *b* Rheinisches Landesmuseum, Bonn/Deutsch Fototek
146: Rheinisches Landesmuseum, Trier
147: *t* The Metropolitan Museum of Art, Purchase 1895, Administrative Funds
149: Phot. Bibl. nat. Paris
150: National Library of Naples
151: The Bettmann Archive
152: *l* Staatsbibliothek, Bamberg; *r* Reproduced by Courtesy of the Trustees of the British Museum
153: Crown Copyright. Victoria and Albert Museum, London
154: Archives Nationales, Paris
155: Deutsches Archäologisches Institut, Rome

Chapter 8
158: Erich Lessing, Magnum Photos, Inc.
160: Courtesy of the Dumbarton Oaks Collection, Washington, D.C.
162: Alinari/Editorial Photocolor Archives
163: Alinari/Editorial Photocolor Archives
164: Reproduced by Courtesy of the Trustees of the British Museum

166: The Bettmann Archive
167: *t* The Metropolitan Museum of Art, Cloisters Collection, 1966; *b* The Metropolitan Museum of Art, Gift of J. Pierpont Morgan, 1917
169: Arabian American Oil Company
171: Courtesy of the Smithsonian Institution, Freer Gallery of Art, Washington, D.C.
173: Courtesy of The American Numismatic Society, New York; *b* The Metropolitan Museum of Art. Bequest of Edward C. Moore, 1891
174: Karen Collidge

Chapter 9
178: Foto Ann Munchow, Aachen
180: Historical Pictures Service, Inc., Chicago
183: Stadtbibliothek, Schaffhausen
185: Millet-Connaissance des Arts, Louvre, Paris
186: *t* Reproduced by Courtesy of the Trustees of the British Museum; *b* Bild-Archiv der Österreichischen Nationalbibliothek, Wien
188: New York Public Library. Astor, Lenox, and Tilden Foundations
190: *t* Swedish Information Service; *b* Statens Historiska Museer, Stockholm
191: Phot. Bibl. nat. Paris
194: *l* Foto Hinz, Basel; *m* The Bettmann Archive; *r* Abbey Archives/Scala/Editorial Photocolor Archives
197: *t* The Metropolitan Museum of Art, Gift of George Blumenthal, 1941; *b* Museo del Castello Sforzesco, Milan
198: Bayerische Staatsbibliothek, Munich
201: Reproduced by permission of the British Library

Chapter 10
205: Giraudon
207: The Bettmann Archive
208: Bodleian Library, Oxford
211: *t* Giraudon; *b* Victoria and Albert Museum, London/From *The Bayeux Tapestry.* Published by Phaidon Press Ltd., Oxford
214: Anonymous Donation
215: The Granger Collection, New York
216: Foto Biblioteca Vaticana, Roma
218: Archives Photographiques, Paris
219: Musée Municipal, Dijon
220: *l* Jean Roubier; *m, r* F. S. Lincoln
221: *l* F. S. Lincoln; *r* Jean Roubier

Chapter 11
228: French Cultural Services
231: Photographie Bulloz, Paris
232: Jean Roubier
234: Reproduced by permission of the British Library
237: *t* The Bettmann Archive; *b* Giraudon

241: The Bettmann Archive
243: Museo di Roma
244: Foto Biblioteca Vaticana, Roma
245: The Bettmann Archive
246: Culver Pictures
248: Alinari/Editorial Photocolor Archives

Chapter 12
252: Master and Fellows of Corpus Christi College, Cambridge
254: All Courtesy of The American Numismatic Society, New York, except second from top, Ashmolean Museum, Oxford
255: Roger-Viollet
256: Reproduced by permission of the British Library Board
258: By Courtesy of the Dean and Chapter of Westminster
259: The Bettmann Archive
261: Foto Biblioteca Vaticana, Roma
262: Alinari/Editorial Photocolor Archives
265: Reproduced by permission of the British Library
267: Reproduced by permission of the British Library
268: Radio Times Hulton/By permission of The British Library
271: Alinari/Editorial Photocolor Archives
272: Phot. Bibl. nat. Paris

Chapter 13
274: Reproduced by permission of The British Library Board
277: The Bettmann Archive
279: Foto Biblioteca Vaticana, Roma
280: The Bodleian Library, Oxford
283: By Courtesy of the Dean and Chapter of Westminster
284: Phot. Bibl. nat. Paris/Roger-Jean Segalat
285: Giraudon
286: A. C. Cooper Ltd., London
289: Musée d'Art et d'Histoire, Geneva
292: *t* New York Public Library. From Lubecker Totentanz, 1489; *b* New York Public Library, Rare Book Division
293: National Gallery, London
294: The Bettmann Archive
295: The Bettmann Archive

Chapter 14
298: MAS, Barcelona
300: Courtesy of the Dumbarton Oaks Collection, Washington, D.C.
301: Reproduced by permission of the British Library
303: The Metropolitan Museum of Art, Rogers Fund, 1913
305: Giraudon
309: Phot. Bibl. nat. Paris
310: Novosti Press Agency, London
312: © 1940 by Macmillan from Michael Prawdin's *The Mongol Empire*

642: The Bettmann Archive
643: Board of Global Ministries, United Methodist Church

Chapter 28

646: The Metropolitan Museum of Art, gift of Frederic H. Hatch, 1926
648: *t* Brown Brothers; *b* London Transport Executive
649: Charts on p. 220 of *Western Civilization,* Vol. II, 2nd Ed., edited by William L. Langer et al. Copyright © 1969, 1975 by Harper & Row Publishers, Inc. Reprinted by permission.
650: Brown Brothers
651: Photographie Bulloz, Paris
652: *t* Reproduced by Courtesy of the Trustees of the British Museum; *b* Radio Times Hulton
653: Gernsheim Collection, Humanities Research Center, The University of Texas at Austin
655: The Granger Collection, New York
656: Phot. Bibl. nat. Paris
657: Roger-Viollet, Paris
658: Radio Times Hulton
659: The Bettmann Archive
660: Gernsheim Collection, Humanities Research Center, The University of Texas at Austin
661: *t* Katherine Young/Archiv für Kunst und Geschichte; *b* Brown Brothers
663: Sovfoto
664: Sovfoto
665: Historical Pictures Service, Inc., Chicago
666: Courtesy of American Museum of Natural History
667: The Bettmann Archive
670: Gernsheim Collection, Humanities Research Center, The University of Texas at Austin
671: The Granger Collection, New York

Chapter 29

674: The Press Association Limited
679: *t* Picture Collection, The Branch Libraries, The New York Public Library; *b* Radio Times Hulton
681: *t* Philadelphia Museum of Art, Louis E. Stern Collection; *b* The Tate Gallery, London
685: *t* United Press International, Inc.
686: Historical Pictures Service, Inc., Chicago
688: Picture Collection, The Branch Libraries, The New York Public Library
690: The Bettmann Archive
692: The Press Association, London
693: United Press International, Inc.
694: Radio Times Hulton

Chapter 30

698: Imperial War Museum, London
700: *t* Imperial War Museum, London;

b Historical Pictures Service, Inc., Chicago
702: Culver Pictures
703: Imperial War Museum, London
704: National Archives, Washington, D.C.
706: *t* "L'Illustration," Paris; *b* The Fotomas Index
707: Sovfoto
709: Imperial War Museum, London
710: U.S. Signal Corps/National Archives, Washington, D.C.
712: Radio Times Hulton
713: Culver Pictures
714: "L'Illustration," Paris
716: The Bettmann Archive
717: Gernsheim Collection, Humanities Research Center, The University of Texas at Austin
718: Wide World Photos
720: *t* The Chase Manhattan Museum of Money of the World; *b* United Press International, Inc.
721: Radio Times Hulton

Chapter 31

724: Dr. Erich Salomon/Magnum Photos, Inc.
726: Library of Congress
728: Culver Pictures
729: Brown Brothers
730: Brown Brothers
731: The Granger Collection, New York
732: Wide World Photos
733: Dr. Erich Salomon
734: Wide World Photos
735: Culver Pictures
736: Topix
737: *t* Earl Leaf, Rapho-Guillumette/PRI; *b* Wide World Photos
738: Marconi Company, London
739: *t* Courtesy of Ford Motor Company; *m, b* © 1973 by National Housewares Manufacturers Assoc. From *The Housewares Story*
740: Clark University Archives
741: Courtesy of Dr. Margaret Mead/ American Museum of Natural History
742: *t* Radio Times Hulton; *b* Brown Brothers
743: On extended loan to the Museum of Modern Art, New York, from the artist's estate

Chapter 32

746: Wide World Photos
748: *t* The Lenin State Library of The U.S.S.R., Moscow; *b* NYT Pictures
749: Sovfoto
750: *t* British Museum/The Fotomas Index; *b* Sovfoto
753: Brown Brothers
757: Library of Congress
758: United Press International, Inc.
759: Gernsheim Collection, Humanities Research Center, The University of Texas at Austin

761: Bildarchiv Preussischer Kulturbesitz, Berlin
762: Frederic Lewis Photos, Inc.
763: Syndication International/Gernsheim Collection, Humanities Research Center, The University of Texas at Austin
764: Brown Brothers
765: Gernsheim Collection, Humanities Research Center, The University of Texas at Austin
768: *t* CBS News; *b* Associated Press Photo, London/Wide World Press
769: United Press International, Inc.

Chapter 33

772: Wide World Photos
774: Wide World Photos
775: *t* Topix; *b* Associated Press Photo, London
777: *t* American Heritage Publishing Co.; *b* Sovfoto
779: National Archives, Washington, D.C.
781: Keystone
782: United States Coastguard Photo
786: Imperial War Museum, London
787: *t* © 1961 *Punch* (Rothco); *b* United Nations
789: Fenno Jacobs, Black Star
791: Wide World Photos

Chapter 34

797: White House Photograph
798: Pictorial Parade
799: Wide World Photos
800: Keystone
801: Pictorial Parade
803: Wide World Photos
804: United Press International, Inc.
805: United Press International, Inc.
806: *t* Wide World Photos; *b* United Press International, Inc.
808: *t* United Nations; *b* A.F.P./Pictorial Parade
809: Erich Lessing, Magnum Photos, Inc.
810: Wide World Photos
812: Eastfoto
813: Fox Butterfield/NYT Pictures
814: *t* Wide World Photos; *b* Jean Guamy/Magnum Photos, Inc.
816: *t* Andrew Bailey, Camera Press/ Photo Trends; *b* Marilyn Silverstone/Magnum Photos, Inc.
818: United Press International, Inc.
821: Camera Press/Photo Trends

Epilogue

824: Bruce Davidson, Magnum Photos, Inc.
826: Popperfoto, London
827: NASA Photo
828: U.S. Department of Energy
829: Daniel S. Brody from Editorial Photocolor Archives
831: Burt Glinn, Magnum Photos, Inc.
833: Charles Harbutt, Magnum Photos, Inc.

Index

Brazil, 397, 399, 401, 408, 440, 632
Breasted, James H.: quoted, 10
Breitenfeld, 432
Brest-Litovsk, Treaty of (1918), 707, 709, 712, 717
Brethren of the Common Life, 279, 375
Brezhnev, Leonid I., 808
Briand, Aristide, 718, 726
Brienne, Lomenie de, 524
Brissot de Warville, Jacques Pierre, 531–33
Bristol, 442
Britain. see England; Great Britain
British Commonwealth, 634, 735–36, 798, 806, 810, 816
British East India Company, 328, 437, 440, 508–09, 518, 613, 634–36
British Empire, 461, 613, 614–15, 625, 633–36, 791, 797–98
British Guiana, 631
British North America Act (1867), 633
Brittain, V.: quoted, 725
Brittany, 17, 206, 239, 366
Brockdorff-Rantzau, Count Ulrich von, 711
Brodsky, Yosif, 809
bronze, 134, 137
Brown, John, 626
Brown v. Board of Education of Topeka (1954), 804
Bruce, Robert, 267
Bruges, 207, 269, 405
Brunanburh, 200
Brunelleschi, Filippo, 355, 356
Bruno, Giordano, 475, 483
Brusilov, Alexei, 702
Brussels, 432, 557; Treaty (1948), 790, 802
Brutus, 75, 76, 265
Bryher: quoted, 100
Bucer, Martin, 382
Bucharest, Treaty of (1913), 692; Treaty of (1918), 707, 709, 712
Buchlau Agreement (1908), 690
Buchner, Ludwig: *Force and Matter*, 665
Budapest, 311, 747
Buddha, the, 127, 130, 132, 136
Buddhism, 124: in China, 128, 130, 136, 138, 140–41, 328–29, 330–31; culture of, 129, 132, 138, 323, 340; Hinayana, 129–30; in India, 122, 127–28, 129–31, 322, 329; in Japan, 130, 333, 340; Mahayana, 129–30; monasteries, 127–28, 340; spread of, 128, 129–31, 141, 323
Bukharin, Nikolai, 749–50, 752
Bulganin, Nikolai, 819
Bulgaria, 676, 677–78, 690, 692, 759; First World War, 699–700, 709, 713; post-Second World War, 787, 789; Second World War, 775–76
Bulgars, 299, 301, 307, 316
Bülow, Bernhard, Prince von, 688
Burckhardt, Jacob: *Civilization of the Renaissance in Italy, The*, 352
Burgenland region, 716
Burgundians, 116, 143, 144, 145, 154
Burgundy, 156, 366; dukes of, 284–85, 288, 289, 293, 294–95, 366, 405
Burke, Edmund, 519; *Reflections on the Revolution in France*, 531, 532, 553
Burma, 130, 323, 639, 684, 783–84, 812–13

business. see capitalism; industrialization; trade and commerce
Bute, John Stuart, 3rd Earl of, 511
Butterfield, Herbert: quoted, 474
Byblos, 17
Byzantine Empire, 166–67, 207, 209; Arab conquests in, 118, 164, 167, 173, 175–76, 299; bureaucracy, 167, 299, 303–04; civil wars, 246; commerce and industry, 176, 179, 300, 307–08; Comneni dynasty, 305; culture, 54, 167, 299–300, 302, 318; decline of, 303–05, 307–08, 309, 316–17; Latin Empire of, 307–08; loss of Italy, 180–81; Macedonian dynasty, 299–304; military of, 167, 303, 307; reconquests of, 299, 305–06; succession problem, 303, 304; Turkish conquests in, 217–18, 305; and western Europe, 217–18, 301, 305–06, 307–08. see also Constantinople; Greek Orthodox Church

C

Cabral, Pedro, 397
Cadiz, 425
Caesar, Gaius Julius, 72–77, 83, 95; *Commentaries on the Gallic War*, 74, 82; military exploits of, 73–74; murder of, 75, 81, 265; as ruler, 74–75, 79
Cairo, 217, 304
Calais, 282, 285, 366, 410
Calcutta, 440
calendars, 10, 75
Calhoun, John C., 624, 627
Calicut, 397
California, 625, 626, 628
Caligula, Roman Emperor, 84
Callaghan, James, 798
calligraphy, 137
Calonne, Charles Alexandre de, 524–25
Calvin, John, 382–83, 385, 388; *Institutes of the Christian Religion*, 382–83
Calvinism, 382, 384, 390, 405–06, 411, 429–30, 433, 434, 465. see also Huguenots
Cambodia, 130, 322–23, 600, 812–13
Cambridge University, 247, 455, 478
Canaanites, 16–17, 19
Canada, 613, 633–34, 790, 800, 806; British, 511, 519, 613, 625, 633; French, 442, 448, 508–09, 511, 633
Canada Act (1791), 633
Canary Islands, 295
Canning, George, 555
Cano, Juan Sebastián del, 399
Canossa, 216
Canterbury, 153
Canterbury, Archbishops of, 153, 210, 237–38, 242, 243, 386–87, 425
Canton, 138, 636–37, 737, 764
Canute, King of Denmark, 201
Cape Colony, 681–82
Capella, Martianus: *Satyricon*, 117
Cape of Good Hope, 397, 399, 408
Capetian dynasty, 239
Cape Verde Islands, 295
capitalism, 390, 591; in agriculture, 364–65, 629, 631; and competition, 574, 578, 591, 630, 667; and competition with communism, 829; cycles in, 731; and Darwin, 667; and industry, 364–65, 571,

652; Marx on, 588–89, 650; monopolistic, 649–50, 667, 685; and trade, 346, 365, 501. see also economy, laissez faire
Caporetto, battle of, 707–08
Capri, 84
Caracalla, Roman Emperor, 88
Carbonari, 557
Caribbean: sugar islands of, 439, 440–41, 511
Carloman, King of the Franks, 182
Carlowitz, Treaty of (1699), 463–64
Carlsbad Decrees, 550
Carlyle, Thomas: *Past and Present*, 590
Carnegie, Andrew: *Gospel of Wealth, The*, 649
Carnot, Lazare, 533, 534
Carolingian dynasty (Franks), 156, 179–91, 192
Carter, Howard: quoted, 15
Carter, James Earl ("Jimmy"), 806, 807, 821, 828, 832
Carthage, 18, 63–64, 65, 175
Cartier, Jacques, 442
Cartwright, Edmund, 573
Casablanca, 781; Conference, 784
Cassiodorus, 145–46; *Introduction to Divine and Secular Literature*, 146
Cassius, 75, 76, 265
Castiglione, Baldassare: *Courtier, The*, 349, 353–54
Castile, 367–68, 402
Castlereagh, Robert Stewart, Lord, 546–48, 549
Castro, Fidel, 807, 820
Catalonia, 368, 432, 434
Catherine II (the Great), Empress of Russia, 469, 505, 512–14
Catherine of Aragon, 386
Catholic Center Party (Germany), 657
Catholic League, 412, 430–32
Catholic Reformation, 388–90, 403. see also Roman Catholic Church
Cato, 66
Catullus, 82
Caucasus, 677, 777
Cavour, Camillo, Count of, 598, 601–04, 612
Cellini, Benvenuto, 349; *Life of Benvenuto Cellini, The*, 349–50, 356
Celts, 61, 73, 116, 122, 143
Central American Common Market, 806
Central Powers, 634, 699–705, 707–13
Central Treaty Organization (CENTO), 814
Ceram, C. W.: quoted, 28
Cervantes, Miguel de: *Don Quixote*, 291, 414
Ceylon, 122, 128, 129–30, 339, 395, 407, 440
Chaldean Empire, 22–23
Chalukya kingdom (India), 320
Chamberlain, Austen, 718
Chamberlain, Joseph, 653, 654
Chamberlain, Neville, 733, 767–68, 773, 774; quoted, 767
Chamberlin, W. H.: quoted, 751
Champagne, 229, 239
Champlain, Samuel de, 442

Duke Ting, 135
Dulles, John Foster, 818
Dumouriez, Charles François, 533
Dunkirk, 744; Treaty of (1947), 790
Dupleix, Joseph, 509
Durham, John George Lambton, 1st Earl of: *Report on the Affairs of British North America*, 633
Dutch East India Company, 407–08, 440
Dying Gaul of Pergamum, 52

E

Eakins, Thomas, 631
East African Community, 817
Eastern Roman Empire, 109, 115, 159–66; architecture, 162; attacked by Persia, 161, 162, 165; Christianity in, 112, 159, 163–64, 166; fiscal conditions, 159, 160, 161, 162; and Germanic kingdoms, 116–18, 143–45, 155, 159, 160–62, 167, 180; Greek influence in, 160, 166; Latin influence in, 160, 166; military of, 159, 160–62, 166; and reconquest of West, 159, 160–62, 165, 175. *see also* Byzantine Empire
Eastern Roumelia, 678
Easter Rebellion (Ireland), 736
East Germany, 800–01; and Soviet Union, 788, 800, 819, 820
East Indies, 394, 396, 399, 439, 440, 737, 783
East Prussia, 700
Ebla, 7
Eddington, Sir Arthur, 742
economy: as cause of revolution, 560; and colonies, 438, 439–40, 443, 633, 643; government regulation of, 437–38; laissez faire, 581–82, 584, 585, 590, 591, 623, 632, 649, 652, 667; and liberalism, 579, 580–82, 584; mercantile, 435–39, 490–91; and natural laws, 490–91; spurred by technology, 295, 363; urban, 437. *see also* Great Depression; individual countries
Edessa, 306
Edict of Nantes (1598), 412, 420; Revocation of, 450–51, 452, 457, 465
Edict of Restitution (1629), 431
Edict of Toleration (313), 107–08
Edinburgh, 485
education: and liberals, 583–84; and printing, 364; public, 537, 584, 621, 648; Renaissance, 345, 350–51, 359; revival in, 279; Rousseau on, 550–51. *see also* scholarship; individual countries
Education Act (1870), 648
Edward I, King of England, 258, 259, 266–68, 270, 281, 287
Edward II, King of England, 281, 287
Edward III, King of England, 275, 281–82, 285, 287
Edward VI, King of England, 387
Edward VII, King of England, 733
Edward (Black Prince), Prince of Wales, 282
Edward the Confessor, King of England, 201, 210, 211
Egypt, 161, 163–66, 636, 709, 819; under Arab Empire, 51, 167, 173, 174, 176, 260; and European imperialism, 679, 680,

689; Mamelukes of, 308–10, 311; under Moslems, 304, 306, 307; Napoleon in, 536; nationalism in, 680, 736, 814; Second World War, 775; under Turks, 317, 556, 680
Egypt, ancient, 3, 14, 19, 26; arts, 11, 15, 42; Assyrian control over, 21–22, 30; Christianity in, 91, 112; civil wars, 11; conquered by Alexander, 50; conquered by Persia, 9, 23, 40, 44–45; decline of, 9, 16; engineers of, 9–10, 11; expansion of, 14–15, 16; government, 8–11, 14; Hebrews in, 18–19; Hellenistic culture in, 52, 54; hieroglyphics, 9; Kingdoms of, 9–12, 14–16, 29; military of, 15, 22; under Rome, 51, 54, 64, 77, 81, 88, 117; science, 8, 9–10, 11, 45; tombs of, 10, 15; trade and commerce, 13, 14, 15, 16, 17, 29, 30, 32, 93, 129
Einstein, Albert, 742
Eisenhower, Dwight D., 781–83, 804, 819
Eisenhower Doctrine, 814, 819
Elba, 542
Eleanor of Aquitaine, 233, 235
Elijah, 20
Eliot, T. S.: *Waste Land, The*, 742
Elisha, 20
Elizabeth, Empress of Russia, 511
Elizabeth I, Queen of England, 387–88, 404, 406, 408–10, 423–24, 425
Emancipation Proclamation, 628
Emerson, Rupert: quoted, 811
"Emperor's Battle," 708
empiricism, 484
Ems, 610
energy crisis, 806, 826
Engels, Friedrich, 586–87, 650; *Communist Manifesto*, 567, 587–89
England, 450, 464, 485, 719; agriculture, 206, 566–67, 572–73, 654; Anglo-Saxon, 116, 143, 145, 152–53, 199–202, 210–11; arts, 233, 492, 551; Black Death in, 280; Catholic Church in, 153, 217, 237, 245, 257–58, 270, 278, 362, 369, 385–88, 408, 456–57; Chartist movement, 566–67; colonies of, 385, 408, 437, 440, 441–43, 454, 499–500, 502–03, 508–11, 517–20; education, 247, 584, 614, 648; Elizabethan, 387–88, 404, 408–10, 414; feudalism in, 195, 202, 211–13, 236–38; fiscal policies, 236, 238, 258, 268, 283, 285, 424–26, 438, 439, 460, 501, 517–18, 654; foreign affairs, 255, 257–58, 266–67, 281, 368, 406, 408–10, 423–26, 427, 453–54, 456, 459–60, 547–49, 550; Glorious Revolution, 457–62; government and politics, 191, 199–200, 202, 208–09, 211–13, 257–59, 267–68, 269, 276, 285–87, 368–70, 422–29, 455–59, 470, 501–03, 558–59, 613–14, 652–55, 725; 798; Hundred Years' War, 281–85, 287–89, 365–66, 368; industry, 231, 285, 409, 542; labor, 567, 578, 584–85, 614, 615, 651–52, 654, 725, 798; law and courts, 200, 201, 211–13, 235–38, 257, 285–86, 413, 425, 426, 558; literature, 200, 233–34, 291–93, 414, 428, 492–93, 670; mercantilism, 435, 437, 438, 440, 442–43, 500, 623, 633;

military of, 200–01, 281–82, 284, 426–28; monarchy, 199–202, 204, 235–38, 239, 245, 256–59, 266–68, 281–87, 344, 365–66, 368–70, 417, 422–29, 455–59; nationalism in, 236, 257, 387–88, 408, 552; nobility, 199–200, 201–02, 238, 257–59, 261, 266–67, 280, 281–87, 368–70, 423, 455, 500, 503; Norman conquest of, 204, 210–13; Peasants' Rebellion, 280, 283; Protestantism in, 363, 383–88, 387–88, 408, 424–28, 455–59, 460, 490; Restoration, 428; Revolution of 1640, 408, 426–28, 461; under Rome, 74, 81, 84, 87, 88, 103; sea power of, 405, 409–10, 427, 460; social reform in, 458, 559, 579, 614, 647, 652–54, 725; society, 279–80, 485–86, 489, 503, 550, 614, 798; trade and commerce, 17, 93, 229, 285, 328, 339, 363, 407, 409, 439–40, 460, 539–42, 720; viking conquests in, 188, 190–91, 199, 201, 211; Wars of the Roses, 285, 368. *see also* Great Britain; Parliament, English
Eniwetok, 783
enlightened despotism. *see* despots, enlightened
Enlightenment, 461, 484–92, 522, 525, 537, 540, 551, 552, 571; liberty, 489, 538; natural law, 488–91; progress, 489; rationalism, 488–89, 493–94, 545, 550, 554, 576; religion, 489–90; social and political thought, 490–91. *see also philosophes*
Entente Cordiale (1904), 689, 692, 695
Enterprise, 827
environment: and Darwin, 667; decay of, 825–26; influences on culture of, 741; and nuclear power, 829; protection of, 805
Epictetus, 96
Epicureans, 53
Epirus, 61, 62–63, 64
equality: and civil rights, 626, 628; and French Revolution, 522, 525, 528–30, 531, 537, 538, 542; and industrialization, 571
Equal Rights Amendment (ERA), 831
Erasmus, 279, 353, 376–77, 380, 405; quoted, 377
Eratosthenes, 53
Erfurt, 659
Erhard, Ludwig, 800
Eritrea, 681, 762
Ermak, 444
Escorial, 412
Estates General, 366; and French Revolution, 524–27; in Middle Ages, 269, 270, 287–89; weakness of, 369, 419
Estonia, 774
Ethelred the Ill-Counseled, King of England, 201
Ethiopia, 81, 661, 681
Ethiopian War, 762–63
Etruria, 61, 64, 93
Etruscans, 57–62 *passim*
Euclid, 53, 300
Eugene of Savoy, Prince, 454, 463
Eugenius III, Pope, 219
Euripides, 43, 46; *Medea*, 44; *Trojan Women, The*, 44

Shafer, Boyd C.: quoted, 552

Shaftesbury, Anthony Ashley Cooper, 1st Earl of, 457, 461

Shakespeare, William, 414, 428; *Julius Caesar*, 75

Shang dynasty (China), 134

Shantung Peninsula, 639, 699, 710–11, 737, 738

Shaw, George Bernard, 650

Sheng, First Emperor of China, 137

Sherman Antitrust Act (1890), 630, 631

Shi-ites, 304

Shimonoseki, Treaty of (1895), 639

Shinto, 340, 641–42

shipping, 285, 295, 339, 435, 574, 575, 613, 622

Shotoku, Prince, 340

Siam, 323, 684

Sibelius, Jan, 743

Siberia, 444, 664, 683–84, 705

Sicily, 18, 31, 32, 47, 63, 65, 68, 190, 209–10, 302, 454, 505; under Holy Roman Empire, 242, 243, 258, 260–62; revolution of 1848, 562; Second World War, 781

Sieyès, Emmanuel Joseph, Abbé, 536; *What Is the Third Estate?*, 526

Sigismund, Holy Roman Emperor, 360

Silesia, 290, 507–09, 511, 516, 574

Simons, Menno: quoted, 384

Sinai Peninsula, 814

Singapore, 813

Sinn Fein movement, 736

Sino-Japanese War, 639, 642, 688, 779

Sinyavsky, Andrei, 809

Sistine Chapel, 356

Sixtus IV, Pope, 362, 374

skepticism: and religion, 483

slavery, 19, 22; abolition of, 548; in ancient Greece, 33, 35, 41; in ancient Rome, 58, 64, 65, 66, 67–68, 71, 91, 92–93; colonial, 400–01, 439, 440, 500; Mamelukes of Egypt, 308–09; trade in, 409, 440, 454, 511, 548; in U.S., 548, 625–28

Slavs, 162, 165, 188, 189–90, 209, 229, 299, 301, 563–64, 605, 615–16, 660, 668, 690, 693, 699, 759

Slovaks, 563

Slovenes, 563

Sluys: naval battle at, 282

Smith, Adam, 435, 485: *Wealth of Nations*, 490–91, 580–82

Smith, Ian, 816

Social Democratic Party: Austrian, 660; German, 659, 726; Russian, 663–64; West German, 800

socialism, 585–90, 668, 833; Christian, 590–91, 652; European, 545, 559, 561–62, 567, 568, 580, 617, 632; international, 651; and labor, 650–51, 652; Marxian (scientific), 579, 586–90, 747; revisionist, 650–51; and rise of totalitarianism, 747; state, 652, 747; in U.S., 586, 621; Utopian, 585–86

Socialist Party: French, 734, 800; German, 657; Italian, 753, 802

Socialist Revolutionaries (Russia), 663–64, 706

social reform: and industrialization, 579–84, 591, 649, 652; and literature, 590, 632, 670–71, 742; U.S. example in, 621; and "welfare state," 652. *see also* individual countries

society: and behavioral sciences, 739–41; under feudalism, 208; and individualism, 482; industrialized, 576–79, 649; Locke on, 484; in nuclear age, 832–34; rationalism in, 488; rising expectations of, 829–34; unrest in Europe of, 412–14. *see also* man; individual countries and social classes

sociology, 670, 740

Socrates, 35, 44, 46, 48, 376

Soissons, Council of (1120), 223

Solferino: battle at, 602

Solomon, King of the Hebrews, 19

Solomon Islands, 685, 783

Solon, 33, 38

Solzhenitsyn, Alexander, 809

Somaliland, 681, 762

Somme, battle of the, 702

Song of Roland, 234–35

Sonnino, Sidney, 710

Sophists, 45–46, 48

Sophocles, 43: *Antigone*, 44; *Oedipus the King*, 44

Sorel, Georges, 755; *Reflections on Violence*, 651

South Africa: Dutch, 383, 682–83, 688; European imperialism in, 681–83, 687–88

South Africa, Republic of, 634, 683, 821; *apartheid* in, 798, 816–17, 830

South America, 701. *see also* Latin America

South Carolina, 627

Southeast Asia, 128, 322, 329, 812–13, 820. *see also* Vietnam War; individual countries

Southeast Asia Treaty Organization (SEATO), 813

South Korea, 787, 793, 796, 813, 818

South Sea Company, 501

South Vietnam, 323, 820, 821

Soviet Union, 715, 717, 724, 756; Allied intervention in, 716, 748; and China, 737, 765, 793, 809–10, 812, 819–20; civil war in, 748; Cold War, 789–92, 793, 796, 803, 817–21; collectivization in, 751, 807; communism in, 714, 719, 747–52, 759, 784–85, 808, 819–20, 821; dissidents in, 832; and eastern Europe, 786–90, 800, 807, 809, 819, 820; economy, 720, 721, 748–49, 751–52, 764, 807; foreign affairs, 717, 719, 747, 749, 752, 761, 767, 768, 769, 799, 801, 804, 805, 807, 808, 810, 817, 818–22; government, 727, 750, 759, 807–09; liberalization in, 808, 818, 819; nationalism in, 751–52; as nuclear power, 792, 796, 810, 818, 828–29; Red army of, 715, 748, 752, 769; repression and terror in, 747, 752, 807, 809; Second World War, 752, 773–74, 776–77, 779–87; space program of, 819, 826–27; trials and Great Purge in, 752, 769; and United Nations, 786, 791, 793; unrest in, 808–09; women in, 831. *see also* Russia

space program: lunar landings, 826; satellites, 827; Soviets, 819, 826–27; U.S., 819, 826–27

Spain: Catholic Church in, 278, 362, 369–70, 375, 388–90, 402–03, 404–06; Civil War, 763–64; culture of, 198, 303, 414; decline of, 405–08, 434; early history, 31, 63–64, 70, 91, 115, 116, 143, 144, 154, 155, 161–62, 175, 183, 189, 194, 204, 208, 259, 302, 304; economy, 368, 403–04, 434, 439; Empire of, 367, 400–08, 409, 434, 439, 440–41, 443, 452–54, 470, 501, 508, 511, 540, 548, 554–55, 628; exploration by, 295, 395, 398–99; foreign affairs, 347, 355, 398, 404, 407, 411–12, 419, 432, 434, 453, 505, 508; and French Revolutionary Wars, 533; government and politics, 259, 369, 557, 759; in Habsburg Empire, 367–68, 370, 402, 404–08, 421, 422, 430, 432, 453; Inquisition in, 367, 389, 552; Italy controlled by, 366, 368, 388, 402, 434; Jews of, 367, 402; mercantilism, 438; military of, 368, 390, 403, 406–07, 410; monarchy, 344, 366–68, 369–70, 402, 412, 417, 503, 547, 549, 609; Moors of, 309, 366–67, 388, 402, 404; under Napoleon, 539, 540–41, 542; nationalism in, 540–41, 557; revolutions of nineteenth century in, 549, 554–55; under Rome, 64, 65, 71, 74, 75, 86, 88, 103; socialism in, 651; Spanish-American War, 621, 631, 685–86; Thirty Years' War, 430, 432, 433; trade and commerce, 363, 404, 802; War of the Spanish Succession, 453–54

Spanish-American War, 621, 631, 685–86

Spanish Armada, 403, 407, 410

Spanish Netherlands, 406, 452–54. *see also* Belgium

Sparta, 35, 37, 40, 41, 47; discipline in, 28, 37–38, 48; Peloponnesian War, 46–47; Persian Wars, 24, 26, 37, 38–39

Spartacus, 68, 71

Spencer, Herbert, 740; *Synthetic Philosophy*, 666–67

Spengler, Oswald, 742; *Decline of the West, The*, 721, 741

Spenser, Edmund, 414

Spice Islands, 397, 399, 440

Spinoza, Baruch: *Ethics Demonstrated in the Geometrical Manner*, 479

Sputnik I, 819, 826

SS troops, 778

Ssu-ma Kuang, 334

Staël, Madame de, 550

Stalin, Joseph, 664, 706, 749–52, 769, 776–77, 781–82, 784–87, 807–08, 818

Stalingrad: siege of, 777, 782

Stalinism, 809

Stamp Act (1765), 518

Standard Oil Company, 630

Stanislaus II (Poniatowski), King of Poland, 513–14

Stanley, Henry Morton, 680

Statute of Westminster (1931), 736

Stavisky scandal, 734

Steele, Richard, 492

Stein, Baron Heinrich vom, 541

Stein, L.: quoted, 735

Stephen II, Pope, 180–81

Stettin, 465

Stimson Doctrine, 760